THE WORDSWORTH
ENCYCLOPEDIA OF
WORLD
RELIGIONS

THE WORDSWORTH ENCYCLOPEDIA OF

WORLD RELIGIONS

WORDSWORTH EDITIONS

This edition first published in Great Britain 1999
by Wordsworth Editions Limited
Cumberland House, Crib Street, Ware
Hertfordshire SG12 9ET

Copyright this edition: © Wordsworth Editions 1999

Text copyright © Concord Reference Books, Inc.

ISBN 1 84022 029 5

Wordsworth® is a registered trade mark of
Wordsworth Editions Limited

Printed and bound in Great Britain
by Mackays of Chatham plc, Chatham, Kent.

THE WORDSWORTH
ENCYCLOPEDIA OF WORLD RELIGIONS

At the onset of the third Millennium AD the
need for a new, up-to-date reference work
covering all major religions in the world has
become increasingly urgent.

Realizing the opportunity for a fresh venture
in this field, a group of publishing houses has
undertaken the task of creating a totally new
dictionary, enlisting the co-operation of
competent scholars in every field of religion
and securing the co-operation of staff members
of the major religious bodies in the world.

The alphabetic section is preceded by a summary
of important entries in the realm of Christianity,
Judaism, Islam, Buddhism and Hinduism.

Major sources of data and material:
- *The New and Old Testament* (Edition of the New York Bible Society)
- *The Jewish Timeline Encyclopedia* (Jason Cantor, Inc.)
- *Encyclopedic Dictionary of Religion* (Corpus Publications, Washington)
- *The Glorious Kuran* (Translation and commentary by Abdallah Yopusuf Ali, University of Cairo)
- *Catechism of the Catholic Church* (Libreria Editrice Vaticana)
- *The Teaching of Buddha* (Buddhist Promoting Foundation, Bukkyo Dendo Kyokai)
- *The Fundamentals of Hinduism* (Satishchandra Chatterjee, New Dehli)
- *Upanisads* (Edition by staff members of the University of Mumbai)
- *Encyclopaedia Britannica Source Library* (Chicago)
- *Encyclopaedia of Islam* (6 volumes, Brill, London)
- *Encyclopedia of Religion and Ethics* (Clark Publishers, Edinburgh)
- *Oxford Illustrated History of Christianity* (Oxford University Press)
- *The National Encyclopedia* (Nat. Encycl. Publishers, Atlanta)
- *Encyclopedie van de Wereldreligies* (Tirion, Baarn)

The authors and editors are very grateful to the following organizations and religious bodies for providing material and data

- World Council of Churches
- Jewish World Congress
- Academia Pontificale (Rome)
- Islamic University Cairo
- Theology Faculty, University of New York
- Religious Seminary, University of New Dehli
- Confucius Institute and Academy, Beijing
- Center for Buddhistic Studies, University of Bangkok
- The Sisters of Saint Joseph, Philadelphia
- Faculty of Theology, University of Zürich
- Faculty of Theology, University of Utrecht

THE WORDSWORTH
ENCYCLOPEDIA OF
WORLD
RELIGIONS

CHRISTIANITY

Selection of important entries

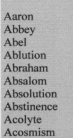

Aaron
Abbey
Abel
Ablution
Abraham
Absalom
Absolution
Abstinence
Acolyte
Acosmism
Act
Action Mass
Acts
Actualism
Adalbert
Adam
Adam and Eve
Adamites
Adiaphorism
Adonai
Adopting Act
Adoptionism
Adoration
Adrian
Advena
Adventism
Advent Wreath
Aërius
Afterlife
Agabus
Agatha
Agility
Agnes
Agnosticism
Agnus Dei
Agrapha
Aitesis
Akathistos
Akolouthia
Alban
Albanian Rite
Albertus Magnus
Albigensians
Aleiptron
Aleppines
Alexander
Almuce
Alphaeus
Altar

Altarbread
Altarpiece
Altarstone
Altarwine
Anabaptism
Anacletus
Anamnesis
Anastasius
Anathema
Andrew
Andronicus
Angel
Angelology
Anglicanism
Anglicans
Aniconism
Annates
Anna
Annulment
Annunciation
Anointing
Anthimus
Anthony
Antichrist
Anticlericalism
Antinomanism
Antioch
Antipas
Antiphon
Antipope
Antonius
Apocalypse
Apocrypha
Apollyon
Apologetics
Apostasy
Apostle
Apostles' Creed
Apostolate
Apostolici
Apparition
Aquinas
Arabia
Aramaic
Ararat
Archangel
Archbishop
Archdiocese
Archonics

Arianism
Aridity
Aristarchus
Ark
Armageddon
Armenian Church
Armenian Rite
Arminianism
Arnobius
Arsenite Schism
Artemas
Ascension
Asceticism
Ashes
Assisi
Assumption
Athanasius
Atheism
Atonement
Attrition
Augsburg
Augustine
Augustinianism
Ave Maria

Baldachino
Ban
Banner
Baptism
Baptistry
Baptists
Baraka
Barbara
Barnabas
Barth
Bartholomew
Bartimaeus
Basil
Basilians
Basilides
Beatification
Beatic vision
Beatitude
Becoming
Beelzebub
Belief
Bell
Benedict
Benediction

Benefice
Benezet
Benjamin
Bernadette
Bernard
Bethlehem
Bible
Bible Vigil
Biretta
Bishop
Black Mass
Blaise
Blessing
Boethius
Bonaventura
Boniface
Brethren
Breviary
Byzantine Church
Byzantine Rite

Caiaphas
Cain
Capital sins
Cappa magna
Cardinal
Carmel
Carmelites
Carpocratians
Carthusians
Cassian
Catacombs
Catafalque
Catachesis
Catechism
Cathechumen
Cathedral
Catherine
Catholic Action
Catholic Church
Catholicism
Catholicity
Catholicos
Cecilia
Celestine
Celestius
Celibacy
Celtic Church
Celtic Rite
Censorship
Certainty
Certitude
Chant
Chapel

Chaplain
Chapter
Charisma
Charity
Charlemagne
Charles
Chastity
Cherubin
Chloe
Choniates
Chorazin
Chrism
Chrism Mass
Chrismation
Christ
Christendom
Christian
Christianity
Christian Myth
Christian Unity
Christmas
Christology
Christopher
Chronicles
Church
Churches
Ciborion
Church Fathers
Cistercians
Clare
Classis
Clemency
Clement
Cleopas
Clergy
Cloister
Codes
Codex
Collegiality
Commandments
Common Prayer
Communion
Community
Concelebration
Conclave
Concomitance
Concordance
Concordate
Confession
Confirmation
Congregation
Conscience
Consecration
Constantine

Constantinople
Contrition
Coptic Church
Corban
Corinthians
Council
Counter-Reformation
Covenant
Creed
Cross
Crucifixion
Crusades
Crypt
Curse
Cyprian

Damascus
Damnation
David
Deacon
Dead
Deesis
Defamation
Dedication
Deism
Deluge
Demas
Demetrius
Demonolatry
Desert Fathers
Devil
Diabolism
Diakonikon
Didache
Diocese
Diocletian
Dionysius
Dioscorus
Disciple
Divination
Divine Healing
Docetism
Doctrine
Dogma
Dominic
Dominicans
Donatists
Dorcas
Dormition
Dositheus
Doxology
Druids
Dyotheletism

Easter
Easter Cycle
Easter Duty
Eastern Churches
Eastern Theology
Ebionites
Ecclesiology
Ecclecticism
Ecstasy
Eucumenism
Eden
Elizabeth
Encratites
Encyclical
Epaphras
Ephesians
Epiclesis
Epiphany
Episcopacy
Epistle
Erasmus
Erastianism
Erastus
Esau
Eschatologism
Eschatology
Edras
Ethiopanism
Eucharist
Eugenius
Euodia
Evangelist
Eve
Evolution
Excommunication
Exodus
Exorcism
Expelling

Fabian
Faculty
Faith
Faith Healing
Fasting
Febronianism
Felix
Filiation
Firstborn
First Communion
Flavian
Flood
Footwashing
Foreteller
Forgiveness

Fortitude
Fortunatus
Franciscans
Francis
Freedom
Fundamentalism

Gabriel
Galatians
Gallican Rites
Gallicanism
Gates of Hell
Gelasius
Genealogy
Genesis
Gennadius
Gentile
George
Germanus
Gethsemane
Gildas
Glorified Body
Glory
Glossolalia
Gnosis
Gnosticism
God
Golgotha
Good Will
Gospel
Gospel Liturgy
Grace
Great Schism
Greed
Greek Orthodoxy
Gregory
Guilt

Hail Mary
Heathen
Heaven
Hedonism
Hegesippus
Helena
Hell
Heresy
Hermas
Hermit
Hermogenes
Herod
Herodion
Heroic Virtue
Hisksites
Hieromonk

High Church
High God
Hilarion
Hilda
Hippolytus
Holiness
Holy Communion
Holy Days
Holy Face
Holy Family
Holy Grail
Holy Innocents
Holy Lance
Holy Orders
Holy Place
Holy See
Holy Sepulchre
Holy Soul
Holy Spirit
Holy Trinity
Holy Water
Holy Week
Holy Year
Homily
Homoeans
Honorius
Hope
Horologion
Humanism
Humanitarianism
Humiliati
Hymenaeus
Hymn
Hypapante
Hyperdulia
Hypostasis

Icon
Icon Veneration
Iconoclasm
Iconology
Iconostasis
Idol
Idolatry
Ignatius
Image
Imaculate Conception
Immersion
Immolation
Immortality
Impeccability
Imprematur
Incarnation
Indulgence

Indult
Infallibility
Innocent
Inquisition
INRI
Inspiration
Installation
Insufflation
Intercession
Irenaeus

Jacob
Jacobite Church
James
Jansenism
Januarius
Jasson
Jehovah
Jeremias
Jerusalem
Jesuits
Jesus Christ
Jesus Only
Jesus Prayer
Joanan
Joanna
John
John Chrysostom
John Climacus
Joseph
Josephists
Judas
Judas Iscariot
Jude
Judgment
Julius
Justification
Justin Martyr
Juvenal

KamisonKanon
Kenosis
Kenotic Theories

Labadists
Lady Chapel
Laicism
Laity
Lamb of God
Lamentation
Lance
Last Days
Last Judgment
Last Supper

Lateran Council
Latin Fathers
Latin Rite
Lauda
Lauds
Laura
Laurentius
Lavabo
Law
Law of Faith
Law of God
Law of Moses
Lawrence
Laxism
Lectionary
Lenity
Lent
Leo
Leontius
Letters
Libellatici
Litany
Liturgical Year
Liturgy
Liudger
Lord's Prayer
Lord's Supper
Lourdes
Loyola
Lucius
Ludmilla
Luke
Luther
Lutheran
Lutheranism
Lydia

Madonna
Magi
Magi Plays
Magisterium
Malachy
Malankar Rite
Mandaeanism
Mandatum
Mandyas
Maniple
Mantelletta
Marcellinus
Marcellus
Marcionites
Margaret
Maria Legio
Marianists

Marinus
Mariolatry
Mariology
Mark
Maronite Church
Maronites
Marriage
Martha
Martin
Martyr
Martyrdom
Mary
Mary Magdalene
Mass
Mater Matuta
Matthat
Matthew
Matthias
Megaloschemi
Meletios
Melkite Church
Mennonites
Menno Simons
Menology
Mercy
Merit
Methodism
Michael
Millenniarism
Miltiades
Ministry
Miracle
Missal
Missions
Mitre

Natural Law
Nave
Nazarene
Nazarenes
Nazareth
Nemesius
Neoplatonism
Neophyte
Nereus
Nestorians
New Covenant
New Testament
Nicaea
Nicene Creed
Nicholas
Ninian
Noah
Nominalism

Nonconformists
Notional Acts
Novena
Novice
Novitate
Nun
Nuncio
Nuptial Mass
Obedience
Observance
Oils
Old Catholics
Oneness of God
Onesimus
Onesiphorus
Opus Dei
Orders
Ordination
Original Sin
Orthodox

Pachonius
Pacifism
Palestine
Palm Sunday
Pantocreator
Papacy
Papal Bull
Papal States
Paradise
Paris Psalter
Parnach
Paschal
Passion
Passion Play
Pastor
Patriarch
Patrick
Patrobas
Patron Saint
Paul
Paulicians
Paulinus
Pelagianism
Pelagius
Penance
Pentecost
Pentecostalism
Pentecost Cycle
Pentekostarion
Perpetual Help
Peter
Philemon
Philip

Philippians
Phoebe
Pieta
Pietism
Pilate
Pilgrimage
Pisida
Pius
Pontianus
Pope
Poverty
Prayer
Preaching
Precept
Predestination
Prelate
Pre-Lent
Presbyterian
Presbyterianism
Priest
Priesthood
Processsion
Profession
Prophecy
Protestantism
Psaltery
Puritanism

Quadratus
Quakers
Quietism

Rabanus Maurus
Rabbula
Rappites
Recollection
Reconciliation
Redemptorists
Reformation
Reformed Church
Relic
Religion
Religious Life
Religious Year
Repentance
Resistance
Resurrection
Revelation
Revivalism
Rhoda
Rites
Romanm Catholic
  Church
Roman Religion

Romans
Romuald
Rosary

Sabbatarianism
Sabinian
Sacrament
Sacramentalism
Sacrifice
Sacristy
Saint
Salvation
Sanctuary
Santa Claus
Sarah
Savior
Scapular
Schism
Scolasticism
Sebastian
Sect
Sergius
Sermon
Shakers
Shrine
Shroud
Shrove Tuesday
Silverius
Simon
Simon Magnus
Simony
Sin
Siricius
Sistine Chapel
Sixtus
Sloth
Socinians
Sophia
Soul
Soul Loss
Spiritism
Spiritual Life
Stanislaw
Stations
Stephen
Stigmata
Stole
Substance
Superstition
Sylvester
Synod
Synoptic Gospel

Tabernacle

Temptation
Tertullus
Thaddeus
Theism
Theocracy
Theodore
Theodosius
Theodotus
Theology
Theophany
Theophilus
Thessalonians
Theudas
Thomas
Thomas Aquinas
Thurstan
Timon
Timothy
Titus
Transcendence
Transfiguration
Trappists
Trent
Trinity

Trophimus
Trusteeism
Tychicus

Ulrich
Unitarianism
United Church
Universalism
Urban
Ursula
Ursulines

Valentine
Valentinus
Validity
Vatican
Vatican City
Vatican Council
Venial Sin
Vernacular
Veronica
Vespers
Vicar
Victor

Virgin Birth
Virginity
Virtue
Vladimir
Vow

Wake
Wenceslas
Wesley
Will
Willebrord
Worship

Youth Ministry

Zaccharias
Zeal
Zebedee
Zenas
Zephyrinus
Zosimus
Zucchetto

JUDAISM

Including the Old Testament. Selection of important entries

Aaron	Ain	Asher
Aaronites	Aleph	Asher b. Jehiel
Abda	Aliya	Ashetite
Abdi	Alleluia	Ashur
Abdiel	Almodad	Ashkenaz
Abel	Almug	Ashkenazim
Abi-Albon	Amalek	Ashtoreth
Abiathar	Amasa	Ashvath
Abib	Amaziah	Asmodeus
Abida	Ammonite	Asrielites
Abidan	Amorites	Asshur
Abigail	Amos	Asylum
Abimael	Amramites	Atarah
Abinadab	Amzi	Athaliah
Abiram	Anah	Attai
Abishag	Anakim	Avera
Abishur	Anamim	Avrekh
Abital	Anan	Avvites
Abiya	Ananiah	Azazel
Abner	Ananias	Azaziah
Abrahamites	Anath	Azel
Absalom	Anathoth	Azgad
Achon	Annas	Azriel
Achor	Anti-Semitism	
Achsah	Aquila	Ba'al
Adah	Ara	Baal-Hermon
Adam	Araba	Baal-Perazim
Adbeel	Arad	Ba'al shem
Adin	Arah	Baal-Tamar
Adlai	Aram	Baana
Adloyada	Aramaic	Baasha
Adonikam	Aramaean	Baal
Adoni-Zedek	Ararat	Babylonian Exile
Adriel	Araunah	Balaam
Adullam	Ard	Bamoth
Aeneas	Areli	Bamoth-Baal
Agadah	Ariel	Bani
Ahab	Arioch	Barabbas
Ahab Ha'am	Ark	Barachel
Aharah	Armilus	Barachiah
Ahasbai	Armoni	Barak
Ahiezer	Arnan	Bar Mitzvah
Ahija	Arubboth	Barnabas
Ahikam	Arvad	Baruch
Ahimelech	Arzah	Barzillai
Ahinadab	Asa	Basemath
Ahira	Asahel	Bath-Rabbim
Ahithophel	Asarel	Bath-sheba
Ahitub	Ashbel	Bavvai

Bazluth
Behemoth
Benedictus
Bene-Israel
Benjamin
Berakhot
Bet-din
Bethlehem
Bible
Bichri
Bildad
Bileam
Bilgai
Binnui
Biziothiah
Black Hebrews
Boaz
Bochim
Borashan
Bozarah

Cabala
Caiaphas
Cain
Calcol
Caleb
Caper berry
Carchemish
Carmel
Chemosh
Chenaniah
Chesalon
Chieftain
Chislev
Chronicles
Cinites
Circumcision
Clan
Cohen
Cohen Gadol
Commandments
Compensation
Congregation
Covenant
Cozeba
Curse
Cush

Daberath
Dalmanutha
Damascus
Dan
Daniel
Dara

Darkon
Dathan
David
Deacon
Dead
Dead Sea Scrolls
Deborah
Dedan
Delaiah
Delilah
Deluge
Demonology
Derasha
Derekh Eretz
Deuteronomy
Devil
Diaspora
Dibbuq
Diblah
Dibri
Dimon
Dinah
Disha
Dizah
Dodo
Doeg
Dophkah
Dor
Dumah
Dungeon

Ebal Mount
Ebed
Ebed-Melech
Ebenezer
Ebron
Ecclesiastes
Ecstasy
Eden
Edom
Edomites
Edrei
Eglaim
Eglon
Ehud
Eker
Ekron
Ela
Elah
Elam
Elasah
Elath
El-Bethel
Eldaah

Eleadah
Elealeh
Eleasah
Eleazar
Eleazer
Elhanan
Eliab
Eliada
Elisaph
Eliathah
Eliel
Eliezer
Eliuh
Elijah
Elim
Elimelech
Elioenai
Eliphal
Eliphet
Elisha
Elishah
Elishama
Elishaphat
Elisheba
Elizaphan
Elizur
Elkesaites
Elnaam
Elohim
Elul
Eluzai
Elzabad
Emek-keziz
Enim
Emmaus
Enaium
Enclave cities
Enoch
Enosh
En-rimmon
En-shemish
En-tappuah
Ephai
Epher
Ephlal
Ephod
Ephraim
Ephratah
Ephron
Er
Esau
Eshban
Essenes
Esther

Etam
Etham
Etan
Ethanim
Ethnan
Ethni
Eunice
Eunuch
Exile
Exodus
Exorcism
Ezbai
Ezbon
Ezekiel
Ezra
Ezrah

Falashas
Firstborn
Flood

Gaal
Gabbai
Gad
Gadarenes
Gaddi
Gaddiel
Gaham
Galilee
Gallim
Gallio
Gamaliel
Gamul
Gazzam
Geba
Geber
Gedaliah
Geder
Gederathite
Gederoth
Gedor
Gehazi
Geloloth
Gemalli
Gemara
Genesis
Gentile
Genubath
Gershom
Gershon
Gershonites
Geshan
Geshem
Geshur

Geuel
Gibbar
Gibbethon
Gibea
Gibeon
Giddalti
Giddel
Gideon
Gidom
Giloh
Ginath
Ginnethon
Girzites
Gob
Gog
Goiim
Golan
Golden Calf
Golem
Goliath
Gomer
Gomorrah
Gagger
Guni

Habaiah
Habakkuk
Hachmoni
Hadad
Haladrimmon
Hadar
Hadassah
Hadlai
Hadrach
Haftara
Hagab
Hagabah
Haganah
Hagar
Haggadah
Haggai
Haggith
Hakkatan
Hakkoz
Halah
Halak
Halakka
Halitza
Hallohesh
Ham
Haman
Hamites
Hammon
Hamonah

Hamor
Hanamel
Hanan
Hanani
Hanaiah
Hanes
Hannah
Hannathon
Hanniel
Hanukkah
Hannum
Harbona
Harbur
Harim
Hariph
Hariphite
Harod
Haruz
Hashabnah
Hashum
Hasideans
Hasidism
Haskala
Hasmonean
Hassenaah
Hauran
Havilah
Hazarmaveth
Hazor
Hazzan
Heaven
Hebrew
Hebrew bible
Hebrews
Hebron
Hegai
Helam
Helbah
Heldai
Heli
Helkath
Hemam
Heman
Hen
Henadad
Hepher
Herod
Heshbon
Hevites
Hezekiah
Hezir
Hezron
High Priest
Hilkiah

Hittite
Hivites
Hobab
Hobah
Hodevah
Hodiah
Holocaust
Horam
Horesh
Horite
Hormah
Hosah
Hosea
Hoshanah Rabba
Hoshea
Hothir
Hukkok
Huldah
Hur
Huram
Husham

Ibhar
Ibzan
Ichabod
Idol
Immanuel
Irpeel
Isaac
Isaish
Ishmael
Ishmaiah
Israel
Issachar

Jaazaniah
Jaaziah
Jaaziel
Jabal
Jachin
Jacob
Jaddai
Jaddua
Jael
Jah
Jahaz
Jahaziel
Jair
Jairus
Jakim
Japheth
Jarib
Javan
Jeberechiah

Jecoliah
Jeconiah
Jediah
Jeduthun
Jehiel
Johoahaz
Jehoiachin
Jehoiakim
Jehoram
Jehoshaphat
Jehovah
Jehu
Jiel
Jephthah
Jerahmeel
Jeremiah
Jeroboam
Jeroham
Jerubbaal
Jerusalem
Jeshaiah
Jeshua
Jethro
Jewish Revolt
Jews
Jezebel
Joab
Joah
Job
Jobab
Jochebed
Joel
Joiakim
Jonah
Jonathan
Joram
Joshua
Josiah
Jozacar
Jubal
Judah
Judaism
Judea
Judges
Judith

Kabbala
Kaddish
Kadmiel
Karaites
Kareah
Kedar
Kedemoth
Kelita

Kenite
Keroith
Keturah
Kiddush
Kings
Kish
Koa
Kol Nidre
Korah

Lag Be-Omer
Lazar
Leah
Lebanah
Lehabim
Lehi
Lemuel
Letushim
Leummim
Levi
Levithian
Levite
Leviticus
Lod
Lois
Lot

Maadiah
Ma'arive
Maaseiah
Maath
Maccabees
Mashbannai
Madmannah
Madon
Magdiel
Mahlah
Mahlites
Mahlon
Maimonides
Malachi
Malchiel
Malchijah
Malchiram
Malchus
Malluch
Manasseh
Manna
Mattan
Mattatha
Matza
Medad
Meded
Megiddo

Melchizedek
Memucan
Menora
Merab
Meraru
Meremoth
Messiah
Methuselah
Mezuzah
Micah
Micaiah
Michal
Midian
Miljamin
Miriam
Mishna
Mitzwa

Naamites
Nabal
Nabateans
Naboth
Nabulus
Nacon
Nadab
Nahash
Nahor
Nashhon
Nahum
Naim
Naphish
Naphtali
Naphtuhim
Nathanael
Nebuchadnezzar
Nehelam
Nehemiah
Nethaniah
Nethinim
Nicodemus
Noah
Numbers

Obadiah
Obed
Og
Oholiab
Old Testament
Onam
Onan

Palestine
Paradise
Parosh

Parthians
Paruah
Pashur
Passover
Patriarch
Pedaiah
Pekah
Pelatiah
Pentateuch
Perez
Pesa
Pharisees
Philistines
Phinehas
Plague
Prisca
Prophet
Proverb
Psalms
Purim

Qodashim
Quarrel
Quartermaster
Quirinius

Raamah
Rabbi
Rachel
Rapha
Raphael
Rebecca
Rechabites
Reform Juadism
Rehob
Rehoboam
Rehoboth
Rehum
Relidion
Reuben
Rezon
Rimmon
Riphath
Rosh Hashanah
Ruth

Sabbath
Sachia
Sadducees
Sallai
Salmon
Salu
Samaria
Samaritans

Samson
Samuel
Sanctuary
Sanhidrin
Sarah
Saul
Sceva
Scribe
Seder
Sefardim
Sefer Torah
Selah
Selihot
Semites
Sephar
Septuagint
Seraiah
Seth
Shabatt
Shadkhan
Shallum
Shammah
Shavuot
Shelemiah
Shem
Sheol
Shimei
Shofar
Siddur
Simeon
Sinai
Sodom
Soferism
Solomon
Sukkot
Synagogue

Tabeel
Tabernacle
Tallit
Talmai
Tamar
Tanhuma
Tarshish
Tartak
Tefillin
Telaim
Telem
Temple
Terah
Teraphim
Tiberias
Timnah
Tiphsah

Tishah Be-Av
Tobiah
Tobit
Tohu
Tola
Tophet
Tubai
Tzedakah

Uel
Ulai
Unni
Ur
Uri
Uriah
Uriel
Urijah
Urim
Uz

Wailing Wall

Wilderness
Yad
Yahweh
Yeshiva
Yiddish language
Yiron
Yom Kippur

Zaanan
Zaanannim
Zaavan
Zabad
Zabbud
Zabdi
Zabud
Zaccai
Zacchaeus
Zaccur
Zadok
Zalaph
Zalmon

Zanoah
Zaphon
Zattu
Zealot
Zebadiah
Zebah
Zebolim
Zeboim
Zebulun
Zechariah
Zedekiah
Zephaniah
Zerah
Zerubbabel
Ziklag
Zillah
Zimri
Zion
Zionism
Zipporah
Zohar

ISLAM

Selection of important entries

Abasa	Black Stone	Fitna
Abbadids	Blue Mosque	Fundamentalism
Abbasids	Bukhari	Furqan
Abd	Buraq	
Abd al-Muttalib	Buruj	Ghaffit
Abu Hanifa	Buyids	Ghanimah
Adham		Ghayba
Adiyat	Chistiyah	Ghaylan b. Muslim
Afrad	Compulsion	Ghoul
Ahmadiyah	Crusades	Ghulam Ahmad
Ahmad Sirhindi		Ghusl
Ahmed	Dahriyah	God
Ahqaf	Da'if	
Ahwal	Dajjal	Hahh
Ahzab	Daqya'il	Hadi
A'ishah	Dawa	Hadid
Al-Ahkam	Dawani	Hadith
Al-A'la	Dawsa	Hadith Nabawi
Alaq	Deobandis	Hadith Qudsi
Al-Amin	Deoband School	Hadra
Al-Anfal	Dervish	Hajar al-Aswad
Al-Ankabut	Dhand	Hajj
Al-A'raf	Dhariyat	Hal
Ali ibin Abi Talib	Dhawq	Hallay
Al-'Iram	Dhimmi	Halqa
Allah	Dhu af-faquar	Hamadhani
Almohad	Dhu 'l-Hijja	Hamdu
Ambiya	Dhu 'l-Qarnayn	Hamza b. al-Muttalib
Amina bint Wahab	Dhu Nowas	Hamzah ibn Ali
Amir	Dikka	Hanafis
Arkan al-Islam	Din	Hanbalis
Aya Sofya	Diya	Hanif
Ayatollah	Duha	Haqiqah
Azhar	Dukhan	Haqq
		Haram
Badr	Fada'il	Haram ash-Sharif
Barzakh	Fajr	Harem
Basmala	Falaq	Harun
Ba'th	Falsalfa	Harut
Batin	Fana'	Hasan
Batiniyah	Farabi	Hasan al-Basri
Bayyina	Fard	Hasane Sabbah
Bid'ah	Fasting	Hashemites
Bila Kayf	Fath	Hashim
Bilal b. Rahab	Fatimids	Hashr
Bilqis	Fatir	Hawwa'
Bka-brgyud-pa	Fatwa	Hejaz
Bka-gdams-pa	Fayd	Hijab
Black Muslims	Fil	Hijr

Hijra
Hisab
Hizb
Hud
Hudayhiyad
Hujurat
Husayn
Husayni

Ibada
Iblis
Ibn Abi as-Rijai
Ibn Abi Asrum
Ibn al-Abdar
Ibn Ezra Moses
Ibn Ishaq
Ibn Jubayr
Ibn Mas'ud
Ibrahim
Ichinen
Ifrit
Ihram
I'jaz
Ijtihad
Ikhlas
Ikhtilaf
Ikhwan
Ikhwan al-Safa
Ilhad
Ilm
Ilm al-hadith
Ilumquh
Imam
Infitar
Injil
Insan
In Sha'a Allah
Inshiqaq
Isa
Ishaq
Isharat al-Sa'a
Islam
Islamic Mysticism
Islamic Philosophy
Islamic Theology
Isma
Isma'il
Isma'iliyah
Isnad
Isra'
Israfil
Istawa
Isra'il

Jabr
Ja'far as-Sadiq
Ja'far ibn Muhammad
Jahannam
Jahiliyah
Jahim
Janna
Jathiyya
Jawhar
Jihad
Jinn
Jinn, al-
Jinni
Jum'a
Jum'ah

Ka'bah
Kafirum
Kafur
Kahf
Kalam
Karmatians
Kasb
Kashf
Kawthar
Khadijna
Khalifa
Kharijites
Khitan
Khorram-dinan
Khutba
Kindi
Koran

Law al-Mahfuz
Layl
Laylat al-Mi'raj
Layat al-Qadr
Laza
Luqman
Lut

Ma-ad
Ma-arij
Madrasah
Mafatih al-ghayb
Mahdi
Mahdi, al-
Mahr
Ma'ida
Maitreya
Maktab
Malamatiyah
Mamluks

Manaf
Maqamat
Marabout
Maryam
Masad
Masih
Masjid
Maturidiyah
Ma'un
Mawla
Mawlawiyya
Mawlid
Mawlid al-Nabi
Maymuna
Mecca
Medina
Mika-il
Minaret
Minbar
Miqat

Nabi
Nafs
Nahl
Najm
Nami
Naqshbandiyah
Nar
Nas
Masikh
Nasr
Nazi'at
Nikah
Nisa
Niyya
Nuh
Nur

Occultation
Omayyads

Pali
Pan-Islamism
Pillars
Polytheism
Prayer
Predestination
Profession
Prophet

Qabil
Qada
Qadar
Qadariyya

Qadi
Qadiriya
Qaf
Qalam
Qamar
Qari'a
Qasas
Qasim
Qibla
Qisas
Qiyama
Qiyas
Qubbat al-Sakhra
Qu'ran
Quraysh
Qurban
Qurra
Qutb

Rabb
Rabi'a al-Adawiyya
Rad
Rafidi
Rahbaniyah
Rahim
Rahman
Ramadan
Rasul
Ra'y
Religion
Riba
Ridda
Ridwan
Rifa'iyah
Rihla
Ruh
Rum
Ru'yat Allah

Sa'a
Saba
Sad
Saffat
Safi od-Din
Safiyya b. Huyay
Sahaba
Sahifa
Sahib

Sa'ir
Sajda
Sajjada
Saladin
Salafiyya
Salat
Saliah
Saljuqs
Sama'
Sariga
Sawm
Shafa's
Shahada
Shams
Shart
Shari's
Shastra
Shath
Shattariyah
Shaykh
Shaytan
Shirk
Shurak
Sifat Allah
Silsila
Sirat al-Mustaqim
Sirhindi
Subhah
Sufi
Sufism
Sulayman
Sunna
Sura
Surah

Tafsir
Taghabun
Taha
Tahannuth
Tahrif
Tahrim
Tahathur
Takbit
Takwir
Talaq
Talha
Tanzih
Taqdir

Taqiyah
Taqlid
Tarawid
Tariq
Tawwuf
Tasbih
Tashbih
Tasnim
Tawba
Ta'ziyah
Tin
Tur
Turban

Umma
Ummah
Umrah

Wahhab
Wali
Wali Allah
Waqf
Waqi'a
Wasil ibn 'Ata
Wird
Wits
Wudu

Yahya
Yajuj
Ya'qub
Yasin
Yawn al-Din
Yawn al-Jum'a
Yawm al-Qiyama
Yunus
Yusuf

Zabaniyya
Zahit
Zahiris
Zalzala
Zaqqum
Ziyarah
Zuad
Zukhruf
Zumar

BUDDHISM

Selection of important entries

Abhaya
Abhidhamma
Abhidhammattha
Abhidharmacosa
Abhijna
Abhiseka
Ablaq
Acintya
Adi-Buddha
Agati
Ahamkara
Ajanta
Ajiva
Akriyavada
Aksobhya
Akusala
Alaya-vijnana
Amarapura
Amaravati
Amitabha
Amrita
Anabhoga
Anagamim
Ananda
Anapana-sati
Anatman
Anatta
Anawrahta
Anguttara
Anicca
Anitya
Annihilation
Antaskarana
Arhat
Arupa
Arupa-loka
Asana
Ascetisicm
Ash'ari
Ash'aris
As if
Asrava
Asura
Atheism
Atman
Authority
Avalokitesvara
Avijja
Ayatana

Ayuthaya

Bala
Balad
Baladhuri
Baqa
Baqara
Baqillani
Beauty
Bhadracarya
Bhagavad-Gita
Bhagavat
Bhakti
Bhava
Bhavana
Bhavanga
Bhikkhu
Bhumisparsa
Bhuta
Birth
Bodhi
Bodhi-citta
Bodhidharma
Bodhisattva
Bodhi Tree
Bön
Borobudur
Brahma Carya
Buddha
Buddha-Carita
Buddha-Dhamma
Buddha-Ghosa
Buddhahood
Buddha-Palita
Buddha Rupa
Buddha-Vamsa
Busddhi
Buddhism
Butsadan

Caitya
Chanda
Compassion

Dai Butsu
Dakhuma
Dakinis
Dana
Darshana

Death
Deva
Devachan
Devadatta
Dge-lugs-pa
Dhamma
Dhammapada
Dharana
Dharma
Dharmacakra
Dharmakaya
Dharmakirti
Dharmapalas
Dhatu
Dhyani-Buddhas
Dispankara Buddha
Ditthi

Eightfold Path
Ekacitta
Ekaggata
Ekayana
Enlightenment
Esoteric
Ethics
Evil
Experience

Four Parts
Four Truths
Free Will

Garbha-dhatu
Gati
Gtor-ma
Guhyasamaja
Guilt

Happiness
Hayagriva
Hell
Hevajra Tantra
Hinayana

Jina
Jnana

Kalacakra Tantra
Kapla

Kama
Kammatthana
Kammavipaka
Karma
Karma-pa
Karuna
Karyapa
Kegon
Kriyatantra
Kshatriya
Kuandalini
Kusala

Lalitavustara
Lama
Lamaism
Lotus
Lumbini

Madhyamika
Maha Maya
Mahamudra
Mahavairocana
Mahavastu
Mahavihara
Mahayana
Manas
Mappo
Mara
Maya
Mediumship

Naga
Nagarjuna
Nembutsuher
Neti, Neti
NidanaNihilism
Nigranthas
Nirmanakaya
Nirodha
Nirvana
Misprapanca
Nivritti
Nivarana

Odantapuri
Om

Padmasambhava
Pamada
Panchen Lama
Pantheism
Paradox
Paramanu

Paramartha
Paramitas
Paravritti
Parikalpita
Parinamana
Parinirvana
Parivarta
Personality
Phag-mo-gru
Phags-pa
Phala
Phasa
Piti
Pradaksina
Prajna
Prajna-paramita
Prajnapti
Prakriti
Pramana
Pranidhana
Pratisandhi
Pratyaya
Pravritti
Precept
Pudgala
Puja
Punna
Purusha

Rahab
Rahula
Ratna
Rebirth
Relics
Religion
Renunciation
Ritual
Rosary
Roshi
Rupa
Rupa-skandha

Sacred
Saddha
Saddharmapunda
Sakra
Sakya
Samadhi
Samantabhadra
Samapatti
Samata
Samatha
Sambodhi
Samgha

Samjna-shandha
Samkya
Samma
Sammatiya
Sampada
Samsara
Samskara
Samudaya
Samvara
Samvrti-satya
Samye Debate
Samyojana
Sangha
Sanghamittha
Sankappa
Samron
Santana
Sarvastivada
Sasana
Sa-skya-pa
Sat
Sati
Sati-Patthana
Sautrantika
Sayadaw
Seal
Shamanism
Shinran
Siddhartha
Siddhas
Siddhi
Sikkha
Smon-Iam
Smrtyupasthana
Soto
Sravaka
Stupa
Subhadda
Sunyata
Sutra
Sutta
Svabhava

T'aigo Wangsa
Taj Mahal
Taimitsu
Tantras
Tariki
Tathagata
Tathata
Telakhon
Tendai
Thera
Theravada

Tiloka
Tirthika
Tisarana
Trikaya
Tripitaka
Tri-ratna
Tri-siksa
Tri-svabhava
Tulku
Tum-mo

Udgita
Uisang Daisa
Ullambana
Upadana
Upasampada

Upaya
Upekkha
Urna
Usual Life

Vada
Vairocana
Vajrapani
Vayama
Vickiccha
Vihara
Vinapti-karman
Vikalpa
Vinaya Pitaka
Vinnana
Virya

Viveka

Wheel of Life
Wonhyo

Yamana
Yana
Yantra
Yidam
Yoga
Yogacara

Zen
Zen Logic

HINDUISM

Selection of important entries

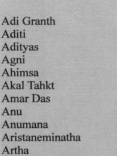

Adi Granth	Digambara	Kanphata Yogis
Aditi	Diwali	Karma
Adityas	Durga	Karma-yoga
Agni	Dvaita	Karttikeya
Ahimsa	Dvija	Khalsa
Akal Tahkt		Krishna
Amar Das	Ganesa	Kubera
Anu	Garuda	Kuvera
Anumana	Gayatri	
Aristaneminatha	God	Laksana
Artha	Gorakhnath	Laksmi
Arthapathi	Gramadevata	Laksmana
Aryans	Grhya-sutras	Laksmi-Narayana
Arya Samaj	Guna	Ligasarira
Asceticism	Gunasthanas	Loka
Asura	Gurdwara	Lokasa
Asvalayana	Guru	Lokapalas
Asvamedha	Guru, Sikh	
Asvins		Madhva
	Hanuman	Mahabalpuram
Bahubali	Hare Ran Hara Krishna	Mahabbharata
Balarama	Haribhadra	Mahakala
Bengal Vaisnavism	Harihara	Mahapurusa
Bhadrabahu I	Hari Krishen	Mahasiddha
Brahma	Harimandir	Maha-sivaratri
Brahma Carya	Henotheism	Mahasukhakaya
Brahman	Hindi	Mahatma
Brahamanas	Hinduism	Maithil Brahmin
Brahamanism	Hinduism Vedas	Mandala
Brahma Samaj	Hindu Musticism	Mandapa
Brahma Vihara	Homa	Manu
Bramin		Marga
Brhaspati	Ishvara	Matsya
Brihadesvara Temple	Istadevata	Matsyendranatha
	Isvara	Meru
Caitanya Movement		
Cakravartin	Jagannatha	Naga
Caran	Jaina Canon	Narasimha
Castes system	Jainism	Nataraja
Chela	Jiva	Natha cult
		Nigranthas
Darsana	Kabir	Nirguna
Dasami sannyasin	Kabitpanthis	Nirjara
Dayananda Sarasvati	Kailasa	Nirmalas
Devadasi	Kaivalya	
Dhanvantari	Kalakacaryakatha	Pancrata cult
Dharma-mangal	Kali	Pandharpur
Dharma-sutra	Kama	Pantheism
Dhyana	Kammavipaka	Parinama

Paryusana
Pisaca
Pramana
Prana
Pranayama
Prapatti
Pratyahara
Pratyeka Buddha

Radha Soami Satsangh
Rama
Ramakrishna
Ramana Maharishi
Ramananda
Ramanandis
Ramatirtha
Ram Raiyas
Ravana
Reincarnation
Rta
Rudra

Sabda
Sadhana
Sadhu
Sadhajiya
Saiva-siddhanta
Saivism
Saktism
Sampradayas
Samskaras

Sangitiparyana
Sankara
Sannyasin
Sanskrit
Saptamatrkas
Sastihi
Sauras
Shakti
Siddha
Sikhara
Sikhs
Sikhism
Sita
Smrti
Srauta-sutras
Sri-Nathaji
Srivaisnavas
Sruti
Sudra

Tagore
Tenkalai
Tilaka
Tirthankara
Tithayatra
Trimurtu
Tri-ratna
Trisala

Upadhi
Upamana

Upallayana
Upavita

Vahana
Vahanasa Vaisnavas
Vaisesika
Vaisana-Sahajiya
Vainavasim
Vaisya
Vallabha
Vamana
Varaha
Varanasi
Varuna
Veda
Vedan
Vedanta
Vedas
Ved-ava
Vedic Chant
Vedic Sacrifice
Vedism
Vetala
Vidyarambha
Vishnu
Vivarta

Yajna
Yama
Yapaniya samgha
Yudhisthira

AACHEN

Historic city in west central Germany, scene of many treaties, partly destroyed in World War II (1944), site of early Christian graves and chapel (5th century), and center of the Carolinian Renaissance. Charlemagne here built a palace and chapel (circa 786) in which 30 German kings were subsequently crowned (936-1531).

AARON

(born circa 1520 BC) The brother of Moses, his senior by three years, and son of Amram and Jochebed of the tribe of Levi. He acted together with his brother in the desperate situation of the Israelites in Egypt and took an active part in the Exodus. Although Moses was the actual leader, Aaron acted as his mouthpiece (Exodus 4:16). Aaron was the first High Priest and his sons were anointed and consecrated to be priests (Leviticus 8:6).

By a seven-day installation ceremony Aaron was invested with his sacred duties by Moses as God's agent, and his four sons were also installed as under-priests. Moses dressed Aaron in beautiful garments of gold, blue, purple and scarlet materials, including shoulder pieces and a breastpiece that were encrusted with precious gems of varied colors. He was not only placed over all the priesthood but was also divinely declared to be the one from whose line or house all future High Priests must come. As High Priest, Aaron was responsible for directing all features of worship at the tabernacle and supervising the work of the thousands of Levites engaged in its service. Aaron's devotion to pure worship was

put to the test early by the death of his sons Nadab and Adihu, who suffered destruction by God for making profane use of their priestly positions. The record says: "And Aaron kept silent." When he and his two surviving sons were instructed not to mourn over the dead transgressors, "they did according to Moses's word" (Leviticus 10:1-11)

During nearly forty years Aaron represented the twelve tribes before God in his capacity as High Priest. While in the wilderness, a serious rebellion broke out against the authority of Moses and Aaron.

Because of a number of incidents and deflections Aaron was not allowed to enter the Promised Land and died on the top of Mount Hor (Numbers 20:22-29).

AARON BEN MEIR

(10th century) Head of a Talmudic academy, prominent in the Jewish calendar controversy of 921. He urged that the timing of the new year should not be deferred.

AARONITES

In Old Testament tradition, the chief priests of ancient Israel, contrasted with Levites, the lesser priests.

AB

The post-exilic name of the fifth lunar month of the Jewish sacred calendar, but the eleventh of the secular calendar. It corresponds to part of July and part of August.

ABADON

Hebrew word for destruction; the word is used in the sense of an angel not of Satan but of God performing his work of destruction at God's bidding.

ABAGTHA

The name of one of seven court officials who ministered to the Persian king Ahasuerus, the husband of the Jewess Esther, in his palace in Shushan, the capital of Persia. The name is evidently Persian, and some connect it with the Sanskrit word

Bagadata and thereby give its meaning as "given by fortune" (Esther 1:10).

ABANDONMENT, Spiritual

An ascetic-mystical term with several not entirely related meanings. In an active sense, it signifies the yielding of self to God's will, not so much as this is expressed in commandment but rather as it is discerned in the unfolding of events manifesting God's will or good pleasure.

In a passive sense, abandonment signifies the dereliction of man by God. This may be real, as when God leaves the sinner in punishment of his sin, or it may be only apparent, as in the experience of passive purification.

ABASA

The title of the 80th sura of the Koran; it means literally "He frowned." The sura belongs to the Meccan period and contains 42 verses. Its title reflects the Prophet Mohammed's impatience on being interrupted by a blind man while the former was expounding the Koran. The sura goes on to stress the honorable, high and pure nature of the Koran before concluding with a survey of some of the gifts which God has bestowed upon man and a warning about the Last Judgment.

ABBA

An aramaic word for father. This familiar form of address was often used by children. Jesus used the intimate address abba when he invoked his father in the greatest crisis of his life (Mark 14:30). Two other New Testament occurrences of abba also are used in the context of prayer (Romans 8:15, Galatians 4:6).

ABBADIDS

Muslim Arab dynasty of Andalusia that arose in Seville in the 11th century, in the period of party kings following the downfall of the caliphate of Cordoba. In 1023 the religious judge Abu al-Qasim Muhammad ibn Abbad declared Seville independent of Cordoba.

ABBA SALAMA

A title originally accorded to St. Frumentius (died circa 383), apostle of Christianity in Ethiopia. It is still used as one of the titles of the head of the Ethiopian Church, the metropolitan of Axum.

ABBASIDS

Major dynasty in medieval Islam which flourished between 750-1258 in Baghdad, and survived as a shadow caliphate in Cairo from 1261 until 1517. The dynasty took its name from the Prophet Mohammed's uncle Al-Abbas.

ABBESS

The title of a superior of certain communities of nuns following the Benedictine Rule, of convents of the Second Order of St. Francis, and of certain communities of canonesses. The first historical record of the name is on a Roman inscription dated circa 514.

ABBEY

Building of a monastic house or religious community, centered on a church. The cloistered life of medieval times grew out of the anchorite, or hermit, communities of Egypt and the Near East in the early Christian era. The first abbey in Western Europe was established in France in 360, and the first in England, Bangor Abbey, in 560. Also in this period such famous Irish abbeys were important centers of culture and the practical arts throughout Western Europe. They served as schools, their libraries were the repositories of classical as well as Christian literature, and their workshops were centers of local industry.

The strictly organized, concentrated abbey is based on the rule of St. Benedict of Nursia, who founded Montecassino Abbey in southern Italy in the 6th century. The standard form of later abbeys was an open quadrangle surrounded by roofed cloister galleries onto which the various buildings of the abbey opened. The abbey church was usually at the northern side of the quadrangle. Other buildings included dormitories, containing sleeping cubicles or cells, the dining hall (refectory) and kitchen, and novice house, the library, the infirmary and perhaps a treasury.

ABBON, Saint

(945-1004) French scholar and monk; from 988, reforming abbot of the Benedictine monastery of Fleury on the Loire River.

ABBOT

The male head or superior of an abbey or monastery. The abbess (superior of a monastic community of nuns) and abbot are elected by the community and have general authority and ordinary jurisdiction over it.

ABBOT, Lay

An abbot who has not received holy orders. The title generally refers to an 8th-11th century abuse, chiefly in the Frankish Empire, whereby a king or someone in authority assigned an abbey and share in its revenues.

ABBOT, Titular

An honorary title found in the Western church (parallel to the title of Archimandrite in the Eastern churches), usually given to a priest in recognition of some special service to a monastic order.

It carries with it the right to receive the abbotial blessing from a bishop or someone else empowered to give it, to wear the garb of prelates including a jeweled cross and ring, and to celebrate pontifically in certain places and circumstances.

ABBOTT GENERAL

The head of certain monastic orders and congregations (for example, The Cistercian Orders, certain Benedictine Congregations) and the superior general of canons regular (for example, the Norbertines).

ABBOTT PRIMATE

The supreme moderator of the Benedictine Confederation of Monastic Congregations. He is also regular abbot of St. Anselms' Abbey, Rome, and president of the Pontifical Academy of St. Anselms.

ABD

In Islam, male slave, servant (of God), man, human being. In the plural, abod, the term is often used to designate slaves, while ibad is used for "servants (of God)." Abd often forms part of a proper name, for example, Abd al-Rahman (Servant of the Merciful God). Slavery was common throughout Islamic history and the institution was governed by a variety of rules established by Islamic jurisprudence. Modern Islam is in favor of the abolition of slavery.

ABDA

In the Old Testament, the father of Adoniram, who was a prince over those conscripted for forced labor during David's and Solomon's reigns, and is evidently the Adoram and Hadoram referred to in other texts (2 Samuel 20:24; 2 Chronicles 10:18). Hence, Abda probably was a contemporary of King David.

ABD ALLAH

(1846-1899) Political and religious leader who succeeded Muhammad Ahmad as head of a religious movement and state within the Sudan.

ABD ALLAH IBN YASIN

(died circa 1060) Islamic scholar and an early leader of the Almpravid reform movement, which spread over North Africa and Spain in the 11th century.

ABDALLAH ZAHIR

(1680-1748) A native of Aleppo, Syria, who became attached to the monastery of Mar Hanna. Living as a lay deacon, he built one of the earliest printing presses for Arabic in the East and devoted himself to the publishing of religious writings.

ABD AL-MUTTALIB

The grandfather, on the paternal side, of the Prophet Mohammed, and father of Mohammed's father Abd Allah. He became head of the clan of Hashim and Mohammed's first guardian after his father's death. Abd al-Muttalib became a prosperous merchant and was the digger of a number of wells; he discovered and restored the well of Zamzam. It is difficult to give precise dates for his birth and death beyond stating that he flourished in the 6th century AD.

ABDI

In the Old Testament, one of the sons of Elam who lived in post-captivity times (Ezra 10:26). They were among those Israelites who had taken foreign wives but who put them away in response to Ezra's exhortation following his return to Jerusalem in the seventh year of Artaxerxes (Ezra 7:8; 10:1-4, 10-12; 26).

ABDICATION

The renunciation of an ecclesiastical office, especially by a pope or patriarch who is normally elected or appointed for a life term.

ABDIEL

In the Old Testament, the son of Guni and the father of Ahi, of the tribe of Gad (1 Chronicles 5:15). He lived in the region of Gilead and Bashan in Transjordan, an area prominent for cattle raising.

ABDON

In the Old Testament, the son of Hillel the Pirathonite of Ephraim (Judges 12:13-15). According to Josephus, his rule of eight years was one of peace, and the Bible record gives no mention of wars during that period. Abdon's 40 sons and thirty grandsons all "rode on 70 full-grown asses," a sign of considerable wealth and rank at that time. At the end of his judgeship Abdon was buried in his native Ephraim.

ABDU, Mohammad

(1849-1905) Religious scholar and liberal reformer, led the late-19th century movement in Egypt and other Muslim countries to revitalize Islamic teachings and institutions in the modern world.

ABDUCTION

As understood in canon law, is the forcible removal of a woman from a place in which she is free and her forcible retention with a view to marriage. The present law of the Roman Catholic Church, in practically the same words as those used by the Council of Trent, provides that no valid marriage is possible between the woman and the abductor as long as she remains in his power.

ABEL

In the Old Testament, second son of Adam and Eve, who was slain by his older brother, Cain. Abel, a shepherd, had offered the Lord the firstborn of his flock, shedding atoning blood (Hebrews 9:22). The Lord respected Abel's sacrifice but did not respect that offered by Cain. In a jealous rage, Cain murdered Abel. Cain then became a fugitive because his brother's innocent blood put a curse on him.

While it cannot be said that Abel has any foreknowledge of the eventual outworking of the divine promise of Genesis 3:15 concerning the promised "seed," yet his offering of the firstlings of his flock certainly was appropriate and undoubtedly was also a factor in God's expression of approval. To the Giver of all, Abel gave as his gift life, even though it was only from his flocks.

In the New Testament the blood of Abel is cited as an example of the vengeance of violated innocence (Matthew 23:35).

The Christian Church honors Abel as the first martyr and as the prototype of faithful innocence.

ABGAR LEGEND

In early Christian times, a popular myth that Jesus had an exchange of letters with King Abgar V of Edessa, situated on the northern fringe of the Syrian plateau. The king reputedly wrote to Jesus, professed belief in his divinity, asked that Jesus cured him of a serious infirmity, and offered his city as a safe refuge from persecution.

ABHAYA

In Buddhism, fearless; as a gesture in an image of the Buddha is that of protection.

ABHDISHO BAR BERIKHA

(died circa 1318) Syrian Christian theologian and poet, who was the last important representative of the Nestorian tradition, a theological school emphasizing a rational, critical interpretation of early Christian doctrine. The sect, centered in ancient Antioch, countered the speculative mysticism then prevalent in Alexandria and Jerusalem.

ABHIBHVAYATANA

In Buddhism, one of the preparatory stages of meditation, in which the senses are completely restrained.
Abhibhvayatana is divided into eight substages during which man comes to realize that physical forms in the external world are different from himself, thus freeing himself from attachment to the sense objects.

ABHIDHAMMA

In Buddhism, the third division of the Canon of the Theravada School. It is largely a commentary on the Sutta Pitaka, the Sermons, and subjects them to analysis. Philosophically and psychologically, it contains an entire system of mind training.

ABHIDHAMMATTHA-SANGAHA

One of the most important Buddhist manuals of psychology and ethics. It is a highly popular primer or digest of the scholastic section of the canon of the Theravada tradition. It was composed in India or in Burma, the chief center of Abhidhamma studies. Written in Pali, it dates from no earlier than the 8th century and probably from the 11th or 12th century.

ABHIDHARMACOSA

An encyclopedic compendium of Abhidharma, the position of which within Buddhism has been likened to that of St. Thomas Aquinas' *Summa theologiae* for Roman Catholicism.

ABHIJNA

In Buddhism, insight attained by the practice of Dhyana; a high state of consciousness when six spiritual powers have been developed. The following spiritual powers have been distinguished:
▲ Power to see what one wills to see, anywhere.
▲ Power to hear and understand all languages.
▲ Power to read thoughts.
▲ Knowledge of former lives (one's own).
▲ Knowledge of former lives (those of others).
▲ The deliverance of mind from passions.

ABHISEKA

In Buddhism, a purificatory or initiatory rite involving sprinkling a candidate with water or other liquid, signifying a change in status. In Tantric Buddhism, the abhiseka rite is a necessary prelude to initiation into mystical teaching or rites.

ABI-ALBON

In the Old Testament, a Benjamite and an outstanding warrior listed among 37 of King David's most valiant fighters (2 Samuel 23:31).

ABIASAPH

In the Old Testament, one of the three sons of Korah the Levite, and a descendant of Kohath (Exodus 6:16-24). It appears that Korah's sons did not join their father in his rebellion, along with Dathan and Abiram, against Moses and

Aaron. Hence, these sons did not die with their father at that time (Numbers 26:9-11).

ABIATHAR

In the Old Testament, son of Ahimelech, priest of Nob. He was the sole survivor of a massacre ordered by King Saul, who attempted to destroy the entire priesthood (1 Samuel 22:18). Fleeing to David, Abiathar remained with him throughout his wanderings and his reign.

ABIB

The original name of the first lunar month of the Jewish sacred calendar and of the seventh month of the secular calendar (Exodus 13:4; 23:15; 34:18; Deuteronomy 16:1). It corresponds, generally, with part of March and part of April. The name is understood to mean "ripening grain" or "green ears," and it was during this month that the barley harvest took place, followed some weeks later by the wheat harvest.

ABIDA

In the Old Testament, a son of Midian, and a grandson of Abraham by his wife Keturah. He had four brothers, named Ephah, Epher, Hanoch and Eldaah (Genesis 25:14; 1 Chronicles 1:33).

ABIDAN

In the Old Testament, the chieftain of the tribe of Benjamin at the time of the census of Israel in the second year of the exodus from Egypt. He was the son of Gideon (Numbers 1:11, 16) He was the head over the 35,400 men of Benjamin over 20 years of age who camped on the western side of the tabernacle (Numbers 2:18-23).

ABIDING IN CHRIST

A scriptural formula expressive of the grace-life of the Christian in virtue of his or her union with Christ, and, through Christ, with the Heavenly Father.

ABIGAIL

In the Old Testament, the wife of Nabal of southern Judah, on whose death she became one of the first wives of David (1 Samuel 25) and the mother of his son Chileab. The name Abigail ("handmaid") was also borne by David's sister (1 Chronicles 2:16), the mother of Amasa, commander of the army of Absalom.

ABIHAIL

In the Old Testament, man of the tribe of Levi and of the family (or clan) of Merari. He was the father of Zuriel, chieftain of the paternal house of the clan at the time of the Exodus (Numbers 3:35).

ABIHU

In the Old Testament, one of Aaron's four sons by his wife Elisheba (Exodus 6:23). Born in Egypt, Abihu as the second son of Aaron, was a mature man by the time of the Exodus, his father then being in his 80s (Numbers 33:39).

ABIJAH

A name borne by nine different persons mentioned in the Old Testament of whom the most noteworthy are:
1 the son and successor of Rehoboam, king of Judah (2 Chronicles 12:16), who reigned about two years (circa 915-916 BC);
2 the second son of Samuel (1 Samuel 8:2), who, with his brother Joel, was judged at Beer-sheba. The elders of Israel made the pair's misconduct a pretext for demanding a king (1 Samuel 8:4).

ABIMAEL

In the Old Testament, a descendant of Shem through Arpachshad. His father was Joktan, whose brother, Peleg, was an ancestor of Abraham (Genesis 10:28; 1 Chronicles 1:17-21). It is likely that Abimael and his twelve brothers were the sources from which thirteen different Arabian tribes developed, settling in the Arabian peninsula.

ABIMELECH

In the Old Testament, either a personal name or an official title of several Philistine kings, similar to the title "Pharaoh" among the Egyptians and "Caesar" among the Romans.

ABINADAB

In Judaism, an inhabitant of the city of Kiriath-Jearim, in the territory of Judah about eight miles northwest of Jerusalem, in whose home the Ark of the covenant was kept for a time. Then the sacred ark was brought up from Beth-shemesh after its disastrous seven-month sojourn among the Philistines, it was deposited in the home of Abinadab, and his son Eleazar was sanctified to guard it. Here in his home the Ark remained for some 70 years, until David arranged to transfer it to Jerusalem. During the transfer another of Abinadab's sons, Uzzah, dropped dead in his tracks when God's anger blazed against him, due to touching the ark in disregard of the command at Numbers 4:15, 2 Samuel 6:1-7; 1 Chronicles 13:6-10.

ABIRAM

In the Old Testament, a Reubenite, the son of Eliab and brother of Dathan and Nemuel. He was a family head and one of the principal men in Israel at the time of the Exodus from Egypt (Numbers 26:5-9).

Abiram and his brother Dathan supported Korah the Levite in his rebellion against the authority of Moses and Aaron. Having gathered a group of 250 chieftains, who were "men of fame," these men accused Moses and Aaron of arbitrarily elevating themselves over the rest of the congregation. Moses dealt separately with them, and their rejection of his call for them to appear before him contains accusations directed solely against Moses, with no mention made of Aaron.

Then, following Moses' call to the rest of the people to withdraw from around the tents of the three ringleaders of the rebellion, God manifested his condemnation of their disrespectful course by causing the ground to open up beneath the tents of these men, swallowing up Abiram and Dathan, and their households (Numbers 16:16-35; Deuteronomy 11:6).

ABISHABIS

Religious movement of the Cree American Indian, originating around mid-1800s. The Methodist missionary James Evans (calling himself Abishabis) applied the name "Jesus" to himself, while a companion became known as Wasiteck, or "light." The two men were believed to have visited heaven and returned with the blessings and teachings for the people. They claimed the ability to draw: "The Track to Heaven" on paper or wood, using the map or chart they created to convey their prophetic message.

The religious movement declined as a result of white opposition to it and because of the waning popularity of Abishabis himself. As he sought more goods for his followers, his support diminished and he returned to his earlier poverty.

ABISHAG

In Judaism, a young virgin from the town of Shunem, north of Jezreel and Mount Gilboa, in the territory of Issachar (Joshua 19:17-23). She was "beautiful in the extreme," and was chosen by David's servants to become the nurse and companion of the king during his final years (1 Kings 1:1-4).

ABISHAI

In the Old Testament, the son of David's sister Zeruiah and brother of Joab and Asahel (2 Samuel 2:18; 12 Chronicles 2:15-16). Abishai came to be more distinguished for his prowess than the thirty mighty warriors over whom he served as chief, his reputation even rivaling those of David's three most mighty men, for he once struck down 300 of the enemy single-handed, but to the rank of the first three he did not come (2 Samuel 23:18-19).

ABISHUR

In Judaism, a descendant of Judah through the family line of Hezron, of the house of Jerahmeel. He was evidently the second son of Shammai and became the father of two sons by his wife Abihail (1 Chronicles 2:28-29).

ABITAL

In the Old Testament, one of the six wives through whom David has sons during the seven and a half years he stayed in Hebron. Her son was named Shephatiah (2 Samuel 3:4; 1 Chronicles 3:3).

ABIUD

The Greekized or Anglicized form of the Hebrew name Abihud. A descendant of Zerrubbabel and an ancestor of Jesus Christ (Matthew 1:13). The term "father" as used by Matthew may suggest that he may have the meaning of "forefather."

ABIYA

In Judaism, the four levels of reality, or the "four worlds," through which a Jewish mystic perceives the outline of the Godhead. The medieval Kabbalists of Safed, Galilee, gave special attention to the concept of abiya, and such famous Kabbalists as Isaac ben Solomon Luria in the 16th century devoted great effort to determining the exact relationship of the four worlds to God. Later Kabbalists claimed that a different Torah was assigned to each world, thus introducing into Judaic thought a religious relativism that was both new and dangerous to established rabbinic traditions.

ABLAQ

In Islam, literally piebald. The word is used as a technical term in Islamic architecture to designate stone, marble or brick decoration in which two colors or tones (often one light and one dark) are used alternately in courses by way of contrast.

ABLUTION

A religiously prescribed washing of part or all of the human body or of possessions such as clothing or ceremonial objects with the intent of purification or dedication. Water, or water with salt or some other traditional ingredient, is most commonly used.

Like most ritual acts, ablution may carry a wide range of meanings to those who perform it. The stain or ritual uncleanness may be felt to be as real as is contamination with unseen germs for the medically minded; or the act of cleansing may be only a gesture, symbolic of desired purity of soul.

In Roman Catholicism, the baptismal bath and the rite of sprinkling holy water on the congregation at the beginning of the liturgy are associated with cleansing from sin.

In liturgy, ablution refers principally to the washing of the hands at Mass by the presider, the purification of the fingers that have touched the sacred species, and the ritual purification with water of the sacred vessels. Ordinarily this is done by pouring wine and/or water over the index fingers and thumbs of the presider into the chalice.

ABNER

In Judaism, the son of New, of the tribe of Benjamin. Abner served as chief of the army for Saul and his fighting force sometimes assumed major proportions, upward to 200,000 men (1 Samuel 15:4). On special occasions he sat next to the kin at the banquet table (1 Samuel 20:25). Though undoubtedly a powerful and valiant man, Abner did not feel himself a match for the towering Philistine Goliath, but stood by and witnessed young David's matchless demonstration of courage in dispatching that formidable opponent (1 Samuel 17:48-58). Later, when David was a fugitive in the wilderness of Ziph, Abner came in for chiding from David for having failed in properly guarding Saul's person as his lord (1 Samuel 26:14-16).

ABO(U) HANIFA

(699-767) Scholar who gave his name to the Hanafi School of Islamic law which was really founded by his disciples rather than Abu Hanifa himself. He was one of the most important jurists and theologians of early medieval Islam, living in al-Kufa and becoming the most distinguished member of the law school there. Towards the end of his life he was imprisoned in Baghdad where he died. His views on jurisprudence were collected and recorded by his disciples.

ABRABANEL, Isaac ben Judah

(1437-1508) Jewish religious writer and statesman who, though in the service of Ferdinand and Isabella, was unable to prevent the expulsion of the Jews from Spain in 1492.

ABRAHAM

("The Father of many nations", born circa 2160 BC) Father of the Hebrew people, first of the patriarchs and regarded as the founder of Israel. He was a descendant of Shem, and son of Terah, being born in Ur of the Chaldees. Called by God to leave his own country and people and journey to an undesignated land, he obeyed unquestioningly and (at 75 years of age) proceed with his barren wife, Sarai, later named Sarah ("Princess"), his nephew Lot, and other companions to the land of Canaan, between Syria and Egypt (Genesis 11:31). He vowed to worship God and was promised that his people should inherit Canaan through his son Isaac. However, as a test of faith and obedience, God commanded Abraham to slay Isaac. Abraham obeyed, and Isaac was spared (Genesis 22:15-19). Through Abraham's faith a covenant of plenty and fecundity was established between God and the Israelites. He died at the age of 175 and was buried next to Sarah in the cave of Machpelah.

While Abraham was still living in Ur, "before he took up residence in Haran," God commanded him to move out to a strange land, leaving behind friends and relatives (Acts 7:2-4; Genesis 15:7). There in that country that He would show Abraham God said he would make out of him a great nation. At the time, Abraham was married to his half-sister Sarah, but they were childless and both were old. So it was great faith to obey, but obey they did.

Terah, now around 200 years old and still the family's patriarchical head, agreed to accompany Abraham and Sarah on this long journey, and it is for this reason that Terah as father is credited with making the move toward Canaan (Genesis 11:31). It appears that fatherless Lot, Abraham's nephew, was adopted by his childless uncle and aunt, and so accompanied them. Northwestward the caravan moved, over 600 miles, until they reached Haran, which was an important junction on the east-west trade routes, located on the Belikh River, more than 65 miles above where it empties into the Euphrates. Here Abraham remained until the death of his father Terah.

The first occurrence of the word "prophet" in the Hebrew scriptures refers to Abraham, though others like Enoch lived before him (Genesis 20:7; Jude 14). The first identified in the scriptures as a "Hebrew" is Abraham (Genesis 14:13).

Abraham, like Abel, Enoch and Noah, was a man of faith. But the first occurrence of the expression "put faith in God" is in reference to Abraham (Genesis 15:6), in agreement with Romans 4:11: "Abraham is the father of all those having faith."

Indeed, this man of unusual faith walked with God and was in constat communication with him by means of visions and dreams, even entertaining his messengers (Genesis 12:1-3; 15:1-8; 18:1-15; 22:15-18). He was well acquainted with the name of God although he had not at that time revealed the full significance of the greatest name in the universe (Exodus 6:2-3). Time after time Abraham built altars and offered up sacrifices in the name of and to the praise and glory of his God (Genesis 12:8; 13:4; 21:33). Jesus and his disciples referred to Abraham more than seventy times in their conversations and writings. Archaeological discoveries have also confirmed many matters related in the biblical history of Abraham.

ABRAHAM, Apocalypse of

A Jewish apocryphal work, written circa 1000 apparently out of reflection upon the destruction of Jerusalem and the Temple in 70 and the effect of this disaster upon the Jewish people.

The work contains an imaginative construction of Abraham's youth influenced by Genesis and rabbinic tradition, that emphasizes his faith in monotheism. It then depicts Abraham as brought to heaven, where he is allowed to view human history, past and future, including the sin of Adam and Eve and the destruction of the Temple.

ABRAHAM, Testament of

A Jewish apocryphal work, written probably in the first century in Hebrew of Aramaic and now extant only in two Greek versions of different length. The work is a mythical story built around Abraham's death. Abraham refuses to surrender his soul in death to the Archngel Michael, requesting a vision of all creation before he dies.

When in the vision he sees the earth filled with sin, he curses the sinners, who expire at his word. Abraham, also sees souls in judgment and succeeds by his prayers in effecting a favorable verdict upon those whose guilt is balanced by their good works.

ABRAHAMITES

An 18th century sect, also called Israelites. They were mostly peasants of Jewish and Protestant background in the vicinity of Pardubice near Prague. Their name came from their claim to be followers of the patriarch Abraham. While denying all Christian teachings, they made use of baptism and Christian wedding services to avoid legal reprisals.

ABRANAVEL, Isaac

(1437-1508) Jewish theologian and statesman. Born in Lisbon, he served King Alfonso V of Portugal in state and financial matters. Forced after the King's death to flee to Spain, he was employed by Ferdinand and Isabella until the Jews were expelled from Spain in 1492. He then lived in various Italian cities, eventually becoming a minister of state in Venice, where he died. He is best known for his extensive commentaries on the Bible.

ABRONAH

In Judaism, the site of one of the encampments of the Israelites on their wilderness trek from Egypt (Numbers 33:34-35).

ABSALOM

(circa 1020 BC) Third and favorite son of David, king of Israel and Judah. He is first mentioned as murdering his half brother Amnon, David's eldest son, in revenge for the rape of his full sister Tamar (2 Samuel 13:28-29). For this deed he was driven into banishment, but he was eventually restored to favor through the good offices of Joab. Later Absalom organized a revolt. For a time he seemed to be completely successful; David, with a few followers and his personal guard, fled across the Jordan, leaving to Absalom Jerusalem and the main portion of the kingdom. The usurper pursued the fugitives with his forces but was completely defeated in "the forest of Ephraim" and killed by Joab, who found him caught by the hair in an oak tree. His body was casted into a pit instead of having a royal burial (2 Samuel 18:17).

ABSALOM'S MONUMENT

A pillar erected by Absalom in the "Low Plain of the King," near Jerusalem (2 Samuel 18:18; Genesis 14:17). The monument was erected by him due to his having no sons to keep his name alive after his death. It thus appears that his three sons mentioned at 2 Samuel 14:27 had died when young. Absalom was not buried at the place of his monument but was left in a hollow in the forest of Ephraim (2 Samuel 18:6, 17).

ABSALON
(1128-1201) Archbishop, statesman, and close adviser of the Danish kings Valdemar I and Canute I. He helped consolidate the Danish monarchy and establish its independence from the Holy Roman Empire.

ABSOLUTION
In the Roman Catholic Church and some other churches, remission of sins by a priest in favor of a penitent.

In keeping with their doctrines of the ministry and of the sacraments, other Christian traditions have confined absolution to prayers for forgiveness and the announcement of God's willingness to forgive all those who truly repent of their sins. Absolution, therefore, is neither act nor a means by which the forgiveness of sins is conferred but is, instead, a statement of divine judgment and divine forgiveness.

ABSOLUTION, Conditional
The conferral of absolution in the sacrament of penance with the proviso that it is intended to be effective only if some specified condition, necessary to the reception of the sacrament, is verified in fact.

ABSOLUTION, General
A term used to indicate both the sacramental forgiveness granted to a group of penitents without private auricular confession and the apostolic blessing given to those in danger of death. In the first sense the term has been extended to include an absolution granted in a penitential service to the group of penitents who participate in it.

ABSOLUTION OF THE DEAD
A name given to the liturgical prayers for the dead that include petitions that the deceased may be absolved, freed by God from his or her sins. In the Roman rite such prayers for the dead are recited at the coffin or catafalque after a requiem Mass.

ABSTINENCE
In Catholic teaching, abstinence is a penitential practice of doing without (abstaining from) meat or another food or drink. According to the Code of Canon Law, "Abstinence from eating meat or another food according to the prescription of the conference of bishops is to be observed on Fridays throughout the year unless they are solemnities" and also on Ash Wednesday and Good Friday.

The National Conference of Catholic Bishops is also entitled "to determine more precisely the observance of fast and abstinence and to substitute in whole or in part for fast and abstinence other forms of penance, especially works of charity and exercises of piety".

ABU, Mount
A mountain of granite peaks in South Rajasthan, India, for 2000 years a place of pilgrimage to elaborate sculptured Jain shrines, temples and tombs, as mentioned in Mahabharata.

ABU BAKR
(circa 573-634) First Muslim caliph of Arabia in 632, following Mohammed;s death. He ordered incursions into Syria and Iraq, thus beginning the Muslim conquests. He was Mohammed's closest companion and adviser.

ABU HANIFA
(699-767) Muslim theologian whose well-defined and farsighted systematization of Islamic legal doctrine was acknowledged as one of the four canonical Islamic schools of law.

ABULAFIA, Abraham ben Samuel
(circa 1240-1291) Messianic Jewish leader and initiator of "prophetic Kabbala" in teaching that the spirit of prophecy can be acquired through contemplation of the Hebrew alphabet.

ABULAFIA, Meir

Castilian Talmudist, who initiated a prolonged controversy within Judaism by repudiating such teachings of Maimonides as that on resurrection.

ABU'L BARAKAT

(1267-1324) Coptic priest and writer in Cairo. He collaborated on a history of Islam, and among his independent works were a Coptic-Arabic dictionary and a theological encyclopedia for the instruction of priests and laity.

ABUNDANTIA

Roman goddess, the personification of prosperity and good fortune. She appeared holding a horn of plenty and distributing grain or money or, in the aspect of Annona or Felicitas, almost exclusively on the coins, as representative of the personal power of the Roman emperor to induce prosperity.

ABU SIMBEL

Site of two temples of Ramses II (circa 1250 BC) in the Aswan governate of Egypt (ancient Nubia), hewn in sandstone cliffs on the west bank of the Nile. Recessed to form facade are four, seated colossi of the king (64 feet high). They were dedicated to the sun gods and so oriented to the east, the morning sun penetrating 185 feet through the great halls to the innermost sanctuary.
In 1968 the seated colossi were cut out of the rock face and precisely reconstructed on a cliff 200 feet above the river bed.

ACACIANS

A moderate Arian sect, also called homoeans, that stemmed from Acacius, bishop of Caesarea in Palestine (340-366). They held that the Son was not consubstantial with, but merely similar to, the eternal Father.

ACACIAN SCHISM

(484-519) Split between the patriarchate of Constantinople and the Roman See, occasioned by the issuance of an edict by the emperor Zeno and the patriarch Acacius which was considered inadmissible by Pope Felix III. The edict omitted reference to two natures of Christ (human and divine) and thus appeared to deviate from the canons of the Council of Chalcedon (451) against the Monophysite heresy (that Christ has only one nature, in which the human had become wholly divine).

ACALA

In Buddhism, the immovable; a stage in the Bodhisattva's career.

ACCESSION

A term used in law and moral theology to signify a special mode of acquiring ownership, namely by addition to property already owned through growth, increase, or labor.

ACCO

Coastal city of Palestine, the medieval Acre, the modern Akka. In the Bible Acco is mentioned in Judges 1:31; elsewhere it is referred to as Ptolemais; the name was received under Ptolemy II Philadelphus (285-246 BC).

ACCULTURATION

The process of socialization which happens when members of diverse cultures come into continuous firsthand contact with the consequences that each culture influences the other and cultural changes take place.
Acculturation is one of the ways in which worship is adapted through accommodation, that is, by making adjustments in the liturgy without necessarily referring to the culture of a people.
Acculturation is also an introductory process in which worship is adapted to a specific culture in an external or a partial way while respecting the singular character of the Roman liturgy. The term also refers to the efforts of missionaries to learn the language and to adapt the customs of a society in order to be more effective in the communication of the faith.

ACEDIA

Spiritual sloth, which is characterized by laziness or indifference in religious matters.

ACHAICUS

In the New Testament, one of the matureassociates of the Corinthian congregation, who, together with Stephanas and Fortunatus, visited Paul while he was at Ephesus (1 Corinthians 16:17-18).

ACHAN

In the Old Testament, the son of Carmi of the household of Zabdi of the family of Zerah of the tribe of Judah. When the Israelites crossed the Jordan, God explicitly commanded that the first-fruits of the conquest, the city of Jericho, "must become a thing devoted to destruction .... it belongs to Jehovah" (Joshua 6:17-19). Achan, however, upon finding a costly garment from Shinar and some money, secretly buried them beneath his tent (Joshua 7:21). Actually he had robbed God. Later he admitted his sin and was executed. He and his family and livestock were first stoned to death, and then burned with fire, together with all his possessions, in the valley of Achor.

ACHERON

A river in Thesprotia, upper Epirus, which, according to legend, with its murky gorges and underground channels, was a waterway to Hades and a likely location for the oracle of the dead mentioned by Herodotos.

ACHILLES

Legendary Greek warrior of the Trojan War, celebrated by Homer. He was dipped in the River Styx by his mother Thetis and made invulnerable except at the point of his heel by which she had held him.

Joining in the Greek attack on Troy, he killed many men including Hector. Achilles was himself killed when the god Apollo guided an arrow from the Trojan Prince Paris into his heel.

ACHIM

In the Old Testament, a royal descendant of David through Solomon and an ancestor of Joseph the foster father of Jesus (Matthew 1:14).

ACHISH

In the Old Testament, a Philistine king of Gath who reigned during the time of David and Solomon. When David became king and warred against Gath Achish apparently was not killed, but lived into Solomon's reign (1 Kings 2:39-41).

ACHOR

In Judaism, a valley or low plain forming part of the north-eastern boundary of the tribal territory of Judah (Joshua 15:7). The valley's name, meaning "trouble," resulted from its being the place where Achan and his household were stoned to death. Achan, by his stealing and hiding booty from the capture of Jericho, had brought trouble on the nation of Israel, including defeat at the first attack on Ai (Joshua 7:5-26).

ACHSAH

In the Old Testament, the daughter of the Judean spy Caleb whom he offered in marriage as a prize to whoever captured the stronghold of Debir in Judah's newly acquired territory. Caleb's nephew Othniel, who evidently became the first judge after Joshua (Judges 3:9-10), captured it and, as a reward, married his cousin Achsah.

ACINTYA

In Buddhism, the inconceivable; beyond the power of mentation.

ACOLYTE

In Roman Catholicism, the office, ministry, or order of clerics who assist at the altar and at other liturgical functions. Since Vatican Council II it designates the ministry into which men are instituted on a permanent or transitory manner to assist the celebrant at Mass and to distribute Holy Communion when necessity dictates.

The term is also commonly used to designate any layman who serves Mass or who assists at other Church services. In this latter capacity, the acolyte's role consists of lighting and carrying candles in the procession and in ministering wine and water at Mass.

ACOSMISM

Philosophical germ denoting the view that God is the sole and ultimate reality and that finite objects and events have no independent existence. Acosmism has been equated with pantheism, the belief that everything is God. Acosmism has also been used to describe the philosophies of Hindu, Vedanta, and Buddhism.

ACOSTA, Uriel

(1585-1640) Freethinking rationalist who became a prototype among Jews of one martyred by the intolerance of his own religious community. He is sometimes cited as a forerunner of the renowned philosopher Benedict Spinoza.

ACROSTIC

An arrangement of words, lines, or verses in which letters or syllables occurring in certain key positions make up, when taken together, a word, name, phrase, or alphabetical sequence. Many examples are found in classical antiquity, and the device is used also in the Bible (for example, in the Alphabetic Psalms).

ACT

A term widely used in scholastic theology and philosophy. From the sense in which it is understood as the operation or activity of a being, or organ, or faculty, it came to signify the being, the perfection, or realization, or fulfillment of a thing.

Thus the act of existence is limited by the essence that it actuates. Such is the Thomastic ontology that postulated a real distinction between essence (passive potency) and existence (act). God, who is pure (unlimited) act, has in himself no element of potentially whatever,

but all creatures are composed of potency and an act of existence limited by that potency.

ACT, First

A term with three meanings in scholastic theology and philosophy.

▲ It is the completely underivative act that is the absolutely independent principle of its own actuality and at the same time gives actuality to all else that is. In this sense the first act is God, who is also called pure act inasmuch as actuality in Him is unmixed with potentiality of any kind.

▲ Philosophical usage also styles as first act an essence or form that itself is actuated by an essenww (or act of existence).

▲ Finally, the term is applied to an agent who is in being (first act) prior to its operation (end act).

ACT OF SUPREMACY

In England the law enacted by Parliament in 1534 under Henry VIII, renewed (it had been repealed by Mary Tudor) and revised in 1559 under Elizabeth I, constituting the reigning sovereign earthly head of the Church of England.

ACTION MASS

Recent term to designate Mass in which the forms for the congregation's active participation would be extensive. These forms usually stress spontaneity and improvisation, for example, dialogue sermons, dancing, newspaper readings, and are sometimes contrary to official liturgical legislation.

ACTIVE ORDERS

Religious orders or congregations whose purpose and daily life entail external activities, especially the temporal and spiritual works of mercy, such as the pastoral ministry, teaching, nursing, and social work.

These orders are often contrasted with contemplative orders and sometimes with mixed orders which unite the active and contemplative life.

Thomas Aquinas maintains that the

highest form of spirituality is "the active life which flows from the fullness of contemplation."

ACTON, Lord

(1834-1902, John Emerich Edward Dalberg Acton) Historian, moralist, and philosopher who became a major proponent of the Christian liberal ethic in England.

After entering into a dispute with Pope Pius IX over the relation of historical studies to church doctrine, he felt that limitations were being placed on the intellectual independence of his journal*Home and Foreign Review*and resigned as its editor. Continuing to advocate his theory of liberalism based on Christianity, he profoundly influenced British politics, particularly through his friend Gladstone, who not only adopted some of Acton's political suggestions, but also recommended that he be raised to peerage (1869).

ACTS

Fifth book of the New Testament, a unique history of the early Christian Church. Written in Greek between 53 and 61 by the evangelist Luke, it is a continuation of Luke's gospel (Acts 1:1-2) and deals mainly with the deeds of the apostles Peter and Paul. Events described include the descent of the Holy Spirit at Pentecost, Stephen's martyrdom, Paul's conversion and journeys. Luke pursues, as a central theme, the spread of Christianity to the Gentile world under the guiding inspiration of the Holy Spirit. The missionary journeys of Paul are given a prominent place, because this close associate of Luke was the pre-eminent apostle to the Gentiles.

The book covers a period of approximately 28 years, from Jesus's ascension to the end of the second year of Paul's imprisonment in Rome circa AD 61. During this period four emperors ruled in succession: Tiberius, Caligula, Claudius and Nero. Since it relates events down to the year 61 it could not have been completed earlier. Had the account been written later than 61, it is reasonable to expect that Luke would have provided more information about Paul; if written after 64, mention surely would have been made of Nero's violent persecution that began then.

The writer Luke accompanied Paul much of the time during his travels, including the perilous voyage to Rome, which is apparent from his use of the first-person plural pronouns "we," "us," and "our" in Acts 16:10-17; 20:5-15; 21:1-37; 28:1-6. Paul, in his letters written from Rome, mentions that Luke was also there.

As already observed, Luke himself was an eyewitness to much of what he wrote, and in his travels he contacted fellow Christians who either participated in or observed certain events described.

ACTS, Apocryphal

Body of early Christian writings not accepted into the New Testament canon, on the lives of the Apostles and their companions.

ACTS, Human

Saint Thomas Aquinas says: "Those acts are called human of which a person is master, and he is master of his actions in virtue of his reason and his will." Actions of human beings are human acts when the person does them deliberately, that is, when the agent is master. An act may be performed less voluntarily when ignorance, passionate desire, or fear are present.

ACTS OF THE APOSTLES

Book of the New Testament, written by the evangelist Luke in 70 to 75. It describes the faith and way of life of the early Christians and the origin and spread of Christian communities circa 30 to 67, but the author is not as much concerned with historical details as he is with the action of God in history, especially through the preaching of the Apostles. He is also concerned with the Church as a human organism compelled to adapt itself to actual circumstances in order to carry out its mission to other places and cultures.

ACTS OF THE MARTYRS

A rather large body of Christian literature composed between the second and
seventh centuries describing the trials
and executions of the early Christians
for their faith. The Acts may be conveniently divided into three different categories:

▲ The Acts proper, transcriptions of the
official court record of a martyr's trial,
usually with the addition of an introduction and conclusion so that the
account could be read at a liturgical
function.

▲ The written reports of eyewitnesses of
a martyr's arrest, trial, and execution.

▲ Legends composed long after a martyr's death for the edification of the
faithful and into which a great deal of
fiction is mingled with a few, even very
few facts.

ACTS OF UNIFORMITY

Successive revisions of the Book of
Common Prayer were accompanied by
Acts of Uniformity requiring conformity to its prescribed rites. The first such
act was adopted in 1549, making the
new Prayer Book mandatory in all religious services.

ACTUALISM

A tendency among certain theologians
to stress the gracious activity of God
toward man to the neglect of any created effect of such activity. It is rather an
attitude than a body of doctrine.

Two facts are to be considered in every
phase of God's activity toward man.
There is God's gracious activity, which
is uncreated grace, and there is the
effect of that activity, which is a created thing, transient or permanent, produced in man himself, more commonly
designated by the term grace.

The gracious activity of God toward
man may be described as event, insofar
as it is a transient activity, but it can not
be adequately understood without
some effect, transient or enduring,
resulting from it in man. This effect is
what is known among Catholic theologians as created grace.

The created effect resulting in man
from God's gracious activity, and
which is improperly called grace, is
neglected by actualism, which distrusts
the Catholic notion of sanctifying grace
as a continuing possession of the justified person.

It sees in this concept only the projection of an abstract mental image in the
place of God. Actualism regards the
religious relationship between God and
man to be always an event, an
encounter between God and man.

AD

Anno Domini, Latin for "the year of
our Lord." The monk Dionysius
Exiguus started a system of reckoning
years in 532, using the year in which
he believed Christ was born as the
beginning of the Christian era. AD
refers to the events that took place after
the birth of Christ and BC (before
Christ) refers to the events that took
place before his birth.

ADA, SCHOOL OF

One of the two chief stylistically
opposed schools producing illuminated
manuscripts which were the finest
achievements of the Carolingian
Renaissance. Themes include figures
of the evangelists, royal portraits, historical initials and ornamental borders
in classical style modified by Celtic
and Near Eastern influences.

ADAD

Great weather god of the Babylonian
and Assyrian pantheon, known to the
Sumerians as Ishkur and to the
Canaanites and Aramaeans as Addu, or
Haddad. The name Adad may have
been brought into Mesopotamia toward
the end of the 3rd millennium BC by
Western Semites.

ADADAH

In the Old Testament, one of the cities
in the southern part of the territory
originally assigned to Judah, lying
toward the border of Edom (Joshua
15:22).

ADAH

In Judaism, the first of Lamech's two living wives. She was the mother of Jabal and Jubal, the founders of nomadic herdsmen and musicians respectively (Genesis 6:19-23).

ADAIAH

A descendant of Levi's son Gershom and an ancestor of Asaph (1 Chronicles 6:39-43).

ADALBERT

(circa 1000-1072) German archbishop, the most brilliant of the medieval prince bishops, and a leading member of the royal administration.King Henry IV granted him extensive powers in Saxony in 1063, but was obliged to dismiss him as royal adviser in 1066 because of the protests of the nobility.

ADALBERT, Saint

(956-997) First bishop of Prague of Czech origin. He promoted the political aims of Bolesav II, prince of Bohemia from 929 to 967, by extending the influence of the church beyond the borders of the Czech kingdom. He tried to improve the standards of church life but found little understanding among his countrymen for his lofty ideals.

ADAM

In Christianity and Judaism, first man and father of the human race. Genesis tells how God made Adam (Hebrew for "man") from adamah (Hebrew for "dust") and Adam's wife Eve from one of his ribs (Genesis 2:21-22). The tale of their temptation, fall and expulsion from Paradise is the basis of such concepts as grace, sin and divine retribution. When creation of man took place is an open question. Paul sees Adam as a forerunner of Christ (Romans 5:12). As Adam initiated the life of man upon earth, so Christ initiates the new life of man. Because of the sin of Adam, death came upon all men; because of the righteousness of Christ, life is given to all men.

After sinner Adam's expulsion from Eden he lived to see murder, murder of his own son, banishment of his killerson, abuse of the marriage arrangement and profanation of God's sacred name. He witnessed the building of a city, the development of musical instruments, and the forging of tools out of iron and copper. He watched and was condemned by the example of Enoch, "the seventh man in line from Adam," one who "kept walking with the true God." He even lived to see Noah's father Lamech of the ninth generation. (Genesis 4:8-26; 5:5-24; Jude 14).

In Islam, Adam is referred to as the first prophet and God's khalifa on earth. After Adam's creation, God ordered the angels to bow down to Adam; all obeyed except Iblis. Adam and Eve were tempted by Iblis in the garden where they tasted the tree and were therefore sent down to each by God. Arabic literature and legend have considerably elaborated the basic Koran portrait of Adam. He also has a special role in the cosmology of the Ismailis, being the first of the seven natiqs. For all Muslims throughout history Adam has had a special significance and symbolism.

ADAM AND EVE, Life of

Most of the numerous versions of the life of Adam and Eve are early Christian in origin, but one in particular,*Vita Adae et Evae,* is a Latin translation of a Greek story that may in turn be based on a Hebrew original, and is in any case of Jewish provenance.

It is closely paralleled by, and indeed in large sections virtually identical with, another Jewish apocryphal work, the inappropriately named*Apocalypse of Moses,* though each of the two contains some material not included in the other. The*Life of Adam*and *Ev* e in particular alludes to the Temple of Herod as still standing, and this, together with certain other factors, suggests that is was written between 20 BC and AD 70.

ADAMITES

A Christian sect of the second century mentioned by Epiphanus and Augustine. Its members attended their religious assemblies in the nude. Sects with similar beliefs and practices appeared in later times in France and Bohemia.

ADAMNAN, Saint

(circa 628-704) Abbot and scholar, particularly noted as the biographer of St. Columba. In 679 he was elected abbot of Iona, the ninth in succession from St. Columba, the founder.

ADAPTATION, Liturgical

The process whereby the liturgy as worship is adjusted to the cultural requirements of different times and places. Liturgical adaptation can be general, adapting the liturgical norms of the universal church to a new cultural era: or particular, making the adjustments required within a particular racial or national setting; or individual, accommodating a specific liturgical celebration to the immediate cultural demands peculiar to the assembled group.

ADAPTATION, Religious

The adjustment made by religious communities to adapt their manner of living, praying, and working to contemporary cultural, social, and economical circumstances and the requirements of their apostolate.

The term should be distinguished from religious renewal: adaptation is concerned with changes demanded by contemporary needs and outward circumstances; renewal refers to the continued interior conversion to Christ, which forms the basis of any exterior modification.

ADAR

The post-exilic name of the twelfth Jewish lunar month of the sacred calendar, but the sixth of the secular calendar (Esther 3:7). It corresponds to part of February and part of March.

Adar is the month in which Governor Zerubbabel finished the reconstruction of the Temple in Jerusalem (Ezra 6:15).

ADBEEL

In Judaism, grandson of Abraham, listed third among the twelve sons of Ishmael, his mother being an Egyptian. He was the chieftain of a tribal clan bearing his name (Genesis 21:21; 25:13-16; 1 Chronicles 1:29).

ADDAI AND MARI, Liturgy of

The customary rite of the Church of the East, or the Nestorian Church; it was the only liturgy of the church before the reform of Mar Aba I (540-552). who is thought to have introduced the Anaphora (the central portion of the eucharistic rite) of Theodore of Mopsuestia and Nestorius to his church. No manuscript of the this rite antedating the 10th-11th century has survived.

ADDI

In the Old Testament, the son of Cosam and father of Melchi. As a descendant of David through Nathan, Addi was an ancestor of Jesus (Luke 3:28, 31).

ADEODATUS

(372-389) Son of St. Augustine and the woman which whom he lived before his conversion., Baptized with Augustine and Alypius at Milan, Adeodatus gave promise of a brilliant future, but died shortly after his return with Augustine to Africa.

ADHAN

In Islam, to call to prayer. This is made five times a day to the Muslim faithful. The call consists of seven main parts, with some variation in the number of repetitions of each part according to madhlab. There are also slight differences between the calls to prayer of the Sunnis and the Shiites. The adhan may be chanted to many different tunes and considerable variations will be heard from city to city and country to country.

ADIAPHORISM

In Christian theology, the opinion that certain doctrines or practices in morals or religion are matters of indifference because they are neither commended nor forbidden in the Bible.

ADI-BUDDHA

In Buddhism, the primordial Buddha of Tibetan Buddhism; the self-existent, unoriginated source of Universal Mind. Its creative power is symbolized in the form of five Dhyani Buddhas, whose active aspects are personified under the Dhyani Bodhisattvas, these in turn being represented on earth as the Manushi or human Buddhas of the Seven Root Races of humanity.

ADI GRANTH

The sacred scripture of the Sikhs, a religious group in India. The book (also known as Granth, or Granth Sahib) is a collection of nearly 6,000 hymns of the Sikh Gurus (religious leaders) and various early and medieval saints of different religions and castes.

The Adi Granth is the central object of worship in all gurdwaras (Sikh houses of worship) and is accorded the reverence paid a living Guru. It is ritually opened in the morning and wrapped up and put away for the night. On special occasions continuous readings of it are held, which last from 2 to 15 days. On the birthdays of the Gurus or anniversaries commemorating Sikh martyrs, the Adi Granth is sometimes taken out in procession.

ADIN

In Judaism, one of the paternal heads of Israel, several hundred of whose descendants returned from Babylonian exile with Zerubbabel (Ezra 2:15). A princely representative of Adin's paternal house was among those who attested to the "trustworthy arrangement" drawn up in the days of Nehemiah (Nehemiah 9:38; 10:1, 16).

ADITI

In the Vedic phase of Hindu mythology, the personification of the infinite, and the mother of a group of celestial deities, the Adityas. As a primeval goddess, she is referred to as the mother of many gods.

ADITYAS

A group of Vedic gods of uncertain number and identity. Varuna is their chief, and they are called like him "Upholders of divine order."

ADIYAT, al-

The title of the 100th sura of the Koran; it means here "The War Horses" or "Chargers." The sura belongs to the Meccan period and contains 11 verses. The title is drawn from the first verse which contains an oath "By the war horses" and which, with the succeeding four verses, evokes the early Arabs' predilection for raiding each other. Man is also reminded that he will be resurrected and judged on the Day of Judgment.

ADJURATION

A solemn command using the authority of the divine or some holy person or thing. As an oath or vow binds him or her who takes it, and an obsecration pleads with a superior, adjuration takes the divine name to command a subject.

ADLAI

In Judaism, father of Shaphat, who served as overseer of the herds of David in the low plains (1 Chronicles 27:29).

ADLOYADA

Term belonging to the Jewish Purim vocabulary. There is a Talmudic saying that one should drink merrily on Purim, until one is so tipsy that one knows not (ad d'lo yada) the difference between Barukh Mordecai ("blessed be Mordecai") and Arur Haman ("cursed the Haman"). This expression has given the name to the annual Adloyada Purim Carnival in Tel Aviv, a gala affair, complete with floats, streamers, costumes and balloons.

ADMONT, Abbey of

Benedictine foundation in Stria, diocese of Graz-Seckau, mentioned in a document of 859. It reached its peak under abbots Gottfried and Irimbert (1138-77) with a scriptorium famous for illumination. After plunderings by Protestants, Turks, Bonapartists, and Nazis, Admont started rebuilding (1945) and restoring its art treasures.

ADNA

In Judaism, an Israelite, descendant of the paternal house of Pahath-moab, who agreed to send his non-Israelite wife away during the cleansing that took place following the counsel of Ezra the priest (Ezra 10:30).

ADON

In Judaism, Hebrew word carrying the thought of ownership or headship. It is used of God and of men, in that both own or are head of others. The word is used in referring to kings (1 Samuel 26:17), government officials (Genesis 45:9), owners of slaves (Genesis 39:2), husbands (Genesis 18:12), and fathers (Genesis 31:35).

ADONAI

Several centuries before the Christian era Jews, out of reverence for the name for God, stopped pronouncing the name of Yahweh and substituted the Old Testament term for God, meaning "Lord" or "my Lord" in its place.

ADONIJAH

In the Old Testament, David's fourth son, born of Haggith in Hebron (2 Samuel 3:4). Though of a different mother, Adonijah was quite similar to Absalom in being "very good-looking in form" and in his ambition (1 Kings 1:5-6). He becomes prominent in the Bible record during David's waning years.

ADONIKAM

In the Old Testament, a founder of one of the paternal houses of Israel. More than 600 members of this family returned to Jerusalem with Zerubbabel after the exile at Babylon (Ezra 2:13; Nehemiah 7:18). An additional 63 members of this paternal house accompanied Ezra to Jerusalem in 468 BC (Ezra 8:13).

ADONIS

In Greek mythology, the handsome youth of Aphrodite the goddess of sensual love. The name "Adonis," however, is derived from the Semitic word "a-dohn," "lord," indicating that his worship did not originate in Greece. This deity has commonly been identified with the Babylonian Tammuz, and it is believed that the worship of Adonis was adopted by the Greeks from the Semites of Syria and Babylonia as early as the seventh century BC.

Various mythological accounts tell of the violent death of Adonis and his return to life. These myths are generally interpreted as representing the death of vegetation in winter and its return to life in the spring.

ADONI-ZEDEK

In the Old Testament, a king of Jerusalem at the time of the Israelite conquest of the Promised Land, who joined with other petty kingdoms west of the Jordan in a consolidated effort to halt Joshua's conquering forces (Joshua 9:1-3).

ADOPTING ACT

A provision in 1729 by Presbyterian clergy at Philadelphia that every entering clergyman or candidate for the ministry should declare the Westminster Confession and the Westminster catechism to be "in all the essential and necessary articles, good forms of sound words and systems of Christian doctrine."

ADOPTION, Supernatural

The assumption of man into divine sonship. Man was created in the image and likeness of God. The fathers of the Church see God reflected especially in human reason, freedom, and creativity. The divine Logos is the pattern by which man was fashioned.

When man is divinized through grace by the surrendering of himself in faith and charity to God's special offer of personal love, he becomes in the fullest sense a replica of the Logos-made man.

ADOPTIONISM

Two Christian heresies; one developed in the second and third centuries and is also known as Dynamic Monarchianism; the other began in the 8th century in Spain and was concerned with the teaching of Elipandus, archbishop of Toledo.

Wishing to distinguish in Christ the operations of each of his natures, human and divine, Elipandus referred to Christ in his humanity as "adopted son" in contradistinction to Christ in his divinity, who is the Son of God by nature. The son of Mary, assumed by the Word, thus was not the Son of God by nature but only by adoption.

Opposition to this view of Christ was expressed, which led Pope Adrian I to intervene and condemn the teaching. Elipandus gained the support of Felix, bishop of Urgel, who eventually engaged in a literary duel with Alcuin of York over the doctrine.

ADORATION

Act whereby man acknowledges God's supreme perfection and domination. Adoration is a conscious act of an intelligent creature by which God alone - infinitely perfect and having supreme domination over nature - is recognized as worthy of supreme worship. Adoration is essentially an act of the mind and will, but is commonly expressed in external acts of sacrifice, prayer, and reverence.

ADORATION OF THE CROSS

In Roman Catholicism, a term with a liturgical and theological significance: liturgically, it refers to a section of the Good Friday services in the Latin rite in which the cross is venerated, or a similar service in some Eastern Churches; theologically, it applies to the homage which Christians have given to relics or images of the cross.

ADORATION OF THE MAGI

A theme in Christian art illustrating the visit to the infant Christ by the Wise Men from the East, who, guided by a stare, came to worship the Child as king of the Jews, bringing gifts of gold, frank incense, and myrrh. The event is described in the Gospel according to Matthew, and it is one of the oldest and most popular themes in Christian art, first appearing in fresco in Roman catacomb decoration of the 2nd century.

The adoration of the Magi often appeared as part of the Nativity scene in Byzantine Churches, but it was especially important as a separate theme in the West, where, in the Romanesque and Gothic periods, its significance as a primary theophany or manifestation of Christ's divinity, was emphasized.

ADORATION OF THE SHEPHERDS

A theme in Christian art depicting shepherds paying homage to the newborn Christ, an event described in the Gospel according to Luke. It is related to the older but less frequently represented annunciation to the shepherds, which shows the same shepherds in the fields receiving from an angel news of the miraculous birth.

The adoration of the shepherds was never treated as a separate theme in the East, and in the West not until the 15th century. At first, in early Christian art in the 4th century, one or more shepherds were included in scenes of the adoration of the Magi, the Wise Men who came from the East to worship the Child.

They were depicted in such scenes because, as the first local people to worship Christ, they symbolize the spreading of Christianity among the Jews, just as the Magi, the first of the Gentiles to see and worship the Child, symbolize the spread of Christianity throughout the pagan world. In early Christian and Byzantine art the annunciation to the shepherds and the shepherds adoring the Child were frequently among the several themes included in the scene of the Nativity.

ADRAMMELECH

A god worshiped by the Sepharvites, one of the subjugated peoples the king of Assyria brought into the territory of Samaria after his taking the Israelites of the ten-tribe kingdom into exile. It was to Adrammelech and Anammelech that the Sepharvites sacrificed their sons in the fire (2 Kings 17:22-24).

ADRIAN I

(718-795)Pope from 772 to 795, who symbolized the medieval ideal of union of church and state in a united Christendom. He strongly opposed adoptionism (dual sonship of Christ), resulting in his condemnation of the teachings of Archbishop Elipandus of Toledo, Spain.

ADRIAN II

(792-872) Pope from 867 to 872. Under his predecessor St. Nicholas I, the papacy had reached a high point that Adrian could not maintain.

ADRIAN III

(809-885) Pope from 884 to 885. His brief pontificate came during troubled times. He died en route to the Diet of Worms after being summoned by the Frankish King Charles II to settle the succession to the empire and discuss the rising Saracen power.

ADRIAN IV

(1100-1159) The only Englishman to occupy the papal throne (1154-59). He crowned Frederick Barbarossa as Holy Roman Emperor in 1155, after Frederick had captured and handed over to him Arnold of Brescia, who had led a revolt in Rome.

ADRIAN V

(1194-1276) Pope for about five weeks in 1276. Elected a successor to Innocent V on July 11, he died a little more than a month later.

ADRIAN VI

(Adrian Florensz Boeyens; 1459-1523) The only Dutch pope from 1522 to 1523. He took up the task of reforming the church with great earnestness, beginning with the curia. An excellent but misunderstood pontiff, his reign was so brief that his real accomplishments seem disappointing.

ADRIEL

In the Old Testament, the son of Barzillai, who was given Saul's oldest daughter Merab as wife, though she had previously been promised to David (1 Samuel 18:17-19).All five of Adriel's sons were later surrendered for execution to help atone for Saul's attempted annihilation of the Gibeonites (2 Samuel 21:8, 9).

ADULLAM

A town south-west of Jerusalem. The earliest reference to Adullam is in the book of Genesis, which tells of the activities of Judah, son of Jacob, in the area. After the exodus from Egypt and the Israelite conquest, Adullam was assigned to the tribe of Judah. It is most famous for its cave in which David hid from Saul (1 Samuel 22:1).

ADULTERY

Sexual relations by a married person with someone other than the spouse. Prohibitions or taboos against adultery, written or customary, constitute part of the marriage code of virtually every society.

ADVAITA

Hindu term meaning non-dual, not two. The Indian doctrine taught by Sankara of a non-duality beyond the pairs of opposites which is more than One, One being only the opposite of many.

ADVENA

A term used in Roman Catholic canon law in its classification of the different statuses of persons in a place with reference to local ecclesiastical jurisdiction. An advena has not yet acquired stable local residence (domicile), but is more stably located than a peregrinus (a visitor who has residence elsewhere) or a vagus (a visitor who has residence nowhere).

ADVENT

From Latin adventus, "coming," a period of preparation for the celebration of the birth of Jesus Christ at Christmas, and also of preparation for the Second Coming of Christ. It begins on the Sunday nearest to November 30 and is the beginning of the church year.

The liturgical readings and prayers place emphasis on the coming (advent, arrival) of Jesus Christ. The first part of the advent highlights his Second Coming at the end of time, and the second part (notably December 17-24) his coming into human history at the time of his birth in Bethlehem. This liturgical season features joy, hope, repentance, expectation, and preparation for the coming of Christ.

ADVENT CHRISTIAN CHURCH

Church organized in 1960, one of the several Adventist Churches that evolved from the teachings of William Miller (1782-1849). Doctrinal emphasis is placed on the anticipated Second Coming of Christ and on the Last Judgment, after which the wicked will be destroyed and the chosen will be resurrected to live in a restored paradise on earth.The church merged with other Adventist Churches in the 1960s.

ADVENTISM

The belief that Christ's second coming, or advent, is at hand to inaugurate the millennium in which the wicked will be annihilated and the kingdom of saints established. In this sense chiliasm, apocalypticism, or millenarianism, as seen in Montanists, Anabaptists, Fifth Monarchy Men, Jehovah's Witnesses, and many other bodies, are forms of adventism.

ADVENTISTS

Christian sects, mainly in the United States, who believe in the imminent advent (Second Coming) of Christ. Adventism grew from the teachings of William Miller, who announced the end of the world would come in 1843. After the failure of Miller's predictions new Adventist Churches arose. The largest is the Seventh-day Adventists, formally organized in 1863, its members observe saturdays as the Sabbath and support an extensive missionary program.

ADVENT WREATH

Form of prayer that uses the emotions or feelings in a positive way to lift up de heart to God in words and silent expressions of loving devotion. It is often called prayer of the heart. Many mystics experienced God in profoundly affective ways; and the Psalms and the Song of Songs are examples of affective prayer. Some types of affective prayer are the loving repetition of the words in the Jesus Prayer or the rosary, praying in tongues as in charismatic prayer or a simple quiet opening of the heart to God's loving presence.

AEGINA, Temple of

(500-480 BC) Supreme example of Doric style of the late archaic severe period, dedicated to Athena Aphaia, who according to Pausanias is related to the Cretan goddess Britomaertis. The supreme pedimental sculptures rank in importance with those of the Parthenon and the Temple of Zeus at Olympia.

AELHEAH, Saint

(956-1012) Celebrated archbishop of Canterbury who became popularly venerated as a martyr after his death at the hands of the Danes.

AELIA CAPITOLINA

Name given by the Romans to the city they founded on the site of Jerusalem (and the Second Temple) after its destruction by Roman forces under Titus in 70. The name was given after the Second Jewish revolt (132-135) and honored the emperor Hadrian and the deities of the Capitoline triad (Jupiter, Juno, and Minerva).

AELRED OF RIEVAUX, Saint

(1100-1167) Historian and outstanding Cistercian abbot who influenced monasticism in medieval England, Scotland, and France.

AENEAS

In the New Testament, a man of Lydda, alongside the plains of Sharon, healed by Peter after being paralyzed for eight years (Acts 9:32-35).

AENON

In the Bible, a place having "a great quantity of water" available, where John the Baptist did baptizing following the Passover of 30 (John 3:23). It was near the apparently better known place named Salim. The abundance of water suggests that the candidates for baptism may have been here immersed, as they were at the Jordan.

AEOLUS

Mythological god and ruler of the winds, which he kept confined in a mountain on his island of Aeolia. In an incident in Homer's Odyssey, Aeolus presented Odysseus with a leather sack containing all the evil winds safely tied up, so that he could sail home to Ithaca.

AEON

One of the order of spirits, or spheres of being, that were said to have emanated from the Godhead. The notion was espoused in the 2nd century by Gnostics, early Christian heretics, who emphasized a religious dualism and generally classified matter as evil and spirit as good, and by Persian Manichaeans, whose dualistic view of religion placed body and mind in conflict with each other.

AËRIANS

Followers of Aërus of Pontus (4th century) once a member of a group of ascetics whose leader was Eustathius of Sebaste, onetime disciple of Arius. Aërius became an Arian, stating that bishops and priests are equal; Easter is to be abolished as a Jewish celebration; prayers and alms for the dead are useless; laws of fasting are relics of the Old Law.

AËRIUS

(fourth century) Priest of Pontus, associated in his early life with Eustathius of Sebaste in the practice of asceticism and ordained by him after he had become Bishop of Sebaste. A rift developed between the two when Aërius embittered by frustrated ambition, began denouncing Eustathius for abandonment of ascetical practices. Aërius attracted some followers, but the sect that bore his name did not long survive him.

AETHELBERT I

(540-616) King of Kent who issued the first code extant of Anglo-Saxon laws, a code that established the legal position of the clergy and many secular regulations.

AETOLUS

In Greek mythology, one of the three sons of Endymion. To determine the succession to the throne, Endymion ordered a foot race to the throne at Olympia between his sons Aetolus, Paeon, and Epeius, of whom Epeius won the race and the crown. Aetolus fled to the Peloponnessos, taking refuge in Aetolia, so called after him.

AETOS

In the Byzantine church a name for either a small round or oval rug depicting a walled city with an eagle soaring above it, or the marble slab fixed in the pavement of a Byzantine Church where formerly the throne of the emperor was set up.

The imperial eagle is now used on the seal of the ecumenical patriarch, and in the Greek Orthodox church it is often seen as a decorative motif, sometimes carved over the royal doors of the iconostasis.

AFFECTIVE PRAYER

A type of mental prayer in which a primarily affective relationship with God is elicited. Through confidence, penitence, humility, and love, affective prayer seeks to respond more fully to the living God.

It differs from discursive mental prayer, characterized by a predominance of reasoning and intellectual considerations, and from contemplative prayer in which the sole affection sought is love.

Since the 17th century, spiritual writers have spoken of affective prayer, and it figures strongly in Carmelite and Franciscan spirituality.

AFRAD

In Islam, a technical term in a variety of fields including that of hadith, criticism. It means literally "single (ones)," "unique ones." In the study of the hadith the afrad are those traditions where the second link in the isnad contains no more than a single name of a tabi (one who did not know the Prophet Mohammed directly but knew one of the Prophet's companions. The terms fard/afrad also have technical meanings in such areas as poetry, astronomy and theology.

AFRICA, Early Christian Church

Christianity probably came to Africa from Rome at the end of the first century, but the earliest records are the acts of the Scillitan martyrs (180) and the passion of the Saints Perpetua and Felicity (203).

Tertullian (197-220) said that the population of the cities in parts of northern Africa (modern Tuniesia, Morocco, Algeria) was almost entirely Christian and that even the small towns had bishops. By the time of St. Cyprian, there were over 100 bishops.

In the second and third centuries the African Church was using a Latin version of the Scriptures and of the liturgy, although Greek was still the official language for the Church of Rome.

AFRICAN BROTHERHOOD CHURCH

Independent African Church founded in Kenya in 1945.

AFRICAN CHRISTIANITY

Roman Christianity in northern Africa was largely destroyed by the Islamic invasions. The major survivors are the Monophysite Coptic Churches of Egypt and Ethiopia. Elsewhere in Africa Christianity was largely produced by later missions. In West Africa, apart from Portuguese Roman Catholicism in the 16th century, most work was done in the 19th century, first by Protestants, then byu Roman Catholics. The areas of activity of the two churches generally corresponded to the religion of rival European trading and colonial powers. The same is true of East Africa after exploration by David Livingstone (1813-73). In southern Africa Dutch settlement from the 17th century produced a local Reformed Church as well as missions. There are numerous African Independent Churches of a messianic, pentecostal type mixed with traditional African religion.

AFRICAN GREEK ORTHODOX CHURCH

A religious movement in East Africa that represents a prolonged church for a Christianity more African and, its adherents say, more authentic that the denominational mission forms.

AFRICAN METHODIST EPISCOPAL CHURCH

Black Protestant denomination akin to but separate from white Methodist denominations. Founded in Philadelphia (1815) by the reverend Richard Allen, it is the largest black Methodist body, with circa 6,500 churches and 2,200,000 members.

AFRICAN METHODIST EPISCOPAL ZION CHURCH

Independent Methodist denomination founded in New York City by African Americans disaffected by white prejudices. They built a church in 1800 and formed the denomination in 1821.

AFRICAN MISSIONS, Society of the

A religious society of pontifical right, founded in France (1856) by Bishop Melchior de Marion-Bresilac, for the evangelization of Africa and its native emigrants.

AFRICANUS, Sextus Julius

(180-250) Early Christian historian who contributed a work on chronology that became highly influential in early church history.

AFTERLIFE

Traditionally, the Christian view of man sees his soul as surviving death. At death an interim judgment is made. This distinguishes between worthy souls destined for heaven, and the unworthy consigned to eternal punishment. Roman Catholicism teaches that most saved souls undergo a period of purification in Purgatory, but Protestantism rejects this.

AGABUS

Christian prophet who, together with the other prophets, came down from Jerusalem to Antioch in Syria during the year of Paul's stay there. Agabus foretold through the spirit "that a great famine was about to come upon the entire inhabited world" (Acts 11:27-28). It appears that the brothers in Antioch understood this prophecy as applying to the land of Palestine, since the next verse (Acts 11:29) states that they determined "to send a relief ministration to the brothers dwelling in Judea." As the account states, the prophecy was fulfilled during the reign of Emperor Claudius I (41-54).

AGAG

In the Old Testament, the king of Amalek who was defeated by King Saul in fulfillment of God's decree (Exodus 17:14; Deuteronomy 25:17-19). However, Saul failed to execute Agag and allowed the people to keep some of the spoil, and this resulted in Samuel's pronouncement of God's rejection of Saul as king (1 Samuel 15:8-29). Agag was then executed by Samuel.

AGA KHAN

Spiritual leader of the Ismaili sect of Shiite Muslims, an hereditary title. His millions of followers are dispersed through the Near East, India, Pakistan and parts of Africa and are descended from 14th century Hindus converted by Persian Ismalis. Aga Khan IV, Prince Karim (1936-) inherited the title in 1957.

AGAMAS

A class of Hindu Tantric writings of medieval India that are sacred texts of the Saivites, or followers of the lord Siva. They are often in the form of a dialogue between Siva and his wife Parvati, during which one sets the questions and the other answers them.

AGAMEDES

In Greek mythology, king of Orchimenus in Boeotia. He and his stepbrother Trophonius were skilled constructors of underground shrines and treasure houses.

AGAPE

Common Greek noun ("love") given special significance in the New Testament, in which it is applied both to God's love for mankind, especially through Jesus Christ, and to man's reciprocal love for God, which necessarily extends to the love of one's fellow man.

The term is used as distinct from philia (love between friends) and eros (sexual love). In its charitable sense agape was used to describe a meal held by early Christians to promote fellowship and benefit the poor; it was a prototype of the Eucharist.

This Greek term occurs in the synoptic

Gospels only twice (Matthew 24:12; Luke 11:42). It is used several times in the Gospel of John and in the letters of John and Paul to refer to love, specifically the love of God for us and our love for God and one another.

AGATHA, Saint

(202-251) Early Christian virgin martyred by a consul named Quintian. He forced her into a house of prostitution and then had her subjected to prolonged torture, during which her breasts were cut off, a circumstance reflected in her iconography. Her feast day is February 5th.

AGATHO, Saint

(557-681) Pope from 678-681. He advocated the doctrine of the two wills. The will, Agatho said, is a property of the nature of Christ, and because he has two natures, divine and human, he also has two wills; but the human will determines itself ever comfortably to the divine and almighty will.

AGATI

In Buddhism, the wrong path as distinct from the right path (to enlightenment).

AGDEN, Council of

A council convened at Agden in southern France in 506 under the leadership of Caesarius of Arles and with the endorsement of the Arian Visgoth King Alaric. Its 47 authentic statutes, written by Caesarius, clarified several matters of ecclesiastical discipline, for example, clerical celibacy, obligation of the laity to receive the Eucharist at Christmas, Easter, and Pentecost, and several regulations concerning monastic life.

AGE, Canonical

In the Roman Catholic and Eastern churches rights are recognized and duties are imposed upon their subjects with a view to their moral and physical stage of development.

Hence, for various provisions of law certain different stages are recognized:

▲ infancy, which embraces those who have not completed their 7th age;
▲ the age of reason, which is presumed to be achieved at the completion of infancy;
▲ puberty, which is presumed to be achieved by the female at the age of 12, and by the male at 14;
▲ adulthood, which is attained under the Latin code at 21.

AGE OF REASON

The time of life at which a person is believed to be morally responsible and able to distinguish between right and wrong, normally at about seven years of age.

AGES, Spiritual

Stages identified by spiritual writers in the growth of the soul as it moves onward toward God. These stages are given names by different writers, and sometimes the classification appears based on the practice of virtue, and sometimes upon the type of prayer that is markedly characteristic of, but not the exclusive preoccupation of, each stage.

AGGADAH

Segments of the Talmud containing history, traditions, legends, proverbs and sayings, mathematics, astronomy and psychology. This material is called Aggadah, making up about one-third of the Talmud.

AGGIORNAMENTO

This Italian word for updating was used by Pope John XXIII when summoning the Vatican Council II. Pope John called it "the opening of the window of the Church to let fresh air enter." Aggiornamento has become synonymous with Church renewal and calls for a new openness on the part of the Church toward the world and other religions and to the internal reform and renewal in its liturgical life.

AGILITY

One of the four qualities with which the glorified bodies of the risen just will be endowed, according to scholastic theology's amplification of Paul's doctrine on the risen body (1 Corinthians 156:42-44). It is commonly interpreted as ability to respond with a swift movement and action to the soul's desire.

AGNES, Saint

4th century virgin martyr of the Roman Catholic Church and patron saint of young girls. For refusing to sacrifice to pagan gods she was disgraced, miraculously saved, and martyred. On her feast day, January 21st, the Pope blesses two lambs in the church of St. Agnes; their wool is used to weave palla (items of ceremonial dress) for archbishops.

AGNETS

The Slavonic word for the square piece cut from the round cake of bread at the prosphora or preparation of the liturgy in the Byzantine rite. The cutting symbolizes the sacrifice of the lamb of God.

AGNI

The fire-god of the Hindus, second only to Indra in the Vedic mythology of ancient India. He is equally the fire of the sun, of lightning, and of the hearth that men and women light for purposes of worship. As the divine personification of the fire of sacrifice, he is the mouth of the gods, the carrier of the oblation, and the messenger between the human and the divine orders.

AGNOSTICISM

In Christianity, the doctrine that one cannot know about things beyond the realm of one's experience, in particular about God. Unlike atheism, which is a rejection of divine order, agnosticism is a skeptical holding back of judgment in the absence of proof.

In Buddhism, the doctrine that man can never know the nature of Ultimate Reality. Buddhism differs from agnosticism that it asserts an innate transcendental faculty in man which by elimination of all elements of defilement may contemplate reality and attain perfect knowledge and enlightenment.

Agnosticism admits differences of degree as well as of object. The absence of certitude that characterizes the agnostic may range from having no more than a merely opinionative judgment to a condition of doubt, either just negative or more positive, that stops short of a definite rejection of religious truth.

Agnosticism has several styles. The reverent agnosticism that hesitates before anthropomorphism or cocksureness about divine things is nobly represented by Moses Maimonides, and indeed by the theologia negativa of a high mystical tradition in Christianity.

Then there is the wistful agnosticism of earnest thinkers who would like to believe but cannot honestly bring themselves to do so; they were prominent in the Victorian era, when the term first came to be widely used.

Finally there is the complacent agnosticism of those who do not bother or do not care to make the effort required to find out about eternal truths. Culpability enters, if at all, only with these last; it may be assessed in accordance with the rules governing the influence of ignorance on moral responsibility, as when one is too lazy to discover what is important, or fears to discover it, lest it prove awkward.

AGNUS DEI

Latin: Lamb of God; designation of Jesus Christ in Christian liturgical usage. It is based on the saying of John the Baptist: "Behold, the Lamb of God, who takes away the sin of the world" (John 1:29).

Agnus Dei refers also to a sacramental that consists of a small disc of wax with an imprinted figure of a lamb representing Christ on one side and the coat of arms of the pope on the reverse side.

These discs are solemnly blessed by the pope on the Wednesday of Holy Week during the first and seventh year of this pontificate and are worn by the recipients as a protection against Satan, temptations, sickness, fires, tempests, and sudden death, and for pregnant women to have safe deliveries.

AGOBARD

(769-840) Archbishop of Lyons, who was active during the reign of emperor Louis I the Pious. He also wrote theological and liturgical treatises.

AGONY OF DEATH

The suffering of body and soul that sometimes accompanies one's passage from this life. Real suffering at the time of death is by no means a universal or necessary phenomenon. In others, suffering is often dulled by coma or drugs. In many instances the dying person welcomes release from his physical troubles, and in a few at least he may long to be dissolved and to be with Christ.

AGRAPHA

In Roman Catholicism agrapha designates words of Jesus not recorded in the four canonical Gospels. The New Testament itself refers to such sayings (Acts 20:35; 1 Thessalonians 4:15-17). Other sources include the Codex Bezae, which departs occasionally from the usual gospel text.

The same is true for the apocryphal gospels (especially the gnostic Gospel of Thomas and other related papyri discovered in Egypt); the works of the Church Fathers; the Talmud, and Mohammedan writings. Much of the material is regarded as dependent in some way upon texts found in the canonical Gospels.

AGRICOLA, Johann

(1494-1566) Lutheran Reformer, friend of Martin Luther, and advocate of antinomianism, a view asserting that Christians are freed by grace from the need to obey the Ten Commandments.

AGUNA

In Orthodox and Conservative Judaism, a woman presumed to be widowed but who cannot remarry because evidence of her husband's death does not satisfy legal requirements.

AGUR

In the Old Testament, the son of Jakeh and writer of the 30th chapter of the Book of Proverbs (Proverbs 30:1). He probably lived sometime during the period from Solomon's reign (1037-997 BC) to Hezekiah's reign (745-716 BC).

AHAB

In the Old Testament, 7th king (reigned circa 874-853 BC) of the northern kingdom of Israel and son of King Omri. His wife Jezebel aroused strong opposition, especially from the prophet Elijah, by her worship of the Canaanite god Baal. Ahab built him a temple and an altar in Samaria, and made a grove for the orgies of the goddess Ashtoreth (1 Kings 16:31-33). He was slain in battle, thus fulfilling the prophecy of Elijah (1 Kings 21:19).

AHAD HA'AM

(1856-1927) Hebrew pen name, meaning "one of the people,"of Asher Ginsberg, Russian Hebrew writer and proponent of "spiritual Zionism." Opposed to political Zionism, he believed that a Jewish nation in Palestine was to be achieved through spiritual rebirth.

Born in Russia in 1856, he spent his childhood in a very pious atmosphere. He wanted more than a religious education and began to study Russian and other languages. In the 1880's he wrote an essay called *This is not the Way,* in which he said that pioneers must be trained to face the hardships before they went to Palestine.

He thought of Palestine as a creative center of Jewish writing, music, dance; there, too, the Jewish ideals of righteousness and learning might flourish best. He died in 1927 in Tel Aviv.

AHAMKARA

In Buddhism, the false belief of individuality, that the self contains some immortal and unchanging faculty or soul.

AHA OF SHABBA

Rabbinical scholar whose *She'eltot* ("Book of Problem") was the first attempt to codify and explicate materials contained in the Babylonian Talmud.

AHARAH

In the Old Testament, third son of Benjamin (1 Chronicles 8:1); probably the same as Ehi in Genesis 46:21 and Ahiram in Numbers 26:38.

AHASBAI

In Judaism, a Maacathite whose "son" Eliphelet was an outstanding fighter for David (2 Samuel 23:34).

AHASUERUS

Name of one Mede and two Persian kings mentioned in the Old Testament. The Ahasuerus described in the Book of Esther was probably the Persian King Xerxes, the invader of Greece, who reigned from 486 to 456 BC. He invaded Greece in 480, and is supposed to have married Esther the following year.

AHAVA

The name given to a river or canal located in Babylonia, north-west of Babylon, where Ezra gathered together certain Jews and held a fast during the trek toward Jerusalem (Ezra 8:15, 21, 31).

AHAZ

King of Judah (circa 735-715 BC) who became an Assyrian vassal. Ahaz assumed the throne of Judah at the age of 20 or 25. Sometime later his kingdom was invaded by Pekah, king of Israel and Rezin, king of Syria, in an effort to force him into an alliance with them against the powerful state of Assyria. Acting against the counsel of the prophet Isaiah, Ahaz appealed for aid to Tiglath-pileser III, king of Assyria, to repel the invaders. Assyria defeated Syria and Israel, and Ahaz presented himself as a vassal to the Assyrian king. He sent him the treasures of the temple and of his own palace, and Assyrian gods were introduced into the Temple of Jerusalem.

AHIEZER

In Judaism, son of Ammishaddai and chieftain of the tribe of Dan selected a year after the exodus (Numbers 1:1, 4, 12). In this capacity he assisted Moses with the census, commanded the rearguard three-tribe division when on the march and presented his tribe's offering on the tenth day of the inauguration of the altar at the tabernacle (Numbers 2:25; 7:66, 71).

AHIJA

Prophet who encouraged Jeroboam to rebel against Solomon (1 Kings 11:29-39). A prophet of Shiloh, he encountered Jeroboam outside Jerusalem and told him that because Solomon had worshiped foreign gods 10 tribes would be taken from his son and given to Jeroboam.

Ahija symbolically tore his garment into 12 pieces and gave 10 of them to Jeroboam. Later disappointed with Jeroboam, he predicted the destruction of his house (1 Kings 14).

AHIKAM

In the Old Testament, son of Shaphan the royal secretary during Josiah's reign. Ahikam was one of the five sent to the prophetess Huldah by Josiah to inquire concerning what they had read in the recently Book of the Law (2 Kings 22:12, 14; 2 Chronicles 34:20). Later he protected Jeremiah's life when it was threatened (Jeremiah 26:24).

AHIMELECH

In the Old Testament, son of Ahitub and great-grandson of Eli; High Priest at the tabernacle located at Nob. Having given aid to David, not knowing he was a fugitive from Saul, Ahimelech, eighty-four other priests of God and the men, women and children of Nob were massacred by the Edomite Doeg at Saul's command.

AHIMSA

The fundamental ethical virtue of the Jainas of India, highly respected throughout the centuries by Hindus and Buddhists as well.

In Buddhism, the term is used in the sense of compassion; especially for animals. Both Buddhish and Jain lay great stress on virtue of ashimsa. The first Buddhist precept enjoins negative compassion by not taking life, and the second of Four Sublime Moods inculcates positive compassion for all life.

AHINADAB

In Judaism, one of the 12 deputies responsible to provide food for Solomon's royal household on a monthly rotation basis (1 Kings 4:7, 14).

AHIRA

In the Old Testament, the son of Enan and the chieftain of the tribe of Naphtali during the wilderness wandering. Following the other chieftains, he made a final contribution on behalf of his tribe at the inauguration of the altar (Numbers 1:15; 2:29; 7:1-3).

AHITHOPHEL

In the Old Testament, one of King David's most trusted advisers whose advice had the authority of a divine oracle (2 Samuel 16:23). He took a leading part in the revolt of David's son Absalom, and Ahithophel's defection was a severe blow to the king. When Ahithophel foresaw the disastrous defeat of Absalom's forces he took his own life (2 Samuel 15:31-37; 16:20-17:23).

AHITUB

In Judaism, a descendant of Aaron's son Ithamar; son of Phinehas and grandson of High Priest Eli (1 Samuel 14:3). Following the death of his father and grandfather on the same day, Ahitub possibly officiated as High Priest (1 Samuel 4:17, 18).

AHL AL-KITAB

Arabic phrase for the People of the Book. The name initially referred to the Jews and Christians whose scriptures like the Torah and the Gospel were completed in Muslim belief by the Islamic revelation of the Koran. The term was later broadened to cover adherents of other religions like Zoroastrianism. Differences on the same subject between the Koran and, for example, the Gospels are accounted for by the doctrine of corruption according to which Christians are believed to have corrupted or distorted the original Gospel text. Koranic references to the People of the Book are a mixture of the friendly and the hostile. In early Islamic history the People of the Book had a protected status provided that they payed the poll tax.

AHL-E HAQQ

Secret religion, doctrinally syncretistic, found in western Iran, with enclaves in Azerbaijan and Iraq. Retaining the 12 spiritual leaders of Shiism (one of the two major branches of Islam) and such aspects of Sufism as the communal feast, the Ahl-e Haqq maintain as central to their religion belief in seven manifestations of God.

AHMADIYAH

A modern Islamic sect and the generic name for various Sufi (mystic) orders. The sect's doctrine, in some aspects, is unorthodox; it is believed that Jesus feigned death and resurrection but in actuality escaped to India, where he died at the age of 120.

AHMAD SIRHINDI

(1593-1624) Indian Muslim theologian and educator, who played a prominent role in re-establishing Muslim orthodoxy after the pantheistic influence of Hindu teaching on Indian and Pakistani Orthodox Muslims and Sufis.

AHMED I

(1589-1617) Succeeded his Father Mohammed III as Sultan in 1603. He brought the wars in Hungary and Persia to an end by the Treaty of Szivatorok (1606), which gave Transylvania its independence and abolished the yearly tribute paid by Austria to the sultan, thus severely jolting Turkish prestige. Under his reign several large mosques were built in Turkey.

AHMED II

(1643-1695) Succeeded his brother Suleiman II as sultan in 1691. Later that year the Turks suffered a resounding defeat at the hands of the Austrians at Slankamen and were expelled from Hungary. In his own country he stimulated the building of mosques.

AHQAF, al-

The title of the 46th sura of the Koran; it means literally "The Sand Dunes." The sura belongs to the Meccan period and has 35 verses. It takes its name from the 21st verse which refers to a place called al-Ahqaf where Hud and the tribe of Ad used to live. The latter part of the sura is full of warnings about what happened to disbelievers in ancient times like the people of Ad.

AHRIMAN

The spirit of darkness and light in the ancient Persian religion Zoroastrianism. Ahriman was the spirit of evil, the embodiment of falsehood and the principle of darkness. He was constantly engaged in a struggle with Ahura Mazda, the creator of heaven and earth and the embodiment of wisdom and good, for the souls of men on earth.

AHURA MAZDA

Supreme god in ancient Iranian religion, especially in the religious system of the Iranian prophet Zoroaster (7th century- 6th century BC). He was worshiped by the Persian king Darius I (552-486 BC) and his successors as Ahura Mazda, greatest of all gods and protector of the just king.

AHWAL

In Islam, literally states. It acquired the technical meaning in tasawwuf of spiritual states which were not, however, permanent but which contained an element of illumination or ecstasy and were achieved only with the help of God. These spiritual states could constitute part of one's progress along the Sufi path. The term was widely used in Sufi writings.

AHZAB, al-

The title of the 33rd sura of the Koran; the name means literally "The Parties" or "The Groups" but is usually translated as "The Confederate Clans" or "The Confederate Tribes." The sura belongs to the Medinan period and has 73 verses. The clans or tribunes of the title were those which banded together with the Meccans to besiege Medina in 627 at the siege and battle of al-Khandaq. The latter part of the sura also refers to the Prophet Mohammed's wives, and provides a considerable amount of ethical instruction for Muslims.

AIDAN, Saint

(484-651) Apostle of Northumbria, monastic founder, first bishop of Lindisfarne, or Holy dland, off the coast of Northumberland. Under his direction and that of his successors, Lindisfarne flourished as one of Britain's leading ecclesiastical centers until the Danish invasions began in 793.

AIMOIN

(960-1010) French Benedictine monk whose history of the Franks was highly esteemed in the Middle Ages.

AIN

In Judaism, a place mentioned by God when setting out the eastern boundary of Israel to Moses (Numbers 34:11).

AINU

Caucasoid people, now numbering between 21,000 and 22,000, of whom about 90 per cent live on the Japanese island of Hokkaido, and the remainder

in Russian controlled Sakhalin.

Originally fierce and warlike tribes, they probably arrived in the Japanese archipelago from northern Siberia. The Ainu once lived on parts of the Japanese main island of Honshu, but in the course of the centuries were steadily driven farther north.

The Ainu worship the forces of nature, and there is some similarity with certain religions of Siberia (worship of bears, shamanism).

AIR SPIRIT

Term used by Inuit, meaning a spiritual power or force permeating the universe, nature, the air, the wind, the weather and open sky. A major deity in some regions, his power includes giving life and healing the sick.

A'ISHAH

(614-678) The third and most favored wife of the Prophet Mohammed, who played a role of some political importance after the Prophet's death.

When Mohammed died in 632, A'ishah was left a childless widow of 18. She remained politically inactive until the time of Uthman (644-656), the caliph, or titular leader of the Islamic empire. During his reign she played a role in fomenting opposition that led to his murder in 656.

AISLE

The walkway along the inside of a church on either side of the nave between the exterior wall and the pillars. An aisle may also run alongside a choir or transept.

AITESIS

In the Byzantine liturgy a series of litany-like invocations recited before the Creed and repeated again in the same form directly before the Lord's Prayer. The invocations ask peace, forgiveness of sin, and repentance; they express hope for a painless and Christian death as well as a good defense at the judgment tribunal.

AJAL

In Islam, the term means appointed time, moment of death, or lifespan. The Koran teaches that no one dies unless God allows; it is He who determines man's term of life. terrestrial and celestial phenomena also have their fixed ajal until the Day of Judgment. Early Muslim theologians spent much time discussing ajal and the problems which they believed surrounded the concept.

AJANTA

In Buddhism, a series of rock-cut caves in the Deccan containing world-famous Buddhist frescoes, mostly of sixth century AD and Buddhist sculptures. Caves cut for Viharas and halls of worship between the second century BC and the seventh century AD and a corresponding development in style.

The paintings, which are of high quality, present a comprehensive record of the development of Buddhism, but the statues are executed in a somewhat more primitive style.

AJAX

Legendary Greek hero of the Trojan War. King of Salamis, he was renowned for his size and physical prowess. According to Homer's Iliad he was, next to Achilles, the bravest of the Greek commanders. He defeated the Trojan hero Hector in single combat and he also rescued Achilles' body from the Trojans.

AJIVA

In Buddhism, livelihood; right livelihood is the fifth step on the Noble Eightfold Path.

AKAL TAHKT

Throne of the Eternal; the chief center of religious authority for the Sikh community of India.

AKASHA

In Buddhism, space, as the spiritual essence of space; the primordial substance. Without cognizable attributes it is the plane of manifestation in which lies inherent the Ideation of the Universe. It lies beyond differentiation and therefore beyond description.

AKASHIC

In occultism, a pictorial record, or "memory," of all events, actions, thoughts, and feelings that have occurred since the beginning of time. They are said to be imprinted on Akasha, the astral light, which is described by spiritualists as a fluid ether existing beyond the range of human senses.

AKATHISTOS

Famous kontakion of the Greek Church. Sung on the eve of the fifth Sunday of Lent, it is one of the most impressive works of the Byzantine rite still performed. An ode of 194 lines based on the gospel account of the Annunciation, it contains two narrative sections, separated by a salution to the Virgin and an Hallelujah.

AKELDAMA

In Judaism, the name applied by the Jews to the plot of land whose purchase resulted from "the wages for unrighteousness" paid to Judas Iscariot for his betrayal of Jesus (Acts 1:18-19).

AKH

In Egyptian religion, concept variously translated as "beneficial," "advantageous," or "glorious." The word akh, whose root meaning may have been "useful efficiency," was used to describe the state of deceased in the next world as an "effective personality or being."

AKHENATON

(1421-1362 BC)Title taken by Amenhotep, King of Egypt of the 18th dynasty, who reigned circa 1380-1362 BC. Son and successor of Amenhotep III, he married his sister Nefertite.
Renouncing the religion of the god Amon-Ra and other Egyptian gods, he started the cult of the sun god Aton thus arousing the hostility of the powerful priesthood.
Changing his name from Amenhotep ("Amon is satisfied") to Akhenaton ("he who serves Aton"), he moved the capital from Thebes, the city of Amon, to Akhenaton. Akhenaton himself probably composed the songs to the sun dating from this period.
In this new religion and in his encouragement of a new naturalism in art he was supported by his queen, Nefertite. After his death the old religion was reestablished by his successors; Akhenaton was abandoned and the king's name was erased from the monuments.

AKHMIN

A discovery made in 1886 by Bauriant in Upper Egypt. This fragment gives us the conclusion of the Passion narrative including the entire story of the Crucifixion and the Resurrection. It claimed special credit by using the name of St. Peter.
Scholars have examined this fragment and shown its faults. It is a radical recasting of the gospel narratives. However, scholars agree there is no trace of doctrinal error. It is an interesting early attempt at Christian theology at the beginning of the second century.

AKIBA BEN JOSEPH

(40-135) Famous Jewish rabbi, one of the greatest compilers of Hebrew law, whose work later formed the basis of the mishnah. After supporting the revolt against the Romans, he was executed as a rebel.

AKKO

Also called Acre or Akka, ancient port city, north-west israel, on the Mediterranean Sea, at the north end of the Bay of Haifa (formerly Bay of Acre). The Bible (Judges 1) states that it did not fall to the Jews under Joshua and his successors; the Canaanites and Phoenicians, Semitic peoples of Palestine and the Levant coast, long held the site.

AKOIMETOS LYCHINA

In a Byzantine church the lamp that usually hangs above or before the royal doors of the iconostasis. Whether the Eucharist is reserved or not, this lamp should never be allowed to go out. It may be fed with oil or, as is commonly the case today, may be electrified.

AKOLOUTHIA

A Byzantine term used to indicate:

▲ the prescribed order of religious rites and ceremonies, especially the parts of the canonical hours in their successive order:
Psalms
Lessons
Hymns, etc.

▲ any Byzantine liturgical ceremony;

▲ the canonical hours of the Byzantine Church. These correspond closely to the Western hours of the Divine Office but are entirely different in their construction and are of great length.

AKRIYAVADA

A set of beliefs held by heretic teachers in India who were contemporaries of the Buddha. The doctrine was a kind of antinomianism that, by denying the orthodox karma's theory of the eppicacy of former deeds on a man's or woman's present and future condition, also denied the possibility of man's or woman's influencing his own destiny through preferring righteous to bad conduct.

AKSOBHYA

In Mahayana Buddhism, one of the five "self-born" Buddhas. Although mentioned in some early Sanskrit texts, which also were translated into Chinese, as lord of an eastern paradise comparable to the western realm ruled over by the Buddha Amitabla, Aksobhya never achieved like popularity. He is usually presented only in company with the other "self-born" Buddhas in paintings, where he faces east.

AKSUM

A village in the northern Ethiopian province of Tigre, once the capital and spiritual center of Ethiopia. According to Ethiopian legend, Aksum was the city of the biblical queen of Sheba, Makade, who bore Solomon a son, Menelik, the founder of the Ethiopian royal dynasty.

The city emerged into Christian history when Saint Frumentius arrived there (circa 320) and began to convert the kingdom. Inscriptions attest to the conversion of King Ezana who appears in one as a pagan and in a later one as a worshiper of the true God. Ezana made Christianity the official religion of the kingdom.

The cathedral of St. Mary of Zion is said to have contained the Ark of the Covenant brought to Ethiopia by Menelik. Ahmed Gran, a Muslim invader, destroyed the original in the 16th century.

AKUSALA

In Buddhism, unwholesome; used of those volitions which are accompanied by greed, hate or delusion and thereby cause undesirable karmic results.

ALABASTRON

In the Byzantine Church a vessel of alabaster, glass, or precious metal used to contain the holy myron (chrism). It is usually kept in the sanctuary area and is similar to the Western ampulla.

ALADURA

A religious movement among the Yoruba peoples of western Nigeria, drawn from the independent prophet-healing churches of West Africa. The movement, which has now several hundred thousand adherents, began circa 1918 among the younger segments in the well-established Christian community. They were dissatisfied with Western religious forms and lack of spiritual power, and were influenced by literature from the small United States divine - healing Faith Tabernacle church of Philadelphia.

The Aladura movement continues to grow and includes many small secessions, ephemeral groups, prophets with one or two congregations, and healing practitioners on a more commercial basis.

A'LA, al

The title of the 87th sura of the Koran; the name, which refers to God, means "The Highest" and occurs in the first verse. The sura belongs to the Meccan period and has 19 verses. The early part of the sura provides a brief list of God's mercies and then instructs the Prophet Mohammed to exhort sinners. It warns that the rogue who ignores all exhortation will burn in hell fire.

ALANS

A nomadic, Iranian people in the South Russian steppes during the early Christian era. Moving westward they came under the domination of the Huns and Visigoths, but in the 5th century, most of them wandered back to the steppes, and some settled in the central Caucasus where they became known as Ossets.

Their conversion to Christianity took place in the 10th century under the guidance of the monk Euthymius, sent from Constantinople. A metropolitan see of Alania was then established, which lasted to the end of the 16th century.

ALAPA

The light touch or pat upon the cheek given by the confirming bishop to the person confirmed after anointing him or her on the forehead. As the accompanying words "Peace be with you" suggest, this is probably a stylized version of the kiss of peace in use before the 12th century.

ALAQ, al-

The title of the 96th sura of the Koran; it means "The Blood Clot". The sura belongs to the Meccan period and has 19 verses. The title is drawn from the second verse which refers to God's creation of man from clotted blood. The sura has a particular place in Muslim affections since it was the first to be revealed by the angel Jibril to the Prophet Mohammed on Hira.

ALAYA-VIJNANA

In Buddhism, the central or universal consciousness which is the womb or "store" consciousness.

ALB

A tunic extending from neck to ankles and gathered at the waist by a cincture, worn at most liturgical functions, generally as an undergarment, by the principal officiating clergy.

ALBAN, Saint

(circa third century) The first Christian martyr in Britain. He was probably born at Verulamium (now St. Albans) in Roman Britain and is said to have served abroad in the Roman army. He returned to Britain in the late 3rd or early 4th century and was martyred during the persecutions of the Emperor Diocletian. He is said to have performed many miracles. A monastery was built in his memory in 795 by the king of Mercia, near the presumed place of his execution. St. Alban's feast day is celebrated on June 17th by the Church of England.

ALBANIAN RITE

One of the 18 Eastern Catholic rites. Byzantine influence was one of the original factors in the Christianizing of Albania. The Orthodox Church of Albania developed with the acceptance of the Byzantine separation from Rome, but the union with the Holy See persisted in the mountain districts until the 17th century.

ALBERT OF SABINA

(early 12th century). He became antipope in 1102. He was bishop of Sabina when elected in February as successor to Antipope Theodoric of Santa Rufina, who had been set up against the legitimate Pope Paschal II by an imperial faction supporting the Holy Roman emperor Henry IV in his struggle with Paschal for supremacy.

ALBERTUS MAGNUS, Saint
(1206-1280) German scholastic philosopher and scientist and teacher of St. Thomas Aquinas. He helped establish Aristotelianism and the study of the natural sciences in Christian thought and he was possibly the first to isolate arsenic. He was bishop of Regensburg in 1260, but soon resigned and returned to his studies and his teaching.

ALBIGENSIAN CRUSADE
(1208-1213) Crusade against heresy in southern France.

ALBIGENSIANS
Members of a heretical sect which flourished in the 12th and 13th centuries. The name is derived from the city of Albi in Languedoc in southern France. The Albigensians believed that the principles of good and evil are in constant struggle, that worldly things represented the force of evil and that the human spirit was good. They attacked the church as the instrument of the devil and condemned marriage and the other sacraments.

The sect increased rapidly from the middle of the 12th century. The nobility and people of Languedoc supported the Albigensians, and it took a crusade, proclaimed by Pope Innocent III in 1208 and led by the French crown, to break the hold of the heresy. A special inquisition was created in 1233 to convert the Albigensians.

ALBO, Joseph
(1380-1435) Spanish-Jewish religious philosopher. Albo, who studied under Hasdai Crescas, defended Judaism at the Disputation of Tortosa (1413-1414). Seeing the need of a better presentation of Jewish religious thought, he produced a work called *Sepher ha-Ikkarium* (Book of Dogmas).

In this he indicated three basic and essential principles that cannot be denied without heresy:
▲ the existence of God,
▲ divine revelation,
▲ reward and punishment.
Other teachings, including that concerning an expected Messiah, are branches and can be called into question without prejudice to orthodoxy. Although his apparent indifference to messianic doctrine gave offense to some, his work achieved wide popularity.

ALBORNOZ, Gil Alvarez Carillo de
(1301-1367) Spanish soldier and cardinal famous for his codification of the laws governing the Papal States and for his paving the way for the return of the papacy to Italy from Avignon (France), where the popes lived from about 1309 to 1377.

ALCANTARA, Order of
Christian military order in Spain founded in 1166 by Don Suero Fernandez Barrientos, and recognized in 1177 by Pope Alexander II in a special papal bull. Its purpose was to defend Christian Spain against the Moors.

ALCHEMIST HERETICS
John XXII's condemnation of alchemists in 1317 seems directed against the fraudulent pretensions of many practitioners of the art rather than against any clearly identifiable doctrinal eccentricity inherent in their teachings.

ALCINOUS
In Greek mythology, king of the Phaeacians, son of Nausitholis, and grandson of the god Poseidon.

ALCMAEON
In Greek legend, the son of the seer Amphiaraus and his wife Eriphyle. After his death Alcmaeon was worshiped at Thebes; his tomb was at Psophis.

ALCOBAÇA, Abbey of

The greatest Cistercian abbey in Portugal, founded by monks from Clairvaux in 1153. It was rebuilt after its destruction by the Moors in 1195.

Its monumental Gothic church, the largest in Portugal, was consecrated in 1252. The abbey, housing 300 monks at the peak of its development in the 14th century, played an important role in the religious, cultural, and economic development of medieval Portugal.

ALCOCK, John

(1430-1500) Bishop and statesman who founded Jesus College, Cambridge, and who was regarded as one of the most eminent pre-Reformation English divines.

ALDEIAMENTO SYSTEM

A method in evangelization and educating Indians in Brazil. In this plan Indians were gathered into mission-settlements (aldeias) and thus kept separated from their pagan fellow tribesmen.

This method, which had some success, was introduced after other plans had been tried and found ineffective. It was analogous to the system for reductions employed by the Jesuits elsewhere in South America.

ALEANDRO, Girolamo

(1480-1542) Cardinal and Humanist who was an important opponent of the Lutheran Reformation.

ALEIPTRON

In the Byzantine Church an instrument for anointing the foreheads of the people with oil or anointing the walls of the church in the rite of consecration. It is sometimes merely a stick tipped with cotton but also may be especially made of metal with a small ball at the end for applying the oil. In the latter form it may be decorated and may form a matched set with the communion spoon and lance.

ALENI, Giulio

(1582-1649) Jesuit missionary who was the first Christian missionary in the province of Kiangsi, China. During his more than 30 years in China, he adopted that country's dress and manners.

ALEPH

The first letter of the Hebrew alphabet. The name assigned to this letter means "bull" (cattle). The letter is also later used outside the Torah as a number and, when so used, denotes unity or one.

ALEPPINES

A name applied to two Eastern catholic religious communities.

1 A Maronite community of Antonian monks known as the Antonian Aleppine Order. It is an offshoot of the older Lebanese Antonian Order.
2 A Melchite community of Basilian monks known as the Aleppine Basilian Order.
   Since 1952 the Aleppines have been considered a non-monastic order. Its members conduct parishes, missionary centers, and schools.

ALEPPO

City in Syria second only to Damascus. Its name occurs early in the second millennium BC. In ancient times Aleppo was a kingdom that witnessed the invasions of Babylonian, Hittite, Egyptian, Mitani, Hurrian, Aramean, Persian, Greek, Roman, and Byzantine troops.

In AD 636 it surrendered to the Muslim Arabs and has stayed in Muslim hands of different races until now. It has over 500,000 inhabitants; 30 percent are Christians of different rites and denominations, a few thousand are Jews, and the rest are Muslims.

ALEXANDER, Saint

Patriarch of Alexandria (313-328) during his episcopate the controversy over Arianism erupted.

ALEXANDER I, Saint

(circa 45-119) Fifth pope after St. Peter and successor to Saint Evaristus. His rule of approximately ten years is attested by Pope St. Eusebius (309). Catholic writers ascribe to him the introduction of holy water and the custom of mixing sacramental wine with water, and he may have made additions to the liturgy.

ALEXANDER II

(1001-1075) Pope from 1061 to 1075. Though he was elected pope, the German court nominated Peter Cadalus of Parma as Honorius III, and Alexander was not recognized by the empire until 1064.

ALEXANDER III

(1105-1181) Pope from 1159 to 1181, a vigorous exponent of papal authority, which he defended against challenges by the Holy Roman Emperor Frederick Barbarossa and Henry II of England.

ALEXANDER VI

(1431-1503) Rodrigo Borgia; a corrupt, worldly, and ambitious pope, whose neglect of the spiritual inheritance of the church contributed to the development of the Protestant reformation.

ALEXANDER VIII

(1610-1691) Pietro Vito Ottoboni; Pope from 1689 to 1691. He initiated measures that led eventually to a solution of the disputes between the papacy and Louis XIV of France.

ALEXANDER OF HALES

(1170-1245) Theologian and philosopher who influenced later thinkers. Basically an Augustinian, to some extent he had taken into account the psychological, physical, and metaphysical doctrines of Aristotle, while discarding popular Avicennian tenets of emanations from a Godhead.

ALEXANDER THE GREAT

Son of Philip II of Macedonia and his wife Olympias, born in Pella circa October 356 BC. Although not mentioned by name in the Bible, his rule of the fifth world empire was foretold two centuries before his birth (Daniel 8:5-7; 20-21).

ALEXANDRIA

Egyptian city and Mediterranean seaport. The Egyptian village of Rhakote existed on the site of the present city from circa 1500 BC. In 332 BC Alexander the Great began the construction there of a great seaport; after his death the work was carried on by the Ptolemies.

It was the Hellenistic center of Egypt and contained a large Jewish population as well. It grew into one of the preeminent centers of learning in the ancient world, having two great libraries, one in the temple of Zeus and the other in the museum.

Its Jewish community produced the Septuagint, and Philo Judaeus, the most noted exponent of Jewish-Hellenistic synthesis in philosophy, was a native of the city.

The city was also a focal place of heresy in the early Christian Church. It was the chief center of Gnosticism, and the city of Arius, founder of Arianism. But Athanasius, indefatigable foe of Arianism, was its bishop from 328 till 373. The patriarchs Theophilus, Cyril and Dioscurus wielded great power in the city and consequently throughout Egypt. In the year 616 it was captured by the Persians and 30 years later was definitively taken and held by the Muslim Arabs.

ALEXANDRIA, Catholic-Coptic Patriarchate of

Primatial see for Coptic Rite Catholics. In 1824 Pope Leo XIII restored the Catholic-Coptic Patriarchate of Alexandria particularly because of the influence of Khedive Mohammed Ali who had supported religious freedom in Egypt.

ALEXANDRIA, Coptic Patriarchate of

Primate see of the Coptic Church (Monophysite). The condemnation of Monophysitism that came from the Council of Chalcedon (451) brought a division within the Egyptian Church. For a time, the patriarchate passed between the Orthodox Melchites and the monophysitic Copts, but since 567 there has been a distinct line of Coptic patriarchs.

ALEXANDRIA, Orthodox Church of

An autocephalous Eastern Orthodox patriarchate, second in honorific rank after the Church of Constantinople. Its patriarch is considered the successor of Mark the Evangelist and heads the Orthodox Church in Africa.

ALEXANDRIA, Patriarchate of

One of the four eminent patriarchates of the Eastern Church. St. Mark is considered the Apostle of Egypt, but the tradition, found no earlier than Eusebius, is doubtful.

The Alexandrian Church, already well-established, emerged into history circa 190 under Patriarch Demetrius. By 389 Christianity had become strong enough to launch a campaign against paganism under Patriarch Theophilus.

The patriarchate passed back and forth between the Dyophysites (called Melchites or King's men) and Monophysites (Copts) until Emperor Justin II recognized both patriarchates (567). From the reign of Peter III to the present there has been an unbroken line of Coptic patriarchates.

ALEXANDRIA, School of

The first Christian institution of higher learning, founded in the mid-second century in Alexandria, Egypt. It became a leading center of the allegorical method of biblical interpretation, espoused a rapprochement between Greek culture and Christian faith.

ALEXANDRIA, Synod of

(362) Official church meeting in Alexandria, Egypt, summoned by the bishop of Alexandria, Athanasius. It allowed the clergy that were readmitted to communion after making common cause with Arians to return to their former ecclesiastical status, provided they had not themselves subscribed to Arianism.

ALEXANDRIAN RITE

The system of liturgical practices and discipline found among Egyptians and Ethiopians of both the Eastern Rite Catholic and independent Christian churches.

The Alexandrian Rite is historically associated with Mark the Evangelist, who traveled to Alexandria, the Greek-speaking capital of the diocese of Egypt and the cultural center of the Eastern Roman Empire. The Liturgy of Mark was originally in Greek but in the 12th century was displaced by the Byzantine Rite.

ALFASI, Isaac ben Jacob

(1013-1103) Scholar of the Talmud who wrote a codification of the Talmud known as Book of Laws (Sefer ha-Halakhot), which ranks with the great codes of Maimonides and Karo.

ALIEN IMMERSION

Among Baptists, signifies a baptism correctly performed, but by a minister authorized in a different denomination, hence an "alien." Such a baptism is recognized by more liberal Baptists groups; conservatives reject it as invalid, but differ as to which ministers are to be considered alien.

ALI IBIN ABI TALIB

(600-601) Son-in-law of Mohammed, the Prophet of Islam, and fourth caliph, reigning from 656 to 661. Adopted by Mohammed, Ali converted to Islam and became devoted to the prophet (whose daughter Fatimah he married). A dispute over his rights to succession followed the death of Mohammed and he retired to a life of religious scholarship.

ALITURGICAL DAYS

In Roman Catholicism, these are the days on which it is not permitted to celebrate Mass. In the Roman Rite, this occurs only during the Triduum on Good Friday when Communion is distributed after a service consisting of the Liturgy of the Word and the Adoration of the Cross. In a sense Holy Saturday is also aliturgical since the one Mass permitted, in the evening, is that of Easter day.

ALIYA

Hebrew word for "going up;" the honor accorded to a Jewish worshiper of being called up to read an assigned passage from the Torah, the heart of the synagogue ritual. Since the passage assigned to each sabbath-morning service is subdivided into a minimum of seven sections, at least seven different persons are called up for these Torah readings. In addition, a final reader is called up to repeat part of the final reading and to recite the Haftara (a reading from the prophetical books of the Bible).

ALLAH

In Islam, word for Deity, formed from the Arabic al-Ilah, which means literally "The God." The name Allah is for Muslims the supreme name. Allah is the eternal and uncreated Creator of the universe and all mankind. The Koran views Him from both a transcendent and an immanent perspective: on the one hand, there is absolutely nothing like Him; on the other, He is closer to man than the jugular vein in his neck.

ALLEGORICAL INTERPRETATION, Biblical

A hermeneutical (interpretive) method used to uncover hidden or symbolic meanings of a biblical text. This method attempts to overcome the difficulties of morally perplexing biblical passages and to harmonize them with certain traditions and accepted teachings of the synagogue or the church.

ALLELUIA

A word of Hebrew origin meaning "praise Yahweh," it is used frequently in the liturgy, especially during the Easter season and at the "alleluia verse" that precedes the reading of the Gospel at the Eucharistic Liturgy.

ALLOUEZ, Claude Jean

(1622-1689) Jesuit priest who worked with Huron and easterm Algonquian Indian groups in Canada and the United States. He mastered both the Huron and Algonquin languages, eventually preparing a prayerbook in those languages. His fluency in these native languages earned him prestige among the different indigenous nations. It is reported that he preached to over twenty-two different tribes and baptized an estimated 10,000 people.

ALL-RUSSIAN CHURCH COUNCIL

Council of the Russian Orthodox Church whose object was to reform Church structures and which was initiated with the support of Tsar Nicholas II and concluded during the turmoil of the Russian Revolution in October 1917.

ALL SAINTS DAY

Religious feast day celebrating all Christian saints, observed by most Christian churches on November 1st. Its present form dates from the reign of Pope Gregory III (731-741).

This feast commemorates all the blessed in heaven, but is especially designed to honor the blessed who have not been canonized and who have no special feast day. All Saints is a holy day of obligation on which Catholics are bound to participate in the Mass.

ALL-SMOKING CEREMONY

Sacred ceremony and religious society among the American Blackfeet Indian nations. It is generally initiated after a request is made, according to the appropriate ritual procedure, to an individual qualified to lead it. Ritual elements include the singing of sacred medicine songs, the preparation of an offering to the sun, the symbolic painting of the person who made the vow along the family members, ritual smoking and consecration.

ALL SOULS' DAY

The day set apart in the Roman Catholic Church for commemoration of the souls of the faithful dead. It falls on November 2nd unless that day is a Sunday, in which case it is observed the next day. The observance of All Souls' Day began in the 10th and 11th centuries and was based on the doctrine that prayers of the faithful on earth may help purify souls in purgatory.

ALL SOULS' DAY

A major Buddhist festival in China and Japan, among whose purposes are the expression of filial piety to deceased ancestors and the release of spirits from bondage to this world.

ALL UNION OF EVANGELICAL CHRISTIANS AND BAPTISTS

A voluntary association of Baptist churches organized in 1944 by uniting the Union of Evangelical Christians and the Russian Baptist Union.

ALMODAD

In Judaism, first of Joktan's 13 sons; fourth generation after Shem; nephew of Peleg, through whom the Messianic lineage is traced. Almodad fathered one of the 70 post-flood families, settling in Arabia (Genesis 10:26, 32; 1 Chronicles 1:20).

ALMOHAD AND ALMORAVID

Two medieval Muslim sects and dynasties originating among North African Berbers. First the Almoravids built an empire covering most of north-west Africa and much of Spain (1063-1142). The Almohads conquered and enlarged the territory (1144-1158), but their empire broke up after 1212 when the combined forces of the Christian kings of Aragon, Castile and Navarre defeat-

ed them at Las Navas de Tolosa in the south of Spain.

ALMOHAD ARCHITECTURE

12th- and 13th century architectural style of Muslin dynasty on the Barbary coast of North Africa, reflected in great mosques of Spain and Morocco.

ALMSGIVING

This act of freely giving material or financial acceptance to a needy person must be motivated by Christian charity. Almsgiving is recognized in the Christian tradition as a corporal work of mercy and is one of the principal forms of penance, especially during Lent.

ALMUCE

A cope lined with fur worn by canons and by the religious of certain orders during choral services. It came into use during the 13th century as a means of keeping the head and neck warm.

ALMUG

In the Old Testament, a tree included by Solomon in his request to Hiram of Tyre for timbers for the construction of the Temple and from which stairs and supports were constructed as well as harps and stringed instruments (2 Chronicles 2:8-9; 1 Kings 10:11-12).

ALPHA AND OMEGA

The first and last letters of the Greek alphabet, used to express the eternity of God (Revelation 1:8). In rabbinic literature the first and last letters of the Hebrew alphabet are similarly used. The word emet ("truth"), composed of the first, middle, and last letters of the Hebrew alphabet, is the seal of God.

In Roman Catholicism is has a slightly different meaning. When the first and last letters of the Greek alphabet are combined they are a symbol of the divinity of Christ, who is the beginning and the end. These words were spoken by Jesus of himself in the scriptures (Revelation 1:8, see also Revelation 21:6; 22:13).

The symbols frequently occur in church art and architecture. During the Easter Vigil the presider cuts the letter Alpha above the cross and Omega below the cross on the paschal candle.

ALPHAEUS

The father of James the Less, the ninth listed of the twelve apostles (Matthew 10:3; Mark 3:18; Luke 6:15). Many authorities are supported by tradition in the general belief that Alphaeus was the same person as Clopas (John 19:25), which would also make him the husband of "the other Mary" (Matthew 27:56; Mark 15:40; Luke 24:10).

ALPHONSUS LIGUORI, Saint

(1696-1787) Italian priest who founded the Congregation of the Most Holy Redeemer (Redemptorist Order), a society of missionary preachers working with the rural poor. He was canonized in 1839.

Alphonsus Liguori had great pastoral concern for the unevangelized poor in the country places outside the city. He founded the Redemptorist Order in 1732 especially to preach the Gospel to these poor people. He wrote over 100 books on the Christian life and is perhaps best known for his monumental four-volume work on moral theology for the guidance of confessors.

His writings were instrumental in opposing the heresy of Jansenism. He was ordained a bishop in 1762 and served the diocese of St. Agatha of the Goths until 1775. He was declared a Doctor of the Church in 1871.

ALTAR

An elevated place on which sacrifices were offered or incense burned to a deity; a table in a church for the celebration of the eucharist.

According to the Code of Canon Law (Roman Catholic Church), an altar may be fixed or movable; it is fixed if it is so constructed that it is joined to the floor and therefore cannot be moved; it is movable if it can be transferred.

According to Catholic custom the table of a fixed altar is to be of stone; nevertheless, even another material, worthy and solid, in the judgment of the conference of bishops also can be used.

A movable altar can be constructed from any solid material appropriate for liturgical use. Moreover, "the ancient tradition of keeping the relics of martyrs and other saints under a fixed altar is to be preserved according to the norms given in the liturgical books."

Until about the 5th century, altars were simple, wooden tables, but it soon became the practice to use a stone altar in which the relics of saints and martyrs were enclosed.

Gradually they became more elaborate. Richly carved marble, bronze statuary, mosaics and magnificent painted altar panels all became part of the usual altar ensemble. During the Reformation a reaction set in, and many altars were removed or destroyed by the Puritans. Roman Catholic altars, however, became still more decorative.

The most elaborate were the astonishing baroque altars of the 17th and 18th centuries, which were immense reredoses (decorated backdrops, usually of carved of painted panels) and baldachins or ciboriums (canopies).

ALTARBREAD

The round, flat wafers used in the Eucharist Liturgy. The unleavened bread is made of pure wheat flour mixed with water and baked between iron molds.

ALTARCLOTH

The fabric, usually of white linen or other suitable material, that covers the entire altar during the celebration of the eucharist. The current legislation (Roman Catholicism) requires only one cloth.

ALTAR OF HEAVEN

Three white marble terraces built in Beijng (Peking) in 1420 by the Yung Lo emperor. It became the site of sacrifices to Heaven offered by Chinese emperors and replaced the earthen mound used by earlier rulers.

ALTARPIECE

Decorated panel or screen, movable or fixed, used for backing an altar. In the various historical styles of art, and particularly in later examples, creators of altarpieces have employed a great variety of materials and techniques, including painting, stone- and wood-carving, metal casting, gilding, and embroidery, tapestry, mosaics and ceramics, to achieve their rich decorative effects.

Although adornments that might be described as altarpieces are found in many cultures (e.g., Buddhist) for enhancing the altar proper or the sanctuary, this artistic form as such is commonly associated with Catholic or Orthodox ritual.

Baroque elaborations of the altarpiece often reached extravagant proportions in combining painting, sculpture and architectural elements with astonishing intricacy and richness of detail.

In Bernini's hands, the altar of St. Peter's, Rome, became just one of the many pictorial devices for expressing the splendor of the Roman Catholic Church. Baroque architects like Bernini and Francesco Borromini used their ornate style of design (which flourished between Mannerism and Rococo) as religious propaganda for the Roman Catholic Counter-Reformation.

In Southern Europe especially the Jesuits, founded by Ignatius of Loyola, embellished their churches with brilliantly colorful paintings and statues of saints and angels to give their congregations a forecast of the glories of Heaven.

ALTAR SOCIETY

A group of the faithful who take it upon themselves to care for the altar and its accessories in the parish church.

ALTARSTONE

The phrase can mean two things. First, it is the large permanent table of the altar consisting of one slab of stone or marble into which are set the relics of two martyrs and is consecrated as one with the rest of the alter.

Second, it may consist of the small square flat stone, consecrated by a bishop, that contains the relics of canonized martyrs or saints that is usually inserted in the center of an altar that is blessed.

ALTARWINE

The wine used for the Eucharist Liturgy must be made from grapes, natural and unadulterated, that is, not mixed with any additives. A small quantity of water is mixed with the wine by the deacon or priest at Mass. Symbolic meanings associated with this action are the union of Christ with the people of God and the union of the human and divine in Jesus.

ALTHUSIUS, Johannes

(1557-1638) Dutch Calvinist political theorist who was the intellectual father of modern federalism and an advocate of popular sovereignty.

Seeking to bring the study of politics into line with Calvinist doctrine, he particularly sought to use the Hebrew Bible in the development of political theory. In effect, his theory was naturalistic and owed little to revelation as it was based logically on the single concept of contrast.

While reflecting Calvinist puritanism, he stressed that each group is to be justified by providing the future and happy life to its members.

ALTIS

In Greek religion, the sacred grove of Zeus, the chief god, or sacred precinct in Olympia, Greece. It was an irregular quadrangular area more than 200 yards on each side. In it were the temples of Zeus and of Hera, his consort; the principal altars and votive offerings; the small treasuries built in various Dorian styles; and the administrative building for the Olympic games, which were held nearby.

ALZON, Emmanuel-Marie-Joseph-Maurice

(1810-1880) Ecclesiastic who founded the order of Augustinians of the Assumption.

AMALEK

In Judaism, son of Esau's firstborn Eliphaz, by his concubine Timna (Genesis 36:12-16). Amalek, a grandson of Esau was one of the fourteen sheiks of Edom (Genesis 36:15-16). The belief of some that the Amalekites were of a much earlier origin and not descendants of Esau's grandson Amalek is not founded on solid factual ground.

AMALTHEIA

In Greek mythology, the goat who nursed Zeus in the Idaean Cave. Out of gratitude the god endowed her horn with the ability to give its possessor all the good things he desired. The horn of Amaltheia is synonymous with plenty.

AMARAPURA

One of the three major Buddhist monastic bodies in Sri Lanka, founded in the 19th century.

AMARAVATI

In Buddhism, site of a magnificent specimen of Buddhist art, near Madras. Sculptures form decorations of a Stupa 138 feet in diameter, and an inner and outer rail surrounding it. The work dates from 200 BC-AD 300 and represents the intermediate stage between ancient Buddhist art and that of the Gandhara period, both symbol and figure being used to depict the Buddha.

AMAR DAS

(1479-1574) Appointed third Sikh Guru at the advanced age of 73, noted for his division of the Punjab into 22 Sikh dioceses and his dispatch of missionaries to spread the faith. Realizing that periodical meetings of all Sikhs would strengthen the faith, he ordered three great festivals a year. He was much revered for his wisdom and piety, and it was said that even the Moghul emperor Akbar sought his food and ate in the Sikhs' castless langar ("free kitchen").

AMASA

In Judaism, son of David's sister Abigail and Jether and cousin of Absalom and Joab (2 Samuel 17:25); 1 Chronicles 2:16-17). Jether is called an Israelite in Samuel and an Ishmaelite in Chronicles, perhaps because he lived in Ishmaelite territory.

AMASAI

In the Old Testament, a Levite of the family of Kohath; son of Eikanah and ancestor of the prophet Samuel and Temple singer Heman of David's day (1 Chronicles 6:25, 35, 36).

AMAZIAH

King of Judah who, in 858 BC, came to the throne at 25 and ruled for 29 years from the assassination of his father Jehoash until his own death in 829. With the kingdom firm in his hand, he executed those that had murdered his father, but heeded the law of Moses not to punish their sons (Deuteronomy 24:16). His reign was marked by some enthusiasm for true worship, but not with a "complete heart" and not without serious shortcomings that brought disaster both to himself and the nation of Judah. The record of his rule deals primarily with two military campaigns (2 Chronicles 25:2).

AMAZONS

In Greek mythology, the daughters of the god of war, Ares and the nymph Harmony. According to some, their kingdom lay in Thrace while in the opinion of others it was in the hills of the Caucasus or even on the left bank of the Don.

The Amazons took part in the Trojan War, on the side of the Trojans with their incredibly beautiful Queen Penthesileia. The Amazons worshiped the goddess Artemis and it is said that the temple at Ephesus, which is dedicated to the goddess was a work of the Amazons.

AMBEDKAR, Bhimra Ramji

(1893-1956) Indian politician who championed his fellow "untouchables," members of the lowest Hindu caste in India. He helped ensure that India's constitution of 1949 banned discrimination against them but failed to eliminate the untouchable castes from Hinduism.

AMBIYA, al-

The title of the 21st sura of the koran; it means "The prophets." The sura belongs to the Meccan period and has 112 verses. It is so-called because of the references to many of the great prophets revered by Islam. These include Musa and Harun, who were given the Torah; Ibrahim, whom pagans attempted to burn to death; and Dawud and Sulayman.

AMINA BINT WAHAB

(died circa 576 AD) The mother of the prophet Mohammed. Through her father she belonged to the Zuhra clan of the tribe Quraysh. She married Abd al-Muttalib who died before the birth of the Prophet. Amina herself died when the Prophet was six years old. The period when she was pregnant with Mohammed, and the latter's birth, have given rise to many miraculous stories.

AMIN, al-

In Islam, the trustworthy. This was a pre-revelation epithet borne by the Prophet Mohammed when he was younger. The title provides some indication of the respect in which Mohammed was held, even before the revelation of the Koran.

AMIR

In Islam, a title which has been variously translated as "Commander of the Faithful," "Prince of the believers" and "Prince of the Faithful," among others. The phrase should really be translated in the light of the historical period under discussion; it acquired greater strength with the passage of time rather like the title khalifa itself. At first Amir al-Mu'minin meant someone given military leadership. The title was then assumed by the second khalifa but with few connotations of real power. From this time onwards, however, it became a title reserved for a caliph alone. It was sometimes used by the sultans in the early period of the Ottomans.

AMITABHA

In Buddhism, the Buddha of Infinite Light. The personification of compassion. In China, Amitabha is the intermediary between Supreme Reality and mankind, and faith in Him ensures rebirth in His Paradise.

AMMONITE

Member of an ancient Semitic people whose principal city was Rabbath Ammon, in Palestine. The "sons of Ammon" were in perennial, though sporadic, conflict with the Israelites. After a long period of seminomadic existence, the Ammonites established a kingdom north of Moab in the 13th century BC. With difficulty, their fortress capital was captured by David. An Ammonite woman, one of many foreigners taken into Solomon's harem, was responsible for inducing the king to worship the Ammonite god Malcom (1 Kings 14:31).

During the reign of Jehoiakim (6th century BC), the Ammonites allied themselves with the Chaldeans, Syrians, and others in an attack on Judah and also harassed the Israelites when they attempted to rebuild the Temple of Jerusalem after the Babylonian Captivity.

AMON

Egyptian deity revered as king of the gods. The Amon cult reached Thebes about 2100 BC. He was sometimes depicted as a human with a ram's head, and sometimes as a ram with large curved horns.

AMORA

A Jewish scholar attached to one of several academies in Palestine, who collaborated in writing interpretations of extensive commentaries on the Mishna (the authoritative collection of Jewish oral laws) and on its critical marginal notes, called Tosefta.

AMORITES

A tribe descended from Canaan, a Semitic-speaking people who dominated the history of Mesopotamia, Syria, and Palestine from about 2000 to about 1600 BC.

AMOS

(8th century BC) Hebrew prophet, the first to proclaim clearly that there was one God for all peoples. A shepherd from Judah, he preached in neighboring Israel, denouncing its corruption until expelled by the king.

The prophet came from the village of Tekoa, near Jerusalem. He left his native Judah to warn the kingdom of Israel against wickedness, evil-doing, and falseness in religion. Israel was prosperous, yet most of its people lived in terrible poverty. Amos believed that Israel should set an example for other nations and he saw that God would use Assyria as a weapon to punish the wickedness of Israel and the other nations.

The probably posthumous biblical Book of Amos is the earliest record of a prophet's sayings and life.

AMOS, Book of

The first Hebrew prophet to have a biblical book named for him. He accurately foretold the destruction of the northern kingdom of Israel. Under the impact of powerful visions of divine destruction of the Hebrews in such natural disasters as a swarm of locusts and fire, Amos travelled from Judah to the neighboring richer, more powerful kingdom of Israel, where he began to preach. The time is uncertain, but the book of Amos puts the date as two years before an earthquake that may have occurred circa 763 BC.

Denunciation of the luxurious living, the idolatry and immorality were the subject of his preachings. After preaching at Bethel, a famous shrine under the special protection of Jeroboam II, Amos was ordered to leave the country by Jeroboam's priest Amaziah.

AMPHITRITE

In Greek mythology, the goddess of the sea, wife of the god Poseidon, and one of the 50 daughters (the Nereids) of Nereus and Doris (the daughter of Oceanus).

Poseidon saw her one day off Naxos dancing with her sister Nereids, fell in love with her and made her his wife.

AMPHITRYON

In Greek mythology, son of Alcaeus, king of Tirns. Heaving accidentally killed his uncle Electyron, king of Mycenae, Amphithryon fled with Alcmene, Electryon's daughter, to Thebes, where he was cleansed from the guilt by Creon, his maternal uncle.

AMPLIATUS

In the New Testament, a beloved Christian brother in the congregation at Rome, to whom the apostle Paul sent greetings (Romans 16:8).

AMRAM BAR SHESHNA

(died circa 875) Head of the Talmudic academy at Sura, Babylonia, traditionally regarded as the first Jewish authority to write a complete domestic and synagogal liturgy of the year.

Amram also composed numerous*responsa* (replies to inquiries about Jewish law), which, touching upon such subjects as dietary restrictions and regulations for sabbaths and holidays, reveal much of the Jewish law and custom of his time.

AMRAMITES

In the Old Testament, the descendants of Amram, the grandson of Levi by Kohath. They composed a subdivision of the family of Kohathites. During the trek through the wilderness they encamped on the south of the tabernacle with all the families of the sons of Kohath. The service assignment of the Kohathites was the ark, the table, the lampstand, the altars and utensils, as well as the screen between the Holy and Most Holy (Numbers 3:27-31).

AMR IBN AL-AS
(died circa 663) The Arab conqueror of Egypt who played a prominent role in the early history of Islam.

AMRITA
In Buddhism, term meaning immortal, deathless; generally used as a term or name for Nirvana.

AMRITANANDA, Thera
Nepalese Buddhist who became a Bhikkhu in Sri Lanka (Ceylon) and then returned to become the leading Buddhist in Nepal.

AMSDORF, Nikolaus von
(1483-1565) Protestant reformer and major supporter of Luther, who stressed the insufficiency of good works in assuring the salvation of sinners. In particular he emphasized that salvation could come only to men of faith and that their efforts to perform good works might even be self-defeating.

AMULET
An object, either natural or man-made, believed to be endowed with special powers to protect or bring good fortune. Amulets are carried on the person or kept in the place that is the desired sphere of influence.

AMZI
In the Old Testament, a Levite of the family of Merari and an ancestor of Ethan, who was one of the singers appointed by David at Jehovah's house (1 Chronicles 6:31, 46).

AN
In Mesopotamian religion, Sumero-Akkadian god of the sky and father of all gods; he was worshiped particularly in Erech in the southern herding region. His name means "sky" and he seems originally to have been envisaged under the form of a great bull, a formlater dissociated from the god as a separate mythological entity.

ANABAPTISM
Movement advocating baptism of adult believers rather than infants. The first group was formed in 1523 by dissatisfied followers of Ulrich Zwingli. Most stressed the dictates of individual conscience, and urged non-violence and separation of church and state.

ANABAPTISTS
("rebaptizers") Radical Protestant sects of the Reformation that sought a return to primitive Christianity. The first group was formed in 1523 in Zurich by dissatisfied followers of Ulrich Zwingli. Denying the validity of infant baptism, they rebaptized adult converts. Most stressed the dictates of individual conscience, and urged non-violence and separation of church and state. Despite widespread persecution their doctrine spread, inspiring the Mennonites in the Netherlands and the Hutterites in Moravia.

ANABHOGA
In Buddhism, term used in the sense of purposeless, effortless, unaware of conscious striving.

ANACLETUS, Saint
(first century AD) Second pope (76-88 or 79-91) after St. Peter. According to Epiphanius and the priest Tyrannius Rufinus, he directed the Roman Church with St. Linus. He died, probably a martyr, during the reign of Domitian.

ANACLETUS II
(1062-1138) Pietro Pierlone; antipope from 1130 to 1138 whose claims to the papacy against Pope Innocent II are still supported by some scholars.

ANAGAMIN
In Buddhism, third of the four stages of the Path. The anagamin does not return

to earth after his death, but is reborn in the highest formless heavens and there attains arhatship.

ANAGI

In Greek mythology, the personification of the forces which made the decisions of Fate imperative. She was considered a wise goddess and according to the Orphic Theogony she and her sister Adrasteia were the nurses of Zeus. For the tragedians she was the supreme force to whom even the gods were obedient.

ANAH

In the Old Testament, a son of Zibeon and the father of Esau's wife Ohoibamah (Genesis 36:2, 14, 18; 1 Chronicles 1:34, 40-41). Anah was the head of a tribe independent of his father, and ranks on an equality of that tribe.

ANAHITA

Ancient Iranian goddess of waters, fertility, and procreation. In Greece, Anahita was identified with Athena and Aphrodite.

ANAKIM

In the Old Testament, a race of people of extraordinary size who inhabited the mountainous regions of Canaan, as well as some coastal areas, particularly in the south thereof. Three prominent men of the Anakim, Ahiman, Sheshai and Talmai, resided at Hebron (Numbers 13:22). It was there that the 12 Hebrew spies first saw the Anakim, and ten of the spies subsequently gave a frightening report of the experience, alleging that these men were descendants of the pre-flood Nephilim and that, by comparison with them, the Hebrews were like "grasshoppers" (Numbers 13:28-33; Deuteronomy 1:28). Their great stature caused them to be used as a standard of comparison in describing even the giantlike men of the Enim and the Rephaim. Their strength apparently produced the proverbial saying: "Who can make a firm stand before the sons of Anak?" (Deuteronomy 2:10-21; 9:1-3).

ANALOGY

A comparison between two things or beings that implies likeness but also dissimilarities. All language about God is based on analogy because we humans can only speak of God from our own limited perspective.

ANALYTICAL INTERPRETATION, Biblical

A hermeneutical (interpretive) method or principle that attempts to reconcile apparent differences between what is conveyed by human language and what is intended by spiritual (i.e., biblical) language. According to biblical interpreters, human words, when applied to divine subjects, do not always have the same meaning; i.e., human and divine words are not univocal.

ANAMIM

In Judaism, Hamitic descendants of Mizraim. Since Mizraim became synonymous with Egypt, it is probable that the Anamim settled there or in that area (Genesis 10:13; 1 Chronicles 1:11).

ANAMMELECH

In the Old Testament, a deity of the Sepharvites that proved unable to deliver them from the Assyrian aggressors. The worship of Anammelech included the revolting practice of child sacrifice (2 Kings 17:31).

ANAMNESIS

The Greek word means remembrance, commemoration, memorial. It refers specifically to the first prayer following the consecration of the Mass that recalls the Passion, Resurrection, and Ascension of Jesus.

ANAN

In Judaism, one of the heads of the people of Israel, whose representative, if not himself, together with Nehemiah and others, sealed the nation's resolution to serve Jehovah faithfully (Nehemiah 10:1, 26).

ANAN BEN DAVID

(second half of the 8th century) Persian Jew, founder of the Ananites, a heretical and antirabbinical order from which the still existing Karaite sect developed.

In 770, Anan wrote the definitive code of his order; Book of Precepts. Its unifying principle is its rejection of much of the Talmud and the rabbinate, which based its authority on the Talmud. Only the Bible is held to be valid, but it is interpreted with a strange mixture of freedom and literalism.

ANANDA

(6th century BC) First cousin of Buddha and one of his principal disciples, known as his "beloved disciple" and devoted companion. He entered the order of monks in the second year of the Buddha's ministry and in the 25th year was appointed his personal attendant. According to the Vinaya Pitaka texts, he persuaded the Buddha, much against the Buddha's own inclination, to allow women to become nuns.

ANANIAH

In the Old Testament, one of the men who stood at Ezra's right hand when he read the law to the people, on the first day of the seventh month. Probably a priest or prince (Nehemiah 8:4).

ANANIAS

In the New Testament, member of the earliest Christian community of Jerusalem, who, with his wife Sapphira, was struck dead for fraud and lying under oath. They had pretended to give their entire wealth to the church but in fact withheld a portion. Afterward, in popular Christian tradition, Ananias became a synonym for an archliar.

ANAPANA-SATI

In Buddhism, term used in the sense of watching over the breathing, in and out. One of the fundamental exercises in "Mindfulness," and the development of higher states of consciousness. Of all subjects fore concentration, and later meditation, it is the most common exercise in all schools of meditation.

ANASTASIUS I, Saint

(319-401) Pope from 399 to 401. He earned the praise of St. Jerome for censuring the work of Origen, one of the most influential theologians of the early Greek Church. In papal letters Anastasius condemned several Origenist writings and disapproved the spreading of Origen's teaching.

ANASTASIUS II

(411-498) Pope from 496 to 498. A confused tradition blamed Anastasius for being led by Photinus into heretical opinions concerning the divinity of Jesus Christ. Because of Photinus, Dante placed the pontiff in hell. Anastasius died before any development occurred in the schism between the sees of Rome and Constantinople.

ANASTASIUS III

(830-913) Pope from 911 to 913. Because his pontificate came during a period when Rome was under the control of the house of Theophylact, he had little authority or freedom of action. In 911 he determined the ecclesiastical divisions of Germany.

ANASTASIUS IV

(1073-1154) Corrado di Suburra; pope from 1153 (July) to 1154 (December). During his brief pontificate he was a peacemaker noted especially for settling two long-standing problems: one regarding Emperor Frederick I Barbarossa and the see of Magdeburg, the other regarding St. William of York and his see.

ANASTASIUS SINAITA, Saint

(7th century) Theologian and abbot of Mount Sinai territory whose writings, public disputes with various heretical movements in Egypt and Syria, and polemics against the Jews made him in his day a foremost advocate of Orthodox Christian doctrine, especially on the person and work of Christ, and provided key documents for the history of early Christian thought. By his leadership and eloquence he won the title "the new Moses" and is revered as a saint by the Byzantine Church.

ANASTASIUS THE LIBRARIAN

(810-878) Language scholar, Roman cardinal, and influential political counsellor to 9th century popes. His intrigues involved him in the imperial faction's nomination for antipope in 855, but his subsequent reconciliation with the Roman Church thenceforth projected his importance principally as an outstanding Papal State secretary, anti-Byzantine theologian, and editor of proceedings of councils.

ANATH

In Judaism, the father of one of Israel's judges, Shamgar (Judges 3:31; 5:6). This was also the name of one of the three principal Canaanite goddesses. She is presented as both the sister and spouse of Baal and a symbol of lustful sex and war.

ANATHEMA

This solemn formula of excommunication or exclusion from the ecclesiastic community was used by the Roman Catholic Church to assert that some position or teaching contradicts Catholic faith and doctrine. Paul used this expression against anyone who preached a false gospel (Galatians 1:8-9 and 1 Corinthians 5:4-5) or rejected the love of Christ (1 Corinthians 16:22). Anathema was abolished by Vatican Council II.

ANATHOTH

In Judaism, one of the heads of the people whose descendant, if not himself, attested to and sealed a trustworthy arrangement in the days of Nehemiah, to walk in the path of true worship of God (Nehemiah 9:38; 10:1, 19).

ANATMAN

In Buddhism, term meaning egolessness. All existence and phenomena in this world do not, ultimately, have any substantial reality. It is very natural for Buddhism, which advocates an impermanence of all existence, to insist that such an impermanent existence could not therefore possess any perpetual substance in it. Anatman may also be translated as non-soul.

ANATTA

In Buddhism, the essential doctrine of non-ego; one the the three signs of Being, with Anticca and Dukkha. It is the doctrine of the non-separateness of all forms of life, and the opposite of that of an immortal and yet personal soul. As applied to man it states that there is no permanent ego or self in the five shandhas which make up the personality.

The Buddha, however, nowhere denied the existence of an ego or soul, but taught that no permanent entity, not subject to Anicca and Dukkha, can be found in any of the human faculties. That which pertains to any human being is not immortal; that which is immortal and unchanging is not the possession of any one human being.

ANAWRAHTA

First king of all of Burma (reigned 1044-1077), who converted his people to Theravada Buddhism. Anawrahta was converted to Theravada Buddhism by a Mon monk, Shin Arahan. As king he strove to convert his people from the influence of Azri, a Mahayana Tantric sect that was at that time predominant in Upper Burma. Theravada became the national religion of Burma and the inspiration for its culture and civilization.

ANCAEUS

In Greek mythology, the son of Zeus and Poseidon and king of the Leleges of Samos.

ANCESTOR SPIRITS

Souls or ghosts of deceased persons or mythical heroes regarded as ancestors, who are believed to have benevolent or malevolent powers and thus to be worthy of veneration. Though far from universal, belief in ancestor spirits has existed in most societies at some stage in their development, especially in preliterate communities in Africa, Asia, and the Pacific area, in many ancient cultures, and in Eastern civilizations; such beliefs, however, have been expunged from the major Western religions (Judaism, Christianity, and Islam).

ANCESTOR WORSHIP

A variety of religious beliefs and practices concerned with the spirits of dead persons regarded as relatives, some of whom may be mythical. Though ancestor worship exists or formerly existed in societies at every level of cultural development, it is far from worldwide.

ANCHOR-CROSS

This symbol combines the anchor, a sign of safety, with the cross, a sign of salvation, to symbolize the Christian hope in eternal salvation.

The early Christians used this figure in the catacombs as a symbol of hope. The theological virtue of hope is said to be the anchor of the soul (Hebrews 6:19-20). The anchor-cross is often associated with St. Nicholas, the patron saint of sailors.

ANDANIA MYSTERIES

Hellenistic Greek mystery cult,held in honor of the earth goddess Demeter and her daughter Kore at the town of Adania in Messenia. Initiation seems to have been open to men, women, and children, bonded and free, and some details have survived as to the costumes to be worn by each class of initiates; all were to be severely plain and of inexpensive material. There was a procession, precedence in which was strictly regulated, and the main ceremonial was preceded by sacrifices to a number of deities.

ANDREW

One of Christ's 12 Apostles and brother of Peter, formerly a fisherman (Mark 1:16) and disciple of John the Baptist (John 1:40). He reputedly preached in what is now Russia and was, by tradition, martyred in Patras, Greece on an X-shaped ("St. Andrew's") cross.

Andrew was first a disciple of John the Baptist (John 1:35, 40). In the fall of 29 he was at Bethany on the east side of the Jordan River and heard John the Baptist introduce Jesus to his residence and was soon convinced he had found the Messiah. He then found and informed his brother Simon and led him to Jesus (John 1:36-41). The two brothers returned to their fishing business, but between six months and a year later, after the arrest of John the Baptist they, along with James and John, were invited by Jesus to become "fishers of men." They immediately abandoned their nets and took up the full-time ministry (Matthew 4:18-20; Mark 1:14, 16-20). In time these four became Apostles, and it is notable that Andrew is always listed as among the first four in all the apostolic lists (Matthew 10:2; Mark 3:18; Luke 6:14).

ANDREWES, Lancelot

(1555-1626) Theologian and court preacher who sought to defend and advance Anglican doctrines during a highly controversial period of the English Church.

Despite his exposure to Puritan influences at Cambridge, Andrewes was a cautious but consistent critic both of Calvinist dogmas and of Puritan reform platforms. His major writings, however, were devoted to anti-Roman Catholic apologetics, in which he combined a critique of distinctly Roman Catholic dogmas with a positive statement of Anglican teaching on such themes as patristic tradition, episcopacy, and the sacraments.

ANDREW OF CARNIOLA

(1399-1484) Archbishop, advocate of councillor rule in the Western church, i.e., the supremacy of a general council of bishops over the papacy. It is generally held that his personal hostility to the pope prompted an erratic behavior that frustrated the effectiveness of his theory.

ANDREW OF CRETE, SAINT

(660-740) Archbishop of Cortyna, Crete, regarded by the Greek Church as one of his greatest hymn writers. In developing the Byzantine liturgy, he is credited with inventing the canon, a new genre of hymnography that consists of nine odes in stanzaic form, each sung in different melody.

ANDRONICUS

In the New Testament, a faithful Jewish Christian in the congregation at Rome to whom Paul sent greetings. Paul calls Andronicus and Junias "my relatives." While the Greek word used here (sygenes) in its broader sense can mean "fellow-countrymen," the primary meaning is "blood relative of the same generation." Like Paul, Andronicus has suffered imprisonment, is now a "man of note" among the apostles, and had become a Christian prior to Paul (Romans 16:7).

ANFAL, al-

The title of the 8th sura of the Koran; it means "The Spoils." The sura belongs to the Medinan period and has 75 verses. Its title is taken from the first verse which refers to questions which will be asked about the spoils gained at the Battle of Badr. The verse indicates that there was some quarrelling among the Muslims over the division of the spoils after the battle.

ANGEL

In Christianity, supernatural messenger and servant of God. Angels serve and praise God, but guardian angels may protect the faithful (Psalm 91:11) against the evil of the Devil, the fallen angel Satan (Ezekiel 28:16). In the Bible, angels appear most frequently in connection with the coming of Christ and his life and death. The hierarchy of angels was said to have nine orders: Cherubim, Seraphim, Thrones, Dominions, Virtues, Powers, Principalities, Archangels, Angels.

In Islam, the term is used for an incorporeal being created from light to render absolute praise, service, and obedience to God. The angels often serve as God's messengers or envoys. The word used in Arabic for angel is malak. The Arabic language does not differentiate between angels and archangels. Each person has two recording or guardian angels who record his or her good and bad deeds.

ANGELOLOGY

In earlier books of the Bible the "angel of Yahweh" appears as the messenger of God to human beings. There are vaguer references to other angels, attending on Yahweh. In post-exile times, possibly under the influence of Zoroastrianism, a hierarchy of angels emerged.

ANGELS, Hierarchy of

An order or ranking of celestial or spiritual beings or entities in Western religions; i.e. Zoroastrianism, Judaism, Christianity, and Islam. Functioning as messengers or servants of the deity or as guardians of individuals or nations, such spiritual beings have been classified into ranks or hierarchies by theologians or philosophical thinkers of the major Western religions, and of sects that have become religions in their own right (for example, the Druzes, a religion that developed from Islam).

ANGLICAN CHANT

Simple harmonized setting of a melodic formula devised for singing prose versions of the psalms and canticles in the Anglican Church.

ANGLICAN COMMUNION

Religious body consisting of national, independent and autonomous Anglican churches throughout the world. The Anglican Communion is united by a common loyalty to the archbishop of Canterbury in England as its titular leader and by a general agreement with doctrines and practices as defined in the 16th-century *Book of Common Prayer.*

ANGLICANISM

The established Church of England became independent of Rome through the Reformation, but contains "Catholic" and Protestant elements. Church government is by bishops; worship is primarily in fixed liturgies: the Book of Common Prayer (1662) and new services since 1965. Doctrine was classically expressed in the Thirty Nine Articles (1563).

ANGLICANS

A word describing the churches united in faith and ecclesial organization to the English See of Canterbury. Anglicanism originated in 1534 with Henry VIII's Act of Supremacy, which declared that the king should be the supreme head of the Church of England. In the United States of America, Anglicans have been called Episcopalians since the Revolutionary War.

The absolute break with the Catholic Church occurred in 1563, when Parliament made the so-called Thirty Nine Articles of religion mandatory for all citizens.

Among the articles:

▲ the Bible contains all that is necessary for salvation;

▲ ecumenical councils are not infallible;

▲ transubstantiation is not acceptable (though today some Anglicans hold views on the Eucharist similar to those of the Roman Catholic Church);

▲ the civil ruler has authority over the church.

The *Book of Common Prayer* is perhaps the most important bond of unity among the Anglican churches.

ANGLO-CATHOLICISM

A movement that emphasizes the Catholic rather than the Protestant heritage of the Anglican Communion. It was an outgrowth of the 19th century Oxford Movement, which sought to renew Catholic thought and practices in the Church of England.

ANGUTTARA NIKAYA

In Buddhism, fourth of the five Nikayas or collections of Discourses of Buddha, into which Sutta Pitaka is divided.

ANICCA

In Buddhism, term meaning impermanence; one of the three characteristics of all existence; the other being Dukkha and Anatta. Buddhism teaches that everything is subject to the law of cause and effect, is the creation of preceding causes and is in turn a cause of after-effect. There is in existence, therefore, no unchanging condition of being, but only an ever-belonging flux.

ANICONISM

Opposition on religious grounds to the depiction in the visual arts of images of living creatures. Such opposition is particularly relevant to the Jewish, Islamic, and Byzantine artistic traditions. The opposition is based on the Second Commandment.

ANIMAL WORSHIP

A term used by Western religionists in a pejorative manner and by ancient Greek and Roman polemicists against religions (e.g., Egyptian) whose gods are represented in animal form. Most examples are given for animal worship of an animal itself. Instead, the sacred power of a deity was believed to be manifested in an epiphany or incarnation of the deity.

ANIMISM

A term first used by E. B. Tylor to designate a general belief in spiritual beings, which belief he held to be the origin of all religions. A common corruption of Tylor's sense is to interpret animism as the belief that all natural objects possess spirits. Piaget has proposed that the growing child characteristically passes through an animistic phase.

In the past the term animism was applied to the belief of less developed peoples that certain plants and material objects have a spirit or soul of their own.

ANITYA

In Buddhism, term meaning transitoriness or impermanency. All existence and phenomena in this world are changing constantly and do not remain the same for even a single moment. Everything has to die or end someday in its future, and such a prospect is the very cause of suffering. This concept should not, however, be interpreted only from a pessimistic or nihilistic viewpoint, because both advancement and reproduction are also manifestations of this constant change.

ANIUS

In Greek mythology, the son of the god Apollo and Rhoeo, a descendant of Dionysus. His mother, when pregnant, had been placed in a chest and cast into the sea by her father; floating to the island of Delos, she gave birth to Anius, who became a seer and a priest of Apollo.

ANKABUT, al-

The title of the 29th sura of the Koran; it means "The Spider." The sura belongs to the Meccan period and has 69 verses. Its name derives from the 41st verse where it is stated that those who take helpers or protectors apart from God do no better than the spider when it builds itself what is always the weakest of house.

ANNA

Jewish prophetess, daughter of Phanuel of the tribe of Asher. Widowed at an early age, she then served God in the Temple by continual prayer and fasting. At the age of 84 she witnessed the presentation of Jesus in the Temple (Luke 2:36-38).

ANNAS

In the Bible, High Priest appointed 6 or 7 BC by Quirinius the Roman governor of Syria, and serving until the year 15 (Luke 2:2). Annas was therefore High Priest when Jesus, at the age of 12, amazed the rabbinical teachers at the Temple (Luke 2:42-49). Procurator Valerius Gratus removed Annas as High Priest, for reportedly overstepping his Roman-assigned jurisdiction. Though he no longer had the official title, yet it was quite evident that he continued to exercise great power and influence as High Priest emeritus and predominant voice of the Jewish hierarchy. Five of his sons were each in turn High Priests.

ANNATES

Term in medieval church history for the first year's income that was paid by new holders of certain church offices to the bishop, or more usually, the pope. The practice was far from uniform and raised considerable protest. Since the 15th century papal annates have gradually fallen into disuse except in Italy.

ANNE, Saint

Mother of the Virgin Mary and wife of St. Joachim. Though not mentioned in Scripture, she was venerated in early Christian times. According to an apocryphal writing of St. James, long after Saint Anne has despaired of bearing a child, an angel appeared to her and foretold the birth of Mary. Often represented in art in such scenes as the Birth of the virgin, Saint Anne is the patron saint of woman in labor. Her feast day is July 26.

ANNE AND JOACHIM, Saints

(1st century BC) According to tradition derived from certain apocryphal writings, the parents of the Virgin Mary. Information concerning their lives and names is found in the 2nd century "First Gospel of James" and the 3rd century "Gospel of the Nativity of Mary." According to these, Anne was born in Bethlehem, Judea. She married Joachim, and, although they shared a wealthy and devout life at Nazareth, they eventually lamented their childlessness. Joachim, reproached at the Temple for his sterility, retreated into the countryside to pray, while Anne, grieved by his disappearance and by her barrenness, solemnly promised God that, if given a child, she would dedicate it to the Lord's service. Both received the vision of an angel, who announced that Anne would conceive and bear a most wondrous child. Messengers announced Joachim's return, and Anne happily met him at the city gate. They rejoiced at the birth of their daughter, whom Anne named Mary.

ANNIHILATION

In Buddhism, misunderstanding of Anatta; this has led to the idea of annihilation as goal of Buddhist endeavor. The only kind of annihilation taught by Buddha was that of the skandhas which form the evanescent part of man.

ANNULMENT

Decree to the effect that a marriage was invalid when contracted. Grounds for annulment include fraud, force and close blood links between the parties. The Roman Catholic Church recognizes annulment but not divorce.

The term annulment is generally used for what is known in the Code of Canon Law (Roman Catholic Church) as a decree of nullity - namely, a declaration by a competent authority of the Church that a marriage was invalid from the beginning because of the presence of a diriment (invalidating) impediment, a basic defect in consent to marriage, or an inability to fulfill the responsibilities of marriage, or a condition placed by one or both of the partners on the vary nature of marriage as understood by the Church.

The annulment procedure may be started at the parish level; the investigation of the facts is usually carried out by a marriage tribunal under the leadership of a bishop.

ANNUNCIATION

In Christian belief, the archangel Gabriel's announcement to the Virgin Mary that she would give birth to the Messiah. The Roman Catholic Church celebrates the annunciation as Lady Day, March 25th. The annunciation appears in many Christian paintings.

ANOINTED, Anointing

Biblical term with slightly different meaning. The Bible indicates a difference between the common practice of rubbing the body with oil and the special anointing with oil of dedicated things and people. This distinction is maintained quite consistently by different original-language words, both in the Hebrew and in the Greek. Some versions of the Bible do not maintain this fine distinction but translate all such words by the one term "anoint."

ANOINTING OF THE SICK

In the Roman Catholic and Eastern Orthodox churches, a sacrament for the seriously ill and the elderly in which the person is anointed with olive oil and prayers are said. According to the teachings of both churches, the rite is a sacrament instituted by Mark (6:13) and recommended by Apostle James (5:14-17). It was evidently practiced in the early church.

ANSELM, Saint

(1033-1109) Archbishop of Canterbury (from, 1093) who upheld Church authority and became the first scholastic philosopher. He endured repeated exile for challenging the right of English kings to influence church affairs. Anselm saw reason as the servant of faith and probably invented the ontological "proof" of God's existence: that our idea of a perfect being implies the existence of such a being.

ANSHAR AND KISHAR

In Mesopotamian mythology, the male and female principles, the twin horizons of sky and earth.

ANTASKARANA

In Buddhism literally "Making an end." In the esoteric analysis of man's principles the path or bridge between the lower mind or personality and the higher mind or reincarnation compound of principles and faculties in which is inherent the power to achieve enlightenment.

ANTHEM

Choral composition with English words, used in Anglican and other English-speaking church services. It developed in the mid-16th century in the Anglican church as a musical form analogous to the Roman Catholic motet, a choral composition with a sacred Latin text.

ANTHIMUS I

(6th century) Greek Orthodox patriarch of Constantinople (reigned 535-536), the last notable Byzantine churchman explicitly to advocate Monophysitism, the largely Eastern Christian heresy of the 5th and 6th centuries that taught a single, divine nature in Christ subsuming his humanity. His political and theological activities on behalf of the Monophysite cause ended in his condemnation and the heresy's suppression.

ANTHIMUS VI

(1790-1878) Joannides; Eastern Orthodox patriarch of Constantinople who attempted to extend his ecclesiastical authority over the independent Bulgarian Orthodox Church, and, with others, wrote an Orthodox encyclical letter repudiating Roman Catholic overtures toward reunion.

ANTHIMUS VII

(1835-1913) Tsatsos; Eastern Orthodox patriarch of Constantinople, theologian, and orator, a leading critic of the Roman Catholic Church. He was the author of a formal Orthodox pronouncement, that rejected papal offers of reunion of the Greek and Latin churches.

ANTHONY III STUDITE

(907-983) Monk and patriarch of Constantinople (reigned 974-979) and advocate of the church's independence from the state. A theological writer, he collaborated in drawing up liturgical literature for Eastern Orthodox worship. The single extant work of Anthony is his Admonition to monks on penance and confession of sins, a treatise that set a standard for Eastern asceticism.

ANTHONY OF EGYPT, Saint

(250-355) Hermit and first Christian monk who subsequently became the founder and father of Christian monasticism. A disciple of Paul of Thebes, Anthony began to practice an ascetic life at the age of 20 and after 15 years withdrew for absolute solitude to a mountain by the Nile called Pispir. In circa 305 he emerged from his retreat to instruct and organize the monastic life of the hermits who imitated him and had established themselves nearby.

ANTHONY OF KIEV

(999-1073) Founder of Russian monasticism through the institution of the Greek Orthodox ideal of the contemplative life. He established the basis for the Russian assimilation of the three elements of Byzantine monasticism: the writings of the early Egyptian and Palestinian monks, the heremitical practices of Mount Athos and the communal spirituality in the rule of Constantinople's Stoudion monastery.

ANTHONY OF PADUA, Saint

(1195-1231) Franciscan friar, theologian and preacher. He was born near Lisbon, but taught and preached in France and Italy. Canonized a year after his death, he is the patron saint of the poor, and his feast day is June 13. He is invoked to aid the discovery of lost objects.

ANTHONY OF TAGRIT

(9th century) Syrian Orthodox theologian and writer, a principal contributor to the development of Syriac literature and poetry.

ANTHONY OF THEBES, Saint

(250-340) Egyptian hermit, considered the founder of Christian monasticism. He founded a desert community of ascetics near Fayum, then lived alone in a mountain cave near the Red Sea and died aged over 100. He supported St. Athanasius in the Arian controversy. His feast day is January 17th.

ANTHROPOMORPHISM

The attributing to God of human traits and characteristics, both physical such as face, mouth, heart, and hands and emotional qualities such as love, compassion, kindness, sorrow, joy, and anger.

To counter the error that can come from a literal understanding of this metaphorical way of portraying God, the Church teaches that God is a pure spirit without physical or spatial dimensions.

ANTICHRIST

The chief enemy of Christ; the antagonist of Christ. The only mention of the name Antichrist is in the letters of John (1 John 2:18-22). John makes a distinction between "antichrist" and "antichrists". In general sense an antichrist is someone who is opposed to Christ as Son of God. The Antichrist, however, appears as a tempter who works by signs and wonders and seeks to obtain divine honors.The concept of a person or power opposed to God can be traced to Jewish tradition.

Roman Catholic writers commonly interpret the term to mean any adversary of Christ and of the church's authority, specifically the last and greatest antagonist of the Christian Church, whose coming will precede the end of the world.

ANTICLERICALISM

Hostility toward the influence of clergy in secular affairs. Anticlericalism emerged in Europe after the Protestant Reformation of the early 16th century. At first it involved attacks on the abuse of secular powers vested in the Roman Catholic Church during the Middle Ages, but as nationalism, liberalism and the study of science and rational philosophy gained ground, anticlericals attacked the Church because its dogmas proved to be scientifically invalid, and because they considered that clerical influence in state affairs was an unwarranted interference in national government.

Developing in France around 1650, anticleralism rapidly gained ground after the French Revolution - spreading through Italy, Spain, Austria-Hungary, Germany and Latin America. In some countries it led to suppression of religious activity. With the lessened political influence of the Church in recent years, anticlericalism has tended to decline.

ANTILOCHUS

In Greek legend, son of Nestor, king of Pylos. One of the suitors of Helen, whose abduction caused the Trojan war, he accompanied his father to the war and distinguished himself as acting commander of the Pylians.

ANTINOMANISM

Doctrine according to which Christians are freed by grace from the necessity of obeying the Mosaic Law. The antinomians rejected the very notion of obedience as legalistic; to them the good life flowed from the inner working of the Holy Spirit. In this circumstance they could and did appeal not only to Martin Luther but also to apostle Paul and Augustine.

ANTIOCH

City founded in 300 BC by the Greeks and was the center of the Seleucid Kingdom until 64 BC, when the Romans made it the capital of their province of Syria. The city was one of the earliest centers of Christianity, serving as one of the refuges of the persecuted disciples after the death of Stephen (Acts 11:19-20).

ANTIOCH, Council of

(341) A non-ecumenical Christian Church council held at Antioch on the occasion of the consecration of Constantine's Golden Church there. It was first of several 4th-century councils that attempted to replace Orthodox Nicene theology with a modified Arianism.

ANTIOCH, Orthodox Church of

An autocephalous (ecclesiastically independent) Eastern Orthodox patriarchate, third in honorific rank after the churches of Constantinople and Alexandria; it is the largest Arab Christian church in the Middle East.

ANTIOCH, School of

A Christian theological institution in Syria, traditionally founded circa 200, that stressed the literal interpretation of the Bible and the completeness of Christ's humanity, in opposition to the school of Alexandria, which emphasized the allegorical interpretation of the Bible and stressed Chirst's divinity.

ANTIOCH, See of

One of the most important centers of nascent Christianity, said to have had st. Peter as its first bishop. By the 4th century it ranked as the third most important patriarchate after Rome and Alexandria.

ANTIOCHENE RITE

Sometimes called West Syrian Rite, the system of liturgical practices and discipline observed by Syrian Monophysites (Jacobites), the Malabar Christians of Kerala, (India), and three Eastern Rite communities of the Roman Catholic Church: Syrians, Maronites, and Malankarese Christians of Kerala.

ANTIPAS

In the New Testament, a martyr of the early Christian congregation at Pergamum in the first century.

ANTIPHON

In Roman Catholic liturgical music, chant melody and text sung before and after a psalm verse, originally by alternating choirs (antiphonal singing). The antiphons of Our Lady are associated with the four seasons:
▲ "Loving Mother of the Redeemer" (Advent);
▲ "Hail Queen of Heaven" (Lent);
▲ "Heavenly Queen" (Paschal season);
▲ "Hail Holy Queen" for the remainder of the year.

Though the antiphons of Our Lady were first sung in association with the psalms, they are now most often heard as independent hymns.

ANTIPOPE

A pretender to the papal throne, elected by faction in the Roman Catholic church or by a secular ruler. The first antipope was Hippolytus (3rd century); the last was Felix V (abdicated 1449). In the great schism (1378) Italy elected Urban VI while France set up court for Clement VII in Avignon. Their successors were deposed by the Council of Constance (1415).

Historically, antipopes have arisen as a result of a variety of causes; the following are some examples:
1   Doctrinal disagreement.
2   Deportation of the pope.
3   Double elections arbitrated by the secular authority.
4   Double elections and subsequent recourse to a third candidate.
5   Change in the manner of choosing the pope.

ANTIQUITIES OF THE JEWS, THE

Original Latin*Antiquitates Judaicae,* an account of Jewish history from its early beginnings to the revolt against Rome in AD 66, written about AD 93 by Flavius Josephus, a Jewish politician, and historian. Josephus sided with Rome against the Jews, and his writings are not always accepted as totally reliable.

ANTI-SEMITISM

Hostility towards Jews, ranging from social prejudice to genocide. Common motives for anti-Semitism include religious opposition to Judaism, national resentment of a people who remain in some ways apart from the life of the country they live in and simpler jealousy of the Jews' material success.

Anti-Semites have often justified their standing by claiming that the Jews' exile and persecution were punishment for their part in Christ's crucifixion. Segregation, expulsion and massacres have dogged Europe's Jewish communities, notably in the Middle Ages, and later in Czarist Russia and in Nazi Germany before and during World War II, when some 6,000,000 Jews were put to death in concentration camps at Auschwitz, Belsen, Buchenwald and elsewhere. Despite the decline of avowed anti-Semitism since World War II, anti-Jewish feelings have increased in Arab lands hostile to the young Jewish state of Israel.

ANTONINUS, Saint

(1389-1459; Antonio Pierozzi) Archbishop of Florence, who is regarded as one of the founders of modern moral theology and Christian social ethics.

ANU

In the differentialist system of Hindu philosophy, the atomic germ of the five elements - ether, air, wood, fire and earth. The elements in their germinal state are without spatial mass and transcendentally independent. In their atomic form, earth, water, and fire are eternal but, in larger aggregates, are transient.

ANUMANA

Second of the means of knowledge in Indian philosophy that enable man to have accurate cognitions.

ANXIETY

In theological terms, fear and apprehension that engender unnecessary doubts about one's faith.

APACHE CEREMONIALISM

Apache ceremonies conducted by people who are channels for spiritual power for healing, locating an animal, finding lost persons and objects, diagnosing illness, protecting from illness and improving luck. Healing ceremonies last one, two, four, or eight nights. Shorter ceremonies are held for diagnostic reasons with longer ceremonies aimed at eliminating illness.

Curing ceremonies have discrete elements, including masked dances, chants, prayers, stylized gestures and the use of ritual paraphernalia and sand paintings.

APADANA

Collection of legends about Buddhist saints, one of the later books of the latest section of the Sutta Pitaka of the Pali canon. This work, which is entirely in verse, presents stories about 547 monks and nuns. For each personage there are tales about one or more previous lives as well as his or her present existence, all the tales presented as the words of the Buddha.

APHEK

Canaanite royal city near the present-day Israeli city of Petah Tiqwa. Conquered by Joshua, it became a Philistine stronghold in the period of the Judges.

APHRODITE

Ancient Greek goddess of sexual love and beauty, identified by the Romans with Venus. Because the Greek word aphros means "foam," the legend arose that Aphrodite was born from the white foam produced by the severed genitals of Uranus (Heaven), after his son Cronus threw him into the sea.

Aphrodite was the patron of love and lovers, and her favorite pastime was causing the gods to fall in love with mortal women. She enjoyed weaving plots and enmeshing the gods in love affairs - especially Zeus, who one finds embroiled in various intrigues at different times.

Nor was Aphrodite herself to be left out of the game. Although married to the lame god Hephaestus, she embarked on an affair with Ares. InThe Iliad,Homer tells us the scandalous tale: Hephaestus found out about Aphrodite's goings on from Helios, the sun god, who saw everything, and decided to lay a trap for her and Ares. He made a magic net which was very complex and pretended to set off for Lemnos. That night, when Artes came to Aphrodite's bed for their assignation, Hephaestus caught then in his net and immobilized them just at the crucial moment. The incident ended in general laughter from the gods. Her union with Ares brought Aphrodite four children: Eros, Deimus, Phobus and Harmony.

APHTHARTODOCETISM

A Christian heresy of the 16th century that carried Monophysitism ("Christ had but one nature and that is divine") to a new extreme: it was proclaimed by Julian, bishop of Halicarnassus, who asserted that the body of Christ was divine and therefore naturally incorruptible and impassible; Christ, however, was free to will his sufferings and death voluntarily.

APIS

Ancient Egyptian bull god, probably originating as a fertility god, but later seen as the reincarnation of Osiris. Worshiped at Memphis, Egypt, in the form of a living bull, Apis was black and white, with distinctive markings. Upon his death, Apis was buried with great pomp in the Serapeum at Memphis and there were wild celebrations at the installation of his successor (a bull with the same distinctive markings and color). Mummified bodied of bulls buried in enormous sarcophagi were discovered at Memphis in 1850.

APOCALYPSE

A prophetic revelation about the end of the world and the ensuing establishment of a heavenly kingdom. Accompanying or heralding God's dramatic intervention in human affairs will be cataclysmic events of cosmic proportions, such as a temporary rule of the world by Satan, signs in the heavens, persecutions, wars, famines and plagues.

Apocalypse means uncovering or revealing. The Apocalypse focused on the visions of events to come and included fearful warnings about crisis-times faced by the earliest Christians.

APOCALYPTIC

A genre of Jewish and Christian literature, called after the Apocalypse, the New Testament Revelation to John. The word means "unveiling," and apocalyptic literature undertakes to disclose matters inaccessible to normal knowledge, such as the mysteries of outer space or those of the future, often in symbolic language.

APOCALYPTICISM

A term used to designate eschatological (end-time) views and movements that focus on cryptic revelations about a sudden, dramatic, and cataclysmic intervention of God in history, the judgment of all men, the salvation of the faithful elect, and the eventual rule of the elect with God in a renewed heaven and earth.

Arising in Zoroastrianism, an Iranian religion founded by the 6th century BC prophet Zoroaster, apocalypticism was developed more fully in Judaic, Christian and Islamic eschatological speculation and movements.

APOCRYPHA

Any writings of dubious authority. The term originally referred to those publications not read publicly, hence "concealed" from others. Later, however, the word took on the meaning of spurious or uncanonical, and today is used most commonly to refer to the eleven additional writings declared as forming part of the Bible canon by the Roman Catholic Church at the Council of Trent (1546). Catholic writers refer to these books as deutero-canonical, meaning "of the second (or later) canon," as distinguished from proto-canonical.

These eleven additional writings are Tobit, Judith, Wisdom (of Solomon), Ecclesiasticus (not Ecclesiastes), Baruch, 1 and 3 Maccabees, supplements to Esther and three additions to Daniel: The Song of the Three Holy Children, Susanna and the Elders, and the Destruction of Bel and the Dragon. The exact time of their being written is uncertain, but the evidence points to a time no earlier than the second or third century BC.

APOLINARIS THE APOLOGIST, Saint

(2nd century) Bishop of Hierapolis, Phrygia, one of the chief apologists of orthodoxy against contemporary heresies, especially Montanism, a doctrine of false prophecy that arose circa 171 in the Christian church in Asia Minor.

APOLINARIS THE YOUNGER

(born circa 310, died circa 390) Bishop of Laodicea who developed the heretical position concerning the nature of Christ called Apollinarianism. He reproduced the Old Testament in the form of Homeric and Pindaric poetry and the New Testament in the style of Platonic dialogues after the Roman emperor Julian had forbidden Christians to teach the classics.

APOLLO

Major deity in Greek and Roman mythology. In the Greek myths, Apollo was the son of Zeus and Leto, and twin of Artemis. Second only to Zeus, he had the power of the sun as giver of light and life. He was the god of justice and masculine beauty, and the purifier of those stained by crime. He was the divine patron of arts, leader of the Muses and god of music and poetry. Apollo was a healer, but could also send disease, and from his foreknowledge he spoke through the oracle at Delphi. The Romans adopted Apollo honoring him as healer and god of the sun.

APOLLYON

Greek name used by the apostle John to translate the Hebrew "Abaddon" at Revelation 9:11. Apollyon means "destroyer," and is given as the name of the "angel of the abyss." Though most reference works apply this name to some evil personage or force, the whole setting of the apocalyptic vision is to the contrary, as it consistently portrays angels being used by God to bring woes upon His enemies.

APOLOGETICS

A branch of theology concerned with the skillful presentation of the reasonableness, truth, and ultimate value of Christian beliefs about God, the Church, Christ, and our common human destiny.

APOLOGISTS, early Christian

Group of writers, primarily in the 2nd century, who attempted to provide a defense of Christianity and criticism of Greco-Roman culture.

The Apologists usually tried to prove the antiquity of their religion by treating it as the fulfillment of Old Testament prophecy; they argued that their opponents were really godless because they worshiped the gods of mythology; and they insisted on the philosophical nature of their own faith as well as its high ethical teaching. Their works did not present a complete picture of Christianity because they were arguing primarily in response to charges of their opponents.

APOLOGY OF THE AUGSBURG CONFESSION

One of the confessions of Lutheranism, a defense and elaboration of the Augsburg Confession, written by the reformer Philip Melanchthon in 1531.

Seven times longer than the Augsburg Confession, the Apology is considered one of the most brilliant of the Reformation theoretical works. About one third of the work is concerned with the problem of justification, while other subjects treated include the church, human tradition, the invocation of saints, marriage of priests, the mass, monastic vows, penitence, and original sin.

APOSTASY

Term used in classical Greek to refer to political defection, and the verb is evidently employed in this sense at Acts 5:37, concerning Judas the Galilean who "drew off" followers. The Greek Septuagint uses the term at Genesis 14:4 with reference to such a rebellion. However, in the Christian Greek

Scriptures it is used primarily with regard to religious defection; a withdrawal or abandonment of the true cause, worship and service of God, and hence an abandonment of what one has previously professed and a total desertion of principles of faith. The religious leaders of Jerusalem charged Paul with such an apostasy against the Mosaic law (Acts 21:21).

APOSTLE

(Greek "apostolos," one who is sent) The 12 disciples closest to Jesus, to whom he chose to proclaim his teaching. The number twelve is related to the twelve tribes of Israel. They were also often called "the twelve" (Matthew 26:14). They were Andrew, John, Bartholomew, Judas, Jude, the two Jameses, Matthew, Peter, Philip, Simon and Thomas (Matthew 10:2). When Judas died, Matthias replaced him (Acts 1:26). Paul and Barnabas became known as apostles for their work in spreading the gospel.

In Islam, the term Rasul is used for apostle, messenger, envoy. Mohammed is called in the Shahaba, the Koran (see verse 40 of Surat al-Ahzab) and elsewhere, "The Messenger of God." His absolute humanity is stressed in the Koran in terms of his being a Rasul and it is stressed in the same verse that there were other messengers before him.

APOSTLES' CREED

A creed ascribed to Christ's apostles and maintained in its present form since the early Middle Ages. The Roman Catholic Church uses it in the sacraments of baptism and confirmation. It is also used by various Protestant denominations.

Apostles' Creed is a summary of Christian faith expressed in 12 articles. Its name came from a popular belief that it was actually written by the 12 apostles; its substance clearly stems from the New Testament.

Historians, however, date the actual text anywhere from 150 to 500. It is clear that at a very early date the Western Church required catechumen (new members) to learn the Apostles' Creed before baptism.

APOSTLESHIP OF PRAYER

This organization, founded in France in 1844, is associated with the League of the Sacred Heart. The members recite the Daily Offering to sanctify their prayers, works, and sufferings of the day by uniting them with the Holy sacrifice of the Mass through the world, and pray for the monthly general and missionintentions recommended by the Holy father.

The association is under Jesuit direction, has centers all over the world, and publishes its magazine the *Messenger of the Sacred Heart* in many different languages.

APOSTOLATE

The work or office of an apostle is the ministry of the Word of God, setting up the church, spreading the faith, and bringing others to Christ.

The apostolate refers to labors done in the name of Christ and for laypersons includes the responsibility to preach Christ in their homes and workplaces and to bring others to him. Participation in the apostolate is an obligation for all the baptized and confirmed.

APOSTOLIC CHURCH

A term used by church historians to designate the earliest form of Christianity, established by Jesus Christ's Apostles in the first century, out of which emerged significant patterns of ecclesiastical organization, the Holy Scriptures, and doctrinal norms.

APOSTOLIC CONSTITUTIONS

Largest collection of ecclesiastical law that has survived from early Christianity. These regulations were drawn up by the apostles and transmitted to the church of Clement of Rome. In modern times it is generally accepted that the constitutions were actually written in Syria circa 380 and that they were the work of one compiler, probably an Arian (believing that Christ, the Son of God, is not divine, but a created being).

The work consists of eight books. The first six are an adaptation of the *Didascalia Apostolorum,* written in Syria circa 250. They deal with Christian ethics, the duties of the clergy, the Eucharistic Liturgy, and various church problems and rituals.

Book 7 contains a paraphrase ann enlargement of the *Teaching of the Twelve Apostles* and a Jewish collection of prayers and liturgical material.

Book 8 contains mainly an elaborate description of the Antiochene liturgy and a collection of 85 canons.

APOSTOLIC DELEGATE

Vatican representative with no diplomatic status and hence no power to deal with civil governments. His relations are with the ecclesiastical hierarchy of a country that maintains no diplomatic relations with the Holy See.

APOSTOLIC FATHERS

Greek Christian writers, several unknown, who were authors of early Christian works dating primarily from the late first and early second centuries. Their works are the principal source of information about Christianity during the two or three generations following the Apostles. They were originally called apostolic men. The name Apostolic Fathers was first applied in the 6th century, after the conception of the authority of the Fathers had been developed.

They include Clement of Rome, Ignatius, Polycarp, Hermas, Barnabas, Papias, and the authors of the *Teachings of the Twelve Apostles, Letter to Diognetus, Letter to Barnabas,* and the *Martyrdom of Polycarp.*

APOSTOLICI

Various Christian sects that sought to re-establish the life and discipline of the primitive church by a literal observance of the precepts of continence and poverty. The earliest Apostolici appeared in Asia Minor about the third century. In the 12th century, certain groups of heretical itinerant preachers called Apostolici were found in various centers in France, Flanders, and the Rhineland.

During the Protestant Reformation, many of the doctrines of the various Apostolici were espoused by the Anabaptists.

APOSTOLIC OVERCOMING HOLY CHURCH OF GOD

African-American Pentecostal church founded in 1916 by Bishop W.T. Phillips in Mobile, Alabama. The founder left the Methodist Church after becoming concerned about the doctrine of holiness.

APOSTOLIC SUCCESSION

A doctrine held by several Christian churches. They believe that Christ's apostles ordained the first bishops and other priests, that these ordained their successors, and so on, forging an unbroken chain of succession reaching to the present day which thereby guarantees their authority. Many Protestants, excepting Episcopalians, reject the doctrine as unproven and unnecessary.

APOSTOLIC SEE

The see of the Bishop of Rome. Since it was founded by St. Peter it is the highest seat of authority in the hierarchy of the Roman Catholic Church. The holder of the

See is the successor of St. Peter, and as Pope or Sovereign Pontiff stands at the head of the Catholic Church.

APPARITION

In the New Testament, specific term used in the two accounts of Jesus' walking over the waters of the Sea of Galilee in a situation when his disciples were in a boat (Matthew 14:26). The frightened disciples are quoted as saying: "It is an apparition!" An apparition is an illusion; something actually not present but temporarily believed due to excited imagination or other causes. Assuring the disciples that such was not the case and that he was real, Jesus said: "It is I; have no fear" (Matthew 14:27; Mark 6:50).

APPARITIONS OF THE BLESSED VIRGIN MARY

An apparition is an extraordinary, visible appearance seen by one or more persons. This manifestation may occur in the form of a supernatural vision or private revelation. The authenticity of apparitions is a matter for inquiry and evaluation by the Church or a skilled spiritual companion.

Recently some Church-accepted apparition sites have become places to which Christian pilgrims and spiritual seekers frequently journey. The places and dates of the apparitions include:

▲ Guadalupe   Mexico   1531
▲ Rue de Bac   France   1830
▲ La Salette   France   1846
▲ Lourdes   France   1858
▲ Fatima   Portugal   1917
▲ Beauraing   Belgium   1933
▲ Banneau   Belgium   1933.

Although the Roman Catholic Church has approved a number of apparitions and shrines, it does not view the messages communicated to persons in supernatural appearance as part of official Catholic doctrine.

APPROACH TO GOD

Specific rules for the approach of a monarch, also applied to God. In an ancient Oriental court any approach to the presence of the monarch by an individual could be made only in accord with established regulations and with the monarch's permission. In most cases an intermediary acted for petitioners desiring an audience with the ruler, introducing them and vouching for the genuineness of their credentials. To enter the inner courtyard of Persian King Ahasuerus without being called meant death; but Queen Esther, when risking her life to gain access to the king's presence, was favored with approval (Esther 4:11; 5:1-3). The action and words of Joseph's brothers illustrate the care employed to avoid causing offense before a king, for Judah said to Joseph: "It is the same with you as with Pharaoh" (Genesis 42:6; 43:15-26).

APSE

The semicircular end of the sanctuary in Romanesque and gothic churches terminates the chancel, aisles, or transepts. The altar is often located in the center of the apse.

AQUAVIVA, Claudio

(1543-1615) Fifth and the youngest general of the Society of Jesus, whom many have considered the order's greatest leader. His generalate was marked by rapid growth of the order from circa 5,000 to more than 13,000 members and from 12 to 32 provinces, with colleges reaching 372. He encouraged the order's theologians and spiritual writers to more profound investigation and to publication.

AQUILA

A natural Jew and native of Pontus in northern Asia Minor. Priscilla, his wife and loyal companion, is always mentioned in association with him. Banished from Rome by Emperor Claudius' decree against Jews as of January 25th, 50, they took up residence in Corinth (Acts 18:1, 2). When Paul arrived there in the autumn of 50, Aquila and Priscilla kindly received him into their home. A very close friendship developed among them as they worked together at their common trade and tentmaking and as Aquila and Priscilla doubtless aided Paul in building up the new congregation there (Acts 18:3).

AQUINAS, Saint Thomas

(1225-1274) Known as the "angelic doctor," major Christian theologian and philosopher who attempted to reconcile faith with reason. Thomism, the philosophy of St. Thomas, has been influential, and his teachings are basic to Roman Catholic theology.

ARA

In the Old Testament, a son of Jether of the tribe of Asher (1 Chronicles 7:30, 38).

ARA COELI

The title since the 14th century of the church of Saint Mary of the Capitoline in Rome. According to an apocryphal legend the Emperor Augustine there erected an altar (ara) to the Redeemer of whose coming he knew through the Sibyline prophecies. The church was given to the Franciscans by Innocent IV in 1250 and houses in its sacristy a celebrated wood carving of the Bambino.

ARA PACIS

Altar of the Peace, dedicated to Augustus, that stood on the Campus Martius, Rome. Raised on a podium, the altar enclosed by a wall, carries a processional frieze depicting Augustus as Pontifex Maximus (High Priest) with members of the imperial family, and senators.

Decorative reliefs show masterly floral patterns, mythological panels of the Earth goddess Tellus with Air and Water, and sacrificial themes.

ARABA

From the Hebrew ha'arabah, meaning desert or plain, the name of the rift valley in which the river Jordan and the Dead Sea lie. It extends from the Sea of Galilee to the head of the Gulf of Aquaba and is part of a great geological fault through the Red Sea all the way to Lake Nyasa in East Africa.

Traces of ancient mining and smelting of iron and copper have been explored in the Araba, especially near Asiongaber, and dated back to Solomonic times.

ARABESQUE

A pattern of endless geometric interlace in Islamic art, and of intricate curvilinear plant and animal design used in late Roman and Renaissance work.

ARABIA

In ancient time, important region of the Asiatic continent, located at its extreme south-western corner. It is bounded on the east by the Persian Gulf and the Gulf of Oman, on the south by the Indian Ocean and the Gulf of Aden, and on the west by the Red Sea, while the Fertile Crescent of Mesopotamia, Syria and Palestine curves around its northern end. Surrounded as it is on three sides by water, in part it resembles a huge island and is commonly called by its people the "Island of the Arabs."

The name Arabia is of Semitic origin and is believed to be drawn from a root word meaning "to be arid" (see Isaiah 21:13).

Arabia eventually became the home of many of the post-flood families listed at Genesis chapter 10. In the Semitic branch, Joktan fathered the heads of some 13 different Arabian tribes; while three of Aram's descendants, Uz, Gether and Mash, appear to have settled in the area of North Arabia and the Syrian Desert. The tent-dwelling Ishmaelites ranged from the Sinai Peninsula, across North Arabia and as far as Assyria (Genesis 25:13-18). The Midianites were located mainly in the north-western part of Arabia just east of the Gulf of Aqabah. Esau's descendants were based in the mountainous region of Edom to the south-east of the Dead Sea (Genesis 36:8; 40-43). From the Hamitic branch several descendants of Cush, including Havilah, Sabtah, Raamah and his sons Sheba and Dedan, and Sabteca, seem to have occupied mainly the southern part of the Arabian Peninsula (Genesis 10:7).

ARABIAN RELIGIONS

The cults of the Arabian Peninsula and adjoining areas among Arabic-speaking peoples that flourished from earliest recorded times until the rise of Islam in the 7th century AD. Because Islam views itself as a new revelation, the earlier religions among Arabic-speaking peoples were rejected as idolatrous and superstitious.

ARABIC

One of the Semitic languages. The Arabic alphabet comprises 28 letters, all consonants, vowels being expressed either by positioned points or, in some cases, by insertion of the letters alif, waw and ya in positions where they would not otherwise occur, thereby representing the long a, u and i respectively. Arabic is written from right to left.

Classical Arabic, the language of the Koran, is today used occasionally in writing, rarely in speech; a standardized modern Arabic being used for newspapers, etc.

Arabic played a large part in the dissemination of knowledge through medieval Europe as many ancient Greek and Roman texts were available solely in Arabic translation.

ARAD

In Judaism, one of the headmen of the tribe of Benjamin who at one time lived in Jerusalem (1 Chronicles 8:15, 28). The name is also used for a city on the southern border of Canaan, whose king attacked Israel as they approached Canaan.

A'RAF, Al-

The title of the seventh sura of the Koran; the word is frequently translated as "The Ramparts," "The Heights" or "The Battlements." The sura belongs to the Meccan period and has 206 verses. The title refers to an apparently intermediate place or state, not in paradise or hell, inhabited by those whose good and bad deeds are equal. One tradition has it that they too will eventually enter paradise.

ARAH

In the Old Testament, head of a family whose members returned to Jerusalem from Babylon with Zerubbabel (Ezra 2:1-5).

ARAM

In the Old Testament, the last son listed of Shem's five sons. Aram and his four sons, Uz, Hul, Gether and Mash, constituted five of the seventy post-flood families, and their descendants were the Aramaeans and Syrians (Genesis 10:22; 1 Chronicles 1:17).

ARAMAIC

An ancient Semitic language having a close relationship with Hebrew and originally spoken by the Aramaeans. With the passing of time, however, it came to embrace various dialects (some of them viewed as separate languages) and enjoyed wide use, especially in south-western Asia. Aramaic was employed particularly from the second millennium BC to about 500. It is named at Ezra 4:7 and Daniel 2:4, and is one of the three languages in which the Bible was originally written. The Aramaic portions of the Bible include Ezra 4:8 to 6:18 and 7:12-26; Jeremiah 10:11 and Daniel 2:4 to 7:28. Aramaic words also appear in Genesis, Esther, Job, certain Psalms, the Song of Solomon, Jonah and the Hebrew parts of Daniel. The Hebrew book of Job is strongly Aramaic and Ezekiel shows Aramaic influences. Quite a number of Aramaic proper and common nouns are found in the Christian Greek Scriptures, and particularly do Aramaic expressions appear in the Gospel accounts of Mark and Matthew.

ARAMAIC LANGUAGE IN LITURGY

Usually the term Aramaic in this context is used inaccurately for Syriac, a language of the Eastern branch of the Aramaic family, distinct from the Western type of Aramaic spoken in ancient Palestine.

Orientals who use Aramaic for the more exact Syriac often do so tendentiously, claiming that their liturgical language is that of Christ. Until the 13th century a Western Aramaic dialect (Christian Palestinian) was used liturgically in certain places in the Orthodox patriarchates of Jerusalem and Antioch.

ARAMAEAN

One of a confederacy of tribes that spoke a North Semitic language

(Aramaic) and, between the 11th and 8th centuries BC, occupied Aram, a large region in northern Syria. In the Old Testament the Arameans are represented as being closely akin to the Hebrews and living in northern Syria around Harran from about the 16th century BC.

ARARAT, Mount

Dormant volcanic mountain in east Turkey, with two peaks (16,950 feet and 13,000 feet) 7 miles apart. Noah's Ark landed upon the mountains of Ararat (Genesis 8:4). The Armenians venerate the mountain as the Mother of the World. The last eruption was in 1840.

Ararat traditionally is associated with the mountain on which Noah's Ark came to rest at the end of the Flood (deluge). The name Ararat, as it appears in the Bible, is the Hebrew equivalent of Urardhu, or Urartu, the Assyro-Babylonian name of a kingdom that flourished between the Aras and the Upper Tigris rivers from the 9th to the 7th century BC. Ararat is sacred to the Armenians, who believe themselves to be the first race of men to appear in the world after the Flood (deluge).

ARATCHINORD

In the Armenian Church, the head of a diocese. He is usually a bishop but may also be a major vardepet, and is, in either case, subject to the catholicos or patriarch on whose jurisdiction the diocese depends.

ARAUNAH

In the Old Testament, the Jebusite owner of the threshing floor purchased by King David for building an altar to God. This action resulted as the divinely indicated means of ending a scourge provoked by David's numbering the people (2 Samuel 24:16-25; 1 Chronicles 21:15-28).

ARCADIUS

(377-408) First Roman Emperor of the East from 395. His father Theodosius I, proclaimed him Augustus when he was only 6 years old and left him in Constantinople in 294 as the sole ruler of the eastern half of the Empire. Upon his father's death Arcadius kept the East while his younger brother Honorius obtained the West.

Arcadius was weak in body and in character and governed largely through his ministers Rufinus and Eutropius. He confiscated the chief pagan temples and forbade heretics from assembling; but his championship of orthodoxy wad dedicated by reasons of state. It was his wife Eudoxia who brought about the exile of St. John Chrysostom.

ARCHANGEL

In Christianity, a special angel, playing a very important role in God's masterplan. In the Bible, archangels are mentioned twice. The first is not mentioned by name (1 Thessalonians 4:16), the second named Michael (Jude 1:9).

In Islam, the word has a different meaning. There is no separate word in Arabic by which to distinguish between the greater angels, known in the West as archangels, from the lesser ordinary angels. The same Arabic word malak or mal'ak, deriving from a verb meaning "to send as an envoy or messenger," serves for both. However, Islam certainly does have its great angels such as Israfil, Munkar, and Nakir. The greatest of all the Islamic angels, of course, is Jibril, since he was the vehicle of the revelation of the Koran from God to Mohammed.

ARCHANGEL CATHEDRAL

(Moscow, Kremlin) According to the legend, back in the 13th century a wooden church of Archangel Michael used to stand at the south slope of Borovitsky Hill.By the beginning of the 16th century Moscow rulers were no longer satisfied by the modest-looking church. In 1505-1508, under Grand Prince Ivan III, the tumbled-down structure was dismantled and a new cathedral built on its site by the Italian architect Alevisio Novy. Another splendid building was added to the

Cathedral square in the Moscow Kremlin.

The Venetian master included some features of Renaissance architecture in his fine, five-domed cathedral, following the style of canons of his time: the facades of the building were decorated with pilasters complete with ornate Corinthian capitals and are separated from each other by decorative arches, the gables of each section of the facade being semicircular and carved in white stone to resemble sea-shells.

In the second half of the 16th century, during the reign of Ivan IV the Terrible, the cathedral was adorned for the first time with monumental paintings (frescoes).

The paintings on the south and north walls of the cathedral devoted to the life and deeds of Archangel Michael are associated with concrete historical events of the epoch of Ivan IV the Terrible.

In 1779-1681 the four-tier iconostasis was made. The sumptuous decoration of its gilded and carved frames is executed in Moscow baroque style, in keeping with the traditions of late 17th century art. The icons were painted by court artists led by well-known icon-painter Fyodor Zubov.

ARCHBISHOP

A metropolitan bishop of the Roman Catholic, Anglican and Eastern churches, and the Lutheran churches of Finland and Sweden, having jurisdiction over the bishops of a church province, or archdiocese, within which he consecrates bishops and presides over synods. Archbishops do not form a separate order of ministry. The term may be applied to bishops of distinguished sees, or patriarchs.

In the Roman Catholic Church the bishop of an archdiocese has limited authority over the bishops of the several dioceses in his territory. The bishops are suffragan bishops and the archbishop is their metropolitan and occupies the metropolitan see.

The title of titular archbishop is given to a prelate who does not have the special duties of an archbishop or who has no bishops under him.

ARCHDEACON

An ecclesiastical dignitary, next in rank below a bishop, who has jurisdiction either over a part of or over the whole diocese.

ARCHDIOCESE

The ecclesiastical territory governed by an archbishop. The archdiocese is the principal diocese within an ecclesiastical province.

ARCHELAUS

In Judaism and the Bible, ruler of Judea; son of Herod the Great by his fourth wife, Malthace. Archelaus became king while young Jesus was down in Egypt with Joseph and Mary. Rather than face his tyrannical rule in Judea on their return, Joseph settled his family outside Archelaus' jurisdiction, up in Nazareth in Galilee (Matthew 2:22-23).

Archelaus was a cruel ruler and very unpopular with the Jews. In quelling a riot, he once had 3,000 of them ruthlessly slain in the Temple grounds; he twice deposed the High Priest; his divorce and remarriage were also contrary to Jewish law. Complaints from the Jews and Samaritans to Augustus finally resulted in an investigation and Archelaus' banishment in the ninth or tenth year of his reign. Judea thereafter was under Roman governors.

ARCHEOLOGY

The branch of learning concerned with study of the material remains of man's past. The discipline has many branches and may be divided by geographical areas of by periods or in some other way. Archaeological investigations are the principal source for all that is known about prehistoric cultures. Biblical archeology is the study of the peoples and events of the Bible through the intriguing record buried in the earth.

ARCHEOLOGY, Christian

Christian archeology is the science of the material remains of Christian antiquity. It studies such objects as religious edifices, cemeteries, liturgical instruments, paintings, sculptures, mosaics, lamps, and gold glasses that can throw light upon the early Christians as individuals and as members of a community.

The period it embraces extends from Apostolic times down to the beginning of the Middle Ages. Christian archeology as a science has its origins in the 16th century and may be traced back to the Renaissance interest in the past, the discovery of a number of lost catacombs near Rome, and, especially to the religious controversies arising from the Reformation.

Both Catholics and Protestants were keenly interested in finding proofs in Scripture, in the Fathers, and in the remains of Christian antiquity to support their own theological positions.

In recent centuries the popes have been strong supporters of archeological studies. In 1757 a Museum of Christian Archeology was added to the Vatican; in 1816 Pius VII founded the Pontificia Academia Romana di Archaeologia; and in 1925 Pius XI, the Pontificio Istituto di Archeologia Christiana for the conferring of academic degrees.

The evidence of early Christian monuments taken alone is of course limited since they were not made to convey information. Nonetheless they do provide concrete support for the doctrines handed down from antiquity through the direct magisterium of the church.

They bear witness to a belief in the particular judgment, the communion of saints, the value of prayers for the living and the dead, the necessity of baptism, the celebration of the eucharist, and the role of Peter as the visible head of the Church.

Though Rome has far more early Christian remains than any other site, there are many other areas in northern Africa, the Near East, and in Europe that are of great significance for their Christian antiquities.

ARCHONTICS

A Gnostic sect of the 4th century, known only from the writings of St. Epiphanius. Peter, a Gnostic anchorite of Palestine, imparted the teachings of Eustachus who spread them to Armenia.

The Archontics rejected all Christian truths. Their bizarre teachings centered upon a system of archons ruling over the seven heavens under the mother of light in the eighth. The God of the Jews, called Sabaoth, presides over the seventh; his son is the devil, who from Eve begot Cain and Abel.

The quest of the soul is to reach the gnosis, then ascend past Sabaoth through the heavens until it reaches the mother of light. The practices of the sect were lifely licentious. They relied heavily on the apocrypha, especially the Assumption of Isaia.

ARCOSOLIUM

Elaborate third century Roman catacomb grave; the burial litter of antiquity was called a solium; by extension the tomb came to be so called. An arcosolium was an elegant wall excavation closed horizontally by a slab above which was a stucco arch frequently decorated with a fresco. Earlier arcosolia were excavated to the floor to receive sarcophagi. Although some arcosolia are along catacomb passages, greater numbers are located in cubicula.

ARD

In the Old Testament, one of the "seventy souls of the house of Jacob who came into Egypt" (Genesis 46:21, 27). In the Genesis account he is called a son of Benjamin, but in view of Numbers 26:40 it seems likely that the meaning here is "grandson." If this is the case, then he is also probably the same ad Addar in 1 Chronicles 2:18.

AREOPAGUS

The name of a rocky hill in Athens north-west of the Acropolis and of the oldest council of Athens which met there. Areopagus means "hill of Ares

(Mars)." In ancient times the council was politically powerful, but when Paul spoke before it (Acts 17:16-34), its influence was confined to educational and religious affairs. Seemingly it was in this capacity that Paul was brought before it, although the place of its meeting was probably not the ancient site but farther north on the Agora.

AREZZO

Italian city important as a religious and cultural center in the Middle Ages; birthplace of Petrarch. Arezzo is capital of Arezzo province in Tuscany, central Italy, and has been the seat of a bishop since the 4th century. St. Satyrus was the first known bishop. The diocese includes the site where St. Francis received the stigmata.

ARELI

In the Old Testament, seventh-named son of Gad, who was one of those who came into Egypt with Jacob's family in circa 1700 BC. He became family head of the Arelites, who were included in the wilderness census shortly before entering the Promised Land (Genesis 46:8, 16; Numbers 26:17).

ARES

The Greek god of war. He was known to the Romans as Mars. Unlike his Roman counterpart, Mars, he was never very popular, and his worship was not extensive in Greece. He represented the distasteful aspects of brutal warfare and slaughter. From at least the time of Homer, who established him as the son of the chief god, Zeus and Hera, his consort, he was one of the Olympian deities, but his fellow gods and even his parents were not fond of him.

ARETAS

The last of several Arabian kings of this name, who controlled Damascus when its governor joined a plot of the Jews to do away with the apostle Paul. Paul escaped in a wicker basket lowered from a window in the city wall (Acts 9:23-25; 2 Corinthians 11:32-33).

ARETHUSA

In Greek mythology, a nymph who gave her name to a spring in Elis and to another on the island of Ortygia, near Syracuse.

ARGUS

The name of a number of figures in Greek mythology. The most important is the son of Inachus. He was appointed by the goddess Hera to watch the cow into which Io (Hera's priestess) had been transformed, but he was slain by the god Hermes.

ARHAT

In Buddhism and Chinese religion, class of disciples of holy men (not deities), who have reached perfection of the Eight Path by rigorous discipline but refrain from Nirvana to sustain others in the law. As Lohans in the Chinese Buddhist imagery of Sung (960-1279), they reached cult proportions.

ARIADNE

In Greek mythology, daughter of Pasiphae and the Cretan king Minos. She fell in love with the Athenean hero Theseus, and with a thread of glittering jewels she helped him escape the Labyrinth after he slew the Minotaur, a beast half bull and half man that Minos kept in the Labyrinth.

ARIANISM

4th-century Christian heresy founded in Alexandria by the priest Arius. He taught that Christ was not coequal and coeternal with God the Father, for the Father had created him. To curb Arianism, the Emperor Constantine called the first Council of Nicaea (325), and the first Nicene Creed declared that God the Father and Christ the Son were of the same substance. Arianism later almost triumphed, but most of the church returned to orthodoxy by the end of the century.

Though checked within the Roman

Empire, Arianism was by no means dead, particularly among the German tribes in the north who has been converted to this type of Christianity by Wulfila and his successors.

During their invasions into Roman lands, they frequently persecuted the native Christians, but they were themselves eventually destroyed or converted. Thus it was the armies of Justinian I that destroyed Arianism among the Vandals in Africa (533) and the Ostrogoths in Italy (540). The Visigoths in Spain were brought into the church through the conversion of their king in 587.

ARIDITY

In Roman Catholicism a term, designating the absence of consolation, emotional warmth or affection in prayer. This is the case when a person often loses enthusiasm for prayer and meditation.

Aridity ranges from the lack of sensible affection to complete desolation. Aridity may come from the good spirit, from one's bodily condition, or from carelessness in one's spiritual life. Spiritual writers advocate patience and faithfulness to prayer even though the feelings of joy or other fruits of prayer are temporarily absent.

ARIEL

In the Old Testament, one of the nine head ones especially used by Ezra in obtaining qualified "ministers for the house of our God." This was in the spring of 468 BC when about 1,500 Israelite males under Ezra were about to depart from the river Ahava for Jerusalem (Ezra 8:15-17, 19).

ARIMINIUM, Council of

(359) One of the several 4th-century councils concerned with Arianism, called by the pro-Arian Emperor Constantinus II. Although the majority of bishop at Ariminium were Orthodox and accepted the faith of Nicaea, the Arian minority included skilled diplomats, who succeeded inundoing the orthodox decision of the majority when it reached the Emperor.

ARIOCH

In the Old Testament, the king of Ellasar who, in league with Chedorlaomer and two other kings, shared in crushing the rebellion of Sodom and Gomorran and carried off Lot and his household. Abraham then overtook the victors, defeated Arioch and his confederates, and rescued Lot (Genesis 14:1-16).

ARISTAEUS

Greek divinity whose worship was widespread but concerning whom myths are somewhat obscure. He was essentially a benevolent deity, who introduced the cultivation of bees and the vine and olive and was the protector of herdsmen and hunters.

ARISTANEMINATHA

Savior of Jainism, a religion of India. He is said to have lived 84,000 years before the coming of the next saint; he is also said to have been a contemporary of the Hindu god Krishna, who was his cousin. He attained release from earthly existence on the Girnar hills in Kathiawar (western India).

ARISTARCHUS

In the New Testament, one of Paul's close associates, a traveling companion and fellow prisoner, a Macedonian from Thessalonica (Acts 2:4; 27:2). He is introduced in the account of Paul's third missionary journey; at the height of the Ephesian riot Aristarchus and Gaius were forcibly dragged into the theater (Acts 19:29). He could have been the "brother" who assisted Paul with the contribution for Judeans that was collected in Macedonia and Greece (2 Corinthians 8:18-20).

ARISTIDES

(2nd century) Athenian philosopher, one of the earliest Christian apologists, his *Apology for the Christian Faith* being the oldest extant apologist document.

ARISTOBULUS OF PANEAS

(born circa 160 BC) Jewish philosopher who, like his successor, Philo, attempted to fuse ideas in the Hebrew scriptures with those in Greek thought. The Stoic technique of allegorizing the Greek myth served as a model for Aristobulus' writings, and for him the Old Testament God became an allegorical figure. In like manner, the Mosaic laws in the Scriptures were translated into allegorical symbols in his system.

ARISTOTELIANISM

The term used in the strict sense to designate the philosophy of Aristotle himself. In a broader sense it is employed to designate the teachings of the philosophers who modified in many ways Aristotle's doctrines and who incorporated into their philosophy elements borrowed from Platonism, Stoicism, and Neoplatonism.

ARISTOTELIANISM, Islamic

The thought and concepts of Aristotle played a significant and diverse role in the development of Islamic philosophy. In particular, the latter absorbed much of the technical metaphysical terminology of Aristotle. The ideas and thoughts which the Arab and Islamic writers knew and absorbed were not always something which Aristotle would have accepted as his own.

ARISTOTLE

(384-322 BC) Greek philosopher, one of the most influential thinkers of the ancient world. He was the son of the Macedonian court physician, and studied at Plato's academy in Athens. In 343 he became the tutor to the young Alexander the Great. In 335 Aristotle set up his own school at the Lyceum in Athens.

Many of Aristotle's teachings survive as lecture notes. His work covered a vast range, including Physics, Metaphysics, On the Soul, On the Heavens, and several works on logic and biology, in both of which subjects he was a pioneer.

In studying such diverse topics as nature, man, soul, Aristotle considered how things became what they were and what function they performed. In doing this he introduced his fourfold analysis of causes (formal, material, efficient and final), and such important notions as form and matter, substance and accident, actual and potential - all of which became philosophical commonplaces.

ARK

Biblical vessel Noah built for protection from the great flood (Genesis 6-9), also, the Ark of the Covenant, the sacred chest of Hebrews. The Ark of Noah was, according to the scripture, built of "copher" wood (the kind of wood is uncertain); it had three decks and measurements equivalent to about 450 feet in length, 75 in width, and 45 in height.

Some scholars think the biblical description was likely patterned after the Ark of Utnapishtim of the Babylonian Flood. Since it was the means through which Noah and his family were saved from God's judgment on the sinful world, the Ark became a symbol of salvation (1 Peter 3:20).

ARK, Coptic

In the Coptic liturgy a cubical box which rests on the altar. The chalice with paten is placed in the ark through a hole in the top before the consecration and remains there until the communion. The sides are covered with paintings. The ark is never used outside the liturgy to preserve the Eucharist.

Among the Ethiopians, the ark (tabot) is solemnly placed on the altar when a church is consecrated. Its origin is unknown and it has no function in the liturgy, although the wooden board on which the sacred gifts rest during the liturgy is called tabot, as is sometimes the whole altar.

ARKAN AL-ISLAM

The five duties incumbent on every Muslim.

ARKITE

Descendants of Ham through Canaan and one of the seventy post-flood families (genesis 10:17; 1 Chronicles 1:15). They settled along the Mediterranean coast west of the Lebanon mountains.

ARK OF THE COVENANT

In the Old Testament, the chest containing the tablets bearing the Ten Commandments received by Moses (Exodus 25:21). The ark rested in the Holy of Holies inside the tabernacle of the ancient Temple of Jerusalem. The Levites (priestly functionaries) carried the ark with them during the Hebrews' wanderings in the wilderness. Following the conquest of Canaan, the Promised Land, the ark resided at Shiloh, but from time to time it was carried into battle by the Israelites (1 Samuel 4:3). Taken to Jerusalem by King David, it was eventually placed in the Temple by King Solomon.

ARMAGEDDON

In the New Testament, place where the kings of the Earth under demonic leadership will wage war on the forces of God at the end of world history. Armageddon is mentioned in the Bible only once, in Revelations (16:16). It is the final battlefield where God's heavenly armies will defeat the demonic forces of evil.

The mountain of Megiddo borders the plain of Esdraelon in present-day Israel. This mountain was the great battlefield of ancient Palestine where the fortunes of kings and nations were decided.

In the New Testament, Armageddon is a symbol of the struggle between good and evil that goes on in the world and in every person. It has become synonymous with the place of the final cosmic battle between God and Satan.

ARMENIAN CATHOLIC CHURCH

An Eastern Rite member of the Roman Catholic Church. The Armenians embraced Christianity in the 3rd century, the first people to do so as a nation. About 50 years after the Council of Chalcedon (451), the Armenians repudiated the Christological decisions of the council and became the Armenian Apostolic (Orthodox) church.

Armenians monks, known as the Friars of Unity of St. Gregory the Illuminator, laid the groundwork for the future Catholic Armenian Church. The church came into being in 1740, when the Armenian bishop of Aleppo was elected patriarch of Sis, in Cilicia.

The head of the Armenian Catholics, who in the early 1990 numbered more than 150,000 faithful, is called patriarch of the Catholic Armenians and katholikos of Cilicia and has always taken the name of Peter. The liturgy continues to be celebrated in the classical Armenian language.

ARMENIAN CHANT

The vocal music of the Armenian Church and the religious poetry that serves as its texts. In its present day performance, Armenian chant consists of intricate melodies with great rhythmic varieties, and the melodies use many intervals not found in European music.

ARMENIAN CHURCH

The national church of Armenia. It evolved as part of the Eastern church and adopted a form of monophysitism. It was the first Christian church to be established.

ARMENIAN LITURGY

The rites and ceremonies of the Armenian Church. When the Armenian Church was organized in the early fourth century, the liturgical practice of Cappadocian Caesarea was introduced along with a certain amount of Syrian practice; only in the reign of the catholicos Sahak I (384-438) were the texts translated into Armenian from Greek to Syriac. The liturgical calendar and the lectionary system reflect the usages of 5th century Jerusalem.

In the fifth century the canonical hours were six:
▲ the Night Office,
▲ the Dawn office,

▲ Tierce,
▲ Set,
▲ None,
▲ Vespers.

In the eighth century were added the Office of Sunrise (Prime) and Repose (Compline), and still later another hour, of Peace, to be said privately before retiring.

Baptism (normally by immersion) is always followed by the anointing of confirmation, and the newly baptized is then taken to the sanctuary to receive Communion; if he or she is an infant, the priest dips his finger in the Precious Blood and with it makes the Sign of the Cross on the infant's lips.

Communion is received under both species (by intinction) among the Gregorians but not necessarily by the Catholics.

ARMENIAN RITE

The system of liturgical practices and discipline observed by the Armenian Apostolic (Orthodox) Church and the Armenian Catholics, Eastern Rite members of the Roman Catholic Church.

The churches are generally devoid of icons and, in place of an iconostasis (screen), have a curtain that conceals the priest and the altar during parts of the liturgy. The Communion itself if given in two pieces, and is other Orthodox churches.

ARMILUS

In Jewish legends, an enemy who will conquer Jerusalem and persecute Jews until his final defeat at the hands of God or the true Messiah. His inevitable destruction symbolizes the ultimate victory of good over evil in the messianic era.

ARMINIANISM

A theological movement in Christianity, a liberal reaction to the Calvinist doctrine of predestination that began early in the 17th century and asserted that God's sovereignty and man's free will are compatible.

In a wider sense, designating a theolog-ical viewpoint, the term Arminianism applies first of all to an emphasis on the freedom to accept grace. The latitu-dinarians of 17th century England were anti-Calvinist and were called "Arminians," but had no link with Dutch Arminianism.

The theology of John Wesley was Arminian, not because of his opposition to Calvinism, but because of his perfectionism.

Arminianism is taken as an anthro-pocentric theological emphasis in the accepted classification of Reformed churches into Calvinist and Arminian. Arminianism characterizes all Wesleyan Methodist groups, the Holiness churches, the United Brethren, the Evangelical Alliance, and the Salvation Army; the Mennonites and the General Baptists, while older than historic Arminianism, also classi-fy their own theology as Arminian.

ARMINIANS

(Remonstrants) Group of Protestant congregations inspired by the Dutch theologian Jacobus Arminius (1560-1609). Arminianism attempted to show that, contrary to John Calvins' free will and God's sovereignty were not incom-patible. The Arminians, though perse-cuted initially, were legally tolerated in the Netherlands from 1630. Arminian theology influenced John Wesley, founder of Methodism.

ARMINIUS, Jacob

(1560-1609) Theologian and minister of the Dutch Reformed church who opposed the strict Calvinist teaching on predestination and who developed his own system of belief known later as Arminianism.

ARMONI

In the Old Testament, one of the two sons born to Saul by his concubine Rizpah. To expiate Saul's bloodguilt, seven of his offspring, including Armoni, were given to the Gibeonites, who put them to death and exposed their corpses on the mountain. Rizpah kept watch, not letting fowl or beast molest them, until David had the bones buried (2 Samuel 21:5-14).

ARNAN

In Judaism, the son of Rephaiah and father of Obadiah; post-exilic descendant of David; fourth generation after Zerubbabel (1 Chronicles 3:19, 21).

ARNI

A person named in the human ancestry of Jesus Christ. Presumably of the Greek equivalent of the Hebrew name Ram; the Hebrew name Ram is rendered Aram (Luke 3:33; 1 Chronicles 2:10).

ARNOBIUS THE ELDER

(4th century) Brilliant early Christian convert who defended Christianity by demonstrating to the pagans their own inconsistencies.

A general defense of Christianity from pagan calumnies (books 1 and 2) is followed by attacks on Neoplatonism, anthropomorphism, and heathen mythology (books 3-5), concluding with worship of images, temples, and ceremonials (books 6 and 7).

ARNOBIUS THE YOUNGER

(circa 460) Christian priest or bishop who was the author of a mystical and allegorical commentary on the Psalms.

ARNOLD OF BRESCIA

(1100-1150) Italian religious reformer and political activist who strongly opposed the temporal power of the pope. Born in Brescia, he was a supporter of Peter Abelard, with whom he was condemned at the Council of Sens in 1140. In 1147 Arnold, a great orator, became leader of the rebellion that had suppressed papal authority in Rome and replaced it by a republic. On the collapse of the republic, Arnold fled to Campania, but was captured, delivered to the pope by Emperor Frederick Barbarossa, and executed as a heretic.

AROERITE

An inhabitant of one of the cities named Aroer. At 1 Chronicles 11:44

Hotham, the father of two of David's mighty men named Shama and Jeiel, is referred to as an Aroerite. His sons' association with David may place their father's home city in the territory of Judah.

ARRICCIO

Rough plaster on a wall in preparation for fresco painting. The finishing coat of plaster on which color is applied, is laid on a base of arriccio.

ARSENITE SCHISM

The withdrawal of the followers of the deposed patriarch of Constantinople, Arsenius Autorianos, from the Patriarchate of Constantinople when Emperor Michael VIII Palaeologus appointed Germanus, bishop of Adrianople, as patriarch (1264) and the latter decided to absolve the emperor from the excommunication which he had received from Arsenius (1267). The schism ended through the conciliatory efforts of Patriarch Niphon (1315).

ARSENIUS AUTORIANUS

(born circa 1200) Patriarch of Constantinople, whose deposition caused a serious schism in the Byzantine Church. Baptized George, he took the name Gennadius on becoming a monk and Arsenius on being appointed patriarch of Nicaea in 1255 by the Byzantine Theodore II Lascaris.

After Arsenius' deposition, the empire was split into two factions known as the Arsenites (followers of Arsenius) and the Josephites (followers of Joseph, Arsenius' second successor).

ARSENIUS THE GREAT

(circa 354-455). Roman noble, later monk of Egypt, whose asceticism among the Christian hermits in the famed Libyan desert caused him to be ranked among the celebrated Desert Fathers and influenced the development of the monastic and contemplative life in Eastern and Western Christendom.

ARTEMAS

A companion whom Paul considered sending to Titus in Crete (Titus 3:12), perhaps as a replacement in order that Titus might join Paul in Nicopolis. Since Paul's choice was to be between Artemas and Tychicus, Artemas was evidently well esteemed, as indicated by Paul's remarks about Tychicus at Ephesians 6:21-22.

ARTEMIS

Virgin goddess of the hunt in Greek mythology. Artemis was Apollo's twin, the daughter of Zeus and Leto. She is usually pictured carrying bow and arrows or a torch. The roles of Artemis, as her legend comes down to us, are often contradictory. Although she presides over the animals, she is primarily known as the goddess of the hunt. And although Artemis is a stern protector of chastity, she also watches over women in childbirth.

She was worshiped at springs, rivers and lakes as goddess of the waters; fruit, grain and domestic animals were sacrificed to her at harvest time; sailors invoked her assistance for fair weather and calm voyages; maidens worshiped her, and mothers thanked her for safe delivery.

She is also sometimes known as the moon goddess, probably through identification with the huntress Diana, Roman goddess of the moon.

ARTHA

In Hinduism, the pursuit of wealth or material advantage, one of the four traditional aims in life. The sanction for artha rests on the assumption that - excluding the exceptional few who can proceed directly to the final aim of moksa, or spiritual release from life - material well-being is a basic necessity of man and his appropriate pursuit while a householder, i.e., the second of the four life stages.

ARTHAPATHI

In Hinduism, the fifth of the five means of knowledge by which man has correct cognitions of the world.

ARTICLES OF FAITH

In Roman Catholicism, those revealed truths which have a specific and proper identity, yet are broad enough to subsume other revealed truths so as to form an organic entity within Christian doctrine.

These truths must be revealed for themselves, and are comparable to fundamental principles within the various branches of science. Thus the Passionand Resurrection of Jesus are distinct articles of faith, whereas the suffering and death of Jesus would be incorporated into the Passion as an article of faith.

Other revealed truths, such as the miracles described in scripture, are not articles of faith since they have not been revealed for themselves but insofar as they have a connection with a broad truth, e.g., the divinity of Christ.

ARTOPHORION

In the Eastern church, a container for the Eucharist when it is reserved.

ARTOTYRITES

Members of a Montanist sect in Phrygia during the second century. They employed bread and cheese in the celebration of their mysteries.

ARUBBOTH

In the Old Testament, a town that served as an administrative center under one of the 12 deputies assigned by King Solomon to provide food for the royal household. The son of Hesed functioned there, heaving oversight over Socoh and the land of Hepher (1 Kings 4:7-10).

ARUPA

In Buddhism, term meaning formless, incorporeal; the highest meditative worlds, where form cognizable by the five senses does not exist, being purely mental.

ARUPA-LOKA

In Buddhism,the highest of the three spheres of existence in which rebirth takes place. The other two are rupa-loka, the world of form, and kama-loka, the world of feeling.

In arupa-loka existence depends on the stage of concentration attained, and there are four levels:

1 the infinity of space;
2 the infinity of thought;
3 the infinity of nonbeing;
4 the infinity of neither consciousness nor non-consciousness.

The rupa-loka which is free from sensuous desire but is still conditioned by form, is inhabited by gods. As superior as is rebirth in the higher worlds, such an existence is still temporary, subject to change, and involves the fundamental conflicts of existence within the limits of transmigration.

ARVAD

In the Old Testament, small rocky island today known as Ruad, lying circa two miles off the coast of northern Syria, some 125 miles north of Tyre. In Ezekiel's prophetic dirge concerning Tyre reference is made of men from Arvad who served as skilled rowers in Tyre's navy and as valorous warriors in her army (Ezekiel 27:8-11).

ARYANS

(Sanskrit for noble or ruler) Name originally applied by the Hindus to Indo-European invaders who moved into the Indus Valley circa 1500 BC. It later became a loosely used linguistic term denoting peoples who speak an Indo-European language. According to the racial definition adopted in Nazi Germany, an Aryan was a person of "nordic," non-Jewish origin, and Nazi propaganda sought to identify German origins with these fierce warriors. As a racial category, the term has no valid basis and has been generally discredited in modern times as an instrument of bigotry.

ARYA SAMAJ

A vigorous reform sect of modern hinduism, founded in 1875 by Swami Dayananda Saraswati, whose aim was to re-establish the Vedas, the earliest Hindu scriptures. He rejected all later accretions to the Vedas as degenerate but, in his own interpretation, included much post-Vedic thought, such as the doctrine of effect of past deeds and of rebirth.

ARZAH

In the Old Testament, steward of the household of Elah, king of Israel (952-951 BC), in whose house in Tirzah the king "was drinking himself drunk" when assassinated by Zimri (1 Kings 16:9-10).

ASA

In Judaism, the third king of Judah following the division of the nation into two kingdoms. Asa was the son of Abijam and grandson of Rehoboam. Since his father's three-year rule began in the 18th year (980 BC) of the reign of Jeroboam, king of Israel, and Asa's began in the 20th year of Jeroboam, apparently Abijam completed that year his third full year and Asa completed that year as an accession period, followed by his forty-one-year rule (977-936 BC; 1 Kings 15:1-10).

ASAHEL

In the Old testament, a son of David's sister or half-sister Zeruiah and the brother of Abishai and Joab; hence, David's nephew (1 Chronicles 2:15-16). Honored as among the thirty outstanding warriors under David, Asahel was particularly noted for his fleetness, "like one of the gazelles that are in the open field" (2 Samuel 2:18; 23:24). At 1 Chronicles 27:7 Asahel is listed as a divisional commander of the month-by-month arrangement of troops.

Asaiah

In the Old Testament, a descendant of Merari, Levi's third son, and a head of a paternal house. He was one of the chief men among the Levites who formed part of the group of 862 chosen to share in bringing up the Ark of the Covenant to Jerusalem at the time of David's second (and successful) attempt (1 Chronicles 6:29-30; 15:6-12).

ASALUHE

In Mesopotamian religion, Sumerian deity, city god ofMu'ar, near Eridu in the south-eastern marshlands region. Asallube was active with the god Enki in rituals of lustrative magic and was considered his son.

ASANA

In Buddhism, a particular posture in meditation; posture with the soles of the feet visible on either thigh, used throughout the East.

ASAPH

In the Old Testament, a son of Levi through Gershom (1 Chronicles 6:39, 43). During King David's reign Asaph was appointed by the Levites as a chief singer and player of cymbals, accompanying the ark as it was brought up from Obed-edom's home to the "city of David" (1 Chronicles 15:17-19; 25-29).

ASARAH BE-TEVET

Significant day of the Jewish calendar. The tenth day of the month of Tevet recalls a sad event in the Jewish history. On that day the Babylonians began their siege of Jerusalem. Thus began a chain of events in which the city was sacked, the Temple destroyed, and an end brought to the First Jewish Commonwealth. That is why many Jews fast on Asarah Be-Tevet.

ASAREL

In the Old Testament, one of the four sons of Jehallelel of the tribe of Judah (1 Chronicles 4:16).

ASAVA

In Buddhism, mental intoxication, defilement. The four asavas are:
1 Kama, sensuality.
2 Bhava, lust of life.
3 Ditthi, false views.
4 Avijja, ignorance of nature of life.
Asavas are erroneous false views which intoxicate the mind so that it cannot contemplate pure truth and attain enlightenment.

ASCENSION

The bodily ascent into heaven of Jesus Christ on the 40th day after his resurrection, described in the New Testament (Acts 1:9). After appearing to the Apostles on various occasions during a period of 40 days, Jesus was taken up in their presence and was then hidden from them by a cloud, a frequent biblical image signifying the presence of God.

Christ's return to the Father in his total humanity occurred otologically in the Resurrection itself, but the very nature of the incarnation economy demands both the clear attestation of the Resurrection, with all its implications, and the manifest glorious completion of his earthly mission.

The cosmological aspects of the Ascension need not detain one: the physical going up of God-made man is a reality, but it is a sign of his return to the Father rather than an indication of where the Father is to be found.

The cloud that receives him is not just a natural phenomenon; in accord with scriptural usage (e.g., the narratives of the Transfiguration), this itself is a manifestation of that divine glory into which Christ is now wholly received.

In this as in other moments of the paschal mystery Christ is our head; in the Ascension mankind makes its return to the father in and through Christ; just as God has raised us with him, so He has "made us sit with him in the heavenly places" (Ephesians 2:6). But this process has to be implemented over the successive centuries until the last day, when Christ's lordship will be fully manifested, the very crown of a redeemed humanity.

ASCENSION, Feast of

The commemoration of Christ's final historical departure from his disciples, his entry into heaven so as to manifest his victory to the good and evil spirits who did not dwell on earth. It is celebrated on the 40th day after Easter as a universal holy day of obligation.

ASCETICAL THEOLOGY

That branch of the science of theology which deals with the attainment of salvation through the disciplined renunciation of personal desires and impulses for religious motives.

The ascetical theology is distinct from moral theology which retreats from these acts that are essential for salvation; since the 17th century, the study of asceticism has also been distinguished from mystical theology which treats of those moral acts resulting from an extraordinary grace leading to infused contemplation.

Some contemporary theologians, however, reject any clear distinction between asceticism and mysticism, and prefer to speak of a spiritual theology that flows out of a truly existential and nonrationalistic dogmatic theology.

ASCETICISM

In religion, the practice of the denial of physical and psychological desires in order to attain a spiritual ideal or goal. The extent to which the practice of asceticism has enabled persons to develop their inner (spiritual) powers over their instinctive urges and the influences of the world has been notable in the history of religions.

In Buddhism, asceticism is defined as the practice for gaining magical powers or propitiating gods in essentially selfish ways. In his first sermon Buddha condemned extreme asceticism as ignoble and useless, and taught a middle way between self-mortification and allurements of senses. Asceticism is permitted as bodily self-control as a method for mental self-control.

In Christianity, Christians under the action of the Spirit have adopted means of self-discipline in order to have greater union with God. True ascesis brings a growth in contemplation and love of God that fosters personal maturity and social responsibility.

ASCETICISM, Eastern

Although some ascetical practices have been present in almost all religions, Hinduism and Buddhism have been especially concerned with the problem of physical and psychological denial in order to attain a distinctive spiritual purpose. Asceticism does not hold a significant place in Chinese and Japanese religions, except in the form of Buddhism.

Hinduism

The fundamental concept that gives direction to the Hindu ascetical ideal is the desire to escape from samsara, the circle of continuous rebirth to which all finite beings are involved, and finally to enjoy moksa or unity with the One beyond all change and materiality.

Buddhism

The origins of Buddhism can be at least partly traced to the Buddha's selection of a "middle path" between the extremes of sexual indulgence and harsh asceticism. After his own lengthy experiments in self-denial, the Buddha reveals in his famous sermon at Deer Park that moderation is the key to existence. Since rigid asceticism is far from moderation, it is unprofitable for the soul. Thus the Buddha encouraged proper care of the body and the usefulness of suffering and painful penance.

Nevertheless, Buddhism is thoroughly ascetical if asceticism is taken to mean discipline, psychological control, and the mastering of selfishness in the effort to attain compassion. In this sense, the Eightful Path of Buddhism whereby the disciple escapes the continually renewed cycle of life's sufferings through ethical conduct is properly regarded as the epitome of ascetical discipline.

Asclepius

In Greek mythology, the god of medicine. The son of Apollo by Coronis, Asclepius spent time in youth with the Centaur Chiron, as did almost all of the important men of his time. The wise Centaur taught him medicine, at which Asclepius became most proficient. In fact, he was credited with the power to raise the dead - an achievement which filled Zeus with the fear that the order of the world might be in danger of being disturbed. He cast a thunderbolt at Asclepius, killing him.

ASENATH

In the Old Testament, the daughter of the Egyptian priest Potiphera of On, given by Pharaoh to Joseph as his wife. She became the mother of Manasseh and Ephraim (Genesis 41:45, 50-52).

ASHAN

In Judaism, a city in the Shephelah or lowland region of Judah. Originally assigned to Judah, it was thereafter given to Simeon, due to Judah's territory being overly large (Joshua 15:42; 1 Chronicles 4:32).

ASH'ARI, al-

(873-936) Muslim Arab theologian noted for having integrated the rationalist methodology of the speculative theologians into the framework of orthodox Islam.

ASH'ARIS

Followers of the 10th century orthodox Muslim theologian al-Ash'arim who held that human reason is incapable of discovering good and evil because of self-interest and that God's will makes acts good or evil.

ASHA VAHISHTA

In Zoroastrianism, one of the Beneficent Immortals, or spiritual entities of Ahura Mazda, the Wise Lord.

ASHAVAN

In Zoroastrianism, a spiritual entity of Ahura Mazda, the Wise Lord.

ASHBEL

In the Old Testament, son of Benjamin, listed third at Genesis 46:21, but second at 1 Chronicles 8:1. The Ashbelites, his descendants, were registered in the census taken on the desert plain of Moab circa 1473 BC (Numbers 26:38).

ASHDOD

One of the five principal cities of the Philistines under their "axis lords" and evidently the religious center of Philistia with its worship of the god Dagon.

ASHDODITE

An inhabitant of the Philistine city of Ashdod (Joshua 13:3). Like the other Philistines, they were descendants of Ham through Mizraim and Casluhim, reaching Canaan apparently from the island of Crete (Genesis 10:6-14).

ASHER

One of the 12 tribes of Israel that in biblical times constituted the people of Israel who later became the Jewish people. The tribe was named after the younger of two sons born to Jacob (also called Israel) and Zilpah, the maidservant of Jacob's first wife, Leah.

ASHERAH

Meaning perhaps "she who treads the sea"; a Canaanite goddess whose cult influenced many Israelites. In the Ugarit texts Asherah is the wife of the supreme god El. She was often confused with the goddess of fertility Ishtar and Anath, the sister of Baal.
Asherah appears in the Old Testament as the consort of Baal (Judges 3:7). The names of these goddesses also appear in Phoenician texts.

ASHER BEN JEHIEL

(1250-1327) Major codifier of the Talmud, the rabbinical compendium of law, lore, and commentary. With the help of Rabbi Solomon ben Sedret, one of the most influential rabbis of his time, he was established as rabbi of Toledo (Spain), where he founded a Jewish academy. He believed that the study of philosophy might endanger the Talmud's authority. He signed a ban forbidding such study to those under 25.

ASHERITE

A descendant of Asher, Jacob's second son by Leah's maidservant Zilpah (Genesis 30:12-13) and a member of the tribe of Asher (Judges 1:31-32).

ASHES

In Roman Catholicism, these symbols of penance and reconciliation are made by burning the palms blessed on the previous Passion Sunday. These ashes are blessed and then the sacramental is used to mark the foreheads of people on Ash Wednesday.

ASHHUR

In the Old Testament, son of Hezron, born after his father's death, and great-grandson of Judah (1 Chronicles 2:4-5, 24). By his two wives he fathered seven sons (1 Chronicles 4:5-7). He is also said to be the father of Tekoa, which some construe to mean that he was the founder of the town by that name.

ASHIMA

A deity worshiped by the people from Hamath whom the king of Assyria settled in Samaria after his taking the Israelites into captivity (2 Kings 17:24, 30). Ashima, according to the Babylonian Talmud, was represented as a hairless he-goat, and for this reason some have identified Ashima with Pan, a pastoral god of fertility.

ASHKELON

One of the five principal cities of Philistia, located on the Maritime Plain north of Gaza. The city was Herod the Great's birthplace and the residence of his sister Salome.

ASHKENAZ

In the Old Testament, the first name of three sons of Gomer, the son of Japheth (Genesis 10:3; 1 Chronicles 1:6). Jeremiah mentions a kingdom of Ashkenaz as allying itself with the kingdoms of Ararat and Minno against Babylon at the time of her downfall (539 BC).

In Jewish writings of medieval times (and thereafter) the term Ashkenaz was applied to the Teutonic race, and more specifically to Germany.

ASHKENAZIM

Those Jews whose medieval ancestors lived in Germany. Persecution drove them to spread throughout central and eastern Europe, and in the 19th and 20th centuries overseas, notably to the United States. Their ritual and Hebrew pronunciation differ from those of Sephardim (Jews of Oriental countries). Up to the beginning of the 20th century most Ashkenazim spoke Yiddish. Most of the Jews in the United States and the majority of the world's Jews are Ashkenazim.

ASHPENAZ

The chief court official, or, more literally, the master of the eunuchs, in Babylon during Nebuchadnezzar's reign (Daniel 1:3). The title in time came to indicate a high official in the royal court who doubtless headed the corps of eunuchs but who himself may not have been a eunuch. Such an official had as one of his duties the training of youths to serve as pages of the monarch.

ASHRAMA

A word which in Hindu religious usage may have several meanings:
▲ a place or hermitage in which austerities are practiced;
▲ the actual performance or practice of austerities;
▲ the four stages of ideal life, to each of which appropriate austerities are attached. These are:
  ▲ Brahman student;
  ▲ householder;
  ▲ hermit;
  ▲ homeless mendicant.

ASHTAROTH

A city in the region of Bashan, generally identified today with Tell 'Ashterah about 20 miles east of the Sea of Galilee. biblical references to it are principally with regard to giant King Og of Bashan, who is spoken of as reigning in Ashtaroth, in Edrei (Deuteronomy 1:4; Joshua 9:10).

ASHTORETH

In biblical times, a goddess of the Canaanites, considered to be the wife of Baal. Ashtoreth is often represented as a nude female with rudely exaggerated sex organs. The worship of this goddess was widespread among various peoples of antiquity, and the name

"Ashtoreth" was common in one form or another. Ashtoreth is thought to be another manifestation of the ancient Babylonian mother goddess of sensual love, maternity and fertility, and has been linked with Ishtar and similar fertility goddesses.

ASHUR

In Mesopotamian religion, city god of Ashur and national god of Assyria. He granted rule of Assyria, supported Assyrian arms against enemies, and even received detailed written reports from the Assyrian kings about their campaigns. He appears a mere personification of the interests of Assyria as a political entity, with little character of his own.

ASHURA

Muslim holy day observed on the 10th of Muharram, the first month of the islamic year. Originally it was a day of fasting. When in the 7th century Jewish-Muslim relations became strained, Mohammed made Ramadan the Muslim month of fasting, leaving the Ashura fast a voluntary observance, as it remained among the Sunnis.

ASHURITE

A people subject to the kingship of Ish-bosheth, Saul's son. At 2 Samuel 2:9 they are listed between Gilead and Jezreel. The name Ashurim is used at Genesis 25:3, but there refers to Arabic descendants of Abraham through Dedam. The identification of the "Ashurites" is therefore conjectural.

ASHVATH

In Judaism, a man of the tribe of Asher, house of Japhet (1 Chronicles 7:33).

ASH WEDNESDAY

In Roman Catholicism, the first day of Lent. On this day, ashes from the burning of palms from the previous year's Passion Sunday are blessed and placed on the foreheads of the faithful as a sign of penance.

ASIA

In the Christian Greek scriptures the term Asia is used as referring, not to the continent of Asia, nor to the peninsula called Asia Minor, but to the Roman province occupying the western part of that peninsula.

ASIA MINOR

Part of Asia, comprising among other countries present-day Turkey. Asia Minor, of which the province of Asia formed only the western part, comprises the entire peninsula bounded by the Black Sea, the Aegean and the Mediterranean on the north, west, and south, and on the east by the mountains lying to the west of the upper course of the Euphrates River.

Asia Minor was the scene of much of apostle Paul's missionary activities, and the names of most of its provinces and regions appear in the Bible account.

ASIEL

Simeonite forefather of Jehu, a chieftain in the days of King Hezekiah (1 Chronicles 4:35-41).

AS IF

Well known concept in Buddhism. It teaches that all manifestation is in the last analysis illusion. Within the field of maya the imagination may be usefully directed to create in thought the condition of the desired mind, and an effort made to behave "as if" this condition has been achieved.

ASKLEPIOS

See Aesculapius.

ASKR AND EMBLA

In Norse mythology, the first man and woman, parents of the human race. They were created from tree trunks found on the seashore by three gods - Odin and his two brothers, Vili and Ve.

ASMODEUS

In Jewish legends, the king of demons, commonly identified with Ashmodai. According to the apocryphal book of Tobit, Asmodeus, smitten with love for Sarah, the daughter of Raguel, killed all seven of her husbands on their wedding nights. Following instructions given by the archangel Raphael, Tobias overcame Asmodeus and married Sarah.

ASOKA Columns

Commemorative, sacred, symbolic edict pillars, erected in various parts of India by the benign Emperor Asoka (273-236 BC), Mauryan conqueror and ruler in northern India, convert from militaristic violence to Buddhism and known as the Constantine of Buddhism.

The tall monolithic pillar shafts of polished sandstone (60 or 70 feet high) carry 3-zoned capitals:

▲ an inverted lotus (symbol of the pure Buddha);
▲ a frieze showing the wheel of the law;
▲ an animal symbolic of the Buddha.

Carved on the shaft is the teaching of the compassionate Buddha, as edicts by Asoka, who also planted fruit trees along India's roads to shade and feed the traveler.

ASPERGES

In Roman Catholicism, in a ceremony, the altar, priest, and people are sprinkled with blessed water. The rite dates at least to the ninth century and is a reminder of baptism. Today the ceremony is the Rite of Sprinkling and an optional replacement for the Penitential Rite.

ASPERGILLUM

In Roman Catholicism, Holy water is sprinkled on persons or things to be blessed with a liturgical instrument consisting of a short handle with a bunch of bristles or a perforated metal bulb at the end. Sometimes the handle is hollow in order to hold more water. A small branch or twig of box, laurel, or other shrub is occasionally used.

ASRAVA

In Buddhist philosophy, the illusion that ceaselessly flows out from internal organs (i.e., five sense organs and the mind), a term synonymous with klesa, affliction. To the unenlightened, every existence becomes the object of illusion or is inevitably accompanied by illusion.

ASRIEL

In Judaism, a male descendant of Manasseh who became the family head of the Asrielites. Numbers 26:29-31 indicates that he was the great-grandson of Manasseh through Machir and his son Gilead.

ASRIELITES

A Manassite family descended from Asriel (Numbers 26:28-31).

ASSEMBLIES OF GOD

Largest of the Protestant Pentecostal denominations in the United States. They were organized as a separate entity in 1914, and later established their headquarters in Springfield, Mo. They now have over 1,000,000 members.

The Assemblies reject sacramentalism and infant baptism; affirm separation from the world and entire sanctification, but as gradual, not instantaneous.

The local church retains autonomy and the power to accept or reject policies of higher bodies. Supreme legislative and executive power resides in the General Council; the working administrative body is the General Presbytery, composed of 16 presbyters

ASSHUR

In the Old Testament, a son of Shem, named second at Genesis 10:22 and 1 Chronicles 1:17. He was the forefather of the Assyrians, and the same Hebrew word is rendered both "Asshur" and "Assyrian."

ASSHURIM

In Judaism, descendants of Dedan, son of Jokshan, one of Abraham's sons by Keturah (Genesis 25:1-3).

ASSIR

In the Old Testament, a Levite born in Egypt who was one of the sons of Korah (Exodus 6:24; 1 Chronicles 6:22).

ASSISI, Saint Francis of

(1181-1226) Italian Roman Catholic mystic, founder of the Franciscans. In 1205 he turned away from his extravagant life and wealthy merchant family to a wandering religious life of utter poverty. With his many followers he preached and ministered to the poor in Italy and abroad, stressing piety, simplicity and joy in creation, and the love of all living things. Given oral sanction by Pope Innocent III, his order expanded beyond the control of its founder; he relinquished the leadership in 1221. His feast day is October 4th.

ASSOCIATE PASTOR

In Roman Catholicism, term from the 1917 Code of Canon Law for a priest assigned to a parish to assist the pastor in parish ministry is replaced in the 1984 code by parochial vicar.

ASSOS

In biblical times, a seaport town in Mysia on the northern shore of the Gulf of Adramyttim, hence within the Roman province of Asia. On his third missionary tour, the apostle Paul was heading back to Jerusalem and had stopped at Troas. From here he sent Luke and others by boat to Assos, where he planned to join them. The boat had to travel out around Cape Lectum to get to Assos (on the other side of the promontory from Troas) and this enabled Paul to walk the shorter distance on foot and still arrive at Assos in tome to board the ship, which then traveled to Mitylene on the island of Lesbos (Acts 20:6, 13-14).

ASSUMPTION OF THE VIRGIN

Official dogma of the Roman Catholic Church (declared by Pope Pius XII in 1950) that the Virgin Mary was "assumed into heaven body and soul" at the end of her life. The feast day of the Assumption is August 15th.

This belief was evident from the very early days of the church. The feast of Mary's Assumption is one of the principal Marian feasts of the church year and is for Roman Catholics a holy day of obligation.

ASSURANCE OF SALVATION

The Christian's certitude that because his life is based on faith, he is saved from sin and numbered among the elect. Luther's strong emphasis on faith as the sole principle of salvation gave prominence to this assurance.

By faith the true believer is comforted with the conviction that God is faithful to his promises; the assurance is absolute. Calvinism grounded such assurance in the sovereign absoluteness of divine election. Roman Catholic teaching in the Council of Trent denied the possibility of an absolute certitude of one's salvation.

Both Roman Catholic and classical Protestant views recognize that salvation does remain an object of hope, and that certitude of salvation is modified by the believer's capacity to fall away from or be unfaithful to God's love.

John Wesley stressed the idea of assurance as a conscious factor in Christian living. In his understanding, assurance is the experience of being able to live without voluntary sin. The idea was developed in the United States in revivalism and the Holiness movement, and assurance in this sense is a characteristic teaching of many churches originating in these movements.

ASSYRIA

Kingdom of northern Mesopotamia that became the center of one of the great empires of the ancient Middle East. It was located in what is now northern Iraq and southeastern Turkey. Famous for their cruelty and fighting powers the Assyrians were also monumental builders, as shown by archaeological sites at Nineveh, Ashur and Nimrud.

ASSYRIAN CHURCH

The contemporary Nestorian Church. The title Assyrian was first applied to the church by Englishmen in the early 20th century. The Archbishop of Canterbury's 19th-century mission of aid to the Nestorians having been known as the "Assyrian Mission," but this name was chosen as more likely to encourage popular contributing support.

Today the Nestorians have come to call themselves Assyrians and their church the Assyrian Church in Western languages, but in their own vernacular Arabic or Soureth, as well as officially in classical Syriac, they continue to speak of "the (Apostolic) Church of the East."

ASTARTE

Great goddess of the West Semitic pantheon and the chief deity of Sidon. Her cult as goddess of fertility and reproduction was widespread throughout Palestine, and she was also worshiped in Cyprus, Sicily, Sardinia, and at Carthage.

ASTERISK

In the Byzantine liturgy a practical accessory instrument to the diskos (paten) made of two intersecting, collapsible, and bent metal bands meeting at right angles and held together by a screw. It is placed on top of the diskos to prevent the veil covering the diskos from touching the bread placed beneath.

The Greek form is usually rounded and forms two intersecting arches while the Slavs often prefer a more squared shape. A metal star is often suspended beneath the intersecting arch.

ASTRAL RELIGION

The worship of the celestial bodies, the sun, moon, planets, stars, and constellations, a widespread practice among primitive peoples and those of higher cultures.

It may be ascribed to man's theopoetic tendency to ascribe preternatural and even divine powers to natural phenomena, especially those intimately connected with his own welfare, but whose origins and movements are shrouded in mystery.

Among primitive tribes the sun and moon are almost universally regarded as being alive and possessing a quasi-human nature. Their sex differs from race to race, but the moon is more commonly regarded as female and the sun as male.

Countless myths have been invented to explain their origin as well as that of the stars, e.g., the belief of the Mantras, that the sun and moon are women who brought forth many children, the stars.

Among more advanced civilizations similar animistic beliefs are to be found. In former times the Chinese, for example, held that the heavenly bodies were the dwelling places of spiritual beings with superhuman powers who were, however, subordinate to Tien, Shang-ti, or God, the sole processor of sovereign might. Sacrifices if not actual worship were offered to these luminaries, to the sun at the vernal equinox, and to the moon at the autumnal.

The ancient Egyptians worshiped a Sun-god Re at Heliopolis along with numerous other divinities. Toward the end of the 15th century BC, Amenhotep IV changed his name to Akhenaton and attempted to establish a new solar theology and worship centered upon Aton, an ancient name for the physical sun, but his efforts to introduce this new, more monotheistic work of worship proved to be ineffectual.

Astral religion found its fullest development among the Babylonians, and it passed form there to the peoples of the West, where it prepared the way for Greco-Roman acceptance of astrology as a science with religious overtones.

Though they worshiped all the celestial bodies as "gods," their principal deities were the sun, moon, and the five visible planets. The sun was Ahamash, the moon Sin, Venus Ishtar, Jupiter Marduk, Saturn Ninib (a war god), Mercury Nebo (a herald), and Mars Nergal (a god of the dead). When the

Greeks and Romans became acquainted with the Babylonian pantheon, they
adopted it for their own use, identifying with some modifications their own
deities with those of the East.

The ancestors of the Hebrews are, like
other Semites, worshipers of the sun,
moon, and stars, but such worship is
condemned in the Old Testament as
idolatrous. Though the stars are at
times personified in the Old Testament,
this was done to stress the sovereignty
of the only true God (seePsalms 18).

ASURA

In Buddhism, elemental forces; projec-
tions of the forces in man's mind.

ASURA

In Hindu philosophy, the enemies of
the gods and of men. In the Vedic age
the asuras and the devas were both
considered classes of gods, but gradually the two groups came to oppose
each other, a development that was
reversed in Iran.

ASVALAYANA

Vedic manual of sacrificial ceremonies
composed for the use of the class of
priests called hotar or hotr, whose main
function was to invoke the gods.
Belonging to the "first tradition" of
hermits and wandering holy men rather
than to that of a priesthood, Asvalayana
is mentioned as a teacher as well as a
sage in Vedic litanies.

ASVAMEDHA

Grandest of the Vedic religious rites of
ancient India, performed by a king to
celebrate his paramountcy. The ceremony involved the sacrifice of a horse,
and served not only to glorify the king
but also to ensure the prosperity and
fertility of the entire kingdom. An
important part of the ceremony
required the chief queen to lie down
beside the sacrificed animal, an act
understood to be symbolic of cosmic
marriage.

ASVINS

Twin deities of Vedic India who perhaps represent the morning twilight or
the morning and evening stars.

ASYLUM, Cities of

Six cities, three on either side of the
Jordan set aside by the Mosaic law to
safeguard the unintentional killer from
blood vengeance (Numbers 35:9-34);
in the earliest legislation, in the Book
of the Covenant apparently any altar
offered such refuge.

Asylum did not dispense with investi-
gation and trial, and in case of an unfa-
vorable verdict the refuge was denied.
In Joshua 20 are found the names of:
Kedesh, Shechem, and Hebron for the
west bank of the Jordan; Bezer,
Ranmoth and Gilead, and Golan for
Transjordan.

It is probable that each of these cities
was chosen because it possessed a
notable place of worship. Scholars also
believe that the institution of the cities
of refuge should be attributed to the
reign of David.

ASYLUM, Right of

Claim to refuge and safety from enemies accorded to fugitives in certain
places. The Mosaic law made certain
cities places of asylum for murderers
(Exodus 21:12-14; Numbers 35:11-29;
Numbers 19:1-13), and under Greco-
Roman influence temples were treated
as places of asylum. In AD 431,
Theodosius II extended the privilege to
all Christian sanctuaries and environs.

Right of asylum became attached to
holy places during the Christian ages
and found its way into canon law in the
12th century. With the rise of the
monarchies and the decline of church
authority, the custom lost common
recognition. Today, right of asylum is
sometimes granted in purely political
context.

ATAD

In biblical times, a place in the region of the Jordan called "the threshing floor of Atad." There Jacob's funeral cortege stopped for seven days of mourning while en route from Egypt to the cave of the field of Machpelah in Canaan.

ATALANTA

In Greek mythology, a heroine, probably a by-form of the goddess Artemis.

ATAR

In Zoroastrianism, the deity of fire, a son of Ahura Mazda; he also oversees and gives his name to the ninth day of the month and the ninth month.
The essence of Atar appears in five forms:

1 the victory or Brahman fire;
2 the life than animates the human body;
3 the spark inherent in wood;
4 lightning;
5 the heavenly fire.

All earthly fires are protected by Asha Vahishta, the archangel of truth and order, who sits between Ahura Mazda and Atar.

ATARAH

In the Old Testament, one of the wives of Jerahmeel of the tribe of Judah and the mother of Onan (1 Chronicles 2:2-5; 25-26).

ATAROTH

In biblical times, a town on the east side of the Jordan, among those requested by the tribes of Gad and Reuben as their possession. The section was considered especially suitable for the livestock of these tribes (Numbers 32:1-5). The town was thereafter rebuilt by the Gadites (Numbers 32:34).

ATER

In Judaism, a man of Israel, 98 of whose sons or descendants returned from Babylonian captivity with Zerubbabel in 537 BC (Ezra 2:1-2, 16).

ATHABASCAN CEREMONIALISM

Traditional religious practices of the Athabascan people (indigenous American nations) revolving around funeral and memorial potlatches, which are community and family expressions of grief. An essential ingredient of the potlatch ceremony is that a young man from the family of the deceased provides moose meat that is shared with the whole family.

ATHAIAH

In the Old Testament, a man of the tribe of Judah, a descendant of Perez, listed with other residents of Jerusalem in Nehemiah's time, after the release from Babylonian captivity (Nehemiah 11:4-6).

ATHALIAH

In the Old Testament, the daughter of Ahab and Jezebel and wife of Jehan, king of Judah. After the death of Ahaziah, her son, Athaliah usurped the throne and reigned for seven years. She massacred all the members of the royal house of Judah (2 Kings 11:1-2), except Joash. A successful revolution was organized in favor of Joash, and she was killed.

ATHANASIAN CREED

Latin creed expounding chiefly the doctrines of the Trinity and the Incarnation, regarded as authoritative by the Roman Catholic and Anglican churches, and also by some Protestant churches. Modern scholars believe it was composed in the 5th century.

ATHANASIUS I

(1230-1310) Byzantine monk and patriarch of Constantinople, who directed the opposition to the reunion of Greek and Latin churches decreed by the second Council of Lyons (1274). His efforts in reforming the Greek Orthodox Church encountered opposition from clergy and hierarchy that eventually demanded his resignation.

ATHANASIUS, Saint

(296-373) Early Christian theologian and Greek Father of the Church. Born in Alexandria, Athanasius was elected archbishop of that city in 328. He was banished to Traves (Trier) in 335 by the Emperor Constantine I for his refusal to compromise with Arianism, but was restored by Constantius II in 338. His writings include On the Incarnation, Five Books against Arius and Life of St. Anthony.

ATHONITE, Anastasius

(about 920-1000) Byzantine monk who founded communal monasticism in the hallowed region of Mount Athos, a traditional habitat for contemplative monks and hermits.

ATHEISM

The denial of God, as reflected either in a theoretical system of thought that excludes the possibility or the necessity of a transcendent first principle or in the way one practically conducts one's private and public life. Atheism is opposed to any religion or worship of God.

In Christianity, the term is used in the sense of denial of the existence of God, distinguished from agnosticism, which holds that the existence of God cannot be proved or disproved but does not necessarily take any position on belief.

Atheism should be distinguished from agnosticism, which denies that God or any transcendent spiritual power is knowable, and from skepticism which suspends judgment in such matters.

In Buddhism, the conception that there is no absolute Personal Deity. Buddhism is not philosophically atheistic as it does not deny Ultimate Reality.

General aspects

Atheism has become an all-purpose word for many forms of rejection of God that are designated variously as misbelief, disbelief, nonbelief, and unbelief. When it closes itself to all concern for the divine, atheism succeeds in rooting out God and the idea of God from human existence, denying

both His transcendence of the world and His action in history.

Because it is surrounded by beliefs of gods and of social forces imbued, however imperfectly, with religious values, atheism must be antitheist and antireligious. Militant atheism is not uncommon among secular humanists, and is not restricted to the ranks of Communism.

Atheism is more than an intellectual position and a spiritual attitude; it is a historical event and occurs only where there has been some recognition and acceptance of the reality of God.

Unbelief in the strong sense is denial, explicit and conscious, and presupposes belief, at least in the social ambiance. From a purely historical perspective atheism points to a pervasive and usually predominant belief in a world other than this one and in some sort of deity.

As a culturally defined and respectable stance, atheism is a newcomer on the scene, with a past as yet rather short. This is not an argument against atheism, which could be conceived as a cultural achievement of modern man, the final victory of man over his anxiety and as a sign of his coming of age.

ATHENA

(Pallas Athena) Greek goddess of wisdom and war who sprang fully-grown from Zeus' head. The patroness of Athens, she protected legendary heroes such as Odysseus. In peacetime she taught men agriculture, law, shipbuilding and all the crafts of civilization. The Romans identified her with Minerva.

The young goddess stood side by side with her father during the Battle of the Giants, where she managed to overcome Enceladus, casting him down and throwing the whole of Sicily on top of him to immobilize him.

Although she was the goddess of war, she was not warlike. Clever and wise, she helped heroes such as Perseus, Achilles and Odysseus - though her love for these figures had nothing erotic about it. Athena and Artemis had decided never to marry - even other gods - and to keep their virginity.

ATHENS

Capital of Greece, on the south-west side of the Attic peninsula. The city was already important by circa 1500 BC, but reached it's political peak after the Persian Wars (490-479 BC). Athens became a major center of art, architecture, philosophy and drama, the home of Sophocles, Euripides, Socrates, and Plato. (Acts 17:16-20).

ATHINGANOI

A religious sect that flourished in central Asia Minor in the 9th and 10 centuries. Often regarded as a branch of the Paulicians, they were really quite distinct. They apparently practiced an exaggerated levitical purity, observed the sabbath, held to adult baptism, and indulged in astrology and black magic. Their reputation for magic and fortune telling caused the name of the sect to be used for the gypsies.

ATHLAI

Son of Bebai; one of the Israelites who dismissed their foreign wives after Ezra came to Jerusalem in 468 BC (Ezra 10:28, 44).

ATHOS, Mount

In northern Greece, an autonomous theocracy of Greek Orthodox monks inhabiting 20 monasteries and dependencies, some of which are larger than the parent monasteries. It occupies the eastermost of the three promontories of Chalcidice peninsula, which projects from Macedonia into the Aegean Sea. The community's present constitution dates from 1924 and forms part of the Greek constitution of 1927.

Besides the larger monasteries, the peninsula is dotted with numerous smaller houses. Asceticism centers chiefly around the liturgical recitation of the Byzantine office, vigils, fasts, and manual labor.

The main monasteries possess rich collections of icons, frescoes, and ancient manuscripts. Before the Russian Revolution there were more than 9,000 monks, but a crisis in monastic vocations has reduced the total number of monks on Mount Athos to little over 1,000.

ATLAS

In Greek mythology, son of the Titan Iapetus and the nymph Clymene and brother of Prometheus (creator of mankind). In the works of Homer, Atlas seems to have been a marine creation who supported the pillars that held heaven and earth apart.

Atlas had seven daughters by Pleione, the Pleiades: Taygete, Electra, Alcyone, Asteroe, Celaeno, Maia and Merope. After their death the Pleiades formed a constellation in the sky.

ATMAN

In Buddhism, term meaning the Supreme Self, Universal Consciousness, or Ultimate Reality. The concept is defined as the divine element in man and woman, degraded into the idea of an entity dwelling in the heart of each man, the thinker of his or her thoughts, and doer of its deeds, and after death dwelling in bliss or misery according to deeds done in the body.

ATOMISM

Theory in medieval Islamic theology according to which absolutely everything (except God) was made up of atoms and perishable accidents. The theory stressed the continuous intervention byu God in the affairs of the world and humanity. It was embraced (though interpreted in its detail in different ways) by many medieval Islamic theologians.

ATON

Egyptian sun god. Originally, Aton was the Egyptian name for the sun, which was also called Khepri, Ra or Atum, according to the position in the sky. Gradually a cult of Aton emerged in which the god represented the sun in its life-giving power. During the religious revolution of the pharaoh Akhenaton, Aton became the supreme god and was worshiped at the new capital Akhenaton. In this period, Aton was represented as a solar disk, whose rays ended in human hands symbolically holding out the gift of life. His cult was soon eradicated by the rulers who succeeded Akhetanon, restoring the old pantheon.

ATONEMENT

In Christianity, the covering over of sin, the reconciliation between God and man accomplished by Jesus Christ. It is an important religious concept whereby rituals, sacrifices and prayers are used in the hope of restoring to mankind a state of "atoneness" with God. In the Old Testament animals were sacrificed as an act of atonement. In medieval Christian thought Anselm of Canterbury refers to Christ as having been sent to earth in order to satisfy divine justice by atoning for mankind's sins.

In Buddhism, the term is used in the sense of vicarious. Primitive Buddhism knows nothing of vicarious atonement; each must work out his own salvation. One may help another by thought, word and deed, but cannot bear results or take over consequences of another's errors or misdeeds.

ATONEMENT, Day of

Specific day of the Jewish calendar; one of propitiation or sin covering, commemorated by Israel on the tenth day of the seventh month of the sacred year, or on Tishri 10th (Tishri corresponds approximately to September-October). On this day Israel's High Priest offered sacrifices as a sin covering for himself, for the other Levites and for the people. It was also a time of cleansing the tabernacle or the later Temples from the polluting effects of sin.

The atonement day was a time of holy convention and of fasting, as is indicated by the fact that the people were then to "afflict their souls". This was the only fast enjoined under the Mosaic law. It was also a sabbath, a time to abstain from regular labors (Leviticus 16:29-31; Numbers 29:7; Acts 27:9). See: Yom Kippur.

ATRAHASIS, Myth of

Old Babylonian myth dealing with mankind's punishment through pestilence and flood.

ATREIDS

In Greek mythology, the major representatives of the House of the Pelopids. Pelops and Hippodameia were the parents of Atreus, Thyestes, Pleisthenes, Pittheus and Niceppe. After the death of Eurystheus, who had succeeded to the throne of his father, Atheneleus, the Pelopids became much more powerful and ruled in Mycenae, Tiryns, Argos and the Argolid.

According to one version of the story, Pelops passed on the scepter of power to Atreus, his first-born. When Atreus died before succeeding and with sons who were not of age, Pelops gave the scepter to his brother, Thyestes. As a good guardian should, Thyestes passed it on in his turn to Agamemnon.

ATREUS

In Greek legend, son of Pelops of Mycenae and his wife Hippodameia, elder brother of Thyestes, and king of Mycenae.

ATRIUM

Roof of early Roman house, partly covered by a roof shedding rain into the impluvium. It became a forecourt in Christian basilicas.

ATROTH-BETH-JOAB

Name appearing among the "sons of Salma" in the genealogy of the tribe of Judah (1 Chronicles 2:54).

ATTAI

In the Old Testament, grandson of Sheshan, a descendant of Judah through Hezron. Sheshan had daughters only, one of whom he gave in marriage to his Egyptian slave Jarha, who fathered Attai. In turn Attai was the father of Nathan (1 Chronicles 2:25, 34-36).

ATTAVADA

In Buddhism, the false belief in the existence in man of a personal soul - Atta - which makes him separate from the other manifestations in one's life. The false belief is an immortal soul.

ATTHAKATHA

A general term designating commentaries on works of Pali Buddhist canon that provide much information on the society, culture, and religious history of ancient India and Sri Lanka.

ATTRITION

In Roman Catholicism, sorrow for sins because they are hateful in themselves or because the person is shamed or fears God's punishment is sometimes referred to as imperfect contrition of attrition. Imperfect contrition is sufficient for the reception of the sacrament of reconciliation.

AUDIANS

Rigorist sect of the 4th century founded by Audius, a Mesopotamian, reacting against the worldliness of the clergy. He officially broke with the church by rejecting the decree of the Council of Nicaea on Easter. Illegally consecrated bishop, Audius was exiled to Scythia where he engaged in missionary activities among the Goths.

After his death the sect dwindled rapidly, although there was still evidence for it in the next century.

AUDIENCE, Papal

A person or a number of persons may have a formal visit with the pope. Public audiences in which a number of persons visit the pope in a group are more common than private audiences in which a single person or a small group is allowed to pay respects to the Holy Father.

AUGEAS

In Greek mythology, son of Helios and king of Elis in the Peloponnese. He had vast herds of cattle, but had been remiss in cleaning out their stables, thus creating two huge problems for his country: on the one hand, the soil was becoming infertile because no manure was being spread on it, and on the other the accumulated filth was in danger of polluting all of Elis.

Here, according to the myth, Heracles was not only acting on instructions from Eurystheus, who assigned him this labor in the hope of humiliating him with such demeaning work, but Augeas, too, who had appealed to him promising him, a part of his kingdom if he could complete the task in a single day.

Heracles hit upon a simple but clever way of performing the work. After digging a channel into the foundation of the stables he was able to change the course of the Peneus and Alpheus rivers whose currents swept out the dung and deposited in on the farmlands of Elis.

AUGSBURG

German town associated with several events of the Reformation and the birthplace of the Holbeins. Located on the Lech River in Bavaria, it was founded in 15 BC under Augustus and named Augusta Vindelicorum. In the 6th century Augsburg became an episcopal see, and in 1276 an imperial city, which later formed part of the Swabian League. It reached a peak in the 15th and 16th centuries when commercial eminence came to the Fuggers, a Catholic family whose loans proved vital to Catholic forces in the Reformation era.

In 1528 Luther appeared in Augsburg before the papal legate, Cajetan, but they were unable to resolve the dispute over indulgences.

A 1527 meeting of Anabaptists in Augsburg came to be called the Martyrs Synod because it sent evangelists out to many places and most of them suffered martyrdom.

In 1530 Lutheran princes stated their position to Emperor Charles V at the Diet of Augsburg in what is known as the Augsburg Confession. It has since been the principal confession of Lutheranism.

AUGSBURG, Diet of

The council, consisting of princes, nobles, and representatives of imperial cities of the Holy Roman Empire, that was convened by Emperor Charles V in 1530 to secure the support of Protestants against the invasions of the Turks.

AUGSBURG CONFESSION

The basic confession of the Lutheran churches, presented June 25, 1530, in German and Latin versions at the Diet of Augsburg to the emperor Charles V by seven Lutheran princes and two imperial free cities. The principal author was the reformer Philip Melanchthon, who utilized earlier Lutheran statements of faith. The purpose was to defend the Lutherans against current misrepresentations and to provide a statement of their theology that would be acceptable to the Roman Catholics in the Holy Roman Empire.

AUGSBURG INTERIM

A temporary doctrinal agreement between German Catholics and Protestants, proclaimed in May 1548 at the Diet of Augsburg (1547-48), becoming imperial law on June 30, 1548. Consisting of 26 articles it primarily reflected a Catholic viewpoint. It did, however, allow clerical marriages and communion in both kinds (bread and wine) for the laity.

AUGURY

The Roman art of discerning the will of the gods with respect to a certain course of action through the interpretation of the auguria, or signs. These could be of a causal nature, or they could be deliberately sought.

They consisted of such diverse things as the creaking of a chair, the spilling of salt, the movement of animals, the sound of thunder, or the flash of lightning. The most significant, however, were those given by birds, either in their cry, their course of flight, or in their manner of eating.

AUGUSTINE OF CANTERBURY, Saint

(556-604) First archbishop of Canterbury and the apostle of England who founded the Christian church in southern England. He tried in vain to unify the British (Celtic) churches of north Wales and the churches he founded. The Christian Celts refused to relinquish their customs for those of Rome or to accept Augustine's pleas of ecclesiastic uniformity.

AUGUSTINE OF HIPPO, Saint

(354-430) Christian theologian and writer, the most prominent of the Latin Fathers of the Church. During the early years in Carthage, northern Africa, he embraced Manichaeism, but in Rome (where he arrived in 383) he was much influenced by Neoplatonism. Moving to Milan, he met and was greatly impressed by St. Ambrose, bishop of Milan, and became a baptized Christian in 387.

Ordained a priest in 389, he became bishop of Hippo in northern Africa in 396. There followed many famous books, including the autobiographical *Confessions* (397-401) and *De Civitate Dei* (413-426), the great Christian philosophy of history.

Having become a Christian, Augustine decided to return to Africa and to lead a kind of monastic life with a few of his friends and pupils. While waiting for his departure, he worked at several books he had planned, including a series on the liberal arts, of which only,*On Music,*has survived.

The death of his mother, which occurred after they had reached Rome and were at the embarkation port of Ostia, delayed his return. For more than a year he remained in Rome, continued to work on his philosophical dialogues, and furthered his knowledge of Christian doctrine and practice.*On the Morals of the Catholic Church and of the Manichaeans,*was written at this time.

It was not until 388 that Augustine with his son and two friends reached

Tagaste. He sold his property, gave the proceeds to the poor, and with his few followers set up a kind of monastery devoted to a life of prayer and study.His son, Adeolatus, who was one of the group and whose education had been a particular care of Augustine's, died in 389.

In 391 Augustine's quiet monastic life was brought suddenly to an end. He happened to be on a visit to Hippo and was attending church when the aged bishop was urging his congregation to find a candidate for the priesthood.

Augustine, despite his protestations, was immediately chosen, and the bishop ordained him as a priest. Later that year he moved his monastery to Hippo and began his sacerdotal duties. Although it was then customary for preaching to be reserved for the bishop, Augustine even as a priest was assigned that task.

He began his sermons on the scriptures, which, transcribed as they were delivered, constitute his many books of commentary on the Bible. He also began the public dispute with the African heretics which were to engage him for the rest of his life.

In 396 Augustine was called upon to assume what he called the "burden of the episcopate." For 35 years as the bishop of Hippo nearly all his energies were given to the defense and promotion of the Catholic Church in northern Africa.

He took an influential part in the many councils and conferences called to deal with various heresies and wrote many works against them, in particular against Manicheism, Donatism, and Pelagianism.

However onerous and varied his duties, Augustine always found time to write. In 397 he wrote the first three books, although On Christian Doctrine, the final book was not completed until 30 years later. At the same time he also began his Confessions, and the completed work seems to have been published by 400.

He had no sooner finished that than he began one of his greatest doctrinal treatises, On the Trinity. Following the sack of Rome in 410, he was drawn into the controversy regarding the responsibility of Christianity for the fall of the "eternal city," and into a correspondence with two Roman officials on the relation of the church and the empire. Out of such reflections he seems to have conceived the City of God, which was begun in 413 and appeared serially for thirteen years.

In 426 Augustine arranged for his successor as bishop of Hippo. Considering it useful "to compile and point out all those things which displease me in my works," he read through all his writings and in his Retractiones noted down what revisions he would make in their doctrine.

In the works as he left it, he comments on 232 separate titles, not including his letters and sermons, which were to have been considered in a separate account.

While Augustine was engaged in this task, North Africa was becoming involved in what amounted to civil war. Vandals from Spain had been invited to Africa, to help in the fight against the Imperial forces, but it was soon evident that they came not to aid but in their own interest.

In 430 the Imperial forces were defeated and sought refuge in Hippo, where they were besieged by the Vandal army. There, when the siege was in its third month, Augustine died, August 28th, 430.

AUGUSTINIAN CANONS

The first religious order of man in the Roman Catholic Church to combine clerical stays with a full common life. Though a number of priests followed the 4th-5th century theologian Augustine's way of life, there is no record of an order being formed until the 11th century.

The order grew and flourished until the Protestant Reformation, during which time many of its foundations perished.

AUGUSTINIAN HERMITS

One of the four great mendicant orders (those orders whose corporate as well as personal poverty made it necessary for them to beg for alms) of the Middle Ages. Dispersed by the Vandal invasion of northern Africa (about 428), a number of congregations of hermits who had been following the rules of St. Augustine founded monasteries in central and northern Italy. These remained independent of one another until the 13th century. when Pope Alexander IV in 1256 established them as one order.

AUGUSTINIANISM

A school of philosophical and theological thought claiming fidelity to the doctrine of St. Augustine of Hippo. The principal tenets of this school were:

▲ There is no autonomous philosophy separate from theology.
▲ The will enjoys a primacy over intellect, with the resulting voluntarist view that beatific vision is formally constituted by man's highest affective power rather than through an act of intellectual contemplation.
▲ The soul knows itself directly and is really identified with its various powers or faculties.
▲ Every created reality, spiritual as well as corporeal, is ultimately constituted of matter and form, with the result that the soul, being a complete substance, is individuated by its own spiritual matter.
▲ To achieve its higher forms of knowledge, including God, the soul requires a special divine "illumination."
▲ Within the structure of every composite reality there are several substantial forms hierarchically ordered, including the form of corporeity, identified with light.
▲ The notion of "seminal reasons," or of a "virtual creation," to describe the causal or potential mode of being imparted at creation to living things that appear progressively in the course of time.
▲ The absolute impossibility of an externally existing world.

AUGUSTINIAN NUNS

Several Roman Catholic religious orders of women, one of which was probably the first solely nursing order in the history of the church. Until 1400 they remained strictly cloistered. From the 17th century the third order members came more to the foreground, and new groups were established as increasing numbers of these women dedicated themselves to the work of schools, hospitals and missions.

AUGUSTINIAN RECOLLECTS

Roman Catholic religious order of men, an offshoot of the Augustinian Hermits. This 16th-century movement in Spain began not as a reform but simply as a desire on the part of some friars for a rule of stricter observance and a return to the heremitic (hermit) ideals of solitude and contemplation.

AUGUSTINIANS

In the Roman Catholic Church, a generic name applied sometimes to the entire group of religious orders and congregations of man and women whose constitutions are based on the rules of St. Augustine.

AUGUSTUS, Caesar

(63 BC-AD 14) Roman emperor, introduced an autocratic regime known as the principate which enabled him, working through institutions that were republican in outward form, to overhead every aspect of Roman life, and to bring stability to the Greco-Roman world.

AUMBRY

This small boxlike recess, set into the wall of the sanctuary, is used for the reservation of the holy oils.

AUREOLE

The gold band, the rays of gold leaf, gilt paint or metal surrounding the figures of the Blessed Trinity and the Blessed Virgin Mary in sacred art, particularly in icons, signifies the sanctity attached to those persons.

In early Byzantine art the aureole appeared as an oval shape behind the person depicted. The Italians gave the name mandorla to this contour because of its almond shape. An aureole is distinct from the nimbus or halo.

AURORA

The Latin word for Eos, the Greek mythological personification of the dawn. According to the Greek poet Hesiod, she was the daughter of Titan Hyperion and the Titaness Theia and sister of Helios, the sun god, and Selene, the moon goddess.

AUTHORITY

In Buddhism, denial of the existence of a particular authority in the sense of one who gives forth doctrine which must be accepted, or who gives authoritative explanation of doctrines. Each Buddhist is his own authority, in the sense that he must learn the truth for himself, by study, self-discipline, and practice. No written teaching or scripture is authoritative in the sense of binding.

AUTOCEPHALOUS CHURCHES

In the modern usage of Eastern Orthodox canon law, churches that enjoy total canonical and administrative independence and elect their own primates and bishops.

Most modern Orthodox "autocephalies" are national churches, but some are limited only geographically and include the territories of several states.

The heads of individual autocephalous churches bear different titles: patriarch, archbishop or metropolitan.

AUTOGENIC CHURCHES

A classification for the numerous, small pseudo-Orthodox bodies that have sprung up in the 20th century, especially in the United States. The designation "autogenic" (self-starting) is applied to such churches to indicate a lack of canonical lineage.

AUXILIARY BISHOP

A bishop acts as an aid to the diocesan bishop who may need assistance because of the amount of work, illness, or age. The auxiliary bishop is appointed by the Holy See and is a titular bishop of an ancient see which has ceased and no longer endures except in records.

He does not have ordinary jurisdiction, nor does he have the right to succession. Canon law recommends that he also be appointed an apicopal vicar or a vicar general.

AVALOKITESVARA

In Buddhism, the self as perceived by Buddhi, the faculty of intuition. The term is also used in the sense of personification of the self-generative creative cosmic force.

AVATAMSAKA-SUTRA

A voluminous Mahayana Buddhist text that some consider the most sublime revelation of the Buddha's teachings and that scholars value for its revelations about the evolution of thought from primitive Buddhism to fully developed Mahayana.

AVATAR

A descent from heaven; the incarnation of the Hindu deities, or their appearance in some manifest shape upon earth.

AVATARA

A manifestation or incarnation of the Hindu God Vishnu. The Buddha is regarded by many Indians as the ninth or latest Avatar, thus keeping the most famous of all Indian teachers within the Hindu pantheon.

AVE MARIA

(Hail Mary) Opening words of the principal prayer in the Roman Catholic Church. The prayer consists of the salution of the archangel Gabriel to the Virgin Mary announcing the Incarnation (Luke 1:28), together with the words addressed to Mary by Elizabeth (Luke 1:42).

AVENGER OF BLOOD

In Hebrew law, term originally applied to the nearest male relative, who was under obligation to avenge the blood of one who has been killed (Numbers 35:19).

The avenging of blood is based on the mandate regarding the sanctity of blood and human life stated to Noah wherein God said: "Your blood of your souls shall I ask back .... from the hand of each one who is the brother, shall I ask back the soul of man. Anyone shedding man's blood, by man will his own blood be shed, for in God's image he made man' (Genesis 9:5-6). A deliberate murderer was to be put to death by the "avenger of blood," and no ransom was to be accepted for such a murderer (Numbers 35:19-21).

AVERA

In Judaism, a moral transgression (or sin) against God or man. It may vary from grievous to slight and is the opposite of mitzwa (commandment), understood in the broad sense of any good deed.

AVERSION

One of the passions which compels a person to turn away from an object. Aversion is the opposite of attachment, and can be either put into the service of spiritual growth or allowed to become destructive.

AVESTA

Sacred book of Zoroastrianism, containing its cosmogony, law, and liturgy,the teachings of the prophet Zoroaster. The extant Avesta is all that remains of a much larger body of scripture, apparently Zoroaster's transformation of a very ancient tradition.

AVIGNON PAPACY

Designation for the period (1309-1377) when the popes took up residence at Avignon (France), instead of at Rome, primarily because of the current political conditions. At that time Avignon was not on French soil but belonged to the vassals of the pope, and, in 1348, became direct papal property.

AVIJJA

In Buddhism, term meaning unwitting, hence ignorance. The term is used in the sense of lack of enlightenment, the fundamental root of evil, and the ultimate cause of the desire which creates the dukkha of existence. It is the nearest approach to "original sin" known to Buddhism. Its total elimination, resulting in perfect enlightenment is the goal of the Buddhist Path.

AVINU MALKENU

The opening words of each verse of a Jewish litany of supplication that is recited in synagogues with special devotion during the Ten Days of Penitence (except on the Sabbath), which mark the beginning of the new religious year.

AVITH

In biblical times, the royal city or home of Hadad, the fourth king of the Edomites, who defeated the Midianites in battle (Genesis 36:35; 1 Chronicles 1:46).

AVREKH

The term of honor and dignity called out before the chariot of Joseph after Pharaoh made him second in the kingdom (Genesis 41:43).

AVVIM

In Judaism, early settlers in that part of the land of Canaan that lay westward toward Gaza. 40 years after the Exodus, Moses told how, for the most part, these Avvim had been dispossessed by the Caphtorim (Deuteronomy 2:23). Shortly before Joshua's death, in about the middle of the 15th century BC, a remnant of the Avvim still remained (Joshua 13:1-3).

AVVITES

In Judaism, inhabitants of Avva, who were among the peoples whom the

Assyrians used to replace exiled Israelites after capturing Samara in 740 BC (2 Kings 17:24). All these transplanted came to be known as Samaritans. The Avvites, though learning the feat of God to some degree, nevertheless, made and worshiped the gods Nibhaz and Tartak (2 Kings 17:29-33).

AXIL LORDS

In the Old Testament, title applied to the five lords ruling the Philistine cities of Gaza, Ashkelon, Ashdod, Ekron and Gath, apparently because of their being in a coalition or alliance.

The axil lords dominated Philistia as rulers of individual city states and as a council of coequals with regard to matters of mutual interest.

AYA SOFYA

Church of the Divine Wisdom in Istanbul (Turkey). Emperor Justinian (527-565) had it built as yet another effort to restore the greatness of the Roman Empire. It was completed in 548 and reigned as the greatest church in Christendom until the conquest of Constantinople in 1453. St. Peter's in Rome is larger than Aya Sofya, but it was built more than 1,000 years later.

Justinian filled the church with gorgeous mosaics. The Byzantine Church and state later went through a fierce civil war (726-787) over the question of whether images were to be allowed or not. When the Turks took Constantinople there was no controversy. The Koran repeatedly rails against idolatry.

Consequently Islamic art is supposed to have no saints's portraits, no pictures of animals, fish or fowl, nor anything else with immortal soul, and the mosaic had to go. Luckily they were covered with plaster rather than destroyed. Restoration work is still going on.

AYATANA

In Buddhism, the 12 bases or sources of mental processes. Six are the five sense organs; the other six are the corresponding sense objects, conceptions or thoughts being objects of mind.

AYATOLLAH

Honorific title meaning "reflection of God" given to the more important Muslim clergymen in Iran. Many of the ayatollahs joined the movement against the Shah in the 1970s. After the Iranian revolution they became the dominant political leaders of the new Islamic republic, occupying most important positions of authority.

AYUTHAYA

Small city north of Bangkok, site of many historic Buddhist temples. Wat Phra Si Samphet was the largest temple inAyuthaya in its time, and it was used as the royal temple/palace for several Ayuthaya kings. Built in the 14th century, the compound once contained a 16 meter Buddha covered with 250 kg of gold, which was melted down by the Burmese conquerors. It is mainly known for the line of three large chedis (stupas) erected in the quintessential Ayuthaya style, which has become to be identified with Thai art more than any other single temple.

AZAZEL

One of the evil spirits thought by the early Hebrews to inhabit the wilderness. On the Day of Atonement, the High Priest sent Azazel a goat supposedly bearing the discarded sins of the people; hence the word scapegoat.

AZAZIAH

In the Old Testament, one of the six harpists in the procession that brought the Ark of the Covenant to Jerusalem (1 Chronicles 15:21).

AZEL

In the Old Testament, a descendant of Saul through Jonathan; he had six sons (1 Chronicles 8:37-38).

AZGAD

In Judaism, the head of a paternal house, some of whose members returned to Jerusalem with Zerubbabel in 537 BC (Ezra 2:12; Nehemiah 7:17).

AZHAR, al-

A university mosque in Cairo, founded in 970 by the Fatimid Dynasty. It influences all Muslim nations through its studies of Arabic, history, the Koran, law and philosophy. Its distinctively turbaned and robed teachers and students are drawn from the entire Islamic world.

AZOR

In the Bible, a post-exilic ancestor of Jesus' foster father Joseph (Matthew 1:13-16).

AZRIEL

In the Old Testament, a household head of the half tribe of Manasseh east of the Jordan, one of the "valiant, mighty fellows" whose descendants were taken captive by the Assyrian king Tiglath-pileser due to worshiping false gods (1 Chronicles 5:23-26).

AZRIKAM

In the Old testament, the "leader of the household" of wicked King Ahaz of Judah. He was killed by the Ephraimite Zichri when King Pekah of Israel battled Judah (2 Chronicles 28:6-7).

AZTEC RELIGION

The religion of north-west Mexican tribe also known as Tenochas. Their name is a derivative of Aztan (white land), their legendary place of origin. Their alternate name Tenochas was in honor of their legendary leader Tenoch. Their empire which was remarkable for its rapid rise in the 14th century was matched only by that of the Incas. They achieved their greatness after the dissolution and decline of the advanced civilization of the Toltecs for whom they probably served as mercenaries. They settled what became their capital of Tenochtitlan on a small island on Lake Texcoco (1325) in the Valley of Mexico.

that the world had four stages of development each dominated by different gods.

▲ Tezcatlipoca reigned over the age of Four Ocelot;

▲ Quetzalcoatl ruled the age of Four Wind;

▲ Tlaloc controlled the age of Four Rain;

▲ Chalchihuitlicue, the age of Four Sun.

The unifying cosmic principle was the quality of life and death, darkness and light, male and female, symbolized by the continuing struggle between Quetzacoatl and Tezcatlipoca, the death god. The calendar, the dates of their ceremonial and solar years were in agreement at 52 year intervals. The end of a cycle was observed by the extinction of all fire and the destruction of idols and pottery,

This was done to prevent Different gods

The Aztecs believed the end of the world. To mark a new era new fires were kindled and temples were redecorated. Divination characterized the ceremonial year and it was a time of great authority for priests as they interpreted omens.

Priests also recorded history in picture writing on folded paper or strips of hide. They accompanied their religious ceremonies with gourd rattles, wooden drums, flutes and pottery whistles.

BAAL

A god worshiped in many ancient Near Eastern communities, especially among the Canaanites, who apparently considered him a fertility deity and the most important god in the pantheon.

Knowledge of Baal's personality and functions derives chiefly from a number of tablets uncovered from 1929 onward at Augured (modern Ras Shamra), in northern Syria and dating to the middle of the 2nd millennium BC. The tablets, although closely attached to the worship of Baal at his local temple, probably represent Canaanite belief generally. Fertility was envisaged in terms of seven-year cycles. In the mythology of Canaan, Baal, the god of life and fertility, locked in mortal combat with Mot, the god of death and sterility. If Baal triumphed, a seven-year cycle of fertility would ensue; but, if he was vanquished by Mot, seven years of drought and famine would ensue.

BA'AL

Hebrew word used with reference to the following persons or situations:

1 Simeonite enclave city within the territory of Judah, apparently the same as Baalath-beer and Ramah of the Negeb (Compare 1 Chronicles 4:32-33; Joshua 19:7-9);
2 A husband as owner of his wife (Genesis 20:3);
3 "owners of the nations" (Isaiah 16:8);
4 confederates (literally, "owners of a covenant") (Genesis 14:13);
5 owners or processors of tangibles (Exodus 21:28; 22:8; 1 Kings 1:8);
6 persons or things having something that is characteristic of their nature,

manner, occupation and the like; for example, an archer (Genesis 40:23);
7 "false gods" (Judges 2:11-13).

At times in Israel's history God was referred to as "Baal," in the sense of being the Lord or Husband of the nation (Isaiah 54:5). Also, the Israelites may have improperly associated God with Baal in their apostasy. The latter appears to be borne out by Hosea's prophecy that the time would come when Israel, after going into and being restored from captivity, would repentantly call God "My Husband," and no more "My owner."

BAALAT

Chief deity of Byblos, often presented with a typical Egyptian hairstyle, headdress, and costume. By the 12th dynasty (1991-1786 BC) she was equated with the Egyptian goddess Hathor.

BAALBEK

A site in Lebanon, in Semitic times dedicated to Baal the sun-god, called by the Greeks Heliopolis. Nero probably began the Temple of Jupiter of which six gigantic Corinthian columns of the peristyle remain. Caracella erected later forms. On the south terrace is the Corinthian Temple of Bacchus and to the east the dramatic small circular Corinthian Temple of Venus (circa 245), a dynamic, baroque syntax of convex and concave forms.

BAAL-BERITH

Canaanite god with a cult centered at Shechem, who was popular among the ancient Israelites in that area (Judges 8:33).

BAAL-GAD

In biblical times, a town in the valley plain of Lebanon at the base of Mount Hermon, on its western side. It is used to describe the most northerly point of Joshua's conquest of the land of Canaan, as compared with the southerly point of Mount Halak in the Negeb (Joshua 11;17; 13:5).

BAAL-HAMON

In the Old Testament, a place mentioned in Song of Solomon (8:11) as the location of a productive vineyard of King Solomon. No indication is given as to its site. While many view it as a literal location, some suggest that it is used in this poetic writing figuratively to represent the realm over which Solomon ruled and which produced great wealth (1 Kings 4:20-21).

BAAL-HERMON

In the Old Testament, name that appears at Judges 3:3 and 1 Chronicles 5:23. In the first instance it describes a point in the region inhabited by the Sidonians and the Hivites who remained unconquered by the Israelites, and it is here referred to as "Mount Baal-Hermon." It is usually identified with Mount Hermon itself, but may refer to the Hermon range in general or to some portion thereof.

At 1 Chronicles 5:23, Baal-Hermon is used along with Senir and Mount Hermon and the region of Bashan to outline the territory occupied by the half tribe of Manasseh.

BAAL OF PEOR

The particular Baal worshiped at Mount Peor by both Moabites and Midianites (Numbers 25:1-6). It has been suggested that Baal of Peor may actually have been Chemosh, in view of the fact that the latter deity was the chief god of the Moabites (Numbers 21:29).

BAAL-PERAZIM

In the Old Testament, the site of a complete victory by King David over the combined forces of the Philistines, sometime after David's conquest of the stronghold of Jerusalem (2 Samuel 5:9-21). The record states that, upon hearing of the Philistines' aggressive approach, David and his men "went down to the place hard to approach," while the Philistines were "tramping about in the low plain of Rephaim."

BA'AL SHEM

A Jewish title for man who reputedly worked wonders and affected cures through secret knowledge of the ineffable names of God. Benjamin ben Zerah (11th century) was one of the several Jewish poets to employ the mystical names of God in his works, thereby demonstrating a belief in the efficacy of the holy name long before certain rabbis and Kabbalists (followers of esoteric Jewish mysticism) were popularly called ba'al shem.

BAAL-TAMAR

In the Old Testament, a site near Gibeah where Israelite fighting men drew up in formation against the tribe of Benjamin in a costly battle provoked by a revolting sex crime. Some of Israel's forces were massed at Baal-Tamar, while others were placed an ambush against the Benjamites (Judges 19:25-28).

BAAL-ZEBUB

The Baal worshiped by the Philistines at Ekron. There are indications that it was a common practice among the Hebrews to change the names of false gods to something similar but degrading. Hence the ending "zebub" may be an alteration of one of the titles of Baal.

The designation "Beelzebub" (possibly meaning "lord of the habitation"), appearing in the Christian Greek Scriptures with reference to the ruler of the demons, may be an alteration of "Baal-Zebub" (Matthew 12:24).

BAANA

In the Old Testament, one of the twelve deputies whom Solomon appointed to secure food for the king's household. Baana's assignment was the fifth-listed district, primarily the fertile valleys of Megiddo and Jezreel. He was the son of Solomon's recorder Jehoshaphat (1 Kings 4:3-12).

BAASEIAH

In the Old Testament, a descendant of Levi through Gershom and ancestor of Temple musician Asaph (1 Chronicles 6:39-43).

BAASHA

In the Old Testament, third king of the 10-tribe kingdom of Israel; son of Ahijah of the tribe of Issachar and of insignificant background.

BAB, the

(1819-1850) Title of Mirza Ali Mohammed, a merchant's son whose claim to the Bab (Gateway) of the hidden imam (the perfect embodiment of Islamic faith) gave rise to the Babi religion and made him one of the three central figures of the Bah'a'i faith.

BABAK

(circa 765-838) Leader of the Iranian Khorram-dinan, a religious sect which arose following the execution of Abu Muslim, who had rebelled against the 'Abbasid Caliphate. Denying that the Abu Muslim was dead, the sect predicted that he would return to spread justice throughout the world. Abu Babak led a new revolt against the Abbasids that as put down in 837.

BABEL

One of the first cities to be built after the Flood. Here God "confused the language of all the earth" (Genesis 11:9). The name is derived from the verb ba-lai, meaning "to mingle, mix, confuse, confound." Local citizens, thinking of their city as God's seat of government, claimed that the name was compounded from Bab (Gate) and El (God), signifying "Gate of God." From antiquity the word "Bab" ("Gate") is the designation given in the Near East to a seat of government.

BABEL, Tower of

In the Old Testament, a tower begun by Noah's descendants to try to reach heaven. God frustrated the builders by making them speak many languages (Babel means "confusion" according to Genesis 11:9).

BABISM

Movement after the Bab, a title assumed by Mirza Ali Mohammed (1819-1850) of Shiraz in 1844, who was finally executed for his beliefs. The Babi sect later gave rise to the Bahá'is.

Originating in 1844 as a movement within Shiite Islam, with some dependence on Shakhism, Babism advocated the abrogation of certain laws of the Koran. Founded in Shiraz, Persia, it came to be considered a threat to Shiism, the official religion of the state. Persecution of the sect began in 1845, and the Babists revolted in 1848 when Nasit-al-Din became shah. The revolt was crushed, and al-Bab executed in 1850 at Tabriz. In 1863 the remaining Babists were expelled to Constantinople. From the group came Baha-Ullah (1817-92), founder of the Bahái Faith.

BABYLON

Ancient cultural region occupying south-eastern Mesopotamia between the Tigris and Euphrates rivers. Babylon is the later name given to Babel. The last ruling Assyrian king was Ashurbanipal, who fought a civil war against his brother, the sub-king in Babylon, devastating the city and its population.

Upon Ashurbanipal's death Nabopolassar made Babylon his capital and instituted the last and greatest period of Babylonian supremacy. His son Nebuchadnezzar II (reigned 605-562 BC) conquered Syria and Palestine; he is best remembered for the destruction of Judah and Jerusalem in 587 BC and for the ensuing Babylonian captivity of the Jews.

BABYLON, Patriarch of

The official title given to the patriarch of the Catholics of the Chaldean rite.

The first Chaldean patriarch, John Sulkaqa (confirmed in Rome in 1553), and his successors were styled patriarch of Mossul or of the East Assyrians. Joseph I, the first of the second series of unionist patriarchs, was made patriarch of the Chaldean nation in 1681. The title of Patriarch of Babylon first appeared with his successor Joseph II in 1696.

BABYLONIA

The ancient land in the lower Mesopotamian valley through which the Tigris and Euphrates Rivers flow, and which corresponds to the southeastern part of modern Iraq. It extends circa 30 miles west of the Euphrates, joining the Arabian Desert. East of the Tigris it is bounded by the Persian hills; on the south-east by the Persian Gulf. Its northern boundary is a natural one marked by a noticeable rise in elevation near Baghdad.

The Amorites were a Semitic-speaking people who came down the Euphrates River from Syria and conquered the northern part of Babylonia. Under the sixth king of the dynasty, Hammurabi (reigned 1792-1750 BC), famous for his code of laws, all of Babylonia, including Sumer, was united into a single state.

Then the Middle Babylonian kings restored native rule, which continued to circa 1000 BC. Thereafter the country came under the domination of a succession of foreign masters, of whom the most important were from Assyria.

After exacting tribute from the Babylonians for many years, the Assyrian kings finally took (729 BC) the title of king in Babylonia. Eventually, a successful revolt against Assyria reestablished (626 BC) Babylonian independence under the so-called Chaldean dynasty, the most notable of whose kings was Nebuchadnezzar II (reigned 605-562 BC). Babylonia owed its long prosperity to its location astride important trade routes

BABYLONIAN EXILE

The forced detention of Jews in Babylonia following the conquest of the kingdom of Judah. King Tiglath-pileser of Assyria introduced this practice of transporting whole conquered nations (2 Kings 15:29). This policy was also followed by kings like Sennacherib and Nebuchadnezzar. The exile formally ended in 538 BC, when the Persian conqueror of Babylonia, Cyrus the Great, gave the Jews permission to return to Palestine.

The term is also used in European history for the period from 1309 to 1377 when, under French domination, the popes resided at Avignon in southern France. Pope Gregory XI returned to Rome in 1377, but after his death the papacy was split by the Great Schism.

BABYLONIAN RELIGION

Babylonian religion took over the complete Sumerian pantheon, in which Anu, Enlil, and Ea are the great gods ruling the universe, heaven, earth, and waters. Marduk became chief god in place of Enlil when Babylon became the capital of Mesopotamia.

An earlier mother goddess was superseded by Ishtar, the most worshiped goddess of the country. Ea was the god of magic, Shamash, the sun god, was protector of justice and morality; Sin, the moon god, was worshiped in Abraham's city of Ur. There were also many evil spirits from which priests protected the people by incantations and spells.

The ritual of Babylonian religion was most important. The chief seasonal feast was Akitu, New Year, held in the spring, the month of Nisan. Because of the agricultural life of the people, the ritual acts for the New Year were directed toward securing fertility and were centered around the victory of Marduk over chaos-dragon Tiamot, an epic of creation.

Consulting omens was also important to the religious life of the Babylonian, for instance, entrails of victims and flights of birds. Religious literature included hymns, prayers to gods, and myths, for instance, the myth of the Deluge in the Gilgamesh epic, the myth of Adapa, the myth of Etana who ascended to Alan on the back of an eagle.

BABYLON THE GREAT

In biblical times, among John's visions recorded in the book of Revelation appear pronouncement of judgment against "Babylon the Great," as well as a description of her and her downfall (Revelation 14:8; 16:19).

In Revelation 17:3-5, Babylon the Great is described as a woman arrayed in purple and scarlet, richly adorned, and sitting upon a scarlet-colored wild beast having seven heads and 10 horns. The luxury and the dominion attributed to Babylon the Great do not allow for simply equating her with the literal city of Babylon in Mesopotamia. After ancient Babylon fell to Cyrus the Persian in 539 BC, it lost its position at a dominant world power, its captives, including the Jews being freed.

BACABS

In Mayan mythology, four gods (also manifestations of a single deity) who, with upraised arms, supported the sky. They were four brothers placed at the points of the compass by the supreme deity. Each was associated with a color: east, red; north, white; west, black; and south, yellow. Each presided over one year and a four-year cycle. The deity Bacab was also patron of bee-keepers.

BACCHUS

In Greek mythology, god of wine and gaiety. Semele was one of the daughters of Cadmus, king of Thebes. Zeus fell in love with her beauty, but their relationship did not escape the notice of the jealous Hera. In order to harm Semele, Hera told her that if she wished to be regarded as Zeus' wife she would have to see him in all his glory, as he had been in the day of his wedding to Hera. Although Zeus tried to dissuade her, Semele fell for Hera's deception and insisted on having this proof of love. But when Zeus gave in and appeared in her chambers mounted on his chariot amidst thunder and lightning, casting his bolts of fire, he set the palace alight and Semele died from a bolt of lightning - or perhaps he just scared her to death.

However, she had been carrying Bacchus (also named Dionysus) in her womb for six months. So that the baby did not burn to death, Mother Earth quickly caused cool ivy to grow and protect him from the flames. Zeus picked up the baby - still in an embryonic state - made an opening in his thigh, and left Bacchus there until it was time for him to be born. When the day came, Zeus broke the stitches, and brought his son Bacchus out into the light.

Bacchus is the god of wine, of green growing things, and of the fertility of the vineyard. The cult dedicated to Bacchus was associated with wine, dance and everything that gets mankind out of its daily rut. The "orgies" were organized festivals with religious rites and included holy works: the word "orgy", which is Greek, originally meant "mystery". The rituals were accompanied by the chanting of the dithyramb, the song in worship of Bacchus.

BACONTHORPE, John

(circa 1290-1346) Theologian and philosopher who, although he did not subscribe to the heterodox doctrine of the great Muslim philosopher Averoes, was regarded in the Renaissance as the prince of the Averoists. He advocated the superiority of reason and philosophy over faith and knowledge.

BADR, Battle of

(624) The Islamic Prophet Mohammed's first military victory, seriously damaging the Meccan prestige and strengthening the political position of Muslims in Medina. It established Islam as a viable force in the Arabian Peninsula.

BAECK, Leo

(1873-1956) German rabbi and theologian of Reform Judaism. Baeck was a leader of German Jewry in the years between the two world wars and was one of the few survivors of Theresienstadt concentration camp. After 1945 he lectured in London and at Hebrew Union College in Cincinatti. Baeck's Essence of Judaism interpreted Judaism as a religion devoid of mythology and concerned with the duty of man.

BAHÁ' ALLAH (1817-1892)

Founder of the Bahá'is. Born into an aristocratic family in Teheran, he became an early disciple of the Bab, though he never actually met him. While in prison in Teheran, he underwent a profound mystical experience. In 1863 Bahá' Allah announced himself as "The Man whom God shall reveal," in fulfillment of a prophecy by the Bab; and later he openly announced his mission in Edirne. He is buried in Haifa in Israel.

BAHA'I FAITH

A religion founded in the mid-19th century by Bah'a Allah, a Persian prophet, that proclaims the necessity and the inevitability of the unification of mankind.

BAHÁ'IS

Members of a new religion, deriving from Babism, founded by Bahá Allah, and propagated by the latter's son Abd

al-Bahá. Bahá'is believe in the utterly transcendent God who has, none the less, manifested Himself through a continuing chain of prophets who include many of the great figures familiar to adherents of the three major monotheistic religions of Judaism, Christianity and Islam. The Bab and Bahá' Allah also have prophetic rank. The Bahá'is believe that all the religions which have prophets posses an intrinsic truth.

BAHUBALI

According to Jaina legend of India, the son of the first Tirthankara, or savior, Rsabhanatha. Tradition relates that he stood immobile for an entire year, meditating the kayotsarga pose.

BAKBAKKAR

In the Old Testament, a Levite who dwelt in Jerusalem after the Babylonian captivity (1 Chronicles 9:3, 14-15, 34).

BAKER, Augustine

(1575-1641) Benedictine monk, who was an important writer on ascetic and mystical theology. He was a Roman Catholic convert who evolved an ascetical doctrine based on his reading and personal experiences.

BALA

In Buddhism, powers; in particular, five of the twenty-two Indriya. They are:

▲ Fath (Saddha).
▲ Energy (Viriya).
▲ Mindfulness (Sati).
▲ Contemplation (Samadhi).
▲ Wisdom (Panna).

BALAAM

In the Old Testament, a son of Beor of the 15th century BC, who lived in the Aramaean town of Pethor in the upper Euphrates valley and near the Sajur River. Though not an Israelite, Balaam had some knowledge and recognition of Jehovah as the true God, speaking of Him in one occasion as "Jehovah My God" (Numbers 22:5, 18).

BALAD, al-

The title of the 90th sura of the Koran; the name most likely means "The City" (i.e. the city of Mecca) or possibly just "The Land." The word al-balad from which the sura derives its name occurs both in the first and second verses. The sura belongs to the Meccan period and has 20 verses. The sura underlines the idea that man has been born to a life of hardship and that he has a choice, either to follow the difficult path of charity and generosity or, in his arrogance and disbelief, forget his fellow man. The sura ends with a warning about hell fire.

BALADHURI, al-

A notable Arab historian. Born, most likely in Baghdad, he studied in a variety of centers of Islamic learning. His two most important historical works were the Muslim Conquest and the Genealogies of the Nobles. Both works are extremely valuable for the early history of Islam and the Arabs.

BALAK

Baal-worshiping king of Moab in the fifteenth century BC; son of Zippor. Balak's people were frightened and filled with a "sickening dread" when they saw what Israel has done to the Amorites.

BALARAMA

In Hindu mythology, the elder half-brother of Krishna, with whom he shared many adventures. Some legends identify him as the incarnation in human form of the serpent Sesa, and he may have originally been an agricultural deity.

BALDACHINO

Umbrella-like structure providing a covering or canopy over the altar. It is composed of metal, stone or wood and is generally dome shaped and supported by chains or columns. Its original purpose was to protect the Sacred Species from dust. The baldachino is absent from many modern churches.

BALFOUR DECLARATION

Statement of British policy issued in 1917 by Foreign Secretary Arthur Balfour. It guaranteed a Jewish national home in Palestine without prejudice to the rights of non-Jews there, but did not mention a separate Jewish state. In 1922 the League of Nations approved a British mandate in Palestine based on the Balfour Declaration.

BALLOU, Hosea

(1771-1852) US clergyman, a leading expert of Universalism. Ballou separated Universalist doctrine from Calvinist influence and introduced aspects of Unitarianism. He was pastor of the Second Universalist Church in Boston 1817-52, and founder-editor of The Universalist Magazine, 1819-28.

BALSAMON, Theodore

(1105-1195) The principal Byzantine legal scholar of the medieval period and patriarch of Antioch (1185-1195). He preserved the world's knowledge of many source documents from early Byzantine theological and political history through his commentary on the nomocanon, the standard annotated collection (since the 6th century) of Eastern Orthodox ecclesiastical and Imperial laws and decrees.

BALTIC RELIGION

So called for the areas it covers (Latvian, Lithuanian, Yatsuage and Old Prussian), a religion similar to Indo-Iranian but later influenced by Finno-Uagric religion.

Extinct for three centuries, the tenets of Baltic religion were reconstructed with the help of folksongs. Baltic folksongs cover every aspect of life; their chief characteristic is gentleness toward mankind and nature.

Even the grass has feelings and should not be thoughtlessly trampled. Absence of aggressive war songs and of bloody sacrifices is noteworthy. Sifting out admixtures of Christian tenets, it appears that the chief god, Dievs, was originally a high god, remote and abstract.

The important thunder god, Perkons or Perkunas, who is associated with fertility, may be another name for him, the sky-god in the process of becoming all-God. Saule, the sun goddess and Meness the moon god are the heroes of song and myth; their children, the morning and evening twilight, carry on charming and poetic love affairs with God's sons - the morning and evening star.

Mother Earth, Laima - goddess of fate - and other goddesses appear in many songs; in Christian times they often became confused with the Virgin Mary. Their cults were associated with feasts and ceremonials connected with agriculture and with important phases of human life. Birth and wedding rites as well as the summer solstice and annual harvest were solemnly observed.

BALTIMORE CATECHISM

Book containing the basic doctrines and practices of the Roman Catholic faith in a question-and-answer format used in the United States for simple religious instructions for young persons and adults. Commissioned in 1884 by the American bishops at the Third Plenary Council of Baltimore, this catechism underwent numerous text revisions.

The Baltimore catechism was the official religious text in Catholic schools and religious education programs until Vatican Council II. Since 1992 this manual has been replaced by the contemporary catechism for the worldwide Christian community - The Catechism of the Catholic Church.

BAMBERG CATHEDRAL

Church of the German High Romanesque architecture dedicated to Sts. Peter and George, the old foundations erected 1002-1012 and the present church, 1185. Most noteworthy is its sculpture (end of the 12th century and first part of the 13th century), stylistically influenced by Naumberg, Reims, and Lombardy. The famous "prophets" from the choir screen show great perception in strong characterization.

BAMOTH

In Judaism, one of the encampment stages of the nation of Israel on its approach to the land of Canaan (Numbers 21:19-20). It is probably a shortened form of Bamoth-baal.

BAMOTH-BAAL

In biblical times, a town in Moab to which Balak, the king of Moab, conducted the prophet Balaam so that he might see the camp of Israel and call a curse upon it (Numbers 22:41). Balak's selection of this location for the enacting of the curse and the accompanying sacrifices may indicate that it was a center for Baal worship, evidently situated in an elevated place (Numbers 23:1-9). Thereafter, Bamoth-Baal and other towns "on the tableland" were assigned to the tribe of Reuben as an inheritance (Joshua 13:15-17).

BAN

Term for the form of excommunication practiced particularly by Mennonites. There are two kinds of ban: exclusion from communion and complete exclusion from membership in the Church.

The prominence of the ban in Mennonite history rests upon the teaching that the church must be kept visibly pure; only by discipline of those who have failed to live up to the decision involved in believer's baptism can this purity be assured.

The ban was one of the points of disagreement between the Swiss Anabaptists and Zwingli; its importance to church life was declared in the Schleitheim Confession (1527) and later in the Dordrecht Confession (1627).

BANGKOK

Capital of Thailand since 1782, established by the first king of the Chakri dynasty, Rama I. Bangkok has dominated Thailand's urban hierarchy since the late 18th century and is today considered a primate city. Such a city is one that is demographically, politically, economically and culturally dominant over all other cities in the country. Bangkok has an assembly of beautiful

Buddhist temples but also Christian churches, Chinese temples, Hindu temples, a Sikh temple and mosques can be found.

BANI

In the Old Testament, a Levite in the line of Merari, and ancestor of the Ethan whom David appointed to temple service (1 Chronicles 6:46). The name is also found for a family head six of whose descendants dismissed their foreign wives and sons in Ezra's time.

BANNER

In its religious use, a ceremonial ensign consisting of a cloth, generally rectangular in shape and marked with some symbol or pictorial design, fastened to a crossbar at the top of a staff that is often tipped with a cross or statue.

The earliest Christian standard was the cross itself, the symbol of Christ's victory, but in Christian art from the 9th century the church and the risen Christ were often depicted holding a banner to symbolize that victory.

In later usage the symbolism was broadened, and banners became popular to identify persons or groups, especially in religious processions.

BANNS OF MARRIAGE

In Roman Catholicism, a public announcement of the promise of marriage. Publication is usually accomplished either through an announcement at Sunday Masses or written in the parish bulletin.

The purpose of the announcement is to discover if any impediments to a marriage exist or if there is any reason why a marriage should be prohibited or postponed.

Canon 1067 leaves the bishops' conference of each country "to issue norms concerning .... marriage banns or other appropriate means for carrying out the necessary inquiries which are to precede marriage."

BAPTISM

Most commonly, a religious rite of initiation that confers purification by the use of water. In Christianity it is a sacrament, but, taken in its broadest sense, it has been practiced in various forms in a wide variety of religions.

In Roman Catholicism, baptism is the first of the seven sacraments, described by the Code of Canon Law in this way: "Baptism, the gate to the sacraments, necessary for salvation in fact or at least in intention, by which men and women are freed from their sins, are reborn as children of God and, configured to Christ by an indelible character, are incorporated in the Church, is validly conferred only by washing with true water together with the form of words."

The following points of Canon 849 should be noted:

▲ baptism may be conferred either by immersion or by pouring;

▲ the water used in baptism should be blessed, but in case of necessity unblessed water is licit;

▲ the required form of words is "I baptize you in the name of the Father, and of the Son, and of the Holy Spirit";

▲ it is recommended that baptism be celebrated on a Sunday or if possible at the Easter Vigil;

▲ the proper place for baptism is a church or oratory, but in case of necessity it may be conferred in a private home or in a hospital;

▲ the ordinary minister of baptism is a bishop, priest, or deacon, but others may be deputed for this function (as often happens in mission territories) and in case of necessity any person can and should confer baptism.

BAPTISM, Christian

An ordinance of admission to the Christian church. The forms and rituals of the various churches vary, but baptism almost invariably involves the use of water and the invocation "I baptize you; in the name of the Father, and of the Son, and of the Holy Spirit." The candidate may be wholly or partly immersed in water, the water may be poured over the head, or a few drops may be sprinkled or placed on the head. Jesus instructed his disciples to baptize new believers (Mark 16:15-16).

Some churches consider the ceremony as the first step to salvation, as a symbolic washing away of man's inherent sinfulness. Others administer baptism, but regard it simply as a confirmation of man's salvation through Christ. Baptism is administered in Catholic and most Protestant churches by sprinkling or pouring water and, in Baptist sects and the Orthodox Church, by immersion. In the Roman Catholic and Eastern churches, and in most Protestant denominations, infants are admitted to baptism, but some Protestant groups, such as the Mormons and the Baptists, admit only those old enough to give credible evidence of Christian experience.

Baptism is usually said to confer three benefits:

▲ the remission of sins;
▲ the infusion of grace;
▲ the incorporation into the church.

When it was administered as part of the process by which one renounced paganism and embraced Christianity, the remission it granted was ordinarily related to the actual sins that the candidate had committed before his conversion.

Baptism and repentance are therefore linked in the New Testament as a break with the sinful past and a renunciation of the dominion of sin. With the advent of infant baptism as the general practice of the Roman Catholic Church, the remission was understood to include original sin as well.

Indeed the practice of infant baptism provided St. Cyprian and above all St. Augustine with powerful evidence for the doctrine of the original sin; for if baptism did reflect remission, this could not apply to actual sins in the case of an infant but had to apply to what he had inherited.

As a means of the infusion of divine grace, baptism has the special importance of emphasizing and documenting the priority of the divine initiative in the establishment of the new relation between God and man. The grace of God is not earned or seized or won but is received when God, though his selected channel, pours it into the baptized.

BAPTISMAL CANDLE

In the Catholic Rite of Baptism there is a section called the "Presentation of a Lighted Candle." A smaller candle is lit from the Easter candle, symbol of Christ as light of the world, and presented to an adult being baptized or, in the case of an infant, to someone in the infant's family (in the absence of a family member, the sponsor), with the admonition to "walk always as a child of the light" and keep the flame of faith alive in your heart.

BAPTISMAL NAME

The name given to an individual at birth, as opposed to his or her family name.

BAPTISMAL PREPARATION

In Roman Catholicism, a period of preparation before baptism. An adult who wishes to be baptized must first "be sufficiently instructed in the truths of faith and in Christian obligations and be tested in the Christian life by means of the catechumate" (Canon 865).

Before the baptism of an infant, the parents (or at least one parent) must give consent to the baptism and must give assurance that the infant will be brought up in the Catholic religion. If such assurance is lacking, the baptism is to be delayed with the hope that the parents will become more aware of their religious responsibilities.

BAPTISMAL REGISTER

A record of a baptism to be completed by the priest or deacon who administers the sacrament; it is kept in the archives of the parish. A copy of this record is usually given to the baptized at the time of the baptism and is available on request.

BAPTISMAL ROBE

In the Catholic Rite of Baptism there is a section called the "Clothing With a Baptismal Garment;" at this time the person being baptized is symbolically covered with a white garment and exhorted to "bring it unstained to the judgment seat of our Lord Jesus Christ so that you may have everlasting life."

BAPTISMAL SPONSORS

Popularly known as godparents, sponsors may play an important part in baptism. In Roman Catholicism, Canons 872-874 give the following norms in reference to baptismal sponsors or godparents:

▲ Insofar as possible one to be baptized is to be given a sponsor who is to assist an adult in Christian initiation, or, together with the parents, to present an infant at the baptism, and who will help the baptized to lead a Christian life in harmony with baptism, and to fulfill faithfully the obligations connected with it;

▲ Only one male or one female sponsor or one of each sex is to be employed;

▲ To be admitted to the role of sponsor, a person must:

1 be designated by the one to be baptized, by the parents or the one who takes their place or, in their absence, by the pastor or minister and is to have the qualifications and intention of performing this role;

2 have completed the 16th year, unless different age has been established by the diocesan bishop or it seems to the pastor or minister that an exception is to be made for a just cause;

3 be a Catholic who has been confirmed and has already received the sacrament of the Most Holy Eucharist and leads a life in harmony with the faith and the role to be undertaken;

4 not be bound by any canonical penalty legitimately imposed or

declared;

5 not be the father or mother of the one to be baptized.

▲ Finally, it should be noted that a non-Catholic may not be a baptismal sponsor for a Catholic, but may serve as a witness to the baptism together with a Catholic sponsor.

BAPTISMAL VOWS

In Roman Catholicism, the renunciation of Satan and all his works and the profession of faith by the one to be baptized or, in the case of an infant, by the parents and sponsor. The solemn renewal of these vows is part of the Easter Vigil. The private renewal of vows is a commendable act of piety.

BAPTISMAL WATER

During the Easter Vigil water is especially blessed for use in baptism. At other times water may be blessed at each baptism by the one who administers the sacrament. The Roman Catholic ritual provides three ritual blessings, two of which involve the symbolic touching of the water by the presider and an interchange of responses by the people.

In case of necessity, ordinary natural water - fresh, salt, warm, cold, clean, dirty - may be used for baptism.

BAPTISM OF BLOOD

Also called baptism of martyrdom. This term refers to the case of a person who freely and patiently suffered death for the Christian faith before he or she could actually receive the sacrament of baptism - not an uncommon encounter in the first three centuries of Christianity and in other times of persecution.

BAPTISM OF CHRIST

In Christian art, a theme illustrating two closely related events from the gospels; Christ's baptism in the waters of the Jordan River by John the Baptist and the subsequent appearance of the Holy Spirit in the form of a dove, as the voice of God the Father publicly declares Jesus to be his Son.

BAPTISM OF DESIRE

In Roman Catholicism, this term refers to the state of those who, in the words of Vatican Council II, "through no fault of their own, do not know the gospel of Christ or his church, yet sincerely seek God and, moved by grace, strive by their deeds to do His will as it is known to them through the dictates of conscience ...."

BAPTISM OF INFANTS

The teaching of the Catholic church on the baptism of infants is this: "From the earliest times, the church, to which the mission of preaching the gospel and of baptizing was entrusted, has baptized not only adults but children as well. Our Lord said: "Unless a man is reborn in water and the Holy Spirit, he cannot enter the kingdom of God."

The Church has always understood these words to mean that children should not be deprived of baptism, because they are baptized in the faith of the church, a faith proclaimed for them by their parents and godparents, who represent both the local church and the whole society of saints and believers .... To fulfill the true meaning of the sacrament, children must later be formed in the faith in which they have been baptized .... so that they may ultimately accept for themselves the faith in which they have been baptized."

Present church law obliges parents to "see to it that infants are baptized within the first weeks after birth;" in danger of death, an infant is to be baptized "without any delay."

BAPTISM OF MARTYRDOM

Also called baptism of blood. This term refers to the case of a person who freely and patiently suffered death for the Christian faith before he or she could actually receive the sacrament of baptism - not an uncommon encounter in the first three centuries of Christianity and in other times of persecution.

BAPTIST BIBLE UNION

Fundamentalist US Northern Baptists, organized in the 1920s.

BAPTISTERY

Hall or chapel situated close to or connected with, a church, in which the sacrament of baptism is administered. The form of the baptistery originally evolved from small, circular Roman buildings that were designated for religious purposes.

BAPTIST FEDERATION OF CANADA

A cooperative agency for several Canadian Baptist groups, organized in 1944 by the United Baptist Convention of Ontario and Quebec, and the Baptist Union of Western Canada.

BAPTIST GENERAL CONFERENCE

Conservative Baptist denomination that was organized in 1879 as the Swedish Baptist general Conference of America; the present name was adopted in 1945.

The Conference is generally considered to be theologically conservative, although the right of individuals to differ in their beliefs is respected.

BAPTIST MISSIONARY ASSOCIATION OF AMERICA

An association of independent conservative Baptist churches, organized as the North American Baptist Association in 1950. The present name was adopted in 1968.

The member churches of the Baptist Missionary Association of America are autonomous and share equally in the cooperative activities of the association. All the churches, however, must subscribe to a strict fundamentalist interpretation of Christian doctrine. They accept the statements of the Bible literally and expect the Second Coming of Christ.

BAPTISTS

Members of many independent branches of the Baptist church, one of the most diverse and distinctive of Protestant denominations. There are more than 35,000,000 Baptists throughout the world, most of whom live in America, where they constitute the largest Protestant group.

The world's Baptist churches are loosely linked in a number of sects or "conventions" and recognition of the relative autonomy of individual churches is one of the denomination's strongest tenets. In general, it is a lay church, for, while Baptist ministers are ordained, there is a "priesthood of all believers," and all members share in the life of the church. The evangelistic and revivalist tradition also emphasizes the influence of laymen.

This independent, individualistic character runs throughout church custom and history. Baptists were influential in establishing the separation of church and state in America and are strong adherents of the same principle in England.

Since there is no special authority claimed by the ministry, a rigid creed characterizing all churches is absent. The Bible is cited as the authority for all doctrine and guidance, and may be read historically and symbolically (modernism) or quite literally (fundamentalism). The strongest underlying principle among all churches is the method of baptism. It is by immersion at the age of reason, usually 12, and its purpose is to form a congregation of truly committed "believers," as opposed to people who are simply born into the faith.

This principle is generally conceded to be the inspiration of John Smyth, the leader of a group of English religious dissenters who had sought refuge in Holland circa 1608. Smyth recommended a merger with the similarly minded Anabaptist Mennonites in Amsterdam, but many of his group turned instead to Thomas Helwys, with whom they returned to England, where they established the first Baptist church circa 1612. This group became known as General Baptists because, although they held to the belief of the early Protestant John Calvin that the fall of Adam represented an original sin staining all mankind, they also believed that Christ's death represented general salvation. The Particular Baptists were formed under the leadership of John Spilsbury and hence to the harsher doctrine that not all men had been redeemed by the crucifixion.

In the emigration following the restoration of the monarchy in England, Baptist churches began to be established in the Colonies. In America, this new denomination was not simply transplanted, but also evolved independently among the variety of Puritan dissenters. As in England, it was the Particular Baptists who predominated, while General Baptist beliefs found sympathy and influence with the Unitarians and Quakers. Roger Williams of Rhode Island was an early Baptist leader, but he later left the faith to follow his own religious vision. John Clarke in Newport, Rhode Island and Shubal Stearns in North Carolina were important early leaders.

In America's 18th century religious revival, the great Awakening, the Baptist evangelical tradition began, and its converts continued to grow along the expanding frontiers. Doctrinal differences created such offshoots as the Separate Baptists, but there was also a growing movement toward unity under such auspices as the American Baptist Foreign Mission Society (1826). The Baptists have placed a great stress on higher education and they founded more than 100 colleges and universities in the 19th century. The denomination had become particular influential in the Midwest and the South by 1845 when a great split occurred over the slavery issue, creating Northern and Southern Baptists.

Following the Civil War, negro churches developed an independent convention, the National Baptist Convention of America (1880). In 1915, a dispute within that membership created another major group, the National Baptist Convention, USA, Inc. In 1955, the Northern Baptists, which include members of all races, formed the American Baptist Convention. The Southern Baptist Convention retained its name but now includes churches beyond the borders of the Old South.

Despite other divisions over such matters as interpretation of the Bible (the United States contains 23 distinct smaller conventions) there has been a growing movement away from sectarianism among Baptists.

In 1944 the Baptist federation of Canada united three conventions. American Baptists are active in The World Council of Churches through the Baptist World Alliance, which was founded in 1905. The European Baptist Congress of 1969 included delegates from every European country, East and West, and held hopes of greater international unity.

BAPTIST UNION OF GREAT BRITAIN AND IRELAND

The largest Baptist group in the British Isles, organized in 1891 as a union of the Particular Baptist and New Connection General Baptist association. These groups were historically related to the first English Baptists, who originated in the 17th century.

BAPTIST WORLD ALLIANCE

An international advisory organization for Baptists, founded in 1905 in London. Its purpose is to promote fellowship and cooperation among all Baptists.

BAQA

In Islam, term meaning remaining, subsistence, abiding, survival, immortality.As a technical term in tasawwuf the word baqa is used to indicate a stage of the mystical experience after Fana, in which the mystic "abides" or "subsists" in God. Baqa, which takes place after death, does not entail a total loss of individuality. The medieval writers realized that the concept was a difficult one to grasp and they therefore wrote parables, like that of Attar entitled "The Speech of Birds", to illustrate exactly what they meant."

BAQARA, al-

The title of the second sura of the koran; the word means "The Cow" and is drawn from the story of the cow which occurs in verses 67-71. This was the first Medinan sura to be revealed. With 286 verses it is also the longest sura in the Koran. After beginning with three of the mysterious letters of the Koran, the sura goes on to deal with, inter alia, with the creation of Adam, the rebellion of Iblis, Musa (including the story of the cow), the change of the qibla from Jerusalem to Mecca, the prohibition on eating pork, fasting in Ramadan, pilgrimage, divorce and the prohibition of riba.

BAQILLANI, al-

(died circa 1013) Distinguished medieval Arab theologian, proponent of Atomism and Maliki jurist and judge. He lived mainly in Baghdad and gained a considerable reputation in lecturing and debate. He wrote works on the Koran, the imamate, miracles and theological problems.

BARABBAS

In the Bible, the imprisoned criminal guilty of robbery, sedition and murder whom Pilate set free in place of Jesus. Pilate did this, "wishing to satisfy the crowd" who clamored for his release at the insistence of the chief priests and older men. The name Barabbas suggests that he may possibly have been the son of a rabbi or Jewish leader (Matthew 27:15-26; Mark 15:6-15; Luke 23:16-25; John 18:39; Acts 3:14).

BARACHEL

In the Old Testament, father of Job's friend Elihu; a Buzite, likely a descendant of Abraham's nephew Buz (Job 32:2).

BARACHIAH

Father of the Zechariah who was murdered "between the sanctuary and the altar" (Matthew 23:35; Luke 11:50-51).

BARAITOT

Ancient oral traditions of Jewish religious law that were not included in the Mishna (the first authoritative codification of such laws), which was given final form early in the third century by Judah ha-Nasi. Baraitot that are found dispersed singly throughout the Palestinian and Babylonian Talmuds are often recognizable by such introductory words as "it was taught" or "the rabbi taught." Other Baraitot are found in independent collections, the best known of which is called Tosefta; in form and content it parallels the Mishna.

BARAK

In Judaism, son of Abinoam of Kedesh in the territory of Naphthali. During an early period in the time of the judges the Israelites fell away from the true worship and so for 20 years God permitted them to be oppressed by Jabin, the king of Canaan.

BARAKA

Blessing, quality possessed especially by holy men in Islam, who can impart it to others. Baraka may also be attached to places and objects. It should never be translated as "grace" in view of the Christian theological connotations of that latter word. In popular Islam, baraka may be gained by visiting the tombs of saints.

BARBARA, Saint

(died circa 200) Virgin martyr of the early church and patroness of artillerymen. According to legend, which dates only to the 7th century, she was the daughter of a pagan, Dioscorus, who kept her guarded to protect her beauty from harm. When she confessed Christianity, he became enraged and took her to the principal prefect, who ordered her to be tortured and beheaded. Dioscorus himself performed the execution and, upon his return home, was struck by lightning and reduced to ashes.

BARBARIC STYLE

Term covering varieties of decoration and ornament in nonfigural and zoomorphic interlace, which entered Western Europe from the first to the ninth centuries through invasions, from the East by Huns, Goths, Celts, Norsemen, Scythians, and Sarmatirans and influenced pre-Carolingian and Carolingian styles.

BARBEAUX, Abbey of

Royal Cistercian abbey near Melun, established in 1146 by Louis VII of France, who was buried there. The abbey was richly endowed and magnificently constructed in Gothic. It was reformed in 1643 by the Cistercian Strict Observance but had only 11 monks at its dissolution in 1790.

BARBERI, Domenico

(1792-1849) Mystic and passionist who worked as a missionary in England. He was already following the growth of the Tractarian movement, and in 1845 he received John Henry Newman (later Cardinal Newman) into the church. He founded four passionist houses in England.

BARBON, Praise-God

(1596-1680) Sectarian preacher from whom the Cromwellian Barebones' Parliament derived its nickname. Opposing the restoration of Charles II, Barbon presented in February 1660 a petition to Parliament depreciating any reconciliation with the Stuarts. Called a Brownist and an Anabaptist by his opponents, Barbon displayed in his writings a toleration unusual in a period of much acrimonious religious controversy.

BARI

(Barensis) Ancient Roman town of Barium founded by Illyrians. Relics of

St. Nicolas of Myra were brought from Lycia (1087) and housed in the Basilica (1108), the foremost monument in Apulia. The cathedral of Bari (San Sabino), built circa 1050 was rebuilt 1170-1178 and restored in 1920. Bari was the medieval point of departure for pilgrims and crusaders and is today the most important port of southern Italy after Naples.

BAR-JESUS

A certain Jew of Paphos on the island of Cyprus in the first century AD, who was "a sorcerer, a false prophet" (Acts 13:6). He held the influential position as court magician and adviser to Sergius Paulus, the Roman proconsul at Paphos. As a "priest" of the divination cult, Bar-Jesus was naturally against Christianity, and, wanting to protect his own lucrative position, he was adamant in his opposition to the preaching of Paul and Barnabas.

BARMAKIDS

Priestly family of Iranian origin from the city of Balkh (now in Afghanistan), who achieved 8th century prominence as scribes and viziers to the early Abbasid caliphs; were also known for their cultural patronage and tolerant religious and philosophical outlook; and who promoted public works but squandered money on magnificent palaces by the Tigris River. Their ancestor was a barmak (a title borne by the High Priest in the Buddhist temple of Nawbahar), but the family had converted to Islam after a move to Basra in Iraq.

BARMEN, Synod of

Meeting of German Protestant leaders at Barmen in the Ruhr region (May 1934). The meeting was meant to organize Protestant resistance to National Socialism. The synod was of decisive importance in the development of the German Confessing church. Representatives came from established Lutheran, Reformed, and United Churches, although some of the church government had already been captured by men loyal to Adolf Hitler. The Pastors' Emergency League, headed by Martin Niemoeller, was the backbone of the active resistance.

BAR MITZVAH

(Hebrew: "Son of the Commandments") Term in the Jewish religion for a boy at the age of 13, when he becomes an adult member of the religious community, responsible for fulfilling the Commandments. In Orthodox and Conservative Judaism the 13th birthday is usually celebrated by a ceremony - also known as Bar Mitzvah - in which the boy is called up to read part of the weekly portion of the Pentateuch or the prophets in the synagogue. Some Conservative congregations have established a similar ceremony for girls, the Bas Mitzvah. Reform Judaism, while often retaining the Bar Mitzvah, also has a joint confirmation ceremony for boys and girls at age 15 or 16.

Originally, every person who was called to the Torah was expected to be able to read his own portion. Later, this task was taken over by the Official Reader, in order not to embarrass whose who were less learned. However, the older custom was preserved in the case of the Bar Mitzvah, and even today, a Bar Mitzvah boy will chant his own portion and sometimes even the entire Sidrah of the week.

Although Bar Mitzvah has gone through many changes in its development through the centuries, and has often indeed been vulgarized, those who stop to think will bear in mind its original meaning. On this day, the boy who has come into possession of this religious heritage of his people has for the first time the right to lead a congregation at services, the duty to recite a passage when called to the Torah, the privilege of being counted as a member of a minyan, and the opportunity to thank God for being a member of the Jewish people.

Reform Judaism replaced Bar Mitzvah, after 1810, with the confirmation of boys and girls together, generally on the feast of Shavuot. In the 20th century, many Reform congregations restored Bar Mitzvah, delaying confirmation until the age of 15 or 16.

BARNABAS

(1st century AD) He was a Jew who joined the Jerusalem church soon after Christ's crucifixion, sold his property and gave the proceeds to the community (Acts 4:36-37). He was one of the Cypriots who founded the church in Antioch, where he preached. After he called Paul from Tarsus as his assistant they undertook joint missionary activity and then they went to Jerusalem in 48. Shortly afterward, a serious conflict separated them, and Barnabas sailed to Cyprus (Acts 15:39).

The portrait of Joseph Barnabas, as painted for us in the Book of Acts, is one of a very warmhearted and generous person, one who did not hesitate to offer both himself and his material possessions willingly for the advancement of the Kingdom interests.

The close association that Barnabas had with Paul, and that extended over the years, had its beginning circa three years after Paul's conversion when he wanted to get in touch with the Jerusalem congregation. How Barnabas knew Paul, whether being an old acquaintance or as a fellow student at the feet of Gamaliel, as certain traditions say, or whether quite by chance in the marketplace, is not revealed, but it was Barnabas who had the privilege of first introducing Paul to Peter and the disciple James (Acts 9:26-27).

In 49 Barnabas and Paul took the burning question of circumcision of non-Jews up to the governing body in Jerusalem, and, with that settled, they were soon back in Antioch preparing for their next missionary tour (Acts 15:2-36). However, because they could come to no agreement over taking John Mark along, they each departed for separate territories. Barnabas took his cousin Mark to Cyprus and Paul took Silas through the districts of Syria and Cilicia (Acts 15:37-41).

BARNABAS, Letter of

An early Christian work written in Greek by one of the so-called apostolic fathers, Greek Christian writers of the late 1st and early 2nd centuries. Ascribed by tradition to St. Barnabas, the Apostle, the writing dates possibly from as late as 130 and was the work of an unknown author who refers to himself in the letter as a teacher.

BARNLEY, George

(1917-1871) Methodist missionary who worked among the Cree Indian tribes of James Bay in Canada. While drilling native people in Methodism he was known to use a stick as a memory-assisting device to remind them of the number of persons needed to recite a given prayer or lesson.

BARONIUS, Caesar

(1538-1607) Ecclesiastical historian and apologist for the Roman Catholic Church. His major work, the *Annales Ecclesiastici* (1588-1607) consists of 12 folios narrating the history of the church down to the year 1198. He is regarded as the father of the ecclesiastical history.

BAROQUE

Art and architecture of Europe and its Latin American colonies in the 17th and first half of the 18th centuries. In a more specific sense, the term refers to the most characteristic of the styles created in that period - that is, to the art that arose in Italy and Flanders soon after 1600, dominated Italian art and architecture until the classical revival of the mid 18th century, and produced echoes of varying intensity in all other countries.

Baroque art at its greatest and most intense is found in Roman Catholic countries, and a close association, if not an ideological link, existed between the style and the Roman Catholic church in the later stages of the Counter Reformation.

For all its dynamism, the baroque style was not absolutely new, in the sense that Gothic art or cubism were new. Formally it owned much to Renaissance art and architecture and it was also influenced by the antique Roman and Greek art and architecture.

What was new in baroque art was the way in which the forms were used or the methods applied. Also new forms were created, of which perhaps the most important was the double curve - inward at the sides, outward in the middle - used for facades, doorways, and furniture.

In architecture the primary features are twisted columns and fantastical pediments. In sculpture, the style is characterized by fluttering draperies, realistic surfaces, and the use of bronze, white and colored marbles, and sometimes other materials in the same work.

The expression of emotion was increasingly emphasized in both painting and sculpture. The result was a style of great richness and flexibility that could encompass effects both on the grandest possible scale and on the scale of a small oil sketch or pen drawing.

BAROQUE THEOLOGY

Baroque Theology can be defined as Roman Catholic and Protestant scholasticism that emerged from the Reformation period and shared in the exuberant humanism characteristic of art and thought until the Enlightenment of the 18th century.

Borrowing the experience of the freedom of faith in a loving God, it was progressive in its openness to new opinion. Rejecting the divisive and debasing elements of a humanism separated from the Christian gospel, it also emphasized continuity with the early church.

This traditional concern spurred the production of patristic and biblical studies and brought a revival of scholastic theology. As a theological

methodology it often reduced itself to historicism.

BARROW

Term for earth-covered burial site, particularly in the British Isles, where a chamber formed by dolmens was covered by a mound of earth. At Sutton Hoo (discovered 1935) the burial chamber was a ship. Similar burials are found in Scandinavia.

BARROW, Isaac

(1630-1677) Classical scholar, theologian, and mathematician, who was the teacher of Isaac Newton. In 1669 he resigned the chair of mathematics at Cambridge in favor of Newton and henceforth devoted himself to the study of divinity.

BARTH, Karl

(1886-1968) Swiss theologian, one of the most influential voices of 20th century Protestantism. He taught in Germany 1921-1935, was expelled by the nazis and spent the rest of his life in Basel. In his "crisis theology," Barth stressed revelation and grace and reemphasized the principles of the Reformation, initiating a movement away from theological "liberalism."

Barth's influence on Protestantism (and mediately on Roman Catholicism, too) seems to have been a strong affirmation of divine transcendence set forth at the onset of the technological revolution. Barth's "faith" was constantly seeking knowledge. His architectonic approach to theology and incredible capacity for system-building, admirable in themselves, opposed the new theological tendencies current in the latter part of his career, especially the emerging theology of the secular and the new humanism.

BARTHOLOMEW

One of the 12 Apostles and generally supposed to have been the same person who, in John's gospel is called Nathanael. According to tradition he preached the Gospel in various parts of Asia Minor and India. He was ultimately martyred in Armenia by being flayed alive.

BARTHOLOMITES

The name of two religious congregations.

1 Armenian Bartholomites, a monastic congregation of Armenian origin which took up residence in Genoa (1307) when their land was attacked by the sultan of Egypt (1296).

2 German Bartholomites, the congregation of priests founded by Bartholomew Holzhauser to improve the training of priests. Named after their founder, they had no relationship with the Armenian congregation.

BARTIMAEUS

A blind beggar whose sight Jesus restored. Bartimaeus and an unidentified companion were sitting outside Jericho when Jesus and a crowd came along. Bartimaeus inquired what the excitement was, and, when told, he began shouting: "Son of David, Jesus, have mercy on me!" Others sternly told him to be silent, but he was even more persistent. When Jesus called, he threw off his outer garment, hurried to the Master, and begged for recovery of his sight. Jesus, discerning the man's faith and moved to pity, cured Bartimaeus, who then followed him, glorifying God (Mark 10:46-52; Matthew 20:39-34).

BARTOLOMMEO, Fra

(1475-1517) Florentine painter, pupil of Cosimo Rosselli and partner of Mariotto Albertinelli. In 1508 he studied the methods of Giovanni Bellini in Venice, and in 1514, those of Michelangelo and Raphael in Rome. On returning to Florence he painted his St. Mark, considered his masterpiece, and St. Sebastian. Most of his works are altarpieces. He was among the first to make skillful use of three-dimensional movement in the human figure.

BARUCH

In the Old Testament, the scribal secretary of Jeremiah. Baruch was the son of Neriah and brother of Seraiah,

Zedekiah's quartermaster who read Jeremiah's scroll alongside the Euphrates (Jeremiah 32:12).

In the fourth year of King Jehoiakim, 635 BC, Baruch began writing in a scroll the prophetic message of Jerusalem's doom, dictated by Jeremiah. In the late fall of the following year, 624, Baruch read the scroll alone "in the ears of all the people" at the entrance of God's house. He was then summoned to read it to an assembly of the princes, who, moved by what they heard and fearing the consequences when the word got to the king's ears, urged Baruch and Jeremiah to hide. Johoiakim, upon hearing the denunciation, burned the scroll piece by piece, and commanded that Baruch and Jeremiah be brought before him, "but God kept them concealed." At Jeremiah's dictation, Baruch then wrote another scroll like the first, but containing "many more words" from the mouth of God (Jeremiah 36:1-32).

BARUCH, Apocalypse of

A pseudo-epigraphical work (a non-canonical writing that in style and content resembles authentic biblical literature) the primary theme of which is whether or not God's relationship with man is just.

Passages in the book indicate that it was written after the destruction of Jerusalem in 70, probably around AD 100. The question of divine justice that preoccupied the Jews after the fall of Jerusalem is discussed in the Apocalypse in a series of prayers and visions.

BARUCH, Book of

A biblical work attributed to Baruch, the prophet Jeremiah's secretary. Relegated to the apocrypha by Protestants, it is included in the Old Testament by Roman Catholics. The book survives in a Greek version, and is probably the work of several authors of Hellenistic times.

BARZAKH

In Islam, literally obstacle, hindrance,

barrier, partition, isthmus. The word came to indicate an intermediate area between hell and heaven, or the place/state between earthly life and the hereafter. It should not be translated, however, as "Purgatory" because, as is the case of al-A'raf, barzakh is not associated with purgation of sin. The word is mentioned a number of times in the Koran.

BARZILLAI

In the Old Testament, a wealthy Gileadite, "a very great man," of the town of Rogelim. Barzillai was one of three who assisted David and his army with supplies of food and bedding during Absalom's rebellion (2 Samuel 17:27-29). When David returned to Jerusalem, Barzillai escorted the party to the Jordan, but due to his age, he declined David's offer to become part of the royal court, sending Chimham in his place.

BASE COMMUNITIES

In Roman Catholicism, small groups of the faithful led by laity gather to participate more effectively in liturgy and sacraments, pastoral ministry, apostolic ministry and personal and social development.

Some groups gather for scripture and Communion services in the absence of a priest; the participants consider the relationship with the scripture to their daily lives and often make social decisions resulting from these reflections.

The concept of base communities originated in Latin America. Where they exist, they contribute to the vigor of parish and diocesan life. They are truly small churches in action and are supported by Pope Paul VI in his letter *Evangelii nuntiandi.*

The apostolic exhortation "On the Mission of the Lay Faithful in the Church of the World" signed by Pope John Paul II in January 1989 provides clear support for building these communities throughout the Catholic world and are a great help in the formation of lay leadership.

BASEL, Confession of

A moderate Protestant Reformation statement of reformed doctrine composed of 12 articles. It was first drafted by John Oecolampadius (1482-1531), the reformer of Basel, and was compiled in fuller form in 1532 by his successor at Basel, Oswald Myconius (1488-1552).

BASEL, Council of

General church council opened in Basel, Switzerland, in 1431, concerned with the heresy of Jan Hus and the continuing struggle over papal supremacy. Pope Eugene IV tried to dissolve the council, but it denied his right to do so, claiming that as an ecumenical council it, rather than the pope, held ultimate authority. Eugene relented, but in 1437 ordered it to move to Ferrara, Italy, to consider reunion with the Eastern church. Most bishops complied, but a small number remained in Basel, deposing Eugene and electing the antipope Felix V in 1439, and continuing to meet until 1449.

BASEMATH

In the Old Testament, a wife of Esau. She was a daughter of Elon the Hittite, therefore either the same person as Adah or her sister. Basemath was "a source of bitterness" to Isaac and Rebekah (Genesis 26:34-35; 28:8).

BASHAN

A large region in northern Transjordan. Bashan was north of Gilead and was bounded on the east by the mountainous region of Jebel Hauran and on the west by the hills bordering the eastern side of the Sea of Galilee (Deuteronomy 3:3-14).

The region of Bashan apparently first enters the Bible record at Genesis 14:5 in the reference to the Rephaim (giants) in Ashteroth-karnaim, who were defeated by the invading kings of Abraham's time. At the time of the Israelite invasion, Og, the king of Bashan and the last-remaining one of the giant-like men of that area, was defeated and slain and the land was occupied by Israel (Numbers 21:33-35). The half tribe of Mannasseh received Bashan as its inheritance, although it appears that a southern portion of it was allotted to the tribe of Gad (Joshua 13:29-31; 17:1-5).

BASIL, Liturgy of

A Syro-Cappadocean Greek liturgy existing in two Greek versions, a shorter Egyptian and a longer Byzantine form, the latter being fairly closely paralleled by a Syriac version, somewhat less so by the oldest Armenian version. That at least part of the liturgy comes from St. Basil the Great is generally accepted by critical scholars, but opinions differ in attributing to him the formation of the primitive text.

The two oldest manuscripts (8th and 10th centuries), containing both the Liturgy of St. Basil and that of St. Chrysostom, suggest by their arrangement that the Liturgy of St. Basil was the one more normally used at that time.

BASIL I

(812-886) Byzantine Emperor, founder of the Macedonian Dynasty (867-1056) who became coemperor (866) and then emperor after murdering Emperor Michael III. When he deposed Photius and restored Ignatius as patriarch of Constantinople, he gained support of Rome.

BASIL II

(958-1025) Byzantine Emperor from 976. His convincing defeat, effected with the aid of Prince Vladimir of Kiev, of the revolt of Bardas Phocas and the Anatolian Guard at Chrysopolis (987-989) made him the sole master of the empire.

BASILIAN MONASTICISM

The form of monasticism practiced in the Eastern Church which takes its spirit from, St. Basil the Great. Among the Orthodox here are no religious orders or societies, but all Orthodox monks acknowledge their debt to St. Basil for his rule.

Orthodox monasticism owes nearly as much to the tradition of the great ascetics and solitaires of the earliest days of Christian monasticism in Egypt. However, when instructing novices and monks, abbots of Orthodox monasteries refer to the Asceticons of St. Basil as a basic consideration for the monastic life.

Elementary manuals designed for the use of monks, while not reproducing all or even most of the rules, quote liberally and often verbatim certain of St. Basil's questions and answers.

BASILIANS

Members of several monastic communities belonging to the non-Latin rites of the Roman Catholic Church, so named because they claim St. Basil the Great as their spiritual father; also the name of a Latin Rite congregation.

BASILICA

In its earliest usage, a type of large public building of ancient Rome. The term came to refer to a building of characteristic rectangular layout, with a central area (nave) separated by rows of columns from two flanking side aisles with high windows. At one or both ends was a semicircular or polygonal apse. The design was adopted as a basic pattern for Christian churches from the time of Constantine. The term "basilica" is also a canonical title for certain important Roman Catholic churches.

The early Christian basilica was approached through an atrium, a colonnaded outer court, or through a simple portico extending across the front of the church. Within the basilica there was a vestibule or narthrex, opening up to the church proper. This consisted of a wide central nave with a raised clerestory and two, four, or even more, narrower aisles along the sides.

The timbered roof was supported by columns and the light coming through the windows in the clerestory and the rows of columns leading toward the rear of the church focused the attention of he faithful upon the altar placed in front of the apse.

Behind the altar were the episcopal throne and rows of benches for the clergy, and in front of it on one or both sides were the ambo or pulpit. Larger basilicas had transepts, and were beautifully adorned with mosaics and colored marble.

BASIL THE GREAT, Saint

(330-379). One of the Great Fathers of the Eastern church, a founder of Greek monasticism and author of the Longer and Shorter Rules for monastic life. As Bishop of Caesarea, he also played a role in subduing Arianism. His brother was St. Gregory of Nyssa.

BASILIDES

(2nd century AD) Founder of an Alexandrian school of Gnosticism, a philosophico-religious system rivalling Christianity, which claimed a gnosis (secret knowledge) of the divine mysteries that were derived in part from Christ's apostles.

In various accounts, Basilides is said to have postulated a succession of spiritual powers emanating from the supreme, unborn God, who exceeds the limit of any categorical description. All activities of mind, thought, wisdom, and power, consequently, issue from His as distinct beings, mediating between Him and the created world.

BASILIDIANS

A Gnostic sect; for instance, a group of religious dualists who believed that matter was evil and the spirit good and that salvation was gained by esoteric knowledge, or gnosis. The sect was named after Basilides, a 2nd century Christian heretic, who held that the world was fashioned by the god Abraxas, who ruled over 365 spheres that separated the human soul from the rightful place with the unknown God.

BASIL'S CATHEDRAL

Russian Orthodox cathedral on the Red Square in the center of Moscow. St. Basil's cathedral was created in 1555-1561, replacing an existing church on the site, to celebrate Ivan the Terrible's taking of the Volga Tsar stronghold of Kazan on 1st October 1552, the feast of the Intercession - hence its official name, the Prkrovsky (Intercession) cathedral.

It owes its usual name to the barefoot holy fool Vasily (Basil) the Blessed, who predicted Ivan's damnation, adding as the army left for Kazan that Ivan would murder a son. Vasily died while Kazan was under siege and was buried beside the church which St. Basil's soon replaced. Later he was canonized.

St. Basil's seeming apathy of shapes hides a fairly simple plan of nine main chapels: the tall tent-roofed one in the center; four big octagonal-powered ones, topped with the four biggest domes, on the north, south, east and west; and four smaller ones in between. A couple of extra tent roofs on the stairways, an extra north-east chapel over Vasily the Blessed's grave, and a tent-roofed south-east belltower were added later. Only in the 1670s were the domes patterned and St. Basil's given its present, highly colorful appearance.

BASMALA

The invocation, or utterance of the common Islamic invocation. Bism 'llah al-Rahman al-Rahim, which means "In the name of Allah, the Merciful, the Compassionate." These words occur at the beginning of every sura of the Koran except the 9th sura.

BATAK PROTESTANT CHRISTIAN CHURCH

A Lutheran church in northern Sumatra (Indonesia) organized as an independent church in 1930; the largest Lutheran church in Asia. It developed from the work of missionaries from the Rheinish Mission Society, established in Barmen, Germany in 1828.

The church is divided into districts, with each district headed by a superintendent. All the superintendents make up the church council headed by an ephorus (bishop), who is elected for a specific term of office.

BA'TH

In Islam, term in the sense of resurrection, sending. Pre-Islamic Arabia believed that the souls of the dead lived on in some kind of shadowy existence beyond the grave. However, there was no concept of any resurrection of the body. The Koran later taught that there would be a resurrection of both bodies and souls, something at which many of the pagan Arabs scoffed. Many Islamic philosophers held, contrary to the teaching of the Koran, that only souls would be resurrected. The Koran contains much information about the Day of Resurrection as well as its terrors and judgments.

The word ba'th also has a technical theological sense indicating the sending out of prophets by God.

BATH-RABBIM

In the Old Testament, in the Song of Solomon the Shulammite maiden's eyes were likened to the pools in Heshbon, by the gate of Bath-Rabbim. Heshbon was a city in the territory of Gad but assigned to the Levites (Joshua 21:38-39).

BATH-SHEBA

In the Old Testament (2 Sam. 11, 12; 1 Kings 1,2) wife of Uriah the Hittite and later of King David. She was a daughter of Eliam and was probably of noble birth. A beautiful woman, she was seduced by David and became pregnant. David then had Uriah killed and married her. The child died, but Bathsheba later gave birth to Solomon.

When David was dying, she successfully conspired with the prophet Nathan to block Adonijah's succession to the throne and to win it for Solomon. Strong-willed and fearless, she occupied an influential position as the queen mother.

BATIN

In Islam, esoteric, inner. Its opposite in Islam and, in particular, in the theology of the Ismailis is zahir. That which is batin belongs to an inner secret dimension of Islam.

BATINIYAH

An Islamic designation for those Muslim sects that interpret religious texts exclusively on the basis of their hidden or inner meanings rather than their literal meanings. Speculative philosophy and theology eventually influenced the Batiniyah, though they remained at all times on the side of esoteric knowledge.

BATTEY, Thomas

(1828-1897) Quaker teacher and Indian agent in American Indian Territory. He was the author of *A Quaker Among the Indians*, published in 1875.

BAU

In Mesopotamian religion, city goddess of Urukug in the Lagash region and, under the name Nininsina, the Queen of Isin, city goddess of Isin, south of Nippur.

BAVVAI

In the Old Testament, a Levite worker on Nehemiah's wall-rebuilding project in Jerusalem. He was from the district of Keilah; the son of Henadad and possibly a brother of Binnui (Nehemiah 3:18, 24).

BAY PSALM BOOK

Name commonly given to the first book printed in Colonial America. *The Whole Book of Psalmes faithfully Translated into English Metre* was published in Cambridge, Mass., in 1640 as a hymnal for the Massachusetts Bay Colony. It was the work of Richard Mather, John Eliot and Thomas Weld and was printed by Stephen Day.

BAYYINA, al-

Title of the 98th sura of the Koran; the word, which means "The Clear Roof," occurs in the first verse. As the second verse shows, this "Clear Roof" may be either a divine messenger or sacred pages. The sura belongs to the Medinan period and has eight verses. It notes at the beginning the request by the People of the Book (Ahl al-Kitab and the polytheists for a "clear roof." The disbelievers in both groups will dwell in hell fire for ever. By contrast, believers and the doers of good deeds will be rewarded in the gardens of Eden.

BAZLUTH

In the Old Testament, a family head whose descendants were among the Nethinim returning to Jerusalem with Zerubbabel in 537 BC (Ezra 2:1, 52; Nehemiah 7:54).

BC

Abbreviation for "before Christ." A date followed by these initials means so many years before the birth of Jesus. This is sometimes called "Before the Christian Era" and is abbreviated BCE.

BEAD

A small, perforated globule of wood, metal, glass, or other hard material, which when strung together with others is used to count prayers, as in the recitation of the rosary. In its earlier form the word was spelled "bede" which meant prayer. From this it was transferred to the counters used to number the prayers said.

BEAN, George Washington

(1831-1897) A pioneering Mormon missionary and interpreter. Unlike other denominations, the Mormons sent missionaries to the field for a limited time. Bean began his service in 1885 at the Mormon Indian mission in Las Vegas, Nevada. His missionary group consisted of 33 men who had a number of challenges to overcome. Besides struggling to maintain themselves in the desert, they anticipated problems with the native people they wanted to convert. As the mission became established, Mormon influence grew. One

writer reported over 50 Indian baptisms. Besides religious work, the missionaries explored the territory for ways to serve and expand mormon interests.

BEAR CEREMONIALISM

The tradition of beliefs, stories, and rituals centering on the bear, practiced by a range of cultures in Europe and in North America, particularly the Algonquians of eastern Canada and the United States. Among the oldest forms of religious practice, bear hunting was conducted according to complex religious procedures. Rites, which varied from group to group, involved ritual appeasement and ceremonial disposal of a slain bear so that other bears would feel honored to be caught and killed.

BEAR-TRACK

(1790-1880) A famous shaman and prophet among the Salish-Kootenai people in North America. His spiritual gifts were said to enable him to locate bisons, to warn against approaching horse thieves, to foresee battles and their outcomes, to tell the location of friendly or unfriendly camps, and to locate missing persons and articles.

BEATIFICATION

Second stage in the process of canonization, in the Roman Catholic Church, whereby a person is named a saint. The beautified person is called blessed, and a limited cult is authorized. A similar practice exists in the Russian Orthodox Church for authorizing local cults.

Beatification is in principal a declaration by the pope that a deceased person lived a holy life and is now in heaven and is worthy of public veneration on a limited (not universal) basis in the church.

This act usually follows upon a process by which the life, virtue, reputation for holiness, ministry, and writings of the person are intensely scrutinized by the congregation for the Causes of Saints in Rome.

BEATIFIC VISION

In Christianity, the final reward of all those who die in God's grace, namely, a direct supernatural knowledge of God Himself.

A Greek patristic tradition represents it as a glorious theophany; to Latin theology, however, it is a direct and immediate insight into the divine essence with no mediating image or concept, enjoyed by the mind strengthened by the light of glory.

Less specifically considered, it includes all the elements of man's final happiness: his beholding the blessed trinity; his love in an eternal response to God's eternal love for him; the torrent of delight which follows; the praise and thanksgiving which well up; and the sharing of all this in the company of the blessed.

BEATITUDE

Any of the blessings said by Jesus in the Sermon on the Mount as told in the New Testament in Matthew and in the Sermon on the Plain in Luke 6:20-23. Named from the initial words (beati sunt, blessed are) of those sayings in the Latin Vulgate Bible, the Beatitudes describe the blessedness of those who have certain qualities or experiences peculiar to those belonging to the Kingdom of Heaven.

BEATITUDES

The promises of Christ concerning happiness or blessedness as proclaimed in the Sermon on the Mount. In the Gospel of Matthew (Matthew 5:3-12) eight are listed; in the Gospel of Luke (Luke 6:20-23) four are stated. They are considered basic qualities of Christian holiness that are generously awarded by God.

BEAUFORT, Margaret

(1443-1509) Mother of King Henry VII of England and founder of St. John's and Christ's colleges. She translated a number of devotional books and was a patron of the English printers.

BEAUTY

In Buddhism, term in the sense of a form of deliverance through the appreciation of beauty. In the pure contemplation of great beauty there is no sense of self, and completely to be free of self is a moment of enlightenment.

BECOMING

In the literal sense of coming into being, a generic term for any process towards existence or a new mode of existence. In classic Greek philosophy the various ways of becoming came to be classified (substantial, quantitative, qualitative, etc.), but in a sense the rudimentary difference between "becoming" and "being" was central to the development of Greek philosophy.

In the history of Christian thought early patristic writings took as a major task the exclusion from the godhead of any form of becoming; this was primarily an assertion that God is not caused and that in Him there is no imperfection.

In classic Catholic systematic theology Aristotle's explanation of becoming as the actualization of a prior potentiality served to articulate key theological themes. The divine transcendence over any form of becoming whatever, in the divine attributes or the divine knowledge and causality, is expressed in the via negativa that disciplines theological statements.

The distinctiveness of the divine act of creation is expressed by contrast with the meaning of becoming: creation does not involve a prior potentiality to existence, but the divine power to bring a total being into existence ex nihilo.

BEDDELL, Harriet M.

(1875-1970) Episcopalian deaconess, who began her missionary career among the Southern Cheyennes Indians in Oklahoma in 1911 and later worked with Alaskan natives before settling among the Florida Seminoles.

BEDE, Saint

(673-735) Also known as "The Venerable." An Anglo-Saxon monk and scholar whose work embraced most of the contemporary learning. His *Ecclesiastical History of the English Nation* is indispensable for the early history of England.

BEECHER, Henry Ward

(1813-1887) Liberal Congregational minister whose oratorical skill and social concern made him one of the most influential Protestant spokesmen of his time. Besides his sermons, Beecher's many works include *Evolution and Religion* (1885); *Life of Jesus Christ (1871-1891); Yale Lectures on Preaching* (1872-1874).

BEECHER, Lyman

(1775-1863) US clergyman and liberal theologian who helped found the American Bible Society (1816). Beecher's sermons against slavery and intemperance made him one of the most influential orators of his time.

BEELZEBUB

Philistine god worshipped by the people of Ekron, whom the Israelites named "lord of the flies." In the New Testament, he is referred to as the chief demon, "lord of dung" (Matthew 12:24).

BEERSHEBA

Biblical town of southern Israel. First mentioned as the site where Abraham, founder of the Jewish people, made a covenant with the Philistine king Abimelech of Gerar.
Beersheba was at the southern edge of permanent agricultural cultivation in ancient Palestine and represented the southern extremity of the Israelite country. The phrase "from Dan to Beersheba" (Judges 20:1) was a saying for "the whole land."

BEGGING DANCE

Dance of the North American tribes performed as an appeal to the Creator to have the people who prospered give to the needy. Gifts were not sought by the dancers themselves but to help other people. The Begging Dance also emphasized that those who shared their prosperity with the poor and helpless would be treated kindly by the Creator.

BEGHERDS

Associations of male laity living in community and practicing charitable and apostolic activities. Their residences were called Begherds. These groups developed chiefly in Flanders and the Low Countries during the Middle Ages.

BEGUINES

Associations of female laity living in community and practicing charitable and apostolic activities. Their residences were called Beguinages. These groups developed chiefly in Flanders and the Low Countries during the Middle Ages.

BEHEMOTH

The powerful march animal described in Job 40:15-24, anciently identified as an elephant, but now commonly as a hippotamus. The passage's point is that man, so feeble next to this monstrous animal made by God, cannot contend in wisdom and strength with God. Later apocalyptic Jewish literature identifies Behemoth as a monstrous beast warring against God who will destroy it at the Judgment.

BEL

An ancient Akkadian god, comparable in status and function to the Sumerian Enlil; the god who governed the earth's surface and therefore living men. When Marduk became Babylon's chief god, he was given the title Bel. Thus the Bel and Merodach (Marduk) of Jeremiah 50:2 are the same god.

BEL AND THE DRAGON

Book of the Apocrypha (Bible). Bel (an idol) and the dragon were worshipped by the Babylonians until Daniel proved that they were not living gods by destroying them.

BEL, Temple of

Main sanctuary of ancient Palmyra (Syria), built AD 32, dedicated to the deities Bel (sky), Iarhibol (sun), and Aglibol (moon), built on a great terrace enclosed by a double row of Corinthian columns with a monumental propylaeum and an additional underground entrance passage for sacrificial animals.

BELGIC CONFESSION

A statement of the Reformed Faith in 37 articles written by Guido de Bres (1522-67), a reformer in Flandren and northern France. It became the standard creed of the Reformed Church of The Netherlands and of reformed churches of Dutch background in the United States.

BELIEF

In Christianity, term used in the sense of faith. In Buddhism, the first step on the Noble Path. Belief in Buddhism must result from apprehension based on reason, not on mental obedience to the authority of another.

BELIEVERS' BAPTISM

The practice among some Protestant denominations, of baptizing adult believers rather than infants.

BELLS

The religious use of bells goes back to antiquity in the Christian Church. Legend, without probable foundation in fact, attributes their introduction to St. Paulinus of Nola. By the 6th century at the latest they were in common use in some places, for Gregory of Tours (died 594) makes frequent mention of them, and there are indications that among the Irish, who attached great importance to bells down through medieval times, they were used for religious purposes as early as the fifth century.

The primary purpose of the bell was to invite the faithful to worship, a function of importance before small clocks and watches came into common use. Bells were also rung - to remind the faithful of certain practices of devotion to be performed at set times;
▲ to ask prayers for a departing soul;
▲ to announce a death or call attention to a burial;
▲ to honor a visiting dignitary;
▲ to celebrate a joyful or solemn occasion.

Special forms of blessing and consecration for church bells have been in use in the Western church since early medieval times.

BELORUSSIAN CATHOLIC CHURCH

An Eastern Catholic church of the Byzantine Rite, in communion with Rome since the Union of Brest-Litovsk in 1596.

BELSHAZZAR

(612-539 BC) Coregent of Babylon at whose feast the prophet Daniel, interpreting the handwriting on the wall foretold the destruction of the city (Daniel 5:4). He was the eldest son of Nabonides, king of Babylon and of Nitocris, who was perhaps a daughter of Nebuchadnezzar.

BEMA FEAST

The principal religious festival of the year in Manichaeism, a dualistic religion founded in the 3rd century by the Persian prophet Mani. The feast was celebrated at the end of a fast of 30 days and occurred either in the final days of February or in March. The primary purpose was to commemorate the death and ascension of Mani.

BENDIGO

(1811-1880) Colorful pugilist and tavern keeper who became a noted Methodist evangelist and who is one of the very few athletes whose name is borne by a city - Bendigo (Victoria).

BENEDICT I

(501-579) Pope from 574 to 579. He ruled the church during a period made calamitous by invasion and famine. While working to solve these problems, he died during a siege of Rome by the Lombards.

BENEDICT II

(604-685) Pope from 684 to 685. During his pontificate he restored several Roman churches. He was buried in St. Peter's church. His feast day is May 8th.

BENEDICT III

(787-858) Pope from 855 to 858. He reprimanded the Frankish bishops, whose inaction he blamed as the source of misery in their empire. He was responsible for the repair of Roman churches damaged by the Saracens.

BENEDICT IV

(831-903) Pope from 900 to 903. He reigned during the darkest period of papal history, and little is known of his life or acts.

BENEDICT V

(891-966) Pope or antipope from May 22nd to June 23nd, 964. Noted for his learning he was called Grammaticus. His election by the Romans on the death of Pope John XII infuriated the Holy Roman Emperor Otto I The Great, who had already deposed John and designated Leo VIII as successor.

BENEDICT VI

(901-974) Pope from January 973 to July 974. His consecration was delayed for the ratification of his protector, the Holy Roman emperor Otto I the Great. He was imprisoned in June 974 and replaced by the deacon Franco, later known as antipope Boniface VII.

BENEDICT VII

(808-983) Pope from 974 to 983. He furthered the cause of monasticism and acted against simony, specifically in an encyclical letter in 981 forbidding the exaction of money for the conferring of any holy order.

BENEDICT VIII

(965-1024) Pope from 1012-1024, the first of several pontiffs from the powerful Tusculani family. He appears to have been more of a feudal baron than a pope; he restored papal authority in the Campagna and in Roman Tuscany by force of arms, he defeated the Saracens attack on northern Italy and he encourage Norman freebooters in their attacks on Byzantine power in the south.

BENEDICT IX

(967-1055) Pope from 1032 to 1045 and from 1047 to 1048. The last of the popes from the powerful Tusculani family, he was notorious for selling the papacy to his godfather and then subsequently reclaiming the office twice.

BENEDICT X

(1001-1080) John Mincius; antipope from April 1058 to January 1059. His expulsion from the throne, on which he had been placed through the efforts of the powerful Tusculani family of Rome, was followed by a reform in the law governing papal elections. The new law, enacted in 1059, established an electoral body, which subsequently became the Sacred College of Cardinals.

BENEDICT XI

(1240-1304) Niccolo Boccasini; pope from 1303 to 1304. His brief reign was taken up with problems he inherited from the quarrel of his predecessor, Boniface VIII, with King Philip IV.

BENEDICT XII

(1269-1342) Jacques Fournier; pope from 1334 to 1342. He was the third pontiff to reign at Avignon, where he devoted himself to reform of the church and its religious orders. He tried to impose stringent constitutions. These rigorous measures aroused much hostility, and most of his reforming work was undone by his successors.

BENEDICT XII

(1649-1730) Pierfrancesco Orsini; pope from 1724 to 1730. He left state affairs almost entirely to the unpopular cardinal Niccolo Cossia, whose abuse of his office to amass riches marred Benedict's reign. He continued the opposition of the papacy to Jansenism -

a Roman Catholic movement of unorthodox tendencies - which had begun in 17th century France, although he allowed the Dominicans to preach the Augustinian doctrine of grace, which broadened the Jansenist teaching.

BENEDICT XIII

(1328-1423) Pedro de Luna; antipope who ruled from 1394 to 1423 as "pope" in Avignon, in opposition to the reigning popes in Rome. His rule occurred during the Great Western Schism, when the Roman Catholic Church was split by national rivalries claiming the papal throne.

BENEDICT XIV

(1675-1758) Prospero Lambertini; pope from 1740 to 1758. His intelligence and moderation won praise even among deprecators of the Roman church, at a time when it was beset by criticism from the philosophers of the Enlightenment and its prerogatives were being challenged by absolutist monarchs. Typical of his pontificate were his promotion of scientific learning and his admonition to those in charge of drawing up the "Index of Forbidden Books" to act with restraint.

BENEDICT XIV

Name of two succeeding counter-antipopes, the only ones in papal history; they represented the last holdout of resistance of the Great Western Schism (1378-1417), a major rent in the Roman Catholic Church caused by multiple claimants to the Holy See.

BENEDICT XV

(1854-1922) Giacomo Della Chiesa; pope from 1914 to 1922. Trying to follow a policy of strict neutrality he abstained from condemning any action of the belligerents during the war of 1914 to 1918. He concentrated the church's efforts initially towards the alleviation of unnecessary suffering. Later he made positive efforts toward re-establishing peace, though hampered by the pro-Austrian sentiments of the majority of cardinals.

BENEDICT, Rule of

A monastic rule of life, probably written in part at Monte Casino by St. Benedict during the latter part of his life (530). It reveals a maturity in spiritual wisdom and experience in government. The Bible was the principal source of the rule; however, it reflects the philosophies of Leo, Cyprian, and Augustine, and earlier monastic rules.

St. Benedict moderated the severity of older rules and often attracted men to prayer and labor in God's service through entire obedience to the abbot and the rule. It has maintained abbatial authority and autonomy of the individual monastery for more than 14 centuries.

One feature of the rule, its remarkable adaptability to a wide variety of cultural and social circumstances, no doubt accounts in large part for the durability of the Benedictine way of life. The rule provides guiding principles for formation, government, and administration of the monastery. It devotes 11 of 73 chapters to the spiritual direction of the monastery. The prologue and chapters on obedience and humility are skillful works of wisdom.

BENEDICT, Saint

(480-546) Hermit at the age of 20; he lived this way of life for some years. He founded a series of monasteries, beginning at Subiaco, Italy; around 525 he founded the monastery of Monte Cassino and there developed his highly acclaimed monastic rule. He is known as "the father of Western monasticism"; his rule is still used not only by his own religious (men and women known as Benedictines) but also by some other religious orders.

BENEDICTINE NUNS

The women's branch of the Order of St. Benedict, which traces its history to the 6th century, when St. Benedict wrote his rule of life for monks, which was later adapted for the use of women. Benedictine nuns count as their patroness Scholastica, the sister of St. Benedict and a dedicated virgin.

BENEDICTINE ORDERS

Order of monks and nuns following the rule of St. Benedict of Nursia. Their motto is "Pray and Work." Stress is laid on a combination of prayer, choral office, study and manual labor under an abbot's supervision. There has been a great revival of the benedictine rule since 1830 in Europe and the United States.

BENEDICTINE RULE

A system of monastic regulations devised by St. Benedict of Nursia in the 6th century for the monastery at Monte Cassino, Italy. It consists of a prologue and 73 chapters. Conceived as a guide to the communal religious life, the rule promoted the ideals of moderation and cooperation as well as regulations that demanded poverty, chastity, obedience, and stability from those who chose the religious life; and it soon became a norm for Western monastic foundations.

BENEDICTINE SPIRITUALITY

The practice of prayer and life developed by the followers of the rule of St. Benedict places great weight on the essential attitudes and methods found in that document. Those who embrace a Benedictine spirituality choose life in a community in which each member supports with the greatest patience the weakness of body and behavior of another, own all goods in common, pray the Liturgy of the hours in community, prayfully reflect on the scriptures and related spiritual reading and prefer nothing other than Christ.

BENEDICTION

A verbal blessing of persons or things, commonly applied to invocations pronounced in God's name by a priest or minister (Numbers. 6:24-26).

BENEDICTUS

A hymn of praise and thanksgiving sung by Zechariah, a Jewish priest of the line of Aaron, on the occasion of the circumcision and naming of his son, John the Baptist. Found in Luke 1:68-79, the canticle received its name from its first words in Latin.

BENEFICE

In Roman Catholicism, this permanent, ecclesiastical foundation consists of a sacred office and the right of the occupant to the annual revenue derived from the endowment. Clergy who hold a benefice have free use of their income, using what they need and spending what is extra for the poor or in good works. Benefices are rare today. In fact, the Vatican Council II and the 1983 Code of Canon Law recommended their suppression.

BENEFIT OF CLERGY

Formerly a useful device for avoiding the death penalty in England and the United States. In the late 12th century, the church succeeded in persuading the royal courts to grant the clergy, accused of a capital offense immunity from trial or punishment in the secular courts. From the 16th century on, however, a long series of statutes made certain crimes punishable by death without benefit of clergy.

BEN-HADAD I

(died circa 840 BC) King of Damascus. In a battle with him King Ahab of Israel was killed. Ben-hadad was murdered by the usurper Hazael.

BENE-ISRAEL

Jews of India who for centuries lived in Bombay and adjacent regions totally isolated from other Jewish influences. Their arrival in India is said to have been precipitated by a shipwreck some 2,000 years ago. Though the Bene-Israel speak Marathi rather than Hebrew and differ little from their Hindi neighbors in appearance, they claim pure Jewish blood.

BENEZET, Saint

(1109-1184) An uneducated shepherd, he claimed that he was divinely commanded to build a bridge where the force of the Rhone was so great it had discouraged even Roman engineers in antiquity. He died four years before the bridge was completed.

BENGAL VAISNAVISM

A devotional and theological movement in Bengali Hinduism, emphasizing the worship of the god Visnu and his incarnations.

BENJAMIN

One of the 12 tribes that in biblical times constituted the people of Israel, and one of the two tribes (along with Judah) that later became the Jewish people. The tribe was named after the younger of two children born to Jacob (also called Israel) and his second wife, Rachel.

BENNO, Saint

(1010-1106) Bishop of Meissen. His canonization (1523) by Pope Adrian VI drew from Martin Luther a violent brochure entitled: *Against the New Idol and the Old Devil About To Be Set Up at Meissen.*

BEN-ZVI, Itzhak

(1884-1963) Russian-born second president of Israel (1952-63). He was active in Jewish pioneer and self-defense groups in Palestine from 1907, and in 1929 was a founder of the Vaad Leumi (National Council of Palestine Jews).

BERAKHA

In Judaism, a benediction that is recited at specific points of the synagogue liturgy, during private prayer, or on other occasions.

BERAKHOT

The first division or tractate of 64 in the Mishnah, a written collection of ancient rabbinical oral rules and regulations governing and guiding moral and doctrinal life. It contains blessings for foods and examines various confessions of Jewish faith and various prayers and rules for saying them.

BERNADETTE DE LOURDES, Saint

(1844-1879) French peasant girl (born Marie-Bernadette Soubirous) who claimed to have had 18 visions of the Virgin Mary in a Lourdes grotto in 1858. The grotto became a shrine, and she was beatified (1925) and canonized 1933). Her feast day is February 19th in France, April 18th elsewhere.

BERNARD OF CLAIRVAUX, Saint

(1090-1153) French theologian and mystic who reinvigorated the Cistercians and inspired the Second Crusade. The founder abbot of Clairvaux Abbey (1115-53), he established 68 religious houses. He was adviser to popes, kings and bishops and was instrumental in Abelard's condemnation (1140). Bernard was canonized in 1174. His feast day is August 20th.

BERNARD OF CLUNY

(mid-12th century) Monk, poet, and Neoplatonic moralist whose writings condemned man's search for earthly happiness and criticized the immorality of his times. He is also noted for his valuable chronicle of monastic customs.

BERNARD OF MONTJOUX, Saint

(996-1081) Founder of hospices at the summits of two Alpine passes, renamed after him the Great and Little St. Bernard passes.

BERNINI, Giovanni Lorenzo

(1598-1680) The greatest sculptor and architect of the Italian baroque. For more than 50 years architect to St. Peter's basilica, Bernini conceived and executed *The Baldacchino* (1624-33), *Scala Regia* (1663-66), the *Cathedra Petri* in the apse (1657-66), and the impressive double colonnade of St. Peter's Square, unifying architecture, sculpture, and ornamentation in overwhelming, dramatic effects expressing the spirit of 17th-century Catholicism. Bernini designed churches, squares, tombs, palaces, and fountains and he gave Rome its baroque character and determined Europe's sculptural style for centuries.

BERRY FESTIVAL

Festival described among the Sandy Lake Cree Indians in northwestern Ontario. Its features included the singing of sacred songs, prayers that sought the help of spirits and a dance in a sunwise movement. The festival was conducted in late summer and fall when berries were available.

BET-DIN

A Jewish tribunal empowered to adjudicate cases involving criminal, civil, or religious law. The history of such institutions goes back to the time God commanded the 12 tribes of Israel to appoint judges and set up courts of law (Deuteronomy 16:18).

BETHANY

Small village and biblical site on the eastern slopes of the Mount of Olives, just outside Jerusalem. Bethany is mentioned frequently in the New Testament. It was the home of Mary and Martha and their brother Lazarus, and the miracle of Lazarus' resurrection took place there (John 11). It was also the home of Simon the Leper (Matthew 26), whom Jesus parted from his disciples from the village (Luke 24:50-51).

BETHEL

Ancient city of Palestine, located just north of Jerusalem. Originally called Luz, Bethel was important in Old Testament times and was frequently associated with Abraham and Jacob. Abraham is said to have build an altar there, and it was in Bethel that Jacob had his dreams of a heavenly ladder. The site was last excavated in 1960.

BETHLEHEM

Hebrew: house of bread. Town in ancient Judah, central Palestine. It is situated in the Judaean Hills, 5 miles south of Jerusalem. David was born in Bethlehem and here he was anointed (1 Samuel 16:1). It was also the birthplace of Jesus Christ, as foretold in the Old Testament (Micah 5:2).

A basilica built by the Emperor Constantine over the grotto of Nativity (326-33) and rebuilt by Justinian I now forms the church of the Nativity, a major attraction for tourists and pilgrims. Long contested by Christians and Muslims, it was taken by israel during the 1967 Six-Day War.

BET SHE'ARIM

Agricultural cooperative settlement and archaeological site in northern Israel, near the western end of the Plain of Esdraelon. Ancient Bet She-arim, circa 3 miles east-north-east of the modern settlement, is frequently mentioned in rabbinic sources. These recount that rabbi Judah ha-Nasi (circa 135-220) presided over the Sanhedrin, or supreme Jewish rabbinical tribunal, and that upon his death his remains were transferred to Bet She'arim for burial.

BETTER GOOD

A term used in theological discussion, designating a good act or deed in the option of a person to whom another or other courses of action, good in themselves but of lesser spiritual value, are also open to choice. Some rigoristic moralists have held that a lesser good, in comparison with a better one, is relatively evil in that its choice involves the deliberate rejection of some measure of spiritual good.

More commonly moral theologians deny this and hold that it is sufficient for a morally good act that an agent's object and intention be good.

BEZA, Theodore

(1519-1605) Author, translator, and theologian who assisted and latter succeeded John Calvin as a leader of the Protestant Reformation, centered at Geneva.

BHADRABAHU I

(350-298 BC) Jaina leader and philosopher who, after a 12-year famine, led an exodus from the Jaia stronghold in north-east India to south-western India, in 310 BC. He was the spiritual leader of the Jainas and became a monk.

BHADRACARYA-PRANIDHANA

A Mahayana (Buddhist) text that also made an important contribution to Tantric Buddhism of Tiber. It presents a universe of totally interdependent phenomena manifesting the Buddha. Its main emphasis is on entering into the full realization of such a universe - or into the Pure Land of Amitabha - through actions conforming to the 10 great vows of the badhisattva.

These 10 vows, understood as the essence of the vows and deeds of all past and future Buddhas, came to be used as daily lessons in Chinese monasteries. In Tibet they were incorporated as utterances in a number of rites, thus influencing the development of Tantric ritualism.

BHAGAVAD-GITA

Song of the Lord, anonymous Sanskrit poem of circa 200 BC, embedded in the Mahabharata epic, a world-famous religious discourse. It consists of a dialogue (700 verses), covering many aspects of Hindu religious
thought, between Prince Arjuna and the god Krishna on a field of battle.

BHAGAVAT

In Buddhism, the Holy Lord, hence the Blessed One. It is a Hindu term used in the invocation of the Buddha which opens Pansil.

BHAKTI

In Buddhism, devotion to a spiritual ideal. Those using this way of development prefer to personify the Ideal and to reach Truth by its service.

In Hinduism, the love toward a Supreme Person. It is much less abstract than the theological systems of the Upanishads or the Vedanta. One school of bhakti began in the southern part of India from the 13th to the 17th centuries. In northern India is another strain of bhakti which depends more on the Gita and the Bhagavata Purana.

Things important to many religious persons were discarded by the bhaktas, such as creeds, dogmas, or sacred books. Even fasting, alms, and the practice of Yoga were for naught in bhakti, unless accompanied by a deep love of God and repetition of his name.

BHAVA

In Buddhism, philosophical term signifying "becoming"; a state of existence (all existence being states of becoming), a life. Bhava is the link between upadana (clinging to life), and jati (rebirth).

BHAVANA

In Buddhism, a term meaning "making-to-become." Self-development by any means, but especially by the method of mind-control, concentration and meditation.

BHAVANGA

In Buddhism, the sub-conscious stream of becoming in which all experience is stored.

BHIKKHU

A member of the Buddhist Sangha; variously translated as monk, mendicant, friar, almsman, priest; all of which are alone inadequate. A Bikkhu is one who has devoted himself to the task of following the Path by renunciation of the distractions of worldly affairs. He relies for his sustenance upon the gifts of the lay disciples, being under no obligation to give anything in return, but often devoting part of his time to secular and religious teaching. A Bikkhu keeps the Ten Precepts and his daily life is governed by 227 rules.

BHUMISPARSA

The mudra (symbolic gesture) in Buddhist art meaning "earth-touching," used by the Buddha under the Bodhi tree during the assault of Mara when calling upon the earth to witness his virtue was confirmed. The Buddha in padmasana (meditation), his right wrist on his right leg, with extended middle finger touches the ground.

BHUTA

In Buddhism, real, reality. The term is used in the sense of the ghost or shell of the dead which exists for a while after the death of the body. It is these "astral" remains (called starry because they are faintly visible to some) which are contacted and often unnaturally used in spiritualistic practices.Hence the Eastern term "Bhuta-worship" applied to those in the West who indulge in these practices.

BIALIK, Hayyin Mahman

(1873-1934) Greatest Hebrew poet of modern times. Born in a little Russian town, he was brought up in the religious home of his grandfather. In 1892, he published his first poem, *To the Bird.* The last period of his life was spent in Palestine, where he lived on Bialik Street - a street named after him - in Tel Aviv. His poetry sings of God and of the Jewish people. It cries out for freedom and justice. It protects against the cruelty suffered in their chains of oppression. His pen-pictures of the European yeshiva student, of the city of Kishinev after Jews were massacred there, and of the house of prayer, have never been excelled. His *Book of Legends* drew the most fascinating stories from the Talmud and cast them into unforgettable language. He wrote nature poems and songs for children.

BIANKI

(1835-1897) Native American dreamer and prophet who became known as Asa'tito'la, "The Messenger," because of his religious ways. He regularly went alone to a mountain to fast and pray for visions, generally in response to those in need of spiritual assistance. Upon his return he would bring messages from departed friends and relatives in the spiritual world or knowl-edge of remedies to use in treating a patient. He revived the beliefs of the Ghost Dance of 1890 including a reunion with departed friends and relatives and a return to traditional ways. His efforts, and those of other former priests of the religious movement, resulted in a revival of the sacred dance among the Kiowa tribe.

BIBLE

Inspired (that is, given by God) book forming the basis for Christian belief and practice. Its 39 Old Testament books, plus the 27 of the New Testament, make up the Bible. Major biblical themes center in God, His creation and care of the world, His righteousness, love, and saving activity. The Bible has had an incalculable influence on the thought, attitudes, beliefs, art, science and politics of Western society. The collection called the Old Testament is substantially the Hebrew Bible, with its three divisions - Law, Prophets, and Writings - amounting in all to 24 (in the traditional Jewish reckoning) or 39 (in the conventional Christian reckoning) documents. The Law, comprising the first five books, is frequently called the Pentateuch (from a Greek adjective meaning "consisting of five scrolls").

The New Testament comprises 27 documents, written within the century following the death of Jesus. These are five narrative works (the four gospels and the Acts of the Gospels), 21 letters (13 of which bear the name of Paul), and the apocalyptic Book of Revelation.

In large measure the New Testament represents the written deposit of first-generation Christian preaching and teaching, in the light of which the Old Testament has traditionally been interpreted in the church.

Books of the Bible - Old Testament

Books of the Bible - New Testament

Standard Proetstant List

- ▲ Genesis
- ▲ Exodus
- ▲ Leviticus
- ▲ Numbers
- ▲ Deuteronomy
- ▲ Joshua
- ▲ Judges
- ▲ Ruth
- ▲ I Samuel
- ▲ II Samuel
- ▲ I Kings
- ▲ II Kings
- ▲ I Chronicles
- ▲ II Chronicles
- ▲ Ezra
- ▲ Nehemiah
- ▲ Esther
- ▲ Job
- ▲ Psalms
- ▲ Proverbs
- ▲ Ecclesiastes
- ▲ Song of Solomon
- ▲ Isaiah
- ▲ Lamentations
- ▲ Ezekiel
- ▲ Daniel
- ▲ Hosea
- ▲ Joel
- ▲ Amos
- ▲ Obadiah
- ▲ Jonah
- ▲ Micah
- ▲ Nahum
- ▲ Habakkuk
- ▲ Zephariah
- ▲ Haggai
- ▲ Zechariah
- ▲ Malachi

- ▲ Matthew
- ▲ Mark
- ▲ Luke
- ▲ John
- ▲ Acts
- ▲ Romans
- ▲ I Corinthians
- ▲ II Corinthians
- ▲ Galatians
- ▲ Ephesians
- ▲ Philippians
- ▲ Collosians
- ▲ I Thessalonians
- ▲ II Thessalonians
- ▲ I Timothy
- ▲ II Timothy
- ▲ Titus
- ▲ Philemon
- ▲ Hebrews
- ▲ James
- ▲ I Peter
- ▲ II Peter
- ▲ I John
- ▲ II John
- ▲ III John
- ▲ Jude
- ▲ Revelation

BIBLE, Authority of

The quality, conceded to be inherent in sacred scripture as the Word of God that makes it a secure norm of religious faith and practice. For centuries before the time of Christ, but at a period difficult to fix precisely, the books of the Old Testament were accepted by the Hebrews or Jews as authored by the spirit of God.

Jesus and the apostles conformed to this Jewish viewpoint on Israel's sacred books (see also Mark 12:36; John 10:35), and the early Christian Church conceived of its own sacred literature in the same manner.

Because it was believed that the human authors of this religious literature, produced within and for the Hebrew and Christian communities, were in a special sense divinely illumined for this purpose, this literature was accepted as the norm of faith. Thus the binding authority of scripture derived from its divine authorship.

BIBLE, Canon of

The word canon, signifying a reed used for measuring, was used figuratively by the second-century Christians to mean a rule of faith, then, a guiding moral principle, then, something unchangeable (e.g., the Canons of the Mass), and, finally, by the fourth century (Athanasius, circa 350) the official list of holy writings commonly accepted by the church as sacred and of divine authorship.

BIBLE CYCLES IN ART

A complex of visual representations illustrating various phases of one subject or many subjects of a single "thematic" idea. First examples found in the catacombs and on early Christian tombs (second and third centuries) are of a narrative and symbolic nature in impressionistic style of the late Roman Imperial painting.

The golden period of Byzantine civilization presents the triumph of cycles in masterpieces of illumination. Following the iconoclastic crisis a Greek stylistic manner determined eighth century Roman frescoes.

Gothic cycles are seen in important portal reliefs at Chartres, Paris, and Nuremberg, in stained glass of extraordinary mastery at Chartres and Reims, and in illuminated manuscripts of France and Bohemia.

The Florentine Renaissance expresses with epic power the new humanistic relation of man and nature which dominated Europe from the 15th to the 17th centuries. Michelangelo's supreme cycle of *Genesis* on the ceiling of the Sistine Chapel was followed by colossal, intense, and imaginative paintings in Venice.

BIBLE SERVICES

In this paraliturgical (Roman Catholic) service, public readings from the scriptures are combined with periods of prayer, singing, and silence. Often a homily or reflection on the themes of readings is included. The Constitution on the sacred Liturgy of Vatican Council II recommended Bible services on the vigils of feasts, Sundays, and holidays and on some Advent and Lenten weekdays.

BIBLE SOCIETY, American

A nonprofit interdenominational organization, founded in New York City in 1816 to encourage the use and promote the wider circulation of the Bible. Incorporated in 1814, the Society is supported mainly by gifts from individuals and churches. To date, the Society has distributed over 800,000,000 in over 180 languages, including many copied in braille and talking records for the blind.

BIBLE VERSIONS

Translations of the Bible, or of any part of it, into a vernacular tongue; a version is distinguished from the text of the Bible, i.e., the written word in manuscripts either in the original languages or in ancient versions made from these languages.

With regard to the Old Testament, four direct versions (i.e., from the original languages) stand out immediately as

the most ancient and important:
- ▲ the Aramaic targums of Onkelos and Jonathan (pre-third century AD)
- ▲ the Greek Septuagint;
- ▲ the Syriac Peshitta;
- ▲ the Latin Vulgate.

The two last named, having been composed by and for Christians, also include the New Testament. These direct versions derive their special critical value from the fact that they were written considerably before the existing Hebrew text was fixed, and consequently bear witness to earlier variants of it that would otherwise be unknown to us.

BIBLE VIGIL

A prayer service based on the reading of the Bible as God's Word and structured according to the traditional principles of worship. Generally it consists of an entrance rite, readings, prayers, and a closing rite, but its format is elastic and adaptable to a variety of circumstances of time, place, and participants.

The theology and form of the service is not new. It is analogous to the synagogue service, and much like the assemblies for reading and prayer out of which the Divine Office developed.

Such services have grown in popularity since World War II as a substitute for repetitious devotions, and growing interest in the Bible has taught people to value the opportunity they provide for a broader exploration of God's Word.

BIBLICAL LITERATURE

The sacred scriptures of Judaism and Christianity, divided into three sections:
1. The Hebrew Bible, or Old Testament, canonical and authoritative to both Jews and Christians;
2. Intertestamental literature, including what is sometimes called the Apocrypha ("hidden" books), deutero-canonical in Roman Catholicism, canonical in Eastern Orthodoxy, and noncanonical in Judaism and Protestantism; the Pseudigrapha (books wrongly ascribed to a biblical author), noncanonical in all groups; and Qumran literature (or the Dead Sea scrolls), also noncanonical;
3. The New Testament, canonical in Christianity only.

BIBLICAL THEOLOGY

A branch of theological study, distinct from both exegesis and speculative theology, in which scriptural revelation is understood and ordered according to the Bible. The task of biblical theology is to examine the revelatory events in their temporal character and within the mental perspectives of those who witness to them in the scriptures in order to identify those events and perspectives within an intelligible pattern of God's self-revelation.

BIBLICAL UNICAL

Type of writing used with the three great early vellum codices of the Bible.

BIBLICISM

The approach to the understanding of the Bible that combines fundamentalism and literalism and insists that the very thought and language of biblical times are the normative sources for Christian faith and for its expression.

BIBLIOTHECA APOSTOLICA VATICANA

Official library of the Vatican, especially notable as one of the world's richest manuscript deposits. The library is the direct heir of the first library of the Roman pontiffs.

BICHRI

In the Old Testament, the Benjaminite father of forefather of the good-for-nothing fellow named Sheba who rebelled against David. In this action the Bichrites supported Sheba (2 Samuel 20:1-2; 14-15).

BID'AH

In Islam, term in the sense of innovation. Its proper opposition is sunna. However, in popular speech bid'ah has come to indicate "heresy" although, if one is to be absolutely correct, it is in fact distinct from heresy, since not all innovation may be bad or hostile to Islam, according to Islamic law.

BIG HEAD RELIGION

Religious movement described as an offshoot of the Bole-Maru Religion, which grew out of the Ghost Dance of 1870 among Native Americans. The Big Head Religion began in Pomo territory and travelled northward to other Californian groups. Ceremonial objects associated with the rituals included big head-dresses, cocoon rattles, a foot drum and split-stick rattles.

BIGOTRY

The fanatical attachment to a cause, coupled with intolerance and contempt of those who oppose it and a blind unwillingness to consider evidence contrary to one's own views. It is often accompanied by paranoid suspicions of one's opponents.

BIGTHAN

One of the two doorkeepers in the Persian palace who conspired against the life of King Ahasuerus. Mordecai learned of the plot, Queen Esther revealed it to the king, Bigthan was hanged, and the incident was recorded in the royal archives (Esther 2:21-23; 6:2).

BIGVAI

In the Old Testament, forefather of some 2,000 "sons of Bigvai" who returned to Jerusalem with Zerubbabel in 537 BC (Ezra 2:14). Later, in 468 BC more of his descendants made the trip with Ezra (8:1, 14).

BIKATH-AVEN

A place or valley plain associated with Damascus and Beth-eden in Amos's prophecy foretelling the exile of the people of Syria (Amos 1:5).

BILA KAYF

In Islam, literally, the phrase means "without (asking) how." It was put forward as a solution in medieval times to the great debate about the attributes of God. According to this Muslims were obliged to believe that God did indeed have real attributes like hands and a face, since these were mentioned in the Koran. Such attributes were to be accepted without asking how they existed.

BILAL B. RAHAB

First muadhdhin appointed by the Prophet Mohammed, who also served in a variety of other ways. He made the Hijra with Mohammed to Medina and later, when the Prophet conquered Mecca, he gave the call to prayer from the top of the Ka'ba. During the conquests, after Mohammed's death, Bilal joined the campaign to Syria.

BILDAD

In the Old Testament, one of Job's three companions, called the Shuahite; a descendant of Shuah, the son of Abraham by Keturah (Job 2:11; Genesis 25:2).

Bildad is introduced as a Shuahite, probably a member of a nomadic tribe dwelling in south-eastern Palestine. His arguments with Job reveal him to be a traditionalist; his wounded orthodoxy provokes the lack of courtesy in his initial reply.

BILEAM

In the Old Testament, a town assigned to the Levites of the family of Kohath, given to them from the territory of the half tribe of Manasseh located west of the Jordan River (1 Chronicles 6:70).

BILGAH

In Judaism, head of the 15th of the 24 priestly service divisions when David reorganized the sanctuary service (1 Chronicles 24:1, 14).

BILGAI

In Judaism, a priest, or forefather of one, who agreed to the covenant Nehemiah arranged (Nehemiah 10:1, 8).

BILHAH

In the Old Testament, one of the maid-servants of Laban's household whom he gave to his daughter Rachel to be her maidservant at the time of her marriage to Jacob (Genesis 29:29).

BILOCATION

Personal presence of an individual in more than one place at the same time; this phenomenon has been recorded of some of the saints.

Physical bilocation would mean that the same atomic body would be simultaneously both here and there, and would seem to be impossible as a contradiction of the principle of identity, that no being can be and not be at once. Therefore reports of bilocation are usually interpreted to mean incidents of apparent bilocation: i.e., that bilocated beings are "seen" in one place while they are known to be "present" in another. For this reason it is difficult to distinguish bilocation from related appearances or visions.

BILQIS

Pre-Islamic queen of Sheba. She is not mentioned in the Koran but the exegetes identify her with the queen in Surat-at-Naml, who vists Sulayman and surrenders with Sulayman to the one true God.

BIMAH

In Jewish synagogues, a raised platform with a reading desk from which, in the Ashkenazi ritual, the Torah and Haftara (a reading from the prophets) are read on sabbaths and festivals. In the Sefardic rite, the entire liturgy is conducted from a platform called a teba.

BINITARIANISM

A classification used especially in England for the belief or doctrine that the Godhead exists in two persons only, the Father and the Son. Thus the Pneumatomachi (Macedonians), who rejected the divinity of the Holy Spirit, were teaching a form of binitarianism.

BINNUI

A forefather in Israel whose descendants over 600 in number, returned to Jerusalem in 537 BC (Nehemiah 7:6).

BIOETHICS

Moral questions arising from the progress made in biological sciences may be of two kinds. First, settling problems such as genetic engineering and artificial insemination created by the rapid technology of the life sciences. Second, studying the possibilities of new developments in ethical procedures compatible with Christian principles of morality, such as natural family planning and organ transplantation.

BIRETTA

The Roman Catholic clergy occasionally wear a stiff square cap with three upright ridges on top and sometimes a tuft in the middle. The priest's biretta is black, a bishop's is purple, a cardinal's is scarlet without a tuft, a Cistercian abbot's is white.

The biretta is worn on entering the church for service and on leaving the church and at certain times during the services. Since the Vatican Council II, the biretta is no longer commonly worn by priests in the United States and Europe, but is still required of all the clerics of the patriarchal basilicas in Rome.

BIRITUALISM

A system in which a priest of the Latin Rite uses the liturgy and offices of the Eastern Rite on the occasion of his work or missionary activities among Catholics or dissidents of the Eastern Church.

BIRSHA

In biblical times, king of Gomorrah whom Chedorlaomer made his subject together with four other nearby kings. He may be the same "king of Gomorrah," though unnamed, whose rebellion against Chedorlaomer 13 years later was crushed, many of his forces having been driven into nearby bitumen pits (Genesis 14:1-11).

BIRTH

In Buddhism, the arising of a state of being in any sphere of existence, the effect of anterior conditions. No coming of existence from previous non-existence.

Under the Mosaic law a woman giving birth to a boy was ceremonially unclean for seven days, with an additional 33 days required for her purification. If the child was a girl, then the mother was considered unclean for 14 days, requiring 66 days more for purification.

BIRTHDAY OF THE CHURCH

The birth of the Roman Church is envisioned in the institution of the eucharist and fulfilled on the cross. The Dogmatic Constitution states "The origin and growth of the Church are symbolized by the blood and water which flowed from the open sides of the crucified Jesus." (See also John 19:34).

This is reiterated in The Constitution on the Sacred Liturgy: "For it was from the side of Christ as he slept the sleep of death upon the cross that there came forth the wondrous sacrament of the whole Church."

BI-SHEVAT

Jewish festival day called New Year of the Trees. The Jewish ancestors set aside the 15th of the month of Shevat as Jewish Arbor Day.It was in the Talmud that the New Year of the Trees received its name. But long before that the Torah showed the way. The Bible, for example, says that fruit trees may not be cut down even in time of war (Deuteronomy 20). The Torah itself is called a "tree of life" (Proverbs 3:18). And King David, in the *Book of Psalms,* says that a righteous man is "like a tree planted by the streams of water" (Psalms 1:3).

BISHLAM

In the Old Testament, an opposer of the post-exile Temple rebuilding who shared in writing a letter of false accusation against the Jews to Persian King Artaxerxes (Ezra 4:6-7).

BISHOP

Highest order in the ministry of the Roman Catholic, Anglican, Eastern and some Lutheran churches. As head of his diocese, a bishop administers its affairs, supervises its clergy and administers confirmation and ordination. Roman Catholic bishops are appointed by the pope, Anglican bishops by the sovereign. In the United States, Protestant Episcopal bishops are elected by both clergy and laity.

BISHOP, Monastic

A title for significant ecclesiastical authorities in the early Irish church. Some historians have interpreted this to mean that all jurisdiction in Ireland was exercised by monastic abbots, but this is an oversimplification. Instead, it appears that the authority of abbots naturally spread from the monastery to the surrounding areas which were dependent upon the monks for their spiritual ministrations.

BISHOP, Ordination of

Vatican Council II called for a revision of the ceremonies and texts of the ordination rites. Pope Paul VI gave approval to the new rites that have been drawn up in accordance with the mandate of the Council. These include new rites for the ordination of bishops, priests, and deacons. So far as the ritual for the ordination (which was formerly more commonly known as the consecration) of bishops is concerned, this ceremony takes place after the Gospel in liturgy, and it includes an exhortation, ritual questions, invitation to prayers, a shortened Litany of the Saints, and the imposition of hands.

BISHOP HILL

A communal colony in Henry County, Ill., established in 1846 by Swedish immigrants who were followers of Erik Janson. He was influenced by the pietist movement in Sweden, which stressed personal religious experience and reform, and he believed that true Christianity could not be found in the traditional Christian churches. After declaring himself a prophet who would restore primitive Christianity, he attracted hundreds of followers. The colony lasted some 20 years. Several of the original buildings were restored in the 1950s.

BISHOPS, Episcopate

According to the Roman Catholic Code of Canon Law, "Through the Holy Spirit who has been given to them, bishops are the successors of the apostles by divine institution; they are constituted pastors within the church so that they are teachers of doctrine, priests of sacred worship and ministers of governance. By the fact of their episcopal consecration bishops receive along with the function of sanctifying also the functions of teaching and of ruling, which by their very nature, however, can be exercised only when they are in hierarchical communion with the head of the college and its members." Bishops are empowered to ordain priests and deacons and other bishops.

BISHOPS, College of

In the Roman Catholic Church, the assembly of bishops is headed by the pope and carries on the teaching authority and pastoral guidance in the church. A person becomes a member of this college upon ordination as a bishop. The college exerts absolute authority in the church when it functions in an ecumenical council or by the collegial action of the bishops around the world in one with the pope.

BISHOPS' BIBLE

(1569) An edition of the Old and New Testament prepared in England under the direction of Matthew Parker, archbishop of Canterbury.

BISHOPS' WARS

Two brief campaigns fought between Charles I and the Scots in 1639 and 1640, caused by Charles' endeavor to enforce Anglican observances in the Scottish church and by the determination of the Scots to abolish the episcopacy.

BISTAMI, al-

(874-877) One of the most famous of all medieval sufis and notorious utterer of such ecstatic phrases as "Glory be to me, how great is my majesty!" He spent most of his life in Bistam where he died.

BITRASHIL

Arabic term, derived from Greek epitrachilion, used by Copts, Maronites, and Arabic-speaking Byzantines for their respective forms of the sacradotal stole.

BIZIOTHIAH

In biblical times, a place listed after Beer-sheba as one of the towns in Judah's inheritance in the Negeb region (Joshua 15:21).

BKA-BRGYUD-PA

Third largest Buddhist sect in Tibet, followers of the 11th century teacher Mar-pa, who distinguished himself as a translator of Buddhist texts while continuing to live the life of a householder.

BKA-GDAMS-PA

A sect of Tibetan Buddhism that followed the teachings of the 11th-century master Atisa; the basis of the later, and now predominant reformist sect, the Dge-lugs-pa.

BKA-GYUR

The collection of Buddhist sacred literature representing "The Word of the Buddha" as distinct from the Bstan-hyur, or collection of commentaries and miscellaneous works.

BLACK CHRISTIANITY

A mid-20th century movement among black Christians, especially those in predominantly white churches of the United States, to develop a form of Christianity expressive of black

thought and responsive to the special needs of the black community. It has developed as a conscious reaction to patterns of life in white churches that are considered racist and harmful to African-American life.

In some ways black Christianity has existed since the days of slavery, when black preachers often addressed congregations of converted slaves in a distinctive style of oratory and the congregations sang spirituals.

BLACK FAST

Only one meal in the evening is allowed on these days of penance. In addition, meat, eggs, dairy products, and alcohol are forbidden. Only bread, water, and vegetables form the diet of such a fast. The black fast no longer exists except in specific religious houses or as a penance of individual devotion.

BLACK FOX

(1812-1895) Native American religious leader among the Eastern Band of Cherokees in North Carolina. He was licensed to preach by the Methodist Episcopal Church South in 1848 and was associated with the Echota Methodist Mission on the Qualla Boundary, where he maintained registers, minutes, letters and reports.

BLACK HEBREWS

Community of (originally) African-Americans in Israel. This community has attracted controversy ever since the first Black Hebrews arrived in 1969. They number around 1300, with most of them living in Dimona. Their claim to be the most authentic descendants of the Jews exiled from Israel 4,000 years ago is disputed, and they have been refused Israeli citizenship. Largely ignored by the authorities, the Black Hebrews are one of the understated fascinations of Israel today. This is due not only to their claims of Jewishness, but also to their communal lifestyle which incorporates such elements as a unique tofu-dominated vegetarian diet, colorful clothing, and the practice of polygamy.

BLACK MASS

In the Roman Catholic Church, a colloquial designation for a requiem mass during which the celebrant wears black vestments; also, a blasphemous and usually obscene burlesque of the true mass performed by satanic cults or by apostates and infidels.

BLACK MONKS

A name sometimes applied to the Benedictines of their totally black habit. The designation originated in the Middle Ages and was used in contrast to the White Monks or Cistercians.

BLACK MUSLIMS

The chief US black nationalist movement, founded in 1930 by Wali Farad. He rejected racial integration, taught thrift, hard work and cleanliness, and foretold an Armageddon where black would crush white. Under Elijah Mohammed, the Muslims proclaimed black supremacy and demanded a Nation within the United States.

BLACK ROAD

(19th century) A venerable holy man among the Oglala Lakota people. As a young man, Black Road had smallpox and was sent to a solitary place by the medicine man who treated him. While he was alone, he received instructions from the Thunder Beings to establish the Sacred Bow Society. After recovering from his illness, he returned home to carry out the teachings he received. The society he formed included sacred, ceremonial and military functions.

BLACK STONE OF MECCA

Stone built into the eastern wall of the small shrine near the Great Mosque of Mecca, probably dating from the pre-Islamic religion of the Arabs. It now consists of three large pieces and some fragments, surrounded by a stone ring and held together by a silver band.

BLAISE, Blessing of

The prayerful placing of two candles on the throats of the faithful on February 3rd, the feast day of St.

Blaise. After his martyrdom, St. Blaise was invoked as one of the 14 Holy Helpers on behalf of those suffering from throat ailments. This devotional practice arose because Blaise saved the life of a boy who was choking on a fishbone.

BLAISE, Saint

Bishop and martyr about whom little is known. His cult became widespread from circa the 8th century and is still popular. According to tradition, Blaise was an Armenian bishop, probably of Sebaste, who is said to have been martyred circa 303. St. Blaise is the patron saint of woodcombers and is invoked against disease of the lungs and throat. His feast day is February 3rd.

BLANE, Saint

(late 6th century) Scots bishop said to have been instructed in religion in Ireland, where he became a monk. He built churches, on the island of Bute, his birthplace and on the Scottish mainland.

BLASPHEMY

Insult or defamation of God by spoken or written word. In religious societies blasphemy is considered a grave sin if committed intentionally, and it has always been punished severely. Mosaic law called for death by stoning as punishment of blasphemy. The biblical concept of blasphemy included blasphemy by deed; that is, in one of its most obvious forms, the deliberate raising of the hand against God.

BLASTUS

The man in charge of the bedchamber of King Herod Agrippa I. Because of his position of influence, the people of Tyre and Sidon first won him over, perhaps by bribery, when they sued for peace with Herod (Acts 12:20).

BLEMISH

A physical or moral defect, imperfection; unsoundness; "anything bad" (Deuteronomy 17:1). In Judaism, soundness, freedom from blemish, was required of the sacrificial animals under the Mosaic law (Exodus 12:5; Leviticus 4:3).

BLESSED SACRAMENT

In Roman Catholicism, the sacrament of the eucharist is called "blessed" because all blessings and graces spring from it. The bread and wine after their consecration in the Mass are often called the Blessed Sacrament.

The Blessed Sacrament in the form of consecrated bread is reserved in Catholic churches in a prominent place or in a special chapel of adoration and is marked by a burning sanctuary lamp.

BLESSING

Act of involving divine favor or, more generally, happiness, upon another or others. In the Catholic, Protestant and Jewish religions, it is a rite by which persons or things are dedicated to a sacred purpose. It can be performed by any priest, minister or rabbi. Special blessings are reserved in the Catholic Church to bishops and the pope. The rite usually consists of a verbal formula and a gesture of the hand.

The term "blessed" is used to indicate man's or woman's state of matchless joy when he or she shares in the Kingdom of God, and it is the title by which Roman Catholics refer to a deceased person who has been beatified and is officially considered worthy of veneration.

BLESSING WAY

Rites of the Navajo people. They are the fundamental ceremonial backbone of the Navajo religion and govern the entire chant way system of ceremonial cures.

Rites include a ritual bath, prayers, songs, sometimes a sand painting of vegetable materials (pollen, meal, crushed flowers) strewn on buckskin spread on the ground, hogan consecration, breathing in the dawn, body blessing and traditional stories.

They are used to maintain harmony, for good luck, to avert misfortune, to invoke positive blessings that people need for a long and happy live, for protection, for increasing possessions, to protect livestock, to protect childbirth, to bless a new hogan, to consecrate ceremonial objects, to consecrate marriage, to instal tribal officers, to protect departing and returning travelers, to bless possessions, to bless daily activities and to dispel fear resulting from bad dreams.

BLOCH, Joseph Samuel
(1850-1923) Rabbi, politician and crusader against anti-Semitism, particularly the canard that Jews use the blood of Christians in the Passover ritual.

BLOOD ATONEMENT
The ancient Israelites' use of blood of animals to obtain God's forgiveness. "The life of a living body is in the blood" (Leviticus 17:11). The blood rite was especially celebrated on the Day of Atonement.

The High Priest entered the Holy of the Holies and sprinkled various objects with blood. This ceremony defined the special power of blood in the expiation of sin. "It is the blood, as the seat of life, that makes atonement" (Leviticus 17:11).

The rite effected forgiveness because it liberated life; this life snuffed out in the act was accepted by God who returned it to the repentant sinner in the form of divine life and restored his friendship.

BLOOD OF CHRIST
Jesus shed his blood on the cross in atonement for the sins of humankind. We share in the life of Christ through the blood of Christ received sacramentally in Holy Communion (1 Corinthians 10:16).

BLUE ARMY
An institute whose full title is the Blue Army of Our Lady of Fatima. Founded in 1946, its purpose is to pray for the conversion of Russia and for world peace as requested by Our Lady of Fatima.

The society has worldwide membership, engages in charitable and educational works, and is headquartered in Washington, New Jersey (USA).

BLUE MOSQUE
Large mosque in Istanbul. Sultan Ahmet I (1603-1617) set out to build a mosque that would rival and even surpass the achievement of Justinian who built the Aya Sofya.

The mosque is a triumph of harmony, proportion and elegance, but it comes nowhere near the technical achievement of the Aya Sofya. The Blue Mosque is the only one in Turkey with six minarets. When it was built, between 1609 and 1616, the sacred Harem esh-Sharif in Mecca had six, and another had to be added so that it would not be outdone.

The layout of the Blue Mosque is the classic Ottoman design as it evolved over the centuries. The forecourt contains an ablutions fountain in its center. The portico around three sides could be used for prayer, meditation or study during warm weather.

The semi-domes and the dome are painted in graceful arabesques. The "blue" of the mosque's name comes from the Iznik tiles which line the walls, particularly in the gallery.

BOANERGES
An Aramaic expression found, with its translation, only at Mark 3:17. Jesus gave it as a surname to the sons of Zebedee, James and John, likely reflecting the fiery enthusiasm of these two Apostles (Luke 9:54). Unlike Simon's new name Peter, Boanerges does not appear to have been commonly used.

BOAZ
In the Old Testament, a landowner of Bethlehem in Judah, "a man mighty in wealth" of about the 14th century BC. Boaz was the son of Salma (Salmon) and Rahab, and the father of Obed (Matthew 1:5). He was a link in the family line of descent from Judah (1 Chronicles 2:3-11; Luke 3:32-33).

BOCHIM

In the Old Testament, a site at which God's angel addressed the Israelites, reproving them for having disregarded God's warning against entering into relations with the pagan inhabitants of the land. The weeping that thereafter resulted among the people gave the place its name (Judges 2:1-5).

BODHI

In Buddhism, a major term meaning enlightenment; the spiritual condition of a Buddha or Bodhisattva. The cause of Bodhi is Prajna' wisdom, and Karuna' compassion. Bodhi is the name given to the highest state of Samadhi in which the mind is awakened and illuminated.

BODHI-CITTA

In Buddhism, a term meaning wisdom-heart; the aspiration of a Bodhi-sattva for supreme enlightenment for the welfare of all. The Bodhi-sattva, by renunciation of all claim to results of individual meritorious deeds, practices compassion to the highest degree of perfection by working ever in the worlds of birth and death for the ultimate enlightenment of humanity.

BODHIDHARMA

(6th century AD) Indian monk who founded the Ch'an (Japanese: Zen) sect of Buddhism. Considered the 28th Indian patriarch in a direct line from Gautama Buddha, Bodhidharma is regarded by the Ch'an as their first patriarch. Because he taught meditation as a return to the Buddha's spiritual precepts, his school was known as the Dhyana (meditation) sect. The word was converted in Chinese to Ch'an and in Japanese to Zen.

BODHISATTVA

In Buddhism, one whose "being" or "essence"; for example, is bodhi, the wisdom resulting from direct perception of truth, with the compassion awakened thereby. Originally, the name was used to indicate Gautama Siddhartha before he had attained the state of enlightenment. After the rise of Mahayana Buddhism, all those who are striving for the Buddhahood have come to be called by this name. Finally, even those who are trying to lead others to the Buddhahood by means of their great compassion while striving themselves for the same goal, have been symbolically personified as Bodhisattvas.

A Bodhisattva is said to be a serene, gentle being with such compassion that he delays his entrance to the state of nirvana and transfers the merit accumulated for his sacrifices and good works to all living beings who are unworthy but suffering. Bodhisattvas are worshiped and can respond to prayer; their generosity and exemplary lives are the subject of many Buddhist legends.

BODHI TREE

The tree under which Buddha attained enlightenment at Buddha Gaya; a fig tree, popularly called Pipal.

BODY

The Hebrew of the Old Testament has no special word for body, but some of the attributes associated with body in the New Testament, especially those of weakness, passivity, liability to death etc., can be expressed by the Old Testament term basar, "flesh." It is in the gospels that the now familiar distinction between body and soul emerges, as for instance when it is stated that the death of the body alone is less to be feared than the destruction of both soul and body alike forever (Matthew 10:28; Luke 12:4).

But it is in the writings of Paul that the concept of body acquires a distinctive theological significance in its own right. Very broadly, it may be defined as the concrete totality of the individual as existing in this physical and earthly sphere, and as subject to its natural conditions. But Paul's conception of the individual body of man is radically conditioned by the fact that he regards it as destined to rise again (1 Corinthians 15:35-44), to be transformed and conformed to the already risen and glorified body of Christ (Philippians 3:21).

BODY, Resurrection of

According to Scripture and the formal teaching of the Roman Catholic Church, the body will be resurrected and reunited to the soul after death. Christ taught the resurrection of the body (see Matthew 22:29-32; Luke 14:14; John 5:29). The doctrine was preached as a fundamental mystery of Christian faith (1 Corinthians 15:20; Revelation 20:12) and was included in all the early creeds.

BODY OF CHRIST

Body is an essential part of the human person; the body is a fundamentally good creation of God; according to Catholic teaching, the body is a temple of God and therefore deserving of respect by oneself and others.

The term Body of Christ refers to the ways that Christ is present to humankind and to the world. It has many meanings that stem from the human body of the historical Jesus. This biblical image and its extension to other images is well developed in the dogmatic Constitution on the Church.

BODY OF THE CHURCH

The visible organized community of the faithful consisting of its human members on earth.

BOETHIUS

(480-524) Anicius Manlius Severinus Boethius; scholar, theologian, and philosopher, who transmitted classical texts and ideals to the Middle Ages. He translated Aristotle's *Organon* but died before he could translate Plato's works and harmonize the philosophies. He applied Aristotelian categories to Trinitarian theology.

BOETHUSIANS

Jewish sect that flourished a century or so before the destruction of Jerusalem in AD 70. Their subsequent history is obscure, as is also the identity of Boethus, their founder. Some scholars tend to view the Boethusians as merely a branch of the Sadducees. Both parties associated with the aristocracy and denied the immortality of the soul and the resurrection of the body, because neither of these doctrines was contained in the written Torah, or first five books of the Bible.

BOHAN

In the Old Testament, a descendant of Reuben after whom a boundary stone for the territory of Judah was named (Joshua 15:6; 18:17).

BÖHM, Jakob

(1575-1624) German mystic and religious philosopher. Claiming divine revelation he argued that all opposites, including good and evil, are reconciled in God. His ideas influenced many late philosophers and theologians.

BOLE-MARU RELIGION

Native American religious movement; an outgrowth of the Ghost Dance of 1870. Its name comes from the Patwin word, bole, and the Pomo word, maru. Both words are said to be associated with the dreamer-prophets who conducted the religious ceremonies as well as with the dream that was recited. One of the originators of the Bole-Maru or Dreamer religion, is believed to be the prophet called Lame Bull. The religious movement spread among Patwin, Pomo and Maidu groups, having its highest development in north-central California. The Bole-Maru leaders were dreamers whose revelations guided the direction of ceremonial activities. They also stressed belief in an afterlife and in a supreme being. Unlike some of the other religious movements stemming from the Ghost Dance, practice of the Bole-Maru form of worship continues today.

BÖN

In Buddhism, the indigenous, pre-Buddhist religion of Tibet. Little is known of it in detail, but it seems to have much in common with the

Shamanism of Mongolia, a form of nature-worship mixed with psychic and sexual practices. At its best it has been influenced to the good by Buddhism; at its worst it has dragged down members of the Dug-pa school to its own level.

BONAVENTURE, Saint

(1221-1274) Italian medieval scholastic philosopher and theologian. He taught principally at Paris and later became master general of the Franciscan order. Called the "Sepharic Doctor," he distinguished between philosophy, based on man's natural knowledge, and theology, which attempts to understand the Christian mysteries.

BONHOEFFER, Dietrich

(1906-1945) German Lutheran pastor and theologian. He was the author of many radical books on ecumenism and Christianity in a secular world. A prominent anti-Nazi, he was arrested in 1943 and executed at Flossenburg concentration camp two years later.

BONIFACE, Saint

(672-745) English missionary, the apostle of Germany. Backed by the Frankish rulers Charles Martel and Pepin the Short, he organized the German church, reformed the Frankish clergy and advanced the conversion of the Saxons. He was martyred by the Frisians.

BONIFACE I, Saint

(345-422) Pope from 418 to 422. His reign was marked by disruption by the faction of the antipope Eulalius. Both Eulalius and Boniface claimed the papacy and the fifth schism that resulted caused chaos in Rome. Boniface became the real pope after a 15-week fight.

BONIFACE I OF MONTFERRAT

(1156-1207) One of the leaders of the Fourth Crusade (1202-1204). After the crusaders conquered Constantinople he became king of Thessalonica, a land including Macedonia, Thessaly, and part of Thrace.

BONIFACE II

(467-532) Pope from 530 to 532. He was the first Germanic pontiff. At the same time Dioscorus was elected pope and an anti-papal schism resulted but was terminated by Dioscorus' death (October 14, 530). Boniface convoked the three Roman synods.

BONIFACE III

(541-607) Pope from February 19th to November 10th. His pontificate is principally known for an edict be obtained from the Byzantine emperor recognizing the See of Rome as the head of all the churches, which doubtless was intended as a limitation on the claims of Cyriacus, patriarch of Constantinople.

BONIFACE IV, Saint

(534-615) Pope from 608 to 615. In 610 he presided over the Council of Rome for the restoration of monastic discipline. His pontificate was plagued, politically and ecclesiastically, by the Monophysites (heretics espousing the doctrine of one nature in Christ), and the heretical bishops cooperated with the invaders of the Byzantine Empire led by Heraclius, patriarch of Africa.

BONIFACE V

(649-625) Pope from 619 to 625. He greatly helped the spread of Christianity in England, by encouraging, through letters, the saintly missionaries evangelizing the Britons.

BONIFACE VI

(911-896) Pope in April 896. A subdeacon when elected to succeed Formosus, Boniface died 15 days later either of gout or by violence, probably murdered by the Spoletan Party, whose candidate, Stephen VI, became the next pope.

BONIFACE VII

(911-985) Antipope from June to July 974 and from August 984 to July 985. A cardinal deacon, he murdered his predecessor, Benedict VI, and was installed by Crescentius I. A reign of intrigue ensued, which ended with Boniface's murder by a vengeful Roman mob.

BONIFACE VIII

(1235-1303) Pope 1294-1303. He steadfastly asserted papal authority over the political leaders of Europe and involved the papacy in a series of conflicts with leading powers. His bull "Unam Sanctam" which called for the subjugation of temporal to spiritual authority, led to a clash with Philip IV of France. In 1303 the king's emissaries attacked Benedict in his palace at Anagni, where he was about to excommunicate Philip; the populace intervened, but Boniface collapsed and died three weeks later in Rome.

BONIFACE IX

(1355-1404) Pietro Tomacelli; pope from 1389 to 1404. He was the second pontiff to reign in Rome during the Great Western Schism (1378-1417). He not only failed to end the breach, but he also aroused hostility by his high-handed methods to raise the large sums of money required for his campaigns.

BONNEY, Mary Lucinda

(1816-1900) A Baptist reformer whose efforts led to the formation of the Women's National Indian Association and to the establishment of missions among native American people.

BOOK OF ABRAHAM

A book published by the 19th century Mormon leader Joseph Smith, and claimed by him to be the translation of an ancient papyrus text.

BOOK OF BLESSINGS

The portion of the Roman Ritual which contains the blessings of persons, places, and things, published by the Holy See in 1984, reflecting the liturgical principles declared by Vatican Council II.
There are six parts of the Book of Blessings.
▲ Part I includes blessings directly pertaining to people.

▲ The blessings in Part II are related to buildings and different forms of human activity.
▲ Parts III and IV present blessings for items used in public and private prayer.
▲ Parts V and VI provide a rich collection of blessings that can be used on the parish level.

BOOK OF COMMON ORDER

Title of three books of worship in Scotland.
▲ The first, by John Knox, called also the Knox's Liturgy, was one of the major documents of the Scottish Reformation. It received official sanction in 1564.
▲ The Euchologion or a Book of Common Order (1867), published after a period of liturgical aridity, by the Church Service Society.
▲ The Book of Common Order (1940) was issued by the General Assembly of the Church, and remains to the present the accepted and authoritative standard of worship in Scotland.

BOOK OF COMMON PRAYER

The official liturgy of the Church of England, including, among others, the services of Morning and Evening Prayer and Holy Communion, and the Psalter, Gospels, and Epistles.

BOOK OF CONCORD

The assembled confessions of the Lutheran Church, published in 1580 at Dresden. Taken together, the confessions published in the Book of Concord constitute the doctrinal standard by which Lutheranism defines itself, the norm to which Lutheran Churches and clergymen are pledged, and the official interpretation of the Lutheran relation both to the Roman Catholic tradition and to other churches.

BOOK OF HOURS

Book of prayers to be said at the canonical hours, widely used by laymen during the late Middle Ages. They were often masterpieces of the miniaturist's art; among the most famous are the Rohan and the De Berry Hours.

BOOK OF KELLS

A copy of the gospels from the late 8th century, completed by the monks of Kells in County Meath, Ireland. Its richly elaborate decoration makes it one of the finest examples of medieval illuminated manuscripts. It is now in the library of Trinity College, Dublin.

BOOK OF MORMON

One of the sources of divine revelation for Mormons. The book was first published in 1830 by Joseph Smith, Jr. In 1823 he claimed that a heavenly personale, the Angel Moroni, son of Mormon, led him to the discovery of a set of golden plates on Mount Cumorah, near Palmyra (NY), where Moroni had buried them more than 1,000 years before.

BOOK OF THE COVENANT

A title in Exodus 24:7 referring to that part of the Sinai legislation given to the people by God through Moses (Exodus 20:22; 23:33), although its basic structure represents a blending of typically Israelite law, together with the more elaborate case-law tradition of some older settled population. This latter group has been identified as Canaanite, but is more probably a primitive settlement not fully assimilated to Canaanite culture and tracing its history to the period of the patriarchs.

BOOK OF THE DEAD

Name given to the papyrus placed in the tomb with the mummy in ancient Egypt. It contained prayers, spells and instructions for the spirit of the deceased to help it on its way through the netherworld. It included the appearance of the sun God Ra out of the water of chaos and his subsequent creation of the world. Written in hieroglyphs, the papyri were often illustrated. Several versions found in Egyptian tombs are still in existence in museums and rare book collections.

BOOTH

A rooflike shelter constructed of tree branches and leaves, sometimes with a wooden floor elevated off the ground. In biblical times, during the annual Festival of the Booth at Jerusalem, booths were built on housetops, in courtyards, public squares, even on the Temple grounds and around the roads near Jerusalem. Branches of poplar, olive and oil trees and the leaves of the palm and the fragrant myrtle were used in their construction. This was to remind Israel that God made them dwell in booths when he brought them up out of Egypt (Leviticus 23:34; 40-43).

BORASHAN

In the Old Testament, one of the places that David and his men frequented during his time as a fugitive (1 Samuel 30:30-31).

BORGIA, Saint Francis

(1510-1572) Founder of the Jesuit College in Granada, which was made a university by papal bull. Under his leadership new colleges and provinces were established in Europe.

BORN-AGAIN CHRISTIANS

Term applied predominantly to Fundamentalist Christians who feel themselves regenerated through the experience of being "born again" (John 3:3). Related to the Calvinist doctrine of election, the experience today assumes a revitalist character. Former American president Jimmy Carter proudly claimed the experience. In the late 1970s, citing a decline in morality, born-again Christians became active in United States politics through such organizations as the moral majority and such evangelists as reverend Jerry Falwell.

BOROBUDUR

One of the largest Buddhist monuments, built in the 7th or 8th century on the island of Java, Indonesia. The pyramid-shaped pagoda is built on a hill, with broad terraces leading up to a huge enclosed pinnacled dome or stupa. The inner and outer terrace walls are decorated with relief scriptures, depicting episodes in the life of Buddha.

Crowning a small hill, the great shrine is constructed on dark-gray volcanic stone and has no interior spaces. It rests on a square base 121 m (430 feet) on each side and consists of eight diminishing tiers of terraces connected by stairways. A huge stupa, or bell-shaped dome, rises over 30 m (100 feet) from the uppermost terrace.

The lower five terraces are square, each bounded by a roofless corridor, the walls of which are lined with intricately carved bands of narrative relief. These illustrate the progress of the Bodhisattva (the Buddha before his enlightenment) - a prototype of ideal royalty - in his thriving for all-embracing compassion.

Each terrace shows a phase in his development: the lower scenes are more mundane and contain moral lessons; the higher are more spiritual and are more severe and static in style. Also depicted are many common objects of secular life.

A sense of opulence and tranquility is conveyed through the gently rounded contours of the relief sculpture bearing the influence of Indian Gupta and post-Gupta art.

The upper three terraces are unwalled and circular, intended to represent the sphere of enlightenment. They carry 72 stupas, enclosed in stone latticework that surround the collosal central stupa. All contain large, stonecut Buddha images.

As a summary, in architecture, of Mahayana Buddhist doctrine, the central stupa symbolizes the axis of the world, source both of the universe created through mind and of enlightenment through total self-abnegation and compassion.

BORROMEO, Saint Charles

(1538-1584) Italian Roman Catholic religious reformer. As secretary of state of Pope Pius IV he influenced the Council of Trent. As archbishop of Milan he developed popular children's "Sunday Schools and priests" seminar-

ies, and set a high personal standard of clerical selflessness.

BOTTICELLI, Sandro

(1445-1510) Florentine painter much admired for his archaic realism in the manner of Verrocchio and the Pollaiuli and for his chaste and melancholic types in elaborately designed and expressive panels (*The Magnificat* and *Madonna of the Pomegranate*). In a mature style, classic and intellectual, Botticelli painted *Saint Augustine* (1480), frescoes in the Sistine Chapel (1481-1482), and many other impressive works.

BOUCHARD, James Chrysostom

(1823-1889; also called Wayonika or Swift Foot) The first Native American to become a Roman Catholic priest in the United States.

BOUCHER, Jonathan

(1738-1804) English clergyman who won fame as a royalist in America.

BOUDINOT, Elias

(1802-1839) Cherokee spokesman and newspaper editor who promoted Christianity among his people and collaborated with the missionary Samuel Austin Worcester on biblical translations.

BOURDALOUE, Louis

(1632-1704) Jesuit, held by many to have been the greatest of the 17th century court preachers. He was called the "king of preachers and preacher of kings." His sermons were logical expositions that contained insight into human nature.

BOURGES CATHEDRAL

(1172-1500) One of the most important French cathedrals, having a crypt and two lateral portals (1172) from the Romanesque period. Bourges attains remarkable height through many-storied elevations cresting over the central nave. Most magnificent 13th-century stained glass fills the many-storied windows of the aisles.

BOURNE, Francis

(1861-1935) Archbishop of Westminster who, although lacking the personal magnetism of his predecessors, was a strong leader of Roman Catholics. He was made archbishop of Westminster in 1903.

BOWING

This liturgical gesture involves either a simple inclination of the head, a medium bend of the upper part of the body, or a profound bend from the waist. Bowing is the normal method of communicating devotion and respect. The gesture is used in the liturgy in reverence to the Blessed Sacrament, the altar, the cross, or some person.

Head bows are made during ceremonies to inform the ministers when they are to perform the action. Bowing is a lesser form of reference than genuflecting.

BOW PRIESTHOOD

American Zuni priests, human representatives of the war gods, appointed by the chief priest; who were leaders in war and protected the village. As the executive arm of the religious hierarchy, they take measures against witches and guard against impurities.

BOX ELDER

(1795-1892) American venerated holy man, warrior and chief. Box Elder was the son of Old Horn, a great holy man of the Suhtai band of the Cheyenne. Besides learning sacred knowledge from his father, he was also instructed by the wolves. He possessed gifts of prophecy as well as the ability to summon the spirits and communicate with them.

BOY BISHOP

Widespread custom in the Middle Ages in which a boy was chosen to act as bishop in connection with the Feast of the Holy Innocents on December 28th.

BOZEZ

One of two rocks of toothlike crags associated with Jonathan's victory over the Philistines recorded at 1 Samuel 14:4-14. Jonathan, looking for a passage to cross over to attack the Philistine outpost, saw the two crags, one on the north facing Michmash (where the Philistines encamped), the other on the south facing Geba (1 Samuel 13:16).

BOZKATH

In biblical times, a town in the inheritance of Judah (Joshua 15:39) and home of King Joshua's maternal grandfather Adaiah (2 Kings 22:1).

BOZRAH

In the Old Testament, a prominent city of Edom, the home of the father of Jobab, an Edomite king in the second millennium BC (Genesis 36:31; 1 Chronicles 1:44). Its prominence is evident from the fact that the prophets Isaiah, Jeremiah and Amos under inspiration referred to it as representative of all Edom, due for desolation (Isaiah 34:5; 63:1-4; Jeremiah 49:12-13; Amos 1:11-12).

BRADY, Nicholas

(1659-1726) Anglican clergyman and poet, author, with Nahum Tate, of a well-known metrical version of the Psalms.

BRAHMA

One aspect of the triune God-head of Hinduism, with Vishnu and Shiva. In the Buddhist scriptures the word is used as an adjective meaning holy or God-like, as in the Brahma Viharas.

BRAHMA CARYA

In Buddhism, the pure or chaste holy life, used of the monk. Also used of a layman who takes eight of the Precepts and interprets the third as a vow of chastity.

BRAHMAN

The name given in the Upanishads (elaborations of the Vedas, the earliest sacred writings in India) to the supreme being.

Though a variety of views are

expressed in the Upanishads, they coalesce in regarding Brahman as eternal, conscious, irreducible, infinite, omnipresent, the spiritual source of the universe of finiteness and change. Marked differences in interpretation of Brahman characterize the various sub-schools of Vedanta, the orthodox system of Hindu philosophy based on the writings of the Upanishads.

In early Hindu mythology Brahman (neuter) is personified as the creator god Brahma (masculine) and placed in a triad of divine functions:

▲ Brahma the creator;
▲ Vishnu the preserver;
▲ Shiva the destroyer.

BRAHMANAS

Prose commentaries attached to the Vedas, the most ancient Hindu sacred literature, explaining the significance of the Vedas as used in the ritual sacrifices, and the symbolic import of the priests' actions.

BRAHMANISM

Indian religion based on belief in Brahma, developed about 500 BC from old Dravidan and Aryan beliefs. Its ritual, symbolism and theosophy came from the Brahmanas, sacred writings of the priestly caste, and from the Upanishads. It developed the "divinaly ordered" caste system and gave rise to modern Hinduism.

BRAHMA SAMAJ

Theistic movement within the fold of Hinduism, founded in Calcutta in 1828 by Rammohan Ray. The Brahma Samaj does not accept the authority of the Vedas, has no faith in avataras ("incarnations"), and does not insist on belief in karma (causal effects of past deeds) or rebirth. It discards Hindu rituals and adopts some Christian practices in its worship. Influenced by Islam and Christianity, it denounces polytheism, idol worship and the caste system. The Brahma Samaj has no authoritative canon of its own and relies more on reason than on faith. The society has had considerable suc-cess with its programs of social reform but has never had a significant popular following.

BRAHMA VIHARA

In Buddhism, a term in this connection meaning lordly, or divine. Vihara here means a state of mind. Hence the four "Divine States of mind" which are methods of meditation in which the mind pervades the six corners of the universe with concentrated thoughts of:
1 Metta (love);
2 Karuna (compassion);
3 Mudiota (sympathetic joy);
4   (serenity).

BRAHMIN (BRAHMAN)

Member of the priestly caste of Hindus. This caste, highest of the four varnas into which Hindu society was traditionally divided, is held to have issued from the mouth of Brahma, the inferior castes having come from lesser parts of his body. Only Brahmans can officiate as priests, and they are permitted to interpret the Vedas, the ancient sacred scriptures of Hinduism. But Brahmans may also enter other professions, as many do, without losing caste, and may marry women of other castes.

BRAMANTE, Donato

(1444-1514) Greatest Italian architect of his generation, engineer of domes, trained earlier as painter by Pietro della Francesca and Montegna from whom no doubt he assimilated the spirit of classical simplicity and harmony furthered by his study of Roman ruins. Most famous was Bramante's plan for St. Peter's, a gigantic domed Greek cross plan.

BRANCH THEORY

The view that although the church is in internal schism, with its main segments not in communion with one another, nevertheless those segments, retaining the historic apostolic succession and holding to the faith of the undivided church continue as living branches of the church.

BRAY, Thomas

(1656-1730) An Anglican clergyman who was instrumental in forming the *Society for Promoting Christian Knowledge, the Society for the Propagation of the Gospel in Foreign Parts,* and *Dr. Bray's Associates.*

BREAD

One of the elements used in the eucharist. The kind of bread varies in different churches. In the 11th century the use of unleavened bread was general in the Western Church, whereas the East retained the leavened. Protestant denominations for the most part adopted leavened bread. Symbolic significance can be advanced in support of both practices. Despite the trouble the divergence of use has occasioned between East and West no doctrinal issue was involved in the controversy.

In the Roman Catholic Church, bread is also used in the liturgy for cleansing the fingers of blessed oil, for the offering of a newly consecrated bishop, for an offering to the pope at a solemn canonization, and for the distribution to the faithful in the form of allege.

Several blessings for bread are to be found in the Roman Ritual, including those in honor of certain saints for protection against various hazards to health.

BREAD, Eucharistic

The altar bread used in the liturgy is an unleavened, round wafer made of wheaten flour. It is consecrated during the Eucharistic Prayer and distributed during the Communion Rite at Mass.

BRECK, James Lloyd

(1818-1876) American Episcopal clergyman who established schools and missions in Wisconsin, Minnesota and California. In the 1840s he turned his attention to Christianizing and "civilizing" Ojibwa people in these regions by opening mission stations with religious, educational and agricultural programs.

BRENDAN, Saint

(484-578) Irish monk who, according to the 8th century Voyages of St. Brendan, may have reached America 900 years before Columbus.

BRETHREN, Church of the

Largest of the Brethren churches, originating in 1708 in Germany, when Alexander Mack (1679-1735) and seven others organized a brotherhood. Beginning in 1719, most of the European Brethren left Germany and settled in Germantown, Pennsylvania.

BRETHREN CHURCHES

A group of Protestant churches, originating in Germany in the 18th century. Influenced by Pietism, a 17th century Lutheran movement, and Anabaptism, a 16th-century radical Reformation movement, the Brethren are found primarily in North America and are considered one of the historic "peace churches" because they generally adhere to the principle of conscientious objection in all wars.

BRETHREN COUNCIL

Denomination organized as the Brethren Church in 1883. They gave up certain church traditions, such as the plain dress worn by members, but maintain the independence of the local congregations, and have an educated clergy.

BRETHREN CHURCHES, National Fellowship of

Formed in 1939 after doctrinal disputes had brought about a division within the Brethren Church. It is strictly congregational in church government.

BRETHREN IN CHRIST

Christian Church in the Unites States and Canada, that developed among European settlers along the Susquehanna River in Pennsylvania. The church stands for equality of all members, though the ultimate authority in policy and doctrine is vested in a general conference held annually.

The teachings of the church are generally conservative. It accepts the Bible as the inspired Word of God and final authority for faith and practice. Adult baptism by immersion, partaking of the Lord's Supper, and washing of members' feet are all practiced.

BRETHREN OF THE COMMON LIFE

Religious community established in the late 14th century by Gerhard Groote at Deventer (the Netherlands). Groote, a well-known preacher of penance, formed the Brethren from among his friends and disciples. They formed two communities, one living in the world and the other monastic; this system became the principal exponent of *devotio moderna,* a school and trend of spirituality stressing meditation and the inner life and criticizing the highly speculative spirituality of the 13th and 14th centuries.

The movement was seriously affected by the religious upheaval during the Protestant Reformation, and the Brethren ceased to exist early in the 17th century.

BRETHREN SERVICE COMMISSION

A social service agency organized in 1941 by the Church of the Brethren, an American Protestant denomination.

BRETON, Nicholas

(1553-1625) Prolific English writer of religious and pastoral poems and essays.

BREVIARY

The book of the Divine Office or "Liturgy of the Hours" of the Roman Catholic Church. Vatican Council II called for a revision of the Divine Office, which had remained substantially unchanged since Pius V, who in 1568 had published a revised version of the 11th century breviary. The new breviary (1971) contains the daily service for the canonical hours. The structure of each canonical hour is basically the same: a short introductory prayer followed by a hymn, three psalms, a lesson and concluding prayers.

At present, the breviary contains:
▲ Office of readings,
▲ Morning Prayer,
▲ Daytime Prayer,
▲ Evening Prayer,
▲ Night Prayer.

Men in holy orders and men and women in solemn vows are required by church law to pray the Liturgy of the Hours; all other members of the church are strongly encouraged to do so.

BRHASPATI

In Vedic mythology, lord of spells. He was the preceptor of the gods, the master of sacred wisdom, charms, hymns and rites, and the sage counsellor of Indra in his war against the titans. As such, he is the heavenly prototype of the caste of Brahmins and, most particularly, of the earthly purohita, or family priest.

BRIDGET OF SWEDEN, Saint

(1303-1373) Patron saint of Sweden, founder of the Brigitine Order, and a mystic whose revelations were influential during the Middle Ages.

BRIEF, papal

A letter from the pope, signed with an impression from the fisherman's ring; generally less formal and of less significance than a papal bull. The distinction between the two dates from the 15th century.

BRIGIT OF IRELAND, Saint

(476-524) Virgin and abbess of Kildare, one of the patron saints of Ireland. She founded the first nunnery in Ireland. Brigit gathered other virgins around her and obtained ecclesiastical recognition of their privileged status. Their community became a double abbey for monks and nuns, with the abbess ranking above the abbot.

BRIHADESVARA TEMPLE

(circa 1000) Temple at Thanjavur, southern India, a beautiful example of Chola dynasty (846-1173) temple architecture, which is notable for its architectonic order, sensitive detail and sculpture. Expressing the imperial grandeur of the Cholas, the temple, 160 feet high and replete with many deities in niches at ordered intervals, further evidences the esthetics achievement of the 10th and 11th centuries by which the mandapa, through a pyramidal superstructure is brought into harmony with the sikhara and its cascade of forms.

BRITISH AND FOREIGN BIBLE SOCIETY

First Bible society in the fullest sense, founded in 1804 at the urging of Thomas Charles and members of the Clapham sect, who proposed the idea to the Religious Tract Society in London.

BRITISH MORALISTS

A classification that includes a considerable number of British philosophers and religious writers who dealt with ethical theory and practice from the 17th into the 19th century. They are usually associated with reaction against empiricism in philosophy that developed as an outgrowth of natural science, or with certain attitudes having roots in the Renaissance and Protestant Reformation, or with an effort to ameliorate social and economic conditions.

BROADSTOLE

Not a stole but the name given to the chasuble worn by the deacon. The broad strip of fabric, either purple or black, is worn over the left shoulder and under the right arm by deacons.

BROOKS, Philips

(1835-1893) Episcopal clergyman who won an international reputation for his sermons, and the hymn "O Little Town of Bethlehem." He taught briefly before going to Philadelphia (1859) to become minister of the Church of the Advent. In a later stage of his life, he was minister of the Trinity church in Boston for 22 years. He was consecrated bishop of Massachusetts in 1891.

BROTHER

A term that from New Testament times has been used to indicate a fellow member of the Christian Church as a whole, Christ being "the first-born of many brethren" (Romans 18:29). More specifically, it has also been applied to members of particular Christian sects, societies, or fellowships. The most pointed example of this has been the use of the term from the earliest days of monasticism in both East and West in reference to members of religious communities of men.

After the distinction between clerical and non-clerical religious became more prominent, popular usage often restricted the term to members of non-clerical orders of man (for instance, Christian Brothers), or to members of essentially clerical orders, who happen not to be priests (e.g., novices clerical students, lay brothers).

BROTHERHOOD WEEK

Week observed during February in the United States, to further understanding and communication among people of all races, religions and ethnic backgrounds. Father McMenamin of Denver first promoted the idea of a Brotherhood Day in 1929. The idea was later extended to include an entire week. In the United States it is sponsored by the National Conference of Christians and Jews.

BROTHERS, Religious

Collective title used for laymen or for members of religious orders who do not become priests. The title brother is sometimes used to designate those who are in various stages of formation within a religious community.

BROTHERS, Richard

(1757-1824) Religious fanatic who believed himself to be a descendant of David, "nephew of the Almighty, the prince of Hebrews," and was the first to preach the theory of British Israel.

BROTHERS OF JESUS

Relatives of Jesus who were reluctant to accept him during his lifetime (Mark 3:21, John 7:5) and therefore probably were not among the Twelve Apostles. However, they were important figures in the early church (Acts 1:14), when "brother of the Lord" was probably a title of honor (Corinthians 9:5).

The New Testament names four of them: James, Jonas (or Joseph), Jude, and Simon (Mark 6:3; Matthew 13:55). With some exceptions, Catholic tradition has denied that they were the sons of Mary and Joseph, and has expressed this conviction in the dogma of the perpetual virginity of Mary, defined at a council held at the Lateran in 649.

Other explanations of the meaning of "brother" have varied. Some ancient authorities regarded them as stepbrothers of Jesus, sons of Joseph from an earlier marriage, despite their hesitation to accept the historical value of the apocryphal Protoevangelicum of James (second century) which made a questionable identification of James the Less, son of Alpheus, with James the brother of the Lord. His conclusion that the brothers were cousins of the Jesus gained acceptance in the Western church and is widely known as "the Catholic position."

Many Protestant exegetes have opposed such theories as contrary to the "natural" sense of the Scriptures and dependent on too little early evidence. The biblical texts themselves, however, have not been clear enough to establish consensus between Catholics and many Protestants.

BROTHERS OF THE CHRISTIAN CHURCH, Institute of the

The first religious congregation of male nonclerics in the Roman Catholic Church to devote itself exclusively to schools, learning, and teaching. Founded at Reims (France) in 1684 for the education of boys, especially of poor families, the congregation in the early 1990s numbered more than 20,000 members and was established on all continents.

BROWN, Amelia

(1868-1979) Traditional leader and shaman from the Smith River Rancheria in California who converted to the Indian Shaker religion when she was 70.

BROWNE, Robert

(1550-1633) English Puritan clergyman, leader of a separatist group, the Brownists. he taught independence of the church from secular government and duty to conscience rather than to outward regulation. His writings are considered the first expression of Congregationalism.

BRUGES

Predominantly Catholic city of northwestern Belgium; a Flemish city serving as capital of West Flanders province. The first recorded preaching of Christianity in the area was circa 650 by Saint Eligius of Noyon-Tournai, and Bruges remained part of the Tournai diocese until Paul IV made it a bishopric in 1559.

BRUGES, Holy Blood of

A relic, supposedly a portion of the blood shed by Christ on the cross, in the Basilica of the Precious Blood in Bruges, Belgium. It was brought by Count Diederik of Alsace from Palestine following a crusade, and has been venerated at Bruges, one of several places that have claimed to possess particles of Christ's blood, since 1158. It is kept in a shrine, and its annual procession has attracted crowds since 1303.

BRUNO OF QUERFURT, Saint

(974-1009) Celebrated missionary to the Prussians, bishop and martyr. During his stay in Hungary, he wrote the best of the three extant biographies of Adalbert. He was so successful in converting the pagan Pechenegs, who inhabited the country bwteen the Don and the Danube, that they made peace with Vladimir and were for a while nominal Christians.

BRUNO THE GREAT, Saint

(925-965) Archbishop of Cologne and
coregent of the Holy Roman Empire.
During Otto's absence in Italy for his
imperial coronation (962), Bruno
shared the responsibilities of government and care of the emperor's son,
Otto II. He died on a mission to France
and was buried at St. Pantaleon.

BRUSSELS

Capital of Belgium and Brabant
province. A predominantly Catholic
city, it became in 1961 an archdiocese
with Mechelen, primatial see of
Belgium since 1559. Saint Gery of
Gaugerius (died circa 625) of Cambrai
is credited with founding Brussels by
building a chapel on an island in the
Senne. In the 10th century the relics of
St, Guduka (died circa 712) were taken
to Brussels, and in 1047 placed in the
church of St. Michael. She became
patroness of the city.

BUBER, MARTIN

(1878-1965) Jewish philosopher, born
in Austria. Editor of a major German-
Jewish journal, Der Jude, 1916-1924,
he was a leading educator and scholar
of Hasidism. An ardent Zionist, he
moved to Palestine in 1938. His central
philosophical concept is that of the
direct "I-Thou" relationship between
man and God and man and man.

BUCHAN, ELSPETH

(1738-1799) Religious fanatic and
founder of a Scottish sect called
Buchanites, proclaimed in 1783 that
the Second Coming of Jesus Christ was
at hand, that she herself was the
woman predicted in Revelation 12, and
that reverend Hugh White of Irvine
was her man-child who would rule the
world with a rod of iron.

BUCHANAN, GEORGE

(1506-1582) The foremost Scottish
Humanist, who was an eloquent critic
of corruption and inefficiency in
church and state during the period of
the Reformation in Scotland.

BUCHIS

In Egyptian religion, black bull sacred
to the war god Mentu, or Mont, and
one of Mentu's favorite incarnations.
He is represented with the solar disk
and two tall plumes between his horns
and special markings upon his body.

BUDD, Henry

(1812-1875) The first North American
Indian to be ordained by the Church of
England in 1853. The native missionary, known as an eloquent preacher in
the Cree language, trained teachers and
established a church government.

BUDDHA

In Buddhism, a title, not the name of a
person. The word is derived from the
root budh, "to wake," and means one
who knows in the sense of having
become one with the highest objects of
knowledge (Supreme Truth). There
have been Buddhas in the past and
there will be others in the future.
Gautama, the historical founder of
Buddhism, was born at Lumbini. His
date of birth is not entirely agreed, but
according to modern historical
research, was 563 BC.
Gautama Siddhartha attained the state
of enlightenment at 35 about 2,500
years ago in India. The final goal for all
Buddhists is, irrespective of their
school or stream, to become a Buddha.
Because of the difference of means as
to how to reach this state, Buddhism
has divided into various sects or
schools. In Mahayana Buddhism,
besides the historical Buddha
Shakyamuni, many Buddhas such as
Amitabha (Amida), Mahavairocana
(Dainichi), Vaisajyaguru (Yakushi),
etc., are generally accepted as symbols
of Buddhist teachings.
Being influenced by the concept of the
Pure Land type of Buddhism in Japan
(one becomes a Buddha after rebirth in
the Pure Land), all those who have
passed away are usually called
"Buddhas," or Hotoke in Japanese.

BUDDHA-CARITA

The poetic narrative of the life of Buddha by the Sanskrit poet Asvaghosa, one of the finest examples of Buddhist literature. The author, who lived in North India in the 2nd century, created a loving account of the Buddha's life and teachings, one that is both artistically arranged and restrained in its handling of miracles.

BUDDHA-DHAMMA

The teaching of the Buddha.

BUDDHA GAYA

One of the four holy places of Buddhism; the place where Buddha attained enlightenment.

BUDDHA-GHOSA

(flourished early 5th century) Indian Buddhist scholar, famous for his Visuddjimagga ("Way of Purity"), a summary of current Buddhist doctrines.

BUDDHAHOOD

The state of enlightenment as a buddha.

BUDDHA JAYANTI, year of

Year extending from June 1956 to May 1957; the 2,500th anniversary (according to Theravada chronology) of the death of the Buddha, a holy year that had important political as well as religious implications in the Theravada Buddhist country of Sri Lanka.

BUDDHA-PALITA

(fl. early 5th century) The founder of the Prasangika school of Buddhism, mainly distinguished by its Socratic-like method of argumentation.

BUDDHA RUPA

An image of the Buddha. For 500 years the person of the Buddha was considered too holy to be depicted in the form of an image. At Sanchi, for instance, the symbols of the vacant throne or the footprint are used. Buddha Rupa represents the Blessed One as seated, standing, or recumbent (lying on the right side).

BUDDHA-VAMSA

A section of the sutta pitaka, a collection of early Buddhist texts.

BUDDHI

The vehicle of enlightenment. The faculty of supreme understanding as distinct from the understanding itself. The sixth principle in the sevenfold constitution of man taught in the esoteric schools of Buddhism, and as such the link between the Ultimate Reality and the Mind.

BUDDHISM

The name given by the West to the teachings of Gautama the Buddha, but usually called by his followers the Buddha Dhamma. Buddhism is a way of life, a discipline; not a system of dogmas to be accepted by the intellect. It is a way to live reality, and not ideas concerning the nature of reality.

The Buddha's teaching was not written down for at least 400 years after his death (then mostly by Ceylonese monks from hearsay and fragments). By this time his message became all but inextricable from developments and additions from pre-existing religions, and already 18 schools had evolved from varying interpretations.

In the 5th century BC a great Buddhist council was held in Rajagaha. It resulted in the Pali Canon, a body of scriptures transcribed from the oral tradition of the

Buddha's teaching, together with his rules for monastic life, a collection of his sermons and a metaphysical analysis of his concepts. At a second council held in Vesali in the 4th century BC there was a dispute over the stringency of the monastic rules for obtaining Buddhahood. From this emerged two separate schools of thought, the Hinayana (surviving as Theravada, "Doctrine of the Elders") which elected to adhere to the rules, and the Mahayana ("Large Vehicle"), which adopted a more flexible and expanding approach.

A third council in the third century BC was called by Emperor Asoka, an ardent convert to Buddhism, and as a result of this, Buddhist missionaries were sent throughout India, as well as to Syria, North Africa, Greece, and Ceylon (Sri Lanka), where, in particular, the Buddha's teaching was immediately successful.

BUDDHIST

Nominally, one born into the Buddhist religion, or one who accepts Buddhism as his or her religion by public recitation or Pensil. Actually, one who studies, disseminates and endeavors to live the fundamental principles of the Bhudda-dhamma.

BUDDHIST MONASTICISM

A movement of Buddhist groups pledged to poverty and chastity and historically forming the organizational center of Buddhism, though lay Buddhist associations have emerged in recent years. Buddha is said to have outlined monastic rules for the men who followed him as disciples, and at the request of his foster mother to have founded an order for nuns.

The community of Buddhist monks is known as the Sangha, with the Buddha and the Dharma (Buddha's teaching) one of the three valued components of Buddhism. For those who joined Buddha's monastic order the traditional caste distinctions were eliminated.

Any male might join, provided he was not sick, disabled, a criminal, a soldier, a debtor, or a minor lacking parental consent. Monks were required to wear the yellow robe, shave their heads, carry the begging bowl, meditate daily, make an initiate's confession, and obey certain precepts.

The monasteries came to be the center of Buddhist life and especially important for Hinayana Buddhism, the prevailing form in Sri Lanka, Burma (Myanmar), Thailand, Laos, Vietnam, and Cambodia.

They have been the intellectual centers of Buddhism, and taking a strong role in society they have sometimes been important political centers.

Prior to the 1950 takeover by China the monks of Tibet held total political power. Generally Buddhist laymen support the monks in return for religious instruction, with laymen commonly spending some months at a monastery.

BUDDHIST MYSTICISM

The sense of direct experience or awareness of divine or cosmic Being in the context of the Buddhist religion; it is characterized by emphasis on knowledge of Being rather that on union or absorption of self into Being. The goal of Buddhist mysticism and all its meditational techniques is to enable the practitioner to come closer to his being, a process that, in its fulfillment, is considered to be an enrichment of the personality with a corresponding loss of fear and anxiety, generally referred to as "liberation." It is a sort of self-actualization that, in its final states, is variously conceived in the different schools of Buddhism.

BUDDHIST MYTHOLOGY

The numerous legends, myths, and tales that have played an essential and all-pervading role in the history of Buddhism. Buddhist mythology, which became very complex in the classical Mahayana period (about 100 BC to AD 800), has included myths concerning the historical Buddha, Sidhartha Gautama, and myths concerning celestial buddhas and bodhisattvas ("buddhas to be"); but fundamental to the mythology is the simple story of Gautama's attainment of enlightenment, or nirvana, despite a variety of temptations brought forth by an evil tempter named Mara.

BUDDHIST PHILOSOPHY

A system of thought and set of ethical norms. In India Buddhism has been regarded as both a philosophy (darsana) and a religion (dharma). Although it was never simply a rationalistic philosophy achieved by ratiocination alone, it developed a variety of speculative systems in various Asian countries.

BUDDHIST SACRED LITERATURE

Religious texts of the major forms of Buddhism. These include what are claimed to be the original discourses of the Buddha, basic doctrinal works and commentaries, regulations for the monastic life, and manuals of meditation techniques.

BUGIA

A small candlestick with a short handle. It is held near the Missal at the Mass of a bishop or of certain other church dignitaries. It came into use at a time when additional candlelight for reading from the book was helpful; its use was abolished from the liturgy in 1968.

BUKA CULT

A Melanesian religious cult founded in the 1930s.

BUKHARI, al-

Very famous compiler of hadith whose collection, entitled the Sahih meaning the sound, true or authentic, was culled from a huge corpus of about 600,000 traditions. Al-Bukhari's Sahih is often esteemed by Muslims as second only to the Koran itself. During his lifetime he travelled throughout much of the Islamic world in search of traditions.

BUKRA

The ordinary word for the East Syrian eucharistic bread, a cake about two inches in diameter and a half inch thick, stamped with a large central cross and four small crosses, leavened, with a little salt and oil added.

BULGARIA, Church of

The territory which was to become Bulgaria was widely Christianized during the early centuries of the church. It embraced numerous episcopal sees, was distinguished by many martyrs, and a famous council was held during the Arian controversy at Sardica (now Sofia) in 343.

But successive waves of invaders from the fifth century to the seventh century practically destroyed Christian life and church organization in the land. A new start was therefore necessary when the territory was settled by Slavic tribes and was consolidated politically by the Proto-Bulgarians (late seventh century), a warrior race of Central Asian origin, akin to the Huns.

Although there was constant contact with Christianity, the formal conversion of the Bulgarian State did not occur until 864 when Khan Boris accepted baptism from Constantinople.

BULGARIA, Orthodox Church of

One of the national churches of the Eastern Orthodox communion. Christianity was introduced to Bulgaria in 864 by King Boris I. While Constantinople refused to grant him a patriarch, it did send an archbishop, and, for several years, St. Clement, a disciple of the missionary saints Cyril and Methodius, trained a large number of Slavs for the ministry, thus preparing the ground for a national church.

After a rather obscure period, the Bulgarian patriarchate was revised in 1235 by Tsar Ivan Asen II, but with the fall of Trnova and Eftimi, was exiled and the patriarchate ceased to exist. Only in the past decade a real survival of an independent Bulgarian Orthodox Church has been noted.

BULGARIAN CATHOLIC CHURCH

An Eastern Catholic church of the Byzantine Rite, in communion with Rome since 1859. In the late 1880s most of the faithful returned to the Orthodox Church of Bulgaria.

BULGARIAN HERETICS

Also known as Bogomils, a dualist sect that began in Bulgaria and spread throughout the Balkans between the 10th and 14th centuries. They took their name from the Bulgarian translation of the Greek Theophile (pleasing to God) and their founder, a certain Jeremiah who called himself Pope Bogomil.

BULL, Papal

The most important document issued by the pope, sealed with a disk of lead called a bulla from which it gains its name. Each bishop is appointed by a papal bull.

BULL CULT

Prehistoric religious practice originating in the western Aegean and extending from the Indus valley of Pakistan to the Danube in eastern Europe. The bull god's symbol was the phallus, and in the east the bull was often depicted as the partner of the great goddess of fertility, thereby representing the virile principle of generation and invincible force.

BULTMANN, Rudolf

(1884-1976) German theologian who advocated "demythologizing" the New Testament and reinterpreting it in existentialist terms. He developed a critical approach to the Gospels, studying the oral tradition behind them.

BUNDAHISHN

A religio-philosophical work written in Pahlavi or Middle Persian dealing with Persian cosmology and cosmogony. It covers the creation of man, animals, and plants, and the long struggle and the stages of the struggle between Ahura Mazda and Ahriman. It includes the destruction of the world, and the rule of Ahura Mazda.

BURAQ, al-

Name of the mount on which Mohammed, in the company of the angel Jibril made his famous isra to Jerusalem; and thence the mi-rah to Paradise, before returning in the same way; the journey was accomplished all in one night. In appearance, al-Buraq resembled a kind of small winged horse and is sometimes portrayed with a human face, for example, in Indian scriptures of the celestial mount, and in some produced in Harat.

BURHANIYYA

Popular sufi order in Egypt, especially in Cairo.

BURIAL, Biblical

The Bible records different methods of burial but in Syria and Palestine inhumation was preferred to cremation. The corpse was washed, anointed, dressed in clothes of everyday life until a later period when the death shroud or linen wrappings became common.

The burial took place within 24 hours because of the danger of rapid decomposition in the warm climate. The corpse was carried by friends amid their lamentations and those of hired mourners. There was no set ritual at the grave with the exception of an occasional eulogy.

The mourning period differed depending upon the rank of the deceased and his or her relationship with the mourners, but it was usually 7 days. Mourners rent their garments and wore outer garments cut and unbound for 30 days, fasted, beat their breasts, sprinkled ashes on their heads, went barefoot and bareheaded.

The fast on the day of burial concluded with a meal called funeral baked meats and in the Old Testament lehem ohnim (bread of mourners). It was also customary to visit the grave and eat a meal there on the sabbath after the burial.

BURIAL, Christian

The interment of a deceased person in consecrated ground after the funeral rites in which "the Church asks spiritual assistance for the departed, honors their bodies, and at the same time brings the solace of hope to the living". Code of Canon Law forbids ecclesiastical burial for certain persons, such as notorious apostates or public sinners, who have not given some signs of repentance.

Ancient Christian

Contrary to the pagan conviction that proper burial was essential for an individual's happiness in the afterlife, the early Christians insisted that this was not so. Nevertheless, out of reverence for the body as a temple of the Holy Spirit and in view of the future resurrection, they were zealous in their care for the dead.

The first Christians naturally followed Jewish burial traditions, but these were later modified under the influence of local practices and Christian hope. When a person died, his eyes and mouth were closed, his body washed, anointed, and wrapped in linen as a sign of immortality. It could then be dressed in the clothes worn during life.

For pagans and Jews death was the occasion for loud and even violent cries of grief. Christians were accustomed to obviate such outbursts by the recitation of psalms.

Burial could take place on the day of death or the following day. A wake could be held at the home, church, or graveside before or after burial. When the time came for the interment, the body was placed on a bier and carried in a kind of triumphal procession to the place of burial, which could be a grave dug in the ground or in a natural or artificial crypt.

An eucology was pronounced either in the church or at the side of the grave by a relative, friend, or cleric. Like the Jews before them, the early Christians never cremated but always buried their dead.

BURIAL, Greco-Roman

Disposal of the dead included both inhumation and cremation but the use of either, varying from age to age, does not seem to have been the result of different eschatalogical beliefs as much as the prevalence of local custom or simply practicality.

What was most important was that the remains of the person, whether cremated or not, had to be covered with earth. The Greek symbolic burial required three handfuls of earth sprinkled on the body; the Roman law stipulated that burial was not official until no bone was showing above the earth or until the body was enclosed in some vault that kept it out or sight.

This practice was thought to assure the passage of the departed to the underworld and prevent the displeasure of the celestial gods whose responsibility for them ceased at the moment of death.

The burial rite for the average Greek or Roman had few variations. Immediately after death, the corpse was cleansed, dressed in everyday attire, placed on a bed, and formally mourned. Then came the funeral procession to some location outside the city designated for burial, for instance, along the side of the road.

In early Rome, the burial place was sometimes on the land worked by the deceased. The deceased was then buried in the ground or in a vault in a coffin or, if cremated, his ashes were interred in a burial urn.

In Greece, offerings at the grave were made on the third and ninth days after burial. In Rome, the period of strict mourning was concluded after the ninth day's offering. In many locales, there was an annual family reunion and meal at the grave to renew by a symbolic, common meal the bond of brotherhood that had existed while the deceased was alive.

More elaborate ceremonies attended the burial of distinguished citizens with differences characteristic of each nation and epoch. Taking part in the funerals of important Roman officials were the general public, invited guests, a long masked retinue representing the ancestors of the deceased, professional women mourners, and musicians. It was the classical belief that for survival in the underworld the deceased have the same material needs as they had while still alive.

BURIAL CUSTOMS

Funeral or burial customs can be traced back some 50,000 years. Neanderthal man was the first to practice careful disposal of the dead. Throughout the ages, the methods and rituals used have been mainly determined by religious beliefs, especially belief in life after death.

Primitive man saw the need to heal the emotional shock suffered by the family or the community on the loss of one of its members; and showed his desire to honor the dead and to assist the swift

The burial of Christ.
"Now in the place where he was crucified there was a garden, and in the garden a new
sepulchre, wherein was never man yet laid" (John 19:41).
Lithograph by Gustave Doré (about 1860).

BURIAL CUSTOMS

passage of the spirit to the world beyond.

By the end of the Old Stone Age, grave-goods (things that might be needed in the next world and on the journey there) were being buried with the dead, a practice reaching its most elaborate form with the ancient Egyptians.

Some people also killed the cattle, slaves and favorite wife of the dead man so that they could serve him in the next world. The Hindu practice of Suttee (the sacrifice of the widow on her husband's funeral pyre) was prompted by the same motive.

In many parts of ancient Europe, carts or chariots were placed in the tombs of kings and chiefs. Scandinavian warriors were often buried in their ships.

BURIAL, Methods of Disposal

Methods of disposal, sometimes influenced by ecological factors, have varied greatly, from burial in a tomb or vault to ritual cannibalism.

In burial, posture and orientation are often important. Muslims are laid on the right side, facing Mecca. The Japanese are sat upright in their tubshaped coffins. In England, Christians are usually buried with their feet to the east.

Cremation, a worldwide practice, is often followed by some secondarily disposal such as scattering the ashes (in the case of Hindus, on a holy river).

Parsees, followers of Zoroastrianism, expose their dead on "towers of silence" where they are eaten by vultures. Some American tribes used similar methods.

Preservation, associated particularly with the ancient Egyptians, is represented today by embalming.

Burial in the earth and cremation are the most common methods of disposing of the dead, although cremation is sometimes opposed on religious grounds, notably by the Roman Catholic Church.

Prayers for the soul of the departed and consolation for the living are the chief features of Christian funeral services. In Jewish services, the beauty and wonder of life, death and the whole of nature are emphasized.

BURSE

The corporal is carried to and from the altar in a small square pocket about 12 inches square covered with the same fabric and color as the vestments. This small square, known as a burse, is not often used today. The corporal is a square piece of linen on which the bread and wine are placed.

BURUJ, al-

The title of the 85th sura of the Koran; it means "The Constellations" or "The Signs of the Zodiac." The sura belongs to the Meccan period and contains 22 verses. The title is drawn from the oath in the first verse. The early part of the sura makes reference to "the people of the pit" who have been variously identified. The sura goes on to warn that those who persecute the believers and do not repent will burn in hell fire.

BUSHNELL, Horace

(1802-1876) Congregational minister and controversial theologian, sometimes called "the father of American religious liberalism." He stood between the orthodox tradition of Puritan New England and the new romantic impulses represented by Ralph Waldo Emerson, Samuel Taylor Coleridge, and especially Friedrich Schleiermacher.

BUSIRIS

In Greek mythology, Egyptian king, son of Poseidon (the god of the sea) and Lyssianasa (daughter of Epaphus, a legendary king of Egypt).

BUTLER, Joseph

(1692-1752) English bishop, moral philosopher, preacher in the royal court, and influential author who defended religion against the nationalists of his time. Among the many thinkers subsequently influenced by his arguments in favor of traditional theology was the Roman Catholic cardinal John Henry Newman (1801-90).

BUTSUDAN

Buddhist family altar found in Japanese homes, usually in addition to the Shinto kamidana ("god shelf"). The Buddhist altar generally contains memorial tablets for dead ancestors and, in accordance with sect affiliation, representations of various Buddhist divinities.

BUYIDS

Major dynasty in medieval Islamic history which flourished in Persia and Iraq between 932 and 1062. Ethnically they were Daylamites; religiously they were Shiite, possible of the Zaydi persuasion. Whatever their own beliefs, however, they exercised a considerable tolerance towards other branches of Islam.

BYBLOS

An ancient seaport in Beirut (Lebanon); it is possibly the oldest continuously inhabited town in the world. Excavations reveal that Byblos was occupied at least by the Neolithic Period (circa 8,000 - circa 4,000 BC).

The crusaders captured the town in 1103 and called it Gibelet, but they later lost it to the Ayyubid sultan Saladin in 1189.

BYZANTINE ART

An amalgam of styles, Christian, Roman, and Greek with strong Eastern modification, developed under royal patronage at Constantinople, new capital of the Roman Empire (330), and distinguished for magnificence of material and excellence of craftsmanship.

The Constantinian Period (330-378) is a synthesis of Hellenism, Christianity, and the Orient with new perforated surface decoration, in lacelike designs.

In the Justinian Period, "First Golden Age" (518-610), painting, mosaic, and sculpture having been destroyed by iconoclasts, evidences are chiefly architectural in the grandiose, domed Aya Sofya (Hagia Sophia) - greatest of Byzantine achievements, the church of Sergius and Bacchus and many other churches.

Manuscripts of importance show classical naturalism in the Vienna Genesis (5th century), and the 7th-century Joshua Roll (Vatican). The Oriental style reached its apogee in silks with a strong Persian influence.

The Macedonian Renaissance (867-1056), a "Second Golden Age," shows Justinian types of Nea Ecclesia, Basil I's court church (881), with central dome and domed cross-arm bays and a synthesis of provincial types smaller, more slender with decorative masonry (Saint Marc's, Venice, Mount Athos).

Most important Paleologan masterworks are frescoes from two major schools in Salonika and Constantinople. At Kariye-Djami (church of the Chora) is the exciting fresco, *The Anastasis* (1310-1320), in a new Byzantine Renaissance. The Byzantine achievement, both worldly and humanistic in nature, was a formative influence in many lands from Greece to Russia.

BYZANTINE CHANT

The monophonic (i.e., single line of melody) liturgical chant of the Greek Orthodox Church during the Byzantine Empire (330-1453) down to the 16th century; in modern Greece the term refers to ecclesiastical music of any period.

BYZANTINE CHURCH

Term often used for churches, singly or collectively, which derive from the church of the Byzantine Empire. In current usage it could refer to the Orthodox Churches united in Constantinople, or incorrectly to the Eastern Catholics of the Byzantine Rite, but more precisely, it applies to the Church that existed in the Byzantine Empire from the fourth century to 1453.

The acceptance of Christianity by Constantine and his establishment of the imperial capital at Constantinople, the "New Rome" (330), mark the beginnings of the Byzantine Church. In the East Roman or Byzantine view, when the Roman Empire became

Christian the perfect world order willed by God had been achieved: one universal empire was sovereign, and coterminus with it was the one universal church.

The patriarch of the imperial capital gradually and by a natural process became the leading bishop in the empire, rescinding from the special position of Rome. Elected by a synod of bishops, he was then officially promoted by the emperor, who had usually already suggested his name.

Often the second person in the state, the patriarch of Constantinople headed a vast curia and other bishops who resided in Constantinople constituted a permanent synod, which became the real governing body of the church.

The Byzantine Church was profoundly affected by the theological conflicts of the early centuries. Arianism was important not so much as a dogmatic deviation but as the precedent it set for constant imperial interference in ecclesiastical matters, most of it occasioned by intriguing bishops. The controversies caused by Nestorianism, Monophysitism, and Monothelitism produced more serious and long-lasting results. While primarily doctrinal, they were complicated by imperial attempts to dictate dogma and rivalry among prominent bishops.

Gradually, the Byzantine Church split into two factions, generally referred to as the moderate and the extremist, a division that plagued the church's history and sometimes led to actual schisms.

The real tragedy of the Byzantine Church seems to be that it became merely the Byzantine Church; it merged itself with the empire not only administratively but also psychologically. Its bishops found it difficult to think in terms of a Christianity without an emperor.

In December, 1452, with the threat of Turkish invasion, one final effort at union was made by the Catholic Emperor Constantine XII and Cardinal Isidore, the papal legate. Despite all opposition they solemnly proclaimed reunion, but six months later the Byzantine Empire fell to the Turks, and Muslim domination divided East from West in a way that fostered the development of two separate churches.

BYZANTINE CIVILIZATION

Byzantine civilization may be defined as the imperial administrative tradition, the social and economic character, the ecclesiastical and monastic influence, and the educational and artistic contributions that accompanied the rise and fall of Constantinople (527-1453).

The policy of Byzantium was marked by a close working interdependence of church and state which is quite evident in its imperial administrative tradition. When crowned by the patriarch of Constantinople, the emperor declared his adherence to orthodox teaching and promised to safeguard the tradition of the church.

The empire was always ruled by a monarch whose authority was a temporal expression of divine power. He was therefore autonomous as lawgiver, judge, administrator, and commander-in-chief. Though originally elected by the people, the army was most often the key to his election. He choose his successor from his own family and could not be removed by rebellion or abdication.

His responsibility to expand the well-being of the church is reflected in the daily court ceremonial. Byzantine law was very much influenced by Roman law, the 6th century collection of Justinian and the 9th century Greek complication, the basilica.

Having survived the difficult theological controversies of the 4th, 5th, and 6th centuries, the patriarch of Constantinople began a very successful missionary program in the 9th century in Central Europe and the Balkans. While Rome was evangelizing the lands of Moravia, Constantinople established the church in Serbia, Bulgaria, and Russia, and had a profound cultural influence on Slavonic peoples.

After the long struggle between Rome

and Constantinople with its continuing schisms the Orthodox Church became autonomous and was the mainstay of Byzantine culture after the empire had succumbed to Turkey.

One of the reasons for this was the impact of monastic life throughout the Orthodox Church. Monks were detached from the temporal order, but their houses gave hospitality to the stranger, cared for the sick, sheltered political outcasts, were schools for future bishops and ecclesiastics, and provided special advice and ideals for the whole empire. This was their greatest strength in resisting invaders from the East.

BYZANTINE EMPIRE

The continuation of the later Roman Empire in the East lasting until 1453, centered around Constantinople and consisting essentially of Asia Minor, the Balkans, Greece, and parts of southern Italy.

The adoption of Christianity and the establishment of the capital at Constantinople by Constantine the Great (330) began a transitional period lasting until the end of the 7th century.

Despite the Western reconquests of Justinian I (527-565), the empire became more oriented toward the East and less Roman in its outlook and institutions. It evolved into a highly centralized, bureaucratic state, Greek in language and culture, and Orthodox Christian in religion.

BYZANTINE LITURGY

The liturgy of the patriarchate of Constantinople, adopted by the 12th century in the other ancient Eastern patriarchates in communion with Constantinople, as well as in the former Orthodox groups now united with Rome and the Italo-Greek communities of Sicily and southern Italy. The composition of the Divine Office, with its hymnody and strophic pieces found now also in the Eucharistic Liturgy, is essentially that which the monks of Constantinople gradually adopted from Palestinian monasteries.

The ritual for the administration of the sacraments, for monastic rites, funerals, blessings, and other ceremonies owes much to the usages of Antioch, but the nuptial rites are essentially Constantinopolitan.

The Eucharistic Liturgies used today are three:

▲ that of St. John Chrysostom (the one usually celebrated);
▲ that of St. Basil (celebrated 10 times a year);
▲ that of the Presanctified (the only liturgy permitted on fast days of Lent).

While the Byzantine priest is behind the iconostasis, he recites most of the liturgical prayers in a low voice, singing only the final words, and outside the screen, the liturgical action continues with the cantors' singing and with diaconal invocations to which the people respond.

The liturgies of St. John Chrysostom and of St. Basil are identical today except for four prayers of the anaphora of which only the ekphoneseis are heard, along with a few changes affecting the deacon and the cantors.

The seven Byzantine sacramental mysteries correspond to the seven Roman sacraments, although the ceremonies are often quite different. Baptism is conferred by a triple total immersion and a declarative Trinitarian formula, and is immediately followed by myroma (the rough equivalent of confirmation), the ceremony being conducted by communion, with wine alone if the neophyte is an infant.

BYZANTINE PHILOSOPHY

The philosophy that flourished in the Byzantine Empire. It was characterized by the study of Plato, Aristotle, and the Neoplatonists in the schools and its application in theology. The 4th century Fathers - Basil, Gregory of Nazianzus, and Gregory of Nyssa - set the pattern for the future by expressing Christian doctrine in philosophical terms, not as apologetic, but to instruct those within the church and to elucidate Trinitarian theology.

Thus the church countered heresies

such as Arianism and later Monophysitism and Monothelitism which were influenced by Neoplatonic concepts of a celestial hierarchy.

BYZANTINE RITE

The system of liturgical practices and discipline observed by the Eastern Orthodox Church, and the Eastern Rite Bulgarian, Greek, Georgian, Italo-Albanian, Melchite, Rumanian, Russian, Rutjenian and Ukranian churches, who are in communion with Rome.

Of the three liturgies in use by Byzantine Rite churches, the liturgy of St. John Crysostom is celebrated most frequently and is the normal church service.

BYZANTINE THEOLOGY

Byzantine theology can be defined as the theology developed in the Byzantine Empire from the Council of Chalcedon (451) to the empire's fall in 1453. The older Syrian and Egyptian theological centers became separated from Byzantium as a result of Chalcedon and, later, because of the Muslim conquests.

The Latin West also gradually lost contact with the empire. Basing itself, then, on its patristic and conciliar heritage, the Byzantine mind created a theology that can be called specifically Byzantine, and which is still viewed as normative for the Orthodox Church.

Byzantine theology tends to regard the visible world as a manifestation, an icon of the invisible world, which alone can satisfy man. This supernatural reality is a mystery and thus incomprehensible to the soul still imprisoned in matter.

There is no place for the rational investigation of the mysteries of revelation. The Byzantines were not interested in speculation nor in positive theological systems, but generally limited themselves to correcting doctrinal distortions. They were reluctant to define dogma unless necessary, but they did hold theologoumena, truths generally accepted without being imposed as articles of faith at all.

The sources of Byzantine theology are scriptures and tradition. Scriptural exegesis is that of the Fathers of the Church, usually preserved in catenae, and is largely typological or allegorical, focusing on the hidden or spiritual meaning of a text. Tradition comprises the creeds, conciliar definitions, certain synods, and the Fathers, to which may be added the liturgy and ascetical works.

C

CABALA

(Hebrew: tradition) A body of esoteric Jewish mystical doctrines dealing with the manifestatioons of God and His revelation. The Cabala attaches mystical significance to every detail in the Torah. Its chief books are the Sefer Yezirah (Book of Creation, 3rd-6th centuries) and the Sefer HaZohar (Book of Splendor; 13th century). The Cabala arose in France and Spain in the Middle Ages and was later a major influence on Hasidism.

CABALLERO, Antonio

(1602-1669) Founder of Franciscan missions in China. Caballero was ordained in 1626, entered China in 1633, left under duress but returned as prefect apostolic in 1649. He baptized about 3,000 converts, established churches throughout Chi-nan and Shan-tung, and was banished in 1665.

CABASILAS, Nicolas

(1320-1391) Noted theologian, liturgist, and spiritual writer of Thessalonica. He studied under his uncle Nilus Cabasilas with whom he is often confused. One of his best known works is a thorough theological commentary on the various rites and ritual formulas of the Byzantine Eucharistic Liturgies.

His *Life of Christ,* consisting of seven books, is a remarkable treatise in ascetical and mystical theology. In it Cabasilas develops the elements and dynamic of spiritual life, treats of the meaning of human cooperation under divine grace, and of the divine causality in the effectiveness of the sacraments.

CABASILAS, Nilus

(1298-1363) Greek orthodox metropolitan, theologian, and scholar, whose treatises critical of medieval Latin theology became classical apologies for the Orthodox tradition of the Byzantine Church. His support of Greek monastic spirituality furthered the ascetical tradition in the Eastern Church.

Cabasilas' principal work was a voluminous *On the Procession of the Holy Spirit,* in which he presented the Greek orthodox speculative view of the Trinity (one God in three persons), emphasizing the question of the Holy Spirit's coming forth from the Father. Rejecting the variant position of the Latin church, as summarized by Aquinas, the book became a standard apologetic text for Eastern Orthodoxy.

CABRERA, Juan Baptista

(1837-1916) Leader of the evangelical movement in Spain, he entered the Clerks Regular of Valencia in 1852 and was ordained in 1862. After teaching for a time he retired to Gibraltar, where he became a Protestant. He returned to Spain to minister after the revolution of 1868 and was consecrated bishop of the Spanish Reformed Church in 1894.

CABRERA, Pablo

(1857-1936) Argentine priest, historian. His knowledge of scholarly material gained through fine historical research made his contribution invaluable. He was a self-taught scholar, considered a genius. Cabrera published 450 books, monographs and articles.

CABRINI, Saint Frances Xavier

(1850-1917) Italian-American nun, first US citizen to be canonized (1946). She founded the Missionary Sisters of the sacred Heart in 1880, and established 67 houses of the order throughout the world. In 1889 she immigrated to New York from Italy.

Her earliest missionary dream was of saving souls in China, but she was sidetracked to the Unites States by her local bishop, who was aware of the desperate needs of Italian emigrants.

CACIQUE

Infigenous American term from the Arawak language meaning a priest-chief. The cacique holds office for life and has a staff as badge of authority.

CADAVERIC COUNCIL

Synod convoked at Rome in 897 at the insistence of Lambert of Spoleto who was infuriated by the coronation of King Arnulf as emperor, which Pope Formosus had performed in 896.

Having reestablished his political power over Rome, Lambert sought to invalidate what the pope had done. The subservient council did as Lambert demanded. It declared the acts of Formosus null and void; it had the body of Formosus, then 9 months dead, exhumed, outraged with a mock trial, and then thrown into the Tiber.

CADMUS

In Greek mythology, the son of Phoenix or Agenor (king of Phoenicia) and brother of Europa. Europa was carried off by Zeus, king of the gods, and Cadmus was sent out to find her. Unsuccessful, he consulted the Delphic oracle, which ordered him to give up his quest, follow a cow, and build a town on the spot where she lay down. The cow guided him to Boeotia, where he founded the city of Thebes.

CADOC, Saint

(505-570) Welsh bishop venerated as a martyr. He is traditionally recognized as the founder of monasteries in Wales and Scotland, the most famous being Llancarfan in Wales. Accounts of miracles and strange happenings abound in the stories told about him. Because of conflicting and frequently unrealistic accounts it is impossible to verify historically anything except some basic facts of his life.

CADOUIN, Abbey of

French Cistercian abbey in Périgord, founded (1115) by followers of Robert d'Arbrissel. It was taken over by Cistercians from Pontigny (1119). The abbey, destroyed during the 15th century, was rebuilt by Louis XI, but languished under commendatory abbots after 1516. Although reformed in 1643, Cadouin numbered only 4 monks when it was suppressed in 1790.

CAECILIAN

(267-344) Bishop of Carthage whose consecration was repudiated by Donatists. Archdeacon of Carthage and successor to Mensurius as bishop after the cessation of the persecution under Diocletian (311), Caecilian met opposition for two reasons: the Numidian bishops led by Donatus, were delayed and thus not able to give their assent to his election, as custom demanded, and his consecrators, especially Felix of Aptunga, were allegedly traditores.

Holding a synod at Carthage, the Numidians elected the lector Majorinus as a rival bishop to Caecilian. Thus began the long Donatist Schism. The Synods of Rome (313) and Arles (314), as well as the imperial government, confirmed Caecilian in his post. Caecilian was the one African bishop present at the Council of Nicaea in 325.

CAEDMON

(628-680) First Old English Christian poet, whose fragmentary hymn to the creation remains a symbol of the great revolution in English vernacular poetry; i.e. the adaptation of the aristocratic-heroic Anglo-Saxon verse tradition to the expression of Christian themes. His story is known from Bede's *Ecclesiastical History of the English People.*

CAEDMON MANUSCRIPT

Old English scriptural paraphrases copied circa 1000, given in 1651 to the scholar Franciscus Junius by Archbishop James Usher of Armagh, and now in the Bodleian Library. It contains the poems *Genesis, Exodus, Daniel,* and *Christ and Satan,* originally attributed to Caedmon because these subjects correspond roughly to the list of subjects described in Bede's *Ecclesiastical History* as having been rendered by Caedmon into vernacular verse.

CAELICOLAE

Heaven-worshippers, the members of a late-4th and 5th centuries cult in North Africa. St. Augustine in 397 mentions encountering them at Tubersicum, and that they had an elder and a new kind of baptism. In 409 the Emperor Honorius passed a law against them. Whether they were Christians, Jews, or did in fact worship the heavens, is unknown.

CAESAREA

Ancient port and administrative city of Palestine, on the Mediterranean coast of Israel south of Haifa. Originally an ancient Phoenician settlement known as Straton's Tower, it was rebuilt and enlarged by Herod the Great, king of Judaea under the Romans, and renamed for his patron, the emperor Augustus Caesar. The city became the capital of the roman province of Judaea in AD 6. Subsequently, it was an important center of early Christianity; in the New Testament it is mentioned in Acts in connection with Peter, Philip the Apostle, and, especially, Paul, who was imprisoned there before being sent to Rome for trial.

CAESARIUS OF ARLES, Saint

(470-542) Abbot, archbishop, who succeeded to the see of Arles (502) after his kinsman Eonus who had ordained him. As vicar of Gaul and Spain, he had proved benevolent and prudent. First Western prelate to receive the pallium (513), in his 40-year episcopate he convoked numerous synods and councils, for which he composed most of their decrees. He introduced the hours of Terce, Sext and None, and encouraged the insertion of hymns in the Office. Caesarius' numerous *Sermons* are well regarded by modern scholars especially for their pastoral concern.

CAESAROPAPISM

The concept of government in which the supreme lay ruler (Caesar) also exercises supreme authority over the church. The term is often, although erroneously, applied to the form of government in the Byzantine Empire. It is true that the Christian emperor was regarded as God's vicar on earth, whose duty it was care for his subjects' temporal and spiritual welfare, which meant that he had to oversee the proper functioning of the church.

He made and enforced ecclestical regulations, convoked synods, appointed and deposed bishops, but was not supposed to intervene in doctrinal or liturgical matters.

Several emperors, however, actually did intrude in doctrinal questions, of which the best and most frequently cited example is Justinian (527-565). But especially after the iconoclastic controversy of the 8th century, the emperors did not so intervene.

CAHENSLY, Peter Paul

(1838-1923) Successful German merchant who helped establish the St. Raphael Society for the purpose of preserving the Catholic faith among European emigrants to the United States of America and other countries. This movement, often referred to as Cahenslyism, was judged, mistakenly, to have as its objective the buttressing of Germanic culture and rule and not the preservation of the faith.

CAIAPHAS, Joseph

High Priest during Jesus' ministry (Luke 3:2). He was the son-in-law of High Priest Annas (John 18:13) and was appointed to office by the predecessor of Pontius Pilate, Valerius Gratus, about AD 18. He held the office until the year 36 or 37, longer than any of his immediate predecessors, this being due to his skillful diplomacy and cooperation with Roman rule. He and Pilate were reportedly good friends. Caiaphas was a sadducee.

CAIN

In the Old Testament, first-born son of Adam and Eve, who murdered his brother Abel (Genesis 4:1-16). Cain, a farmer, became enraged when the Lord accepted the offering of his brother Abel, a shepherd, in preference to his own. He murdered Abel and was banished by the Lord from the settled country. He built a city and named it Enoch for his son (Genesis 4:17).

According to St. Irenaeus and other early writers, a Gnostic sect called Cainites existed in the second century AD. They believed that Cain derived his existence from the superior power, while Abel derived his existence from an inferior power.

CAINITES

An heretical Gnostic sect - i.e., a group of religious dualists who believed that matter was evil and the spirit good and that salvation was attained by esoteric knowledge, or gnosis, taught by Christ. The sect flourished during the second century AD, probably in the eastern area of the Roman Empire. The Christian theologian Origen (2nd-3rd century) declared that the Cainites had "entirely abandoned Jesus." Their reinterpretation of Old Testament texts reflected the view that Yaweh (the God of the Jews) was evil because his creation of the world was perversely designed to prevent the reunion of the divine element in man with the unknown perfect God.

CAITANYA MOVEMENT

An intensely emotional form of Hinduism, that has flourished from the 16th century, mainly in Bengal and eastern Orissa. The possible feelings of a worshipper toward the Lord were classified into five progressively superior states of feeling:

1 santa, characterized as calm meditation;
2 dasya, a servitude, the kind of faithfulness felt by a servant for his master or a younger relative for his elder;
3 sakhya, or friendship, the emotion aroused when the deity is considered as a friend;
4 vatsalya, the sentiment of a parent for a beloved child;
5 madhurya, the feelings of a woman towards her lover.

The sect's present leaders, called gosvamins are (with some exceptions) the lineal descendants of Caitanya's early disciples and companions. The ascetics are known as vairagins.

CAITYA

(Sanskrit for chaitya) In India a sacred spot - a single tree, often small groves of trees, or tumuli where earth-spirits (Yakshas, Nagas) dwelt accessible to simple folk. Buddha and his followers revered the cult of caitya near to which lived holy men and later, Buddhist monks built monasteries.

CAJETAN OF THIENE, Saint

(1480-1547) Priest who cofounded the Theatines and became an important figure of the Catholic Counter-Reformation. Cajetan created at the church of St. Paul Major (1538) a center of Catholic reform. He was canonized by Pope Clement X in 1671. His feast day is August 7.

CAKRAVARTIN

The ancient Indian conception of the world ruler, derived from Sanskrit cakra, "wheel." A cakravartin may be interpreted as a king or emperor whose wide rulership is the result of abiding in the wheel of dharma, "righteous conduct," or as a sovereign whose chariot wheels roll everywhere. In Buddhism, the cakravartin is seen as the secular counterpart of the Buddha who set in motion the dharma-cakra, or wheel of law, for spiritual enlightenment.

CALAMY

(1600-1666) English Presbyterian theologian who contributed significantly to Smectymnuus (1641), the pen name of the Calvinists' famous reply to the

Anglican apology for bishops and liturgical worship in the church.

CALAS, Jean
(1698-1762) French Calvinist and successful cloth merchant of Toulouse. Calas reared all his seven children in the Calvinist faith. When his eldest son Marc Antoine, 28, declared his proposed conversion, his father's rage was felt in and out of the house. Shortly after, in 1761, Marc Antoine was found hanged, and his father was charged with the murder. Unfortunately, his vacillating testimony helped to incriminate him, although he protested his innocence up to his execution. The whole affair was the occasion for anti-Calvinist manifestations.

CALATRAVA, Order of
The oldest military and religious order in Spain, founded in 1158 by two Cistercian monks who proclaimed a holy crusade to defend the city of Calatrava against the Moors.

CALCED
An adjective derived from the Latin calceus, meaning shoe. This word is used to distinguish the branches of some religious orders. The calced are those that wear shoes or boots as opposed to the discalced, the branch that wears sandals or goes barefoot.

CALCHAS
In Greek mythology, a seer who was extremely adept at interpreting bird flight and knew the past, the present and the future in great detail. Apollo had given him the power of prophecy. Calchas was the prophet who followed the Achaeans to the Trojan War.

CALCOL
In Judaism, one whose wisdom, though great, was exceeded by King Solomon's possibly the same as the descendant of Judah through Zerah.

CALDERWOOD, David
(1575-1650) Scottish Presbyterian minister and historian of the Church of Scotland. He was banished to Holland by King James VI of Scotland for refusing to divulge the names of Presbyterian clergy signing the remonstrance against royalist-episcopal control of the church.

CALEB
In the Old Testament, one of the spies sent by Moses from Kadesh in south Palestine to spy out the land of Canaan. Only Caleb and Joshua advised the Hebrews to proceed immediately to take the land; for his faith Caleb was rewarded with the promise that he and his descendants should possess it. The stories of Caleb probably represent the movements of a clan that invaded Palestine from the south, settled in the region of Hebron and southward, and eventually became absorbed in the tribe of Judah.

CALENDAR
A method of reckoning days and months of the year. The first calendars were probably used for religious and agricultural purposes. The earliest calendars were based upon the phases of the moon. It is from the name "moon" that we get the word "month." The first day of each month was the day of the new moon.

CAO DAI
Highly eclectic modern Vietnamese religious sect with a strongly nationalist political character. The sect draws upon ethical precepts from Confucianism, occult practices from Taoism, theories of karma and rebirth from Buddhism, and a hierarchical organization from Catholicism, including a pope. Its pantheon of saints include such diverse figures as the Buddha, Confucius, Jesus Christ, Joan of Arc, the 19th century social writer Victor Hugo, and the founder of the republic of China, Sun Yat-sen. The sect numbers more than 2,500,000 members.

CAODAISM

A politico-religious movement developed by Le Van Trung in South Vietnam about 1920 and officially declared a formal religion in 1926. It is primarily a syncretic movement and claims to sum up and surpass all the local religions as well as to draw on all the major religions, Islam excepted.

CAPER BERRY

Hebrew term with different interpretations. Some translations of Ecclesiastes 12:6 render this term as "desire" so that the passage is made to read "and desire fails." However, many modern translators consider that the writer of Ecclesiastes, in this chapter describing the conditions of man in his old age, used a metaphor, and refers to the caper berries stimulating desire or appetite.

CAPERNAUM

Ancient city on the north-western shore of the Sea of Galilee, Israel. It was Jesus' second home and, during the period of his life, a garrison town, an administrative center, and a customs station. Jesus chose his disciples Peter, Andrew, and Matthew from Capernaum and performed many of his miracles there.

CAPGRAVE, John

(1393-1464) English Augustinian historian and theologian. Augustinian provincial (1453-1457), he wrote the first vernacular chronicle of England to 1417. He also wrote Latin commentaries on almost all books of the Bible.

CAPITAL SINS

In Roman Catholicism, popularly referred to as "the deadly sins", they are the chief sinful tendencies of fallen human nature, the main sources from which other particular sins arise; traditionally, they are:
- ▲ pride,
- ▲ avarice,
- ▲ lust,
- ▲ envy,
- ▲ gluttony,
- ▲ anger,
- ▲ sloth.

CAPITO, Wolfgang Fabricius

(1478-1541) Christian humanist and Catholic priest who, breaking with his Roman faith, became a primary reformer at Strassburg. He corresponded with Marten Luther and, being a distinguished Hebraist, became a diligent biblical scholar, editing the psalter in Hebrew. He remained friendly to the Anabaptists, the radical wing of the Reformation, and other dissenters disturbing the Strassburg reformation, until 1534, when he clearly repudiated them. His most important work is considered to be *Berner Synodus* with church discipline and pastoral instruction.

CAPITOLINE HILL

Rome, symbolic hill of importance from ancient Roman times, the site of numerous temples to Jupiter's many powers, crowned by the monumental, magnificent design (1537-1539) of Michelangelo (finished according to his plans after his death).

CAPITULANT

A member of an ecclesiastical voting unit, e.g., a cathedral chapter. The orders, properly so defined, provide for a chapter (voting body) in each religious house.

CAPPADOCIA

Large inland region in the eastern part of Asia Minor. The natives of Cappadocia were evidently Aryans of Jephetic stock, but Jewish settlements were in evidence by the second century BC. Jews from Cappadocia were present at Jerusalem on Passover of AD 33 (Acts 2:9). Likely as a result of this, Christianity spread into Cappadocia at an early date, and Cappadocian Christians were among those addressed by Peter in his first letter.

CAPPADOCIANS

Three famous natives of the Province of Cappadocia:

▲ Basil the Great,
▲ Gregory of Nazianus,
▲ Gregory of Nyssa.

Basil and Gregory of Nyssa were brothers; Gregory of Nazianus was their personal friend. They expanded the theological insights of Athanasius in the dispute with Arianism and prepared the way for the definitions of Nicaea.

CAPPA MAGNA

A nonliturgical vestment worn on ceremonial occasions by cardinals, bishops, and certain other prelates of the Roman Catholic Church. It is a long cloak of silk or wool with a large hood lined with silk or ermine.

CAPPEL, Louis

(1585-1658) French Huguenot, theologian and Hebrew scholar. Cappel was the first to conclude that vowel points and accents were not an original part of Hebrew but were inserted by the Masoretic Jews of Tiberias, not earlier than the 5th century AD.

CAPRARA, Giovanni Battista

(1733-1810) Roman Catholic churchman and diplomat who negotiated between the Vatican and Napoleon Bonaparte. Caprara committed himself to respect the Gallican liberties (the relative autonomous status of the French church), and he agreed to compromises unacceptable to the Vatican.

CAPREOLUS, John

(1380-1444) Dominican theologian, entitled "the Prince of Thomists", and probably the most celebrated of the Middle Ages. The work for which he is famous is his commentary on the four books of Sentences, which in effect systematically takes up a position against the Avicennist Augustinianism.

CAPTAIN OF THE TEMPLE

The officer, second in dignity to the High Priest (Acts 4:1), who had charge over the officiating priesthood and the Levites who were organized under lesser captains to guard the Temple in Jerusalem and to keep order (Luke 22:4, 22:52). There were 24 divisions of the Levites, which divisions served a wheel at a time in rotation, twice a year. Each division likely also had a captain over it, with several captains of smaller groups.

The captains were men of influence. They conspired with the chief priests in hiring Judas to betray Jesus. They brought their forces along with the priests to arrest Jesus (Luke 22:3-4). It was the Temple captain who lent official favor to the arrest of Peter and John in the Temple (Acts 4:1-3).

CAPTIVITY

In biblical history a number of different captivities are mentioned (e.g., Numbers 21:29; 2 Chronicles 29:9; Isaiah 46:2). However "The Captivity" generally refers to the great exiling of Jews from the promised land in the eighth and seventh centuries BC by the Assyrian and Babylonian powers, and is also called the "Exile" and "Deportation" (Ezra 6:11; Matthew 1:17).

CAPUCHINS

Roman Catholic order of friars and an independent branch of the Franciscans. Founded (1525) by Matteo di Basico, a Franciscan who sought to return to the simplicity of St. Francis' life, the order is distinguished by the pointed hood, or capuccino.

CARA

Center for Applied Research in Apostolate, a research and development agency about the Roman Catholic Church's worldwide religious and social mission. CARA's purpose is to gather information, evaluate it, then promote and apply modern techniques and scientific information for practical use in an effective and coordinated approach to the social and religious mission of the church in today's world.

CARAN

A Hindu caste of hereditary genealogists located in western India. They have a reputation of preferring death to breaking a promise.

CARBONARI

Members of a secret revolutionary society in Italy in the early 19th century. Organized in lodges with a ritual that combined Freemasonry with Christianity, the Carbonari made their first appearance in southern Italy about 1806 and then spread to northern Italy. Ideologically heterogenous, they were united by a common hatred of reaction and clericalism.

CARCHEMISH

In the Old Testament, important trade center situated on the west bank of the upper Euphrates. Carchemish figures in the biblical account at Isaiah 19:9 where God foretold the Assyrian attack against Israel and Judah.

CARDINAL

Hierarchically high-ranking official of the Roman Catholic Church, whose principal duties include the election of the pope, counseling the papacy and administrating church government. Cardinals are chosen by the pope, and have the title of Eminence. Their insignia consists of scarlet cassock, sash, biretta (skullcap) and hat, and a ring.

There are three orders: cardinal bishops of the sees of Rome; cardinal priests (cardinal archbishops) with responsibilities outside the district of Rome; and cardinal deacons, who have been titular bishops since 1962. Cardinal bishops and cardinal deacons are members of the Curia, the central administrative body of the church. The head the tribunals, the courts of the church.

Together, the cardinals form the cacred college, which elects the pope. The cardinalate originated in early 6th century Rome. The term cardinal is derived from Latin cardo, meaning hinge, reflecting the essential working relationship between this institution and the papacy.

CARDINAL BISHOP

The highest of the three ranks within the College of Cardinals. The office is held by those cardinals who are the ordinaries of the neighboring dioceses of Rome.

CARDINAL CANONS

Priests who hold the seven canonries at the shrine of St. James of Compostela in Spain. They are the only priests permitted to offer Mass at the shrine and may wear the mitre and cassock of a cardinal.

CARDINAL DEACON

The lowest of the three ranks within the College of Cardinals. The office was originally held by seven deacons in the Roman church, each of whom was closely associated with the bishop of Rome.

CARDINAL PRIEST

The middle of the three ranks within the College of Cardinals. The designation is an ancient one, although its meaning has undergone considerable change. Most members of the College of Cardinals today are cardinal priests who also function as ordinaries of dioceses throughout the world.

CARDINAL SINS

A designation sometimes used for the capital sins. A parellel with the cardinal virtues is implied with some justification. The cardinal virtues are concerned with the principal areas of virtuous living; the capital sins are bent upon the principal sinful enticements to human appetite.

CARDINAL VIRTUES

Prudence, justice, fortitude, and temperance are called the cardinal (from the Latin word cardo meaning "hinge") virtues because all the other virtues hinge on or are related to them.

CARGO CULTS

Religious movements common among

the natives of New Guinea and Melanesia, who believe that by aping in ritual the European society they do not understand, they can persuade supernatural powers to give them European material wealth - "cargo." Often worshiping John Frum, a messianic figure, the cults have even involved building airstrips to receive the "cargo."

CARITAS CHRISTI

An institute of pontifical right, established for lay women at Marseilles, France, in 1937. Its members are dedicated to a rule that includes the vow of chastity and promises of poverty and obedience, and they perform apostolic tasks in the environment of their secular professions.

CARLO ALLE QUATTRO FONTANE, San

St. Charles at the Four Fountains, influential Baroque church in Rome designed by Francesco Borromini. It was commissioned in 1634 and built from 1638-1641.

CARMEL, Mount

Mountain range, north-western Israel; the city of Haifa is on its north-eastern slope. As a "high place" it was long a center of idol worship, and its reference in the Bible is as the scene of Elijah's confrontation with the false prophets of Baal (1 Kings 18:21-46).
Traditionally the mountain is believed to have been, at least at some periods, a favored location of schools of prophets. Some Carmelites have attempted to trace their order's beginnings back through such schools of Elijah himself. The word carmel is also used sometimes to designate a monastery of Carmelite nuns.

CARMELITE MARTYRS

A group of 16 Carmelite nuns executed during the French Revolution (July 17, 1794). The antireligious fury of the revolutionary government of France was nowhere more evident in its senselessness than in the guilloting of the community of Carmelite nuns from Compiègne.

CARMELITES

First of Our Lady of Mount Carmel, a religious order of the Roman Catholic Church. It is named for Mount Carmel, in Israel, where it originated about 1150. The Carmelites' strict rule was based on silence and solitude but it was slightly relaxed by the English prior, St. Simon Stick (died 1265).

CARMELITES, Discalced

An order of cloistered women who follow the primitive Carmelite rule and follow the contemplative way of life. After a period of decline St. Teresa of Avila initiated a reform in 1562, a reform that spread throughout the world.

CARMELITES, Sisters

The Order of Carmelite Sisters was established in 1452. St. Theresa of Avila and St. John of the Cross were members. In 1593 a separate branch, the Discalced (Barefoot) Carmelites, was founded. The order's typical clothing consists of a brown habit and scapular, with a white mantle and black hood.

CARMEN ADVERSUS MARCIONEM

Longest work of Tertullian, which is the principal source of information about the Gnostic ascetic movement initiated by Marcion and active from the 2nd century to the 7th century, which rejected the Old Testament and belief in Christ as God incarnate.

CARNAC

On the southern coast of Brittany, France, site of 3,000 table stones (dolmens) 16 feet tall in three parallel rows, over 3 miles in length. The stones were erected for ritual purposes at the end of the Neolithic Age.

CARNESECCHI, Pietro

(1508-1567) Controversial Humanist and reformer executed because of his sympathy for an affiliation with the Reformation. At Naples he joined the circle of the influential Spanish religious writer Juan de Valdes, whose distinctive Christianity was a nonsacramental, undogmatic religion that stressed the immediacy of Inner Light (i.e, a divine presence to enlighten and guide the soul) yet was taught and practiced within the context of Catholicism. It aroused the fury of the Roman inquisitors.

CARNIVAL

Term used in many countries for any festive season with processions and masquerades and particularly for the period preceding Lent. Historically, carnival can be traced back at least to the Dionysian festivals of Athens in the 6th century BC, when a float dedicated to the god was escorted through the city, and to the Saturnalia of ancient Rome. The word carnival may have been derived from the Latin carnem levare (to put meat aside), a reference to Lenten abstinence. The Christian church, unable to suppress the traditional pagan festivals entirely, had to adapt and recognize them.

CARO, Joseph Ben Ephraim

(1488-1575) Outstanding codifier of Jewish law. A scholar of Jewish law second only to Maimonides. Caro included in his works not only the collections of previous codifiers but also his own opinions on disputed points.

CAROL

Broadly, a song, characteristically of religious joy associated with a given season, especially Christmas; more strictly, a late medieval English song with uniform stanzas, or verses.

CAROLINE DIVINES

Anglican theological writers who, especially in the 17th century, stressed Roman Catholic elements in Anglicanism as essentials. They defended episcopacy, ritual, and the doctrine of the Real Presence.

CAROLINGIAN DYNASTY

The great dynasty of Western Europe (754-987). The family rose to power as mayors of the palace under the Merovingian Kings. In 751 Charles Martel's son, Pepin the Short, deposed the puppet ruler and made himself king with the pope's approval. Government was personal and primitive and reflected the policy and will of the monarch himself. The unity of Charlemagne's empire was shattered by civil wars and new barbarian invasions.

CAROLINGIAN LEGENDS

Epic poems chiefly from the 12th and 13th centuries, expressing the idealized life and deeds of Emperor Charlemagne (742-814). These legends began as early as Charlemagne's own lifetime and were largely fostered in religious houses claiming Carolingian foundation.

CAROLINGIAN REFORM

A century-long reform movement (circa 740-840) in the Frankish realm. It aimed at correcting clerical corruption, ignorance, immorality, pagan survivals, the great diversity in religious observances, and widespread seizure of Church property in the Frankish kingdom.

CAROLINGIAN RENAISSANCE

An aesthetic and intellectual revival of Latin classicism emphasizing education and church reform, which was initiated by Charlemagne (742-814) and carried through in the 9th century.

CARON

(1515-1593) French painter, best known for church windows. His figures, often long and exaggerated, with twisted postures and tapering arms and legs, frequently are found in large spaces.

CARPOCRATIANS

Sect of Christian Gnostic heretics - i.e., a group of religious dualists who believed that mater was evil and spirit good and that salvation was gained by esoteric knowledge, or gnosis. The sect flourished in Alexandria, Egypt, and was named after its founder, Carpocrates. They revered Jesus as an ordinary man whose uniqueness flowed from the fact that his soul had not forgotten that its origin and true home was within the sphere of the unknown perfect God. In other words, Jesus was to them a fellow Gnostic and as such a model for imitation.

CARPOCRATUS

Gnostic of the 2nd century, who taught in Alexandria. Some modern authorities deny his existence and claim that people of the sect were followers of the Egyptian god Horus-Harpacrates.

CARPUS

A Christian residing at Troas, with whom Paul had left his cloak. Likely Carpus was Paul's host when the apostle visited there.

CARR, John H.

(1812-1899) Methodist missionary in Indian Territory (present-day Oklahoma). In 1845 he joined the Indian Mission Conference.

CARROLL, John

(1735-1815) First Roman Catholic bishop of the United States of America. Carroll had to contend with ecclesiastics in France who schemed to bring the church in America under a French vicar apostolic. Because he understood the need for a native clergy, he established (1789) a college at Georgetown, later consigned to the Jesuits.

By the time of his death, Carroll had achieved his objective of an American Church free from foreign domination but loyal to the Holy See, an accepted influence in the life of the republic, and a church ready to assimilate the great waves of immigrants about to engulf American catholicism in the mid-century.

CARSTARES

(1649-1715) Presbyterian theologian and statesman who headed the Church of Scotland (1688) and University of Edinburgh. He successfully maintained the independent Presbyterian nature of the Church of Scotland.

CARTESIANISM

A philosophic term referring either to the system of thought advanced by the French philosopher René Descartes (1596-1650), or to any of a number of attitudes developed by thinkers influenced by his doctrines.

Insisting upon the importance of method in speculation and adopting skepticism as its point of departure, the Cartesian view posed a universal and systematic doubt on everything not yet established as true beyond doubt - this is the hope at arriving ultimately at certainty in knowledge rather than mere conjecture.

He aspired to end much controversy by proving on solid grounds the existence of God, the reality of the external world, the immortality of the human soul, etc., at the same time to provide a firm foundation for the natural sciences.

CARTHAGE

City founded by the Phoenicians in the 9th century BC on the coast of northern Africa 12 miles north-east of the modern city of Tunis. As a Christian city it was second only to Rome in the West. Many important councils were held there, the first recorded in 220 under bishop Agrippinus. It resisted the early onslaughts of the Muslims but finally fell to them in 698.

CARTHAGE, Councils of

Synods held in the city of Carthage, in North Africa. Christian Carthage from the 3rd century until the 6th century held ecclesiastical primacy in North Africa. The most important councils of Carthage were those held under bishop Aurelius (391-429) with the active participation of St. Augustine. Some of them dealt with the Donatists, especially on the rebaptism of those who had been baptized by heretics.

CARTHUSIAN SPIRITUALITY

Because the Carthusian Order is heremetical and contemplative, its spiritual doctrine rests on the necessity of silence and solitude as paths to mystical union with God.

CARTHUSIANS

Contemplative and austere Roman Catholic monastic order founded in France in 1084 by St. Bruno. Each monk spends most of his life in solitude in his private cell and garden. Lay brothers prepare the Chartreuse liqueur which has made the order famous.

The Carthusians spread slowly, but, by 1521, the order numbered 195 houses in every country in Catholic Europe. It is the one form of communal religious life that has never required and never experienced reform.

CARTWRIGHT, Thomas

(1535-1604) Leader of the Elizabethan Puritans and the chief exponent of Presbyterianism in England. Should the Church fail to reform itself, he taught, the magistrate must assume the enforcement of godly discipline.

CARVAJAL Y MENDOZA, Luisa de

(1568-1614) Missionary who, moved by the execution of the Jesuit Henry Walpole in 1595, decided to devote herself to the cause of the faith in England.

CASA, Giovanni della

(1503-1556) Bishop, poet, and scholar, who is remembered chiefly for his popular and widely translated treatise on manners, *Galateo*.

CASE

(Latin casus) A term used in Roman Catholic moral theology and canon law to indicate a particular and concrete situation of some perplexity that is to be resolved by the application of appropriate general principles of law and morality.

CASE, Shirley Jackson

(1872-1947) Canadian-US theological scholar and educator, who studied the social and environmental influences on the historical evolution of the Christian religion. Among his writing are *Jesus: A New Biography* (1927) and investigations in Christian mysticism.

CASE, William

(1780-1855) Minister who became known as the father of the early Methodist Indian mission work in Upper Canada. Recognizing the effectiveness of native religious leaders among their own people, Case carefully selected and trained a number of them for service in the mission field.

CASIPHIA

A place evidently situated in Babylonia and apparently near the gathering point of the exiles returning with Ezra to Jerusalem in 469 BC (Ezra 8:17-20).

CASSANDRA

In Greek mythology, the daughter of Priam, the last king of Troy, and his wife Hecuba. Cassandra was loved by the god Apollo, who promised to bestow on her the spirit of prophecy if she would comply with his desires. Cassandra accepted the proposal, received the gift, and then refused her favors. Apollo revenged himself by ordaining that her prophecies should never be believed.

CASSIAN, Saint John

(360-435) One of the most revered abbots and theologians of his time and the first monk to introduce his rules of Eastern monasticism to the West. He also was a leading exponent of semi-pelagianism: the heretical belief in the power of man's innate will to seek God, concurrently believing in Augustine of Hippo's concept of the universality of original sin as a corruptive force which without God's grace cannot be overcome.

CASSIODORUS

(490-585) Historian, and monk, who helped to save the culture of Rome at a time of impending barbarism. He wrote extensively on the nature of the soul and life after death, and an encyclopedia of pagan learning regarded as indispensable for understanding the Bible.

CASSOCK

A long, close-fitting long-sleeved robe or coat, worn both as an ordinary dress and as the garment under liturgical vestments by Roman Catholic, Eastern Orthodox, and some Anglican and other Protestant clergy. In the Roman Catholic Church the color corresponds to the wearer's ecclesiastical rank: black for priests and lesser clergy, purple for bishops and monsignori, red for cardinals, and white for the pope.

CASTAGNO, Andrea del

(1421-1457) Early Renaissance painter known for his naturalistic treatment of religious subjects, an important figure in the development of Florentine art.

CASTE, Christian

A social stratification that overrides religious egalitarian doctrine, denoting endogamous segments among the Christians in India that are commensal and share certain observances. The Christians of the Malabar Coast, who belong to the Syrian Church, are divided into different groups that may dine together but may not intermarry; the converts of Protestant and Roman Catholic missionaries each form their own separate units. Among the Roman Catholics, converts from "untouchable" castes have their own churches.

CASTE, Islamic

The distinctive social stratification that developed among Muslims in Pakistan and India as a result of the proximity of Hindu culture. Most of the South Asian Muslims were recruited from the Hindu population; despite the egalitarian axioms of Islam, in their habits they kept accommodating to Hindu usage. Hindus, in turn accommodated the Muslim ruling class by giving it a status of its own.

CASTES SYSTEM

The division of society into closed groups, primarily by birth, but usually also involving religion and occupation. The most caste-bound society today is probably that of Hindu India; caste systems are mentioned in the Rig Veda, dating from 3000 BC, and have not been discouraged until recently.

The hierarchy consists of four Varnas (graded classes) with various subdivisions:

▲ Brahman (priests);
▲ Kshatriyas (warrior);
▲ Vaisyas (merchants and farmers);
▲ Sudras (menials and laborers).

There was also a classless element, the outvarnas or untouchables, who performed the lowest tasks. The system solidified social structures by fixing from birth social contacts, thought, diet, ritual, occupation and marriage. Western influences weakened the Indian system in the 19th century. In India today caste has been drastically modified but not destroyed, despite corrective legislation in the second half of the 20th century.

CASTLE

In the Old Testament, the Hebrew word bi-rah is defined as "citadel, acropolis, castle, fortified town, temple," and occurs only in the books of Daniel, Esther, Chronicles and Nehemiah, which were completed between 536 and sometime after 443 BC following the Babylonian exile.

Writing in the language of his day. Ezra records David's calling Solomon's Temple a "castle" when he encouraged the people fully to support its construction (1 Chronicles 29:1, 19).

CASTLE (CASTEL) SANT'ANGELO

Also called the Sepulcrum Antoniorum, originally the mausoleum of the Roman emperor Hadrian. It was built AD 135 to 139 and converted into a fortress in the 5th century.

In 590 Pope Gregory the Great, conducting a penitential procession to pray for the end of a plague, had a vision of the Archangel Michael sheathing his sword over the castle, signifying the end of the plague; from that incident came the structure's modern name and marble statue of the Archangel that surrounds the building.

CASTOR AND POLLUX
In classical mythology the sons of Leda, also called Dioscuri, "Sons of Zeus," indicating both to the offspring of Zeus, who was worshipped as the supreme deity of the Greeks. Castor and Pollux were venerated by both the Greeks and the Romans.

CASUISTRY
The art and practical science of resolving issues of conscience when there is a question of doubt, the bringing to bear of the principles and conclusions of moral theology on particular instances where it appears that there is a conflict of duties or that circumstances alter cases.

CATACOMBS
Name given to underground cemeteries, particularly those of the early Christians. The best known and most extensive are at Rome. The oldest of the catacombs, those of St. Sebastian and St. Priscilla, date from the 1st century. They also served as a refuge from the religious persecutions of the Roman emperors. Construction was freely permitted provided they were situated outside the city walls. The catacombs extend through rocky soil at depths between 20 and 65 feet sometimes at several levels,the oldest catacomb usually being uppermost.
They form a labyrinthine network of narrow passages, the sides of which are lined with tiers or recesses and frequently decorated with pictorial and written symbols. After a body had been placed in its recess, the opening was sealed with an inscribed slab of marble or terracotta.

Catacombs are by no means a Christian or an exclusively Roman invention. The custom of burying the dead in underground rock chambers goes far back into antiquity, probably originating as a mimetic reproduction in permanent form of prehistoric house burials. Catacombs are found all over the Mediterranean world.

CATAFALQUE
A temporary structure set up in church to hold the coffin of a deceased person or, in the commoner use of the term, to take the place of the coffin when the body of the deceased is not present.

CATALDO, Joseph M.
(1837-1928) Italian Jesuit missionary who worked among Indians of the Pacific North-west for more than 60 years. He entered the Society of Jesus at the age of 15 years and he sailed for America in 1862. In 1967, he introduced Catholicism to the Nez Perce people in Idaho territory and remained with them off and on for 60 years.

CATECHESIS
Instruction and formation in the Catholic faith, both for those who are preparing to be baptized and for those who are already baptized but in need for continuing instruction and formation according to their age and their level of maturity in the Christian life.
Proclamation is supported by another element of the catechetical task, namely, that of disposing people for a right listening and understanding of the word of God. Hence it is a question of calling forth fundamental questions regarding man's life in general.
It is concerned with the existential elements of the formation of personality and human existence that consciously or unconsciously influence the growth to maturity in surrender to God's love. These are essential aspects of the human situation which spontaneously lead to questions that catechesis can answer on the basis of revelation.

CATECHESIS, Missionary

The prebaptismal process involved in introducing the nonbeliever to the Christian message, and in guiding him to a proper understanding and full acceptance of it.

CATECHETICAL SCHOOL

A term referring to the organization of religious instruction as the official form of religious teaching for all the children of a determined ecclesiastical territory.

CATECHETICS

The science or art devoted to structuring the principles of religious teaching. Its concern is the engagement of the whole person with all his faculties; it views Christian education as a progressive teaching or initiation into a new life; it seeks an integration of the individual's personality with those types of behavior identified as Christian.

CATECHISM

Manual of religious instruction arranged in question and answer form. This first catechismal manuals, as they are known today, appeared in the 8th and 9th centuries and were widely used during the Middle Ages. During the Reformation, Martin Luther, John Calvin, and other reformers wrote catechisms to promulgate their doctrines. In 1566 the Council of Trent authorized a Roman Catechism to be translated for use by the clergy. In the Anglican Church the catechism is included in the Book of Common Prayer. Till recently the Baltimore Catechism (1885) was used by Roman Catholics in the United States. The Roman Catholic Church published a revised edition of the catechism in 1992.

CATECHISM OF THE CATHOLIC CHURCH

A universal text summarizing the doctrines of the Catholic Church which was first published in French in October 1992. It was prepared by a Vatican commission and is intended to help bishops in formulating local cate-

chism programs adapted to the cultural and other concerns of their locales. It is seen as the organic presentation of the Catholic faith in its entirety.

CATECHUMEN

Someone under immediate preparation for baptism. In the early church this preparation included a series of exorcisms as well as actual teaching.

CATECHUMENATE

The period of instruction and involvement in the Catholic faith in preparation for the baptism of adults or for the reception of baptized non-Catholic Christians into the Catholic Church; the basic elements of the catechumates are explained in the Rite of Christian Initiation of Adults.

CATENA, Biblical

An early form of scriptural commentary. After the golden age of exegesis in the Greek church creative work in this field declined, and interpreters came to rely increasingly on the interpretations of the Fathers and other ancient writers. Greek catenae, notably those of Procopius of Gaza (died 538) appeared from the 5th century onward. Of the Latin catenae the most famous is the *Catena aurea* of St. Thomas Aquinas.

CATHARI

Name properly applied to full-fledged members (Perfecti) of several neo-Manichaean sects that appeared in Western Europe during the 12th century, but generally employed as a collective designation for the sects themselves.

CATHARISM

The most widely diffused of all medieval heresies, being not only anticlerical and antisacramental, but also anti-Christian and antisocial.

Its creed combined elements of Manichaeism, Docetism, Monarchainism, Gnosticism, and Hinduism. Doctrinal unity was lacking among the various Cathar groups, but all of them professed some form of dualism.

CATHEDRA

The chair, throne, or stool of a bishop in his cathedral church.

CATHEDRAL

The principal church of a diocese, in which the bishop has his cathedra, his official seat or throne. A cathedral need not be particularly large or imposing, though its importance as a major center led to the magnificent structures of the Gothic and Renaissance periods. By its prominent position and size, a cathedral often dominated a city and served as the focus of its life. In Europe, most of the older cathedral cities were already important centers in Roman and early Christian times.

In the Eastern Orthodox Church the cathedral is the main church of a city where the bishop resides and where he celebrates the liturgy on festival occasions. In Russia, where the dioceses have always been few and have covered a vast area, the main church in any large town became known as a cathedral (sobor), even though no bishop was in residence there. The principal church of a big monastery also assumed the same name.

After the 16th century Protestant Reformation, cathedrals where bishops rejected became simple churches. In Sweden the cathedral continued to be the seat of the Lutheran bishop. In the Church of England, where the order of bishops was retained, the cathedrals remained as the seat of the bishop.

CATHEDRAL, Early Christian Style

The sites of early cathedrals are historically interesting. In Gaul pagan sanctuaries in wood were replaced by Roman altars in stone placed at the boundaries of Gallo-Roman villas.

Upon these sites many of the first Christian shrines were built, frequently orientated toward the east, a custom surviving from primitive times, to which Christians also attached a mystical significance.

Merovingian basilicas were heavy and dark, their exterior walls decorated with gems and metals set in barbaric abstractions, black against white, red against yellow. None of these ancient Merovingian cathedrals survived the invasions, wars, and fires.

CATHEDRAL, French Gothic

France is the homeland of Gothic, and the best French Gothic was built within a 50-mile radius of Paris at Amiens, Laon, Reims, Sens, Orléans, Chartres, Beauvais, and Rouen. The greatest French Gothic is at Chartres (11th-12th centuries), consecrated 1260 in the presence of King Louis IX.

Chartres is a miracle of proportion in the rigorous nave where each rib is functionally engaged. The most beautiful piers occur at the transept crossing, rising in a fine unbroken ascent.

The stained glass at Chartres is the most beautiful medieval glass in the world. Irregularities produced by bubbles and blisters in the glass enhance its effect by multiplying and varying refractions. Stained glass was placed according to theories of color interplay, in an imaginative, highly decorative, and utterly nonrepresentative way. Medieval glass-setting in many small pieces was not a fluid technique; images attained a fixed, linear style proper to the medium.

The 15th century developed Flamboyant Gothic, introducing the ogee arch, its compound curve an example of decoration that denies structure. Facades became cluttered and confused, as in the cathedrals of Rouen and Louviers, where many details are completely unrelated and mutually destructive.

CATHEDRAL, Gothic Style

Gothic expresses the logical French mind when it discovered the precise point of strain along the haunch of the arch and placed against it those fingers of the stone, the flying buttresses, now out in the open, freeing the areas of wall between the expanses of fragile glass.

Gothic is rather space than form, heaviness is alien to it. Whereas Romanesque depicts the God of majesty, Gothic offers the Beau Dieu of Amiens and the radiant faces of the dead rising at Bourges (1270).

Yet everything takes its place in the medieval dialectic of a preconceived order. Thus the sculpture is architectural, correctly restricted to the pillar shape, more ordered and coherent in earlier facades; later in a new materialism, it loses a little decorum and some nobility.

Italian Gothic

French Gothic is foreign to the classic tradition of Italy. The cathedrals of Siena and Florence pay lip service to the French style. Pointed facades and splayed doors are decorative nonstructural at Sienna and Orvieto.

It is only in details of tracery and pinnacles that the Gothic spirit is evident. The cathedral of Milan (begun 1386) is a French design built in Italy by two German architects, its marble luxury remarkably ornamented by 3,159 statues.

German Gothic

By temperament Germans were not attuned to the lightness of Gothic; they referred to it as the "French style." The cathedral of Cologne (1248) imitated Amiens; Limburg (consecrated 1235), Bamberg (1237) and Naumburg (after 1250) were inspired by the French, while stone tracery at Minden is reminiscent of Tuscan wheel windows.

Gothic churches built in red brick were a German innovation, the white plastered vaults often delicately edged with foliate patterns between the red brick ribs.

English Gothic

The English cathedral, set in a park, is low with double transepts, square apse, and rectangular towers. The facades present screen-like forms of somewhat unrelated parts. The specific development of English Gothic was an elaboration of the ceiling through a multiplication of decorative, nonfunctional ribs. The Westminster chapel of Henry VII (died 1509) and the cloisters of Gloucester exploit the intricacies of fan vaulting.

Later, English windows are frequently colorless except for heraldic patterns set at intervals. In the lead tracery of windows as in vaulting, the English concentrated on decorative elegance of line.

Spanish Gothic

Spain was an artistic province of France, as were most countries as regard to Gothic. The cathedral of Burgos was begun by Bishop Mauritio in 1221; it has a west front that is lavishly ornamented, its spires designed by Master Hans of Cologne.

At Toledo (1227) moldings and piers are very decrivative of Chartres. In the South, roofs are not steeply pitched and clerestories are omitted. Decorations is exuberant in ceilings, choirs, and altars, combining Moorish and Christian motifs.

CATHEDRAL, Renaissance

Interest in nature and life in this world culminated in Renaissance individualism and secularization. Flamboyant Gothic gave way before Greek and Roman forms which were noble, reserved, and dignified. The Renaissance built with aplomb. Contrary to the Gothic in which form and structure was absolutely functional, the Renaissance architect concealed structure in the interest of an ideal effect.

Florence

The cathedral of Florence, begun (1296) as Tuscan Gothic by Arnolfo di Cambio, is lavishly inlaid with colored marble. Over the crossing of the heavy and austere nave that is feeble Gothic in its pointed arches, rises Brunelleschi's impressive dome.

The elliptical lines of the dome add grace and lightness; the dome dominates the church as well as the Florentine skyline, Its dimensions are fast: 140 feet in diameter and 180 feet in height. Its support is concealed within the base of the dome, a second, inner shell serving as ceiling.

Rome

In Rome, St. Peter's old (4th century) basilica was demolished in the 16th century, to make room for a

Renaissance basilica of enormous scale. As many as 14 architects were engaged upon the project between 1450 and 1667.

Michelangelo, finally put in charge (1546), designed a church on a central Greek cross plan with short, compact arms to serve as a pedestal for the magnificent dome. Giacomo della Porto completed the great dome in elliptical lines. The dynamism of the dome derives from its three-dimensional movement in space.

London

St. Paul's cathedral in London (1675-1710) has a two-storied pedimental facade similar to Perrault's wing at the Louvre (1665), well chosen by Christopher Wren for strong emphasis in London mists. St. Paul's boasts one of the great Renaissance domes.

CATHEDRAL, Romanesque Style

Romanesque cathedrals are stone constructions; they tend to be heavy and ponderous, but have richly textured surfaces and a good concentration of architectural carvings around necessary doorways.

Romanesque architects preferred vaulting in stone for insurance against fire but particularly for the beauty of the vault itself. A vault is a thing alive, sustaining weight, transferring it, and persistently stabilizing the pressures.

Romanesque builders experimented with a variety of vaults. Romanesque was truly Roman in its consistent use of the Roman arch, engaged piers, and arcades, but French Romanesque decoration combines Greco-Roman, Byzantine, Persian and barbaric motifs.

French Romanesque

In Provence cathedrals in town originally Roman are characteristically classical with draped statues and friezes, with ropes aligned along the edges as in the Arch of Constantine.

The tympanum of Arles is framed in concentric arches, varied and unadorned as were Roman string courses. But their Corinthian supports rest upon fantastic beasts and Persian animals.

In the north of France Norman Romanesque churches, austere and unornamented, were achievements in vaulting. Predecessor of Gothic, their prophetic buttressing was often cautiously hidden within the masonry, as at Caen.

Few French cathedrals of the 11th and 12th centuries have remained unaltered. Nevertheless important Romanesque portions remain at Arles, Bourges, Cahors, Poitiers, Chartres (where the Romanesque crypt constructed by bishop Fulbert, the royal portal with lancets, and areas of the ground stage survived).

Italian Romanesque

The Italians provided organic structure in the most important constructional discovery of the Middle Ages. They concentrated support upon ribs, transverse, longitudinal, and diagonal, each of which was supported by individual members of the clustered piers along the nave. In a system of semicircular arches, diagonal ribs thrust higher than longitudinal and transverse ones, leaving a darkened vault.

The Lombardy band confirmed and enhanced structural lines; Lombardy facades were decorated with compound arches and thin pilasters; the small Lombardy porch consisted of a pediment advanced upon two columns supported on fantastic caryatids (Parma). The elaborate lacework of open arcadings upon slender colonnettes is distinctive of Pisa.

English Romanesque

The Normans brought to England the Romanesque of St. Etienne and La Trinité of Caen. The cathedrals of Durham (begun 1093), Ely (begun before 1094), and Canterbury (11th-19th century) are massive and sturdy, with heavy rectangular towers at facades and over transept crossings. Pillars and soffits of arches are cut in abstract patterns for instance, zigzags and diamonds.

German Romanesque

Distinctive of German Romanesque are double aspes with eliminate the central portal, and polygonal and rhomboid towers as at Speyer (12th century, but rebuilt five times after fires).

The famous bronze doors at Hildesheim cathedral are the work of the artist-bishop Bernward. The sumptuous metalwork of Ottoman artists, for instance, from the school of goldsmiths established at the Abbey of Essen, appeared in splendid jeweled chalices, croziers, and gospel books, maintaining a unity of style between architecture and minor arts in the Romanesque period.

CATHEDRAL SCHOOLS

Medieval European schools run by cathedral clergy. Originally their function was to train priests, but later they taught lay students as well.

CATHEDRAL SQUARE

Artistic, historical and layout center of the Kremlin in Moscow. The architectural ensemble of Cathedral Square has retained its original medieval aspect in which traditions of early Moscow architecture and local Russian architectural schools are successfully combined with Italian achievements.

These monuments (e.g.: cathedral of the Assumption, Cathedral of the Annunciation, Archangel cathedral, church of the Deposition of the Robe) surround the Kremlin's main square which witnessed all the major events in the country's life. In old documents it was called just a square or a courtyard between the cathedrals and the Kremlin Palace.

CATHEDRA PETRI

Decorative setting by Gian Lorenzo Bernini (1657-66) for the traditional papal throne located in the apse of St. Peter's basilica, Rome. The gilot bronze encased throne is supported by four bronze statues of the doctors of the early church.

CATHERINE, Saint

(1522-1590) Italian Dominican mystic, who entered the dominican convent at the age of 13, becoming prioress from 1560 to 1590. She was famous for her visions of the Passion and her stigmatization. She was canonized in 1746. Her feast day is February 13th.

CATHERINE OF ALEXANDRIA, Saint

(early 4th century) One of the most popular early martyrs. According to the legend, she was an extremely learned young girl of noble birth who protested the persecution of Christians under the Roman Emperor Maxentius. The spiked wheel by which she was sentenced broke, and she was then beheaded.

CATHERINE OF BOLOGNA, Saint

(1413-1463) Poor Clare abbess whose spiritual writings were popular in Italy until the end of the 18th century. Throughout her life Catherine had visions and revelations. She was canonized in 1712, and her feast day is March 9th.

CATHERINE DE GENOA, Saint

Italian mystic. After several years of unhappiness she led a life of pleasure for a time, but was converted by a mystical experience in 1473, which marked the beginning of her life of close union with God. This she combined with the assiduous service of the sick in a hospital at Genoa. She was beatified in 1737, and her name was added to the Roman martyrology, with the title of saint, by Benedict XIV. Her feast day is September 15th.

CATHERINE OF JESUS CARMELITE

(1589-1623) French mystic. While quite young, Catherine was attracted to a life of penance in imitation of St. Catherine of Siena. At the age of 20, she arrived at the mystical stage, suffering of Christ's Passion, and eventually on the Blessed Trinity. She was even tormented by the devil. During all her trials, she never succumbed to melancholy but bargained for souls in France and in foreign missions.

CATHERINE OF SIENA, Saint

(1347-1380) Patron saint of Italy who was regarded as the greatest of the 14th century mystics. She became a tertiary (a man or woman member of a monastic third order who takes simple vows and many remain outside a convent or monastery) of the Dominican Order. She rapidly gained a wide reputation of her holiness and her severe asceticism.

CATHERINE THOMAS, Saint

(1533-1574) She expressed early a desire for the religious life and after overcoming obstacles imposed by her guardian, she entered the convent of St. Mary Magdalene in Palma as a canoness Regular of St. Augustine. Her great sanctity and the extraordinary spiritual gifts with which she was endowed were known, even during her lifetime.

CATHOLIC

From a Greek word meaning "general" or "universal." The commonest uses of it by Christians are:
1 to describe "orthodox" as distinct from "heretical" Christianity;
2 as the term preferred by Roman Catholics to describe themselves;
3 in contrast to Protestantism for churches such as Roman Catholicism, the Orthodox Church, Old Catholics and Anglicanism, which emphasize church tradition, episcopal ministry, and sacraments in continuity with the early church.

CATHOLIC

In Catholicism, part of the official title or designation given to the body of Christian communities in union with the bishop of Rome (the pope); it was used to describe the Church by St. Ignatius of Antioch in approximately 107: Wherever the bishop shall appear, there let the people be, even as where Jesus is, there is the Catholic Church.

CATHOLIC ACTION

A term that arose in the early 20th century to designate the organized work of the laity that is performed under the direction of mandate of the bishop in the fields of dogma, morals, liturgy, education, and charity. In 1927 Pope Pius XI gave the term its classical definition as "the participation of the laity in the apostolate of the hierarchy."

CATHOLIC ACTION, General

Organizations such as the Holy Name Society or the Legion of Mary, open to all Catholics, working in the fields of dogma, morals, liturgy, education and charity under the mandate of a bishop.

CATHOLIC ACTION, Specialized

Groups limited to members of a given profession or interest group, such as workers, students, doctors, lawyers, or married couples who participate in committees of dogma, morals, liturgy, education and charity under the mandate of a bishop. The most famous of the specialized groups is the joists, an organized association of factory workers.

CATHOLIC APOSTOLIC CHURCH

Religious community established in England in the 1830s, trying to restore the office of the 12 Apostles in anticipation of the imminent Second Coming of Christ. When speaking in tongues and prophecy began occurring in some Church of England and Independent congregations, the group decided that the Second Coming was near and that the apostolic church must be formed to prepare for it.
Churches were established throughout Europe, North America, and Australia. In the early 1960s there were few ministers remaining, most churches were closed, but some members still cherished their hope.

CATHOLIC ASSOCIATION

Irish Catholic organization formed in 1823 to gain for Catholics in Ireland the same political and civil rights enjoyed by Protestants.

CATHOLIC CHURCH

The common name for the Roman Catholic church. The word "catholic" derives from the Greek meaning "universal," and was used in this sense in the early years of the second century to describe one of the characteristics of the church. Gradually the meaning of the term changed to indicate adherence to the original structure and doctrines of the church founded by Christ and propagated by the apostles. Luther and the reformers denied that the term necessarily signified "orthodox," and held that it should be applied to the entire body of Christians, including the Protestants. The use of the word to distinguish the Roman Catholic Church became common during the 16th century. Members of the Anglican, Eastern Orthodox and Byzantine churches call themselves Catholics.

CATHOLIC DAUGHTERS OF AMERICA

A charitable organization of women founded by the Knights of Columbus in 1903, with membership in the mid-1990s of over 200,000. The purpose of this organization is the preservation and propagation of the faith, the spiritual and intellectual development of Catholic womanhood, and the promotion of charitable projects.

CATHOLIC DOCTRINE

The basic doctrines, or dogmas, of the church are the verbal expression of what God has revealed about the relationship with God. The key characteristic of the church's dogmas is that they agree with sacred scripture.

The teachings spell out the unchangeable content of revelation, translating it into the changeable thought - forms and languages of people in every new era and culture.

A dogma is a statement of truth, a formulation of some aspect of the Catholic faith. The purpose of each dogma is to bring Jesus Christ to our attention from a particular point of view. As a coherent set of teachings, Church dogma is a faithful interpretation of God's self-communication to humankind.

CATHOLIC EMANCIPATION

Movement in Britain and Ireland in the late 18th and early 19th centuries to secure full civil and political rights for Roman Catholics.

CATHOLIC EMANCIPATION ACT

British law enacted on April 13, 1829, removing most of the civil disabilities imposed on British Roman Catholics. A controversial measure, it was introduced by Sir Robert Peel, after considerable pressure from Irish campaigners headed by Daniel O'Connell.

CATHOLIC LEAGUE

Association of German Catholic princes and prelates in the 17th century. Established by Maximillian of Bavaria in 1609, it was created to offset the Protestant Union. During the Thirty Years' War, the Catholic League was victorious in the Battle of the White Mountain (1620) and subjugated the Bohemians. In 1631, at the Battle of Leipzig, the League was severely defeated.

CATHOLIC SOCIAL GUILD

An English organization that owes its inception (1909) and early development to Charles D. Plater, SJ; it soon became an adult education movement centered at Oxford where it maintains the Catholic Workers College at Plater Hall.

CATHOLIC TRADITIONALIST MOVEMENT

Educational organization founded in 1964 by Reverend Gommar A. DePauw to provide the Catholic laity with all information necessary for the correct understanding and implementations of the Vatican Council II's decisions in full conformity with the traditional doctrine and practices of the Roman Catholic Church.

CATHOLICATE

The territory under the jurisdiction of a catholicos. In some instances the jurisdiction may be autocephalous and extend to an entire country, as in the catholicate of Georgia, or a catholicate may depend on a primatial see, as in the Armenian Church.

CATHOLICISM

The universal community formed by the teaching, worship and practice of the Catholic Church, usually understood of the Roman Catholic Church, which tightens the meaning of the term to intercommunion within a common obedience and discipline. Unlike catholicity, which refers to a quality, Catholicism refers to a system.

CATHOLICITY

The quality or the characteristic of universality. Though not of scriptural origin, the adjective "Catholic" has been considered properly descriptive of the Church as a whole since the time of Ignatius of Antioch (died circa 110); by the third century it was commonly accepted as part of the Church's title; from the fourth century it has been incorporated in the principal creeds.

CATHOLICOS

The title of certain ecclesiastical superiors in Eastern Christian Churches. In earlier times (Greek katholikos, "universal" bishop) had occasionally been used of a superior abbot; but the title eventually came to designate a bishop who, while head of a major church, was still in some way dependent on his patriarch. The titles catholicos and patriarch later became synonymous and were applied to the heads of the Armenian, Nestorian (Assyrian) and Georgian churches.

CAUDA

An island off the south-west coast of Crete passed by the apostles Paul and Luke on the voyage to Rome in the fall of 58. Having lifted anchor at Fair Havens their chip hugged the south coast of Crete until, likely after rounding Cape Matala, they were caught and driven by a tempestuous wind that could have forced the boat into the quicksands off the shores of North Africa. However, they came into the shelter of "a certain small island called Cauda" and the island's position evidently broke the force of the wind, providing them with smoother waters (Acts 27:13-17).

CAUSALITY, Divine

The exercise of divine causality must be an eternally free act of creation, producing finite existents from nothing but the infinite power of a divine fiat exercised in the creatural duration of time. Creation explains both the limitation and multiplicity of finite being.

CAUSE

The notion of causality is understood, taken for granted, and acted upon by people in the ordinary living of their lives; by it they understand the influence or sum of influences that bring an effect about.

CAUSE, First

A term that is applied to God insofar as is considered as the ultimate explanation of all created reality; it is analogous to the designation of God as the maker of everything in scripture.

CAUSES OF THE SAINTS, Congregation for

The congregation or department of government in the reorganized Roman Curia responsible for procedures and decisions in matters pertaining to the beatification and canonization of servants of God.

CAVALIER D'ARPINO

(1568-1640) Painter of the post-Renaissance school known as Mannerist. He executed extensive decorations in the church of St.. Martino, Naples. Perhaps his best work is the four incidents from the life of St. John the Baptist in the church of San Gionanni in Laterano, Rome. During his long career, he also created the designs for the mosaics of the cupola of St. Peter's; the frescoes of the Cappella Paolina of the church of St. Maria Maggiore, and the fine murals of the Ogliate chapel.

CAVE

An underground hollow or cavern with an opening to the surface. Caves abound in the limestone of Palestine; Mount Carmel and the vicinity of

Jerusalem, for example, were undermined with many caves. Accordingly, they were frequently mentioned in Scripture, sometimes in a figurative sense. Some of them were so large as to hold hundreds of persons, and were used for permanent dwellings, as at Petra, or as temporary shelters, burial sites, cisterns, stables and storehouses. Many valuable artifacts have been recovered from these natural shelters.

Caves provided refuge in times of danger. The first mention of such a place concerns Lot and his two daughters living in a cave after leaving Zoar because of fear (Genesis 19:30).

The dead were often buried in caves. The very rocky soil in much of Palestine made digging graves difficult. The Bible's second mention of a cave is concerning the one of Machpelah at Hebron that Abraham bought and used as a burial site, and where Sarah, Abraham, Isaac, Rebekah, Jacob and Leah were all buried (Genesis 23:7-20; 25:9-10; 49:29-32; 50:13).

CECILIA, Saint

(2nd or 3rd century) Virgin and patroness of music, one of the most famous Roman martyrs of the early church. She is often represented in art playing the organ. Her feast day is November 22th.

CECROPS

In Greek mythology, the mythical king of Attica, son of Mother Earth, a man from the waist up while the rest of his body was that of a serpent. During the time of his reign, the competition took place between Athena and Poseidon to determine who would finally take Athens. Cecrops, and Cranaus, who later succeeded him, played the role of arbiters.

CEDD, Saint

(602-664) English Benedictine bishop, brother of St. Chad. Cedd was born in Northumbria and educated at St. Aidan and the Irish monks of Lindisfarne. He was consecrated bishop of the East Saxons by St. Finan at London in 654. In 644 Cedd participated in the Whitby conference to settle the Easter controversy. The conference ultimately decided whether the church in England should remain linked with the Celtic Church or with Rome.

CELEBRANT

In Roman Catholicism, the bishop, priest or deacon who officiates at a liturgical ceremony. Because liturgical services are not private functions, but a celebration of the church in which all actively participate, each in his own capacity (as discussed at the second Vatican council), all can in a sense be said to celebrate them together. In order to highlight the communal character of such celebrations, many have come to prefer the term president in place of celebrant.

CELEBRATIONS IN CATECHETICS

The celebration in catechetics has become an organic part of the catechesis of children since the 1950s. It was initiated by French catechesists and perfected by the Higher Institute of Catechetics in Paris.

The catechetical celebration has three essential parts:

▲ the recalling of a historical event by means of gestures meaningful to the children;

▲ the turning to the mystery being explored by placing the children before the mystery itself and by leading them to a sincere religious attitude before God, and

▲ the communal profession of faith by means of procession, song, gestures, prayers, and silence enacted together.

CELESTINE I, Saint

(345-432) Pope from 422 to 432. His pontificate is noted for its vigorous attack on Nestorianism, the unorthodox teaching of patriarch Nestorius of Constantinople, which stressed that Christ's human and divine natures were independent and which denounced the Virgin's title Theotokos (God-bearer). He also minimized the role of divine grace in man's salvation. In the Roman martyrology, Celestine is commemorated on July 27th, but Ireland observes his feast day on April 6th.

CELESTINE II

Elected Pope 1124, he resigned a few days later, and is not counted in the official of popes. He studied under Abelard and became a cardinal priest and staunch supporter of Innocent II. As pope he reappraised the treaty of Innocent II with Roger II of Sicily.

CELESTINE III

(1106-1198) Pope from 1191 to 1198. On the day of his consecration he was ordained priest and the day after his consecration he crowned King Henry VI of Germany as Holy Roman Emperor. The pope and Henry died within a few months of each other. Celestine's conciliatory and temporizing policy towards Henry was probably caused not by senile weakness, as has been asserted, but rather by moderation and patience.

CELESTINE IV

(1172-1241) Pope during 1241. He was the first pope to be elected in a conclave, which had been set up by the senator of Rome, Matthew Orsini. Celestine, an old and sick man, was consecrated on October 28 and died two weeks later amidst papal struggle with the Holy Roman Emperor Frederick II.

CELESTINE V, Saint

(1209-1296) The first pope to abdicate. He founded the Celestine Order. Formally a Benedictine, he became a hermit and lived in the Abruzzi Mountains, near Sulmona. His rigorous asceticism, comparable to that of the Eastern desert fathers, attracted followers, and he became head of a group of hermits. Celestine was in his 80s when he was elected pope in 1294. He accepted only because of the perilous situation of the church.

CELESTINES

A congregation within the Benedictine Order founded by Peter of Morrone (Celestine V) about 1240. In the 15th century the order had about 150 houses, mostly in Italy and France. The Celestines ceased to exist as an order under the suppressions of anticlerical governments in the late 18th and early 19th centuries.

CELESTIUS

(354-429) One of the first and probably the most outstanding of the disciples of the British theologian Pelagius, proponent of Pelagianism, a heretical doctrine minimizing the role of divine grace in man's salvation, which caused dissension in the Christian church for more than a century.

Although it did not specify which of Celestius' opinions it was censoring, the Council of Ephesus (431) condemned him, perhaps for his alleged denial of original sin and for his doctrine that grace of God is given to a man in accordance with his merits.

CELIBACY

Voluntary abstinence from marriage and sexual intercourse. The term is mostly used in the sense of being unmarried, usually in connection with a religious official, specialist, or devotee. Applied only to those for whom the unmarried state is the result of a sacred vow, act of renunciation, or religious conviction, celibacy has existed in some form or another throughout man's religious history and in virtually all the major religions of the world.

Celibacy of the clergy of the Roman Catholic Church was instituted by Pope Siricius (384), but abandoned by Protestants during the Reformation. In the Eastern Church, married men can be ordained as priests, though bishops must be celibates or widowers. Recently there has been opposition to celibacy among some Catholics.

In the face of the widespread and sometimes obstreperous criticism of the law of celibacy, Paul VI in 1967 published his encyclical *Sacerdotis celibatus,* in which he reaffirmed the position taken by Lateran II and Trent, pointed to the values of celibacy, and denied that the exceptions admitted in the contemporary practice of the church represent a weakening of the ideal or a true mitigation of the law itself.

No discussion of the problem of celibacy as a whole has been permitted at Vatican Council II. After the council, however, those eager to press forward with the work of reform have included celibacy among the established institutions and practices they think should be questioned.

In the new climate of dialogue, ecclesiastical authority, especially at local and regional levels, has been hesitant - or perhaps unable - to stifle discussion. In any case, the pastoral problems raised by the scarcity of vocations, coupled with an unprecedented increase in the number of priests giving up their ministry, has caused the celibacy issue to clamor for attention.

CELIBACY, Clerical

In the Eastern churches the praise of virginity in the New Testament led to the practice of voluntary clerical celibacy in the Christian East. It became obligatory first for married bishops (5th century), who were required to separate from their wives.

The canonical discipline among the Eastern Catholic Churches is identical with that of their Orthodox counterparts, with these exceptions:

▲ Celibate candidates can become secular priests without entering the monastic state.

▲ The Chaldeans have not followed the Nestorians in permitting widowed priests to remarry.

▲ All groups favor celibacy in various degrees.

CELL, Monastic

The monk's private place, where he prays, reads, meditates, studies, and sleeps. At certain periods cenobites, living a more common life, did without cells properly so called. When their common dormitory was partitioned to give some privacy during sleep, these divisions were called cells.

CELLARER

An official in a monastery, originally in charge of wine and spirits, who came in later times to be assigned the duties of procurator or bursar in many monasteries.

CELTIC CHURCH

Churches organized along monastic lines in areas of Celtic settlement (Scotland, Ireland, Wales and Britannia) between about the 5th century and the Norman Conquest. They differed from Rome only in superficial matters, and were responsible for converting large areas of Europe.

Presided over by the Druids (the priestly order), Celtic religion presents beliefs and practices similar to those of ancient Indian culture, thus indicating an ancient common heritage.

CELTIC RELIGION

Celtic religion, traces of which have been found from Ireland to Asia Minor, was basically a form of nature worship. Dominated by anthropomorphic chief deities, it abounded in cults of minor divinities also. Greek and Roman authorities, from the 3rd century BC on, clouded the picture by providing the names of their own deities in substitution for those of Celtic gods.

CELTIC RITE

A name given not so much to a single uniform rite as to a variety of rites or eclectic collections of liturgical practices used in the ancient churches of Ireland, England, and Wales. The rite was Gallician in its main characteristics but was much modified by local and, increasingly as time went on, by Roman influences.

The rite was marked by its difference in determining the date of Easter and the manner of administering baptism. The chalice was prepared before Mass, a litany and other prayers were inserted between the reading of the epistle and gospel, and there was a commemoration of the dead and a reading of the diptychs before the preface.

CEMETERY

A burial place for the dead which is not a churchyard. The term was used by early Christians to describe the areas situated beyond city walls which they set aside for burials. At that time, and for many centuries afterwards, burial in churches or churchyards was unknown. Today, cemeteries may be termed an alternative to overcrowded churchyards. As large cities grew, resulting in high population density,the problem of burial became acute. More land had to be set aside for this purpose. Consequently, burial in cemeteries outside cities became more common.

Cremation, or the practice of burning the dead, is becoming mow widely preferred among Americans and Europeans and has greatly alleviated the overcrowding of many large city cemeteries.

Apart from community cemeteries, there are also special cemeteries. Certain religious denominations, such as the Jews and Catholics, maintain their own cemeteries, as do members of Masonic lodges and other similar fraternal organizations. Certain cemeteries are places of honor, such as Arlington National Cemetery near Washington, and the war graves maintained in Europe and elsewhere by former combatants of the two World Wars.

CENACLE

The upper room where the Last Supper was celebrated (Luke 22:12). An Israeli shrine of King David's tomb (based on a late tradition) occupies the first floor. It is located on the hill of Zion to the south-western of the present walls of Old Jerusalem.

CENCHREAE

The account of Acts 18:18 relates that in Cenchreae Paul had his hair clipped because he had made a vow, and afterward he apparently sailed from

Cenchreae to Ephesus accompanied by Priscilla and Aquila (in the spring of 52). Writing to Rome about four years later, the apostle referred to "the congregation that is in Cenchreae." Paul's letter to the Romans may have been carried to its destination by Phoebe of the city of Cenchreae.

CENOBITE

A word derived from two Greek words meaning common life. It designates a monk, or one who lives in community, as contrasted with a hermit living separately from others.

CENOBITIC MONASTICISM

A form of monasticism based on "life in common," characterized by strict discipline, regular worship, and manual work. St. Pachomius of Egypt (circa 290-346) was the author of the first cenobitic rule. Cenobitic monasticism was introduced in the West by St. Benedict (died 547) and became a norm of the Benedictine Order.

CENSER

A container, usually covered and suspended by chains, in which incense is burned at liturgical services. It is mentioned frequently in the Bible (e.g., Exodus 27:3, 1 Kings 7:50; Revelation 8:3-5). It was introduced in the Christian liturgy about the 4th century. In its present form it is usually covered and suspended from one or more chains.

CENSOR OF BOOKS

Ecclesiastical official appointed to judge the soundness of a book dealing with faith or morals before publication. The Roman censors, charged initially with the census, became also guardians of public morality. Roman Catholic canon law requires appointment from among the clergy, secular and religious, of competent official censors.

The censor of any work must base his judgement on objective norms of Catholic teaching, not on his private preferences; he may also judge on the timeliness of any work.

CENSORSHIP

Supervision or control exercised by anybody in authority over public communication, conduct or morals. Early censorship in the Greek city states curbed conduct insulting to the gods or dangerous to public order. In Rome the censor dictated public morality.

Censorship of books was not widespread (although some books were publicly burned) until the invention of printing in the 15th century. The first *Index of Prohibited Books* was drawn up by the Catholic Church in 1559 in an effort to stop the spread of subversive literature. Similar tactics were employed by Protestants and secular authorities in one period or another.

CENSURE, Ecclesiastical

In Roman Catholicism, an ecclesiastical penalty for a grave sin. Excommunication, interdict, and suspension are three types of censure. Censures fall into two general classes. Those called the *latae sententiae* censures are incurred ipso facto by the commission of the act to which the penalty is attached. Others, known as *ferendae sententiae* censures, are incurred if competent ecclesiastical authority inflicts them when the violation of the law or precept becomes known.

A censure supposes the penalized individual to have been delinquent and contumacious in his violation of the law, and it is not incurred when certain extenuating circumstances, attached to the law, diminish his responsibility or the contumacity of his transgression.

CENSURE, Theological

An unfavorable judgment made by ecclesiastical authority upon propositions or statements held to be detrimental in some way to faith or morals. Since medieval times these condemnations have been expressed in terms that indicate the degree or measure in which the proscribed doctrine stands, or appears to stand, opposed to Catholic teaching.

CENTAURS

In Greek mythology, monsters, half human (from the waist up) and half horse. They had a human head, the arms and torso of a man and the four legs of a horse. Chiron and Pholus stood apart among the Centaurs because they did not have the savage character of the others. Chiron was wise and operated a school on Mount Pelion where generation after generation of heroes studied.

CENTRAL CONFERENCE OF AMERICAN RABBIS

Federation of Reform rabbis (oldest rabbinical association in the US) formed in 1889 by Rabbi Isaac Mayer Wise as the final step in the organizational structure of American Reform Judaism. The purpose was to promote uniformity of Reform practice and decide such practices as the appointment of rabbis.

CENTURION

The principal professional officer in the armies of ancient Rome and its empire. The centurion was the commander of a century (companies of 100 men). The centurions were key men and served a most important function in the legion. While they were under the authority of the tribunes and responsible for carrying out their orders, the army officer was the real and immediate head of the soldiers. On a number of occasions army officers appear in the New Testament.

CERDO

(2nd century) Gnostic teacher who taught in Rome (circa 140) and is known only through the writings of Irenaeus, Epiphanius and Hippolytus. From these sources it seems that Cerdo's teachings are reflected in those of Marcion.

CEREAL OFFERING

A Hebrew grain offering to God made up of fried or baked grits, flour, cake, or bread (Leviticus 2:1-16). Frankincense and olive oil were poured over these offerings; part was burned as a token to God, and the remainder was eaten by the priests. Salt was used for seasoning; the use of fermented foods such as honey or leaven was forbidden.

CEREMONIES, Congregation of

Former congregation of the Curia Romana, in charge of papal and cardinalatial ceremonies and also of matters of diplomatic protocol.

CERTAINTY, Moral

An objective thing, a quality of propositions which are supported by such evidence that the mind cannot reject them. The term moral certainty is often used loosely to mean virtual or practical certainty, a type of certainty that exists when the truth of a proposition cannot be strictly demonstrated beyond all possibility of doubt.

Moral theologians use the term to indicate the highest type of certainty attainable in moral judgments, especially when these concern propositions dealing with variable and contingent matters.

CERTAINTY, Theological

A qualifying note applied to a proposition deduced from a formally revealed truth and a second premise naturally known and held to be certain. The reasoning involved need not be strictly syllogistic, but must accord with the deposit of faith. It this way theology contributes not to the multiplication of dogmas, but to the progressively clearer understanding of the unique mystery of God's saving relationship with man.

CERTITUDE, Moral

An attitude of mind in assenting to a proposition which appears to be beyond doubt and to exclude all fear of error. Different kinds of either certainty or certitude are distinguishable on the basis of the type of evidence seen as supporting the truth of a proposition.

CERTITUDE OF FAITH

Firmness of mind in assenting to the truth of what is believed by theological faith; different from assurance of salvation. Faith's certitude, for instance, adherence without fear of being wrong, rests on two supports.

The first is proper to the mind itself, as the virtue empowers it to give cognitive assent; faith gives the power to accept God as He "speaks," for instance, guarantees the truth of matters of belief.

A second sort of certitude is derived from the will: what faith assents to means eternal life. The will's firm cleaving to God as loved above all redounds upon the mind's act of faith and gives it a subjective certitude that quietens its restless pondering.

CERUNNOS

An archaic, powerful, and widely worshipped pagan Celtic deity. Cerunnos may have had a variety of names in different parts of the Celtic world but his attributes were generally consistent. Animals often surrounded Cerunnos, and his role was clearly that of "lord of wild things." He was worshipped primarily in Britain, although there are also traces of his cult in Ireland.

CESSATION OF LAW

Concept in canon law, used regarding circumstances under which a law ceases to bind. This may occur through repeal (called extrinsic cessation) or by the change of conditions making the law harmful or devoid of purpose (intrinsic cessation). A law which through changing circumstances has become unreasonable is assumed to have lapsed, even if not repealed.

CETANA

In Buddhism, volition; a factor of consciousness. Nearest Buddhist term for will. The Sankharas have been called Karma-producing impulses or volitions.

CHACS

Maya gods of rain and, hence, of crop fertility. The major god of the Maya peasant since antiquity, the giant snakelike deity was at once a single god and four gods associated with the points of the compass.

CHAD, Saint

(601-672) Monastic founder, abbot, first bishop of Lichfeld, who is credited with the Christianization of the ancient English kingdom of Mercia.

CHAFF

The thin protective covering or hunk on the kernels of cereal grains such as barley and wheat. Though the biblical references to chaff are figurative, they reflect the threshing practices common in ancient times. After harvesting, this inedible membrane covering of the valuable grain was useless, and hence was an appropriate symbol of something light, worthless and undesirable, something to be separated from the good and disposed of.

The worthless chaff was often gathered and burned to prevent it from blowing back and contaminating the piles of grain. Similarly, John the Baptist foretold the coming burning destruction of the wicked false religionists - the Thresher, Jesus Christ, will gather in the wheat, "but the chaff he will burn up with the fire that cannot be put out." (Matthew 3:7-12; Luke 3:17).

CHAIN PRAYERS

A name given to anonymous prayers or a system of praying in which directions are given to recite certain prayers a particular number of times and to pass the practice on without to fail to a definite number of persons.

CHAIR OF PETER

A theological expression that signifies the authority and doctrinal power that resides in the bishop of Rome, the successor of St. Peter. In early times the bishop presided over his people and instructed his flock on the Word of God from his official chair.

CHAJANG YULSA

(7th century AD) Buddhist monk who attempted to make Buddhism the Korean state religion. Appointed to the highest post in the official Buddhist hierarchy of his native state of Silla, one of the three kingdoms into which Korea was then divided, he propagated the theory that Silla was the exemplary Buddhist land and that the other Korean kingdoms should humbly follow Silla's lead.

CHAKRA

Wheel or disc, referring especially to Buddha's Wheel of the Law (dharmacakra), its eight spokes symbolizing the Eightfold Path by which man, extinguishing desire, attains to liberation and eternal bliss (nirvana).

CHALCEDON, Council of

Fourth ecumenical council of the Christian Church, held in Chalcedon (Turkey) in 451. Convoked by the emperor Marcian, it was attended by about 520 bishops or their representatives and was the largest and best documented of the early councils. It approved the creed of Nicaea (325), the creed of Constantinople (381; subsequently known as the Nicene Creed); two letters of Cyril against Nestorius (which insisted on the unity of persons in Christ), and Pope Leo I's *Tome* (confirming two distinct natures in Christ against the Monophysites). The council then explained these doctrines in its own confession of faith.

CHALCIUTLICUE

Aztec goddess of rivers, lakes, streams, and other freshwaters. Chalchiutlicue means She Who Wears a Jade Skirt; she was also called Matlalcueye (She who wears a green skirt). Wife of the rain god Tlaloc, in Aztec cosmology she was the fourth of the previous suns.

CHALDEA

Name for South Babylonia, after its occupation by the Chaldeans in the 10th century BC. The Chaldeans were accomplished astronomers and astrologers, and ancient writers often used their name as a synonym for "magician". In 626 BC Nabopalassar founded the Chaldean Neo-Babylonian Empire, which held sway over the area until the death of Nebuchadnezzar in 561 BC.

"Chaldean" also was used by several ancient authors to denote the priests and other persons educated in the classical Babylonian literature, especially intraditions of astronomy and astrology.

CHALDEAN CATHOLIC CHURCH

An Eastern-rite member of the Roman catholic Church, numbering in the early 1990s about 220,000 faithful in Iraq, Iran, and Lebanon.

Christianity in Iraq and Iran dates from the late second century. In the fifth century, the Church of the East embraced Nestorianism, a heresy that declared Christ to be man and God the son to be his divine counterpart. The church prospered and expanded into China, the steppes of Mongol Asia, and the Malabar Coast of India until the 14th century, when the Mongol leader Tuimur completely destroyed the Nestorian Church east of Iraq, except in India.

CHALDEAN LITURGY

The liturgy used by Catholics of the Chaldean Rite, chiefly in Iraq. It begins like other Eastern liturgies with an enarxis after the model of an office, abbreviated somewhat at the low Masses which Catholics have introduced with the custom of daily Mass. The elements are prepared during the lakhumira, a chant at the end of this with prayers corresponding to the Byzantine prothesis, and (at solemn Masses) a blessing of incense. The Prophecy is read only on Sundays and feasts and in some penitential seasons, but there is always an Old Testament lesson and two from the New Testament before the Gospel.

CHALDEAN RITE

The system of liturgical practices and discipline historically associated with the Church of the east, or Nestorian Church, and also used today by the Catholic patriarch of Babylon of the Chaldeans, where it is called the East Syrian rite.

The Chaldean Rite, in comparison with other Eastern rites, is simpler in form, lacking, for instance, a detailed lectionary of scriptural verses and commemorating fewer saints. The liturgy is sometimes accompanied by symbols and triangle and is always chanted.

CHALICE

A cup containing the wine which in the Eucharistic sacrifice is changed into the precious blood of Christ. It must be constructed of appropriate materials and should be blessed by a bishop or priest.

CHALK

The only occurrence of the Hebrew word se'redh in the Bible is at Isaiah 44:13, and it has reference to the red chalk used by wood craftsmen for marking purposes.

CHALK, Blessing of

A blessing given after the Ephany Mass over the chalk to be used in the blessing of the homes on this day. After blessing the home the initials of the legendary kings, Gaspar, Melchior, Balthasar, are written with white chalk on the inside of the door together with the year.

CHALKSTONE

Outcroppings of this very soft, easily powdered rock are found in various parts of Palestine. Because it is so readily crumbled and pulverized, the prophet Isaiah used it in an effective simile to show what must be done to the idolatrous altars of Israel if forgiveness was to be attained (Isaiah 27:9).

CHALLONER, Richard

(1691-1781) Leader of the Roman Catholics in the 18th century whose revision of the Reims-Douai translation of the Bible - an English version from the latin Vulgate for Roman Catholics - became the authorized edition for English Catholics. Challoner is the author of numerous devotional books, including *The Garden of the Soul* (1740), a popular manual of prayer.

CHALMERS, James

(1841-1901) Scottish Congregationalist member of the London Missionary Society. Having facilitated the establishment of British rule in northern New Guinea, he strove to form an indigenous church free of westernized culture but was killed by tribesmen at Dopima.

CHALMERS, Thomas

(1780-1847) Presbyterian preacher, theologian, author, and social reformer, first moderator of the Free Church of Scotland. Chalmers adopted the evangelical position that stresses the importance of faith for salvation.

CHAM

Religious masked dances of Tibet, annually performed in the open air at most Buddhist monasteries and - until the Chinese Communists assumed rule in 1959 - at the great New Year festival in Lhasa to exorcise evil.

CH'AN

A form of Mahayana Buddhism that arose in China and that emphasized the direct, intuitive awareness of one's own Buddha nature; in modern times it is most widely known through its development in Japan, where it is called Zen.

CHANCEL

That part of the church designated for the clergy. The term is from the Latin cancellus (lattice), and arose from the custom in the early centuries of the church of separating the area by a low lattice-work or railing. In the Middle Ages the chancel came to be separated from the nave by a choir screen or rood screen. Orthodox churches continue to use screens separating the two areas, but most Western Churches now use no more than a low railing.

CHANCELLOR

A priest appointed by the bishop of a diocese to be in charge of the diocesan governing office.

CHANCERY, Apostolic

The bureau of the Roman Catholic Curia (the papal administrative office) that is responsible for the preparation and preservation of official documents, such as decretal letters of canonization, various papal bulls and papal correspondence.

CHANCERY, Diocesan

Governing office of the diocese that includes persons who assist the bishop in the administration and discipline of the diocese and the execution of justice. The chancellor keeps the archives of the diocese.

CHANDA

In Buddhism, a term approximate to will; intention, desire, but desire which is still under some control and can be directed downward, becoming Tanha or upward, to liberation.

CHANEL, Peter

(1803-1841) French missionary and martyr. As a member of the Marist Fathers, Chanel was assigned to Futuna Islands, Oceania, where he lived among a group of primitive and savage peoples. Although circumstances prolonged his stay, his missionary work among the people seemed fruitless. Baptism was administered to only a few, but his faith and strong character supported him as he suffered persecution and finally a martyr's death. Not many years after his death, the entire island converted to Catholicism. Chanel was canonized in 1954.

CHANGING WOMAN

The principal deity called by some the "mother" of the Navajos in the United States. She created Earth Surface People, whom Navajos recognize as their ancestors. She gave the Blessing Way rites, the fundamental ceremony and backbone of the Navajo religion, to the Navajos.

CHANG KUO-LAO

One of the eight Immortals of Taoism. In art he is depicted carrying a phoenix feather and the peach of immortality. In later time his picture adorned nuptial chambers for the reputed bestowing of children on newly married couples.

CHANG LING

(born ? 34, died ? 156) The founder and the first patriarchate of the Taoist religion in China. He began as a faith healer whose patients paid him a fee of five pecks of rise a year. Hence his cult became popularly known as the Way of the Five Pecks of Rice. It was known officially as the Way of the Celestial Master or the Taoism of the Celestial Master. Chang promised longevity and physical immortality to his followers. Chang Lu even succeeded in establishing a Taoist theocratic state in Hanchung.

CHANNING, William Ellery

(1780-1842) US theologian, writer and philanthropist, leader of the Unitarian movement in New England. He led the Unitarian withdrawal from Congregationalism in 1820-25. Active in anti-slavery, temperance and pacifist causes, he believed that moral improvement was man's prime concern.

CHANT, Ecclesiastical

A simple melody, usually characterized by single notes, used in liturgical services. The Western church uses the Gregorian chant of which the Ambrosian, Dominican, and Carthusian are various forms.

CHANTAL, Saint Jane Frances de

(1572-1641) Cofounder of the Visitation Order. The Order had 86 houses at her death. She was canonized by Pope Clement XIII in 1767, and her feast day is August 21st.

Members of the order included both young girls and widows striving to imitate the contemplative spirit of the Magnificat by their prayer and the active mercy of the Visitation by their visits to the sick.

CHANTRY

A chapel, generally within a church, endowed for the singing of masses for the founder after his death. The foundation of chantries or chantry chapels goes back to the 13th century.

CHAPEL

Subordinate place of Christian worship, usually located in a compartment or chamber within a church, it is separately dedicated and devoted to special services. A chapel may also be a separate building. Deriving from the Latin cappella ("short cloak"), the word originally referred to the shrine containing the cloak of St. Martin. It eventually came to mean any sanctuary containing relics, and then, later, all places of worship excluding cathedrals and churches. The Sistine Chapel in the Vatican is probably the best known.

In the Middle Ages, the cult of the Virgin Mary was such that by the close of the 14th century, most major churches in western Europe had a Lady Chapel. Such extradevotional chapels were largely introduced by the religious orders, secular clergy in parochial and cathedral churches quickly following their example.

CHAPLAIN

An ordained clergyman who is assigned to a special ministry. The title dates to the early centuries of the Christian church. In the 4th century, chaplains were so called because they were in charge of St. Martin's half cloak (Latin cappella).

In modern usage, the term chaplain is not confined to any church or denomination. Clergymen appointed to a variety of institutions and corporate bodies, such as prisons, hospitals, schools, universities, and the armed services, are called chaplains.

Protestant, Roman Catholic, and Jewish chaplains have served with the armed forces of the United Kingdom and the United States.

CHAPLET

A circular string of beads for keeping count of prayers.

By extension the word is also applied to the devotion whose prayer parts are counted on such beads.

CHAPTER, Cathedral

An organized group of clergy attached to a cathedral. The institution reached its peak of influence in the High Middle Ages. In the early centuries of the church, all clergy generally lived with the bishop and served the cathedral church. In the Middle Ages the cathedral clergy acquired personal property and separate houses. The cathedral chapter therefore became an entity separate in some ways from the bishop and at times was in contest with him.

At the Reformation chapters were abolished in the Lutheran and Calvinistic churches.

CHAPTER, Collegiate

The clergy attached to a collegiate church. Such a church, often supported by endowments, is one served by a group of clergy who share responsibility. It differs from the cathedral in having no bishop.

CHAPTER, Conventual

A meeting held periodically or upon special occasions in some religious orders or congregations at which the professed members of a monastery, convent, or house are in attendance. At such meetings important announcements are made, prayers are offered for benefactors and the deceased, and votes are taken regarding matters concerning which superiors are obliged to hear the views of their subjects before taking decisions.

CHAPTER, General

A canonical assembly of provincials and other delegated members of a religious order or congregation, who meet at regular intervals to discuss and legislate on matters of general importance to the institute and of specific concern to the individual members.

CHAPTER, Provincial

A conference of superiors and other members delegated to represent the religious in a certain territory or province. They assemble to discuss, improve, or change the rules pertaining to their local province, and to elect provincial officials.

CHARGE

In Methodism, the local church (station charge) or a group of local churches (circuit charge). It is the basic unit of Methodist organization.

CHARIOT CITIES

Cities of ancient times set apart as places to station chariots, particularly chariots of war (2 Chronicles 1:14; 9:25). Solomon had various of such cities (2 Chronicles 8:5-6).

CHARISMA

(Greek: gift of divine grace), the attribute of awesome and almost magical power and capacity ascribed by followers to the person and personality of extraordinarily magnetic leaders. Such leaders may be political and secular as well as religious.

It is also a New Testament term from the Greek for the gifts of the Holy Spirit, imparted to members of the church to promote God's Kingdom and enabling Christians to serve the Church of Christ (1 Corinthians 12:7-11).

CHARISMATIC GIFTS

Spiritual, preternatural gifts given for the work of ministry in the church (Ephesians 4:12). The New Testament gives various lists (e.g., Romans 12:6-8; Corinthians 12:4-10; Ephesians 4:11).The charismatic serve the activities of teaching, governing, and sanctifying in the Church.

CHARISMATIC PRAYER

The nonliturgical but communitary prayer characteristic of the charismatic renewal.

CHARISMATIC RENEWAL MOVEMENT

Also known as the Catholic Pentecostal Movement, this movement originated in 1967, and believes there is new outpouring of the Holy Spirit in the Catholic Church, a need to reawaken Catholics to the gifts of the Holy Spirit and to the baptism of the Holy Spirit, that is, to a personal experience of the graces already sacramentally received.

Generally, charismatic communities have weekly meetings consisting of scripture readings and teachings, prayer, singing of hymns, sharing of experiences, and fellowship.

CHARITY

(From Greek agape, love) The highest form of love, signifying the reciprocal love between God and man that is made manifest in unselfish love of one's fellow men. Paul's classical description of charity is found in the New Testament (1 Corinthians 13).

In Christian theology and ethics, charity is most eloquently shown in the life, teaching, and death of Jesus Christ. Augustine summarized much of Christian thought about charity when he said: "Charity is a virtue which, when our affections are perfectly ordered, unites us to God, for by it we love Him." Quoting this definition, the medieval theologians, especially Thomas Aquinas, placed charity into the context of the other virtues and specified its role as "the foundation or root" of them all.

Although the controversies of the Reformation dealt more with the definition of faith than with either hope or charity, the Reformers identified the uniqueness of God's agape for man as unmerited love; therefore they required that charity, as man's love for man, be based not upon the desirability of its object but upon the transformation of its object through the power of divine agape.

CHARITY, Brothers of

A religious community of brothers founded at Ghent, Belgium, in 1807 by Canon Peter Joseph Triest. The apostolate comprises primarily charitable and educational works.

CHARITY, Sisters of

A religious order of sisters, which includes numerous individual congregations in Europe and the United States. Probably the earliest of these was founded in France in 1633 by Vincent de Paul and Louise de Marillac.

CHARLEMAGNE

(742-814) King, emperor, son of Pepin III and Bertha. he succeeded his father in 768 with his brother Carloman. Carloman's death in 771 left him sole ruler of Frankland.

In recognition of his extensive domain as well as of his special relation to the Church he was crowned as emperor by Pope Leo III in Rome on Christmas Day, 800. Charlemagne, concerned for spread of the Roman rite and Gregorian chant, took himself seriously as eldest son and protector of the Church.

CHARLES V, Holy Roman Emperor

(1500-1558) Through his parents Philip of Burgundy and Joanna (third daughter of Ferdinand and Isabella), he became an emperor (1519-1556) and a ruler of envied political strength.

Charles' reign was above all a struggle to defend the Catholic faith and maintain his power as universal emperor in an era disturbed by the religious and political force of the Reformation. He strongly insisted on a general council to deal with the issues raised by the Reformation, but was in continuous conflict with the popes over the progress and program of the Council of Trent.

CHARLES, Thomas
(1755-1814) Welsh religious leader, a founder of Calvinistic Methodism in Wales and an inspirer of missionary activities. He compiled a dictionary of the Bible and edited a quarterly magazine, both in Welsh; he composed a catechism in Welsh and English.

The rapid growth of Methodist societies and associations as a result of his labors led, insensibly yet inevitably, to the demand for a separate organization with its own ministers. Charles, who like Wesley never repudiated his own episcopal orders, long opposed this, but in 1811 he drew up a form of ordination and himself ordained eight lay preachers.

CHARM
In the Old Testament, the Hebrew word has the meaning of favor, charm, or elegance, in form and conduct and is generally rendered favor (Genesis 6:8). Divine wisdom and understanding can be a real ornamental charm (Proverbs 3:21-22; 22:4-7), as is also true of proper speech. When the Jews returned from exile in Babylon, Governor Zerubbabel was encouraged to press forward with the Temple building, being assured that with the laying of a headstone, "there will be shoutings to it: How charming! How charming."

CHARON
In Greek mythology, the son of Erebus and Nyx (Night), whose duty it was to ferry over the Rivers Rtyx and Acheron those souls of deceased who had received the coin that was placed in the mouth of the corpse.

CHARONTON, Enquerrand
(1410-1479) Late Gothic religious painter, famous for his "Coronation of the Virgin." He is full of imagination, creating very original types of Virgin and saints; his drawing is precise and graceful, his composition majestic and rich.

CHARRON, Pierre
(1541-1603) Roman Catholic theologian and major contributor to the new thought of the 17th century, remembered for his controversial form of Skepticism and his separation of ethics from religion as an independent philosophical discipline.

CHARTER OF CHARITY
Early constitution of the Cistercian Order, attributed to the Englishman Stephen Harding, third abbot of Cîteaux (1109-1133). The initial version, modified and added to, was completed in the late 12th century. It granted legislative and judicial power to the annual general chapter at Cîteaux attended by all the abbots of the order.

CHARTOPHYLAX
In many eparchies of the Byzantine Church a position equivalent to the Western chancellor. Since the small size of many dioceses did not warrant the appointment of a syncellus (vicar-general), the chartophylax was in charge of the executive office of the bishop, including the care of the archives.

CHARTRES CATHEDRAL
Great French High Gothic cathedral unsurpassed in sculpture and glass, setting the standard for Gothic architecture of Europe. Following a fire (1134) the face (1150), brought flush with the towers, was enriched by the sculptured Royal Portal (1145-1170), one of the greatest achievements of the 13th century in calm and monumental grandeur. The magnificently modeled and restrained figures preserve a perfect relationship with the architectural whole. The entire complex of figures of Old and New Testament reference, together with martyrs, princes of the church, and calendar designs, confirm

the lofty Scholasticism of the school of Chartres, which stressed humanism under bishops Fulbert and John of Salisbury with Bernard de Chartres.

CHASTITY

Abstention from unlawful sexual intercourse, or total abstention from sexual intercourse - most commonly for religious motives. Members of Christian religious orders vow chastity as an outward expression of their religious dedication.

Chastity is regarded as the virtue that moderates and regulates the sexual appetite according to the principles of right reason and the law of God; this virtue applies to all, both married and single, but is expressed differently according to one's state of life. The vow of chastity is one of the evangelical councils (Matthew 19:11) and one of the three vows (together with obedience and poverty) professed by religious in the church.

CHASUBLE

A liturgical vestment, the outermost garment worn by Roman Catholic priests and bishops and by some Anglicans and Lutherans when they celebrate the Eucharist.

CHATZINARIANS

An Armenian sect of the 7th century who were essentially iconoclasts, venerating only the cross. They claimed falsely the authority of St. Gregory the Illuminator for a doctrine on the dual nature of Christ which seemed to postulate two persons: one suffering on the cross and the other separately contemplating the suffering Christ.

CHEDORLAOMER

King of ancient Elam who, prior to Abraham's entry into the Promised Land some 2,000 years BC had extended his power westward to the borders of Egypt.

Among Chedorlaomer's captives was Abraham's nephew Lot, who had been living nearby. Abraham, learning of this, quickly set out in hot pursuit with 318 of his armed servants. At Dan they surprised the enemy's far superior forces, and, successfully pursuing them as far as Hobah north of Damascus, recovered Lot and his possessions (Genesis 14:1-17).

CHEEK

The Bible speaks of striking the cheek, not so much to inflict physical harm, but to chastise, reproach or insult. Job was reproachfully struck on the cheeks by those who disrespected and ridiculed him during his trial at Satan's hands (Job 16:10).

The prophets Isaiah and Micah prophesied relative to the Messiah's being struck on the cheek and the hair being pulled from the cheeks, all significant of the bitter reproach that the enemies would heap upon him (Isaiah 50:6).

CHEESEFARE SUNDAY

Term used among Eastern Christians for Quinquagesima. For those keeping the strict Lent fast, cheese but no meat may be eaten from the Monday preceding Quinquagesima until the Monday following, after which even cheese is excluded.

CHEKE, Sir John

(1514-1557) Humanist and supporter of the Reformation. Through his teachings he made Cambridge the center of "new learning" and the Reformed religion.

CHELA

The disciple or follower of a Guru, a spiritual teacher.

CHELAL

In the Old Testament, a former exile of the sons of Pahath-moab among those who put away their foreign wives at Ezra's instruction (Ezra 10:16-17).

CHEMOSH

Ancient West-Semitic deity, revered by the Moabites as their supreme god. King Solomon of Israel built a sanctuary to him east of Jerusalem (1 Kings 11:7), the shrine was later abolished by

King Josiah (2 Kings 23:13). The goddess Astarte was probably the cult partner of Chemosh.

CHENANIAH

In Old Testament, a Levite contemporaneous with King David. "Chenaniah the chief of the Levites in carrying" was an expert, qualified to instruct others concerning the proper handling of the sacred ark (1 Chronicles 15:22, 25-27).

CHENEY, Charles Edward

(1836-1916) Controversial clergyman who helped found the Reformed Episcopal Church. He became rector of Christ Church, Chicago, 1860, the year he was ordained a priest in the Protestant Episcopal Church. A pronounced evangelical, he joined others in signing the "Chicago Protest" against "unprotestantizing" tendencies in the church.

CH'ENG HUANG

In Chinese mythology, the spiritual magistrate and guardian deity of Chinese cities. Because dead spirits reputedly inform the god of all good and evil deeds that take place within his jurisdiction, there is a popular belief that devout prayers offered in Ch'eng Huang's temple will be liberally rewarded. The wide popularity of this cult is also due in part to imperial appropriation. In 1382 his temples were appropriated by the government and people were directed to offer sacrifices to the protector of their city.

In practice, a Ch'eng Huang is often a deceased local official who has been deified because he served his community with distinction in bygone days.

CHERUBIKON

Hymn of the Cheribim. This Eastern hymn is sung prior to the Great Entrance during which the hymn is interrupted and continued only after the Great Entrance is completed. It reminds the faithful to put aside earthly cares and prepare themselves to receive the heavenly King worthily. While the first part of the hymn is being sung, the priest prays for purity of mind that he may consecrate the gifts of bread and wine worthily.

CHERUBIM

Celestial winged being with human characteristics. Old Testament descriptions of the cherubim emphasize their supernatural mobility and their role as throne bearers of God, rather than intercessory functions. In the New Testament cherubim are ranked among the higher order of angels and, as celestial attendants of God, continually praise Him.

CHESALON

In Old Testament, a city mentioned with Mount Jearim and serving to mark part of the northern boundary of Judah (Joshua 15:10). It is today commonly identified with Kesia, located about 11 miles west of Jerusalem, and its situation on a mountain ridge may help explain its biblical name.

CHESIL

Name of a town appearing in the list of places within the territory of Judah (Joshua 15:21).

CHEVALIER, Jules

(1824-1907) Priest, author, and founder of the Missionaries of the Sacred Heart of Jesus (Missionarii Sacratissimi Cordis Jesu), a Roman Catholic congregation of men originally dedicated to restoring the faith in the rural sections of France and later expanded to world missions, teaching and promoting devotion to the Sacred Heart of Jesus Christ.

CHEVERUS, Jean-Louis Lefebvre de

(1768-1836) First Roman Catholic bishop of Boston. Arriving in Boston (1796), he assisted at Holy Cross Church and served Indian missions in Maine. His courage and charity during the yellow fever epidemic of 1798 and his eloquent preaching attracted many Protestants. In 1808 the diocese of Boston was created with Cheverus as its bishop.

CHIAO

Chinese term for religion, ritual, sect, or church; it may also mean teaching, education, or training.

CHICHÉN ITZÁ

Village in Yucatán state, Mexico, site of the ancient Mayan city of that name. From the 12th to the 15th centuries it was the Mayan ceremonial center and its architecture rose to new heights, including the largest pre-Columbian Ball Court, the imposing pyramid of Kukalcán, the Temple of Warriors and the Temple of Jaguars with important murals. The principal temple, the so-called Castillo, covers an acre of ground and rises 100 feet above the plain.

CHICOMECOATL

Aztec goddess of sustenance and hence, of maize (corn). A very ancient goddess of Nahua-speaking peoples, she was one of the several maize deities.

CHIDON

The name of the owner of the threshing floor or the threshing floor itself where Uzzah was struck down by God when an attempt was made to move the ark of the covenant in an improper manner from Kirath-jearim to the city of David (1 Chronicles 13:6-14).

CHIEF RABBINATE

In Judaism, a supreme religious authority whose decisions bind all those under its jurisdiction. The prototype of the chief rabbinate was the Great Sanhedrin of Jerusalem, which, until the destruction of the Second Temple in AD 70, issued legislation and interpreted Jewish Law for all the Jewish people. The most important chief rabbinate today is that in Israel. It had two rabbis, one representing the Sefardic community, the other the Ashkenazi Jews.

CHIEFTAIN

In the Old Testament, a man in a ruling position, such as the hereditary head of a tribe or a paternal house. The Hebrew word is variously translated in Bible versions as "prince," "leader," "ruler," "chieftain." The heads of the twelve paternal houses or tribes of Israel were termed "chieftains." (Numbers 1:16; Joshua 22:14). The term is also applied to the heads of the 12 clans springing from Ishmael (Genesis 17:20; 25:16). The high standing that Abraham had as the family head with God is indicated in his being called a "chieftain of God," by the Hittites (Genesis 23:6).

CHIH NU

In Chinese mythology, the heavenly maiden who used clouds to spin seamless robes of brocade for her father, the Jade Emperor.

CHILDREN'S CRUSADE

(1212) Sad attempt by 30,000 children to conquer the Holy Land after their elders had failed. Defying kings, priests and parents, they set out from France and Germany, led by the youths Stephen of Vendome and Nicholas of Cologne. Those who survived disease, starvation and the gruelling journey over the Alps were mostly sold into slavery by unscrupulous sea captains when they reached the Mediterranean ports.

CHILEAB

In the Old Testament, David's second son born in Hebron. His mother Abigail was the former wife of Nabal (2 Samuel 3:2-3).

CHILIASM

The belief, based chiefly on the literal interpretation of Revelation chapter 20, that Christ will come to rule visibly upon earth for 1,000 years before the end of the world. It is used as a synonym for millennarianism, but it is less proper to identify it with any but the premillennarian variety of millennarian thought since chiliasm, insofar as it has a distinctive meaning, expects the personal corporeal reign of Christ upon earth for 1,000 years.

CHILION

In the Old Testament, son of Naomi and Elimelech and the brother of Mahlon the husband of Ruth. In Moab, where the family had moved from Bethlehem, in Judah, to escape a famine after the death of his father, he married the Moabitess Orpah. Both he and his brother died childless in Moab (Ruth 1:1-5; 4:9-10).

CHIMERA

In Greek mythology, a fire-breathing female monster resembling a lion in the forepart, a goat in the middle, and a dragon behind. Born of Typhon and Echidna, it is said to have had many goat's heads. Terrible in appearance, flames shot from its mouths and its nostrils. It plundered crops and did great damage. The Chimera was so dangerous that lobates believed he had sent Bellerophon to certain death by asking him to exterminate it.

CHINA, Nestorian Church in

China received the first knowledge of Christianity in the 7th century during the Tang Dynasty, when a Nestorian monk from Syria or Palestine settled near Siam. An important source of knowledge comes from the uncovering in 1625 of the famous marble monument of Sianfu. The inscription gives the main points of Christian doctrine of the Nestorian Church in China from 635 until 781 and the names and titles of 70 Western missionaries.

CHINA, Orthodox Church in

The first Orthodox church was built in Beijing in 1685 for Russian prisoners. Bishop Innocent Figurovsky was responsible for translating the liturgical books into Chinese at the turn of the 20th century, the period of greatest evangelizing effort and most rapid growth.

CHINERETH

Probably the early name of the Sea of Galilee (Numbers 34:11). Associating the name with the Hebrew word for harp (kin-nohr), some suggest that it is applied to the lake because of the harp-shaped form of this body of water. Gennesaret, probably the Greek form of the name, was used when Jesus was on earth (Luke 5:1), as well as the names Sea of Galilee and Sea of Tiberias (John 6:1).

CHINESE PHILOSOPHY

The development of Chinese philosophy is marked by four distinct phases:
▲ the ancient, which lasted until 221 BC,
▲ the middle (221 BC - AD 960);
▲ the modern (960 - 1900);
▲ the contemporary.
The so-called 100 schools, among which are the Confucianists, the Taoists, the Moists, the Logicians, the Yin Yang school, and the Legalists, all held that man is of primary concern and central to their philosophy.
For all, man was important as an individual and a member of society. For this reason one finds that Chinese philosophy is marked by the humanistic, moral, and legal considerations upon which it is grounded.

CHINESE RELIGION

The complex of beliefs and practices of the traditional folk religion and great religions (Taoism, Confucianism, and Buddhism) of China. It is best regarded as an integral expression of Chinese culture rather than as comprising separate systems of dogma. The veneration of ancestors is the dominating preoccupation of Chinese religion.

CHINESE RITES CONTROVERSY

Dispute within the Roman Catholic Church over retention by Chinese converts of such customs as honoring Confucius and family ancestors, and the use of certain terms of Chinese thought for Christian concepts such as T'ien for heaven and Shang-to for God. The controversy developed from a decision in 1603 by the Jesuit missionary M. Ricci (1552-1610) to allow the usages.
The papacy has taken an increasingly tolerant position in the 20th century, holding that rites formerly associated

with heathen practices now signify no more than respect for ancestors and patriotic regard for the nation.

CHIRON
In Greek mythology, one of the centaurs, the son of the god Cronus and Philyra, a sea nymph. Chiron dwelt at the foot of Mount Pelion and was famous for his wisdom and knowledge of medicine. Many Greek heroes were brought up and instructed by him.

CHIROTHESIA
In the administration of sacraments of confirmation and holy orders, the imposition of hands by the bishop.

CHIROTONIA
The act of extending the hands in bestowing a blessing or praying in a person's behalf.

CHISHTIYAH
Islamic Sufi (mystic) order in India and Pakistan, named after Chisht, the village in which the founder of the order, Abu Ishaq of Syria, settled. Great emphasis is placed by the Chishtis on the Sufi doctrine of the unity of being, oneness with God; thus, all material goods are rejected as distracting from the contemplation of God; absolutely no connection with the secular state is permitted; and the recitation of the names of God, both aloud and silently forms the cornerstone of Chishti practice.

CHISLEV
In Hebrew, the post-exilic name of the ninth Jewish lunar month, which falls within November and December. It corresponded with the third month of the secular calendar.

CHLOE
In the New Testament, woman through whose household Paul received reports concerning the dissensions existing in the Corinthian congregation (1 Corinthians 1:11). Though Paul's letter did not state that Chloe was a Christian residing at Corinth or at Ephesus where the letter was penned, in view of the apostles's reference to this household by name, evidently at least some members thereof, either family members or slaves, were Christians known to the Corinthians.

CHOIR
Members of the church who assist in the liturgy through the ministry of song. Although the choir underwent a period of neglect in some countries, immediately following the introduction of liturgical changes after Vatican Council II, the beginnings of a renaissance soon became apparent as new choral music of high quality began to appear.

CHOIR MONK
A member of a religious institute or order of man with solemn vow, obliged to recite the Liturgy of the Hours (Divine Office) daily in common, for instance, in choir.

CHOIR NUN
A member of a religious institute or order of man with solemn vow, obliged to recite the Liturgy of the Hours (Divine Office) daily in common, for instance, in choir.

CHOIRS OF ANGELS
The nine ranks of angels, from the lowest to the highest:
▲ angels,
▲ archangels,
▲ principalities,
▲ powers,
▲ virtues,
▲ dominations,
▲ thrones,
▲ cherubim,
▲ seraphim.

CHONIATES, Michael
(born circa 1140) Byzantine humanist scholar and archbishop of Athens whose extensive classical literary works provide the principal documentary witness to the political turbulence

and academic decline of 13th century Greece after its devastation by the Western crusaders.

CHONIATES, Nicetas

(1140-1213) Byzantine statesman, historian, and theologian whose chronicle of Byzantine's invasion by the Third and Fourth Crusades (1189-1204) and whose anthology of 12th century writings constitute the authoritative historical sources for this period.

CHORA

Name of a famous Byzantine church and monastery of the historical Constantinople (now Istanbul), well-known for its magnificent mosaics and frescoes. The name chora means land, country, a suburb or suburban area, as it lied outside the city walls built by the Emperor Constantine. It was rebuilt by Maria Dukaena (after being destroyed by an earthquake), the mother-in-law of the Emperor Alexis I.

During the 57 years long duration of the occupation of Istanbul by the Latins from 1204 up to 1261, although all the churches in Istanbul were in ruins, this church was not even occupied.

CHORALE

Metrical hymn tune associated in common English usage with the Lutheran Church in Germany. Martin Luther himself composed, or caused to be composed, many hymn tunes that were known at once as chorales because they were designed for congregational singing.

CHORAZIN

In the New Testament, city among those reproached by Jesus and located in the north-western end of the Sea of Galilee (Matthew 11:21). It is usually identified by geographers with Khirbet Kerazeh, only about 2 miles north of the suggested site of Capernaum, the city that Jesus apparently used as a base of operations during his great Galilean ministry of over two years' duration. Jesus pronounced coming "woe" for the Jewish inhabitants of Chorazin who, during that period, were witnesses of "powerful works" that would have moved the pagans of Tyre and Sidon to repentance, yet who failed to act on Jesus' message.

CHOREPISCOPUS

A title used in the Western church in the 10th century. At first a person so designated received episcopal ordination, and his function was to serve as an archdeacon, a title that came to displace that of chorepiscopus. Among Catholics of the Syrian, Chaldean, and Maronite Rites, the title is honorific, and those who possess it generally perform the function of vicars general.

CHOSEN PEOPLE

The notion that the Jewish people are the special elect of god. The idea is a recurring theme in Jewish liturgy and is expressed in such passages of scripture as "For you are a people holy to the Lord your God, and the Lord has chosen you to be a people of his own possession, out of all the nations that are on the face of the earth" (Deuteronomy 14:2).

CHRISM

A mixture of olive oil and balsam used for anointing in the ritual of Eastern and Roman Catholic Churches.

CHRISM MASS

The Mass on Holy Thursday at which the holy oils are blessed. According to Hippolytus, the blessing of the oils in the early church took place just before the baptism of catechumens, therefore as part of the Easter Vigil, but by the 6th century at the latest it was transferred, probably to reduce the accumulation of liturgical events on that occasion.

CHRISMATION

In Eastern Orthodox and Christianity, the sacrament that, together with baptism, introduces new members into the church. A priest anoints the forehead, eyes, nostrils, mouth, ears, breast, hands, and feet of the newly baptized with chrism, a mixture of oil and perfumes blessed by a patriarch, and recites at each anointment, "The seal of the gift of the Holy Spirit." The sacrament may also be administered to certain non-Orthodox Christians whose baptisms are recognized as valid when they are admitted into Orthodoxy.

CHRIST

(Greek Christos, anointed one). Translation from the Hebrew Mashiah or Messiah. The term, under various forms, was used in the Old Testament of kings (1 Samuel 24:6-10), priests (Exodus 28:41), patriarchs (Psalms 105:15), and even the nation (Habakkuk 3:13).

Eventually the designation was reserved especially for the expected descendant of David, the Messiah or Christ of Jewish hope. As the primary messianic title, its roots run deep in Judaism and the Old Testament. Of particular importance is the oracle of Nathan promising David an eternal dynasty (2 Samuel 7:5 - 16:1; Psalms 89:20-38). The sufferings of Jewish national life from the exile through the Seleucid domination made of this promise the bedrock of national hope.

The primitive church did not hesitate to confess Jesus as "the Christ" (Acts 2:36; 3:20; 4:26; 8:5; 9:22; 17:3; 18:5; 26:23). But expansion of the gospel to peoples unaware of Jewish tradition behind the title inevitably meant that it would lose its messianic force and gradually take on the properties of a personal name: Jesus Christ, Christ Jesus, or simply Christ.

Paul uses it predominantly in this sense (e.g. 1 Corinthians 1:13; Romans 1:1-8) as does the rest of the New Testament. Liturgical usage is also reflected in such combinations as Christ Jesus, the Lord Jesus Christ, Our Savior, Christ Jesus (2 Timothy 1:10; Titus 1:4). Thus the word evolved in the early church from simply a messianic title to a personal and even cultic name for Jesus.

CHRIST, The Great Sacrament

A theological view of Christ as the personal embodiment of God's desire to save all men. The mystery of God is his plan of salvation in which he communicates himself to men in a sacramental way, that is, in a way consonant with the nature of men by means of a visible intervention.

The church as sacrament and the seven sacraments are extensions of the primordial sacrament that is Christ. Man, by responding to the church and the sacraments, responds to Christ and realizes his saving encounter with God. Thus the mystery of God is realized in and by means of Christ.

CHRISTADELPHIANS

A sect founded in 1848 by J. Thomas (1805-1871). He refused to describe himself and his followers as Christian because that term had become corrupted by the connotation of apostasy; in its place he choose the name Christadelphians, i.e. brethren of Christ.

The brethren:
▲ reject the doctrine of the Trinity and the existence of hell;
▲ call for a revival of primitive Christianity;
▲ look to the second coming of Jesus Christ to reign for 1,000 years;
▲ claim that only baptism by immersion is effective; and
▲ teach conditional immortality, that only those who hold the divine truth as recognized by the Christadelphians will be saved.

CHRISTENDOM

The whole body of members of the Christian church; all countries professing Christianity as opposed to those professing other religions. In its early use the term was contrasted with "heatheness" and it came to have a geopolitical meaning, in which sense it means the Christian domain, or the countries professing Christianity.

CHRISTENING

Christian ceremony of baptism of infants, including giving a name.

CHRIST GIVING THE KEYS

A theme in Christian art illustrating the historical event of Christ entrusting his earthly church to St. Peter; the transfer of authority is symbolized by Christ presenting Peter with the keys to heaven.

CHRIST GIVING THE LAW

A theme in Christian art showing Christ delivering the new law to his Apostles. A symbolic rather than historical subject, it was particularly important in early Christian (2nd-6th centuries) art, frequently decorating the domed semicircular apse at the end of the nave of basilicas.

CHRISTIAN

The Latinized Greek term Khristianos, found only three times in the New Testament, designated followers of Jesus Christ (Acts 11:26; 26:28).

"It was first in Antioch that the disciples were by divine providence called Christians" (Acts 11:26). It is possible, then, that this name was used as early as the year 44 when the events surrounding this text occurred, although the grammatical structure of this phrase does not necessarily make it some; some think it was a little later. At any rate, by 58, in the city of Caesarea, nearly 300 miles south of Antioch, the term was well known and used even by public officials, for, at that time, King Agrippa II said to Paul, "In a short time you would persuade me to become a Christian" (Acts 26:28).

CHRISTIAN AND MISSIONARY ALLIANCE

A missionary and evangelistic movement that developed from the work of Albert B. Simpson (1852-1919), a Presbyterian minister who left that church to become an independent evangelist in New York City.

Theologically conservative, it stresses Christ as "Savior, Sanctifier, Healer, and Coming King." It concentrates on sending missionaries to parts of the world neglected by other Christian groups.

In the United States congregations are independent but are joined together in a general conference that meets annually.

CHRISTIAN ATHEISM

A concept associated with the death-of-God thinking of some American Protestants and, more specifically, with the writing of Thomas J. Altizer. The concept has emerged from a disturbing encounter of this thinking and events and forces of contemporary culture. The dissolution of the Christian era is proclaimed, together with a dawning awareness that the totality of human experience points to the death of God.

CHRISTIAN BROTHERS

Roman Catholic teaching order founded in 1802 by Edmund Ignatius Rice at Waterford, Ireland, to care for poor Catholic boys. The order now has schools and colleges in many countries.

CHRISTIAN CATHOLIC CHURCH

Conservative Christian sect founded in Chicago in 1896 by John Alexander Dowie (1847-1907), who established a tabernacle and "healing rooms" in Chicago, where he attracted a large following. With many of his followers Dowie established an exclusive Christian community in Zion, Illinois, a city that he planned and that was controlled and governed by church officials. In later years, the church remained strong in Zion, but the city eventually welcomed other businesses and churches.

CHRISTIAN CHURCH

A Protestant sect that developed on the American frontiers, known until 1968 as the Disciples of Christ. A separate body of independent congregations differs from the Disciples of Christ on matters of church organization. Known as the Churches of Christ, it has circa 2.8 million members.

CHRISTIAN CIVIC ALLIANCE

Alliance of the Swiss Cantons that officially adopted the religious reforms of Zwingli (1484-1531).

CHRISTIAN DEMOCRACY

A term that has had different meanings at different times and places. Generally speaking, it refers to those movements that are inspired by Christian principles and organized by laymen in the pursuit of political and socio-economic objectives. Historically, the most important Christian democratic movement developed in Italy as an immediate consequence of the church-state quarrel that accompanied political unification in the 19th century.

CHRISTIAN ENDEAVOR

International youth organization established in 1881 by the reverend E. Clark in Portland, Maine. Its purpose is to promote the observance of Christian virtues among young people. The interdenominational movement has adherents throughout the world. Members pledge to read the Bible daily and to attend society prayer meetings.

CHRISTIAN FAMILY MOVEMENT

An apostolic organization founded in 1943 to promote the Christian way of life in the family, and in the families of the community, and in institutions that affect the family by servicing, educating, and representing the family.

CHRISTIAN FELLOWSHIP

A unity of persons that results from the shared life of the Spirit. Today this term describes the experiences of those who pray together in the Spirit, help each other, and enjoy each other's company for the sake of Jesus Christ, and who share the eucharist as the best expression and source of their oneness.

CHRISTIAN FRONT

American anti-Semitic and pro-Nazi organization active from circa 1938 until the United States entered World War II. It openly encouraged boycotts of Jewish merchants; used the slogan "Buy Christian;" and published the Christian Index, a directory of non-Jewish merchants in parts of New York City.

More responsible Catholic spokesmen,including Cardinal Mundelein of Chicago, strongly opposed such anti-Semitic manifestations.

CHRISTIAN GREEK SCRIPTURES

So designated to distinguish them from the pre-Christian Greek scriptures, that is, the Greek Septuagint translation of the Hebrew scriptures (Hebrew Bible). It is a common practice to call this latter portion of the Bible the New Testament.

CHRISTIANITY

Religion founded on the life, death and resurrection of Jesus Christ. The central Christian proclamation is that by the grace of God people are saved through faith in Christ, their sins are forgiven, and they receive new and eternal life. Arising out of this are the various aspects of Christian life and teaching, broadly divided into worship, theology, mission and personal and social obedience to God's will - that is, the practice of righteousness, love and mercy. The whole church regards the Bible as authoritative.

It is one of the world's great religions and the single most powerful influence in the history of Western civilization. Though it is a universal creed and the church now exists throughout the world (nearly 1,8 billion people, or one third of the human race, are identified as being associated with Christianity), half its members are found in Europe and the bulk of the remainder in North and South America. Christianity had its beginnings when a small band of Jews recognized Jesus of Nazareth, who died circa 33 as the Messiah - the Christ - come to fulfill the Messianic prophecies that abound in the Old Testament. The Christian faith has its roots in Judaism, and it was to the Jews that Jesus, and later the Apostles, first preached the new law of love of God and charity toward one's neighbor.

CHRISTIANITY, Church of England

Because it was based on a political rather than a religious dispute, church reform in England came about in a different way. After the pope has refused to annul his first marriage, King Henry VIII had declared the Church of England to be free of papal jurisdiction; but the Anglican Church at first retained much of Roman Catholic liturgy and doctrine. Only later, under Edward VI and Elizabeth I, did it become truly Protestant; its tenets were set forth in the Thirty-nine Articles of 1576. The Puritans considered these doctrinal reforms inadequate, however, and sought a form of worship based strictly on the scriptures. Puritan sects later gave rise to the Baptist and Congregational Churches and to the Religious Society of Friends, or Quakers.

The discovery and colonization of the New World offered great opportunities for expansion to the European Christian churches. The settlements founded throughout the American colonies by dissenting members of Protestant churches gave impetus to the development of independent American church bodies, such as the Protestant Episcopal Church, an offshoot of the Church of England. Roman Catholic colonists settled Maryland, where they practiced religious toleration. Some distinctly American churches afterward sprang up, among these the Church of Jesus Christ of Latter-Day Saints (Mormons), founded in 1830, and the Church of Christ Scientist (Christian Science), founded in 1882. In all there are more than 220 branches of the Christian Church in the United States.

During the 18th century John Wesley, who turned from Calvinism to a more traditional Christian view, founded the Methodist Church.

CHRISTIANITY, Counter-Reformation

The Catholic Church responded to the Reformation with a movement known as the Counter-Reformation, a period of extraordinary religious activity and vigor, during which various former abuses were corrected, several new religious orders were formed, and a spirit of Christian mission was fostered among the faithful. It was a highly active era for proselytizing the faith and a period of great creativity in religious matters.

The social ills of the 18th and 19th centuries spurred Protestant and Catholic groups alike to a new social consciousness, which has developed further in the 20th century and become characteristic of much Christian activity, particularly with regard to more secular social concerns. Work with those who live on the margins of modern society - minority groups, the poor and the under-privileged all over the world - has become a cause that unites Christians.

One of the most significant developments in the continued growth of the Christian church in this century is the ecumenical movement. Although still in an early phase, with its progress often slowed by the many and complex organizational and doctrinal difficulties involved, ecumenicism has caught the imagination of a majority of the clergy and the faithful, who envision a future in which the Christian church will again be one universal body, as it was established by Christ.

CHRISTIANITY, Early centuries

The early centuries of the church were troubled by doctrinal disputes. In order to settle these differences and establish the basic tenets of Christianity, Constantine called the first ecumenical council at Nicaea in 325. The Nicene creed, adopted at this council, stated the basic truths of the Christian Church; any departures from this statement of faith were thereafter regarded as heresy.

From earliest times the preeminence of the bishop of Rome, as direct successor of St. Peter, was recognized by the entire Western church. However, many disputes arose from the fact that the Eastern church, headed by the patriarch of Constantinople, had traditionally retained jurisdiction over organizational and doctrinal matters in its own sphere. The question of papal authority led to the Great Schism in 1054, when the patriarch of Constantinople refused to recognize the pope as head of the entire church, and the Eastern church broke its ties with the West. As the Eastern Orthodox church, it has since maintained its organizational and jurisdictional independence, while much of its doctrine and liturgy reflect its common origin with the Western church in early Christian rites.

CHRISTIANITY, Early development

Immediately after the crucifixion of Jesus, christianity counted only a few hundred members, among them the Apostles, who followed Christ's teachings and preached his gospel, particularly as it concerned the life, sufferings, death, resurrection and divine nature of Jesus. The Christian community had its center in Jerusalem but soon spread into Asia Minor, Syria, Macedonia and Greece. While St. Peter was the leader of the Jewish Christian community, Saul of Tarsus (later known as St. Paul the Apostle) was preeminent in the task of converting the gentiles and establishing churches in the Greco-Roman world. Although there may have been some differences in form or ritual between the Jewish and gentile communities of Christians, both professed the same fundamental tenets of the faith, bearing witness to Christ's resurrection and commemorating his sacrifice in the sacrament of the Eucharist, which he himself had instituted at the Last Supper when he broke bread and drank wine with his Apostles.

CHRISTIANITY, Ecclesiastical structure

As the faith spread and greater numbers of converts swelled the ranks of the faithful, an ecclesiastical structure evolved. The meetings of the faithful were conducted by bishops, who replaced the Apostles as celebrants of the ritual of the Eucharist. They were assisted by presbyters, or elders, who eventually were given the right to perform the sacred duties connected with the Eucharist, while the bishops retained the right of consecrating the presbyters and of confirming the faithful. Various regions were organized into dioceses and provinces; the bishop who was known as the metropolitan, had authority over the other bishops of the province. The Council of Nicaea affirmed the preeminence of the metropolitans of Rome, Alexandria and Antioch, who, together with the bishops of Jerusalem and Constantinople, came to be called patriarchs.

Within three centuries, despite persecutions (the last, and most severe, was under Diocletian in 303), the Christian religion had become so firmly established that, in 313, Emperor Constantine proclaimed freedom of worship throughout the empire and, in 324, he established Christianity as the official religion.

CHRISTIANITY, Popes

The popes emerged as influential rulers in Western Europe during the Middle Ages, contending with the Holy Roman Emperors for temporal power as well as spiritual authority. Now that Christianity had become a dominant political force, disputes arose concerning papal succession, and popes and antipopes, supported by rival kings and princes, fought for the right to rule with the authority of the Holy See. The entire structure of the church was shaken by this discussion, and abuses such as simony and the sale of indulgences that had grown up within it cried out for reform.

CHRISTIANITY, Reformation

The reformation, which begin in the 16th century, was spearheaded by the Englishman John Wycliffe and the Bohemian reformer Hans Hus, who preached individual interpretation of the Bible, and it was fulfilled by Martin Luther, who gave decisive form to the revolt against the system of Christianity as it was then understood. Luther denied the supreme authority of the pope and rejected all but two of the seven sacraments, retaining only baptism and the Eucharist. Positively, he affirmed the supreme authority of the Bible in all matters of faith - hence his espousal of the doctrine of the priesthood of all believers and justification by faith alone. From that time on, there have existed, two main currents of Christianity, Protestantism and Roman Catholicism. The Eastern Orthodox Church has always been the most unchanging and conservative of Christian religious bodies.

In reaction to the religious abuses that had engendered it, Protestantism sought a greater purity of religion, a more austere spiritual code and a return to godliness in the life of the individual. Lutheranism spread rapidly in Germany and Scandinavia; in Switzerland the Reformation was lead by Zwingli and Calvin. Calvinism, which teaches the predestination of the elect and which was adopted by the French Huguenots, forms the basis of modern Presbyterianism and the Reformed churches.

CHRISTIAN METHODIST EPISCOPAL CHURCH

Methodist church in the United States, organized in 1870 as the Colored Methodist Episcopal Church; it adopted its present name in 1954. The church originated from a movement begun in 1866 within the Methodist Episcopal Church, South, to organize the African-American members into an independent church. The church is Methodist in church government and doctrine.

CHRISTIAN METHODIST EPISCOPAL CHURCH

A denomination that has its roots in a proposal made in 1866 by the General Conference of the Methodist Episcopal Church, South, when faced with desertion of its African-American members. The Conference voted to organize black members into "separate missions, churches, charges, districts, and Annual Conferences of their own."

CHRISTIAN MYSTICISM

The sense of direct contact with the divine reality, involving in its higher forms the experience of union with God, in the context of the Christian faith. Although the value of mysticism has been questioned by church authorities, it has played an important role in the history of the Christian religion beginning with the "Christ-mysticism" (union with Christ) in the writings of Paul and John and continuing through the major branches of Christianity to the present time.

CHRISTIAN MYTH

Sacred and edifying stories based on the motifs of earlier Jewish and Greek myths and legends and those of peoples with whom Christians later interacted or dominated. Aiding Christians to understand their origins, identities, and destinies and to emulate religious personages who have led exemplary lives, Christian myths and legends have exerted a significant influence on the political theory, economic thought, visual arts, music, popular piety, and science of Western civilization.

CHRISTIAN OF PRUSSIA

(1178-1245) Cistercian missionary, first bishop of Prussia. He preached successfully among the Prussians and was consecrated bishop in 1215.

CHRISTIAN OF STABLO

(819-880) Benedictine exegete. Scholar of the Carolingian Renaissance, he had a fine knowledge of Greek and is best known for his commentary on St. Matthew which demonstrates 9th century methods of compiling scriptural expositions and monastic teaching.

CHRISTIAN PERFECTION

The spiritual goal of individual Christians, progressively acquired by striving to live in ever more perfect accord with the precepts of Jesus Christ; e.g., to love one's enemies and to repay evil with good. Such perfection was most fully exemplified in the lives of the saints.

CHRISTIAN PHILOSOPHY

A family of systems of movements of thought conditioned by the presuppositions, tenets, and commitments of the Christian faith. Although Christian philosophy was at first identified with Christian theology, the medieval Scholastics gradually came to distinguish philosophy, with its universally accessible truths, from the revealed theology derived from the Bible. Christian philosophers have argued that if one believes that the world is the creation of God and that the person is a unitary body-soul whose lost freedom can be restored only through the grace of God, then his or her philosophy will reflect these truths. Others have held that there can be no philosophy that is distinctively Christian.

CHRISTIAN PREACHING CONFERENCE

An organization of priests and ministers dedicated to a more effective proclamation of the Word. The conference's charter convention was held in New York in 1958.

CHRISTIAN REFORMED CHURCH

Protestant denomination founded in 1857 by Dutch immigrants in the United States who separated from the Protestant Dutch Church (now the Reformed Church in America). Originally known as the True Holland Reformed Church, the present name was adopted in 1890.

CHRISTIAN SCIENCE

A religious movement, the major tenet of which is the belief in the power of Christian faith to heal sickness. It was founded by Mary Baker Eddy. who organized the first "Church of Christ, Scientist" at Boston, Mass. in 1879. There are now many affiliated churches throughout the world. The Christian Science Monitor is a widely respected international daily newspaper.

Christian Science is regarded by its adherents as the restatement of primitive Christianity with its full gospel of salvation from all evil, including sickness and disease as well as sin. According to its adherents, Christian Science healing is brought about by the operation of truth in human conscience. There is no ordained priesthood, but there are public practitioners of Christian Science healing who are officially authorized.

CHRISTIAN SOCIAL EDUCATION

A constructive study and training in a program of social action based largely on papal encyclicals. It is designed to inculcate in youth a better understanding of temporary society; to awaken them to their responsibilities to their fellow men and society at large; and to help them to acquire a grasp of Christian doctrine relative to social problems emerging from social evolution and an understanding of their role in the solution of such problems.

CHRISTIAN SOCIALISM

19th century movement of social reform based on Christian ideals rather than on secular socialist class struggle. The movement has differed from the socialism of the First and Ssecond International by its stress on the right to private property, and from communism by its order of priorities; the first has tended to scorn it as offering mere palliatives, the second to suppress it or give it the kiss of death.

CHRISTIANS OF SAINT THOMAS

Four major Christian groups - Syro-Malabar, Syro-Malankara, Syrian Orthodox (Jacobite), and Mar Thomite - living in the state of Kerala (formerly Malabar), along the south-west coast of India, who claim to have been Christianized by the Apostle Thomas.

The origins of the so-called Malabar Christians are uncertain, though they seem to have been in existence before the 6th century and probably derive from the missionary activities of the East Syrian (Nestorian) Church - which held that, in effect, the two natures of Christ were two persons, somehow joined in a moral union - centered at Ctesiphon. Despite their geographic isolation, they retained the Chaldean liturgy and Syriac language and maintained fraternal ties with the Babylonian (Baghdad) patriarchate; their devotional practices also included Hindu religious symbolism, vestiges of their early religion.

CHRISTIAN UNION
A Pentecostal group formed in North Carolina in the late 19th century.

CHRISTIAN UNITY
In the early church, the ideal of spiritual harmony among believers through the suppression of petty jealousies and strife that tended to set one Christian church (or individuals within the same church) against another; more recently, the positive goal of various Christian churches to work together, despite doctrinal differences, in the hope of eventually finding a means by which all the churches can be reunited.

CHRISTIAN UNITY, Secretariat for Promoting
A Vatican office created by Pope John XXIII with the immediate aim of facilitating fruitful participation of the Orthodox and other Christian churches in Vatican Council II, and with the broader aim of working with those churches toward unity.

CHRIST IN MAJESTY
Theme in Christian art showing the resurrected Christ enthroned as a sovereign. The subject originated in Roman Early Christian art of the 5th century and was current in western Europe through the 12th century.
The standard iconography of the theme emphasized different theological aspects of Christ. His figure usually framed by a mandorla or almond-shaped aureole, Christ holds in his left hand a book or the gospels containing the new law and with his right hand makes a gesture of speech - benediction or admonition. He is thus both the lawgiver and the word of God.

CHRISTMAS
Christian festival celebrated in the Western world on December 25, commemorating the birth of Jesus Christ. It is a public holiday in Christian countries, usually marked by the exchange of gifts - tokens of the gifts of the three wise men to the infant Jesus. Many of its customs have a non-Christian origin and were adapted from celebration of the winter solstice. The choice of the date near the winter solstice owed much to missionary desire to facilitate conversion of members of older religions, which held festivals at the same time of the year.
The Christmas cycle extends from the first Sunday of Advent through the Advent season to Christmas Eve, through Christmastide and the feasts associated with the Epiphany, down to the Sunday after the Epiphany when the last echoes of the Christmas mystery are heard in the liturgy.

CHRISTMAS CONFERENCE
Meeting of Methodist preachers in Baltimore (USA) in 1784, which organized the Methodist Episcopal Church

CHRISTMAS PLAYS
A genre of medieval liturgical drama flourishing in the 11th and 12th centuries, consisting at first only of the shepherds" visit to the manger but gradually acquiring other related incidents like the offering of the Magi and the slaughter of the Holy innocents.

CHRISTMAS TREE
An evergreen tree decorated with lights, ornaments, etc. For Christmas the tree and decorations are reminders of Christ, who is the tree of life and the light of the world. The Christmas tree was first used by the people of Germany. It was a combination of two earlier customs: the paradise tree (11th century) and the Christmas light.

CHRIST-MYSTICISM
An approach to union with God through union with Jesus Christ, classi-

cally exemplified in the writings of Paul the Apostle and John the Evangelist; it is distinguished from mysticism that seeks union with God as a transcendent being.

CHRISTOCENTRISM

A characteristic of any approach to theology, spirituality, or history by virtue of which such an approach accords a central role to Jesus Christ in his human nature - or to God precisely as incarnate.

CHRISTOLOGICAL CONTROVERSIES

Conflicts in the early Christian centuries between orthodox and heterodox explanations of how Jesus Christ is true God and true man. Ignatius of Antioch in the first century condemned Docetism, the denial that Christ had a genuine, physical body.

Irenaeus combated the same error against various uses in Gnosticism. The Council of Nicaea I condemned Arianism and sanctioned the term homoousion (consubstantial) to describe Christ's oneness in nature with the Father.

CHRISTOLOGY

Teaching concerning the person of Jesus Christ. In Christian theology, the term is used in the sense of the study of the doctrines concerning the divine-human nature of Jesus of Nazareth, the Christ, and his relationship to the Father and the Holy Spirit within the divine Trinity of God the Father, Son, and Holy Spirit.

CHRISTOPHER, Saint

(3rd century) By tradition a Christian martyr and patron of travelers because, according to a popular legend, he once carried the Christ child across a river. The Roman Catholic Church has removed Christopher from its calendar of saints for lack of historical evidence as to his existence.

CHRISTOPHER MOVEMENT

A challenge in line with Christian principles to raise standards of human endeavor. Inaugurated (1945) by Maryknoll priest, J. Keller, it evokes individual responsibility and motivates human initiative engagements at all levels, especially in five vital fields:
▲ government,
▲ education,
▲ entertainment,
▲ industrial relations,
▲ labor management.

CHRISTOTOKOS

Nestorius' theological term for Mary as the mother of Jesus; he held that Mary was the "Christ-bearer" but could not be called the mother of God. The Council of Ephesus (431) excommunicated him, deposed him as bishop of Constantinople, and formally declared that Mary was Theotokos, the "God-bearer."

CHRIST'S THORN

Common name for any of several prickly or thorny shrubs, of the buckthorn family.

CHRIST THE KING, Feast of

Celebrated in the Roman Catholic Church in honor of Christ. It was established by Pope Pius IX in 1925 and was celebrated on the last Sunday in October.

CHRONICLES, Books of

Two Old Testament books, concerning the history of priestly worship from the death of Saul to the Babylonian Captivity. It is probably written by Ezra, around 400 BC.

The material of the chronicles may be divided as follows:
▲ lists of genealogies from Adam to King Saul (1 Chronicles 1-2);
▲ the death of Saul and the reign of King David (1 Chronicles 10-29);
▲ the reign of King Solomon (2 Chronicles 1-9);
▲ division of the monarchy into the northern and southern kingdoms to the end of the Babylonian exile (2 Chronicles 10-36).

The Chronicler used the Old Testament books of Samuel and Kings as sources for his historical account running from Saul to the exile. These sources, however, were freely modified to bring them into line with the chronicler's own interests and point of view.

CHRONISTA

Liturgical term designating the person (properly a deacon) who chants the narrative portions of the four gospels of the Passion when they are sung solemnly during Holy Week.

CHRYSOPHRASE

A semiprecious translucent gemstone, an apple-green variety of chalcedony. The color is caused by a trace of nickel oxide in the mineral. The only biblical reference to chrysophrase is in Revelation, where it is mentioned as constituting the 10th foundation of the wall of "the holy city, New Jerusalem" (Revelation 21:2, 20).

CHTHONIA

In Greek mythology, the founder of the Temple of Demeter in the Peloponesian city of Hermione.

CHTHONIC DEITIES

Divinities of the underworld associated with vegetation rites. They include the Greek goddess Demeter (called Chthonia, or earth goddess) and her daughter Kore, the Egyptian fertility god Osiris, and the Baltic goddess Zemes mate (earth mother), whose functions were later assumed by the Virgin Mary under the influence of syncretism after the Christianization of the Baltic lands in the 15th and 16th centuries.

CHU KI-CHOL

(1897-1944) Presbyterian minister who suffered martyrdom because of his opposition to Japanese demands that Christians pay reverence at Shinto shrines.

CH'UN CH'IU

The first Chinese chronological history, one of the Five Classics of Confucianism. In subtle ways, the book passes moral judgment on many events, as when Confucius deliberately omits the title of a degenerative ruler.

CHUNG YUNG

One of the four Confucian texts, meaning "Doctrine of the Mean."The text in 33 chapters that average circa 200 characters each, makes difficult reading because of its style, its brevity, and the richness of its concepts. Taoists and Buddhists profess to detect mystical meaning in the text and have studied it with special interest.

CHURCH

The community of Christian believers. The church as the body of Christ began on the day of Pentecost when the Holy Spirit arrived with his spiritual gifts.

The term is used both for the universal church (all Christians) and for its national and local expressions (the various denominations). Governed and served by its ministry, the church is established by the Holy Spirit through the Bible and the ordinances. Its life, ideally characterized by holiness, is expressed in worship, teaching, mission and good works.

St. Augustine proposed that the real church is an invisible entity known only to God. Martin Luther used this theory to excuse the divisions of the church at the Reformation, holding that the true church has its members scattered among the various Christian bodies but that it is independent of any organization known upon earth. The majority of Christians, however, have believed that Jesus intended to found one visible church here upon earth. In the 20th century, the ecumenical movement has worked to restore the unity of the church.

CHURCH ARCHITECTURE

As buildings for Christian worship, the earliest churches were no more than simple rooms devoid of architectural features. After the recognition of Christianity in the Roman Empire (313), churches came to be built in the style of secular Basilica. Eastern

churches followed the Byzantine style. In the West, the basilica was greatly modified during the Romanesque and Gothic periods. Later, in England, the basilica was adapted by Sir Christopher Wren and other of his school including James Gibbs. Both these architects influenced church architecture in colonial America.

During the 19th century, the historical styles were revised, and there were also eclectic architects who gave strongly personal interpretations, such as the American Bertram Grosvenor Goodhue (churches St. Thomas and St. Vincent Ferrer, New York).

Among the pioneers of modern church architecture was the French architect Analone de Baudot, whose St. Jean de Montmartre, Paris, was the first reinforced concrete church. Impressive modern churches include Notre-Dame du Haut, at Ronchamp, France, by Le Corbusier (1950-54), and the shell concrete church of the Miraculous Virgin, in Mexico City, by Felix Candela (1954).

CHURCH, Body of Christ

The image of the church as the body of Christ is found in the New Testament writings of Paul. In chapter 10 of 1 Corinthians, Paul says that our communion with Christ comes form "the cup of blessing," which unites us in his blood, and from "the bread that we break," which unites us to his body. Because the bread is one, all of us, though many, are one body. The eucharistic body of Christ and the church are, together the (Mystical) Body of Christ.

CHURCH ARCHITECTURE

As buildings for Christian worship, the earliest churches were no more than simple rooms devoid of architectural features. After the recognition of Christianity in the Roman Empire (313), churches came to be built in the style of secular Basilica. Eastern churches followed the Byzantine style. In the West, the basilica was greatly modified during the Romanesque and Gothic periods. Later, in England, the basilica was adapted by Sir Christopher Wren and other of his school including James Gibbs. Both these architects influenced church architecture in colonial America.

During the 19th century, the historical styles were revised, and there were also eclectic architects who gave strongly personal interpretations, such as the American Bertram Grosvenor Goodhue (churches St. Thomas and St. Vincent Ferrer, New York).

Among the pioneers of modern church architecture was the French architect Analone de Baudot, whose St. Jean de Montmartre, Paris, was the first reinforced concrete church. Impressive modern churches include Notre-Dame du Haut, at Ronchamp, France, by Le Corbusier (1950-54), and the shell concrete church of the Miraculous Virgin, in Mexico City, by Felix Candela (1954).

CHURCH ARMY

Organization of lay evangelists within the Anglican Church, founded in the slums of London in 1882 by Wilson Carlile, primarily concerned with social work and rehabilitation. After a two-year residential course of training, students are commissioned as officers of the church Army; the men are called captains, and the women sisters.

CHURCH ASSEMBLY

The national assembly of the church of England, established by the Enabling Act of Parliament in 1919. The Assembly is composed of three divisions:
▲ the House of Bishops, including all the members of the Upper Houses of the two Convocations;
▲ the House of Clergy, including all members of the Lower House of the Convocations;
▲ the House of Laity, consisting of laymen and women elected by the dioceses of both Convocations for 5-year terms.

CHURCH AUTHORITY

The nature and event of the right of ecclesiastical hierarchies, at whatever levels of responsibility, to enact and enforce laws affecting members under their jurisdiction, or that affect nonbelievers, for example, who form a minority group in a state having an established religion.

CHURCH COMMISSIONERS

In the Church of England, established in 1947 by the amalgamation of two corporations, Queen Anne's Bounty and the Ecclesiastical Commissioners, to help with the expenses of poor parishes.

CHURCH DISCIPLINE

Christian regulations for religious and moral life including systems of canon law. This developed from the rules of the early councils, and popes, later elaborated as in Roman Catholicism's *Corpus juris canonici*. Most churches have developed rules administered through hierarchies of church courts.

CHURCH DOCTORS

Saints whose writings in Christian doctrine have special authority. The four great doctors of the Eastern church are saints Athanasius of Alexandria, Basil the Great of Caesarea, Gregory of Narianzus, and John Chrysostom. The four great doctors of the Western church are saints Ambrose, Augustine, Gregory the Great (Pope Gregory) and Jerome. The West has 20 other doctors, including Sts. Thomas Aquinas, Bonaventure, Catherine of Sienna and Teresa of Avila. The last two were declared doctors by papal decree.

CHURCH FATHERS

Eminent bishops and teachers of the early Christian Church. They were known for their sanctity, learning and wise judgment; and their doctrinal writings were regarded by their successors as having decisive authority when dogmatic and other controversies arose.

The great age of the fathers was in the first six centuries of christianity, and respected Christian writers of the succeeding six centuries are also regarded as church fathers. The eight great early church Doctors of East and West have a special place among the Church Fathers. They are also the so-called "Apostolic Fathers" such as St. Clement of Rome (1st century), St. Ignatius of Antioch (died 107) and St. Polycarp of Smyrna (born circa 70). The unknown authors of the Didache, an invaluable work on the primitive church, and the allegorical Shepherd of Hermas, are also regarded as Apostolic Fathers.

CHURCH MEETING

A distinctive element of the congregational policy of Congregationalists and Baptists, the gathering of the entire congregation to consider material or spiritual concerns of the local church.

CHURCH OF CHRIST

US religious denominations based on the primitive church. It holds that the Church of Christ was founded at Pentecost and refounded by Thomas Campbell (1763-1854). There are over 18,000 independent churches and over 3 million members.

The Churches of Christ have no creed. They believe in the manifestation of God in Christ, the all-sufficiency of the Bible, with the primacy of the New Testament, as the revelation of the will of God and the only rule of faith and practice. They do not take part in interdenominational activities.

CHURCH OF CHRIST, Scientist

Christian Science, a religious body founded by Mary Baker Eddy in 1875 as the Christian Science Associated and chartered in 1879 as the Church of Christ, Scientist. Mrs. Eddy laid down the fundamental truths that were to guide the followers.

▲ There is no such thing as matter.
▲ Eternal mind is the source of all being.
▲ The apparent dualism of mind and matter is an error.
▲ Our senses are fallible and sense-

impression does not convey true knowledge.

▲ Disease is caused by mind alone, and the appearance of disease conveyed to the senses is an error of incorrect thinking.

Christian Science is the wisdom of Eternal Mind revealed through Jesus Christ, who taught the power of Mind to overcome the illusions of sin, sickness, and death. What is the key to understanding of God? It is that God, infinite Love, is Mind.

CHURCH OF CHRIST IN CHRISTIAN UNION

Protestant denomination in the United States, formed in 1909 by a group of dissenters in the Christian Union Church.

CHURCH(ES) OF GOD

Several Pentecostal churches that developed in the US South from the late-19th and early 20th-century Latter Rain revival, based on a belief that a second rain of the gifts of the Holy Spirit would occur similar to that of the first Christian Pentecost. They adhere to an ultraconservative theology, including holiness as a work of grace subsequent to conversion or justification, and "speaking in other tongues as the Spirit gives utterance."

CHURCH OF ENGLAND

The English national church. Its doctrine is basically Protestant and its hierarchy and ceremony are rooted in Catholic tradition. The church broke with Rome in 1534 when Henry VIII assumed the title of head of the church. In the 16th and 17th centuries the church was troubled by Puritan agitation and later by nonconformity. But it remains the established state church with a nominal membership of 25-30 million (active members perhaps total only 20 percent of this figure). The 26 senior bishops (lords spiritual) sit in the House of Lords, and are led by the archbishop of Canterbury.

CHURCH OF GOD

Christian fellowship that considers itself a "reformation movement" among Christians and not a church or sect; it accepts its title for identification purposes only. Its members believe that they have organized themselves to carry on the work of the church, but they don't believe they have organized the church, which is made up of all Christians and cannot be limited to human organizations.

Despite the movement's stated beliefs, it functions as a denomination. It has a congregational system of church government, and ministers belong to state and regional assemblies.

CHURCH OF GOD IN CHRIST

African-American Pentecostal church, established in 1897 by C.P. Jones and C.H. Mason. The founders emphasized entire scarification and speaking in tongues. Its organizational structure, which it believes is based on the Bible, consists of bishops, apostles, prophets, pastors, elders, deacons, evangelists, teachers, and missionaries.

CHURCH OF IRELAND

Official title of the autocephalous church in both Eire and Northern Ireland that is in full communion with the see of Canterbury and the other churches of the Anglican Communion.

CHURCH OF ROME

Very little is known about the origins of the church in Rome. It may well have been founded by the "visitors from Rome" (Acts 2:11) who were among those baptized by the Apostles on the first pentecost.

A rather late tradition places the arrival of Peter in Rome (circa 42), though this is probably too early. Some years later (circa 49), the Emperor Claudius expelled the Jews from Rome for disturbances which seem to have been occasioned by the presence of Christians in their midst.

CHURCH OF SCOTLAND

The Scottish national church, based on Presbyterianism. It is governed by the General Assembly, which is elected from the presbyters. Parishes are presided over by kirk sessions elected by the congregations. Membership totals some 1.4 million.

CHURCH OF THE NAZARENE

Protestant evangelical denomination created in its present form in Texas in 1908 when three groups merged. Its headquarters is in Kansas City, Missouri.

CHURCH OF THE NEW DISPENSATION

Hindu social group formed by Keshab Chandra Sen in 1881. The denomination is also known as Naba Bidhan or Nava Vidhana.

CHURCH OF THE NEW JERUSALEM

Religious organization based on the writings and philosophy of Emanuel Swedenborg.

CHURCH OF THE SEVEN COUNCILS

A term sometimes applied to the Orthodox church, signifying the church at the stage of doctrinal development it had reached after the seventh ecumenical council, the Council of Nicaea II (787). Because of the later split between the Eastern and Western church, that is the last council accepted as ecumenical by the East.

CHURCH SUFFERING

The souls in purgatory. According to Roman Catholic theology, the souls that must be cleansed of sin prior to their admittance into heaven are purged by suffering in the intermediate state. In the past the suffering has often been portrayed as physical, but it is now more generally interpreted as spiritual. Christians also speak of the Church Suffering on earth as it imitates Christ in accepting opposition and persecution (Mark 8:31).

CHURCHWARDEN

A lay officer in the churches of the Anglican Communion. Since early medieval times in England, churchwardens (usually two) have been appointed in every parish to take care of the temporalities. Though the rector has control of the church edifice and its appurtenances, the wardens are responsible for its repair and for providing the furnishings necessary for the performance of divine service. They are also required to maintain order in the church and churchyard, and have the power to arrest offenders.

Shortly before the Reformation, and continuing after, they assimilated the originally distinct office of sidemen or questmen, who represented the parish in diocesan synods or visitations and were responsible for presenting offenders against ecclesiastical law to the ordinary.

CHURCHYARD

The plot of ground in which the church building is set. Since churchyards, or an area within them, have often been set apart as a place for burials, the term has sometimes been considered almost equivalent to cemetery.

CIARAN OF CLONMACNOISE, Saint

(516-549) One of the most influential and illustrious founders of monasticism in Ireland. He founded an abbey in 548 at Clonmacnoise that subsequently developed into one of the most famous Irish monastic cities; by the 9th century it was a great center of learning.

CIBORION

In Eastern church architecture, a canopy of wood, stone, or other material supported on four or more columns and placed over the altar table.

It is the equivalent of the Western baldacchino or ciborium. If a eucharistic dove is used as an artophorion, it is usually suspended by a chain from the interior of the ciborion dome.

The canopy came into use as a special sign of reverence for the altar beneath and as an architectural device to concentrate attention upon it.

CIBORIUM

A term that in its earliest ecclesiastical use was applied to the dome or canopy supported by pillars that began in the 6th century to be placed above the altar; its purpose was to accent the altar.

From the late Middle Ages onward it was also used in reference to a rectangular box, enshrining the pyx with the reserved eucharistic bread. With the increase of devotion to the Eucharist there was a corresponding development in the vessels used in connection with the sacrament.

Today, when the practice of giving communion with hosts consecrated at the Mass attended by the communicants is spreading, smaller ciboria are more appropriate when the number of communicants is not too large.

CILICIA, Armenian Kingdom of

Also known as Lesser Armenia. From 1089 to 1375, the Armenian kingdom of Cilicia perdured, largely through alliance with the crusaders. Cilicia was fearful of both the Turks and the Greeks and depended upon Latins for support against these enemies.

Through the friendly relations with the crusaders, Roman influence was strengthened. King Leo II held his title from Emperor Henry VI and was crowned by a representative of Pope Celestine II in 1911.

CINITES

A non-Israelite seminomadic group, considered one of the indigenous tribes of Palestine (Genesis 15:19) and living in the Wadi 'Arabah region (Numbers 24:21-22) and as far south as Midian. Moses married a Cinite (Judges 4:11). Chronicles connects the Cinites and Rechabites (1 Chronicles 2:55). These wandering smiths probably influenced Israel but the hypothesis that Israel borrowed the worship of Yahweh from the Cinites is unproved.

CINNAMON

Spice from the cinnamon tree. Cinnamon was used in the preparation of the holy anointing oil as one of the "choicest perfumes" (Exodus 30:23). It was sprinkled on beds, was figuratively used in describing the beloved Shulammite girl, and is included among the products its traveling merchants sold to "Babylon the Great" before her destruction (Revelation 18:11-13).

CIRCASSIANS

Independent group in the Muslim community of Israel numbering some 5000. They originated in the Caucasian Mountains of Russia, immigrated to Palestine in the 1890s. Mostly loyal to the State of Israel, the community is concentrated in two villages in Galilee.

CIRCE

In Greek legend, a famous sorceress, the daughter of Helios, the sun god, and the ocean nymph Perse. She was able by means of drugs and incantations to change human beings into wolves, lions, and swine.

CIRCUIT

A term used more often in early Methodism than today, signifying a group of churches served by one minister, sometimes with the help of one or two associates, who traveled among the churches.

Geographically a circuit was quite large in early Methodism, sometimes comprising 10 or more churches. The preachers often used horses to travel their circuits and thus were called "circuit riders."

CIRCUMCELLIONS

Bands of Donatist peasants who terrorized Upper Numidia and Mauretania in the 4th and 5th centuries. Their name was derived from the attacks they made upon the settlements about which they roamed (circum cellas vagatur, Psalms 132:3).

The movement began as a protest against Roman landlords and an attempt to secure the abolition of debts and the liberation of slaves, but it later took on the character of a religious war.

CIRCUMCISION

The operation of cutting away all or part of the foreskin (prepuce) of the male organ. For the Jews it represents the fulfillment of the covenant between God and Abraham (Genesis 17:10-14), the first divine command of the Pentateuch, that every male child shall be circumcised. Christians are said to be circumcised in Christ, a spiritual rite and not physical (Colossians 2:11).

At whatever age performed, circumcision usually signifies the formal admission of the individual into his group or the achievement of a certain status, thus fixing his social position, right and status. Among the Ethiopians, the Muslims, and the Christians, as well as in traditional societies all over the world, the operation is regarded as having the profoundest religious significance.

CIRCUMCISION OF OUR LORD

An observance of Jewish law that took place at home 8 days after birth (Luke 2:21). In the case of Jesus, the act was presumably performed by St. Joseph. The rite incorporated Our Lord in the Jewish community and was the occasion for the bestowal of the sacred name Jesus ("Yahweh saves") who as Savior of the world belongs to the race of Abraham.

CIRCUMINCESSION

The technical theological term for the interpenetration of the three Persons of the Trinity. The doctrine was stated at the Council of Florence (1442): "Because of this unity (of the Godhead) the Father is totally in the Son, and totally in the Holy Spirit; the Holy Spirit is totally in the Father, and totally in the Son."

CIRCUMSTANCES, Moral

The variable situational factors affecting the moral goodness or evil of a concrete human act. Examples of such factors would be the agent's motive, his condition or state in life, the time, place, or manner in which he acts, the means he employs, and the effects of his action.

Thus, among other ways, circumstances may bear on morality: by adding a radically new moral character to an act, as when a cup of cold water is given to a little one because he is a disciple, or when a murder is committed in a cathedral.

CISTERCIAN ART

Primarily a noble and austere architecture rooted in the rules and Apologia of St. Bernard. The earliest churches were distinguished by structural simplicity and lack of ornamentation because of St. Bernard's reforms.

Stained glass was prohibited and windows of clear glass were enhanced by intricate interlacing arabesques of lead. But in all these fields Cistercian austerity ultimately relaxed, and immense baroque churches, rich illumination, and representational window glass expressed the styles of successive ages.

CISTERCIAN NUNS

Several Roman Catholic communities of cloistered, contemplative nuns who adopted the customs of the Cistercian monks, including silence, abstinence, and much outdoor labor. The first Cistercian monasteries for women were founded as early as 1120.

CISTERCIANS

White Monks, Roman Catholic religious order founded at Citeaux, France, in 1098 by St. Robert of Molesme and at its height in the 12th and 13th centuries. Cistercians eat and work in silence and abstain from meat, fish, and eggs.

CITY OF GOD

Translation of *De Civitate Dei,* a philosophy of history written by St. Augustine of Hippo after the sack of Rome by the barbarian Visigoths in 410. It was a reply to pagan critics that

Rome's acceptance of Christianity was the cause of the imperial city's disaster.

CITY RECORDER

A scribe, a man of letters. In the municipal government of the free cities in Asia Minor under the Roman Empire, the city recorder was the most important public officer. He was apparently elected to office by the people and functioned as the leading member of the municipal government. He may be compared to a modern-day mayor, as some translations render the term. Consequently, he was very influential in city affairs, and his dignified office was held in esteem by the people to a greater degree than is implied by the word "clerk" or "town clerk," as used in several biblical translations at Acts 19:35. The influence the city recorded wielded is shown by that manner in which this official in Ephesus quieted the mob that gathered against Paul and his companions (Acts 19:35-41).

CIVIL ALLEGIANCE

The obedience citizens are conscience-bound to give to political authority when it is legally exercised within the limits of morality and on behalf of the common good. The general principles that civil law obliges in conscience is found in Romans 13 and 1 Peter 2. The Fathers of the church and the social encyclicals have called for civil allegiance.

CIVIL CONSTITUTION OF THE CLERGY

During the French revolution, an attempt to reorganize the Roman Catholic Church in France on a national basis. It caused a schism within the French church and made many devout Catholics turn against the Revolution.

CIVIL RELIGION

The acceptance and, to varying degrees, the institutionalization of a set of values, symbols and rituals, based upon universal and transcendent truths, which serve as the cohesive force and center of meaning for a nation.

Although the truths of a civil religion have a transcendental value, their transmission and symbolic expression are through the history of a particular people.

CLAN

A large social group having a common inheritance, and resembling a tribe in magnitude. In all three instances where the Hebrew word "um-mah" occurs, it refers to a large group of non-Israelites and is translated "clan." Descendants of Ishmael's 12 sons, for example, are described as "clans" early in the history of that ethnic group (Genesis 25:16). The same is true of the descendants of Midian (Numbers 25:15). The term is also found in Hebrew poetry at Psalm 117:1, where it appears in a parallelism with "nations."

CLAPHAM SECT

An appellation by Sydney Smith (1764-1840) that stuck to an informal group of Anglican evangelists, who in the late 18th century worshiped at Clapham parish church and shared a sense of social responsibility and the conviction that religion should be manifested in good works.

CLARE, Saint

(1194-1253) Italian founder of the poor Clares. She was born at Assisi, and was influenced by St. Francis of Assisi. She was canonized 1255.

CLARENDON, Constitutions of

16 regulations set forth by Henry II of England in 1164 at a council held at Clarendon Park, Wiltshire. They were designed to assert the authority of the royal over the ecclesiastical courts and to forbid appeals to Rome without the king's consent.

CLARENI

A group of Franciscan Spirituals founded by Liberatus of Macerata and later given brief legal existence by Celestine V. This pope granted them immunity from the authority of the minister general of the Friars Minor in 1294; they are therefore referred to as

Poor Hermits of the Lord Celestine, or simply as Celestines.

CLARETIANS

Missionary Sons of the Immaculate Heart of Mary, community of priests and brothers organized in Spain in 1849. In the 19th century the Claretians have extended their apostolate to include teaching and parish work.

CLASS

In Methodism, a small subdivision (at first about 12 persons and a leader) within an early Methodist society. Each member of the society was placed in a class; leaders supervised the lives of the class members, who met each week for prayer and spiritual exhortation. A few Methodist bodies still have class meetings.

CLASS DISTINCTION

Preferential status of one group over another in a society on the grounds of race, lineage, wealth, or some other real or claimed privilege. Diversity of gifts or advantages is a fact of human society.

CLASSIS

An ecclesiastical governing body for a particular geographical district in Reformed churches. Presbyterian denominations apply the term presbytery for the same body.

Classis membership consists of the clergymen and representative elders of the district. The classis ranks in authority above that of the Reformed consistory (Presbyterian church session) and below that of the particular or regional synod and the general synod (Presbyterian general assembly).

CLAUDIA

A Christian women at Rome whose greetings Paul included in his second letter to Timothy (2 Timothy 4:21).

CLAUDIUS

Fourth emperor of Rome; son of Drusus the brother of Tiberius, and uncle of Caligula, whom he followed to the throne in January of 41. Claudius ordered all the Jews to depart from Rome, issuing his decree on January 25, 50, in the ninth year of his reign. The Latin historian Suetonius corroborates this banishment of Jews from Rome. As a consequence, two Christian Jews, Aquila and Priscilla, left Rome for Corinth, where not long after their arrival he met the apostle Paul upon his reaching there in the fall of the year (Acts 18:1-3). Toward the beginning of his reign, Claudius had been favorably disposed toward the Jews, even ordering toleration in their behalf and granting them various freedoms throughout the empire. It appears, however, that numerous Jews in Rome were rather riotous, resulting in Claudius' expelling them from the city.

CLAUDIUS LYSIAS

Military commander of the Roman garrison at Jerusalem when the apostle Paul last visited there, circa 56. Claudius Lysias figures in the account of Acts because of his dealings with the apostle Paul. He and the soldiers and army officers with him rescued Paul from death at the hands of a rioting mob. Taking hold of Paul, Claudius Lysias directed that the apostle be bound and, when unable, because of the tumult, to ascertain through inquiry the nature of the accusation against him, commanded that the apostle be brought to the soldiers' quarters located in the fortress of Antonia (Acts 21:30-34).

CLEAR VISION, Doctrine of

The theory, originally proposed by Uthred of Boldon, that the soul at the moment of death has a clear vision or full realization of divine truth and the nature of sin, and thus illumined makes a final acceptance or rejection of God. Uthred's theory was censured in 1368. A similar opinion was revived in the 19th century.

CLEMENCY

A virtue disposing in authority to temper justice with mercy when imposing punishment upon violators of the law. As a virtue, this disposition stands between two extremes. It is equally removed from an unreasonable leniency that will allow the common good to suffer by failure to use adequate severity in dealing with offenders, and from a cruelty too ready to insist upon exacting the last farthing of retribution from a wrongdoer.

CLEMENT I, Saint

(Clement of Rome; died end of first century AD) First Apostolic Father, pope from 88-101, supposed third successor to St. Peter. His martyrdom is legendary, and he has been hypothetically identified with the Clement mentioned in Phil. 4:3.

CLEMENT II

(971-1047) Pope from 1046-47. In 1047 Clement convoked the Council of Rome that passed strong decrees against simony (for instance, the buying or selling of a church office) and began a period of reform that was carried on by his successors.

CLEMENT III

(1025-1100) Paolo Scolari; antipope from 1080 to 1100. When Clement became the Italian leader of the imperialist faction opposing the Gregorian reform, Gregory excommunicated him. He was elected antipope in 1080, by a synod convoked by Henry at Brixen, which declared Gregory deposed.

CLEMENT IV

(1197-1268) Guido Fulcodi; pope from 1265 to 1268. Clement executed the plan of Pope Urban IV, his successor, in a century-old battle between the papacy and the German Hohenstaufen family. Clement's participation in the political affairs of Italy and Germany, however, brought peace neither to Rome nor to Italy.

CLEMENT V

(1260-1314) Bertrand de Got; pope from 1305 to 1314, who in choosing Avignon (France) for the papal residency - where it flourished until 1377 became the first of the Avignonese popes. The Council of Vienna convened in 1311. Clement approved the council's decision to charge heresy against the Spirituals, Franciscan extremists who observed absolute material poverty.

CLEMENT VI

(1291-1352) Pierre Roger; pope from 1342 to 1352. He considered the crusade against the Ottoman Turks as the pope's first duty. In 1344 he was responsible for a crusader naval expedition that took Smyrna, ending its piratical raids in the eastern Mediterranean. Clement helped secure the election in 1346 of the German king Charles IV, who allied with the papacy.

CLEMENT VII

(1478-1534) Giulio de Medici; pope from 1523 to 1534. A weak, vacillating pope in the political rivalries of King Francis I of France and the Holy Roman Emperor Charles V for the domination of Europe, Clement supported first one and then the other under pressure of events. Clement's incapacitation complicated the English King Henry VIII's request for an annulment of his marriage to Catherine of Aragon.

CLEMENT VII

(1342-1394) Robert of Geneva; he was the first antipope of the Great Western Schism that troubled the Roman Catholic Church for 40 years. He was a leader of the cardinals who declared the unpopular Italian pope Urban VI's election invalid and was chosen antipope in 1378.

CLEMENT VIII

(1536-1605) Ippolito Aldobrandini; pope from 1592 to 1605, the last pontiff to serve during the Counter-Reformation. He encouraged the Counter-Reformation efforts of St. Francis de Sales, whom he made bishop of Geneva, and was responsible for printing of the Vulgate (the standard version of the Latin Bible) and other key liturgical books. In 1597 Clement established a commission to investigate a controversy between the Jesuits and the Dominicans on divine grace and free will, but the issue was not resolved until after his death.

CLEMENT IX

(1600-1669) Giulio Rospiglosi; pope from 1667 to 1669. A distinguished man of letters, Clement wrote poetry but gained fame through his dramas with religious themes and several libretti. He clashed with King Louis XIV of France, who was determined to eliminate any religious divergence he saw as a threat to the unity of his kingdom and who revived the condemnation of Jansenism, a heretical doctrine de-emphasizing freedom of the will and teaching that redemption through Christ's death is limited to some but not all.

CLEMENT X

(1590-1676) Emilio Altieri; pope from 1670 to 1676. Despite his advanced age, Clement held out against French arrogance. Like his predecessor, he failed to rouse Europe against the Turks, who were menacing the Mediterranean. Well loved and deeply spiritual, he canonized the celebrated Cajetan of Thiene, Francis Borgia, and Rose of Lima.

CLEMENT XI

(1649-1721) Giovanni Francesco Albani; Pope from 18700 to 1721. Like his preceding popes Clement IX and X, he was embroiled in the French problems of Gallicanism, an ecclesiastical doctrine that advocated restrictions of papal power, and Jansenism, a heretical doctrine de-emphasizing freedom of the will and teaching that redemption through Christ's death is open to some but not all.

CLEMENT XII

(1652-1740) Lorenzo Corsini; pope from 1730 to 1740. Despite ill health and total blindness (from 1732), he worked diligently to halt the decline of papal influence. He aided large missionary enterprises, as exemplified in his sending Franciscans to Ethiopia. In 1738 he promulgated his bull *In Eminenti,* which condemned Freemasonry, the beliefs and observances of which were considered pagan and unlawful by the Roman Catholic Church.

CLEMENT XIII

(1693-1769) Carlo della Torre Rezzonica; pope from 1758 to 1769. The Jesuit issue dominated Clement's pontificate and that of his successor, Clement XIV. He did everything in his power to save the Jesuits from the Bourbon Absolutionists, who confederated with the Jansenists (advocated of a heretical doctrine de-emphasizing freedom of the will and teaching that redemption through Christ's death is open to some but not all) and the Freemasons, whose beliefs and observances were considered pagan and unlawful by the Roman Catholic Church.

CLEMENT XIV

(1705-1774) Giovanni Vincenzo Antonio Ganganelli; pope from 1769 to 1774. He was forced to dissolve the Society of Jesus (Jesuits), asserting that he did so because the Society could no longer attain its original ends as well as to restore true peace to the church.

CLEMENT, First Letter of

Originally entitled Letter to the church of Corinth; a letter to the Christian church in Corinth from the church of Rome, traditionally ascribed to and almost certainly written by Clement I of Rome (circa 96). It is extant in a second century Latin translation, which is possibly the oldest surviving Latin Christian work.

The Letter was an important influence on the development in the church of the episcopal orders of the ministry, and it has been used to support the doctrine of the apostolic succession, according to which bishops represent a direct, unbroken line of succession from the Apostles.

CLEMENT OF ALEXANDRIA

(circa 150-215) Theologian of the early Christian church. His most important work is the trilogy *Exhortation to the Greeks,* the *Tutor* and *Miscellanies.* Born in Athens, Clement spent most of his life as a teacher in Alexandria.

CLEMENTINAE

A collection of the legislation of Clement V and of the Council of Vienne (1311-1312), important to the history of canon law.

CLEMENTINE INSTRUCTION

An instruction issued by Pope Clement XII in 1731 regulating the Forty Hours Devotion, setting down in minute detail the rubrics for the services. The present rubrics for Benediction and exposition of the Blessed Sacrament (1973) considerably modify former observance of this instruction

CLEOPAS

One of the two disciples, neither of whom were apostles, who traveled to Emmaus on Jesus' resurrection day. When Jesus joined them as a stranger and asked what they were debating, Cleopas replied: "Are you dwelling as an alien by yourself in Jerusalem and so do not know the things that have occurred in her in these days?" After Jesus explained many scriptures to them and then identified himself, Cleopas and his companion, instead of staying overnight in Emmaus, hastened back to Jerusalem and reported these things to the others (Luke 24:13-35).

CLERGY

Ordained ministers of the Christian churches. In the Roman Catholic Church the term clergy includes the orders of bishops, priest, and deacon, and, more freely used, it includes also members of the religious orders. A distinction may be made between diocesan clergy, that is, those ordained for a particular diocese and committed in obedience to a particular bishop; and regular (or religious) clergy, that is, those who belong to a religious institute in the church and owe primary obedience to their religious superiors as well as pastoral obedience to the bishop in whose diocese they exercise their ministry.

CLERGY, Congregation of the

The congregation or department of the Catholic Church government in the reorganized Roman Curia that replaces the older Congregation of the Council. It exists to deal with matters concerning the pastoral ministry of priests and deacons throughout the world.

CLERGY, Indigenous

Priests who fulfill their sacramental apostolate in their native land. Vatican Council II (Act 16) states that the church's work is more effectively carried out when the orders of bishop, priest, and deacon are assumed by an indigenous clergy. From apostolic times to the 16th century it was the church practice to ordain indigenous priests for new Christian communities whenever possible. With the establishment of missions among non-Western peoples and continuing until relatively recent times, however, this practice was often reduced to a mere aspiration, an ultimate but unattained goal.

But a new vision of modern missionary action and the insistence of Leo XIII and his successors caused a renewed thrust toward the actual nativization of the clergy in mission areas.

CLERGY, Marriage of

The Eastern Orthodox Churches know only a celibate religious clergy or a married secular clergy. Unmarried candidates before receiving ordination must either enter the religious state by monastic profession or be married.

Once ordained, deacons, priests, and bishops are prevented from marrying by the diriment impediment of sacred orders, which continues to bind them even if they have become widowers.

CLERGY RESERVES

Lands formerly set aside for the Church of England in Canada; a cause of controversy in 19th-century Canadian politics. Established by the Constitutional Act of 1791 "for the support and maintenance of a Protestant clergy," the Clergy reserves amounted to one-seventh of all land grants.

The system was finally secularized in 1864. At the same time, a large cash payment was made to the Church of England, the Church of Scotland, the Roman Catholic Church, and the Wesleyan Methodists as acknowledgments of their "vested interests" in the Clergy Reserves.

CLERICALISM

A term originating in the latter half of the 19th century, and generally used in a pejorative sense, signifying domination of civil government and temporal affairs by the church. Its meaning has been broadened by some to apply to all attempts of churches to influence special and economic aspects of life.

CLERKS REGULAR

Communities of priests bound by the vows of the religious life and living a common life under a rule. They differ from canons regular by the fact that they are dedicated primarily to the active ministry and are excused from choral obligations.

In most such communities the priests are expected to cultivate the sacred sciences in addition to their priestly ministry. They generally observe a uniformity of clerical dress.

CLERMONT, Councils of

Two councils bear the name, held in that city in 535 and the other in 1095. The latter is the more important. There Pope Urban II delivered an address that inspired the First Crusade (1096-1099). Urban pleaded for help for the Eastern Christians and for the recovery of Jerusalem from non-Christian hands.

CLOISTER

A court surrounded by vaulted and arcaded passageways supported by columns. Usually adjoining an abbey or church, the cloister served as a sheltered access to the surrounding buildings and was mainly used for recreation and exercise. An essential feature of Romanesque and Gothic churches and monasteries since the 11th century, cloisters exist throughout Europe.

Vatican Council II decreed that Roman Catholic cloisters should be maintained by those in the contemplative life but adjusted to conditions of time and place by those engaged in the active apostolate.

CLOPAS

The husband of one of the Mary's that stood beside Jesus as he hung on the cross (John 19:25). Presumably he was the husband of the "other Mary," and father of the Apostle James the less and his brother Joseph (Matthew 27:56; 28:1; Mark 15:40; Luke 6:15). That Clopas was a brother of Joseph, the foster father of Jesus, is a conjecture based entirely on tradition.

CLOSED COMMUNION

Restriction by a Roman Catholic Church of participation in the Lord's Supper to its own members; the opposite of open communion, the more general practice among Protestant churches. While the term is not used, closed communion is in fact the law in the Roman Catholic Church.

Closed communion has been particularly associated with Baptist history. Until the 20th century, most Baptists practiced closed communion, for instance, refused to share in the Lord's Supper with pedobaptists.

Today most Baptists in the northern part of the United States practice open communion, a minister usually announcing that all Christians are welcome to the Lord's Table.

In the Southern Baptist Convention there is a diversity of practice; the tendency in the south-west is strongly toward closed communion, but in the south-east many churches practice open communion.

CLOUD OF UNKNOWING

A 14th century English masterpiece of the spiritual life, distinguished by beauty of phrasing, skillful use of scriptural language and imagery, profound thought and simplicity of style. The unknown author, writing with force and originality, gives direct, practical instruction on the life of mystical prayer to a disciple who finds himself "between a cloud of forgetting (of creatures) and a cloud of unknowing (of God)."

CLUNIAC ART

Reached its zenith 1090-1150 under Abbots Hugh of Cluny and Peter the Venerable, when the third abbey church of Cluny, the greatest of Romanesque churches, was built. The Cluniac monastery and church contained some of the best Romanesque sculpture.

CLUNY, Abbey of

Roman Catholic monastic congregation founded in Burgundy in 910; it played a major role in reforming Christian monasticism during the early Middle Ages. The abbey was an important center of ecclesiastical reform in the 10th-12th centuries. Both the latest church (completed 1113) and the monastery were monumental examples of Romanesque architecture and elaborate sculpture.

COBRA

An extremely poisonous snake of Asia and Africa. The cobra mentioned in six passages in the Bible is undoubtedly the Egyptian cobra or asp, one commonly used in snake charming, both in Bible times and today. The Israelites were well acquainted with this snake, not only while they were in Egypt, but also during their wandering through the wilderness. Moses, in addressing the Israelites in the wilderness, referred to the cobra's venom, "the cruel poison of cobras" (Deuteronomy 32:33).

COCKCROW

Name given to the third watch period of the night, according to the Grecian and the Roman division (Mark 13:35). It corresponded to the time from midnight to three o'clock in the morning.

There has been some discussion of the subject of cockcrowing owing to Jesus' reference to it in connection with his prediction of Peter's denying him on three occasions (e.g., Matthew 26:34, 74-75; Mark 14:30; Luke 22:34). On the basis of the statements made in the Jewish mishnah, some argue that cocks were not bred in Jerusalem, since they caused ceremonial uncleanness by their scratching up the ground. They say that the cockcrowing mentioned by Jesus actually refers to the Roman gallicinium, a time signal said to be made with bugles by the Roman guard stationed on the ramparts of the castle of Antonia in Jerusalem that sounded out at the close of the third night watch.

CODE OF CANON LAW

The official systematized collection of the universal legislation by which the Latin church is governed. The Code was completed while Benedict XV was pope. He officially promulgated it on May 27, 1917, and it went into effect on May 19th of the following year. After Vatican Council II part of the Code has been revised and more revisions are now in progress.

CODES, Biblical

Ancient Hebrew law collections found in various places in the Old Testament. Archaeologists have uncovered law codes of ancient Near Eastern monarchs - as the Code of Hammurabi, an 18th-17th century BC Babylonian king; and the Code of Lipit-Ishtar, a 20th century BC king of the Mesopotamian city of Eshnunna - that predate, but are similar to, the codes found in the Old Testament.

CODEX

In biblical studies, a manuscript of the Bible or part of the Bible, the leaves of which are assembled in book form, not rolled together in a scroll. The codex supplanted the scroll or roll early in the Christian era.

CODEX ALEXANDRINUS

A Greek manuscript, thought to have been compiled 400-450, containing the Septuagint, the New Testament, and 1 and 2 Clement. In scholarly works on the biblical text it is designated by the letter A or the numerals 02, and is regarded as one of the most important of the biblical manuscripts.

CODEX AMIATINUS

A manuscript of the Vulgate. Generally considered the best witness to the Vulgate text, it was produced circa 700 and contains the whole Bible, including the Apocrypha. Amiatinus was produced for Ceofrid, abbot of Wearmouth and Jarrow, Northumbria, England.

CODEX BEZAE

A manuscript dating from the 5th or 6th centuries that contains the gospels (in the order traditional for Latin manuscripts - Matthew, John, Luke, and Mark), Acts, and a small fragment of 3 John. It is named for T. Beza (1519-1605) who made some use of it in his annotated editions of the New Testament. It was in the monastery of St. Irenaeus in Lyons, France, and came into Beza's possession after Lyons was sacked by the Huguenots in 1562.

CODEX EPHRAEMI RESCRIPTUS

5th-century Greek manuscript of the Bible, regarded as among the most important for establishing the biblical text. The name derived from the fact that the leaves were erased and a 12th-century Greek translation of sermons by St. Ephraem the Syrian written over them.

CODEX PALIMPSESTUS SINAITICUS

Old Syriac text of the gospels, discovered in 1892 in the monastery of St. Catherine at Mount Sinai.

CODEX VATICANUS

4th-century Greek manuscript of the Bible. Scholars rank it as one of the most important sources for reconstructing the original text of the Septuagint and the New Testament.

The Vatican library has possessed the manuscript since before the first cataloguing of the library (1475). One conjecture of its presence in the Vatican library is that it was brought to Italy from Alexandria following the Arab conquest and later came into the possession of Cardinal Bessarion, who obtained many Greek manuscripts from the Greek monasteries in Italy.

CODICES, Biblical

Ancient manuscripts, often fragmentary, that exist in various languages and aid scholars in reconstructing the original version of the Bible.

COERCION

In moral theology, force applied to someone to make him do what he does not want to do, a matter of interest to moralists because of its bearing upon the voluntariness and moral imputability of what is done under its influence.

COERCIVE POWER

A form of administrative or executive power by which a superior who is vested with it is entitled to enforce his will on a person subject to his authority.

COGITATIVE POWER

In scholastic philosophical psychology a sensory power of comparative perception of the concrete objects of experience. The function of the cogitative power is particularly important to the exercise of the mind in its practical decisions in the moral order, since moral actions deal with concrete situations of human living.

COHEN

(Hebrew: priest) Jewish priest, descendant of Zadok, founder of the priesthood of Jerusalem when the First Temple was built by Solomon (10th century BC) and trough Zadok related to Aaron, the first Jewish priest.

COHEN GADOL

(Hebrew: High Priest) According to the Old Testament, a priest heading a priestly hierarchy. He had many privileges but was also bound by numerous restrictions. Until the time of King Josiah (7th century BC), the High Priest was anointed with oil before assuming office, and he alone could enter the Holy of the Holies once a year to offer sacrifice on Yom Kippur.

COINCIDENCE OF FEASTS

The occurrence of two or more feasts on the same day, When this happens the feat of higher rank takes precedence and the lesser feast is commemorated, transferred to another day, or is not observed.

Since Sunday is the Roman Catholic Church's celebration day, of the paschal mystery and thus the nucleus of the liturgical year, it takes precedence over all feasts except those of truly overriding importance.

COLET, John

(1466-1519) Theologian, founder of St. Paul's school, who, as one of the chief Tudor Humanists, promoted Renaissance culture in England. He adopted as his philosophy the Neoplatonism of the 3rd century philosopher Plotinus. He was appointed dean of St. Paul's cathedral in 1504.

COLETTE, Saint

(1381-1447 Abbess, reformer of the Poor Clares and founder of the Colettine Poor Clares. She was orphaned at 17 and entered the third order of St. Francis, living in a hermitage given her by the abbot of Corbie. She was canonized in 1807; her feast day is March 6th.

COLHOZEH

An Israelite whose son Shallun assisted in repairing Jerusalem's wall in Nehemiah's days (Nehemiah 3:15).

COLIGNY, Gaspard II de

(1519-1572) Admiral of France and leader of the Huguenots during the early years of the Wars of Religion (1562-98), whose growing influence over King Charles IX of France in 1572 so strongly threatened the former regent, Catherine de Medicis, that she precipitated the massacre of Protestants on St. Bartholomew's Day.

COLLECT

In Roman Catholicism, a short prayer which usually concludes the entrance rite at Mass. It is generally addressed to God the Father through Christ, and embraces the petitions of the congregation.

COLLECTIVE RESPONSIBILITY, Biblical

The notion of corporate responsibility was characteristic of archaic societies including those of the ancient Orient. Hammurabi's law code (1868-1728 BC) prescribes instances in which an offender's children must bear the punishment of their father's crime.

The classic Old Testament example of collective responsibility is that of Adam and Eve, whose sin is imputed to all their descendants, as also the promise of eventual victory (Genesis 3:15).

COLLECTIVISM

An economic system by which property is owned by the state. The church views unrestricted collectivism as undetermining the autonomy of the individual.

COLLEGE OF CARDINALS

According to the Code of Canon Law, the cardinals of the Holy Roman Church constitute a special college whose responsibility is to provide for the election of the Roman pontiff in accord with the norm of special law;

the cardinals assist the Roman pontiff collegially when they are called together to deal with questions of major importance; they do so individually when they assist the Roman pontiff especially in the daily care of the universal church by means of the different offices which they perform.

COLLEGIALITY

In Roman Catholicism, this term refers to the fact that all the bishops of the church in union with and subordinate to the pope, the bishop of Rome, possess supreme teaching and pastoral authority over the whole church.

This authority is exercised most clearly in ecumenical councils, but also in other ways sanctioned by the pope. Collegiality is considered an essential element of the church as instituted by Christ; it is explained at length in Vatican II's Dogmatic Constitution on the church.

In a wide sense, this term is often used to describe other forms of correspondibility in various ecclesiastical communities, such as the diocese, the parish, or the religious community.

COLLIER, Jeremy

(1650-1726) Bishop of the nonjurors (clergy who refused to take the oaths of allegiance to William III and Mary II in 1689). Collier favored the 1549 Book of Common Prayer and regretted that later editions omitted certain usages from the communion service. His *Reasons for Restoring Some Prayers* (1717) recommended the reintroduction of the oblatory prayer, the invocation, the mixed chalice, and the petition for the faithful departed.

COLLUTHIANS

A sect that arose in Alexandria during the Arian disturbances. Colluthus was one of the first to agree with Bishop Alexander in condemning Arius (320-321). But when Athanasius became bishop (328) Colluthus withdrew from his jurisdiction and formed his own party.

COLOSSAE

City in Phrygia, situated near an important trade route. The city was destroyed by earthquake in the ninth year of Nero and rebuilt.

COLOSSIANS, Letter to

New Testament writing addressed to Christians at Colossae, Asia Minor, written by Paul from his Roman imprisonment (circa 60). The Colossians were adopting views and practices that were incompatible with the knowledge of God's mystery (Colossians 2:2-3).

Paul exhorts the Christian community to put away anger, malice, and foul talk and to show kindness, meekness, patience, forgiveness, and love in imitation of Christ. Every Christian according to his state in life, should fulfill his duties.

COLUMBIA, Saint

(521-597) Missionary to Scotland. After founding Irish monasteries at Derry and Kells, he made the island of Iona the base for the conversion of North Scotland.

COMB, Liturgical

A hair comb made of ivory, metal, or wood, used extensively in the liturgy of the Middle Ages. Today the comb is used only at the ordination of a bishop to smooth his hair after the chrism has been wiped away.

COMMANDMENTS OF GOD

A term often applied to the Decalogue or Ten Commandments as given by God to Moses on Mount Sinai (Exodus 20:1-21 and Deuteronomy 5:2-33) and interpreted by Jesus Christ (Matthew 5:17-48). As given in the Book of Exodus, the Ten Commandments are as follows:
▲ I am the Lord your God .... You shall have no other gods before me ...
▲ You shall not take the name of the Lord your God in vain.
▲ Remember the sabbath day, to keep it holy ....

- ▲ Honor your father and your mother ....
- ▲ You shall not kill.
- ▲ You shall not commit adultery.
- ▲ You shall not steal.
- ▲ You shall not bear false witness against your neighbor.
- ▲ You shall not covet your neighbor's house ....
- ▲ _ You shall not covet your neighbor's wife ....

Theologically, the giving of the Decalogue represented another gracious act of God. Covenant and Decalogue are so connected as God's gift and man's response that in the Commandments the covenant comes to expression. The observance represents the obedience implicit in the covenant relationship of fidelity.

COMMANDMENTS OF THE CHURCH

In its widest sense, the laws by which people of God live in a communion of order with one another and with ecclesiastical authority. Thus all the canons of ecclesiastical law, both in and outside the Code or other authorized collection, could be considered the commandments of the church.

COMMENDATION OF A SOUL

The prayers contained in the Roman Ritual for use at the bedside of a dying person. Originally the person whose soul was commended in this service was not dying but already dead, but since the 9th century the prayers have been offered for the soul before its departure.

The 1972 Rite of the Pastoral Care of the Sick provides readings from the scriptures that may be added or omitted according to circumstances. There are special prayers as death nears and for the moment after death occurs.

COMMENTATOR, Liturgical

A cleric or layman appointed to explain the rites and prayers of the liturgy to the faithful and to direct and lead them in their participation. The office of commentator was introduced into the liturgy in the 20th century, when the liturgical movement was directing attention to the need of a more active and intelligent participation on the part of the faithful.

COMMITMENT

An act of committing oneself to a cause or a course of action. This is a relatively new understanding of the term. From its still common meaning of a legal warrant to place someone in custody, it later entered religious (mainly Protestant) literature as fidelity to Christ.

In current usage, it means spiritual dedication on a permanent basis to a way of life that demands above-average generosity and requires more than ordinary grace of God.

COMMON GOOD

A broad concept that may be described as the sum total of social conditions that allow individuals, families, and organizations to achieve complete and efficacious fulfillment.

COMMON LIFE

A manner of living that invokes a group of individuals who participate in common activities to attain a common goal. In religious life it is "dwelling together in a canonically erected house and contributing toward and sharing in a common fund," as well as submitting to a rule and a superior and carrying out certain activities together such as prayer and meals.

COMMON ORDER, Book of

First Reformed manual of worship in English, introduced by John Knox in 1556, adopted by the Scottish reformers in 1562, revised in 1564. The norm of public worship followed in the book is the ancient service of word and sacrament. The book aims at securing a common pattern of worship without making specific verbal forms compulsory, and the prayers are almost entirely to be said by the minister.

COMMON PRAYER, Book of

Liturgical book used by the churches of the Anglican Communion, first authorized for use in the Church of England in 1549, radically revised in 1552, with subsequent minor revisions in 1559, 1604, and 1662. The prayer book of 1662 has continued as the standard liturgy of the Anglican Communion and is used with minor changes in most countries of the British Commonwealth.

COMMUNAL MOVEMENTS

Non-monastic communities motivated by religious or ethical ideals, which to some extent own property in common; sometimes called communistic settlements of intentional communities. Already found in several civilizations and religions, the communal movement most typical in Western society has generally originated from a deliberate attempt to revive the structure of the primitive Christian community of Jerusalem, which "held all the things in common" (Acts 2:44, Acts 4:32).

COMMUNAL PENANCE

A term applicable either to an ecclesial community's expressing together their exercise of the virtue of penance; or to its receiving together the sacrament of penance.

The theological significance, stressed by the Decree of the Congregation of Divine Worship, (1973), promulgating the new Rite of Penance, is the ecclesial dimension of sin and repentance.

The Latin church is a union of its members in the bond of charity that unites each to Christ and so to each other; sin is an injury to that bond; penance is a healing of the injury, and the reconciliation of each member with God is also a restoration of the bond of the community itself.

COMMUNICATION OF IDIOMS

The theological term for the mutual predication of properties or attributes of the two natures in Christ of the one person. Because the Word of God is the one ultimate subject or person of both the divine and human natures, qualities or attributes of both natures may be predicated of this person. Because the two natures remain distinct and unmixed, the qualities of one nature do not belong to the other nature.

COMMUNION

From the Latin communio, meaning participation, the term used by Christians to describe the act of taking part in the sacrament of the Lord's Supper. The sacrament, which includes the eating of bread and the drinking of wine, is a spiritual repetition of the original Last Supper before Christ's crucifixion, when he said to his disciples, "Take, eat. This is my body .... This is my blood .... This do in remembrance of me." Since only those holding the faith of the Christian church are admitted to this rite, the word communion has come to be used to describe the body of all those people united by belief in the tenets of a particular denomination; hence one speaks of the Roman Communion, Lutheran Communion, etc.

COMMUNION, Spiritual

In Roman Catholicism, a deep desire to receive the Blessed Sacrament when one is actually unable to do so.

COMMUNION FAST

In Roman Catholicism, the conditions for receiving Holy Communion are the state of grace (freedom from mortal sin), the right intention (not out of routine or human respect, but for the purpose of pleasing God), and observance of the Communion fast.

The fast means that you must not eat anything or drink any liquid (other than water) one hour before the reception of Communion. However, the sick and aged, even those not confined to bed or a home (and those caring for them who wish to receive Communion but cannot fast for an hour without inconvenience), can receive Holy Communion even if they have taken something during the previous hour.

COMMUNION OF SAINTS

In Christian theology, the fellowship of those united in Jesus Christ in baptism;

the phrase is first found in the 5th-century version of the Apostles' Creed by Nicetas of Remesiana.

In medieval Western Christianity, special emphasis was placed on the benefits to be derived from the living through the intercession of the saints in heaven with God; the dead who were not yet perfected were also believed to be the beneficiaries of prayers said in their behalf. Protestant reformers denied the intercession of the saints.

COMMUNION OF THE SICK

The distribution of the Eucharist to persons unable to attend church because of illness. In the Roman Catholic Church it is considered obligatory for a person in danger of death to receive communion if it is morally possible for him to do so. Apart from any imminent danger of death, sick persons (and others impeded from getting to church) are encouraged to seek communion at least occasionally.

COMMUNION TABLE

A place designated for the faithful to receive communion. In early times communion was received at the altar. Gradually a rail, often fairly wide and of stone, separating the sanctuary from the nave, came to symbolize the communion table. In the 16th century the communion rail was mandated. Since Vatican Council II the trend has been to eliminate the communion rail altogether.

COMMUNITY

A collectivity of people united by all or most of the following characteristics:
▲ spatial proximity;
▲ shared goals and values;
▲ an acceptance of significant interdependence;
▲ some structure of government or authority;
▲ a degree of permanence.

The term is commonly used analogously within a neighborhood, a religious association or order, or even to all of humankind (the community of man).

COMMUNITY CHURCHES

Local churches, independent of denominational connections, that accept members from any Protestant denominations. They vary in patterns of organization, worship, and membership conditions, but usually have a doctrinal basis broad enough to admit Christians of all persuasions, who, as members of these churches, may still retain their own denominational loyalties.

Community churches originated in villages and rural areas that could not support more than one church, but are common today in newer suburban areas where religious pluralism exists along with a minimizing of denominational distinctions.

Although these churches are independent, they sometimes belong to the loose association called the National Council of Community Churches, organized in 1950. This organization has no jurisdiction and serves primarily to provide fellowship and a channel of missionary outreach. In 1995 circa 550 of 4,200 known community churches were associated with this Council.

COMPANY OF MARY

A community of sisters dedicated in the Christian education of youth, founded (1607) at Bordeaux, France, by St. Jeanne de Lestonnac. The general motherhouse is in Rome.

COMPARATIVE SYMBOLICS

The branch of theological studies that treats the various Christian creeds and public confessions of faith (symbols); it investigates the origin, nature, and contents of such statements, in comparison with other confessions or symbols.

COMPASSION

In Buddhism, the supreme Buddhist virtue, being based on the fundamental principle of the unity of all life. It is the second of the four sublime moods - karuna - identifying oneself with the suffering of others and so creating affection. It is the only form of vicarious sacrifice known to Buddhism.

COMPENSATION

Under the law given to Israel through Moses, compensation was demanded where there was injury or loss in any field of human relations. Compensation also had to be made for work done or services rendered. Hired laborers, whether Israelites or alien residents or others were to be paid their wages on the same day (Deuteronomy 24:14-15).

COMPENSATIONISM

One of the moral systems, and consisting in the position that in the case of a doubt whether a law prohibits an action, the action may be pursued if there is a good and sufficient reason. Such a reason compensates for the possible violation of law if in truth it does prohibit the action at issue.

The casuistic kind of moral theology to which the moral systems belong is now widely deplored for its negative conception of morality and law, and for its neglect of the true meaning of Christian prudence.

COMPREHENSION

A theological term with two senses. The first is cognitional; it is the knowing of an object as much as it can be known; and thus God is comprehended by Himself alone. The second is appetitional; in this sense it is the relation of will to a good really present and held in the mind and therefore enjoyed.

COMPULSION

An emotional, frequently irresistible drive towards an action that neither in itself nor for the compulsive person is reasonable or explainable.

Compulsion is one of the basic principles of Islam that one's religion should be held freely, and this point is enshrined in the Koran.

COMPULSORY SERVICE

Translation of the Hebrew word se'vel, which had to do with a literal or figurative load, an enforced burden, or burdensome labor. Associated with the word se'vel is sabbal, meaning burden

bearer. After taking a census of the men who were temporary residents in Israel, Solomon put them in service, and 70,000 of their number became burden bearers (2 Chronicles 2:2, 17-18). Many years later King Josiah repaired the temple, and "the burden bearers" were among those doing the work (2 Chronicles 34:12, 13).

CONCELEBRATION

The celebration of any liturgical action by several ministers, or the congregational participation in the celebration of the liturgy. Concelebration can mean the simultaneous saying of Mass by more than one priest where all consecrate the same bread and wine. This practice was common in the West until the Middle Ages, and was restored in modern time by Vatican Council II.

CONCILIARISM

In the medieval Roman Catholic Church, a theory that a general council of the church has greater authority than the pope, and may, if necessary, depose him. Conciliarism has its roots in discussions of 12th and 13th century canonists who were attempting to set juridical limitations on the power of the papacy. The First Vatican Council in 1870 explicitly condemned conciliarism.

CONCLAVE

A word used to describe the meeting of cardinals to elect a pope or to the place of election, a sealed-off area in the Vatican. Initiated by Pope Gregory X in 1274, the process of election today is governed by the regulations issued by popes Pius XII, John XXIII, and Paul VI.

Fifteen days after the death of a pope, an election is held in an area cut off from all outside contacts. The cardinal camerlingo presides, assisted by three senior cardinals.

The customary method of election is by secret ballot, a tho-thirds majority required for election. Ballots are cast, two in the morning and two in the afternoon, until a majority is achieved.

No cardinal over the age of 80 may take part in the conclave and the number of cardinals involved may not exceed 120.

CONCOMITANCE

In the theology of the Eucharist, the manner in which under the appearance of the bread, the blood of Christ; under the appearance of wine, the body of Christ; under the appearance of both, the soul of Christ are really present. Concomitance is taken in distinction from real presence "by virtue of the sacrament;" the theological point implied is that each sacrament directly brings about what the sacramental action and words signify.

CONCORD, Book of

Collective doctrinal standards of the Lutheran Church, published in German (1580) and in Latin (1584). It was not adopted in total by all Lutheran churches, but it has remained the standard of orthodox Lutheran theology.

CONCORDANCE

An alphabetical list of words in the Bible, arranged to show the location and context of each individual occurrence.

CONCORDAT

Agreement between a pope and a secular government regulating religious affairs within that state, for instance, the appointment of bishops and the status of church property. The first concordat was the Concordat of Worms, in 1122. The Lateran Treaty (1929), recognized Vatican City as a sovereign state and established Roman Catholicism as Italy's only state religion.

CONCORDAT OF 1801

Agreement between Napoleonic France and the papacy defining the status of the Roman Catholic Church in France and ending the breach caused by the church reforms enacted during the French Revolution.

CONCUBINAGE

A term given to the cohabitation of two persons without benefit of marriage.

CONCUBINE

In the Bible, a genuine wife above the rank of a mere slave but not enjoying all the privileges of the legal wife. Her husband did not have to support her; she could remain in her father's house where her husband went to her for sexual relations (Judges 15:1). Abraham (Genesis 25:6), Jacob (Genesis 35:22), Saul (2 Samuel 3:7), David and Solomon all had concubines.

CONCUPISCENCE

A tending toward sin, an inordinate desire for material things.

CONDITIONAL IMMORTALITY

The teaching that the human soul is inherently mortal and receives immortality only as a gift of grace or on condition that a person has lived an upright live. The term is often used interchangeable with annihilationism, because the teaching usually concomitant to conditional immortality is that the souls of the wicked are annihilated. Annihilationism strictly speaking, however, presupposes that the soul is immortal; total extinction is a punishment for sin.

CONFESSING CHURCH

Movement for revival within the German Protestant churches that developed out of their resistance to Hitler's attempt to turn the churches into an instrument of Nazi propaganda and politics. In 1948 it ceased to exist when the German territorial churches formed the reorganized Evangelical Church in Germany.

CONFESSION

Admission of sin, an aspect of repentance and thus required for absolution. General confession may be made in a congregation; private confession may be made to God, or also to a priest. The latter is a sacrament of the Roman

Catholic and Eastern Churches, also observed in some Lutheran and Episcopal Churches.

In modern times, the Roman Catholic Church teaches that penance is a sacrament, instituted by Christ, in which a confession of all serious sins committed after baptism is necessary. The doctrine of the Eastern Orthodox churches concerning confession agrees with that of the Roman Catholic Church.

CONFESSIONAL
In Roman Catholic churches, box cabinet or stall in which the priest sits to head the confessions of the penitents.

CONFESSIONS, Book of
Prepared by a committee of the United Presbyterian Church in the United States and adopted by the church in 1967. It includes the Nicene Creed, the Apostles' Creed, the Scots Confession (1560), the Heidelberg Catechismus (1562), the Second Helvetic Confession (1566), the Westminster Confession and the Westminster Shorter Catechismus (1648), the Barmen Declaration (1934) and the New Confession (1967).

CONFESSOR
A title of honor used in sanctoral classification to designate those male saints who do not fall within the category of martyrs but who proclaimed the faith by their way of life. The name has an exceptional broad extension, including popes, bishops, ascetics, monks, priests, religious, and laymen.

CONFESSOR, Regular
A priest to whom a penitent with deliberate regularity opens his conscience and makes his confession.

CONFIRMATION
A rite of certain Christian churches, usually administered in adolescence. The candidates confirm the promises made at their baptism and the bishop lays his hands on them, invoking the Holy Spirit upon them. In the Roman Catholic and Eastern churches confirmation is a sacrament.

After the Reformation, Anglicanism and Lutheranism retained a form of confirmation. Other Protestant bodies sometimes use the term confirmation for acceptance of baptized members into full membership of the church, including the right to receive Holy Communion.

CONFUCIANISM
Philosophy based on the thinking of Confucius (551-479 BC), the great Chinese philosopher and moralist.

Confucianism teaches a moral and social philosophy and code of behavior based on certain abstract qualities and strengths, such as love, peace, harmony, order, humanity, wisdom, courage, and fidelity, without appealing to any ultimate higher authority or god. Heaven is the highest state to which a man can attain, although no actual God-personality exists. Man arrives at this perfect state by cultivating virtues such as curiosity, knowledge, patience and sincerity and by developing a personality based on the harmony between man and the universe. Thus man takes his place in the universal pattern of creation, and immortality is won by those whose good name lives after them. The typical Confucian tries to be a scholar and a gentleman.

Confucianism also has a strong social and political message. It teaches that the individual must not only cultivate

himself, but must also enrich other people's lives. This derives essentially from the principle that man is a social being.

Confucians believe that the individual's peace of mind spreads from him into the family, and from the family to the state - which is conceived as a huge family - and from the state to the world as a whole. Confucius was a social reformer as much as a religious teacher. In his code of "right living," religion, education and artistic concepts all contribute towards the creation of a more harmonious world.

CONFUCIUS

(K'ung-Fu-Tzu; 551-479 BC) China's most famous teacher, philosopher and political theorist whose ideas have influenced the civilizations of all of eastern Asia.

Confucius was deeply disturbed by the political and social conditions of his times. Unable to obtain an official position to implement his ideas of reform, he spent the greater part of his life educating a small group of disciples. He was not a religious leader in the ordinary sense, for his teaching was essentially a social ethics.

CONGREGATION

An assembly of persons, especially a body assembled for religious worship or attending a particular church. The word occurs more than 350 times in the Bible, but only one of these references is in the New testament (Acts 13:43). As it is used in the Old Testament, congregation sometimes refers to the entire Israelite community, and at other times it means a gathering or assembly of people.

In Protestant churches, a congregation usually means the assembly of worshippers gathered in a church at a particular service. But among English Nonconformists and American Protestants, it has been increasingly used to designate the members of a local church, often only the lay people of a local church, and it has become virtually synonymous with parish.

CONGREGATIONAL CHRISTIAN CHURCHES, General Council of

A Protestant church in the United States organized in 1931 by a merger of the National Council of the Congregational Churches and the General Convention of the Christian church. It was merged into the United Church of Christ in 1957. At that time circa 1.5 million members were reported.

The Christian church developed from three independent groups that had withdrawn from the Methodist, Baptist, and Presbyterian denominations in the late 1700s and early 1800s. The three groups began cooperating a few years later. The Bible was the only rule of faith, church government was congregational, and complete freedom of belief was allowed.

CONGREGATIONAL CHRISTIAN CHURCHES, National Association of

Association of churches organized in Detroit, in 1955 by ministers and laymen of Congregational Christian Churches who did not wish to take part in the merger of the Congregational Christian Churches and the Evangelical and Reformed Church that formed the United Church of Christ. Several commissions oversee various key functions, including Christian education, the ministry, youth and women's work, and publications.

CONGREGATIONAL CHURCH OF ENGLAND AND WALES

National organization of Congregational Churches, established in 1832 and known for many years as the Congregational Union of England and Wales; the present name was adopted in 1965. The churches established several academies and colleges and have been active in ecumenical movement.

CONGREGATIONAL CHURCHES

Protestant churches which hold that each local church (congregation) should have complete autonomy, though they may form loose associations. In the 16th century Robert

Browne first stated Congregational doctrine. In the 17th century Congregationalists established churches in the New England colonies and founded Harvard and Yale universities. Most US Congregationalists merged (1931) within the Christian church and then with the Evangelical and Reformed Church (1957) to form the United Church of Christ.

CONGREGATIONAL COUNCIL FOR WORLD MISSION

English Congregational missions organization, formed in 1966 by merger of the Commonwealth Missionary Society and the London Missionary Society.

CONGREGATIONALISM

Churches historically emphasizing government through officers elected by the membership, and the independence of each local church. In later times associations of churches developed for cooperation.

CONGREGATIONALISTS

Also called Independents; members of a group of churches that arose in England in the late 16th and early 17th centuries, emphasizing the right and duty of each congregation to make its own decisions about its affairs, independently of any higher human authority. Congregationalists accept the basic beliefs of Protestant Christianity but do not grant binding authority to any creedal statement, stressing freedom of conscience and voluntary adherence.

CONGRUISM

In Roman Catholic theology, a theory attempting to reconcile the efficaciousness of grace and the freedom of the human will.

CONSCIENCE

In Christianity and Judaism, the consciousness that a proposed act is or is not right, manifesting itself in the feeling of obligation and duty. It implies moral sense to discern both good and evil (Hebrews 5:14) and a feeling of responsibility. The apostle Paul expresses the operation of his conscience in this manner: "My conscience bears witness with me in holy spirit" (Romans 9:1).

In Buddhism, nothing is known of an "inner monitor" implanted by a deity as an infallible guide to right conduct. Conscience is thus the quality of the mind resulting from past experience. One's state of moral development depends on one's response to experience in past lives, and in the present life. There is no absolute right and wrong; there is a gradual growth towards the highest morality: utter unselfishness.

CONSCIENCE, Examination of

The act of reflecting upon one's moral state and its conformances to the will of God; a preliminary to confession.

CONSCIENCE, Manifestation of

In canon law for religious, a subject's giving an account of matters of conscience (failing, doubts, temptations, etc.) to a superior. Superiors are strictly enjoined from doing anything, even indirectly, to exact such a manifestation of conscience.

CONSCIOUSNESS

A psychological concept, defined as early as 1690 by the English philosopher John Locke as "the perception of what passes in man's own mind." That consciousness depends on the function of the brain has been known from ancient times.

In Buddhism, it is a term with various meanings and levels of interpretation. Consciousness is divided into two classes: phenomenal and transcendental. Phenomenal consciousness is the relation between subject and object and the inferences drawn therefrom. It depends for its expression on the sense organs and mind, and is personal.

Transcendental is independent of sense organs and of the relation of subject and object. The action of the former is ratiocinative, of the latter intuitive. These two aspects are united in an ultimate identity which will be realized at the goal of the Eightfold Path.

The dynamic consciousness represents the union of the two aspects of consciousness, in which individual consciousness is not lost, but is transcended in the union with universal consciousness.

CONSECRATION

The act of making a person, place, or thing holy and sacred, and setting it aside for the service of God: the bread and wine are consecrated at Mass, a permanent church building is consecrated, as are those who receive holy orders.

CONSECRATION, Personal

An act by which a person is dedicated, or dedicates him- or herself, to the service of God. Theologians recognize that every Christian is, in effect, consecrated to the service of God by the reception of baptism and again by confirmation. Priests and bishops in the sacrament of orders are consecrated for the special service of God at the altar.

CONSISTORY

A gathering of ecclesiastical persons for the purpose of administering justice or transacting business, particularly meetings of the Sacred College of Cardinals with the pope as president.

In the Church of England the consistory court is the bishop's court for administering church law in his diocese. In some Presbyterian churches the consistory court is the lowest court, consisting of the minister and elders of the congregation.

CONSISTORY COURT

In some Presbyterian churches a church court corresponding to the session (in Scotland kirk session) or, as in French Reformed Churches, to the presbytery.

CONSOLATION, Spiritual

In a wide sense, the relief experienced after a period of spiritual desolation, aridity, or suffering; in a narrower and more exact sense, the delight that accompanies certain exercises and practices of the spiritual life or the joyful feeling God sometimes bestows on faithful souls as an incentive or a reward.

CONSTANCE, Council of

16th ecumenical council of the Roman Catholic Church (1414-1418). Following the election of two rival popes (Gregory XII in Rome and Benedict XIII in Avignon, France) and the attempt at the Council of Pisa in 1409 to resolve the schism by the election of a new pope, the church found itself with three popes instead of one. Under pressure from the Emperor Sigismund, John XXIII, the successor of the Pisa pope, summoned a council at Constance principally to reunite Christendom but also to examine the teachings of John Wycliffe and Jan Hus and to reform the church.

CONSTANTINE I, The Great

(280-337) The first Christian Emperor of Rome. In 325 Constantine became sole ruler of the Roman World. He had striven to promote Christian unity, although he continued to tolerate paganism. The rejection of the heresy of Donatism by his council at Arles (314) heralded a bloody attack on Donatists (317). Another, and much more threatening heresy, Arianism, prompted the Council of Nicaea (325), the first ecumenical council and an important step in the unification of the church. In the same year, he put to death his son Crispus and Fausta, his wife, for reasons that remain obscure. His new capital of the East, called "New Rome" and named Constantinople for its founder, was inaugurated in 330.

Constantine was an absolute ruler. He separated the civil from the military administration, created a centralized bureaucracy, and introduced enlightened legal reforms. Whether he was sincere in his Christianity remains debatable. He seemed to have destroyed the concept of divided rule, but, before his death, military control was divided among his three sons and two nephews, and the scene was thus set for a further bloody struggle.

CONSTANTINOPLE

(modern Istanbul) Capital of the Byzantine Empire from 330 to 1453 and residence of the ecumenical patriarch. The history of the Empire is largely the history of Constantinople. From the beginning the strongly Christian character of the city was evident. Churches and monasteries were erected on a magnificent scale, and their relics made it a center of pilgrimages. The bishop soon came to be the most important in the East and as patriarch was recognized as second only to the Roman pope.

The city was the site of four ecumenical and many local councils. Through most of the Middle Ages Constantinople was the most significant Christian cultural, intellectual, and artistic center and, even in its decline, played a key role in the transmission of classical Greek learning to the West. In 1453, it was taken by the Turks and became the capital of the Ottoman Empire.

CONSTANTINOPLE, Councils of

Four councils of the Christian church, all recognized by the Roman Catholic Church as ecumenical; the Eastern Orthodox church recognizes only the first three.

The first Council of Constantinople (381) established the Nicene Creed and fully defined the Trinitarian doctrine of the equality of the Holy Spirit with the Father and the Son.

The second Council of Constantinople (553) rejected Nestorianism by defining the unity of the Person of Christ in two distinct natures.

The third Council of Constantinople (680-681) condemned the Monothelites by asserting that Christ had two wills and two operations corresponding to his two natures, one divine and one human.

The fourth Council of Constantinople (869-870) excommunicated Photius, patriarch of Constantinople and prohibited lay interference in episcopal elections.

CONSTANTINOPLE, Orthodox Church of

Honorary primacy of the Eastern Orthodox autocephalous (ecclesiastically independent) churches.

CONSUBSTANTIALITY

The term used in Christian tradition mainly to express that then three persons of the Trinity have one and the same divine nature.

CONSULTATION ON CHRIST UNION

Commission studying a merger of various Protestant Churches, proposed in 1960 by Eugene Carson Blake. Discussions are still underway.

CONTEMPLATION

A form of interior, affective prayer in which one admires or rests in the knowledge and love of God. In the word of St. John of the Cross: "Contemplation is the science of love, which is an infused knowledge of God." It its purest form contemplation is a gift of the Holy Spirit.

CONTEMPLATIVE LIFE

A distinction should be made between the psychological and theological sense of the term on the one hand and its ecclesiological or canonical sense on the other. The first calls for unmitigated approval, the second for reverent yet not uncritical appraisal.

CONTEMPLATIVE ORDER

A religious community which engages exclusively, or almost exclusively, in activities directly ordered to contemplation. Such groups, made up of men (e.g., Carthusians, Trappists) or of women, (e.g. Poor Clares, cloistered Carmelites and Dominicans) live in monasteries generally removed from the ordinary activities of life, where they may achieve silence and recollection.

CONTINGENCY

One of the four modes of being, is applied to being which can be or not-be, and can sustain contrary possibles. In contradiction, necessary being cannot not-be; possible beings can be; impossible beings cannot be. Both the contingent and possible denote a capacity for being; the necessary implies actuality; the impossible excludes both real and potential actuality.

CONTRITION

In the words of the Council of Trent, contrition is "heartful sorrow and aversion for the sin committed along with the intention of sinning no more." In the sacrament of penance, contrition is the most important act of the penitent.
A theological distinction may be made between perfect contrition and imperfect contrition. Perfect contrition is sorrow for sin arising out of the motive of love of God, while imperfect contrition is sorrow for sin arising out of some lesser motive, such as fear of the anticipated loss of heaven or condemnation to hell.

CONVENT

Term used to designate a monastic community of monks, friars, or nuns. Today it usually applies solely to the residences of nuns, or, in the case of "convent schools," to girls' schools that are closely associated with convents.

CONVENTION

A gathering or meeting together of people for a specific purpose; an assembly. In the Bible the term "convention" is a translation of the Hebrew word migra, meaning "a calling together." Bearing out its basic meaning is its use in Numbers 10:2 to convey the thought of convening the assembly of Israel.

CONVERSION

In the New Testament the Greek word metanoia, often translated as conversion or repentance, means something very profound and personal: not merely a change of manners but a change of heart, a turning away from sin, a return to the Father's love.

CONVOCATIONS OF CANTERBURY AND YORK

Ecclesiastical assemblies of the provinces of Canterbury and York of the Church of England. They meet a number of times a year concerning themselves particularly with the reform of the canons of ecclesiastical law. They legislate by passing canons, but their powers are limited. The influence of convocation, however, is considerable in reaching and expressing the common mind of the church and in giving a lead in the affairs of the church.

COPE

A semicircular cloak reaching to the feet and having a hood or a vestigial hood in the form of a shield-shaped piece of material. It evolved during the 10th century from the cloak worn by choir monks during the celebration of the Divine Office.

COPTIC ART

The folk art of the Coptic-speaking Christians of Egypt. Coptic art is distinct from the "official"art of the Roman-Byzantine Empire and from the folk art of the Egyptian Hellenistic colonies. Coptic art has its source in the ordinary life of fellahin and of monastic society drawn from the fellahin. It flourished from the 4th to the 7th centuries.
Statues, friezes, and capitals tend toward two-level relief with designs giving a cutout appearance. Human figures have outsized heads, simple garments with the folds merely incised, and unnatural stances.

COPTIC CATHOLIC CHURCH

Eastern Catholic Church of the Alexandrian Rite in Egypt, in communion with Rome since 1741, when Athenasius, a Monophysite (acknowledging only one nature in the person of Christ) Coptic bishop, became a Roman Catholic.

The Coptic Church was a Monophysite Church, dating from the latter part of the third century when a large number of Coptic-speaking Christians existed in Egypt. It was a subculture with the Greek-dominated patriarchate of Alexandria.

COPTIC CHANT

Liturgical music of the descendants of ancient Egyptians who converted to Christianity prior to the Islamic conquest of Egypt in the 7th century. Much of the Coptic chant consists of melody types, or melodic formulas that serve as starting points for improvisation by singers, which is produced within fairly well understood limits for individual expression.

COPTIC CHURCH

Chief Christian church in Egypt, led by a patriarch in Cairo and 12 diocesan bishops. Services are held in Greek, Arabic, and the otherwise dead language Coptic. The Copts broke from the Roman Catholic Church when the Council of Chalcedon in 451 rejected their doctrine of monophysitism. After the 7th-century Arab conquest many Copts became Muslims. The Ethiopian Church derives from the Coptic.

CORBAN

In the New Testament, a gift dedicated to God (Mark 7:11). The word is also used in Leviticus and Numbers and applied both to offerings containing blood and those that are bloodless. By the time of Jesus Christ's ministry on earth, a culpable practice had developed in connection with corban, it especially being fostered by the Pharisees. They taught that money, property or anything dedicated to the temple as "corban," or a votive gift, thereafter belonged to the temple and could not be used for some other purpose.

CORD

A sash or cincture worn to honor some saint or to serve as a reminder of symbol of some virtue one seeks to practice, e.g., humility, mortification, chastity. The use of such cords by members of devout societies was popular in the Middle Ages, and some examples of confraternities of this kind have continued down to the present time.

COREDEMPTION

In Roman Catholic theology, the Blessed Virgin Mary's active share in the redemptive work of her son Jesus Christ, during his life on earth.

CORIANDER

Annual plant with parsley-like leaves and umbelliferous pink or white flower clusters. The fruit consists of globular seeds, of a grayish-white color and about the size of peppercorn. The manna eaten by the Israelites in the wilderness was said to be "white like coriander seed" (Exodus 16:31), evidently resembling it not only in color but also in general appearance.

CORINTH

Commercial city, south of the isthmus connecting central Greece with the Peloponnesus. Its strategic location made it a very important trade center between East and West.

The city has a prehistoric legendary foundation, but its origin is traceable to the Ionic and Doric peoples. It was the wealthiest city in ancient Greece. Excavations unearthed the remains of many of the buildings described by Pausianus. The Temple of Apollo, dating from the 6th century, was the most prominent brought to light.

CORINTHIANS, First Letter to

Addressed from Paul to the Christian community that he had founded at Corinth, Greece. The first letter, probably written circa 54-54 at Ephesus, Asia Minor, deals with problems that arose in the early years after Paul's initial missionary visit (circa 50-51) to Corinth and his establishment there of a Christian community. Saddened by reports of dissension among the converts of various Apostles, Paul begins his letter with a reminder that all are servants of Christ and stewards etc. (4:1) Then, while answering questions sent from Corinth, he addressed questions of immorality, marriage and celibacy, the conduct of women, the propriety of eating meat offered to idols, and the worthy reception of the Lord's Supper.

Then (chapter 13) the apostle explains to his fellow Christians that no gift of God has meaning unless it is accompanied by love. He also reaffirms the reality of Christ's Resurrection - doubted or denied by some - as the very foundation of Christian faith.

CORINTHIANS, Second Letter to

This letter was written from Macedonia in circa 55. It refers to an upheaval among the Christians there, during the course of which Paul had been insulted and his apostolic authority challenged. Because of this incident, Paul resolved not to go to Corinth again in person. Instead he evidently wrote an intervening letter (2:3-4, 7:8, 12), now lost, in which he told the Corinthians of his anguish and displeasure. Presumably, he sent a fellow worker Titus to deliver the letter to the community at Corinth.

In the second letter Paul expresses his joy at the news, just received from Titus, that the Corinthians had repented, that his authority among them had been reaffirmed, and that the troublemaker had been punished. After expressing his happiness and relief, Paul urges the Corinthians to respond generously to his plea for contributions to assist the poor of Jerusalem.

The last four chapters of the letter are a sharp and vigorous defense of Paul's apostolic authority.

CORNELIUS, Saint

(178-253) Pope from 251 to 253. His pontificate was complicated by a schism, one cause of which was the self-appointment of the Roman priest Novatian as antipope; and the second, the dispute over the church's attitude toward Christian apostates. His feast day is September 16th.

CORONATION OF THE VIRGIN

A theme in Christian art illustrating the Virgin Mary's coronation in heaven following her assumption, or bodily elevation into heaven. In almost all representations of the subject, the Virgin is shown seated at the right side of Christ.

CORPUS CHRISTI

A doctrinal feast established in honor of Christ present in the Eucharist. Its purpose is to instruct the people in the mystery, faith, and devotion surrounding the Eucharist. The celebration of the feast evolved during the 13th and 14th centuries.

CORRECTION

The act of prudently admonishing a sinner in order to encourage a change in behavior. This reproof must be done out of charity; and there must be a reasonable chance that the admonition will do some good and that no one else can or will give it.

COS

The capital city at the north-eastern end of an island bearing the same name and off the south-western coast of Asia Minor. Though the apostle Paul apparently sailed past this city when traveling from Ephesus to Caesarea at the conclusion of his second missionary journey in the spring of 52 (Acts 18:21-22), it was not until the close of his third tour, about four years later, that the island received mention by name in Acts (21:1).

The island of Cos is reputed to have long been a Jewish center in the Aegean. It was a free Roman state in the province of Asia and, according to Tacitus, was granted immunity from taxation by Claudius in 53.

COSAM

A seventh-century BC descendant of David's son Nathan; son of Elmadam and father of Addi; and ancestor of Jesus' mother Mary (Luke 3:28).

COSIN, John

(1594-1672) Bishop of Durham, theologian, and liturgist whose scholarly promotion of traditional worship, doctrine, and architecture established him as one of the fathers of Anglo-Catholicism in the Church of England.

COSMOGENESIS

The process of evolution which accounts for the origin of the universe. The process, according to Teilhard de Chardin, began with layers of cosmic dust in a state of expansion. The explosive force of the universe expanding placed great pressure on the subatomic particles of cosmic dust causing them to unite and condense, forming more complex structures. Within this process of expansion and condensation, our universe with its suns and planets came forth.

COSMOLOGY, Biblical

The biblical view of the universe. The Babylonians, Egyptians, Sumerians, and Phoenicians as well as the Hebrews accepted the same general, popular, and unscientific world picture, based on visual experience.

The Hebrews, however, were unique in claiming that the world was the creation of God and as such belonged to him.

COUGHLIN, Charles Edward

(1891-1969) American Roman Catholic priest, who became famous for his vitriolic sermons which were broadcast by radio from his Shrine of the Little Flower at Royal Oak, Michigan. Styling himself the spokesman for "White, Christian America," he upheld isolationism, attacked President Roosevelt, and preached anti-Semitism. he also disseminated his reactionary views through his magazine, Social Justice.

COUNCIL

In the Christian church, a meeting of bishops and other leaders to consider and rule on questions of doctrine, administration and discipline. An ecumenical or general council is a meeting of bishops of the whole church; local councils representing such areas as provinces or patriarchates are often called synods.

COUNCIL, Ecumenical

An assembly of the Catholic bishops from around the world called by the pope who sets the council's agenda and approves its decisions. These meetings are held to consider matters of concern to the universal church.

COUNCIL OF BISHOPS, Methodist

An official body composed of all bishops of all the Jurisdictional and Central Conferences. The Council of Bishops was not a traditional constitutional body within Methodism, but was instituted at the Uniting Conference of the three major American Methodist bodies in 1939.

COUNCILS, Early Buddhist

Assemblies convened in the centuries immediately following the death of the Buddha in circa 483 BC to recite approved texts of scriptures and to settle doctrinal disputes. The first council, held at Rajgir (India), is said to have taken place during the first rainy season following Buddha's death. The second council, held in Vaisali circa a century later, was called to settle a dispute regarding the relaxed rules of discipline followed by the monks of Vaisali. The third council, held during the reign of the emperor Asoka at his capital, Patna, circa 247 BC, may have been confined to an assembly of the Theravadas. The assembly discussed the different interpretations of monastic discipline.

COUNCILS OF THE CHURCH

Official meetings of bishops and others at various levels of the church to settle doctrine or discipline; at lower levels usually called "synods." General (Ecumenical) Councils represent the whole church. In Roman Catholicism they are considered valid and infallible if summoned and confirmed by the papacy.

COUNSEL

One of the seven gifts of the Holy Spirit whose effect is to enable one to identify what is the right course of action in a given circumstance and to urge a person to pursue that right action.

COUNSELS, Evangelical

These are the counsels of perfection: poverty, chastity, and obedience. These counsels, based on the words and examples of Christ, differ from the Commandments or precepts binding on all for salvation; counsels are embraced freely for a more perfect fulfillment of the command to love God and neighbor wholeheartedly. The counsels are practiced both privately and in community forms of religious life.

COUNTER-REFORMATION

A reform movement in the Roman Catholic Church during the 16th and 17th centuries, in part a reaction against the Reformation, a more extreme reform movement which resulted in the independence of the Protestant churches. Since the 14th century there had been repeated calls for reform of the abuses that plagued the church. Corruption, simony (the buying and selling of church offices) and ignorance among the clergy had given rise to confusion and mistrust which spurred two divergent movements. One, the Reformation, attacked the church as it existed in the early 16th century and in the end offered as an alternative the independent Protestant churches founded by Luther and Calvin. The Counter-Reformation, on the other hand, proposed to reform the church from within.

One of the first moves towards religious reform was the founding of the Oratory of Divine love in 1516, an assembly of pious churchmen intent upon official and authoritative action against reform.

The movement gained impetus with the founding of several new religious orders that emphasized simplicity and austerity. The most important new order was the Society of Jesus (Jesuits) founded by Ignatius Loyola in 1540. The Jesuits were militant and zealous teachers, scholars and missionaries, who carried the spirit of revival to their missions around the world, winning new members for the church to make up for those lost to Protestantism.

The spirit and methods of the Counter-Reformation were enunciated by the Council of Trent, which reaffirmed the doctrines of the faith, reorganized ecclesiastical administration, set educational requirements and moral standards for the clergy, and condemned sodomy.

The popes of this period lent their authority and support to the strengthening and reorganization of the church. It moves to combat heresy, Paul III revived the medieval institution of the Inquisition in Italy and Spain and Paul IV authorized the *of Forbidden Books.*

The spiritual revival was particularly intense in Spain, where Teresa of Avila and John of the Cross combined a profound mysticism that renewed the spiritual life of the church with active contributions toward reform of the religious orders. The renewal of Catholicism was expressed as well as aided by the dramatic forms of Baroque architecture and by the religious music of Palestrina.

COVENANT

A binding promise of far-reaching importance in relations between individuals, groups, and nations. As the biblical notion also meaning the pact between God and man.

Covenant is a term meaning a formal agreement, pact, or contract, in religious terms it describes the special relationship between God and his people. The Old Testament gives many examples of God's covenant with the

Israelites, for example with Abraham (Genesis 15:1-10), with Noah (Genesis 6:18), with Moses (Deuteronomy 5-7). In the covenant, God promised to be faithful to His people; and they, in turn, promised to be faithful to Him, to worship Him alone, and to keep His Commandments. One of the dominant themes of the Old testament is that while God is always faithful to His part of the covenant, the Israelites are not always faithful to theirs.

The New Testament describes the new covenant: that is the special relationship between God the father, Jesus His beloved Son, and each Christian in and with Jesus. The new covenant does not annul but, in Jesus, brings it to fulfillment. In the new covenant, Jesus expresses unconditioned love for his people, instructs them, forgives them, and lays down his life for them, thus sealing the new covenant in his blood.

COVENANT, Abraham

Major covenant, recorded in Genesis, chapter 17. This covenant was unconditional: Abraham was blessed with the promise that he would be the father of many nations and that he and his descendants would be given everlasting possession of the land of Canaan. The seal, or sign, of this covenant was the requirement that every male be circumcised at the age of eight days. Those not circumcised were to be cut off from the community as covenant breakers.

COVENANT, David

The covenant with David, the 10th-century BC king of Israel, involved a promise that the throne of David's kingdom would last forever; and when David's dynasty was destroyed in the 6th century BC, the hope of a Davidic messiah (salvatory figure) kept the knowledge of the covenant alive.

COVENANT, Law

Covenant between God and the nation of natural Israel, made in the third month after leaving Egypt. (Exodus 19:1). It was a national covenant. One born a natural Israelite was, by birth, in the law covenant, and was thus in this special relationship with God. The law was in the form of a code, arranged in an orderly way, its statutes grouped together. The law, transmitted through angels by the hand of a mediator, Moses, was made operative by a sacrifice of animals at Mount Sinai (Gal. 3:19; Hebr. 2:2; 9:16-20).

COVENANT, Moses

Most significant covenant between God and Moses; given by God to Israel through Moses. Moses was the 13 century BC leader and law giver of the Israelites. The covenant made at Mount sinai (Exodus, chapter 20) contains the famous apodictic laws known as the Decalogue, or the Ten Commandments. In the Sinai covenant, Yahweh, the God of Israel, is identified as the covenant giver and the deliverer of the Israelites from bondage in Egypt, a God whom the people can either accept and obey or reject and disobey - the consequences of which would be a loss of the covenant community.

COVENANT, New

The idea of a new covenant - especially one alluded to by the 7th-6th century BC prophet Jeremiah, who wrote a covenant written in the hearts of men rather than one on stone - was reinterpreted by New Testament writers. The Last Supper of Jesus before his crucifixion and Resurrection was identified as the new covenant. The believers in Christ thus viewed themselves as the new covenant community, the new Israel.

COVENANT, Noah

God made a covenant with Noah, who represented his family, with regard to God's purpose to destroy the wicked world (Genesis 6:17-21). At the time God revealed this purpose to Noah, his sons were grown and married. Noah, on his part, was to build the Ark and take in his family, animals and food; God was to preserve flesh on earth, both of man and animals. Noah's obediently keeping the terms of the covenant resulted in God's preservation of human and animal life.

COVENANT, Rainbow

Covenant between God and all flesh, as represented by Noah and his family, in the mountains of Ararat. God stated that He would never again destroy all flesh by means of a flood. The rainbow was then given as a sign of the covenant, which endures as long as mankind lives on earth, that is, forever (Genesis 9:8-17; Psalms 37:29).

COVENANT, Tribe of Levi

Covenant of God with the tribe of Levi that the tribe should be set aside to constitute the tabernacle service organization, including the priesthood. This occurred in the wilderness of Sinai (Exodus 40:2, 12-16). Aaron and his sons, of the family of Kohath, were to be priests, the remaining families of Levi taking care of other duties, such as setting up the tabernacle, moving it, and other matters (Numbers 3:6-13). Later, they served likewise at the Temple (1 Chronicles chapter 23).

COVENANT RELATIONSHIPS

In the ecumenical movement a bond between parishes of different churches that unites them, short of intercommunion, in prayer, social ministry, study, and dialogue. Synchronization of liturgical prayers and reading is often another uniting element.

COVENANT THEOLOGY

Not so much a separate system as an idiom used to explain the mystery of the election and perseverance of the saints, within the framework of the Calvinist tradition.

The covenant idea and covenant thinking greatly influenced theological development on both sides of the Atlantic among Presbyterians and Congregationalists; the concept of covenant also regulated the interpretation of church order and of the socio-political order, especially in some eastern states of the United States.

COVENANTERS

16th and 17th century Scottish Presbyterians pledged by covenants to defend their religion against Anglican influences. They were suppressed, both by Cromwell and the Stuart kings. Their savage persecution after the Restoration was known as the "killing time."

COVENANTS, Biblical

Sacred and solemn contracts, promises, or agreements between God and individuals, between individuals or between God and Israel and sanctioned by an oath. Originally political instruments that may have reached back to prehistoric times to maintain social and political order, by the Late Bronze Age covenants took the form of treaties between nations.

COVENTRY, Cathedral

The first building was erected (1053) by Leofric and Lady Godiva as a minister church for the Benedictine monastery, and raised to cathedral status in 1100 in the joint Diocese of Coventry and Lichfield.

In the mid-16th century Henry VIII dismantled the cathedral and Coventry ceased to be a see for nearly 400 years. In 1918 a new Diocese of Coventry was founded and the central and beautiful St. Michael's church, built as a parish church in 1326, became the cathedral.

In 1940 German bombing completely gutted and destroyed all but the tower. Some 20 years later the cathedral was rebuild according to a new, visionary, imaginative, and wildly controversial plan of Basil Spence, conceived in dramatic contemporary style of glass, steel, and concrete and enhanced by the work of leading artists and craftsmen of the age.

COW

Animal that filled an important role in the Old Testament. Besides serving as a draft animal, the cow was valued for its production of milk, from which other common items of diet were prepared, including cheese, butter and buttermilk (Numbers 19:2).

Cows or heifers were at times sacrificed (Genesis 15:9). The ashes of an entire red cow, burned outside the camp, came to be an ingredient in Israel's "water for cleansing" (Numbers 19:2-9). In the case of unsolved murder, the representative older men of the town nearest the slain one were required to kill a young cow in an uncultivated torrent valley and then wash their hands over the carcass while testifying to their innocence of the crime (Deuteronomy 21:1-9).

COWL

The most characteristic and proper garment of the monk. It is usually a long, flowing garment with ample sleeves and a hood, conferred on a monk when he makes his solemn vows. For many Benedictines it is usually black, while the Cistercians and some groups of Benedictines wear a white cowl.

COZEBA

A site in Judah where descendants of Shelah the son of Judah resided (1 Chronicles 4:21-22). Most authorities consider Cozeba to be the same as Achzib. The men of Cozeba are apparently included in the expression "they were the potters" (1 Chronicles 4:23).

CRANMER, Thomas

(1489-1556) Prelate and servant of King Henry VIII, who was the first reformed archbishop of Canterbury and drew up *The Book of Common Prayer.* He promoted the publication of an English Bible and in 1545 composed a litany for the reformed church of England.

CRASHAW, Richard

(1613-1649) Poet famed for religious verse of vibrant ornamentation and brilliant wit. He prepared the first edition of *Steps to the Temple Sacred Poems, With other Delights of the Muses* in 1646. These were religious and secular poems in Latin and English.

CREATION

The act of creating or causing the existence of someone or something, or the state or fact of having been created or brought into existence. Throughout the Bible God is identified as the Creator. He is "the Creator of the heavens, ... the Former of the earth and the Maker of it" (Isaiah 45:18). He is "the Former of the mountains and the Creator of the wind" (Amos 4:13), and is "the One who made the heaven and the earth and the sea and all things in them" (Acts 4:23; 14:15).

CREATION ACCOUNT

A term sometimes used of the theological exposition of creation in Genesis 1:1-2. The Bible begins with this exposition, one of the last to be written for the Pentateuch. It is the result of a long development from its origins in Mesopotamian myth, from which it borrowed and against which it was directed.

CREATION OF MAN

The biblical creation account is a religious teaching that explains the origin of sin and misery; as God created the world and mankind they were good; man was made to the image and likeness of God. This is the main point of Genesis's accounting for man's origin.

CREATIONISM

Theory held by fundamentalist Christians that the earth and living beings were created as described in Genesis rather than through a process of evolution, such as is accepted in modern geology and biology. In the United States, creationists have survived numerous setbacks, including the Scopes trial in 1925, the push in the 1960s to improve science education, and a Supreme Court ruling in 1977 striking down a Tennessee law requiring discussion of Genesis in schools. In a 1980 court decision a law requiring the teaching of creationism in Arkansas was overturned as unconstitutional.

CREATION MYTHS

Various explanations given by different cultures as to how the world and universe came into existence. Such stories vary from country to country, yet there are many features that they have in common. Most creation myths begin with the world consisting of a watery mass. The Babylonian creation story explains the origin of matter from the combination of sweet water and salt water. In the Greek version the beginning of matter was Chaos, surrounded by water and darkness. In Japanese accounts, a male and female deity rose up spontaneously from a watery mass. The idea of a male and female god working together is widespread.

In the Babylonian epic, in a conflict between the older and younger generations of the gods, Marduk, the chief god, fought Tamiat, goddess of Chaos or of salt water, and made heaven and earth from, the two halves of her body.

In the Mayan creation story Hurakan and Gucumatz cooperated to give life to the world. Like the biblical account, they said "earth" and earth appeared, and they fashioned man out of the various substances.

In the Chinese version the mountains were made from parts of the body of the first man. In one Egyptian account man and animals emerge from, the mud of the Nile River. In the Finnish creation story, heaven and earth were formed by an egg laid by a duck or an eagle. The yolk of the egg is the sun, the white the moon, the spots stars, and the black specks, clouds.

CREDENCE TABLE

A side table on which the chalice, cruets, basin and towel are laid out for use in the Eucharistic Liturgy.

CREDO

First word of the Nicene Creed, the third part of the Ordinary of the Mass.

Although part of the Mozarabic liturgy as early as 589, the Credo was not finally admitted as part of the Ordinary until 1014 at the insistence of Henry II.

CREED

Formal summary of beliefs, usually of a religious nature. The Christian creed had its historical origins in confessions of belief at the time of baptism. The Apostles' Creed, now universally used in the West at the baptismal rite, is traditionally attributed to the Apostles, but its origins are probably later (mid-2nd century). A more formal type of creed was promulgated by the Council of Nicaea (325) as a basic statement of the Christian faith, and came to be known as the Nicene Creed.

The Athanasian Creed (4th or 5th century) was widely used by the Protestant reformers and has been retained by the Church of England. Among the Protestant creeds are the Augsburg Confession (1530) of the Lutheran Church; the Thirty-nine Articles (1563-1571) of the Church of England and (as revised in 1801) of the Protestant Episcopal Church in the United States; and the Calvinist Westminster Confession (1645-1647), which is the definite statement of Presbyterian beliefs.

CREED AND CONFESSION

Authoritative formulations of the beliefs of religious communities. Historically called "symbols," creeds (brief affirmations of faith employed in public worship or initiation rites) and confessions (longer, more detailed than doctrinal declarations) contain the specific teachings or articles of faith of religious communities.

CREMATION

The reducing of corpses to ashes by fire. Some pagan societies in antiquity, e.g., the Roman Empire, practiced cremation. In apostolic times Christians followed the Jewish practice of burial, often risking their lives to recover the corpses of martyrs before they were cremated.

Jesus falling beneath the cross.
"And they compel one Simon a Cyrenian, who passed by, coming out of the country, the father of Alexander and Rufus, to bear his cross" Mark 15-21).
Lithograph by Gustave Doré (about 1860).

CREMATION

Nailing Christ to the cross.
"Where they crucified him, and two other with him, on either side, and Jesus in the midst" (John 19:18).
Lithograph by Gustave Doré (about 1860).

CREMATION

CRESCENS

In the New Testament, one mentioned by the apostle Paul in his second letter to Timothy as having gone to Galatia (2 Timothy 4:10).

CRESSY, Hugh Paulin

(1605-1674) Benedictine monk, apologist, and spiritual writer noted for his editorship of writings by Counter-Reformation mystics.

CRETAN-MYCENAEAN RELIGION

Though there are numerous archeological remains that once pertained to Cretan rites and beliefs, they are not easily interpreted. The Minoans of Crete built no separate temples but worshiped in caves or in small chapels within their homes or palaces. One of their most popular cult objects was a bare-breasted goddess holding in her hands a pair of snakes.

Minoans worshiped a multiplicity of gods, even though the majority are females. There is evidence also that they worshiped trees and pillars and believed in demons and monsters.

CRETE

Mediterranean island lying midway between Syria and Malta. The Cretans were known for being good sailors and having skill in archery.

CRISPIN AND CRISPINIAN SAINTS

(third century AD) Patron saints of shoemakers, whose legendary history dates from the 8th century. Their feast day is October 25th, when in medieval France it was the occasion of solemn processions and merrymaking in which guilds of shoemakers took the chief part.

CRISPUS

The presiding officer of the synagogue at Corinth whom the apostle Paul personally baptized and whose entire household became Christians (Acts 18:8; Corinthians 1:14).

CRONUS

In Greek mythology, a member of the first generation of gods, the only son of Mother Earth to help her in taking revenge on his father Uranus. After taking revenge on Uranus, Cronus took his place and cast his brothers, the Hundred-handed Ones and the Cyclopes, into Tartarus, where their father had already imprisoned them.

Then Cronus married his sister Rhea, but tried to ensure that none of their children would live, as his parents has told him that he would lose power to one of his own offspring.

As soon as the children were born, Cronus devoured them: Hestia, Demeter, Hera, Pluto and Poseidon, one after the other. As soon as Rhea realized she was pregnant again (with Zeus), she fled to Crete and bore the baby secretly. She left the baby to be brought up by the Oceanid Metis, giving Cronus a stone wrapped in swaddling clothes which he took for the newborn child and ate. So it happened that Zeus was saved.

CROSS

A structure consisting essentially of an upright and a crosspiece, used in ancient times for executions by crucifixion. It is now the principal symbol of the Christian religion. There are four basic forms of the cross: the Latin cross, in which the upright is longer than the transverse beam that crosses it near the top; the Greek cross, an upright crossed at right angles at its center by a beam of the same length; the tau, or Anthony's cross in the form of a T; and Andrew's cross in the form of an X.

CROSS, Hand

In the Eastern churches a cross with the lower bar ending in a handle, prescribed by the rubrics at certain times for blessing the people or some object of sacred use. In East and West Syrian churches it has a thin veil attached, and is used only by a bishop.

In the Armenian Rite it is held with a small cloth of silk. In the Coptic Liturgy, when the priest incenses the altar on each side, the deacon holds the hand cross aloft and moves from side to side, facing the celebrant.

CROWN, Episcopal

Headgear of Eastern bishops or higher prelates. It is embellished with religious images and mounted by a cross.

CROWN OF THORNS

An instrument of torture and mockery, used by Jesus' executioners (Matthew 27:29). Most likely taken from the kindling at hand, the exact material is not known; nor whether the crown was a cap or a circlet.

CRUCIFIX

A cross bearing an image of Christ crucified, sometimes also depicted in paintings. The earliest known crucifix dates from the 5th century. Some earlier crucifixes showed Christ in a king's robes and crown, but after the 13th century his suffering is depicted more realistically. A crucifix usually bears a scroll above Christ's head with the initials INRI, standing for the Latin of "Jesus of Nazareth, King of the Jews."

CRUCIFIXION

Execution by being nailed or tied to a cross by the limbs or, more specifically, the execution in this manner of Jesus Christ (Matthew 27:32-41). Many countries of the ancient world used it as their most painful method of execution. For Jews it was even more horrible, regarding the curse in Deuteronomy (Deut. 21:23). According to custom victims were watched by soldiers to prevent them from being taken down. Fracture of the legs could hasten death, but was not done to Christ (John 19:32-34).

CRUSADES

In general, wars sanctioned by the pope and directed against anyone considered the enemy of Christianity. Specifically, a series of wars in the Middle Ages under papal authority against the Muslims for the recovery of the Holy Places, and particularly Jerusalem. The initial impetus for the Crusades was a revival of religious enthusiasm in Western Europe during the 11th century. Though it was strong during the First Crusade, the religious fervor gradually weakened during the later Crusades as more mundane considerations triumphed; for there was a strong element of conquest underlying the Crusades - much like the imperialism of the 19th century - as Western Europe, recovering from the confusion of the Dark Ages and growing in wealth and population, began to expand beyond its frontiers, and particularly towards the East.

In the Muslim lands the crusaders came up against a relatively enlightened and urbane culture. The end result was not only an interchange of ideas, but a rapid enrichment of the material culture and the trade of Europe, leading directly to the growth of Western civilization in later centuries.

CRYSTAL

As used in the Bible, crystal denotes a clear transparent mineral, probably the variety of quartz presently called rock crystal. The comparative worth of rock crystal in Job's day may be suggested by his appraisal of it along with coral and pearls, and yet he considered them all to be of less value than wisdom (Job 28:18).

CRYPT

A vault, partly or wholly underground, especially that under the sanctuary of a church. The church crypt derived from the custom of building a church over the burial place of a saint or martyr; however, crypts were not always burial vaults but could also be repositories for the church's relics and treasures. In some cases the crypt was an underground church. It was usually placed under the choir. The crypt of St. Mark's, Venice and that of

The descent from the cross.
"Joseph of Arimathaea, an honorable counsellor ... bought fine linen, and took him down"
(Mark 15:43, 46).
Lithograph by Gustave Doré (about 1860).

Canterbury cathedral in England, are notable for their size and sumptuous decoration.

CUCKOO
Bird that occurs only once in the Bible, at 1 Kings 4:23 where the list of daily provisions of food for Solomon's court includes "flattened cuckoos."

CUCUMBER
In the Old Testament, among the foods of Egypt for which the complaining Israelites and mixed crowd, now tired or the daily diet of manna, expressed great longing were the cucumbers, along with watermelons, leeks, onions and garlic (Numbers 11:5).

CULT
A term that in modern times refers to particular religious or semireligious groups noteworthy for esoteric beliefs, and practices.

Generally, cult is a term denoting either worship or a certain type of religious body. In the first sense cult is the act of worship, a specific set of worship forms, or the veneration of God or the saints under some particular title.

Because of its deviant beliefs and the problems of succession following the death of a leader, the cult tends to be of short duration, and unlike the sect it is not apt to become transformed into a denomination.

CUMBERLAND, Richard
(1631-1718) Theologian, Anglican bishop, and highly influential philosopher of ethics who is sometimes called the father of English Unitarianism, a school of thought stressing happiness as a goal of moral action.

CUMMINGS, George David
(1822-1876) Dissident clergyman who founded and became the first bishop of the Reformed Episcopal Church. He became a distinguished preacher and served several important parishes of the Methodist Episcopal Church in the eastern United States and Chicago. After a dispute over ritual, he organ-

ized the Reformed Episcopal Church.

CUPBEARER
In the Old Testament, an official of the royal court who served wine or other drinks to the king (Genesis 49:1, 2, 11). The duties of the chief cupbearer sometimes included testing wine by tasting it before giving it to the king. This was because the possibility always existed that an attempt might be made on the king's life by poisoning his wine.

The fact that cupbearers are often present in ancient illustrations indicates the importance of their position. The queen of Sheba was greatly impressed by Solomon's "drinking service and their attire" (2 Chronicles 9:4).

CURIA ROMANA
The aggregate of the congregations, secretariats, courts, special commissions, which assist the Roman pontiff in the government of the Roman Catholic Church

CURSE
The desiring, threatening or pronouncing of evil upon someone or something is the basic idea of a number of Hebrew and Greek words in the Bible that are translated by the word "curse," or similar expressions.

The first curse employed was, logically, at the time of the Edenic rebellion, and was directed by God against the instigator of the rebellion through the agent that was employed, the serpent (Genesis 3:14-15). The curse was to end in his destruction. At the same time the ground was cursed on Adam's account, resulting in its producing thorns and thistles but not in its destruction (Genesis 3:17, 18; 5:29). The curse that God placed on Cain condemned him to a fugitive life (Genesis 4:11-12). Following the Flood, the first curse pronounced by a human was that which Noah directed against Canaan, son of Ham, condemning him to slave for Shem and Japheth, a curse that saw its major realization some eight centuries later with the conquest of Canaan by the Shemite nation of Israel (Genesis 9:25-27).

CURSILLO MOVEMENT
An intense, three-day experience of Christian renewal involving community living, presentations on Christian doctrine by laypersons and priests, participating in group discussions, liturgical prayer, and the like.

The Cursillo is followed by a post-Cursillo program focusing on weekly meetings of small groups and larger reunions in which participants share prayer and insights. The Cursillo movement originated in Spain in 1949.

CUSH
In the Old Testament, the first-named son of Ham and father of six sons (Genesis 10:6-8; 1 Chronicles 1:8-10). Cush and his named descendants are included among those from whom "the nations were spread about in the earth after the deluge" (Genesis 10:32). Thus, while no details are given concerning Cush as an individual in the Genesis account, his name is used throughout the Old Testament as representing his descendants and the land or region that they settled.

CUSHAN-RISHATHAIM
King of Mesopotamia from whose domination Othniel liberated the Israelites after eight years of servitude. he is also called "the king of Syria" (Judges 3:7-11).

CUSTODY
The care and keeping of anything. The term is also used in the sense of the detainer of a man's person by virtue of lawful process or authority. The biblical law most clearly explains the responsibilities of a custodian (as outlined in Exodus 22:10-13), involving animals entrusted to another. This law, undoubtedly based on an earlier patriarchal law (Genesis 31:39) states: "In case a man should give his fellow .... any domestic animal to keep, and it does die or get maimed or gets led off while nobody is looking .... the other is not to make compensation. But if they should for a fact be stolen from him, he is to make compensation to their owner. If it should for a fact be torn by a wild beast, he is to bring it as evidence. For something torn by a wild beast he is not to make compensation" (Genesis 30:31). At Galatians (3:19-25), a spiritual application of the term "custody" is made. Paul says that "the scripture delivered up all things together to the custody of sin."

CUTH
Original home of a people moved by the king of Assyria to the cities of Samaria after Israel's exiling in 740 BC.

CUTHBERT, Saint
(634-687) Bishop of the great Benedictine abbey of Lindisfarne, one of the most venerated English saints, who evangelized Northumbria and was posthumously hailed as a wonder-worker.

CYBELE
The great mother-goddess of Anatolia, worshiped in conjunction with the youthful lover Attis, whose annual death and resurrection were reflected in the changes of the seasons. In Greece, where her cult had spread by the 5th century BC, Cybele was variously identified with Rhea, Ge, and Demeter. In Rome, where she was officially introduced in 205-204 BC, she was known as the "Magna Mater," or Great Mother.

CYDONUS, Prochorus
(1330-1369) Eastern Orthodox monk, theologian, and linguist, who wrote a famous work called *On the Essence and Activity of God.* Cydonus denounced the "light mystique" as a grossly materialistic concept of God and challenged others to refute him.

CYMBALS
In biblical times, a percussion instrument similar to modern cymbals, used to accompany the harp, trumpet and

other instruments (1 Chronicles 15:28; 2 Chronicles 5:12-13). According to 1 Chronicles 15:19 the cymbals for the Temple were made of copper.

CYPRIAN, Saint

(200-258) Early Christian theologian and bishop of Carthage. He became involved in a dispute with Stephen, bishop of Rome, in 254 when Spanish congregations appealed to him against a decision by Stephen. Cyprian summoned a council that decided in favor of the congregations. He was executed in 258, the first bishop-martyr of Africa.

CYPRUS, Orthodox Church of

One of the oldest autocephalous or ecclesiastically independent churches of the Eastern Orthodox communion. Its independence, first recognized by the third ecumenical Council of Ephesus (431), was reaffirmed by the Council in Trullo (692) and was never lost, not even during the occupation of the island by the crusaders.

CYRENE

In Greek mythology, a nymph, daughter of Hypseus and Chlidanope. One day Cyrene wrestled a lion that had attacked her father's flocks. Apollo, who was watching, fell in love with her and carried her off from Mount Pelion, in Thessaly, to Libya. There he founded the city of Cyrene and made her his queen.

CYRIL AND METHODIUS, Saints

(827-868 and 825-884) Greek missionaries, apostles to the Slavs, who deeply influenced Slavic culture. Invited to Moravia, from 863 the brothers rivaled Latin-speaking German missionaries in the Danube region, preaching in the local Slavic tongue, pioneering the Glagolitic script (precursor of Cyrillic) and translating biblical texts into Old Church Slavonic. Their feast day is July 7.

CYRIL OF JERUSALEM, Saint

(315-386) Bishop of Jerusalem and Doctor of the Church who fostered the development of the "holy city" as a pilgrimage center for all Christendom. Cyril's primary surviving work is a collection of 23 catechetical lectures delivered to candidates for baptism. The first 18, based on the Jerusalem baptismal creed, were given during Lent, and the concluding 5 instructed the newly baptized during the week after Easter.

CYRUS II

Also known as Cyrus the Great, (590-529 BC) Conqueror who founded the vast Persian empire, centered on Persia and comprising the Near East from the Aegean Sea to the Indus River. He is also remembered as a tolerant and ideal monarch who was called father of his people by the ancient Persians and in the Bible as the liberator of the Jews captive in Babylonia (Ezra 1:1-4).

CZESTOCHOWA, Our Lady of

A wooden icon of Mary and the Child traditionally believed to have been painted by St. Luke on a tablet held by St. Joseph for the Holy Family in Nazareth. Most likely the icon dates from the 9th century and is Greek or Greek-Italian in origin, with 13th century overpaintings.

D

DABERATH

In biblical times, a city mentioned in the boundary list of Zebulun (Joshua 19:10-12), b ut considered as belonging to the neighboring tribe of Issachar when later apportioned with its pasture grounds to Levites of the family Gershon (Joshua 21:27-28; 1 Chronicles 6:71-72).

DADUPANTHIS

(Followers of the 16th century saint Dadu, born in 1544, who settled at Naraina, near Jaipur (India). He rejected the authority of the Vedas (earliest Hindu scriptures), caste distinctions, and all diverse, distinct forms of worship, such as visits to temples and pilgrimages. Instead he concentrated on Japa; repetition of the name of God, i.e., Rama. Both Hindus and Buddhists were admitted as his disciples.

DAEDALA

Ancient festival of Hera, consort of the supreme Greek god Zeus, in which a wooden image dressed as a bride was carried in procession, then burnt with sacrificed animals on a wooden altar. A myth existed that Zeus had won back the estranged Hera by arousing her jealousy with such an image.

DAEDALUS

In Greek mythology, a member of the royal family of Cecrops, first king of Athens. He was an artist of the greatest importance, he produced sculptures, works of architecture and some of the greatest inventions of his day.
He found himself in the service of King Minos of Crete for whom, among other marvels he constructed the famous Labyrinth, a palace whose corridors were so complicated that it was impossible to retain one's bearings. It was in this maze that Minos enclosed the Minotaur.
When Theseus came to Crete in order to kill the Minotaur, it was Daedalus who showed Ariadne how best to advise the hero on entering and leaving the Labyrinth. When Minos found out what he had done, he was so furious that he shut the artist and his son up in the Labyrinth themselves. There, in prison, Daedalus never ceased to think about ways in which he could escape from Crete. One day the thought of wings struck him. He stuck the feathers together with wax and fitted them to the shoulders of himself and Icarus, and the two set off on their incredible journey.

DAENA

In Iranian religion, one of several spiritual forces that are roughly equivalent to elements of the human soul.

DAEVAS AND AHURAS

(Terms applied to certain Persian divinities. The opposition between the two terms is similar to the opposition of devas and asuras in India, but with different values. In India the notion of asura deteriorated because of emphasis on its occult side, which led to the asura's being regarded as evil or malevolent. The asuras in India accordingly were reduced to the rank of demons. In Iran, on the contrary, the ahuras were exalted into higher divine beings, while the daevas suffered a corresponding decline. It is quite possible that Zoroaster was responsible for giving the higher values to the ahuras.

DAGDA, the

(One of the leaders of the Irish people, the Tuatha De Danann (People of the Goddess Danu). He was credited with many powers and possessed a magical caldron of plenty.

DAGON

West Semitic god of crop fertility, worshipped extensively throughout the ancient Near East. Dagon was the Hebrew and Ugaritic common noun for "grain" and the god Dagon was the legendary inventor of the plow.

DAHRIYAH

In Islam, the unbelievers who contend that the course of time is all that governs their existence. They were so called because of a reference to them in the Koran, in which they are repudiated for saying, "There is no other than our present life; we die and we live and nothing but the course of time destroys us."

DAI BUTSU

The Great Buddha at Kamakura, a figure of Amida in meditation. Erected in 1252 of bronze plates welded together, it is 52 feet high. The monastic building which once housed it was destroyed in a tidal wave, and the great image now stands amid the trees of an old monastery garden.

DAIGAK GUKSO

(1055-1101) Buddhist priest who founded the Ch'ont'ae sect of Son, or Zen, Buddhism. Ch'ont'ae became a Buddhist at the age of 11 and started to study the Garland Sutra. He went to the Sung court in China and stayed a year and a half studying and collecting Buddhist literature. After his return home he applied himself to the collection of the writings of Liao and Silla priests. While working as a master priest at Hungwang-sa (temple), he published some 4,750 books of Buddhist scriptures he had collected.

DA'IF

In Islam, term in the sense of weak. Used as a technical term in hadith criticism to characterize the lack of strength and reliability of a tradition. There are various grades of weak tradition.

DAIKOKU

In Japanese mythology, one of the Seven Gods of Luck; the god of wealth and the guardian of farmers. He is depicted in legends and art as dark complected, stout, carrying a wish-granting mallet in his right hand, a bag of precious things slung over his back, and sitting on two rice bags.

DAIMBERT

(1029-1107) First archbishop of Pisa, who, as a patriarch of Jerusalem, played a major role in the First Crusade. He accompanied Pope Urban II to France in 1095 to preach the First Crusade. In 1096 he raised a crusading fleet that sailed for the Holy Land in 1098. In 1100 he arrived in Jerusalem at the head os his own expedition. The same year he became patriarch of Jerusalem. He was driven from Jerusalem in 1102.

DAJJAL, al-

Term to signify an Islamic "anti-Christ." A huge amount of tradition has grown up around this eschatological figure. The bare bones of these indicate that he will arrive on earth during the last days of which he himself will be a major sign. He will preside over 40 years (or forty days) of injustice and license, after which Isa will destroy him and the entire world will convert to Islam.

DAKHMA

Parsee funeral tower erected on hills for the disposal of the dead according to Zoroastrian rite. Such towers are circa 25 feet high, built of brick or stone, and contain gratings on which the corpses are exposed.

DAKINIS

In the Buddhist mythology of Tibet, female divinities of lesser rank, invoked for the superhuman powers, or aiddhi, which they grant. Some are fierce, others pleasing in their appearance, some are animal-headed, but all are usually shown nude and dancing.

DALAI LAMA

Religious and political leader of Lamaism, or Tibetan Buddhism. He is regarded as the spiritual and temporal head of Tibet. Regarded as the earthly manifestation of Chenresi, the "Precious Protector." The word Dalai, "Great Ocean," is Mongolian, and was a title granted to the third Grand Lama of the Gelugpa School in 1587 by Gusri Khan, a Mongol Prince whom the Lama had called into Tibet to help him quash rival attempts for supreme power. There have been 14 Dalai Lamas. The present, fourteenth, Dalai Lama was born in Amdo on 6 June 1935, and was approved, brought to Lhasa and enthroned in 1940. He visited India in 1956 for India's Buddha Jayanti celebrations, and then returned to Tibet. In 1959 he was forced into exile by Chinese Communists. Pending his return he lives at Dharmsala in the Punjab.

DA'LETH

(The fourth letter of the Hebrew alphabet. Later, outside the Hebrew scriptures, as a number, it denoted four. In the Hebrew Bible, this fourth letter is used as the initial letter in the first word of each of the eight verses of Psalm 119:25-32.

DALMANUTHA

(In the Old Testament, an area to which Jesus retired by boat with his disciples after the miraculous feeding of 4,000 men near the Sea of Galilee (Mark 8:1-10). Though various sites have been suggested for Dalmanutha, the name is not referred to in other biblical or non-biblical sources, so its exact location remains unknown.

DALMATIA

An area in the mountainous region east of the Adriatic Sea in what is today the Balkan. Paul's companion Titus departed for Dalmatia sometime prior to the apostle's execution, assumed to be circa 65 (1 Timothy 4:6-10). In the same verse in which Demas is said to have "forsaken" Paul Titus is mentioned as going there.

DALMATIC

(The outer liturgical garment worn by the deacon. In its present form it usually has wide short sleeves, is open at the sides, and reaches below the knees. This vestment was originally a garment of wool or linen that originated in the Greek province of Dalmatia. It was adopted by the Romans of the upper class and became a distinctively clerical garment when it passed from secular use.

Probably it was worn first only by the pope, but the privilege of wearing it was extended to deacons in Rome by the fourth century. By the 12th century it was distinctive of diaconal rank.

The earlier dalmatic was usually white with two vertical red stripes (clavi) running the length of the garment in both front and rear, one over each shoulder. Sometimes in later dalmatics the clavi were joined together with a horizontal stripe.

By the 12th century the color of the garment varied with the liturgical occasion on which it was worn. In modern times the dalmatic has often been indistinguishable in its style and design from the subdeacon's tunicle, although it is desirable that the tunicle should have narrower sleeves and either have no clavi, or at least have its clavi unjoined.

DAMASCENES

(The inhabitants of Damascus (2 Corinthian 11:32). Paul used the term when recounting his narrow escape from that city circa 20 years after it occurred, as narrated in Acts 9:23-25.

DAMASCUS

Capital of Syria, located in the southwestern part of the country. It has been known by its present name since at least the 15th century BC. Being very fertile and being situated on the natural highway from the east to the west, it became important in biblical times.

Damascus is a leading Middle Eastern market center, exporting agricultural produce and importing basic industrial products, machinery and automobiles.

Damascus was probably founded over 4,000 years ago and under the Arameans became a leading caravan center around 1000 BC. Conquered by Alexander the Great, it came under Greco-Macedonian and later Roman control. In 635 the then Christian city was captured by Muslim Arabs and under the early Omayyad caliphs became the capital of the vast Arab empire (till 750). It remained a starting point for pilgrims traveling to Mecca. Devastated by the Mongols under Tamerlane, it was rebuilt as a part of the Ottoman Empire and enjoyed several centuries of peace and prosperity until captured by British and Arab forces in 1918. It was then the seat of a short-lived Syrian kingdom, the capital of French controlled Syria, and after revolt against French administration it finally emerged as the capital of Syria in 1946.

DAMASCUS I, Saint

(304-384) Pope from October 366 to December 384. During his rule the primacy of the Roman see was asserted. He was active in suppressing heresy. In two synods (368 and 369) the unorthodox teachings of Bishop Macedonius of Constantinople and of Bishop Apollinaris of Laodicea were condemned.

Damascus was the first pope to refer to Rome as the apostolic see, to distinguish it as that established by the apostle Peter, founder of the church.

DAMASCUS II

(978-1048) Pope during 1048. His brief reign, delayed by a local claimant to the papal throne, occurred during a period when the German emperors and factions of the Roman nobility vied for control of the papacy. He died of malaria after reigning only 23 days.

DAMASCUS DOCUMENT

(One of the most important extant works of the Essene community of Jews at Qumran in Palestine. The Essenes fled to the Judean desert wilderness around Qumran during Antiochus IV Epiphanes' persecution of Palestinian Jews from 175-163 BC. Two medieval manuscripts dating from the 10th and 12th centuries were discovered in 1896-97 in the Geniza (storeroom) of the Ezra synagogue in Cairo. The subsequent discovery of extensive Hebrew fragments from caves IV and VI at Qumran confirmed the fact that the document was indeed one of the major doctrinal and administrative codes of the Essene sect.

The Damascus document consists of two major sections. The "exhortation" set forth the sect's religious teaching, emphasizing fidelity to God's covenant with Israel and strict observance of the sabbath and other holy days.

The second section contains a list of statutes dealing with vows and ritual purity, guidelines for community assemblies, the selection of judges, and the duties of the Guardian, who controlled the admission and instruction of new members.

Though a precise date for the composition of the Damascus document has not been determined, it must have been written before the great Jewish revolt of 66-70, which forced the Qumran community to disband. Most scholars date the document sometime during the 1st century BC.

DAMIAN, Saint Peter

(1007-1072) Pier Damiani; cardinal and doctor of the church, an original leader and a most forceful figure in the 11th century reform movement. A conservative in political and theological controversies, he often used strong language, thus reminding his contemporaries of St. Jerome.

DAMIEN, Father

(1840-1889) Priest who devoted his life to missionary work among the Hawaiian lepers. In 1884 he contracted leprosy and refused cure because it would have necessitated his leaving the lepers.

DAMNATION

A term used in Roman Catholicism for the judgment of condemnation to hell that will be pronounced by Christ, the supreme judge, on the wicked end of the world (Matthew 25:41-46); but the word itself is hardly used with this meaning in sacred scriptures.

As the objective result of a condemnatory action, damnation signifies the state of the damned, primarily of those condemned to eternal punishments. In this meaning it includes the pain of sense as well as the pain of loss.

Though the terms damned and damnation are used in the strict sense of those condemned to the punishments of hell, they might be in a limited way be applied to the souls in purgatory. Though this usage is rare, if found at all in Catholic speech and writings, it could be justified on the ground that these should do positively suffer because of the temporary loss of God that they know to be due to their unforgiven venial faults and unremitted temporal punishment of serious sins committed in this mortal life.

DAMU

(In Mesopotamian religion, Sumerian deity, city God of Girsu on the Euphrates River near Ur in the southern orchards region. He was a vegetation god, especially of the vernal flowing of the sap of trees and plants.

DAN

One of the 12 tribes of Israel that in biblical times comprised the people of Israel who later became the Jewish people. The tribe was named after the first of two sons born to Jacob (also called Israel) and Bilhah, the maidservant of Jacob's second wife, Rachel. Nine of the other 11 tribes were also named after sons of Jacob, while two bear the names of Jacob's grandsons, children of Joseph.

The great hero of the Danites was Samson, who, until his betrayal by Delilah, used his mighty strength against the Philistine invaders.

DANA

In Buddhism, the virtue of alms-giving to the poor and needy; also, making

gifts to a Bhikkhu or community of Bhikkhus.

DANAUS

(In Greek legend, son of Belus, king of Egypt,and twin brother of Aegyptus. Driven out of Egypt by his brother, he fled with his 50 daughters (the Danaids) to Argos, where he became king. Soon thereafter the 50 sons of Aegyptus arrived in Argos, and Danaus was forced to consent to their marriage with his daughters. Danaus, however, commanded each daughter to slay her husband on the marriage night. They all obeyed except Hypermnestra. In punishment for their crime the Danaids were condemned to the endless task of filling with water a vessel that had no bottom.

DANCE OF DEATH

A medieval allegorical concept of the all-conquering and equalizing power of death, expressed in the drama, poetry, music, and visual arts of Western Europe mainly in the late Middle Ages. The concept of the dance of death lost its awesome hold in the Renaissance, but the universitality of the theme inspired its revival in French 19th century Romantic literature and in 19th and 20th century music.

DANCING, Religious

(Man has ever searched for more expressive forms of communication with the transcendent. Thus, religious dance has been found to supplement, even replace, speech.

Throughout the East, sacred dancers were a prominent feature in religious worship; in Egypt, colleges of female dancers and singers were annexed to certain shrines. Many of these religious dances consisted of slow and stately processions through the streets of the city or around the altar.

In the Old Testament, dancing was an adjunct of worship, a practice probably borrowed from neighboring people. "Thus Miriam took a timbrel and danced" (Exodus 15:20-21). And David on the recovery of the ark "danced with all his might before the Lord" (2 Kings 6:14). It is also clear from many passages in the psalms that dancing formed part of the liturgy of the Temple.

In early Christian times dancing was a part of the celebration of the vigils of martyrs as the people thus expressed their joy in the church or at the martyr's tomb.

In the Middle Ages the practice developed in combining more closely dance and formal worship, especially during the chief liturgical seasons. Even until the present, dancing before the high altar in Seville cathedral takes place on the feasts of the Immaculate Conception, Corpus Christi, and in Shrovetide.

DANDOLO, Enrico

(1107-1205) Doge of Republic of Venice (1192-1205), noted for his promotion of the Fourth Crusade, which overthrew the Greek Byzantine Empire and further aggrandized Venice.

DANGERFIELD, Thomas

(1650-1685)Informer who falsely accused Roman Catholics of conspiracy during the panic created by the fictitious "Popish Plot" of 1678.

DANIEL

1   In the Old Testament, second Son of David, born to him at Hebron by Abigail (1 Chronicles 3:1). With the slaying of the firstborn, Amron, he could feel in line for kingship after David, but no mention is made of a usurpation, suggesting either that he respected the God-given appointment of Solomon of that he died before his father.

2   In Judaism, the name of an outstanding prophet of the tribe of Judah; the writer of the book bearing his name. Very little is known of his entire life, but he tells of being taken to Babylon, likely as a teen age prince, along with other royal offspring and nobles (Daniel 1:3-6).

DANIEL, Additions to

(Three independent stories that were not part of the original Hebrew or Aramaic biblical texts but were inserted in the Book of Daniel in the Latin (Vulgate) and Greek (Septuagint) biblical canons. Neither the date, place, or language of these works has been definitely determined.

DANIEL, Book of

A book of the Old Testament, its first half (chapters 1-6) contains stories about the experiences of Daniel and his friends under Kings Nebuchadnezzar II, Belshazzar, Darius I, and Cyrus II; the second half contains reports of Daniel's three visions (and one dream). The book takes an apocalyptic view of history; the end time is vividly anticipated when the reign of God will be established and the faithful, through a resurrection of the just, will be relieved of their suffering. The book exhorts its hearers and readers to endure, even to the point of martyrdom. It is one of the earliest examples of Jewish apocalyptic literature.

DANTE ALIGHIERI

(1265-1321) Theological and philosophical poet, a man who represents, perhaps better than any other, the climax of the Middle Ages. Not only was he a poet, but he was also a philosopher, theologian, soldier, politician, traveler, and, in some sense, mystic as well.

The factors behind his formation include:
▲ the political vitality of the Italian communes;
▲ - the piety to be found in the religious orders;
▲ - the apex of the development of Scholasticism in the universities;
▲ the coming to flower of poetry in Florence and Sicily.

The *Divinia Commedia*, originally called the *Comedy* because it begins in sorrow and concludes in joy, was his supreme masterpiece. It is a spiritual odyssey, profoundly religious from beginning to end.

It is now recognized that Dante is profoundly influenced by the thought of St. Thomas Aquinas, but the *Divinia Commedia* is more than religious in the narrow sense; it is a poetic compendium of medieval history, science, and culture.

DANU

(Pagan Celtic goddess, the earth mother or female principle; she was honored under various names from eastern Europe to Ireland. Possibly a goddess of fertility, of wisdom, and of wind, she was believed to have suckled the gods.

DAPHNE

(In Greek mythology. the personification of the laurel, a tree whose leaves, formed into garlands, were particularly associated with Apollo.

DAPHNEPHORIA

In Greek religion, festival every ninth year at Thebes in Boeotia in honor of Apollo Ismenius or Apollo Chalazius (god of hail). It consisted of a procession in which the chief figure was a boy of good family, whose parents were still alive. In front of the boy walked one of his nearest relatives, carrying an olive tree hung with laurel, flowers, and bronze balls and twined round with ribbons.

Then followed the daphnephoria, laurel bearer, i.e., a young priest of Apollo Ismenius.

DAQYA'IL

In Islam, name of little-known angel responsible in one account for the guardians of hell.

DARA

(In the Old Testament, a descendant of Judah through Zerah (1 Chronicles 2:4-6); possibly the same as the Darda, whose wisdom, though great, was not equal to Solomon's (1 Kings 4:31).

DAR AL-ISLAM

Literally "The abode (or House) of Islam." The term is used, particularly in Islamic jurisprudence, to denote the totality of those regions or countries which are subject to Islamic law.

DAR AL-MAI AL-ISLAMI

Literally, "The House of Islamic Wealth." This is the name borne by the largest Islamic financial institution in the world. It was established in 1981 with the specific purpose of co-ordinating, implementing and emphasizing Islamic Banking undertaken in accordance with Shari'a law.

DARA SHIKOH

(1615-1659) Persian prince, Muslim scholar, and theological in India during the Mughal period. He wrote a treatise on the technical terms of Hindu pantheism and their equivalents in Sufi theology and directed Persian translations of several Hindu scriptures.

DARDANUS

(In Greek legend, the son of Zeus and the Pleiad Electra, mythical founder of Dardania on the Hellespont. He was the ancestor of the Dardans of the Troad and, through Aeneas, of the Romans.

DARIUS

Darius I, Darius the Great (550-486), king of Persia in 522-486 BC one of the greatest rulers of the Achaemenid dynasty, who was noted for his administrative genius and for his great building projects.

DARK AGES

(A pejorative designation of a period in European history, the terminal dates of which depend on the interpreter. The Renaissance designation of a "middle age" was a scornful dismissal of the period from the 6th to the 16th centuries as unbrightened by the pursuit of classical learning.

Well into the 19th century, a politically and religiously polemical reading of history made the Dark Ages and the Middle Ages coterminous. A fairer evaluation of the contributions of the 12th and 13th centuries in all areas of knowledge, in the arts, in education, set the Dark Ages back to the period from the 5th to the 11th centuries.

The designation may be most accurately applicable to the chaotic times of the barbarian invasions and following on the fall of Rome.

DARKNESS, Biblical

Darkness is a theme joined with manifestation of divine power in biblical thought patterns that appear to have disparate mythological origins sometimes difficult to identify. Darkness is closely associated with God's own awesome presence (2 Samuel 22:12); here the imagery refers to the storm clouds.

In other texts, darkness is more directly related to the failure of the heavenly bodies to shine because they have become paralyzed at the approach of the warrior God who fights for His people (Isaiah 13:10). This darkness came to be applied to the beginning of a new world order (Mark 13:24; Acts 2:20), in which finally there would be no darkness of any need for the sun (Revelation 22:5).

It becomes difficult to distinguish such thought from a third context, the darkness of the original world chaos, which has the vestigial characteristics of an independent being (Genesis 1:2; Isaiah 45:19; Job 38:19) totally subject to God's creative activity (Genesis 1:4-5). The darkness appears closely related to that in the land of the dead (Job 10:21-22; Psalms 86:13); both are in fact identified in a discussion of the ninth plague in Egypt (Exodus 10:22; Acts 13:11). The attempt to explain this plague and some other of the above texts through actual cosmic disturbances involving Venus and Mars has not won acceptance.

DARKON

(In Judaism, one whose descendants were represented among "the sons of Solomon" returning with Zerubbabbel from Babylonian captivity (Ezra 2:1-2, 55).

DARSANA

(In Hindu worship, the beholding of an auspicious deity, person, or object. The experience results in a blessing of the viewer. The boon conferred may differ according to the deity and the circumstances, time and place, of the viewing.

DARSHANA

In Buddhism, term meaning seeing; objectively, a display, a splendid sight, the reverence roused by that sight. Subjectively, the term is meant to denote the inward understanding.

In Hinduism, the term may mean a philosophical view, a school of thought.

DASAMI SANNYASIN

A Hindu saiva ascetic who belongs to one of the 10 orders established by the philosopher Sankara in the 8th century and still flourishing in India today. The 10 orders are:

▲ Aranya,
▲ Asrama,
▲ Bharati,
▲ Giri,
▲ Parvata,
▲ Puri,
▲ Sarasvati,
▲ Sagara,
▲ Tirtha,
▲ Vana.

On initiation each sannyasin (an ascetic, specifically, one who pays particular devotion to the god Siva) takes a new name, which includes as its suffix the name of one of the ten orders, indicating either the order to which his preceptor belongs, the center at which he was initiated, or the one to which he is attached.

DATHAN

(In the Old Testament, son of Eliab of the tribe of Reuben and the brother of Abiram and Nemuel. Dathan and Abiram supported the Levite Korah in his rebellion against the authority of Moses and Aaron and, in effect, challenged God.

DAUGHTERS OF CHARITY

A Roman Catholic religious congregation founded at Paris in 1663 by St. Vincent de Paul and St. Louis de Marillac. The congregation was a radical innovation by 17th century standards; it was the first noncloistered institute of women religious devoted to active charitable works, especially in the service of the poor. Numbering circa 50,000 members in the early 1990s, the Daughters of Charity comprise the largest congregation of women religious.

DAVENPORT, Christopher

(1598-1680) Franciscus a Sancta Clara; Franciscan priest and theologian who hoped for the reunion of the English Church with Roman Catholicism and attempted to reconcile the Thirty-nine Articles of Anglicanism with Roman Catholic teaching.

DAVID

(died circa 960 BC). Second of the Israelite kings (after Saul), reigning circa 1000-960 BC. who established a united kingdom over all Israel, with Jerusalem as its capital. A Judean from Bethlehem, he became arms bearer to King Saul of Israel (1 Samuel 16:21), and an intimate friend to Saul's son Jonathan (1 Samuel 20:17). David killed the Philistine giant Goliath (1 Samuel 17:50) and his subsequent popularity aroused Saul's envy and wrath. After years as an outlaw, he was chosen king of Judah on Saul's death, soon extending his authority over the northern tribes. David then seized Jerusalem, making it the religious and political capital of Israel and of a large empire. His highly prosperous reign lasted 40 years. David was the proto-type of the Messiah through whom God mediated his blessing to Israel, and an ancestor of Jesus Christ (Matthew 1:17). He is the author of many of the psalms.

For many years David led the life of an outlaw, sometimes fighting for his former enemies, the Philistines. When Saul and Jonathan were defeated and killed by the Philistines, David was chosen King of Judah, the southern kingdom, and on the death of Ishbaal, Saul's successor, the northern kingdom decided to join Judah under David's rule. David then seized Jerusalem from the Canaanites and made it the religious and political capital of a united Israel. Thereafter he extended his kingdom widely to the east and north.

David's reign began circa 1000 BC and is said to have lasted 40 years. His infatuation with Bathsheba and the revolt and death of his son Absalom tarnished the later years of his reign. Nevertheless, Israel experienced its golden age under David, especially in literature. Many of the psalms in the Bible are attributed to David, and a few may actually have been composed by him. David was succeeded by Solomon, his son by Bath-sheba.

In Islam, the name is spelled Dawud or Daud. He is one of the prophets mentioned in the Koran, sometimes in conjunction with Sulayman. David is specifically called one of God's khalifas in Surad Sad and he is also the recipient of a book of revelation. The Koran shows that David has been endowed with special gifts of justice and wisdom. In an extended Koran passage (verses 21 and following of Surat Sad) both qualities are displayed in full measure where David gives judgement between two disputants and then, feeling guilt for a perceived sin of his own, asks God's forgiveness, which he receives.

DAVID, City of

(In Judaism, the name given to the "stronghold of Zion" after its capture from the Jebusites (2 Samuel 5:6-9). This section is understood to be a spur or ridge that runs south from Mount Moriah. It thus lay south of the site of the temple later built by Solomon. Today this narrow southern plateau is considerably lower than Mount Moriah, Josephus claimed that the Maccabees removed the crest of the hill in the second century BC so that it would not appear to rival the height of the Temple area. So, it is possible that in ancient times its height may have been more comparable, though still beneath the height of the Temple site.

The name "city of David" resulted from David's making his royal residence there, after ruling for seven and a half years in Hebron. Here, with contributions from Hiram of Tyre, David's "house of cedars" was built (2 Samuel 5:5-11; 7:2). David had the ark of the covenant brought from the house of Obed-edom up to the city of David, his wife, Michal, being able to see the procession approach from a window of David's house (2 Samuel 6:10-16). Upon his death, the king was buried in the city, a custom followed with many other monarchs of the Davidic line (1 Kings 2:10).

DAVID, Saint
(circa 520-600) Patron saint of Wales. He founded many monasteries and churches in the 6th century. His feast day is March 1st.

DAVIDSON OF LAMBETH
(1848-1930) Anglican priest, chaplain, confidant of Queen Victoria, and archbishop of Canterbury. Noted as a common sense moderate, Davidson sought to reconcile extremists in the disputes between 1902 and 1906 over religious instruction in schools and the amount of ritual appropriate for worship service.

DAVIES, Samuel
(1723-1761) Presbyterian preacher who defended religious dissent and helped lead the Southern phase of the religious revival known as the Great Awakening.

His work during the Great Awakening centered at Hanover, Virginia, where Presbyterians were persecuted as Nonconformists by the established church leaders, and he became the chief defender of Dissidents. He argued their cause before the Virginia general court and enlisted support of prominent English and Scottish Dissenters.

DAWA
In Islam, call, propaganda, invitation, invocation, missionary movement, missionary call.

DAWANI
(1427-1502; Muhammad Ibn Jalal Ad-Din Dawani) Jurist and philosopher who was chiefly responsible for maintaining the traditions of Islamic philosophy in the 15th century.

He attempted to demonstrate that there need to be no conflict between the mystical and philosophical view of the world, that they could coexist but that, because a mystic reaches his conclusions through faith based on divine grace, he is superior to a philosopher, who is motivated by human knowledge and possibly doubt.

DAWSA
In Islam, literally treading or trampling underfoot. The term was used in tasawwuf to refer to a ceremony which used to be enacted in Cairo in which the Shaykh of the Sa'di order would ride a horse over several hundred members of the order without apparent injury to these adherents.

DAYANANDA SARASVATI
(1824-1883) Hindu ascetic and social reformer, founder of the Arya Samaj, a Hindu reform movement advocating a return to the temporal and spiritual authority of the Vedas, the earliest scriptures of India.

DAY OF ATONEMENT
(Yom Kippur) One of the best-known Jewish feasts, introduced in late Old Testament times and continuing in modern Judaism as the prime day of

expiation and penance. In the Hebrew of the Old Testament the feast is called, yom hakkippurim, "the day of expiations," while in Acts 27:9 it is simply "The Fast."

The feast is observed on the 10th day of the 7th month of Tishri (September-October). Its origin is probably later since it is not mentioned in pre-exilic or even early post-exilic texts. When Ezekiel tells of the reconstructed Temple liturgy, he includes a rite of atonement (Ezekiel 45:18-20), but the rite is not identical with that of this feast, and furthermore it was observed on the 1st and 7th day of the month.

The Old Testament ritual is described in Leviticus 16:1-34. As it now stands the rite can be divided into three parts.

▲ First the High Priest sacrificed a bull as a sin offering for his own sins and those of the Aaronite priesthood. It was during this ceremony that he entered the Holy of the Holies - the only occasion in the year that this was done; he placed incense before the mercy seat and sprinkled the bull's blood on and before it. In later times two distinct entrances were involved, one with incense and the other with blood, although this is not clear from the text.

▲ The High Priest made another sin offering, this time a male goat for the sins of the people, and he again entered the Holy of Holies to sprinkle the mercy seat. When the blood of both the bull and the male goat had been sprinkled the High Priest than purified the Holy of Holies, the Tent of Meeting, and finally the altar by putting some of the blood on the horns of the altar. All this was done to cleanse them from the uncleanenesses of the people.

▲ The third element involves the scapegoat. Toward the beginning of the ceremony, the High Priest cast lots upon two male goats, one lot for the Lord and the other lot for Azazel. The goat upon which the lot for the Lord was used was the sin offering above, but the one for Azazel was presented alive before the Lord, while the High Priest placed his hands upon its head and confessed over it all the iniquities of the people. The last part of the ritual has parallels among the Babylonians.

DAY OF RECOLLECTION

A practice of setting aside specific days on which priests, religious, and/or lay people come together for special prayer, conferences, or discussions aimed at heightening their spiritual consciousness and promoting their spiritual development. It serves much the same purpose as a retreat, especially for those who cannot spare the time for more extended exercises.

DAY OF THE LORD

A term whose development in richness of meaning extended over a period of history from the conquest into New Testament times. In the wide sense it indicates a time when Yahweh will reveal his judgment or manifest his punitive justice through calamities.

In the narrow sense it is an eschatological idea indicating the time of long-awaited salvation after judgment is passed on all things hostile to Yahweh.

In a total view of history, the term designates Yahweh's solemn intervention in the course of history. Originally the phrase referred to military victory in favor of the people of God, a day of vindication for the oppressed people over an enemy through Yahweh's saving help.

From this national and political meaning, the term came to have the more spiritual content of freeing men from the bondage of the sin so that Yahweh might have complete dominion over this world.

The prophet Amos was the first to confront the people concerning their naïve assumption that Yahweh would be with them at all cost. He informed them that the Day of the Lord for them would not be what they thought - a day of victory and glory - but rather a day of wrath and vengeance. The people must learn to keep the covenant with the Lord.

The New Testament borrows the same concept with its Christian overtones. Some of the writers use the term as does the Old Testament to speak of the Day of Judgment and Purification in which the heavens and the earth will be cleansed and renewed to make a new world of love and justice (2 Peter 3). This Day is identified in 1 and 2 Thessalonians with the second coming of Christ.

Thus the apocalyptic sections of the synoptics really speak of this day as understood in Christian teaching.

DEACON

(Greek diakonis, "servant") Assistant to the clergy in the Christian church. deacons form a minor holy order in the Roman Catholic Church and an important class of clergy in the Orthodox church. In Protestant churches deacons are usually laymen given special church responsibilities.

In the early church, deacons were members of a basic but subservient ministerial order that helped with the practical and charitable functions of the Christian community. Later in the Roman Catholic, Eastern Orthodox, and Anglican churches the diaconate almost entirely lost its original independent status as one of the major orders. Instead, it became a transitional probationary period for ordination to the priesthood, usually lasting one year. Since the second Vatican Council (1962-65) in the Roman Catholic Church, however, provision has been made for a permanent office of deacon to be filled by both celibate and married men.

Especially in Germany and Scandinavia, special diaconal institutes, first founded in Germany in 1833, train deacons for social service and youth work in the parishes.

Several Protestant churches in Asia and Africa have revived the permanent diaconate.

DEACONESS

A woman involved in the pastoral, social, or teaching ministry of the Anglican, Lutheran, Methodist, Presbyterian and Reformed, and some other Protestant churches.

In the New Testament, a deaconess of the church at Cenchreae is mentioned (Romans 16:1), but little is known of the actual functions of such women in the church until the 4th century. They acted as doorkeepers in churches and as assistants to the clergy in baptizing of women.

Their ordination resembled that of deacons and conveyed no sacerdotal powers or authority, but it was partly fear that they would usurp priestly functions that led to their decline. The order of deaconesses was abolished by the Councils of Epaon (517) and Orleans (533).

After the Reformation, some deaconess work was introduced among some Reformed groups in the 16th century. The modern deaconess movement began in the 19th century, first in Germany, and later in other countries. The deaconesses in modern times have varying education, duties, and powers, depending on the church and the country in which they serve. They do not promise to remain deaconesses all their lives.

DEAD

The biblical notions on the condition of the dead evidence a slow development. The ancient Hebrews held the same notions about life and death as the Canaanites among whom they lived. These notions were derived from observation of phenomena.

They noted that life, a movement from within and the ability to accomplish things, ceased with man's last breath and that man's lifeless body crumbled to dust. Hence they looked upon a breathing man as a "living-being," or a "living soul," constituted of God-given breath and God-molded dust (see Genesis 2:7). A corpse, on the other hand, was considered a "dead soul" (Numbers 6:6; Leviticus 21:11).

The notion of a distinction between soul and body, therefore, was something unintelligible to the ancient Hebrew, and he did not look upon death as the separation of these two elements.

Yet death was not regarded as annihilation. As long as the body continued to exist and as long as the bones at least remained, the soul continued to exist, like a shade, in extreme weakness in the abode of the dead (Isaiah 14:9; Psalms 88:11). Hence the dead were called the "weak ones" (Job 26:5; Isaiah 14:9).

The rise of an awareness of individual responsibility (see Ezekiel 14:12-20) and the realization that occasionally, at least, evil persons die unpunished led to the introduction of a notion of punishment after death. Thus Ezekiel 32:20 assigns enemy leaders to the deepest part of the pit (Sheol), the place reserved for those slaughtered and uncircumcised, a position of disgrace.

This seems to be the starting point of the teaching or retribution for sins after death. The notion of disgrace transforms the worms of the grave, referred to in Isaiah 14:11 as a blanket covering the corpse, into worms that do not die or cease eating and a fire that refuses to be put out (Isaiah 66:24, Mark 9:48).

Finally, under the influence of the Grecian anthropology, through the Greek speaking Jews of Alexandria, the notion of immortality was introduced. But an immortal soul existing independent of the body by which man is existentially man may be only a temporary condition if the afterlife is to be truly human.

Hence resurrection of the body is demanded (see 1 Corinthians 15). In this framework, the Day of Yahweh gives way to a particular judgment at the moment of death, in and through which man is awarded and joy in the bosom of Abraham, paradise or heaven (Luke 16:22-25; Luke 23:43) or punishment in the pit of flames.

The general judgment on the last day, the Day of the Lord, becomes the occasion for the proclamation of Yahweh's victory and moment of the resurrection of the bodies of the dead to glory (1 Corinthians 15:1; Revelation 21:2-5).

Here more than in any other area of religious thought, the condescension, the humanization or adaptation of divine revelation to the cultural milieu of the recipient is seen.

DEAD, Care of the

The special treatment required by religious custom and law in the disposal of the human body after death. Some special observance is practiced by almost all religions for reasons associated with the beliefs peculiar to each.

Although for Christians burying the dead was not included among the works of mercy mentioned by Jesus in the eschatological discourse on the judgment (Matthew 25:35-36), the special practices adopted at an early date are not without scriptural warrant.

In the Old Testament Tobit was praised by the angel (Tobit 12:13) for his work, and in the New Testament Jesus commended the women who anointed him at Bethany, which he took as done to prepare him for burial (Matthew 26:12).

Two theological considerations support Christian practice in this matter:

▲ the body as part of the human person is "the temple of the Holy Spirit" (1 Corinthians 6:19);

▲ concern for the decent disposal of the dead may witness to the core Christian belief in the resurrection of the dead to another life in Christ.

DEAD, Mass for the

The Eucharistic Sacrifice offered on behalf of a deceased person. From the early centuries of the church, it has been customary to offer Mass for one who has died on the third day after his death. Originally this probably concluded a watch kept at the grave. In the West it later became common to celebrate Mass either at the grave or in the church on the occasion of the funeral itself. Masses are also offered on the 7th and 30th days after death and upon the anniversary of the death date.

In the East the funeral Mass did not become part of the burial rite, but Masses were offered on the third, 19th and 40th days after death and upon the anniversary day.

The liturgy of the burial rite and Masses for the dead originally reflected two themes: one of joy at the deceased's completion of his earthly pilgrimage and his union with Christ, and the other of hope that his survivors might help him to his rest by the suffrage of prayer and Eucharistic sacrifice.

The natural sadness of the occasion appears to have been deliberately muted by early Christians in order to affirm their faith in the resurrection and to disavow pagan attitudes toward the fact of death.

DEAD, Prayers for the

From apostolic times the church has cherished the belief that the souls of the departed can be helped by the prayers of the living. In this sense 2 Maccabees 12:39-45 is conclusive: after a battle, Judas had expiratory sacrifices offered for the slain Jewish soldiers. A specific doctrine was sanctioned by the Council of Trent in 1563, which banned as superstitious the custom of offering for the dead a fixed number of Masses.

The theological basis of the doctrine is the communion of saints, understood originally as a living communion in holy things rather than of holy persons. The living and the dead are all members of the same church with the possibility of exercising a mutual salutary influence.

DEAD, Worship of the

Worship of the dead are the historically ambivalent forms of interaction with and commemoration of the dead found in most cultures and religions. Such interaction may be said to be positive when help is extended to the dead by providing an adequate tomb, effective rituals, food offerings, prayers, and the observance of mourning period.

It is negative when the dead, like other spirits, ghosts, and demons with whom they often merge, are considered a threat to the living. In this case rituals, offerings, prayers, and magical techniques are aimed at restraining the dead from acts of destruction and revenge.

Often both attitudes coexist side by side. Worship of the dead was prevalent in those primitive societies which engaged in sun-worship since they believed that the sun carried the dead into the underworld at sunset and could restore them to the light at dawn. Its complexity seems to grow with both economical and social differentiation.

In general it is less developed among gatherers and hunters. It becomes very complex among the sedentary cultures of planters, for whom the identity of the village, the fertility of the field, and their magico-religious interpretation are in many respects substantialized in the mystique of birth and death and the rituals that refer to them.

Finally it culminates in archaic high cultures with their emphasis on social status as expressed in the burial customs such as existed in Ancient Egypt, China, America, and some of the ancient African kingdoms.

In ancient Greece, food offerings were laid at a crossroad every month for Hecate, the goddess of the underworld, and for the ghosts of those who could not rest in their graves.

In the Old Testament, traces remain of sacrifices offered to or for the dead, and of the practice of furnishing them with food even though this was condemned by official Judaism (Deuteronomy 26:14).

DEAD SEA

Landlocked salt lake between Israel and Jordan, the lowest body of water on Earth at approximately 1,321 feet below sea level. The waters of the Dead Sea are extremely saline, it excludes any animal or vegetable life except bacteria. It has been associated with biblical history since the time of Abraham (progenitor of the Hebrews) and the destruction of Sodom and Gomorrah. These two cities were destroyed by fire from heaven because of their wickedness. The city sites are now possibly submerged in the southern part of the Dead Sea.

DEAD SEA SCROLLS

A group of Hebrew and Aramaic manuscripts discovered in caves near the northwestern coast of the Dead Sea in the late 1940s and 1950s. The scrolls, which were preserved in clay jars, were documents of a Jewish sect of ascetics who lived in Qumran in the area around the first century BC. Little is known about the group, which is usually identified with the Essenes, but it is thought to have been suppressed by the Romans following the Jewish revolt in 67-70. Many of the scrolls are books of the Old Testament, dating from the third century BC to the first century AD, far older than the oldest biblical manuscripts previously known. Their main interest lies in the remarkable degree of which they agree with the traditional text of the Hebrew Bible.

The most important of the biblical scrolls is the complete text of Isaiah. Among the non-biblical texts is one describing the "war of the sons of light against the sons of darkness," a work which is believed to be an allegory on political events of the time. Another important work was the "Manual of discipline," which tells us most of what we know about the group. Because many of their beliefs were similar to those of the early Christians and because their way of life resembled that later followed by Christian monks, it is often suggested that they had some connection with or influence on early Christianity.

The scrolls also speak of a "teacher of righteousness" who is opposed byu a "wicked priest." The "teacher of righteousness," who may have been the leader of the group, is thought by some to refer to Jesus, but this is unlikely. The scrolls also show a great similarity to a manuscript known as the "Damascus document," telling of a similar group that has been forced to more from Jerusalem to Damascus. Found in 1896, in an old Cairo synagogue, the authenticity of the Damascus document has now been established because of its resemblance to the Dead Sea scrolls. The scrolls illuminate the great diversity of Jewish religious beliefs and literature at this period, and the religious background of Jesus and his early followers.

DEATH

The cessation of all functions of life, hence the opposite of life (Deuteronomy 30:15, 19). In the Bible the same original-language words for "death" or "dying" are applied to humans, animals, and plants (John 12:24; Jude 12; Revelation 16:3). However, for humans and animals the Bible shows the vital function of the blood in maintaining life, stating that the "soul of the flesh is in the blood" (Leviticus 17:11, 14; Genesis 4:8-11; 9:3-4).

In Buddhism, death is regarded as the last of the chain of the 12 Nidanas; the abandonment of the body and other sheaths or bodies which alike dissolve at death. To the Buddhist it is a recurrent phenomenon.

DEATH, Theology of

The Paschal Mystery, Christ's Passion, death, and Resurrection, is the criterion of a Christian theology of death. Such a theology can recognize consideration abstractly antecedent to the concrete history of salvation. Thus death and physical deterioration are natural consequences of human nature's material composition, the union of soul with body.

There is, as well, a possibility to demonstrate by philosophical reasoning the immortality of the soul on the basis of its having a level of existence and activity transcending the bodily level. The soul's manner of separated existence and final, natural destiny can be speculated to be a state of imperfect survival (since the natural condition of the soul is to be the united with the body) and to be a state of reward or punishment corresponding to a person's relationship to the First Cause and Final End of all creation.

There can also be a recognition that innate in human nature is a natural desire to see God and correspondingly a natural dread of death not simply as a physical phenomenon, but as it looms in spite of philosophical arguments for immortality, as the absurd negation of personal existence, consciousness, and desire for transcendence.

Christian theology, however, must see such considerations as abstractions displaced by the concrete divine economy of salvation revealed in Jesus Christ.

DEATH OF GOD MOVEMENT

Radical Christian (mainly Protestant) theological school that arose in the United States during the 1960s, evoking extraordinary publicity, response, and controversy. Although thinkers of many varied viewpoints have been grouped within this school, basic to practically all of them is the conviction that belief in God is impossible or meaningless in the modern world, and that man's fulfillment is to be found in the secular life in this world.

DEATH OF THE VIRGIN

A theme in Christian art illustrating the central event in apocryphal accounts of the last days of the Virgin Mary. According to these immensely popular accounts, after the archangel Gabriel had announced to Mary that she was about to die, the Apostles, scattered throughout the world, were miraculously transported to her deathbed. Christ came down from heaven and received her soul as it left her body. The Virgin was buried and remained dead for three days, after which her body was resurrected and reunited with her soul; soul and body were than elevated to heaven in the Assumption of the Virgin.

DEBIR

In biblical times, the king of Eglon, one of the four petty kingdoms allied with the king of Jerusalem to attack the city of Gibeon for making peace with Joshua. Gibeon's surrender to Joshua caused fear since it likely weakened any united front against Israel (Joshua 9:1-2).

DEBORAH

Prophetess and heroine in the Old Testament (Judges 4, 5), who inspired the Israelites to a mighty victory over their Canaanite oppressors. The song of Deborah (Judges 5) is universally regarded as a masterpiece of Hebrew poetry. After the battle at Mount Tabot, in which the Canaanites were routed, Deborah sang a song of victory, a lusty poem of victory, dedicated to the God of Israel, and is one of the oldest examples of Hebrew poetry in the Bible.

DÉCADI, Cult of

A patriotic cult observing every ten days in the calendar of the French Republic; an attempt to substitute the Christian Sunday for a naturalistic, nonreligious service. The Décadi was a ceremonial with bonfires, chants, and imprecations prescribed for certain feasts, as, for example, youth, age, knowledge.

In 1797 the Second Directory promulgated the Décadi as the national official cult. Penal legislation insisted on the suspension of court and government business, schools, factories, and shops. Many bishops suffered imprisonment and death for resisting the suppression of Sunday observance and that of Christian marriage. Napoleon reopened the closed churches in 1799 and officially dissolved the cult in 1805.

DECAPOLIS

In biblical times, league or confederation of ten cities, or the region in which most of these cities were centered (Matthew 4:25).

DECIUS

(201-251) Roman emperor (249-251) who fought the Gothic invasion of Moesia and instituted the first organized persecution of the Christians throughout the empire. Before Decius' reign, persecution of the Christians in the empire had been sporadic and local, but around the beginning of January 250 he issued an edict ordering all citizens to perform a religious sacrifice in the presence of commissioners. A large number of Christians defied the government, which responded by striking at their leaders. The suppression strengthened rather than weakened the Christian movement, for public opinion condemned the government's violence and applauded the passive resistance of the martyrs.

DECLARATION OF NULLITY

In Roman Catholicism, the official pronouncement that a putative marriage was not a true, Christian marriage at all. The declaration is made by the Roman Rota or by a diocesan tribunal after thorough official investigation and interrogation. Ground for a finding of nullity may be a defect that negated the ostensible matrimonial consent either because of the deceit of an undiscovered or undisclosed diriment (invalidating) impediment; the fact that the canonical forms of marriage (for instance, contraction before an authorized priest and two witnesses) was not observed.

DECREE

In the theology of predestination, a term to describe the act of God's will putting into effect the plan or economy of salvation. The term has the connotation of an ordered and discerning choice.

Traditional Roman Catholic theology affirmed a positive decree of predestination, but not reprobation; strict Calvinism equivalently maintained a positive decree predestining the elect and reprobating thenonelect.

DECREE (CANON LAW)

A formal pronouncement of the Holy See, having the force of a command or prohibition. The term has the connotation of being a decision binding either on the whole church or on the addressee. In the ordinary workings of the Holy See a decree is issued usually by a congregation of the Curia Romana with the pope's approval. Vatican Council II among its documents issued nine classified as decrees, four as dogmatic constitutions, three as declarations.

DECREE ON ECUMENISM

The pastoral document of Vatican Council II that sets forth for all Roman Catholics the guidelines and methods by which they may respond to the grace of the Holy Spirit calling for "restoration of unity among all the followers of Christ."

Recognizing that the present division among Christians "contradicts the will of Christ, scandalizes the world, and damages that most holy cause, the preaching of the Gospel to every creature," the Decree notes that among "our separated brethren" a movement for the restoration of unity "fostered by the grace of the Holy Spirit" has increased day by day. The chief advances made by the Decree on Ecumenism are the acceptance of this ecumenical movement and the encouragement given to Catholics to participate in it according to their Catholic principles. The Decree also makes an important contribution to the beginnings of a new ecclesiology. For the first time in a Roman Catholic ecclesiastical document, religious bodies tracing their origins from the Reformation are called churches, with ecclesiastical gifts and sacred actions capable of giving birth to the life of grace and admission to the community of salvation.

DECRETALS

Letters of papal decision on matters of discipline and teaching that indicate the growth in power of the medieval papacy and mark the development of canon law. Papal issuance of mandatory letters is clearly dated from at least the pontificate of Siricius, but the practice had its greatest significance in the Middle Ages.

Increase of papal power is evident in the marked increase in the number of decretals. Their meaning and status as law came to be more clearly defined: they are strictly speaking rescripts in response to questions submitted for papal decision. In modern practice the term decretal usually is restricted to documents on canonization or dogmatic teaching.

DEDAN

In the Old Testament, a descendant of Abraham through Jokshan (Genesis 25:3; 1 Chronicles 1:32). The Dedanites descending from Jokshan apparently settled south and south-east of Palestine in the same general vicinity to which Abraham sent all his offspring through Keturah (Genesis 25:6).

DEESIS

In the Orthodox church a tripartite icon showing Christ flanked on his right side by the Holy Mother of God and on his left by John the Baptist. The side images face toward the central figure of the enthroned Christ and extend their hands toward him in a gesture of prayer and entreaty.

Sometimes these attendant figures are extended by the addition of other saints, which usually include the archangels Michael and Gabriel. the saints Peter and Paul and the saints Basil, Chrysostom, Gregory of Nazianzus and Nicholas.

DEFAMATION

The general term used in Roman Catholic moral theology for an act that unjustly deprives another of his good name or reputation. The term includes both calumny, which takes away another's reputation by lies, and detraction, which tells the truth but without necessity (as in the revelation of another's secret faults), whether these offenses are committed in their more blatant and obvious forms, or by exaggerations and insinuations that reflect discreditably on another.

Defamation is considered a sin against both charity and justice, and when it does, or is seen as likely to do, notably harm, it is said to be a serious sin, but various circumstances such as the quality and character of both the defamer and the defamed, the publicity that may or may not attend the defamatory words.

DEFENDER OF THE FAITH

A title belonging to the sovereign of England (as from the 16th century) in the same way as *Christianissimus* ("the most Christian") belonged to the king of France.

DEFENSOR PACIS

Work by the Italian Franciscan Marsilius of Padua (1324), translated as *Defender of the Peace,* holding that power resided within a community. It was used by supporters of the Holy Roman Emperor Louis IV as propaganda against papal supremacy over the empire.

DEFINITION, Dogmatic

A solemn and authoritative judgment of the Roman Catholic Church in the area of doctrine. It is not identical with revelation of the original expression of it found in scripture, but is a statement of faith held by the church as a result of a living reflection on the revealed mysteries.

DEFINITION, Infallible

In the Roman Catholic Church, a solemn declaration by the church witnessing to religious truth with divine assurance of certitude and of preservation from error. While most definitions are concerned with things that are divinely revealed, they can also be ideas or facts merely connected with revelation.

DEIFICATION

Making or being made like God, a descriptive term for transformation and regeneration through grace. The term is particularly related to the expression in 2 Peter 1:4, "becoming sharers of the divine nature."

DEISM

A religious attitude that flourished in England from the late 17th to the mid 18th century. It was influenced by the writings of Lord Herbert of Cherbury and John Locke in the 17th century, and its "bible" was Matthew Tindal's *Christianity as old as the Creation* (1730). Deism influenced Voltaire and the Encyclopedists in France, and was later influential in Germany and the

United States, where many of the "Founding Fathers", including Washington, Adams and Jefferson, the first three presidents, could be considered Deists.

The Deists, reflecting the rationalism of the times, recognized the existence of God on the evidence of nature and reason, but rejected supernatural revelation as traditionally presented by Judaism and Christianity. Their God created the worlds and then withdrew from it. This belief led to a new interpretation of the Bible in terms of reason rather than supernatural.

DEKER

In Judaism, father of one of Solomon's 12 deputies. Deker's son provided food for Solomon and his household one month out of the year apparently from the region of southern Dan (1 Kings 4:7-9).

DELAIAH

In the Old Testament, an Aaronic priest of David's time designated by lot as the head of the twenty-third priestly division (1 Chronicles 24:1, 5, 18).

DELATION

Canonical term for reporting to ecclesiastical authority a doctrine or work evidencing unorthodoxy; it is a form of denunciation.

DELILAH

In the Old Testament (Judges 16) she was a Philistine who, bribed to entrap Samson, coaxed him into revealing that the secret of his strength was his long hair, whereupon she took advantage of his confidence to betray him to his enemies. Her name has since become synonymous with a voluptuous, treacherous woman.

DELPHI

Site in ancient Greece. Famous as the site of the temple and oracle of Apollo, it is located on the lower slopes of Mount Parnassus. In ancient Greece an oracle was the place where a divinity made known his will or purpose to the person consulting him. There were several of these oracles, each with its own ritual, but the most famous of all was the oracle of Delphi. Here Apollo is supposed to have revealed his wishes and decisions through a priesteress by means of vapors rising out of a crevice in the earth.

Delphi remained an important cultural and religious center throughout the fifth and fourth centuries BC. The oracle was finally closed by the Christian Emperor Theodosius in 390.

DELPHI, Oracle of

An oracle of Apollo and the principal oracle of ancient Greece. It was located at what was thought to be the center of the earth, marked by the sacred navel-stone, or omphalos, on the southern slope of Mount Parnassus.

The first oracles of the god were given through the interpretation of natural signs such as the song and flight of birds. Later they were uttered through the mouth of a frenzied virgin priestess, the Pythia.

The oracle gave responses to questions of a religious and secular nature, to individuals and to official embassies, to Greeks and to foreigners. Frequently ambiguous and politically opportunistic, the oracle nevertheless played an important role in Greek colonization, giving advice on the choice of a site and patron deity.

DELUGE

In the Old Testament, the catastrophic destruction of men and animals by an overwhelming flood in the days of Noah (circa 2300 BC). According to biblical records, this greatest cataclysm in all human history was sent by God because wicked men had filled the earth with violence. The survival of righteous Noah and his family, eight souls in all, together with selected animals, was by means of a huge Ark or chest (Genesis 6:9-9:19).

DEMA DEITIES

A collective name given to ancestral beings by the Marind-Anim of southern New Guinea. The decisive act in the dema myths is the slaying of a dema deity by the dema. This act brings about the transition from the previous ancestral world to the present human one.

DEMAS

A Christian who was with Paul, when he was a prisoner in Rome. He later deserted Paul and went off to Thessalonica.

DEMETER

In Greek religion, daughter of the deities Cronus and Rhea, sister of Zeus (the king of gods), and goddess of agriculture. He name means either "grain mother" or "mother earth." Demeter appeared most commonly as a corn goddess.

Persephone, Demeter's only daughter, grew up to be a happy child in the company of her mother and the other goddesses, until one day Pluto fell in love with her and abducted her.

Persephone was picking lilies in a field, when suddenly the earth opened beneath her feet and Pluto carried her off to the underworld. When Demeter discovered that her daughter was missing, she began to search for her. She wandered anxiously and sadly, day and night, across the entire known world, but no one could tell her anything.

When Helios, the sun god, eventually revealed the truth to her, Demeter was so angry that she left her post and duties on Olympus and, changed into an old woman, entered the service of Celeus, king of Eleusis. While she was absent in Eleusis, the earth was barren, the crops withered, no plant blossomed or bore fruit and mankind suffered from starvation.

It was then that Zeus ordered Pluto to send Persephone home, since Demeter was threatening to prevent the earth from bearing even a single stalk of wheat. Pluto agreed to send his wife back to her mother in the upper world - but before doing so, he cunningly made her eat a pomegranate seed, which was enough to bind her to the underworld

for ever. And so a contract was made with Pluto: for eight months of the year Persephone would live in the upper world with her mother, and for four months she would stay in Hades, with her husband.

DEMETRIA

Obscure Greek festival or rite of Demeter, goddess of agriculture, in which the participants beat each other with whips of twisted bark, a well-known fertility charm.

DEMETRIUS

In the New Testament, a Christian mentioned favorably by the Apostle John in a letter to Gaius, circa 98. Demetrius may have delivered the letter to Gaius. John's recommendation of Demetrius may have been to encourage hospitality on the part of Gaius, as it seems to have been a custom of the congregations to assist in providing food and lodging for the faithful brothers who traveled in behalf of the good news (3 John 1,12).

DEMON

In biblical terms, an invisible wicked spirit or creature, sometimes called "a fallen angel," having superhuman powers. The demons as such were, according to biblical records, not created by God. The first to make himself one was Satan the Devil, who became the ruler of other angelic sons of god who also made themselves demons (Matthew 12:24-26). In Noah's days these disobedient angels materialized, married women, fathered a hybrid generation known as Nephilim, and then dematerialized when the Flood came (Genesis 6:1-4). However, upon returning to the spirit realm they did not regain their lofty original position, for Jude 6 says: "The angels that did not keep their original position but forsook their own proper dwelling place He has reserved with eternal bonds under dense darkness for the judgment of the great day" (1 Peter 3:19-20). So it is in this condition of dense spiritual darkness that they must now confine their operations. Though evidently restrained from materializing, they still have great power and influence over the minds and lives of men, even having the ability to enter into and possess human and animals, as well as to use inanimate things such as houses, fetishes, charms, and so forth (Matthew 12:43-45; Luke 8:27-33).

DEMONIC

In Christian theology, the power of evil and destruction embedded in the structure of things, which may take possession of men and which is conquerable by divine grace. This concept, which played an important role in the New Testament and in traditional Christian thought, fell into disrepute in modern times until its renewal in the 20th century by the German-American theologian Paul Tillich. His analysis and interpretation of the demonic made it a familiar term in contemporary theological and cultural discussion, and it was applied to social and psychological as well as religious phenomena.

DEMONOLATRY

Worship of demons. Belief in the power of demons to inflict evils of various kinds has sometimes led to attempts at winning their favor through rites and prayers. Strongly condemned by orthodox religion, the practice may express rebellion against God and a survival of pagan practices. It has had a revival in the late 20th century.

DEMONOLOGY

In Judaism during the Hellenistic period there is a belief in individual demons, controlled by a hierarchy. The influence of Zoroastrianism may easily be recognized. In the Enoch literature the demons are identified with the "sons of god," who (according to Genesis 6:2,4) were attracted by the beauty of the "daughters of men."

DEMON POSSESSION

The captive control and influence of a person by an invisible wicked spirit. In biblical times demonized persons were afflicted in various ways; some were dumb, some blind, some acted like lunatics and some possessed superhuman strength. All were woefully mistreated by these invisible bullies (Matthew 9:32; Mark 5:3-5; Luke 8:29; Acts 19:16). Men, women and children were their victims (Matthew 15:22; Mark 5:2). Sometimes the agony was compounded when many demons gained possession of a person at the same time (Luke 8:2, 30). When the demon was expelled, the person returned to a normal, sane state of mind. There is a difference between demon possession and ordinary physical sickness and disease, for Jesus cured both types of disorder (Matthew 8:16-18; Mark 1:32-34).

DEMONS, Hierarchy of

An ordering or ranking of malevolent celestial or spiritual beings especially noted in Western religions; for instance, Zoroastrianism, Judaism, Christianity, and Islam. Arranged in ranking counterposed to the hierarchy of angels, the various demonic hierarchies are headed by a prince of evil who generally is designated by the term devil.

DEMOPHON

In Greek mythology, the son of Celeus, king of Eleusis. The goddess Demeter, wandering in search for her daughter Persephone, became Demophon's nurse. As an act of kindness to those who sheltered her, she attempted to immortalize him by burning out his mortal parts but was surprised in the act by his mother, who thought that she was harming the body. Incensed, Demeter quickly withdrew the child from the fire, thus leaving him susceptible to death.

DEMOTIC SCRIPT

Term used since the time of Herodotus (5th century BC) for the Egyptian style of writing that, beginning in the 6th century BC, succeeded the hieratic script for nonreligious matters.

DEMYTHOLOGIZING

A method of biblical criticism concerning itself with the cultural religious expressions of myths used by the biblical authors to convey their religious message, the kerygma or proclamation. Myth has a technical meaning - the human expression of religious experience. This definition does not concern itself with the truth or falsity of the myth. It simply defines the way religious man expresses his experience. This understanding of myth is valid whether the human expression be the etchings on the caves of Neanderthal man, or the biblical writing of the Old and New Testaments, or a religious proclamation today. Demythologizing concerns itself with the kerygma of the Scriptures.

DENIS, Saint

(3rd century) Patron saint of France and first bishop of Paris. According to tradition, Denis was really Dionysius, a missionary sent from Rome to convert the Gauls. As Bishop of Paris he was arrested by Roman officials and beheaded. The abbey of St. Denis, the burial place of French kings, was erected in the 7th century on the supposed site of his martyrdom. His feast day is October 9th.

DENOMINATION

In a broad sense a synonym for a sect or for any church body composed of local congregations united in belief and government. It may also be defined as a religious group accommodated to the prevailing culture, willingly accepting itself as one among many other denominations, stressing practical cooperation, and minimizing distinctive theological differences.

DENOMINATIONALISM

A term used in several senses:
▲ a synonym for sectarianism in all its senses;
▲ a view of the church that allows and even favors the coexistence of many differing church bodies;
▲ the theory and practice that joins many local churches in one ecclesiastical body, united by belief and government.

DEOBANDIS

Members of a fundamentalist Indian Muslim group of reformers originally centered in an academy of theology started in a town called Deoband, in 1867. The object of the academy was the training of future ulama who would be devoted to the reform of Islam. Deobandis have a particular reverence for the figure of the Prophet Mohammed, and at Deoband the teaching placed special emphasis on the study of hadith.

Many of the early ulama held a variety of Sufi beliefs and performed practices such as dhikr. For them the highest state of mysticism was the most successful emulation of the Prophet Mohammed. However, intercession with God via the saints was frowned upon as was pilgrimage to their tombs. Presumably because of their attempts to purge Islam of what were regarded as Sufi abuses, the Deobandis were later characterized by some as "anti-Sufi" and contrasted as such with Barelwis.

DEOBAND SCHOOL

The leading Muslim theological center of India, second in prestige in the Muslim world only to al-Azhar University of Cairo. It was founded in 1867 by Muhammed Abid Husayn. The theological position of Deoband has always been heavily influenced by the 18th century Muslim reformer Shah Wali Allah and the early 10th century Indian Wahhabis, giving it a very puritanical and orthodox outlook.

DEPOSING POWER

Power of the pope to excommunicate and dethrone princes. In the Middle Ages it was generally accepted that the power of the Roman pontiff was above that of all sovereigns. In addressing the Academy of Catholic Religion (1871), Pope Pius IX said: "No one now thinks any more of the right of deposing princes, which the Holy See formerly exercised; and the supreme pontiff even less than any one."

DEPOSITION

A term usually applied to a theme in Christian art, also called the descent from the cross, that illustrates the taking down of the dead Christ from the cross. The deposition was not illustrated until the 9th century because it is a purely narrative scene with no symbolic or liturgical function and was thus not well suited to the iconographic schemes of church decoration in earlier periods.

DEPOSIT OF FAITH

A term used to describe the sum of revelation and tradition entrusted to the Roman Catholic Church and its teaching office (magisterium) to be safeguarded and explained to the people of God.

"The Roman Pontiff and the bishops, by reason of their office and the seriousness of the matter, apply themselves with zeal to the work of enquiring by every suitable means into this revelation and of giving apt expression to its contents; they do not, however, admit any new public revelation as pertaining to the divine deposit of faith" (Dogmatic Constitution on the church, paragraph 25).

DERASHA

In Judaism, a homily or sermon generally preached by a rabbi in the synagogue. Often a Jewish boy delivers a derasha as part of the ceremony (Bar Mitzva) that formally acknowledges his religious adulthood.

DEREKH ERETZ

(Hebrew: "correct conduct") The decorum dignified behavior, and gentlemanly conduct that should characterize a Jew at all times. Rabbinic scholars have applied the notion, for example, to all aspects of family life and marriage, to the qualities expected of a scholar, and to relationships between friends.

For Jews, Derekh Eretz is not only postulated in the Torah; without it, the Torah itself is rendered sterile.

DERVISH

Member of the Muslim religious fraternity, sometimes mendicant, resembling in some respects a Christian religious monastic order. Within the fraternity, organized in the 12th century, an established leadership and prescribed discipline obliged the dervish to learn the chain of reputed spiritual descent of his fraternity to which he was bound through his initiating teacher.

Dervishes could be either resident in community or lay members, both groups generally drawn from the lower classes. In the Middle Ages, dervish communities played a vital role in religious, social, and political life in the central Islamic lands, but their monasteries now are often under government control.

DESECRATION

A form of sacrilege, consisting in profanation or violation of the sacred. The sacred means any reality or person dedicated to the service or worship of God; irreverence towards it, then, is contrary to the virtue of religion by which due reverence is shown to God.

The seriousness of the sin corresponds to the sanctity of the person, place, or object violated. Thus abuse of a person consecrated to God is worse than one against a holy place or object.

DESERT FATHERS

Early Christians who retired into the solitude of the Egyptian deserts to lead a life of prayer and mortification. This ascetical movement, which began about the mid-third century, flourished particularly in the 4th century as a reaction to the secular triumphs of Christianity after it had obtained its freedom and the favor of the emperors. The first Desert Fathers were not philosophers but simple fellahin of the Nile valley.

DESIRE

In Buddhism, thirst for separate existence in the worlds of sense. "Desire" in itself is colorless, but selfish desire is the cause of suffering. The "will to live" must be transmuted into "aspiration" for the welfare and ultimate enlightenment of all beings.

DESOLATION

In the spiritual life, an experience of being alone; sometimes an element in spiritual abandonment, part of the purification of the spirit. The exemplar of this experience is Christ and his feeling on the cross of abandonment by the Father. St. John of the Cross, as well as other mystical writers, maintains that the night of the senses and the night of the soul include such experience.

DEUCALION

In Greek legend, the son of Prometheus (the creator of mankind), king of Phthia in Thessaly, and husband of Pyrrha; he was also the father of Hellen, the mythical ancestor of the Hellenic race.

DEUEL

In the Old Testament, one whose son Eliasaph served as the chieftain of the tribe of Gad during Israel's wilderness wanderings (Numbers 1:14; 7:42-47).

DEUSDEDIT, Saint

(645-618) Pope from 615-618, chiefly noteworthy for an unsuccessful resumption of the Byzantine war against the Lombards in Italy and for a reversal of the policy of Popes Gregory I and Boniface IV, who favored monks over the secular clergy.

DEUS EX MACHINA

(Latin: god from the machine), in ancient Greek and Roman drama, the timely appearance of a god in the sky by means of a crane to unravel and resolve the plot.

DEUS OTIOSUS

(Latin: "neutral god") Term used in the history of religions and philosophies to designate a high god who has withdrawn from the immediate details of the governing of the world.

DEUTERONOMIST

Abbreviated D, name given by scholars to the supposed author or authors of one of the sources of the Pentateuch, especially Deuteronomy, as well as Joshua, Judges, Samuel, and Kings. D has a distinctive style of exhortation and vocabulary, calling for Israel's conformity with YWHW's covenant laws and stressing His election of Israel as His special people.

DEUTERONOMY, Book of

Fifth book of the Old Testament, a testament left by Moses to the Israelites about to enter Canaan, it is primarily a recapitulation of moral laws and laws relating to the settlement of Canaan.

The speeches that comprise this book recall Israel's past, reiterate laws that Moses had communicated to the people at Horeb (Sinai), and emphasize that observance of these laws is essential for the wellbeing of the people in the land they are about to possess.

A large part of the precepts of Deuteronomy are of a moral rather than a spiritual nature. It is thought that this was the book of the law found in the Temple during the reign of Josiah II (2 Kings 22:8) and responsible for extensive reforms. The humanitarian, liberal outlook of Deuteronomy is echoed by such prophets as Jeremiah.

DEVA

In Buddhism, celestial things, good, bad or indifferent in nature. The devas may inhabit one of the three worlds. They correspond to the angelic powers of Western theology.

DEVACHAN

In Buddhism, the subjective heaven state in which an individual lives between two earth "lives" after the death of the gross physical bodies and the separation of the kama-rupa.

DEVADASI

A disappearing caste of women connected originally with great temples in southern India, where they dedicated themselves to the service of its patron god. The caste appears to date from the 9th and 10th centuries, the great period of temple building in south India.

DEVADATTA

(6th century BC) Cousin of the Buddha who made an unsuccessful attempt to supersede him as head of the sangha (the Buddhist monastic community) and to impose a stricter code of life on it.

DEVIL

(From Greek "diabolos," slanderer or accuser) The chief spirit of evil and commander of lesser evil spirits or demons. The devil, Satan, who opposes God and tempts mankind. The devil's main task is that of tempting man to reject the way of life and redemption and to accept the way of death and destruction (Matthew 4:8-11).

Dualistic systems (notably Zoroastrianism, gnosticism, and Manichaeism) have regarded the devil as the uncreated equal of God, engaged in an eternal war for evil against good. Such beliefs have appeared sporadically in connection with the occult and devil worship. In Judaism, Christianity, and Islam, the devil, Satan, is a fallen angel, powerful but subordinate to God, but is to be utterly defeated and bound at the Last Judgment (Revelation 19:20'.

In post-biblical Judaism and Christianity, Satan became known as the "prince of devils" (Matthew 25:41) and assumed various names: Beelzebub (the lord of flies) in Matthew 12:24-27, sometimes corrupted to lord of the dung and Lucifer (the fallen angel of Light) in the interpretations of the early church Fathers of the words of Jesus in Luke 10:18: "I saw Satan fall like lightening from heaven," as a reference to the fall of the Day Star (or "shining one") from heaven in Isaiah 14:12-17.

DEVIL AND SIN

The reality of the devil is associated with the causing of sin (Ephesians 6:12).

DEVIL DANCE

Ceylonese Buddhist masked dance of exorcism performed in Sri Lanka to cure a person afflicted with disease or bad fortune.

DEVIL WORSHIP

The practice of offering homage to some personified force of evil hostile to God, which is conceived as having at least limited dominion over the world. As a belief it is usually based on the dualism of two counterbalancing and universal forces of good and evil, but may, as with the Uezidis of Armenia and Caucasus, hold that Satan or Iblis will be ranged under God in the end.

It takes various forms and includes practices, squalid and bizarre, sometimes intentionally sacrilegious or blasphemous on the part of Christian believers - they fall rather flat otherwise.

But diabolism, in the sense of devil-dealing, is not necessarily devil worship, nor is it traffic with demons, black magic, and suchlike sorts of superstition. Some blood-curdling legends are not to be credulously entertained: the informed theologian will not judge Voodoo, for instance, as altogether benighted, and the Christian traveler will find the devil-worshiping villages at the foothills of the Caucasus composed of honorable people, through out to propitiate a very present power.

DEVOTION

In religion, the adoration of God or the sacred through prayer, sacrifice, or other religious practices. It is often distinguished from service as the other aspect of worship, comprising life-disciplines, ethical acts, and good works. Bhakti in Hinduism and Hasidism in Judaism are notable examples of devotional movements.

DEVOTIONAL LITERATURE

Spiritual writings intended for private reading and study. Christian works of this type greatly increased after the Protestant Reformation.

DEVOTIONS

In the singular, devotion means primarily the quality or condition of being devoted or given earnestly to God's worship and service, the essence of religion taken as a virtue. A manual of devotions is a book of prayer designed for private as distinguished from formal public or liturgical worship.

In a similar sense, among Protestants, organizational meetings at a local church may be preceded by devotions, for instance, a short period of devout reflection that usually includes a hymn, a scripture reading, and a prayer.

Popular devotions, in Roman catholic usage, is a term covering a wide variety of optional prayers and practices, often peripheral to the central themes of Christian worship, that people find helpful as means of arousing devotion in the primary meaning of the term.

DGE-LUGS-PA

Since the 17th century a center of the predominant Buddhist order in Tibet; the sect of the Dalai Lamas and the Panchen Lamas.

DHAMMA

In Buddhism, any teaching set forth as a formulated system; the guiding principles accepted or followed by a man; the teachings of the Buddha.

DHAMMA-CAKKA-PAVATTANA-SUTTA

In Buddhism, the setting in motion of the wheel of the law. The term is sued for the sermon of the foundation of the Kingdom of Righteousness; the first discourse of the Buddha after his enlightenment.

DHAMMAPADA

In Buddhism, the path or way of the Buddha's Dhamma or teaching. It is a collection of 423 verses comprising a noble system of moral philosophy.

The book is very popular in Buddhist countries of both Theravada and Mahayana traditions. In Sri Lanka it has been used for centuries as a manual for novices, and it is said that every monk can recite it from memory from beginning to end. Its verses frequently serve also as sermon texts. In its teachings on the Buddhist life, the Dhammapada often contrasts behavior that leads toward Nibbana (Sanskrit Nirvana) with that which leads away from it.

DHAND

In Islam, term denoting sin, crime. Despite the latter meaning the word technically denotes a minor sin or fault, rather than a major crime or offence. Sin has been variously categorized by the jurists; some, for example, developed a scheme of venial and mortal sins. Perhaps the best known are those which attracted the death penalties. The remedy for all sin in Islam is sincere repentance to God who will always forgive the repentant sinner. Islamic moral theology, like the Christian, stresses the place of intention in all actions. God will judge a man by his intentions, and a death-bed repentance or final good deed will bring a sinner to Paradise.

DHANVANTARI

In Hindu mythology, the physician of the gods. According to the legend, the gods and the demons sought the elixir amrta by churning the milky ocean, and, as a result, Dhanvantari rose out of the waters bearing the cup filled with the elixir amrta. The Ayurveda, a traditional system of medicine developed from a text known as Atharvaveda, was, according to legend, communicated to Dhanvantari by the lord Brahma, and Dhantanvari was deified as the god of medicine.

The name has also been applied to other semi-legendary or historical physicians, and to a legendary king.

DHARANA

In Buddhism, intense concentration upon one interior object to the complete exclusion of all else. In one sense can be practiced throughout the day.

DHARIYAT, al-

The title of the 51st sura of the Koran; the Arabic title indicates "The Scattering Winds." The sura belongs to the Meccan period and has 60 verses. It takes its title from the first verse which begins with the oath "By the scattering winds ...." which are but one of the bounties of God. The sura goes on to warn of the punishment which will befall the evildoers and the joys of Paradise which await the pious and those who do good. At the end of the sura God stresses that both jinn and men were created for His worship.

DHARMA

In Buddhism, term in the sense of true teaching. This is the teaching taught by the Enlightenment One, the Buddha. There are three types of canons in the teachings:

1 Sutras (teachings taught by Buddha himself);
2 Vianayas (disciplines provided by Buddha);
3 Abdidharmas (commentaries and discussions on the Sutras and Vinayas by scholars in later periods).

These three are called the Tripitaka. Dharma is one of the three treasures of Buddhism.

The Dharma is the doctrine, the universal truth common to all men at all times, proclaimed by the Buddha. Dharma together with the Buddha and the community, make up the tri-ratna, or threefold refuge, the primary statement of Buddhist belief. In Buddhist metaphysics the term in the plural (Dharmas) is used to describe the interrelated elements that make up the empirical world.

In Jaina philosophy, dharma, in addition to being commonly understood as moral virtue, also had the meaning - unique to Jainism - of the eternal "substance," the medium that allows being to move.

DHARMACAKRA

Mudra or iconographic position of hands of Buddha signifying teaching or turning the wheel (cakra) of the Law (dharma). The hands are against the chest, the right palm out, the left palm in, fingers counting off the Noble Eightfold Paths.

DHARMAKAYA

In Buddhism , the body of the law; the Buddha as the personification of truth.

DHARMAKIRTI

(7th century) Indian Buddhist philosopher and logician, who elaborated the Indian system of syllogistic thought by introducing finer distinctions in predicating abstract and concrete terms, and distinguished varieties of inferences from negative premises and interferences leading to negative results.

DHARMA-MANGAL

In Hindu sacred literature a variety of Middle Bengali literature (1300-1500), a major branch of literary genre known as mangal-kavya.

Originally a kind of oral narrative, with much in common with folk song and probably recited on the occasion of the religious ceremonies and festivals, in the late 15th or early 16th century, Dharma-mangal became fashionable as a subject for written composition. It is a folk epic concerned with eulogy of the merits and activities of the folk god, Dharma-Thakur. According to literary tradition, such a text is to be comprised of 12 parts (since 12 is an auspicious number in the worship of the deity). The epic narrates the way in which the worship of Dharma as the supreme deity was introduced to the world. It is largely concerned with the exploits of its human hero, Lau Sen, whose birth, life, and adventures demonstrate the powers and majesty of his divine protector.

Chief among many incredible exploits

of Lau Sen is the causing of the sun to rise in the west in order to demonstrate the limitless power of Dharma-Thakur. The text also contains an account of the creation of the world.

DHARMAPALAS

Tibetan Buddhist divinities who, though benevolent, represented as hideous and ferocious in order to instill terror in evil spirits.

Worship of dharmapalas was initiated in the 8th century by the magician-saint Padmasambhava, who is said to have conquered the malignant deities in Tibet and forced them to take an oath promising to protect Buddhists and the Buddhist faith.

The dharmapalas are usually worshipped in the mgon khang, a subterranean monastery room, the entrance of which is often guarded by stuffed wild yaks or leopards. Priests wear special vestments and use ritual instruments often made of human bone or skin. Worship includes the performance of religious masked dances.

DHARMA-SUTRA

Hindu manuals of human conduct, the earliest source of Hindu law.

DHATU

In Buddhism, root, in the sense of elements. Used in several senses in Buddhist scriptures, of the four elements, of the three basic planes of existence and so on.

DHAWQ

In Islam, literally "taste." The word is used in a technical sense in tasawwuf to indicate experience of (divine) truth or a certain refined sensitivity illuminated by the light of the Divine.

DHIMMI

Arabic word indicating one whose life was regulated according to "an agreement of protection." Such persons, known collectively as People of (the agreement of) Protection, were free non-Muslims who lived in Muslim countries and were guaranteed freedom of worship and security by the state from any form of harassment, provided certain taxes were paid.

The term is also used for all nonbelievers in Islamic states; also designating the "protected people," or "peoples of the book" - for instance,Christians and Jews.

DHU AL-FAQUAR

In Islamic mythology, the two-pointed magical sword that has come to represent 'Ali, fourth caliph and son-in-law of Mohammed.

As 'Ali's legendary status grew, the importance of his association with Dhu-al-faquar also increased. Particularly in myths surrounding the Battle of Siffin (657), Dhu-al-faquar, the two points of which were useful for blinding an enemy, is credited with enabling 'Ali to perform phenomenal military feats, decapitating or halving over 500 men.

DHU 'L-HIJJA

In Islam, the month of pilgrimage, which is the last month of the Muslim lunar calendar.

DHU 'L-KIFL

One of the prophets mentioned by name in the Koran. He has been variously identified with Hizqil (= Ezekiel) and a Bishr, son of Ayyub, but other identifications have been made as well.

DHU 'L-QARNAYN

In Islam, literally, "He with the Two Horns". This is the name of an important figure who appears in verses 88-98 in Surat al-Kahf of the Koran and has been identified as Alexander the Great by Muslim commentators and others. The reason for endowing Alexander with the title Dhu 'l-Qarnayn are unclear and a number of possibilities have been mooted. The Koran portrays him as a recipient of earthly power from God and one who promises punishment for wickedness and reward for goodness. He travels to the West and the East and builds a barrier to protect people against Gog and Magog.

DHU NOWAS

Pre-Islamic South Arabian king who adopted Judaism, ruled, traditionally for 38 years, and persecuted the Christians of Najran, notably 524-525. He is of interest to Islam because of the reference in the Koran to "the people of the pit" in Surat al-Buruj.

DHYANA

A stage of yoga. In Hinduism dhyana is meditation or concentration of mind that leads to the final stage of contemplation, total absorption in the object in mind.

DHYANI-BUDDHAS

In Buddhism, the personification of aspects of the one Adi-Buddha which appear in meditation. It is also a term used to denote a group of five Buddhas. The concept of these five "self-born" celestial Buddhas who have always existed from the beginning of time appears to have been known in Nepal and Tibet, in medieval Java, and to some extent in Japan.

Scholars in recent years have claimed that the term Dhyani-Buddha does not appear in the original texts, but the nomenclature continues to be commonly used, particularly in describing groups of images composed of five meditating Buddhas.

In order to counter any tendency towards polytheism suggested by the five-fold scheme, some sects elevated one of the five, usually Vairocana, to a position of first or primal Buddha.

DIABOLIC OBSESSION

The prolonged harassment of a person by the devil; the devil's laying siege to a person from the outside. In Roman Catholicism, the best-known case in the life of a modern saint (as distinct from the fathers of the Egyptian desert in the third and fourth centuries, whose constant troubles from devils lack consistent historical basis) is the activity by which the devil made the life of St. John Vianney uncomfortable and his sleep sometimes impossible.

These manifestations were to some extent similar to those of poltergeists in haunted houses. While completely accepting the possibility, the church has always been skeptical of alleged instances of diabolic intervention in human affairs.

Accordingly, it demands a rigorous examination of phenomena before accepting that causes other than natural ones are required as adequate explanation of them.

DIABOLIC POSSESSION

A condition in which a demon or evil spirit is in control of some of a person's faculties and activities. There is mention in the Old Testament of something like possession in the affliction of Saul by an evil spirit (1 Samuel 16:14; 1 Samuel 18:10): soothsaying was understood to imply a kind of transitory possession (Leviticus 20:27); and certain illnesses were attributed to the activity of evil spirits (Tobit 3:8).

The number of cases of possession referred to in the New Testament is astonishing when judged in the light of later ideas concerning the prevalence of this affliction. One explanation is that notion of possession played a greater part in the thinking of the Jewish people among whom Jesus lived.

They made much of the connection between sin and suffering (see John 9:2), and they attributed psychic disorders, as well as other kinds of sickness, to the direct action of evil spirits.

Jesus' cure of these disorders could have been interpreted by the populace as an expulsion of demons, and Jesus simply made no attempt to teach them otherwise, any more than he corrected the many other false scientific notions they entertained.

He thus accommodated his words and deeds to their popular beliefs, not only because the correction of errors of that kind was beyond the scope of his mission, but also because toleration of their errors was in the matter pedagogically useful inasmuch as it enabled him to direct their attention more effectively to the truth he came to teach.

DIABOLISM

The practice of communicating or having commerce with the devil, especially when this is intended to do him homage or service, or includes working in alliance with him. Diabolism appears to derive from superstitious belief in the possibility of gaining temporary advantages from its practice or of avoiding misfortunes the devil might bring about.

DIAKONIKON

In the Eastern Churches a small room, classically apsidal in form, at the far end of the south aisle (as one faces east) in a Byzantine church, opening, however, not into the aisle but into the presbytery behind the iconostasis.

It is traditionally cared for by deacons (hence the name). In it is kept vestments and sacred vessels. In former times the records and library of the church were also kept there. The diakonikon is also found in Armenian, East and West Syrian, and Coptic traditions, but the name, in the various languages concerned, is often applied to a sacristy whose place varies in modern churches.

DIALOGUES CONCERNING NATURAL RELIGION

A skeptical review of religious beliefs and philosophical arguments about God, by the Scottish philosopher David Hume; posthumously published in 1779 and probably written in the 1750s.

DIAMPER, Synod of

Council that formally united the ancient Christian church of the Malabar Coast (modern Kerala), India, with the Roman Catholic Church. In was convoked in 1599 by Aleixo de Meneses, archbishop of Goa. The synod renounced Nestorianism, the heresy that believed in two persons rather than two natures of Jesus Christ, as the Indians were suspected of being heretics by the Portuguese missionaries. The Syrian Chaldean patriarch was then removed from jurisdiction in India and replaced by a Portuguese bishop. The forced Latinization and disregard for local tradition elicited a violent reaction from the Christians. In 1653 most of them broke with Rome.

DIANA

In Roman religion, originally a woodland goddess, later identified with the Greek Artemis. With strong associations as a fertility deity she was invoked by women to aid conception and delivery.

DIASPORA

The term used to describe Jewish settlements outside Palestine. The name first referred to the Jewish community exiled to Babylonia in the 8th century BC and later included all Jews living outside the Holy Land. The largest Diaspora center in early Jewish history was in Alexandria in the first century BC. Many modern thinkers have stressed the positive aspects of dispersion. They point out that the synagogue as an institution developed in Babylonia and that Judaism was broadened as a result of its confrontation with other cultures. Others maintain that life in the Diaspora has been primarily a continuous history of persecution.

Jews still hold widely divergent views about the role of Diaspora Jewry and the desirability and significance of maintaining a national identity. While the vast majority of Orthodox Jews go so far as to oppose Israel as a Godless and secular state, defying God's will to send his messiah at the time he proclaimed.

Although Reform Jews still commonly maintain that the Diaspora is a valid expression of God's will, they now support the establishment of a Jewish homeland.

DIASPORA, Russian

A collective term for the dispersed Russians who for one reason or another have left their homeland and have taken up residence and often citizenship in another country. The first wave of the diaspora was made up of poor people seeking a better livelihood and included some sectarians fleeing religious persecution by the czarist government; the latest of Russian, principally Orthodox, fleeing from the Communist regime. In recent years many Jew migrated to Israel.

Between World War I and II there were large Russian enclaves in Manchuria and in various Chinese cities. The Russian Orthodox community in Manchuria flourished with its own hierarchy, monastic communities, seminary, press, and other necessities for ecclesiastical life.

DIATESSARON

A Syriac edition of the four New Testament Gospels compiled as a single narrative by Tatian in the late second century. It was the standard gospel text in the Syrian Near East until circa 400, when it was replaced by the four separated Gospels. No ancient Syriac manuscript now exists, though quotations from the Diatessaron appear in ancient Syriac literature.

DIBBUQ

(Hebrew: "attachment") In Jewish folklore, a disembodied human spirit that, because of former sins, wanders restlessly until it finds a haven in the body of a living person. Belief in such spirits was especially prevalent during the 16th and 17th centuries in eastern Europe. Often persons suffering from nervous or mental disorders were taken to a miracle-working rabbi, who alone, it was believed, could expel the harmful dibbuq through a religious rite of exorcism.

DIBELIUS, Martin

(1883-1947) German biblical scholar, one of the originators of form criticism in New Testament studies, who tried to get at the oral traditions behind written gospels and particularly studied early Christian ethical teaching.

DIBLAH

In the Old Testament, a site mentioned by Ezekiel (6:14) when recording God's prophecy of the desolation to come upon the land of Israel as recompense for its idolatrous worship. Any ancient location by this name is unknown, and most modern authorities, therefore, hold that Diblah is a copyist error for Riblah, the initial Hebrew letter R being easily mistaken for the Hebrew letter D. If this is the case, it may be identified with the biblical Riblah (modern Ribleh) at the Orontes River, in the land of Hamath (2 Kings 23:33).

DIBON

In the Old Testament, a city east of the Dead Sea, wrested from the Moabites by Sihon the Amorite, but later taken from him by Israel at the time of the Israelite entry into the land under Moses (Numbers 21:25-30).

DIBRI

In Judaism, an Israelite of the tribe of Dan whose daughter Shelomoth married an Egyptian. Shortly after the exodus from Egypt, the son of this union was stoned to death for abusing God's name (Leviticus 24:10-16).

DICTATUS PAPAE

A document composed by the pope himself, though the term has come to refer specifically to an entry in the Register of Gregory VII (1073-1085) which asserts official papal supremacy in spiritual and temporal matters throughout Christendom. Nearly all of the 27 titles in the register deal with principles of ecclesiology with special emphasis upon the primacy of the Roman Catholic Church and the bishop of Rome in the universal church.

DIDACHE

The oldest surviving Christian church order, probably written in Egypt or Syria in the second century. In 16 short chapters it deals with morals and ethics, church practice, and the eschatological hope (of the Second Coming of Christ at the end of time) and presents a general program for instruction and initiation into the primitive church.

The Didache is not a unified and coherent work but a compilation of regulations that had acquired the force of law by usage in scattered Christian communities. Evidently several pre-existing written sources were used and were compiled by an unknown editor.

Chapters 1-6 give ethical instruction concerning the two ways, of life and death, and reflect an early Christian adaptation of a Jewish pattern of teaching in order to prepare catechumens (candidates for Christian baptism). Chapters 7-15 discuss baptism, fasting, prayer, the Eucharist, how to receive and test traveling apostles and prophets, and the appointment of bishops and deacons. Chapter 16 considers the signs of the Second Coming of the Lord.

DIDYMUS THE BLIND

(circa 313-398) Eastern church theologian who headed the influential Catechetical School of Alexandria.

Didymus' biblical commentaries (supposedly on nearly all the books of the Bible) survived in fragments only, and those on the so-called Catholic Letters are of dubious authenticity. Treatises on the Trinity and on the Manichaeans (believers in a 3rd century Persian religious dualism teaching the release of the spirit from matter through ascetism) have been attributed to him.

DIETARY LAWS

Laws laid down by priests or religious leaders, particularly in the religions of antiquity, which described clean and unclean foods, thus distinguishing what was acceptable for eating and what was not.

The Israelites apparently had many such laws as part of their religious traditions and heritage, but it remained for the great lawgiver Moses and later the priesthood to codify these laws and give them legal and moral force.

A curious method for distinguishing those animals which are clean and unclean is found in Deuteronomy 14:4-8 and Leviticus 11:26-28. Clean was the animal "that parteth the hoof ....

and cheweth the cud." These included the ox, the sheep, the goat, the hart, the roe-buck, etc.

Animals were unclean that did not part the hoof or did not chew the cud or that "go upon their paws." These included the camel, rick-badger, hare, swine, etc. Among the fish the clean were distinguished by fins and scales, but those which like the eel resembled reptiles were unclean. Birds of prey like the eagle, vulture, raven, owl, night hawk, etc., were unclean because they were carnivorous and fed on carrion or filth.

The Israelites were taught that "the life of the flesh is in the blood" (Leviticus 17:11) and that God has "given it to you upon the altar to make an atonement for your souls." It was therefore not to be eaten but to be offered solely unto God.

Among Christians dietary laws fell into rapid disuse. St. Peter in Acts 10:9-43 was warned by God against them; and Paul always staunchly opposed laying Jewish customs on Christian shoulders. In Acts 15:20 the only dietary law for the Christian is to abstain from things strangled and from blood.

DIGAMBARA

In Jainism, one of the two principal sects. whose ascetics, shunning all property, do not wear clothes. The ascetics of the other sect, the Svetambara, wear only simple white loincloths or robes.

The philosophical doctrines of the two groups never significantly differed and their members have continued to intermarry. Since the northern and southern branches lived at a distance from one another, however, variations in their ritual, mythology, and literature did arise. The most serious issue, the question of whether it was possible for a monk who owned property (e.g., wore clothes) to achieve mosa (spiritual release), led to the division into two sects 80.

DIKKA

Raised platform in a mosque, often positioned near the Minbar. On Friday at the congregational worship the muadhdhin used the dikka to give the final call to prayer. It is also used by one or more prayer "leaders" other than the principal Imman who is directly in front of the mihrab when a large crowd is present in the mosque; these lead the vocal responses and the dikka also enables their ritual gestures and prostrations to be seen by the whole congregation so that all can pray together in unison.

DIKLAH

In the Old Testament, a descendant of Shem through Joktan (Genesis 10:21; 1 Chronicles 1:17-20). Some geographers believe his tribe settled in south Arabia, perhaps occupying part of present-day Yemen.

DIKSA

The rite of consecration that preceded the Vedic sacrifice in ancient India; in later and modern Hinduism, the initiation of a layman by his guru (spiritual guide) into a religious sect.

In modern Hinduism, rites of consecration and initiation show many regional and sectarian variations. They are generally preceded by preparatory fasting, bathing, and dressing in new clothes and include in the act of initiation the placing of special marks on the body or forehead, taking on a new name, receiving from the preceptor a selected mantra (prayer formula) and worship.

DIMON

In the Old Testament, a site mentioned in Isaiah's pronouncement of doom upon Moab; the slaughter of the Moabites causes the waters of Dimon to become "full of blood" (Isaiah 15:9).

DIMONAH

In biblical times, a southern city of Judah near the border of Edom (Joshua 15:21-22). It is suggested by some to be the same as "Dibon" mentioned at Nehemiah 11:25, and while its exact location remains uncertain, some geographers would identify it with el-Qebab between Beer-sheba and the Dead Sea.

DIN

Arabic word for faith, religion, the area of that which concerns the spiritual. In Islamic writings, the din (of Islam) is often contrasted with al-dunya (the world).

DINAH

In the Old Testament, daughter of Jacob by Leah. Dinah may have been six years old when Jacob returned to Canaan and settled at Succoth, she having been born at Haran when her father was residing there (Genesis 3):21-22). At the time Jacob and his family were tenting outside the city of Shechem, Dinah unwisely made it a practice to visit the Canaanite girls there. On one of these visits she was violated by Shechem the son of Hivite chieftain Hamor. Shechem fell in love with her, and Dinah remained in his home until avenged by her full brothers Simeon and Levi (Genesis 34:1-31).

DIOCESE

In some Christian churches, a territorial area administered by a bishop. The original unit of ecclesiastical administration was the parish, which in the Eastern Orthodox Church still remains the designation of the area administered by the bishop, whereas the diocese is the larger area administered by the patriarch. The use of these terms was still fluid in the West in the 9th century; but, by the 13th century, diocese meant the territory administered by a bishop.

In the Roman Catholic Church, only the pope can divide or merge dioceses or create new ones. All dioceses are divided into parishes,each with its own church; dioceses are also sometimes divided into rural deaneries, which contain several parishes.

The writings of Vatican Council II defines a diocese as "that portion of God's people which is entrusted to a bishop to be shepherd by him with the cooperation of the presbytery."

While certainly not of divine institution, territorial division of the church is attested to in the first century. An urban

Christian community was organized under its bishop whose authority gradually expanded to cover the rural areas. These communities, or territorial divisions, were at first called simply churches. The term diocese, already used in the fourth century did not become the exclusive term to designate territorial divisions until the 13th century.

DIOCLETIAN
(circa 245-313) Emperor of Rome 284-305. Of humble origin, Diocletian held important military commands and was chosen as Emperor by the army. Once established, Diocletian reorganized the empire into a tetrarchy (four-man rule) including a co-emperor (Maximilian) and two vice-emperors. Each ruler had a separate capital. This reorganization was intended to secure the defense and efficient administration of the empire. Diocletan also changed the tax structure, reorganized the army and reformed the currency.

He upheld the old Roman religion and ordered a general persecution of Christians throughout the empire that began in 303. Diocletian abdicated and retired in 305.

DIODATI, Giovanni
(1576-1649) Swiss Calvinist pastor known for his translation of the Bible into Italian. A leader of the reformers, he was an eloquent, bold, and fearless preacher and a rigid Calvinist. He was also the author of a translation into French and of biblical annotations and polemical treatises.

DIOGENES OF SINOPE
(400-325 BC) Founder of Cynicism. Brought to Athens at an early age by his father, he lived in poverty and, either under the influence of the teachings of Antisthenes of Athens (445-360 BC) or independently, he rejected all conventions. He held that happiness is attained by satisfying one's natural needs in the cheapest and easiest way possible, stressing self-sufficiently, training of the body to reduce its needs to the bare minimum, and shamelessness.

DIOGNETIUS, Epistle to
A Christian apology of unknown authorship and date, erroneously classified by custom among the writings of the Apostolic Fathers. This work was cited by no ancient or medieval writer, and only a single manuscript copy of it, dating from the 13th or 14th centuries, has ever been discovered. Addressed apparently by an inquiring pagan, it is like other apologies in its ridicule of idol worship and its exposition of the inadequacy of Jewish religion. In contrast it gives a sketch of Christian belief and indicates the dignity of the role of Christians in the world, for they are to the world as the soul to the body.

DIOMEDES
The name of two figures in Greek legend. Diomedes, son of war god Ares and king of the Thracian Bistones, was the owner of mares to which he fed human flesh. Diomedes, son of Tydeus, was commander of 80 Argive ships and one of the most respected leaders in the Trojan War.

DIONYSIA
In Greek religion, festivals of Dionysus, the wine god. The most famous of these were at Attica and included the Little or Rustic Dionysia, characterized by simple, old-fashioned rites; the Lenaea, the chief rites of which were a festal procession and dramatic performance.

DIONYSUS
Greek God of wine. Known as Bacchus to the Romans, he was the son of Zeus and Semele. Dionysius was said to have gone around planting vines and teaching men how to make wine. The Dionysia were Athenian festivals held in honor of Dionysus. The ceremonies included comedies and tragedies performed in the god's honor.

DIONYSIUS, Saint
(201-268) Pope from 259 to 268. He faced the urgent task of reorganizing the church. In response to charges of triethism (for instance,separating the

members of the Trinity as three distinct deities) against Bishop Dionysius of Alexandria, the pope convened a Roman synod (260) and demanded an explanation from the bishop; this became known as "the affair of the two Dyonisii."

DIONYSIUS EXIGUUS

(circa 500-560) Celebrated 6th century canonist who is considered the inventor of the Christian calendar, the use of which spread through the employment of the new Easter tables. Highly reputed as a theologian and as an accomplished mathematician and astronomer, Dionysius was well versed in the Holy scriptures and in canon law. Credited to him are a collection of 401 ecclesiastical canons - including the apostolic canons and the decrees of the councils of Nicaea, Constantinople, Chalcedon, and Sardis - and a collection of the decretals of the popes from St. Siricius (384-399) to Anastasius II (496-498).

DIONYSIUS TELMAHARENSIS

(773-845) Patriarch of the Syrian Jacobite Church and author of "The Chronicles," an important source document on Eastern Christianity between the reigns of the Byzantine emperors Mauricius and Theophilus.

DIONYSIUS THE AREOPAGITE

(1st century) Early Christian converted by apostle Paul at Athens. In the second century he was held to have been the first bishop of Athens, and in the 9th century he was identified with St. Denis of France.

DIONYSIUS THE CARTHUSIAN

(1402-1471) Theologian and mystic, one of the important contributors to, and propagators of, the influential school of Rheinish spirituality originating in the 14th century.

This school was influenced by Neoplatonism, the theology of St. Thomas Aquinas, and the teaching of Pseudo-Dionysius, whose works especially inspired late medieval mystics.

DIONYSIUS THE GREAT, Saint

(circa 200-265) Bishop of Alexandria, then the most important Eastern see, and a chief opponent of Sabellianism, a heresy teaching that the Trinity is indivisible. A Christian convert, he studied in Alexandria at the catechetical school headed by Origen.

During the persecution of Christians (250-251) by the Roman emperor Decius, he was forced to flee to the Libyan Desert, and he was again exiled in the Valerian persecution (257-260).

On his return to Alexandria circa 260, Dionysius favored readmitting penitent apostles to the church in opposition to those who wanted to exclude them permanently. He denied that the Book of Revelation was written by John the Evangelist and denounced the millennarians, who, basing their argument on a literal reading of Revelation, believed that after 1,000 years Jesus Christ would return and establish his kingdom on earth.

DIOSCORUS

(circa 479-530) Pope for 23 days in 530. A deacon in the Alexandrian Church, he clashed with the Monophysites (Christians teaching that Christ has only one nature, rather than two - for instance, human and and divine) and went to Rome. Denying Boniface II as pope, the majority of the Roman clergy appointed Dioscorus as the successor of Felix. Discord followed; Dioscorus' sudden death, however, ended the schism, and his partisans then supported Boniface, who in the following December convoked a Roman synod that anathematized Dioscorus.

DIOTREPHES

In the Bible, a man mentioned by apostle John in his letter to Gaius. In addition to being ambitious, proud, disrespectful of apostolic authority, rebellious and inhospitable, Diotrephes tried to hinder those desiring to show hospitality to the brothers and to expel these from the congregation (3 John 9,10).

DIPLOMACY, Papal

The pope maintains formal diplomatic relations with most of the states of the world. In return these states accredit their own ambassadors (or ministers plenipotentiary) to the Holy See in Vatican City. This exchange is conducted under the rules of international law and practice. The nuncios, or pronuncios, as the papal envoys are styled, enjoy full diplomatic privilege and immunity where they are stationed.

DIPLOMATICS, Ecclesiastical

Diplomatics is a term used to describe those studies that deal with public documents, charters, private and public records, and juridical and legal documents. Within the church these critical studies deal with similar content. Ecclesiastical diplomatics primarily denotes papal documents, but the term applies as well to papers and documents of private individuals in the church as well as to persons of rank.

DIPTYCHS

A small folding tablet of wood or metal, with ornamental outside surfaces and inner surfaces bearing an inscription on wax or engraved. Their liturgical use, both in the East and the West, was connected with the practice of remembering in the Eucharistic Liturgy those whom the community honored or for whom they prayed: the martyrs, the deceased, those sharing in Christian community; such names and also those of catechumens were recorded on the diptychs and read off by one of the liturgical ministers.

DIRAR

(late 8th-early 9th century) Leading early theologian who lived mainly in Basra and wrote a book on Aristotelian metaphysics. He was an upholder of - and, indeed, may have originated - the idea of kasb and he played an important role with his followers in the early development of kalam in all its varied forms.

DIRGE

In biblical terms, a composition, lyrical or musical, such as the grief occasioned by the death of a friend or loved one; an elegy.

DISCERNMENT OF SPIRITS

A classical formula in ascetical theology to indicate the activity whereby a person comes to understand his own interior spiritual state and the phenomena (spiritual activity, psychological motivations, inclinations to act, etc.) that manifest that state. The term is adopted from the New Testament, "Beloved, do not believe every spirit, but test the spirits to see whether they are of God" (1 John 4:1; 1 Corinthians 12:10) where Paul speaks of the gift of distinguishing between spirits.

These sections seem to proceed from Jewish belief at that time in good and evil spirits which regularly influenced human actions. This emphasis continued into the patristic period when the distinction between diabolical illusion and the promptings of the Holy Spirit was continually a matter of concern.

DISCIPLE

Any founder of a school must have followers. The gospels mention disciples of the Pharisees and disciples of John the Baptist as well as the disciples of Jesus Christ. Jesus had many disciples in addition to the Apostles whom he selected from their ranks. On one occasion he sent out 70 of them, two byu two, on a preaching and healing mission. The disciples later formed the nucleus of the church, in which "disciple" became synonymous with "Christian."

DISCIPLES OF CHRIST

(now known as the International Convention of Christian Churches). A Protestant sect, active mainly in the western and central United States. The group, which bases its belief on simple adherence to the Bible alone, was initiated by Thomas Campbell in western

Pennsylvania in the early 19th century. Its membership grew rapidly in frontier America. It is now active in missionary work throughout the world. By the early 1990s the group numbered more than 1,500,000 in the Unites States.

DISCIPLINE, Ecclesiastical

Like discipline in general, it may be understood as:

▲ a set of rules governing conduct, or
▲ the formation envisaged by such rules,
▲ the orderly conduct that ensures from the observance of such rules.

Currently the discipline as it affects the Latin church is embodied largely in the Code of Canon Law, which took effect in 1918.

DISCIPLINE OF THE SACRAMENTS, Sacred

Congregation for An administrative office of the Roman Catholic Church charged with supervising the discipline of the seven sacraments. Among its most important functions are matters of the validity of marriages and sacred orders.

DISCIPLINE OF THE SECRET

A custom in the early Christian church of concealing certain doctrines and religious practices from the catechumens and pagans as a safeguard against persecution and profanation. It was in use mostly during the first 5 centuries and was reflected in the custom of not admitting catechumens to the Mass of the Faithful in the Eucharistic celebration. Symbolic reminders were the fish, the lamb, and the shepherd found in the ancient catacombs.

DISHAN

In Judaism, a Seirite, a sheik of the Horites in the land of Edom (Genesis 36:20-21).

DISHON

The name of one or possibly two different men in the genealogies recorded at Genesis 36:20-28 and 1 Chronicles 1:38-42.

At Genesis 36:20-21, seven sons of Seir the Horite are listed as sheiks. Then, in verses 22 to 28 each of the seven sheiks is listed with his sons. Others, however, believe the account to present the seven sheiks merely as descendants of Seir, not of the same generation, hence "sons" in the broad sense of the word.

DISKOS

The plate used in the Byzantine divine liturgy to hold the bread that is offered and sanctified in the divine liturgy. Equivalent to the Roman paten, it too is made of gold or silver or at least gilded metal. It was originally a large tray or platter on which the deacon bore the consecrated bread, as can still be seen in many magnificent specimens of the fifth and sixth centuries.

The modern diskos is rarely larger than circa eight inches in diameter and has a rim and concave inner surface. The Russian style adds an attached base or foot to facilitate its carrying in procession and this style is usually found among the Greeks and other Byzantines.

DISMAS, Saint

Traditionally, the good thief who was crucified with Christ. Luke relates that of the two thieves condemned to die with Christ, one, whom tradition has called Dismas, asked Christ to remember him. Christ assured him with the words, "Today thou shalt be with me in paradise."

DISPANKARA BUDDHA

In Buddhism, the luminous; the only one of the predecessors in office of Gautama the Buddha of whom there are any details in the scriptures. It was he who taught Gautama Siddhartha in previous births, and prepared him for his future achievement.

DISPARITY OF CULT

The name given in Roman Catholic canon law to a diriment impediment to marriage between a baptized Roman Catholic and an unbaptized person. Unless a dispensation from this impediment is granted by competent authority, the impediment renders the marriage null and void and illicit.

DISPENSATION

Term applied in ecclesiastical law to the action of a competent authority in granting relief from the strict application of a law.

DISPERSION OF THE APOSTLES

The feast - not universally observed - commemorating their departure on their missionary journeys. Through the endeavors of the Apostles to spread the gospel to all nations, God's will was carried out for the conversion of the world, substituting a new diaspora for the Jewish one. Peter (1 Peter 1:2) and Luke (Acts 1:1-11) speak about forming a new people of God in order to lead dispersed mankind back into the unity of faith.

DISSENT, Theology of

The theological ground for resisting lawful authority; the term as such is linked with the unrest in the 1960s, with movements of civil disobedience, but the issues it denotes are perennial.

DISSIDENT

In a religious sense a term used of groups that reject the established church. More commonly employed on the Continent, it is equivalent to dissenter, the more usual term in Britain. Even churches that have official status in their own areas, such as some of the Orthodox churches, have been considered dissidents by Roman Catholics. With growing secularism altering the status of all churches, and the changed atmosphere of an ecumenical age, the term is less frequently employed.

DISTRACTION

In prayer, the alien images or thoughts, often affectively toned, that intrude on its attention or divert its inattention. In the second case they stop the prayer; in the first case, especially when they are not really wilful, though they may detract from the effect of spiritual refreshment, prayer still continues effectively and meritoriously.

Talking with God is not, after all, the same thing as closely following a discussion or arguing a case, and though there is a disciplined art of mental prayer, there are schools and masters to bid us take it easily and without straining at it. Some fluctuation of attention does little to hold down the lifting of the mind to God.

DITTHI

In Buddhism, views; right view is the first step of the Noble Eightfold Path.

DIVINA COMMEDIA

The towering Christian epic composed by Dante Alighieri and completed circa 1317 in Ravenna where Dante lived in exile. It consists of 100 cantos in three major sections: Inferno, Purgatorio, and Paradiso. In Dante's vision he is led by Virgil, representing human philosophy and human virtue, through hell, then purgatory. Beatrice, his lifelong love, leads him through the natural paradise to the true paradise illumined by the sight of God. Here St. Bernard becomes his guide who leads him to the Blessed Virgin.

DIVINATION

Prediction of future events by means of oracles, omens or signs. Familiar examples include omens such as the dog baying at the moon, supposed to foretell a death; dreams in which departed souls appear and which are interpreted as messages; the red moon, supposed to presage a disaster.

Practitioners of divination believe that superhuman gods reveal the future to those trained to read and interpret certain signs and omens, which, they say, are communicated in various ways: by celestial phenomena (the position and movement of stars and planets, eclipses, meteors), by terrestrial physical forces (wind, storms, fire), by behavior of creatures (howling of dogs, flight of birds, movement of snakes), by patterns of tea leaves in cups, by oil configurations on water or the direction falling arrows take, by the appearance of the liver, lungs and entrails of sacrificed animals, by the lines in the palm of the hand, by the casting of lots, and by the "spirits" of the dead.

Certain fields of divination have been given specific names. For example:

- ▲ augury, popular with the Romans, is a study of birds in flight;
- ▲ palmistry predicts the future from lines on the inside of the hand;
- ▲ hepatoscopy inspects the liver;
- ▲ haruspication inspects entrails;
- ▲ axiomancy divines with ax heads;
- ▲ belomancy divines with arrows;
- ▲ oneuromancy is divination by dreams;
- ▲ necromancy is a purported inquiring of the dead.

DIVINE, Father

(George Baker, 1880-1965) African American religious leader. He was the founder of the Peace Mission movement, a nonsectarian, interracial church that worked to promote justice, peace, and an end to poverty. The movement began in Harlem and won the support of many people throughout the United states. Deified by his devotees, Father Divine was harshly criticized by others for his lavish life-style.

DIVINE HEALING

A cardinal belief and practice in Pentecostalism. Divine healing differs from the mental or metaphysical healing of Christian Science, New Thought, or Spiritualism,. Nor is it like faith healing, in which a cure may come about simply through the internal belief of the sufferer.

Divine healing is rather a gift or charisma (see Acts 4:30) from the power of the Holy Spirit to impart health to others. Healing is practiced through the laying on of hands (Mark 16:18), the observance of the prescriptions in James 5:14-18 and often with the use of anointed handkerchiefs or aprons (see Acts 19:12).

With the exception of some extremists, most Pentecostals do not reject medical science; they rather see divine healing as a superior way to health. The basis for viewing healing as part of the foursquare gospel is that bodily ills are a curse connected with sin, and that as Jesus atoned for all sin, so he delivers from all bodily infirmity.

DIVINE OFFICE

In Roman Catholicism, the name formerly used for the public prayer of the church designed to sanctify the hours of the day. The revision of this prayer is known as the Liturgy of the Hours.

DIVINE PERSON

One of the three subsistences in the Holy Trinity. That God is personal is a truth attainable to reason, for all the perfections implied in the concept of person are found in him in an infinite degree. But that God is three Persons is known only through revelation. Person is not a biblical term; nevertheless the New Testament witnesses to the personhood of Father, Son, and Spirit.

The concept of person, as distinct from nature, is of Christian origin. The need for a clear conceptual expression of the mystery of the Trinity forced upon the mind of the Fathers of the church this distinction unknown to the philosophies in their time. While in man's experience individual nature and person coincide in all cases, this is not true where the mystery of God is concerned.

DIVINE SCIENCE

A religious movement in the United States that emphasizes the omnipresence of God and spiritual healing, begun in the 1880s by Malinda E. Cramer in San Francisco, and by three sisters Brooks. The teachings of Divine science are essentially those of most New Thought groups. Unlike Christian Science, Divine science does not deny the reality of disease but teaches that right thinking brings health and prosperity.

DIVINE UNION

In Christian mysticism, a supernatural communion with God through love, the final goal of the mystical journey.

DIVINE WORD, Society of the

A Roman Catholic religious organization, composed of priests and brothers, founded in 1875 at Steyl by Arnold Janssen to work in the foreign missions. Its members are engaged in all places of missionary activities, from teaching in schools and universities to working among primitive peoples.

DIVINITY OF CHRIST

In Roman Catholicism, the solemn teaching of the church that Jesus Christ is a divine Person, true God as well as true man, the second Person of the Blessed Trinity.

DIVORCE

In Roman Catholicism, the teaching of the church, based on the teaching of Christ himself (Mark 10:2-12, Luke 16:18), is that "a ratified and consummated marriage cannot be dissolved by any human power or for any reason other than death" (Canon 1141).

Thus, although civil law may claim to dissolve the bond of marriage and render a person free to marry again, the church maintains that the civil law has no power to do this. For serious reasons (such as adultery, serious danger to spirit or body of the other spouse or of the children), a spouse may have a legitimate cause for separation "in virtue of a decree of the local ordinary, or even in his or her own authority if there is danger in delay" (Canon 1153).

DIWALI

One of the major religious festivals in India, celebrated over a five-year period from the 13th day of the dark half of Asvina (September-October) to the second day of the light half of Kartika (from part of October to part of November). It is an important festival among members of the Jaia community, many of whom belong to the merchant class. In a special ceremony special lamps are lighted, and this lighting of the lamps is explained as a material substitute for the light of holy knowledge that was extinguished with the passing of Mahavira, an important saint.

DIYA

In Islam, term denoting blood money, indemnity or compensation for injury or death. The Koran in verse 45 of Surat al-Ma'ida drwas attention to the Judaic law which is stated to have enjoined a life for a life, an eye for an eye, a nose for a nose, an ear for an ear, a tooth for a tooth, and retaliation for inflicted wounds. The verse also indicates that the wronged party could forego what was due. Islam continued the Arabs substitution of money, or goods which could, for example, be camels, in place of any rigid application of a lex talionis. Today, in those areas where Islamic law prevails, modern practice defines the diya as a variable quantity of money.

DIZAHAB

In the Old Testament, a site, each of the Jordan River, where Israel was camped at the time Moses delivered his farewell address (Deuteronomy 1:1).

Docetism

An early Christian heresy affirming that Christ did not have a real or natural body during his life on earth but only an apparent or phantom one. Though its incipient forms are alluded to the New Testament, such as in the first latter of John, Docetism became more fully developed as an important doctrinal position of Gnosticism, a religious dualist system of belief arising in the 2nd century which held that matter was evil and the spirit good and claimed that salvation was attained only through esoteric knowledge, or gnosis.

More thoroughgoing Docetists asserted that Christ was born without any participation of matter and that all the acts and sufferings of his life, including the crucifixion, were mere appearances.

DOCTOR OF THE CHURCH

A title conferred on ecclesiastical writers of eminent learning and outstanding holiness because of their contribution to the explanation and defense of Catholic doctrine. There are presently 32 such Doctors of the church, including two women, St. Catharine of Siena and St. Teresa of Avila.

DOCTRINAL STANDARD

A statement used by a church as its authoritative understanding of the Christian faith, and as a guide by which it is distinguished from other churches. Doctrinal standards are sometimes ranked in a hierarchy of importance, but all are generally considered subordinate to revealed truth as originally given in Christ and the scriptures and are regarded as attempts to outline the fundamental truths of revelation.

Normally individual members of the church are expected to accept the standard, and clergy and teachers, to confirm their teaching to it.

DOCTRINE

That which is taught. In classical Greek thought, the word is common and means the teaching of a wise man or philosopher. Its meaning changes, however, in the Bible: in the plural it denotes the uncertain theories of men (Isaiah 29:13), whereas the singular is always used to convey the sense of divine instruction (Romans 12:7). Thus scripture establishes an opposition between absolute and unequivocal revelation of God and the fleeting thoughts of men. Moreover in the New Testament, especially in the Pastoral Epistles, the word is connected with the historical revelation of God in Jesus (1 Timothy 4:13; 2 Timothy 3:16), and it becomes the church's mission to proclaim that historical doctrine.

DOCTRINE, Development of

One of the most difficult problems of fundamental theology. It was the main issue in the modernist controversy and remains very much to the fore. Christianity has from the start recognized the historical and evolutive character of revelation. Therefore, although it is based on the assumption that the epoch of objective revelation in which the deposit of faith has been constituted came to an end, it has always been open to the idea that there may be a growth in the objective understanding of that tradition of the church.

That which is objectively revealed in a given epoch may not from the start be objectively understood in the fullness of its content. Objective understanding is contradistinguished from subjective understanding. The latter is a progress in the depth and firmness of realizing faith and is always personal.

DOCUMENTS, Papal

The pronouncements of the Holy See, classified broadly into those issued by the pope and those issued by the Curia Romana with the pope's approval. Those issued by the pope are subdivided into:

▲ apostolic constitutions, on points of grave doctrinal or disciplinary concern;
▲ de motu proprio, issued by the pope "on his own" in regard to disciplinary issue of secondary importance;
▲ letters:
▲ apostolic - on canonizations, episcopal appointments, establishment of a new diocese;
▲ pontifical - addressed to an individual or some specific occasion;
▲ encyclical - issued to the whole hierarchy on social or theological matters;
▲ chirocraphi, i.e. written in the pope's own hand to a cardinal on some point of discipline.

DODAVAHU

In the Old Testament, a man from Maresha whose son Eliezer prophesied disaster for the ships of Jehoshaphat that were built in partnership with wicked King Ahaziah of Israel.

DODO

In Judaism, an ancestor, probably the grandfather of Judge Tola of the tribe of Issachar (Judges 10:1). The name is also given to a descendant of Benjamin through Alohi. Dodo's son Eleazar was one of David's three mighty men (2 Samuel 23:9; 1 Chronicles 11:12).

DOEG

In the Old Testament, an Edomite serving as King Saul's principal shepherd, a responsible position of oversight (1 Samuel 21:7; 22:9). Doeg evidently was a proselyte. Because of being "detained before Jehovah" at Nob, possibly on account of a vow, some uncleanness or suspected leprosy, Doeg witnessed High Priest Ahimelech's providing David with shewbread and the sword of Goliath. Later, when Saul, in addressing his servants, voiced the opinion that they were conspiring against him, Doeg revealed what he has seen at Nob. After summoning the High Priest as well as the other priests of Nob and then questioning Ahimelech, Saul ordered the runners to put the priests to death. When these refused, Doeg, at Saul's command, unhesitatingly killed a total of 85 priests. After this wicked act, Doeg devoted Nob to destruction, slaughtering all its inhabitants, both young and old, as well as the livestock (1 Samuel 22:6-20).

DOGMA

A teaching or doctrine authoritatively and explicitly proposed by the church as revealed by God and requiring the belief of the people of God. A dogma may be proposed by the church in a solemn manner (for instance, the dogma of the Immaculate Conception) or through the ordinary magisterium (for instance, the truth that innocent human life is inviolable).

In Roman Catholicism, a dogma is a truth that the church requires the faithful to accept as a doctrine revealed by God. In the early centuries, the term was used more frequently to describe a norm of Christian morality than to describe a principle of faith.

Since the time of Cyril of Jerusalem and Gregory of Nyssa, the meaning of dogma as a truth of revelation began to prevail, and from at least the 17th century, it has referred exclusively to an article of Catholic belief as distinct from a premise of ethical conduct.

Two elements constitute a dogma. It is a truth immediately (formally) revealed by God in Scripture or tradition, whether explicitly (e.g., Christ's divinity) or implicitly (e.g., Mary's bodily assumption).

It is also promulgated by the church as a revealed truth. This can be done either solemnly by papal definition or the pronouncement of an ecumenical council or, more commonly, by the church's ordinary and universal teaching authority.

Speaking of this common practice of making dogmas known in the church, Vatican Council II explained that the bishops "proclaim Christ's doctrine infallibly whenever, even though dispersed throughout the world, but still maintaining the bond of communion among themselves and with the successor of Peter, and authentically teaching matters of faith and morals, they are in agreement on one position as definitively can be held."

Consequently a dogma may be taught by the church quite apart from an official definition.

DOGMA AND DOCTRINE

The explications and officially accepted versions of religious teachings. Having significantly affected the traditions, institutions, and practices of the religions of the world, doctrines and dogmas have also influenced and been influenced by the ongoing development of secular history, science, and philosophy.

DOGMATIC CONSTITUTION ON THE CHURCH

One of the ecclesiastical constitutions of the second Vatican Council, promulgated in 1964.

DOGMATIC FACT

The designation whereby revealed truth is applied to doctrinal matters or to persons and events connected with doctrine. Thus the church defines as dogmatic facts those factual statements so related to its faith as to be necessary for its proper explanation, acceptance, or defense. These facts may be historical, such as the legitimacy of a pope or an ecumenical council, or doctrinal, as the unorthodox character of a given writing.

DOGMATIC THEOLOGY

The theological science treating of religious, especially Christian dogma, the object of which is the whole of divine revelation. As part of Christian and especially Catholic, theology, it is a scientific (i.e., reflexive, methodical, and systematic) finding, penetration, and presentation by the believer (i.e., in the light of faith) of all the divinely revealed salvational truths, or of the salvific self-revelation of the triadic god, which are witnessed to by the whole church and are implicitly or explicitly proposed by the church's teaching authority.

DOGMATISM

A term used to discredit as presumptuous any proposal of philosophical or religious truth as certain, absolute, or authoritative. In modern philosophical usage, the term has become widespread since Immanuel Kant claimed that existing systems of thought accepted their presuppositions uncritically.

In a religious context, Christians are charged with dogmatism because they accept their tenets as revelation. Among the churches those espousing authoritative creeds or official teaching have been accused of dogmatism by nonauthoritarian or anticreedal churches.

Contemporary insistence upon the relativeness and inadequacy of all human concepts and language leads to the view that any theology claiming to be a valid formulation of divine revelation is dogmatism.

DOKYO

Popular or religious Taoism, as distinguished from philosophical Taoism, introduced in Japan from China, the source of many widespread folk beliefs and practices of divination and magic, some of which persist in modern times.

DOME OF THE ROCK

Shrine in Jerusalem that is the oldest extant Islamic monument. The Dome was built over a rock that is sacred to both Muslims and Jews. To the former, it is the site from which the prophet Mohammed, founder of Islam, ascended to heaven; to the latter, it is the site at which Abraham, the first patriarch and progenitor of the Hebrew people, prepared to sacrifice his son Isaac. The Dome of the Rock was built between 685 and 691, not as a mosque for public worship but as a shrine for pilgrims.

DOMINATIONS

One of the classes of supernatural beings, or angels, mentioned by Paul in Colossians 1:16 and Ephesians 1:21, the only places that are specifically spoken of in the New Testament. They are always referred to in the plural.

DOMINATIVE POWER

In its primary canonical usage, the power of a religious superior to govern the subjects who are bound by vow to obey. The pleonastic qualifier "dominative" has as its reason the fact that in religious life the superior can command an act of obedience (not simply external compliance) because the subject is vowed to obedience in all that belongs to religious life according to the community's constitution.

The special term is also used to distinguish this power from the power of jurisdiction, which in its proper sense is hierarchical, requiring sacred ordination and concerned with the public good of the whole church as such.

The term in a wider sense may describe the ruling power of a superior in any society that is not a complete, self-contained unit; then it means the power to require compliance with a command: e.g., the domestic power of parents in the family; the ruling power of a teacher in the school.

DOMINIC, Saint

(1170-1221) Spanish-born founder of the Dominican order. Sent by Pope

Innocent III in 1205 to Languedoc (southern France) to convert the Albigensian heretics, Dominic and his band of priests proved their usefulness and in 1226 he was given papal support for the new order he had established. Dominic was noted for his disciplined living and steadfastness in the face of adversity. He was canonized in 1234 and his feast day is August 4th.

DOMINICAL LETTER

In calendars, providing a means of finding the day of the week for any given day of the year. Because the number of whole days in a year is not exactly divisible by the number of days in a week, succeeding years must begin in different weekdays,

Early Christians, calculating the proper date for the celebration of Easter, adopted the devise used in the Roman calendar of calculating market days by assigning letters to days. In the ecclesiastical calendar, each day of the week was allotted a letter, beginning at the commencement of the year, January 1st being denoted by A, January 2nd by B, and so on. After January 7th (G, the cycle repeats with January 8thj being assigned the letter A.

DOMINICAN NUNS

Several communities of Roman Catholic women religious that are affiliated to the Dominican friars by reason of their rule of life, their government, and their religious habit, or dress. The communities are divided into groups; the second order, of strictly cloistered, or enclosed, contemplative nuns; and the conventual third order, usually dedicated to works of the active apostolate (religious activity). The latter group is far more numerous and includes many congregations that are of recent origin.

DOMINICAN RITE

Because of the scholarly nature of their apostolate, the Dominicans early felt the need of a Mass rite short enough to permit suitable time for study and preaching and at the same time one that could be used uniformly in their many European convents.

Thus in 1220 the Dominicans constructed their own rite from available sources. For 25 years they used this rite until the liturgical revolution sweeping Rome caused the Dominicans to revise their original rite.

The new one was marked by beauty and simplicity; other religious orders and dioceses adopted it as their own. A few of the characteristics of the Dominican Rite include:

▲ the water and wine were put into the chalice at the beginning of Mass;
▲ the Gloria and Credo were read from the Missal;
▲ the host and the chalice were offered up in a single oblation and with a single prayer.

The Mass of the Friar Preachers survived 7 centuries with only minor changes.

DOMINICANS

Full name Order of the Friar Preachers, one of the four great mendicant orders of the Roman Catholic church, founded by St. Dominic in 1205.

From the beginning the order has been a synthesis of the contemplative life and the active ministry. The members live a community life, observe the diet and fasts traditional to monks (although in recent years these observances have been mitigated), and recite the liturgical office in choir, but dispensations for study and preaching are explicitly allowed in the constitutions of Dominic.

The Dominican Order has continued to be noted for an unswerving orthodoxy, based upon the philosophical and theological teaching of Aquinas, and has steadfastly opposed novelty, opportunism, or accommodation in theology. Nevertheless, several Dominicans have been active in the reform of the Catholic church during and following the second Vatican Council.

DOMINICAN SPIRITUALITY

The type of spirituality characteristic of the Dominican tradition; it can be described as Christological, theocentric, contemplative, and evangelical. St. Dominic went beyond what was common in monastic institutions of his time to Dominican spirituality. Consecrated by the vows, sustained by the common life, pivoting around the choral liturgy, and continuing in individual prayer, the spiritual life of the Dominican reaches out to souls, atones for sins, testifies by word and example, and begs that the Spirit may come into the hearts of those who hear the Word.

DOMINION

Originally a Roman law notion, and meaning the juridical power of disposing of and using an object as one freely wills. God alone has supreme and total dominion, yet properly speaking he is not a juridical person, for he transcends all such categories. Consequently if we speak of human beings possessing full dominion, this is in no absolute or unlimited sense, but only within a legal frame of reference.

DOMOVOY

In Slavic mythology, a household spirit appearing under various names and having its origin in ancestor worship. A domovoy dwells in each home in any number of places; near the oven, under the doorstep, in the heart. He never goes out beyond the boundaries of the household.

The domovoy sees to it that the various traditional properties are observed. He can foresee the future, and his groans and weeping or singing and jumping are interpreted as portents of evil or good.

DON, Children of

In Celtic mythology, one of two warring families of gods; Don, known from Welsh tradition, was akin to the Irish goddess Danu. According to one interpretation, the Children of Don were the powers of light, constantly in conflict with the Children of Llyr, the powers of darkness. Others interpret the conflict as a struggle between indigenous gods and those of an invading people. Although Don and other Welsh deities had Irish analogues, the stories surrounding them differed, and the Welsh mythology has only partially survived.

DONATELLO

(1386-1466) Sculptor of Florence, one of the most influential figures in the establishment of Renaissance art. His works are distinguished by their vital realism, their exploration of perspective effects, and, in heroic subjects, by the grandness of their pathos.

The large majority of his works represent Christian subjects. They are animated by a keen sense for the drama of the life of the Savior and the heroic aspects of sainthood, and are deeply moving.

DONATION OF CONSTANTINE

Medieval forgery purporting to give the pope spiritual authority over the entire church and temporal authority over Rome and Italy. Probably originating in the 8th century, it was supposed to have been given by Constantine to an early pope in thanks for his conversion and his having been cured of leprosy. The first recorded use was by Pope Leo IX in 1054. It became the subject of a vast controversy in the 15th century, when its authenticity was questioned. The church finally admitted the falsity of the document in the 18th century.

DONATION OF PEPIN

(754) Promise made by the Carolingian king Pepin III to win for Pope Stephen II lands in Italy; it was later (756) embodied in a document that became the origin of papal rule over central Italy, which lasted until the 19th century.

DONATISTS

Named for their leader Donatus, a Christian group in North Africa that broke with the Catholics in 312 over the election of Caecilian as bishop of Carthage. Historically, they belong to the tradition of early Christianity that produced the Montanist and

Novatianist movements in Asia Minor and Melitians in Egypt. They opposed state interference in church affairs, and, through the peasant warriors called Circumcellions, they had a program of social revolution combined with eschatological hopes. Martyrdom following a life of penance was the goal of the religiously minded Donatist. The Donastist church survived until the extinction of Christianity in North Africa in the early Middle Ages.

DOORS, Church

Impressive in monumental concepts, church doors of wood and metal in varied themes reflect iconographic and stylistic changes throughout the ages. The wooden doors of St. Sabina on the Aventine in Rome (circa 432) with Oriental stylistic elements in 28 panels of the Old Testament and New Testament show one of the earliest examples of the crucifixion.

Metal doors inlaid with niello, silver and gold (St. Paul-outside-the-Walls in Rome) show faces in thin silver plate with delicately engraved features.

DOORS, Holy

Special entrance doors to the four major basilicas in Rome: St. Peter, St. Paul-outside-the-Walls, St. John Lateran, and St. Mary Major.These doorways are walled up except during a Holy Year when they are opened by the pope and three cardinals in simultaneous ceremonies.

DOPHKAH

In Judaism, the first stopping place for the Israelites after leaving the wilderness of Sinai on their way to the Promised Land (Numbers 33:12-13). The Bible does not include the exact geographical location. However, many scholars associate Dophkah with the Egyptian mafkat, a district named for the turquoise mined since ancient times around Serabit el-Khadim about 20 miles each of modern-day Abu Zenima on the Sinai Peninsula.

DOR

One of the Palestinian cities allied with Canaanite King Jabin of Hazor to fight against Joshua (Joshua 11:1-2) and summarily defeated (Joshua 11:12). Though Dor and its dependent towns actually lay in Asher's territory, these were given to the tribe of Manasseh, who proved unable to dispossess the inhabitants remaining there (Joshua 17:11-13); 1 Chronicles 7:29). Later, the territory of Dor, overseen by one of Solomon's sons-in-law provided food one month of the year for the king's household (1 Kings 4:11).

DORCAS

In the New Testament, a Christian woman in the Joppa congregation abounding in "good deeds and gifts of mercy," evidently including the making of inner and outer garments for needy widows (Acts 9:36, 39). "Dorcas" corresponds to the Aramaic "Tabitha," both names meaning "gazelle." Possibly Dorcas was known by both names, as it was not uncommon for Jews, especially those living in a seaport such as Joppa with its mixed population of Jews and gentiles, to have a Hebrew name as well as a Greek or Latin name.

At her death the disciples at Joppa prepared her for burial and, on learning that Peter was in Lydda, just a few miles south-east of Joppa, sent for him. Undoubtedly they had heard about Peter's healing the paralytic Aeneas there and this may have given them a basis for reasoning that the Apostle might resurrect Dorcas. On the other hand, they may have turned to Peter simply for consolation (Acts 9:32-38).

DORÉ, Gustave Paul

(1832-1883) French artist, painter, and sculptor, acclaimed in the 19th century for drawings, book illustrations, and caricatures. After 1862 he made sketches that were transferred photographically to blocks, effecting dramatic illustrations for his most ambitious and successful project - an illustrated Bible (1865).

DORMITION OF THE VIRGIN

A phrase used to refer to Mary's death. Although it is never mentioned in Scripture, a body of legends concerning Mary's death gradually arose in Christian apocryphal literature. These legends are called the *Transitus Mariae* literature, and the earliest dates back to the second half of the fifth century. Although highly imaginative, they reveal a strong early Christian desire to discover everything possible about Mary's death, and a belief that something quite extraordinary attended that event.

DORNER, Isaak August

(1809-1884) Protestant theologian who sought to interpret Kantian and post-Kantian thought in terms of traditional Lutheran doctrine. The best known of the English translations of his many works is *of the Development of the Doctrine of the Person of Christ* (1861-63).

DORT, Synod of

An assembly of the Reformed Church of the Netherlands that met at Dordrecht (Dort) from November 1618 to May 1619. It was the purpose of the synod to settle disputes concerning Arminianism, the theological movement that developed from the teachings of Jacobus Arminius. They rejected the strict Calvinist doctrine of predestination, the doctrine that God elects or chooses those who will be saved.

DOSITHEUS

(1641-1707) Patriarch of Jerusalem, an important church politician and theologian of the modern Greek Church who staunchly supported Eastern Orthodoxy over that of Rome. He interpreted his patriarchate as including the entire Orthodox Church. To prevent Protestantism from influencing the Greek Church, in 1672 he convoked the Synod of Jerusalem, which is considered to be the most important Orthodox Eastern Church council council in modern times. Rejecting unconditional predestination and justification of faith alone, Dositheus' synod was the culmination of a controversy of the plan of Patriarch Lucaris of Constantinople to reform the Orthodox Church on Calvinistic lines.

DOSSAL

A reredos-like curtain hung behind the alter or suspended from the canopy. Before the change of the altar's position this curtain, with two others, one at each side, was hung from rods fastened on the wall or rested on four pillars erected at each end of the altar. Often the pillars were surmounted by angels holding candelabra lighted on festive occasions.

DOTHAN

A city figuring in two Biblical narratives. Dothan is today identified with Tell Dotha, situated on a hill in a small basin-like plain lying between the hills of Samaria and the Carmel range, ten miles northeast of Samaria.

DOUAI BIBLE

The first English translation of the Bible authorized for Roman Catholics. It is a translation of the Latin Vulgate Bible of St. Jerome. The name is taken from the town of Douai in France where the translation was prepared at a seminary for exiled English Catholics. The New Testament was completed in 1582 and the Old Testament appeared in 1609 and 1610.

DOUBLE PREDESTINATION

The teaching that God predistines some men to certain salvation and reprobates others to damnation. There are two forms:

▲ supralapsarianism holds that there is an effective twofold divine plan of salvation and damnation anterior to God's foreknowledge of the Fall;

▲ infralapsarianism holds that the plan is subsequent to foreknowledge of the Fall.

In both forms, double predestination implies the positive reprobation of some to damnation. In this sense it is rejected by Roman Catholic and Lutheran doctrinal standards.

DOUBLE TRUTH THEORY

A philosophical position according to which there can coexist two truths, one for faith and one for reason, both true yet contradictory. It is not established that such doctrine was ever actually held by a particular thinker, though individuals and groups have been alleged to have held it during the Middle ages.

DOUKHOBORS

Members of a communal, mystical movement that originated in the 18th century Russia as a protest against the State and the Russian Orthodox Church. Rejecting the doctrine of the Trinity and the authority of the Bible, these peasants, who originally called themselves Christians of the Universal Brotherhood, taught that Christ was simply a man and reappears periodically in chosen men; that the soul is mortal and undergoes metempsychosis; and that those led by the Spirit are incapable of sin.

Because of their opposition to government, private property, schools, war, and oaths, Doukhobors were periodically persecuted by the tsars and expelled by the Cossacks from their villages.

DOVE

A common symbol for the Holy Spirit who appeared in the form of a dove at our Lord's baptism.

DOWIE, John Alexander

(1847-1907) Evangelist and faith healer who founded the Christian Catholic Church and Zion City. The church emphasized spiritual healing but otherwise differed little from the more millennialist of the Protestant churches. He established Zion City in 1901 on the shore of Lake Michigan, with about 5,000 of his followers. In the same year, he proclaimed himself Elijah the Restorer and later, first Apostle of the church. He ruled the community as a theocracy. Various industries were begun and the town prospered, Dowie in sole control of the businesses. He was removed in 1906 and replaced by Wilbur Voliva.

DOXOLOGY

An expression of praise to God. In Christian worship there are three common doxologies:

1 The greater doxology, or Gloria, used in the Roman Catholic liturgy, the Eastern Orthodox liturgies, and in many Anglican, Lutheran, and Protestant worship services.

2 The lesser doxology, or Gloria Patri, used in most Christian traditions at the close of the psalmody.

3 Metrical doxologies, usually variations upon the Gloria Patri.

DRAGON

In the Bible and other Near Eastern literature a symbol of the forces of evil. It is identified with Rahab in the poetic parallelism of Isaiah 51:9. The primeval monster overcome by Yahweh is elsewhere called Leviathan (Psalms 73: 13-14), sea monster (Job 7:12) and Bashan (Psalms 68:22).

The dragon also became an eschatological symbol of evil God would destroy to accomplish the new creation (Isaiah 27:1; Revelation 20:2).

DRAVYA

A fundamental concept in the Jaina philosophy of India. The Jaina assume the existence of five so-called astikayas, or eternal categories of being, which together make up the dravya, or "substance."

DRUIDS

An order of ancient Celtic priests in Gaul (France), Britain and Ireland. The Druids as a class were revered as elders and sages as well as priests and their influence united the separate Celtic groups. Their wide range of functions included prophesying the future and dispensing justice. Druidic learning was a mixture of astronomy, medicine and jurisprudence; and they were entrusted with the education of young noblemen. Little is known of their religious rites, but it is thought that the oak and mistletoe were sacred to them.

The earliest sources of information about the Druids are the writings of Julius Caesar and of Strabo. Because of their power, the Druids were feared and persecuted by the Romans.

DRUMMOND, Henry

(1786-1860) Writer and member of Parliament who helped found the Catholic Apostolic Church. In 1826 he and several clergymen and laymen held the first of five annual conferences on the prophetic scriptures at his Albury home. From these meetings the organization of the Catholic Apostolic Church evolved.

DRUSE

Adherent of a religion which developed originally from the 11th century Isma'ilis in Egypt. Druse is an anglicized form of the Arabic word durzi which in turn derives from the last element of the proper name Mohammed b. Isma'il al-Darazi. The latter, who must be accounted one of the founders of the drusen, taught that the 6th Fatimid caliph, al-Hakim was divine. Al-Hakim disappeared in mysterious circumstances in 1021 and the Drusen teach that he is not dead. Druse doctrine is highly complex and secretive but it is clear that the religion has been influenced both by Neoplatonism and Gnosticism. They are to be found today mainly in the Lebanon, Israel and Syria.

DRUSILLA

The third and youngest daughter of Herod Agrippa I, born circa AD 38; sister of Agrippa II and Bernice. Before she was six years old, her marriage to prince Epiphanes of Commagene was arranged, but it never materialized due to the refusal of the king-to-be to embrace Judaism. A Syrian king, Azizus of Emesa, met the terms of circumcision, and Drusilla became his bride at the age of 14.

Aggravated by his cruelty, and nettled by the envy of her less attractive sister Bernice, Drusilla was easily induced to divorce Azisus, contrary to Jewish law, and marry Governor Felix about 54. Perhaps she was present when prisoner Paul "talked about righteousness and self-control and the judgment to come," which proved to be most disquieting subjects for Governor Felix. After two years, when Felix turned the governorship over to Festus, he left Paul in chains "to gain favor with the Jews," which some think was done to please his youthful wife, who was a Jewess (Acts 24:24-27). Drusilla's son by Felix was another Agrippa, reportedly killed in the great eruption of Mount Vesuvius in 79.

DUALISM

A system of belief which holds that the universe is the work of two opposing principles, Good and Evil, Light and Darkness, locked in eternal conflict.

DUALISM, religious

Belief in two supreme opposed powers or gods, or sets of divine or demonic beings, that control the world. It may be absolute or relative (in which one principle is derived from the other); and dialectical (involving an eternal tension); or eschatological (looking to a final resolution of the dualism).

DUFF, Alexander

(1806-1878) First Presbyterian foreign missionary of the Church of Scotland, highly influential on later missionary endeavors through his promotion of higher education.

DUHA, al-

The title of the 93rd sura of the Koran; it means "The Forenoon." The sura belongs to the Meccan period and has 11 verses. Its title comes from the oath in the first verse "By the forenoon." The sura begins by assuring the Prophet Mohammed (who is the "you" in the third verse) that he is not been abandoned by God (simply because there has been a hiatus in the Revelation). The sura reminds Mohammed of God's favor to him when the Prophet was orphaned and urges that other orphans should not be suppressed.

DUKHAN, al-

The title of the 44th sura of the Koran; it means "The Smoke." The sura belongs to the Meccan period and has 59 verses. Its title comes from the 10th verse which talks of a day when Heaven shall bring forth evident smoke, which will cover the people. The reference may either be eschatological or to later events in Mecca. The sura begins with two of the Mysterious Letters of the Koran and continues with references to Pharaoh, the deliverance of the Children of Israel and the divine purpose behind creation. Mention is also made of the Tree of al-Zaqqum and the pains of hell, as well as the pleasure of paradise.

Dukkha

In Buddhism, suffering or ill, ordinarily set in opposition to Sukha, ease and well-being. It signifies disease in the sense of discomfort, frustration or disharmony with the environment. Dukkkas is the first of the Four Noble Truths and one of the three Signs of Being, or Characteristics of Existence.

DULIA

The reverence given to saints and angels on account of their union with God. Dulia is distinguished from Iatria, which is the adoration due to God, and hyperdulia, which is the special honor given to the Blessed Virgin Mary.

DUMAH

In the Old Testament, the sixth in the list of Ishmael's twelve sons. By the marriage of his sister Mahalath, Dumah became the brother-in-law to his half-cousin Esau. Dumah also became a chieftain and head of a clan or nation, in fulfillment of God's promise to Abraham (Genesis 17:20; 25:14-16).

DUMUZI

In Mesopotamian religion, important deity in the Sumero-Akkadian pantheon, city god of Badtibria in the central grasslands region. Dumuzi was the god of fertility and the production of new life.

DUMUZI-ABZU

In Mesopotamian religion, city goddess of Kinirsha near Lagash in the south-eastern marshlands region. She represented the power of fertility and new life in the marshes.

DUMUZI-AMAUSHUMGALANA

In Mesopotamian religion, deity especially popular in the southern orchard regions. He was the young bridegroom of the goddess Inanna, the Lady of the Date Clusters, and as such he represented the power of growth and new life in the date palm.

DUNGEON

In Judaism, name applied to David, when he felt as though he was in a dungeon at the time he was hiding in a cave as an outlaw refugee from King Saul. His circumstances looked very dark, with his life constantly in danger, traps in his pathway and no other place to flee. He prayed to God for liberation (Psalms 142:7).

DUNS SCOTUS, John

(1266-1308) Influential Franciscan Realist philosopher and Scholastic theologian. His theology survives in hundreds of manuscripts and was followed many Catholic theologians until the 18th century.

DUNSTAN, Saint

(924-988) Celebrated archbishop of Canterbury, and a chief adviser to the kings of Wessex, who is best known for the major monastic reforms that he effected. He introduced the Rule of St. Benedict and restored monastic life in what is generally considered to be the first revival of English monasticism after the Danish invasions.

DUNSTER, Henry

(1609-1659) English-born Baptist minister, scholar, and the first president of Harvard College.

DURA

The plain where Nebuchadnezzar set up a golden image (Daniel 3:1).

DURANDUS OF SAINT POURCAIN

(1270-1334) Bishop, theologian and philosopher known primarily for his opposition to the ideas of St. Thomas Aquinas.

In some of his differences with Aquinas, Durandus took a position similar to Nominalism (the view that only individual things exist and not universal classes such as man, tree, animal, etc.). This approach had theological implications that sometimes brought on Furandus the censure of church authorities.

DURGA

In Hindu mythology, one of the many forms of Sakti (the goddess), and the wife of Siva. Her best-known feat was the slaying of the buffalo-demon Mahisasura.

DUTCH REFORMED CHURCH

The largest and oldest Protestant Church in the Netherlands, to which 25 percent of the population belong. In the United States it was the first reformed church of Continental European origins to establish itself in North America. In South Africa is it the dominant church among whites.

DVAITA

An important school in the orthodox Hindu philosophical system of Vedanta. Its founder was Madhva (probably 1199-1278). Already during his lifetime he was regarded as the incarnation of the wind god Vayu, who had been sent to Earth by the Lord Vishnu to save the good, after the powers of evil had sent Sankara, the teacher of Nondualism (Advaita). He wrote 37 treatises that have been preserved.

DVIJA

In the Hindu social system, members of the tree upper social classes
1 the Brahmana (priests and teachers);
2 Ksatriya (warriors);
3 Vaisya (merchants).
The initiation ceremony invests the male caste members with a sacred thread, a loop worn next to the skin over the left shoulder and across the right hip.

DYOPHYSITE

One who maintains the Chalcedonian doctrine that full deity and full humanity exist in the person of Jesus Christ as two natures united without confusion or change. The Council of Chalcedon (451) condemned the monophysite doctrine of Eutyches, which held that the substantial union of the Logos with the humanity formed one nature only (physis) in which the humanity was completely absorbed by the divinity.

DYOTHELETISM

The theory that Christ had both a human and divine will. It was held in opposition to Monotheletism, a Christological heresy condemned by the Council of Constantinople III (680-681). The council declared that since Christ had a human and divine nature, he thereby possessed two wills that were free but never in conflict.

DZIADY

In Slavic religion, all the dead ancestors of a family, the rites that are performed in their memory, and the day on which those rites are performed. Dziady takes place three or four times a year; though the dates vary in different localities, dziady are generally celebrated in the winter before the beginning of Advent and in the spring on the Sunday of Doubting Thomas.

DVIN, Synod of

(505/506) Armenian church council held at Dvin, in ancient Armenia, which rejected the decisions of the Council of Chalcedon.

EARLY CHRISTIAN ART AND ARCHITECTURE

The period of Christian art from around the 4th century to the mid-6th century, particularly the art of Italy and the western Mediterranean. The Christian religion was part of a general trend in the late Roman Empire toward mysticism and spirituality, and Christian art arose naturally from the artistic climate of that "late antique" period. Except for differences in subject matter, Christian and pagan artworks looked very much the same; in fact, it is possible to show that the same workshop sometimes produced sculpture for both Christian and non-Christian purposes.

The art of this period has its roots in the classical Roman style, but it developed into more abstract, simplified artistic expression whose ideal was not physical beauty but spiritual feeling. The human figures thus became types rather than individuals and often had large, staring eyes, "the windows of the soul." Symbols were frequently used, and compositions were flat and hieratic, in order to concentrate on and clearly visualize the main idea. Although the art of the period was not naturalistic, it had great power and intimacy.

The earliest extant examples of Christian art are the wall paintings and sarcophagi (stone coffins) of the catacombs in Rome, dating from as early as 180. These frescoes are very similar in style to contemporary pagan painting, but their subjects are often drawn from the Old Testament. Representations of Jonah, Daniel and Noah were frequently used to symbolize the Christian promise of salvation.

The Emperor Constantine's Edict of Milan (313) marked official acceptance of the new religion. Christians had previously met secretly in private houses, but in the 4th and 5th centuries, when Christianity became the state religion of the Empire, monumental churches of the basilica type began to be constructed. The Christians continued to use Roman secular forms in their architecture, as in their painting. The basilicas were large roofed buildings divided by columns into three or sometimes five aisles. At one end of the central aisle was a projecting semicircular area, the apse, which was often a tribunal for judges or public officials. In Christian basilicas the apse was the site of the altar, and a transept was sometimes added to the plan to achieve the cross-shaped design typical of later churches. Although the basilica is most characteristic of Rome, where many examples are still standing, remains of these earliest churches are common throughout the Mediterranean.

The exterior of the church was simple and undecorated, but the interior was covered with resplendent wall mosaics. The early Christians raised the mosaic to a major art, an art which illustrates the complicated development of Christian symbolism. Rome, Ravenna and Istanbul still have magnificent examples of this art form, but probably all basilicas were richly decorated with glass mosaics and colored marble. One of the earliest known mosaics covers the domed aspe of Sta. Pudenziana in Rome. Depicting the enthroned Christ as judge, it echoes the older judicial and magisterial functions of the pagan basilica.

EARLY MONASTICISM

The first appearance of Christian monasticism can be traced to some authorities to St. Anthony who retired to the Egyptian desert in the third century to live a solitary life. He drew several disciples who imitated his austerity and evangelical dedication thus making Lower Egypt an eremetical center.

In Upper Egypt St. Pachominius (290-346) shifted the monastic way of life from the eremitic to the cenobitic by grouping his disciples under one roof near Tabennesi.

EARTH, BLESSED

Earth blessed and sometimes placed in small quantity into the coffin at private services for the dead; sometimes it is scattered on the coffin as it is lowered into the grave. Sprinkling the coffin with holy water has been derived from this practice. The term also refers to the blessed ground or cemetery plot in which a Roman Catholic should be buried.

EARTH, MOTHER

In Greek mythology, Mother Earth was the leading protagonist in cosmogony. It formed a union with Sky to make the first divine couple. The first-born Oceanus fathered with Tethys the Rivers and the Oceanids. Hyperion and Theia sired Helios (sun), Selene (moon) and Eos (dawn).

In the beginning Sky and Mother Earth were united but they later separated. After the Sky (Uranus) was mutilated by its terrible child Cronus, Mother Earth formed a union with Pondus and their union brought the world Thaumas, Phorces, Ceto, Eurybia and Nereus.

EASTER

Principal festival of the Christian church Year, celebrating the resurrection of Jesus Christ on the third day after his crucifixion. Its origins go back to the beginnings of Christianity, and it is probably the oldest Christian observance after Sunday, which came to be regarded as the weekly celebration of the Resurrection.

The festival of Easter occurs on a particular Sunday, but its importance is emphasized in the worship of the church by the long preparation of Lent; by the Holy Week, with its solemn services; and by the following seven weeks until Pentecost (Whitsunday). Easter is central to the whole Christian year; not only dies the entire ecclesiastical calendar of movable feasts depend upon its date but the whole liturgical year of worship is arranged around it. In the liturgical texts the emphasis is laid on its being the Christian Passover (the time of redemption).

EASTER CYCLE

The liturgical season embracing the period of preparation for Easter, beginning with Septuagesima and extending through Lent and Holy Week; the celebration of Easter itself; and the prolongation of the Easter celebration through Pentecost and its octave.

With the promulgation of the revised liturgical calendar in 1969, fulfilling the directives of Vatican Council II's call for such a revision, the season now embraces a period of 50 days from Easter Sunday to Pentecost.

In its earliest observance Easter itself was the celebration of the whole of the paschal mystery, including Christ's death, Resurrection, Ascension, and the sending of the Spirit, but gradually specific aspects of the mystery began to be given special attention on distinct days.

EASTER DUTY

In Roman Catholicism, a popular term for the obligation thus described in the Code of Canon Law: "All the faithful, after they have been initiated into the Most Holy Eucharist, are bound by the obligation of receiving Communion at least once a year." "This precept must be fulfilled during the Easter season unless it is fulfilled for a just cause at some other time during the year."

EASTER ISLAND

Eastermost Polynesian island, renowned for distinctive huge volcanic stone carvings of heads and figures. Thirty feet high, these "cult" forms, solemn and monumental, probably do not antedate the 15th century. Driftwood has been used for recent skeleton-like ancestor figure.

EASTERN CHRISTIANITY, INDEPENDENT CHURCHES OF

The Christian churches originating in the apostolic or subapostolic age that do not recognize the authority of the pope in Rome or the ecumenical patriarch in Istanbul. Tracing their heritage back to the earliest centuries of the church, these churches contributed to the popular, intellectual, and national life and thought in the areas in which they developed.

EASTERN CHURCHES

Eastern churches are those that developed in the Eastern half of the Roman Empire. Subsequent to its political division, made first by Diocletan (193) and again by the sons of Theodosius I, namely Arcadius in the East (395) and Honorius in the West, the ecclesiastical division into Eastern and Western churches was affected as well.

The boundary ran between Italy and Greece, more precisely along the Sava, Drina and Zeta rivers down to the city of Budva and to the Adriatic Sea. All lands west of the line belonged to the Latin or Western church, while lands to the east belonged to Eastern churches.

Viewed in retrospect, the circumstance that its patriarchate was central in administration of the early church gave the pentarchy - Rome, Alexandria, Antioch, Constantinople, Jerusalem - its importance.

Originally at the Council of Nicaea (325) there were the first three patriarchates. Further conciliar legislation formed the two others, Constantinople in 381 and 431 and Jerusalem in 451. Since these councils a division was delineated so that Western Christendom is identified with the Roman patriarchate and all churches that have broken away from it. All the others, with schismatical bodies formed from them, make up the Eastern half.

All Eastern churches evolved from the Patriarchates of Constantinople, Alexandria, and Antioch, and the churches of Persia and Armenia, which developed outside the Roman Empire. All the daughter churches dependent on these three Eastern Patriarchates embraced the rite and came under the jurisdiction of their mother churches, namely the Byzantine, Alexandrian, and Antiochene (Syrian) Rites respectively.

Historic ruptures between East and West

The rupture between East and West came about, not at certain specific dates, but gradually; it was brought about in good faith, against the desire of both sides, the result of conjectures of historical circumstances rather than ill will.

The Eastern churches have no consciousness of having broken with their own past or with apostolic tradition, or of having denied anything whatever in it. The epithets "schismatic" and "heretic" are deeply resented by the Eastern churches; and Rome in official pronouncements and documents refers now always to the separated Eastern brothers simply as dissidents.

Vatican Council II not only promulgated a special decree on the Eastern churches, but also included in this decree and in the Decree on Ecumenism a special reference to the Eastern churches separated from Rome.

These decrees express great esteem for the institutions, liturgy, and traditions of the Eastern churches. The first decree speaks of the local Eastern churches, of the preservation of their spiritual heritage, of the venerable institution of the patriarchate; it speaks also of the sacramental discipline, the celebration of feasts, of contact and intercommunion with the separated Eastern churches. This change of attitude is being reciprocated, and thus hope for reunion is increased. It is right and proper that the Westerns should value the rights and usages and traditions and glorious history of their own, while they should also value those of Eastern churches by accepting them as part of the whole which is to come.

EASTERN CHURCHES, CATHOLIC

These are Catholic churches (whose members number approximately 12,000,000 throughout the world) who follow Eastern Rites. Vatican Council II, in its Decree on Eastern Catholic Churches, says: "The Catholic Church values highly the institutions of the Eastern churches, their liturgical rites, ecclesiastical traditions and their ordering of Christian life. For in these churches, which are distinguished by their venerable antiquity, there is clearly evident the tradition which has come from the apostles through the fathers and which is part of the divinely revealed, undivided heritage of the Universal Church."

EASTERN ORTHODOX CHURCH

The second largest Christian communion in the world today, the Eastern Orthodox Church (also designated as the Greek Orthodox) has a following which is variously estimated at between 150 and 250 million; exact figures are still unavailable for Eastern European countries. Encompassing the majority of the Christian population in the Middle East, the Balkans, and Russia, it has more recently expanded, either through immigration or missionary activity, to America, Western Europe, East Africa, and the Far East.

As apostles of Jesus preached throughout the Eastern Mediterranean world, communities or local churches were established in most urban centers of the area, which were then under the control of the Roman Empire. In 324, Emperor Constantine transferred the imperial capital from Rome to Byzantium on the Bosphorus. The city was renamed "Constantinople-New Rome" and soon became not only the political capital of the Empire, but also the center of the Eastern Christian civilization.

A leading role to be exercised by the bishop of Constantinople among his colleagues was sanctioned by the Councils of Constantinople (381) and Chalcedon (451). In the sixth century, he assumed the title of "ecumenical patriarch" and occupied the second position after Rome in a system of five patriarchs: Rome, Constantinople, Alexandria, Antioch, Jerusalem - were considered as the main centers of the Christian world.

Their role was decisive in the solution of doctrinal controversies which were debated at the councils of

▲ Nicea I (325);
▲ Constantinople I (381);
▲ Ephesus (331);
▲ Chalcedon (451);
▲ Constantinople II (553);
▲ Constantinople III (680);
▲ Nicaea II (787).

These seven councils are the ones recognized as ecumenical by the Orthodox church today.

Starting with the ninth century, the church of Constantinople undertook a major missionary expansion among the Slavic nations of Eastern Europe. Following the tradition of earlier missionaries, the Scripture was translated into the vernacular language of the Slavs. In 864 Bulgaria was converted to Christianity, followed, in 988, by Russia. Controversies on points of doctrine and discipline began between East and West in the early Middle Ages. The Christian East refused to recognize a specific form of papal supremacy. The date of 1054, generally quoted as the date of the schism between Rome and Constantinople, represents, in fact, only an incident in a long process of estrangement.

Today, the Orthodox church consists of 14 independent or autocephalous churches, united in faith, sacraments, and canon law. These churches include the patriarchates of Constantinople, Alexandria, Antioch, Jerusalem, Russia, Georgia, Serbia, Romania, and Bulgaria, and the autocephalous churches of Cyprus, Greece, Poland, Czechia and Slovakia, and America. All recognize the honorary primacy of the ecumenical patriarch of Constantinople.

EASTERN ORTHODOXY

Eastern Orthodoxy is one of the three major doctrinal and jurisdictional groups of Christianity characterized by its continuity with the apostolic church, its liturgy, and its territorial churches. Known officially as "the Orthodox Catholic Church," Eastern Orthodoxy follows the faith and practices that were defined by the first seven ecumenical councils.

EASTERN RITE CHURCHES

Eastern Christian churches originating in various ancient national or ethnic Christian groups that are in union with the Western Catholic Church under the jurisdiction of the papacy at Rome. The Eastern Rite churches, often known as uniate churches, differ from the Western Latin Catholics in their allowance of a married clergy, celebration of their own liturgies, and other ancient established traditions.

EASTERN THEOLOGY

The theology of the Eastern churches. Its tradition of thought, roots in special cultural areas, milieu, and general mentality account for its distinctive quality. Although Eastern theology takes its point of departure from the same transcendent reality as Western theology, it is complementary because of the diversity of its conceptualization and formulation. Eastern theology today is gradually rediscovering its proper genius. Among the outstanding characteristics of this theology is its mystical bent, or integration with the spiritual life of man. The Greek Eastern fathers conceived theology as the loftiest degree of the spiritual life, consisting of a quasi-experimental knowledge (contemplation) of the Trinity.

Hence it is Trinitarian, having the Trinity for its origin, center, and eschatological goal. Because it is prone to accentuate the role of faith and is distrustful of reason and philosophy, it is an experimental theology.

EASTER VIGIL

Called the "mother of all holy vigils," the Easter Vigil is celebrated after sundown on the night before Easter. The Easter Vigil service includes ceremonies that were held in the early Christian communities and highlights some of the most precious symbols of the church. The Vigil consists of four parts:

- ▲ Service of the Light;
- ▲ Liturgy of the Word;
- ▲ Liturgy of Baptism;
- ▲ Liturgy of the Eucharist.

EASTER WATER

The water that is blessed at the Easter Vigil celebration. It is used for the renewal of baptismal promises and in some places is taken home to be used by the faithful in private devotions.

EBAL

The third-named son of the Horite sheik Shobal descended from Seir (Genesis 36:23; 1 Chronicles 1:40). The Horites dwelt in Seir before being dispossessed and annihilated by the sons of Esau (Deuteronomy 2:12).

EBAL MOUNT

In biblical times, a mountain now identified as Jebel Eslamiyeh, situated in the district of Samaria. Mount Ebal is opposite Mount Gerizim, these mountains being separated by a beautiful narrow valley, the Vale of Shechem, in which nestles the city of Nablus, not far from ancient Shechem. The possible meaning of the name fits the characteristics of the mountain, for only its lower slopes sustain such vegetation as vines and olive trees, the higher elevations being quite barren and rocky.

Moses told the Israelites that when God brought them into the land that they were going to possess they "must also give the blessing upon Mount Gerizim and the malediction upon Mount Ebal" (Deuteronomy 11:29-30). He also instructed that great uncut stones be selected, whitewashed with lime and set on Mount Ebal. An altar was to be erected there, upon which sacrifices were to be presented to God. Moses also said: "You must write on the stones all the words of this law, making them quite clear" (Deuteronomy 27:1-8).

EBBO OF REIMS

(circa 775-851) Controversial German archbishop whose pioneering missions to the North helped prepare the Christianization of Denmark and who exercised significant influence on contemporary arts.

EBED

In Judaism, father of Gaal, the one who led the landowners in an unsuccessful rebellion against Abimelech (Judges 9:26, 29, 39-41).

EBED-MELECH

In the Old Testament, an Ethiopian eunuch in the house of King Zedekiah who, by his course of action, demonstrated that he was in full agreement with the work of God's prophet Jeremiah. He was assured by God, through Jeremiah, that he would not perish during the Babylonian siege but would be furnished an escape (Jeremiah 39:15-18).

EBENEZER

In the Old Testament, a site near which Israel was twice defeated by the Philistines, not only resulting in he death of 34,000 Israelites, including Hophni and Phnehas, but also in enemy capture of the ark of the covenant. News of this latter event precipitated the death of Eli the priest (1 Samuel 4:1-11). Bible geographers tentatively place Ebenezer at Majed Yaba, some two and a half miles south-east of the suggested site of Ephraimite Aphek (where the Philistines were encamped, and eleven miles east of modern Tel Aviv).

EBIONITES

An early Christian ascetic sect that retained and exaggerated the Jewish emphasis in Christianity. Explicit mention of them is first found in the works of Irenaeus (circa 185) and they were known to still exist in the 4th century. They evidently left Palestine and settled in Transjordan and Syria and were later known to be in Asia Minor, Egypt, and Rome.

Most of the features of Ebionite doctrine were anticipated in the teachings of the earlier Qumran sect, as revealed in the Dead Sea scrolls. Evidently, the Ebionite movement arose after the destruction i Jerusalem in 70 and for a time had some association with Jewish Christianity. When they rejected apostle Paul, however, the Ebionites were not following the example of the Christian church in Jerusalem. Finally, they found even Matthew's Gospel unsatisfactory, and they developed their own literature, including the gospels of the Ebionites and of the Nazarenes.

EBRON

In Judaism, the name of a boundary city apportioned to Asher (Joshua 19:24-28). Since many Hebrew manuscripts read "Abdon," most scholars generally consider "Ebron" to be an erroneous spelling of the name.

ECCE HOMO

(Latin: "Behold the Man!") A theme in Christian art showing Christ presented by Pontius Pilate to the Jews, bearing signs of the flagellation and wearing a crown of thorns and a purple robe. The subject became frequent in Western Europe in the 15th century, when popular concern with the pathetic aspects of Christ's life was widespread; it remained current through the 17th century.

ECCLESIA

(Greek: "gathering of those summoned") The most general word for an assembly of citizens in a Greek citystate, and among early Christians it became the word for "church." Its roots lay in the Homeric agora, the meeting of the people. The Athenian Ecclesia, for which exists the most detailed evidence, was already functioning in Draco's day (circa 620 BC). In the course of Solon's codification of the law (circa 594 BC), the ecclesia became coterminous with the body of male citizens 18 years of age or over.

Christian usage of ecclesia as "church"

was probably derived from the Septuagint, where it renders the Hebrew qahal ("gathering"). In Acts it refers to pagan or Christian gatherings and the Christian community as a whole.

ECCLESIASTES

Book of the Old Testament; canonical text both accepted by the Jewish and the Christian churches. It is in agreement with other portions of the Bible that treat the same subject. For example, it agrees with Genesis on man's being made up of a body composed of the dust of the ground and having the spirit or life force and the breath that sustains it from God (Ecclesiastes 3:20-21; 12:7; Genesis 2:7). It affirms the Bible teaching that man was created upright but willfully close to disobey God (Ecclesiastes 7:29).

The Hebrew name fittingly described the role of the king in a theocratic government such as Israel enjoyed (Ecclesiastes 1:1, 12). It was the responsibility of the ruler to hold the dedicated people of God together in faithfulness to their true king and God (1 Kings 8:1-5). For that reason, whether a king was good or bad for the nation was determined by whether he led the nation in the worship of God or not.

The congregator, who was Solomon, had already done much congregating of Israel and their companions, the temporary residents, to the temple. In this book he is sought to congregate God's people away from the vain and fruitless works of this world to the world worthy of the God to whom they as a nation were dedicated.

Since the book mentions the building program of Solomon, it must have been written after that time but before he "began to do what was bad in the eyes of God" (1 Kings 11:6). The book was therefore written before 100 BC in Jerusalem. That Solomon would be one of the best qualified men to write the book is supported by the fact that he was not only the richest but probably one of the best informed kings of his day, his sailors and tradesmen as well

as visiting dignitaries bringing news and knowledge of people of other lands (1 Kings 9:26-28; 10:23-25).

ECCLESIASTICAL COURTS

Tribunals set up by religious authorities to deal with disputes among clerics or with spiritual matters involving either clerics of laymen. Although such courts are found today among the Jews and among the Muslims as well as the various Christian sects, their functions have become limited strictly to religious issues and to governance of church property. During earlier periods in history, ecclesiastical courts often had a degree of temporal jurisdiction, and in the Middle Ages the courts of the Roman Catholic Church rivalled the temporal courts in power.

In England today the ecclesiastical courts exercise jurisdiction in civil cases concerning church buildings and in criminal cases in which clergymen are accused of ecclesiastical crimes.

ECCLESIASTICAL HISTORY

Series of book written by Eusebius, bishop of Caesarea, the primary source for the history of Christianity from the time of the Apostles until 324. It is essentially an apologetic work that demonstrates the victory of the Christian church over her enemies. Probably first completed circa 303, it consisted of seven books, but it was enlarged in successive editions to 10 books, which included contemporary events.

ECCLESIASTICAL LAW

In England, a body of law concerned with the constitutional position of the established church of England in relation to the rest of the state and with the church's internal constitution with the appointment, rights, and obligations of its ministers and other officers, with the functioning of the church's courts, with forms of service, and with the proprietary rights so far as the church's property is concerned. It is administered largely by the ecclesiastical courts.

ECCLESIASTICAL PROVINCE

A name given to a group of neighboring dioceses under the supervision of a metropolitan archbishop. The bishops of these groupings can meet in synods or provincial councils.

ECCLESIASTICUS

An apocryphal work (noncanonical for Jews and Protestants) that was incorporated into the Greek Bible (Septuagint) but excluded from the Hebrew biblical canon. It is an outstanding example of the "wisdom" genre of religious literature that was popular in the early Hellenistic period of Judaism (3rd century BC to 3rd century AD).

Like other major wisdom books (Proverbs, Ecclesiastes, Job, and Wisdom of Solomon), Ecclesiasticus contains practical and moral rules and exhortations, frequently arranged according to subject matter; e.g., hypocrisy, generosity, filial respect.

Wisdom, personified as Sophia, or Lady Wisdom, delivers an extended discourse on her eternal relationship with God (Chapter 24) and is identified with the Mosaic Law.

The text, the only apocryphal work the author of which is known, was written in Hebrew in Palestine around 190 BC by a certain Jesus ben Sirach, who was probably a scribe well-versed in Jewish law and custom.

ECCLESIOLOGY

The theology or study of the church in any or all of its aspects; e.g., its nature, its authority, its divine mission. Although ecclesiology did not appear as a distinct branch of theology until the Reformation, reflections on the nature of the church are to be found in the New Testament and the earliest patristic traditions. The Pauline doctrine of the mystical body of Christ, e.g., exposes a definite theological insight into the nature of salvation and the communal relationship established thereby.

Among the earliest Church fathers (Clement of Rome, Polycarp, Ignatius of Antioch), the church was seen as the new Israel, composed of divinely chosen members of Christ. The distinction between the church as visible and invisible was not yet used. Irenaeus speaks of the church as the great body of Christ in which the Spirit works and insures its key characteristics, especially its possession of the truth.

Clement of Alexandria and Origen stress the universal reality of the church as the gathering of all the elect rules by the Word, even those not present in the visible society of believers.

Augustine of Hippo played an important role in the development of ecclesiology. He used the Pauline image of the church as the mystical body of Christ, and underlined the significance of its unity of belief and charity. Augustine also distinguished between the church's perfect essence and its imperfect embodiment. It is perfect in essence because it is constituted by Christ who establishes its holy people; it is imperfect in embodiment insofar as it is a visible congregation of sinners.

ECHTERNACH GOSPELS

Manuscript illuminated circa 710 in the hibero-Saxon style at the monastery of Echternach, Luxembourg.

ECKEHART, MEISTER

(1260-1328) German Dominican and great speculative mystic whose teachings contributed to the future development of Protestantism, Romanticism, Idealism and Existentialism.

From 1314 his main activity was preaching to a group of contemplative nuns while residing in Strassburg. In both his Latin and German works Eckehart describes the four stages of union between the soul and God as dissimilarity, similarity, identity and breakthrough.

ECLECTICISM

In theology and philosophy, the practice of selecting doctrines from different systems of thought without adopting the whole parent system for each doctrine. It is distinct from syncretism - the attempt to reconcile or combine systems - inasmuch as it leaves the contradictions between them unresolved. In the sphere of abstract thought, eclecticism is open to the objection that insofar as each system is supposed to be a whole of which its various doctrines are integral parts, the arbitrary juxtaposition of doctrines from different systems risks a fundamental incoherence. In practical affairs, however, the eclectic spirit has much to commend it.

ECLOGUE

A short pastoral poem, usually in dialogue, on the subject of rural life and the society of shepherds, depicting it as enjoying a freedom from the complexity and corruption of more civilized life. Some types of eclogues have a religious background.

ECONOMY, DIVINE

The eternal and intellectual plan of the triadic God concerning the order of nature and of grace, which is revealed and executed by His act of creation (theological and cosmological aspects), sanctification and divinization of the Holy Spirit (pneumatological aspect), self-revelation through the history of salvation (historical and ecclesiological aspects), and consummation, i.e., final and eternal fulfillment through a participation in His inner life and love (eschatological aspect).

Strictly speaking the divine economy denotes the economy of salvation in which the fruits of Redemption are applied by God as the primary cause and through the creatures as secondary agents (for instance, Christ, priest, sacrament). Essentially it is the mystery of reality. Oriental Christianity understands economy of the church as a benign application of its canonical power.

ECONOMY OF SALVATION

The great plan of God by which his will and work is accomplished even without the help of human beings. This plan of salvation is described in Ephesians 1:3-14.

ECSTASY

A term used in mysticism to describe its primary goal: the experience of an inner vision of God or one's relation to or union with the divine. Various methods have been used to achieve this goal.

The most typical is the four stages:
1 purgation (of bodily desire);
2 purification (of the will);
3 illumination (of the mind);
4 unification (of one's being or will with the divine).

In certain ancient Israelite prophetic groups, music was used to achieve the ecstatic state, in which the participants, in their accompanying dancing, were believed to have been seized by the hands of Yahweh, the God of Israel.

The goal of ecstasy and its effects are best known from the writings and activities of the mystics of the world's great religions.

ECSTASY OF ST. TERESA

Life-size, white marble sculpture group over the altar of the Coronaro chapel in the church of Maria della Vittoria at Rome. The sculpture, as well as the design of the chapel, was executed from 1645 to 1652 by Gian Lorenzo Bernini.

ECUMENICAL COUNCIL

In the Christian church, a general council of the church. Its decisions (called canons) are considered to have official authority, although they have not been invariably accepted and, in the Roman Catholic Church, require ratification by the Pope. The ecumenical council was held at Nicaea (325), and there have since been 20 more, but not all are universally accepted as ecumenical. The Eastern church recognizes the first seven, and also the Trullan Synod (692) at which the basis of Eastern Canon Law was established. The Roman Catholic Church ignores the Trullan Synod, but recognizes 14 later councils as ecumenical.

Protestants consider that such councils are fallible in their decisions, and do not regard their utterances as binding.

But Protestant observers have attended the most recent councils. The earlier councils were chiefly concerned with matters of discipline and morals. One of the most important topics at Vatican 2 (1962) was the reunion of other churches with the Roman Catholic church. Christian unity is also the aim of the Protestant Ecumenical movement.

ECUMENICAL CREEDS

Creeds so called because of universal or widespread acceptance or use. The Nicene, Athanasian, and Apostles' creeds have received this designation. Only the Nicene (Niceno-Constantinopolitan) creed can be called ecumenical in the full sense, since it has been professed and used liturgically in both West and East.

The Roman Catholic Church has employed the three creeds in teaching and liturgy. The Reformation churches for the most part have accorded recognition in these creeds, but the Apostles' creed has had its widest use.

The Lutheran churches (in the Formula of Concord) and the Church of England (in the Thirty-nine Articles) have explicitly adopted the three as doctrinal standards. The Protestant Episcopal Church omitted the Athanasian creed from its adaptation of the Articles and the Book of Common Prayer.

Those who designate these creeds as ecumenical regard them as a possible basis for Christian unity. The epithet "ecumenical," however, is not acceptable to all, not even to some who acknowledge the creeds in question.

ECUMENICAL MOVEMENT

A movement among the Christian churches in the 20th century, for greater cooperation and unity among themselves. The word "ecumenical" is derived from the Greek word oikoemene, meaning the whole inhabited world.

The modern movement has evolved out of the 19th-century Christian attempts to cooperate across denominational barriers. Particularly in the field of missionary work throughout the world, the churches felt that their Christian witness was greatly weakened by denominational divisions. The World Council of Churches, comprising more than 200 Protestant, Eastern Orthodox, and Old Catholic bodies, has become the main manifestation of the modern ecumenical movement.

The missionary impulse of the 19th century led to the World Missionary Conference held in Edinburgh in 1910, which is considered the birthplace of the modern ecumenical idea. The Edinburgh conference led to three movements. The International Missionary Conference was formed to coordinate and aid missionary work throughout the world. In an effort to foster united Christian action in social and political justice, the Life and Work movement was organized at Stockholm in 1927. The third movement, Faith and Order, was set up to study doctrinal and ecclesiastical differences among the churches.

In 1938, the Life and Work and Faith and Order movements, meeting in Utrecht, proposed the formation of the World Council of Churches. World War II however, prevented the immediate implementation of this proposal. In 1948, representatives of 147 churches throughout the world met in Amsterdam and approved the formation of the World Council of churches. Since then other Protestant and Eastern Orthodox churches have joined the Council. While the Roman Catholic Church is not a member of the Council, it participated in several joint study commissions. Theologically, the member churches believe that the unity of the Christian churches is based on their common confession of one Lord. The movement seeks ways to manifest this unity in the life and work of the churches.

ECUMENICAL PATRIARCH

The title assumed by John IV the Faster, bishop of Constantinople (582-595) under Emperor Maurice (582-

602). Since the term oikoemene was used in the East to designate the Christian world, ideally ruled by a single Roman emperor, the title emphasized the political origin of Constantinople's primacy and the role of its bishops as main advisors of the emperor in church affairs.

The title and office of ecumenical patriarch continued to be used even after the fall of Constantinople to the Turks (1453), when the bishop of Constantinople was granted civil authority over all Christians in the Ottoman Empire; it is still carried by the present archbishop of Constantinople (Istanbul).

ECUMENISM

A term of recent origin denoting in an admittedly vague manner the awakened conscience of the Christian church its universal aspects and its renewed sense of mission and service. Historically rooted in the beginnings of the church and especially noted in the ecumenical councils of the distant past, ecumenism in modern times represents a movement toward church unity.

According to Vatican Council II "The term ecumenical movement indicates the initiatives and activities encouraged and organized, according to the various needs of the church and as opportunities offer, to promote Christian unity."

EDEN

According to biblical records, a region in which the Creator planted a garden-like park as the original home of the first human pair. The statement that the garden was "in Eden, toward the east," apparently indicates that the garden occupied a portion of the region called Eden (Genesis 2:8). However, the garden is thereafter called "the garden of Eden" (Genesis 2:15), and, in later texts, is spoken of as "Eden, the garden of God" (Ezekiel 28:13), and "the garden of Jehovah" (Isaiah 51:3).

EDEN, GARDEN OF

In the Old Testament Book of Genesis, earthly paradise inhabited by the first created man and woman, Adam and Eve, prior to their expulsion for disobeying the Commandments of God.

The biblical Eden is described as being watered by the Euphrates, the Tigris, and two lesser known streams, the Gihon and the Pishon. Thus its location was probably in ancient Mesopotamia (modern Iraq). However, its importance lies more in its symbolizing a natural state of perfection before Adam and Eve sinned. Its name is often synonymous with paradise.

EDER

In Judaism, a descendant of Beriah of the tribe of Benjamin who dwelt in Jerusalem (1 Chronicles 8:1, 15-16).

EDOM

In biblical times, land bordering ancient Israel, in what is now southwestern Jordan, between the Dead Sea and the Gulf of Aqaba. The Edomites probably occupied the area about the 13th century BC. Though closely related to the Israelites (they were descendants of Esau), they had frequent conflicts with them and were probably subject to them at the time of the Israelite Kingdom (11th till 10th century BC).

EDOMITES

Descendants of Esau, basically a Semitic race, but with a strong Hamitic strain (See: Edom).

EDDY, MARY BAKER

(1821-1910) American Founder of Christian Science. Born near Concord, New Hampshire, as a young woman she suffered from ill health and unhappiness and came to believe that the cure for her condition must be spiritual. In 1866, having been seriously injured in a fall, she made a sudden and unexpected recovery which she attributed to the illumination given her by the Bible. In the next few years she developed her discovery, and in 1875 published *Science and Health with Key to Scripture*. In 1877 she married Dr. Asa Gilbert Eddy, one of her earliest followers, and two years later she organized the first Church of Christ, Scientist in Boston.

EDMUND, SAINT
(1175-1240) Distinguished scholar, outspoken archbishop of Canterbury, one of the most virtuous and attractive figures of the church in England, whose literary works strongly influenced subsequent spiritual writers in England.

One of the various writings ascribed to him, the one assuredly authentic includes *Speculum Ecclesiae,* a widely known devotional treatise (belonging to the end of his career), considered a major contribution to medieval theology.

EDMUND THE MARTYR
(circa 841-870) King of the Anglo-Saxon kingdom of East Anglia, who, for defending Christianity against heathenism, was murdered by the Danes.

EDREI
In the Old Testament, one of the cities of residence of Og, king of Bashan (Joshua 12:4; 13:12). After defeating Sihon the Amorite, the Israelite forces under Moses' direction "went up," that is, went northward, until they encountered Og's military force in "the battle of Edrei," at what was apparently Bashan's southern frontier. Though Og was the last of the giant-like Rephaim and may have presented a formidable army, the Israelites, advised by God to be fearless, wiped out Og, his sons and people, taking possession of his territory (Numbers 21:33-35; Deuteronomy 3:1-10). The city was later granted to Manasseh as part of his inheritance (Joshua 13:31).

EDUCATION, EARLY CHRISTIAN
The earliest centers of Christian education wee catechetical in purpose, intended for the education of neophytes. The scriptures, the articles of faith, liturgy, and the music of liturgy constituted the curriculum. The training of clerics introduced new elements as the cathedral schools taught philosophy, the liberal arts, and language in addition to scriptures.

Great teachers of Alexandria included Clement, Hippolytus, and Origen. The cathedral school was an outgrowth of the apostolic rule of community living where the bishop and his clergy lived a common life.

Such centers as Rome, Antioch, and Alexandria provided educational centers for training clerics. Augustine in his see of Hippo, established a quasi-monastic community which undertook the education of clergy, in the late fifth century.

EDWARDS, LEWIS
(1809-1887) Minister of the Calvinistic Methodist Church of Wales whose literary and theological essays greatly influenced Welsh culture. Through his influence his denomination adopted a more Presbyterian form of church government on the Scottish model.

EDWARDS, THOMAS CHARLES
(1837-1900) Welsh separatist churchmen, who became the first principal of the University College of Wales at Aberystwyth (1872-91). He wrote several biblical commentaries related to the theologies of Christ.

EDWARD THE CONFESSOR, SAINT
(circa 1003-1066) King of England from 1042 to 1066. His reputation for piety preserved much of the dignity of the crown. He was canonized in 1161.

EDWARD THE MARTYR, SAINT
(circa 963 to 978). His reign was marked by a reaction against the promonastic policies of his father and predecessor, King Edgar (ruled 959-975).

EGEDE, HANS
Norwegian Lutheran missionary and explorer, the first man to preach the gospel to the Eskimos in Greenland.

EGLAIM

In the Old Testament, the mother of King David's sixth son Ithream, born to him in Hebron (2 Samuel 3:5; 1 Chronicles 3:3).

EGLATH-SHELISHIYAH

A term used by Isaiah (15:5) and Jeremiah (48:34) in their pronouncement of doom against Moab, apparently referring to a site in that nation. Some told that there were three towns in one vicinity with the same name, and that the third, is here the target of the prophet's utterances.

EGLON

In Judaism, a king of Moab in the in the days of the judges, who oppressed Israel for 18 years, "because they did what was bad in God's eyes" (Judges 3:12-25). Eglon was head of the confederacy of Moab, Ammon and Amalek in their assault upon Israel. His downfall came when left-handed Ehud, after presenting the customary tribute said: "I have a secret word for you, O King." In the privacy of his cool chamber atop the flat roof of his palace, Eglon, after dismissing his attendants, rose up from his throne to receive what Ehud said was "a word of god." Thereupon Ehud thrust into Eglon's fat belly a double-edged sword so that "the handle kept going in also after the blade."

EGO

A conscious thinking subject or the part of the mind that reacts to reality and has a sense of individuality.

In Buddhism, term with a very specific meaning. Buddhism denies an ego in the sense of a self in man ultimately separate from the self in every other man. The belief in an ego creates and fosters egoism and desire, thus preventing the realization of the unity and the attainment of enlightenment.

EGYPT

Country located in the north-eastern corner of Africa, divided into two unequal, extremely arid regions by the landscape's dominant feature, the northward-flowing Nile River. It is one of the world's oldest continuous civilizations, in ancient times ruled by a pharaoh. Jacob and his sons had gone down into Egypt in time of famine (Genesis 46:6). After a 430 year-year sojourn the Hebrews left Egypt, circa 1441 BC. Egypt and its inhabitants are referred to over 700 times in the Bible.

EGYPT, EARLY CHRISTIANITY

Though there is no direct evidence for the existence of Christianity in Egypt in the first century, the prominent position which the land occupied in the Greco-Roman world and the large numbers of Jews living there are adequate reasons for believing that it was an early object of Christian missionary activities.

The tradition that the church at Alexandria was founded by St. Mark is hardly credible, since it is not mentioned by Clement or Origen and first appears in Eusebius. It is even less likely that a letter of the Emperor Claudius to the Alexandrines refers to the presence of Christians in their city. On the other hand, since there were Jews from "Egypt and the parts of Libya about Cyrene" (Acts 2:10) who heard the Apostles preaching in tongues on the first Christian Pentecost, it is possible that they were converted and brought the new faith back with them to Egypt when they returned home.

The Catechetical School of Alexandria was the first important institution of religious learning in Christian antiquity. It was founded in 190 by Pantanaeus, a Christian scholar who is believed to have come to Alexandria approximately 10 years earlier. Its scope was not limited to theological subjects, because science, mathematics and the humanities were also taught there. Significantly, the emergence of the school coincides with the first direct attacks by the Romans on the Christians of Alexandria.

Clement (160-215), a convert from paganism who succeeded Pantanaeus, is regarded as an early apostle of Christian liberalism and taught in Alexandria for more than 20 years. He was succeeded by Origen (185-253) the theologian and writer who is regarded as the greatest of the early Christian apologists.

Gnosticism

The origin of the Gnostic communities is still obscure. The Gnostics were hounded into silence, in the name of orthodox Christianity, from the fourth century onward and their writings were burned whenever they could be found. Recently found codices contain a gospel of Thomas, a compilation of sayings attributed to Jesus and apocrypha (sacred books) related to Zoroastrianism and Manichaeism.

Neoplatonism

A more formidable rival to Christianity in the long run came directly from pagan thought: Neoplatonism. Coalescing in Alexandria during the third century, this philosophical school revived and developed the metaphysical and mystical side of Platonic doctrine, explaining the universe as a hierarchy rising from matter to soul, soul to reason, and reason to God, conceived as pure being without matter or form.

Neoplatonists understood reality as the spiritual world contemplated by reason and allowed the material world only a formal existence.

Religious persecution

The first systematic attempts to put an end to Christianity by depriving the church of both its leaders and followers took place under the Emperor Decius (249-251), who ordered Egyptians to participate in pagan worship in the presence of Roman officers and to submit certificates of sacrifice.

Those who refused were declared to be self-avowed Christians and were tortured. Some Christians sent in false certificates; others managed to escape to the solitude of the desert. Many, however, were willing to die rather than abjure their faith; and their martyrdom further accelerated the Christian movement.

Monasticism

St. Paul the Theban, orphaned as a youth, and St. Antony, who came from a family of landowners with a certain status in society, were two of Egypt's earliest and greatest spiritual leaders. Both lived lives of meditation and prayer at about this time.

St. Jerome credits St. Paul the Theban with being the first hermit. In both Coptic and Western tradition, however, St. Antony, whose fame spread as a result of the biography written after his death by Athanasius in 350, holds a more prominent position.

Conversion

The famous revelation of the Emperor Constantine in 312, which resulted in his conversion to Christianity, was followed by the Edict of Milan, according to which Christianity became the favored religion throughout the Roman Empire. It was at last safe to admit to being a Christian in Egypt. Unfortunately, the theological disputes that had plagued the early Christian movement became even fiercer in the fourth and following centuries.

EGYPT, PRIMITIVE GODS

Throughout its history there was always a difference between the official religion, popular folk-religion, and the religion of the occult. Furthermore, the Egyptian pharaoh was himself a god and retained this divine character to the days of the Ptolemies.

A particular phenomenon is the spread of Egyptian religion in the Greco-Roman world: here the syncretism of the times took old Egyptian divinities with those of other provenance (e.g., Osiris with Serapis from Sinope), infusing the rites with Hellenistic piety, reinterpreting them as Hellenistic mysteries or as philosophical cults.

The primitive local gods seem to have had animal forms for the most part; their human behavior led to typically Egyptian representation of such gods in human form with the original animal head or a symbolic part thereof. Some gods, apparently abstract in origin, where always represented in human form. The nature of the gods was expounded by myth; either by the cosmogonic myths produced by the learned activity of clerical circles, or by the popular myths, full of often earthly narrative color, telling of the vicissitudes of well-known divinities. The popular myths, especially those of the Osirian cycle, were subject to constant variation and development, according to the shifting trends of popular preference and the creative imagination of men in different times and places.

The more learned cosmogonic myths, once established, tended to remain stable. The latter type fixed the hierarchical relation of gods to another; such relations, being constructed on the natures of the various divinities concerned, constituted a kind of Egyptian theodicy.

The earliest systems were those of:

▲ Heliopolis, which. reckoning with an Ennead of nine gods and goddesses, explained the origins and perdurance of the universe, admitted select gods into the Ennead's prominence, and gave supremacy to Re (the Sun) as absolute first principle.

▲ Hermopolis, which reckoned with an Ogdoad of four abstract, divine couples at the origins of the world, with Re himself created by them. The rise of Thebes to hegemony (circa 2000 BC) led to a Theban construction placing Amon at the head of the pantheon, but the prevailing solar trend of Egyptian religion brought a blending of Re and Amon.

In the 4th century BC the solar cult itself took a radical turn, when Amenophis IV (Akhenaten) introduced a cult in which the solar disk itself (aten), devoid of all human or animal traits, was worshiped, to the practical exclusion of other gods and the explicit exclusion of the national cult of Amon. The aten cult was monotheistic, but it was neither typical nor successful. The universal character of Re or Amon-Re returned.

EGYPT, ROOTS OF RELIGION

The religion of the ancient Egyptians presents a bewildering complexity in the realm of religious thought, relieved only by a certain unity of religious practice.

The earliest inhabitants of the Nile Valley were hunters who tracked game across northern Africa and eastern Sudan, later joined by nomadic tribes of Asiatic origin who filtered into Egypt in sporadic migrations across the Sinai peninsula and the Red Sea. Late Paleolithic settlements (circa 12,000 BC to 8,000 BC) reveal that both these newcomers and the indigenous inhabitants had a hunting and food-gathering economy.

As a certain rhythm formed in their lives, they observed that the gifts of their naturally irrigated valley depended on a dual force: the sun and the river. The life-giving rays of the sun that cause a crop to grow could also cause it to shrivel and die. And the river that invigorated the soil with mineral-rich deposits could destroy whatever lay in its path or, if it failed to rise sufficiently, bring famine.

These two phenomena, however, shared in the pattern of death and rebirth that left a profound impression on the people: the sun that "died" on the western horizon each evening was "reborn" in the eastern sky the following morning; and the river was directly and unfailingly responsible for the germination or "rebirth" of the crop after the "death" of the land each year. This natural sequence of rebirth after death undoubtedly lay at the root of the ancient Egyptian belief in the afterlife.

Slowly, assimilation took place. Some villages may have emerged as their boundaries expanded; or small groups of people may have gravitated towards larger ones and started to trade and barter with them. Later, the affairs of various communities became tied to major settlements, which undoubtedly represented the richest and most powerful of them.

The tendency towards political unity occurred in both Upper and Lower Egypt. Unification of the two lands has been ascribed to Narmer (Menes) 3100 BC, who set up his capital at Memphis, at the apex of the delta. He stands at the beginning of Egypt's ancient history, which was divided by an Egyptian historian into 30 royal dynasties from Menes to Alexander the Great. The dynasties were subsequently grouped into three major periods:

▲ the Old Kingdom or Pyramid Age (2686-2181 BC);
▲ the Middle Kingdom (2133-1786 BC);
▲ the New Kingdom (1567-1080 BC).

EGYPT, TEMPLES OF

As elsewhere in the Ancient Near East, the earthly house of a god was a temple. The vast temple complexes of the New Kingdom (latter second millennium) and the Ptolemaic period (after 304 BC) show a plan in which a gate led through the massive frontal pylons into a large open court surrounded by porticoes, where the ordinary people gathered on festive occasions.

Beyond this was a dim hall with a roof supported by multiple columns (hypostyle hall) where certain rites were performed in the presence of a privileged few. Further beyond, in darkness, were the god's living quarters, with the shrine containing the divine statue.

The statue was not simply identified with the god: it was vitalized by magic rites which brought about its occupancy by the god's ba, a vital force that enabled its processor to move about and to take on various aspects.

The daily ritual comprised rites based materially on the services performed for a king by his courtiers - a morning wakening, washing, perfuming, incensing, clothing, and the offering of food trice daily.

The words to be spoken and the ritual directives, however, endowed the actions with a sense of recalling and reenacting events in Egyptian mythology, a sense which was even more pronounced in festive liturgies with their mythological drama and mimes celebrating events in the lives of the gods.

Sacrificial offerings (vegetables, fruit, bread, meat, as food for the god), are also shown by ritual words and symbolic actions to have been permeated with mythological and magical concepts.

Certain elements in the cult of the god recur in Egyptian rites having to do with the care of the dead. Offerings of food to the dead were made to the accompaniment of ritual words and gestures analogous to those accompanying offerings of food to a god.

In both cases, however, a statue of the dead person or of the god was magically animated to enable him to receive his food, and in both cases mythology of the Osirian cycle exerted a certain influence in ritual symbolism.

EGYPT, TORRENT VALLEY OF

In Biblical terms, a long wadi (or ravine) marking the God-ordained southwestern boundary of the Promised Land, that is, the "land of Canaan" (numbers 34:2; 1 Kings 8:65). While this torrent valley was not actually in Egypt, that nation's domain apparently extended, at least in certain periods, up to that point (2 Kings 24:7). The valley is usually identified with Wadi el-'Arish, which starts circa 136 miles inland on the Sinai Peninsula, near Jebel et-Tih.

EHUD

In the Old Testament, son of Gera, the Benjaminite, Israelite hero who delivered Israel from 18 years of oppression by the Moabites. A left-handed man, Ehud tricked Eglon, king of Moab, and killed him. He then led the tribe of Ephraim to seize the fords of the Jordan, where they killed circa 10.000 Moabite soldiers. As a result, Israel enjoyed peace for circa 80 years.

EIGHTFOLD PATH

The doctrine taught by Gautama Buddha in his first sermon at the deer park near Benares (Varanasi). Together with the four noble rules of which it forms a part, it sums up the whole of Buddhist teaching.

The eightfold path consist of:

1 right understanding - faith in the Buddhist view of the nature of existence in terms of the four noble truths;
2 right thought - the resolve to practice the faith;
3 right speech - avoidance of falsehoods, slander, or abusive speech;
4 right action - abstention from taking life, stealing, and improper sexual behavior;
5 right livelihood - rejection of occupations not in keeping with Buddhist principles;
6 right effort - avoidance of bad and development of good mental states;
7 right mindfulness - awareness of the body, feelings, and thought;
8 right concentration - meditation.

EIGHT SAINTS, WAR OF THE

(1375-2378) A conflict between Pope Gregory XI and an Italian coalition headed by Florence, which occasioned the papacy's return from Avignon to Rome.

EILEITHYIA

Pre-Hellenistic goddess of childbirth. The earliest evidence of her cult is at Amnisus, in Crete, where excavations indicate that she was worshipped continuously from Neolithic to Roman times.

EKACITTA

In Buddhism, the "one thought-moment" out of time, in which the Zen monk experiences non-duality, that state before the one became the many, before thought was borne.

EKAGGATA

In Buddhism, one-pointedness of mind, rather in limiting sense of reducing other factors in consciousness.

EKAYANA

In Buddhism, a concept that has been interpreted differently within the various schools of Buddhism. In general, the concept is regarded as the distinctive teaching of the Lotus Sutra, which declares that the three customary yanas are merely expedients for imparting instruction to those of differing mental capacities and inclinations.

EKER

In the Old Testament, a son of Ram, Jerahmeel's firstborn, of the tribe of Judah (1 Chronicles 2:4-9).

EKRON

Ancient Canaanite and Philistine city, one of the five cities of the Philistine pentapolis (league of five cities), and currently identified with Tel Miqne, south of the settlement Mazkeret Batya, central Israel.

Ekron was a Philistine stronghold in David's time. During the time of king Ahaziah of Israel, it was associated with the worship of the deity Beelzebub.

EL

The name of the chief deity of the West Semites. In the Old Testament, el was used both as a general term for "deity" and as a synonym for "Yahweh."

ELA

In the Old Testament, father of Shimei, one of Solomon's twelve deputies who provided food for the king and his household (1 Kings 4:7, 18).

ELAH

In Judaism, an Edomite sheik who likely occupied the village of Elath (Genesis 36:40-43). The name is also applied to the fourth king of the northern ten-tribe kingdom of Israel. Elah came to the throne on the death of his father Raasha and ruled in Tirzah for parts of two years circa 952-951 BC (1 Kings 16:8). While Elah was drunk, Zimri, the chief over half the chariots, put him to death to get the kingship for himself and then went on to wipe out all of Raasha's house, to fulfill God's prophecy (1 Kings 16:1-14).

ELAM

In the Old Testament, one of the five sons of Shem from whom descended families, according to their tongues, in their lands, according to their nations (Genesis 10:22; 1 Chronicles 1:17). The names of Elam's sons are not specified; his name, however, designates both a people and a region on the south-western border of Mesopotamia.

The first biblical mention of Elam as a country or nation is in the time of Abraham, when Chedorlaomer "king of Elam" marched with an alliance of the kings against a Canaanite coalition of kings in the Dead Sea region (Genesis 14:1-3). This period of Elamite power in Babylonia was upset and terminated by Hammurabi and it was not until the latter part of the second millennium BC that Elam was able to conquer Babylon and again established control for a period of some centuries. It is believed that it was during this time that a stele bearing the famous Code of Hammurabi was taken from Babylonia to Susa, where modern archaeologists discovered it.

ELAM DEITIES

Principally Inshushinak, Kirrishna, Nahhunte, and Huban, gods of the ancient country of Elam in south-western Iran.

ELASAH

In the Old Testament, the son of Shaphan who with Gemariah, was sent by Zedekiah to Nebuchadnezzar in Babylon. The prophet Jeremiah on that occasion sent his letter to the exiles in Babylon by the hand of Elasah and of Gemariah (Jeremiah 29:1-3).

ELATH

In biblical times, a sit first mentioned in Moses' recapitulation of the Israelites' 40 trek through the wilderness (Deuteronomy 2:8). Elath is mentioned along with Ezion-geber and lay on the shore of the Red Sea in the land of Edom (1 Kings 9:26). This points to a location on the northeastern arm or branch of the Red Sea known as the Gulf of Aqaba. Modern biblical geographers basically agree with Jerome, of the fourth and fifth centuries, who identified Elath with the city then known as Aila, associated with the Nabataeans. This would place Eliath at or near the present-day Arabic city of Aqaba situated at the north-eastern corner of the gulf (the modern Jewish city called Elath being at the north-western corner).

EL-BETHEL

In the Old Testament, the name given by Jacob to the spot where he erected an alter in obedience to God's command (Genesis 35:1,7). It was in this area some twenty years earlier that God revealed himself to Jacob in a dream, promising to protect him. At that time the patriarch was moved to respond, "Truly God is in this place." (Genesis 28:10-22) Since this was the case, when later naming the altar site, Jacob was saying in effect, "God is in Bethel" (Genesis 33:20).

ELDAAH

In the Old Testament, a son of Midian the fourth-named son of Abraham by Keturah (Genesis 25:1-4; 1 Chronicles 1:33).

ELDAD

In the Old Testament, one of the 70 older men selected by Moses to assist him in carrying the load of the people. Because of murmuring on the part of the mixed crowd and also the Israelites about the manna and not having meat to eat, Moses voiced the feeling that the load was too heavy for him alone. Therefore God directed Moses to gather 70 older men and take them to the tent of meeting. Two of these older men, Eldad and Meldad, however, did not go to the tent of meeting but, undoubtedly for a valid reason, remained in the camp. God then proceeded to take some of the spirit that was upon Moses and put it upon the older men; these, in turn, began to prophesy. The spirit also settled upon

Eldad and Meldad and they began to act as prophets in the camp (Numbers 11:13-29).

ELDAD (BEN MAHLI) HA-DANI

(late 9th century) Jewish traveller and philologist who was generally credited with the authorship of a fanciful narrative that exerted an enduring influence throughout the Middle Ages and possibly gave rise to the legend of Prester John, the mighty priest-potentate of fabulous wealth and power.

ELDER

Any of various church officers. The term was derived from the Israelites, who shared it with other Semitic peoples. Moses appointed 70 elders as intermediaries between himself and the people (Numbers 11:16). In the New Testament, elders are mentioned together with bishops (episcopal) as leaders of local churches.

ELDERS

In the Old Testament period prior to the monarchy, the rulers of the tribes; later the rulers or authoritative persons in various localities were so designated, and with the priestly representatives formed the Sanhedrin of Jerusalem.

ELEADAH

In the Old Testament, one of Epharim's descendants (1 Chronicles 7:20).

ELEALEH

In Judaism, a site regularly mentioned with Heshbon and located in the pastoral country east of the Jordan. The tribe of Reuben "built" the city soon after its conquest (Numbers 32:3-5).

ELEASAH

In the Old Testament, son of Helez and father of Sismai, a descendant of Judah through Jerahmeel (1 Chronicles 2:33-40).

ELEAZAR

In Judaism, the third-named son of High Priest Aaron by his wife Elisheba. Eleazar was of the family of Kohath the son of Levi (Exodus 6:16-23). Aaron and his sons, Nadab, Abihu, Eleazar and Ithamar, constituted the priesthood at the time of the installation of Moses. The second year after leaving Egypt, when the tabernacle had been set up, Eleazar is mentioned as being chief of the Levites (Numbers 1:1; 3:32). He must have been 30 years of age at the time, inasmuch as he was performing priestly duties (Numbers 4:3).

ELEAZER

In the Old Testament, a descendant of Parosh among those having taken foreign wives but who followed through on Ezra's exhortation to dismiss them (Ezra 10:25, 44).

ELEAZAR BEN AZARIAH

(late first and early second centuries) Rabbinic scholar whose practical maxims constitute some of the best-known sayings of the Talmud.

ELEAZAR BEN JUDAH OF WORMS

(1160-1238) Rabbi, mystic, Talmudist, and codifier, whose voluminous works are the major extant documents of medieval German Hasidism (a fervent ultrapious sect that stressed prayer and practical mysticism as a means of attaining to God).

ELECTION

In theology, God's free choice of a certain group, or of certain individuals, for an unmerited glorious destiny. Election has thus been applied to the Jewish people as recipients of the Torah and to those who are said to have been predestined to eternal salvation.

ELECTION OF POPES

In the first centuries of Christianity, the pope or bishop of Rome was chosen by the clergy and faithful of that city. The choice became restricted to the higher clergy because of the interference of the Roman Emperors, however; and in 1179 Alexander III formally limited the right of election to the cardinals, establishing at the same time the rule of two-thirds majority for a valid election. The procedures for papal elections have been modified as a result of various experiences and abuses, such as outside political pressures and excessively long conclaves. In modern times, papal elections have been held in Rome, except for the conclave that elected Pius VII in Venice. In the 19th century, several conclaves were held in the Quirinal palace, then the main papal residence, but since 1846 all conclaves have taken place in the Sistine chapel of the Vatican Palace.

The papal conclave, according to existing canons, must open within 15 or at most 18 days after the pope's death, A cardinal elector may be accompanied by an assistant, or perhaps two if his health should require. Radios, telephones, faxes, telegraph, and presumably tape-recorders are forbidden.

All participants are held to secrecy as to the course of voting, even after the conclave, unless the newly elected pontiff should decide otherwise. Balloting takes place twice each day, with two votes taken on each occasion. Cardinals are forbidden from making any preconclave agreement or promises, and any such promises, if made, are declared null and void.

The result of the balloting is indicated to those outside the conclave by black or white (at the time of election) smoke which emerges from a chimney built into the chapel. When the candidate receiving the two-thirds vote formally accepts the decision of the cardinals, he becomes from the minute bishop of Rome, i.e., pope, though the coronation takes place only later.

ELEUSIAN MYSTERIES

In ancient Greece, the secret rites, originally performed in Eleusis but taken over by Athens circa 600 BC, marking the departure to the underworld and return to earth of Persephone (winter and spring). Little is known of the ceremonies, but they seem to have included fasting, ritual purification and sacred "performances."

Before leaving Eleusis, Demeter taught its kings to honor her. The ceremonies connected to the Eleusian Mysteries were only taken part in by the initiates and they kept their secret from the rest of the world. But those who managed to become initiates had a better fate when they went to Hades. Besides the large Eleusian Mysteries performed in Eleusis, Demeter was also honored in smaller ones held in Athens.

ELEUTERIUS, SAINT

(111-189) Pope from circa 175 to 189. During his pontificate the church was involved in a controversy over Monotanism, a movement that arose in Asia Minor among Christians who believed that no spiritual revelations could be achieved through the ecstatic trances of their prophets.

ELEVATION OF MAN

As understood in Roman Catholic theology, the raising of the human creature, perhaps at the time of his creation, perhaps at a later moment, in a state in which it is possible to reach the vision of God.

ELF

In Germanic mythology, diminutive being, usually in tiny male form. Often mischievous, elves caused diseases and evil dreams, stole children, and substituted changelings (deformed or weak elf or fairy children) for them.

EL-GOD

Generic name for the divinity in the ancient Semitic world and title of the supreme god of the Ugaritic pantheon. The name served as a vehicle for God's manifestation of Himself to the Hebrew patriarchs (Genesis 16:13).

ELHANAN

In the Old Testament, the son of Jahr who, in war with the Philistines, struck down Lahmi the brother of Goliath the Gathite (1 Chronicles 20:5).

ELI

In Judaism, a High Priest of Israel; evidently a descendant of Aaron's fourth-named son Ithamar (1 Kings 2:27; 1 Chronicles 24:3). In addition to serving as High Priest, Eli judged Israel for 40 years. Samuel began to be a prophet during his lifetime.

ELIAB

In the Old Testament, son of Helon of the tribe of Zebulum; one of the 12 chieftains designated by God to aid Moses and Aaron in numbering the sons of Israel for the army (Numbers 1:1-4). In addition to sharing in the group representation made by the chieftains after the setting up of the tabernacle, chieftain Eliab thereafter represented his tribe individually in presenting an offering on the third day for the inauguration of the altar (Numbers 7:1-3; 24-29).

ELIAB

One of King David's mighty men; son of Ahithophel (2 Samuel 23:34).

ELIADA

In biblical times, a son of David born at Jerusalem (2 Samuel 5:13-16).

ELIAKIM

In Judaism, son of Hilkiah; chief administrator of the affairs of the house of Hezekiah the king of Judah at the time of the Assyrian king Sennacherib invasion of Judah in 732 BC.

ELIAS OF CORTONA

(1180-1253) Disciple of St. Francis of Assisi and a leading participant in the early history of the Franciscan Order, which he twice governed.

ELIASAPH

In Judaism, son of Deuul of the tribe of Gad; one of the 12 chieftains whom God selected to assist Moses and Aaron in taking the sum of the males for the army (Numbers 1:1-4). Eliasaph was over the army of his tribe, which was a part of the three-tribe division of the camp of Reuben (Numbers 2:10-15). Besides sharing in the group presentation made by the chieftains after the setting up of the tabernacle,

Eliasaph thereafter represented his tribe individually in presenting an offering on the sixth day for the inauguration of the altar (Numbers 7:1-2; 42-47).

ELIATHAH

A son of Hemon who, during the rule of King David, was designated by lot to be a musician in the 20th service group at the house of God (1 Chronicles 25:1; 4-6).

ELIEL

In the Old Testament, one of the heads of the half tribe of Manasseh. Like the other heads, Eliel was a valiant, mighty fellow, a man of fame (1 Chronicles 11:26).
The name is also applied to a Levite of the family of the Kohathites and an ancestor of the prophet Samuel (1 Chronicles 6:33-34).

ELIEZER

In the Old Testament, a man of Damascus and the apparent heir of childless Abraham. Abraham referred to him as "a son of my household" (Genesis 15:2-3). Archaeological discoveries, such as the tablets from Nuzi, shed light on why Abraham considered Eliezer as his heir. Often childless couples adopted a son who would then care for them in old age and arrange for their burial at death, thereupon inheriting the property. It was stipulated, however, that, in the event a son was born to them after the adoption, the real son would become the principal heir.

ELIUH

In the Old Testament, the son of Barachel the Buzite of the family of Ram. As a descendant of Buz, Elihu was evidently a distant relative of Abraham (Job 32:1-6); Genesis 22:20-21). Likely Elihu listened carefully to the entire debate between Job and his three would-be comforters. But, out of due respect for their age, he remained silent until all had finished speaking.

ELIJAH

Hebrew prophet of the 9th century BC, mentioned in the Old Testament book of Kings. He fought against the worship of Baal introduced from Phoenicia during the reign of King Ahab of Israel by his queen, Jezebel. During his own lifetime he had a number of supernatural events ascribed to him including restoring a dead child to life. Elijah was finally taken to heaven in a whirlwind.

In the New Testament Elijah appears with Christ at the Transfiguration.

ELIJAH BEN SOLOMON

(1720-1797) The outstanding authority in Jewish religious and cultural life in 18th century Lithuania.

ELIJAH'S CUP

In Judaism, the fifth ceremonial cup of wine poured during the Seder dinner on Passover. It is left untouched in honor of Elijah, who, according to tradition, will arrive one day as an unknown guest to herald advent of the Messiah.

ELIM

In biblical times, the second encampment location of the Israelites after crossing the Red Sea (Exodus 15:27; Numbers 33:9-10). Although the exact location is not certain, it is traditionally identified with Wadi Gharandel on the Sinai Peninsula, circa fifty-two miles south-south-east of Suez.

ELIMELECH

In the Old Testament, a man of Bethlehem who, because of a famine in the days of the judges, left Judah along with his wife Naomi and their two sons Mahlon and Chilion, and took up alien residence in Moab, where he died (Ruth 1:1-3).

ELIOENAI

In the Old Testament, a son of Neariah and a descendant of King Solomon through Zerubbabel. Elioenai was the father of Hodaviah (1 Chronicles 3:10; 23-24).

ELIPANDUS

(717-808) Archbishop of Toledo, who propounded a doctrine known as adoptionism, that Christ was not the son of nature but by adoption.

ELIPHAL

According to biblical records, the son of Ur among the mighty men of David's military forces. Eliphal may be the Eliphelet of 2 Samuel 23:24 (1 Chronicles 11:26).

ELIPHAZ THE TEMANITE

In the Old Testament book of Job, one of three friends who sought to console Job, who is a biblical archetype of unmerited suffering. The word Temanite probably indicates that he was an Edomite, or member of a Palestinian people descended from Esau.

ELIPHELET

In the Old Testament, son of Ahasbai; one of David's mighty men (2 Samuel 23:34). Eliphelet possibly is the Eliphal of 1 Chronicles 11:35.

ELISHA

Hebrew prophet, a disciple of and successor to Elijah (circa 856 BC). He was plowing when Elijah called him by throwing his mantle on him, a token of investiture. Greatly gifted as a prophet and healer, he was successful in driving out Baal worship from the northern state of Israel.

Like Elijah he acted as the Hebrew King's conscience and managed to engineer the downfall of the dynasty of Omri and the rise of the house of Jehu.

ELISHAH BEN ABUYAH

(circa 100) Jewish free thinker regarded in later years as a prototype of the heretic whose pride of intellect betrays him into infidelity to Jewish laws and morals.

ELISHAH

According to biblical records, son of Javan and a family head whom the "population of the isles of the nations was spread about" (Genesis 10:4-5). The only other biblical mention of Elishah is in the dirge pronounced against Tyre, where the name appears as that of a land or region trading with Tyre.

ELISHAMA

In the Old Testament, son of Ammihud of the tribe of Ephraim; grandfather of Joshua (Numbers 1:10; 2:18; 1 Chronicles 7:26-27). Elishama was one of the 12 chieftains designated by God to assist Moses and Aaron in registering the sons of Israel for the Army. He was also over the army of his tribe (Numbers 1:1-4; 2:18). Besides sharing the group presentation made by the chieftains after the setting up of the tabernacle, Elishama thereafter represented his tribe individually in presenting an offering on the seventh day for the inauguration of the altar (Numbers 7:1-5; 48-53).

ELISHAPHAT

In the Old Testament, one of the chiefs of 100s whom Jehoiada the priest took into covenant and who was among those afterward sent throughout Judah to collect the Levites and the heads of the paternal houses of Israel (2 Chronicles 23:1,2). Elishaphat gave his support to Jehoiada in securing the kingship for Jehoash the rightful heir to the throne and deposing the usurper Athaliah.

ELISHEBA

According to biblical records, one of the sons born to King David in Jerusalem (2 Samuel 5:15; 1 Chronicles 14:5).

ELIZABETH, SAINT

Mother of John the Baptist, wife of the priest Zachary, and relative of Mary. The couple was old and childless when an angel announced to them that Elizabeth was to bear a son. Her feast day is November 5.

ELIZABETH OF HUNGARY, SAINT

(1207-1231) Princess of Hungary whose devotion to the poor (for whom she relinquished her wealth) made her an enduring symbol of Christian charity. Among the best known legends about Elizabeth is the one often depicted in art showing her meeting her husband unexpectedly on one of the charitable errands; the loaves of bread she was carrying were miraculously changed into roses.

ELIZABETH OF PORTUGAL, SAINT

(1271-1336) Daughter of Peter III of Aragon, wife of King Denis of Portugal. She was known for her devout habits and charitable establishments. She was canonized in 1625; her feast day is July 8.

ELIZAPHAN

In the Old Testament, the son of Aaron's uncle Uzziel, who, along with his brother Michael, at Moses' direction, carried the bodies of Nadab and Abihu outside the camp (Exodus 6:22; Leviticus 10:4). Elizaphan was the ancestral head of a Levitical family, members of which are specifically mentioned in the Bible as serving during the reigns of David and Hezekiah (1 Chronicles 15:8; 2 Chronicles 29:13).

ELIZUR

In the Old Testament, a Levite identified along with Assir and Abiasaph as sons of the rebellious Korah, but who did not share the fate of their father (Exodus 6:24; Numbers 26:11).

ELKESAITES

A Judaeo-Christian sect that began in the first century and existed in Palestine and Syria. The name is of Syrian origin, from Elxsai or Elkesai. Whether this was the name of a real person or an esoteric symbol is uncertain. Neither is it clear that in the beginning the Elkesaites were

Christian at all. Nothing is known of them except through the Philosophoumena of Hippolytus, which reports the preaching of Alcibiades, who brought the *Book of Elkesai* to Rome (circa 200).

By this time their doctrine was a mixture of Jewish, Christian, astrological, magical, and Gnostic elements. They practiced circumcision, placed great emphasis on religious ablutions (including repeated baptisms), took a mitigated view of penance, rejected virginity and continence, made marriage mandatory for all, insisted on God's oneness, and denied the divinity of Christ and of the Holy Spirit.

ELLASAR

A kingdom or city over which Arioch reigned in the time of Abraham and Lot (Genesis 14:1).

ELNAAM

In the Old Testament, the father of Jeribai and Joshaviah, two mighty men of David's military forces (1 Chronicles 11:46).

ELNATHAN

According to biblical records, the father of King Jehoiachin's mother Nehushta (2 Kings 24:8).

ELOHIM

A plural of majesty, the term Elohim is usually employed in the Old Testament for the one and only God of Israel, whose personal name was revealed to Moses as YHWH, or Yahweh.

The term Elohim is also used when referring to idol gods. Sometimes this plural form means simply "gods" (Exodus 12:12; 20:23). At Psalms (83:1-6) the term is used for man, human judges in Israel.

ELOHIST SOURCE

One of the four sources that, according to the documentary hypothesis, comprise the original literary constituents of the Pentateuch. It is so called of its use of the Hebrew term Elohim for God.

ELTEKEH

According to biblical records, a city of Dan (Joshua 19:44) given with its pasture ground, to the Kohathite Levites (Joshua 21:20-23).

ELUL

The post-exile name of the sixth Jewish lunar month of the sacred calendar, but the 12th of the secular calendar, corresponding to part of August and part of September.

ELUZAI

In the Old Testament, one of the ambidextrous Benjamite mighty men who joined David at Ziklag while he was still under restrictions because of King Saul (1 Chronicles 12:1-5).

ELVIRA, COUNCIL OF

The first known council of the Christian church in Spain, held early in the 4th century at Elvira, near modern Granada. It is the first council of which the canons have survived, and they provide the earliest reliable information on the Spanish church. The exact date is disputed, but some scholars believe it was held either circa 300-303 or in 309.

ELYMAS

The professional name or title of a certain man, a srocerer, a false prophet, named Bar-Jesus, a Jew who lived on the island of Cyprus in the first century (Acts 13:6-8).

ELYSIAN FIELDS

In Greek mythology the eternal abode to which the blessed were taken after death to dwell in perfect happiness. This place was variously represented as a lovely meadow (Homer) at the western end of the earth, or as the Islands of the Blessed (Hesiod). Much later Elysium came to be regarded as the part of the underworld where the souls, or shades, of the blessed dead remained eternally, as in the Hades described in Virgil's *Aeneid.*

ELYSIUM

Elysian Fields.

ELZABAD

In the Old Testament, one of the swift and courageous men of the tribe of Gad who joined themselves to David in the wilderness while he was still under restriction because of King Saul. The last of these Gadites is described as equal to a 100 and the greatest to a 1,000 (1 Chronicles 12:1; 8-14).

EMANATIONISM

A philosophical and theological theory that sees all of creation as an unwilled, necessary, and spontaneous outflow of contingent beings of descending perfection - from an infinite, undiminished, unchanged primary substance.

Hints of this doctrine occur in the first two centuries in the writings of Philo, a Hellenistic Jewish philosopher, and of Basilides and Valentius, both founders of Gnostic schools; but its classic formulation is found in Neoplatonists such as Plotinus and Proclus.

Emanationism was also a feature of Gnosticism, which in some cases posited a large number of emanations, and creation of the world by a lower, imperfect being. A consequence of the theory was that man's plight was understood as his involvement in the material world, rather than as his sin. Redemption, consequently, was seen as escape from the material world and reascent to God.

It has also influenced Jewish and Muslim thought. It was expressly condemned by Vatican Council I.

EMBALMING

The treatment of a body so as to sterilize it or to protect it from decay by means of spices (Genesis 50:2).

The Egyptians seem to have regarded the preservation of a person's mummy as essential to an eventual reunion of his body with his soul, which they believed to be immortal, this reunion being mentioned in the Egyptian Book of the Dead. They also appear to have thought that survival of an individual's soul was dependent upon the preservation of his body.

There are only two cases specifically called embalming in the Bible and both of these took place in Egypt. It was there that Jacob died and after relating Joseph's expression of sorrow over his father's demise, the following statement can be read: "After that Joseph commanded his servants and the physicians to embalm his father. So the physicians embalmed Israel, and they took fully 40 days for him, for this many days they customarily take for the embalming, and the Egyptians continued to shed tears for him 70 days" (Genesis 50:2-3). Joseph died at the age of 110 years, "and they had him embalmed, and he was put in a coffin in Egypt" (Genesis 50:26). Being faithful Hebrews, Jacob and Joseph knew that humans do not possess an immortal soul (Genesis 2:7; 3:17-19). Hence, they did not share Egyptian false religious views associated with embalming and the soul. In Jacob's case the principal purpose appoarently was [preservation until his burial in the Promised Land. Joseph's prominence may have been the reason in this case (Genesis 49:29-32; Exodus 13:18-19; Joshua 24:32).

EMBER DAYS, EMBER WEEKS

In the Roman Catholic and Anglican churches, four "times" set apart for special prayer and fasting for the ordination of the clergy. The Ember Weeks are the complete weeks following

1 Holy Cross Day (September 14);
2 The Feast of St. Lucy (December 13);
3 The first Sunday in Lent;
4 Pentecost (Whitsunday).

The current practice is to compute the Ember Days as the Wednesday, Friday, and Saterday following the third Sunday of Advent, the first Sunday of Lent, Pentecost Sunday, and the third Sunday of September.

EMBURY, PHILIP

(1728-1775) Preacher and one of the founders of Methodism in the United States. Converted after a religiuous experience on Christmas Day, 1752, he was soon recognized as a potential leader and was licensed as a local preacher. He organized the first Methodist society north of New York City in Camden and continued until his death to preach and to act as the civil magistrate.

EMDEN, JACOB ISRAEL

(1679-1776) Rabbi and Talmudic scholar primarily known for his distinguished writings that fall into two categories; those of a polemic nature, in which he attacked Sabbataian heresies, and religious commentaries. His diary is revealing as a record of Jewish thought in his time, and his critical study of the Zohar, a part of the influential body of Jewish mystical writings known as the Kabbala, made clear that it was the work of several hands.

EMEK-KEZIZ

According to biblical records, a Benjamite city (Joshua 18:21). The meaning of its name and its mention along with Jericho in the Jordan valley may indicate a location in that vicinity.

EMIM

In the Old Testament, a tribe or people that dwelt in the terrritory east of the Dead Sea. They are described as being great, numerous and tall "like the Anakim" (Deuteronomy 2:10). This comparison with the sons of Anak indicates that the Emim were giantlike in stature and fierce.

EMINENTLY

A scholastic term qualifying the higher mode of existence that certain created predicates, e.g., goodness, truth, justice, have as they are attributed to the divine being.

EMMANUEL

Name given to Christ by Matthew (Matthew 1:23) after Isaiah 7:14. Emmanuel ("God-man") refers to the human nature and the divine in Christ.

EMMAUS

According to biblical records, a village toward which Cleopas and a fellow disciple were journeying when they were joined by the m,aterialized Jesus Christ on the day of the resurrection. It was not, however, until after they reached Emmaus and Jesus "was reclining with them at the meal" that they recognized him. Following Jesus' subsequent disappearance the two disciples returned to Jerusalem that same evening (Luke 24:13-33).

EMOTIONALISM

Here understood as an excessive emphasis upon emotions in religion. Wih the rise of revivalism in the 18th century, emotionalism became a controversial factor in mainstream American Protestantism. Earlier Puritans had stressed inward experience as a sign of regeneration, but this experience did not commonly include a loss of emotional control.

The Great Awakening (18th century), however, introduced a type of preaching that often included anxiety and deplored such displays of feeling. In the 20th century, Billy Sunday was criticized for his use of sensational methods; the revivals of Billy Graham are much more moderate and controlled. Today there is little evidence of emotionalism in most Protestant services, but in Pentecostalism glossolalia (tongues-speaking) and other outward manifestations are regarded as evidence of the Holy Spirit's presence.

Debates continue over the line between appeals to emotions that are essential to the religious experience of human beings and "emotionalism."

EMSER, HIERONYMOUS

(1478-1527) Theologian remembered for his long public controversy with Martin Luther at the onset of the Reformation.

ENAIM

In the Old Testament, a site near which Tamar, disguised as a prostitute, cohabited with Judah, resulting in the birth of Perez and Zerah (Genesis 38:14-16; 29-30). Enaim was apparently situated between Adullam and Timnah (Joshua 15:34).

ENARXIS

A term applied in the Byzantine Church to:
▲ the beginning of any ceremony or ecclesiastical office;
▲ the section of the liturgy between the preparation of the gifts and the little entrance consisting of three diaconal litanies by a variable antiphon sung by the choir and/or people. The celebrant meanwhile silently recites the antiphon at the altar. This foreliturgy which precedes the liturgy of the word was inserted circa the ninth century.

ENCLAVE CITIES

In biblical times, cities of a particular people or tribe that are enclosed within the territory of a different tribe.

In the division of the Promised Land among the 12 tribes, there were cities within the general territory of one tribe that were held by another tribe. According to Joshua 16:9, "the sons of Ephraim had enclave cities in the midst of the inheritance of the sons of Manasseh" (Joshua 17:8-9). Soms of the sons of Manasseh resided in towns within the boundaries of Issachar and Asher (Joshua 17:11; 1 Chronicles 7:29).

Simeon's inheritance consisted of cities all of which were located in Judah's territory, because the latter's allotment "proved to be too large for them" (Joshua 21:3-41).

ENCOUNTER

A concept that in contemporary theology is particularly associated with Emil Brunner (1889-1966), for whom the source of religious truth was God's personal act of meeting with man.

Those who stress the personal encounter also understand the response demanded from man to be personal, a decision to repent and to act in accordance with the command of God. This is in contrast with the view that would understand man's proper response to be primarily the intellectual acceptance of propositional statements, or, by subjectivists, the full realization of his own nature.

Belief is understood by those who stress encounter as an attitude that is revealed in personal obedience rather than in acceptance of doctrinal statements about God and His nature. The emphasis upon encounter is a reaction against both the objectivity of orthodoxy and its emphasis on right belief and against the subjectivity of Pietism and its emphasis upon inner feelings.

Encounter seeks to correlate in the manner of dialectical theology the objectivity of the word of God and the subjectivity of faith, maintaining the fully personal character of both.

ENCRATITES

A gnostic sect - i.e. a group of religious dualists who believed that matter was evil and the spirit good and that salvation was gained by esoteric knowledge, or gnosis.

The Encratites were led (perhaps even founded) by Tatian, a second-century Syrian rhetorician who converted to Christianity while studying in Rome under the Christian apologist Justin Martyr.

ENCYCLICAL, PAPAL

In modern times a circular letter addressed by the pope to the bishops of the Roman Catholic Church. Papal encyclicals are statements concerned with the general welfare of the faithful and usually set out guidelines for the application of the theological and social teachings of the church. Catholics are bound to accept any doctrinal teachings they may contain. Encyclicals are known by their opening words.

EN-DOR

In biblical times, a plains city located in the territory of Issachar but assigned to Manasseh. The Cannanites there were not entirely dispossessed but came under forced labor (Joshua 17:11-13). En-dor is usually identified with the modern site of the same name, about midway between Megiddo and the southern end of the Sea of Galilee.

ENDOWMENTS

Among Mormons the name for the secret temple rites in which only Mormons in good standing participate. Among those is the celebration of Mormon celestial marriages.

ENDYMION

In Greek mythology, the son of Aethlius and king of Elis. He was loved by Selene, goddess of the moon by whom he had 50 daughters.

EN-EGLAIM

Specific site mentioned in the Old Testament. In a symbolic vision given to Ezekiel the salt-laden waters of the Dead Sea were to be "healed" and fishers were to stand on its shore from En-gedi up to En-eglaim (Ezekiel 47:8-10).

ENERGIES, DIVINE

In Byzantine theology, the term describing the presence and action of God-in-self-revelation, or God-outside-Himself, as opposed in the existence of God-in-Himself. The distinction between the divine energies and the divine essence of God, although constant in the Eastern patristic tradition, was formulated with greatest precision by Gregory Palamas (died 1359).

According to Gregory, whose doctrine was officially adopted by the Orthodox Church, the essence of God is absolutely unknowable and totally incomprehensible to creaturely understanding.

Both in this age of God's kingdom, as well as in the ages to come, man, as well as the angelic powers, can never know the essence of God.

Nevertheless, God is known by creatures. Even in this world the knowledge of God is possible for men, and union with divine reality is given. This is so because of the divine energies of God through which He Himself becomes accesible to creatures both in this age, through Christ and the Holy Spirit, as well as the kingdom to come.

The divine energies are substantial and natural, i.e., they are of the substance and nature of God. They are eternal, uncreated, and inseparable from the Godhead. They are countless in number, and, unlike the divine essence, they are communicable, distinguishable, separable, namable, and accesible to men.

Thus, they are not created entities, symbolic manifestations or fabricated signs of God's presence. They are the presence of God himself. When a man is in union with God and has a knowledge of Him through the divine energies, it is indeed God Himself who is met and is known, and nothing else. Through the divine energies, he grants and redeems the world.

Through the energies, He grants to creatures the deifying life in union with Himself and His own divine and uncreated nature. Therefore, in and through the divine energies, the essential unknowability of God is preserved, while the genuine communion which He desires for all creation with Himself is made possible.

In theological literature, synonyms for the divine energies are divine actions, operations, emanations, outpourings, manifestations, powers.

ENERGUMEN

Literally, one who is agitated; a term used in the early church for a person thought to be possessed by the devil and in need for exorcism.

EN-GANNIM

In biblical times, a Judaean city in the Shephelah or lowlands mentioned in the same group as Adullam at Joshua 15:33-35.

ENGLAND, CHURCH OF

The English national church that traces its history back to the arrival of Christianity in Britain during the second century and the original church of the Anglican Communion since the 16th century Protestant Reformation. As the successor of the Anglo-Saxon and medieval English church, it has valued and preserved much of the traditional framework of medieval Catholicism in church government, liturgy, and customs, while it also has usually held the fundamentals of Reformation faith.

EN-HADDAH

In biblical times, a city of Issachar, likely near En-gammin (Joshua 19:17-21). It is generally identified with el-Jaddetheh, six miles east of Mount Tabor.

EN-HAZOR

A fortified city of the tribe of Naphtali (Joshua 19:32-37).

ENLIGHTENMENT

A movement of thought and belief concerned with the interrelated concepts of God,reason, nature, and man that claimed wide assent among European intellectuals in the 17th and 18th centuries; its basic conviction was that through reason mankind could find knowledge and happiness.

Buddhism rests historically on the fact that Gautama Siddhartha became Buddha, a word meaning (fully) enlightened or awakened. Both meanings imply freedom from the mind's limitations, and the expansion of this mind until one with All-Mind and commensurate with the universe. This is the goal of every Buddhist, to break through the barriers of thought to the non-duality which lies beyond the One and the Many, and all others of the "pairs of opposite."

ENLIL

A divinity in the Mesopotamian pantheon; originally a god of wind or air, then a mountain god, then the god of earth and a member of the great cosmic triad along with Anu and Enki, or Ea. Evidence suggests that he even tended to rival Anu in supremacy in the pantheon, but he normally remained second in rank.

Enlil was the god who presided over the government and ordering of the earth, upheld earthly laws, and punished those guilty of breaking them.

ENMITY

A sin of the flesh, cataloged in the Letter to the Galatians, that prevents a person from inheriting the kingdom of God.

ENOCH

According to biblical records, the son born to Jared at the age of 162' the seventh man in the genealogical line from Adam. In addition to Methuselah, who was born to him when he was 65 years old, Enoch had other sons and daughters. Enoch was one of the "so great a cloud of witnesses" who were outstanding examples of faith in ancient times. Enoch kept walking with the true God (Genesis 5:18; 21-24). As a prophet, he foretold God's coming with His holy myriads to execute judgment against the ungodly (Jude 14, 15). Likely persecution was brought against him because of his prophesying. However, God did not permit the opposers to kill Enoch.

Enoch is not the writer of the Book of Enoch. This is an uninspired, apocryphal book written many centuries later, probably sometime during the second and first centuries BC.

ENOCH, FIRST BOOK OF

A pseudepigraphical work (one in style and content authentic biblical literature, but noncanonical). Enoch, the seventh patriarch in the book of Genesis, was the subject of abundant apocryphal literature, especially during the Hellenistic period of Judaism (3rd century BC to 3rd century AD). At first revered only for his piety, he was later believed to be the recipient of secret knowledge from God.

ENOCH, SECOND BOOK OF

A pseudepigraphical work, based on an old Jewish work written sometimes in the first century AD. The first part of the book (chapters 1-21) deals with Enoch's journey through the seven tiers of heaven; it thus invites comparisons with descriptions of the heavenly spheres and their inhabitants in *The Testament of Levi*.

The second section (chapters 22-38) is an explication of the tradition of Enoch's reception of secret wisdom from God. The final section (chapters 39-68) includes Enoch's advice to his sons and an account of his life, including his final ascension.

ENOSH

In the Old Testament, the son of Seth, born to him at the age of 105. Enosh was 90 years old when he became father of Kenan, and lived, according to biblical records, a total of 905 years (genesis 5:6-11). His name is also listed in the genealogies at 1 Chronicles 1:1 and Luke 3:38.

EN-RIMMON

In biblical times, a city of Judah mentioned after the captivity as being inhabited by sons of Judah. Its name may be a combination of Ain and Rimmon, mentioned at Joshua 15:32 and 1 Chronicles 4:32.

EN-ROGEL

A spring or well near Jerusalen that marked the boundary between Judah and benjamin (Joshua 15:7). David's spies waited at Enrogel for intelligence concerning Absalom's rebellion (2 Samuel 17:17). Near here David's other rebellious son Adonijah later held a feast to enlist support for his unsurpation of the throne (1 Kings 1:9).

EN-SHEMISH

In biblical times, a site on the boundary between the territorial inheritances of Benjamin and Judah (Joshua 15:1-7). It is generally identified with Ain el-Hod circa three miles east of Jerusalem, the last spring found on the Jerusalem-Jericho road before eaching the Jordan valley.

EN-TAPPUAH

In biblical times, name given to a spring by the city of Tappuah, used as a point of definition of the boundary between the inheritance of the tribe of Manasseh and that of Ephraim (Joshua 17:7). The name may have been also used for the city of Tappuah itself (Joshua 17:8).

ENTRANCE, GREAT

In the Eastern churches originally a procession in which the clergy moved from the nave into the sanctuary for the Liturgy of the Faithful. In the Byzantine and Armenian liturgies it has evolved into the procession in the early part of the Liturgy of the Faithful. The priest and deacon, accompanied by the lesser ministers, carry the bread and wine from the table of prothesis down the side aisle, where the gifts are laid on the altar.

ENTRANCE, LITTLE

In the Eastern churches originally the entrance of the clergy into the church for the beginning of the liturgy. Today, in the Byzantine liturgy, it has been transformed into a short procession in which the priest, the deacon carrying the gospel book, and the lesser minsters come from the north door of the iconostasis and move directly to the central door, through which the priest and deacon enter the sanctuary, where the deacon places the book on the altar.

EPAENETUS

A Christian in the congregation at Rome whom Paul mentions by name and to whom he sends personal greetings (Romans 16:5).

EPANAGOGE

Legal code compiled circa 879, during the reign of the Byzantine emperor Basil I (867-886), intended to be the introduction to a comprehensive collection of laws to be published in Greek. Its chief importance lies in its exposition of the theory of the separation of the powers of church and state.

EPAPHRAS

A faithful minister of Christ who, by preaching the good news, acquainted the Collosians with the undeserved kindness of God, and thus very likely was instrumental in establishing the congregation at Collosae. At the time of apostle Paul's first imprisonment, Epaphras came to Rome, bringing an encouraging report in regard to the love and steadfastness of the Collosian congregation.

EPAPHRODITUS

A trustworthy member of the Christian congregation at Philippi, Macedonia, who was sent with a gift to apostle Paul, then a prisoner at Rome circa 60-61 (Philippians 3:25; 4:18).

EPARCHY

A term used in the Eastern church to signify a diocese.

EPHAI

In the Old Testament, a Netophathite (Jeremiah 40:8) of the tribe of Judah (1 Chronicles 2:50-54) whose sons were among the chiefs of the military forces who were not taken into Babylonian exile in 607 BC.

EPHER

In the Old Testament, one of the seven heads of the half tribe of Manasseh. These family heads are described as valiant, mighty men. Their descendants were unfaitful toward God and therefore God allowed the king of Assyria to take them into exile (1 Chronicles 5:23-26).

EPHESIANS, LETTER TO

New Testament book written by Paul probably during his first imprisonment in Rome circa 62. The letter points out that the Christian gospel of salvation, first revealed to the Apostles, is the source of true wisdom and that salvation through Christ is offered to Jews and Gentiles alike. Paul affirms that there is but one Lord, who united all things in Christ, through whose death all men are redeemed (4:5-6). The author exhorts his readers - parents and children, masters and slaves - to lead exemplary Christian lives and to arm themselves with the shield of faith, helmet of salvation, sword of the spirit in order to resist the devil (6:16-17).

EPHESUS

The most important Greek city in Asia Minor located on the banks of the Cayster and circa forty miles south-east of Smyrna. It was the capital of pro-consular Asia. The city became famous through its connection with the nearby sanctuary of the goddess Artemis (Diana). The original temple (Artemisium) was destroyed in 356 BC and was rebuilt even more sumptuously, to becomen one of the seven wonders of the Ancient World. Under the Romans, Ephesus became the chief port and trading center of Asia Minor and the residence of the pro-consul. Between 55 and 58 the Apostle Paul used Ephesus as the base for his proselytizing activities. Excavations in the late 19th century have uncovered important parts of the ancient Greek temple and city.

EPHESUS, COUNCILS OF

Three assemblies held in Asia Minor to resolve the problems of the early Christian church.

In 190, Polycrates, bishop of Ephesus, convened a synod to establish the 14th of Nisan (the date of the Jewish Passover) as the official date of Easter.

In 431 Pope Celestine I commisioned Cyril, patriarch of Alexandria, to conduct proceedings against Nestorius, his longtime adversary, whose doctrine of two persons in Christ the pope had previously condemned.

In 449 Emperor Theodosius II convened a council in Ephesus to uphold the Monophysite Eutyches in his battle against Flavian, who, as patriarch of Constantinople, championed the doctrine of two natures of Christ.

EPHLAL

In Judaism, the son of Zabad of the family of Jerahmeel and the father of Obed. Ephlal was a descendant of Perez, a son of Judah by Tamar. His great-great-grandfather was an Egyptian, Jarha, to whom his master Sheshan gave his daughter as wife, inasmuch as Sheshan had no sons (1 Chronicles 2:4-9; 34-37).

EPHOD

Part of the ceremonial dress of the High Priest of ancient Israel described in the Old Testament (Exodus 28:6-8). It was worn outside the robe and probably kept in place by a girdle and by shoulder pieces, from which hung the breast piece (or pouch) containting the sacred lots, Urim and Thummim.

A similar vestment, made of linen, was worn by persons other than the High Priest. Samual wore the ephod when he served before the tabernacle at Shiloh, as did David when he danced before the ark at its entry into Jerusalem.

EPHPATHA

An Aramaic expression used by Jesus at the time he healed a deaf man with a speech impediment (Mark 7:32-34).

EPHRAEM SYRUS, SAINT

(born circa 306) Christian theologian, and Doctor of the Church who, as doctrinal consultant to Eastern churchmen, composed numerous theological-biblical commentaries and polemical works that, in witnessing to the common Christian tradition, have exerted widespread influence on the Greek and Latin churches. He is recognized as the mosty authorative representative of 4th century Syriac Christianity.

EPHRAIM

One of the 12 tribes of Israel that in biblical times comprised the people of Israel who later became the Jewish people. The tribe was named after one of the younger sons of Joseph, himself a son of Jacob.

In 930 BC the tribe of Ephraim led the 10 northern tribes in a successful revolt against the south and established the Kingdom of Israel, with Jeroboam I, an Ephraimite, as king.

EPHRAIN

A city taken by King Abijah of Judah in his battle against Jeroboam of Israel (2 Chronicles 13:19). It was evidently in the territory of the tribe of Ephraim mentioned at 2 Samuel 13:23 and also at John 11:54.

EPHRATA COMMUNITY

Protestant monastic settlement in the United States, an offshoot of the Germantown Dunkers, founded in 1732 by Johann Conrad Beissel on Cocalico Creek in Lancaster County, Pannsylvania. In the Ephrata cloisters the members, both men and women, were celibate, worked hard, ate a mainly vegetarian diet, and lived in tiny cells, where they slept on benches with wooden blocks as pillows, interrupting their sleep for lengthy prayer vigils. In the 1810s the members reorganized themselves as the Seventh Day Baptists. In the late 20th century the church had three churches and circa 200 members.

EPHRATAH

In the Old Testament tradition, the wife of Caleb son of Hezron of the tribe of Judah. She married Caleb during the Egyptian captivity after the death of his wife Azubah. Ephratah became the mother of Hur and in time the great-grandmother of Bezalel, the skilled craftsman so famous in the building of the tabernacle (1 Chronicles 2:9-19; Exodus 35:30-35).

EPHRON

In the Old Testament, a Hittite son of Zohar who owned a field in Machpelah in front of Mamre, that is, in Hebren. In circa 1880 BC Abraham purchased this field from Ephron, together with the cave located in it, as a burial place for his wife Sarah (Genesis 23:3-20).

EPICLESIS

In Eastern Orthodoxy, the special invocation of the Holy Spirit in the Christian eucharistic prayer. In the Western church, the term denotes an intercessory prayer in which the priest asks God the Father to send down the Holy Spirit so that the bread and wine at Mass may be changed to the body and blood of Jesus Christ.

EPICTETUS

(born circa 55). Philosopher associated with the Stoics, remembered for the religious tone of his teachings, which commended him to numerous Christian thinkers.

EPICUREANS

Followers of the Greek philosopher Epicurus.

EPICURUS

Greek philosopher who lived from 341 to 270 BC. The philosophy, flourishing for over seven centuries, was characterized by a complete absence of principle. Lawbreaking was counseled against simply because of the shame associated with detection and the punishment it might bring. Living in fear of being found out and/or punished would take away from pleasure, and this made even secret wrongdoing inadvisable. To the Epicureans, virtue in itself had no value and was only beneficial when it served as a means to gain happiness. Reproducity was recommended because it paid off. Friendships rested on the same selfish basis, that is, the pleasure resulting to the possessor. While the pursuit of pleasure formed the focal point of the philosophy, paradoxically Epicurus referred to life as a "bitter gift."

The Epicureans believed in the existence of gods, but that they, just like everything else, were made of atoms, though of finer texture. It was thought that the gods were too far away from the earth to have any interest in what man was doing, so it did not do any good to pray or to sacrifice to them. The gods, they believed, did not create the universe, nor did they inflict punishment or bestow blessings on anyone, but they were supremely happy, and this was the goal to strive for during one's life. However, the Epicureans contended that the gods were in no position to aid anyone in this, that life came into existence by accident in a mechanical universe, and that death ends everything, liberating the individual from the nightmare of life. Although it was believed that man has a soul, the soul was thought to be composed of atoms that dissolved at the death of the body, just as water spills out of a pitcher that breaks.

EPIPHANIUS, SAINT

(circa 315 - circa 403) Bishop noted in the history of the early Christian church for his struggle against beliefs he considered heretical.

EPIPHANY

(from Greek epiphania, manifestation). Feast of the church year held on January 6th. Originating in the third century in the Eastern church, where it commemorates Christ's baptism, it came into the Western church in the fourth century anmd there celebrates the manifestation of Christ to the gentiles, represented by the Magi.

EPISCOPACY

In some Christian churches, the office of a bishop and the system of church government based on the three orders, or offices, of the ministry: bishops, priests, and deacons. The origins of episcopacy are obscure, but by the second century it was becoming established in the main centers of Christianity. It was closely tied to the idea of apostolic succession, the belief that bishops can trace their office in a direct, uninterrupted line back to the Apostles of Jesus.

EPISCOPAL CHURCH, PROTESTANT

Religious denomination in the United States, formed as a successor to the Church of England in the American colonies, it remains a member of the

Anglican communion, an association of 19 self-governing Anglican churches around the world. The church was brought to the Virginia Colony in 1607 and became a separate denomination in 1789 when it adopted a constitution at Philadelphia, calling itself the Protestrant Episcopal Church. With a membership of over 4 million, organized in over 8,000 congregations divided into more than 100 dioceses, it is served by an administrative body in New York known as the Executive Council and governed by a triennial General Convention of clergy and layman.

Like the Church of England, the Episcopal Church is distinctively Protestant in its teaching concerning the Bible, but retains its pre-Reformation heritage in many other respects, for example in much of its liturgy.

The denomination adheres to the *Book of Common Prayer*, and accepts the Apostles' and Nicene Creeds, and the Thirty-nine Articles. Baptism and Communion are the two essential sacraments, and the Bible is recognized as the final authority in all matters and doctrines. The episcopate remains the symbol of unity in the church and of the unbroken succession of the church's ministry.

EPISCOPAL CONFERENCE

In the Roman Catholic Church, a gathering of the bishops of a given region or nation at fixed times to discuss matters of common interest, to formulate collective statements, to coordinate service agencies of the church in the region, and in some circumstances to legislate.

EPISCOPIUS, SIMON

(1583-1643) Also called Simon Biscop, bishop of bishops, Dutch theologian, the systematizer of Arminianism, a liberal reaction to the doctrine of predestination asserting that God's sovereignty and man's free will are compatible.

EPISCOPI VAGANTES

In Christianity, bishops without authority or without recognition in any major Christian church; it is a Latin term meaning "wandering bishops." Such bishops have been properly consecrated but were not assigned to a diocese or were deprived of their diocese for some reason or were excommunicated by their church; or they may have received an irregular consecration by another bishop.

EPISTLE

Originally simply a letter, it later came to signify a special, formal letter of which the best known examples are the 21 epistles in the New Testament. Of these, 14 are attributed to Paul, two to Peter, three to John, one to James and one to Jude. Those ascribed to Paul are known as Pauline epistles, while the others are called Catholic or general epistles, as those in the ancient world generally, in that they are documenmts arising out of special circumstances but treated in such a manner as to expound general principles.

In the post-apostolic age, the epistles written by the Christian fathers Cyprian, Ambrose, Augustine and Jerome were between churches rather than individuals. In classical times the epistle came to have the additional meaning of imperial decree; in poetic form epistles reached a height in the moral and philosophical epistles of Horace. In modern times their greatest literary exponent was Alexander Pope in his verse epistles.

EPITAPH

Originally an inscription on a tomb or memorial, but now also any commemorative lines or verse. The earliest examples, consisting of name, status and a prayer, are on Egyptian sarcophagi.

EPONA

In Roman religion, goddess of horses, asses, and mules. The cult of Epona was probably not introduced into Rome before imperial times, when she was often called Augusta and invoked on behalf of the emperor and of the imperial house.

EQUANIMITY

In Buddhism, one of the aims of meditation.

ER

In the Old Testament, Judah's firstborn son by his Canaanite wife. His father took Tamar as a wife for him, but, because Er proved to be wicked in the eyes of God, He put him to death before he was able to father any offspring (Genesis 38:1-7).

ERASMUS, SAINT

(died circa 303) Early Christian bishop, martyr, and one of the patron saints of sailors. He is reported to have been bishop of Formia, where he was martyred, probably during the persecution of Christians by the Roman emperor Diocletian.

ERASTIANISM

Doctrine that the state should have complete control over the affairs of the church. It is named for Erastus who, in fact, believed only a Christian state could administer church discipline.

ERASTUS

A Christian who ministered to apostle Paul on his third missionary tour and whom Paul sent from Asia to Macedonia along with Timothy (Acts 19:22). Likely he is the Erastus who remained in Corinth at the time Paul wrote his second letter to Timothy (2 Timothy 4:20).

ERASTUS, THOMAS

(1524-1583) Swiss physician for whom Erastianism was named. An adherent of Zwingli, he clashed with the Calvinists, particularly over the practice of excommunication, which he opposed.

ERATO

In Greek religion, one of the nine muses, the patron of lyric poetry or hymns.

She was traditionally the mother of the Thracian poet Thamyris who, after boasting that he could surpass the Muses in song, was at once struck blind and dumb by them.

ERECH

One of the four cities constituting the "beginning of Nimrod's kingdom" in the land of Shinar (Genesis 10:10). Erech is today represented by a cluster of mounds at the site called Warka by the Arabs and known as Uruk to the ancient Akkadians of Mesopotamia.

ERESHKIGAL

In Mesopotamian religion, goddess who was the Lady of the Great Place (i.e., the abode of the dead) and in texts of the third millenium BC wife of the God Ninazu.

ERIDU GENESIS

In Mesopotamian religious literature, ancient Sumerian epic primarily concerned with the creation of the world, the building of cities, and the flood. After the universe was created out of the primeval sea, and the gods were given birth, the deities in turn fashioned man from clay to cultivate the ground, care for flocks, and perpetuate the worship of the gods.

ERIGONE

In Greek mythology, daughter of Icarus, the hero of the Attic deme (township) of Icaria.

ERINYES

In Greek mythology, the name given to the demons of vengeance. They were probably personified curses, but possibly in origin they were ghosts of the murdered; in Roman literature they were called furies.

ERIS

In Greek mythology, the personification of strife, daughter of Night, and sister and companion of Ares. Eris is best known for her part in starting the Trojan War.

EROS

In Greek religion, god of love. He was a primeval god, son of Chaos, the original primeval emptiness of the universe; but later tradition made him the son of Aphrodite, goddess of sexual love and beauty, by Zeus, Ares, or Hermes.

The naked boy with gold wings on his shoulders, curly hair and the bow from which he shoots his magic arrows, was for the ancient Greeks the son of Aphrodite and Ares long before he became the darling of the poets, painters and sculptors.

The wounder of the hearts of gods and men was regarded as the most beautiful of the gods because he inspired in them the finest feeling and helped to unite couples. Right from the beginning, Eros could soften the hardest heart and the roughest character among men, bringing beauty and meaning to life.

ESAGILA

Most important temple complex in Babylon, dedicated to the god Marduk, the tutelary deity of that city.

ESAR-HADDON

In Biblical times, a younger son and successor of Sen-nacherib, king of Assyria. In one of his inscriptions Esarhaddon confirms the scriptural account of his father's death (Isaiah 37:37-38), saying: 'A firm determination fell upon my brothers. They forsook the gods and turned to their deeds of violence, plotting evil... To gain the kingship they slew Sennacherib their father."

ESAU

Also called Edom, in the Old Testament (Genesis 25:19-34) son of Isaac and Rebekah, elder twin brother of Jacob, and the ancestor of the Edomites. At birth, Esau was red and hairy, and he became a wandering hunter, while Jacob was a shepherd. Although younger, Jacob dominated him by deception.

ESCHATOLOGICAL ETHICS

Moral preaching charged with eschatos, the furthest, or news of the "last things," death, judgment, heaven, hell, the end of time, the second coming of Christ.

Judaic teaching held that history was moving toward an end when men would be brought suddenly to salvation and condemnation. This was the background for the Christian teaching.

Three stages can be distinguished in eschatological ethics.

▲ First, the attitude towards life and the manner of living of Christians who expected the end at once.

▲ Second, when the sense of impending doom lifted, Christians grew aware of the gift given them in the power and promises of Christ and began to live their lives accordingly.

▲ Finally, and now more prevalent, it means how each Christian should stand and live, in view of the fact that each will die soon enough and some before judgment and that "we have here no lasting home" (Hebrews 13:14).

ESCHATOLOGICAL THEOLOGY

The theology named for its orientation is eschatology, the doctrine concerning the final outcome of the universe and humanity. As a result of the revival of biblical studies, it is one of the emphases that have characterized theology in the first half of the 20th century. The term was widely used by the historians of religion when they spoke of the beliefs of the Egyptians, Babylonians, Persians, Greeks, Romans, etc.

In Roman Catholicism, some authorities feel that Christianity is carried along toward the future and the coming of Christ by a powerful dynamism, though some think the future bodes ill for the universe. Others hold that human progress can be turned into good or evil, depending upon the use Christians make of it.

ESCHATOLOGISM

The interpretation of the gospels as proclaiming the imminent eschaton, the end time when the Kingdom of God is to be established on earth. The Gospel message shows that Jesus fits into the setting of Jewish apocalyptic myth at this period as one who became gradually conscious of his messianic and apocalyptic mission.

The message proclaiming the imminence of the kingdom is world-negating, the proclamation being unfulfilled; future Christians can still learn both its world negation and the world affirmation contained in Jesus' ethic of love.

ESCHATOLOGY

A theological term indicating the "doctrine of last things." In the Old Testament, this concept of the end of days is only introduced in the later prophets, such as Ezekiel and Isaiah. There it is spoken of vaguely as a time when everyone would come to believe in God, when justice would reign, and all the earth would live in peace. The concept was made more specific in the Book of Daniel and in the post-biblical writings, when, concerned by Roman oppression, the Jews conceived of a divine redemption that would come in their time. This was also the position of the early Christian church whose members looked forward to the imminent Second Coming of Christ. Often the belief in the end of days was accompanied in both Judaism and Christianity by the belief that it would be preceded by a terrible cataclysm in which all the wicked would be destroyed. In modern times, with the exception of some Protestant sects and Jewish Hasidism, the end of days is held to be in the indeterminate future.

ESCOBAR Y MENDOZA, ANTONIO

(1589-1669) Jesuit preacher and moral theologian who was derided for the support of probabilism, the theory that when the rightness or wrongness of a course of action is in doubt, any probable right course may be followed, even if an opposed course appears more probable.

ESDRAS, FIRST BOOK OF

An apocryphal work (noncanonical for Jews and Protestants) that was included in the canon of the Septuagint (the Greek version of the Hebrew Bible) but is not part of the modern biblical canons.

The work is textually more closely related to the Old Testament than other books of the Apocrypha, for it traces portions of Israel's history from 621 BC to 444 BC by summarizing 2 Chronicles 35:1-36:23, the whole of the canonical Book of Ezra, and Nehemiah 7:73-8:12. The only new material is the *Tale of the Three Guardsmen,* a Persian folk story that was slightly altered to fit a Jewish text.

ESDRAS, SECOND BOOK OF

An apocryphal work (noncanonical) printed in the Vulgate (Latin Bible) as an appendix to the New Testament. The central portion of the work (chapters 3-14), consisting of seven visions revealed to the seer Salathiel-Ezra, was written in Aramaic by an unknown Jew around 100. In the mid-second century, a Christian author added an introductory portion (chapters 1 and 2) to the Greek edition of the book, and a century later another Christian writer appended chapters 15-16 to the same edition. It is possible that the whole Greek edition was redacted by a Christian author, since there are passages in the central Jewish section that reflect Christian doctrines on original sin and Christology.

ESEK

In biblical times, a well of fresh water dug by Isaac's servants in the torrent valley of Gerar (Genesis 26:20). The Philistine shepherd of that area, however, claimed the well as theirs and the resultant "quarrelling" between the two parties gave the site its name (Genesis 26:12-20).

ESHBAN

In the Old testament, the second-named son of Sheik Dishon; a descendant of Seir the Horite. The Horites were the inhabitants of the land of Seir before the sons of Esau dispossessed and annihilated them (Genesis 36:20, 26; 1 Chronicles 1:38-41).

ESHEK

In the Old Testament, a descendant of King Saul. The biblical record mentions that this Benjaminite had three sons and that the sons of his firstborn, Ulam, came to be valiant, mighty men, bending the bow, and having many sons and grandsons, a 150 (1 Chronicles 8:1; 33-40).

ESLI

A postexile ancestor of Christ; the son of Naggai and the father of Nahum (Luke 3:25).

ESOTERIC

In Buddhism, term with two meanings: secret and symbolic. Secret in the sense of teaching not revealed to those unworthy or unfit to receive it. Such teaching may refer to phenomenal or spiritual matters. Symbolic in the sense of the inner or spiritual meaning underlying the final surface meaning. Spiritual truths are apprehended by the intuition and cannot be revealed or explained except to those whose inner development enables them to grasp them.

ESOTERICISM

Restriction of religious doctrine or ritual participation to initiates; also the cultivation of occult doctrines and practices. Esotericism was first connected with the Greek mysteries, then with a distinction between the teachings given by philosophers to the many and those given to an inner circle.

As a religious or quasi-religious phenomenon, it is present in the case of the secret fraternal orders and in such religio-philosophic systems as theosophy, spiritualism, and anthroposophy.

Certain esoteric aspects may be seen in early Christianity, with the distinction between the Mass of catechumens, open to all, and the Mass of the faithful, restricted to the baptized.

The mysteries of the New Testament, however, are not items of esoterica, but are proclaimed as the wonders of God's gracious action saving man.

Esotericism may be rooted in a primitive fascination with the magical. It does represent an attitude that sacred things are profaned by the presence of unbelievers or that the benefits bestowed by sacred things are rightly restricted to committed disciples.

ESRAELON, PLAIN OF

Also called Valley of Jezreel, lowland in northern Israel, dividing the hilly areas of Galilee in the north and Samaria in the South.

ESSENCE AND EXISTENCE

The potentiality-actuality composition of all beings other than God. The term essence can suggest that the actuality of a being is mere factuality, as though there were real essences, some of which adventitiously receive a further predicate, "existence."

The composition of essence and esse means rather than in an actual existence, esse is the ultimate and integrated actuality of the being that is.

The being exists as the subject actualized, this as the potentiality in reference to its actuality, esse, and as such as other than, but identical with, its own actuality.

ESSENES

Ascetic Jewish sect that flourished prior to 70. Living in their own communities, usually in or near the wilderness, they practiced communal ownership of property. In a period of political upheavals, the Essenes withdrew completely from public life, appearing only occasionally to warn others that the end of the world was at hand. The discovery of the Dead Sea scrolls has led to a long debate on whether the Qumran sect were Essenes.

ESTABLISHED CHURCH

A church recognized by law as the official church of a state or nation and supported by civil authority. Though not strictly created by a legal contract, the religious establishment is more like a contractual entity than like anything else and, therefore, ordinarily cannot be varied or repudiated by one party to it.

ESTHER

A Jewish orphan girl of the tribe of Benjamin, a descendant from among those deported from Jerusalem along with King Jehoiachin in circa 617 BC (Esther 2:5-7). She was the daughter of Abigail, the uncle of Mordecai.

ESTHER, BOOK OF

Old Testament book. It tells of Esther, formerly named Hadassah, a Jewess, queen of the Persian King Ahasuerus who prevented the king's favorite, Haman, from massacring all Persian Jews. Instead the Jews' enemies were slain.

The book which is read by Jews on the festival of Purim, was only reluctantly accepted into the canon of the Bible because of its non-religious character.

ESUS

One of three powerful Celtic deities mentioned by the Roman poet Lucan in the first century AD; the other two were Taranias ("Thunderer") and Teutates ("God of the People"). Esus' victims, according to later commentators, were sacrificed by being ritually stabbed and hung from trees.

ETAM

In biblical times, a settlement of Simeonites within the territory of Judah (1 Chronicles 4:24, 32).

ETHAM

The second campsite listed by Moses in Israel's march out of Egypt (Exodus 13:20; Numbers 33:3-7). It was at Etham, "on the edge of the wilderness," that the Israelites made a change in their direction, "turning back" toward Pharaoh where the crossing of the sea took place (Numbers 33:7-8).

ETHAN

In the Old Testament tradition, one of four men whose wisdom, though great, was exceeded by Solomon. Ethan is singled out as being the Ezrahite, whereas the other three, Henan, Calcol and Darda, are referred to as sons of Mahol (1 Kings 4:31). This Ethan may be the writer of Psalm 89, for the superscription identifies Ethan the Ezrahite as its writer.

ETHANIM

Seventh lunar month of the sacred calendar of the Israelites, but the first of the secular calendar (1 Kings 8:2). It corresponds to part of September and part of October. Following the Babylonian exile it was called Tishri, a name that does not appear in the Bible record but which is found in postexilic writings.

ETHBAAL

In biblical times, king of the Sidonians, the father of Jezebel the wife of king Ahab (1 Kings 19:31). By giving his daughter in marriage to Ahab, Ethbaal entered into a political alliance with him. Ethbaal is evidently the Ithobalus mentioned in Josephus' quotation of historian Menander as being the priest of the goddess Astarte. This priest got the kinship by murdering Pheles, a descendant of Hiram the king of Tyre with whom Solomon had dealings in connection with the building of the Temple.

ETHELDREDA, SAINT

(circa 630-679) Daughter of Anna, king of East Anglia. She built a doubler monastery on the west bank of the Ouse and ruled as abbess until her death from plague.

ETHICAL FORMALISM

A generic description of any theory of morality tending to stress the formal aspects of the moral act, usually at the expense of the material ones. The formal considerations are the moral law itself and the intention or motivation of the agent in acting, whereas the material considerations are the content of the act, i.e., that it is that is done and the consequences of what is done.

ETHICS
In Buddhism, system based on the doctrine of Anatta; every quality encouraging altruism is therefore considered a virtue, and every opposite quality a vice. The Buddhist moral code is set forth in the Noble Eightfold Path and in the Precepts.

ETHIOPIAN CATHOLIC CHURCH
An Eastern Catholic Church of the Alexandrian Rite in Ethiopia, in communion with Rome. Since they were Christianized in the mid-5th century, the Ethiopians have been Monophysites (believers in one nature in the person of Christ) under the authority of the Coptic patriarch of Alexandria and hence independent of Rome. In the 1050s the church was organized into a metropolitanate with Addis Abada as its metropolis.

ETHIOPIAN CHANT
Vocal music of the Ethiopian Christians in East Africa. The musical notation for Ethiopian chant was introduced in the 16th century and is called meleket and consists of characters from the ancient Ethiopian language Ge'ez, in which each sign stands for a syllable of text.

ETHIOPIAN CHURCH
An independent Monophysite Christian patriarchate in Ethiopia - that is, one which holds that Christ has one nature but he is perfectly human as well as perfectly divine.

ETHIOPIANISM
A religious movement among sub-Saharan Africans that embodied the earliest stirrings towards religious and political freedom in the modern colonial period. The movement was initiated in the 1880s, when South African mission workers began forming independent all-African Churches, such as the Temby tribal church (1884) and the Church of Africa (1889).

The mystique of the term Ethiopianism derived from its occurrence in the Bible (where Ethiopia is also referred to as Kush or Cuch), and from the history of the ancient independent Christian kingdom of Ethiopia that had defeated the Italians at Adowa in 1896. The word therefore represented Africa's dignity and place in the divine dispensation and provided a charter for free African Churches and nations of the future.

ETH-KAZIN
In biblical times, a site marking the boundary of Zebulun (Joshua 19:10-13).

ETHNAN
In the Old Testament, a son of Ashur by his wife Helah. Ethnan was of the tribe of Judah and of the family of Hezron (1 Chronicles 2:3-5).

ETHNI
In Judaism, a descendant of Levi through his son Gershom; the son of Zerah and the forefather of the musician Asaph (1 Chronicles 6:39-43).

ETIMASIA
An explanation, often in story form, for the origin or cause of a personal or place name, custom or institution found in the Bible. This explanation may at times possess genuine historical value, but is often based on popular etymologies of folklore.

EUBULUS
One of the Christian brothers in Rome at the time of the apostle's Paul's last imprisonment and who is mentioned as sending greetings of Timothy (2 Timothy 4:21).

EUCHARIST
The chief sacrament and central act of Christian worship (also called Holy Communion, Lord's Supper, and Mass). Jesus Christ at his final meal

with his disciples blessed bread and wine with the words; "this is my body," "this is my blood." Debate has centered mainly on the nature of the "presence" of Christ in the rite, and its character as a Christian "sacrifice."

The literature of Vatican Council II gives the following description: "The Most Holy Eucharist is the most august sacrament, in which Christ the Lord himself is contained, offered and received, and by which the church constantly lives and grows. The Eucharistic Sacrifice, the memorial of the death and resurrection of the Lord, in which the sacrifice of the cross is perpetual over the centuries, is the summit and the source of all Christian worship and life; it signifies and effects the unity of the people of God and achieves the building up of the Body of Christ. The other sacraments and all the ecclesiastical works of the apostolate are closely related to the Holy Eucharist and are directed to it."

EUCHARISTIC ADORATION

The worship of Iatria, due only to God, which is directed to the Eucharist because of the belief that Jesus Christ, the God-man, is in some way present in the bread and wine. The practice of eucharistic adoration, therefore, necessarily depends upon a comprehensive eucharistic theology, and would not be found in those Christian churches which deny the Real Presence.

Because of Roman Catholic belief that Christ is completely and substantially present under the appearances of bread and wine, the Eucharist is adored not only during Mass but also outside Mass when the Host is reserved for Viaticum and for the adoration of the faithful.

EUCHARISTIC CELEBRATION

The central celebration of the church's life by which the sacrifice of Christ on the cross is made present.

EUCHARISTIC CONGRESS

A national or international conference held to promote devotion to the Holy Eucharist.

EUCHARISTIC MINISTERS

Persons who preside or assist at the Eucharistic assembly. Christ is always the principal agent of the Eucharist, but priests acting in his stead represent him. Other Eucharistic ministers include readers, those who bring up the offerings, and those who give Communion.

EUDES, SAINT JOHN

(1601-1680) Founder of the Congregation of Jesus and Mary (Eudist Fathers), an order dedicated to the training of candidates for the priesthood and to the preaching of missions. He was canonized in 1925, and his feast day is August 19th.

EUGENIKOS, JOHN

(mid-15th century) Greek Byzantine theological polemicist, classical scholar, who was a proponent of an anti-Roman ecclesiastical policy and the author of a celebrated tragic ode on the fall of Constantinople to the Ottoman Turks in 1453.

EUGENIKOS, MARKOS

(1392-1445) Greek Orthodox metropolitan of Ephesus and theologian whose leadership of the anti-unionist party in the Eastern Orthodox Church and polemics against the Latin church, both at the general Council of Florence (Italy) in 1539 and throughout Byzantium, prevented any lasting reconciliation between Eastern and Western Christendom.

EUGENIUS I, SAINT

(583-657) Pope from 654 to 657. He was elected while his predecessor, Pope St. Martin I, was still alive in exile. Little is known about his achievements.

EUGENIUS II

(756-827) Pope from 824 to 827. He opposed a revival in the Eastern Church of the Iconoclastic Controversy, a long-standing theological dispute over the worship of icons.

EUGENIUS III

(1187-1153) Pope from 1145 to 1153. The first Cistercian pope, a disciple of St. Bernard of Clairvaux, and abbot of the monastery of Vincent and Anastasius. He concluded the Treaty of Constance (1153) with the Holy Roman Emperor Frederick I Barbarossa, fixing conditions for his imperial coronation.

EUGENIUS IV

(1383-1447) Pope from 1431 to 1447. His pontificate was dominated by his struggle with the Council of Basel (1431-1437), which assembled to effect church reform.

EUNICE

A believing Jewess, the daughter of Lois. She was the wife of an unbelieving Greek and the mother of Timothy (Acts 16:1). Very likely the apostle Paul met Eunice at Lystra in Asia Minor on his first missionary tour, and it was then, as a result of his preaching, that she and her mother Lois became Christians (Acts 14:4-18). Although married to a pagan husband, she was exemplary in teaching her son Timothy the "holy writings" from his "infancy" and, upon becoming a Christian she doubtless instructed him accordingly (2 Timothy 3:15). Since Eunice's husband was a Greek, Timothy's parents had not had him circumcised (Acts 16:3).

EUNUCH

The Hebrew word saris and the Greek word eunoukhos, when used in a literal sense, apply to a human male who has been castrated. Such were appointed in royal courts as attendants or caretakers of the queen, the harem and the women (Esther 2:3, 12-15). Due to the closeness to the king's household, eunuchs of ability rose to high rank.

In a broad sense the term also denoted any official assigned to duties in the court of the king, not indicating that these men were literal eunuchs.

God comfortingly foretold the time when eunuchs would be accepted by Him as servants and, if obedient, would have a name better than sons and daughters. With the abolition of the law by Jesus Christ, all persons exercising faith, regardless of their former status or condition, could become spiritual sons of God (Isaiah 56:4-5; John 1:12; 1 Corinthians 7:24).

EUODIA

A woman in the Christian congregation at Philippi who had fought side by side with rhe apostle Paul and others "in the good news." Euodia was apparently having some difficulty in resolving a problem that had arisen between her and Syntyche, and apostle Paul admonished these Christian women "to be of the same mind in the Lord" (Philistines 4:2-3).

EUPHRATES RIVER

The largest river of western Asia, rising on the Armenian plateau in Turkey and flowing generally south-eastward across Syria and southern Iraq, where it joins the Tigris River to form the Shatt al-arab, which empties into the Persian Gulf. The river irrigated the country making the desert to become a garden of fertility.

EUROPA

In Greek mythology, the beautiful daughter of Agenora and Telephassa, who was among the young women Zeus fell in love with. The maiden was playing with her girl friends on the shore at Sidon and her charms made the father of gods and men fall in love with her. In order to get near her he transformed himself into a pure white bull and went and lay at her feet.

As Europa took courage, she began to sport with the bull. But as soon as she sat on his back he leapt up and plunged into the sea. She cried for help in vain. The bull swam further and further from the shore.

Europa took firm hold of his horns to keep from falling off and in that way they reached Crete. At the spring of Cortys the couple made love under the shadow of the plane trees. Since that time the trees have never shed their leaves because they covered the love of a god. Zeus and Europa had three sons: the legendary Minos, the brave Sarpedon and the just Radamanthys.

Europa stayed on Crete, married its king Asterionas, who adopted her children and gave her name to a continent.

EUSEBIUS

(circa 260-340) Christian scholar and ecclesiastical historian. He became bishop of Caesarea circa 314. His *Chronicles,* based upon the now lost writings of previous historians and his greater work, *History of the Christian Church,* are the primary sources of informatrion on early Christianity up to 324.

EUTHEMERISM

The theory (first proposed by Euthemerus, a Greek) that mythological gods are simply deified humans and that mythological events represent historical happenings.

EUTALIUS

(357-423) Antipope from December 418 to April 419. He was an archdeacon set up against Pope St. Boniface I by a clerical faction. The rivalry that ensued led to the first interference of the temporal authorities in papal elections.

EUTYCHUS

A young man in Troas who is the last person reported in the Bible as having been miraculously restored to life. Upon apostle Paul's visit to Troas on his third missionary tour, he prolonged his discourse to the brothers until midnight. Overcome by tiredness and possibly by the heat of the many lamps and the crowded condition in the upper chamber, Eutychus feel into deep sleep and tumbled down from a third-story window. The physician Luke, the writer of Acts and apparently an eyewitness of what happened, reports that Eutychus was not merely unconscious, but "was picked up dead." Following a procedure similar to that of Elisha in resurrecting the Shuanammite's son, Paul threw himself upon Eutychus and embraced him. Paul's words, "Stop raising a clamor, for his soul is in him," indicated that life has been restored to Eutychus (Acts 20:7-12).

EVANGELICAL

Word derived from the Greek for gospel and used today of groups in Protestantism claiming to declare this with special fidelity.

EVANGELICAL ALLIANCE

Now called World's Evangelical Alliance, an association of churches, Christian societies, and individual Christians of different denominations.

EVANGELICAL AND REFORMED CHURCH

Protestant church formed by the union of the Reformed Church of America and the Evangelical Synod of North America; since 1957 part of the United Church of Christ.

EVANGELICAL CHURCHES

Broadly denominating all Christian churches preaching the gospel, less broadly, many classical Protestant churches and their offshoots, and more narrowly, certain Protestant churches maintaining fundamentalist tenets. In its broadest meaning the term evangelical churches includes Roman Catholic, Eastern Orthodox, Eastern Independent and Protestant Churches.

The term also has been used to designate or define certain classical Protestant churches or those derived from them, such as the Evangelical and Reformed Church, the Evangelical Church in Germany, the Evangelical Lutheran Church, the Evangelical United Brethren Church and the Evangelical Friends Alliance.

EVANGELICAL CHURCH IN GERMANY

A federation of Lutheran, Reformed, and United territorial churches in Germany, organized in 1948.

EVANGELICAL COVENANT CHURCH OF AMERICA

Protestant church organized in Chicago in 1885 as the Swedish Evangelical Mission Covenant of America; the present name was adopted in 1957.

EVANGELICAL FREE CHURCH OF AMERICA

A fellowship of independent Christian churches organized in 1950 that developed from several free-church groups made up of members of Scandinavian descent.

EVANGELICAL FRIENDS ALLIANCE

Federation of four Friends yearly meetings: Kansas, Ohio, Oregon and Rocky Mountains. This group generally holds a Fundamentalist interpretation of the Bible. They hold church services similar to those of other Protestant churches, rather than the traditional unprogrammed Friends meeting.

EVANGELICALISM

Meaning "pertaining to the gospel," is the name applied to a theological movement, found in most Protestant denominations, that emphasizes the primary authority of the Bible. Among the basic emphases of evangelicalism are personal conversion and expository preaching. Evangelical doctrine includes the depravity of human nature, justification of faith alone, and the working of the Holy Spirit in conversion. Among the denominations using the name are the Evangelical Lutherans; the Evangelical and Reformed Church, which joined the Congregational Christian Churches in 1961 to form the United Church of Christ; the Evangelical Covenant Church of America; the Evangelical United Brethren.

The same biblical theology is also found within the Anglican communion and other Protestant denominations that do not. in their entirety, identify with evangelicalism. The name was applied to the movement led by John Wesley in the 18th century which eventually separated from the Church of England to become the Methodist Church.

EVANGELICAL LUTHERAN CHURCH

Organized in the United States in 1917 as the Norwegian Lutheran Church by merger of three synods comprised of members of Norwegian descent; the name was changed in 1946.

EVANGELICAL REVIVAL

In England, an 19th century religious revival that brought forth the Methodists, founded by the Wesley brothers, and other evangelical Free Churches, such as the Baptists, that spread to the United States, and also brought into being reactions that eventuated in the formation of Unitarian groups in both England and the United States.

EVANGELICALS, ANGLICAN

Those who emphasize biblical faith, personal conversion, piety, and, in general, the Protestant rather than the Catholic heritage of the Anglican Communion.

EVANGELICAL UNITED BRETHREN CHURCH

Protestant Church formed in 1946 by the merger of the Evangelical Church and the Church of the United Brethren in Christ. Both of these churches were essentially Methodist in doctrine and church government, and both originated among German-speaking people in Pennsylvania, Maryland, and Virginia after the American Revolution.

EVANGELIST

Designation in the New Testament for a person sent out to preach the gospel; latterly anyone who preaches the Gospel to those outside the church. From the 3rd century on the term is used for the writers of the gospels: Matthew, Mark, Luke and John. In church history the term is applied to an itinerant preacher who travels from place to place, as distinct from a pastor or teacher who remains in one place. The best-known evangelists in English and American history are John Wesley and George Whitefield; while the most famous living evangelist is the American, W. F. (Billy) Graham.

EVANGELICAL UNITED BRETHREN

Protestant church, essentially Methodist, formed by the merger (1946) of the Evangelical Church and the Church of the United Brethren in Christ. In 1948 they became part of the United Methodist Church.

EVE

The first woman, wife of Adam, from whose rib God created her. According to the account of creation in the book of Genesis, Eve is the mother of the human race. Genesis tells of the creation of Adam (the Hebrew word for the dust, or earth, of which Adam was formed by God, is Adammah) and his wife Eve. their temptation, fall and expulsion from the garden of Eden. The story forms the basis of such concepts as sin, grace, and divine retribution in Christianity and Judaism.

EVIL

In Buddhism, term with a specific meaning. Buddhism is not dualistic, and therefore does not divide phenomena into absolute good and evil. It recognizes evil as limitation, and therefore purely relative. There is therefore "no problem of evil" as in theistic systems of thought. All evil is traced to desire for self. The basic evil is the idea of separateness, and the Buddhist goal is the removal of evil by the eradication of all sense of separate selfhood.

EVIL-MERODACH

In biblical times, the oldest son of the Babylonian king Nebuchadnezzar and his immediate successor to the throne in 580 BC. Evil-merodach received mention in the Bible for the kindness he extended, in the year of his becoming king, to Jehoiachin the king of Judah by releasing him from the house of detention in the thirty-seventh year of his exile in Babylon and granting

him a position of favor above all the other kings who were in captivity in Babylon (2 Kings 25:27-30; Jeremiah 52:31-34). Josephus claims that Evil-merodach viewed Jehoiachin as one of his most intimate friends.

EVOLUTION

A theory explaining the appearance of life on earth and the process by which living organisms have acquired their present form. In the mid-19th century the British naturalist Charles Darwin proposed his theory of evolution.

Despite the dominance of Darwin's theory - that human beings evolved from lower life forms over millions of years - theologians and religious leaders have yielded relatively little ground on what for them is a fundamental doctrine of faith. The three major Western religions - Christianity, Judaism and Islam - all teach that the universe is the handiwork of a divine creator who has given humanity a special place in that creation, although the details of just how and when it all occurred are widely disputed.

The apparent conflict between religious and scientific explanations of creation and evolution has left a century-old legacy of suspicion and outright acrimony. While few experts suggest an actual convergence of the two views is possible, and some question whether it is desirable, creative dialogue is on the upswing. New organizations are forming and others expanding whose aim is rapprochement between science and religion. More than 100 organizations worldwide, many in the Unites States, now provide forums for creative exchange of religious and scientific perspectives.

EXECRATION

In biblical terms, a severe and even violent denunciation of that which is viewed as detestable and worthy of cursing. The word (in Hebrew qa'van) appears only in the account of King Balak's futile efforts to get the prophet Balaam to execrate the nation of Israel and thus represent that nation before God as worthy of his curse (Numbers 22:11, 17; 23:11-13; 24:10).

EXCOMMUNICATION

Ecclestical censure, common to all Christian denominations, usually denoting formal exclusion of an offender from sharing in the communion of the church. In the Roman Catholic Church an excommunicate may not attend mass or receive the sacraments and is denied a Christian burial. Excommunication was important in the Middle Ages as a punishment meted out of ecclesiastical courts. It was sometimes used to force temporal rulers to submit to papal authority.

EXEDRA

Semicircular or rectangular niche with a raised seat; more loosely applied, the term also refers to the apse, or projection at the end, of a church or to a niche therein.

EXEGESIS AND HERMENEUTICS, BIBLICAL

The critical interpretation and the science of interpretive principles of the Bible. Used by both Jews and Christians throughout their histories, the subject's most common purpose has been to discover the truths and values of the Old and New Testaments by means of various techniques and principles aften arrived at because of the exigencies of certain historical conditions.

EXILE, BABYLONIAN

The forced detention of Jews in Babylonia following the conquest of the kingdom of Judah in the 6th century BC. The exile formally ended in 538 BC, when the Persian conqueror of Babylonia, Cyrus the Great, gave the Jews permission to return to Palestine (2 Chronicles 36:22-23).

Historians agree that several deportations took place, that not all Jews were forced to leave their homeland, that returning Jews left Babylon at various times, and that some Jews chose to remain in Babylonia - thus constituting the first of numerous Jewish communities living permanently in the Diaspora. The exile began with a series of deportations during the reigns of the Judean kings, Jehoiakim (609-598 BC), Jehoiachin (598 BC) and Zedekiah (598-587 BC). After the destruction of Jerusalem by Nebuchadnezzar (587 BC) the kingdom of Judea ceased to exist as a political entity. Although there were settlements in Egypt, the exiles in Babylonia who maintained the historic Jewish faith and provided the nucleus which returned to Judea subsequent to the decree of Cyrus.

Although the Jews suffered greatly and faced powerful cultural pressures in a foreign land, they maintained their national spirit and religious identity. Elders supervised the Jewish communities and Ezekiel was one of several prophets who kept alive the hope of one day returning home.

EXODUS

The liberation of the people of Israel from slavery in Egypt in the 15th century BC, under the leadership of Moses. Also the second book of the Old Testament, written by Moses. Chapters 1-18 narrate the history of the Egyptian bondage, the exodus from Egypt, and the journey to Mount Sinai under the leadership of Moses. The second half of the book tells of the Covenant that was established between God and Israel at Sinai and promulgates laws for the ordering of Israel's life.

During the period of the exodus to the founding of Solomon's Temple, the only continuous biblical era is the era of the Exodus. With regard to a crucial date expressed in this era, the best approximation is described in 1 Kings 6:1 - "In the 480th year after the people of Israel came out of the land of Egypt, in the fourth year of Solomon's reign over Israel, in the month of Ziv, which is the second month, he began to build the house of the Lord." Solomon began the building of the Temple in his fourth year of kingship (1034 BC).

The last plague - the death of firstborn - signalled the beginning of the exodus. The Israelites ate the Passover meal in haste, ready to depart from Egypt. The opening of the Red Sea by the "strong east wind" was the means by which God brought His people out of Egypt in the wilderness where, for a period of 40 years, they were miraculously sustained.

EXODUS, BOOK OF

The second book of the Bible. the English name of which derives from the Septuagint usage where "exodus" was chosen to designate the deliverance of the Israelites from Egyptian bondage and their safe passage through the Sea of Reeds (Red Sea).

Chapters 1-18 narrate the sacred history of the Egyptian bondage, the Exodus from Egypt, and the journey to Mount Sinai under the leadership of Moses. The second half od the book (chapters 19-40) tells of the covenant that was established between Israel and God at Sinai and sets down the laws promulgated for the ordering of Israel's life.

EXORCISM

The expulsion of demons from places or persons, common in pagan religions, and found also in Judaism and Christianity. In the New Testament, Jesus cast out demons from the possessed by a word, and the apostles did likewise in his name. In the early church anyone gifted could exorcise; in the third century exorcism was restricted to ordained clergy, in particularly a minor order, called exorcists, finally suppressed in 1972.

Now somewhat controversial, exorcism is practiced as a last resort and with medical advice. Regulated by canon law and requiring episcopal permission, it is a ceremonial rite with set prayers. An exorcism to ward off evil (not presupposing possession) forms part of the Roman Catholic service of baptism.

EXPELLING

The judicial excommunication or disfellowshipping of delinquents from membership and association in a community or organization. With religious societies it is a principle and a right inherent in them and is analogous to the powers of capital punishment, banishment and exclusion from membership that are exercised by political and municipal bodies. In some religious denominations, it is exercised to maintain the purity of the organization doctrinally and morally. The exercise of this power is in such cases necessary to the continued existence of the organization, and particularly so the Christian congregation. (See also Revelations 2:5; 1 Corinthians 5:5-6).

EXPERIENCE

In Buddhism, term with a specific meaning. Buddhism is not so much a religion as a way of life. Even the scriptures have little value compared with actual experience of the doctrines they describe. The is why Buddhism claims no authority for any doctrine and professes complete tolerance for differing opinions. Satori is described as a personal yet impersonal, direct, intuitive experience of the non-relative. It is unmistakable and unforgettable, but being beyond the plane of the intellect incommunicable in words. This experience, large or small, is the goal of Zen training.

EXPOSITION OF THE BLESSED SACRAMENT

A ceremony of scripture readings, hymns, prayers, and silent meditation in which the consecrated host is displayed, usually in monstrance, for all the faithful to see. Exposition of the Blessed Sacrament has traditionally been part of Benediction, Corpus Christi processions, perpetual adoration, and Forty Hours devotion.

EXUPERANTIUS

Third-century Christian martyr, servant of the Christian missionaries Felix and Regula, who died with them on the site of the present-day Zurich, Switzerland.

EZBAI

In the Old Testament, the father of Naarai, one of the mighty men of King David's military forces (1 Chronicles 11:26, 27).

EZBON

In the Old Testament, a son of Gad and the grandson of Jacob (Genesis 46:16). The parallel account in Numbers 26:16 lists Ozni as the forefather of the Oznites instead of Ezbon, suggesting that both names apply to the same person.

EZEKIEL

(6th century BC) Hebrew priest and prophet, author of the third of the major prophetic books of the Old Testament, which bears his name. Deported to Babylon by Nebuchadnezzar, Ezekiel became a prophet to the exiles. His predictions of Israel's national restoration include the celebrated vision of a "valley of dry bones" being restored to life.

EZEKIEL, BOOK OF

One of the major prophetical books of the Old Testament. Ezekiel received his prophetic call in the fifth year of the first deportation to Babylonia (592 BC) and was active until at least 571 BC. Most of the time was spent in exile. Ezekiel's mission was one of comfort to the captives in Babylon. His prophecies demonstrated that God was justified in permitting the captivity of His people.

EZEM

In biblical times, one of the Horite sheiks in the land of Seir (Genesis 36:20-30). The Horites were later dispossessed and annihilated by the sons of Esau (Deuteronomy 2:22).

EZRA

(5th century BC) Babylonian Jewish priest and religious leader, whose teachings are recorded in the Old Testament Book of Ezra. He advocated an exclusive and legalistic doctrine, prohibiting marriages between Jews and Gentiles.

EZRA, BOOK OF

Old Testament book written by the 5th century Jewish priest and religious leader Ezra, who lived in Babylon. He was allowed by King Artaxerxes to go to Jerusalem, taking circa 1500 Jews with him. In Jerusalem he forbade the marriages of Jews and heathens, teaching statutes and judgments. The book treats the return of the exiles and the rebuilding of the Temple of Jerusalem. The first six chapters of Ezra are taken up with the decree of the Persian King Cyrus freeing the Jews from the Babylonian captivity, with the return of the exiles, and the rebuilding of the Temple in Jerusalem. The last four chapters relate the life of Ezra, who reformed Jewish religious rites.

EZRA AND NEHEMIAH, BOOKS OF

Two Old Testament books that together form a sequel to the books of the Chronicles.

EZRAH

In the Old Testament, a name appearing in a list of Judah's descendants. Jether, Mered, Epher and Jalon are identified as the sons of Ezrah (1 Chronicles 4:1, 17).

EZRAHITE

A person belonging to the family of Ezrah, or possibly Zerah, as this is almost the same Hebrew form.

EZRI

In biblical times, son of Chelub and overseer of the cultivators of the king's fields during David's reign (1 Chronicles 27:26).

F

FABIAN, Saint
(189-250) Pope from 236 to 250. Martyred during the persecution of the Roman Emperor Decius, he was buried in the catacomb of St. Calixtus; his body was later moved to St. Sebastian's, where his tomb was found in 1915. His feast day is January 15th.

FABIOLA, Saint
circa 325-399) Christian noblewoman credited with founding the first public hospital in western Europe.

FACULTIES, Apostolic
Those faculties granted by the pope with regard to powers reserved to himself. They are to be interpreted like all privileges; for instance, following strictly the terms of their concession.

FACULTIES OF THE SOUL
The operative potencies or powers of the soul. These potencies are usually designated as vegetative, sensitive, and rational or intellectual.

FACULTY
As a canonical term a faculty is an empowerment granted to another by a superior to whom the power belongs by office or law. There is a general usage of the term and a narrower usage, referring to apostolic faculties.

▲ In the broader usage the term has applications. In regard to the sacrament of penance it is used to designate a confessor's competence to absolve from sin or ecclesiastical censures. In this usage it is equivalent to a delegated jurisdiction. The power to absolve is conferred by priestly ordination; its exercise belongs to the realm of jurisdiction in the church. A priest must receive faculties from the competent authority in order to absolve validly those who are subject to the ordinary. Such faculties are granted not only for absolving from sin, but also from censures and from reserved sins.

▲ In a second broad usage of the term and one that in practice is often linked with a confessor's faculties is the faculty to preach. The ministry of preaching belongs by office to the pope as universal pastor throughout the church, to the bishop as first pastor to the diocese.
The ministry of preaching can be exercised lawfully by no one else except on receiving the canonical mission from the pope or from the competent ordinary.

FADA'IL
Arab term denoting excellences, merits, virtues. Fada-'il literature is a genre in Arabic which vaunts the excellent qualities in things, people, places, and, indeed, sacred books; a branch of early fada'il literature, for example, concentrated on praising the numerous merits of the Koran.

FA-HSIEN
(399-414) Chinese Buddhist monk whose pilgrimage to India initially began Sino-Indian relations and whose writings gave important information about early Buddhism.

FAIR HAVENS
In biblical times, a harbor near the city of Lasea identified with the bay on the south coast of Crete that still bears the same name in modern Greek, Kalous Limionas (Acts 27:7-8). In 58 the apostle Paul, as a prisoner, was sailing from Myra (on the southern coast of Asia Minor) via Cnidus en route to Rome. The more direct way from Cnidus to Rome would have been to the north of Crete. But evidently adverse winds, probably from the northwest, forced the mariners to take a southerly course from Cnidus to Crete and then sail

under the shelter of the island's south coast, finally reaching Fair Havens with difficulty (Acts 27:5-8).

FAITH

In Christianity, the divinely inspired human response to God's historical revelation through Jesus Christ and, consequently, of crucial significance. The Christian first letter to the Corinthians similarly asserts that faith is a gift of God (1 Corinthians 12:8-9), while the letter to the Hebrews (11:1) defines faith as "the assurance of things hoped for, the conviction of things not seen".

In Buddhism, faith is not the acceptance of doctrinal beliefs, but confidence in the teacher and his teachings as a way to a goal desired. There is no reliance on the authority of another's spiritual achievement, however great, and the Buddha so taught in words.

Faith is being regarded by Roman Catholics as one of the three theological (God-given and God-directed) virtues or powers, infused into the soul with sanctifying grace, by which, in the words of Vatican Council I, "a person is enabled to believe that what God has revealed is true - not because its intrinsic worth is seen with the rational light of reason - but because of the authority of God who reveals it, that God who can neither deceive not be deceived."

This definition is amplified by the description of faith given by Vatican Council II: "The obedience of faith (see Romans 1:5; Romans 16:26; 2 Corinthians 10:5-6) must be given to God as He reveals himself. By faith man freely commits his entire self to God, making "the full submission of his intellect and will to God who reveals," and willingly ascending to the revelation given by Him. Before this faith can be exercised, man must have the grace of God to move and assist him; he must have the interior helps of the Holy Spirit, who moves the heart and converts it to God, who opens the eyes of the mind and "makes it easy for all to accept and believe the truth."

Faith is assenting knowledge. To cite the most extreme case, the New Testament ascribes "believing" even to the demons: "You believe that God is one; you do well. Even the demons believe - and shudder" (James 2:19). In such a context, presumably, to believe is to know a religious truth and to accept it as true, for the demons do not obey or trust even though they are obliged to acknowledge that monotheism is an accurate theory about the divine.

FAITH, Act of

In the general grammar of assent, the significance of the Act of Faith is indicated in Hebrews 1:1. Accordingly, to speak of its cognitive element, as an act convinced of the truth of its judgment, it differs from doubt, a suspense of assent, and from opinion, an assent mixed with some uncertainty. Yet because the object is its assent is neither evident in itself not inferred from evident premises it differs respectively from insight and from holding by scientific proof.

Catholic theologians in general insist that such a faith is more than a feeling, or just a gamble, but a firm act of mind, based on, though not to be resolved into, thorough reasonable ground for belief. Nevertheless so far does the object transcend the subject, that certitude, while remaining intact, may periodically or even constantly suffer a diminution of its assurance, as holy people, not only waverers, are well aware from experience.

FAITH IN PROTESTANTISM

In Protestantism, faith is trust. In Luther's formula, which every major Christian theologian would affirm, "a God is that to which we look for all good and in which we find refuge in every time of need. To have a God is nothing else than to trust and believe him with our whole heart."

The paradigm for this kind of faith in Scripture is Abraham, who is thus "the father of us all" because "in hope he believed against hope, that he should become the father of many nations"

(Romans 4:16-18). In his trusting faith Abraham: "obeyed when he was called to go out to a place which he had received as an inheritance; and he went out, not knowing where he was to go" (Hebrews 11:8).

Here the knowledge of faith is clearly subordinated to the obedience of faith and to the trust of faith. He who believes in God is one who has confidence that God can be relied upon even in times and places that are still unknown.

Faith is therefore "the assurance of things hoped for, the conviction not of what awaits it but the certainty of who awaits it." The certainty and confidence of such a faith have been well summarized in the words of 2 Timothy 1:12: "I know whom I have believed, and I am sure that he is able to guard until the day that has been entrusted to me."

Sometimes, in reaction to the sort of intellectualism described in the preceding paragraph, theologians, especially in the Protestant and existentialist traditions, have attempted to restrict faith to trust and to regard other aspects of it, particularly the aspect of assenting knowledge, as alien or at least subordinate. Distorted though such a view is, it does make the valid point that in the Bible trust is central to faith.

FAITH, Loss of

A term commonly but inexactly used to describe the process through which one decides to remove or annul the commitment by which he or she has assented to the teachings of Jesus and his church. As by the acts of faith one assent to those teachings, so by its opposite, called loss of faith, one dissents from the same teachings.

The popular use of the term "loss" to describe the passage from belief to disbelief reflects an assumption that replacement of assent by dissent is an event that happens to a person rather than an event which the person brings about.

Loss of faith is taken to be a privation over which one has no control, like the loss of eyesight from an injury. While, however, the power to believe is given tp the soul by God and each use of the power, being an act of faith, is supported by God's helping grace, man's deliberative powers are used in each commitment or act of faith he makes.

He can not believe without God's help but God does not believe for him; man does the believing. So, too, if there is disbelief he does the disbelieving; it does not just happen to him. At every point in his life a man or womanwith faith has the grace to use it. But, at any point in his or her life the same man or woman has the power to resist the grace offered him or her.

FAITH, Professions of

Summaries and symbols of the essential elements of the church's principal truths. The first profession of faith is made at baptism. Different articulations of faith, or creeds, have been formulated in different eras; for instance, the Apostles' Creed, the Nicene Creed, the Athanasian Creed.

FAITH, Roman Catholic Theology

The act of believing God; the gift of grace empowering the recipient for such an act; and the truths believed, as in the phrase "Faith of our Fathers."

Faith in the Old Testament and the New Testament is the fundamental and all-pervasive condition of man's relationship with God. The Old Testament meaning is brought out in contexts that, whether in regard to Israel or to the individual, express God's faithfulness and truthfulness in his promises, and a human response that acknowledges God's fidelity.

The Synoptic gospels place faith as the condition of trust in his claims that Jesus imposes for discipleship (Matthew 8:10; Mark 4:36; Luke 8:25). John's gospel expresses the object of belief, that Jesus is from God (John 16:30); the Messiah (John 11:27); that his own words are to be believed (John 2:22; John 5:47; John 8:45). In Acts the disciples identified themselves simply as believers, and believers in Jesus as

Lord, having salvation through his grace.

God does not address man in faith in order to provide him with information, but with the invitation to salvation. Man is empowered by God's love to respond in love, and belief is indeed part of that response.

Not only is faith not just a matter of knowledge like other knowledge, nor merely a pondering; it is a pondering with assent. The God who speaks to the believer is the God who loves him and whom he loves in return. The assent is the act of the mind that cleaves to God's word, because it is the beloved Father who speaks. In its integration within the whole relationship of the person to God, belief is a believing God, a believing in God, and a believing unto God.

FAITHFUL, Liturgy of the

The second part of the worship service in the early Christian church, comprising the mystery of the Eucharist (the thanksgiving, or Holy Communion), which was reserved for baptized Christians only.

FAITH HEALING

Spiritual healing, the curing of disease by means of prayer, often accompanied by anointing or the laying on of hands. The phenomenon is common in primitive societies, where faith healing is practiced by shamans and with doctors. In more highly developed societies, cures seemingly effected by means of faith alone have been recorded at shrines such as Lourdes in France, and as a result of the activity of pentecostal preachers, who consider faith healing an important part of their ministry.

FAITH MOVEMENT

Indian reformist or renewal movement based on Sufi teachings and principles, founded by Mawlana Mohammed Ilyas. He believed that Muslims should genuinely feel that they are Muslims and this involved a real study of the religion of Islam. The dhikr was used with a preference for individual prayer rather than communal recitation and the movement stressed the need for simplicity of life. One of the more unusual aspects of the movement's principles was that of donation of time for preaching. The Faith Movement started in 1927 in Mewat, South of Dehli, and has continued to expand.

FAJR, al-

The title of the 89th sura of the Koran; it means "The Dawn." The sura belongs to the Meccan period and has 30 verses. Its title comes from the oath of the first verse "By the dawn." The first verses remind man of the divine punishments inflicted on the tribe of 'Ad, Iram of the Pillarts, the tribe of Thamud and Pharaoh. Man will remember God when he sees the terrors which precede the Last Judgement.

FALAQ, al-

The title of the 113th sura of the Koran; it means "The Daybreak." The sura belongs to the Meccan period and has 5 verses. It is the penultimate sura of the Koran. Its title is drawn from the first verse where God is referred to as "The Lord of the dawn." The whole sura is a plea for protection by God from a variety of evils including darkness, vicious women (or witches) and envies.

FALASHAS

Ethiopians of Jewish faith calling themselves House of Israel (Beta Israel), claiming descent from the Queen of Sheba and King Solomon's son, Menelik I. More likely their ancestors were Agau natives converted to Judaism about the time of the Second Commonwealth. First discovered by Joseph Halevy in 1867, some 20,000 or more Falashas now live mostly in the regions north of Lake Tana and generally remain aloof from other Ethiopians. In the 1990s several thousands of them have moved to Israel.

FALSALFA

Arab term for philosophy. The word derives from the Greek philosophia. Perhaps the most notable legacy of Greek philosophy to Islamic philosophy was Aristotelian philosophical vocabulary and Greek logic. Islamic philosophy was much influenced by Aristotelianism, Neoplatonism and, to a lesser degree, Platonism, but it would certainly be untrue to say that Islamic philosophy is merely an amalgam or synthesis of other foreign philosophies. It may rightly claim to be a system of thought in its own right. Down the ages the Islamic philosophers were frequently suspected of heterodoxy and heresy.

FALSE DECRETALS

A 9th century collection of ecclesiastical legislation containing some forged documents. The principal aim of the forgers was to free the church from interference by the state and to maintain the independence of the bishops against the encroachments of the archbishops, who were attempting to extend their power.

FAMILY, Christian

Considering the family from a Christian viewpoint, Pope John Paul II, in his encyclical *Familiaris consortio* (On the Family), points out that the family is:

▲ a community of persons; a community which must strive for ever deeper communication through the power of love;

▲ a school of humanity where each member learns to take care of the others and where mutual service is highlighted;

▲ a place of reconciliation where conflict and division can be healed;

▲ a vital cell of society where young citizens learn the values of justice, respect, and charity.

FAMILY, Rights of

The family is a natural society in its own right. As such it possesses certain fundamental rights which should be respected by both other natural societies and by individuals. After the Roman Synod (1981), at which bishops from different parts of the world shared their views on the family, Pope John Paul II issued "a charter of family rights". These rights are as follows:

▲ The right to exist and progress as a family, that is, the right of every human being, even if he or she is poor, to found a family and to have adequate means to support it.

▲ The right to exercise its responsibility regarding the transmission of life and to educate children.

▲ The right to the intimacy of conjugal life.

▲ The right to stability of the bond and the institution of marriage.

▲ The right to believe in and profess one's faith and to propagate it.

▲ The right to bring up children in accord with the family's own traditions and religious values, with the necessary instruments, means, and institutions.

▲ The right, especially of the poor and sick, to obtain physical, social, political, and economic security.

▲ The right to housing suitable for living family life in a suitable way.

▲ The right to form associations with other families and institutions in order to fulfill the family's role suitably.

▲ The right to wholesome recreation of a kind that also fosters family values.

▲ The right of the elderly to a worthy life and a worthy death.

▲ The right to emigrate as a family in search of a better life.

FAMINE

An extreme food shortage; also, a scarcity of hearing the words of God, that is, a spiritual famine (Amos 8:11). Famine is one of the plagues to come upon symbolic Babylon the Great.

FANA'

In Islam, term denoting extinction, cessation, annihilation, passing away. It is a technical term in tasawwuf; the word fana' being used to indicate a stage in the mystical experience before baqa in which all the mystic's imperfections and earthly ties are annihilated or extinguished, and he is absorbed into the Deity losing consciousness of the self and those things which impede his spiritual imperfection. To put it another way, fana' means that the mystic "dies to himself" so that he may be "born in God" and "God be born in him". Fana' does not, however, mean that the mystic's individuality is totally lost.

FARABI, al-

(870-950) One of the great Islamic philosophers and a leading proponent of Islamic Neoplatonism. he became known as "The Second Master" (i.e. after Aristotle). He made a major contribution to Islamic metaphysics with his development of the doctrine of essence and existence. His writings describe God through both negative and positive propositions and epithets.

FARD

In Islam, term denoting religious duty. Except among the Hanafis fard and wajib are considered to be exactly the same. Islamic law makes a distinction between those duties incumbent upon individuals and those incumbent upon the entire community, which may be fulfilled by a representative number of persons from that community.

FAREL, Guillaume

(1489-1565) Reformer and preacher primarily responsible for introducing the Reformation to French-speaking Switzerland, where his efforts led to John Calvin's establishment of the Reformed Church in Geneva.

FARMER, Herbert Henry

(1892-1871)English philosopher and theologian, noted as a lecturer in the philosophy of religion and professor of systemic theology at Cambridge University (1935-60). Among his writings, which present a critical although traditional view of the intellectual basis of theism, are The World and God (1935) and Revelation and Religion (1954).

FAST, Eucharistic

Extreme starvation sometimes resulting in death. The acceptance of human society of widespread famine is a grave injustice.

FASTING

Abstinence from food or drink or both for religious purposes. Fasting is common to many religions, ranging from that practiced by indigenous Americans to the Jewish, Islamic and Christian faiths. It is an act of repentance and mortification that takes various forms. Jews refrain from, all food and drink on Yom Kippur, the Day of Atonement; Roman Catholics limit their consumption of food on so-called "fast days" during Lent and in the Eucharistic fast, the strict fast observed before taking Communion. The Eastern churches practice strict fasts, and the Anglican Church also observes fasts during Lent. Muslims fast during the daylight hours of the month of Ramadan.

FASTING, Eastern Church

Although the ancient rules in the East that permitted on a fast day only one or two meals consisting solely of cooked or uncooked vegetables have been abandoned, the Christian East has preserved a certain rigor by excluding on fasting days any food deriving from a warm-blooded animal (meat or meat products, together with eggs, milk, butter, and cheese). However, it is not required that one's consumption of other kinds of food be diminished; hence the distinction between fast and abstinence has become practically obsolete. The Orthodox faithful do not regard themselves strictly obliged to observe the fast with all rigor, but according to their specific circumstances. Among Catholic Orientals the regulations of fast have been interpreted strictly, but their requirements have been so reduced, that they do not differ from those of the Latin church.

FASTING, Comparative Perspective

In religions and dogmas other than Islam, the observer of a fast abstains from certain kinds of food or drinks or material substances, but he is free to substitute for that and fill his stomach with alternative foods or drinks.

In Islam one abstains from the things of material nature - food, drink, smoking etc., in order to have spiritual joys and moral nourishment. The Muslim empties his stomach of all the material things: to fill his soul with peace and blessings, to fill his heart with love and sympathy, to fill his spirit with piety and faith, to fill his mind with wisdom and resolution.

The purpose of fasting other than in Islam is invariably partial. It is either for spiritual aims, or for physical needs, or for intellectual cultivations; never all combined. But in Islam it is for all these gains and many other purposes, social and economic, moral and humanitarian, private and public, personal and common, inner and outer, local and national - all combined together as mentioned above.

The non-Islamic fasting does not demand more than partial abstinence from certain material things. But the Islamic type is accompanied by extra devotion and worship, extra charity and study and of the Koran, extra sociability and liveliness, extra self-discipline and conscience-awakening. Thus the fasting Muslim feels a different person altogether.

Even the timetable of the Islamic fasting is a striking phenomenon. In other cases the time of fasting is fixed at a certain time of the year in a most inflexible way. But in Islam the time comes with the month of Ramadan, the ninth month of the year.

The Islamic calendar is a lunar one, and months go according to the various positions of the moon. This means that over a period of a limited number of years the Islamic fasting covers the four major seasons of the year and circulates back and forth between the summer and the winter through the fall and the spring in a rotating manner.

The nature of the lunar calendar is such that the month of Ramadan falls in January, for example, in one year and in December in another year, and at any time in between during the succeeding years. In a spiritual sense, this means that the Muslim enjoys the moral experience of fasting on various levels, and tastes its spiritual flavors at variant seasons of variant climates, sometimes in the winter of short and cold days, sometimes in the summer of long and hot days, sometimes in between.

But this variety of experience remains at all times an impressive feature of the liveliness of the Islamic institution. It also stands as an unfailing expression of readiness, dynamism and adaptability on the part of the Muslim believer.

FASTING IN ISLAM

Fasting in Islam means to abstain "completely" from foods, drinks, ultimate intercourses and smoking before the break of dawn until sunset, during the entire month of Ramadan, the ninth month of the Islamic year. Some important points of the Islamic fasting are:

▲ It teaches man the principle of sincere love; because when he observes the fasting he does it out of deep love for God. And the man who lives God truly is a man who really knows what love is.

▲ It equips man with a creative sense of hope and an optimistic outlook on life, because when he fasts he is hoping to please God and is seeking his grace.

▲ It imbues man with a genuine virtue of effective devotion, honest dedication and closeness to God, because when he fasts he does so for God and for His sake alone.

▲ It cultivates in man a vigilant and sound conscience, because the fasting person keeps his fast in secret as well as in public. In fasting, especially, there is no mundane authority to check man's behavior or compel him to observe the fasting. He keeps it to please God and satisfy his own conscience by being faithful in secret and in public. There is no better way to cultivate a sound conscience in man.

▲ It indoctrinates man in patience and unselfishness, because when he fasts he feels the pains of deprivation but endures patiently. Truly this deprivation may be only temporary, yet there is no doubt that the experience makes him realize the severe effects of such pains on others, who might be deprived of essential commodities for days or weeks or probably months together. The meaning of this experience in a social and humanitarian sense is so that such a person is much quicker than anybody else in sympathizing with his fellow men and responding to their needs, and this is an eloquent expression of unselfishness and genuine sympathy.

▲ It is an effective lesson in applied moderation and willpower. The person who observes his fasting properly is certainly a man who can discipline his passionate desires and place his self above physical temptations. Such is the man of personality and character, the man of willpower and determination.

▲ It provides man with a transparent soul to transcend, a clear mind to think and a light body to move and act. All this is the never-failing result of carrying a light stomach. Medical instructions, biological rules and intellectual experience attest to this fact.

▲ It enables man to master the art of mature adaptability. We can easily understand the point once we realize that fasting makes man change the course of his daily life. When he makes the change, he naturally adapts himself to a new system and moves along to satisfy the new rules. This, in the long run, develops in him a wise sense of adaptability and a self-created power to overcome the unpredictable hardships of life. A man who values constructive adaptability and courage will readily appreciate the effects of fasting in this respect.

▲ It originates in man the real spirit of social belonging, of unity and brotherhood, or equality before God as well as before the Law. His spirit is the natural product of the fact that man fasts; he feels that he is joining the whole Muslim society in observing the same duty in the same manner at the same time for the same motives to the same end.

▲ It is a Godly prescription for self-reassurance and self-control, for maintenance of human dignity and freedom, for victory and peace. These results never fail to manifest themselves as a lively reality in the heart of the person who knows how to keep the fasting. When he fasts in the proper manner, he is in control of himself, exercises full command over his passions, disciplines his desires and resists all evil temptations. By this course, he is in a position to reassure himself, to restore his dignity and integrity and to attain freedom from the captivity of evil. Once he obtains this, he has established inner peace, which is the source of permanent peace with God and, consequently, with the entire universe.

FAST OF 17TH OF TAMMUZ

Jewish fast day marking the Roman destruction of Jerusalem's city walls. Observant Jews fast during the daylight hours.

FAST OF NINGH OF AV

Jewish fast day remembering the destruction of the First and Second Temples.

FATEH SINGH, Saint

(1911-1972) Sikh religious leader and foremost campaigner for Sikh rights against the dominant Hindu and Muslim communities, notable for his work in securing a greater voice among the Sikhs for the rural population.

FATES

The goddess of destiny in Greek and Roman mythology, called Moirai by the Greeks and Parcae by the Romans. There are three Fates who are said to rule man's lives: Clotho, who spins the thread of life; Lachesis, who decides its length and Atropos, the inevitable, who cuts the thread. They are spoken of as the daughters of Zeus and of

Themis, goddess of justice, and also as daughters of the night. Fate comes from the Latin fatum, "that which has been spoken."

FATH, al-

The title of the 48th sura of the Koran; it means "The Victory." The sura belongs to the Medinan period and contains 29 verses. Its title comes from the first verse in which God tells Mohammed that He has given him an evident victory in 628 and/or the coming conquest of Mecca by Mohammed in 630. The sura was revealed around the time of al-Hudaybiyya and is dominated by the thought of this treaty and the coming conquest of Mecca.

FATHERS OF THE CHURCH

Saintly, orthodox writers of the early church (from the first to approximately the end of the seventh century); their writings had a major impact on the doctrinal development of the church. They are usually divided into the Latin Fathers, including such giants as
▲ St. Irenaeus (130-200);
▲ St. Ambrose (340-397);
▲ St. Augustine (354-430);
and the Greek fathers, including:
▲ St. Clement of Alexandria (150-215);
▲ St. Athanasius (297-373);
▲ St. John Crysostom (347-407).

FATIHA, al-

The title of the first sutra of the Koran; it means "The Opening" in reference to its being the opening chapter of the sacred text. The sura belongs to the Meccan period and has 7 verses. It constitutes both a hymn of praise to God (who is the Lord of all being as well as of the Last Judgement and who is worshipped and prayed to for assistance) as well as a plea for guidance onto the right path, a path for the virtuous rather than the wicked. The Fatiha is recited many times a day during the Muslim's daily prayers.

FATIMA

(605-633) The daughter of the Prophet Mohammed and Khadija bint Khuwaylid. Of all the daughters of the Prophet Mohammed, she has been without any dispute the most respected and revered by Muslims down the ages. Her name has become enveloped with much legend but the following historical points are worthy of note: she was immensely fond of her father and looked after his wounds after the battle of Uhud; she married Ali after Hijra and accompanied Mohammed at the surrender of Mecca. She was present at his death bed.

FATIMIDS

Major dynasty in medieval Islamic history which flourished in North Africa (from 908) and later in Egypt (from 969-1171). It derived its name from Fatima, the daughter of Mohammed and its caliphs claimed descent from Fatima and Ali b. Abi Talib.

FATIR, al-

The title of the 35th sura of the Koran; it means "The Creator" and the reference is, of course, to God Himself. The sura belongs to the Meccan period and has 45 verses. Its title is drawn from the first verse which opens by praising God, Creator of the Heavens and the earth and the One who has made the angels His envoys or emissaries. This reference here to the angels has also led some commentators to give the title "The Angels" to this sura. It calls on men to remember God's generosity of provision to them. Hell fire awaits the disbeliever but God's true believers will enter the garden of Eden. The partners whom the unbelievers associate with God, and invoke, are incapable of creation. God sustains the heavens and earth in existence.

FATWA

Technical term used in Islamic law to indicate a formal legal judgement or view.

FAYD

In its philosophical sense, term used by Islamic philosophers meaning emanation. The contrast often posed was between a world created ex nihilo at a moment in time by God, and a world which emanated eternally from the Deity. The latter position was frequently condemned as heretical by the ulama.

FEAR

As commonly used, fear means an expectation of harm or pain, generally a painful emotion characterized by alarm, dread, disquiet. However, fear may also mean a calm recognition or consideration of whatever may injure or damage, such recognition causing one to exercise reasoned caution and intelligent foresight.

The Bible shows that there is a proper fear and an improper fear. Thus, fear may be wholesome, causing the individual to proceed with due caution in the face of danger, thereby averting disaster, or it may be morbid, destroying hope and weakening a person's nervous stamina, even to the point of bringing about death.

According to biblical records, the fear of God is healthful; it is an awe and profound reverence for the Creator and a wholesome dread of displeasing Him because of an appreciation of His loving kindness and goodness together with the realization that He is the Supreme Judge and the Almighty, with the power to inflict punishment or death upon those who disobey Him. Proper fear also includes due respect for secular authority, the Christian knowing that just punishment from the authority for a crime would be an indirect expression of God's anger (Romans 13:2-7).

Adam and Eve failed to exercise a proper, healthful fear of God and therefore disobeyed Him. This caused them to hide from God's presence. Adam said: "Your voice I heard in the garden, but I was afraid" (Genesis 3:10). Adam's son Cain felt a similar fear after murdering his brother Abel, and this fear may have been a contributing factor in his deciding to build a city (Genesis 4:13-17).

At Genesis 9:2 the word "fear" is used in connection with the animal creation. God told Noah and his sons, "A fear of you and a terror of you will continue upon every living creature of the earth."During the year that Noah and his family were inside the ark, the animals and birds penned up therein had a fear toward these humans and this helped to restrain them. Accordingly, when they emerged from the ark after the flood, God gave Noah assurance that this fear would continue.

At Hebrews 12:28 Christians are instructed to have godly fear: "Let us continue to have undeserved kindness, through which we may acceptably render God sacred service with godly fear and awe." An angel in midheaven having everlasting good news to declare opened his declaration with the words: "Fear God and give Him glory" (Revelation 14:6-7). Jesus contrasted the wholesome fear of God with fear of man, saying, as recorded at Matthew 10:28: "Do not be fearful of those who kill the body but cannot kill the soul; but rather be in fear of Him that can destroy both soul and body in gehenna." At Revelation 2:10 he also counsels Christians, "Do not be afraid of the things you are about to suffer."

The wise man, after making a careful study of mankind and man's occupations and calamitous experiences, said "The conclusion of the matter, everything having been heard is: Fear the true God and keep his Commandments. For this is the whole obligation to man" (Ecclesiastics 12:13).

FEAST DAYS

In Roman Catholicism, a day set aside to honor God, Mary, the saints, or angels. In liturgical terms, a feast is one category of liturgical observance, with a solemnity being a festival of higher observance, and a memorial being a lower order of observance.

FEBRONIANISM

A German religio-political doctrine expounded by Bishop Johann Nikolaus von Hontheim in his *The State and the Church and the Lawful Power of the*

Roman Pontiff (1763). The doctrine imposed severe limitations on the pope, making him subject to the total church and to a general council of bishops, and strengthened both the state and the national bodies of bishops. The movement collapsed by the end of the 18th century.

FELICITAS

Roman goddess of good luck, encountered from the mid-2nd century BC. The Roman emperors made her prominent as symbolizing the blessings of the imperial regime.

FELIX

The Roman governor before whom Paul was brought for trial at Caesarea. He kept Paul in prison for two years, hoping for a bribe.

FELIX, Bishop

(738-818) Bishop of Urgel (Spain), one of the chief proponents of Adoptionism, a heresy teaching that Christ was the Son of God only by adoption and not by nature. This doctrine abated after his death but temporarily re-emerged in the 12th century through the teaching of the celebrated French theologian and philosopher Peter Abelard and his followers.

FELIX I, Saint

(199-174) Pope from 269 to 274. He was the author of an important dogmatic letter on the unity of Christ's person. He was buried in the catacomb of St. Calixtus and mistakenly called a martyr. His feast day is May 30th.

FELIX II

(301-365) Antipope from 355 to 357. He was irregularly installed as pope in 355 after the Roman Emperor Constantius banished the reigning pope, Tiberius, to Thrace, in northern Greece. The true pope was recalled in 357. The Emperor planned to have Felix and Liberius rule jointly, but Felix was forced to retire to Porto when Liberius returned.

FELIX III, Saint

(413-492) Pope from 483 to 492. He excommunicated Patriarch Acacius of Constantinople in 484 for publishing a document favoring Monophysitism. In this way the 35-year Acacian Schism was created.

FELIX IV, Saint

(477-530) Pope from 526 to 530. He ended the controversy on grace at the second Council (529) of Orange (France). To avoid a disputed succession, Felix named the archdeacon Beniface as his successor.

FELIX DE VALOIS, Saint

(1127-1212) Hermit who with his disciple St. Jean de Matha founded the Trinitarians (Order of the Most Holy Trinity) to free Christian slaves from the Muslims.

FENG-HUANG

A Chinese mythological creature whose rare appearance is said to indicate some great event or bear testimony to the greatness of a ruler.

FERDINAND III (THE SAINT)

(circa 1201-1252) King of Castile from 1217 to 1252 and of Leon from 1230 to 1252. He was a religious zealot and, perhaps urged on by his first wife, Beatrice of Swabia, set about destroying Moorish rule in Andalusia with a vigor and a crusading zeal that were new in Spanish Christian relations with the Moors.

FERIAE LATINAE

In Roman religion, the Festival of Jupiter Latiaris, held in the spring and fall of each year on Mons Albanus.

FERRARA-FLORENCE, Council of

Ecumenical council of the Roman Catholic Church (1438-1445)in which the Latin and Greek churches tried to reach agreement on their doctrinal differences and end the schism between them. Doctrinally, the council is of interest because of the exposition of the Catholic doctrines of purgatory and of the primacy and plenary powers of the pope set out in *Laetentur Caeli*.

FERTILITY

In religion, the procreative power active in nature and believed to be sacred. It is particularly celebrated or supplicated in vegetation cults among agricultural societies, but its sway extends also to the animal world and man. Phallic symbols and other expressions of human sexuality play an important role in fertility rites.

FERTILITY CULTS

Sets of practices, beliefs, and customs with religious or mystical significance and pertaining to the fertility of the soil, have existed in primitive societies the world over; traces of them remain in various peasant folkways. Concerned as they were with agriculture - linked by ritual magic with the passage of the seasons and vegetable growth - they were a means of explaining the miracle of a seeds's development from the planting (in the source of all life, the Earth-Mother) to harvest. Ancient rites, calculated to encourage the soil's fertility and therefore a bountiful harvest, all have, despite their diversity in various cultures, the common denominator of sacred fecundity.

For example, women of the Finnish peasantry once scattered their breast-milk over furrows prior to the crops being sown. The soil (identified with woman, the womb, and sexuality) was supposedly made fertile by the magic practices of the farmer.

Death also played an important role in fertility cults; the burial of the dead in the soil was viewed as a completion of the cycle in which life arose from and returned to the earth.

Gods and divinities of fertility are common in the most diverse religions. They include a mother goddess figure and her mate - also, sometimes, her son - who are united in a sacred marriage. The Hindu Durga is a goddess of fertility as well as of the dead. The Greek Demeter's name, changed to the Roman Ceres, was given to the grain once sacrificed to her. The consort of a fertility goddess may be Dumuzi, Tammuz, Adonis, Dionysos, etc. The German Odin, usually associated with the dead, was a fertility god also.

FESTUS

Governor of the Roman province of Judea after the recall of Felix to Rome (Acts 24:27).Three days after Festus arrived in Caesarea he journeyed to Jerusalem, evidently to familiarize himself with the problems of the people he was to govern. The Jewish chief priests and principal men wasted no time in requesting that Paul, in Caesarea as a leftover prisoner from Felix's administration, be sent for, hoping to ambush him and kill him on the way. Instead, Festus decided on a retrial for Paul and ordered the accusers to appear before his judgment seat in Caesarea. After the "trial" Festus was convinced of Paul's innocence and later confessed to King Agrippa II "I perceived he had committed nothing deserving of death" (Acts 25:25).

FETIALES

Roman priestly officials who were concerned with various aspects of international relations, such as treaties and declarations of war.

FIDEISM

A philosophical view extolling theological faith by making it the ultimate criterion of truth and minimizing the power of reason to know religious truths. Strict fideists assign no place to reason in discovering or understanding fundamental tenets of religion. For them blind faith is supreme as the way to certitude and salvation.

FIDES

Roman goddess, deified "good faith." She was closely connected with Jupiter, and her temple at Rome, dating from 254 BC was located on the Capitol near his.

FIL, al-

The title of the 105th sura of the Koran. It means "The Elephant." The sura belongs to the Meccan period and has five verses. The title is taken from the first verse which asks whether the actions of God with the men of the elephant have not been noticed. The reference here is to the attack on Mecca by Abraha which, as the rest of the sura shows, was unsuccessful.

FILIATION

The relation of the Second Person of the Trinity to the Father as a result of the generation of the Word. There are four Trinitarian relations, for instance, the ordering of one person to another. Filiation expresses the relationship or order of the Son to the father because the Son is generated; paternity expresses the relationship of the Father to the Son whom He generates. The notion is a speculative precision and is not contained in scripture.

FIQH

Arab term meaning Islamic jurisprudence. Originally the word meant "understanding" or "knowledge."

FIRE

In Buddhism, symbolized as the flames of undesirable forces in the mind. Thus the three fires of hatred, lust and Illusion which must be allowed to die for lack of fueling.

FIRE-BAPTIZED HOLINESS CHURCH

One of the Pentecostal churches that merged in the early 20th century to become part of the Pentecostal Holiness Church.

FIRE WORSHIP

This has been practiced through the ages in many continents and appears in all mythologies. Fire was often associated with the sun, and its sanctity was also a recognition of its purifying and protective powers. Among the ancient Hebrews, during the later kingdom, the worship of Moloch, god of fire, was accompanied by the sacrifice of children, a horrible custom sternly condemned by the prophets. Moloch was also venerated by the Assyrians, and, as Baal-Ammon by the Phoenicians, whose religion was also observed in Carthage. In ancient Rome virgins tended the sacred fire of Vesta, goddess of the heart. In the New World, the Aztecs worshipped Xiutecuhtli, the fire god, and Chantico, goddess of volcanoes. Hinduism has the Vedic fire-god Agni, and fire worship is a prominent feature of Zoroastrianism, the religion of the Parsees, to whom fire represents Ahura Mazda, the supreme spirit of universal knowledge. Fire is also sacred to many primitive peoples, including the Ainu of the northern Japanese archipelago.

FIRSTBORN

The oldest son of a father (rather than the firstborn of the mother); the beginning of the father's generation (Deuteronomy 21:17).

From earliest times the firstborn son held an honored position in the family and was the one who succeeded to the headship of the household. He inherited a double portion of the father's property (Deuteronomy 21:17). Reuben was seated by Joseph at a meal according to his right of firstborn (Genesis 43:33). But the Bible does not always honor the firstborn by listing sons according to birth. The first place is often given to the most prominent or faithful of the sons rather than to the firstborn (Genesis 6:10; 1 Chronicles 1:28).

The firstborn came into considerable prominence at the time that God delivered his people from slavery in Egypt. Among the Egyptians, the firstborn were dedicated as sacred to the sun-god Amon-Ra, the supposed preserver of all the firstborn. The tenth plague that God brought upon the Egyptians served to discredit this god and showed up his inability to protect the firstborn. By obeying God's instructions concerning the slaying of the lamb and the splashing of its blood on the doorposts and upper part of the doorways of their houses, the Israelites did not lose their firstborn in death, whereas all the first-born of the Egyptians, both of man and beast, were slain (Exodus 12:21-23). Evidently the firstborn son of each household is meant in most cases and not the head of the household, who may have been a firstborn. Pharaoh himself was probably a firstborn and yet his life was not taken. However, it may be that not every Egyptian house-hold had a literal firstborn son, and in view of the statement in Exodus 12:30, "there was not a house where there was not one dead," the destruction could have included the chief one in the house occupying the position of first-born.

Since the firstborn sons among the Israelites were those in line to become the heads of the various households, they represented the entire nation. God, in fact, referred to the whole nation as His "firstborn," it being his firstborn nation because of the Abrahamic covenant (Exodus 4:22).

FIRST CHURCH OF CHRIST, Scientist

In Boston, the Mother Church of Christian Science, first established by Mary Baker Eddy in 1879, re-estab-lished as an international organization by Mrs. Eddy in 1892. The church building was constructed in 1895; a domed extension was added later (1903-1906).

FIRST COMMUNION

In Roman Catholicism, the solemn observance of one who is receiving the Eucharist for the first time. For chil-dren, this usually occurs on reaching the age of reason.

There are two movements that have gained momentum in recent years in connection with first communion. The first concerns the involvement of the sacraments in the preparation of the child for first sacramental participa-tion, a custom developing from the cur-rent realization of the centrality of the role of the parents in the child's reli-gious formation.

A second development concerns that of first confession. Many had been advo-cating the traditional coupling of these events in the training of children. It was argued that a child of 7 is rarely if ever in spiritual need of the sacrament of penance because he or she normally lacks the moral development necessary for grave sin, and because he or she can be better introduced to the practice of confession at a somewhat later age. Permission was granted by Rome for a period of experiment in which, where local bishops permitted, children could be given their first communion before being trained in the practice of sacra-mental confession.

FIRST FRIDAYS

In Roman Catholicism, a devotion in honor of the sacred Heart in which a person receives Holy Communion for nine consecutive first Fridays of each month. According to a promise made to St. Margaret Mary Alacoque, a person following this observance will have the grace of a final repentance.

FIRST SERMON

The Buddha's enlightenment at Buddha Gaya whence he moved slow-ly across India until he reached the Deer Park near Benares, where he preached to five ascetics his First Sermon. It sets forth the Middle Way between all extremes, the Four Noble Truths and the Noble Eightfold Path.

FISCHER, Saint John

(1469-1535) English cardinal, as bish-op of Rochester (1504-34), he refused to recognize the divorce of Henry VIII from Catharine of Aragon, was impris-oned in the Tower, and later beheaded. Canonized in 1935, his feast day is June 22.

FITNA

In Islam, term denoting temptation, enchantment, civil war, strife. It is a term often used in islamic history with the specific historical sense of Civil War, particularly with reference of the era of conflict between Ali b. Abi Talib and Mu'awiya b. Abi Sufyan. The word fitna also appears frequently in the Koran where man's wealth and children are described as a temptation.

FIVE BOOKS OF MOSES
Pentateuch.

FIVE POINTS OF CALVINISM
Designation for the basic tenets of strict Calvinism as contained in the canons of the Synod of Dort (1618-19). The five points can be indicated by the mnemonic t-u-l-i-p:
▲ total depravity of man;
▲ unconditional predestination and reprobation;
▲ limitation of the Redemption to the elect;
▲ irresistibility of divine grace;
▲ perseverance in grace assured to the elect.

FIVE POINTS OF FUNDAMENTALISM
Tenets of conservative Protestant faith, also referred to as the five fundamentals:
▲ the inerrancy of the Bible, Jesus Christ's divinity;
▲ virgin birth;
▲ substitutionary atonement;
▲ resurrection;
▲ future second coming.
They were formulated at the Niagara Bible Conference of 1895. While many denominations described as fundamentalist do adhere to such teachings, the so-called five points cannot be taken as an adequate reflection of fundamentalism.

FLAVIAN I OF ANTIOCH
(circa 320-404) Bishop of Antioch from 381 to 404, whose election perpetuated the Meletian Schism, a crucial division in the Eastern church over the nature of the Trinity. Flavian defended the Nicene Creed against Arianism.

FLAVIAN II OF ANTIOCH
(circa 450-518) Patriarch of Antioch from 498 to 512. He accepted the decree of union between the Monophysites and the Orthodox. He was later forced to abdicate and banished to Petra in Arabia, where he died.

FLESH (IN THE BIBLE)
A term not to be thought of as synonymous with the body, nor as the material component joined with soul and thus forming man. Flesh indicates man as a psychophysical whole and has a variety of meanings in the Old Testament.

It can mean the soft, meaty parts of animals and men and therefore what is capable of movement as contrasted with dead material, or it is sometimes applied to the entire body of man or beast, or is used to designate blood relationship.

"All flesh" is used to include mankind and all living things collectively. It particularly signifies what is characteristically human as compared to God and what is divine. It defines relationship of dependence and a state of transitoriness (Isaiah 40:6; Psalms 78:). It is the relationship of creature to Creator. In the New Testament flesh has all the connotations of the Old Testament. Moreover, it indicates humanity without God and His spirit (Matthew 16:17).

FLEURY, Claude
(1640-1725) French ecclesiastical historian, Cistercian abbot, who was appointed confessor to the young Louis XV. He wrote a famous *History of the Church* in 1414.

FLOATING PARISH
A name coined to describe any group of Christians who choose to form their own worship community apart from the conventional, i.e., territorial parish. The name also connotes the practice frequently followed by varying the place for each gathering of the groups. The floating parish is inspired by the desire to create a more dynamic Christian community than the participants find in the established local church or parish.

The group is usually made up of whole families. Liturgical experimentation and spontaneity are prominent features, but an intense concern for social problems is also a mark of such groups.

FLOOD

The phenomenal world-engulfing event, caused by the wickedness of man (Genesis 6:5-7).

FLOWERS, Symbolism of

Christian art is abundantly provided with flowers symbolically interpreted, especially in the Middle Ages and Renaissance. A partial list includes the following with the figurative meanings:

▲ crocus   joy;
▲ fleur-de-lys   the Virgin and possibly the conventional form of the Annunciation lily;
▲ daisy   the innocence of the Christ Child;
▲ hyacinth   Christian prudence, peace of mind;
▲ iris   the sorrow of Mary at the Passion of Christ;
▲ lily   purity;
▲ pansy   remembrance and meditation;
▲ violet   humility;
▲ poppy   sleep, fertility, extravagance;
▲ rose   pride and triumphant lover;
▲ narcissus   selfishness and self-love.

FOLLOWING OF CHRIST

Taking Christ in his humanity as the model and exemplar of the Christian life. The theme in its theological interpretation means that Jesus Christ is the way of salvation, not only as the one who accomplished redemption, but as the model and exemplar of all sanctification as well.

Imitation of Christ includes the truth that the grace of sonship by hypostatic union in Jesus is the exemplar of others' adoptive sonship by grace, that as the image of the father, Jesus is the ideal according to which is fashioned the image of God in all who live by grace of Christ.

His exemplarity means that grace is Christian, giving the recipient an identity as a member of Christ; this is particularly the effect of grace received through the sacraments, so that, for instance, the one receiving baptism shares in Christ's Passion as though he himself were the one who suffered and died.

FOOT, Symbolism of

References to the foot in the Scriptures. The foot is a symbol of humility, willing service, and penitence. These are demonstrated by Christ's washing the feet of his disciples (John 13:4), and by the woman's bathing his feet with her tears and drying them with her hair in repentance (Luke 7:38).

The human foot is also said to symbolize humility, because it touches the dust of the earth. Victory and subjection are represented by an conqueror's placing his foot on the neck of the vanquished or using him as a footstool (Joshua 10:24).

FOOTWASHING

A practice, based on John 13:4-20 and 1 Timothy 5:10, observed as an ordinance by some Protestant bodies; it is also observed in some Eastern and Roman Catholic Churches on Holy Thursday.

Early Lutherans strongly repudiated the rite as a Roman abomination. The Anabaptists and Mennonites gave prominence to the practice to signify brotherhood and humility; it has been observed by them as equal in significance to the Lord's Supper.

FOREKNOWLEDGE

Knowledge of a thing before it happens or exists; also called prescience. In the Bible it relates primarily, though not exclusively, to God the Creator and His purposes.

FORENSIC JUSTIFICATION

An understanding of the process of man's being made righteous usually ascribed to Martin Luther and his disciples. "Forensic" here means "by a legal act" i.e., by a declaration; accordingly, righteousness is imputed to man by God without man's being thereby inherently affected. This is doubtless the sort of theory against which the Council of Trent formulated canon 2 of the decree on justification. It is questionable, however, whether Luther himself ever took so gross a position.

FOREORDINATION

The ordaining, decreeing or determining of something forehand; or the quality or state of being forehand.

FORERUNNER

One who goes in advance to prepare for the coming of another. This might include scouting and spying, clearing the way, proclaiming and giving notice of another's approach, or showing the way for others to follow.

In biblical times, it was the Oriental custom that runners go before the royal chariot and announce the king's coming and to assist him generally (1 Samuel 8:11). Absalom and Adonijah, in imitation of such regal dignity and to add prestige and seeming sanction to their respective rebellions, placed 50 runners before their personal chariots (2 Samuel 15:1; 1 Kings 1:5).

FORETELLER OF EVENTS

A person claiming ability to forecast what will take place in the future, among whom the Bible names magic-practicing priests, spiritistic diviners, astrologers and others. Some of these possessed occult powers by virtue of contact with the demons, the wicked angelic enemies of God under Satan the devil, the ruler of the demons (Luke 11:14-20). In ancient times various methods were employed by these prognosticators in obtaining their messages of prediction; stargazing (Isaiah 47:13); examination of the liver and other viscera of sacrificed animal victims (Ezekiel 21:21); interpretation of omens (2 Kings 21:6); consultation with the so-called "spirits" of the dead, and so forth (Deuteronomy 18:11).

FORGIVENESS

The act of pardoning an offender; ceasing to feel resentment toward him because of his offense and giving up all claim to recompense.

According to God's law given to the nation of Israel, in order for one who had sinned against God or against his fellow man to have his sins forgiven, he first had to rectify the wrong as the Low prescribed and then, in most cases, present a blood offering to God (Leviticus 5:5-7). Hence, the principle stated by Paul: "Yes, nearly all things are cleansed with blood according to the law, and unless blood is poured out no forgiveness takes place" (Hebrews 9:22).

It is proper to pray for forgiveness in behalf of others, even an entire congregation. Moses did so respecting the nation of Israel, confessing their national sin and asking forgiveness, and was favorably heard by God (Numbers 14:19-20).

FORMER PROPHETS

Also called the First or Earlier Prophets; the Books of Joshua, Judges, Samuel, and Kings; modern scholars refer to them as Deuteronomic history, The distinction between Former and Latter Prophets is from the division of the Hebrew Bible into Torah, Prophets, and Writings. The latter Prophets include the Books of Isaiah, Jeremiah, Ezekiel, and the 12 minor prophets.

FORMSTECHER, Solomon

(1808-1889) Jewish idealist philosopher who wrote *The Religion of the Spirit* which is considered the most complete exposition of his philosophy and a thorough systematization of Judaism.

FORSYTH, Peter Taylor

(1848-1921) Congregational minister whose numerous and influential writings anticipated the philosophy of the Swiss Protestant theologian Karl Barth. By bringing the word grace back into Protestant theology and by showing anew the sovereignty of God as

revealed in Christ's love Forsyth anticipated many insights characteristic of
Karl Barth.

FORTITUDE

One of the four cardinal (or "hinge")
virtues and one of the gifts of the Holy
Spirit; it is courage in doing good
despite the dangers or difficulties that
stand in one's way.

Fortitude complements the cardinal
virtue of courage, which may be steadfast to endure and brave to tackle the
difficulties and dangers in the human
scene, even including the ultimate
challenge of death, but is given a
superhuman strength when it reaches
into the darkness beyond to the goal of
eternal life, a high courage that "neither things present nor things to come,
nor height nor depth, nor anything else
in all creation will ne able to separate
us from the love of God (Romans
8:39).

FORTITUDE, Virtue of

In the wide sense, the virtue regulates
the emotions of fear and boldness so as
to dispose a man to act reasonably in
situations of danger.

The Christian virtue of fortitude finds
its distinctive expression in martyrdom, the willing acceptance of death
from persecutors as the price of steadfastness in the warfare of Christian witness.

The gospel does not overlook the frequent necessity of resisting evils; but it
does extol endurance, rather than the
willingness to do battle, as the most
characteristic act of Christian fortitude.

FORTUNATUS

One of the mature members of the congregation in Corinth who, together
with Stephanas and Achaicus, visited
Paul at Ephesus (1 Corinthians 16: 8,
17-18). From these men Paul may have
learned of the disturbing conditions
about which he wrote, and they were
possibly the one who delivered Paul's
first canonical letter to the Corinthians
(1 Corinthians 1:11; 5:1).

FORUM IN CANON LAW

The sphere in which the power of jurisdiction is exercised. The internal forum
means conscience, which is subject to
sacramental jurisdiction in the sacrament of penance or to extrasacramental
but private and spiritual jurisdiction.

Matters belonging to the internal forum
concern the state of a person's soul
before God. The external forum means
the public governmental sphere of the
church's life, which is subject to the
public exercise of disciplinary jurisdiction. Matters belonging to the external
forum concern the juridical status (guilt
or innocence) of the members of the
church, for instance, matters dealt with
by the penal power of the church.

FOSDICK, Harry Emerson

(1878-1969) Liberal Protestant minister, teacher and author, an early practitioner of pastoral counselling and of
the church's cooperation with psychia-
try.

FOUNTAIN, Spring

Generally, a natural source of water
(Exodus 15:27), in contrast to wells
and cisterns that were usually dug
(Genesis 26:15); also used with reference to a source of something other
than waster. Since springs were cleared
and deepened at times, this may
explain why "fountain" and "well" are
sometimes used interchangeable for the
same water source (Genesis 16:7, 14;
24:11-13; John 4:6).

@NORMAAL:FOUNTAIN OF THE BIG SNAKE

The Hebrew expression, carrying the
thought of a fountain, spring or well of
a land or sea monster. This water
source was located along the route
Nehemiah took on his first inspection
of Jerusalem's broken-down walls
(Nehemiah 2:12-13). Since this name
is not found again in the Bible, the
fountain or well, if elsewhere referred
to, must be under a different designation.

FOUR HORSEMEN OF THE APOCALYPSE

In the New Testament (Revelation 6:1-8), four allegorical figures: the rider of the red horse representing War; of the black, Famine; of the "pale horse," Death. The first to appear, riding a white horse and carrying a bow, has been variously interpreted, but is usually believed to represent Christ and the victory of his word.

FOUR LAST THINGS

Death, personal judgment, heaven, and hell, along with purgatory in the Roman Catholic tradition, make up the personal aspects of eschatology. These are realities that define the limit of man's personal history as an individual before God, culminating in either fulfillment in all dimensions of his existence or in final personal loss.

They are distinguished from the eschatological realities connected with the cosmic fulfillment of mankind which include the parousia, resurrection of the flesh, and general judgment.

FOUR NOBLE TRUTHS

In Buddhism, the basic truths as set forth by the Buddha in his first sermon. They are:

1 Dukkha: There can be no existence without suffering.
2 Samudaya: The cause of suffering is egoistic desire.
3 Nirodha: The elimination of desire brings the cessation of suffering.
4 Magga: The way to the elimination of desire is the Noble Eightfold Path.

FOUR PATHS

In Buddhism, the four stages on the Path to liberation. These four paths or stages are:

1 Sotapanna: He who has entered the Stream. At this stage he is free from the first three of the ten Fetters.
2 Sakadagamin: He who will return once only to this world before attaining liberation.
3 Anagamin: He who will never return to this world, being utterly free from these five Fetters.

4 Arahat: The Worthy One, who attains Nirvana. Such a one has cast off the five higher Fetters.

FOURTEEN FUNDAMENTAL BUDDHIST BELIEFS

The 14 points compiled at the Council organized at Adyar, Madras, in 1891.

FORTY HOURS DEVOTION

In Roman Catholicism, an approximately three-day period of worship before the Blessed Sacrament as it is exposed in a monstrance and displayed on an altar or reservation. The 40 hours commemorate the length of time that Jesus lay in the tomb. Forty Hours devotion originated in Milan circa 1527.

FOXE, Richard

(1448-1528) Ecclesiastical statesman, one of the chief ministers of King Henry VII and founder of Corpus Christi College, Oxford.

FRANCISCAN CROWN

A rosary of seven decades introduced in 1422, and said in honor of the seven joys of the Blessed Virgin. This rosary is also known as the seraphic rosary.

FRANCISCAN NUNS

Numerous communities of Roman Catholic religious women who are affiliated to one of the branches of the Franciscan friars by reason of their rule of life, their customs and their religious habit, or dress.

The communities are divided into two groups: the second order, of strictly cloistered, or enclosed, contemplative nuns; and the regular third order of sisters, devoted primarily to active works such as teaching, nursing, foreign missions, and a wide variety of charitable works. The latter group is far more numerous and includes many congregations that are of recent origin.

FRANCISCANS

Orders of mendicant friars founded by St. Francis of Assisi in 1208. In addition to the usual vows of poverty, chastity and obedience, the Franciscans emphasize preaching and ministering the poor. As the first order began to acquire property, a dispute arose over the strict observance of Francis' insistence upon absolute poverty. The resulting division in the order led to the establishment of three branches: the Friars Minor, or Minorites, have retained the strict rule; the Friars Minor Conventual own property in common; and the Friars Minor Capuchin, or Capuchins, are a reform branch of the first. Known as the Gray Friars during the Middle Ages for the color of their habits, the Franciscans now wear hooded brown robes and sandals. The Franciscan second order of nuns is known as the Poor Clares, after their foundress, St. Clare.

FRANCISCAN SPIRITUALITY

The spirituality that bears the name of St. Francis is purely Christian, being drawn from the gospel without addition or subtraction. It was the intensity of the love, joy, enthusiasm, and thoroughness with which Francis imitated his observance of the gospel truly unique. St. Francis was deeply conscious of God's dominion and his own creaturehood.

Franciscan spirituality is not a theological construction evolved by a theorist. The adjectives customarily employed to describe it include:

▲ evangelical;
▲ Christocentric;
▲ apostolic;
▲ seraphic;
▲ ecclesial;
▲ Marian;
▲ mendicant.

It never occurred to Francis, who instinctively thought and spoke in concrete, personal, gospel terms, to organize the complex of elements designated by these words into a precise system. The Franciscan doctors, especially St. Bonaventure and John Duns Scotus, gave some of these elements theological explication, and the Franciscan saints gave them practical exemplification; but the efforts of those less gifted

with wisdom and holiness to systematize them have not met with universal acceptance.

FRANCIS DE SALES, Saint

(1567-1622) French nobleman, Roman Catholic bishop of Geneva-Annecy from 1603. Author of popular works such as *Introduction to the Devout Life* (1608), he is even respected by the Calvinists for his good nature and humility. He helped found the Order of the Visitation (1610). He was canonized in 1665. His feast day is January 29th.

FRANCIS OF ASSISI, Saint

(1182-1226) Italian Roman Catholic mystic, founder of the Franciscans. In 1205 he turned away from his extravagant life and wealthy merchant family and entered a religious life of utter poverty. He was given oral sanction by Pope Innocent III to form an order or friars in 1209. With his many followers Francis preached and ministered to the poor in Italy and abroad, stressing piety, simplicity, and the life of all living things. Eventually the order expanded beyond control of its founder; Francis relinquished the leadership in 1221. His feast day is October 4th.

FRANCIS DE MEYRONNES

(1285-1328) Franciscan monk, one of the principal philosopher-theologians of 14th century Scholasticism and a leading advocate of the subtle system of Realism proposed by the eminent English Scholastic John Duns Scotus.

FRANCIS OF PAOLA, Saint

(1416-1507) Founder of the Minim Friars, a severely ascetic Roman Catholic order that does charitable work and refrains from eating meat, eggs, or dairy products.

FRANCIS XAVIER, Saint

(1506-1552) Spanish missionary. A friend of St. Ignatius of Loyola, he was a founder member of the Jesuits. In 1541 he set out as a missionary, reaching the East Indies, Goa, India, and Ceylon. In 1549 he established a Jesuit mission in Japan and in 1552 sought to extend his work to China, but died before he reached there. His feast day is December 3th.

FRANCKE, August Hermann

(1663-1727) Protestant religious leader, and social reformer, who was one of the principal promoters of Pietism, a devotional revival of personal Christianity that reacted to academic Lutheranism.

FRAVASHIS

In Zoroastrianism, pre-existing external higher souls or essences of man. Associated with Ahura Mazda, the supreme divinity, since the first creation, they participate in his nature of pure light and inexhaustible bounty. Each man's fravashi, distinct from his incarnate soul, subtly guides him in life toward the realization of his higher nature.

FREE CHURCH FEDERAL COUNCIL

Organization of free churches (not part of the Church of England) of England and Wales, including Methodist, Baptist, Congregationalist, Presbyterian, and some other churches. It was formed in 1940.

FREEDMAN, Freeman

During Roman rule, one who was emancipated from slavery was called a "freedman," whereas a "freeman" was free from birth, possessing full citizenship rights, as did the apostle Paul (Acts 22:28).

Formal emancipation granted the freedman Roman citizenship, but such a former slave was not eligible for political office, although his descendants were, in the second or at least the third generation. Informal emancipation, however, merely gave practical freedom to the individual, not civic rights.

Since the freedman was viewed as belonging to the family of his former master, a mutual obligation rested upon the two parties. The freedman either remained in the home and in the employ of his former master or received a farm and capital to get started in making his own living. The patron buried his freedman in the family tomb and took charge of any surviving minor children, and inherited the property if there were no heirs. On the other hand, if the patron suffered financial reverses, his freedman was required by law to care for him. But the rights of a former master in relation to his freedman could not be passed on to his heirs.

It has been suggested that those who belonged to the "Synagogue of the Freedman," were Jews who had been taken captive by the Romans and then later were emancipated. Another view is that these persons were freed slaves who had become Jewish proselytes (Acts 6:9).

As indicated in the Bible, although a Christian may be a slave to an earthly master, he is actually Christ's freedman, liberated from bondage to sin and death, but having bought with a price, Jesus' precious blood. A Christian who is a freedman in a physical sense is a slave of God and of Jesus Christ, obligated to obey his commands. This indicates that for humans freedom is always relative, never absolute. Therefore, from God's viewpoint, in the Christian congregation, there is no difference between slave and freedman. Moreover, the freedom, possessed by a Christian does not entitle him to use this as a blind for moral badness (1 Corinthians 7:22-23; Hebrews 2:14-15).

FREEDOM

In general, the state or condition of one not subject to constraint in the exercise of his capacity to determine for himself what he shall think, believe, or do. It is not the same thing as free will, which is a natural endowment shared by all normal men, and it cannot be taken from them (although its use may be influenced or impeded in various ways; e.g, by drugs); whereas freedom, is something that must be achieved.

FREEDOM, Human

According to Roman Catholicism, the human person, made in the image and likeness of God, is not subject to determinism but possesses true moral freedom of choice; that is, the human person, when acting in a truly human way, is able to choose or not to choose a certain course of action.

The importance of human freedom is emphasized in the writings of Vatican Council II: "Only in freedom that man can turn himself toward what is good .... But that which is truly freedom is an exceptional sign of the image of God in man .... Man's dignity therefore requires him to act out of conscious and free choice, as moved and drawn in a personal way from within, and not by blind impulses in himself or by mere constraint."

FREEDOM, Religious

In matters of religious conviction and worship of God the human person should be free to follow the dictates of his or her conscience and should not be forced by civil authority to act against these dictates nor be restrained from acting in accord with them, provided there is no serious danger to the common good.

Vatican Council II in its Declaration on Religious Liberty says that the right to religious freedom in civil society "means that all men should be immune from coercion on the part of individuals, social groups and every human power, so that, within due limits, no body is forced to act against his or her convictions nor is anyone to be restrained from acting in accordance with his or her convictions in religious matters in private or in public, alone or in association with others."

FREEDOM, Spiritual

The liberty from sin and spiritual death which Christ has won for mankind and in accordance with which the Christian acts. Spiritual freedom may be spoken of in a cosmic sense, designating the fundamental Christian vision of the world expressed in Paul's Epistle to the Romans according to which all men having sinned were under the power of death until their redemption could be secured by Christ.

In this sense, Paul speaks of man lacking freedom while he is under the law. To this notion of the cosmic freedom granted by Christ must be added that of the personal freedom within which a Christian may make his moral decisions.

This implies a liberating death to sin and an orientation of the will under grace to accomplish only what is good. Thus the person is freed from the slavery of a will constructed by selfishness and opened to the Spirit so that he may achieve the goals which he recognizes as good.

FREEDOM OF CHRIST

Christ underwent his Passion and death under the mandate of his Father. The Greek term entole (command or precept) used by John's gospel with reference to Christ's death (John 14:31), leaves no doubt as to the binding character of the Father's will.

This mandate and the obedience due to it raise the delicate theological problem of the nature of Christ's human freedom. Did the Father's precept leave room in him for the exercise of that faculty? More precisely, how can Christ's human liberty be combined with his absolute and intrinsic impeccability on the one hand and the Father's mandate on the other.

The solution of the antinomy seems to lie in a correct conception of liberty. The essence of freedom does not consist in the faculty of choice, but in the power of self-determination, such as in fact the human freedom of Christ. The immediate vision of the Father showed him the goodness of the Father's will. Christ embraced it in an act of perfect self-determination. While submitting to the Father's will, he claimed to lay down his life of his own will.

FREEDOM OF CONSCIENCE

The dignity of the human person consists in the fact that he or she can intelligently and freely choose God's will and God's law. On a practical level, conscience plays a critical role in this choice. Conscience should be free from all external constraints and force. According to the writings of Vatican Council II " ... man sees and recognizes the demands of the divine law. He is bound to follow this conscience faithfully in all his activity so that he may come to God, who is his last end. Therefore he must not be forced to act contrary to his conscience. Not must he be prevented from acting according to his conscience, especially in religious matters."

FREEMASONS

Members of those fraternal organizations that follow the principles, usages and rites known as Freemasonry. Freemasons trace their origins to medieval stonemasons, who were called free masons because they worked on free stone; these artisans, were working or operative masons.

In England these fraternities of working masons, which had a religious and mortal purpose, gradually admitted non-working, honorary, members. When the building of churches stopped after the Reformation, the lodges came to be made up largely of non-working Masons, and the tools and terms of he trade took on a purely symbolic nature. Modern Freemasons have their origin in the Grand Lodge of England, formed from four lodges there in 1717. After 1721 the Freemasons accepted many members from the royalty and nobility, and the lodges grew in size. From England the organization moved to continental Europe and America.

Freemasonry has a religious content. In Anglo-Saxon countries the deism connoted by the designation of God as Great Architect and the general naturalism signify a neutral and non-denominational attitude rather than the hostility to religion prevalent to Freemasons of France and the Latin countries. The anti-Catholicism associated with Masonry was more a part of the religious antipathy between Protestants and Catholics than an essential of Freemasonry.

FREE METHODIST CHURCH

United States denomination founded in 1860 by members excluded from the methodist Episcopal Church for trying to restore Wesleyan principles. The church follows the teachings of John Wesley.

FREE WILL

The human faculty to choose among several courses of action and thus the underlying basis for moral responsibility.

In Buddhism, determinism, in the sense that human action is determined by forces independent of the will. This is classed in Buddhism as an erroneous conception. It asserts that the will of man is not bound by external causes, but is free in the sense that all fetters are of man's own making, and may be by man himself cast off. In other words, will per se is free, but is limited by the results of its own previous acts.

FREE WOMAN

A woman who is not in slavery. This term is used with reference to Abraham's wife Sarah and "the Jerusalem above." From the time God liberated the Israelites from Egyptian bondage and gave them the Law at Mount Sinai till the days when Jesus Christ was on earth, God treated the nation of Israel as a secondary wife (Jeremiah 3:14, 31:31-32). However, the Law did not give the nation of Israel the status of a free woman, for it showed them up as under subjection to sin, hence slaves. Most appropriately, therefore, apostle Paul compared the enslaved Jerusalem of his day with the servant girl Hagar, Abraham's concubine, and Jerusalem's "children" or citizens with Hagar's son Ishmael. In contrast, God's original wife, the heavenly Jerusalem, has, like Sarah, always been a free woman and her children are likewise free. To become a free child of the Jerusalem above, having "her freedom," it is necessary to be set free from the bondage of sin by the Son of God (John 8:34-36).

FREYJA

Most renowned of the Norse goddesses, the sister and female counterpart of Freyr, in charge of love, fertility, battle, and death.

FREYR

In Norse mythology, the son of the fertility god Njord and himself a ruler of peace and fertility, rain, and sunshine.

FRIAR

A member of one of the mendicant orders who pursue an ideal of poverty. Friars are distinct from monks because they pursue a pastoral ministry and can move around according to need. Dominicans and Franciscans are examples of orders of friars.

FRIDAY

The sixth day of the week. Its name comes from "Frigg's day," after Frigg, the Teutonic goddess of love. The Romans called it the day of Venus, after their own goddess of love, and this is the origin of such names as the French vendredi and the Spanish viernes.

FRIDOLIN, Saint

(6th century) Irish missionary, first mentioned by the monk Balther Saeckingen (circa 1000) as apostle of the Alamanni on the upper Rhine and founder of Saeckingen in the time of Clovis I.

FRIEND OF GOD

Among the divine blessings bestowed upon Abraham was the privilege and honor of being called "God's friend." This was by reason of Abraham's outstanding faith, which he demonstrated to the greatest degree possible in his willingness to offer up his son Isaac as a sacrifice (Isaiah 41:8; 2 Chronicles 20:7).

FRIEND (COMPANION) OF THE KING

In using this expression, the Bible does not indicate that it had more than the usual connotation of one who is friendly or a companion. Neither does it directly describe the specific functions of the friend of the king as an official title. However, based on the customs of other lands, it may be that the expression designated a court official who was a confidant, a personal friend and companion to a king and who at times executed confidential orders (Genesis 26:26).

Among Solomon's court dignitaries, listed at 1 Kings 4:1-6, are two sons of Nathan. One is mentioned as being "over the deputies," whereas the other, Zabud, is called "the friend of the king." In the reign of Solomon's father, King David, Hushai the Archite is spoken of as having this relationship to King David, being called "David's companion." At David's request Hushai returned to Jerusalem to frustrate the counsel of Ahithophel when Absalom conspired to usurp the throne (2 Samuel 15:32-37; 16:16-19).

FRIEND OF THE BRIDEGROOM

In ancient times, a man of the bridegroom's close acquaintances acted as a legal representative of the bridegroom and took the primary responsibility in making arrangements for the marriage. He would sometimes arrange the bride price to the father and gifts to the bride. He was viewed as bringing together the bride and groom. The bridal procession would arrive at the house of the bridegroom's father or the bridegroom's house, where the marriage was consummated. At the feast, on hearing the bridegroom speak to the bride, the friend of the bridegroom was happy, feeling that his duty was successfully concluded.

John the Baptist, who , according to biblical tradition, prepared the way for the Messiah, introduced the first members of the "bride" to Jesus Christ, to whom she was espoused (2 Corinthians 11:2, Revelation 21:2, 9).

"Friends of the bridegroom" are mentioned at Matthew 9:15. Here reference is made to other friends who joined in the marriage procession and who were invited to the marriage feast.

FRIENDS OF GOD

A medieval Christian fellowship that originated during the early part of the 14th century in Basel, Switserland, and then spread to Germany. Primarily a lay, middle class, and democratic movement espousing a Christian life of love, piety, devotion and holiness, the Friends of God presaged the 16th century Reformation.

FRIENDS OF THE TEMPLE

A religious body that originated in Germany for the purpose of bringing about the kingdom of Christ on earth in their autonomous communities. The founder, Württemberg Pietist Christoph Hoffmann (1815-1885), envisaged the restoration of the Temple and a theocracy at Jerusalem.

Together with George David Hardegg (1805-1879) and Christian Paulus, he set out to found other temple communities, first in Germany and then in various places of the Holy Land. Usually good schools and hospitals were connected with each community, and the Friends thus became known for their cultural and social contributions.

The Friends of the Temple spread to Russia and North America (1905), where they became closely associated with the Unitarians.

FRUMENTIUS, Saint

(4th century) Syrian apostle who introduced Christianity into Ethiopia and, as first bishop of its ancient capital, Aksum, near modern Adwam structured the emerging church in the orthodox theology of the Alexandrian school during the 4th century Trinitarian controversy.

FUGITIVE

In canon law, a member of a religious order or of any clerical society who disobediently leaves his community, without permission and for a considerable period of time, but with the intention of returning.

During his absence, he remains bound by all his religious obligations, including that of rejoining the community. The fugitive automatically incurs deprivation of the office, and if a cleric, suspension. He cannot, however, be reconciled unless he regrets his flight and undertakes to return as soon as possible to submit himself to the authority of his superior.

FUGITIVENESS, Land of

A land "east of Eden," in which the condemned murderer Cain took up residence (Genesis 4:16). The Hebrew word nohdh is derived from the same root (nudh) as is the word "fugitive" used in verses 12 and 14. The location of the land is unknown.

FU HSING

In Chinese mythology, the Star God of Happiness, the first of three stellar divinities known collectively as Fu-Shou-Lu. He is but one of many Chinese gods who bestow happiness on their worshippers.

FUKKO SHINTO

A school of Japanese religion prominent in the 18th century that attempted to uncover the pure meaning of ancient Shinto thought through the philosophical study of the Japanese classics. The school has a lasting influence on the development of modern Shinto thought.

FULANI EMPIRE

Muslim theocracy of the Western Sudan that flourished in the 19th century. The Fulani, a people of obscure and controversial origins expanded eastward in the 14th century. The Empire reached its zenith under Muhammad

Bello, who administered it according to the principles of Muslim law. The decay of this system was to aid the establishment in the late 19th century of British rule in what was later to be known as Northern Nigeria.

FULBERT OF CHARTRES, Saint

(circa 960-1028) Bishop of Chartres who developed the cathedral school there into one of Europe's chief centers of learning. His extant works include sermons, letters, and poems. His feast day is April 10th.

FULCHER OF CHARTRES

(circa 1059-1127) French chaplain and chronicler of the First Crusade whose account is among the most reliable in regard to the European journey to the Holy Land and the early years of the Kingdom of Jerusalem.

FULGENTIUS OF RUSPE, Saint

(467-533) Bishop of Ruspe and theological writer who defended orthodoxy in 6th century Africa against Arianism, the heretical doctrine that Christ was neither equal with God nor eternal.

Eight of the numerous, essentially polemical writings ascribed to him are known to be authentic. All of his works elaborate orthodox views. He was such a fervent disciple of St. Augustine that he has been called the "abbreviated Augustine."

FUNDAMENTAL ARTICLES OF BELIEF

Those principles of the Christian religion in which belief is necessary, according to some, for church membership and salvation. This notion caused much discussion in the 17th century and was the subject of a noted controversy between Bossuet and Jurieu.

Jurieu, a Protestant, maintained that Christian unity could be achieved if the various churches recognized that certain unessential doctrines have been attached to the faith, and that those who have retained the fundamental articles of faith contained in the earliest creeds are in fact united in Christ's one church.

FUNDAMENTAL THEOLOGY

The study of revelation as a possible act of God, its transmission in time and event, and man's ability to receive it. It is the foundation of theology in that it asks the basic preliminary questions:

▲ How can God's words be revealed to men?

▲ What and where is divine revelation?

Although the authority of God revealing is motive and foundation of the act of faith, yet it is knowledge of the credibility of revealed truth that justifies this response intellectually.

As a means of salvation, revelation must validate itself and answer man's hesitancy and doubts. Fundamental theology, therefore, weighs the credentials of revelation so that its acceptance may be seen to be reasonable, even obligatory.

Moreover, since revelation cannot be substantiated by appeal to faith and revealed truth, metaphysics must provide the criteria and history must establish its actual occurrence. Thus in Christian faith, scripture proclaims itself credible testimony confirmed by "signs" (John 20:30-31), and the preaching of Jesus and his Apostles focuses on God who reveals Himself in His Word (Hebrews 1:1) and in man who comes to the revealing God by faith that is reasonable.

Here fundamental theology functions as a bridge between theology and philosophy. Ultimately it can draw conclusions regarding the personal nature of God, man's openness to freely given revelation beyond what nature discloses, and the relation of faith to god.

FUNDAMENTALISM

Conservatist Protestant movement, upholding evangelicalism against modernism. The movement has flourished, particularly in the south of the United States, since the early 20th century. Its chief doctrines, set out in a series of pamphlets, *The Fundamentals* (1910-12), are Christ's virgin birth, the substitutionary theory of atonement, and the absolute infallibility of the Bible. The last has led to a denial of evolution. Leading advocates of the movement include W. J. Bryan and the theological John Cresham Machen. Modern Protestant fundamentalism is mostly dispensationalist, and revivalist.

Fundamentalism should be understood primarily as an attempt to protect essential elements (fundamentals) of the Christian faith from the eroding effects of nationalism and naturalism. It was not a monolithic movement, but has a variety of expressions.

Although it emerged as a party in the fundamentalist-modernist controversy after World War I, its roots so back into the 19th century, when evolution, biblical criticism, and other intellectual currents began to challenge old assumptions concerning the authority of biblical revelation.

As fundamentalism developed, most Protestant denominations in the United States felt the division between liberalism and fundamentalism. The Baptists, Presbyterians, and Disciples of Christ were more affected than others. Nevertheless, talk of schism was much more common than schism itself.

Preoccupations with the Depression of the 1930s and World War II curtailed fundamentalism's appeal. By 1950 it was either isolated and muted or had taken on the more moderate tones of Evangelicalism. In the 1970s and 1980s, however, fundamentalism again became an influential force in the United States.

FUNDAMENTALISM, Biblical

A religious movement which developed independently in different Protestant denominations towards the end of the 19th century. The biblical teachings on the virgin birth, the physical resurrection of Christ, the substitutionary atonement of his sacrifice, and his second coming were advanced as touchstones of orthodoxy.

To unify their efforts, the World's Christian Fundamental Association was founded in 1919 and enlarged in 1948 to the International Council of Christian Churches and World Evangelical Fellowship.

FUNDAMENTALISM, Islamic

Desire to return to an "ideal" Islam, perhaps that of the ages of Rashidun. Many Islamic fundamentalists believe that the Islam of the modern era, and the so-called "Islamic" states, as they perceive them, have been corrupted. They desire a return to "true" Islam, shorn of any modern compromises with secularism. This has sometimes engendered a profound hostility towards the West which is often perceived as secular and even atheistic. The spirit of Islamic fundamentalism has imbued many Islamic groups.

FUNDAMENTALIST AND EVANGELICAL CHURCHES

A mixed group of theologically conservative Protestant churches that arose in the United States in the 1920s. Derived from a group of dissenters who called themselves Fundamentalists, these churches have claimed to defend the standards of orthodox Christianity against the liberals or Modernists; i.e., those Protestants who incorporated biblical criticism into their theologies and attempted to make the church relevant to the social dilemmas of the era.

FUNERAL CUSTOMS

Customs related to funerals can be traced back some 50,000 years. Neanderthal man was the first to practice careful disposal of the dead. Throughout the ages, the methods and rituals used have been mainly determined by religious beliefs, especially belief in life after death.

Primitive man saw the need to heal the emotional shock suffered by the family or the community on the loss of one of its members; and show his desire to honor the dead and to assist the swift passage of the spirit to the world beyond.

By the end of the Old Stone Age, grave-goods (things that might be needed in the next world and on the journey there) was being buried with the dead, a practice reaching its most elaborate form with the ancient Egyptians. Some people also killed the cattle, slaves and favorite wife of the dead man so that they could serve him in the next world. The Hindu practice of Suttee (the sacrifice of the widow on her husband's funeral pyre) was prompted by the same motive.

In many parts of ancient Europe, carts or chariots were placed in the tombs of kings and chiefs. Scandinavian warriors were often buried in their ships.

Methods of disposal, sometimes influenced by ecological factors, have varied greatly, from burial in a tomb or vault to ritual cannibalism. In burial, posture and orientation are often important. The Japanese are sat upright, Muslims are laid on the right side, facing Mecca. Christians are usually buried with their feet to the east.

Cremation, a worldwide practice, is often followed by some secondary disposal such as scattering the ashes (in the case of Hindus, on a holy river). Parsees, followers of Zoroastrianism, expose their dead on "towers of silence" where they are eaten by vultures. Some American tribes used similar methods. Preservation, associated particularly with the ancient Egyptians, is represented today by embalming.

Burial in the earth and cremation are two most common methods of disposing of the dead, although cremation is sometimes opposed on religious grounds, notably by the Roman Catholic Church. Prayers for the soul of the departed and consolation for the living are the chief features of Christian funeral services. In Jewish services, the beauty and wonder of life, death and the whole of nature are emphasized.

FURQAN, al-

The title of the 25th sura of the koran,. meaning literally "The Distinguisher between Good and Evil" or "The Proof." The title of the sura is drawn from verse 30. A major theme of this chapter is the foolishness of the polytheists and unbelievers. The sura also stresses the humanity of God's messengers and the coming punishment for idolaters, polytheists and disbelievers. By contrast, paradise will be the reward of the Godfearing.

FURSEY, Saint

(567-650) Monk, celebrated visionary, one of the greatest early medieval Irish monastic missionaries to the Continent; his renowned visions had considerable influence on dream literature of the later Middle Ages.

G

GAAL

In the Old Testament, the son of Ebed who, along with his brothers, came to Shechem and gained the confidence of the landowners there (Judges 9:26). These landowners had previously strengthened the hand of Abimelech to kill the 70 sons of Jerubbaal (Gideon) and then had proceeded to make him king over them (Judges 9:1-6). Apparently Abimelech constituted Zebul as resident prince of Shechem, while he himself personally loved in Arumah. In time a bad spirit developed between the landowners of Shechem and Abimelech. So Gaal and his brothers now incited the city to revolt against Abimelech. Zebul, hearing of this, at once sent word to Abimelech, with a recommendation on how to cope with the situation that was developing. Gaal and those with him were defeated in the ensuing battle with King Abimelech and fled back to the city. Finally Zebul drove Gaal and his brothers out of Shechem (Judges 9:22-41).

GAASH

The name of a hill in the mountainous region of Ephraim, sough of Timnah-heres (Joshua 24:30). The torrent valleys of Gaash, mentioned in 2 Samuel 23:30 and 1 Chronicles 11:32, apparently refer to ravines in the vicinity of that hill.

GABAR

Name formerly applied to members of the small Zoroastrian minority in Iran. In the early 1990s they numbered 22,000. They are noted gardeners, and many have become prosperous merchants.

GABBAI

In biblical times, a Benjaminite jurisdictional district head whose name appears in a listing of those residing in Jerusalem in Nehemiah's days (Nehemiah 11:3-8).

GABRIEL

One of the archangels. Gabriel was the heavenly messenger sent to announce the birth of John the Baptist to Zachariah and to announce the birth of Jesus to Mary.

Gabriel, meaning man of God in Hebrew, is chiefly known from the Gospel according to Luke. In the Old Testament he interpreted Daniel's visions. In the Koran, Gabriel is the medium of revelation to Mohammed.

GAD

One of the 12 tribes of Israel that in biblical times comprised the people of Israel who later became the Jewish people. The tribe was named after the elder of two sons born to Jacob and Zilpah, a maidservant of Jacob's first wife, Leah.

The tribe's warriors numbered 45,650 in the second year of the exodus from Egypt (Genesis 46:16; Numbers 1:1-3). Gad was in the three-tribe division with Reuben and Simeon. Their campsite was to the south of the tabernacle (Numbers 2:10-16). When on the march Judah's division was first, followed by the Levites of the families of Gershon and Merari carrying the tabernacle and, after them, the division of which Gad was a part.

GADARENES

In biblical times, name applied to the inhabitants of an area where Jesus Christ expelled demons from two men. According to what is considered to be the best available manuscript evidence, Matthew originally used "country of the Gadarenes," whereas Mark and Luke, in relation to this event, employed "country of the Geradenes" (Matthew 8:28; Mark 5:1; Luke 8:26). Both countries are shown to lie on "the other side," that is, the east side, of the Sea of Galilee. The designation "country of the gadarenes" possibly applied to the district radiating from the city of Gadara, situated about five miles southeast of the Sea of Galilee.

GADDI

In Judaism, son of Susi of the tribe of Manasseh; one of the 12 chieftains Moses sent out from the wilderness of Paran to spy out the land of Canaan (Numbers 13:2-11).

GADDIEL

In Judaism, son of Sodi of the tribe of Zebulun; one of the twelve chieftains sent out by Moses from the wilderness of Paran to spy out the land of Canaan (Numbers 13:2-10).

GAEA

Mother Earth, personified as a goddess, the most ancient of the Greek divinities. According to Greek myth, Gaea emerged by her own power out of Chaos and, in turn, produced the sky, seas, and mountains. By her union with Uranus (heaven), she brought forth the Titans, Cyclops, and Giants; hence in literature and art she is sometimes sees as the enemy of Zeus. The equivalent of the later Roman deity Tellus, Gaea was the universal nurse and mother from whom all life sprang and to whom, in death, it returned.

GAHAM

In the Old Testament, a son of Abraham's brother Nahor by his concubine Reumah (Genesis 22:23-24).

GAHANBARS

In Zoroastrianism, six festivals, occurring at irregular intervals throughout the year, which celebrate the seasons and possibly the six stages of the creation of the world:
▲ the heavens;
▲ water;
▲ the earth;
▲ the vegetable world;
▲ the animal world;
▲ man.
Each of the festivals lasts five days.

GAIUS

A Christian from Derbe in Asia Minor who is listed along with six others as accompanying the apostle Paul on his last missionary tour. Gaius and these others evidently separated from Paul and then went on to Troas, on the west coast of Asia Minor, where they waited for him (Acts 20:4-5).

GALATIA

Central region of the peninsula of Asia Minor. Its limits were frequently changing. It contained towns like Antioch, Iconium, Lystra and Derbe.

GALATIANS, LETTER TO

Ninth book of the New Testament (circa 52 AD), a letter written by Paul to the Christians in Galatia to counter the influence of Judaizers. The members of this faction taught that Christian converts were obliged to observe circumcision and other prescriptions of the Mosaic Law. Paul reaffirmed his former teaching that the Mosaic Law is obsolete. But though Christians have a new freedom, they have no license to sin; rather, they assume a responsibility to live lives in accord with the Spirit of God.

GALEED

The place in the mountainous region of Gilead each of the Jordan where the patriarchs Jacob and Laban concluded a covenant (Genesis 31:43-48). The latter came from "Galeed," the name originally given to the spot where, according to biblical tradition, these events occurred circa 1760 BC.

GALILEE

Hilly region of northern ancient Palestine between the Sea of Galilee and the Jordan River. It was the homeland of Jesus, who was sometimes referred to as the Galilean (Matthew 26:69). The first three gospels are

The miraculous draught of fishes (Galilee).
"And he said unto them. Cast the net on the right side of the ship, and ye shall find. They cast therefore, and now they were not able to draw it for the multitude of fishes" (John 21:6)
Lithograph by Gustave Doré (about 1860).

occupied largely with Christ's ministry in Galilee.

The region's revival in modern times is a result of Zionist colonization. Beginning with the village of Rosh Pinna in 1882, a string of settlements were set up; these proved the key bargaining point in the inclusion of all Galilee in the British mandate (1920).

GALILEE, Sea of

Also called lake Tiberias, lake in northern Israel through which the Jordan River flows. The only body of fresh water in Israel, it has been a fishing center since biblical times. Many sites on its shores are associated with Jesus' ministry. Many Bible stories, such as Jesus's transformation of water into wine, are set along this sea. Ruins of ancient cities lie along its northern shores.

GALL, Saint

(550-645) Monk and disciple of the Irish missionary St. Columba, who helped introduce Christianity to western Europe.

GALLICAN CONFESSION

A statement of faith adopted in 1559 in Paris by the first National Synod of the Reformed Church of France. Based on a 35-article draft of a confession prepared by John Calvin, which he sent with representatives from Geneva to the French synod, the Gallican Confession consisted of 40 articles divided into four sections concerning God, Christ, the Holy Spirit, and the church. If affirmed that the Bible is the only rule of faith. It also included an exposition on predestination, the doctrine that God elects or chooses who will be saved, and stated Calvin's doctrine of the Eucharist.

GALLICAN RITES

The name under which the diverse liturgical forms in use in the first millennium in western Europe excepting Rome, are grouped. Many of these rites were to be found in Gaul, but the term is not narrowly restricted to those rites

only. Their origins are uncertain, especially since they do not present a single form of worship but are remarkable for their diversity.

The rites grouped loosely under the designation Gallican, include certain more specific types of rite. Among these are:

▲ The Ambrosian rite, now thoroughly Romanized, which is still to be found in use in the ecclesiastical province of Milan where it was once prominent.

▲ The Celtic rite used among the Irish and Scots until the seventh century.

▲ The Gallican rites (in a narrower sense) found in the Frankish kingdom.

▲ The Mozarabic liturgy which prevailed in Spain until the 15th century.

In evident contrast to the starkness of Roman liturgical rites; the Gallican liturgies evidence a marked ceremonial splendor. They contain a number of liturgical characteristics, for instance, the chanting of the Trisagion and Benedictus, and the use of the diptych for the dead during Mass. They also manifest a feature peculiarly their own, the addition of variable prayer forms to the central eucharistic proclamation. In this last respect, they are known to have influenced subsequent forms of the Roman Mass.

GALLICANISM

A 19th century term for various assertions of the freedom of the French church from papal authority. Exponents of Gallicanism held that the power of the pope in France, particularly in temporal matters but also in matters of doctrine and discipline, should be limited. Though the theory was formulated in the fourteenth century, it was claimed to have historical basis in ancient privileges. The most consistent advocate of the doctrine was the Paris Parlement, which after 1418, despite variations by both king and clergy, never relaxed its support.

In the last years of the 14th century and the beginning of the 15th century so-called ecclesiastical Gallicanism developed. Appointments to benefices and bishoprics were declared free from papal control in an attempt to end the Great Western Schism and bring Reform to the French church by restoring election of these positions. After the Napoleonic era, Gallicanism lingered in France. The discussions and declarations of Vatican Council I clearly marked its incompatibility with Roman Catholic teaching.

Although the ideological content of Gallicanism varied with time and group, its main points included the following:

▲ The pope has no temporal power within France. He cannot prevent the legal heir from ascending the throne, release the French from obedience to the king, interfere with the rights of the crown or the exercise of duties by royal officials, or exercise absolute authority over the French clergy.

▲ The king is the only head of the state. He is the protector of the church, can convoke councils to handle discipline and temporal affairs, can reform or suppress religious communities.

▲ In the spiritual realm the king has power to decide whether or not papal pronouncements are in accord with those of former councils already accepted in France.

▲ Gallicans also claimed that a general council was superior to the pope, whose judgments are not irreformable; truths of faiths are guaranteed by the consent of the faithful.

▲ Gallican bishops claimed the right to be judges of doctrine and discipline in their own domains, independent of the pope.

GALLIM

In the Old Testament, the home of Palti, to whom Saul gave his daughter Michal as his wife after David was outlawed (1 Samuel 25:44). It is possibly the same as the Gallim whose inhabitants, centuries later, cried out in lamentation over the approaching Assyrian army under Sennacherib (Isaiah 10:24, 30). Gallim is placed at Khiorbet Kabul, three miles northeast of Jerusalem, by most modern geographers.

GALLIO

In biblical times, the proconsul of Achaia, before whose judgment seat the Jews accused Paul of leading men into another persuasion in worshiping God. Gallio dismissed the case on the basis that it did not involve a violation of Roman law. Thereupon the crowd went to beating Sosthenes the presiding officer of the synagogue, but Gallio chose not to concern himself with this either (Acts 18:12-17).

GAMALIEL

In the Old Testament, a son of Pedahzur of the tribe of Manasseh and the chieftain of this tribe (Numbers 1:10-16). Gamaliel was one of the 12 chieftains designated by God to aid Moses and Aaron in numbering the sons of Israel for the army, from 20 years old upward (Numbers 1:1-4, 10). He was over the army of his tribe, which was a part of the three-tribe division of the camp of Phraim (Numbers 2:18-20). After the setting up of the tabernacle the chieftains made their presentations, directed by God to be used for carrying on the service of the tent of meeting. Gamaliel also represented his tribe in presenting his offering on the eighth day for the inauguration of the altar (Numbers 7:1-5).

GAMBLING

In Catholic moral theology, gambling is considered a kind of contract (technically, an aleatory contract, from the Latin word alea meaning "chance"). It is a contract by which the participants in gambling or games of chance agree that the winner receives a certain prize or sum of money.

Though some Christian churches condemn gambling absolutely, the Catholic tradition has held that it may be morally justified provided the following conditions are observed:

▲ the stakes belong to the one who gambles and may be freely used by him;

▲ there is no fraud or deceit involved, such as marked cards, loaded dice, collusion with the operator;

▲ there is equal risk and equal opportunity for all participants;

▲ there is no just prohibition by civil authorities.

At the same time, Catholic moralists warn that gambling may give rise to serious abuses, especially for those who are compulsive or addictive gamblers.

GAMMADIAE

Originally the series of Gammadion traced on the garments of Christ and the saints in early Christian iconography. By the eighth century the term designated the same symbols woven in purple or gold on vestments.

GAMUL

In the Old Testament, an Aaronic priest in David's time who was chosen by lot to act as chief of the 22nd priestly division in connection with the service at the sanctuary (1 Chronicles 24:1-3).

GANESA

Elephant-headed Hindu god, the son of Shiva and Parvati. Since Ganesa is considered the remover of obstacles, he is the first god invoked at the beginning of worship or a new enterprise, and his image is often seen at the entrance of temples or houses.

He is a patron of letters and learning, and is the legendary scribe who wrote down the Mahabharata (Great Epic of the Bharata dynasty).

Genasa is usually depicted colored red, pot-bellied, one tusk broken, and with four arms that varyingly hold a noose, goad, pot of rice or sweetmeats, and his broken tusk, or bestow boons or protection.

Some authorities suggest that the elephant head on the human body symbolizes the union of man with the divine (here represented by the enormous size and power of the animal).

GAON

Title of the heads of Jewish academies at Sura and Pumbeditha in Babylonia (from 589 to 1040). The geonim, generally elected by the members of the academy or appointed by the exilarch (the civic leader of Babylonian Jewry) were thus honored for their contribution to the development and interpretation of the Talmud and were regarded as supreme authorities in religious matters.

GARBHA-DHATU

Buddhist concept of one of the two realms of Buddha. The garbha-dhatu mandala is a ritual drawing used in the worship of the Japanese Shingon sect.

GARBHAGRHA

Shrine room in a Hindu temple. It is a Sanskrit term meaning "womb chamber" and indicating the innermost, most holy shrine room marked exteriorly by the Sikhara or tower erected over the sacred spot in Hindu temples of northern or Indo-Aryan style.

GARDEN OF EDEN

The most celebrated garden of history. According to biblical tradition, it seems to have been an enclosed area, bounded, no doubt, by natural barriers. The garden, "located in Eden, toward the east," had an entrance on its eastern side. It was there that cherubs were stationed with the flaming blade of a sword to block men's access to the tree of life in the middle of the garden (Genesis 2:8; 3:24). The garden was well watered by a river flowing throughout it and parting to become the headwaters of four large rivers. This park-like "paradise of pleasure" (Genesis 2:8) contained every tree desirable to one's sight and good for food, as well as other vegetation, and was the habitat of animals and birds. Adam was to cultivate it and to keep it and eventually to expand it earth wide as he carried out God's command to "subdue" the earth. It was a sanctuary, a palace where God representatively walked and communicated with Adam and Eve, a perfect home for them (Genesis 2:9-10, 15-18; 3:8-19).

GAREB

In the Old Testament, one of David's mighty men, an Ithrite of the tribe of

Judah (2 Samuel 23:8; 1 Chronicles 2:4-5).

GARTH

An archaic term, the center garden within the surrounding cloister walk in a church or monastery.

GARUDA

In Hindu mythology the bird and the vahana (mount) of the god Visnu. In the Regveda (a collection of Vedic hymns addressed to the deities) the sun is compared to a bird in its flight across the sky, and the association of the kite-like Garuda with Visnu is taken by scholars as another indication of Visnu's early origins as a sun deity.

The mythological account of Garuda's birth identifies him as the younger brother of Aruna, the charioteer of the sun god, Surya. His mother was held in slavery by her co-wife and her sons, who were nagas (serpents), to which is attributed the lasting enmity between the eagle-like kite and the serpents.

The nagas agreed to release his mother if he could obtain for them a drink of the elixir of immortality, the amrta. Garuda performed this feat with a certain amount of difficulty and on his way back from the heavens met Visnu and agreed to serve him as his vehicle and also as his emblem.

GASTER, Moses

(1856-1939) Jewish scholar who achieved distinction as the hakham ("wiseman"), or chief rabbi, of the English Sefardic communities. He was also a folklorist, a literary historian, and a Zionist.

Many of the meetings between English government officials and Zionists leading up to the Balfour Declaration (1917), the British document supporting a Jewish homeland in Palestine, took place in his home in England.

Gatam

The fourth-named son of Esau's first-born Eliphaz. Gatam became one of the sheiks of the sons of Esau (Genesis 36:10-16; 1 Chronicles 1:36).

ATEKEEPER

In ancient times gatekeepers, also called doorkeepers, served at various places, such as city gates, temple gates, even at the gateways or doorways of homes. Gatekeepers of city gates were appointed to see that the gates were closed at night, and acted as watchmen at the gate. Other watchmen might be posted as lookouts on top of the gate or in a tower where they could get a wide range of view and could announce those approaching the city. They cooperated with the gatekeeper (2 Samuel 18:24). It was a very responsible position inasmuch as the safety of the city depended on the gatekeeper to a considerable degree, and he was an instrument of communication between those outside the city and those inside (2 Kings 7:10-11). The doorkeepers of King Aharuerus, two of whom plotted to assassinate him, were also called court officials (Esther 2:21-23).

GATE OF HEAVEN

An explanatory term used in Genesis 28:17 in relation to the sanctuary of Bethel. Such a high place served, according to the ancient conception, as a point of contact between earth and heaven (John 1:51).

GATES OF HELL

An expression, found only once in the New Testament, that has claimed the attention of exegetes and theologians because it occurs in the theologically important Petrine text: "And on this rock, I will build my church and the gates of Hell shall not prevail against it " (Matthew 16:18).

It has been suggested that "gates" is merely pleonastic, that the sense is simply "hell shall not prevail against it." Many exegetes, however, feel that the word gates adds something by symbolizing power and strength, since in ancient times the gates of city or citadel were specially fortified and at the gates political and social power was exercised when judgments were there handed down.

Exegetes have long disputed whether by hell is to be understood the place or region of the dead (the older biblical sense) or of the damned and of Satan (as suggested by the New Testament use of the word). In the first interpretation then, "death shall not overtake the Church"; in the second, "the power of evil shall not lay it low."

In any case there appears to be a promise if indefectibility for the church; in the first interpretation explicitly, in the second implicitly, for Our Lord would scarcely have made a solemn promise of abiding protection from external forces, if he foresaw that the church was to succumb to processes of internal decay and disintegration.

GATH

One of the five royal cities of the Philistines, the exact location is unknown. The name occurs several times in the Old Testament, especially in connection with the history of David. Goliath, the Philistine champion, came from Gath.

GATI

In Buddhism, a course of existence, gate, entrance, way of going. The term is also used in the sense of the conditions of sentient existence.

GAUNILO

(11th century) Benedictine monk at the Marmoutier Abbey near Tours (France). He wrote a famous critique of the rationality of Anselm's assertion that the concept of "that than which nothing can be greater" (for example, God) implies God's existence. He argued by apology, pointing out that one's concept of a "perfect island" does not imply that such a place exists.

GAYATRI

Famous Hindu mantra, or invocation, addressed to Savitr, the sun god.

GAZA

Largest city of the Gaza Strip, in south-west Palestine. After 300 years of Egyptian occupation, one of the Sea Peoples (Philistines) settled the city and surrounding area. Gaza became an important center of the Philistine Pentapolis (league of five cities). There the biblical hero Samson perished while toppling the temple of the god Dagon. In the New Testament it is known for Philip's service (Acts 8:26).

GAZITES

Inhabitants of Gaza, the word applying in both of its occurrences to Philistines (Joshua 13:2-3; Judges 16:1-2).

GAZZAM

In the Old testament, forefather of some Nethinim who returned from Babylonian exile with Zerubbabel (Ezra 2:1-2, 43-48).

GCOD-PA

Tibetan meditational practice brought to Tibet by the Indian teacher Phadam-pa, and practiced by the Zhi-byed-pa.

GEBA

In the Old Testament, a city of Benjamin given to the Kohathites; one of the 13 priestly cities (Joshua 18:21-24; 1 Chronicles 6:54-60). Geba apparently was situated by the northern boundary of the kingdom of Judah. The ancient city is usually identified with the modern village of Jeba, circa six miles north-east of Jerusalem. A steep valley separates the site from the suggested location of ancient Michmash.

GEBAL

A Phoenician city on the Mediterranean seacoast, identified with modern Jebeil, 20 miles north of Beirut. Historians consider Gebal, the Byblos of the Greeks, to be one of the oldest cities of the Near East.

God included "the land of the Gebalites" among those regions yet to be taken by Israel in Joshua's day (Joshua 13:1-5). Gebalites helped Solomon in the 11th century BC with the preparation of the materials for the temple construction (1 Kings 5:18).

GEBER

In the Old Testament, one of Solomon's twelve deputies who had the responsibility of providing food for the king and his household one month out of the year. Geber is identified as the son of Uri, and it is probable that his son also served as a deputy (1 Kings 4:7-19).

GEDALIAH

In the Old Testament, a Levite singer who, in David's time, was designated by lot to be in charge of the second of the 24 service groups of 12 musicians each (1 Chronicles 25:3, 31).

GEDALIAH, Fast of

Jewish fast day; the day after Rosh Hashanah. Gedaliah was a governor appointed to rule the Jews of Judea by Nebuchadnezzar some 2,500 years ago. On this day, Gedaliah was assassinated, and wicked Nebuchadnezzar instituted a reign of terror against the Jewish inhabitants of Palestine. Tzom Gedaliah has since then been considered one of the minor fast days in the Jewish calendar.

GEDER

In the Old Testament, a town in Canaan, whose king was of the thirty-one conquered by Joshua (Joshua 12:13). Its location was probably on the western side of the Jordan and its being mentioned (Joshua 12:7-8) next to Debir may place it in the Shephelah region.

GEDERATHITE

In Judaism, a designation applied to Jozabad, an ambidextrous Benjamniite warrior associated with David, and apparently identifying him as being from Gederah of Benjamin (1 Chronicles 12:1-4).

GEDEROTH

In the Old Testament, a city in the Shephelah assigned to Judah (Joshua 15:20) and one of the places taken by the Philistines during the reign of King Ahaz (761-745 BC).

GEDOR

In the Old Testament, a son of Jeiel of the town of Gibeon. A member of the tribe of Benjamin, he was a great-uncle of King Saul (1 Chronicles 8:29-31).

GEERTGEN TOT SINT JANS

(1465-1495) Dutch painter of religious subjects, notable for his harmonious fusion of the elements of the landscape. His "Nativity" in the National Gallery in London, is a night scene remarkable for its rendering of chiaroscuro.

GE-HARASHIM

In biblical times, a valley named for the community of craftsmen living there (1 Chronicles 4:14). The community was "fathered" or founded by Joab, though evidently not the Joab of David's time. It was settled by Benjamites after the Babylonian exile (Nehemiah 11:31-35).

GEHAZI

In Judaism, the attendant of the prophet Elisha. When Elisha wondered what could be done for a hospitable Shunammite woman, it was Gehazi who called to the master's attention that she was childless and that her husband was old. Accordingly, Elisha told her that she would be rewarded with a son. Years later the miraculously given boy became ill and died. The Shunammite thereupon came riding to see Elisha at Mount Carmel, and took hold of his feet. On seeing this, Gehazi tried to push her away but was admonished to let her alone. After she finished speaking, Elisha at once sent Gehazi ahead to the boy, while Elisha and the women followed. On their way there Gehazi met them, bringing back the report that, although he had placed Elisha's staff on the boy's face, "the boy did not wake up." But shortly after arriving, Elisha resurrected the Shunammite's son (2 Kings 4:12-37).

GEHENNA

Originally was a valley west and south of Jerusalem, where children were burned as sacrifices to the Ammonite god Moloch. This practice was carried out by the Israelites during the reigns of King Solomon in the 10th century BC and king Manasseh in the 7th century BC and continued until the Babylonian Captivity in the 6th century BC. In later times Gehenna became synonym for hell.

GELASIUS I, Saint

(died circa 496) Roman Catholic pope elected 492, noted for his letter 494 to Byzantine Emperor Anastasius I setting forth the relationship between spiritual authority and secular power. He contended that the power of the popes stood above that of secular leaders.

GELASIUS II

(1043-1119) Pope from 1118-1119. He was elected pope on January 24, 1118, as successor to Paschal II, whose pontificate had been damaged by the dissension from the "investiture controversy," an administrative struggle between the popes and the Holy Roman emperors over the right to grant titles to ecclesiastics.

GELILOTH

A site listed in connection with the boundary of Benjamin (Joshua 18:17). The location is described as "in front of the ascent of Adummim," and matches that of Gilgal (Joshua 15:7).

GEMALLI

In Judaism, a Danite whose son Ammiel represented his tribe as one of the spies sent into Canaan (Numbers 13:12-16).

GEMARA

Important Jewish religious book. There are two Gemaras. One was completed circa 1,500 years ago by Jewish scholars in Babylonia, the other a hundred years earlier by scholars in Palestine. The Mishnah (one of the two parts of the Talmud, containing all the Jewish laws that had been written since the time of the Bible) plus the Babylonian Gemare is called the Babylonian Talmud (Talmud Bavli); the Mishnah together with the Palestinian Gemara is known as the Palestinian Talmud (Talmud Yerushalmi).

The Palestinian Talmud is circa one-third the length of the other. From the beginning, it was never used as much as the Babylonian Talmud. That was chiefly because Babylonia was the real center of Jewish life at the time and it lasted as such much longer than the community in Palestine; from which the Jews were exiled again in 70. When the name Talmud is mentioned, the Babylonian Talmud is meant.

GENEALOGIES, Biblical

Lists of ancestors that determined a man's rights and privileges in his clan and tribe. These were important to the Israelites for civil and religious reasons. Legal inheritance depended on one's position in the ancestral line. A priest or Levite established his role in temple worship and his right to tithes and other support through them. As a literary form they have the dullness of the registry of births and deaths, but one must realize that the civil and the religious spheres were inseparable, essentially, in the Ancient Near East.

In the priestly traditions of the Bible and in Chronicles copious genealogies served to fill in gaps between narratives pertaining to different ages. The Chronicler seemed to have intended the nine chapters of genealogies at the beginning of his work to play down the history of Israel before the glorious King David and the establishment of God's covenant with his line, just as he leaves out of his story of David anything that would tarnish the glorified image of the Davidic messianic hopes.

GENEALOGY OF JESUS

Two genealogies of Jesus, different in theology and details, are present in the New Testament, Matthew's (Matthew 1:1-17) and Luke's (Luke 3:23-38). The former emphasizes the messianic identity of Jesus as the heir to God's promises to David and Abraham. Three sets of 14 names symbolize Davidic fulfillment (D-V-D in Hebrew = 4 + 6

+ 4 = 24); to get 14 names in set 3 one counts Mary or Christ as the ultimate completion of the promises.

The symbolism of the four women in the list is obscure; if all four were originally gentiles, they point to the risen Christ's universal mission (Matthew 28:19). David's crime of adultery and murder, evoked by "Uriah's wife", underlines Jesus' mission to save from sins (Matthew 1:21).

Luke's aim is more patently universal; he goes back from Jesus - just revealed as God's unique son (Luke 3:22) - past Abraham all the way to Adam, "the son of God", thus alluding to Jesus as the new Adam, the image of God, who fathers a new humanity (Pauline themes).

That Luke's names total 77 may symbolize the plentitude in Christ (seven meant fullness in Luke's mind).

Various attempts to reconcile the diverse names in the two lists, which agree on only two from David to Joseph, have not received wide acceptance. Matthew's lineage of kings supports his fulfillment intent. Luke may have the more authentic line through Nathan. No hard evidence is extant to explain how they could differ about even Joseph's father. What is clear is that theological purposes were paramount in their treatment of whatever human evidence they had.

GENERAL ASSOCIATION OF GENERAL BAPTISTS

An association of Baptist churches organized in 1870. It traces its history to the beginning of Baptist movement in England and Holland in the early 1600s and to the church establishment in Providence, Rhode Island by Roger Williams in 1639.

The early General Baptists in America, who believed in a general salvation available to all, were soon outnumbered by the Baptists who were Calvinists; for example, who believed that salvation was limited to those elected to be saved. The early General Baptist churches in America died out or were absorbed by the Calvinist Baptists. In 1823, however, a General Baptist church was established in Evansville, Ind. From that church the movement spread, other churches were established, and in 1870 the General Association was formed.

GENERAL ASSOCIATION OF REGULAR BAPTIST CHURCHES

An association of independent, conservative Baptist churches, organized in 1932 after 22 Baptist churches withdrew from the Northern (later American) Baptist Convention. They withdrew because they felt that the Northern Baptists were accepting the teachings of the Modernists, or Liberals, those who accepted biblical criticism and attempted to make the church relevant to social problems. They also felt that the Northern Baptist Convention was assuming too much control over the local churches and that the independence of the local church was being threatened.

GENERAL BUDDHIST ASSOCIATION OF VIETNAM

20th century organization established to unite all various Buddhist associations of Vietnam.

GENERAL CONFERENCE OF THE MENNONITE CHURCH

Religious conference organized in Iowa, in 1860, by three Mennonite congregations as the General Conference of the Mennonite Church of North America. The present name was adopted in 1953.

The movement grew, and eventually Mennonites from a variety of church backgrounds were members, including most of the 19th century Mennonite immigrants from Poland, Prussia, Russia, and Switzerland.

From its beginning this church has stressed missions, education, and publication. It varies little from the other Mennonite groups in doctrine, but it does advocate autonomy for the local congregation and freedom for individual members from the requirement to wear traditional plain Mennonite clothing.

GENERAL CONFESSION

A confession in which the penitent makes mention of the sins of his past life or of a certain period of his past life, even though in some cases these sins had been previously confessed and forgiven. A general confession is necessary when a mortal sin has been knowingly concealed in a past confession or when a past confession was invalid because the penitent lacked sorrow.

In such a case, the general confession must include all moral sins mentioned in the original bad confession and in any subsequent confessions. A general confession can be spiritually useful when made in the decisive moments of life, for instance, before reviving holy orders, making religious vows, or receiving the sacrament of matrimony.

GENERAL SYNOD

In the polity of Reformed and some Lutheran Churches because it is a concern for rights and duties of a person as a member of a general, collective whole, society; and because it brings into its service acts of other particular virtues, including commutative and distributive justice, to advance the collective good.

GENEROSITY

In Roman Catholicism. generosity is regarded as one of the 12 traditional fruits of the Holy Spirit as listed in Galatians. Generosity encourages a sense of values and a willingness to do what may not be popular.

GENESIS, Book of

(Greek: origin or generation) The first book of the Old Testament, written by Moses (before 4000 BC). It tells of the creation, the fall, the flood, the origins of the Hebrews, and the early patriarchs with whom God made his Covenant. The book accounts for the Israelites' presence in Egypt, and so leads into Exodus.

All the information contained in the book of Genesis relates to events that took place prior to Moses' birth. It could have been received directly by divine revelation.It is obvious that, according to biblical tradition, someone had to receive the information relating to the events prior to man's creation in that way, whether Moses or someone prior to him (Genesis 1:1-27; 2:7-8). This information and the remaining information, however, could have been transmitted to Moses by means of oral tradition.

Scholars have identified three literary traditions in Genesis, designated by the letters J, E and P. The J strand, so called because it used the name Yahweh (Jehovah) for God, is a Judaean rendition of the sacred story, perhaps written as early as 900 BC.

The E strand, which designated God as Elohim, is traceable to the northern kingdom of Israel and was written 900-750 BC. The P (Priestly) strand, so called because of its cultic interests and regulations for priests, is usually dated in the 5th century BC and is regarded as the law upon which Ezra and Nehemiah based their reform.

Because each of these strands preserves materials much older than the time of their incorporation into a written work, Genesis contains extremely old oral and written traditions.

GENESIS APOCRYPHON

A pseudepigraphical work (a non-canonical writing that in style and content resembles authentic biblical literature), one of the most important works of the Essene community of Jews, part of whose library was discovered in 1947 in caves at Qumran, near the Dead Sea.

The scroll, the last of seven scrolls discovered in Cave I, is also the least well preserved. It is a collection of apocryphal embellishments on leading figures in Genesis and not, as was first suspected, the long lost "Apocalypse of Lamech." The contents of the scroll comprise four major sections:
▲ the story of Lamech (columns 1-5);
▲ the story of Noah (columns 6-15);

▲ the story of the Peoples (columns 16-17);

▲ the story of Abraham (columns 18-22).

GENEVA BIBLE

A conservative English translation of the Bible, published in 1560 by English Puritan exiles in Switzerland. It is also called the Breeches Bible because of its terminology for the first clothing used by Adam and Eve.

GENEVA CATECHISM

A doctrinal confession prepared by John Calvin to instruct children in Reformed theology. Recognizing that his first catechism (1537) was too difficult for children, Calvin rewrote it. He arranged the Geneva catechism (1542) in questions and answers in an effort to simplify doctrinal complexities.

GENNADIUS I OF CONSTANTINOPLE, Saint

(circa 401-471) Byzantine theologian, and patriarch, a champion of Christian Orthodoxy who strove for an ecumenical statement of doctrine on the person and work of Christ to reconcile the opposing Alexandrian (Egyptian) and Antiochan (Syrian) theological traditions.

Only part of Gennadius' biblical commentaries on the Old Testament book of Genesis and Letter of Paul to the Romans are extant, preserved in several series of collected patristic texts.

In the Eastern Orthodox Church Gennadius is revered as a saint, and several legends exist concerning his moral influence and wonder-working.

GENNADIUS II SCHOLARIUS

(1405-1473) Foremost Greek Orthodox Aristotelian theologian. After his patriarchate of Constantinople (1454-1464) he produced in monastic seclusion a wealth of theological and philosophical literature, including commentaries, unique for Byzantines, on the works of Western Christendom's most celebrated theologians, among them Thomas Aquinas.

GENNADIUS OF MARSEILLES

(late 5th century). Theologian-priest whose work *On Famous Men* constitutes the sole source for biographical and bibliographical information on numerous early Eastern and Western Christian authors.

GENOCIDE

The extermination of a people, or ethnic minority which is an unprincipled and inexcusable act.

GENTILE

Person who is not Jewish; word used in the Old Testament to refer to people who are not Jewish. In modern times the term is often used, incorrectly, to mean "Christian." Muslims and members of the Church of Christ of Latter Day Saints also refer to non-members of their faith as gentiles.

In the New Testament it is clear that Jesus first directed his disciples to preach the Good News only to the "lost sheep of the house of Israel" (Matthew 10:6), but generally extended their mission to the gentiles - "all nations" - as well (Matthew 28:19). The extension of the church to gentiles is spoken of in the Acts of the Apostles (see chapters 8-12) and in many of the New Testament letters.

GENTLENESS

Word with a special meaning in biblical contexts. The word is closely related to humanity, meekness, mildness and reasonableness. Gentleness is mildness of disposition or manner. To "gentle" is to mollify, appease or placate, or to calm whatever one is doing, such as speaking, playing music, acting on a matter, and so forth.

Gentleness in tone or manner, for example, being soft-spoken, does not always prove true gentleness. It is a quality that, to be thoroughly genuine, must come from the heart.

While the ancient servant of God, Job, was suffering at the hands of Satan in a test of his integrity to God, he was verbally attacked by three companions. They charged Job with secret sin, wickedness and stubbornness, intimating also that he was apostate and that his sons has met death at God's hands because of their wickedness. Yet one of the three, Epiphaz, said to Job, "Are the consolations of God not enough for you, or a word spoken gently with you" (Job 15:11). Thus, some of their speech at least may have been in a soft tone, yet it was harsh in content, hence not truly gentle.

GENUBATH

In the Old Testament, son of Edomite prince Hadad. When army chief Joab occupied Moab during the reign of David, Hadad fled to Egypt. There he gained the favor of Pharaoh, whose sister-in-law he was given as a wife. By her, Hadad fathered Genubath, who was raised with the sons of Pharaoh (1 Kings 11:14-20).

GENUFLEXION

A bending of the knee as a sign of adoration and reverence; it is a Catholic practice to genuflect when entering a church where the Blessed Sacrament is reserved or when passing before the Blessed Sacrament.

GEORGE, Saint

(late 11 century) Martyr who enigmatically became the patron saint of England. He has been known in England at least since the 8th century, and no doubt returning crusaders popularized his cult (he was said to have been seen helping the Franks at the Battle of Antioch in 1098).

GEORGE THE MONK

Byzantine historian, author of a world chronicle that constitutes the prime documentary source for mid-9th century Byzantine history, particularly the Iconoclast movement.

The chronicle, comprising also data on the growing Islamic-Christian turbulence, enjoyed widespread diffusion among the neighboring Slavic peoples throughout the medieval period.

GEORGE THE PISIDIAN

(early 7th century) Byzantine epic poet, historian and cleric whose classically structured verse lyricizing the military, philosophical, and religious themes of his day was acclaimed as a model of medieval Greek poetry.

GEORGIA, Orthodox Church of

One of the most ancient Christian communities in the world. The Georgians adopted Christianity through the ministry of a woman, St. Nino, early in the 4th century. Since that time Georgia remained in the ecclesiastical sphere of Antioch and also under the influence of neighboring Armenia. Its autocephaly, or ecclesiastical independence, was probably granted by Emperor Zeno (474-491) with the consent of the patriarch of Antioch.

GERAR

A site near Gaza mentioned in the earliest record of the boundaries of Canaanite territory (Genesis 10:19).

GERIZIM, Mount

Mountain in Samaria, central Palestine, just south of Nablus and the site of biblical Shechem. It is mentioned in the Old Testament as the site where God was to pronounce blessing on the Jewish people. The Samaritans, a small Jewish sect, built a shrine there during the early second Temple period (4th century BC) and directed their prayers there, instead of Jerusalem.

GERMAN CHRISTIANS

Protestants who attempted to subordinate church policy to the political exigencies of Nazi Germany. The German Christians' Faith Movement, organized in 1932, was nationalistic and so anti-Semitic that extremists wished to repudiate the Old Testament and the Pauline Letters because of their Jewish authorship. After World War II the German Christian church party was banned.

GERMANIC RELIGION AND MYTHOLOGY

The mythology, religious beliefs, and cults of the Germanic-speaking peoples before their conversion to Christianity. Germanic culture extended from the Black Sea to Greenland and beyond, but despite its important role in European development, vivid memories of Germanic religion have survived only in Scandinavia.

GERMAN REQUIEM

Musical work for solo voices, chorus, and orchestra by Johannes Brahms, composed 1857-1868. The work was based on free adaptations from Scripture rather than on the liturgical text of the Roman Catholic service, and it was intended more for the solace of mourners than for the repose of the dead or as a work to performed in the church.

GERMANUS I, Saint

(634-732) Byzantine patriarch of Constantinople and theologian who led the Orthodox opposition to the Iconoclastic heresy (the destruction of religious images). His writings also fostered the doctrine and devotion to the Virgin Mary.

Because his writings were ordered burned by Leo III, only a few of Germanus' works survived. A strong advocate of Marian devotion, Germanus' work is a source for the theological development of her role as mediator of supernatural blessings.

GERMANUS OF AUXERRE, Saint

(378-448) Important Gallic prelate who was twice sent on crucial missions to England that helped effect the consolidation of the British church.

GERMANUS OF GRANFEL, Saint

(610-675) Abbot who was martyred for remonstrating against royal oppression of the poor. At that time, Cathic launched an aggressive policy against monasticism while concurrently extorting the peasants. Germanus bravely opposed him, pleading on behalf of the oppressed poor. Cathic killed him and his prior Randoals in the midst of a mass plundering.

GERMANUS OF PARIS, Saint

(496-576) Abbot, bishop, one of France's most reverend saints, who was an important, though unsuccessful, mediator in the fratricidal conflicts and civil wars among several Merovingian kings.

GERSHOM

In the Old Testament, the first-listed son of Levi the son of Jacob. He was the father of Libni and Shimei (1 Chronicles 6:16-20). He is also called Gershon (Genesis 46:11, Exodus 6:16-17).

GERSHOM BEN JUDAH

(960-1040) Eminent rabbinical scholar who proposed a far-reaching series of legal enactments that profoundly molded the social institutions of medieval European Jewry. At synods of community leaders he proposed his taqqanot, which included the prohibition of polygamy (permitted by biblical and talmudic law but already mostly unpracticed), interdiction of the husband's right to divorce without the wife's consent, prohibition of reading another's mail without his consent, and prohibition against taunting Jews who had been forcibly converted to another religion and had then returned to Judaism.

GERSHON

The first listed of Levi's three sons. Gershon's descendants were called Gershonites and "sons of Gershon" (Exodus 6:16; Numbers 3:17-21).

GERSHONITES

The descendants of Gershon, or Gershom, the first named of the three sons of Levi, through his two sons Libni and Shimei (1 Chronicles 6:1, 16-17). The Gershonites constituted one of the three divisions of the Levites. At the first census in the wilderness they numbered 7,500 males from a month old and upward. Those from 30 to 50 years of age who served at the tabernacle, numbered 2,630 males (Numbers 3:21-22). The service of the Gershonites in the wilderness included caring for the tent cloths of the tabernacle and the tent of meeting, the screen of the entrance of the tent of meeting, the hangings of the courtyard and the screen of the courtyard entrance (Numbers 3:23). When the chieftains of Israel presented six covered wagons and 12 bulls for tabernacle service, Moses gave two wagons and four bulls to the sons of Gershon (Numbers 7:1-7). When moving camp the Gershonites marched with the Merarites between the leading three-tribe divisions of Judah and the three-tribe division of Reuben (Numbers 10:14-20).

GESHAN

In the Old Testament, the third-named son of Jahdai of the tribe of Judah. Geshan is listed among the descendants of Caleb (1 Chronicles 2:47).

GESHEM

In biblical times, an Arabian, who, along with Sanballat and Tobiah, opposed nehemiah in the rebuilding of Jerusalem's wall. These enemies first derided Nehemiah and his co-workers (Nehemiah 2:19). Then they conspired and plotted against Nehemiah, to no avail. Finally these opposers sent a letter to Nehemiah and the Jews were scheming to rebel and that he was becoming a king to them. In this, too, these enemies failed (Nehemiah 6:5-7). Their quoting of Geshem in the letter seems to indicate that he was a man of influence.

GESHUR

An Aramaean kingdom bordering on the Argob region of Bashan east of the Jordan River. Its northerly neighbor was Maacath. Although Israel's early conquests extended as far as Geshur, the region itself was not taken (Deuteronomy 3:14; Joshua 12:1). It was to Geshur, the realm of his mater-

nal grandfather Talmai, that Absalom fled after murdering his half-brother Amron. There he continued in banishment for three years, until brought back to Jerusalem by Joab (2 Samuel 3:2-3; 13:28-38).

GESHURITES

The inhabitants of Geshur, a territory east of the Jordan (Deuteronomy 3:14; Joshua 12:4-5).

GESU, Church of

Mother church in Rome of the Jesuit order, designed by Giacomo da Vignola in 1568, except for the facade, which was the work of Giocomo della Porta.

GETHSEMANE

(from Hebrew "gat semanim," oil press) The garden across the Kidron valley, on the Mount of Olives, East of the old city of Jerusalem, where Jesus prayed on the eve of his crucifixion, and was betrayed (Mark 14:32). Gethsemane was probably an olive grove in New Testament times; its precise location is disputed.

The "Grotto of the Agony," near the Brook of Kidron, is one possible location, while another is marked by a Franciscan church. But the Latin, Russian, Greek and Armenian churches place the site at various olive groves on the hill.

Though the exact location of Gethsemane cannot be determined with certainty, Armenian, Greek, Latin, and Russian churches have accepted an olive grove on the western slope of the Mount of Olives as the authentic site, which was so recognized by the empress Helena, mother of Constantine (the first Christian emperor, early 4th century).

GEUEL

In the Old Testament, son of Machi of the tribe of Gad; one of the 12 chieftains sent out by Moses from the wilderness of Paran to spy out the land of Canaan (Numbers 13:2-16).

GEZER

Ancient royal Canaanite city, 18 miles north-west of Jerusalem. The site was strategic since it guarded one of the few roads of access from Jaffa to Jerusalem.

GHAFIR

The title of the 40th sura of the Koran; it means "Forgiver," i.e. God. The sura belongs to the Meccan period and has 85 verses. Its title is drawn from verse 3 which refers to God as Forgiver of sin and Acceptor of repentance. The sura is one of seven which begin with the Mysterious Letters of the Koran. The sura stresses God's unity and power and provides considerable detail about the life of the prophet Musa and his dealings with Pharaoh.

GHANIMAH

In the early Islamic community (7th century AD), booty taken in battle in the form of weapons, horses, prisoners, and movable goods.

GHAYBA

In Islam, term meaning occulation, absence, concealment, invisibility. The best-known occulation is that of the 12th Imam Mohammed al-Qua'im.

GHAYLAN B. MUSLIM

(died 8th century) Leading early proponent of free will who lived in Damascus and was a contemporary of the Christian John of Damascus.

GHAZALI, al-

(1058-1111). One of Islam's greatest theologians, a major sufi and an outstanding scholar of Islamic philosophy, though by no means an original philosopher. He was also very well versed in the doctrines of the Isma'ilis which he refuted. He came to hold the belief that he would be the Renewer of Islam for the new Islamic century.

GHENT ALTARPIECE

The Adoration of the Lamb, masterpiece of Late Gothic Flemish painting commissioned by Jodocus Vyt, the mayor of Bruges, and painted by the brothers Hubert and Jan van Eyck in oil and tempera (completed by 1432).

GHOST

Soul or specter of a dead person, usually appearing as living being or as a nebulous likeness of the deceased and, occasionally, in other forms. Belief in ghosts is based on the ancient notion that a man's spirits separable from his body and may maintain in existence after his death.

GHOST DANCE

The name of a number of distinct cults in a complex of late-19th century religious movements that represented the last attempt of Indians in the western United States to rehabilitate traditional cultures shattered through conquest by the whites.

The cults helped to reshape traditional shamanism (a belief system based on the healing and psychic transformation powers of the shaman, or medicine man) and prepared for further Christianization and accommodation to white culture.

GHOUL

Demonic being believed to inhabit burial grounds and other deserted places. The name was originally applied to cannibal jinn (spirits) who roamed the desserts in Arab countries. They were considered the offspring of Iblis, the Muslim prince of darkness.

GHULAM AHMAD, Mirza

(1839-1908) Indian Muslim who formulated a synthesis of religious thought in the face of Western cultural influences that were penetrating India.

GHUSL

Major ritual Islamic washing of the whole body to achieve a state of purity, before visiting a mosque and after such occasions as childbirth, menstruation, sexual intercourse, contact with a dead body, or before events such as formal admission to the Islamic faith.

GIAH

In Biblical times, a site near "the hill of Ammah" mentioned in describing the pursuit of Abner by Joab and Abishal (2 Samuel 2:24). The context suggests to some that Giah was north-east of Gibeon in Benjamin's territory.

GIANTS

In Greek mythology, children of Mother Earth. When Zeus punished the Titans, Mother Earth was angry that some of her children had been punished in this way, for, according to another version, because she did not think the gods were doing her enough honor.

To take revenge, she gave birth to the Giants. These were huge creatures with the hair of snakes and bodies whose lower parts were those of dragons. Their appearance inspired terror, and they were almost invincible.

As soon as they were born they launched their attack on the gods of Olympus, hurling lighted torches, a rain of boulders and entire flaming trees. The mountains shook, and the air and sea were a hell of fire. The Olympian gods were thus forced to go to war once more, with Zeus and his thunderbolts in command, flanked by comrades capable of standing any test: Poseidon, Apollo, Hephaestus, the Fates, Dionysos and his retinue, and all the others.

But the leading role in this battle was played by Athena, who was born during the course of the war, springing fully-armed from the Head of Zeus. She immediately killed the Giant Pallas and took up her position by her father's side.

The Battle of the Giants was prolonged, and would never have ended if Fate had not fulfilled itself as a mortal and fought side by side with the gods to bring them victory. This was Heracles, with whose help the Giants were killed off one by one.

GIBBAR

In the Old Testament, the name of a family head 95 of whose "sons"

(descendants) returned with Zerubbabel from Babylonian captivity in 537 BC (Ezra 2:1-2). However, in the parallel passage of Nehemiah 7:25 Gibeon is listed instead of Gibbar. Hence "the sons of Gibbar (Gibeon), 95," may have reference to the descendants of the former inhabitants of Gibeon, inasmuch as other place-names appear in Ezra 2:21-34, for example "the sons of Bethlehem."

GIBBETHON

In the Old Testament tradition, a city originally assigned to the tribe of Dan (Joshua 19:40-44) but later given to the Kohathites as a Levite city (Joshua 21:20-23). Centuries later Gibbethon was in the hands of the Philistines, and it was while Israel's King Nadab attempted to wrest the city from them that the conspirator Baasha assassinated him (1 Kings 15:27). Gibbethon was under Philistine control some 24 years later when Omri, army chief of Israel, encamped against it. Acclaimed as king by the Israelite camp there, Omri broke off the siege of Gibbethon to attack the rival Israelite King Zimri (1 Kings 16:15-18).

GIBBONS, James

(1834-1921) Archbishop of Baltimore and second Roman Catholic cardinal of North America. His experiences as a missionary bishop made him aware of the need for a simple and concise statement of Roman Catholic doctrines. He wrote *The Faith of Our Fathers* (1876), which became one of the most popular volumes of Roman Catholic apologetics published in the United States.

GIBEA

In the Old Testament, a descendant of Caleb of the tribe of Judah (1 Chronicles 2:42-49); or, possibly, the city of Gibeah (Joshua 15:57), "fathered" or founded by one of Caleb's offspring.

GIBEAH

Ancient town of the Israelite tribe of Benjamin, located just north of

Jerusalem. During the time of King Saul, it served as the first royal residence of Israel. Later becoming insignificant, it was finally destroyed in 70.

GIBEATH-HAARALOTH

The place where all the Israelite males born in the Egyptian exile (wilderness) were circumcised after crossing the Jordan. The place was near the city of Jericho and came to be called Gilgal (Joshua 5:3-10).

GIBEATHITE

An inhabitant of "Gibeah of Benjamin" (1 Chronicles 12:1-3); the term is applied to Shemaah whose "sons" served in David's army.

GIBEON

Place linked with el-Jib six miles north-west of Jerusalem. Numerous earthware jar handles, bearing the name "Gibeon" in ancient Hebrew characters, have been found there. Located on a hill that rises some 200 feet above the surrounding plain, the ancient site covers circa 16 acres.

In Joshua's time Gibeon was inhabited by Hivites, one of the seven Canaanite nations in line for destruction (Joshua 9:3-7; Deuteronomy 7:1-2). The Gibeonites were also called "Amorites," as this designation appears at times to have been applied generally to all the Canaanites (2 Samuel 21:2). Unlike the other Canaanites, the Gibeonites realized that, despite their military strength and the greatness of their city, resistance would fail, because God was fighting with Israel. Therefore, after the destruction of Jericho and Ai, the men of Gibeon, apparently also representing the three other Hivite cities of Chepirah, Beeroth and Kiriath-jearim (Joshua 9:17), sent a delegation to Joshua at Gilgal to sue for peace.

GICHTEL, Johann

(1638-1710) Protestant visionary and theosophist, who promoted the quasi-pantheist teaching of the early-17th century Lutheran mystic Jakob Boehme and compiled the first complete edition of his works.

GIDDALTI

In the Old Testament, a son of Heman; a Levite singer who in David's time was designated by lot to serve as the head of the 22nd of the 24 service groups of twelve musicians each (1 Chronicles 25:1, 4, 29).

GIDDEL

In Judaism, the paternal head of one of the families of "the sons of the servants of Solomon" who are listed among those who returned to Jerusalem and Judah in 537 BC (Ezra 2:1-2, 55-56; Nehemiah 7:58).

GIDEON

One of Israel's greatest judges. His heroic acts concerning the fight of the Midianites and destruction of the altars of Baal are described in the book of Judges. Being offered Israel's kingship, he refused on religious grounds (Judges 8:22).

Gideon was secretly threshing his crop when God's angel called to him to rescue Israel from the Midianites, one of Israel's greatest enemies at that time. To make sure that the call was from God he put it to a test. Twice God gave him the sign he asked for.

Gideon chose 300 men from the thousands who followed him. These were divided into three groups. Armed with an empty pitcher, a torch and a trumpet, they surprised the enemy at night with a tremendous shout, "the sword of the lord and of Gideon." Panic broke out in the army of Midian. They turned on each other and then fled, with the Israelites in hot pursuit. Victory was complete and Gideon gave the land peace for 40 years until his death. (Judges 6:11-23, 26-39; 7:1-23).

GIDEONI

In the Old Testament, father of Abidan the chieftain of the tribe of Benjamin in the time of Moses (Numbers 1:11-16).

GIDOM

A Biblical site mentioned in Judges 20:45. Following a gross sex crime by Benjaminites, the other Israelite tribes pursued the Benjaminites as far as this point. Its exact situation is unknown.

GIFTS OF MERCY

In Judaism, things given to one in need to relieve the situation. While "gifts of mercy" are not directly referred to as such in the Hebrew scriptures, the law gave specific directions to the Israelites about their obligations toward the poor. They were not to be close-fisted but generous, in dealing with their needy brothers (Deuteronomy 15:7-10).

GIFTS OF THE HOLY SPIRIT

According to Roman Catholic teaching, the gifts of the Holy Spirit are supernatural graces freely given to the soul with sanctifying grace and enable the graced person to respond freely and promptly to the inspiration of God. The seven gifts are:
▲ wisdom;
▲ understanding;
▲ counsel;
▲ fortitude;
▲ knowledge;
▲ piety;
▲ fear of the Lord.

GIFT OF TONGUES

The ability to speak in a language that is not known to the speaker. Mentioned in Acts and Corinthians, speaking in tongues is a means of praising God and an indication of his approval.

GIHON

According to Biblical tradition, one of the four rivers that branches out from the river issuing out of Eden, described as "encircling the entire land of Cush" (Genesis 2:10-13).

GILALAI

One of the Levite musicians in the procession arranged by Nehemiah at the inauguration of the rebuilt wall of Jerusalem in 455 BC (Nehemiah 12:27-31).

GILBERT FOLIOT

(1110-1187) Cluniac monk who became archbishop of Hereford and later of London, and who was an unsuccessful rival of Thomas Becket for the archbishopric of Canterbury and afterward was Becket's opponent in ecclesiastical and secular politics.

GILDAS

(502-570) British saint and historian of the Anglo-Saxon conquest of Britain. A monk, he founded a monastery in Britanny known after him as St. Gildas de Rhuys.

GILEAD

Area of ancient Palestine east of the Jordan. The name Gilead first appears in the biblical account of the last meeting of Jacob and Laban (Genesis 31:21-22). The "balm of Gilead" (Genesis 37:25) used medicinally in antiquity was the mastic obtained from Pistachia Lentiscus.

GILGAMESH, Epic of

Babylonian poem constituting one of the chief masterpieces of the Akkadian language and one of the oldest epics in existence.

Composed in southern Mesopotamia before 2000 BC it is a collection of tales centering around the story of Gilgamesh, the most famous of Sumerian heroes. The tale has been described as "an Odyssey of a king who did not want to die," and may in fact have influenced the Greek Odyssey. It also influenced an account bearing some similarity to the story of Noah and the flood in Genesis. The manuscript, part of a much larger whole, was discovered in 1872 in the remains of an Assyrian library of clay tablets at Nineveh.

GILOH

In Biblical times, a city in the mountainous region of Judah (Joshua 15:48-51) and the home of the traitor "Ahithophel the Gilonite" (2 Samuel 15:12). Though its exact location is unknown, some geographers tentatively identify Giloh with Khirbet Jala, somewhat less than seven miles northwest of Hebron.

GILONITE

An inhabitant of Giloh. This term is usually applied to Ahithophel, David's counselor (Joshua 15:51; 2 Samuel 15:12).

GILPIN, Bernard

(1517-1583) One of the most conscientious and broad-minded upholders of the Elizabethan church settlement that ordered recognition of the English sovereign, rather than the pope, as head (supreme governor) of the English church.

GIMZO

A city of Judah that, with its dependent towns, was captured by the Philistines during the reign of Ahaz (2 Chronicles 28:18-19). It is usually identified with Jimzu, a large village circa 13_ miles southeast of modern Tel Aviv.

GINATH

In Judaism, father of Tibni the unsuccessful rival of Omri for the kingship over the ten-tribe kingdom of Israel (1 Kings 16:21-22).

GINNETHOI

In the Old Testament, one of the heads of the priests who returned from Babylon with Zerubbabel in 537 BC (Nehemiah 12:1-7); he may be the same as Ginnethon at Nehemiah 12:16).

GINNETHON

In the Old Testament, a paternal house of priests headed by a certain Meshullam during Nehemiah's governorship (Nehemiah 12:12).

GINSBURG, Christian David

(1831-1914) Hebrew and biblical scholar, the foremost authority in England on the Masorah (authorative Jewish tradition concerning the correct text of the Hebrew Bible).

GINZBURG, Louis

(1873-1953) One of the great Judaic scholars of modern times, who wrote the most comprehensive study of Jewish biblical lore yet published. Ginsburg's best known works are his seven-volume *Legends of the Jews* (1909-1938) and his monumental three-volume *Commentary on the Palestinian Talmud* (1941).

GIRALDUS CAMBRENSIS

(1146-1223) Historian and vigorous opponent of Anglo-Norman authority over the Welsh church. Although he was primarily an ecclesiastic distinguished for his zeal, Gerald was a prolific writer.

GISLEBERTUS

(early 12th century) Sculptor who made major contributions to the cathedrals of St. Lazarus in Autun and several Burgundian churches in a short but productive period from 1125-1135.

Girzites

In Biblical times, a people who were among the victims of a raid that David and his 600 men made during their sixteen-month stay with the Philistines. David took much livestock as spoil, but did not preserve any of the Girzites alive. Probably nomads, the Girzites lived in the territory south of Judah in the general direction of Egypt (1 Samuel 27:2-9).

GITTITE

A term often applied to an inhabitant or native of the Philistine city of Gath (Joshua 13:2-3). Giant Goliath was a "Gittite" (2 Samuel 21:19; 1 Chronicles 20:5).

GITTITH

A musical expression of uncertain meaning, appearing in the superscriptions of Psalms 8, 81 and 84. The term seems to be derived from the Hebrew word gath, which is also the name of a town located on the border of Judah and Philistia. Gittith probably is making reference to a musical instrument or a melody originating at Gath. Another possibility is that Gittith denotes a tune associated with vintage songs, since gath denotes a press for wine or oil.

GIUNTA PISANO

(1201-1260) Italian painter, a native of Pisa, who painted in the upper church of Assisi, notably a "Crucifixion" dated 1236, with a figure of father Elias, the general of the Franciscans, embracing the cross.

GIUSTINIANI, Agostino

1479-1536) Statesman, scholar, and Dominican priest, who became a leading authority in Eastern studies and held an influential position in the intellectual circles of his day.

An acquaintance of two leading Renaissance scholars, Erasmus and Thomas More, Giustiniani himself wrote several works, including a history of Genoa and translations of the Bible.

GLABER, Radulfus

(985-1047) Monk and chronicler whose works are useful as historical documents because there are so few sources from this period.

GLAS, John

(1695-1773) Presbyterian clergyman denounced by his church for opposing the concept of national religious establishment; founder of the Glasites.

GLASTONBURY THORN

Originally a hawthorn tree at Glastonbury Abbey that, according to the legend of the abbey's foundation by Joseph of Arimathea, sprouted form his staff. Thorn trees in England that bear the name are from slips taken from the tree at Glastonbury, which was uprooted as part of Cromwell's destruction of the abbey because it was a place of pilgrimage.

The Glastonbury thorn is unique in that it flowers twice a year, in spring and in fall, often at Christmas time. Botanists call it a "sport," or random development, because it does not reproduce naturally but must be budded and grafted.

GLAUCUS

In Greek mythology, a sea god who was originally a man, but was later transformed into a sea spirit. His form was human while his torso was covered with shells and seaweed.

GLEANING

The process of gathering whatever portion of a certain crop the harvesters had intentionally or unintentionally left behind. God's law to Israel specifically directed his people not to reap the edges of their fields completely, not to go over the boughs of the olive tree after having harvested the crop by beating the tree, nor to gather the leftovers of their vineyards. Even if a sheaf of grain was inadvertently left in the field, this was not to be retrieved. Gleaning was the God-given right of the poor in the land, the afflicted one, the alien resident, the fatherless boy and the widow (Leviticus 19:9-10; Deuteronomy 24:19-21).

GLORIFIED BODY

The human body of the just endowed with the preternatural qualities it will have after the general resurrection. These qualities are given in 1 Corinthians 15:42-44. It will enjoy a splendor or glory (doxa), which is primarily the glory of God in the face of Christ (2 Corinthians 4:6) but which passes through him to the blessed (2 Corinthians 3:18), who will shine like the sun in the kingdom of their Father (Matthew 13:43).

Corruption was the result of sin (Romans 5:12). When sin is entirely conquered, the just lives for God, like Christ (Romans 6:120). Death is absorbed into life, and as a consequence all concomitant needs like nutrition (1 Corinthians 6:13) and procreation (Matthew 22:30) will cease.

It will have power for it is the immense power of God (Ephesians 1:19) that will transform the human body, and, according to the constant law of Pauline soteriology, that which is characteristic of the cause passes into the effect. It will be spiritual.

GLORY

Biblical term with varying meanings in the Old Testament and New Testament.

Old Testament

In its primary significance the Hebrew word kabod, usually translated by glory, signifies weight or worth. From this comes to mean the outward expression of a man's importance, his standing among his fellows, and the respect in which he is held. By a further derivation it is used to signify that which causes to be so esteemed, the wealth or substance he has gained. It is with this sense in mind that the pious Israelite confesses that Yahweh is his glory.

A more important aspect of glory comes to the fore when it is the glory of Yahweh himself that is in question. In the Priestly tradition the visible expression of Yahweh's presence to his people is the cloud of radiant fire, and this, too, is called the glory (Kabod). The kabod advances before the people at the exodus and comes down to rest upon the "mercy-seat," the ark-throne in the tabernacle in their midst, creating a radiant sphere of holiness about itself in which the people constantly dwell.

New Testament

In three episodes in the Gospels Jesus appears as the focal point of the divine glory or kabod:

▲ at his birth, when the brilliant light illumines the heavens above Bethlehem (Luke 2:9);

▲ at his Transfiguration, when the light appears to shine out of his own countenance and person (Luke 9:31-36);

▲ in the prediction of the Parousia, when he will come "in the glory of his Father with his angels" (Matthew 16:27), "on the clouds of heaven with great power and glory" (Matthew 24:30), and "take his seat upon the throne of glory" (Mark 8:38; Luke 21-27).

The Johannine writings offer a new and almost unprecedented insight, in which the Passion, death, and Resurrection of Jesus are taken as a single event and said to be his "glorification" (John 12:23; 13:31; 17:1-5).

The glory he thereby achieves is imparted to his Disciples also when the Spirit is given to them and they are enabled to understand the significance of his words (John 7:39; 12:16).

GLOSSOLALIA

Ecstatic speaking in tongues. In Pentecostalism tongues-speaking is regarded as the manifestation of baptism with the Holy Spirit. The occurrence of this charismatic gift in the early church is attested by Acts 2:4-21; 8:9-24; 10:46; 1 Corinthians 12-14). Pentecostal authors point to the recurrence of the phenomenon in the case of some medieval groups and the Camisards, the Jansenists, American revivalists, and the Catholic Apostolic church.

In no form of Christianity since apostolic times, however, has glossolalia been stressed to such a degree, or so claimed to be part of the ordinary Christian life, as in Pentecostalism.

Some distinguish glossolalia as a sign, initial evidence of Spirit baptism, and glossolalia as a more permanent gift or grace to be exercised as witness to the Spirit-filled character of the Pentecostal message.

Glossolalia is usually in the form of unintelligible sounds or utterances, although cases of xenoglossy (or xenolalia, ecstatic speaking of a language by a person who had no previous knowledge of that language) have been cited. Consequently, for glossolalia to be profitable to others the gift of interpretation (1 Corinthians 14:10) is required; often the interpreter restricts himself to conveying a comprehensive meaning of what the tongue-speaker has said. Abuse of glossolalia has caused many Pentecostals to point to the need for control over its use. Some Pentecostal bodies seem to have deemphasized its importance.

GLUTTON

A selfish, greedy person given to excessive indulgence, especially overeating. Gluttony in any form is diametrically opposed to Bible precepts and principles.

The Mosaic law struck at the root of the matter in that parents of an incorrigible son who was a glutton and a drunkard were to bring him to the older men of the city, who would have him stoned to death (Deuteronomy 21:18-21).

GLUTTONY

One of the capital or deadly sins, it is an unreasonable, disordered desire for food and drink, usually expressed by eating and drinking to excess.

GNESIO-LUTHERANISM

Name given circa 1700 to the conservative segment of second-generation Lutheranism led by M. Flacius Illyricus (1520-75) which claimed to be the defender of genuine Lutheranism, even among those who called themselves disciples of Luther. The controversies belonged to two principal categories. First, the doctrine of justification had to be defended against the synergists, who tended to compromise with the doctrine of the church of Rome concerning the necessity of good works for salvation. Second, the Gnesio-Lutherans were concerned with the doctrine called Crypto-Calvinism, concerning the person of Christ and the Lord's Supper.

GNOSIS

A term used in the religious philosophy of Gnosticism, a belief system in which matter is viewed as evil and the spirit as good and in which salvation was believed to be gained by esoteric knowledge or gnosis. Gnosis was of the divine nature and its emanations.

GNOSIS, Christian

A special knowledge of divine things, concerning which a doctrine was developed by early Christian writers. Indeed there is some probability (but no certainty), that some passages in the New Testament are directed against one or another form of Gnosticism. There is, however, also a doctrine of Christian Gnosis, to be distinguished from heretical Gnosticism as well as from Jewish Gnosticism, that is undoubtedly found in Paul and John. To the former, as to the latter, knowledge of God, not knowledge of self, is most important. This knowledge of God is primarily knowledge of Christ. In dignity it is less than the love of God. Among earlier Christian writers Clement of Alexandria and Origen significantly developed the doctrine of Gnosis.

GNOSTICISM

A religious sect in early Christianity and other contemporary religions. It combined mystical elements from various Hellenistic and Eastern sources, and like all mystical religions, laid great stress on individual salvation. This was to be achieved by elaborate rituals and spells. An accurate grasp of these observances was considered vital, hence the name gnosis, which is Greek for knowledge. Gnostic groups found their way into Christianity and were strongly attacked as heretics by Paul and the Fathers of the church. After the third century, gnosticism declined and was displaced by the new and similar movements of Manichaeism.

GOAH

A site, now unknown, named with the hill of Gareb in Jeremiah's prophecy concerning the rebuilding and extending of Jerusalem (Jeremiah 31:38-39).

GOB

In the Old Testament, a site where David's men twice struck down giant warriors of the Philistines' forces (2 Samuel 21:18-19). The parallel narrative at 1 Chronicles 20:4 lists the place of the first encounter as "Gezer," while leaving the place of the second encounter unnamed (20:5). Both accounts, however, show that a third encounter took place at "Gath" (2 Samuel 21:20; 1 Chronicles 20:6) and therefore many scholars have assumed that "Gob" is a scribal error for "Gath."

GOBAT, Samuel

(1799-1879) Second Anglican bishop of Jerusalem, missionary, and linguist, who was appointed by King Frederick William IV of Prussia to head the joint Anglican, Lutheran, and Eastern Orthodox mission in Jerusalem.

GOD

The Supreme Being. Man has always conceived of the existence of spirits or gods that controlled the world of nature and governed such natural phenomena as the sun, the rain, birth, death and fertility. Among early peoples there were also many minor deities presiding over springs, rivers, trees and other natural objects. This polytheism is still common in primitive societies.

Gradually, as in the Greek and Roman pantheons, one of these gods - called Zeus among the Greeks and Jupiter among the Romans - came to be regarded as the ruler of all others.

The Hindu pantheon also reflects this hierarchy by regarding Brahman as the supreme being, although other gods are worshiped as aspects of this being.

True monotheism emerged in the religion of the Hebrews, whose one God Yahweh, is a personal being with whom the Hebrews established a covenant.

The Christian concept of God is based on the Hebrew tradition, which is expanded to include the doctrines of the divine nature of Jesus Christ and the Trinity of three persons on one God. Another monotheistic religion, Islam, worships Allah as its one true God.

The major religions of the Far East - Buddhism, Shintoism and Confucianism - are philosophical, moral and contemplative, but they are not essentially monotheistic. There are many gods in the Buddhist and Hindu pantheon, but none is absolute or beyond the "wheel of life."

Theology and Philosophy

The principal arguments developed in the West to prove the existence of God are

▲ the ontological, put forth by Anselm of Canterbury, based on the idea of a perfect being;

▲ the cosmological, best stated by Thomas Aquinas, arguing from the principle of causality;

▲ the teleological, inspired by the order of the universe;

▲ the moral, enunciated by Immanuel Kant, based on man's inherently moral nature.

Another school of thought refutes these traditional arguments in favor of the belief that God reveals Himself directly to man through a mystical experience.

Philosophers have often conceived of God as a transcendent and impersonal being that shows Itself in the world and the universe but creates no personal relationship with man. This concept of God as the Prime Mover, or the force behind all reality, or the sum total of historical necessity, has been proposed by philosophers through the ages from Aristotle to Spinoza and Hegel. The pantheists, and those following their view, believe that god is the sum of the universe and that all things, including man, are therefore part of God. Deists see God expressed in the rational pattern of the universe but withdrawn from the events of the world. This view was popular among the philosophers of the 18th century.

Both the industrial and scientific revolutions have had far-reaching effects on the nature of belief in God. For many people, materialism and skepticism have replaced the earlier certitude of religion. Considerable numbers of people are agnostic, with a smaller group professing to be atheist. But the vast majority of the world's people retain a belief in a power beyond themselves and beyond the objective unfolding of historical, biological and economic forces. In addition, the old opposition of science and faith has lessened, as science has uncovered more mystery in the universe and religion has shown itself less dogmatic about the nature of the objective world. Thus, while particular concepts of God may have lost their former authority, the fundamental notion has shown itself to be enduring.

GOD, Catholic Teaching

Catholic teaching on the nature of God and His divine attributes is admirably expressed in the writings of Vatican Council I; "The holy, Catholic, apostolic Roman Church believes and professes that there is one true, living God, the Creator and Lord of heaven and earth. He is almighty, eternal, beyond measure, incomprehensible, and infinite in intellect, will and every perfection.

"Since He is one unique spiritual substance, entirely simple and unchangeable, He must be declared distinct from the world, perfectly happy in Himself and by His very nature, and inexpressibly exalted over all things that exist or can be conceived other than Himself."

In the fullness of revelation, moreover, it is known that the one God subsists in three equal persons, the Father and the Son and the Holy Spirit.

GOD, Classical arguments of existence

In philosophy, three arguments for God's existence that have been prominent in the philosophy of religion since the Middle Ages. The three arguments are:

1 the nature of perfect being;
2 the contingency of the world;
3 the purposiveness of the world.

Ontological arguments, defining God as the most perfect being conceivable, hold that if God did not exist, it would still be possible to conceive of a being like God in every respect but who does exist. But this being would be more perfect than God because he would possess all of God's attributes plus existence as well.

GOD, Intuition of

The created mind's unmediated vision of God as He is. "Intuition" here means, not a swiftly felt, unreasoned conviction, but, like the Latin intuitus,

a gazing or looking upon. Because the bodily sense of sight apprehends objects immediately present to the beholder, words referring to vision become metaphors for the cognitive union of mind with God as He is immediately present to it.

The knowing is termed an intuition because it involves no mental image, concept, or idea as medium; only the eternal Word, no created representation, expresses the divine being as It is, and the cognitive union intended is directly with God Himself.

The beatific vision is the only certain instance of the intuition of God; theology speculates about biblical references to Moses (Exodus 33:11; Numbers 12:8; Deuteronomy 34:10-11); and about the theoretical possibility of the created mind's being elevated to the intuition of the divine being.

GOD, Islamic view of

According to the Islam, Allah is the name God gave Himself when he revealed Himself to Moses through the burning bush (Sura 20:14; Exodus 3:4-6). The name, Allah, is found scores of times in the Koran, and with it begins the great Koranic leit-motiv: "In the name of God, Most Gracious, Most Merciful," which opens each sura. The Arabic word Allah is a shorted version of al-ilah, "the god."

In pre-Islamic times, Allah certainly was a creator god, and possibly the supreme deity of the Meccan pantheon. In the Koran Mohammed preached an absolute monotheism. No systemic exposition on the nature and the attributes are found in the Koran, but there emerge from it many ideas which constitute the ground of such a treatise.

The first and foremost idea the Koran insists upon, is the Oneness of the Godhead. The Koran gives to Allah a good number of attributes out of which the Muslims have put together the 99 "most beautiful names" of God. They express either God's immanent qualities, like Immortal, Supreme, The Living, or his activities ad extra like Creator, Omnipotent, Supreme Judge,

Avenger, Guide, The Merciful, The Protector.

When the Muslim divines began to rationalize their faith in theology (ilm al-kalam), they came upon some particularly difficult passages in the Koran that described God in anthropomorphic terms ascribing to him eyes, hands, a face, and portraying him as speaking and sitting on a throne (Sura 2:254-7:54).

The philosophers (falasifa) developed a rationalistic theology whereby the existence of God is proved by the contingency of the world. God is being, necessary and perfect, supreme intelligence and supreme love.

GOD, Knowledge of

Intellectual or experiential apprehension of God that some claim can be gained through the use of natural reason and others contend can be comprehended through religious experience or through God's self-disclosure.

GOD, Nature of

The being or essence of the Supreme Being that is variously conceived by different religious traditions. Even within a given tradition, the conception of God's nature has a tendency to evolve with the development of the religion. This evolution has been held by many scholars in the past to begin with animism (belief in souls), to progress to polytheism (belief in many gods), and finally to develop into a belief in one God (monotheism).

GOD, the Name

As a proper name it translates the biblical words Yahweh, Elohim, Theos. The labor of etymologists to trace precisely the origin and meaning of either the Greek theos of the Latin deus has yielded little. Thus it would be difficult to substantiate an etymological grounds that "God" means for all who use it a being, who has universal presidence over things.

The basis in human experience for applying any name to the divine can only be effects of divine activity; then the referent become the being to whom the action belongs.

Thus in the case of "God" in its theoretically possible origin it signifies action, particularly providence; in its reference it signifies the divine nature: it is used to mean something that is above all that is and that is the source of all things and distinct from them all.

GODLY DEVOTION

In Christianity, reverence, worship and service to God, with loyalty to His universal sovereignty. The prime example of Godly devotion is Jesus Christ. The apostle Paul wrote to Timothy: "Indeed, the sacred secret of this Godly devotion is admittedly great." He was made in flesh, was declared righteous in spirit, appeared in angels, was preached about among nations, was believed upon in the world, was received upon in glory (1 Timothy 3:16). Adam, the perfect man, had not set the perfect example of Godly devotion. None of his children, born imperfect, could do so.

According to Biblical tradition, Jesus Christ was the one man to manifest Godly devotion perfectly, in every sense, proving that man in the flesh can certainly maintain such devotion. Jesus was, at the end of his earthly course under severe trials, "loyal, guileless, undefined, separated from the sinners" (Hebrews 7:26).

GOD, Kingdom of

The spiritual realm over which God reigns as king, of the fulfillment on earth of God's will.

GOD OF GOOD LUCK

In Isaiah's time the worship of deities evidently involved setting a table of food and drink before them (Isaiah 65:11). Arabic tradition identifies the planet Jupiter with the "greater good luck" and the planet Venus with the "lesser good luck." Hence, it has been suggested that the god of Good Luck (Gad) may be identified with Jupiter, and the god of Destiny with Venus.

GOD THE GOD OF ISRAEL

After Jacob's encounter at Peniel with the angel of God, as a result of which he was given the name "Israel," and after a peaceable meeting with his brother Esau, Jacob dwelt at Succoth and then Shechem. Here he acquired a tract of land from the sons of Hamor and pitched his tent upon it (Genesis 32:24-30; 33:1-4, 17-19). After that he set up an altar and called it "God the God of Israel" (Genesis 33:20). This was Jacob's first altar in Palestine (Genesis 33:20). In identifying himself by his newly given name "Israel" with the name of the altar, Jacob indicated his acceptance and appreciation of that name and of God's guiding him safely back into the Promised Land. The expression occurs only once in the Bible.

GOG

Name found in chapters 38 and 39 of Ezekiel, applied to the leader of a storm-like, multinational assault against God's people. The attack comes after God has gathered his people out of the nations and restored them to the previously devastated "mountains of Israel." Because they dwell in security, with no visible signs of protection, and because they enjoy abundant prosperity, Gog is drawn into waging a vicious, all-out attack upon them. He congregates a vast army from many nations for this purpose. But the assault sets off God's rage and brings terrible defeat and destruction upon Gog and his entire crowd. Their carcasses become food for birds and beasts and their bones are buried in the valley that thereafter is called the "Valley of God's crowd."

GOIIM

In the Old Testament, the domain of a Canaanite King defeated by Joshua. He is spoken of as "the king of Goiim in Gilgal" (Joshua 12:7, 23).

OLASECCA

Site of cremation cemeteries of the Early Iron Age, located on the Somma plateau at the southern end of Lake Maggiore, north-west of modern Milan. Each tomb contained a jar-shaped burial urn covered with an inverted bowl; the urns held the ashes of the dead together with small accessories and weapons. The Golasecca civilization, dating circa 650-500 BC, is closely connected with that of the Comacines.

GOLAN

In the Old Testament, a city of Bashan in the territory of Mannasseh, selected as a city of refuge (Deuteronomy 4:41-43; Joshua 20:2-8). The Gershonite Levites were given the city for their dwelling (Joshua 21:27). Most geographers consider its probable modern location to be Jaulan, a little more than 17 miles each of the Sea of Galilee. A district of the same name is somewhat closer to the Sea of Galilee.

GOLAN HEIGHTS

One of the three cities of refuge on the east of Jordan. It became the head of the province of Gualanitus, one of the four provinces into which Bashan was divided after the Babylonian captivity.

GOLDEN CALF

The image made, according to Exodus 32, in connection with the worship of Yahweh. The term refers to the young bull or cow. Calves were slaughtered for sacrifice (Leviticus 9:2-3) and for food (1 Samuel 28:24). A golden calf, probably a wooden core overlaid with gold, was made by Aaron at the request of the people (Exodus 32:4-8; Deuteronomy 9:16; Nehemiah 8:18). The calf, a figure of strength and usefulness, was meant to be a visible representation of their God. Jeroboam later erected two golden calves in Bethel and Dan to affirm the unity of the northern kingdom (1 Kings 12:26-33). Such practices, being superstitious and idolatrous, were severely condemned by Moses (Exodus 32:19-30) and the prophets.

GOLDEN RULE
The precept stated by Jesus in the sermon on the mount (Matthew 7:12). The name, implying that this is the chief ethical principle, has been used since the 16th century.

GOLDSMID, Isaac Lyon
(1778-1859) Financier, England's first Jewish baronet, whose work for Jewish emancipation in that nation made possible passage of the Jewish Disabilities Bill of 1859, granting basic civil and political rights to Jews.

GOLEM
In Jewish folklore, an image endowed with life. The term is used in the Bible (Psalms 139:16) and in Talmudic literature to refer to an embryonic or incomplete substance. It assumed its present connotation in the Middle Ages, when many legends arose of wise men who were able to bring effigies to life by means of a charm.

GOLGOTHA
(Greek "kranion", skull) Jerusalem hill site of the crucifixion of Jesus (Matthew 27:33).

The "Church of the Holy Sepulchre" located within the present walls of Jerusalem, stands on the traditional site of Golgotha and Jesus' tomb. There is doubt whether this site actually was outside the walls of Jerusalem in the days of Jesus' earthly ministry.

Another location that has been suggested is "Gordon's Calvary" situated on a cliff circa 250 yards north-east of the Damascus Gate. The cliff somewhat resembles a skull. Circa 100 yards to the west of "Gordon's Calvary" lies a very large garden, the north end of which is bounded by a hill. A tomb containing only one finished grave is cut out of a huge stone protruding from

the side of this hill. Although this site would fit the biblical record, it cannot be stated dogmatically that this is the correct location.

GOLIATH
According to the Old Testament account, was a Philistine warrior nearly 10 feet tall, who challenged the Israelites to send out a champion to engage him in single combat. The challenge was taken up by the youthful David, armed only with a slingshot. David, confident of his cause and expert with his simple weapon, struck his heavily armed adversary with a single stone between the eyes and cut off his head. Once their champion was killed, the Philistines were quickly put to flight.

GOMER
In the Old Testament, grandson of Noah and first-named son of Japheth, born after the Flood (Genesis 10:1-2; 1 Chronicles 1:4-5). He and his sons, Ashkenaz, Riphath and Togarmah, are listed among "the families of the sons of Noah according to their family descents" from whom the nations were spread about after the Deluge (Flood) (Genesis 10:3, 32).

The nation that descended from Gomer is historically associated with the ancient Cimmerians, an Aryan race called Gimmirrai in the Assyrian inscriptions and who settled in the region north of the Black Sea. The Crimea (the peninsula of the southern Ukraine extending into the northern portion of the Black Sea) evidently derives its name from this basically nomadic people.

GOMORRAH
In biblical times, one of the "cities of the District" probably located near the southern end of the Dead Sea (Genesis 13:12). Sodom and Gomorrah were apparently the chief of these cities. The ruins are believed to be presently submerged under the waters of the Dead Sea, which now cover what in

Abraham's time was described as "a well-watered region ... like the garden of God" (Genesis 13:10).

GONZAGA, Saint Aloysius

(1568-1591)Patron of Roman Catholic youth whose characteristic chastity, holiness, heroism, and enthusiasm for the Christian ideal has made him one of the most venerated saints.

GOOD, The Supreme

The superlative in respect to all created goods and to human desire. As the first and universal object of appetite, it is signified in the abstract as "pure goodness" by contrast with any particular kind of goodness, and in the concrete as the subsisting good, by contrast with the derivative good.

Theological language attributes both terms to God, who embraces in Himself the whole range of good through infinitely transcending His creation. The supreme good belongs to the being who in his own whole, not to the whole of created things.

Usage in speaking of God as the supreme good can be twofold. It is sometimes metaphorical, as often in the scriptures, when an essentially creaturely perfection is projected into God on the principle that every effect somehow reflects its cause. The term also centers with special force into moral philosophy and theology as the ultimate end of the human will. It charges every intention and choice of intermediate objects with the value and delight of what is final and paramount for human beings, namely happiness.

GOOD FRIDAY

Two days before Easter, the Friday in Holy Week on which the yearly commemoration of the crucifixion of Jesus Christ is observed. As early as the second century, there are references to fasting and penance on this day by Christians, who, since the time of the early church, had observed every Friday as a fast day in memory of the crucifixion.

In the Roman Catholic Church it is the one day of the year on which Mass is not celebrated; the three-part Good Friday ceremony consists of the reading of the Passion from the gospel of John, the Veneration of the Cross, and a Communion service. The Eucharist consumed on Good Friday was consecrated on Holy Thursday.

GOOD NEWS

In Christianity, this phrase refers to the news of the kingdom of God and of salvation by faith in Jesus Christ. It is called in the Bible "the good news of the kingdom" (Matthew 4:23), "the good news of God" (Romans 15:16), "the good news about Jesus Christ" (Mark 1:1), "the good news of the undeserved kingness of god" (Acts 20:24).

The apostle Paul made the strong declaration that the good news committed to the apostles was the only good news; that if the apostles themselves or even an angel out of heaven were to declare as good news something beyond what the apostles had declared as good news, "let them be aroused." He then gave the reason, namely, that the good news is not something human, not from man, but through revelation by Jesus Christ. This strong declaration was necessary, for even then there were some who were trying to overthrow the true faith by preaching "another good news" (2 Corinthians 11:4).

GOOD SHEPHERD SISTERS

A Roman Catholic order of religious devotion particularly to the care, rehabilitation and education of girls and young women who have demonstrated delinquent behavior. The congregation traces its history to an order founded by St. John Eudes in 1641 at Caen (France).

The sisters work with delinquent girls, problem children, persons who are serving sentence imposed by civil courts, and alcoholics.

GOOD WILL

Both the Hebrew and Greek nouns and related forms of these words have reference to that which pleases or to one's being pleased, and are translated "delight," "pleasure," "pleased," "good pleasure," "liking," "approval," and so forth.

In the Bible these terms are used with regard to the pleasure, approval or good will of God (Psalms 51: 18; 106:4). God sets forth clearly what is required to please Him, and He determines whom He will accept as his friends, as recipients of His good will. Those rejecting His word or rebelling against Him do not receive His good will, but, rather, experience His displeasure (Psalms 2:5; Hebrews 3:16-19).

GOODWIN, Thomas

(1600-1680) Puritan clergyman and a chaplain to Oliver Cromwell who helped draft a confession of faith for Congregationalism.

GOOD WOMAN OF SETZUAN, The

Title of a play by Bertolt Brecht about three gods who, in order to justify their existence, descend to earth to find one really good person.

GORAKHNATH

(late 10th early 11th century) Hindu master yogi, commonly regarded as the founder of the Kanphata Yogis, an order of ascetics that stresses the physical and spiritual disciplines of Hatha Yoga.

Gorakhnath's work *Goraksasataka* is a fundamental text among yogis. The most orthodox of his followers regarded him as an incarnation of the god Shiva, and thus eternal, and he is said to reside still in a cave in the Himalayas.

GORDON, Judah Leib

Lithuanian Hebrew poet, the leading essayist of the Hebrew Enlightenment, whose use of biblical and post-biblical Hebrew resulted in a new and influential style of Hebrew poetry.

GORYO

In Japanese religion, vengeful spirits of the dead. In the Heian period (794-857) goryo were generally considered to be spirits of nobility who had died as a result of political intrigue and who because of their ill will for the living brought about natural disasters, diseases, and wars.

Belief in the power of goryo has survived, particularly among the rural population of Japan, and special memorial services continue to be performed to appease victims of untimely death.

GOSHEN

A region in Egypt where the Israelites resided for circa 215 years (1728-1513 BC) (Genesis 45:10; 47:27). While the exact location of Goshen is uncertain, it appears to have lain in the eastern part of the Nile Delta, the entrance of Egypt proper. This is indicated by the fact that Joseph, leaving his Egyptian quarters, met his father (who was traveling from Canaan) at Goshen (Genesis 46:28-29).

GOSPEL

From the Anglo-Saxon term godspell, meaning "good story" or "good telling;" the term gospel thus encompasses the Christian proclamation of the life, works, death, and Resurrection of Jesus of Nazareth and his salvific significance for man.

It is customary to describe the gospels of Matthew, Mark, and Luke as "synoptic Gospels" because they give a "synopsis" or similar view of the life and teaching of Jesus; the gospel of John reflects a different apostolic tradition. The gospels are held in high esteem by the church; passages from them are read in the Eucharist Liturgy and in the formal celebration of the sacraments.

GOSPEL LITURGY

A section from the four gospels customarily read or sung as the most prominent part of the Liturgy of the Word in Roman and other Christian worship services. Lectionaries containing such sections, determined for daily Mass, feasts, and Sundays, are borne in solemn procession to a prominent place in the church, are venerated by an incensation before being read by no one of lower rank than a deacon, while the congregation stands out of respect for God's Word being proclaimed.

GOSPELS

(Greek: evangelion, "a good message") First four books of the New Testament, named for their authors: Matthew, Mark, Luke and John. Each is a collection of the acts and words of Jesus. Didactic in intention rather then biographical, they were written to help spread the gospel ("good news") of Christian salvation. All broadly cover the key events of Jesus' life, death and resurrection, but narrative styles and details, and intended readership differ. Matthew shows the prophesied King, Mark presents him as a servant, Luke, as a man, John, as the Son of God. These are four portraits of one person, namely Christ.

GOTHIC ART

An artistic phase originating in the 12th century northern France and spreading throughout Western Europe from the 13th through the 15th century. First developed in ecclesiastical architecture, the Gothic structure is characterized by an ogival construction (raising of all ribs to equal height) of ribbed vaults, clustered piers and flying buttresses.

This skeletal system carried the heavy masonry load, thus opening the walls for large areas of stained glass and raising vast other-worldly interiors in the great cathedrals of Chartres (1194), Amiens (1220) and Reims (1211).

Along with this, new religious themes and devotional images emerged in sculptural ornamentation, manuscript illumination, tapestries, textiles, embroideries, and virtually all the arts and produced a rich variety of regional and national styles ranging from Early to Late "Gothic" art.

GOTHIC REVIVAL

18th century romantic revival of Gothic architectural forms introduced in English domestic buildings of exotic charm and playfulness; e.g. the pseudo-Gothic Houses of Parliament.

GOTTSCHALK OF ORHAIS

(803-868) Monk, poet, and theologian whose teachings on predestination shook the medieval Catholic church in the 9th century.

Holding that Christ's salvation was limited and that his power of redemption extended only to the elect, Gottschalk taught that the elect went to eternal glory and the reprobate went to damnation.

GOVERNMENT, Divine

The execution of the plan of divine providence for the universe through the causal workings toward their ends of all things set in being by divine creation and maintained by divine conservation. "It is thy providence, O Father, that steers the course" (Wisdom 14:3). That God is the first cause, efficient, final, and exemplar, of all activity is the key notion; that creatures themselves are true causes has to be made compatible with this.

A Dionysian tradition takes biblical references to God's being jealous in the sense less of His tolerating no unfaithfulness than of His zealous cherishing of the natures he has created so that His governing respects and fosters their own proper activities.

The thought that divine Wisdom "reaches mighty from one end of the earth to the other and orders all things sweetly and well" (Wisdom 8:1) runs throughout the classical treatises on divine government, which do not agree with some authors that the first cause is the unique cause and that creatures are only occasions for its productive action.

GOVERNOR

Authority, who in biblical times, generally had military and judicial powers and was responsible to see that the tribute, tax, or revenue to the king of the superior ruler was paid by the jurisdictional districts or provinces that the

Cathedral of Orvieto; an example of Gothic architecture of the 12th century.

governor ruled (Luke 2:1-2). Often they put a heavy load on the people to supply food for themselves and their large body of attendants (Nehemiah 5:15-18).

King Solomon appointed governors over the districts of Israel. They are mentioned at 1 Kings 10:15, and may be the same as the 12 deputies of 1 Kings 4:7-19, whose duty it was to provide food for the king and his household, each for one month in the year.

GOZAN

A name seemingly applied both to a place and to a river. At 2 Kings 19:12 and Isaiah 37:12, Gozan appears to embrace an area larger than a city, for its inhabitants are listed among the "nations" conquered by the Assyrians. Many scholars, evidently basing their conclusions on word similarities, believe that Gozan may correspond to Gausanitis, a district of Mesopotamia referred to by Ptolemy and considered to be the same as the "Guzana" mentioned in Assyrian records. Guzana is commonly linked with modern Tell Halaf on the upper Khabur River, circa 365 miles north-east of the Sea of Galilee.

GOZZOLI, Benozzo

(1420-1497) Celebrated early Renaissance painter whose masterpiece, a fresco cycle in the chapel of Palazzo Medici-Riccardi, Florence, reveals a new interest in nature and in the representation of human features as definite portraiture. He painted a number of beautiful altarpieces.

GRACE

In Christian theology, a term that conveys the concept of the divine initiative displayed supremely in God's gift of salvation. The English term grace is a translation of the Greek charis which occurs around 150 times in the New Testament. Ever since the apostle Paul used the term grace to convey a sense of the unmerited favor of God, the major Christian theologians -

Augustine, Aquinas, Martin Luther, Karl Barth - have regarded themselves as expositors of divine grace. Grace is also used colloquially to mean a verbal thanksgiving to God for a meal about to be eaten.

According to Catholic teaching grace is a supernatural gift of God bestowed upon a person with a view of salvation and sanctification. Understood in this sense, there are three kinds of grace:

▲ uncreated grace refers to the abiding presence of the Holy Trinity in the souls of the just;

▲ created or sanctifying grace is a created sharing or participation in the life of God Himself;

▲ actual grace is a transient help of God which enlightens the mind and strengthens the will to do good and avoid evil.

Grace is given to human beings through the merits of Jesus Christ and is communicated by the Holy Spirit. The principal means of growing in grace are prayer, the sacraments (especially the Eucharist), and good works. Sanctifying grace is lost by the commission of mortal sin.

GRACE, Actual

The divine help given to a person, prompting those acts of mind and will that belong to salvation. The term actual serves to distinguish it from sanctifying grace, which later scholastics referred to as habitual grace; it denotes the help as given at the moment of the exercise of a concrete action of mind or of will.

Against Pelagianism Augustine emphasized continual dependence upon this divine help, both for the beginning and completion of justification, and for the subsequent process of salvation; the strongest church declaration on this dependence was given by the Council of Trent.

GRACE, Baptismal

The sanctifying newness effected through the sacrament: rebirth into adopted sonship and liberation from all sin, original and, in the case of adults, personal; incorporation into Christ and thereby into the church, Christ's body.

The baptismal liturgy and theology both seek to express the Pauline teaching of a complete death to sin and a resurrection to new life in Christ (Romans 6:3). Baptismal grace, though not the sacramental character, is received extrasacramentally by Baptism of desire or of blood.

GRACE, Consciousness of

An experienced awareness of the presence and working of grace in oneself. Grace empowers a person to live a life of knowing and loving God; self-awareness, a concomitant reflexiveness, is characteristic of such vital actions. Even as in the case of purely natural knowing and willing, the concomitant consciousness is first of all of the acts themselves; then and thereby of their objects, i.e., uncreated grace, the Divine Persons present, and of their inner source, i.e., created grace, the gifts of God abiding in the soul.

The cognitive quality of this consciousness, however, is limited by faith, the objects of which always remain believed, not evident; thus awareness of grace is not equivalent to assurance of salvation. The awareness, however, is more intense and more interior than simply a moral certitude about one's state of soul derived, e.g., from an examination of conscience.

GRACE, Created

A gratuitous gift of God to a created intellectual being. This grace may be external, i.e., something outside the one to whom it is given; e.g., the church or the sacraments in relation to man. It may also be internal, i.e., a special effect produced by God in the substance or the powers of a rational creature.

To be a grace this effect must be supernatural, that is, beyond the power of nature to produce or attain and not due to nature as such. Instances of created internal graces are sanctifying grace, a habit produced in the soul by God, and actual grace.

Illuminations of the mind concerning things that pertain to salvation are actual graces, so also impulses of the will toward some supernatural good. The habit that will be infused into the soul of the just man after death, called the light of glory and also the act of seeing God face to face, called the beatific vision, are created graces.

The word created does not mean, according to the more common opinion of theologians, that the grace is created in the strict sense of that word, that is, produced by God out of nothing. The word is used rather to express the fact that the supernatural effects of God's action are distinct from God himself and caused by Him in the rational creature.

GRACE, Efficacious

A term used to signify a grace that infallibly moves a man to perform an act leading to salvation while leaving him perfectly free to consent or resist. It is an actual grace, i.e., a help conceived of as an impulse or a movement bestowed on the recipient. An efficacious grace not only gives a man the power to act but unfailingly secures the free use of that power. It is efficacious, therefore, not merely in the event of man's cooperation but from the moment it is given by God, before man's consent is given.

The difficult problem of grace that efficaciously brings about the will's consent and still leaves the freedom of the will intact has vexed theologians for many centuries. Some authors say, the grace is efficacious because imparted by God in the light of man's foreknown consent; i.e., by the foreknowledge called scientia media God has foreseen the effect it will have, the grace is said to be efficacious before it is actually conferred; once given, it cooperates with the act of the will consenting, and the salutary is performed.

The Roman Catholic Church grants full freedom for the teaching of these and other theories provided two truths are safeguarded: the dominion of God over man's actions and the freedom of the will.

GRACE, External

In a broad sense, any objective divine gift external to man, not demanded by his nature or constitution. Riches, power, and such things fall under this definition. In the strict theological sense this gift must be a supernatural one, ultimately directed to salvation.

External grace may be something supernatural in itself or at least supernatural in the manner in which it is produced. Again this grace may consist of a created gift or it may be God's self-donation objectively considered.

From the viewpoint of man's perfection, external grace has relevance only inasmuch as it is conductive to the production and increase of internal sanctifying grace. More in particular, external graces are objective realities, initially perceived by the senses, that make their way under the influence of internal grace to the mind and the will to stir up supernatural life.

The proclamation of the gospel, which according to the Scripture, is the beginning of salvation (Romans 10:14), is the classical example. Other external created graces are works of supernatural providence ordained for man's salvation, such as the church and the sacraments.

GRACE, Natural

Any endowment of nature, especially of human nature, so designated because it is an effect of God's causal goodness, and as such a gift freely given; distinguished against grace in its proper sense, the gift of God's love drawing man above the natural to share in the divine life. Natural endowments or experiences can also be called graces in all of God's causality over man related to His saving love.

GRACE, Sacramental

In Roman Catholic theology grace can mean only one concrete reality, the divine gift given through Jesus Christ the Savior. To speak of sacramental grace involves the presuppositions that grace is a created gift interiorly affecting the being and the acting of the recipient and that this gift is conferred through the sacraments, both teachings of the Council of Trent (1545-1563).

There is also, by contrast, a further implication, "extrasacramental grace," i.e., that grace is given in ways other than through the sacraments. A recent (Vatican Council II) and to-be-treasured church statement on this point is that catechumens - not yet baptized - are already in many cases living the life of faith, hope, and charity.

Classical theology has inquired, consequently, into the precise meaning of grace as it is received in virtue of the sacraments. There is a first, general response that applies to all sacraments. The sacraments are signs witnessing the union in faith with Jesus Christ in his Passion, death and Resurrection; their effectiveness consists in and is derived from Christ as the universal and first saving Mediator.

In serving as signs of faith the sacraments bring about what they signify. They are signs of the past, the Paschal mystery of Christ, of the actual effectiveness of that mystery here and now, and of the future, final sharing in the fruits and purpose of that mystery. All sacramental grace then, is a gift conforming a participation in its effectiveness, and promising future glory.

Each sacrament is a distinctive form of witnessing and of being conjoined with the paschal mystery. The further theological issue, then, is the nature of the grace given by each of the seven sacraments. Centuries of theological discussion have developed a variety of categories, usually scholastic in origin, to classify the quality of grace proper to each sacrament (e.g., that each confers a right to the actual graces needed to carry out the essential meaning of the sacrament).

A more contemporarily fruitful evaluation may be seen in the documents of Vatican Council II and in their subsequent implementation with the revised liturgical rites. The general instructions for the new liturgical rites contain a rich theology that directs the rites to be carried out in such a way as to manifest more clearly how each sacrament brings about a special mode in which the recipient is enabled to live as a sharer in Christ's priestly, paschal mystery. Sacramental grace so understood is not taken as static and objectified. The sacraments and their graces point to an abiding manner of living, the life of the faithful as such. Even the graces given that were traditionally referred to as "actual graces" as well as the charisms, are to be seen as related to sacramental grace, in the sense that they are gifts to those who are constituted as a priestly community by the grace of the sacraments.

GRACES

Greek goddesses of fertility, who also personified charm, gentleness and beauty. They were usually three sisters: Aglaia ("the Radiant"), Euphrosyne ("Joy") and Thalia ("the Flowering"). The Graces were the daughters of Zeus and Eurynome and sometimes attended Aphrodite, the goddess of love. With the nine Muses and Apollo they joined in a chorus on Mount Olympus and hence were sometimes associated with music and arts. They were frequently depicted in flowing white and transparent garments, dancing together holding hands.

GRAETZ, Heinrich

(1817-1891) Jewish historian who taught at the Jewish Theological Seminar of Breslau, Germany and at the University of Breslau. It took him twenty-two years to complete his 11-volume work on the history of the Jews. It was translated from German in many languages.

Graetz surpassed all previous Jewish history writers because of his tireless and painstaking research, his scientific approach, his warm manner, and his clear style. He searched through the Talmud to find out about the history of that time.

GRAGGER

Jewish word belonging to the Purim vocabulary. Noisemaking at the mention of Haman's name in the reading of the Scroll of Esther is an old custom. The gragger has been in use since the 13th century in France and Germany. It combines two primitive instruments: the "bull-roarer" consisted of a long stick at the top of which was attached a string and at the end of the string a thin board. When this was twirled, it made a strange noise. The "scraper" was notched shell or bone which was scraped with a stiff object. The gragger combines both these objects.

GRAHAM, Sylvester

(1794-1851) Clergyman whose advocacy of a health regimen emphasizing temperance and vegetarianism.

GRAHAM, William Franklin

(1918-) American evangelist, known as Billy Graham. Born near Charlotte, North Carolina and ordained a Southern Baptist minister in 1940, he first achieved national prominence on the revivalist circuit circa 1949 and is probably the Western world's best-known leader of mass religious rallies.

GRAMADEVATA

A type of folk deity widely worshipped in rural India. They may have originated as agricultural deities, existing side by side with the Brahmanical deities of modern Hinduism.

GRAUN, Karl Heinrich

(1704-1759) Composer of operas and sacred music, known especially for his Passion oratorio Der Tod Jesu.

GREAT AWAKENING

Intense and widespread religious revival in 18th century North America, forming part of the international evangelical revival. Starting in New Jersey (1726), the movement quickly spread across New England. In reaction to the prevailing rationalism and formalism, its leaders - notably Jonathan Edwards and George Whitefield - preached evangelical Calvinism and discouraged excessive emotionalism. The 1740s saw the zenith of Awakening, which led to the rapid growth of the Presbyterian, Baptist and Methodist churches, continuing to the end of the century. A similar revival beginning in the 1790s is known as the Second Great Awakening.

GREAT BOOK OF ORGANUM

Translation of *Magnus liber Organi,* medieval collection of liturgical polyphonic settings arranged for the entire church year.

GREAT CHURCH

In the Byzantine tradition, the church Aya Sofia (Hagia Sophia); then also the patriarchate itself of Constantinople, because of its pride of place in the history of Eastern Christendom.

GREAT MOTHER OF GODS

Ancient Oriental-Greek-Roman deity from circa the 5th century BC onward. The Great Mother was especially prominent in the art of the empire. She usually appears with mural crown and veil, seated on a throne or in a chariot, and accompanied by two lions.

Mother goddess figures are found in almost every ancient religion, but these figures, who were usually only goddessesh of fertility and reproduction in general, should not be confused with the Great Mother of Gods, who was regarded as the giver of life to gods, men, and beasts alike.

GREAT SCHISM

The occurrence and development of two divisions in the Christian church. The first was the breach between the Eastern and Western churches. Longstanding divergences in tradition, combined with political and theological disputes, came to a head in 1054 when Pope Leo IX sent legates to refuse the title of Ecumenical Patriarch to the patriarch of Constantinople and to demand acceptance of the filioque ("and from the Son") clause in the Nicene Creed.

The patriarch refused and rejected the claim of papal supremacy. Reciprocal excommunications and anathemas followed. Later councils were unsuccessful in healing the breach.

The second Great Schism was the division within the Roman Catholic Church (1378-1417) when there were 2 or 3 rival popes and antipopes, each with his nationalistic following. The Council of Constantinople ended the schism by electing Martin V as sole pope.

GREECE, Orthodox Church of

One of the largest and most important autocephalous (ecclesiastically independent) Eastern Orthodox churches. During the Byzantine Empire and the subsequent Turkish occupation, the church of Greece was under the administration of the ecumenical patriarch of Constantinople. It was declared autocephalous by the Council of Navplion in 1833 and recognized by the ecumenical patriarch in 1850.

Orthodoxy as a popular religion still retains a powerful hold on the countryside, and the transition to a church of the modern secularized world has proved a major problem. Several monastic communities, chiefly the monastic republic of Mount Athos, are the main strongholds of the traditional forms. The recruitment for the monastic communities is poor.

GREED

Inordinate or rapacious desire; covetousness. Greed can manifest itself in love of money, desire for power or gain, voraciousness for food and drink, sex, or other material things. The Bible warns Christians against this degrading trait, and commands that they should avoid association with anyone calling himself a Christian "brother" who practices greediness (1 Corinthians 5:9-11).

GREEK ART AND ARCHITECTURE

Ancient Greek art developed and flourished between circa 1000 and 31 BC in mainland Greece and in the Greek colonies of the eastern Mediterranean, southern Italy, Sicily, and the Aegean. The earlier date is associated with the transitional period following the decline of the prehistoric Minoan and Mycenean civilizations. The battle of Actium in 31 BC represents the time of transition into Roman art. Greek art developed within the framework of the Greek city states.

The Doric, Ionic, and Corinthian orders, which had profound influence on the history of architecture, developed in monumental Greek religious and civic architecture. Greek sculpture progressed from stylization to naturalism and from naturalism to realism, creating some of the greatest works in the history of Greek art. Painting developed in two channels: monumental painting and painting on pottery.

Because little remains of the former type, scholars rely mainly on vase painting to trace the development of Greek drawing. The earliest study of Greek art, which was seen mainly through the works of Roman copyists, had enormous influence in 16th century Italy and was of fundamental importance in the development of Renaissance art and architecture.

Monumental Greek architecture began in the archaic period (7th-6th century BC), flourished through the classical and Hellenistic periods (5th-2nd century BC) and saw the first of many revivals during the Roman Empire.

The roots of Greek architecture lie in the tradition of local Bronze Age houses and palaces, the megaron of the Mycenean princes, with its columned porch, forehall, and throne room, which provided the basic plan of the Greek temple.

GREEK ORTHODOX CHURCH
Eastern Orthodox Church.

GREEK RELIGION
The complex beliefs and religious practices of the ancient Greeks in numerous communities throughout Greece proper and the Mediterranean and Pontic world from pre-Homeric times down to the disappearance of paganism in the fifth and sixth centuries AD.

Knowledge of this religion is derived from both literary and archeological sources. The writings of Homer, Hesiod, the elegiac, lyric, and tragic poets, and the historians and philosophers contain numerous references to, and descriptions of, various rites and a great many myths.

Excavations at Athens, Eleusis, Olympia, Delphi, Epidauros, and elsewhere have turned up numerous temples, statues, treasuries, altars, and inscriptions containing calendars, lists of priests, oracles, and sacred decrees.

The assessment of material is frequently difficult, not simply because of the differences of time and place, but also because of the character of Greek religion itself. It has no specifically sacred books such as the Bible or the Koran, no dogmas or creeds, that is, a prescribed body of doctrine, no powerful priestly castes, no code of ethics, and no theology in the sense of a rational investigation of the data of religious experience or revelation.

Nevertheless, the Greeks were an essentially religious people (see also Acts 17:22), and their interpretation of life and of the world about them was definitively religious. This may be seen in their faith in the power and omniscience of the gods, their trust in them, their gratitude for favors, and their joy and enthusiasm in honoring them, particularly during the public festivals.

In contrast with the Judaeo-Christian tradition, Greek religion was to a large extent amoral and in its mythology even in the minds of some Greeks themselves at times, quite immoral. This deficiency was to an extent remedied by the reflections and ethical teachings of Pindar and the tragedians, particularly Aeschylus and Sophocles, and by the philosophizing of the Greek sages, of Socrates, Plato, Aristotle, and the Stoics, all of whom subscribed to the religion of the state but taught at the same time a more or less perfect kind of monotheism.

The separation in the cities of the public worship of the gods from its agrarian foundation, the decline of the city states in the fourth century BC, the rationalizations of the philosophers, and the disappointment of personal hopes as the result of constant civil and foreign wars that plagued the Greeks, weakened the influence of traditional religion and turned the minds of men to more personal types of worship that would at the same time give promise of a happy immortality.

Already in the classical period the Eleusian mysteries and those connected with Orpheus and Dionysus promised purification and survival after death to their initiates. The feeling for the importance of the individual is also reflected from the fifth century on the popularity of Aesclepius, the god of healing, the worship of Tyche, the goddess Fortune, during the Hellenistic Age, and the widespread cult of such foreign deities as the Egyptian Isis and the Persian Mithras under Roman rule.

Probably the most lasting achievement of Greek religion was the profound influence it had on the whole of Hellenic art - the painting of vases, the engraving of gems and coins, the carving and casting of exquisite statues, the erection of altars such as that of Zeus at Pergamum and hundreds of temples throughout the Mediterranean world.

GREEK RELIGION, Early period

Though Greek religion retained traces of more primitive practices, a worship of rocks, trees, and animals, a belief in taboos and magic, and the conducting of fertility rites, in its developed form it was essentially an anthropomorphic polytheism.

This was brought about through a fusion of a belief in sky gods and the use of bloody sacrifices that belonged to the Indo-European invaders of Greece with earlier belief in chthonic deities and the offering of unbloody sacrifices on the part of the peoples already living there. To these were later added other gods borrowed, particularly from the East, and other rites such as the ecstatic dancers in honor of Dionysus (Bacchus) and the temple-harlotry of Aphrodite at Corinth.

GREEK RELIGION, Olympic Gods

By the time of Homer, the Greek deities had already been associated into a kind of clan with Zeus, "the father of gods and men," exercising a kind of patriarchal authority over the rest of the Olympians.

Among these latter were his wife Hera, his daughters Artemis and Athena, and his sons Ares and Apollo. Associated with these gods were the heroes, men such as Heracles who had been divinized for their noble deeds.

In contrast with these celestial deities were those of the Lower World, particularly Hades and his wife Persephone. As Gods of the dead rather than the living, they received little worship. When an animal was offered to them in sacrifice, it was always an appropriate black.

Over all these gods and their mortal clients there reigned, however, in some mysterious fashion Destiny, at times in conflict with the gods but far more frequently expressive of their will.

GREEK RELIGION, Oracles

Greek literature, particularly in Homer and in the tragedians, portrays the role of individual men such as Calchas and Tiresias who, as seers or prophets, proclaimed the will of the gods. Much more important than such diviners, however, were the oracular shrines at Dodona, Delos, Didyma, and above all at Delphi.

There through the medium of a priest or priestess, the will of the gods could be discovered with respect to the advisability of proposed courses of action. The oracle at Delphi could be consulted by individuals, as it was by Socrates, or by cities with regard to the founding of colonies and the waging of war.

It could even be consulted by foreigners such as Croesus, king of Lydia, and the Roman Senate. Its answers were frequently ambiguous and occasionally partial; but because of the respect in which it was held, it was probably the most important unifying element among the Greeks in religion as it was in politics.

GREEK RELIGION, Prayers and Sacrifices

In antique Greece, prayers and sacrifices were offered to the gods by individuals, families, the members of a clan or phratry, and especially by the city states, for Greek religion was essentially of a communal nature.

Prayers addressed to the gods usually consisted of an invocation, the reasons why it should be heard, and the actual petition. In the official festivals these prayers would be accompanied by hymns, processions, and sacrifices.

One of the most famous of these festivals was the Great Panathenaea held every four years at Athens, a vivid presentation of which is given in the lengthy frieze that surrounded the cella wall of the Parthenon. Religious in character also were the Panhellenic games held at Olympia, Delphi, and Corinth.

GREGORAS, Nicephorus

(1295-1360) Byzantine philosopher and theologian. He was the author of the Platonist polemics against Aristotelian thought, against Hesychism, a form of monastic contemplative prayer, and the ecclesiastical claims of the papacy.

GREGORIAN CHANT

Monophonic (single line of melody) music of the Roman Catholic Church, used to accompany the official Latin texts of the mass and the canonical hours (divine office).

GREGORIAN REFORM

An 11th century attempt by Pope Gregory VII to reform the medieval Western church, especially by prohibiting lay investiture. In addition to strengthening the church temporally and spiritually, Gregory also brought about internal ecclesiastical reforms through innovations in canon law.

GREGORY I, Saint

(540-640) Pope from 590-640, architect of medieval papacy, a people's pope, and an administrative, social, liturgical, and moral reformer. He formulated ideas of a Christian society that became formalized in the Middle Ages. Among his accomplishments were a reform of the mass from which came the Gregorian chant. Since the 8th century he has been regarded as a doctor (teacher) of the church.

GREGORY II CYPRIUS

(1241-1290) Patriarch of Constantinople (1283-1289) who led Byzantine Christendom in determined opposition to union with the Roman church of the West and who engaged in speculative theology that occasioned his downfall.

GREGORY II, Saint

(669-731) Pope from 715-731, held office at a time of increasing conflict between Rome and Byzantium (Constantinople), and eventually excommunicated Patriarch Anastasius of Byzantium.

GREGORY III, Saint

(669-741) Elected pope (731-741) by acclamation, but his pontificate was one of the most critical in papal history. He was immediately confronted with the Iconoclastic Controversy. He encouraged the Christianizing of the German tribes and appointed (732) St. Boniface, organizer of the Frankish church, as metropolitan of Germany.

GREGORY IV

(773-844) Pope from 827 to 844. He is chiefly remembered for his mediation in the struggle between King Lothair I of the Franks and the Holy Roman Emperor Louis the Pious.

GREGORY V

(972-99) The first German pope (996-999), whose pontificate was among the most turbulent in history.

GREGORY VI

(972-1048) Pope from 1045 to 1046. He was accused of simony at the Council of Sutri (Italy) held by the Holy Roman Emperor Henry III in

1046. He abdicated on December 20, retiring to Germany with his chaplain Hildebrand, later Pope Gregory VII.

GREGORY VII

(circa 1025-85) Pope from 1073 to 1085. One of the great medieval reform popes, he attacked corruption in the church, and insisted on the celibacy of the clergy and on the sole right of the church to appoint bishops and abbots. These reforms threatened the power of the German monarchy, leading to disputes and war between Henry IV of Germany and the papacy. In 1084 Henry seized Rome, forcing Gregory to flee.

GREGORY VIII

(1127-1187) Pope during 1187. He began reforms in the Curia and took immediate measures to restore Jerusalem to the Christians by initiating the Third Crusade but died during an effort to reconcile the rival Italian seaports of Pisa and Genoa in order to expedite shipments to the Holy Land.

GREGORY IX

(1170-1241) One of the most vigorous of the 13th century popes, reigning 1227-1241. He promulgated the *Decretals* in 1234, a code of canon law which remained as the fundamental source of ecclesiastical law for the Catholic Church until after World War I.

GREGORY X

(1210-1276) Pope from 1271-1276, who created the assembly of cardinals that elects the pope. In 1270 he joined the future King Edward I of England on a crusade to the Holy Land. He succeeded in saving the Holy Roman Empire from disassembly by promoting the election of Rudolf I of Habsburg as emperor.

GREGORY XI

(1329-1378) Pope from 1370-1378. Although not a priest, he was unanimously elected pope at Avignon to succeed Urban V. As pope, he immediately considered returning the papacy to Rome to conduct negotiations for reuniting the Eastern and Western churches, and to maintain papal territories against a Florentine revolt being led by the powerful Visconti family.

GREGORY XII

(1325-1417) Pope from 1406 to 1415, the last of the Roman line during the Great Western Schism (1378-1417), when the papacy was contested by antipopes in Avignon and in Pisa.

GREGORY XIII

(1502-85) Pope from 1572-85, promoted the Counter-Reformation through his pledge to execute the decrees of the Council of Trent. A patron of the Jesuits, he is remembered for the calendar reform he sponsored and for his lavish building program, which emptied the papal treasury. He celebrated the massacre of the Huguenots on St. Bartholomew's Day, 1572, with a Te Deum.

GRENFELL, Wilfred Thomason

(1865-1940) Medical missionary who was a tireless benefactor of the Royal National Mission to Deep Sea Fishermen.

GRESSMANN, Hugo

(1877-1927) German Old Testament scholar who was a prominent advocate of the religio-historical approach. He advanced the new theory that eschatology was not a late phenomenon in Israel but pre-exilic, and its popular form can be traced to Old Testament passages.

GRHYA-SUTRAS

Hindu religious manuals detailing the domestic (grhua) religious ceremonies by the householder over his own fire. The manuals describe the ceremonies which mark each stage of man's life, from the moment of his conception to his final death rites; the five daily sacrifices; seasonal ceremonies; and those observed on special occasions, such as house building or cattle breeding.

GRIESBACH, Johann Jakob

(745-1812) Rationalist Protestant theologian, the earliest biblical critic to subject the Gospels to systematic literary analysis. He originated the term synoptic to designate the first three Gospels and rejecting the traditional view, held that Mark was derived from Matthew and Luke.

GRUNDTVIG, Nikolai Frederick Severin

(1783-1872) Danish bishop and poet, founder of a theologian movement that revitalized the Danish church.

GTOR-MA

Sacrificial cakes used as offerings to deities in Tibetan Buddhist ceremonies. The cakes form part of the phyi-mchod, or seven offerings of the five senses, which are considered internal worship.

GUARDIAN ANGELS

Celestial or spiritual beings regarded as protectors and guides of individuals, groups, or nations in Judaism, Christianity, and Islam. Developing out of Persian angelology and in consequence of an increased emphasis of the transcendence of God, the notion of guardian angels became significant in post-exilic (after 538 BC) Judaism. In the Old Testament (Daniel 4:14), the Irin, or "watchers," may refer to such guardian spirits.

GUARDIAN SPIRITS

Supernatural teachers, frequently depicted in animal form, who guide an individual in every important activity through advice and songs; the belief in guardian spirits is widely diffused among the North American Indians.

GUHYASAMAJA TANTRA

The oldest and one of the most important Buddhist Tantras. These are the basic texts of the Tantric - an esoteric and highly symbolic - form of Buddhism, which developed in India and became dominant in Tibet.

GUILT

In its common and fundamental notion, guilt involves two closely associated elements: first, misdirected human action, i.e., a failure or a sin in general terms and a moral fault more specifically; and second, a condition of being deficient or of lacking some integrity in oneself, or of being displaced with respect to one's environment.

Under this latter aspect it approaches the notion of being penalized. The first of these elements is presupposed to, rather than constitutive of, guilt as it is generally understood.

Guilt is thus less the wrongdoing than the resulting condition of dislocation. In this condition we may distinguish between the dislocation itself and the being held responsible and having the fault imputed for blame. Though guiltiness is commonly blurred with culpability, both in popular speech and in theological rhetoric, it seems that the two should at least be separately discerned.

In Buddhism, guilt is a term with a specific meaning. The Buddhist born has no feeling of guilt in the sense of fear of a God who will punish him for his wrong-doing. But he knows that he will by the law of Karma receive the effects of his wrong-doing and in this way suffer the effects of his sin.

In Christianity, guilt is a state or condition of mind and soul that follows upon a personal, free, deliberate transgression of God's law; awareness that one has done wrong gives rise to what are often referred to as "guilt feelings," that is, feelings of spiritual unrest and discomfort.

Guilt feelings, in their turn, urge the sinful person to repent and to seek reconciliation, and thus once again to experience inner peace. In contrast to true guilt which follows upon actual sin, false or neurotic guilt seems to arise from a general lack of self-worth or a scrupulous conviction that one is almost always in sin.

GULLOTH-MAIM

In the Old Testament, a site requested by Caleb's daughter at the time of her marriage to Othniel (Joshua 15:17-19; Judges 1:13-15).

GUNA

The three Gunas pertaining to Hindu philosophy. They are:
1 Sattva, spiritual happiness or bliss.
2 Rajas, restless energy with the implication of violence.
3 Tamas, inertia.

GUNASTHANAS

According to Jainism the 14 stages of spiritual development through which a soul passes on its way to moksa (spiritual liberation). The progression is seen as one of decreasing sinfulness and increasing purity, freeing the individual from the bonds of karma (merit and demirit) and the cycle of rebirths.

GUNI

In the Old Testament, the second-named son of Naphtali, included among those of Jacob's household in Egypt (Genesis 46:24-26).

GURBAAL

A place inhabited by Arabs in King Uzzaiah's time (2 Chronicles 26:3-7). Although the exact site is unknown, some would connect it with Jagur in southern Judah (Joshua 15:21).

GURDWARA

The place of worship of the Sikhs, a religious group in India. The gurdwara contains - on a cot under a canopy - a copy of the *Adi Granth,* the sacred scripture of the Sikhs. It also serves as a meeting place for conducting the business of the congregation, holding wedding and initiation ceremonies, and, in the more historically important gurdwaras, as a center of pilgrimage during festivals. A free kitchen and frequently a school for Sikh children are attached to the gurdwara.

GURU

In Hinduism, a personal spiritual teacher or guide who has himself attained spiritual insight. From at least the time of the Upanisads (ancient commentaries on the sacred scriptures), India has stressed the importance of the tutorial method in religious instruction.

GURU, Sikh

The title assumed by the first ten leaders of the Sikhs, a religious group originating in the Punjab district of northern India. The word Sikh is derived from the Sanskrit sisya ("disciple"), and all Sikhs are disciples of the Guru (spiritual guide or teacher). The first Sikh Guru, Nanak, established the practice of naming his successor before his death (1539), and from the time of Ram Das, the fourth to reign, the Gurus all came from one family. Guru Nanak also emphasized the mystical transference of the personality of the Guru from one individual to another "as one lamplight to another," and many of his successors used as a pseudonym the name Nanak.

H

HAAHASHITARI

In the Old Testament, a descendant of Judah, son of Ashhur (1 Chronicles 4:1-6).

HABAIAH

In Judaism, a priest whose descendants returned from exile in Babylon. But as his "sons" were unable to establish their genealogy, they were barred from the priesthood and were not permitted to "eat from the most holy things until a priest stood up with Urim and Thummim" (Ezra 21:1-2; Nehemiah 7:63-65).

HABAKKUK

One of the minor prophets of the Old Testament. Some authorities believe that Habakkuk lived in the late 600s BC, writer of the Bible book bearing his name. Evidence in the book of Habakkuk seems to indicate that he prophesied early in the reign of Jehoiakim, before the Judean king became vassal to Babylon in 620 BC (2 Kings 24:1).

HABAKKUK, Book of

The 8th of 12 Old Testament books bearing the names of minor prophets, dated probably 7th century BC. Habakkuk probably was a Levitical member of the Temple choir (3:19). The first part explores the problem of God using the evil Chaldeans to punish Judah, and includes the influential statement "The righteous will live by his faith" (2:4). The final chapter is a psalm.

HABBAKUK

18th century Eskimo prophet who led a religious revival in a south Greenland Christian community in 1790.

HABAZZINIAH

In the Old Testament, a descendant of Jonadab the son of Rechab. He was one of the Rechabites tested by the prophet Jeremiah in the days of King Jehoiakim (Jeremiah 35:1-6).

HABIRU

Bands of seminomadic peoples, widespread in the Fertile Crescent from lower Mesopotamia to Egypt in the second millennium BC, to whom the ancient Hebrews may have been related. The Habiru are first mentioned in texts from the Third Dynasty of Ur (2050 BC), and from then on are mentioned in documents from all the important archives of the Near East: Babylonia, Mesopotamia, Mari, Syria, and Phoenicia.

The ancient text found in the narrative of Genesis 14, in which Abraham is depicted drawn into the battles between different confederations of kings, refers to Abraham "the Hebrew." The text may date from a period in which the word Hebrew retained its class meaning of mercenary fighter recruited from the bands of seminomads. The words Habiru and Hebrew would than have evolved in a way similar to that of the word Canaanite, which originally meant merchant before it acquired its ethnic meaning.

HABIT

A disposition to some thought or act facilitated by repetition. Habit makes resistance to the performance of an act more difficult and thus is one of the factors to be taken into account in evaluating the morality of an act.

HABIT, Religious

The distinctive garb worn by members of religious communities that commonly serves as a means of identifying the religious organization to which an individual belongs. The custom of a special mode of dress for religious was begun by St. Pachomius (died 346) and adopted by St. Basil (died 397) and promoted by his rules, which were widely influential in both East and West.

HACELDAMA
Name of a potter's field near Jerusalem whose purchase is connected in the New Testament with Jesus' betrayal by Judas (Acts 1:18; Matthew 27:6-9). According to a 4th century tradition it was located on the southern side of Hennom Valley but this is suspect (Jeremiah 19:11).

HACHILAH
In biblical times, a hill in the wilderness of Ziph, where David and his men concealed themselves from King Saul (1 Samuel 23:19; 26:1-3). Today its exact location is unknown.

HACHIMAN
One of the most popular Shinto deities of Japan; the patron deity of the Minamoto clan and of warriors in general; often referred to as the god of war. Hachiman is commonly regarded as the deification of Ojin, the 15th emperor of Japan. He is seldom worshipped alone however, and Hachiman shrines are most frequently dedicated to three deities, the emperor Ojin, his mother the empress Jingo, and the goddess Hime-gami.

HACHMONI
In the Old Testament, ancestor of Zabdiel and his son Jashobeam. The latter was the head of one of David's top three mighty men and is called "the son of a Hachmonite" (1 Chronicles 11:11).

HADAD
In the Old Testament, one of the twelve sons of Ishmael the son of Abraham and his concubine Hagar (Genesis 25:12-15; 1 Chronicles 1:28-30).)

HADAD
West Semitic god of storms, thunder, and rain. The bull was the symbol animal of Hadad, as of the Hittite deity Teshub, who was identical with him.

HADAD III
(10th century BC), prince who restored the independence of Edom, which had been under Israelite rule during the reign of David. As a child he escaped an Israelite massacre of Edomite males by fleeing to Egypt and coming under the protection of the Pharaoh.

HADADRIMMON
In the Old Testament, a location in the valley plain of Megiddo (Zachariah 12:11). The "great wailing" at Hadadrimmon mentioned in Zachariah's prophecy perhaps alludes to the lamentation over King Josoah, killed in battle at Megiddo (2 Kings 23:29). But some associate this lamentation with ritualistic mourning ceremonies like those for the false god Tammuz, and consider Hadradrimmon to be the composite name of a god.

HADAR
In the Old Testament, successor to the kingship of Edom after the death of Baal-hanan; also called Hadad (Genesis 36:31, 39; 1 Chronicles 1:43-51).

HADASSAH
In Judaism, the cousin of Mordecai who replaced Persian Queen Vashti, better known by her Persian name Esther, meaning "fresh myrtle" (Esther 2:7).

HADD
In Islam, literally edge, boundary, limit. The term denotes God's limits and the punishment for certain crimes which are mentioned in the Koran. There are five of these:
1 fornication or adultery (stoning or 100 lashes);
2 false accusation of unchastity (80 lashes);

3 wine drinking (80 lashes);
4 theft (amputation of hands and/or feet);
5 highway robbery (execution if homicide occurs).

HADES

Realm of the dead in Greek mythology. The name was originally only that of the god of the underworld, but eventually came to refer to the underworld itself. It was first pictured as a gloomy, dismal place, but later Greeks, especially the Orphics, initiated a concept of reward and punishment after death. Entrance to Hades was said to be a ferry across the river Styx.

In his kingdom of darkness, Hades was harsh and ruthless. None of the inhabitants of the underworld was permitted to return to the land of the living. He had various demons and servants, such as Charon, who as ferryman took souls across the river Acheron in his boat, to the kingdom of the dead on the other side.

HADI, al-

(reigned 785-786) The fourth caliph of the Abbasids dynasty, whose persecution of the Alids, the minority Shiite sect of Islam, precipitated a Meccan rebellion against his rule.

HADID, al-

The title of the 57th sura of the Koran; it means "The Iron." The sura belongs to the very late Medinan period and has 29 verses. It is so-called after the reference to the iron which God has sent down for the use of man, in verse 25. The sura begins by praising God the omniscient Creator and stresses later that the life of this world is as transient as the green plants which follow a fall of rain.

HADITH

Arabic term with such meanings as speech, report, narrative. It also has the very important specialist sense of tradition, i.e., a record of the sayings and doings of the Prophet Mohammed and his companions, and as such is regarded by Muslims as a source of Islamic law, dogma and ritual second only in importance to the Koran itself.

A hadith is traditionally supported by an isnad or chain of authorities. It contains a main text and may conclude with a moral.

HADITH NABAWI

In Islam, term in the sense of prophetic tradition. *See* Hadith Qudsi.

HADITH QUDSI

In Islam, a sacred, or holy, tradition. It is the name given to a tradition which records God's own utterances as opposed to those of the Prophet Mohammed. The latter type of tradition is called in arabic by the term Hadith nabawi, meaning prophetic tradition.

HADLAI

In the Old Testament, father of the Amasa who was one of the heads of the sons of Ephraim in the days of King Pekah of Israel and King Ahaz of Judah (2 Chronicles 26:6-16).

HADORAM

In the Old Testament, a son of Joktan and descendant of Shem, listed among the founders of the post-flood families (Genesis 10:21-27). This family settled in Arabia, possibly in Yemen.

HADRA

In Islam, literally presence. The word has acquired a technical meaning in tasawwuf and come to indicate the dhikr recited communally, often on a Friday.

HADRACH

In biblical times, a land against which God expressed a pronouncement through his prophet Zachariah (9:1). A consideration of the pronouncement suggests that it is directed against Damascus, Hamath, Tyre, Sidon and the Philistine cities of Ashkelon, Gaza, Ekron and Ashod (Zechariah 9:108). Hence, although various identifications have been suggested and many would like Hadrach with the Hatarikka mentioned in Assyrian texts, it may well be a symbolic name designating the territory in which these many cities were located.

HAFTARA

A selective reading from Old Testament prophets, recited in Jewish synagogues during the morning service on sabbaths and on festivals (but during the afternoon service on fast days).

Though Haftarot (plural of Haftara) vary with various rites and no longer follow recommendations of the Mishna (the lawbook section of the Talmud), selections are generally chosen that relate to the Torah reading that immediately precedes.

HAGAB

In the Old Testament, ancestor of a family of Nethinim temple slaves. "The sons of Hagab" are mentioned among those returning with Zerubabbel in 537 BC from captivity in Babylon (Ezra 2:1-2, 43-46).

HAGABAH

In the Old Testament, ancestor of a family of Nethinim. "The sons of Hagabah" are mentioned among those returning in 537 BC from exile in Babylon (Ezra 2:1-2; 43-46).

HAGANAH

Zionist military organization representing the majority of the Jews in Palestine after World War I. Organized in 1920 to combat the revolts of Palestinian Arabs against the Jewish settlement of Palestine, it early came under the influence of the Histadrut (General federation of Labor). Although it was outlawed by the British Mandatory authorities and was poorly armed, it managed effectively to defend Jewish settlements.

HAGAR

In the Old Testament, Abraham's secondary wife and the mother of his son Ishmael. Purchased in Egypt, she served as a maid to Abraham's childless wife, Sarah, who gave her to Abraham. Circa 14 years after the birth of Ishmael, Isaac, Abraham's son with whom God had promised to make a covenant, was born to Sarah.

HAGGADAH

Usually refers to the ritual narration of the events of the Exodus from Egypt which forms part of the traditional Seder or Passover feast celebrated by Jews.

The Haggadah is an kind of "guide book" for the celebration of Passover.It has directions on how to conduct the Seder, explanations for the Pesah symbols, selections from Psalms (113-118), interesting stories, children's folk songs, riddles and prayers.

The Haggadah has a long history. It is more than 2,000 years old. Even before it was written down, the father of the family would tell the story of Pesah at the Seder table. The very term Haggadah comes from the Hebrew word "haged," which means "to tell."

As time went by, more parts were added to the Haggadah, which was still not written down - prayers, hymns, selections from the Mishnah. By the Middle Ages so much has been added that it was necessary to record the Haggadah. But even then the Haggadah was not a separate book, but a part of the prayer book. Soon after the Middle Ages the Haggadah became a book in its own right.

It is in the Haggadah that the Jews learn the use of the sacrificial lamb (Pesah), unleavened bread (matzah) and bitter herbs (maror). It interrupts the thanksgiving (Hallel) with the meal, and at last ends with the songs of Adir Hu and Had Gadya.

One of the most stirring parts of the Haggadah is recited at the beginning of Seder, beginning with Ha-Lahma Anya, "This is the bread of affliction." The head of the house rises, lifts the plate of matzah in his hands, and recites, "This is the bread of affliction which our fathers ate in the land of Egypt. Let all who are hungry come and eat. Let all who are in need come and celebrate Pesah with us. Now we are here. Next year may we be in the land of Israel. Now we are slaves. Next year may we be free men."

Ha-Lahma Anya is one of the oldest sections of the Haggadah. It is written in Aramaic, a language spoken by the Jewish ancestors in Israel almost 2,000 years ago. It was once customary for the head of the house to step out into the street and recite Ha-Lahma Anya. Today the invitation to the poor is recited within the home - but the spirit of hospitality remains the same.

HAGGAG, Shaykh Yusuf al-
A local Muslim saint whose mosque is part of the temple at Luxor in Egypt.

HAGGAI
Jewish prophet and author of an Old Testament Book. In 520 BC, 18 years after King Cyrus had permitted the Babylonian exiles to return to Judah, very little work had been done on the rebuilding of the Temple. The unfriendly Samaritans had interfered with the work and the Israelites had lost their courage and determination. Haggai urged the returning exiles to be of good cheer and to build the Temple anew. His words gave spirit to flagging souls and the weary exiles bent their energies to the task.

HAGGAI, Book of
The tenth of the Old Testament minor prophets, dated 520-519 BC. It consists of four prophecies urging the returned Babylonian exiles to rebuild the Temple at Jerusalem and predicting the glories of the Messianic Age.

HAGGITH
In the Old Testament, a wife of David and the mother of Adonijah, who schemed to get the kingship over Israel (2 Samuel 3:2-4; 1 Kings 1:5; 1 Chronicles 3:1-2).

HAGIA SOPHIA
Cathedral built at Constantinople under Justinian I's direction, a unique building, still one of the world's great monuments despite time's ravage. A domed basilica, it was built in the amazingly short time of some six years, being completed in 537.

HAGIASMA
In the singular, water that has been blessed in the manner prescribed by the Roman Catholic Church. In the plural (hagiasmata) it is used of anything consecrated or blessed by the church as bread, holy water, and even the consecrated Eucharist.

HAGIOGRAPHY
Research into and writing about the lives of saints.

HAGIOLOGY
The branch of historical studies dealing with the lives of the saints and the devotion paid to them throughout the centuries. The need for this specialized study was created by the special nature of the documents concerned: acts of the martyrs; lives of saintly monks, bishops, princes, or virgins; and accounts of miracles taking place at their tombs or in connection with their relics, icons, or statues.

HAGIORITIC TOME
Book compiled in Greek in the 14th century that contains the doctrines of St. Gregory Palamas.

HAI BEN SHERIRA
(939-1038) Last outstanding Babylonian gaon, or head, of a great Talmudic academy, remembered for the range and profundity of an exceptionally large number of responses, authoritative answers to questions concerning interpretation of Jewish law.

HAIL MARY
In Roman Catholicism, the best-known and most popular prayer in honor of the Blessed Virgin Mary. It is composed of verses from the gospel of Luke (see Luke 1:28, 42) and a centuries'-old petition formulated by the church.

"Hail Mary, full of grace. The Lord is with thee. Blessed art thou among women, and blessed is the fruit of thy womb, Jesus. Holy Mary, Mother of God, pray for us sinners, now and at the hour of our death. Amen."

HAJAR, al-Aswad

In Islam, term for the Black Stone, set in the Ka'ba. Those pilgrims near enough to it will attempt to kiss the Black Stone during their circumambulation of the Ka'ba during the Islamic pilgrimage. Tradition associated the stone with Adam and Ibrahim.

HAJJ

In Islam, pilgrimage. This is one of the five arkan or Pillars of Islam. All Muslims, provided a number of conditions including good health and financial ability are present, have a duty to make a pilgrimage to Mecca at least once in their lifetimes. This major pilgrimage must be made in the Month of the Pilgrimage, the last month of the Muslim lunar calendar, between the 8th day of the month and the 12th or 13th. Before arriving in Mecca the pilgrim dons white garments during which he or she will abstain from sexual intercourse, perfume, the wearing of sewn garments and the cutting of hair and nails. A number of ritual ceremonies are undertaken in Mecca including the sevenfold circumambulation of the Ka'ba and a sevenfold running between al-Safa and al-Marwa. On the 9th day of the pilgrimage month occurs the standing in the Plain of 'Arafa outside Mecca. This is an essential part of the pilgrimage and if it is omitted, the pilgrimage is considered invalid. Prayers are said at 'Arafa and pilgrims listen to a sermon. On the 10th day pilgrims sacrifice an animal at Mina imitating the projected sacrifice of Ibrahim of Isma'il and this day constitutes one of the great feast days of the Muslim calendar.
After the pilgrimage proper, pilgrims frequently include a visit to the tomb of the Prophet Mohammed at Medina. The Koran provides a considerable amount of detail about the pilgrimage, especially in verses 199-200 of Surat al-Baqara and verses 26-30 of Surat al-Hajj.
Those who undertake the pilgrimage are entitled to bear the honorific title hajj, expressed colloquially as haggi.

HAKKATAN

In the Old Testament, father of the Johanan of the family of Azgad who, accompanied by 110 males, returned from Babylon with Ezra (Ezra 8:1, 12).

HAKKOZ

In Judaism, an Aaronic priest and head of the paternal house that in David's time was constituted the seventh of the twenty-four priestly divisions (1 Chronicles 24:3-7). After returning from Babylon in 537 BC, "sons of Hakkoz" were among those who were disqualified from the priesthood because of being unable to establish their genealogy. They were among those forbidden to eat from "the most holy things until a priest stood up with Urim and Thummim" (Ezra 2:61-63; Nehemiah 7:63-65).
A descendant of Hakkoz is specifically referred to as sharing in rebuilding the walls of Jerusalem (Nehemiah 3:21).

HAKUIN

(1685-1768) Priest and writer who helped revive Zen Buddhism in Japan. In contrast to the haughty priests who served the shogunate, or ruling feudal government, he lived in great poverty among his peasant parishioners; and his spirituality, humility, and contentment attracted a large following that became a new foundation for Zen in Japan.

HAL

In Sufi (Muslim mysticism)terminology, a spiritual state of mind that comes to the Sufi from time to time during his mystical journey toward God.

HALAH

In the Old Testament, a place to which Assyrian monarchs transported Israelite captives (2 Kings 17:6; 1 Chronicles 5:26).

HALAK

In biblical times, a mountain marking the southern geographical limit of Israel's conquest of the Promised Land under the leadership of Joshua (Joshua 11:16-17). Halak is generally identified with Jebel Halaq, the last western Palestinian height on the road from Beer-sheba to the Aqabah. The range that begins with Jebel Halaq divides the pastureland on the east from the sandy desert on the west.

HALAKHA

The totality of laws and ordinances that have evolved since biblical times to regulate religious observances and the day-to-day life and conduct of the Jewish people. Quite distinct from Jewish laws written in the Pentateuch (first five books of the Bible), Halakha purports to preserve and represent oral traditions stemming from the revelation on Mount Sinai or evolved on the basis of it.

HALF-WAY COVENANT

Religious-political solution adopted by 17th century New England Puritans that allowed the children of baptized but unconverted church members to be baptized and thus become church members and have political rights.

HALHUL

In biblical times, a city in the mountainous region of Judah (Joshua 15:20, 48, 58). The same name is still attached to a village and a conspicuous hill, a little more than three and a half miles north of Hebron.

HALI

In biblical times, a town on the boundary of Asher, named between Helkath and Beten (Joshua 19:24-25).

HALIMA BINT ABI DHY'AYB

Foster mother and wet nurse of the Prophet Mohammed for his first two years of life.

HALITZA

Jewish ritual whereby a widow is freed from the biblical obligation of marrying her brother-in-law in cases where her husband died without issue. To enable a widow to marry a "stranger," the ritual of halitza has to be performed in a precise prescribed manner.

HALL, Joseph

(1574-1656) Bishop, moral philosopher, and satirist, remarkable for his literary versatility and innovations. He took part in the literary campaign between Anglicans and Puritans at the opening (1642) of the English Civil War.

HALL, Robert

(1764-1831) English Baptist minister, writer, and social reformer in Cambridge and Leicester, who became famous for his commanding oratory and liberal views on religious liberties, freedom of the press, and the French Revolution.

HALLAY, Al-

(857-922) Muslim mystic and saint, commonly recognized as one of the greatest of Muslim mystics. Devoted to the ascetic life from an early age, he followed first the teaching of Sal al-Tustari and later, at Basra, became a disciple of Amr al-Makki and al-Junaid. At his first, year-long, pilgrimage to Mecca he gave up the usual Sufi custom of secrecy and later the wool tunic also, in order to be able to reach more people in his preaching.

Basically his doctrine was one of the bond of love that unites God and the believer, and of the value of faith for the interior life of the soul. After considerable court intrigue, he was crucified, decapitated, and cremated at Baghdad. Though condemned by many, he had a large following and many have considered him a saint.

HALLEL

In the Bible, a song of praise to God. Psalms 113 to 118 constitute what is known in Jewish writings as the "Egyptian Hallel." According to the Mishnah, this Hallel was sung at the Temple and in the synagogues on the occasion of the Passover and the festivals of Pentecost, Booths and Dedication.

At the celebration of the Passover in the home, the first part of the Hallel (either Psalm 113 or Psalms 113 and 114) was recited after the second cup of wine had been poured and the significance of the Passover explained.

The Hallel was brought to a conclusion over the fourth cup of wine. The "Great Hallel" (variously considered to be Psalm 136 only, Psalms 120-136, or Psalm 135:4-136:26) is said to have been sung on joyful occasions and by those who used a fifth cup of wine at the celebration of the Passover.

HALLELUJAH

Exclamation of joy and thanksgiving, meaning "praise God". The word has been taken untranslated from the Psalms (Psalm 111:1).

HALLER, Bertold

(1492-1536) Religious reformer who was primarily responsible for bringing the Reformation to Bern.

HALLOHESH

In the Old Testament, one of the headmen of the people whose descendant, if not himself, attested to the confession contract drawn up in the days of Nehemiah; possibly the same as the father of Shallum (Nehemiah 9:38; 10:1).

HALO

Nimus, whether as circle behind the head or oval behind the whole figure, is widely found in Buddhist art. It presumably represents the effulgence of light around the holy figure produced by his spiritual development.

HALQA

In Islam, term meaning circle, link, ring. The term has a number of technical meanings in tassawwuf; it can mean, for example, a group of students studying with a sufi, or the circle of Sufis formed to perform a dhikr.

HAM

In the Old Testament, one of Noah's sons (Genesis 5:32; 7:6; 11:10). He was possibly the youngest son; however, he is listed in second place at Genesis 5:32.

He married before the flood and survived the flood, along with his wife, his father and mother and his two brothers and their wives (Genesis 6:18; 7:13). Ham's sons were born after the flood. Sometime later he became involved in an incident that brought him a curse on his son Canaan. Noah had become intoxicated with wine and he uncovered himself in his tent. Ham saw his father's nakedness, and instead of showing the proper respect for Noah, the family head and the servant and prophet whom God had made an instrument in the preservation of the human race, Ham told his two brothers of the discovery. Shem and Japheth exhibited the proper respect by walking backwards with a mantle to cover Noah, so that they would not bring reproach by looking on their father's nakedness. Noah, on waking, uttered a curse, not on Ham, but on Ham's son Canaan. In the accompanying blessing of Shem, which included a blessing for Japheth, Ham was passed over and ignored; only Canaan was mentioned as cursed and was prophetically foretold to become a slave to Shem and Japheth (Genesis 9:20-27).

HAMADHANI, al-

(1098-1131) Famous Sufi who was born in Hamadhan. He immersed himself in the religious sciences from an early age and also became a Sufi in his youth. His teachings and ecstatic utterances aroused the wrath of the orthodox; he was brutally executed in 1131 for heresy.

HAMAN

In the Old Testament, son of Hammedatha, the Agagite. The designation "Agagite" may mean that Haman was a royal Amalekite (Esther 3:1). If, indeed, Haman was an Amalekite, this in itself would explain why he harbored such great hatred for the Jews, for God had decreed the eventual extermination of the Amalekites (Exodus 17:14-16). This was because they showed hatred of God and his people by taking the initiative to sally forth in attack on the Israelites when they traveled through the wilderness (Exodus 17:8).

HAMANN, Johann Georg

Protestant thinker, fidelist, and friend of Immanuel Kant whose distrust of reason led him to conclude that a child-like faith in God was the only solution to vexing problems of philosophy.

HAMANTASHEN

Jewish pastry, eaten at the celebration of Purim. They are three-cornered little cakes filled with poppy seeds of plum jam. Some say that the name comes from mohntashen, or "poppy seed pouches;" others claim that the cakes resemble Haman's hat.

HAMARTIOLOGY

A term for the theological study of sin; hamartia in the Greek New Testament means sin (Matthew 7:2-5; Acts 7:60; Romans 5:12; 2 Corinthians 5:21).

HAMATH

Capital of a small Canaanite kingdom in Syria during the early history of Israel.

HAMATH-ZOBAH

A place apparently conquered by King Solomon and thus figuring in his only military engagement alluded to in the Bible (2 Chronicles 8:3).

HAMDU (-AL) LI 'LLAH

In Islam, very commonly used Muslim invocation meaning "Praise be to God" or "Thank God."

HAMITES

In ancient tradition, the descendants of Ham, Noah's second son, who is represented (Genesis 10) as the father of Canaan (Palestine), Cush (Ethiopia), Mizraim (Egypt) and Put (Libya or Somalia). Today, the term is sometimes applied to members of a brown-skinned people of eastern, northern and northeastern Africa.

HAMMADETHA

An Agagite; father of Haman, who plotted the extermination of the Jews in the days of Mordecai and Esther (Esther 3:1-6).

HAMMON

In the Old Testament, a city on the boundary of Asher (Joshua 19:24-28). It is generally identified with Umm el-Awamid, on the Mediterranean sea-coast, circa eight miles south of Tyre.

HAMONAH

According to biblical tradition, a symbolic city in the vicinity of the valley in which the king and his crowd are to be buried, after their combined attack on God's people ends in defeat and mass slaughter. The city derived its name from that circumstance, as a memorial of God's victory over these foes (Ezekiel 39:16). A city implies an organized body of persons, here apparently relating to the organization for bone disposal described in Ezekiel 39:11-15.

HAMOR

In the Old Testament, a Hivite chieftain; father of Shechem. It was from the sons of Hamor that Jacob purchased a tract of land where he pitched his tent and then later set up an altar. After Shechem violated Jacob's daughter Dinah, Simeon and Levi, in avenging their sister, killed both Hamor and his son (Genesis 33:18-20).

HAMUL

In the Old Testament, the younger son of Perez and grandson of Judah, from whom the Hamulites descended (Genesis 46:12; Numbers 26:21).

HAMZA B. AND AL-MUTTALIB

(died 625) Famous uncle of the Prophet Mohammed on his father's side. At first Hamza opposed the new islamic faith but later became one of its most valiant adherents.

HAMZAH IBN ALI

(11th century) One of the founders of the Druze religion. Hamzah claimed to be representing not just another sect but rather an independent religion, one that superseded traditional Islam. Hamzah's teachings served as an ideological foundation for many peasant revolts in Syria.

HANAFIS

Adherents of one of the four main law schools of Sunni Islam, named after the famous jurist Abu Hanafa.

HANAMEL

In the Old Testament, son of Shallum the paternal uncle of the prophet Jeremiah. It was from Hanamel that the prophet bought the field that was in Anathoth at the time the Babylonians were laying siege to Jerusalem (Jeremiah 32:1-12).

HANAN

In the Old Testament, one of the Levites who assisted Azra in explaining the Law to the congregation of Israel assembled in the public square before the Water Gate of Jerusalem (Nehemiah 8:1, 7).

HANANI

The seer or visionary who rebuked King Asa of Judah for making an alliance with the king of Syria instead of relying upon God, and who was put in the house of stocks because the king took offense at what he said (2 Chronicles 16:1-3, 7-10). Hanani apparently was the father of Jehu, the prophet who rebuked Baasha the king of Israel and Jehoshaphat the king of Judah (1 Kings 16:1-4; 2 Chronicles 19:2-3).

HANANIAH

In the Old Testament, son of Azzur; a false prophet from the Benjaminite city of Gibeon who opposed God's prophet Jeremiah. During the reign of King Zedekiah of Judah, while Jeremiah encouraged the people to bring their necks under the yoke of the king of Babylon and thus keep living (Jeremiah 27:12-14), Hananiah prophesied that Babylon's power would be broken within two years, the Jewish exiles there would be released and all the confiscated utensils of the Temple would be returned. To illustrate his point, Hananiah removed the wooden yoke from off Jeremiah's neck and broke it. God then commanded Jeremiah to inform Hananiah that the yoke bar of wood was to be replaced by an iron yoke, and that Hananiah's death would occur within that year. True to the prophecy, the false prophet died in that year (Jeremiah, chapter 28).

HANBALIS

Adherents of one of the four main law schools of Sunni Islam, named after the distinguished jurist and theologian Ahmad b. Hanbal.

HANES

In the Old Testament, a site mentioned at Isaiah 30:4 in God's denunciation of those seeking help from Egypt (Isaiah 30:1-5).

HAN HSIANG

In Chinese mythology, one of the eight Immortals of Taoism; he desired to make flowers bloom in an instant and to produce fine-tasting wine without using grain.

Han Hsiang usually is depicted holding a bouquet or basket of flowers, a hoe, and a mushroom of immortality. He is said to have been converted to Taoism (circa 9th century AD) by Lu Tung-pin, another Immortal, but all attempts to convert his wife ended in failure.

HANIF

In Islam, term meaning monotheist. The word occurs several times in its singular and plural forms in the Koran. Here it basically indicates those who were neither Christians nor Jews but were monotheists.

HANIWAH FIGURES

Third-century clay images around early Japanese mounded tombs, representing men, women, animals, and buildings, and considered both ritualistic and practical. The hollow, expressive forms, grave and serene, inserted by pin-extensions at the base rise three and four feet high.

HANNAH

(11th century BC) Mother of Samuel, the Jewish judge. Childless as one of the two wives of Elkanah, she prayed for a son, promising to dedicate him to God. Her prayers were answered, and she brought her child Samuel to Shiloh for religious education.

HANNATHON

In the Old Testament, a boundary city of Zebulun (Joshua 19:10-14). Most geographers tentatively identify Hannathon with Tell al-Bedeiwiyeh, a little more than six miles northwest of Nazareth.

HANNIEL

In the Old Testament, a chieftain selected by God to represented the tribe of Mannasseh in dividing the land west of the Jordan among the 9_ Israelite tribes settling there. Hanniel was a son of Ephod and a descendant of Joseph (Numbers 34:13-17).

HANUKKAH

Jewish holiday which falls in December and celebrates the rededication of the Temple after the victory of Judas Maccabeus over Antiochos IV, Epiphaneus in 165 BC, observed for eight days, one candle on the first night, two on the second, and so forth. The oldest historical sources that deal with the festival of Hannukah are ancient works known as the Books of the Maccabees. They tell how Judah and his brothers came to the desolate Temple, how they cleansed it and rededicated it on the 25th day of the month of Kislev. Slowly, the custom of lighting Hannukah candles in every Jewish home was developed until Hanukkah became the widespread festival that it is today.

A favorite Hannukah food is latkes, or potato pancakes. Originally, the pancakes were made of cheese. From the custom of eating cheese delicacies grew the custom of eating pancakes of all kinds. During the Middle Ages, Jews explained this custom by connecting it with the story of Judith which they linked with the story of Hannukah. Judith, according to legend, was a daughter of the Hashmoneans. She fed cheese to the leader of the enemies of the Jews. He was made thirsty by the cheese and began to drink much wine. When he grew quite drunk, she cut off his head. For this reason, it was said, Jews ate cheese delicacies on Hannukah.

HANNUN

In the Old Testament, son of and successor to the throne of Nahash the king of Ammon. Because of the loving kindness Nahash had exercised toward him, David sent messengers to comfort Hannun over the loss of his father. But Hannun, convinced by his princes that this was merely a subterfuge on David's part to spy out the city, dishonored David's servants by shaving off half their beards and cutting their garments in half to their buttocks, and then sent them away. When the sons of Ammon saw that they had become foul-smelling to David because of the humiliation meted out to his messengers, Hannun took the initiative to prepare for war and hired the Syrians to fight against Israel. In the ensuing conflicts the Ammonites and the Syrians were completely defeated by Israel;

David subjected the surviving Ammonites of Rabbah to forced labor (2 Samuel 10:1-11; 1 Chronicles 19:1-20).

HANUMAN

In Hindu mythology the divine monkey chief, a central figure in the great Hindu epic the Ramayana. Hanuman is the child of a nymph by the wind god, and accompanied by a host of monkeys, he aided Rama in recovering his wife, Sita, from the demon Ravana.

HAN YONG-UN

(1879-1944) Buddhist poet and religious and political leader. Han early developed a deep concern for his country and people and participated in the famous Tonghak Revolt in 1894, a social reform movement directed by leaders of the apocalyptic Tonghak sect.

HAN YU

(768-824) Outstanding poet and first proponent of what later came to be known as Neo-Confucianism, which had wide influence in Japan and China.

HAN YUAN TI

(75-33 BC) Ninth emperor of the Han dynasty, who ardently promoted and helped firmly establish Confucianism as the official creed of China.

HAOMA

In Zoroastrianism, sacred plant and the drink made from it. The preparation of the drink from the plant by pounding and the drinking of it are central features of Zoroastrian ritual. It is believed to bestow essential vital qualities - health, fertility, husbands for maidens, even immortality.

HAPPINESS

A state of well-being characterized by relative permanence, by dominantly agreeable emotion ranging in value from mere contentment to deep and intense joy in living, and by a natural desire for its constitution. The happiness described in Psalms and Proverbs, and particularly those spoken of by Jesus Christ in his sermon on the Mount, are often called "beatitudes" or "blessedness."

In Buddhism, happiness is regarded as a by-product of right living, and never an end in itself. The sense of happiness and unhappiness are both transcended in the course of development of the mind. In this respect, happiness should not be confused with spiritual states of consciousness such as Samadhi or Prajna.

HAPU

19th century religious cult in Hawaii named after the prophetess Hapu.

HAQIQAH

In Sufi (Muslim mystic) terminology, the knowledge the Sufi acquires when the secrets of the divine essence are revealed to him at the end of his journey toward union with God.

HAQQ, al-

The title of the 69th sura of the Koran; it may variously be translated as "That Which is Inevitable," "The Calamity" or "The Resurrection," but whichever one chooses the reference is clearly to the Last Day. The sura belongs to the Meccan period and contains 52 verses. Its title is drawn from the first three verses. The punishments which overtook 'Ad and Thamud are also mentioned at the beginning. The sura continues with a description of the Day of Judgement and its judgement with books; the man who is given the book itemizing his deeds on earth in his right hand will taste the joys of Paradise, but he who receives his book in the left hand will be consigned to hell.

HARA

In biblical times, a site to which Assyrian King Tiglath-pilsener transported Israelite captives (1 Chronicles 5:26).

HARAI

Purification ceremonies, an important element in the Shinto religion of Japan.

Harai rites (and the purification exercises using water referred to as misogi) return the individual to a condition of prior purity that enables him to approach the kami (god or sacred power). Salt, water, and fire are the principal purification agents.

HARAM

In Islam, term denoting a sanctuary. The Arabic word indicates an area of a particularly sacred nature. Examples include Mecca and Medina, both of which are forbidden to non-Muslims. The term is also used in the sense of that which is forbidden and unlawful, also sinful.

HARAM (AL-) ASH-SHARIF

In Islam, the Noble Sanctuary; the third holiest sanctuary in Islam after Mecca and Medina, situated in the Temple area of Jerusalem.

HARAN

Ancient city of strategic importance, now a village, in south-eastern Turkey. It lies along the Balikh River, 24 miles south-east of Urfa. The town was located on the road that ran from Nineveh to Carchemish and was regarded as of considerable importance by the Assyrian kings. Being a center of the moon god cult, it is frequently mentioned in the Bible. Abraham's family settled there when they left Ur of the Chaldeans (Genesis 11:31-32).

HARARITE

The designation of certain of David's mighty men (2 Samuel 23:8; 1 Chronicles 11:26-35). They were perhaps from the hill country of Judah.

HARBONA

In the Old Testament, one of Ahasuerus' seven court officials sent to convey to Queen Vashti the king's word for her to appear before him. Then, at the time that Haman's scheme to exterminate the Jews was exposed, Harbona's mentioning the fifty-cubit stake Haman had made for Mordecai prompted Ahasuerus to order that Haman himself be hanged on it (Esther 1:10-12).

HARDOUIN, Jean

(1646-1729) Jesuit scholar who edited numerous and ecclesiastical works, most notably the councils of the church.

HAREM

A name applied to that part of a house in Muslim countries set apart for the women. Mohammed did not originate the idea of the harem or of the veiling and seclusion of women; he borrowed it from older Semitic cultures; but he sponsored it, and wherever Islam spread, this institution went with it, with its religious sanctions.

HARE RAM HARA KRISHNA

Religious organization that originated in India and was founded by Swami A.C. Bhaktivedanta.

HARHUR

In the Old Testament, ancestral head of a family of Nethinim temple slaves. "The sons of Harbur" are listed among those returning with Zerubbabel from Babylon in 537 BC (Ezra 2:1-2; Nehemiah 7:43, 56).

HARIBHADRA

(8th century) One of the most famous Jaina authors, known for his works in Sanskrit and Prakrit on Jaina doctrine and ethics and for his brilliant commentaries.

HARIHARA

In Hinduism, a syncretic deity, combining the two major gods, Visnu (Hari) and Siva (Hara). Images of Harihara began to appear in the classical period. This occurred after sectarian movements, which elevated one god as supreme over the others, had waned sufficiently for efforts at compromise to be attempted.

HARI KRISHEN

(1656-1664) Eighth Sikh Guru who was installed at five years of age and reigned for only three years yet was apparently possessed of vast wisdom and amazed visiting Brahmins by his great knowledge of Bhagavadgita.

HARIM

In the Old Testament, an Aaronic priest selected by lot to head the third of the 24 priestly divisions organized by David (1 Chronicles 24:1-8). "Sons (or descendants) of Harim" are mentioned among the post-exile priests; 1,017 returned from Babylon in 537 BC (Ezra 2:1-2; Nehemia 7:42).

HARIMANDIR

The chief gurdwara, or house of worship, of the Sikhs of India and their most important pilgrimage site; it is located in Amritsar, in the Punjab state. The Harimandir was built in 1604 by Guru Arjun, who symbolically had it placed on a lower level so that even the humblest had to step down to enter it, and with entrances on all four sides, signifying that it was open to worshippers of all castes and creeds.

HARIPH

Head of a Hebrew family of which 112 males returned from Babylonian exile in 537 BC; also called Jorah (Nehemiah 7:6-7). The name Hariph is again listed among the heads of the people, evidently being represented by a descendant, who attested by seal the confession contract made during Nehemiah's governorship (Nehemiah 9:38; 10:1).

HARIPHITE

In the Old Testament, a designation applied to a Benjamite, Shephatiah, who joined David at Ziklag while David was still under restrictions because of Saul. Shephatiah's being called a Hariphite may mean that he was either a native of Hariph or Hareph (a place of unknown location) or a descendant of a certain Hariph or Hareph (1 Chronicles 12:1-5).

HARNAK, Adolf von

(1851-1930) Leading scholar on the early Church fathers, theologian, and historian.

HAROD

In biblical times, a well in the vicinity of which the Israelite army under Gideon's leadership, encamped and where, later, the reduced force of 10,000 was put to the proof. Subsequently 300 men were selected to rout the Midianites. The earlier departure of 22,000 Israelites because of their being "afraid and trembling" may have been the reason for giving the well its name (Judges 7:1-7).

HARODITE

In biblical times, a resident or native of Harod. The term is applied to Shammah and Elika, two of David's mighty men (2 Samuel 23:8, 25).

HARP

Stringed instrument in which the resonator, or belly, is perpendicular, or nearly so, to the plane of the strings. Harps were widely used in the ancient Mediterranean and Middle Eastern civilizations. Depictions survive from Egypt and Mesopotamia from circa 3000 BC.

HARPIES

In classical mythology, fabulous creatures, probably wind spirits. Their presence as tomb figures, however, makes it possible that they were also ghosts.

HARUMAPH

In the Old Testament, father (or forefather) of the Jedaiah who helped Nehemiah rebuild Jerusalem's wall (Nehemiah 3:10).

HARUN

The Aaron of the Koran. Here Aaron is portrayed as an associate and brother of Musa who stands beside him before Pharaoh. At one point Musa scolds

Harun because of the calf worship which has taken place in Musa's absence. The death of Harun attracted the attention of later Muslim commentators who wove much legend around the event.

HARUSPICES

Ancient Etruscan diviners, whose art consisted primarily in deducing the will of the gods from the sacrificial animal. They also interpreted all portents or unusual phenomena of nature, especially thunder and lightning, and prescribed the expiatory ceremonies after such events.

HARUT AND MARUT

Two angels mentioned in verse 102 of Surat al-Baqara of the Koran. They either taught men sorcery or hope to avoid sorcery. Commentators further explain that they came to earth, having accepted God's challenge to behave better then sinful man. However, they committed murder and fornication and, in choosing to make reparation on earth, they were imprisoned and tormented in a Babylonian well.

HARUZ

In the Old Testament, a man from Jotbah; the grandfather of King Amon of Judah and the father of Meshullemeth the wife of King Manasseh (2 Kings 21:19-20).

HASADIAH

In the Old Testament, one of Zerubbabel's sons. The fact that the sons of Zerubbabel are listed in two different groups (the first two names being separated from the other five by the mention of Shelomith in the genealogy of King David's descendants) may mean that they were sons of different mothers (1 Chronicles 3:1, 19-20).

HASAN

In Islam, term denoting fair or good. The word is used to indicate in hadith criticism regarding relative strength and reliability of a tradition. A hasan tradition was not regarded as quite as strong as one which was sahih, but it was better than those which were da'if or saqim.

HASAN, Sayyid Muhammad ibn Allah

(1864-1920) Dervish religious fanatic and nationalist leader who for 20 years led armed resistance to the British, Italian, and Ethiopian colonial forces in Somalia.

HASAN AL-BASRI, al

(642-728)Deeply religious ascetic Muslim of the early Islamic community, traditionally regarded as a founder of the two most important schools of early Sunni (traditionalist) Islam.

HASANE- SABBAH

(1154-1124) Leader of an extremist Islamic sect, the Nizari Ismailis. He wrote a number of cogent theological treaties, stressing in particular the need to accept absolute authority in matters of religious faith. His expression of this doctrine became widely accepted by contemporary Nizaris.

HASAN IBN ALI IBN ABI TALIB

(624-680) A grandson of the Prophet Mohammed and considered by many of his contemporaries to be rightful heir to Mohammed's position of leadership.

HASHABIAH

In the Old Testament, a Levite whose descendants resided in Jerusalem after the Babylonian exile (1 Chronicles 9:2-3, 14). The name is also mentioned for one of the priests whom Ezra entrusted with the transporting of precious materials from Babylon to Jerusalem in 468 BC (Ezra 8:24-30).

HASHABNAH

In the Old Testament, one of the eight Levites who called upon the sons of Israel to bless God and his glorious name and then reviewed God's dealings with Israel before the attestation by seal to the confession contract made during Nehemiah's governorship (Nehemiah 9:5, 38).

HASHEMITES

The Arab descendants, either direct or collateral, of the prophet Mohammed, from among whom came the family who created the 20th century Hashemite dynasty. Mohammed himself was a member of the house of Hashim, a subdivision of the Quraysh tribe.

HASHIM

Great grandfather of the Prophet Mohammed whose name was borne by the Prophet's own clan. Hashim was responsible for provisioning pilgrims and is also credited with having dug a number of wells. The term is also used to indicate the Meccan clan to which the Prophet Mohammed belonged; it was part of the tribe of Quraysh.

HASHMONAH

In the Old Testament, an Israelite camping site, apparently between Mithkah and Moseroth (Numbers 33:29-30).

HASHR, al-

The title of the 59th sura of the Koran; it means "The Gathering" but also "The Exile." The sura belongs to the Medinan period and has 24 verses. Its title is drawn from a phrase in verse 2 which has been variously interpreted. Mush of the sura concerns Jewish-Muslim relations and, in particular, the breaking of the Jewish tribe of al-Nadit of a treaty of neutrality which it had made with Mohammed. Verse 21 uses a most striking image in which God tells his people that if the Koran had been sent down on a mountain, they would have seen that very mountain submissive and cleft open in fear of God.

HASHUM

Ancestral head of a family of Israelites, members of which returned from Babylon with Zerubbabel in 537 BC (Ezra 2:1-2; Nehemiah 7:22). Upon Ezra's arrival in Jerusalem in 468 BC, seven men of the "sons of Hashum" dismissed their foreign wives (Ezra 10:33). The family representative or one bearing the name Hashum stood to the left of Ezra as he read the book of the law to the Israelites assembled at the public square before the Water Gate of Jerusalem (Nehemiah 8:1-4).

HASIDEANS

Pre-Christian Jewish sect of uncertain origin noted for uncompromising observance of Judah Law. Its members joined the Maccabean revolt against the Romans (2nd century BC) to fight for religious freedom and against the tide of paganism. They had no interest in politics as such.

HASIDISM

The beliefs and religious practices of the Hasidim, a word designating at least three pious Jewish sects. Hasidim are identified with the Assideans (Hasideans), a sect devoted to strict Judaism about the 3rd century BC which formed the nucleus of the 2nd century BC Maccabaean revolt of the Jews.

The Hasidim of medieval Germany were a mystical sect that flourished in the 12th and 13th century. Another group known by this name was founded in Poland in the 18th century by Israel ben Eliezer, called Baal Shem Tov, or Master of the Holy Name. His teachings emphasized simple piety, joyful celebration and mystical faith in God. After the death of the founder each group had its own leader, a rabbi known as zaddik. Thousands of Hasidim still carry on their traditions today, mostly in the United States and Israel.

HASKALA

A late 18th century and 19th century social and cultural movement among the Jews of central and eastern Europe. Though it owed much of its inspiration and values to the European Enlightenment, its roots, character, and development were distinctly Jewish.

Early proponents of Haskala were convinced that Jews could be brought into the mainstream of European culture

through a reform of traditional Jewish education and a breakdown of ghetto life.

Orthodox Judaism opposed the Haskala movement from the start because its repudiation of the traditional Jewish way of life threatened to destroy the tightly knit fabric of Judaism, to undermine religious observance, and ultimately to adulterate Jewish identity. There was particular distrust of a rationalistic ideology that seemed to challenge rabbinic orthodoxy and the important role of Talmudic studies in Jewish education.

HASMONEAN

Name of a distinguished family of Jewish leaders active from the 2nd century BC. Mattathias was the founder of the family. He had several sons, the most famous of whom was the soldier Judas Maccabaeus (Judas the hammerer) who led the revolt against Antiochos IV of Syria in 165 BC and restored the Temple worship. Simon, his brother, became ruler of Judea in 141 after securing the kingdom's political independence, and his descendants carried on the dynasty. The last Hasmonean leader, Antigonus, was executed by the Roman Mark Antony in 37 BC.

HASSENAAH

In the Old Testament, "the sons of Hassenaah" rebuilt the fish gate at the time Jerusalem's walls were being repaired under Nehemiah's direction (Nehemiah 3:3).

HASSHUB

In the Old Testament, son of Pahath-moab; one of those who did repair work when the wall of Jerusalem was being rebuilt under Nehemiah's direction (Nehemiah 3:11).

HASUPHA

In the Old Testament, the forefather of a family of Nethinim, members of which returned from Babylon with Zerubbabel in 537 BC (Ezra 2:1-2, 43).

HATANA SEIICHI

(1877-1950) Scholar whose pioneering works on Christian and Western philosophy continue to be studied in Japanese universities. He did a series of studies on Christianity, which, in place of the usual polemics, attempted a serious philosophical approach.

HATCHMENT

Heraldic memorial to a deceased person. The hatchment is placed first over the doorway of the house and then moved to the church of burial.

HATRED

In moral theology, hatred is deliberately desiring harm or evil on another person. It is contrary to charity, indeed the direct opposite of love of one's neighbor and love of one's enemies as taught by Jesus in the Sermon of the Mount (see Matthew 5:44-45).

HAUHAU MOVEMENT

A religio-military cult among the Maori of New Zealand that arose during the Maori Wars of the 1860s.

A mixture of Jewish, Christian, and Maori religious tenets with the practice of cannibalism, the cult, known as Pai Marire, held that the Maori were a new chosen people.

Ultimately unsuccessful in its endeavor, the Hauhau Movement kept hostility blazing until 1872, when active Maori resistance ended. The movement than dwindled, and in the 20th century only a few Maori claimed adherence to the cult.

HAURAN

In the Old Testament, a boundary site in Ezekiel's vision of Israel's inheritance (Ezekiel 47:13-18). According to some scholars it embraced approximately the same area earlier covered by the term "Bashan."

HAVILAH

According to biblical tradition, a land "encircled" by the Pishon, one of the four rivers branching off from the river issuing out of Eden. It is further identified as a land of good gold, bdellium gum and the onyx stone (Genesis 2:10-12). In as much as the Pishon river is no longer identifiable, the location of the land of Havilah remains uncertain. The description of its resources is considered by some to be typically Arabian and it is often associated with a region in south-western Arabia.

HAWWA'

Name given by Muslim authors to Eve, the wife of Adam. In The Koran text Eve is referred to as spouse of partner. She joined with Adam in his disobedience and was accordingly cast out with him. Later, after an initial separation, Eve encountered Adam again at 'Arafa. Her name, like that of her husband, has become embroidered with much legend. Eve's tomb was traditionally located in what is now the Red Sea Arabian port of Judda, known to the West as Jeddah. The name has been held by some to derive from the Arabic jadda or jidda meaning "grandmother," in reference to Eve, but this has been denied by others.

HAYAGRIVA

In northern Buddhism, a fierce protective deity, usually shown with a horse's head in its hair.

HAZAEL

(9th century BC) King of Damascus. Hazael became king after he killed king Benhadad I, under whom he was a court official. He ruled for many years, during which time he fought the kings of Judah and Israel with some success, capturing all Israel's possessions east of the Jordan.

HAZAR-ADDAR

In the Old Testament, a city on the southern border of Judah, perhaps the same as the Addar near Kadesh-barnea (Numbers 34:4; Joshua 15:3).

HAZAR-ENAN

In biblical times, a site on the northern boundary of "the land of Canaan" (Numbers 34:2, 7-10). Ezekiel referred to Hazar-enan along with Damascus and Hamath, in his forevision of the territory of Israel (Ezekiel 47:13; 48:1).

HAZAR-SHUAL

In the Old Testament, an enclave city of Simeon in the southern part of Judah (Joshua 15:21-28; 1 Chronicles 4:28). It was reoccupied after the Babylonian exile (Nehemiah 11:25-27).

HAZAR-SUSAH

In the Old Testament, a Simeonite enclave city in the southern part of Judah (Joshua 19:1-5).

HAZARMAVETH

In Judaism a descendant of Noah through Shem and Joktan (Genesis 10:1, 21-16). It is generally believed that Hazarmaveth's descendants settled the Hadhramaut region in south Arabia.

HAZOR

In the Old Testament, a chief city of northern Canaan at the time of Israel's conquest under Joshua (Joshua 11:10). Jabin the king of Hazor led the united forces of northern Canaan against Joshua, but suffered a humiliating defeat. Hazor itself was burned, the only city in that area built on a mound to be so treated (Joshua 11:1-13).

HAZZAN

In Judaism, the official who directs liturgical prayer in the synagogue and leads the chanting. He may be engaged by a congregation for the entire year or merely to assist at the ceremonies of Rosh Hashana and Yom Kippur.

HEALING

The cure of bodily ills by religious means, a teaching and practice that appear in various forms among Christian bodies. Besides Jesus' own ministry of healing, the New Testament attests to the charisma of healing given to the Apostles and to the early church (Matthew 10:1; Acts 3:1-16; 1 Corinthians 12:28-30) and to the connection between bodily ills and sin (John 9:2-3).

The instruction in James 5:14-16 was followed in the early church in both liturgical anointings and prayers for the sick. The Roman Catholic Church came to regard the anointing of the sick as one of the seven sacraments, and its meaning as a sacrament for the sick has been affirmed in recent times (Vatican Council II).

Besides this sacramental healing, private blessings and prayers for the sick, sometimes involving the use of relics, have continued in Roman Catholic practice.

Other christian bodies, while not recognizing a sacrament for the sick, still have retained the use of prayers, blessings, laying on of hands, and anointing as profitable for bodily health.

Particular importance have been attached to it in revivalism, the Holiness Churches, and as part of the foursquare gospel message that healing is an essential part of the Christian message; that as Jesus saves from sin, so also he heals the body from the consequences of sin.

In Pentecostalism charismatic, divine healing is regarded as an essential part of the Christian life, connected with baptism with the Holy Spirit.

HEALTH

In moral theology, a basic moral principle is that the human person has a moral responsibility to take reasonable care of his or her health; health is used in the holistic sense, that is, the care of and harmony between one's physical, mental, and spiritual capacities.

HEART DOCTRINE

In Buddhism, wisdom of teachings. The diction between the Eye Doctrine and that of the Heart is basic for oriental wisdom. The former contains the doctrines and practices of a teaching; the latter its wisdom which cannot be written down.

HEATHEN

One who is not a believer in God of the Bible, or one who is neither Jewish, Christian, nor (in some usages) Muslim. The term probably derives from "heath" and is related to the fact that the first Christians lived in the towns, while the country people continued to worship pagan deities. The word came to have the derogatory implication of not living by Christian moral standards, and sometimes meant more broadly one uncultured and unenlightened.

HEAVEN

The firmament surrounding the earth in which the sun, moon and stars circulate and which is traditionally believed to be the home of the deity.

Hebrew-Christian view

Heaven is regarded as the residence of God, angels and the righteous after death. Heaven is the eternal home of true believers, or the state of living in full union with Christ, which the perfected soul enters after death (1 Peter 1:4).

In the Old Testament God, who dwells in heaven, also transcends it. Not until late Judaism was heaven generally regarded as the abode of the righteous. In Christian thought heaven is the eternal home of true believers or the state of living in full union with Christ, which the perfected soul enters after death.

Other religions

Among ancient civilizations, the Sumerians and early Egyptians believed heaven to be a distant land to which the dead traveled and which was ruled by a benign supreme being.

The ancient Greeks regarded heaven as the Elysian Fields, located in the underworld, the place where the great and good lived on in after-life. The Norse conceived of heaven as Valhalla, a place of pleasure and feasting; the Zoroastrians, a realm of eternal light.

In Islam heaven is viewed as a garden where faithful Muslims may seek the face of God.

In the Eastern religions of Buddhism and Hinduism heaven consists of many levels that must be achieved over many lifetimes until a soul attains the eternal state of nirvana.

HEBREW

The designation "Hebrew" is first used for Abraham, distinguishing him thereby from his Amoritish neighbors (Genesis 14:13). Thereafter, in virtually every case of its use, the term "Hebrew(s)" continued to be employed as a contrasting or distinguishing designation - the one speaking is of a non-Israelite nation (Genesis 39:14-17; Exodus 1:16; 1 Samuel 4:6-9), or is an Israelite addressing a foreigner (Genesis 40:15; Exodus 1:19), or foreigners are mentioned (Genesis 43:32; Exodus 1:15).

As the above texts show, the designation "Hebrew" was already familiar to the Egyptians in the 18th century BC. This would seem to indicate that Abraham, Isaac and Jacob had become quite well known over a wide area, thus making the appellative "Hebrew" a recognizable one.

HEBREW

A Semitic language with a rich literary heritage which includes the Old Testament. While the Bible is a major source for ancient Hebrew, there is an extensive literature of post-biblical Hebrew, even though, until recently, Hebrew was widely spoken only in the biblical period. The earliest Hebrew writings date from as early as the 12th century BC and the language has produced a continuous literature right down to the present, in spite of the general neglect of the spoken language in the post-biblical period.

It is generally believed that Hebrew is of north-west Semitic origin, with the local Canaanite dialects playing a significant part in its development. In a later period another Semitic language, Aramaic, strongly affected the development of Hebrew, and it is due to this influence that much of the distinctive nature of classical Hebrew grammar was lost. During this period the older cursive script was replaced by the square Aramaic or "Assyrian" letters still in use. While the Jews had stopped speaking Hebrew even during the end of the biblical period, scholars contin-ued to write it and even the common people used it in their liturgy. It continued to be a sacred tongue as well as a common language for Jews from different countries.

HEBREW BIBLE

The 24 books accepted by modern Jews as the sacred scripture (some reckon the books as numbering 22, like the letters of the Hebrew alphabet, by counting Jg-Ru and Jer-Lam as single books). The Hebrew acronym TNK is based on the conventional division into the Law (Tora), the Prophets (Nebi'im) and the Writings (Ketubim).

The acceptance of them as *the books* (greek biblia) in an absolute sense was a gradual process. The Law, the five books of the Pentateuch, was the first to receive this status. Much later the same sacredness was attributed to the prophets, divided into the former prophets (Joshua, 1-2 Samuel, 1-2 Kings), and the later prophets (Major - Isaiah, Jeremiah, Ezekiel, and the 12, the minor prophets, taken as a single book Hosea, Joel, Amos, Obadiah, Micah, Jonah, Nahum, Habakkuk, Zephaniah, Haggai, Zechariah, Malachi).

The Writings, comprising Psalms, Proverbs, Job, the five Megilloth or scrolls - Song of Solomon, Ruth, Lamentations, Ecclesiastes, Esther - Daniel, Ezra-Nehemiah, and 1-2 Chronicles were almost certainly the last to receive acceptance.

HEBREW UNION COLLEGE

The oldest Jewish seminary in the United States for the training of rabbis, long a stronghold of American Reform Judaism. It was founded in 1875 at Cincinnati, Ohio, by Rabbi Isaac Mayer Wise.

HEBREWS

Any member of an ancient northern Semitic people that were the ancestors of the Jews. The term Hebrew always occurs in the Old Testament as a name given to the Israelites by other peoples, rather than one used by themselves.

HEBREWS, Letter to

Inspired letter of the Christian Greek scriptures. The letter was addressed to a Christian community whose faith was faltering because of strong Jewish influences. To fortify their beliefs, the author describes the perfect priesthood of Christ, who, unlike the Jewish High Priest, offered but one sacrifice as God's own Son, thereby redeeming all of mankind once and for all. The Christians are warned against apostasy and the expectation of judgment that awaits the enemies of God (10:27-29). They are urged to persevere in their faith following the heroic example of others well known to them.

HEBREW SCRIPTURES

According to a specific classification, the 39 inspired books from Genesis to Malachi, according to the popular present-day arrangement, constituting the major portion of the Bible.

HEBREW UNION COLLEGE

The oldest Jewish seminary in the United States for the training of rabbis, long stronghold of American Reform Judaism. It was founded in 1875 at Cincinnati, Ohio, by Rabbi Isaac Mayer Wise.

HEBRON

City in the southern Judaean Hills, south-south-west of Jerusalem. An ancient Canaanite royal city, Hebron was founded "seven years before Zoan in Egypt" (Numbers 13:22) and Zoan, later Tanis, has been dated to the 18th century BC.

King David (circa 10th century BC) was ordered by God to go to Hebron; he was anointed king of Israel there, and made it his capital for 7.5 years, until the taking of Jerusalem.

HEBRON

In the Old Testament, son of Mareshah and father of Korah, Tappuah, Rekem and Shema; a descendant of Caleb of the tribe of Judah (1 Chronicles 2:43-44).

HEBRONITES

A Levite family descended from Kohath's son Hebron (Exodus 6:16-18; Numbers 3:27). King David assigned 1,700 capable Hebronites to serve in administrative capacities over the region west of the Jordan and 2,700 over the territory east of the Jordan (1 Chronicles 26:30-32).

HEDONISM

A general philosophical theory that holds that pleasure is the greatest good. Although the term is usually popularly employed to refer only to sensual pleasure, most philosophers have also included the pleasures resulting from art, religion, scholarship, friendship or fame.

Moral hedonism has been attacked by many philosophers, beginning with Socrates. Psychological hedonism has been most effectively criticized by Joseph Butler, who argued that most pleasure comes as a bonus after a human desire has been fulfilled and is rarely a satisfying goal for its own sake. Thus, when I am hungry I desire to eat. But if I eat when I am not hungry, purely for pleasure, it is less satisfying than if I were to eat to satisfy my hunger.

HEGAI

In biblical times, a eunuch of King Ahasuerus' court; the guardian of the women who prepared Esther with special beauty treatments before she was taken to the king (Esther 2:3-15).

HEGESIPPUS

(circa 340-399) Supposed author of a free Latin adaptation of the *Jewish War* of Josephus. The seven books of Josephus are compressed into five. The name Hegesippus itself appears to be a corruption of Josephus, unless it was purposely adopted as reminiscent of Hegesippus, the father of ecclesiastical history (2nd century).

HEGESIPPUS, Saint

(2nd century AD) Greek Christian historian and champion of orthodoxy who opposed Gnosticism, a heretical, dualist religious philosophy advocating salvation through secret knowledge.

HEIDELBERG CATECHISM

A Reformed confession of faith that is used by many of the Reformed churches. It was written in 1562 primarily by Caspar Olevianus (1536-87), the superintendent of the Palatinate church, and Zacharias Ursinus (1534-83), a professor of the theological faculty of the University of Heidelberg.

The authors based their work on earlier catechetical works by themselves and others, and they attempted to prepare a catechism acceptable to all. In discussing the sacraments they sought to bring their Reformed statements as near to the moderate Melanchthonian-Lutheran position as they could.

HEILER, Johann Friedrich

(1892-1967) Religious writer and scholar in the history of religions, converted from Roman Catholicism to the Lutheran Church (1919), who led the German High Church movement, including the introduction of monasticism.

HEJAZ

The Holy Land of Islam, an area of the Arabian Peninsula adjacent to the Red Sea. It contains the holy cities of Mecca and Medina, as well as the port of Jeddah. The hashimite emir rules the country until 1924, when it was conquered by the Wahabite Ibn Saud and made a part of Saudi Arabia. Hejaz was always a center of Muslim pilgrimage.

HEL

In Norse mythology, originally the name of the world of the dead; it later came to mean the goddess of death. Hel was one of the children of the trickster god Loki, and her kingdom was said to lie downward and northward.

HELAM

In the Old Testament, the site where David's army defeated the military forces of Syrian king Hadadezer under his army chief Shobach (2 Samuel 10:15-19).

HELBAH

In the Old Testament, a city in the territory of the tribe of Asher. It is mentioned as being one of the towns from which the tribe of Asher did not drive out the Canaanite inhabitants (Judges 1:31-32).

HELDAI

In Judaism, the head of the 12th monthly service group that David organized; a descendant of Othniel (1 Chronicles 27:1,15).

HELENA, Saint

(248-328) Roman empress who was the reputed discoverer of Christ's cross. Before 337, it was claimed in Jerusalem that Christ's cross had been found during the building of Constantine's church on Golgotha. Later in the century Helena was credited with the discovery. Many subsequent legends developed, and the story of the "invention," or the finding of the cross, enhanced by romances and confusions with other Helena, became a favorite throughout Christendom.

HELI

According to biblical tradition, the father of Mary and maternal grandfather of Jesus Christ (Luke 3:23). Joseph's being called "the son of Heli" is understood to mean that he was the son-in-law of Heli. While not listing her, Luke evidently traces the natural descent of Jesus' mother Mary from David (Luke 3:31).

HELIOS

In Greek mythology, the god of light or the sun. Helios was older that the gods of Olympus. The son of the Titan Hyperion and the Titaness Theia, he was descended from Uranus and Mother Earth. Io (the dawn) and Oceanus were his brother and sister, and he had a number of famous children: the sorceress Circe, Aetes the king of Colchis, Pasiphae, the wife of Minos, and Perses.

Helios is shown as a handsome man whose golden locks are crowned with the gold rays of the sun. He is depicted driving across the sky in his fiery chariot, drawn by horses of unsurpassed speed.

The sun god is above the Earth and the Ocean, in his chariot all day, using a craft like a huge, deep cup to cross the sea. Helios sees everything, and in various myths is a witness to acts of good and evil.

HELKATH

In the Old Testament, a city listed among the boundary sites of the tribe of Asher (Joshua 19:24-31), later assigned to the Gershonites as a Levitical city (Joshua 21:27-31).

HELL

In several religions, abode of evil spirits and of the wicked after death, usually thought of as an underworld or abyss. In Christian theology, those damned by God are sent to hell for eternity. The New Testament describes hell as a place of corruption and unquenchable fire and brimstone, images which have often been taken literally. Usually hell is regarded as ultimate separation from God, the confirmation of the sinner's own choice.

In the old Norse Hel the lost souls suffer in cold and darkness. The hell of the Icelandic Eddas is considered to have been influenced by Christian concepts. The ancient Greeks believed in Hades, either a gloomy netherworld or a distant island.

The Jewish Sheol was a dark place where the souls of all men, not just Jews, dwelt in misery. Jews at the time of Christ believed in Gehenna, a place of punishment after death.

In Buddhism, there is no hell in the sense of endless torture. The hells described and depicted in Buddhist countries are temporary states of purgatory, of which Avici is the lowest. The period of suffering is measured by the acts of the Gaya, which is the site of the Enlightenment.

The hell of Islam is much like that of Christianity, while the hell of the Far East religions is usually a place of temporary suffering.

In Roman Catholicism, hell is the dwelling place of Satan and the evil spirits of all those who die deliberately alienated from God. The primary punishment of hell is the pain of loss: the deprivation of the face-to-face vision of God and eternal happiness with Him. There is also the pain of sense caused by an outside agent, described as fire in the New Testament (*see* Matthew 25:41, Mark 9:43).

Hell is the dire destination for one who freely chooses his or her own will against the will of God.

HELL, Christian

A primarily Buddhist conception of the realm of punishment and expiation after death, accepted and modified by Taoism in China.

HELL SCROLL

12th century Japanese emaki showing the eight Buddhist hells, each with 16 minor hells attached, illustrating the Six Roads of Reincarnation. The small paintings depict vividly the torments and terrors of the damned. The dynamic lines of the flames have been compared with the calligraphic curves of Botticelli.

HELLEN

In Greek mythology, king of Phthia and grandson of the god Prometheus. He was the eponymous ancestor of all true Greeks, called Hellenes in his honor.

HELLENISM

A term that may signify:
1 a complex of religious and social ties and cultural achievements that united the ancient Greeks (Hellenes) into a distinctive and recognizable group; or
2 the adoption of salient features of the Hellenic civilization by other ethnic groups in the East and West to constitute a richly varied and widely diffused

Hellenistic culture;

3 a contemporary enthusiasm for the art, literature, and philosophy of the ancient Greeks.

HELLENISTIC JUDAISM

Judaism as it developed outside Palestine in Greek-speaking areas of the ancient world, notably in and near Alexandria, Egypt, from about the 4th century BC onward.

HELLENISTIC RELIGIONS

The religious cults of the Hellenistic Age (circa 300 BC to 300), a time of spiritual revolution in the Greek and Roman empires, when old cults died or were fundamentally transformed and when new, vital religious movements arose.

Among the many religions or religious movements that were transformed or arose during this period were mystery religions (centered, for example, on veneration of Isis, Mithra, Cybele, Sarapis, or Dionysus), Judaism, Gnosticism; prophetic and healing cults, religious philosophies, Manichaeism, and Christianity.

HELL-FIRE

The principal physical punishment or pain of sense suffered by the damned. Along with pain of loss it described the dual aspects of eternal punishment as elaborated by scholastic theology. The New Testament description of punishment by fire was influenced by Jewish writing concerning Gehenna and reflects contemporary apocalyptic language. The Synoptics, for example, speak of a place of punishment for sinners where fire is eternal and unquenchable (Matthew 5:22; Matthew 18:8-9). In the same vein the final state of the wicked in Revelation is the pool of fire which is a second death (Revelation 19:20; Revelation 20:1-5). Christian tradition has no definite statement on the kind and quality of the pains of hell. From the patristic era, theologians have questioned whether hell-fire is real or metaphorical. Until relatively recent times, the majority opinion was that the fire was material and real, but it seems to be commonly held today that it is a metaphor which, along with other apocalyptic expressions, helps describe the final state of loss which is possible for man, a condition of alienation not only from God but from creation as well.

HELVETIC CONFESSIONS

Two confessions of faith officially adopted by the Reformed Church in Switzerland. The First Helvetic Confession was composed in 1536 by Heinrich Bullinger and other Swiss delegates, assisted by Martin Buber of Strassbourg.

In 1562 Bullinger wrote a lengthy theological statement of 30 articles, which he later revised and attached to his will. This document became known as the Second Helvetic Confession and was published in 1566 as the official creed of the Swiss cantons.

HEMAM

In the Old Testament, son of Lotan and descendant of Seit the Horite (Genesis 36:20-22).

HEMAN

One of four wise men whose wisdom, though great, was surpassed by that of King Solomon. Heman, Calcol and Darba are designated as the "sons of Mahol," an expression thought by some to refer to an association of dancers or musicians (1 Kings 4:31). This Heman appears to be further identified at 1 Chronicles 2:3-6 as a descendant of Judah through Zerah.

HEN

In the Old Testament, son of a certain Zephaniah (not the prophet); one who returned from captivity in Babylon. He is mentioned in connection with the grand crown that was to be placed on the head of Joshua the High Priest and which would afterward come to belong to Hen and three others as a memorial in the Temple of God (Zechariah 6:11-14).

HENADAD

A Levite whose descendants apparently served as supervisors in connection with the rebuilding of the Temple by Zerubbabel (Ezra 3:8-9). Two of Henadad's descendants are specifically referred to as sharing in the repair of Jerusalem's wall, and one of his descendants attested by seal the confession contract made during Nehemiah's governorship (Nehemiah 3:17-24).

HENDERSON, Alexander

(1583-1646) Presbyterian clergyman primarily responsible for the preservation of the Presbyterian form of church government in Scotland, who was influential in the defeat of Charles I during the Civil War of 1642-51.

HENGSTENBERG, Ernst Wilhelm

(1802-1869) Theologian who defended Lutheran orthodoxy against the rationalism pervading the Protestant churches. He wrote many biblical commentaries, opposing the growing reliance upon historical-critical interpretation and following the traditional method of reading the Old Testament as a Christian book filled with prophecies of the Messiah fulfilled by the coming of Christ.

HENOTHEISM

The worship of but one god without denying the existence of other gods. One supposes that in the Vedic and other religions there was a process in which worship and all divine attributes were centered successively in a single one of the gods. One called this kathenotheism or simply henotheism. Henotheism is also used to denote to signify the exclusive worship given to the god of a nation or people; the religion of Israel during the Mosaic period has been so described by some scholars, The term may also connote concentration, within a monotheistic system, on some particular divine attribute.

HENRY OF GHENT

(1217-1293) Scholastic philosopher and theologian, one of the most illustrious teachers of the time, who was a great adversary of St. Thomas Aquinas and whose controversial and occasionally unique writings influenced his contemporaries and followers, particularly post-medieval Platonists.

HENSON, Herbert Hensley

(1863-1947) Controversial Anglican bishop of Durham and author of many theological studies attempting to modernize Christian doctrine.

HEPHAESTUS

In Greek mythology, the god of fire and patron of craftsmen. Son of Zeus and Hera, Hephaestus was the husband of Aphrodite. The Romans identified him with the god Volcan or Vulcan. He was associated with Athena, goddess of the arts, and the festival Chalkeia was celebrated in Athens in their honor.
Hephaestus' workshop was on Lemnos, but all places where there were volcanoes and fire belonged to him. He was strong of arm, like any other blacksmith who spends all day with hammer and anvil, but his legs were weak.
In addition, Hephaestus was lame, a fact for which there were two explanations: according to one, Zeus was quarreling with Hera one day when the young Hephaestus dared to intervene on his mother's side. In his rage, Zeus picked Hephaestus up by the leg and hurled him from Olympus. He fell to earth on Lemnos, where the Sintians, a Thracian people who had emigrated to the island, took care of him - but he was left with a lame leg.
The other tale says that he was born lame, and that it was Hera, who decided to throw him off Olympus. He fell into the Ocean, where Tethys and Eurynome saved him and brought him up in a sea cave.

HEPHER

In the Old Testament, a son of Gilead and great-grandson of Manasseh; ancestor of the Hepherites (Numbers 26:29-32). Hepher was the father of Zelophehad, known for having no sons but five daughters whose case set a legal precedent in handling hereditary possessions when there was no male offspring (Numbers 26:33; Joshua 17:2-3).

HERA

In Greek mythology, queen of the Olympian Gods and sister and wife of Zeus. Hera is the goddess of marriage and birth. A jealous and quarrelsome wife, she often persecuted those who rivaled her for Zeus' affections. She was the patroness of the cities of Argos, Sparta and Mycenae and the island of Samos. Her sacred symbols were the cow and the peacock. Hera is often represented as a regal figure wearing a bridal dress, or carrying a scepter, or with a wreath on her brow. The Romans identified her with the goddess Juno. A supporter of the Greeks against the Trojans in Homer's Iliad, she was also the protectress of heroes.

HERACLES

In Greek mythology, a demi-god who is identified with power, heroism and majesty. He became a symbol as his fame reached every corner of the then known world and he represented a true superman.

There was no "labor" that was beyond the power of Heracles. The problems which appeared in nearly all Greek societies, as well as outside it, could only be solved by one man and that was Heracles. He did battle with villains, monsters, armies, gods, natural forces, illness and was even a victor over death.

Heracles was a demi-god, endowed with supernatural gifts but also with human weaknesses. He belonged to the Perseid family, and was born at Thebes, supposedly to a mortal father, Amphitryon, and Alcemene. However, his real father was Zeus, who took advantage of Amphitryon's absence one night to impersoniate him and sleep with Alcemene.

HERALDRY, Ecclesiastical

Arms associated with the church's administrative and collegiate bodies. Abbeys, priories, and dioceses have their own arms, and high ecclesiastics have always impaled these with their personal arms.

HERCULES

Roman version of Heracles. Hercules was set 12 seemingly impossible tasks, known as the Twelve Labors. These "labors," celebrated in ancient legend and art, were said to symbolize the difficult road to virtue.

HEREM

Hebrew word for isolating or barring a Jew from his community for improper conduct. It was a potent force for ensuring orthodox behavior when Jewish communities were confined to ghettos.

HERES

In biblical times, a mount where Amorites kept dwelling despite Israel's conquest of Canaan. It is associated with the territory of the tribe of Dan (Judges 1:34-35). Most scholars consider it the equivalent of Ir-shemesh mentioned at Joshua 19:41.

HERESY

Denial of an officially defined doctrine of the church. The term is used in the sense of an opinion that dissents from an established creed of the church or other generally accepted beliefs. From early times both Christians and Jews attacked heresy as a willful, subversive divergence from established faith.

In Roman Catholicism, heresy is the deliberate and obstinate denial by a baptized person of any truth which must be believed as a matter of divine and Catholic faith; it is a grave sin and incurs the penalty of excommunication.

Reference is sometimes made to "material heresy" as the condition of those baptized persons who, in good faith and through no fault of their own, accept heretical doctrine; but, since they are in good faith, in reality there is no sin and no excommunication.

Since the Reformation not only did the

Roman Catholic Church continue in its rejection of heresy, but confessional churches of the Reformation shared in the same zeal of orthodoxy. The Lutheran and Reformed confessions of faith reject as heresy teachings that are contrary to the gospel.

In modern times the notion of heresy is often ridiculed. This is in part explained by the minimizing of dogma, rooted in rationalism and in theological liberalism, and in part by the widespread acceptance of the adage "deeds not creeds."

Yet many of the churches continue to recognize the possibility of heresy, the need to resist it, and have juridic processes for those accused of heresy. There is also, however, a healthy contemporary restraint from use of the word heresy both by Catholics and Protestants.

The term is less frequently used to impugn the genuineness of the belief of fellow Christians. This involves a recognition of past polemical exaggeration and a hesitancy to accuse others of consciously preferring their own opinion over what is known to be the authentic word of God. Heresy in its strict meaning would be such a choice.

HERM

In Greek religion, a sacred object of stone connected with the cult of Hermes, the fertility god.

HERMAS

One of the Christians in the congregation at Rome to whom Paul sent personal greetings (Romans 16:14).

HERMENEUTICS, Biblical

The part of theological science that treats the principles of biblical interpretation applied in actual practice by exegesis. Hence it deals with the meaning of the scripture. Hermeneutics presupposes that the Bible has been written by men in human fashion, but under the inspiration of the Spirit of God (2 Timothy 3:16); as a result it contains the Word of God in the words of men.

The literal sense of scripture is the meaning God intended to be conveyed, to men at all time. To ascertain this meaning, the text and the oral and written traditions that lie behind it must be studied with the help of philology, archeology, history, textual and literary criticism. Attention must also be paid to the unity of the Bible, for each word, sentence, section, or book processes its complete meaning only as part of a larger whole - namely, the progressive revelation of God in the history of salvation culminating in the New Testament.

HERMES

Ancient Greek God, usually identified as the messenger of the gods. Hermes corresponded to the Roman god Mercury. He was also said to guard the roads and highways, and travelers set up shrines in his honor. In addition, he was the patron of all those whose work involved skill or cunning, including thieves. In his role of divine messengers, Hermes led the souls of the dead to the underworld. He was the most benign of the gods; his statues (herms) were to be found everywhere.

HERMES, Georg

(1775-1831) Roman Catholic theologian, originator of the controversial theological system called Hermesianism, which attempted to demonstrate the rational necessity of Christianity.

HERMIT

One who lives alone, usually in the wilderness, and pursues a contemplative religious life. Hermits were common among the early Christians of the late 3rd century, especially in Egypt. St. Anthony of Egypt, who founded monasticism, and St. Simeon Stylites were noted ascetics. The hermit is distinguished from the cenobite - one who shares his life of monasticism with others, The term hermit is now applied to men who live alone in remote spots to avoid contact with others.

HERMOGENES

One of the two Christians in he district of Asia specifically mentioned by name as having turned away from Paul, possibly because of the violent persecution launched by Nero against the Christians after the burning of Rome in 64 (2 Timothy 1:15).

HERMON, Mount

Snowcapped ridge on the Lebanon-Syria border west of Damascus. It rises to 9,232 feet and is the highest point on the east coast of the Mediterranean Sea. A sacred landmark in Hittite, Palestinian, and Roman times, it represented the north-western limit of Israelite conquest under Moses and Joshua.

HEROD

Name of a family of political rulers over the Hebrews. They were Idumaeans, Edomites. They were nominally Jews, for the Idumaeans had had circumcision forced upon them by the Maccabean ruler John Hyrcanus in 125 BC, according to Josephus.

HEROD AGRIPPA I

(10 BC-AD 44) Grandson of Herod the Great, king of Judaea 40-44. He was a clever diplomat who through his friendship with the Roman imperial family obtained the kingdom of his grandfather. In Judaea, Agrippa zealously pursued orthodox Jewish policies, earning the friendship of the Jews and vigorously repressing the Jewish Christians. He imprisoned Peter the Apostle and executed James, son of Zebedee (Acts 4:1-3).

HEROD AGRIPPA II

(AD 27-100) Son of Herod Agrippa I, last important ruler of the Herodian dynasty. Lacking his father's tact in the treatment of the Jews, he contributed to their discontent, and sided with the Romans in the Jewish revolt 66-70.

HEROD ANTIPAS

(21 BC-AD 39) Son of Herod I the Great, who became tetrarch of Galilee and ruled throughout Jesus' ministry. He was tricked by his wife and her daughter Salome into having John the Baptist executed (Mark 6:22-26). When Jesus was arrested in Jerusalem, Pilate, the Roman procurator of Judaea, first sent him to Antipas because Jesus came from Antipas' realm (Luke 23:11).

HEROD ARCHELAUS

(22 BC-AD 18) Son and principal heir of Herod I the Great as king of Judaea, deposed by Rome because of his unpopularity with the Jews (AD 6). Named in his father's will as ruler of the largest part of the Judaean kingdom -Judaean proper, Idumaea, and Samaria- Archelaus went to Rome (4 BC) to defend his title against the claims of his brothers Philip and Antipas before the emperor Augustus. Augustus confirmed him in possession of the largest portion but he did not recognize him as king, giving him instead the lesser title of ethnarch to emphasize his dependence on Rome. In the account of the gospel according to Matthew (2:22), it was fear of Archelaus' tyranny that led Jesus' family to settle outside his domain at Nazareth in Galilee.

HEROD THE GREAT

(73 BC-4 BC) Roman-appointed king of Judaea (37-4 BC). Although an able ruler and generous builder (especially the Temple at Jerusalem) he was hated for his ruthlessness. He was responsible for the deaths of many of his family and, according to the New Testament, ordered the massacre of the infants of Bethlehem (Matthew 2:13).

HERODIAS

The wife of Herod Antipas, who was tetrarch (ruler appointed by Rome) of Galilee, in northern Palestine. She conspired to arrange the execution of John the Baptist. Her marriage to Herod Antipas (himself divorced), after her divorce from his half-brother was censured by John as a transgression of Mosaic law. According to Mark

(6:19,20) she would have had John killed but could not because Herod feared the man. On Herod's birthday celebration she seized the opportunity in having John killed (Mark 6:22-26).

HERODION

One to whom apostle Paul sent personal greetings in his letter to the Christian congregation at Rome. Paul refers to Herodion as "my relative" (Romans 16:11). Some suggest that this may simply mean that Herodion was a fellow Jew rather than an immediate member of Paul's family, in view of the apostle's use of the designation "relatives" at Romans 9:3. However, since Paul does not refer to all the Jews to whom he sent greetings as "my relatives" (compare Acts 18:2), likely a close relative is meant.

HEROIC ACT OF CHARITY

In Roman Catholicism, the offerings to God of a person's works, prayers, and sufferings for the benefit of the souls in purgatory.

HEROIC VIRTUE

Human virtue, whether moral or theological, in a superlative degree, even to an extreme that may somewhat baffle a sober and rational moral theologian. The notion, though not the term, appears in the *Summa theologiae* of Thomas Aquinas; he was well aware that although the moral virtues of living according to right and Christian reason observe a measure between the two extremes of excess, or too much, and of defect, or too little, no such middle course is prescribed for faith, hope, and charity which go out unreservedly to God Himself.

Now the heroic will be variously exemplified in different cultures: styles and mannerisms vastly admired by one may strike another as affected or eccentric. The hagiographical models which appealed to the taste from the Renaissance to the post-Baroque were caught up in the miraculous and ecstatic when they were not presented as practitioners according to a very spe-

cialized routine.

Some saints were too roughly themselves, too racy, and too implicated in human history to conform to the convention, which was admirable when expressed with the zest of Bernini or the imagery of Crashawe, but less so in the more pedestrian exercises of religious repository art.

One effect was that the saints came to be considered as experts in a special and professional style of living that was not for the ordinary people of God, who on the whole were prepared to admire and even to humor what sometimes was felt to be really either all rather odd or all rather prim.

HERZL, Theodor

s impossible even for Western Jews and that Jews must therefore organize a state of their own.

HERZLIYYA

City, west central Israel, on the Plain of Sharon and the Mediterranean Sea, at the north of Tel Aviv metropolitan area. Founded in 1924 with the financial backing of American Zionists, named for Theodor Herzl, the founder of modern political Zionism.

HERZOG, Isaac Halevi

Scholar and religious philosopher, chief rabbi of Palestine (Later Israel) from 1936. He made significant contributions to reconciling the necessities of modern living with the demands of the Talmud.

HERZOG, Johann Jakob

(1805-1882) German Protestant theologian, authority on the Hussite-Waldensian church. He edited the theological reference work *Encyclopedia of Religious Knowledge* (13 volumes).

HESCHEL, Abraham Joshua

(1907-1972) American Jewish theologian and philosopher, noted especially for his presentation of the prophetic and mystical aspects of Judaism, and his attempt to construct a modern philosophy of religion out of the ancient and medieval Jewish tradition.

HESED

In biblical times, an Israelite, whose son was one of Solomon's twelve deputies, each being responsible to provide the king and his household with food for one month in the year (1 Kings 4:7-10).

HESHBON

In biblical times, a place identified with modern Heshban, a ruined city situated circa 15_ miles east of the Jordan River at a point almost parallel with the north coast of the Dead Sea. It lies nearly midway between the Arnon and Jabbok Rivers (Joshua 12:2).

The Amorite king Sihon captured Heshbon from the Moabites and made it his royal residence. The Moabite defeat even provided the basis for a taunting proverbial saying, either of Amorite of Israelite origin. In the event this saying stemmed from the Amorites, it mocked the Moabites and memorialized King Sihon's victory. But, if originating with the Israelites, it signified that just as Sihon had wrested Heshbon from the Moabites, so Israel would take this and other cities from the Amorites. The taunt would then be that the victory of Sihon paved the way for the Israelites to take possession of land to which they would otherwise not have been entitled (Numbers 21:26-30; Deuteronomy 2:9).

HESTIA

In Greek mythology, the goddess of family peace. As her name ("hearth") indicates, Hestia was the personification of the family home. The eldest daughter of Cronus and Rhea, Hestia asked her brother Zeus to let her remain a virgin, despite the fact that both Poseidon and Apollo wanted her for a wife. The serenity of Hestia's life on Olympus and the stability of her position there meant that she played little part in the events and her presence is confined largely to the world of ideas.

HESYCHISM

A type of Eastern Christian monastic life, the purpose of which is to achieve divine quietness (Greek: hesychia) through the contemplation of God in universal prayer. The practice flourished in the 13th and 14th centuries.

HESYCHIUS OF JERUSALEM

(382-450) Priest-monk, renowned in the Eastern church as a theologian, biblical commentator, and preacher. He played a prominent role in the 5th century Christological (on the nature of Christ) controversy and was acclaimed as having annotated the whole of sacred scripture.

HEVAJRA TANTRA

A ritual text, in the Vajrayana tradition of Buddhism predominant in Tibet. The text contains numerous rituals, organized primarily in terms of the mandala (ritual drawing), which appears repeatedly throughout the text.

HEVITES

A term that appears in the Old Testament in the stereotyped lists of peoples expelled from Canaan by the Israelites; however, it is not found in any extrabiblical source. Many scholars think the name is a synonym of "Horrites" (Hurrians), probably to distinguish them from the Horrite pre-Edomite population.

HEXAPTERYGON

In Eastern churches a disk fashioned in the form of an angel's head surrounded by six wings. Mounted on a pole, it is borne in liturgical processions; it is one of the instruments passed to the deacon at ordination as a sign of office. In its functional origin it was a fan to brush away flies from the gifts during the Eucharistic canon.

HEXATEUCH

The first six books of the Old Testament.

HEZEKIAH

(8th and 9th centuries BC) Son of Ahaz, a descendant and 13th successor of David as king of Judah at Jerusalem. Reigning at a time of Assyrian supremacy, Hezekiah rooted out the Assyrian and Canaanite cults. He is also famous for the steps he took to supply fresh water within the city walls of Jerusalem (2 Kings 20:20), trying to achieve a degree of political independence. His attempt to gain political independence led to the fall of all Judah to King Sennacherib. Only Jerusalem was miraculously saved (2 Kings 18-21).

HEZION

Grandfather of the first King Benhadad of Syria mentioned in the Bible (1 Kings 15:18).

HEZIR

In the Old Testament, the priest whose paternal house was chosen by lot for the 17th of the 24 priestly service divisions organized toward the end of David's reign (1 Chronicles 24:1-7).

HEZRON

In the Old Testament, son of Perez and family head of the Judean "Hezronites"; ancestor of King David and of Jesus Christ (Genesis 46:12; Numbers 26:20-21; Matthew 1:3; Luke 3:33).

HEZRONITES

In the Old Testament, this designation is applied to both the family descended from Reuben's son Hezron (Genesis 46:9) and to the one descended from Judah's grandson Hezron (Genesis 46:12; Numbers 26:21).

HICKSITES

A label attached to those Quakers who accepted the interpretation of Quakerism given by Elias Hicks, and beginning in 1827, separated from the orthodox or evangelical Quakers. The name still connotes the lineage of Quaker bodies that originated in that separation.

HIDDAI

In the Old Testament, one of the mighty men in David's army. Hiddai was from the torrent valleys of Gaash in the mountainous region of Ephraim (2 Samuel 23:8).

HIDDEKEL

In biblical times, one of the four rivers branching off from the river issuing out of Eden (Genesis 2:10-14). The Hiddekel was known in the Assyro-Babylonian language as the Idiqlat and in Old Persian as the Tigra, from which latter form comes the Greek name for the Tigris River. It is called by some the "twin river" of the Euphrates and, together with this river, it waters the plains of Mesopotamia. It was on the banks of the Tigris River that Daniel received the vision concerning the power struggle to be waged by the "king of the north" and the "king of the south" (Daniel 10:4-1; 11:5-6).

HIEL

In the Old Testament, a Bethelite who rebuilt Jericho during Ahab's reign in the 10th century BC. In fulfillment of the oath Joshua had pronounced at the destruction of Jericho over 500 years earlier, Hiel laid the foundation of the city at the forfeit of Abiram his firstborn and put up its doors at the forfeit of Segub his youngest child.

HIERACITES

Egyptian ascetics and followers of Hieracas (3rd century), a native of Leontopolis and a man learned in the scriptures as well as in the science and literature of the day. He interpreted the scriptures in an allegorical fashion, denied the reality of the terrestrial paradise, and maintained that there would be no resurrection of the body. He held that the body was nothing more than a prison from which the soul would be liberated and a resurrection would only mean a new imprisonment for the soul.

HIERAPOLIS

A city in the province of Asia. Among its pagan residents lived a group of first-century Christians in whose behalf Epoaphras "put himself to great effort" (1 Corinthians 16:8). It was located on the northern edge of the Lycus valley of Asia Minor, circa six miles north of Laodicea. Although the apostle Paul apparently never visited Hierapolis, the effects of his long work at Ephesus (from the winter of 52 until after Pentecost in 55) (1 Corinthians 16:8) radiated all "over Asia" (Acts 19:1, 10).

Christianity appears to have reached Hierapolis through the "efforts" of Epoaphras. Tradition also credits the apostles John and Philip with laboring there. While the city lacked political importance, it became prosperous in the peaceful Roman period as a center of devotion to Cybele. Her worship there was enhanced by two natural phenomena, mineral springs and the Plutonium, or so-called "Entrance to Hades," a deep, narrow chasm that entitled deadly fumes.

HIERARCHY, Ecclesiastical

In various Christian churches, a term denoting the bishops of the entire church (the episcopate) or of a particular nation or region. In a more technical sense, it applies to those churches in which the office of bishop is believed to be derived from the uninterrupted succession of bishops from the Apostles.

HIERARCHY, Roman Catholic

This term, as applied to the systematic arrangement of authority within the Catholic church, is used in two ways:
▲ the hierarchy of holy orders: namely, those ordained as bishops, priests, or deacons to carry out the sacramental and pastoral ministry of the church;
▲ the hierarchy of jurisdiction: namely, the pope and the bishops in communion with him to carry out, by divine institution, the teaching and governing office of the Vatican.

HIEROGLYPHICS

An ancient Egyptian style of writing with signs or pictures, so-called from the Greek for "sacred carvings." A myth of origin attributes their invention to the god Thoth. Strictly, hieroglyphics are limited to picture writings on Egyptian temples and monuments, but the term is commonly extended to picture writing in other cultures.

Traces of hieroglyphics are preserved from the end of the fourth millennium, and the most recent example dates to 394. Knowledge of the hieroglyphics decreased as Christianity promoted the use of Greek in Egypt in the second and third centuries.

HIEROGNOSIS

A form of spiritual clairvoyance enabling the recipient to recognize the holiness (or its opposite) of another person, a place, or thing. It is a gift in the same class as the reading of hearts and was manifested in the lives of many saints. Authors differ, however, on whether it invariably is a gift given only to those who are in God's grace.

HIEROMONK

In the Eastern church a monk who has been ordained to the priesthood. According to Eastern practice the majority of monks do not receive holy orders.

HIERON

Sacred place or temple, or the enclosure containing the temple. A wall surrounding the sacred precinct, entered by gateway or propylaeum, often embraced further auxiliary shrines, groves, and treasures, as at Olympia and Delphi.

HIEROPHANTES

In ancient Greece, chief of the Eleusinian cult, the best known of the mystery religions of ancient Greece. His principal job was to chant demonstrations of sacred symbols during the celebration of the mysteries. At the opening of the ceremonies, he proclaimed that all unclean persons must stay away - a rule that he had the right to enforce.

HIEROPHANY

A manifestation of sacred or holy reality, for instance, a sacred stone, plant, or animal. Anything may become an expression of the sacred in a particular context: non-living things, living beings and processes, and human activities and appurtenances.

HIEROS GAMOS

(Greek: sacred marriage) Term referring primarily to the sexual relations of fertility deities in myths and rituals that are widely distributed among cereal agriculturists, especially in the Near East. At least once a year, divine persons (for instance, humans representing the deities), engage in sexual intercourse, which guarantees the fertility of the land, the prosperity of the community, and the continuation of the cosmos.

HIGH CHURCH

A term first used in 17th century England as a descriptive phrase for persons or movements that emphasized the continuity and authority of the Church of England and its sacramental life. As with low church, the phrase has had different connotations during its 2 or 3 centuries of use, sometimes referring to political matters, such as the divine right of kings, and sometimes identifying, very often pejoratively, mere ceremonial usages.

HIGH GOD

A term applied by anthropologists and historians of religion to one type of supreme deity found among many primitive peoples. The adjective "high" is primarily a locative term. The most basic description of a high god is that he is up there, beyond the sky. He is utterly transcendent, removed from the world that he originally created.

HIGH MASS

A term to indicate a form of the former Tridentine Mass in the Roman rite celebrated and sung by one priest accompanied by a chanter, choir, and/or the entire congregation.

HIGH PRIEST

The chief religious functionary in the Temple of Jerusalem, whose unique privilege was to enter the Holy of Holies (inner sanctuary) once a year on Yom Kippur, the Day of Atonement. Since AD 70 there has been no Jewish High Priest, for national sacrifice was permanently interrupted with the destruction of the second Temple.

Apart from the normal priestly vestments, his ceremonial robes consisted of an embroidered coat, miter and a sacred breastplate of four rows of three precious stones, inscribed with the names of the Twelve Tribes of Israel. The office was hereditary, originating with Aaron, elder brother of Moses. The office existed until the destruction of Jerusalem and the Temple by the Romans in 70.

The Bible does not specifically state the age of eligibility for High Priest. While it gives a retirement age of 50 years for Levites, it does not mention any retirement for priests, and its record indicates that the High Priest's was a lifetime appointment (Numbers 8:24-25). Aaron was 83 years old when he went with Moses before Pharaoh. His anointing as High Priest apparently took place in the following year (Exodus 7:7). He was believed to be around 120 years of age at the time of his death. During all that time he served, with no retirement (Numbers 20:28; 33:39). The provision of the cities of refuge takes account of the lifetime tenure of the High Priest, in requiring that the unintentional manslayer remain in the city until the death of the High Priest (Numbers 35:25).

HIJAB

Veil, worn by many Muslim women out of modesty; also a striking symbol of pride in being a Muslim which many younger Muslims, as well as the older generation, are pleased to wear, contrary to popular belief.

HIJR, al-

The title of the 15th sura of the Koran; a place name. Some commentators associate it with the tribe of Thamud, but others with the people of Salih. The sura belongs mainly to the Meccan period and contains 99 verses. It describes among other things the disobedience of Iblis after creation of Adam.

HIJRA, al-

Arabic word for migration; in Islamic religious history, the emigration of the Prophet Mohammed from Mecca to Medina in 622, which became Year 1 of the Muslim lunar calendar. The was one of the great seminal events of Islamic history and paved the way for the conquest of Mecca by Mohammed and the final settlement of Islam in Arabia from whence it would emerge to become a major world religion.

HILARIA

In Roman religion, day of merriment and rejoicing in the Cybele-Attis cult and in the Isis-Osiris cult.

HILARION, Saint

(circa 291-370) Monk and mystic who founded Christian monasticism in Palestine modelled after the Egyptian tradition. He came from non-Christian parents and studied under a grammarian at Alexandria, where he became a Christian. He also came under the influence of the renowned desert ascetic Anthony of Egypt and followed his discipline for two months. He observed the strict ascetical regimen of fasting and chanting the Old Testament psalm prayers, and, like the Egyptian hermits, he wove baskets of rushes to earn his subsistence, possessing only a monk's garb.

HILARY OF ARLES, Saint

(401-449) Bishop of Arles who is often regarded as providing the occasion for extending papal authority in Gaul. He wrote a memorial sermon on Honoratus.

HILARY OF POITIERS, Saint

(315-367) Doctor of the Church who as bishop of Poitiers was a champion of orthodoxy against Arianism (heresy teaching that Christ was not equal to God) during the 4th century and was the first Latin writer to introduce Greek doctrine to Western Christendom.

HILDA, Saint

(614-680) Founder of Strenaneshalch Abbey and one of the foremost abbesses of Anglo-Saxon England.

HILDESHEIMER, Azriel

(1820-1899) Jewish scholar who founded the Berlin Rabbinical Seminary (1973) to promote Neo-Orthodoxy and to counter the growing influence of Reform Judaism.

HILKIAH

In the Old Testament, a Levite gatekeeper of the family of Merari who received this assignment in David's time; a son of Hosiah (1 Chronicles 26:10-12).

The name is also applied to the High Priest in the days of King Josiah; son of Shallum and father of Azariah; apparently a forefather of Ezra the copyist (2 Kings 22:3; 1 Chronicles 6:13; Ezra 7:1). Hilkiah, as High Priest, figured prominently in the restoration of true worship undertaken by Josiah. During the course of the Temple repair work, Hilkiah found the very "book of Jehovah's law by the hand of Moses." What made the find outstanding was most likely the manuscript's being the original book written by Moses. Hilkiah gave it to Shaphan the secretary, who took the manuscript to the king. Upon hearing Shaphan read the book, King Josiah dispatched a delegation headed by High Priest Hilkiah to Huldah the prophetess to inquire of God in his behalf and in behalf of the people (2 Kings 22:3-14; 2 Chronicles 34:14).

HILL, Rowland

(1744-1833) English evangelist and writer; after being denied Anglican priestly orders, he built Surrey Chapel, London (1783), developed an extensive Methodist-like program of religious education, and helped found the Religious Tract Society.

HILLEL

(circa 70 BC - AD 10) Jewish scholar and leader. Born in Babylonia, Hillel came to Palestine to study and soon rose to a position of intellectual leadership, becoming an authority on biblical law and attracting many pupils. Stressing humanitarism, he led the moderate school which, while insising on observance of religious law, made the law more suitable to existing conditions. He was President of the Sanhedrin, the Hebrew high court, for 40 years. He is regarded as one of the great founders of rabbinic Judaism.

HILLEL BEN SAMUEL

(1220-1295) Physician, Talmudic scholar, and philosopher who defended the ideas of the 12th century Jewish philosopher Maimonides during the "year of controversy (1289-1290), when Maimonides work was challenged and attacked.

HINAYANA

Buddhist tradition in ancient India adhering to the more orthodox, conservative schools. The name reflected the Mahayanists" evaluation of their own tradition as a superior method, surpassing the others in universality and compassion; but the name was not accepted by conservative schools as referring to a common tradition.

HINDI

National language of India, spoken by more than 200 million people. Two main branches of Hindi, an Indo-European language, are usually recognized: West and East Hindi. Both have numerous dialects. Hindi is related to Hindustani and was the standard language used by British government officials in the 19th century. India's written language is known as High Hindo, grammatically similar to Urdu, the language of Pakistan, but derived from Sanskrit. Hindi uses the Devanagari alphabet.

HINDUISM

Chief religion of India, embracing all types and classes of the population, from the learned Brahman to the illiterate peasant. In terms of adherents it is the third greatest of the world's religions. The words "Hinduism" and "Brahamism" (the latter used to describe the abstract philosophy of the religion rather than its ceremonies and customs) are Western: in India the word used is dharma, which implies not only religion but law and order, justice and right, duty and accepted custom.

HINDUISM, Buddhism and Jainism

Between circa 800 and 500 BC Hinduism began to change under the impact of two new, rival religions - Buddhism, which preached personal salvation through righteous living, and Jainism, which advocated fanatical self-denial, an ascetic life and the practice of abimsa, reverence for life in all its forms, animal, plant and human. Buddhism took a strong hold in the north of India, Jainism in the south. But Hinduism never lost its grip on the popular mind, in developing more elaborate ceremonies, and gradually discarding the older mythological gods. It absorbed village and tribal gods into a Pantheon dominated by the trio of Brahma (the creator), Vishnu (the preserver) and Shiva (the destroyer).

HINDUISM, Modern developments

Hinduism has to some extent adapted itself successfully to a rapidly changing world. A number of the sects it has given birth to are preoccupied with social problems. Elaborate ceremonial is gradually being rejected in favor of Vedic simplicity. Ahimsa, the reverence for life in all its forms, continues to be widespread and strong; cows in particular are revered as sacred creatures.

The true Hindu, whether Brahman or peasant, pours out a little water each day in the name of the sub-cult because, from earliest times, water has been regarded as a manifestation of the essence of gods. A little bowl of water may be worshiped at any time as a proxy for the god.

Pilgrimages to holy places are still made, and the Brahman is still respected as the "custodian of knowledge."

HINDUISM, Sub-cults

Hinduism has sub-cults, of which those of Shiva, Vishnu, Krishna, Shakti and the Matris are the most important. Shiva, god of nature and reproduction, is both creator of the universe (to the ascetic Brahman) and, more humbly, a god of fertility, whom farmers worship in the symbolic form of a linga, or phallus. Fanatical Shivites once lay on beds of nails as expression of devotion, but such manifestations are rare nowadays. The cult of Vishnu, the god who was reborn 10 times out of pity for human suffering, emphasizes the doctrine of reincarnation. The modern acceptance of democratic ideas and the attempted abolition of the caste system have given this cult a wider appeal than ever before.

The cult of Krishna, which stresses the delights of social life, grew up relatively recently, in the 15th century. The cult of Shaki and the Matris (mother goddesses) was widely publicized, and misunderstood, by Christian missionaries who were appealed by the bloody sacrifices and sexual rites of the worshipers at these shrines, who celebrated in physical union the principle of eternal life renewed in eternal ecstasy.

HINDUISM, Vedas

Hinduism is based on unquestioning reverence for the words of the 3,000 year-old Vedas, which comprise the Rig-Veda (or Hymn Veda) with its 1,068 hymns, the Sama-Veda (or Chant veda) which contains tunes for the hymns, the Yajur-Veda (a collection of prayers) and the Atharva Veda, a priestly compilation of 20 books of magic formulae or incantations (known as mantra) relating to such diverse things as the curing of baldness, the anointing of kings and the overthrowing of rivals. The religion of the Vedas is animistic, being mainly based on the belief that the powers of Nature are divine and should be worshiped as such. They may also be placated and controlled by appropriate sacrifices and ceremonies. The chief god of the Rig-veda is Indra, to whom a quarter of the hymns in that book are directly addressed. He is a warrior, huge and strong, with a tawny beard (and a bulging belly acquired from overeating). Fighting from his chariot, he overcomes all his enemies. The other ancient Vedic gods were Varuna (god of earth), Agni (god of fire) and Surya (god of the sun). These survive, but others have been discarded. All, however, were regarded as kindly, opposed to demons and at war with evil.

HINDU MYSTICISM

Union, or desire for union of the individual self with the divine principle or Reality in the context of the Hindu religion. The forms of Hindu mysticism show great diversity, ranging from the notion of identity with the impersonal principles called Brahman to the intensive devotionalism to a personal God called by a variety of names.

HINDU MYTHOLOGY

The stories of the gods, the myths, and the tales that have played an essential and all-pervading role in the history of Hinduism. Hindu mythology, which has a continuous documented history dating from circa 1400 BC, is rich and varied, ranging from the vague personifications of natural phenomena to an intricate mythical architecture of space and time; it can provide a grand cosmogonic design describing the origin of the universe and man's place in it or a simple story explaining the holiness of a river ford.

HINDU SACRED LITERATURE

The numerous oral traditions and written texts that in the course of their gradual development and composition have become the sources of Hindu religion and the foundations of Indian society.

Because the sacred for Hindus is not only that which bears upon the divine but also that which bears upon man's place in the family and in society and upon his relations with others, Hindu sacred literature includes much that might be considered secular in other religious traditions.

HINNOM, Valley of

In biblical times, possibly called "the low plain of the carcasses and of the fatty aches" at Jeremiah 31:40. The individual after whom the valley may have been named is unknown, as is also the meaning of the name Hinnom. The valley is located on the west and south-west of Jerusalem and runs south from the vicinity of the modern Jaffa Gate, turns sharply east at the southwestern corner of the city and runs along the south to meet the Tyrepean and Kidron valleys at a point near the south-eastern corner of the city.

The valley of Hinnom formed a part of the boundary between the tribes of Judah and Benjamin, Judah's territory being to the south, placing Jerusalem in Benjamin's territory, as outlined at Joshua 15:1-8. The valley is now known as the Wadi er-Rababi.

HIPPOLYTUS, Canons of Saint

A collection of 38 canons, preserved in an Arabic translation. These canons are neither the authentic work of St. Hippolytus nor the oldest church order but are a later adaptation of the *Apostolic Tradition* of St. Hippolytus. The unknown author of the canons generally follows the order of his source and treats the same subjects: ordination, catechumenate, baptism, prayer, and discipline of the Christian community.

HIPPOLYTUS OF ROME, Saint

(170-235) Controversial theologian, martyr and first antipope (218-235), who was the first Roman priest to produce a theologico-philosophical work on dogma.

HIRAM

Also called Huram, Ahiram. Phoenician king of Tyre (reigned 970-936 BC) who appears in the Bible as an ally of the Israelite kings David and Solomon. He maintained friendly relations with Israel, supplying Solomon with men and materials for the construction of the Temple at Jerusalem and cooperating with him in Mediterranean and Red Sea voyages. Solomon gave him tribute and Galilean territory in return.

HIRAM-ABI

An appellation applied to the "skillful man" whom the king of Tyre sent to make the furnishings of Solomon's Temple. It evidently indicated that Hiram was "father" in the sense of being a "master workman" (2 Chronicles 2:13).

HIRAM-ABIV

A term used in reference to the "skilled craftsmen" whom the king of Tyre sent to make the furnishings of Solomon's temple. It evidently indicated that Hiram was "father" in the sense of being a "master workman" (2 Chronicles 4:16).

HIRATA ATSUTANE

(1776-1843) Thinker, and leader of the Revival Shinto school, which tried to free native Shinto from Buddhist and Confucian influences. His thought, stressing the divine nature of the emperor, exerted a powerful influence on royalists who fought for the restoration of imperial rule during the second half of the 19th century in Japan.

HIRSCH, Samson Raphael

(1808-1888) Major Jewish religious thinker, founder of Trennungs-orthodoxie (separatist orthodoxy), or Neo-Orthodoxy, a theological system that helped make Orthodox Judaism viable in Germany.

HIRSCH, Samuel

(1815-1889) Religious philosopher, rabbi, and a leading advocate of radical Reform Judaism. He was among the first to propose holding Jewish services on Sunday.

HISAB, al-

In Islam, term meaning literally reckoning. The Day of Judgement is called in Arabic "The Day of Reckoning" (Yawm al-Hisab). The Koran gives a considerable amount of detail about the Day of Judgement; in particular two types of judgement, with scales and with books, are mentioned.

HISTORICITY

In its common use by exegetes, the historical validity of the words and events in the New Testament, especially regarding the person of Jesus Christ. The New Testament itself verifies Christianity as a historical religion. Luke began his gospel by explaining that, "after carefully going over the whole story from the beginning," he would "write an ordered account," in order to show "how well founded the teaching is that you have received" (Luke 1:2-4).

John said he was writing of events "that we have heard, that we have seen with our eyes; that we have watched and touched with our hands " (1 John 1:1).

Roman Catholicism recognizes the unique character of New Testament history, yet one that squares with empirical observation. The sacred authors selected some things in preference to others from the many words and events which were handed on by word of mouth or in writing; they reduced certain facts to a synthesis.

HITO-GAMI

A way of distinguishing certain characteristics of Japanese religion by focussing on the close relationship between a deity and his transmitter, such as a seer or a medicine man.

HITO-NO-MICHI

A Japanese religious sect founded by Miki Tokuharu (1871-1938). He taught that the sufferings of his followers could be transferred to him by divine meditation and that he would vicariously endure their troubles.

HITTITE

Member of an ancient Indo-European people who appeared in Anatolia at the beginning of the 2nd millennium BC; by 1340 BC they had become one of the dominant powers of the Near East. They were among the inhabitants of Canaan but were not driven out (1 Sam. 26:6).

Abraham had some dealings with the Hittites, who resided in Canaan prior to his moving there in circa 1940 BC. When his wife Sarah died, he bargained with Ephroin the son of Zohar the Hittite at the gate of the city of Hebron, for the cave of Machpelah, which was in Ephron's field. Ephron refused to sell the cave by itself (Genesis 23:1-10). Before this time God had promised to give to Abraham's seen the land of Canaan, inhabited by nations one of which was the Hittite nation. However, God told Abraham that "the error of the Amorites (a term often used generally for the nations in Canaan) has not yet come to completion" (Genesis 15:16). Therefore Abraham rejected the Hittite ownership of the land (Genesis 15:18-21).

HIVITES

In the Old Testament, a people descended from Canaan the son of Ham (Genesis 10:5, 15, 17; 1 Chronicles 1:13-15). Hivites inhabited the city of Shechem in the days of the patriarch Jacob. The sons of Jacob, led by Simeon and Levi, killed every male and plundered the city because Sechem the son of Hamor the chieftain had defiled their sister Dinah (Genesis 34:1-19).

When Israel entered the Promised Land the Hivites constituted one of the seven Canaanite nations that God promised to drive out before them (Exodus 3:8, 17; 33:2; 34:11). These nations were said to be more populous and mighty than Israel (Deuteronomy 7:1). Moses commanded the Israelites to devote them to destruction, leaving none alive when capturing their cities, because of their detestable practices and their pagan gods. Otherwise they would prove to be a snare and would cause Israel to come into God's disfavor (Leviticus 18:27-18; Deuteronomy 18:9-13).

HIWI AL-BALKHI

(late 9th century) Jewish Bible scholar, who wrote a work containing 200 queries on the Bible. Although the book itself is lost, quotations show its author to have been a controversial freethinker who attempted to explain biblical miracles naturally and who detected later additions in biblical texts.

HIZB

Arabic word with a number of specific meanings. It may designate a prayer of particular efficacy. Perhaps the most famous hizb of all is the "Prayer (or Litany) of the Sea", often sung during a Sufi hadra. The word hizb was also used in another sense to mean a 60th part of the Koran.

HIZKIAH

In the Old Testament, one of the three sons of Neariah, a descendant of King Solomon (1 Chronicles 3:10, 23).

HOBAB

In Judaism, Moses' brother-in-law; son of Reuel (Jethro) and a Midianite of the tribe of Kenites (Numbers 10:29; Exodus 3:1; Judges 1:16). When the time came for the Israelites to move from the region of Mount Sinai toward the Promised Land, Moses requested that Hobab accompany them so as to serve as "eyes" or as a scout for the nation because of his familiarity with the area. Although Hobab declined at first, apparently he did accompany the Israelites, for his descendants, the Kenites, took up dwelling in the wilderness of Judah to the south of Arad and are mentioned as still living in that area in the time of Saul and David (Numbers 10:29-32; Judges 1:16; 1 Samuel 15:6).

HOBAH

In the Old Testament, a site north of Damascus to which Abraham pursued the defeated armies under Chedorlaomer (Genesis 14:13-17). The biblical location is associated by certain scholars with Hoba, a spring on the road between Palmyra and Damascus, where at least the ancient name appears to be preserved. Hoba, like other large springs near the desert, may have once had a village standing nearby.

HOBART, John Henry

(1775-1830) Educator, author, and bishop of the Protestant Episcopal Church whose emphasis upon the discipline of orthodoxy during the inchoate post-Revolutionary period in American history helped Anglicanism to expand in a new nation without compromising its traditions.

HOD

According to biblical tradition, son of Zophah of the tribe of Asher. Hod was probably the head over one of the larger divisions of the army having other chieftains under him (1 Chronicles 7:36-37).

HODAVIAH

In Judaism, a Levite family head, seventy-four of whose "sons" (descendants) returned from Babylon in 537 BC and some of whom, if not all, served as supervisors in connection with the rebuilding of the Temple (Ezra 2:1-2; 3:9).

HODEVAH

Forefather of certain Levites among those returning from Babylonian exile (Nehemiah 7:6-7).

HODGE, Charles

(1797-1878) Conservative biblical scholar and a leader of the "Princeton School" of Reformed, or Calvinist, theology. He stressed the verbal infallibility of the Bible.

HODIAH

In the Old Testament, a Levite who assisted Ezra in explaining the law of God to the congregation of Israel assembled before the Water Gate at the public square of Jerusalem, and evidently one of those who called upon the sons of Israel to bless God and His glorious name and then reviewed God's dealings with the people (Nehemiah 8:1-7).

HOFBAUER, Saint Clement Mary

(1751-1820) Patron saint of Vienna. He established a monastery and sought government approbation for Redemptorist houses.

HOFMEISTER, Sebastian

(1476-1533) Swiss religious reformer who was a prominent figure in the debates of the early Reformation.

HOGLAH

In the Old Testament. the third listed of Zelophehad's five daughters. Since her father had no sons, his inheritance was divided among the five daughters with the stipulation that they marry inside their own tribe of Manasseh, in order "that their inheritance might continue together with the tribe of the family of the father" and "not circulate from one tribe to another" (Numbers 36:1-12; Joshua 17:3-4).

HOHAM

In biblical times, king of Hebron; one of the five kings who went up to war against Gibeon because it had made peace with Joshua and the Israelites. The five kings were defeated when Joshua came to the aid of the Gibeonites. After being put to death, they were hung upon stakes until the evening and were thereafter thrown into a cave (Joshua 10:1-27).

HOL HA-MO'ED

Jewish semi-holidays, the four days following the first two days of Sukkot. The Hallel prayers are recited at the morning service, and the procession with etrog and lulav takes place. When one of the days of Hol Ha-Mo'ed falls on the Sabbath, the book of Kohelet, or Ecclesiastes, is read before the portion of the Torah.

HOLDHEIM, Samuel

(1806-1860) Rabbi who was a founder and leader of Reform Judaism. His theological positions, sometimes radical even within the Reform movement, offer an extreme example of the movement's attempt to keep Judaism viable in modern times.

HOLINESS

Literally: setting apart. It is a general term to indicate separation from all that is sinful, impure or imperfect. In Roman Catholicism, holiness is regarded as a state of spiritual progress that is marked by an ever more intimate union with Christ. All Christians are called toward this fullness of Christian life.

HOLINESS, Code of

A collection of secular, ritualistic, moral, and festival regulations in the Old Testament Book of Leviticus, chapter 17-26. The division, designated "H" in scholarly circles, was so named by a German biblical scholar, A. Klostermann, in 1877, because of its concern for sanctity ("Sanctify yourself and be holy").

HOLINESS, Law of

Name given to chapters 17-26 of Leviticus, which are characterized by the frequent exhortation, "Be holy, for I, Yahweh your God, am holy." Purportedly" the laws, customs and rules the Lord laid down between himself and the sons of Israel on Mount Sinai through the meditation of Moses" (Leviticus 26:46), these chapters probably attained their present form during the Exile.

HOLINESS CHURCHES

A group of Protestant churches that arose in the 19th century in the United States and that stress a doctrine of sanctification centering on a post-conversion experience, enabling the believer to live a sinless, perfect, holy Christian life.

HOLINESS METHODISTS

Methodist bodies or denominations that were originally formed or that broke away from other Methodist bodies because of their belief that the denominations in general, and the Methodist denominations in particular, were not placing sufficient stress in the doctrinal emphasis on personal holiness.

HOLINESS MOVEMENT

A post-Civil War (USA) emphasis on entire sanctification that led to the emergence of the Holiness Churches. John Wesley's doctrine of Christian perfection was the immediate inspiration of the teaching elaborated during the course of the Holiness Movement.

HOLOCAUST DAY

Jewish memorial day. The 27th day of Nissan was set aside in 1951 as a day of mourning for the Holocaust victims. The occasion also serves as a reminder of the potential for similar evils to come. Throughout Israel on this day, sirens blast to begin a period of respectful silence. It is an effective symbol, with traffic stopping, drivers and passengers getting out of their vehicles to stand to attention.

HOLON

In the Old Testament, a city in the mountainous region of Judah assigned to the priestly Kohathites (Joshua 15:21; 21:9-19); apparently called Hilen at 1 Chronicles 8:58. Holon of Judah is tentatively identified with Khirbet 'Alin, circa ten miles north-north-west of Hebron.

HOLY ALLIANCE

A 19th century European collective security arrangement created in the wake of the upheavals of the French Revolution and Napoleonic wars. The Alliance was formed when Czar Alexander I of Russia, Francis II, Emperor of Austria and King Frederick William of Prussia signed an Agreement at Paris on September 26, 1815. The original signatories were later joined by all the other European sovereigns, except those of Britain and Turkey, and the pope.

The Alliance's avowed aim was to unite the respective governments to conduct their relations with one another on Christian principles.

HOLY COMMUNION

A term used by many churches for the celebration of the Eucharist, or Lord's Supper. It is often called simply communion or the communion service. Although disagreements about the meaning of the rite have been numerous and deep among Christians, they generally agree that one of its meanings is the unity that people of diverse backgrounds have through Christ; they therefore regard the existence of separate churches not in intercommunion as an anomaly to be overcome.

HOLY CONTRIBUTION

In the Old Testament, a portion of land in Ezekiel's vision of the division of the Promised Land. Each of the 12 tribes with the exception of Levi was given an allotment running east and west across the land. South of the portion for Judah, which was the seventh allotment from the northern extremity, was the "holy contribution" (Ezekiel 48:1-8). The northern border os this strip ran along the southern border of Judah's allotment; it was bounded on the south by Benjamin's portion, which was the fifth allotment from the southern extremity. The holy contribution was 25,000 cubits (6.9 miles) wide from north to south. It was to be given by the people for governmental use.

HOLY DAYS OF OBLIGATION

In the Roman Catholic Church, religious feast days on which Catholics must attend mass and refrain from unnecessary work. Although all Sundays are sanctified in this way, the term holy days usually refers to other feasts that must be observed in the same manner as Sunday.

According to the Code of Canon Law, Sunday is the day on which the paschal mystery is celebrated in light of the apostolic tradition and is to be observed as the foremost holy day of obligation in the universal church. Also to be observed are:

▲ the day of the Nativity of Our Lord Jesus Christ;
▲ the Epiphany;
▲ The Ascension and the Most Holy Body and Blood of Christ;
▲ Holy Mary Mother of God and her Immaculate Conception and Assumption;
▲ St. Joseph;
▲ the apostles Sts. Peter and Paul, and finally
▲ All Saints (Canon 1246).

The Code than goes on to note this practical principle: "However, the conference of bishops can abolish certain holy days of obligation or transfer them to a Sunday with prior approval of the Apostolic see."

The obligation of Catholics on these days is as follows: "On Sundays and other holy days of obligation the faithful are bound to participate in the Mass; they are also to abstain from those labors and business concerns which impede the worship to be rendered to God, the joy which is proper to the Lord's Day, or the relaxation of mind and body" (Canon 1247).

HOLY FACE

The image of Christ which, according to various medieval legends, was impressed on a linen cloth or veil belonging to St. Veronica. Such a cloth received great devotion in the Middle Ages; in Rome from as early as the 10th century, where one such cloth, now almost completely faded, is preserved as a relic at St. Peter's basilica.

HOLY FAMILY

A subject used by many artists to portray Jesus, Mary and Joseph. Byzantine mosaics portray various events in the lives of the family, medieval church panels show the family together with saints and angels, and Renaissance painters and sculptors, including Michelangelo, produced many works reflecting their symbolic meaning. Raphael and Titian were among the best-known artists who used the Holy Family as themes for their work.

HOLY GHOST FATHERS

A Roman Catholic society of men founded in 1703 at Paris by Claude Poullart des Places. Originally intended only for the training of seminarians, the congregation gradually began to take an active part in missionary work. The congregation pioneered in the resumption of African missions in the 19th century.

HOLY GRAIL

A legendary object, thought to be a much sought after chalice, which has been the subject of numerous literary works since the 12th century. Exactly what it was, if indeed it existed, has fired the imagination of writers, poets and archaeologists. It is known that the word graal, meaning wide-mouthed cup, originated in France in the 12th century.

A religious significance is given to the Holy Grail by Robert de Borron, who wrote a history of it in the late 12th century. He linked it with an early Christian story which identifies the Grail as the vessel from which Jesus drank during the Last Supper, and was used by Joseph of Arimathea to catch the last drops of blood as he died on the cross.

HOLY GROUND RELIGION

Apache millennial religious movement founded by Silas John Edwards in 1921.

HOLY INDIFFERENCE

A quality in a person's love for God above all that excludes preference for any person, object, or condition of life. The possibility of such an attitude is implicit in the totality that measures charity and so the determination at the commandment of charity must be fulfilled by loving nothing to the exclusion of God, but may be more fully fulfilled by loving nothing except in direct relation to the love of God.

HOLY INNOCENTS, Feast of the

Festival celebrated in the Christian churches in the West on December 28 and in the Eastern churches on December 29, commemorating the massacre of the children by King Herod in his attempt to kill the infant Jesus (Matthew 2:16-18).

HOLY LANCE

A relic discovered in June 1098 during the First Crusade by Christian crusaders at Antioch, in Syria. It was said to be the lance that pierced the side of Christ at the crucifixion.

HOLY OF HOLIES

Most sacred part of the Israelite sanctuary. In the desert tabernacle of Moses, it was the innermost part, containing the tablets of the covenant. When the Temple of Jerusalem was built, it was again the innermost part. In the second Temple, the Holy of Holies was empty, as the sacred tablets had been lost.

In later Judaism this inner sanctum was entered only once a year by the High Priest on the Day of Atonement (Leviticus 16:15-16), on which occasion alone, of all Jews, he was allowed to pronounce the sacred name of Yahweh in his prayer for forgiveness of sins. In the Letter to Hebrews this ritual became a symbol of Jesus' entering once for all time into heaven with the atoning value of his own sacrifice for the sins of all men (Hebrews 9:11-18).

HOLY ORDERS

The steps or grades of ordained members of the clergy of the Roman Catholic, Eastern and Anglican churches. The church established the three major orders of priest, deacon and subdeacon, and the minor orders of porter, lector, exorcist and acolyte. The minor orders, including the subdiaconate, are not sacramental but are preliminary steps towards the priesthood. In most churches, a candidate for holy orders must be of a specified age and education and have been baptized. In the offices above deacon, such as priest and bishop, all must be ordained and consecrated.

In the Roman Catholic Church, the Holy Orders is one of the seven sacraments of the church. It is defined thus in the Code of Canon Law: "By divine institution some among the Christian faithful are constituted sacred ministers through the sacrament of orders by means of the indelible character with which they are marked; accordingly they are consecrated and deputed to shepherd the people of God, each in accord with his own grade of orders, by fulfilling in the person of Christ the Head the functions of teaching, sanctifying and governing" (Canon 1008).

HOLY PLACE

A term applied in the Bible in several ways.

(1) In general, it could be applied to the camp of Israel, the people of God, and to Jerusalem and the holy places within it;
(2) the sanctuary including the courtyard and the entire tent of meeting of the later Temple;
(3) only the two compartments of the tabernacle or Temple building itself;
(4) the first interior room of the tabernacle, as distinguished from the most holy compartment.

HOLY PLACES

The sites in Palestine and its environs connected with the life of Christ. Several are associated with Christ's Passion and Resurrection:
▲ the Upper Room;
▲ the Garden of Gethsemane;
▲ the Way of the Cross;

- ▲ Calvary;
- ▲ the Holy Sepulcher;
- ▲ site of the Ascension.
  Others are linked with the public life of Christ:
- ▲ the Jordan River;
- ▲ Sea of Galilee;
- ▲ the site of Transfiguration;
- ▲ the Temple of Jerusalem.
  The care and the custody of most of the holy places has been exercised by the Friars Minor since the 13th century, although the Eastern Orthodox care for some.

HOLY ROLLERS

A derogatory nickname for religious groups whose meetings are characterized by high emotionalism, manifested by physical agitation. In particular, the name has been attached by Pentecostal groups.

HOLY ROMAN EMPIRE

A traditional European institution dating from the 8th century until 1806. The Roman imperial title, which had lapsed in western Europe in the 5th century, was revived in 800 by Pope Leo III and conferred on Charlemagne, king of the Franks. After another lapse when the Carolingian line died out, the title was borne by successive dynasties of German kings almost continuously from the mid-10th century until its abolition.

HOLY SEE

A term used to designate the pope as head of the universal church and all those associated with him who assist in its administration. Originally the word see was applied to the five great centers of Antioch, Alexandria, Jerusalem, Constantinople, and Rome. The last name was regarded as the primary see of Christianity. Though in theory and in fact, with several notable exceptions, the pope and curia reside in Rome, it is not necessary that they do so. Wherever the pope and his officials are, technically is the Holy See.

HOLY SEPULCHRE

(officially, Church of the Resurrection), a church in Jerusalem located on which is traditionally believed to be the site of the tomb of Jesus. The first church, built by Constantine the Great circa 336 was destroyed by the Persians in 614, rebuilt, again destroyed in 1009 and restored by the crusaders in the 12th century. The present edifice was rebuilt in 1810.

HOLY SOUL

According to Roman Catholic teaching, those who depart this life in the grace of God but who are not yet free from all imperfection are called holy souls. In a state of purgatory, they make expiation for the temporal punishment due to venial and mortal sins that have already been forgiven and, probably, for unforgiven venial sins. In this they can be helped by the intercession of the faithful.

HOLY SPIRIT

The third Person of the Trinity, proceeding from the Father and the Son (Matthew 28:19). In the Old Testament shows the Spirit as God in action (Genesis 1:2), both in creation and in man. The Spirit, bringing wisdom and holiness, was bestowed especially on the prophets (Isaiah 61:1), and was promised to dwell in the Messiah. The New Testament shows the Holy Spirit as empowering Jesus Christ throughout his life, and at Pentecost descending on the Apostles, filling them with power. By the title "Paraclete" (Greek parakletos) the Holy Spirit is described as a comforter or advocate (John 14:26).

HOLY TRINITY

In Roman Catholicism, the most sublime and central doctrine of the Christian faith, namely, that there are three persons - Father, Son, Holy Spirit - in one God. This doctrine is indicated in the scriptures (see for example, Matthew 28:18-20) and expressed in all of the Christian Creeds. The Catholic Church celebrates the feast of the Holy Trinity on the Sunday after Pentecost.

HOLY WATER

In the Roman Catholic, Greek Orthodox and Episcopal churches, water that has been blessed by a priest or minister and symbolizes the washing away of sins. Since biblical times water, as a symbol of God's pure spirit, has been used for sanctifying and cleansing. Holy water is used in many sacraments in the church. Probably the most widely known is baptism, and the blessing of devotional articles, churches and houses.

HOLY WEEK

Final week of Lent, just before Easter Sunday. It is the yearly focal point of church solemnity in preparation for the celebration of Christ's resurrection. Beginning with Palm Sunday, each day is intended to commemorate the most important events in the life of Christ; his triumphal entry into Jerusalem, Judas' betrayal, the Last Supper and the crucifixion. The events are marked by special services in all Roman Catholic, Anglican, Eastern Orthodox and some Protestant churches.

HOLY YEAR

In the Roman Catholic Church it is held once every 25 years. It is for the faithful to make special pilgrimages to Rome and other designated places to pray for the pope's hopes for the church. The ceremony begins when the pope opens the holy door of St. Peter's on Christmas Eve, and ends 12 months later, when the special door is bricked up. The custom began in 1300, and at that time it was decreed that Holy Year would be held every 100 years. Since then is has been held every 25 years, so that Catholics can make the pilgrimage once in their lifetime.

HOMA

In Hindu worship, a libation made with ghee (clarified butter) and poured into the sacred fire as an offering to the gods. A sacrifice so made is said to be carried to heaven by the smoke of the sacred fire. Homa offerings were a characteristic part of Vedic sacrifice in ancient India and continue to be a common feature of Hindu worship today.

HOMILY

In Roman Catholicism, an integral part of the Mass; it is an instruction or sermon preached after the readings from scripture; its purpose is to explain the Word of God and also to make application of that word to the lives of people today.

The term, in its original sense, meant familiar conversation, applied in early Christianity to the explanation of sacred scripture preached at liturgical services. Jews had observed a similar practice in the synagogue, after reading the sacred writings. Jesus himself is reported as having done this in the synagogue of Nazareth (Luke 4:16-20), and the Apostles adopted the custom at the gatherings for the breaking of the bread (Acts 2:42).

HOMOEANS

In the Trinitarian controversies of the 4th century Christian church, the followers of Acacius, bishop of Caesarea. They taught a form of Arianism that asserted that the Son was distinct from, but like (homoios), the Father, as opposed to the Nicene Creed, which started that the Son is of one substance (homoousios) with the Father.

HOMOOUSIOS

(Greek: of one substance) A nonscriptural word used in a technical, theological sense at the Council of Nicaea (325) to express the equality of God the Son with God the Father.

HOMUNCIONITAE

Those teaching that it is the body, not the soul, that makes man the image of God. In his attempt to match a list of heresies to a list of heresiarchs Filaster probably invented a sect professing such a teaching.

HONORIUS I

(died 638) Pope from 625 to 638. A disciple of St. Gregory the Great, Honorius I was an able administrator and fostered the development of the Church in England and Ireland. In 681, the third Council of Constantinople condemned Honorius as a heretic because he had not opposed Monothelitism.

HONORIUS II

(Died 1072) Antipope from 1061 to 1072. He opposed church reform and claimed the papacy against Alexander II, the reform candidate. He installed himself in Rome but was shortly forced to abandon the throne and lived in obscurity for the rest of his life.

HONORIUS III

(died 1227) Pope from 1216 to 1227. Successor to Innocent III, he continued that pope's peaceful and inspiring reign, revitalizing church life. He recognized the Dominicans, Franciscans and Carmelites and helped secure the crown for Henry III of England.

HONORIUS IV

(circa 1210-1287) Pope from 1285 to 1287. Grandnephew of Honorius III, he was elected Pope at an advanced age and reigned only two years. He intervened in the dispute over Sicily against Aragon and promoted the study of oriental languages in hopes of unity with the Eastern church.

HONOS

Ancient Roman deified abstraction of honor, particularly as a military virtue. The earliest shrine of this deity in Rome was not earlier than the 3rd century BC and was located just outside the Colline gate.

HOPE

In Christian thought, one of the three "theological virtues," the others being faith and charity (love). It is distinct from the latter two because it is directed exclusively toward the future, as fervent desire and confident expectation. According to St. Augustine, "hope deals only with good things, and only with those which lie in the future, and which pertain to the man who cherishes the hope." When hope has attained its object, it ceases to be hope and becomes possession.

HOPE OF SALVATION

The theological virtue of hope insofar as it is ordered to man's trusting expectation of final deliverance from the powers of evil. In the Old Testament, this notion underwent a gradual development. At the time of the Judges, Israel's hope was rooted in Yahweh as the one who would continue to give his people military victories over their enemies (Judges 15:18).

Among the pre-exilic prophets, however, a longing for a salvation greater that political security emerged. These Prophets condemned the nation's confidence in their temporal kings, and warned that a day of wrath was approaching when only a remnant, the poor and humble servants of the Lord, would be saved from destruction (Isaiah 2:6-21; Zephaniah 1:14-18).

The post-exilic prophets expanded this vision even further; the fact that some exiles did return to Jerusalem is clear evidence that Yahweh is still the savior of the people. Through this pious remnant, the Lord's dominion will be exercised over all the world (Isaiah 45:22) - a time of justice and joy will dawn upon the earth.

The New Testament brings this hope for salvation to its ultimate conclusion in Jesus. The kingdom of God that Jesus proclaimed is in the future, but it is a future that breaks into the present because of Jesus' actions. He comes to bring deliverance from sin and death (Matthew 8:17, Luke 7:11-17), and his resurrection is the pledge that this salvation is granted to all who believe in him (Acts 2:37-41).

HOPHNI

In the Old Testament, one of High Priest Eli's sons. Hophni and his brother Phinehas were "good-for-nothing men," guilty of sacrilegious conduct and gross immorality (1 Samuel 1:3; 2:12-17). Because of this unfaithfulness while serving as priest at God's sanctuary in the 12th century BC, God judged Hophni worthy of death, which befell him at the time the Philistines captured the sacred ark (1 Samuel 2:34; 4:4.-17).

HOPHRA

In biblical times, king of Egypt in the time of Zedekiah king of Judah and Nebuchadnezzar king of Babylon. It is believed to be Pharaoh Hophra with whom Zedekiah formed an alliance for protection against Nebuchadnezzar, contrary to the commands that God had given years beforehand through isaiah the prophet, warning Israel not to look to Egypt for help (Isaiah 30:1-5; 31:1-3). Nebuchadnezzar came up to Jerusalem in 609 BC, but lifted the siege temporarily because of news that a military force was coming out of Egypt. The Egyptians disappointed Zedekiah, being forced to withdraw, and the Babylonians returned to destroy the city (Jeremiah 37:5-10).

HOPKINS, Samuel

(1721-1803) Theologian and writer who was one of the first Congregationalists to oppose slavery and who shared a mutually influential association with Jonathan Edwards, the outstanding Puritan theologian of the 18th century.

Hopkin's belief in the need and the desirability of social service is implicit in a number of his works. His system, which became popular as "Hopkinsianism," reflected many of Edward's views on the relation of God to man.

HOR

The mountain near Moserah on the border of Edom where Aaron died shortly before Israel's entry into the Promised Land. With the assembly of Israel watching, Aaron, Moses and Aaron's son Eleazar ascended Mount Hor. On the mountaintop Moses removed Aaron's priestly garments and clothed Eleazar with them. After this, Aaron died, and Moses and Eleazar probably buried him there (Numbers 20:22-29; Deuteronomy 32:50).

HORAE

In Greek and Roman mythology, the Seasons. Traditionally they were the children of Zeus, the king of the gods, and Themis, a Titaness, and their names - Eunomia (Good Order), Dike(Justice), Eirene (Peace) indicate the extension of their functions from nature to the events of human life.

HORAM

In the Old Testament, one of the 31 kings defeated by the Israelites under the leadership of Joshua during the conquest of the Promised Land. Horam and all his host were killed when they came to the aid of Lachish at the time of Joshua's campaign against that city (Joshua 10:33; 12:7-24).

HORESH

In the Old Testament, a site in the wilderness of Ziph where David hid from Saul. Here also Jonathan acknowledged David as the next king of Israel and the two men "concluded a covenant" of mutual support (1 Samuel 23:15-19). Horesh is usually identified with modern-day Khirbet Khoreisa, circa 5_ mile south-south-east of Hebron.

HORITE

In the Old Testament, a people inhabiting the mountains of Seir in patriarchal times. They are called in the Bible "the sons of Seir the Horite" (Genesis 36:20-30). The Edomites "proceeded to dispossess them and to annihilate them from before them and to dwell in their place" (Deuteronomy 2:12-22).

HORMAH

In the Old Testament, most probably a city in the southern part of the territory of Judah (1 Chronicles 4:30).

Following the return of the 12 Israelite spies to Kadesh (Numbers 13:26), the

Israelites at first refused to attempt an invasion of Canaan. Then, following God's condemnation of their rebellious attitude and lack of faith, they decided to attempt it contrary to His instructions. They "got up early in the morning" to go up to the place that God mentioned. The record speaks of their endeavoring to "go up to the top of the mountain" (Numbers 14:40). However, their statement about going up "the place that Jehovah mentioned" may indicate the "mountainous region of the Amorites" referred to by Moses in his restatement of the events, rather than a particular mountain (Deuteronomy 1:19-21; 41-43). The record does not indicate how far they traveled, nor does it specifically indicate whether the actions described took place during one day or not; but the text seems to indicate events occurring within a relatively short space of time.

Whatever was the case, the record shows that they were met by the Amalekites and Canaanites (at Deuteronomy 1:44, "Amorites," a term used to refer to the people of Canaan), and these defeated the Israelites, scattering them "as far as Hormah" (Numbers 14:45). The account in Deuteronomy 1:44 says they were scattered "in Seir as far as Hormah." Seir was the territory of the Edomites, and their dominion then seems to have extended west of Wadi Arabah into the Negeb region (Joshua 11:17). Following this defeat, the Israelites returned to Kadesh (1:45-46).

HORMISDAS, Saint

(451-523) Pope from 514 to 523, who resolved the Acacian Schism (484-519), which was the first official break between the Holy see and the East. His great achievement was to reunite the Eastern and Western churches, separated since the excommunication of Patriarch Acacius of Constantinople (484).

HORN

Any of several wind instruments sounded by vibration of the player's tensed lips against a mouthpiece and primarily derived from animal horns blown at the truncated narrow end.

HORNS OF THE ALTAR

The most sacred parts of the altars of holocaust (Exodus 27:2; Exodus 38:2) and of incense (Exodus 30:2, Exodus 37:25). They extend the four top corners. The blood of victims was rubbed on then in rites of expiation (Leviticus 4), and a fugitive could gain asylum by grasping the horn of the altar (1 Kings 2:28). The altar itself was a symbol of Yahweh's presence; the horn a symbol of power and strength.

HOROLOGION

A liturgical term used in the Orthodox Church to signify a Byzantine liturgical book that contains the ordinaries for the canonical Hours, together with a supplement that includes votive canons and hymns and various prayers, and an appendix with rules for the computation of the liturgical calendar and a paschal table.

HORONAIM

In the Old Testament, a place in Moab included among those against which God's judgment was directed (Isaiah 15:1-5; Jeremiah 48:1-5). Its exact location is uncertain. However, the possible meaning of its name ("two caves, holes") has led some geographers to identify Horonaim tentatively with el-Arak ("cave"), situated more than 1,000 feet below the level of the Moabite plateau and some eight miles east of the southern end of the Dead Sea.

HORONITE

In the Old Testament, a designation applied to Sanballat, one of the men opposing the work of nehemiah (Nehemiah 2:10). Some scholars think that Sanballat may have been from the Moabite city of Horonaim (Isaiah 15:5; Jeremiah 48:3) and, in support of this, call attention to his being mentioned with Tobiah the Ammonite and Geshem the Arabian. But the view generally favored is that "Horonite" probably means a native or inhabitant of Beth-horon. Both Upper and Lower Beth-horon were located in territory originally assigned to Ephraim (Joshua 16:1-5).

HORST, Fenton

(1828-1829). British New Testament scholar and authority on early Christianity, who produced with Bruce Foss Westcott, in a lifelong project, one of the principal critical editions of the Greek New Testament.

HOSAH

In the Old Testament, a Mearite gatekeeper for the tent in which the ark of the covenant was put by David (1 Chronicles 16:1; 37-38).

HOSANNA

In modern speech and liturgical usage, a cry of praise to God. It has acquired this meaning through the assumption, perhaps correct, that it was so meant by the multitude who hailed Jesus on Palm Sunday.

HOSEA

Hebrew prophet and writer of the Book of Hosea; identified merely as the son of Beeri. He served as God's prophet during the reigns of Kings Uzziah, Jotham, Ahaz and Hezekiah of Judah and Jeroboam II of Israel, in the late ninth century and the first part of the eighth century BC. Prophets of the same period included Amos, Isaiah and Micah (Isaiah 1:1; Micah 1:1).

HOSEA, Book of

The first of the Old Testament minor prophets. Hosea began his prophetic activity during the reign of Jeroboam II (787-747 BC). His prophetic announcements indicate that he was active until near the fall of the northern kingdom of Israel, the scene of his entire ministry. The book compares God's abiding love for idolatrous Israel to Hosea's love for his prostitute wife, whom he divorced but remarried. He compared the pagan worship of many Israelites to the sinning of a wayward wife. Just as he said that God continued to love Israel despite its sinning, so Hosea, though hurt, continued to accept his unfaithful wife.

HOSHAIAH

In the Old testament, father of Jezaniah, who was a contemporary of prophet Jeremiah (Jeremiah 42:1-2).

HOSHANAH RABBA

Jewish phrase meaning great help. They mark the seventh day of Sukkot (festival of tabernacles). It is the day when the palm fronds and the willow and myrtle will be given to the children. They will make rings and bracelets, bows and tassels out of the palm fronds.

But more important to the children than the charms is the midnight of Hoshanah Rabba, for exactly at midnight, it is said, the skies open, and anyone who makes a wish exactly at that moment when the skies open will have the wish come true. During the seven days of Sukkot, after the morning prayer, special prayers called Hoshanot are recited. On Hodhanah Rabba, the Hoshanot are much longer. Seven times around the synagogue the Jews march, varying lulav and etrog. Each person holds a little bunch of willows called Hoshanot, and at the close of the service, these willows are beaten on the benches until all or most of the leaves have fallen off. Symbolically, one tries to rid himself of all his sins.

HOSHEA

In the Old Testament (2 Kings 15:30) son of Elah and last king of Israel. He became king through a conspiracy in which his predecessor, Pekah, was killed. The Assyrian king Tiglath-pileser III claimed that he made Hoshea king, and Hoshea paid an annual tribute to him. After Tiglath-pileser died, Hoshea revolted against the new Assyrian king, Shalmaneser, who then invaded Israel, took Hoshea prisoner, and besieged Samaria. When the city fell three years later, many of

Israel's citizens were deported to Assyria (BC 721), and the Assyrians ruled in Israel.

HOSPITALITY, Biblical

The cordial and generous reception and entertainment of guests or strangers. In patriarchal times, though Egyptians and others practiced hospitality, the Semites were most notable for this quality. Care for the traveler was viewed as an integral part of living, and great was the courtesy extended to the visitor, whether a stranger, friend, relative, or invited guest.From the Bible account it is learned that hospitality was customarily extended to a traveler. He was greeted by a kiss, particularly if a relative (Genesis 29:13-14). His feet were washed by a member of the household, usually a servant (Genesis 18:5), and his animals were fed and cared for (Genesis 24:15-25). He was often asked to stay for the night and sometimes even for several days (Genesis 24:54). The visitor was considered to be under the householder's protection during his stay (Genesis 19:6-8). On departure. he might be escorted part way on his journey (Genesis 18:16).

The importance with which the extending of hospitality was viewed is seen in Reuel's remarks when his daughters spoke of the "Egyptian" traveler (actually Moses) who had helped them watering their flock. Reuel exclaimed: "But where is he? Why is it that you have left the man behind? Call him, that he may eat bread" (Exodus 2:16-20).

HOST

The Eucharist bread, so called because it is Christ's body "given up for us" as victim in the sacrifice of the Cross. Sometimes the unconsecrated communion wafers are called "hosts" in distinction from the consecrated Eucharistic bread.

HOSTS, Lord of

An ancient designation for Yahweh. It stands for the fuller title, the God of the Hosts of Israel (1 Samuel 17:45). Israel is considered an army with Yahweh as its leader. The designation is later used most frequently by the Prophets, especially Isaiah, Jeremiah, and Zechariah.

HOTEI

In Japanese mythology, one of the Seven Gods of Luck. He is depicted as a cheerful, contended Buddhist monk, with a large exposed belly, frequently shown in the company of children.

HOTHAM

In the Old Testament, son of Heber from the tribe of Asher (1 Chronicles 7:30-32); likely the same person as the Helem mentioned in 1 Chronicles 7:35.

HOTHIR

In the Old Testament, one of the fourteen sons of Heman who served under the direction of their father as musicians at the sanctuary. In David's time Hothir and his sons and brothers were constituted the 21st of the 24 service groups of musicians (1 Chronicles 25:1-6).

HOU CHI

In Chinese mythology, Lord of Millet Grains, worshipped for the abundant harvests that he graciously provided for his people. The Chinese honored him not only for past favors but in the hope that devotion to the deity would guarantee continued blessings.

HOURIS

Anglicized version of the Arabic huriyya. The houris are the virginal female companions of the blessed in Paradise. They appear several times in the Koran. For example, in verse 20 of Surat al-Tur the blessed are told that they will be wed to houris as one of the many delights of Paradise.

HOUSE

In biblical terminology, word with several meanings:
1 a household or all the offspring of one man (Genesis 12:1);
2 a dwelling house (Genesis 19:2-4);

3 a jail or, figuratively, a country of enslavement (Genesis 40:4; Exodus 13:3);
4 a dwelling place of animals and birds (Job 39:6);
5 a spider's web (Job 4:14);
6 a royal residence or palace (2 Samuel 5:11);
7 a priestly line (1 Samuel 2:35);
8 God's tabernacle or Temple, both literal and spiritual (Exodus 23:19; 1 Kings 6:1);
9 a royal dynasty (1 Samuel 25:28);
10 the dwelling place of God, heaven itself (John 14:2);
11 the sanctuary of a false god (Judges 9:27);
12 the corruptible physical body of humans (2 Corinthians 5:1);
13 the incorruptible spiritual body (2 Corinthians 5:1);
14 the common grave (Job 17:13);
15 an association of workers engaged in the same profession (1 Chronicles 4:21);
16 a building for housing official records of state (Ezra 6:1).
A form of the Hebrew word for house, ba'yith often constitutes part of a proper name as in Bethel (house of God) and Bethlehem (house of bread).

HOUSE OF PRAYER
The term in a generic use refers to a center with a core community intended to provide an experience of prayer within an interpersonal setting. It refers to a center, then, where Christians, whether laity, clergy, or religious, may pass a period of retreat or retirement to share in this experience.

HOUSELING CLOTH
A white linen cloth spread before communicants to prevent the host or crumbs from falling to the floor. The cloth is held by the altar boys, or is attached to the altar rail, or is clipped along the top of the pews, possibly to give the impression of a prepared table. Its use originated in the Middle Ages and in some places continues at the present time.

HOU T'U
In Chinese mythology, the Spirit of the Earth, first worshipped in 113 BC by Wu Ti, a Han dynasty emperor. At various times and in various places Hou T'u seems also to have had a cult as the spirit of humanity, as the national earth god, and as the spirit of deceased emperors and empresses.

HO YEN
(circa 178-249) cofounder of the famous Ch'ing-t'an or Pure Discussions, philosophical school, a group of scholars who used Taoist terms and concepts to give new meanings to Confucian texts, at the same time that they utilized Confucian moral and social philosophy to politicize Taoist thought.

HSIEN
In Chinese Taoism, an immortal, one who has reached the beatitude of a higher existence by following the teachings of Lao-tzu and his disciples.

HSI K'ANG
(223-262) Taoist philosopher, and poet who was one of the most important members of the free-spirited, heavy drinking Seven Sages of the Bamboo Grove, a coterie of poets and philosophers who scandalized Chinese society by their iconoclastic thoughts and actions.

HSIN HSUEH
Chinese term for Neo-Confucian Idealism as developed in the 15th and 16th centuries by Wang Yang-ming. It was an extension of the philosophy of Lu Hsianh-shan, a contemporary and opponent of Chu Hsi and his school of Rationalism.

HSIUNG SHIH-LI
(1885-1971) One of the outstanding figures of contemporary philosophy. His philosophical system is an original synthesis of Buddhist, Confucian, and Western motifs.

HSI WANG MU

In Taoist mythology, queen of the immortals in charge of female genies (spirits) who dwell in a fairyland.

HSI-YU CHI

Comic novel based on the actual 7th century pilgrimage of the Buddhist monk Hsiian-tsang (602-644) to India in search of sacred texts.

HSU

In Chinese Taoism, a great void from which all things take form and the source of all potentiality.

HU, Sia, AND HEH

In Egyptian religion, deified abstractions personifying respectively creative command, perception and eternity. They were all essential forces in the creation and continuance of the universe.

HUACA

Ancient Inca religious concept variously used to refer to sacred ritual, the state of being after death, or any sacred object.

HUBB 'UDHRI

In Islamic secular and religious poetry, the classical theme expressing the living man's desire to die on the path to his beloved.

HUBERT, Walter

(1156-1205) Archbishop of Canterbury, papal legate, an administrator whose position in church and state was unmatched until the time of Cardinal Wolsey in the 16th century.

HUBMAIER, Balthasar

(1485-1528) Early Reformation figure, one of the foremost leaders of the Anabaptists, who practiced a primitive Christianity and opposed infant baptism.

HUBRIS

In classical Greek ethical and religious thought, overweening presumption suggesting impious disregard of the limits governing men's actions in an orderly universe. It is the sin to which the great and gifted are most susceptible, and in Greek tragedy it is usually the basic flaw of the tragic hero.

HUD

The title of the 11th sura of the Koran; the proper name of a prophet sent to the people of Ad. The sura belongs to the Meccan period and has 123 verses. The story of the prophet Hud, from which the title of the sura derives, occupies verses 50-60. It tells how Hud goes to the people of Ad to warn them. They reject him and accuse Hud of not bringing them a clear proof. Disaster, in consequence, overtakes the tribe of Ad.

HUDAYHIYAD, Pact of al-

Compromise reached between Mohammed and Meccan leaders (628), in which Mecca gave political and religious recognition to the growing community of Muslims in Medina.

HUDRA

East Syrian liturgical book containing the older proverbs of the Mass and Office; complemented for the Night Office by the gazza.

HUDUD

In the Druze religion, the five supreme ministers, who are emanations of God, the One. The system of emanations was ultimately derived from Neoplatonism and more immediate from Ismailism, an esoteric Ismailic sect strongly influenced by hellenistic philosophy, from which the Druzes evolved.

HUGHES, John

(1797-1864) First Roman Catholic archbishop of New York, who became one of the foremost American Roman Catholic prelates of his time.

HUGH OF CLUNY, Saint

(1024-1109) Abbot of the Benedictine monastery of Cluny (1049-1109) and head of its extensive monastic network

throughout Western Europe, who expanded medieval monasticism to its apogee.

HUGH OF LINCOLN, Saint

(1140-1200) Bishop of Lincoln who became the first Carthusian monk to be canonized.

HUGH OF LINCOLN, Little Saint

(1245-1255) A Christian child allegedly tortured and crucified for ritual purposes by a Jewish group led by one named Koppin.

HUGH OF SAINT CHER

(1200-1263) Cardinal and maker of an early biblical concordance.

HUGH OF SAINT-VICTOR

(1096-1141) Eminent scholastic theologian who began the tradition of mysticism that made the School of Saint-Victor (Paris) famous throughout the 12th century. His mystical treatises were strongly influenced by Bishop St. Augustine of Hippo, whose practical teachings on contemplative life Hugh blended with the theoretical writings of Pseudo-Dionysius the Areopagite.

HUGUENOTS

Name given since the beginning of the 16th century to the Protestants in France. The early Huguenots were part of the religious Reformation whose members followed the teaching of John Calvin. Within a short period the Huguenot movement spread to all sections of the French people - nobility, bourgeoisie, peasants and workers.

From the reign of Francis I on the Huguenots were persecuted. After 1562 religious wars broke out between the Protestant and Roman Catholic factions, and reached their bloodiest point on August 24, 1572. On that day Catherine de Medicis, the queen mother and regent for her son Charles IX, carried out the Massacre of St. Bartholomew's Day in which the Huguenot leadership was cut down and thousands of Huguenots murdered. In 1574 Charles IX was succeeded by the unpopular Henry III, during whose reign a Holy League was created to crush the Huguenots.

HUI-NENG

(638-713) The sixth great patriarch of Zen Buddhism, who founded the Southern School, which became the dominant school of Zen, both in China and Japan.

HUI-YUAN

(333-416) A celebrated early Chinese Buddhist priest, who formed a devotional society of monks and lay worshippers of the Buddha Amitabha.

HUJURAT, al-

The title of the 49th sura of the Koran; it means "The Rooms" or "The Chambers." The sura belongs to the Medinan period of has 18 verses. The title comes from a reference in verse 4 to the Prophet Mohammed's rooms (in his house) and a belligerent visit by some of the tribe of Tamim to the adjacent mosque of the Prophet. The sura warns against contempt for others and backbiting. It was revealed not long before Mohammed's death.

HUKKOK

In the Old Testament, a border city of Naphtali (Joshua 19:32-34). Whereas some consider it to be too far north and east, modern Yaquq is usually identified with ancient Hukkok. This site lies some 5_ miles west of the northern end of the Sea of Galilee and overlooks the fertile plain of Gennesaret.

HUKOK

In the Old Testament, a border city in the territory of Asher that was assigned to the Gershonites of the tribe of Levi (Joshua 19:25; 1 Chronicles 6:74-75).

HULDAH

In biblical records, the wife of Shallum; a prophetess residing at Jerusalem in the second quarter during the reign of faithful King Josiah of Judah. When Josiah heard the reading of "the very book of the law" found by

Hilkiah the High Priest during the Temple repair work, he sent a delegation to inquire of God. They went to Huldah, who, in turn, relayed the word of God, indicating that all the calamities for disobedience recorded in the "book" would befall the apostate nation. Huldah added that Josiah, because of having humbled himself before God, would not have to look upon the calamity but would be gathered to his forefathers and taken to his graveyard in peace (2 Kings 22:8-20).

HUMAN ACT

In scholastic moral theology, an act deliberately willed. It is called human because the source of such an act is the powers of mind and will that set the human apart from lesser creatures. The distinctive name also implies that in a person's activity some actions are not human in the full sense. Every action belongs to the one who acts, but some are purely physical phenomena, biological or sentient, some are reflexes, some are unthinking.

The greater number of human acts are choices. To be fully human these must be acts of will that correspond to a sufficient mental evaluation of the good chosen. The same basis for distinguishing a human act from other sorts of human activity ("acts of man") is also a basis for recognizing acts that are only partially human, i.e. that lack sufficient mental awareness and evaluation, and complete willingness.

The possibility of morality, i.e., of any moral good or evil requires the capability for making deliberate choices. To deny such possibility is not only to deny the possibility of sin, but also of moral good.

HUMANISM

The attitude of mind which stresses the dignity and importance of man. Humanism has come to indicate the prevailing attitude of the Renaissance which developed in Western Europe from the 1300s to the 1500s. Its origins are associated with the rediscovery of Greek and Roman classicism which had sought to understand and interpret the whole meaning of human life and existence. Among the giants of this movement, now known as Renaissance humanism, were the Italians Petrarch and Boccacio, the Englishman Sir Thomas More and the Dutch scholar, Erasmus. Each of these tried to combine high ideals with a realistic recognition of man's nature and potential.

Against the background of the teaching of the Medieval Christian church, which insisted that man's life on earth was only significant in so far as it affected his future after death, the humanists underlined man's intrinsic value now and his present potential. So profound was this change in attitude that humanism was to affect the whole of Western culture - its art, education and government - right down until the present time. While the early humanists, such as Erasmus and More were religious, the trend became irreligious, and by the 18th century Enlightenment the leading humanist figures, such as Voltaire, Diderot and Rousseau, were specifically non-religious.

In the 1800s one of the most articulate non-religious and original humanists was the Englishman Matthew Arnold, whose ideal man combined knowledge with an appreciation of beauty and the ability to exercise moral judgments. In the 20th century many people think that the greatest threat to the values of humanism is to be found in an excessive preoccupation with science and technology leading to a neglect of man and humane values.

In recent years the term humanism has been used to refer to value systems that emphasize the personal worth of each individual but that do not include a belief in God.

HUMANITARIANISM

The advocacy and action of promoting the welfare of mankind at large, often associated with schemes of organized philanthropy, and sometimes professed as a "religion of humanity," as though this chiefly or wholly comprised human duty.

Yet its positive aspiration should be effectively integrated in Christianity. In fact, for many centuries it was under the aegis of the church that hospitals for the sick and homes for orphans, the aged, the friendless, and strangers were founded; the history of European medicine takes it back Medieval religious sources.

However, with the widening separation between the sacred and the secular from the time of the Renaissance and Reformation, and in the climate first of the Enlightenment, then of Positivism, then of moral indignation with the inhuman after-effects of industrial capitalism, the cause of humanitarianism has been presented in non-confessional terms. Widespread and effective campaigns of social reform, extending even to the human treatment of animals, have been conducted without appeal to religion.

HUMANITY OF CHRIST

A dogmatic theme, the genuineness and completeness of Christ's human nature as well as its hypostatic union with the Word are matters of faith. The denial of the reality of his humanity is the heresy of Docetism; the denial of his humanity from Christ's divinity, united only by excellence or holiness to divinity, is the heresy of Nestorianism.

As a theme in spiritual theology, the humanity of Christ, i.e., the events and examples of his life, death, and Resurrection, is a central emphasis in the following of Christ as the model for Christian life.

HUMAN SACRIFICE

The offering of the life of a human being to a deity. The occurrence of human sacrifice can usually be related to the recognition of blood as the sacred life-force in man.

Human sacrifice is found primarily among agricultural societies and in archaic cultures. The Aztecs, for instance, offered thousands of prisoners of war to the sun, which was thought to be strengthened by human blood, symbolized in the still beating heart torn out of the breast of the victim. These rituals symbolized man's fight with the earth, the fertilization of the earth and its continuous renewal.

The Mayas sacrificed young girls by drowning them in a deep well, and the Incas celebrated the initiation of a new ruler with a human sacrifice.

In some of the African kingdoms a king sacrificed himself or was slaughtered when his term was ended, when his health declined, or when land and people were endangered by a catastrophe.

A very common form of human sacrifice is the mortuary band. Human beings were offered, occasionally voluntarily, to provide a guide, servant, or messenger for the king, or just to honor and strengthen the deceased by the life of the living. Sometimes a widow was burned on the pyre to accompany the deceased husband.

Other occasions for human sacrifice were crisis situations (famine, war, etc.), when the best possession was offered, for instance, a child to Moloch, to please the godhead; or when the fertility of man, cattle, and crops has to be secured; of when, as in Greece, a crime had to be expiated.

The ideology of human sacrifice revolves around two poles: that of the demi-godhead, who by death provides life through plants, food supply, etc., and that of the ruler godhead, whose lordship cannot be pleased except by man's most precious possession, life.

HUMAZA, al-

The title of the 104th sura of the Koran; it means "The Slanderer." The sura belongs to the Meccan period and contains 9 verses. Its title is drawn from the first verse which commences a severe warning to every money-grabbing and miserly slanderer; he will be thrown into the fire of hell.

HUMILIATI

First a lay fraternity, than a religious order for man and women, inspired by the ideal of apostolic poverty and simplicity. Members were also called Berettini from their attire of undyed, grayish wool (Italian, beretto). Their origins are unknown but they existed in Lombardy as early as the mid-12th century.

They were another manifestation of the desire of laymen of the time to restore the church to simplicity and to remove the abuses of the clergy. The Humiliati began to preach in public for reform in the church; in 1179 Pope Alexander III ordered them to cease; when they continued, they were excommunicated by Lucius III in 1184.

Many rejoined the church in 1202, and they became effective counter-agents against groups of similar inspiration who were attacking the church, especially the Cathari. The many houses of the order were suppressed in 1571 by Pius V.

HUMILITY

The moral virtue by which one recognizes his or her absolute dependence on God, appreciates all of one's abilities and talents as gifts of God, and strives to use them in accord with His will and purpose.

HUMTAH

According to biblical records, a city in the mountainous region of Judah (Joshua 15:20).

HUPHAM

In the Old Testament, a "son," probably a later descendant, of Benjamin, and ancestral head of the Huphamites (Genesis 46:8).

HUPPAH

In the Old Testament, head of the 13th of the 24 priestly divisions David organized (1 Chronicles 24:1-3).

HUPPIM

In the Old Testament, a "son" of Benjamin included in the list of those who came into Egypt with Jacob's household in 1728 BC or were born there during Jacob's lifetime (Genesis 46:8).

HUR

In the Old Testament, a descendant of Judah; son of Caleb and Ephrath; grandfather of the craftsman Bezalel. Some of Hur's descendants may have settled in Bethlehem (Exodus 31:2; 35:30).

HURAI

In the Old Testament, one of David's mighty men; from the torrent valleys of Gaash (1 Chronicles 11:26-32).

HURAM

In the Old Testament, probably either a grandson or a great-grandson of Benjamin through Bela and Ir; apparently also called Huppium (1 Chronicles 7:6-12).

HUSAYN, al-

(626-680) Third Shiite Imman, known among the Shiites as the "Prince of the Martyrs,", one of the grandsons of the Prophet Mohammed and the son of the 4th caliph Ali b. Talib and Fatima. Al-Husayn is greatly revered by both the Sunni branch of Islam and the Shiites alike. A notice hanging on one of the walls of the al-Husayn mosque reads: "The Prophet of God, blessing and peace be upon him."

HUSAYNI, Amin al-

(1893-1987) Mufti of Jerusalem and Arab nationalist figure who played a major role in Arab resistance to Zionist political ambitions in Palestine.

HUSHAH

In the Old Testament, either a "son" of or a city "fathered" or "founded" by Ezer of the tribe of Judah (1 Chronicles 4:1-4). If Hushah designates a city, then it was likely the home of one of David's mighty men, Sibbecai, who was probably also called Mebunnai (1 Chronicles 27:11). Those who regard Hushah as the name of a city generally identify it with Husan, circa four miles west of Bethlehem.

HUSHAI

In Judaism, a loyal Archite friend of King David who helped thwart

Absalom's rebellion (1 Chronicles 27:33). Hushai, with his robe ripped and dirt on his head, met the fleeing king on the Mount of Olives. He followed David's suggestion that he go back into the city, feign loyalty to Absalom, endeavor to frustrate Ahithophel's counsel, and keep David informed through the priests Zadok and Abiathar (2 Samuel 15:30; 32-37). At first Absalom was suspicious, but Hushai succeeded in winning his confidence (2 Samuel 16:16-19). When Absalom called for Hushai's opinion concerning the best military strategy, Hushai spoke contrary to Ahithophel and recommended a course that would in fact allow David time to get organized. Hushai presented his idea in a way that made it appear better for Absalom and his associates that Ahithophel's advice to attack immediately not be followed; Hushai then informed the priests of what happened (2 Samuel 17:1-6). Hushai's counsel frustrated that of Ahithophel, just as David had petitioned God, and thus "Jehovah brought calamity upon Absalom" (2 Samuel 15:31).

HUSHAM
In the Old Testament, a native of the land of the Temanites who succeeded Jobab as king of Edom (Genesis 36:31-35). This was "before any king reigned over the sons of Israel" (1 Chronicles 1:43).

HUTTERITES
Members of a strict Protestant sect known as the Hutterian Brethren, most of which members live in South Dakota, Montana and Canada. They believe in common ownership and all goods and are pacifists. The sect originated in 1529 as a branch of the Anabaptists in Moravia and takes its name from its martyred leader, Jacob Hutter. The denomination has circa 20,000 members.

HUWASI STONE
In Hittite religion, a standing stone sacred to a particular deity and situated in the open air, frequently in a grove of trees or wooded area. At any cult center, those deities who could not be provided with their own temples were worshipped at a Huwasi stone; in fact, as many as 21 such stones are attested at a single village.

HUYNH PHU SO
(1919-1947) Philosopher, founder of the religion Phat Giao Hoa Hoa, in Vietnam. The religion is an amalgam of Buddhism, ancestor worship, animistic rites, elements of Confucian doctrine, and indigenous Vietnamese sorcery.

HYADES
In Greek mythology, the five sisters of the Pleiades who nursed the infant wine god, Dionysus, and as a reward were made the five stars in the head of the constellation Taurus, the bull.

HYDROMANCY
A form of divination using water. In some cases springs or fountains are observed for signs, particularly after casting in offerings. If the water refuses to accept the offering, that is, if the offering floats, the outlook is unfavorable.

Hydromancy has also been practiced with water in a basin, sometimes watching globules of oil in the water or the ripples caused by droppings in a pebble.

HYDROPARASTATE
A name given to Christians who used water instead of wine in the Eucharist. The custom was observed by Ebionites, Tatianites, Marcionites, and Manichaeans. The practice of substituting water appears also to have been resorted to in certain circumstances without heretical intent.

Thus Cyprian relates that some Christians celebrated a Eucharistic SService in the morning without wine, and again in the evening with wine. The custom evidently arose in the time of persecution, for Christians were daily communicants and could be detected by the smell of wine, which pagans would not have used in the early morning.

HYGEIA

In Greek mythology, the most important daughter of Asclepius; the personification of psychic and bodily health. There is no specific myth related to her. She belonged to the assembly of Asclepius and was worshipped together with him.

HYLOZOISM

In philosophy, any system that views all matter as alive, either in itself or by participation in the operation of a world soul or some similar principle. Hylozoism is logically distinct from early forms of animism, which personify nature, and from panpsychism, which attributes some form of consciousness or sensation to all matter.

Hymenaeus

An apostate from Christianity during the first century, who was identified by apostle Paul as a blasphemer, full of "empty speeches that violate what is holy." In his deviation from the truth, Hymenaeus, along with a certain Philetus, taught false doctrine, subverting the faith of some. One of the false teachings was that "the resurrection had already occurred" in their day. Evidently this was their teaching: that the resurrection was merely a spiritual one, of a symbolic kind, and that the dedicated Christians had already had their resurrection, that this was all there was to the matter and there was no further resurrection in the future under God's Messianic kingdom.

In Paul's first letter to Timothy, Hymenaeus' name is associated with another apostate, Alexander. The apostle states that he had handed Hymenaeus and Alexander "over to Satan," evidently referring to Paul's expelling or disfellowshipping them from the congregation. This constituted discipline or training for the Christians who had been acquainted with these apostate men, as a warning not to follow their blasphemous course (1 Timothy 1:18-20; 2 Timothy 2:16-18).

HYMN

Sacred song in praise of gods or heroes, found in almost all churches, ancient and modern. Jewish psalms, sung in the temple worship, were adopted by the early Christian church and supplemented by distinctively Christian hymns such as the canticles.

The 150 poetic Hebrew hymns known as the Psalms have been adopted by Christians, as have the seven canticles from the Old Testament. In addition, the Christian liturgy contains three canticles from the New Testament (Magnificat, Benedictus, and Nunc Dimitiis). The Roman breviary and missal has 184 hymns of ancient, medieval or modern origin.

During the Reformation Martin Luther wrote and adapted many hymns for congregational singing. English-language hymn writing dates from the 17th century. Famous hymn writers include Isaac Watts and Charles and John Wesley in 18th century England, and in the United States John Greenleaf Whittier, Julia Ward Howe and Phillips Brooks.

The gospel hymns of the United States, evangelical songs set to simple tunes, are a unique form of hymn and are associated with the names of D.L. Moody and Ira Sankey.

In Islam, term denoting the truth of the Divine truth. It is a word of immense significance in the intellectual and linguistic development of Islam. It is also used as an attribute and name of God. As such it is not to be borne by any human being.

HYPAPANTE

In the Byzantine liturgy the name given to the feast of the Presentation (February 2). It commemorates the first public appearance of Christ in the Temple and thus his first formal encounter with the chosen people.

HYPERDULIA

The special honor given to the Blessed Virgin Mary in her role as the mother of God. It is distinguished from latria, the worship only due to God, and dulia, the veneration given to the saints and angels. The distinction reflects the difference between the Almighty God and Mary, a creature, but also emphasized her unique holiness which surpasses that of all other creatures.

HYPOSTASIS

A term used to describe the substance of the Holy Trinity wherein the Father, Son, and Holy Spirit are distinct but united. Originally the term referred somewhat ambiguously to concrete reality and was open to various developments. The Greek and Latin traditions evolved it in opposite directions. The Greek tradition understood hypostasis in the sense of person and preferred it to prosopon because it expressed more clearly the ontological reality of the subject.

The Latin tradition took substantia to mean nature. Not before the ambiguity of terminology was clarified could the Trinatarian and Christological faith of both traditions appear clearly identified. The Council of Constantinople II (553) is a clear witness to the understanding arrived at between the two traditions.

HYPOSTATIC UNION

Theologically speaking, a term indicating that the two natures of Jesus Christ (the divine and the human) are united to form one person.

HYPSIPYLE

In Greek legend, daughter of Dionysus' son Thomas, king of the island of Lemnos.

HYPSISTARIANS

A 4th century sect that worshiped God as all high ruler, but not as Father, and that is known only from the writings of Gregory Nazanzus.

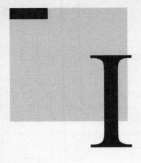

I

IACCHUS

A minor deity associated with the Eleusian Mysteries, the best known of the ancient Greek mystery religions. He is identified as the son of Kore or of Dionysus. In art Iacchus was portrayed holding a torch and leading the celebrants.

I AM MOVEMENT

Religious movement in the United States that taught that the Mighty I Am is the source of power and of all things necessary for everyone. The movement was started in the 1930s by Guy Ballard (1878-1939), a mining engineer, and his wife Edna. The name of the movement came from the Bible verse (Exodus 3:14) in which God replies to Moses, "I am who I am."

IAPETUS

In Greek mythology, son of Uranus (Heaven) and Ge (Earth), one of the Titans, and father of Atlas, Prometheus, Epimetheus, and Menoetius.

IBADA

In Islam, term denoting worship, devotional action, observance required by the Islamic faith.

IBHAR

In the Old Testament, one of the sons born to King David in Jerusalem after he transferred his residence there from Hebron (2 Samuel 5:13-15).

IBLEAM

In biblical times, a city in the territory of Issachar but assigned with its dependent towns to Manasseh. The Manassites, however, failed to dispossess the Canaanites from Ibleam (Joshua 17:11-13). Undoubtedly Ibleam is the same as the Bileam in Manasseh given to the Kohathite Levites (1 Chronicles 6:70). Many scholars believe that Ibleam corresponds to Ybr'm, a city listed among the Palestinian conquests of the Egyptian Pharaoh Thutmose III.

IBLIS

In Islam, term, denoting the devil. The Arabic word may derive from the Greek word diabolos. Made out of fire, he was cast down by God for refusing, alone of all the angels, to bow down and acknowledge God's new creation Adam, who was made out of clay. The story of Iblis may be constructed from the considerable detail about him which is given in the Koran. In the Paradise Iblis tempted Adam and Eve and precipitated their downfall. He is also called the Satan.

IBEIAH

In the Old Testament, son of Jeroham; a Benjaminite head of a paternal house returning from Babylonian exile (1 Chronicles 9:1-9).

IBN ABI AR-RIJAI

(1620-1681) Yemeni scholar and theologian who was a noted commentator on the esoteric Islamic Zaydi sect of Yemen.

IBN ABI ASRUM

(1099-1189) Scholar who became a leading theologian and chief judicial officer of the Ayyubid caliphate. He taught religious subjects in Damascus and became an administrator of religious endowments. During his lifetime six religious colleges were built in his honor.

IBN AL-ABDAR

(1199-1260) Historian and theologian who became one of the most famous students of Islamic Spain.

IBN AL-ATHIR

(1160-1233) Influential Arab historian and theologian. His chief work was a history of the world, starting with the creation of Adam.

IBN EZRA MOSES

(1060-1139) Hebrew critic and poet. He was one of the first Jewish poets to write secular verse. Both his sacred and secular poetry are generally considered to be unsurpassed in mastery of the Hebrew language. His later works were mostly penitential prayers of an introspective, melancholy cast.

IBN ISHAQ

(704-767) Biographer of the Prophet Mohammed whose book is one of the most important sources of the Prophet's life.

IBN JUBAYR

(1145-1217) Native of Muslim Spain known for a book recounting his travels on pilgrimage to Mecca.

IBN MAS'UD

(died circa 653) Notable companion of the Prophet Mohammed and very early convert to Islam. He was among the migrants to Ethiopia but later joined the Prophet in Medina and witnessed the Battles of Badr and Uhud.

IBN SHEM TOV

(1380-1441) Jewish mystic who vociferously opposed the teachings of Jewish rationalist thinkers, especially Maimonides, advocating instead the study of the Kabala (Jewish mysticism), which he considered the correct interpretation of Jewish tradition.

IBRAHIM

Arabic word for Abraham, a great Islamic prophet, patriarch and ardent proponent of monotheism who figures prominently in the Koran. In Surat al-Imran Ibrahim is described as being neither a Jew nor a Christian but a hanif and a muslim. The Koran retails several major incidents from his life: Allah brings four birds to life for him; angels forecast the birth of his son; he is compassionate towards his father Azar and prays for him, despite the latter's idolatry; he is cast into a fire by a ruler whom the commentators call Nimrod and saved by God, according to some commentators by the intercession of the angel Jibris; and he is commanded by God to sacrifice his son, but the son is saved at the last moment by God.

IBRAHIM

The title of the 14th sura of the Koran; the reference is to the great prophet and patriarch Ibrahim. The sura belongs to the Meccan period and has 52 verses. It bears the name Ibrahim because verses 35 and following make considerable reference to him. The sura begins with three of the Mysterious Letters of the Koran and refers to the signs conveyed by Musa as well as warning what happened to the people of Nuh, Ad and Thamud. The tyrant will enter Jahannam and be given pus to drink which will be very difficult to swallow.

IBRI

In the Old Testament, son of Jaaziah; a Merarite Levite of King David's time (1 Chronicles 24:27-31).

IBZAN

In Judaism, the one who succeeded Jephthah as judge of Israel. Ibzan was the father of 30 sons and 30 daughters, indicating that he was a polygamist and evidently also a man of some means. He procured thirty daughters as wives for his sons. After judging for seven years Ibzan died and was buried in his native city of Bethlehem, likely the Bethlehem in Zebulun (Judges 12:7-10; Joshua 19:10-15).

ICARUS

In Greek mythology, the son of Daedalus, with whom he was imprisoned in the Labyrinth by King Minos of Crete. To escape Minos' wrath, they attached feathered wings to their shoulders with wax and flew away. Icarus, however, flew too high; the sun melted the wax, and he plunged into the seas and was drowned.

ICELAND, National Church of

Established (state-supported) Church of Iceland, changed from the Roman Catholic to the Lutheran faith during the 16th century Protestant Reformation. The outstanding Icelandic Reformer was Gudbrandur Thorlaksson (1541-1627), bishop of Holar for 56 years. He worked to educate the clergy and people in the new faith and wrote or prepared for publication many religious works in the Icelandic language, including the Bible.

ICHABOD

In Judaism, posthumous son of Phinehas and brother of Ahitub; grandson of High Priest Eli. The name Ichabod, given to him by his dying mother while giving birth, signified that glory had gone away from Israel in view of the capture of the ark and the deaths of Phinehas and Eli (1 Samuel 4:17-22).

ICHINEN

Term of Zen Buddhism meaning one thought, or mental event. When this first happens the mind is said to be "disturbed," and there arises an awareness of duality, or true and untrue, good and evil. A mind which can revert to the state of "no-mind", before this so-called disturbance occurs, is free from anxiety, fear and desire which all thought produces.

ICHIJO, Kaneyoshi

(1402-81) Japanese eclectic philosopher, who tried to reconstruct Shinto according to an idealistic monism (the idea that there is only one kind of substance).

I CHING

An ancient Chinese text, one of the Five Classics of Confucianism. Though the book was originally used for divination, its profound impact on Chinese minds and its universal popularity is due to a system of cosmology that involves man and nature in a single system.

ICON

Generally any image or portrait. The term usually refers to pictures of sacred personages or events, usually painted on wood or ivory, and venerated in the Eastern Orthodox Church. Figures of Christ, the Virgin or saints are often represented. Icons play an important role in the Orthodox liturgy. They originated in the Byzantine period and are still common today in the Slavic countries and Greece.

In Christian art, the term icon refers to images of the savior, the Trinity, the Mother of God, angels, saints, as well as sacred events and theological mysteries. Icons, usually portable, are to be distinguished from statues and also from idols that had cultic purposes in pre-Christian Hellenism and other Near East religions.

Generally they are made of slabs of wood, but at times the Romans used glass, and there have been small portable icons of mosaic. On these surfaces the iconographer, following rules ecclesiastically established, sketches the outlines of the figures he wishes to depict. He then lays down the background in paint or goldleaf.

When this is completed, the figures are filled in with paints generally prepared from vegetable colors mixed with egg whites. The finished product is coated thoroughly with linseed oil which makes the colors appear brilliant for a time, but they soon darken.

In the 17th century metal covering (in Russia, a riza), began to be used to cover the entire icon except the face and hands of the figures. This was done partly to preserve the icon and partly to express veneration. These coverings were often of silver or gold and further enhanced by having precious stones inserted into them in decorative patterns such as crowns and necklaces.

ICON PAINTER

Icons ideally are painted by monks or nuns who live contemplating the persons and mysteries they depict for the veneration and instruction of their fellow Christians.

The iconographer is an evangelist in paints; in his work he hopes to be moved by a kind of inspiration analogous to that enjoyed by the writers of the scripture. He begins his work with fasting and prayer, and by his painting he seeks to concretize his own vision of the transfigured cosmos through Christ, the Trinity, the Mother of God, the angels, and saints.

For this reason the genuine icon is never naturalistic or sentimental, but always strives to make the glorified state of its subject shine through its earthly portrayal, so that the worshiper may behold the presence of the world to come.

A special liturgy consecrating the icons for church use is prescribed and the wording of the prayers shows traces of the controversies over iconoclasm.

ICON VENERATION

Icons are venerated by bows, or pratratations, during which the worshiper continually makes the sign of the cross. They are also kissed and the forehead is pressed against them as gestures of respect and honor. Lamps and candles burn before them both during liturgical services and in private devotion.

During the liturgy the holy icons are incensed by the celebrant or deacon three times in veneration of the church, both earthly and heavenly. They are borne in procession on certain feast days, and blessings are given with them at the end of some services.

On certain occasions the faithful are anointed with oil from the lamp burning before an icon. The icon is venerated as an extension of the incarnation of the savior; the image is believed to participate in Christ as the Image of God, and is an expression of man as the image of God, who is renewed and deified by the redemptive incarnation.

Icons mediate to man the presence of those whom they depict in much the same way that the words of the gospels mediate the message of salvation.

ICONIUM

An ancient city of Asia Minor lying circa 2,320 feet above sea level. Iconium is presently known as Konya, located circa 150 miles south of Ankara on the southwestern edge of the central Turkish plateau. In the surrounding area, watered by streams flowing from mountains a few miles to the west, grain, sugar beets and flax are cultivated. Although given the title Claudiconium during the rule of Emperor Claudius, not until Hadrian's time (in the second century) was the city constituted a Roman colony.

In the first century BC Iconium was one of the principal cities in the Roman province of Galatia and lay astride the main trade route from Ephesus to Syria. The city had an influential Jewish population. Paul and Barnabas, after being forced to leave Pisidian Antioch, preached in the city of Iconium and its synagogue and there aided many Jews and Greeks to become believers. But when an attempt was made to stone them, they fled from Iconium to Lystra. Soon Jews from Antioch and Iconium came to Lystra and stirred up the crowds there so that they stoned Paul. Thereafter Paul and Barnabas went to Derbe and then courageously returned to Lystra, Iconium and Antioch, strengthening the brothers and appointing "older men" to positions of responsibility in the congregations established in these cities (Acts 13:50-52; 14:1-7).

ICONOCLASM

A heresy that arose in the eighth century declaring that the religious veneration of pictures and images was sacrilegious and advocating "image breaking" as a solution to the problem.

ICONOCLASTIC CONTROVERSY

Christian dispute over the popular use of icons within the Eastern Orthodox (Byzantine) Church. With public support from Emperor Leo III, the iconoclasts (Greek for "image breakers") succeeded (726) in destroying works of art and in persecuting icon worshippers for idolatry and heresy. Under Empress Irene, icon veneration was officially restored (787), an event still celebrated in the Eastern Church as the Feast of Orthodoxy.

Combined Jewish and Islamic influence resulted in some Christian opposition to veneration of sacred images, and Paulician heretics in Constantinople claimed the support of certain Catholic bishops. In 730 Emperor Leo III the Isaurian ordered the destruction of all holy icons. The patriarch Germanus. who was opposed to this policy. was deposed, and Leo's attempts to force the Pope to accept iconoclasm led to a serious rupture in relations between Rome and Byzantium.

Emperor Constantine V Copronymos, seeking ecclesiastical condemnation of images, summoned 340 bishops to a synod in Hieria (754). Here they decreed that the Eucharist alone could be held to be a lawful representation of Christ. Publicly denounced were patriarch Germanus, St. John Damascene, and George of Cyprus, staunch iconodules. Constantine, the new patriarch, and all the bishops were required to sign the new synodal Acts. The emperor then embarked on a savage persecution of the iconodules, particularly the monks.

At the seventh General Council, convoked at Nicaea (787), the bishops repudiated the synodal decrees of Hieria (754). The doctrinal decree defining the veneration of images included the theological distinction between the terms latria and dulia. On abjuration of their error patriarch Tarasius admitted former iconoclastic bishops to their original status.

Renewed persecution continued under the Emperors Michael II (820-829) and Theophilus (829-842). Theodora, imperial regent (842-856), named Methodius (842-846) to replace the iconoclastic patriarch and at a synod in March 843, the decrees of the Council of Nicaea were reinstated and unrepentant iconoclasts excommunicated. The first Sunday of Lent is still kept by the Eastern churches as the Sunday of Orthodoxy in commemoration of the triumph over heresy.

ICONOGRAPHY

The illustration of a subject by drawings or figures. St. Thomas Aquinas (1225-1274) justified reference to images, arguing that worship is directed to the reality symbolized. Protestantism generally reacted violently against images, although Luther allowed the crucifix. Anglo-Catholics allow for the use of images.

ICONOLOGY

The investigation and interpretation of meaning in a work of visual art. It is distinguished from iconography, which is the study and identification of symbols, themes, and subject matter in art, in that it seeks, partially through a consideration of these elements, to determine the total meaning of the work and to comprehend it in its historical context.

Iconology considers the cultural context of symbols and images as a means of interpreting their content. Thus a 15th century Italian Virgin Mary, though in subject the same as a 12th century Byzantine representation, reflects from a different time and place significant cultural differences.

Iconology investigates the complex stylistic and cultural relationship that converges to shape the symbolism and imagery of a given artist or artistic period. Although the term was used as early as the late 16th century for a manual of symbols, allegories and personifications, it was not used in reference to the interpretive study until modern times.

ICONOSTASIS

A solid screen of stone, wood, or metal that usually separates the sanctuary from the nave in Eastern Christian churches of Byzantine tradition.

After the resolution of the iconoclast controversy (726-843 AD), the way was open in the East for the proliferation of iconographic art. This activity was eventually focused on and reached its zenith in the embellishment of the iconostasis.

Basically, the iconostasis is a screen, usually of wood, that separates the sanctuary from the main body of the church. The oldest known form of chancel screen was a simple affair which did not restrict the worshipers' view of the altar or the frescoes and mosaics in the sanctuary.

Such early screens, approximately 3 to 4 feet in height, on which was placed a single row of icons, were first introduced in Byzantium. Although in Kievan Rus (11th-13th century) the iconostasis was of comparable size to its Byzantine models, it was ultimately among the Russians that the most lavish and ornamental screens were produced.

Opinions vary as to the date of the first solid iconostasis, reaching from floor to ceiling and serving to display three to five tiers of icons. However, such screens which date from the 14th century, have survived to the present. Russians in particular, regarded the sanctuary as a shrine within a shrine and the sacred mysteries performed therein as suitable only to be witnessed by the clergy.

Whatever the case, the fact remains that in medieval Russia the Eucharist was surrounded by a very ascetic theology, and the liturgy witnessed a growth in the number of secret prayers. It was logical to expect that in such conditions the sanctuary would be progressively closed to the congregation. As a direct result of this, the importance of icons grew, both as objects for veneration and as worthy of great artistic effort.

The iconostasis of the tradition described above is pierced by three doors. In the center is the double-gated Royal Door, behind which stands the altar, which is visible when the gates are open and the curtain is drawn aside, as in the case at certain moments during the liturgy.

The left door, as one faces the apse, leads to the side altar at which the rite of preparation or prothesis is accomplished. The right door leads to the diakonikon where the Book of Gospels and the vestments are kept. These doors are used for various purposes, such as the procession of the gifts, the proclamation of the gospel, and the distribution of communion. Laymen are not permitted behind the iconostasis, except as acolytes, and only an officiating priest may stand between the altar and the Royal Door.

The arrangement of icons on the iconostasis is according to a precise pattern. Those on the lowest tier are the largest and most important. They are called the "local icons." To the right side of the Royal Door is the icon of Christ, holding the gospels in one hand and giving his blessing with the other. To the left is an icon of the Mother of God holding the infant Jesus.

On the Royal Door itself are six small icons: the two in the center depict the Annunciation, and the four others, the Evangelists. The Archangels Michael and Gabriel are shown on the two side doors.

The remaining icons of the first tier include the patron saint or feast of the church and other popular and national saints. The second row, just above the doors, commemorates the 12 principal feasts or holy days of the church. A third row contains the icons of the prophets, facing the Virgin, seated in the center.

Above this are the Apostles, headed by Peter and Paul, all facing a central group of Deisis (Christ seated as judge, with the Virgin and John the Baptist at his sides).

IDDO

According to biblical tradition, a visionary whose writings were consulted by the compiler of the Chronicles for information concerning the affairs of Kings Solomon, Rehoboam and Abijah. Iddo's writings are referred to as "exposition." a "commentary" or a "mihrash" (2 Chronicles 9:29; 12:15).

IDOL

An image, representation of anything or a symbol that is an object of passionate devotion, whether material or imagined. God's law not to form images (Exodus 20:4-5) did not rule out the making of all representations and statues. This is indicated by God's later command to make two golden cherubs on the cover of the ark and to embroider representations of cherubs on the inner tent covering of ten tent cloths for the tabernacle and the curtain separating the Holy from the Most Holy (Exodus 25:18; 26:31-33). Likewise, the interior of Solomon's Temple, the architectural plans for which were given to David by divine inspiration (1 Chronicles 28:11-12) was beautifully embellished with engraved carvings of cherubs, palm-tree figures and blossoms.

These representations, however, were not idols for worship. Only the officiating priests saw the representations of the tabernacle interior and, later, of the Temple interior. No one but the High Priest entered the Most Holy, and that normally but once a year on the Day of Atonement (Hebrews 9:7). Thus there was no danger of the Israelites' being ensnared into idolizing the golden cherubs in the sanctuary. These representations primarily served as a picture of the heavenly cherubs (Hebrews 9:24-25). That they were not to be venerated is evident from the fact that the angels themselves were not to be worshiped (Revelation 19:10; 22:8-9).

The scriptures do not sanction the use of images as a means to address God in prayer. Such a practice runs counter to the principle that those seeking to serve God must worship Him with spirit and truth (John 4:24). He tolerates no mixing of idolatrous practices with true worship, although the Israelites had attached his name thereto (Exodus 32:3-10).

IDOLATRY

The veneration, love, worship or adoration of an idol. It is usually practiced toward a real or supposed higher power, whether such power is believed to have animate existence (as a human or animal god or an organization) or whether it is inanimate (as a force or lifeless object of nature). Idolatry generally involves some form, ceremony or ritual.

IDUMAEA

In Maccabean and Roman times the geographical boundaries of Idumaea did not include the heartland of ancient Edom east of the Arabah but embraced parts of what had formerly been Simeonite and Judean territory.

It is reported that the Idumaeans suffered a crushing defeat at the hands of Judas Maccabeus (1 Maccabees 5:3). Later, according to Josephus, John Hyrcanus subdued all the Idumaeans, allowing them to remain in the land on condition that they submit to circumcision and adhere to Jewish law. Rather than leave the country, the Idumaeans complied with this condition. Inhabitants of Idumaea, were among those who personally came to Jesus upon hearing of the "many things he was doing" (Mark 3:8).

IFRIT

In Islamic mythology, a class of infernal jinn (spirits below the level of angels and devils) noted for their strength and cunning.

IGNATIUS OF ANTIOCH, Saint

(died circa 100) Christian bishop of Antioch, condemned to death in Trajan's reign. Ignatius wrote seven letters (now precious early church documents) in which "catholic church" was first used to denote Christians everywhere and in which he tried to prove that Docetism, a doctrine which held that Christ's bodily sufferings were only "appearance," was heresy.

IGNATIUS OF LOYOLA, Saint

(1491-1556) Spanish founder of the Society of Jesus. Having spent his youth as a Basque nobleman and soldier, Loyola became converted to the religious life in 1521 while recovering from a serious wound. He wrote the famous *Spiritual Exercises* (begun 1522-23), and later went to Paris where, with St. Francis Xavier, he formed the Society of Jesus (1534). Loyola was its first general, and the author of its *Constitutions* (1547-50).

IHRAM

In Islam, term denoting the state of ritual consecration and purification during the Hajj, symbolized by the wearing of two, usually white, garments by male pilgrims (one of which may later be used as their shroud), and the observance of certain taboos. The Arabic word ihram is also used to designate the garments themselves as well as the state of consecration.

I'JAZ

In Islam, term denoting inimicability, especially of the Koran. The sacred text challenges those who oppose it to produce it like.

IJON

One of the places taken by the military forces of Syria's King Ben-hadad I circa 962-961 BC during the reign of Baasha (1 Kings 15:20-21). Nearly two centuries later Assyrian King Tiglath-pileser III conquered Ijon and exiled its population (2 Kings 15:29).

IJTIHAD

In Islam, term denoting independent or original interpretation of problems not precisely covered by the Koran.

IKHLAS, al-

The title of the 112th sura of the Koran; it means literally "loyalty" or "sincerity" and has been variously translated as "Pure (or Sincere) Religion" and "Purity of Faith." The sura belongs to the Meccan period and, like the other suras towards the end of the Koran. It is extremely short having only 4 verses. The title of the sura reflects the general orientation of these verses. The first two stress the Oneness and eternal nature of God while the second two stress that He has neither father or son nor equal. The sura is sometimes called The Sura of Unity and is said to encapsulate the essence of the whole Koran.

IKHTILAF

In Islam, term in the sense of difference, indicating the differences between and within the four Schools of Islamic law.

IKHWAN

In Islam, term denoting brethren; a title born by a variety of groups from medieval to modern times.

IKHWAN AL-SAFA

In Islam, phrase denoting Brethren of Purity; a group of Arab philosophers, theologians and intellectuals who flourished most probably in Basra in the 10th or 11th centuries. They produced a famous corpus of 52 Epistles which were encyclopedic in range, covering such subjects as diverse music, astronomy, embryology and philosophy. The Epistles are highly syncretic and draw on the Christian and Judaic traditions for material, as well as the Islamic. Their view of God is by turns the Unknowable One of Plotinus on the one hand, and the Creator God of the Koran, who operates directly within and on man's history, on the other. No attempt is made by the Ikhwan to reconcile these two opposing views.

ILHAD

In Islam, term meaning deviation from the correct path.

ILLUMINATED MANUSCRIPT

The decoration by hand of a written text with ornamental designs and illustrations, often in gold, silver and bright colors. Traditionally, illumination appears around the margins and often includes elaborate decoration of raised initials. Illustrated manuscripts existed in scroll form in ancient Egypt, an example being the celebrated *Book of the Dead.* The Celtic *Gospel Books* of the late 8th century AD, especially the Irish *Book of Kells,* are characterized by their extravagantly interlacing designs.

ILLYRICUM

A Roman province with varying boundaries that roughly corresponded to what today is the former Yugoslavia on the Adriatic Sea. After three years of fighting, Emperor Tiberius completely subdued the Dalmatians in 9 BC, and Dalmatia, Iapydia and Liburnia became the Roman province of Illyricum.

At Romans 15:19 the apostle Paul speaks of preaching in a circuit "as far as Illyuricum." Whether the original Greek is to be understood to mean that Paul actually preached in or merely up to Illyricum cannot be established with certainty.

ILM

Arabic word for knowledge, learning, science. A tradition from the Prophet Mohammed enjoins that knowledge should be sought even as far as China. Travel in search of knowledge became a popular and well-recognized scholarly activity in the Islamic Middle Ages.

ILM AL-HADITH

The science established by Muslim traditionalists in the 9th century to determine the validity of Mohammed's statements, actions, and approbations as reported by various authorities.

ILMARINEN

One of the chief deities of the Finnic peoples, who functions in the twin capacity of creator deity and weather god.

ILUMQUH

Arabian god of pre-Islamic times who is associated with the moon and is greater that the two other principal astral deities of South Arabia: the goddess Shams and the god Athtar who are associated with the Sun and the planet Venus, respectively.

ILUS

In Greek mythology, the founder of Ilium (Troy).He has been identified as the brother of Erichthonius or as the son of Tros and grandson of Erichthonius.

ILYAS, Mawlana Mohammed

(1885-1944) Founder of the Faith Movement in India. He became profoundly interested in tasawwuf early in life and was a member of the Cishtiyya order. After two pilgrimages to Mecca he concluded that he had a vocation to preach to those Indian masses who had little or no proper knowledge of their Islamic faith. He suffered from poor health throughout his life but this did not prevent him from much travel and teaching.

IMAGE

Representation of the external form of an object, e.g., a statue (especially of a saint etc. as an object of veneration). Whereas references to images in the Bible frequently refer to idolatry, this is not always the case. God, in creating man, said first "Let us make man in our image, according to our likeness" (Genesis 1:26-27). Since God's Son stated that his Father is "a Spirit," this rules out any physical likeness between God and man (John 4:24). Rather, man has qualities reflecting or mirroring those of his heavenly Maker, qualities that positively distinguished man from the animal creation. Though in the image of his Creator, man was not made to be an object of worship or veneration.

There is a myth that the representation of the human form in Islam is forbidden by the Koran; this is not the case. It was the hadith literature which instituted such a prohibition, advising that the artist would receive severe punishment on Judgement Day. What the Koran specifically forbids is the worship of idols; otherwise it shows Sulayman causing the jinn to build him statues. Although the hadith prohibition held sway in the Islamic Middle Ages, it was often ignored at the caliphal courts during this and later times. Sometimes, however, the artist would portray Mohammed with his face blanked out, as happened in some illustrated volumes of the life of the prophet Mohammed. This dislike of representing the human form is seen most clearly today in the mosque where the decoration is usually calligraphic or mosaic or arabesque. Similarly, one would not find the representation of the human form in a copy of the Koran; here the decoration is mainly calligraphic, often of the most beautiful kind.

IMAGE OF GOD

The theological description of man based on Genesis 1:26. Theology has taken this description both as the key to the makeup of man's being and as the revelation of the fulfillment towards which God's loving care is moving him. Latin theology's understanding of the imaging of the divine was strongly dependent on Pseudo-Dionysius's theme, the dynamic likening to the divine that constitutes the hierarchic governance of angels and men in the going forth from and return to God.

The later Greek elaboration of the concept, which makes man's higher intelligence and will the specification of the imaging of God, is more dependent on Greek than on Hebrew anthropology and actually shifts the imaging from man's closeness to God to his superiority over animals.

IMAM

Arabic word with a variety of meanings. Its primary meaning in Islam is that of prayer leader. Islam has no priests and thus the imam attached to the mosque is not ordained. However, any male Muslim may lead the pray in the absence of a mosque imam. The 12 early leaders of the Ithna Asharis are referred to as the Twelve Imams. The Isma'ilis acknowledge seven early Imams and the concept of imam plays a key role in the complex doctrines of Isma'ilism. In early Islamic history the title Imam was associated with the caliph.

IMITATION OF CHRIST

A Christian devotional book written between 1390 and 1440, linked to the name of Thomas a Kempis.

IMMACULATE CONCEPTION

In Roman Catholicism, a belief of ancient origin defined as a dogma in 1854 by Pope Pius IX in these words: "We declare, announce, and define that the doctrine which states that the Blessed Virgin Mary was preserved, in the first instant of her conception, by a singular grace and privilege of God omnipotent and because of the merits of Jesus Christ the Savior of the human race, free from all stain and original sin, is revealed by God and must be believed firmly and with constancy by all the faithful." The feast of Mary's Immaculate Conception is celebrated on December 8th and is a holy day of obligation for the Roman Catholic Church.

IMANNA AND BILULU

Ancient Sumerian myth probably originally used in southern Mesopotamia during the annual lamentation rites for Dumuzi, a fertility god who was believed to go through a yearly death and resurrection cycle.

IMMANENCE

In philosophy and theology, the fact or condition of residing or operating entirely within something. In its most important use, God is conceived as existing in and throughout the created universe, not as outside and separated from it.

IMMANUEL

Name first mentioned by the prophet Isaiah (7:14; 8:8), during the reign of Ahaz (761-745 BC). In Matthew 1:23, the only other occurrence, Immanuel is a name-title applied to Christ the Messiah.

IMMER

In the Old Testament, a descendant of Aaron designated head of the 16th priestly division in David's time (1 Chronicles 24:1, 6, 14). Apparently 1,052 of his descendants returned with Zerubbabel from Babylon in 537 BC (Ezra 2:37). Two of the "sons of Immer" were among those putting away their foreign wives in Ezra's time (Ezra 10:20).

IMMERSION

The most ancient manner of baptizing, i.e., by submerging the candidate, still the practice of the Eastern Churches. Baptism so received is the allusion of Paul (Romans 6:3-4) to being buried together with Christ. The other forms of baptizing are by sprinkling (aspersion) and by pouring (effusion) the water. Baptism by sprinkling is not allowed, although to baptize in this way would not invalidate the sacrament.

IMMOLATION

In its primary theological usage the distinctive element in sacrifice. The Christian theology of the Old Testament ceremonial precepts, was developed in relation to Christ's Passion and death and to Eucharistic teaching.

Sacrifice, an act of the virtue of religion, is one form of offering (obligation) by which the spiritual sacrifice of interior submission to God, is expressed, the offering distinctive of sacrifice, however, is one in which there is a living victim or a burning or pouring forth of the fruits of the earth.

Immolation particularly refers to the victim-offering; Christ's sacrifice is his immolation on the cross. Of the Eucharist the Council of Trent teaches that in the sacrifice of the Mass the same Christ is contained and is immolated bloodlessly who one for all offered himself bloodily once the altar of the cross.

IMMORTALITY

A belief in the continued life of the human being after death is found in both primitive and advanced societies. It is common to many religions and philosophies.

Belief in the immortal soul is fundamental in Christianity and to Islam, and is generally accepted in Judaism. Hinduism, Buddhism and Jainism do not recognize individual immortality, but believe that souls can be reincarnated several times until they reach ultimate and eternal bliss.

Pythagoras, Plato and other Greek philosophers believed in immortality, but Anaximenes and the Greek atomists did not believe in the existence of the soul and rejected it as a meaningless concept. This view was shared by later philosophers, including Thomas Hobbes and David Hume in England and William James and John Dewey in the United States. Others, like John Locke and Immanuel Kant agreed that the soul's existence could not be proved but argued that belief in the soul's immortality was justifiable on moral grounds.

IMMORTALITY OF THE SOUL

In Roman Catholicism, that characteristic of the soul by which it is free from death. The immortal or undying soul, reunites with the body at the final resurrection, and both share the eternal life of those who have been saved by the same sacrifice.

IMMUTABILITY OF GOD

A negative divine attribute, the impossibility of God's changing, "in whom there is no change or shadow of alteration" (James 1:17). Theology explains this attribute, a constant of biblical belief in God, on the basis that change connotes perfectibility.

Change in its first sense is proper only

to material things, subject to coming to be and to passing away, or subject to material alteration; by an analysis of change Aristotle concluded to the necessity of there being an absolutely unmoved (unchangeable) mover (Acts 17:27-28).

Change in a wider sense is the process towards achieving an unrealized potentiality. Since God can neither be material nor lack any actuality, there can be no change of any kind in the divine being. The consideration of the eternity of God, as He is absolutely and all at once, as it were, all that He is, is an attempt to give positive expression to the divine changelessness.

IMNAH

In the Old Testament, first-named son of Asher and forefather of the Imnites (Genesis 46:17; Numbers 26:44).

The name is also applied to the Levite whose son Kore was the gatekeeper to the east in temple service, in charge of the voluntary offerings of God, in Hezekiah's time (2 Chronicles 31:14).

IMPALEMENT

In the literal sense, the fastening of a victim either dead or alive to a stake. The execution of Jesus Christ is the best-known case (Luke 24:20; John 19:14-16; Acts 2:23-36). Impalements by nations in ancient times were carried out in a variety of ways.

It was Jewish law that those guilty of such heinous crimes as blasphemy or idolatry were first killed by stoning, beheading or by some other method, then their dead bodies were exposed on stakes or trees as warning examples to others (Deuteronomy 21:22; Joshua 8:29; 2 Samuel 21:6-9). The Egyptians may also have first killed their criminals before fastening them to stakes, as indicated by Joseph's prophetic words to Pharaoh's chief baker: "Pharaoh will lift up your head from off you and will certainly hang you upon a stake" (Genesis 40:22; 41:13).

IMPARTIALITY

Freedom from bias or favoritism; fairness. The Hebrew and Greek words used in the Bible for "partial" or "partiality" have the sense of viewing and judging from the outward appearance; respect of persons. Impartiality, therefore, is a matter of not letting the person or that which appears materially, such as his position, wealth, power or other influence, or a bribe (or, on the other hand, sentimentality for a poor person) sway one's judgment of actions in favor of the individual. Impartiality sees that all are treated in harmony with what is fair and just, according to what each deserves and needs (Proverbs 3:27).

IMPECCABILITY

Not merely the absence of sins committed by a free agent but also the impossibility of sinning. In Roman Catholic theology this quality is said to extend to three categories of existent free agents:
▲ the triune God;
▲ the humanity of Jesus and his mother;
▲ the blessed in heaven.

The question of sin obviously cannot apply to the Triune God. In regard to the humanity of Jesus, Scripture (John 8:46; Hebrews 7:26) and church teaching maintain that Jesus was sinless in fact and impeccable in theory.

A common objection is that the inability to sin destroys the concept of human freedom. Yet human freedom is a faculty (power or ability) designed to enable man to orient himself properly toward life's purpose.

IMPEDIMENTS TO MARRIAGE

In Roman Catholicism, an impediment is an obstacle; according to the Code of Canon Law there are certain obstacles to a valid marriage. These are called "diriment impediments." The Code defines a diriment impediment in this way: "A diriment impediment renders a person incapable of contracting marriage validly" (Canon 1073).

The Code lists these impediments in Canons 1083 to 1094. Ordinarily, a person may receive a dispensation from impediments arising from ecclesiastical (church) law, provided there is sufficient reason, by requesting it from one's diocesan bishop; in several cases, however, only the Holy see can grant a dispensation. Impediments arising from natural law (for example, impotence) cannot be given a dispensation.

IMPREMATUR

In the Roman Catholic Church, a permission, required by canon law and granted by a bishop, for the publication of any work on scripture; dogmatic, moral, or ascetical theology; or, in general, any writing containing something of peculiar significance to religion or morality.

IMPURITY

A term used for unlawful acts of sexual pleasure. Sins against purity can be committed in thought or action.

IMRAH

In the Old Testament, son of Zophah; a paternal head and also a head of chieftains of the tribe of Asher, a valiant, mighty man (1 Chronicles 7:36-40).

IMRAN, al-

The title of the third sura of the Koran; it means "The Family of Imran." The sura belongs to the Medinan period and has 200 verses. The title is drawn from the verse 33 which makes reference to Adam, Nuh, Ibrahim, and Al' Imran. Muslims identify the Imran in this verse as the father of Musa. However, Imran was also the name borne by the father of Maryam.

INADVERTENCE

Unintentional lack of knowledge occurring when one knows a thing but is not able to think of it in the circumstances. Inadvertence can diminish a person's responsibility for an act.

INCARDINATION

The act by which a cleric is subordinated to his diocese and bishop or a religious to his community superiors.

INCA RELIGION

An admixture of complex religious ceremonies, practices, animistic beliefs, varied forms of fetishism, and nature worships of the peoples ruled by the last pre-Columbian conquerors of the Andean regions of South America.

Inca religion is a Peruvian system deeply concerned with ritual and the organization of life and society during the Imperial Inca Period which began circa AD 1440 with the Inca conquests and declined with the coming of the Spanish.

Reflecting a subdued interest in mysticism and spirituality, ritual worship of the supreme deity, Viracocha, the creator, was less important than prayer to the lesser, more accessible deities, the huacas. These were associated with the food supply, significant places, physical cures, and the agricultural lunar calendar.

Viracocha, though represented in human form, was considered too distant and withdrawn from the world to be approached by any but members of a royal cult. Of major importance, however, was the sun, protector of crops and the personal ancestral god of the ruling family. Represented by a golden disk with rays around the face, the Sun shared his temple in Cuzco with other astral deities - stars, Moon, and the Weather-god.

In contrast to most Mesoamerican religion, the concept of the four directions of the universe had little significance for the Inca. During the Inca conquests, idols of conquered peoples, were sent to Cuzco along with priests to attend them, making Cuzco an important religious site.

Many special places, passes, summits, springs, bridges, as well as outstanding rock formations were considered dwelling places for natural powers.

Evil spirits were feared but not worshipped, since they could do no good.

The temples served to store images and ritual objects and to house priests and chosen women. They were maintained by produce of land assigned as the Sun's portions, official religious land as distinct from land reserved for government rulers and for the people.

The major public ceremonies were linked to the agricultural lunar year and were held in the open air. Ritual cleanliness was required of all participants in the services, thus making confessions of transgressions to a confessor, penance, and purification in running water, ideally at the confluence of rivers, an important feature of religious practice.

Magical and religious methods were used to cure injuries and disease, since maladies were considered to be of supernatural origin. A broken bone, for example, might have been caused by the anger of the spirit at the place where the bone was broken; thus sacrifice to the spirit was considered an essential part of the cure.

INCARNATION

The essence of the incarnation is that the Son of God (John 3:18) took human nature and was born as Jesus Christ, who was thus fully God and fully man (1 John 5:20). By the incarnation, redeemed mankind is in Christ united to God.

Buddhists hold that the 6th century BC Gautama was the embodiment of divine virtue and that other divinities also reveal themselves to man in human form, as in the Dalai Lamas of Tibet. The fullness of the divine and human natures in Jesus Christ was the subject of much controversy in early church, but was officially defined by the Council of Chalcedon (451).

INCENSE

A grainy substance made from resins of various plants that gives off an aromatic odor when burned; used in divine worship as a symbol of the ascent of prayer to God.

INDEPENDENCE DAY, Jewish

The fifth day of Lyyar (14 May); in 1948 Israel became an independent state and since then the day has been celebrated by Jews worldwide.

INDEPENDENTS

English Christians in the 16th and 17th centuries who wished to separate from the Church of England and form independent local churches composed only of Christian believers.

INDEX LIBRORUM PROHIBITORUM

Index of forbidden books; official list of books banned by the Roman Catholic Church as being in doctrinal or moral error. A book could be removed from the Index by expurgation of offending passages, and permission could be given to read prohibited books. The Index ceased publication in 1966.

INDIANS, Religion of North American

Although religious practices among North American Indians varied from tribe to tribe, there was a widespread belief in a divine supernatural power. To the Iroquois, it was orenda, to the Algonquian tribes it was manitu and to the Sioux it was wakonda. Another general characteristic of Indian religion was its close relationship with the world of nature. Animals were frequently personified and given human characteristics. Individuals could be guided by spirits in the guise of animals or birds. Many tribes had special spiritual ties with particular "totem" animals which dominated their tribal mythology.

The major gods were usually associated with the sky. The sun god was the central figure in the religion of the Pueblos, the tribes of the Northwest Coast, Plains and South-eastern Woodlands. Priests and religious leaders called shamans performed sacred ceremonies. They were sometimes called medicine men, since their duties included the treatment of the sick. For this they used herbal remedies or performed ritual calculated to exercise the spirits causing the illness. In some areas, shamans formed medicine societies in which each member had a particular status. The Mediwiwin of the Algonquians and the False Face Society of the Iroquois were two such organizations.

Religious ceremonies were closely tied to Indian mythology, to beliefs about the origins of the universe and the values and teachings of the individual societies. The sun dance of the Plains tribes, which sometimes included self-torture, emphasized tribal unity and the fertility of nature and of man necessary to survive. The Bison Dance ensures success before the great Bison hunts. The Pueblo kachina dancers performed in planting ceremonies and visited homes to punish or reward the behavior of children. Other Pueblo rituals dramatized stories from Pueblo mythology.

INDIAN SHAKER CHURCH

The most Christianized prophet cult among North-west American Indians; it is unconnected with the Shaker communities developed from the teachings of Ann Lee.

In the 1880s the Shaker Church was founded and the believers replaced shaman curing by its spiritual healing through shaking and dancing rituals. Christian elements include belief in the Trinity and Sunday worship in plain churches furnished with a prayer table, handbells, and many crosses. Christian sacraments and festivals are not observed.

INDULGENCE

In the Roman Catholic Church, a remission of the temporal punishment (on earth or in purgatory) that remains due for sin even after confession, absolution and doing penance. In consideration of prayers and good works, the church may grant plenary (full) or partial indulgences

According to church dogma the merits of Christ and the saints have created a reserve of grace than can be drawn upon to grant remission of such debts.

Indulgences are usually obtained by special prayers. Abuses in the practice of granting or selling indulgences were denounced by Martin Luther and outlawed by the Council of Trent (1562).

INDULT

Special permission given by the Holy see, usually for a specific period of time, to bishops or others to do something not usually permitted by the general laws of the church.

INERRENCE OF SCRIPTURE

The teaching of the Roman Catholic Church concerning the truth of the Sacred scriptures, expressed by Vatican Council II in this way: "Since, therefore, all that the inspired authors, or sacred writers, affirm should be regarded as affirmed by the Holy Spirit, we must acknowledge that the book of Scripture, firmly, faithfully, and without error, teaches that truth which God, for the sake of our salvation, wished to see confided to the sacred scriptures."

INFALLIBILITY

In Roman Catholicism, a doctrine of the church, that the church, through the power of God, is preserved from the possibility and liability of error in teaching matters of faith and morals. This charisma is present in a singular way in the bishop of Rome - the pope - and in the college of bishops. The doctrine is carefully described by Vatican Council II in its Dogmatic Constitution on the church:

"This infallibility, however, with which the divine redeemer wished to endow his church in defining doctrine pertaining to faith and morals, is co-extensive with the deposit of revelation, which must be religiously guarded and loyally and courageously expounded. The Roman pontiff, head of the college of bishops, enjoys this infallibility in virtue of his office, when, as supreme pastor and teacher of all the faithful - who confirms his brethren in the faith (see Luke 22:23) - he proclaims in an absolute decision a doctrine pertaining to faith or morals.

"For that reason his definitions are rightly said to be irreformable by their very nature and not by reason of the assent of the church, in as much as they were made with the assistance of the Holy Spirit promised to him in the person of blessed Peter himself; and as a consequence the are in no way in need of the approval of others, and do not admit of appeal to any other tribunal.

"For in such a case the Roman pontiff does not utter a pronouncement as a private person, but rather does he expound and defend the teaching of the Catholic Church as the supreme teacher of the universal church, in which the church's charisma of infallibility is present in a singular way. The infallibility promised to the church is also present in the body of bishops when, together with Peter's successor, they exercise the supreme teaching office. Now, the ascent of the church can never be lacking to such definitions on account of the same Holy Spirit's influence, through which Christ's whole flock is maintained in the unity of the faith and makes progress in it."

INFITAR, al-

The title of the 82nd sura of the Koran; it means "The Cleaving" or "The Splitting." The sura belongs to the Meccan period and has 19 verses. Its title is drawn from the first verse which refers dramatically to heaven being cleft, one of the signs of the beginning of the Day of Resurrection. The sura goes on to remind man of the Recording Angels (called her "Keepers" or "Guardians"), and that man's deed will determine his ultimate fate; the pious will go to heaven while the debauched will burn in hell.

INFUSED VIRTUES

In Roman Catholicism, the virtues of faith, hope, and charity that are infused in the soul through sanctifying grace. These virtues are not acquired by any human effort so that even baptized infants possess the infused virtues.

INJIL, al-

Arabic term for the gospel. The word is mentioned several times in the Koran. Islam believes that at one time there was a proto-gospel which accorded with all the data of the Koran. However, according to the doctrine of tahrif, that gospel has been or become corrupted; hence the present disparity between the gospels as Christians have them today and the message of the Koran.

INNEN

Term of Zen Buddhism used to describe a feeling of causal link or relationship of sympathetic affinity between a speaker and some other person, as though coming from past Karma.

INNER LIGHT

The distinctive theme of the Friends, the direct awareness of God that allows a person to know God's will for him. It was expressed in the teachings of George Fox (1624-91), founder of the Friends, who had failed to find spiritual truth in the English churches, and who finally experienced a voice saying: "There is one, even Christ Jesus, that can speak to thy condition."

INNOCENT I, Saint

(346-417) Pope from 401 to 417, who condemned Pegagianism, a heresy concerning the role of grace and free will. His papacy was endangered by the Visigothic chief Alaric, who besieged Rome (408-410) because the West Roman Emperor Flavius Honorius refused to appease him. His acknowledgment of Alexander as bishop of Antioch (414) restored communications between the sees and ended the Meletian schism, a complex 4th century controversy about the nature of the Trinity.

INNOCENT II

(Georgio Parareschi Dei Guidone; 1065-1143), Pope from 1130 to 1143. He confirmed the rule and customs of

the Templars, one of the three orders of Knighthood during the Crusades. During his pontificate he dealt chiefly with two struggles. He fought for church independence when the Romans established a commune with a senate free from papal authority. He also placed France under the interdict - a denial of the sacraments - when King Louis VII of France refused to accept the papal choice for archbishop of Bourges.

INNOCENT III, Saint

(circa 1161-1216) Pope from 1198. Under him the medieval papacy reached the summit of its power and influence. In an assertion of temporal power he forced King John of England to become his vassal and had Emperor Otto deposed in favor of Frederick II. He initiated the Fourth Crusade (1202) and supported the Crusade against the Albigenses (1208). He presided over the Fourth Lateran Council (1215), culmination of the entire medieval papacy.

INNOCENT IV

(Sinibaldo Fieschii; 1176-1254) One of the great pontiffs of the Middle Ages, whose clash with Holy Roman Emperor Frederick II formed an important chapter in the conflict between papacy and empire. He believed in the universal dominion of the papacy and belief in universal responsibility of the papacy that led him to attempt the evangelization of the East and the unification of Christian churches.

INNOCENT V

(Peter of Tarentaise; 1224-1276) Pope during 1276 and the first Dominican pontiff. During his short pontificate he tried to initiate a crusade, reunite the Greek and Roman churches, and pacify Italy's warring states.

INNOCENT VI

(Etienne Aubert; 1288-1362) Pope from 1352 to 1362. He prohibited the granting of innumerable benefices to one recipient, urged prelates to reside in their sees, and reformed the Papal Curia at Avignon, where the papacy resided from 1307 to 1377.

INNOCENT VII

(Cosimo Gentile de Migliorati; 1336-1406) Pope from 1404 to 1406. His election was opposed at Rome, where it caused considerable strife, and at Avignon (France), where the Great Western Schism (1378-1417) was perpetuated by the rival election of Antipope Benedict XIII.

INNOCENT VIII

(Giovanni Battista Cibo; 1432-1492) Pope from 1484, was worldly and unscrupulous. He fomented the witchcraft hysteria and meddled in Italian politics. For a fee he kept the brother and rival of Sultan Bayazid II imprisoned.

INNOCENT IX

(Giovanni Antonio Facchinetti; 1519-1591) Pope for two months during 1591. He assumed practically all administration under the ailing pope Gregory XIV, whom he was chosen to succeed as pope on October 29, 1591. He died two months later.

INNOCENT X

(Gian Battista Ramphili; 1574-1655) Pope from 1644 to 1655. In theological matters he intervened in the quarrel between the Jesuits and the Jansenists and in a bull of 1653 condemned five propositions by Bishop Cornellius Jansen, the founder of Jansenism. A century of controversy with the Jansenists ensued, which was particularly damaging to the French church. By the time of Innocent's death, papal prestige had seriously declined.

INNOCENT XI

(Benedetto Odescalchi; 1611-1689) Pope from 1676. An opponent of Quietism he favored toleration of Protestantism, and over this and the issue of papal power clashed with Louis XV of France.

INNOCENT XII

(Antonio Pignatelli; 1615-1700) Pope from 1691 to 1700. He is best known for the breaking up of the politico-religious deadlock between King Louis XIV of France and the Holy See by influencing Louis to disavow the four Gallician Articles of 1682 issued against Innocent XI.

INNOCENT XIII

(Michelangelo Conti; 1655-1724) Pope from 1721 to 1724. He recognized James (the Old Pretender) as the king of England and promised him subsidies conditional upon the re-establishment of Roman Catholicism in England. Distrusting the Jesuits and their missionaries in China, who modified Christian usage to attract converts, Innocent commanded the Society of Jesus to obey Clement's bull of 1713, which prohibited these rites and practices.

INQUISITION

A medieval agency of the Roman Catholic Church to combat heresy, first made official in 1231, when Pope Gregory IX appointed a commission of Dominicans to investigate heresy among the Albigensians of South France. It aimed to save the heretic's soul, but a refusal to recant was punished by fines, penance or imprisonment, and often by confiscation of land by the secular authorities. Later the penalty was death by burning.

Torture, condemned by former popes, was permitted in heresy by Innocent IV (died 1254). The accused was not told the name of his accusers but could name his own enemies so that their hostile testimony might be discounted. Often the Inquisition was an object of political manipulation. In 1542 it was reconstituted to counter Protestantism in Italy; its modern descendant is the Congregation of the Doctrine of the Faith.

The Spanish Inquisition, founded in 1478 by Ferdinand V and Isabella, was a branch of government and was distinct from the papal institution. Its first commission was to investigate Jews who has publicly embraced Christianity but secretly held to Judaism. Under the grand inquisitor Torquemada, it became an agency of official terror - even St. Ignatius of Loyola was investigated. It was extended to Portugal and South America and not dissolved until 1820.

INRI

An abbreviation formed of the initial letters of the title Pilate had affixed to the cross on which Jesus was crucified: *Jesus Nazarenus Rex Iudaeorum,* according to the vulgate version of John 19:19. This abbreviation is often used in Western art in representations of the crucifixion.

INSAN, al-

The title of the 76th sura of the Koran; the Arabic word means "Man." The sura belongs to the Medinan period and has 31 verses. Its title is drawn from the reference to man in the first verse. The sura begins by dividing mankind into the grateful and their opposite, reiterating the reward for each. The rewards for the good are outlined in considerable detail. The end of this sura provides encouragement for Mohammed in his mission.

IN SHA'A ALLAH

Very common Muslim expression, the equivalent of the Latin Deo Volente. Verses 23 and 24 of Surat al Kahf counsel that one should not say that one will do something tomorrow but rather "If God wills."

INSHIQAQ, al-

The title of the 84th sura of the Koran; it means "The Splitting Apart." The sura belongs to the Meccan period and has 25 verses. Its title is taken from the first verse which refers to "heaven" being split apart. This may be compared with the opening of Surat al-Infitar. The sura goes on to mention the judgment with books on the Last Day; the sinner will receive his book behind his back and be consigned to hell.

INSPIRATION

The apostle Paul stated at 2 Timothy 3:16: "All Scripture is inspired of God." The phrase "inspired of God" translates the compound Greek word theopneustos, meaning, literally, "God-breathed" or "breathed by God."

This is the only occurrence of this Greek term in the scriptures. Its use here clearly identifies God as the source and producer of the Sacred Scriptures, the Bible. Their being "God-breathed" finds some parallel in the expression found in the Hebrew scriptures at Psalm 33:6: "By the word of God the heavens themselves were made, and by the spirit (or breath) of his mouth all their army."

INSPIRATION, Biblical

The teaching of the Roman Catholic Church, as expressed in Vatican Council II, that "the divinely revealed realities, which are contained and presented in the text of sacred scripture, have been written down under the inspiration of the Holy Spirit. For Holy Mother Church relying on the faith of the apostolic age, accepts as sacred and canonical the books of the Old and the New Testaments, whole and entire, with all their parts, on the grounds that, written under the inspiration of the Holy Spirit (see John 20:31; 2 Timothy 3:16; 2 Peter 1:19-21, 2 Peter 3:15-16), they have God as their author, and have been handed on as such to the church herself. To compose the sacred books, God chose certain men who, all the while he employed them in this task, made full use of their powers and facilities so that, though he acted in them and by them, it was as true authors that they consigned to writing whatever he wanted written, and no more."

INSTALLATION

In biblical terminology, the induction of the priesthood into office. Aaron and his sons were taken from the Kohathite family of the tribe of Levi to serve as the priesthood of Israel (Exodus 6:16-20; 28:1). Their installation occupied seven days, apparently falling on Nisdnan 1-7, circa 1512 BC, while Israel was encamped at the foot of Mount Sinai in Arabia (Exodus 40:2, 12, 17). The tent of meeting had just been completed and set up on the first day of the month; the priestly family had been chosen by Hod, and now Moses, the brother of Aaron, as mediator of the Law covenant was commanded to perform the ceremony of their sanctification and installation. Instructions for the procedure are given in Exodus chapter 29 and the record of Moses' carrying out the ceremony is in Leviticus chapter 8.

The Bible gives no record of an installation ceremony for the successors of Aaron. Evidently the one installation service was sufficient to place the Aaronic house and all its male offspring in their priestly office once and for all, to continue to time indefinite, down until the installation in office of the true and everlasting High Priest Jesus Christ (Hebrews 7:12, 17, 9:11-12).

INSTITUTES OF THE CHRISTIAN RELIGION

Theological masterpiece of John Calvin; a summary of biblical theology that became the normative statement of the Reformed faith. First published in 1536, it was revised and enlarged by Calvin in several editions before the final and definitive edition was published in 1559.

The final edition is organized into four books concerning Creator, Redeemer, Spirit, and Church. The dominating themes deal with God's sovereignty, His grace, and His redemption of undeserving sinners.

INSTITUTIONAL CHURCH

A term used in two senses.

1 A description of any church as organized with some structural form of authority, pursuing a special mission and accepting set means of sanctifica-

tion and modes of worship.

2 An instrument of the Social Gospel movement. The term was applied to churches that also sought to be agencies for social service on behalf of the urban poor.

INSTRUMENTAL CAUSE

An efficient cause that in its use of a principal cause, produces an effect greater than itself. The qualities and function proportionate to the instrument enter into the makeup of the final effect, but that effect matches the genius or power of the user of the instrument.

Theology uses the meaning of instrumental causality in assigning the function of Christ's human powers with regard to divine effects, e.g., miracles; or the function of the sacramental signs.

INSUFFLATION

A blowing or breathing upon a person or thing to symbolize the giving of the Holy Spirit and the expulsion of an evil spirit (John 20:22). This ritual action is used in exorcism, the stages of the catechumate, and in the blessing of chrism. As this action signifies the expulsion of an evil spirit, it is sometimes referred to as exsufflation.

INTEGRITY OF CONFESSION

An obligation imposed upon the penitent to insure that the confession of sins, a necessary part of the sign of the sacrament of penance, is entire and complete. It requires the penitent to confess all serious sins not yet remitted by the power of the keys, thereby submitting them to the judgment of the church. This means that the penitent must avow all serious sins committed since baptism which have either never been confessed, or which were confessed but were not forgiven because of some obstacles such as ill-deposition on the part of the penitent, which prevented the sacrament from being effective.

INTERCESSION

Prayers offered on behalf of others. The term bears on one meaning of impetration: that prayer is addressed to the saints, not as though they have power to answer it - that kind of prayer is offered to God alone - but to obtain their supportive petitioning, their intercession. The most important meaning of intercession, however, is that it is an inherent element in the communion of saints, i.e., the vital communication existing in the mystical body of Christ.

INTERCOMMUNION

An agreement between two religious bodies that permits participants to receive communion in either denomination regardless of doctrinal differences.

INTERCONFESSIONALISM

Movements of thought and action relating to churches that have different confessions of faith. With the rise of the ecumenical movement the importance of Christian unity has made it seem necessary for Christians to seek some way of securing a united witness despite their differences of doctrinal expression.

INTERFAITH DIALOGUE

Conservation between representatives of different communions with the aim of developing greater understanding and finding a basis for greater cooperation. It is distinguished from debate in which representatives try to prove that the position of their communion is right and the others are wrong.

INTERNATIONAL CHURCH OF THE FOURSQUARE GOSPEL

Pentecostal denomination established by Aimee Semple McPherson in Los Angeles in 1927. It developed from McPherson's work at the Angelus Temple (opened January 1, 1923), where she regularly preached to large crowds, held healing sessions, and dispensed charity to the poor.

INTERNATIONAL MISSIONARY COUNCIL

Cooperative organization linking numerous national and regional Protestant mission associations, formally organized in 1921 at Lake Mohonk, New York; as an early expression of ecumenism, it united with the World Council of Churches in 1961 and became the Division of World Mission and Evangelism.

INTERTESTAMENTAL LITERATURE

Jewish literature which appeared in the last two or three centuries BC and provides a background to the New Testament. It includes most of the apocryphal books (mainly found in the Septuagint but not in the Hebrew Bible) and the pseudepigrapha, works of later date ascribed to ancient authors like Enoch, the patriarch, and Moses. The volume of extant intertestamental literature has been greatly amplified by the discovery of the Dead Sea scrolls at Qumran.

INVASATI

A sect, probably related to the Turlupians, that arose in Germany and spread into France during the 14th century. Adherents engaged in obscene dances while invoking the demons. For these practices and for their antinomianism they were condemned by Gregory IX in 1373.

INVESTITURE CONTROVERSY

Conflict between European rulers and the papacy in the 11th and 12th centuries. Originally a dispute about the appointment of bishops and abbots, it became a power struggle between church and state. In England a compromise was reached in 1107; in Germany the issue was resolved in 1122 by the Concordat of Worms.

INVISIBLE CHURCH

A description to designate the true church, a spiritual, eschatological community, as a reality distinct from the visible church, an empirical, imperfect, organized institution.

INVOCATION OF SAINTS

Praying to those who have reached eternal life, because of their nearness to God and so their special powers of impetration and intercession. The antiquity and constant sanctioning of the practice was declared by the Council of Trent against the reformers' charge that it was a form of idolatry.

IO

In Greek mythology, daughter of Inachus, the river god of Argos. Under the name of Callithia, Io was regarded as the first priestess of Hera, the wife of Zeus.

IOB

In the Old Testament, third-named son of Issachar (Genesis 46:13).

IONA COMMUNITY

A missionary group of clergy and laymen within the Church of Scotland. In was founded in 1938 by George MacLeod, a parish minister in Glasgow, who hoped to infuse a new vitality into Christianity.

The members of such a community adhere to a community "rule" of prayer and Bible study rather than to any particular ritual. Christian groups, young people, and individuals of all denominations visit Iona every summer for recreation of body, mind, and spirit.

IPHIGENIA

In Greek mythology, daughter of Agamemnon and Clytemnestra, and sister of Orestes and Electra. Agamemnon was ordered to sacrifice Iphigenia. On the pretext of marrying Iphigenea to Achilles, Agamemnon summoned his daughter from Mycenae. However, at the last moment before the sacrifice the goddess Artemis put a stag in her place and had Iphigenia carried off in a cloud to the land of Tauris. The story of Iphigenia is the subject of a tragedy by Euripides and works by such later writers as Racine and Goethe.

IPHTAH

In the Old Testament records, a city of Judah in the Shepheliah (Joshua 15:20), circa six miles north-north-west of Hebron.

IRA

In the Old Testament, a Jairite listed among King David's leading officers as "a priest of David" (2 Samuel 20:26). Ira perhaps was a descendant of the Jair mentioned at Numbers 32:41 and, therefore, in this case the designation "priest" may signify "chief minister." There is no biblical evidence that the Jairites were Levites.

IRELAND, John

(1838-1918) First archbishop of St. Paul, Minnesota; head of the liberal Roman Catholic clergy who promoted the integration of predominantly immigrant parishes into the life of the United states church (and society as a whole) - in opposition to the separatist tendency of many ethnic groups to preserve their European-style churches, with priests of their own nationalities.

IRENAEUS, Saint

(circa 139-200) Theologian and Father of the church. After going to Gaul as a missionary, he was made bishop of Lugdunum (Lyons) in 178. A major defender of the early Christian church, he wrote several theological works. The most important is *Against Heresies,* in which he refutes gnosticism.

IRENE

(752-803) Byzantine ruler and saint of the Greek Orthodox Church who was instrumental in restoring the use of icons in the Eastern Roman Church. The wife of the Byzantine emperor Leo IV, Irene became, on her husband's death in September 780, guardian of their 10 year-old son, Constantine VI, and co-emperor with him. Irene's zeal in restoring icons and her patronage of monasteries ensured her a place among the saints of the Greek Orthodox Church.

IRI

In the Old Testament, son of Bela; a paternal head and valiant, mighty man of Benjamin (1 Chronicles 7:7).

IRIS

In Greek mythology, the personification of the rainbow and a messenger of the gods.

IRISH CROSSES

An important body of sculptural and monumental art, some 50 examples of which date from AD 800. The series continues into the Romanesque age. Starting with pillars and roughly hewn stones, the series includes upright cross-bearing slabs, closely analogous in form and ornament to the monuments of the Christian Picts, and culminates in high wheel-headed crosses such as those of Moone and Muiredach. Such crosses were probably set up as preaching-stations in the countryside, and were also regularly erected in and around monasteries and churches. Elaborate iconography of biblical and lay scenes and rich Celtic ornament were developed.

IRPEEL

In biblical times, a city of Benjamin (Joshua 18:21-27). Some geographers suggest as a possible identification Rafat, a village circa six miles north-west of Jerusalem.

IRRELIGION

A positive refusal to offer the worship due to God.

IRU

In the Old Testament, the first-names son of Caleb the spy; of Judah's tribe (1 Chronicles 4:15).

IRVING, Edward

(1792-1834) Minister of the Church of Scotland whose teachings became the basis of the religious movement known as Irvingism, later called the Catholic Apostolic Church. Formed shortly after his death by several disciples and associates, the sect thought to emphasize the unity of all Christians in a universal church, and to prepare for the Second Coming. The church flourished until the end of the 19th century.

ISA

Arabic name for Jesus. He is regarded as a major prophet for Muslims who has a prominent place in the Koran. Islam regards Jesus as purely human and not as the Son of God. Muslims thus have no concept of salvation history associated with Jesus. The latter's annunciation by Jibril and subsequent birth is described in some detail in Surat Maryam. Jesus performs the miracle of the table in Surat al-Ma'ida and he is not crucified but rather taken up by God in Surat al-Nisa. Jesus is frequently called "Son of Mary" in the Koran and he is portrayed speaking in the cradle in Surat Maryam.

ISAAC

In the Old Testament (Genesis), second of the patriarchs of Israel, only son of Abraham and Sarah, father of Esau and Jacob. Although Sarah was past the age of childbearing, God promised Abraham and Sarah that they would have a son, and Isaac was born. The story of Abraham's obedience to God's command to sacrifice Isaac was used as an example of faith (Hebrews 11:27).

ISAAC BEN JOSEPH OF CORBEIL

(1209-1280) Codifier of Jewish religious law and author of the once extremely popular Sefer Mitzwat Gajan.

ISAAC BEN MOSES OF VIENNA

(1180-1250) Codifier of and commentator on Jewish religious law whose frequently quoted "Light is Sown" is also valued for its descriptions of Jewish life in Europe.

ISAAC OF ANTIOCH

(389-460). Syrian writer, probably a priest of an independent Syrian Christian church and author of a wealth of theological literature.

ISAAC OF NINEVEH

(623-700) Syrian bishop, theologian, and monk whose writings on mysticism became a fundamental source for both Eastern and Western Christians.

ISAAC OF STELLA

(1100-1169) Monk, philosopher, and theologian, a leading thinker in 12th century Christian humanism and proponent of a synthesis of Neoplatonic and Aristotelian philosophies.

ISAAC THE GREAT, Saint

(345-439) Spiritual head of the Armenian Orthodox Church, principal advocate of Armenian cultural and ecclesiastical independence and collaborator in the first translation of the Bible and varied Christian literature into Armenian.

ISAIAH

Hebrew prophet, after whom the Old Testament Book of Isaiah is named. The greatest and most eloquent of the Hebrew prophets, Isaiah preached in the second half of the 8th century BC. He warned Judah against foreign alliances, and told of the coming of a Messiah.

ISAIAH, Ascension of

A pseudepigraphical work (a non-canonical writing that resembles in style and content authentic biblical literature) the title of which is derived from the 5th-7th century Ethiopic edition, the only complete extant version. It contains a description of the tiers of heaven paralleling that found in the Second Book of Enoch and in the New Testament.

ISAIAH, Book of

One of the major prophetical writings of the Old Testament. The superscription identifies Isaiah as the son of Amos and his book as "the vision of Isaiah..." concerning Judah and Jerusalem in the days of Uzziah, Jotham, Ahaz, and Hezekiah, kings of Judah. Isaiah was a great Hebrew prophet of the 8th century BC. He condemns the decadence of Judah, foretelling coming disaster; he warns against trusting in foreign alliances rather than in God and heralds the Messiah (Matthew 12:17-21). When Jesus entered a synagogue in Nazareth and got up to read they handed him a scroll of Isaiah (Luke 4:16-21).

ISHAQ

Arabic word for Isaac, the son of Ibrahim (Abraham) and younger brother of Isma'il. Muslim commentators often identify Ishaq as the reward given to Ibrahim after the latter's obedience with Isma'il.

ISHARAT AL-SA'A

In Islam, the signs of the Hour (i.e. of the Last Day). There are a large number of signs given both in the Koran and the hadith literature. The former talks of the darkening sun, boiling seas and moving mountains; the latter chronicles a general breakdown in morals followed by the arrival of such figures as al-Dajjal, Isa and the Mahdi. Gog and Magog will also appear as cannibals to terrify the earth.

ISHI

In the Old Testament, a descendant of Judah; son of Appaim and father of Sheshan (1 Chronicles 2:3, 31). The name is also applied to a Simeonite whose four sons are noted in the Chronicles for having led 500 to victory against the Amalekites living in Mount Seit (1 Chronicles 4:42-43).

ISHKUR

In Mesopotamian religion, god of the rain and thunderstorms of spring. He was the city god of Bit Khakhuru in the central grasslands region.

ISHMA

In the Old Testament, an early descendant of Judah (1 Chronicles 4:1-3).

ISHMAEL

In the Old Testament, son of Abraham and Hagar, his Egyptian concubine.

Sarah, Abraham's wife, feared she was too old and gave him her slave. Hagar. But later, when Isaac was born to Sarah, Hagar and Ishmael were driven into the desert, where a spring created by God miraculously saved their lives. Ishmael became a famous warrior and fathered 12 sons. The 12 Arab tribes were called Ishmaelites after him. Muslims venerate Ishmael as a patriarch.

ISHMAEL BEN ELISHA

(2nd century AD) Jewish Talmudic teacher who completed the thirteen hermeneutical rules for interpreting the Torah, contributed to the commentaries on the law, and founded a school that wrote the legal commentary called Mekhilta.

ISHMAELITE

A descendant of Ishmael, the firstborn son of Abraham by Hagar, the Egyptian handmaid of Sarah (Genesis 16:1-4).

In the course of the time it is quite likely that intermarriage between Ishmaelites and descendants of Abraham through Keturah (Genesis 25:1-4) occurred, resulting in the race of Arabs that occupied sections of Arabia. In the seventh century Mohammed, the founder of Islam, claimed to be an Ishmaelite descendant of Abraham.

ISHMAIAH

In the Old Testament, an outstanding Gibeonite warrior who joined David's army at Ziklag before Saul's death (1 Chronicles 12:1-4). In this early list of David's "thirty" leading warriors, Ishmaiah is called their head, but the absence of his name in later lists suggests that he may have died in the meantime (2 Samuel 23:8-19).

ISHPAH

In the Old Testament, a head of the people among the Benjaminites living in Jerusalem; son or descendant of Beriah (1 Chronicles 8:1, 16).

ISHVARA

Sanskrit divine title ("Supreme Lord") used in two separate contexts.

1 In the Yoga system, Ishvara becomes an object of the student's concentration and thereby facilitates the eventual achievement of samadhi or liberation.

2 In one version of the Vedanta system, Ishvara is the title given by Shankara to Brahman (God) as personified, as involved in the universe and knowable by humans (as opposed to Brahman which transcends personality and which is beyond knowledge).

In another version, that of Ramanuja, the Ishvara whom humans can know and especially love is the transcendent Lord himself.

ISIDORE OF SEVILLE, Saint

(560-636) Theologian and Father of the Church, who wrote an encyclopedia of divine and human subjects and the canon law of the Spanish church.

ISIHAN

In the Old Testament, a Benjaminite son or descendant of Shashak; one of the heads of the people living in Jerusalem (1 Chronicles 8:22-28).

ISHTOB

In biblical times, one of the small kingdoms that provided fighting men for the sons of Ammon to use against David. The forces from "Ishtob" and their allies were defeated (2 Samuel chapter 10).

ISHVAH

In the Old Testament, the second of Asher's four sons (Genesis 46:17; 1 Chronicles 7:30). Since he is not listed in the families of Asher, it is possible that he had no sons or that his line of descent soon died out (Numbers 26:44).

ISHVI

In the Old Testament, third-listed son of Asher and founder of the Ishvite family in that tribe (Genesis 46:17; Numbers 26:44).

ISIS

Worshiped by the ancient Egyptians as the universal mother goddess and the goddess of nature and fertility. She was also the lawgiver, the queen of the underworld and protector of the welfare of the state and man. Isis was the sister and wife of Osiris, and mother of Horus. She was always pictured in human form. After 100 BC the cult was observed throughout Greece, and later in Rome. It survived into the 6th century AD.

ISLAM

One of the world's great monotheistic religions. The word means literally "submission" (to the will of God). Islam was founded by the prophet Mohammed in the seventh century as a result of the revelation of the Koran which he received via the angel Jibril from God.

Islam is the youngest of the three monotheistic religions to develop in the Middle East. It incorporates many elements of Judaism and Christianity, which preceded it by hundreds of years. The religion is sometimes incorrectly called "Mohammedanism," with the mistaken implication that Muslim's worship Mohammed himself, rather than follow the religion he preached.

The holy book of Islam is the Koran which sets forth the fundamental beliefs of Islam as revealed by God to Mohammed. These include the five basic duties of every Muslim, and the rules that govern moral behavior and social life.

Muslims also look to Mohammed's way of life for guidance in their daily lives. His teachings, called Sunna, are collected in the hadith, which means "traditions." Together, the Koran and the Sunna provide instructions governing all aspects of the personal and communal life of Muslims. A system of law, the Shari'a, has been developed on the basis of the Koran and the Sunna. At various times, the Shari'a had been the law of many Muslim countries.

In Islam, public worship is held in

buildings called mosques. Muslims must ritually wash themselves in the courtyard. The mosques are usually elaborately decorated, but no representations of animal of human figures are permitted because of proscriptions against idolatry. Decoration consists of abstract or floral patterns. When praying, five times during the day, Muslims face in the direction of their holy city Mecca.

Muslims do not have ordained priests. Worship is led by a lay religious leader called an imam. Traditionally, Muslims are called to prayer by a muezzin, who chants from a rooftop or from a minaret, a tall tower attached to the mosque. Other leaders in Muslim communities include the ulema (or ulama), authorities in the Shari'a, whose duties may include giving guidance, opinions or even deciding legal disputes.

ISLAM, Basic duties of

Also known as the Pillars of Islam; to be performed regularly and correctly with an awareness of their relevance to practical life. This brings the Muslim's life into line with Allah's wishes. It also enables the believer to fit neatly into the system of Islam which aims at the establishment of truth and the eradication of untruth.

Ash-Shahadah

The first and most fundamental of the five basic duties, is to pronounce the first declaration of faith; There is no God except Allah, and Mohammed is Allah's messenger.

Salah

These are compulsatory prayers, offered five times a day, either individually or in congregation. They are considered to be the practical demonstration of faith and to keep believers in constant touch with their Creator. This makes them conscious of the basic duty to work for the establishment of a true order in society and to remove untruth, evil and the undecent. Salah should induce qualities of self-discipline, steadfastness and obedience to the truth, making Muslims honest and courageous.

Zakah

This welfare contribution is a compulsory payment from a Muslim's annual savings. The rate of payment is 2.5 percent on cash, jewelry and precious metals, with another rate for animals and agricultural products. It is neither a charity donation nor a tax. Zakah is an act of worship and it is one of the Islamic economy's fundamental principles, designed to develop an equitable society where everyone has a right to contribute and share.

Sawn

From dawn to sunset every day during ramadan, the ninth month of the Islamic calendar, Muslims should refrain from eating, drinking, smoking and sexual relations. It is a means of achieving self-control, designed to raise a person's moral and spiritual standards above selfishness, laxity and other vices. Sawn is an annual training program to refresh Muslims' determination to fulfil their obligation to Allah.

Hajj

This pilgrimage to the "House" of Allah is obligatory at least once in the life of all Muslims who can afford to undertake it. It is a journey to Al-Ka'bah, in Mecca, Saudi Arabia, where the Prophet Mohammed was born.

Hajj symbolizes the unity and equality of mankind and is the annual assembly of the Muslim community. It also stands as the peak of Muslims' obligatory duties as it should lay bare to them that they belong to no-one but Allah.

ISLAMIC ART

The principal achievement of Islamic religious art is the mosque, and its most exclusive achievement is the development of calligraphy as a decorative style. The mosque reflects the integral relationship between the social organization and the religious faith of Islam.

It is marked by great congregational space, orientation toward Mecca, the tall minaret for summoning to prayer, and a pulpit-like place within for the imam who leads prayers.

Types of mosques include the Romano-

Byzantine, as in Syria (Damascus); the great hall with columns, as in Egypt and Spain (Cordoba); the courtyard with vaults and arcades, as in Iran (Isfahan); and the central plan, derived from Christian churches after 1453. In recent years, new architectonic styles have resulted in beautiful mosques such as the one in Casablanca for some 25,000 Muslims.

The basic design of a court surrounded by halls derived from the house of the Prophet in Medina. The huge outer gates of some mosques show the direct influence of palace architecture.

Islamic art has expressed itself also in small mosques, educational institutions, and memorials, among the earliest of which is the Dome of the Rock in Jerusalem. The most spectacularly lovely architectural form of impressive grandeur is the Taj Mahal in India.

Decoration of architecture and religious articles with words and phrases from the Koran, beautifully and intricately inlaid, evidence the preeminence of calligraphy as a decorative art deriving principally from Muslim reverence for the text of the holy Koran.

ISLAMIC MYSTICISM

The aspect of Islamic belief and practice in which Muslims seek to find the truth of divine love and knowledge through direct personal experience of God. Islamic mysticism, called Sufism in Western languages, consists of a variety of paths that are designed to help the mystic ascertain the nature of man and of God and to facilitate his experience of the presence of divine love and wisdom in the world.

ISLAMIC PHILOSOPHY

In Arabic termed falsafa, the philosopher being called failasuf (plural falasifa), though frequently the terms hikma (wisdom) and hakim are used in the same sense.

In Islam falsafa is distinct and separate from speculative theology as the two rest upon quite different sources and are developed in comparative independence, representing quite divergent attitudes in almost all fundamental matters.

The falsalfa is rooted in Greek philosophy which was transmitted and, for the most part, translated by Christians, most significantly those of the school of the Nestorian Hunain ibn Ishaq (801-878).

Filtered as it was through the end of the Hellenistic age, the Greek philosophical tradition was presented to Islam as a single, basically unified system, Aristotelian in its form but containing a heavy admixture of Neoplatonism and already adapted to theological perspectives.

The Muslims, thus, viewed philosophy as a single system elaborated by Plato, perfected by Aristotle, and further elaborated in matters of detail by successive generations of commentators.

Because of its apparent unity as presented in the contemporary tradition, they saw philosophy as giving the rational, analytic structure of the universe, i.e., as the one (and so necessary and true) description of the nature of the universe discovered by reason or mind without the aid of divine revelation.

The Muslim falasifa then began to study and carry on this tradition with an Islamic context to which certain of its elements and vocabulary have inevitably to be adapted; the system was in some respects, however, inseparable from the basically Greek view of the universe; and a thoroughgoing commitment to the system in its unity demanded a proportionate commitment to a universe, some of whose essential structures and underlying principles were altogether alien to the native Arab and Islamic institution of the nature of being and the universe, which was elaborated in the classical kalam.

The system which had the widest and most profound influence within Islam is that elaborated by al-Farabi (died 950) and Ibn Sina (died 1037). Following Neoplatonic conceptions of the nature of the intellect and of God's unity, God's action was conceived as absolutely simple, necessitated by His nature from which there flows eternally first one and then a growing multitude of ever more complex beings in a descending ontological hierarchy.

ISLAMIC THEOLOGY

The speculative theology that is native to Islam and is referred to in Arabic by the term kalam (discourse), a word taken, in its technical sense, from Greek dialexis, as it was used by the Stoa.

The earliest theological debates in Islam centered around the questions of faith (which involves the notion of belonging to the Muslim community) and of the imamate (Imam), which was the focus of the contentions of the Shiites and the Kharijites.

From the beginnings, the various systems that were attempted show a building of diverse elements, eclectically chosen from past traditions, Greek and Christian, tending in the main to follow a fundamentally Stoic pattern in their conception of created (i.e., material) reality and a more Aristotelian or Neoplatonic conception of the being of God and His attributes.

The history of the kalam can be divided into three periods, that of its formation up to the end of the ninth century, the classical period, embracing the 10th and 11th centuries, and the period of its Hellenization from the 12th century until the demise of the kalam.

The main schools of kalam of the classical period, opposing the Aristotelian and Neoplatonic character of late Hellenistic philosophy, considered all being other than God to be material, composed of an atomistic substrate with its inherent qualities or accidents. Considerable attention was devoted to the problem of reasoning by analogy from the (material) phenomenal to the (immaterial) non-phenomenal. Except in the doctrine of the imamate the theology of the moderate Shiites tends to follow the Mutazilites very closely. There have been, since the 19th century, a number of attempts by various authors, all of whom have been much influenced by modern Western thought, to revive theological thought in Islam, but it is not yet possible to speak of a coherent trend in modern Muslim religious thought.

ISMA

In Islam, term to denote infallibility. This is a quality attributed by the Shiites for their Imams. Isma also embraces the idea of sinlessness, and a number of Shiite traditions relate to the sinlessness of the 12 Imams as well as that of figures like Mohammed and Fatima.

ISMACHIAH

In the Old Testament, one of the Levites selected as a commissioner in connection with the contributions for Temple service during Hezekiah's reign (2 Chronicles 31:13).

ISMA'IL

Major Islamic prophet, son of Ibrahim (Abraham) and Hajar. He is identified by most commentators with the son who is nearly sacrificed by Ibrahim out of obedience to God. On being cast out by Ibrahim (after the birth of Ishaq), Isma'il, together with Hajar, found themselves on the site of present-day Mecca. Hajar frantically ran backwards and forwards between two small hills called al-Safa and al-Marwa trying to find water to quench her son's thirst. This event is commemorated by the sevenfold sa'y between the two points during the Hajj.

ISMA'ILIYAH

A sect of the Shi'ah (one of the major branches of Islam), most active as a religophilosophical movement in the 9th-13th centuries through its subsects, the Fatimids, the Qarmatians and the Assassins.

ISNAD

In Islam, chain of authorities at the beginning of a hadith. Medieval Islam developed a highly complex science of Isnad criticism.

ISRA'

In Islam, word meaning night journey.It refers to the famous night journey in Islam that was made by the Prophet Mohammed through the air, mounted on al-Buraq from Mecca to Jerusalem; thence he made the Ascension through the Seven Heavens, borne by Jibril and entered God's presence. The Night Journey and the Mi'rau are together celebrated in the Islamic world on the 27th day of the Islamic month of Rajab.

ISRA, al-

The title of the 17th sura of the Koran; it means literally "The Night Journey." The sura belongs to the Meccan period and contains 111 verses. The title of the sura is derived from verse 1 which refers to the Night Journey of the Prophet Mohammed. One widely recorded tradition associates the practice of praying five times a day with the Night Journey, Mohammed having been initially commanded by God to pray 50 times a day but finally managing, on the advice of Musa, to have the number reduced to five.

ISRAEL

Israel is a Jewish republic in southwest Asia, at the eastern end of the Mediterranean Sea, founded in 1948. It is bordered on three sides by Arab countries. The country has been vitally affected by a majority of its citizens being immigrants, as well as by a constant tension between Israel and Syria, which supports terrorist groups in Lebanon. In 1967, in the course of a brief conflict familiarly known as "the Six Day War," victorious Israel occupied large areas of surrounding Arab lands, in Sinai, Jordan and Syria. In the course 80s and 90s the situations with the surrounding Arab countries and the PLO headed by Yassar Arafat has significantly changed. In, 1993 the PLO was granted semi-autonomy in the Gaza Strip and Jericho, and the war between Jordan and Israel was officially ended in 1994. Negotations with Syria are still continuing.

ISRAEL HISTORY, Exile and Restoration

Period from 587-538 BC. Though the deportation to Babylon evoked reactions of despair and disbelief on the part of some, others realized that in it the warnings of the prophets had been fulfilled to the letter. Thus a new and even higher premium was set upon the revealed Word of God (this being taken to include both the Law and the prophets).

Inspired by this the Jewish exiles survived as a relatively united people still clinging to faith and hope in Yahweh who, through the mouth of the prophets had promised them a future restoration. In 538 Cyrus, the conqueror of the short-lived Babylonian Empire, authorized and even actively encouraged the return of the Jews to Jerusalem, and this was naturally hailed as the fulfillment of the prophets and the inauguration of a new and more glorious epoch in Jewish history.

ISRAEL HISTORY, Exodus and Moses

Period from circa 1280-1260 BC. Though the exact historical details are difficult to recapture, it is clear that as a result of events subsequently interpreted as divine portents Moses was enabled to lead a specific ethnic group of the semi-nomadic Semites, known to the Egyptians as the hapiru, out of Egypt to Mount Sinai. Here, in a striking experience the precise nature of which cannot be reconstructed from the biblical text, the God of their fathers manifested himself to them, bound them to himself in covenant and revealed his will to them.

Subsequently, during a period of sojourning centered upon Kadesh-barnea, the implication of this central experience seems to have been drawn out to a point where Israel came to realize more fully her destiny as a chosen people consecrated in a unique sense to the God of the Patriarchs.

They pledged themselves to the task of achieving His glory and their own happiness by faithfully fulfilling His will for them as revealed at Sinai and as expressed in His laws. Thus Israel as a people in the true sense was born.

ISRAEL HISTORY, Joshua and the Judges

Period from circa 1260-1040 BC. Canaan, the land promised by Yahweh to his people, seems to have been weakened by internal conflicts and by invasions from the West by elements of the "sea peoples" shortly before the Israelites themselves made their incursion from the East. Thus extraneous factors contributed to the limited degree of success the Israelites achieved under Joshua in acquiring a firm foothold in the land.

The judges were charismatic leaders raised up from the individual tribes to deal with particular moments of crisis in the form of onslaughts from external foes. Their authority seem to have been limited to particular tribes or groups of tribes.

ISRAEL HISTORY, Maccabeans and Hasmoneans

Period from 167-63 BC. The attempt of Antiochus to erect a statue of Zeus Olympus in the Temple, to abolish circumcision, and to force the Jews to eat unclean food instigated the Maccabean revolt under the three brothers Judas (166-160), Jonathan (160-142) and Simon (142-134).

This movement, brilliantly daring and successful as it was, was initially purely religious in inspiration but came progressively to be dominated by political motivations.

In their struggle against the Seleucids, the Maccabean leaders turned to Rome for help, thereby, though unwittingly, taking the first step towards subsequent domination by Rome.

The descendants of Simon, the Hasmoneans as they are called, ruled Judah until Pompey's conquest of Judah and Jerusalem in 63 BC. Largely secular in outlook and ambitious, the greatest of them, Alexander Jannaeus, succeeded in regaining the lost territories and extending his domain almost to the boundaries of the ancient kingdom of David.

The reign of the Hasmoneans was ended by a dynastic dispute between two brothers, Hyrcanus II and Aristobulus, each of whom appealed to Pompey for arbitration. When Aristobulus refused to accept Pompey's decision, the latter attacked and took Jerusalem in 63 BC and made Judea part of the Roman province of Syria.

ISRAEL HISTORY, Patriarchs

Texts discovered at Nuzi and Mari attest the fact that many of the social customs and institutions ascribed to the patriarchs Abraham, Isaac and Jacob in Genesis 12-50 were indeed practiced by semi-nomadic people of precisely their type during the Middle Bronze Age (circa 2000-1500 BC) and not at any later stage.

Even on natural grounds, therefore, it seems reasonable to infer that the biblical accounts are substantially accurate. The message of these, reduced to its barest essentials, is that Israel's forbearers originated in Mesopotamia and thence journeyed to Palestine where they established themselves to some limited extent. Later some of them went to Egypt where, after an initial period of prosperity, their descendants were reduced to forced labor by the Egyptians.

ISRAEL HISTORY, Persian and Hellenistic Period

Period from 538-167 BC. Under the tolerant rule of the Persians the state of Judah was reconstituted and the Temple and walls of Jerusalem itself were rebuilt. At this time a new danger arose to Israel, that of allowing the purity of its religion to be contaminated by intermarriage with inhabitants of mixed race who had occupied its territories during the Exile. Further religious and social reforms were carried out by Ezra and Nehemiah.

Thus the Diaspora was born, with its special emphasis on the synagogue form of worship developed during the Exile, and on the written word of God (as distinct from the Temple cult) as the center of Jewish religious practice.

By 331 the Persian empire had suffered a crushing defeat at the hands of Alexander, but it was not until circa 300 BC, when Alexander's empire was divided among his successors, that more trouble began.

In 198 Palestine finally fell to the Seleucids and the reigning representative of these, Antiochus IV Epiphanes, began to seek by every means in his power to force Greek cultural practices and Greek religious beliefs upon his Jewish subjects.

ISRAEL HISTORY, Reign of Solomon and Successors

Period from 961 to 587 BC. The enormous prosperity which accrued to Solomon and his kingdom was owing in no small measure to the position of his kingdom on the route between Egypt and Phoenicia; but in that period Israel was also influenced by the culture and politics of Egypt and Phoenicia.

A new class of merchants and capitalists emerged together with a new class of civil servants, professional administrators and professional soldiers of the king's personal army.

The attempts of Solomon's son King Rehoboam to maintain, and even to intensify these developments led to the 10 northern tribes breaking away from Judah and Benjamin in the south, choosing their own king Jeroboam, and eventually setting up their own independent capital at Samaria.

Judah did not escape the savagery of the Assyrian attacks, but Jerusalem itself was spared by what appeared to be a miraculous dispensation. However, under the two worst of her kings, Amon and Manasseh, she seems very largely to have succumbed to Assyrian influence in the religious sphere.

The successor to Amon, Josiah, undertook a far-reaching religious reform, and this seemed at first to bring blessing on the nation. His successes in warfare came to an abrupt end with his death in battle at Megiddo in 609. The remaining history of Judah is a story of petty and disastrous intrigues against the new Babylonian power, culminating in the final defeat and sacking of Jerusalem in 587 and the deportation of the king and many of the people to Babylon.

ISRAEL HISTORY, Saul and David

Period from circa 1040-961 BC. The introduction of kingship, regarded as un-Israelite and offensive to Yahweh by one important current of Israelite thought, entailed special difficulties for a people whose previous formation and development left so little room for this institutional type of leader.

In attempting to maintain and ameliorate his position as king, Saul transgressed the covenant customs and laws and so, in spite of initial successes, failed to establish a lasting dynasty to survive him when he fell victim to the Philistines.

Where Saul had failed David succeeded. He established a lasting dynasty and made kingship a permanent institution in Israel. He conquered the Philistines and founded a sort of miniature empire, in which the small nations surrounding Judah were forced to pay tribute to him and accept some degree of subordination to him. Above all he conquered the Canaanite stronghold of Jerusalem which Joshua has failed to overcome. He succeeded in making it the shrine of the ark, the symbol and focal point of Yahweh's covenant with the tribes.

David survived a number of rebellions and intrigues on the part of his own sons, but his dynasty survived as kings of Judah for more than 400 years.

ISRAEL, People

The majority of Israel's citizens are Jews and of these the greater number are immigrants. While Jewish presence in the area has been continuous since biblical times, repressive measures from the Roman era onward caused a steady decline in their numbers. Only at the end of the 19th century did large-scale Jewish immigration begin again. At that time most of the settlers came from eastern Europe, fleeing from the recurrent pogroms. After 1945 large numbers of immigrants came from central and western Europe. They were followed by Jewish immigrants from the other countries of the Middle East and from North Africa. The last group now forms the largest identifiable ethnic community among Israeli citizens. More recently there has been an influx of tens of thousands of Jews from Russia, bringing new technological skills.

The largest minority group, constituting over 15 percent, is of Arabs, who live for the most part in self-contained rural communities, following a pattern of life more traditional than that of the Jews. Other minority groups include Druses, Circassians and Samaritans. In contrast to the Arabs, whose attitude towards the Jewish state ranges from indifference to open opposition, most members of these other groups are active supporters of the state.

The official language of Israel is Hebrew, but because most immigrants arrive without a knowledge of Hebrew, the government has set up special schools, known as Upanim, which teach the language. Nonetheless, many Israelis remain more literate in languages other than Hebrew. The second most dominant language is Arabic, and many native-born Israeli Jews speak it.

ISRAEL RECENT HISTORY

Throughout the centuries, Jews had never given up hope of a return to the Holy Land. Small groups of Jews lived in the holy city of Jerusalem, in Hebron, Safad and Tiberias; others dwelt in villages in Galilee. The new settlers coming from eastern Europe were quite different in social outlook, however. Spurning the charity of older residents, they attempted to earn a living from the soil and bought land that others would not have. Their first efforts often failed.. The newcomers found themselves reduced by cholera, malaria or simply starvation. Then the Zionist Organization was founded, in 1897, by Theodore Herzl. This group advocated political activity in order to convince the great powers of the need for a Jewish homeland in Palestine. These early efforts failed, but Jewish settlement continued, organized generally on socialist lines.

A major change came in 1917, when the British government issued the Balfour Declaration supporting the Zionist claims. The Balfour Declaration aroused the opposition of most Arabs throughout the Middle East. After World War I, the British government was given an international mandate over Palestine. The immediate results were increased Jewish immigration, increased Arab hostility and increased British indecisiveness. Attempts were made to curtail Jewish immigration. This aroused such strong opposition, especially in the light of the rise of Nazi Germany with its policy of exterminating the Jewish populace of Europe, that a mass program of illegal immigration was organized by the Jewish community.

Opposition to the British mandate continued in three forms. The overwhelming majority of Palestinian Jews aimed at a settlement on a political level. The military arm, the Haganah, was concerned with self-defense only. A militant minority, the terrorist group Irgun, Zva'i Leumi or Etzel, concentrated on active disruption of the British administration and retaliation against Arab attacks. A third group, Lehy or the "Stern Gang," followed an even more extreme terrorist policy of bombing and shooting.

In 1947 Britain placed the issue before the United Nations, which voted to partition Palestine into separate Jewish and Arab states. This was welcomed by the Jews but bitterly opposed by the Arabs in Palestine and by the surrounding Arab states. As the British forces withdrew, the Arabs began to attack Jewish settlements. Arab armies also entered the country in an effort to eradicate the new state of israel. The Jews not only defeated their attackers but captured large areas that had been assigned to the Arab state.

Fighting was bitter. Members of Etzel and Lehy massacred inhabitants of the Arab village of Deir Yassin. Arab leaders forced Arabs to desert their homes in order to leave their forces unhampered in their attacks on the Jews. Consequently, many Arabs fled behind the lines of fire. When, in 1949, a truce was agreed upon, these thousands of Arab refugees were housed in temporary camps. Many are still there. Without work and supported by charity and the United Nations, they have constituted a persistent social and political problem.

At this time Israel held all of Palestine with the exception of Samaria and Judea, which were held by Transjordan, and the Gaza Strip, held by Egypt. The City of Jerusalem was divided, with Israel holding the so-called New City. The area held by Transjordan was incorporated into the state, which then became simply Jordan (1949); Egypt continued to administer the Gaza Strip. The Arab state proposed in the original plan was never formed. A peace treaty was never signed, and Israel's major problem was the antagonism of its neighbors. Meanwhile immigrants flooded into the country, many of them from Arab countries, with little understanding of a modern technological society.

In 1956, following Egyptian nationalization of the Suez Canal. Israel joined Britain and France in an attack on Egypt.Israeli forces overran the Gaza Strip and the Sinai Peninsula, then were forced to pull back by international pressure, but not before Israel had secured the right to sail its ships through the straits of Tiran into the Red Sea.

The situation remained relatively quiet until May 1967, when Egypt's President Nasser demanded that the UN force leave the area and at the same time closed the Straits of Tiran to Israeli shipping. A brief conflict ensued, in which Egypt was joined by Syria and Jordan. Within six days Israel had occupied all of the Gaza Strip and Sinai Peninsula, all of Jordan west of the Jordan River, and the Golan Heights, an area of Syria north-east of the Sea of Galilee. At the same time the Old City of Jerusalem was annexed by Israel.

On October 6, 1973 (Yom Kippur; the Jewish Day of Atonement) Egyptian and Syrian forces caught Israel unprepared in a fresh war fought to recover their lost territories. At first the Arab armies seemed likely to thrust Israel from the Golan Heights and Sinai, but Israeli defense hardened, and after heavy losses on both sides fighting ended in a stalemate.

From then on the relations with the neighboring countries and the PLO of Yassar Arafat have slowly changed. In 1975 Egypt's President Sadat visited Israel and a peace treaty was signed and most of the Sinai Peninsula returned to Egypt. In 1993 a treaty was signed between Israel and the PLO, granting semi-autonomy to the Gaza Strip and Jericho and in 1994 a peace treaty was signed between Israel and Jordan.

ISRAEL, KINGDOM OF

Hebrew kingdom, first as united under Saul, David and Solomon circa 1020-992 BC, and then the breakaway state in the North founded by Jeroboam I in the territory of the 10 tribes. In 721 BC this was overrun by the Assyrians; the tribes were killed, enslaved or scattered.

ISRAELITE

In the broadcast sense, a Jew, a descendant of Jacob, whose name was changed to Israel (2 Samuel 17:25; John 1:47). As determined by the context, in the plural the term refers to the following:

1 Members of all the twelve tribes before the split in the kingdom (1 Samuel 2:14; 13:20);

2 those of the ten-tribe northern kingdom (1 Kings 12:19);

3 non-Levitical Jews returning from Babylonian exile (1 Chronicles 9:1-2);

4 Jews of the first century AD (Acts 13:16; Romans 9:3; 2 Corinthians 11:22).

ISRAEL OF GOD

Expression found only once in the Bible. referring to spiritual Israel rather than to racial descendants of Jacob, whose name was changed to Israel (Genesis 32:22-28). The apostle Paul, when using the expression "the Israel of God," shows that it has nothing to do with whether one is a circumcised descendent of Abraham or not.

ISRAFIL

One of the great Islamic angels. He is often called "The Lord of the Trumpet" because it is his task to sound that instrument on the Day of Resurrection. In Islamic art he is often portrayed poised, ready to blow the trumpet on the Last Day at God's express command. Israfil is not mentioned by name in the Koran but there is much tradition about him. For example, the spirits of some of the dead who wait for Resurrection inhabit the holes in the mighty trumpet of Israfil. What is actually mentioned in the Koran is the actual sounding of the trumpet at the end of time.

ISSACHAR

In the Old Testament, the ninth son of Jacob and the fifth of Leah's seven children born in Paddan-aram. Leah viewed this son as God's reward or wages paid for her having allowed a maidservant to bear sons by her husband during a period when she was barren (Genesis 29:30-32; 35:23-26).

ISSHIAH

In the Old Testament, one of the headmen of the tribe of Issachar whose descendants helped make that tribe very numerous (1 Chronicles 7:1-4).

ISSHIJAH

In the Old Testament, one of the Levites who responded to Ezra's urging to send away their foreign wives and sons.

ISTADEVATA

In Hinduism, the particular deity or manifestation of a deity selected by a worshipper as the primary object of his devotion and attention. The selection of an Istadevata in no way excludes belief in, or worship of, other Hindu gods.

ISTAWA

Arabic phrase, meaning "to be straight," to stand erect," "to sit down," "to mount."

ISVARA

The Lord or Overlord in the Hindu pantheon. Esoterically the term is used in the sense of the highest Self.

ITALO-ALBANIAN CHURCH

An Eastern-rite member of the Roman-Catholic Communion, comprising the descendants of ancient Greek colonists in southern Italy and Sicily and 15th century Albanian refugees from Ottoman rule. Although heavily influenced by Latin usages in their churches, calendar, and feast days, they have made some attempt to restore the purity of the Byzantine liturgical rites.

IVO OF CHARTRES, Saint

(1040-1116) Bishop of Chartres who was regarded as the most learned canonist of his age. He wrote 8 books and 288 letters revealing contemporary political, religious and liturgical questions.

IZRA'IL

Principal Islamic angel of death with a reputation in tradition for toughness and ruthlessness. He is mentioned in the Koran as "The Angel of Death" rather than by name. He is of gigantic size and has a roll with the names of all mankind inscribed upon it. He does not know, however, when each person will die. An individual's death is signalled by a leaf falling from the tree beneath God's throne on which the fated person's name appears. It is then Izra'il's task to separate that person's soul from his or her body.

JAAKOBAH

In the Old Testament, one of the chieftains of Simeon who, in the days of Hezekiah, extended their territory into the fertile valley of Gedor by striking down its inhabitants (1 Chronicles 4:24; 36-41).

JAALAH

In Judaism, the founder of a family of Solomon's servants, some of whom, along with the Nethenim, returned from the Babylonian exile with Zerubbabel (Ezra 2:2; 55-58).

JAARESHIAH

In the Old Testament, a family head in the tribe of Benjamin; son or descendant of Jeroham. He and his household lived in Jerusalem (1 Chronicles 8:1; 27-28).

JAASIEL

In the Old Testament, one of the mighty men of David, listed only in Chronicles; a Mezabaite (1 Chronicles 27:21-22).
The name is also applied to the prince of a tribe of Benjamin during David's reign. He was the son of Abner, therefore probably a cousin of King Saul (1 Chronicles 27:21-22).

JAAZANIAH

In biblical times, a rather common name toward the end of the kingdom of Judah. All four men mentioned in the Bible by this name lived within the same short period of time. The name is applied, among others to:

1 A leader of the Rechabites when the prophet Jeremiah tested their integrity by offering them wine, which they refused. Jaazaniah was the son of another Jeremiah (Jeremiah 35:3-6).
2 Son of Shaphan; the only individual named in Ezekiel's vision of the 70 men who offered incense before carved idolatrous symbols in the temple at Jerusalem (Ezekiel 8:1-11).
3 Son of Azzur; one of the 25 men seen in Ezekiel's vision at the eastern gate at the temple (Ezekiel 11:1-4).
4 A military chief of Judah in the brief period immediately following the destruction of Jerusalem by the Babylonians (2 Kings 25:23).

JAAZIAH

In the Old Testament, a Merarite Levite, four of whose sons or descendants served during David's reign (1 Chronicles 24:26-31).

JAAZIEL

In Judaism, a Levite musician in the second division that accompanied the ark of the covenant when it was transferred from Obed-edom's house to Jerusalem (1 Chronicles 15:18).

JABAL

According to biblical tradition, a descendant of Cain; son of Lamech and his first wife Adah (Genesis 4:17-20).

JABESH

In biblical times, a town in the northern section of Gilead; it is mentioned in the history of the judges and kings (Judges 21:8; 1 Samuel 11:1).

JABESH-GILEAD

An ancient town in the tribal territory of Gad east of the Jordan. The first mention of this town was in the days of the judges, in connection with the retribution dealt out to the neighboring tribe of Benjamin for its condoning of gross immorality (Judges 21:8). On that occasion when the Israelites practically exterminated the entire tribe of Benjamin (only 600 males escaped), it was found that not a man of Jabesh-gilead had participated in meting out this justified punishment. It was therefore determined that every man, woman and child of Jabesh-gilead, with the exception of the virgins, should be put to death. The 400 virgins that were thus spared were then given as wives to the fugitive Benjaminites so as to prevent extinction of the tribe (Judges 20:1; 21:14).

JABLONSKI, Daniel Ernst

(1660-1741) German theologian who worked for a union of Lutherans and Calvinists, and attempted an unsuccessful reform of the church of Prussia.

JABNEEL

In biblical times, a Judean boundary site (Joshua 15:1, 11), probably the same as the Jabneh that King Uzziah (829-777 BC) wrested from the Philistines (2 Chronicles 26:6).

JABNEH

A walled Philistine city that suffered defeat at the hands of Judah's King Uzziah (2 Chronicles 26:6). It is probably the same as Jabneel (Joshua 15:11).

JABNEH, Synod of

Synod in circa 100 to decide which writings were to be included in the Hebrew canon of the Bible.

JABOTINSKI, Vladimir

(1880-1940) Controversial Zionist leader, who founded the militant Zionist Revisionist movement that played an important role in the eventual establishment of the State of Israel.

JABR

In Islam, term denoting compulsion, predestination, fate, determinism, determination. It was a word of considerable theological significance in the debates of medieval Islam.

JACHIN

In the Old Testament, the fourth son of Simeon (Genesis 46:10). The name is also applied to the priest whose paternal house was selected by lot to care for the 21st of the 24 priestly divisions that David organized (1 Chronicles 24:7, 17). One or more of the descendants (or another priest of the same name) resided in Jerusalem after the Babylonian exile (1 Chronicles 9:3-10).

JACOB

In the Old Testament, son of Isaac and Rebecca, ancestor of the Israelites. He fled after tricking his elder brother Esau out of his birthright; he settled in Mesopotamia, where he married, then returned to Canaan. In a vision he wrestled with and overcame an angel, and was honored with the name Israel. Jacob had 13 children, 10 of whom were founders of tribes of Israel. Leah bore him his only daughter Dinah, and six sons, Reuben, Simeon, Levi (who did not found a tribe, but was the ancestor of the Levites), Judah, Issachar, and Zebulun. Leah's maidservant, Zilpah, bore him Gad and Asher. Rachel's maidservant, Bilhah, bore him Dan and Naphtali. Rachel's sons were Benjamin and Joseph (who did not found a tribe, but whose sons founded the tribes of Manasseh and Ephraim).

In a time of famine he migrated to Egypt, where he died, after a period of staying with his favorite son Joseph.

The prophets often used "Jacob" in a figurative sense as the nation descended from the patriarch (Isaiah 9:8; 27:9; Jeremiah 10:25; Ezekiel 39:25; Amos 6:8; Romans 11:26). Jesus Christ, on one occasion, used the name Jacob figuratively when speaking of those who would be "in the kingdom of the heavens" (Matthew 8:11).

JACOBITE CHURCH

Syrian Orthodox church, Christian church of Syria, India and Iraq. One of the Monophysite churches, it was founded in the 6th century in Syria by Jacobus Baradaeus. Its head is the patriarch of Antioch, who now resides at Damascus, and its ritual language is Syriac. An offshoot of the Jacobites is the Syrian Catholic Church, one of the uniate churches.

JACOB JOSEPH OF POLONNOYE
(1708-1782) Noted disciple of the Ba'al Shem Tov, founder of Jewish Hasidism. As a writer he contributed significantly to the spread of Hasidism by propagating the teachings of Ba'al Shem Tov.

JACOB OF EDESSA
(578-640) Theologian, who became bishop of Edessa. His strict discipline giving offense, he retired and devoted himself to study and teaching. He wrote significant commentaries on the Old and New Testament.

JACOB OF SERUGH
(451-521) Syriac writer described for his learning and holiness as "the flute of the Holy Spirit and the harp of the believing church." He has been regarded as orthodox, but four of his letters prove his Monophysitism, the belief in the existence of one, divine nature of Christ.

JACOB'S FOUNTAIN
The "well" or "fountain" where Jesus Christ, while resting, conversed with a Samaritan woman (John 4:5-30). It is considered to be Bir Ya'qub, situated about a mile and a half south-east of Nablus. It is a deep well, the water level of which never rises to the top.
The Bible does not directly state that Jacob dug the well. However, it does indicate that Jacob had property in this vicinity (Genesis 33:18-20; Joshua 24:32; John 4:5).

JACOPONE DA TODI
(1230-1306) Religious poet, author of more than 100 mystical poems of great power and originality.

JADA
A descendant of Judah through Jerahmeel. Jada is listed as a son of Onam, and father of Jether and Jonathan (1 Chronicles 2:3, 25-32).

JADDAI
In the Old Testament, a son of Nebo; one of those who took non-Israelite wives but sent them away at the urging of Ezra (Ezra 10:43-44).

JADDUA
In ancient times, one of the headmen of Israel whose descendant, if not himself, sealed the resolution of faithfulness during Nehemiah's governorship (Nehemiah 10:1, 14, 21).

JADON
In the Old Testament, a Meronothite who helped Nehemiah rebuild Jerusalem's wall in 455 BC; he was apparently from the vicinity of Mizpah (Nehemiah 3:7).

JAEL
In Judaism, the wife of Heber the Kenite and slayer of Canaanite army chief Sisera. Though living at Kedesh, the point where Barak and Deborah rallied to fight against Sisera, Heber was at peace with the Canaanite oppressors (Judges 4:10-11; 17-21). After Sisera was defeated at Israel's hand, he fled to Heber's neutral encampment, where Jael invited him into her tent. She then covered him with a blanket. He was then killed by "the hand of a woman," as Deborah foretold (Judges 4:9; 17-22).

JA'FAR AS-SADIQ
(700-767) Religious leader of the Shi'i, an Islamic sect, that split into two divergent groups after Ja'far's death. He was widely respected as a religious leader whose teachings conveyed divine guidance.

JA'FAR IBN MUHAMMAD
(699-765) The sixth imam, or spiritual head of the Shi'ah branch of Islam and

the last to be recognized as imam by all the Shiite sects.

JAGANNATHA

The form under which the Hindu god Krishna is worshipped at Puri, one of the most famous religious centers in India. The Sanskrit name means "lord of the world."

JAH

(Hebrew: Yah) A poetic shortening of Jehovah (Yahweh), the name of God (Exodus 15:1-2). This abbreviated form is represented by the first half of the Hebrew tetragrammation YHWH; the tenth and fifth letters of the Hebrew alphabet respectively.

Jah occurs fifty times in the Hebrew scriptures, twenty-six times alone, and twenty-four times in the expression "Hallelujah," which is literally a command to a number of people "to praise Jah."

JAHANNAM

In Islam, one of the seven ranks of hell. The word has connotations in Arabic for "depth" and is very commonly used in the Koran to designate hell,. appearing 77 times. Tradition consigned unrepentant wicked Muslims to this layer of hell to suffer for a while until their eventual transfer to Paradise.

JAHAZ

In biblical times, a city east of the Jordan and evidently situated north of the Arnon. It was probably wrested from the Moabites by Amorite King Sihon (Numbers 21:23-26). At Jahaz the Israelites defeated the forces of Sihon, and the city itself became a Reubenite possession (Deuteronomy 2:32-33; Joshua 13:15-18). Subsequently Jahaz was designated as a Levite city for the Merarites (Joshua 21:34-36). Later in Israel's history the city came under Moabite control (Isaiah 15:1-4).

JAHAZIEL

In the Old Testament, third-listed son of Hebron, a Kohathite of the tribe of Levi (1 Chronicles 23:6, 12, 19). The name is also applied to the Levite who was empowered by God's spirit to speak words of encouragement to King Jehoshaphat and the congregation when they were threatened by a superior force of the enemy (2 Chronicles 20:14-17).

JAHDAI

In the Old Testament, a father of six sons listed among the descendants of Judah's great-grandson Caleb. Jahdai's exact relationship to Caleb is not given (1 Chronicles 2:3; 42-47).

JAHDIEL

In Judaism, one of the household heads of the half tribe of Manasseh residing east of the Jordan. His descendants "began to act unfaithfully" toward God, leading to eventual exile by the Assyrians (1 Chronicles 2:3, 42, 47).

JAHILIYAH

In Islam, term meaning state of ignorance. The Arabic word is used to designate the pre-Islamic period. The term has a positive connotation only in literature, because pre-Islamic Arabic poetry is esteemed by Muslims for its precise and rich vocabulary, sophisticated metrical structures, and fully developed system of rhyme and thematic sequence.

JAHIM, al-

In Islam, one of the seven ranks of hell. The word appears 25 times in the Koran and is in the region of hell to which tradition consigns idolaters.

JAHZEEL

In the Old Testament, the first-listed son of Naphtali and founder of the Jahzeelite family in that tribe (Genesis 46:24).

JAINA CANON

The sacred texts of Jainism, a religion of India. Lists of works vary from one sectarian group to another. The canon is written in a dialect called Prakrit, though from the Gupta period Jaina writers have used Sanskrit when they wished to establish communication with a wider audience.

JAINISM

Indian religion founded in the 6th century BC as an offshoot of Hinduism. It is based on the belief that man's ideal state is to be found in the soul's original purity, free from the physical sufferings of life and death. The term comes from the Sanskrit jina, or conqueror, for a Jain strives to overcome physical suffering in order to concentrate on purity of soul.

The spiritual teachings of Jainism are highly sophisticated. Jains believe the world is eternal and unchangeable and was neither created nor affected by any supreme being. Jainism is this atheistic. Events in the world are believed to be the result of action between the two eternal substances, soul and matter. Matter permeates the pure substance of soul, driving out its purity and introducing ignorance and suffering. Jainist teaching aims to free the soul from the body, and emphasizes the sacredness of all living things and the observance of asceticism and chastity.

Numerous beautiful temples in India are dedicated to Jainism. Because of their reverence for all life, Jainists also maintain animal hospitals. Jains number approximately 3 million and are found predominantly among the merchant classes of India.

JAIR

In the Old Testament, a descendant of Judah through his grandson Hezron. Hezron married out of his tribe to a woman of Manasseh (1 Chronicles 2:21-22). Jair is reckoned as a descendant of Manasseh rather than Judah, likely because of his exploits in the territory of Manasseh, having captured a number of tent cities and naming them after himself, which name they kept for many generations (Numbers 32:41; Deuteronomy 3:14).

JAIRUS

In biblical times, a presiding officer of the synagogue (probably in Capernaum) whose only daughter Jesus resurrected (Matthew 9:18).

When, in late 31 or early 32, Jairus' twelve-year-old daughter became so ill that she was expected to die, her father sought out Jesus, fell at his feet and implored him to come and cure her before it was too late. While leading Jesus to his home, Jairus surely must have been greatly encouraged by witnessing Jesus heal a woman subject for 12 years to a flow of blood. But how disheartening to receive word from messengers that his own little daughter had already died. Nonetheless, Jesus urged Jairus not to fear, but to exercise faith. Passing amidst the noisy mourners who ridiculed Jesus' remark that the child was only sleeping, Jairus, his wife and three apostles accompanied Jesus inside, where Jesus restored the girl to life. As might be expected, Jairus and his wife were "beside themselves with great ecstasy" Mark 5:21-43; Matthew 9:18-26; Luke 8:41-56).

JAKIM

In the Old Testament, a descendant of Benjamin through Shimei, included in a list of heads of fathers' houses residing in Jerusalem (1 Chronicles 8:1; 19-28).

The name is also applied to the priest whose paternal house was selected by lot for the 12 of the 24 divisions of priestly temple service under David's reign (1 Chronicles 24:3-5).

JALAM

In the Old Testament, a son of Esau by his wife Oholibamah. Jalam was born in Canaan but was soon taken to Edom, where he eventually became a sheik (Genesis 36:6-18).

JAMES, Brother of Jesus

Probably James and his brothers and sisters were sons and daughters of Joseph and Mary (Matthew 13:55). Though he was not one of the 12 disciples, he later became the leader of the church in Jerusalem (Acts 21:18). James wrote the letter, bearing his name.

JAMES, Brother of John the Evangelist

The son of Zebedee and a fishermen when he was called by Jesus. Together with his brother John and Peter he was one of the most intimate disciples of Jesus. James and his brother were called "Boanerges" ("sons of thunder") by Jesus. James was the first of the Apostles to suffer martyrdom, being killed under King Herod in 44 (Acts 12:2).

JAMES, Letter of

A letter directed to Jewish Christians (1:1) or Christians in general, dated circa 62 AD. James' letter is mainly an interpretation of the Old Testament in the light of Christian gospel. It emphasizes the responsibility of a Christian, both in word and action (3:13).

JAMES, Liturgy of Saint

A eucharistic service based on the Antiochene Liturgy, said to be the most ancient Christian Liturgy. The liturgy has the following order of service:

1 readings from scriptures;
2 a sermon from the bishop;
3 a dismissal of the catechumens;
4 a prayer for the faithful;
5 the kiss of peace and words of greeting from the bishop;
6 the washing of hands;
7 the offering of gifts;
8 the Eucharist - prayer, preface, Sanctus, words of institution, remembrance of the dead, invocation of the Holy Spirit, prayers for the church, for the living, and for the dead.
9 the final blessing from the bishop.

JAMIN

In the Old Testament, the second-listed son of Simeon (Genesis 46:10; Exodus 6:15). He founded the family of the Jamenites (Numbers 26:12).

JAMLECH

In Judaism, one of the chieftains of the tribe of Simeon who, in the days of King Hezekiah, extended their territory into the valley of Gedor (1 Chronicles 5:11-12).

JANNA, al-

In Islam, literally meaning "The Garden." It is the most common name by which Paradise is referred to in the Koran. Though paradise, like hell, is described in the Koran in very physical terms, some have preferred to interpret these descriptions allegorically or metaphorically. A well-known hadith holds that Paradise may best be characterized as a state which has not been seen by the human eye nor heard by the human ear. Basing themselves upon the Koran, later traditions identified seven heavenly gardens, which contrast neatly with the seven divisions of hell.

JANNES

In the Old Testament, a resister of Moses with whom Paul compares apostles who resist the truth (Timothy 3:8-9). Jannes and Jambres, whose "madness became plain at all," and not identified in the Hebrew scriptures, but it is generally agreed that they were two of the leading men in Pharaoh's court, perhaps the magic-practicing priests who resisted Moses and Aaron on their numerous appearances there (Exodus 7:11-12; 8:17-19).

JANOAH

In biblical times, a city in the ten-tribe kingdom taken by Tiglath-pileser during Pekah's reign (circa 778-758 BC).

1

Its inhabitants were deported to Assyria (2 Kings 15:29).

JANSEN, Cornelius Otto

(1585-1638) Leader of the Roman Catholic Reform movement known as Jansenism. After receiving the degree of doctor of theology, he became rector of the University of Louvain in 1635 and bishop of Ypres in 1636. He wrote biblical commentaries and pamphlets against the Protestants. His major work was *Augustinus,* published by his friends in 1640. Although condemned by Pope Urban VII in 1642, it was of critical importance in the Jansenist movement.

JANSENISM

A movement in Roman Catholicism named after Cornelius Jansen (1585-1638), Bishop of Ypres, who promoted St. Augustine's severe doctrines of God's grace. Their severe moral theology was opposite to Jesuit casuistry. Condemned by the papacy in 1653 and 1713, its influence continued in moral severity and resistance (sometimes political) to papal authority.

Jansenism was a complex movement, based more on a certain mentality and spirituality, than on specific doctrines. It was an attempt, in line with that of the reformers, to reform the church in the spirit of early Christianity. It opposed what, it its view, was a compromising approach to true Christian theology and practice but was rejected by the church as an exaggerated and unorthodox position.

The followers of Cornelius Jansen became extreme rigorists, taught that the average Catholic cannot keep some of the Commandments and is practically always unworthy of receiving Holy Communion. This harsh and inhuman heresy was condemned by Pope Innocent X in 1653, but it exercised a strong negative influence on the pastoral life of the church for centuries to come.

JANUARIUS, Saint

(245-305) Bishop of Benevento and patron saint of Naples, believed to have been martyred during the persecution of the Roman emperor, Diocletian in 305. His fame rests on the relic, allegedly his blood, which is kept in a glass phial in the Naples cathedral. Of solid substance, it liquifies 18 times each year. While no natural explanation has been given, the phenomenon has been tested frequently and seems genuine.

JAPAN, Orthodox Church of

An autonomous body of the Eastern Orthodox Church, in canonical relation with the patriarchate of Moscow, which confirms the election of the metropolitan of Tokyo.

JAPANESE RELIGION

The concept of religion as a distinct category in social and psychological life is not native to Japan. The Japanese language contained no word corresponding to the Western "religion" until contact with the West in the 19th century led to the adaptation of many words, including shukyo for religion, to meet the sort of categories in which foreign investigators thought.

One can still encounter arguments that Shinto or Buddhism are not religions, meaning religions in some Western sense. The argument, being highly semantic, is usually sterile.

The modern phenomenological approach to comparative studies detects, contrariwise, an almost embarrassing richness of forms in traditional Japan which play the role of religion as generally defined cross-culturally. Acts of awareness of the numinous or sacred techniques of spiritual rebirth, and human commerce with superhuman forces provide fundamental contexts for family, community, or sect activities of coinherence.

The two major religions of Japan are Buddhism and the native Shinto, but they are not mutually exclusive since many Japanese observe practices of both - often having a Shinto shrine and a Buddhist family altar. Religion is nonetheless a vital part of their life.

Buddhism came to Japan from China

to Korea in the 6th century, and the Mahayana variant soon established its supremacy over rival religions - becoming virtually a state religion by the 9th century. In the 12th and 13th centuries, new Buddhist sects arose in Japan which appealed more to the masses, and Buddhism has remained the religion of the common man. About the same time, Zen Buddhism came to Japan from China. Adherents to Zen stress meditation, rather than reason, as the source of enlightenment. In all, there are close to 100 million Buddhists in modern Japan, most of whom also serve Shinto.

Shinto - "the way of Gods" - was strongly influenced and overshadowed by Buddhism until the Meiji Restoration of 1868, when Shinto was promoted as a purely Japanese and nationalistic religion. The new constitution of 1947 disestablished Shinto as the state religion and guaranteed freedom of worship. Shinto is based on the worship of nature and one"s ancestors and attempts to maintain the traditions of national life. Christians in Japan comprise less than one percent of the population.

JAPHETH

In the Old Testament, a son of Noah and brother of Shem and Ham. Although usually listed last, Japheth appears to have been the eldest of the three sons (Genesis 10:21).

Japheth and his wife were among the eight occupants of the ark, thereby surviving the flood (Genesis 7:13). Remaining childless until after the flood, they thereafter produced seven sons (Genesis 10:1-2). These sons and also some grandsons are the ones from whom "the population of the isles of the nations (coastal people) was spread about in their lands, each according to its tongue, according to their families, by their nations" (Genesis 10:3-5).

JAPHIA

In ancient times, a king of Lachesh who joined forces with four other Amorite kings to punish Gibeon for making peace with Israel (Joshua 10:3-5). Gibeon's call for help brought Joshua's forces on a rescue mission from Gilgal. During the ensuing battle the Israelites trapped Japhia and his allied kings in a cave at Makkedah. Later he and the others were executed and their dead bodies hung on stakes until sunset, after which they were thrown into the cave where they had sought refuge (Joshua 10:6-27).

JAPHLET

In the Old Testament, a descendant of Asher through Beriah and Heber. Three "sons of Japhlet" are included in the genealogy (1 Chronicles 7:30-33).

JAPHLETITES

An ancient people occupying territory on Ephraim's boundary when the Israelites moved into the Promised Land (Joshua 16:3). There is no evidence linking the Japhletites with the descendant of Asher named Japhlet (1 Chronicles 7:30-32).

JARED

In the Old Testament, father of Enoch and a pre-Flood ancestor of Jesus Christ; the fifth generation after Adam (1 Chronicles 1:2; Luke 3:37).

JARHA

An Egyptian slave of Judah's descendant Sheshan. Since Sheshan had no sons, he gave his daughter in marriage to Jarha, enabling Jarha to father Attai and thus preserve Sheshan's family line through him (1 Chronicles 2:34-35).

JARIB

In the Old Testament, a son of Simeon (1 Chronicles 4:24). The name is also applied to one of the nine headmen whom Ezra sent to encourage Levites and Nethinim to come to the river Ahava and join the others on the journey to Jerusalem (Ezra 8:15-20).

JARMUTH

In biblical times, one of the five Amorite cities involved in the attempted punitive expedition against the Gibeonites. Its king, Piram, and his allies were defeated by Joshua. Thereafter the city of Shephelah was assigned to Judah (Joshua 10:3-5; 23-25). After the Babylonian exile Judeans again resided at Jarmuth (Nehemiah 11:25, 29). Khirbet Yarmuk, some 16 miles southwest of Jerusalem, seems to be the ancient site. Situated on a hilltop, it overlooks the coastal plains as far as Gaza by the Mediterranean Sea.

JASHOBEAM

In the Old Testament, the head one of David's three most outstanding mighty men. Jashobeam once used his spear to fight off several hundred of the enemy and was also one of the three to force their way into the Philistine camp to get water for David from the cistern of Bethlehem (1 Chronicles 11:11, 15-19). In the course of events Jashobeam was appointed head of the first monthly division of 24,000 (1 Chronicles 27:1-2).

JASON

A prominent early Christian in Thessalonica who had "received Paul and Silas hospitably" on their first journey into Macedonia. A mob of jealous Jews set about to take Paul and Silas from Jason's home, but, not finding them there, they took Jason instead, and made him the principal defendant in charges of sedition against Caesar. Jason and the others with him were released after giving "sufficient security," perhaps in the form of bail (Acts 17:5-10).

In Paul's letter to the Romans, written from Corinth on his next trip through Macedonia and Greece, Jason is one whose greetings are included (Romans 16:21).

JASON

In Greek mythology, leader of the Argonauts and son of Aeson, king of Ioclos in Thessaly. After many adventures Jason abducted the Golden Fleece with the help of the enchantress Medea, whom he married.

JATHIYYA, al-

The title of the 45th sura of the Koran; it means literally "The Kneeling." The sura belongs to the Meccan period and has 37 verses. Its title is drawn from verse 28 which refers to every nation kneeling. The sura begins with two of the Mysterious Letters of the Koran and reiterates a number of ways in which God has provided for man. Then, by contrast, the pains of Jahannam are threatened for those who reject God's signs and blessing. Reference is made to God who has sovereignty over the heavens and the earth and who will assemble all mankind on the Day of Resurrection. The sura ends with a hymn of praise to God.

JATHNIEL

In the Old Testament, one of the Levitical gatekeepers for the house of God; the fourth son of Meshelemiah, a Korahite (1 Chronicles 26:1-2).

JATTIR

In ancient times, a priestly city in the mountainous region of Judah (Joshua 15:20; 1 Chronicles 6:54-57). It was to Jattir that David sent a portion of the spoils of victory taken from Amalekite raiders. Perhaps this was in appreciation for hospitality and friendship accorded to him, a fugitive from King Saul (1 Samuel 30:17-20).

JAVAN

In the Old Testament, fourth-listed son of Japheth and the father of Elishah, Tarshish, Kittim and Dodanim. As post-flood descendants of Noah, they are included among those populating the "isles of the nations," which phrase can also refer to the coastlands and not simply to islands surrounded by water (Genesis 10:2-5). Historical evidence indicates that the descendants of Javan and his four sons settled in the islands and coastlands of the Mediterranean Sea from Cyprus (Kittim) to perhaps as far west as Spain.

JAWHAR

Arabic word meaning substance. It derives from the Aristotelian metaphysical terminology and is an Arabic translation of the Greek word ousia.

JAZER

In ancient times, an Amorite city with dependent towns, located east of the Jordan. In the time of Moses, the Israelites took Jazer and the surrounding region (Numbers 21:25). Originally granted to Gad and fortified by that tribe, Jazer was subsequently assigned to the Levites (Numbers 32:1-5; Joshua 13:2-25).

It was one of the places mentioned in connection with the route followed by Joab and the chiefs of the military forces when taking the census that David had ordered without having divine authorization (2 Samuel 24:4-5). Toward the close of David's reign certain mighty men of the Hebronites residing at Jazer were assigned administrative duties in Israel's territory east of the Jordan (1 Chronicles 26:31-32).

JEBERECHIAH

In the Old Testament, father of Zechariah who witnessed Isaiah's writing the prophetic name Maher-shalal-hash-baz, that of the prophet's own son, on a tablet (Isaiah 81:1-2).

JECOLIAH

Mother of Judah's King Uzziah, whom she bore in circa 845 BC. Jecoliah, wife of Amaziah, was from Jerusalem (2 Kings 15:1-2).

JECONIAH

In ancient times, king of Judah for only three months and the days before being taken captive to Babylon by Nebuchadnezzar in 617 BC; son of Jehoiakim and grandson of good King Josiah (1 Chronicles 3:15-17).

JEDIAH

In the Old Testament, a priest, or possibly members of a paternal house of priests selected by lot for the second of the 24 priestly groups into which David divided the priesthood (1 Chronicles 24:1-7).

JEDIAEL

In the Old Testament, a son of Benjamin. Jediael's descendants at one time numbered 17,200 valiant, mighty men (1 Chronicles 7:6-11). He is probably the same as Benjamin's son Ashbel (Genesis 46:21).

JEDIAH

In the Old Testament, wife of Amon and mother of King Josiah, whom she bore in 667 BC; daughter of Adaiah from Bozkath (2 Kings 21:24-26).

JEDIDIAH

The name given by the prophet Nathan to the second child of David and Bathsheba (2 Samuel 12:24-25). The name reflected God's love and acceptance of the newborn infant, in contrast with His rejection of their earlier adulterine child, which died soon after birth (2 Samuel 12:13-19).

JEDUTHUN

In Judaism, a Levite musician. He and his family of musicians participated in several; celebrations when "thanking and praising God" was in order (1 Chronicles 25:3); for example, when the ark of the covenant was brought to Jerusalem (1 Chronicles 16:1, 41-42). One of the twenty-four divisions into which David's organization separated the sanctuary musicians, the second, fourth, eighth, tenth, twelfth and fourteenth lots fell to the six sons of Jeduthun, all working under their father's direction (1 Chronicles 25:1-21). The sharing of these duties by Jeduthun, Asaph and Heman meant that each of the three main branches of Levites was represented among the Temple musicians (1 Chronicles 6:31-37).

JEGAR-SAHADUTHA

In biblical times, the Aramaic expression that Laban used to designate the heap of stones on which he and Jacob ate a covenant meal.

JEHIEL

In the Old Testament, a Levite descendant of Gershon through Ladan; a "headman" (1 Chronicles 23:6-8). Toward the close of David's reign, Jehiel and his sons (or the paternal house called by his name) took care of the treasury belonging to God's house of worship (1 Chronicles 26:21-22).

JEHIELI

In the Old Testament, a Gershonite Levite who apparently served as an overseer of the sanctuary's treasury (1 Chronicles 26:20-22).

JEHOAHAZ

King of Israel; son and successor of King Jehu. For 17 years Jehoahaz reigned, from 876 to circa 860 BC (2 Kings 10:35; 13:1). When he succeeded his father to the throne, much of the realm was controlled by Syrian King Hazael of Damascus, who had seized from Jehu all of Israel's territory east of the Jordan River (2 Kings 10:32-34). Upon his death Jehoahaz was buried in Samaria and was succeeded on the throne by his son Jehoash (2 Kings 13:8-9; 2 Chronicles 25:17).

JEHOASH

1 King of Judah for 40 years, from 898 to 858 BC. He was the youngest son of Judah's King Ahaziah; his mother was Zibiah from Beer-sheba (2 Kings 12:1; 1 Chronicles 3:11).
2 King of Israel; son of Jehoahaz and grandson of Jehu. He ruled for 16 years in the middle of the ninth century BC. During the first part of the reign of this Jehoash (son of Jehoahaz) over the northern kingdom of Israel, Jehoash (son of Ahaziah) was king over the southern kingdom of Judah (2 Kings 13:10).

JEHOHANAN

In the Old Testament, father of the Ishmael who stood up with Jehoiada and other chiefs to depose Athaliah and put Jehoash on Judah's throne (2 Chronicles 23:1-3).

JEHOIACHIN

In the Old Testament (2 Kings 24) king of Judah, son of King Jehoaiakim. He came to the throne at the age of 18 in the midst of the Chaldean invasion of Judah and reigned three months. He was forced to surrender to Nebuchadnezzar II and was taken to Babylon (597) along with 10,000 of his subjects. Nearly 37 years later Nebuchadnezzar died, and his successor released Jehoiachin.

JEHOIADA

In the Old Testament, father of the Benaiah who was one of David's mighty men and also Solomon's army chief (2 Samuel 23:8-23). He is connected with the priesthood, being called "the chief priest". He is referred to as "the leader of the sons of Aaron" and was among those flocking to David when he became king over all Israel at Hebron (1 Chronicles 27:5; 12:27).

JEHOIAKIM

In the Old Testament (2 Kings 23:34-24:17), king of Judah (circa 609-598 BC), being a vicious and irreligious man. When Josiah died at Megiddo, his younger son, Jehoahaz, was chosen king by the Judahites, but the Egyptian conqueror Necho took Jehoahaz to Egypt and made Jehoiakim king. When the new Chaldean Empire under Nebuchadnezzar II defeated Egypt, however, Jehoiakim changed his allegiance from the Egyptian king to Nebuchadnezzar. Later he revolted against Nebuchadnezzar. After several battles and invasions, Nebuchadnezzar led the decisive invasion against Judah and besieged Jerusalem (598 BC).

JEHOIARIB

In the Old Testament, the priest whose paternal house was selected by lot at first of the 24 priestly divisions organized during David's rule (1 Chronicles 24:1-7). Some of the post-exilic descendants of this paternal house, or another priest with the same name, lived in Jerusalem (1 Chronicles 9:3-10).

JEHONADAB

In the Old Testament, David's nephew; son of his brother Shimeah. He was a "very wise man" but crafty and shrewd. After inducing David's son Amnon to disclose to him his passion for his half-sister Tamar, Jehonadab proposed the scheme by which Amnon violated her. After her full brother Absalom had Amnon killed in revenge, the report came to David that Absalom has killed all the king's sons, but Jehonadab was on hand to give assurance that Amnon alone was dead (2 Samuel 13:3-5; 28-33).

JEHORAM

1 One of two contemporary Old Testament kings. Jehoram, the son of Ahab and Jezebel and king (853-842 BC) of Israel, maintained close relations with Judah. Together with Jehoshaphat, king of Judah, Jehoram unsuccessfully attempted to subdue a revolt of Moab against Israel. As had his father, Jehoram later endeavored to recover Ramoth-gilead from Hazael, king of Damascus. In this matter he was aided by his nephew Ahaziah, then king of Judah. Wounded during the fighting at Ramoth-gilead, Jehoram retired to Jizreel in Judah. During his convalescence a revolution took place and Jehu was anointed king at Ramoth-gilead. Jehu then put to death all the members of Ahab's family including Jehoram, Jezebel, and Ahaziah.

2 Jehoram, son of Jehoshaphat and king (850-843 BC) of Judah, married Athaliah, daughter of Ahab, and was thus brother-in-law of the Jehoram of Israel. On ascending the throne Jehoram massacred his kinsmen. He had to face a successful revolt by Edom, a revolt by Libnak, and an invasion of Philistines and Arabs.

JEHOSHAPHAT

King (circa 875-850 BC) of Judah during the reigns in Israel of Ahab, Ahaziah, and Jehoram, with whom he maintained close political and economic alliances. Jehoshaphat aided Ahab in his unsuccessful attempt to recapture the city of Ramoth-gilead. He helped Jehoram in his battle with Moab, and married his son and successor, Jehoram, to Athaliah, a daughter of Ahab. In Judah he reorganized the army and attempted to centralize political power through a series of religious and legal measures.

JEHOSHEBA

In the Old Testament, wife of High Priest Jehoiada; daughter of King Jehoram of Judah, though not necessarily by his wife Athaliah. After the death of her half-brother of brother King Ahaziah, she took her infant son Jehoash into hiding to escape Athaliah's slaughter of the royal offspring. Jehoiada and Jehosheba kept their nephew hidden in their temple quarters for six years before Jehoiada brought him out to be proclaimed king (2 Kings 11:1-3; 2 Chronicles 22:10-12).

JEHOVAH

Variant of the Old Testament personal name for God. The sacred name YHWH, probably pronounced "Yahweh", was not used by the Jews after circa 300 BC for fear of blaspheming. Hence in reading the Hebrew Bible "Adonai" (Lord) was substituted. Medieval translators combined the consonants of one name with the vowels of the other, arriving at "Jehovah".

JEHOVAH'S WITNESSES

Religious movement founded in 1872 by Charles Taze Russell in Pittsburgh, Pa. There is no formal church organization. Their central doctrine is that the Second Coming is at hand; they avoid participation in secular government which they see as diabolically inspired. Over two million members proselytize by house-to-house calls and through publications such as The Watchtower and Awake, issued by the Watchtower Bible and Tract Society. The Jehovah's Witnesses are known for their defiance of the state, especially in refusing to show allegiance to a sovereign other than Jehovah by not saluting the flag and by rejecting military service.

JEHU

King (circa 842-815 BC) of Israel. He was a commander of chariots for the king of Israel, Ahab, and his son Jehoram, on Israel's frontier facing Damascus and Assyria. During Jehoram's rule, Jehu accepted the prophet Elisha anointing him as king and overthrew the dynasty of Omri (2 Kings 9-10). He did not, however, overturn the golden calves worshipped in Bethel and Dan. For this it was foretold that his dynasty should only extend to four generations.

JEHUCAL

In the Old Testament, a prince sent by King Zedekiah to ask Jeremiah to pray for Judah (Jeremiah 37:3). This son of Shelemiah and three other influential princes had Jeremiah put into the miry cistern because his preaching was, as they put it, "weakening the hands of the man of war," as well as the hands of the people in general (Jeremiah 38:1-6).

JEHUZABAD

In the Old Testament, an accomplice in the slaying of King Jehoash of Judah. Jehizabad and Jozacar, servants of Jehoash, put the king to death on account of his murdering Jehoiadah's son Zechariah. They themselves were killed by Jehoash's son and successor Amaziah. Jehuzabad was the son of a Moabitess named Shimrith (2 Kings 12:20-21; 2 Chronicles 24:20-22).

JEIEL

In Judaism, a Levite, both a gatekeeper and a musician, who participated in the musical celebration when the ark was first brought to Jerusalem and thereafter played in front of the tent that contained it (1 Chronicles 15:17-28).

JEKEMEAM

In the Old Testament, the fourth son of Hebron, a Kohathite Levite, and founder of a Levitical paternal house that survived at least until David's reign (1 Chronicles 23:12-19).

JEKUTHIEL

In the Old Testament, a descendant of Judah and "father of Zanoah" (1 Chronicles 4:1). Zanoah is the name of a city rather than a person in its other occurrence (Joshua 15:56-57), so Jekuthiel as its "father" was likely the father of those who settled there, or was himself its founder or chief settler.

JEMUEL

In the Old Testament, the first-named son of Simeon and one of the "seventy" numbered among Jacob's household "who came into Egypt" (Genesis 46:10; Exodus 6:15).

JEPHTHAH

A judge or regent of Israel who dominates a narrative in the book of Judges, where he is described as an example of faith for Israel in its commitment to God. Of the Israelite tribe in Gilead, he was banished from his home and became the head of a powerful band of brigands. Oppressed by the rapacity of the non-Israelite peoples of Hauran and Ammon, he successfully overcame the enemy. Trying to keep his rash promise that he should offer his only daughter in case of victory, he set her apart for God, remaining virgin.

JERAHMEEL

In the Old Testament, the firstborn of Judah's grandson Hezron. The royal and messianic lineage passed through Jerahmeel's brother Ram. An extensive genealogy is included for Jerahmeel's descendants, some of whom inhabited the southern part of Judah (1 Chronicles 2:4-15; 1 Samuel 27:10; Luke 3:33).

JERAHMEELITES

The descendants of Judah through Jerahmeel son of Hezron (1 Chronicles 2:4, 25-27). The Jerahmeelites lived in the southern part of Judah, apparently in the same general region as the

Amalekites, Geshurites and Girzites whom David raided while residing among the Philistines as a fugitive from King Saul.

JEREMIAH

(circa 650 - circa 570 BC) Prophet of Judah, and the primary author of the Old Testament Book of Jeremiah, a collection of his oracles. Because he foretold the downfall of Jerusalem and recommended submission to Babylon, Jeremiah was branded a traitor and persecuted. Nevertheless he continued to preach the moral regeneration of his people despite the political and military turmoil around him.

JEREMIAH, Book of

One of the major prophetical writings of the Old Testament. Jeremiah foretold the subjugation of Judah by Babylon and the destruction of Jerusalem and the Temple, and called for submission to the conquerors as God's agents in punishing idolatry. An unusual feature of this book is the "confessions" of Jeremiah, a group of individual lamentations, reflecting the personal struggles in the prophet's role as the spokesman of a message so unpopular that it evoked imprisonments and threats to his life.

Jeremiah's most important prophecy concerning the future is that regarding the new covenant (Jeremiah 31:31-34). He prophesied of a time when God would make a covenant with Israel, superseding the old Mosaic covenant; God would write His law upon the hearts of men (rather than on tables of stone) and all would know God directly and receive his forgiveness. It is quoted in the letter to the Hebrews and lies behind words of Jesus at the Last Super: "This cup is the new covenant in my blood."

JEREMIAH, Letter of

An apocryphal work (noncanonical for Jews and Protestants) placed after the Lamentations of Jeremiah in two of the major editions of the Septuagint (Greek Bible).

The work is supposedly a letter sent by Jeremiah to Jews exiled to Babylon by King Nebuchadnezzar in 597 BC, but it is not a letter, nor was it written by Jeremiah. It is rather a polemic against the worship of idols, developed around the only verse in Jeremiah written in Aramaic (10:11), which states that false gods shall perish.

JEREMIAS II

(1530-1595) Patriarch of Constantinople, theologian, who commissioned a celebrated statement of Eastern Orthodox doctrine addressed to German Lutheran theologians.

JEREMOTH

In Judaism, son of Mushi and grandson of Merari in the tribe of Levi. The paternal house founded by this person was included in David's rearrangement of the Levitical service organization (1 Chronicles 23:21-31). The name is also applied to a son of Heman in the Levitical branch of Kohathites. During David's reign, Jeremoth was selected by lot to head the 15th of the 24 divisions of sanctuary musicians (1 Chronicles 6:33; 25:1-9).

JERICHO

Village on the west side of the Jordan River valley. Dating possibly from 9000 BC, it was captured from the Canaanites by Joshua in 1400 BC. It has regularly been destroyed and rebuilt; Herod the Great built a Jericho near the Old Testament city.

JERIMOTH

In the Old Testament, a son of David whose daughter married King Rehoboam (2 Chronicles 11:18). As Jerimoth is not mentioned in the listings of David's sons by his named wives, he might have been a son by a concubine or an unnamed wife (2 Samuel 5:13).

JEROBOAM

Name of two kings of ancient Israel, whose reigns were separated by some 130 years.

1 First king of the ten-tribe kingdom of Israel. The son of Nebat, one of Solomon's officers in the village of Zeredah; of the tribe of Ephraim. Apparently at an early age Jeroboam was left fatherless, to be raised by his widowed mother Zeruah (1 Kings 11:26).

At some time, Jeroboam fled to Egypt, and here under the sheltering protection of Pharaoh Shishak he remained until the death of Solomon (1 Kings 11:40). The ten tribes appointed Jeroboam as their king. The newly installed king immediately set about to build up Shechem as his royal capital, and east of Shechem, on the other side of the Jordan, he fortified the settlement of Penuel, the place where Jacob had wrestled with an angel (Genesis 32:30-31).

2 King of Israel; son and successor of Jehoash, and great-grandson of Jehu. As the 14th ruler of the northern kingdom Jeroboam II reigned for 41 years, from circa 843 to 802 BC (2 Kings 14:16-23). Like so many of his predecessors he did what was bad in God's eyes by perpetuating the calf worship of Jeroboam I (2 Kings 14:24).

JEROHAM

In the Old Testament, a Benjaminite of Gedor whose two "sons" were named among David's "helpers in the warfare" while he was at Ziklag under Saul's restrictions (1 Chronicles 12:1-7).

JEROME, Saint

(347-420) Biblical scholar, one of the first theologians to be called a Doctor of the Christian church. After being educated in classical studies he fled to the desert as a hermit in 375 to devote himself to prayer. He was subsequently papal secretary and translated the Old Testament into Latin and wrote New Testament commentaries.

JERUBBAAL

In the Old Testament, the name given to Gideon' son of Joash the Abi-ezrite after he had torn down his father's altar to Baal and the wooden sacred pole by it; then on an altar built to Jehovah, Gideon sacrificed a bull belonging to his father, using the pieces of the sacred pole as fuel (Judges 6:11, 25-27).

JERUSALEM

Capital of Israel, located near the center of Israel, circa 15 miles west of the Dead Sea and 35 miles east of the Mediterranean Sea. Jerusalem is the pivotal city of the Bible and the holy city of Christians, Jews, and Muslims. The name is of Semitic origin, and through the centuries such meaning as "the city of peace," "vision of peace," "possession of peace" are more popular than exact.

Most probable the name means "City of Shalem," Shalem being a well-known Semitic god who appears in the texts of Urgarit. Today the Arabs call the city el-Quds (The Holy City), while in the State of Israel it is called Yerushalayim.

The city is situated on Palestine's central limestone plateau, at an elevation of 2493 feet above sea level. The northern part of the city is a continuation of the central plateau, but the city itself generally slopes downward toward the south.

Jerusalem is skirted on three sides by protecting valleys, the Kidron to the east and the Hennon (whence Gehenna) on the west and south. These two valleys meet at En-Rogel whence they work their way south-eastward to the Dead Sea as one valley.

The city is divided into two hills by another, smaller valley, called the Tyropoen Valley by Josephus, which has accumulated from 40 to 70 feet of filling in the course of centuries. The two hills are cut through with other depressions so that the terrain of the city is quite uneven.

The southern narrow extremity of the east hill is the Ophel (City of David) and to the north is the site of several temples in the general area of the present Mosque of Omar. The Basilica of the Holy Sepulcher containing Calvary, and the Cenacle are located on the larger, western hill.

No doubt, the water sources determined the location of the city originally. The most interesting is the spring located low on the eastern slope of the Ophel which the Bible calls Gihon (1 Kings 1:33) (today: Spring of the Mother of the Steps" of "Spring of Lady Mary"). Even before David captured the city, this spring was artificially blocked up so that the water could be reached through a shaft from within the city above. Joab captured the city through this shaft, for David (2 Samuel 5:8).

Water flowed through canals from this spring into two pools at the lower end of the Ophel until King Hezekiah's engineers cut a tunnel through the rock so that the flow of water would not be exposed to enemies. The reservoir at the end of the tunnel is called the Pool of Siloe.

Further to the south where the Kidron and Hennon Valleys join is another, but poorer spring, En-Rogel. In the northern part of the city, a large pool near the Sheepgate served the city in later times. This is Bethzatha with five porticoes (John 5:2) which has been located near the church of St. Ann. Today Jerusalem's main water supply comes from Wadi el-Fara, 10 miles to the north-east.

JERUSALEM, Council of

A conference of the Christian Apostles in Jerusalem, circa 50, which decreed that Gentile Christians did not have to observe the Mosaic Law of the Jews. It was occasioned by the insistence of certain Judaic Christians from Jerusalem that Gentile Christians from Antioch in Syria obey the Mosaic custom of circumcision. A delegation, led by the apostle Paul and his companion Barnabas, was appointed to confer with the elders of the church in Jerusalem.

JERUSALEM, History of

Jerusalem dates from possibly the 4th millennium BC. In circa 1000 BC King David captured the city from the Jebusites and made it his capital. The great Temple was built by his son Solomon circa 970 BC. David's dynasty was ended in 586 BC by the invasion of King Nebuchadnezzar, who sacked the Temple and deported most of the Jews to Babylon.

The Jews were allowed to return by Cyrus II of Persia, and the Temple was rebuilt. Jerusalem subsequently became part of Syria, but in 165 BC Judas Maccabeus freed the city, and it was ruled by the Hasmonean dynasty.

From 37 BC the Herod family led the state under the aegis of the Roman Empire. The city was destroyed in AD 70 by the Romans, and its inhabitants were massacred. Subsequently the Romans rebuilt the city.

When Constantine the Great made Christianity the official imperial religion in the 4th century, a concentrated effort was made to locate and mark the places sacred to Christianity. Of special importance was the church of the Holy Sepulchre, marking the tomb of Christ. In the 5th century, Jews were again allowed to live in the city and to worship at the western wall of the courtyard of the Temple (the Wailing Wall), all that remained of Herod's Temple.

Byzantine rule continued, then the city was taken by the Persians (614) and finally was lost to the Arabs under Omar. Muslim rule was one of tolerance towards the Jews, and at first also to the Christians. Chief among the Arab building programs were construction of the Dome of the Rock and the El Aqsa mosques, both in the Temple area. The Western Christians of the First Crusade succeeded in capturing Jerusalem in 1099, and for many years the history of the city was that of alternating Christian and Muslim rule, with massacre and destruction by both groups until it fell to Saladin in 1187. The city later fell to the hands of the Mamelukes, who held it until they succumbed to the Ottoman Turks in 1517. The Turks possessed the city until 1917.

The city grew rapidly in the 19th century owing to an influx of Jews, at first motivated by religious piety and later

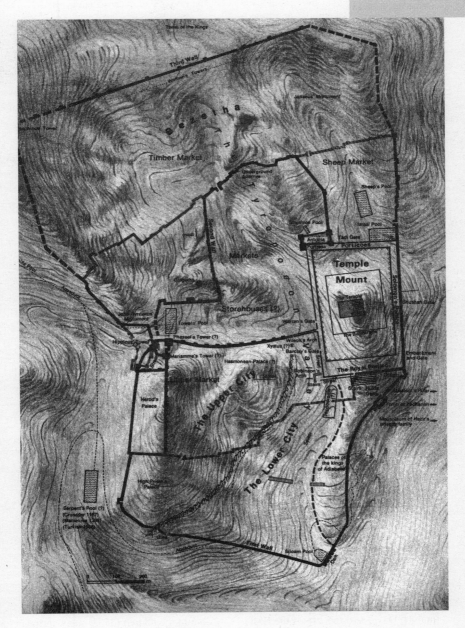

Map of Jerusalem at the time of Jesus.

by political Zionism. It was at this time that the first neighborhoods were built outside the city walls. World War I brought with it British conquest. Jerusalem was made the capital of Palestine by the British and continued to grow. According to the 1947 United Nations' resolution partitioning Palestine, Jerusalem was to be an international city under UN supervision. In the war that followed in 1948, however, Arab (Jordanian) forces captured the Old City, while Jewish forces held the New City, thus partitioning the city. Israel made Jerusalem the official capital. In the Arab-Israeli War of June 1967, the Old City of Jerusalem was captured by Israel, which immediately took steps to incorporate the whole city into the state.

The Old City is divided into four quarters: Muslim, Jewish, Christian and Armenian. The Muslim quarter lies to the east, adjacent to the ancient Temple area and where the Dome of the Rock and El Aqsa mosques are situated. The Dome of the Rock, built in the 7th century and decorated in part by Byzantine craftsmen, is judged an architectural masterpiece. From the rock over which it was built, according to Muslim belief, Mohammed ascended to heaven.

The Jewish quarter, which bordered on the Wailing Wall, was largely destroyed in 1948 and is being rebuilt. The quarter now shows beautiful archaeological excavations. The Christian quarter surrounds the Church of the Holy Sepulchre. First built in 4th century and rebuilt many times, this church incorporates the traditional sites of both the crucifixion and tomb of Christ. Another tomb lying outside the city, known as the Garden Tomb, is the site accepted by most Protestants. Also in the Christian quarter, ending at the church of the Holy Sepulchre, is the Via Dolorosa, a long winding street on which the Stations of the Cross are located. Other sites of religious significance include the Mount of Olives, outside the city walls to the east, the tomb of David and the site of the Last Supper (on what is now known as Mount Zion, just south of the city walls), the Tower of David on the wall itself, and the Byzantine Monastery of the Cross, said to mark the spot where the tree of Jesus' cross had grown.

JERUSALEM, Council of

A conference of the Christian Apostles in Jerusalem, circa 50, which decreed that Gentile Christians did not have to observe the Mosaic Law of the Jews. It was occasioned by the insistence of certain Judaic Christians from Jerusalem that Gentile Christians from Antioch in Syria obey the Mosaic custom of circumcision. A delegation, led by the apostle Paul and his companion Barnabas, was appointed to confer with the elders of the church in Jerusalem.

JERUSALEM, Kingdom of

Kingdom formed in 1099 from territory in Palestine wrested from the Muslims by European Christians during the First Crusade and lasting until 1291, when the two surviving cities of the kingdom succumbed to attacks by Muslim armies.

JERUSALEM, Orthodox Church of

An autocephalous (ecclesiastically independent) Eastern Orthodox patriarchate, fourth in honorific seniority after the churches of Constantinople, Alexandria, and Antioch. Since the beginning of Muslim rule in the 7th century, it has been the main custodian of the Christian holy places in Jerusalem.

JERUSALEM, Patriarchate of

One of the four eminent patriarchates of the Eastern church. Ecclesiastically speaking, the patriarchate can be traced to the Apostle James the Less, first bishop of Jerusalem. In spite of its religious importance, the city did not receive the recognition it deserved and was merely a suffragan see to Caesarea in Palestine, itself under the patriarchate of Antioch.

After Constantine the Great gave freedom to the church (313), many shrines and monasteries were erected in and around Jerusalem, thus making it a pilgrimage center. The Council of Nicaea I (325) conferred honorary precedence upon Jerusalem after Rome, Alexandria, and Antioch, although, jurisdictionally, it was still subordinate to the metropolitan see of Caesarea in Palestine.

Ultimately the Council of Chalcedon (415) elevated the Holy City to the status of a genuine patriarchate, independent of Antioch which ceded 58 dioceses. The elevation was achieved mainly through the persistence of Juvenal, bishop of Jerusalem (422-458).

During the Monophysite conflict, the patriarchate remained Orthodox, but there were sufficient Monophysites in Palestine for the Jacobite patriarch of Antioch to appoint Seberus bishop for Jerusalem.

The prosperity that had grown from the 4th to the 7th centuries ended with the Persian and Arab invasions in 614 and 637, respectively. The Latin kingdom established through the Crusades (1099-1187) brought with it a Latin hierarchy that displaced the Melkite patriarchate.

The Melkite patriarch took up residence in Constantinople and the ecumenical patriarch of the imperial city actually ruled the Jerusalem patriarchate until the dissolution of the Latin kingdom.

During this difficult era, the patriarch of Jerusalem followed Michael Cerularius in his break from Rome (1054). Temporary reunion was achieved by the patriarchs of Jerusalem, Antioch, and Alexandria, after the Council of Florence (1439).

But before the end of the 15th century, relations between Rome and the Orthodox patriarch of Jerusalem were completely severed. In 1838 the Catholic Melkite patriarch of Antioch, Maximos III Mazlum, received the title of Patriarch of Jerusalem and Alexandria with authority over Catholic Melkites in these jurisdictions.

In 1847, the Latin patriarchate was restored. Jerusalem is also claimed as an Armenian patriarchate. From the beginning of the 20th century, cooperation between Greek and Arab members of the Orthodox church has been greatly strained. The Orthodox patriarchate resides in Jerusalem itself and governs some 100,000 faithful in three eparchies.

JERUSALEM, Synod of

Synod held in 1672, important council of the Eastern Orthodox Church. In was convened by Dositheos, patriarch of Jerusalem, in order to reject the *Confession of Orthodox Faith* (1629), by Cyril Lucaris, which professed most of the major Calvinist doctrines. In its 18 canons the synod repudiated Lucaris's confession article by article and accepted the *Orthodox Confession* of Peter Moglia.

JESHAIAH

In the Old Testament, a Levitical descendant of Moses through Eliezer and an ancestor of the Shelomoth whom David appointed one of his treasurers (1 Chronicles 23:12, 24-26). The name is also applied to a Levite musician of "the sons of Jeduthun,"; selected by lot to head the eighth of the 24 Davidic musical groups (1 Chronicles 25:1-3).

JESHANAH

In Judaism, a place mentioned along with Mizpah as indicating the location of the stone that Samuel set up and called "Ebenezer" (2 Samuel 7:12). Jeshanah was one of the cities captured by Judean King Abijah (980-977 BC) from Jeroboam the king of Israel (2 Chronicles 13:19).

JESHEBEAB

In the Old Testament, the priest whose paternal house was selected by lot for the 14th course when David had the priestly services divided up (1 Chronicles 24:6, 13).

JESHUA

In the Old Testament, an Aaronic priest in David's time. The ninth of the 24 divisions of the Aaronic priesthood as arranged by David was assigned to the house of Jeshua. Probably the same house is listed among those returning with Zerubbabel from Babylonian exile in 537 BC (1 Chronicles 24:1-11; Ezra 2:1, 36).

JESHUA BEN JUDAH

(1012-1078) Jewish law interpreter and minor philosopher of the Karaite sect that rejected the oral law, especially the Talmud, the rabbinical compendium of law, lore, and commentary.

JESIMIEL

In the Old Testament, one of the Simeonite chieftains who, in King Hezekiah's day, extended their territory to the east of the valley of Gedor (1 Chronicles 4:24, 34-41).

JESSE

In the Old Testament, father of King David of the tribe of Judah; grandson of Ruth and Boaz and a link in the genealogical line from Abraham to Jesus (Ruth 4:17, 22; Matthew 1:5-6; Luke 3:31-32). Jesse fathered eight sons, one of whom apparently died before producing any sons of his own, which may account for the omission of his name from the genealogies of Chronicles (1 Samuel 16:10-12); 1 Chronicles 2:12-15). The two sisters of David, Abigail and Zerulah, are nowhere called Jesse's daughters, but one is called "the daughter of Nahash" (1 Chronicles 2:16-17).

JESUIT ESTATES CONTROVERSY

A Roman Catholic-Protestant dispute in 19th century Canada. When the Society of Jesus was suppressed by the papacy in 1773, its extensive land holdings in Canada were transferred to the British Government with the stipulation that the revenue derived from them should be applied to educational purposes. After the Jesuits returned to Canada, the Jesuit's Estates Act regulated a compensation of $400,000 for the loss of their estates.

JESUITS

Name commonly given to the members of the Society of Jesus, founded by Saint Ignatius Loyola in 1534. It is a missionary order dedicated to the defense of Christian principles, to education and yo foreign missions. Jesuits live under the Constitutions of Ignatius (1558), and their training, based upon Ignatius' *Spiritual Exercises,* is long and arduous. The order is directed by a vicar-general in Rome, and members take the usual vows of poverty, chastity and obedience as well a fourth vow of obedience to the pope.

The Jesuits were notably active in the mission field. As early as the 1540s Francis Xavier, a cofounder of the order, made many converts in India and Japan while later Jesuits penetrated China. Others carried Christianity to the people of the Americas, and many of the black-robed fathers were martyred for their faith. During the Counter-Reformation the Jesuits led the van of those opposing, the Protestants, and contributed to a revival of Christianity in Central Europe.

Nevertheless by the 18th century the Jesuits had aroused the animosity of those rulers of Catholic Europe who sought to free themselves from the influence of the Holy see. They were banned from country after country, and in 1773 were disbanded by Pope Clement XIV, except in Russia and Prussia.

At the beginning of the 19th century the order was revived in some countries, especially in the United Sates, and in 1814 it was reinstated by the Pope, The number of Jesuits throughout the world today is circa 35,000. Among them are some of Catholicism's most esteemed scholars and theologians. The order is responsible for the Gregorian university in Rome. Jesuits continue to emphasize the importance of sound secondary and university education and have adapted mass communication methods - including radio stations and more than 1,000 periodicals of various types - to the purpose of their apostolate.

JESUS CHRIST

Being both God and man, Jesus always exists, but as a human he was born in Bethlehem Judaea, to Mary (John 1:10-13). His public life was inaugurated when he was baptized in the Jordan River by John the Baptist (Mark 1:9). For the next three years he journeyed, mainly in Galilee, gathering a band of disciples. He preached to large crowds and healed the physically and mentally ill. His message concerned the coming of the Kingdom of God and his mission was to prepare men for it. His sermon on the mount transformed the application of the Mosaic law (John 1:17). Introducing God as a loving Father, he antagonized the scribes and Pharisees. The latter finally got him crucified (AD 33, Mark 15:25-32). But after three days he rose from the dead. He appeared several times before he went to heaven, the so-called Ascension (Acts 1:3). Thereafter his followers, strengthened by the Holy Spirit, spread the gospel throughout the world. Many people came to accept him as Messiah, Lord and Son of God and as the Savior who by dying redeemed mankind (John 3:16).

Although only a few references to Jesus occur in ancient non-Christian sources, the varied writings of early Christianity all proclaim Jesus as the Messiah. The main sources of events in the life and teachings of Jesus are the four gospels - Matthew, Mark, Luke and John - and the epistles of the New Testament. From the numerous details given by the gospels, it is possible to form a vivid picture of Jesus. The writers of the gospels sifted and arranged the material that was known to them in order to provide manuals for the preaching and spread of Christianity. Thus the numerous sayings of Jesus and the events in his life are reported not so much as historical statements, but rather to characterize him as a servant of God and the instrument through whom God worked.

JESUS ONLY

Movement of believers within Pentecostalism who hold that true baptism can only be "in the name of Jesus" rather than in the name of the Trinity.

JESUS PRAYER

A characteristic form of Eastern Christian spirituality, consisting in a mental invocation of the name of Jesus Christ, repeated continuously. The most widely accepted form of the prayer is "Lord Jesus Christ, Son of God, have mercy on me." It reflects the biblical idea that the name of God is sacred and that its invocation implies a direct meeting with the divine.

JETHER

In the Old Testament, father of David's onetime army chief Amasa (1 Kings 2:5).

JETHRO

In the Old Testament, priest of Midian of the Kenite clan, with whom Moses took refuge after he killed an Egyptian and whose daughter Moses married (Exodus 3:1).

After the Exodus, Jethro visited the Hebrews encamped at the "mountain of God" and brought with him Moses' wife and sons. He suggested that Moses appoint able men to assist him in judging his people, thus founding the Hebrew judiciary (Exodus 18). Jethro's Kenite descendants settled in Judaean territory in the Negev and were on friendly terms with the Hebrews in the time of Deborah, Saul, and David.

JETUR

In the Old Testament, a son of Ishmael (Genesis 25:13-15) and forefather of a people against whom the Israelites warred (1 Chronicles 5:18-19). It is possible that Jetur's descendants were the Ituraeans (Luke 3:1).

JEUL

In the Old Testament, a Levite who helped in cleansing the temple during Hezekiah's reign; a descendant of Elizaphan (2 Chronicles 29:13-16).

JEUZ

In the Old Testament, a family head in the tribe of Benjamin; son of Shaharaim by his wife Hodesh (1 Chronicles 8:1, 8-10).

JEWISH AGENCY

An international body representing the World Zionist Organization, created in 1929 by Chaim Weizmann, with head-quarters in Jerusalem.

With the establishment of an Israeli state in 1948, the agency devoted itself primarily to problems of immigration, settlement, the Youth Aliyah, propa-ganda, and the cultural education of Jews outside Israel.

JEWISH MYTH AND LEGEND

Stories transmitted over the past 3,000 years in Hebrew and vernacular dialects spoken by Jews in various parts of the world. The stories have played an important role in Jewish reli-gion and culture, and those in the Old Testament have become part of general Western culture and have had an important influence on Western litera-ture and art.

JEWISH RELIGIOUS YEAR

The cycle of sabbaths and holidays commonly observed by the Jewish reli-gious community all over the world; in Israel the major holidays are also observed officially by the secular com-munity.

JEWISH REVOLT, First

Major uprising (66-70) being the result of a long series of clashes in which small groups of Jews offered sporadic resistance to the Romans, who respond-ed with severe counter-measures. In 66 the Jews combined in revolt, expelled the Romans from Jerusalem, and over-whelmed in the pass of Beth-Horon a Roman punitive force under Gallus.

JEWISH REVOLT, Second

Major uprising (132-135) of the Jews against the Romans. The misrule of Tinnius Rufus, the Roman governor of Judaea, combined with Emperor Hadrian's intention to found a Roman colony on the site of Jerusalem, roused the last remnants of Palestinian Jewry to revolt. With the fall of Jerusalem in 135, Jews were thenceforth forbidden to enter Jerusalem.

JEWS

Jew is a name first applied to the tribe of Judah, in distinction from the seceding ten tribes, the Israelites. From the time of the Babylonian Captivity it became the appellation of the whole nation. The descendants of Abraham being called "Hebrews," the word "Jews" later became more or less synonymous.

Jews are the followers of the Jewish religion, a group held together by a shared faith and a common history and culture reaching back more than 3,000 years. Since the 19th century, when the Jews were emancipated from the ghetto and religion no longer regulated every aspect of daily life, there has been no single definition to which even all Jews can agree. The Jews are variously been defined as a nation, a people, an ethnic or cultural group, or the adherents of Judaism. A Jew may express his sense of belonging in many ways besides religious practice, and this identifica-tion has been reinforced by the experi-ence of persecution and discrimination to create a sense of unity, a community sharing a single fate. But while it seems impossible to find a common denominator of "Jewishness," there continues to be a group of people who call themselves Jews and are consid-ered Jews by the world around them.

One thing however is clear - Jews in no way form a separate race. Jewish groups throughout the world differ far more from each other than they do from populations around them. Even in the days of the Old Testament the Jews were a racially mixed people, and today this is nowhere more apparent than in Israel, where more than four

Jesus and the women taken in adultery.
"Jesus stopped down, and with his finger wrote on the ground ... and said unto them. He that is without sin among you, let him first cast a stone at her" (John 8:6,7).
Lithograph by Gustave Doré (about 1860).

million Jews from some 70 countries represent virtually every racial type in existence. The recent controversies in Israel over the issue of who can claim to be a Jew indicate that most Israelis accept that virtually anyone who declares himself to be Jewish must be accepted as such.

JEWS, Beginnings

According to the Old testament, the history of the Jewish people begins with the Hebrew patriarchs, Abraham, his son Isaac and his grandson Jacob, also named Israel. Abraham left his home at Ur in Mesopotamia, and led his family to Canaan (Palestine). The story of the sons of Jacob, Joseph and his brothers, tells how the children of Israel migrated to the land of Goshen in north-eastern Egypt at a time of famine and drought. A pharaoh reduced the Israelites to slavery until Moses finally led his people out of Egypt in the Exodus. After 40 years of wandering in the wilderness, the Israelites finally reentered Canaan circa 1200 BC.

Under their leaders, the Judges, the Israelites were engaged in constant warfare with their neighbors in Canaan, but the threat of the Philistines forced the Twelve Tribes to unite into a monarchy, with Saul as their king.

Saul's reign ended when the Israelite army was defeated by the Philistines, but his successor David brought prosperity and peace, expanding the kingdom and establishing a long-enduring dynasty. David conquered the city of Jerusalem and made it the capital and chief religious shrine. His son Solomon built the Temple at Jerusalem, but the grandeur of the reign came at the price of oppressive taxes, and under his son Rehoboam the kingdom split in two: the southern monarchy, Judah, continued to be ruled by the descendants of the house of David; the northern kingdom, Israel, suffered repeated dynastic upheavals.

The monarchies ended with the defeat and destruction of Israel in 721 BC by the Assyrians and the defeat of Judah and destruction of the Temple by the Babylonians in 587 BC. Many of the inhabitants of Israel and Judah were deported. The exiles from Israel soon lost their identity in captivity; they became the "Ten Lost Tribes."

The Jews of Judah kept, however, their individuality while in exile in Babylonia. During the period of the Babylonian captivity the synagogue, a place of study and prayer, was introduced to replace the Temple and its sacrifices. When Babylonia was conquered by Cyrus the Great, King of Persia, he granted the Jews permission to return to their homeland in 538 BC. The Temple was rebuilt, and the Pentateuch, the first five books of the Bible, received their sacred character.

After weathering the conquest of Alexander the Great, Judah was soon to suffer from his successors, the Seleucid kings of Syria. Antiochus IV Epiphanes began to impose Greek culture on the country and to force the Jews to give up their religion. A rebellion led by Mattathias the Hasmonean, and later by his son Judas Maccabaeus, finally restored an independent Jewish state in 142 BC. The Hasmoneans established a new dynasty of rulers and High Priests, but their dominion was to be shortlived.

JEWS, Middle Ages

The rise of Christianity brought with it ever-increasing harassment of the Jews, persecuted for rejecting Christ. The restrictions placed on Jews became increasingly severe, and during the Middle Ages in many countries they were confined to ghettos, excluded from trades and professions and barred from owning land. In Palestine the Jews had been an agricultural people, but now trade and money-lending were the only occupations open to them. Rulers frequently found the Jews useful to them as sources of loans, seldom repaid; but beginning at the end of the 12th century, at the time of the Crusades, a new wave of persecution began and one by one the nations of western Europe expelled the Jews from their territory. When the Moors had ruled Spain, Jewish scholarship and culture had enjoyed a golden age, but in 1492 the Jews of Spain were expelled by the Christian rulers Ferdinand and Isabella, and by the end of the Middle Ages only small parts of Germany and Italy still allowed Jews within their borders.

Many of the exiles perished; others, the descendants of the Spanish Jews, the Sephardim, found refuge in the Ottoman Empire, where under Muslim rule they were granted a large measure of tolerance.

The Inquisition forced the Jews remaining in Spain to abandon their faith, but many of these converts, or marranos, continued to practice Judaism in secret. The descendants reestablished Jewish communities in England, France and the Netherlands in the 17th century. In 1654, 23 Dutch Jews founded the first Jewish congregation in what is now the United States, at New Amsterdam (New York City).

The descendants of the German Jews, or Ashkenazim, found refuge in eastern Europe, in Poland and Lithuania. But increasingly a segment of Eastern European Jewry found itself trapped in a life of poverty and persecution in the lands that came under Russian rule. One form of escape from their condition was through mysticism and religious fervor, such as that displayed by the Hasidim in the 18th century.

As intolerance slowly lessened in western Europe, especially after the French Revolution, the Jewish communities there grew in size. But most Jews continued to live in the areas of the east that remained in the dark ages of intolerance until the 20th century.

JEWS, Modern world

For the Jews of western Europe, the advances of the Enlightenment proved to be both a religious and social challenge. Rights long withheld were suddenly granted and traditional Judaism found itself unprepared to face the new relationships that came with the end of enforced separatism and ghetto life.

Some communities reacted by introducing religious reforms, and many individuals became completely assimilated and converted Christianity. While some expected the Jews to give up all that had made them unique as a group, at the same time a new movement arose which, for the first time, attacked Jews as a race rather than as members of a religious group. The seeds of hatred planted by the bigotry of the Middle Ages bore a bitter pseudo-scientific fruit in various manifestations of anti-Semitism.

One reaction to this phenomenon was Zionism. Many of the founders of the movement at the end of the 19th century, men like Theodore Herzl, came from the emancipated communities of western Europe. They found mass support among the Jews of eastern Europe, motivated by merciless oppression and the historical Jewish yearning to return to Palestine. The harsh conditions of Jewish life in eastern Europe caused a steady stream of Jews to leave their homes. In the period 1881-1914 one-third of all Jews of eastern Europe emigrated, and 90 percent of this total of two million settled in the United States. In the 1930s all other Jewish problems were overshadowed by the advent of Nazism in Germany, with its virulent anti-Semitism. The tragic result was the killing of more than 6 million Jews during the war in concentration and death camps.

Reaction to the catastrophe of World War II led to establishment of the state of Israel in 1948, the first Jewish state since the Roman conquest of Jerusalem in 70.

JEWS, Roman conquest

As the Roman Empire expanded, it easily absorbed the Hasmonean state, and puppet rulers of the house of Herod were installed in Jerusalem. This period was marked by strife and controversy between the two major religious groups, the Pharisees and the Sadducees, and sects such as the Essenes grew up on the fringes of orthodox Judaism. Oppressive Roman rule led the people to believe that help would come from God in the form of a Messiah, who would restore the glory of Israel and bring peace. In this era, various individuals appeared who claimed to be the Messiah, and it is in this context that the Romans crucified Jesus of Nazareth as a threat to the security of their rule.

The Jews rose against the Romans in 66 and when the revolt was put down four years later with the conquest of Jerusalem, the city and the Temple were destroyed. Until the creation of the state of Israel in 1948, there was to be n0 independent state in Palestine. Jewish communities outside Palestine, particularly in Egypt, were already well established and with the destruction of their homeland, Jews moved to all parts of the Roman Empire.

Another futile revolt took place in 132-135 but the Temple was never to be rebuilt, and this had significant consequences for Judaism. Feeling that the religion was in danger of being lost, scholars codified the unwritten traditions known as oral law into the text of the mishnah and the later commentary, the gemara, which together form the Talmud, second only to the Bible in its authority.

JEZANIAH

In the Old Testament, a chief of the Judean military force among those submitting to Gedaliah's brief administration in 607 BC (Jeremiah 40:8-9).

JEZEBEL

In the Old Testament (Kings 1 and II), the wife of king Ahab, who ruled the kingdom of Israel (ninth century BC). By the introduction of idolatry, disregarding the rights of the common man, and defying the great prophets Elijah and Elisha, she provoked the internecine strife that enfeebled Israel for decades. She has come to be known as an archetype of the wicked woman.

JEZER

In the Old Testament, the third-listed son of Naphtali; founder of the family of Jezerites (Genesis 46:24; Numbers 26:48-49).

JEZERITES

A family of Naphtali that sprang from Jezer (Numbers 26:48-49; 1 Chronicles 7:13).

JIBRIL

In Islam, name for the angel Gabriel. he is one of the greatest of all the Islamic angels since he was the channel through which the Holy Koran was revealed from God to the Prophet Mohammed. He is mentioned by name three times in the Koran and elsewhere referred to by names like "The Spirit." Much tradition has accumulated in Islam around the figure of Gabriel; for example, he showed Nuh how to build the Ark and lured Pharaoh's army into the Red Sea. He pleaded with God for, and tried to rescue, Ibrahim when the latter was on the point of being burned to death by Namrud.

JIDLAPH

In the Old Testament, the seventh listed of the eight sons born to Nahor by his wife Milcah. Jidlaph was therefore a nephew of Abraham and an uncle of Isaac's wife Rebekah (Genesis 22:20-23).

JIGOKU

The Japanese Buddhist Hell, popularly believed to be composed primarily of eight hot and eight cold regions, located under the earth; ruled over by Emma-o, the Japanese equivalent of the Indian lord of Death, Yama.

JIHAD

In Islam, term denoting Holy War. The word derived from an Arabic root meaning basically "to strive." Jihad is sometimes considered by some groups to be a sixth pillar of Islam. Of course, all Muslims are obliged to wage the spiritual jihad in the sense of striving against sin and sinful inclinations within themselves; this is the other major sense of jihad.

The jihad is counted as one of the five

legitimate form of war recognized by fundamental Islamic doctrine. According to Sunnite doctrine the term is not applicable to warfare carried on against other Muslims, even schismatics, while for the Shiites, who consider other Muslims as non-believers, it is allowed.

JINA

Literally, the conqueror; one of the many terms used to describe the Buddha, though more usually applied to the Jains who have adopted it as a special title for their own leaders.

JINJA

In Japanese religion, a Shinto shrine; the place where the spirit of a deity is enshrined.

JINN

In Islam, term denoting intelligent, often invisible, beings made from flame (by contrast with the angels, made from light, and mankind, made from dust). The jinn also have the ability to assume various kinds of perceptible forms. They are mentioned in the Koran and, like man, some will be saved and go to Paradise since there are good as well as bad jinn, and jinn who help men as well as those who hinder and harm as they meddle in the lives of men.

The mission of Mohammed was both to mankind and to the jinn. Iblis is described in the Koran as both one of the jinn and an angel. A huge amount of folklore and tradition has grown up about the jinn in the Near and Middle East.

JINN, al-

The Title of the 72nd sura of the Koran; it means "The Jinn." The sura belongs to the Meccan period and has 28 verses. Its title is drawn from the references to the jinn in the first eight verses, which describe the jinn listening to the Koran and accepting its message. Stress is placed on the principal mission of Mohammed; whoever disobeys either the Prophet or God will burn in the fire of Jahannam forever.

JINNI

In Arabic mythology, general term for a supernatural spirit below the level of angels and devils.

JI-SHU

A branch of the Jodo-shu of Japanese Buddhism emphasizing devotion to the Buddha Amida through the chanting on hymns and dance.

JIVA

According to the Jaina philosophy of India, "living substance" or "souls" as opposed to ajiva, or "non-living substance."

JNANA

In Buddhism, term denoting wisdom, higher intellect. The term is flexible and sometimes means no more than worldly knowledge.

JOAB

(circa 1000 BC) In the Old Testament (2 Samuel), a Jewish military commander under king David, his mother's brother. He played a leading part in many of David's victories and led the loyal force that crushed the rebellion of David's son Absalom. Utterly devoted to David, Joab believed that he knew David's interests better than David himself did; hence he killed Absalom, although David had commanded that his life be saved.

During David's last days, Joab supported the abortive bid for the throne by David's son Adonijah and was executed by the successful Solomon.

JOACHIM OF FIORE

(1132-1202) Cistercian abbot and visionary. Five years after he was ordained as bishop of Corazzo (1177) he resigned this office to devote himself to biblical study and contemplation. In 1190 he obtained permission to found a community of hermits at Fiora (Flora) in Calabria for the more austere observance of the Cistercian Rule.

The religious ideas of Joachim centered on biblical prophecy as applied to the future reform of the church and his speculation displayed a clear tendency toward illuminism.

JOACHIMISM

A name given to an apocalyptic theology of history and a reform spirit derived from writings of Joachim of Fiore, or from Joachimite apocrypha. During his lifetime Joachims's orthodoxy was hardly questioned, but after his death zealous enthusiastics gave his eschatological theories interpretations that inspired as a whole spectrum of reformers, ranging from fervid idealists to crass opportunists.

JOAH

In the Old Testament, one of the Levitical gatekeepers assigned in David's day to guard duty over the storehouses; the third son of Obededom (1 Chronicles 26:1-4).

The name is also applied to one of the committee of three sent by King Hezekiah to the Assyrian messenger Rabshakeh but who were not to answer his charges and brags. Joah and his two companions did, however, ask Rabshakeh to speak to them in the Syrian tongue, which they themselves understood, rather than the Jews' language in the hearing of others on the city wall.

JOAN, Pope

Legendary female pontiff who supposedly reigned, under the title of John VIII, for slightly more than 25 months, from 855 to 858, between the pontificates of Leo IV and Benedict III. It has subsequently been proved that a gap of only a few weeks fell between Leo and Benedict and that the story is entirely apocryphal, though it has some historical inspiration.

JOANAN

An ancestor of Jesus' mother Mary; listed apparently as grandson of Zerubbabel (Luke 3:23-27).

JOAN OF ARC, Saint

(1412-1431) French heroine of the Hundred Years' War, a peasant girl from Domremy, Lorraine, who heard "voices" telling her to liberate France from the English. Given command of a small force by the Dauphin Charles, she inspired it to victory at Orleans and in the surrounding region in 1429. She stood beside the Dauphin when he was crowned Charles VII that year, but failed to relieve beseiged Paris because he denied her adequate forces. Captured at Compiegne (1430), she was tried for heresy by French clerics who sympathized with the English, and burnt her at the stake. The trial was an important political issue, because the English were determined to break her almost magical hold over the French people. Thus she was tried by church authorities rather than as a military prisoner. Records of the trial show that it was unjust in its procedures. Evidence was obtained from her confessor and Joan was often tricked into seemingly heretical answers on complex and difficult theological points.

Twenty years later Charles VII asked the pope to reassess the trial, and a new one was ordered 24 years after Joan died. She was pronounced innocent. In 1909 she was beautified and in 1920 canonized as St. Joan.

JOANNA

One of several women whom Jesus Christ cured of some infirmity and who then became his followers, ministering to him and his Apostles from their own possessions (Luke 8:1-3). Joanna was apparently with those present at Jesus' impalement and, having prepared spices and oil to take to his tomb, was among the first to find that he had been resurrected. The 11 Apostles, however, found their report thereof difficult to believe (Luke 23:49).

JOASH

In the Old Testament, the father of Judge Gideon; an Abierite of the tribe of Manasseh (Judges 6:11, 15). Joash was evidently a man of considerable means and influence in the community, possessing an altar dedicated to Baal, also a "sacred pole," and having a household of servants.

The name is also applied to one of the mighty men of the tribe of Benjamin that joined David's forces at Ziklag when the latter was outlawed by Saul; son or descendant of Shemaah (1 Chronicles 12:1-3).

JOB

Principal figure in the Old Testament book of Job, one of the finest literary masterpieces in the Bible. Job lived in the land of Uz (Job 1:1). Through the prophet Ezekiel, God pointed to Job as an example of righteousness (Ezekiel 14:14-20). His patient endurance of suffering is set before Christians as a pattern and his happy outcome is pointed to as magnifying God's affection and mercy. The account of his trial some experience gives great comfort and strength to Christians, and many Bible principles are highlighted and illuminated by the book bearing his name.

JOB, Book of

A dramatic poem, taking its name from its chief character, Job (probably 10th century BC). It shows that suffering need not be God's penalty for sin. God permits Satan to torment the virtuous Job with the loss of family, wealth and health. Finding small comfort in wife and friends, Job is bitterly questioning but remains faithful, and is restored to good fortune in old age.

JOBAB

In the Old Testament, a descendant of Shem through Joktan (Genesis 10:21, 25-29); 1 Chronicles 1:23). The exact region settled by the offspring of Jobab is not known today. Some would associated his name with Juhaibab, a town in the vicinity of Mecca.

JOCHEBED

In Judaism, a daughter of Levi who married Amram of the same tribe and became the mother of Miriam, Aaron and Moses (Exodus 6:20; Numbers 26:59). Jochebed was a woman of faith and trust in her God. In defiance of Pharaoh's decree she refused to kill her baby later named Moses, and after three months, when he could no longer be concealed in the house, she placed him in an ark of papyrus and put it among the reeds along the bank of the Nile. Pharaoh's daughter found the baby and claimed him for herself, but, as it worked out, Moses' own mother was asked to nurse him. As the child grew, Jochebed, together with her husband, was very diligent to teach her children the principles of pure worship, as reflected in their later lives (Exodus 2:1-10).

JODO

Japanese term for the Buddhist Paradise, associated with the teaching of the Amitabha and rebirth in his Western Paradise. The Jodo (Pure Land) sect had a strong following in China (third century) and Japan (10th century). The Raigo concept (joyous descent of the Amitabha and bodhisattivas) inspired magnificent sculpture and paintings.

JOEL, Book of

(8th century BC) Second of 12 Old Testament minor prophets. The book's central theme is that salvation will come to Judah and Jerusalem only when the people turn to God. In the prophecy a terrible plague of insects is made the occasion of great prophetic significance (1:13-14) adumbrating the Day of the Lord. The prophetic imagery foreshadows the end time of the present age, that is the "times of the Gentiles" (Luke 21:24). The prophecy about pouring out of the Holy Spirit preceding God's kingdom has been fulfilled after Jesus' ascension (Acts 2:16-21).

JOELAH

In the Old Testament, one of the warriors who joined David at Ziklag when he was still under restrictions due to Saul; a Korahite (1 Chronicles 12:1-6).

JOGBEHAH

In biblical times, one of the fortified cities with stone flock pens that was built or rebuilt by the Gadites before their crossing the Jordan to assist in the conquest of Canaan (Numbers 32:34-36). At a later period Judge Gideon's forces passed Jogbehah prior to their surprise attack on the Midianite camp at Karkor (Judges 8:10-11).

JOHANAN

In the Old Testament, firstborn son of King Josiah (1 Chronicles 3:15). Since he is nowhere mentioned in connection with succession to the throne of Judah, as are his three younger brothers, he must have died before his father's death (2 Kings 23:30-34).

JOHN

Son of Zebedee and Salome, and brother of James, is the author of three New Testament letters, the fourth gospel and the Revelation to John in the New Testament. He was a fisherman, though not of the poorer class (Mark 1:20). John and his brother James were among the first disciples called by Jesus. In the gospel according to Mark he is always mentioned after James and was no doubt the younger brother. James and John were called by Jesus "Boanerges" or "sons of thunder". John and his brother, together with Simon Peter, formed an inner structure of intimate disciples. In the fourth gospel, the sons of Zebedee are mentioned only once, as being at the shores of the lake of Tiberias, when the risen Lord appeared. John is probably meant by "the disciple whom Jesus loved" (John 19:26).

JOHN

(9th century, Italy) Antipope during January 844. A Roman archdeacon well liked by the populace, he was elected by them on January 25 against the nobility's candidate, Sergius II. John withdrew to the Lateran Palace, his stronghold for a brief period. Concurrently, Sergius was consecrated pope at St. Peter's without imperial sanction.

JOHN (THE BAPTIST)

(died circa AD 30) Preacher who proclaimed the coming of Christ and urged repentance, baptizing his followers in the Jordan River (Matthew 3:5). His miraculous birth, his sober life and the expectation that some great one was about to appear, served to attract many people; for John did no miracle (John 10:41). An account of his birth is given in the gospel of Luke.

After baptizing Jesus he pointed out Jesus as the one he announced. He denounced Herod Antipas for marrying Herodias, wife of Herod's brother, and was beheaded at her instigation (Mark 6:18).

JOHN, Gospel of

The fourth gospel in the New Testament, written circa 90 by John the Apostle. It emphasizes Jesus' deity and is spiritual and theological in tone. John's gospel differs from the others. The major difference lies in John's overall purpose. The author tells us that he has chosen not to record many of the symbolic acts of Jesus and has instead included certain episodes in order that his readers may believe that Jesus is the Son of God and they may obtain eternal life (20:30).

JOHN, Letters of

Three New Testament writings, all composed around 90-100, by John, son of Zebedee and disciple of Jesus. The first letter urges the Christian community to hold fast to what they had been taught and to repudiate false teachings. Christians are exhorted to persevere in leading a moral life, which means imitating Christ and loving one another.

The second letter exhorts a church called "the chosen lady and her children" (2 John 1:1-5) to boycott heretics who deny the reality of Jesus being both God and man.

The third letter is addressed to a certain Gaius, its main theme is "the truth", by which John means the body of revealed truth, the scriptures.

St. Peter and St. John at the beautiful gate.
"Then Peter said. Silver and gold I have none; but such as I have give I thee: In the name
of Jesus Christ of Nazareth rise up and walk" (Acts 3:6).
Lithograph by Gustave Doré (about 1860).

JOHN I, Saint

(451-523) Pope from 523 to 526, who ended the Acacian schism, thus reuniting the Eastern and Western churches by restoring peace between the papacy and the Byzantine emperor Justin I. He is honored as a martyr and his feast day is May 27.

JOHN II

(461-535) Mercurius; pope from 533 to 535, who opposed Nestorianism, one of the principal early Christian heresies. Nestorianism separated the divine and human natures of Christ and denied the Blessed Virgin Mary the title God-Bearer or Mother of God.

JOHN III

(501-574) Catelinus; pope from 561 to 574; no significant achievements are known of his Pontificate.

JOHN IV

(567-642) Pope from 640 to 642. He defended the highly controversial orthodoxy of Pope Honorius I, who has held that Christ's human and divine natures were indivisible and that the Son's will was not different from that of the Father.

JOHN V

(615-686) Pope from 685 to 686. He condemned the Monotheilite heresy; the view that Christ had only one will, divine. He was a man of learning and generosity, who made liberal donations for the poor.

JOHN VI

(639-705) Pope from 701 to 705. In his only extant letter, he ordered the restoration of the deposed bishop St. Wilfrid of York, Northumbria.

JOHN VII

(632-707) Pope from 705 to 707. He was noted for his devotion to the Virgin Mary and for his energetic restoration of Roman churches. He did not recognize the decrees of the Council of Trullo, which included disapproval of such Roman customs as celibacy of the clergy and rules for fasting.

JOHN VIII

(812-882) Pope from 872 to 882. He solved a controversy over orthodoxy between the Holy see and the East by recognizing in 879 the heretofore condemned Photius as patriarch of Constantinople. Always plagued by intrigues of Roman enemies and by the Saracens, John was murdered in a local conspiracy.

JOHN IX

(834-900) Pope from 898 to 900. He held councils at Rome and Ravenna to exculpate Pope Formosus, who had ordained John a priest. He condemned Stephen's synod and destroyed its acts and restored the clergy.

JOHN X

(854-928) Pope from 914 to 928. He approved the severe rule of the Benedictine Order of Cluny. His rule was characterized by attempts to drive the Saracens (Muslim enemies) from southern Italy.

JOHN XI

(910-935) Pope from 931 to 935. He was consecrated when only 21 years old. John served his mother's political ends. In 933 he was confined to the Lateran and remained a prisoner until his death.

JOHN XII

(937-964) Octavian; pope from 955 to 964. He was the only son of Duke Alberic II of Spoleto, Italy, then ruler of Rome, who ordered Octavian's election as pope when he was only circa 18 years of age. The young pope changed his name to John, and he crowned the German king Otto I the Great and his wife Adelaide as Holy Roman emperor and empress in 962. He died in 964 in the arms of his mistress.

JOHN XIII THE GOOD

(704-972) Pope from 965 to 972. John was chosen pope on October 1st, 965, by Emperor Otto I. Although John was a pious and learned man, the Roman nobles opposed Otto's choice and kidnapped John (December 965). In 966 Otto and took escaped and savage vengeance on his enemies.

JOHN XIV

(911-984) Pietro Canepanova; pope from 983 to 984. His election was opposed by the powerful Roman Crescentii family, which supported Antipope Boniface. After the death of Emperor Otto, Boniface imprisoned John in the Castel San Angelo, Rome, where he was murdered, either by starvation or poison.

JOHN XV

(926-996) Pope from 985 to 996. He carried out the first solemn canonization in history by papal decree. He became pope in one of the darkest periods in papal history, shadowed by the murders of popes Benedict VI and John XIV by the antipope Boniface VII.

JOHN XVI

(945-1013) Giovanni Filagato; antipope from 997 to 998. His pontificate was marked by quarrels and wars. The Emperor Otto III imprisoned or confined him to a monastery after blinding and mutilating John since he objected to a number of his measures.

JOHN XVII

(945-1003) Giovanni Siconne; pope from June to December 1003. Chosen by the patrician John Crescentius II, he was merely a puppet of the Crescentiti, then the most influential family in Rome.

JOHN XVIII

(939-1009) Giovanni Fasana; pope from 1004 to 1009. More independent of the powerful Italian Crescentii family than John XVII, he eventually abdicated and died shortly thereafter at the Abbey of St. Paul-Outside-the-Walls, Rome.

JOHN XIX

(961-1032) Romano of Tusculum; pope from 1024 to 1032. A member of the Tusculani family that followed the powerful Crescentii as rulers of Rome, he was a layman when he succeeded his brother Pope Benedict VIII in 1024. Generally considered inept as pope because of his greed, John consented to be paid for recognizing the patriarch of Constantinople.

JOHN XXI

(1210-1277) Peter Juliani; pope from 1276 to 1277. One of the most scholarly pontiffs in papal history. He was the author of one of the most widely used medieval textbooks on logic.

JOHN XXIII

(1881-1963) Angelo Guiseppe Roncali; pope from 1958-1963. Of peasant stock, he was an army chaplain in World War I. He was made a titular bishop in the Vatican diplomatic corps 1925-1935 and nuncio 1925-1953, serving in Turkey, the Balkans and Franc. Made cardinal in 1953, he was elected pope in 1958. He revolutionized the church, promoting cooperation with other Christian churches and other religions in the face of world problems; the encyclical *Mater et Magister* (1961) advocated social reform in underdeveloped areas of the world. In 1962 he called the influential Second Vatican Council.

JOHN CHRYSOSTOM, Saint

(347-407) Father of the early Christian church. He was born in Antioch, Syria, and was converted to Christianity in his youth. In 398 he was made patriarch of Constantinople. As a result of his attempts to reform the church and the imperial court, he was exiled by the emperor. His *Homilies* are well known.

JOHN CLIMACUS, Saint

(579-649) Byzantine monk and author of "The Ladder of Divine Ascent", a handbook on the ascetical and mystical life that has become a Christian spiritual classic.

JOHN HYRCANUS II

(died circa 30 BC) High Priest of Judaea from 76 to 40 BC, and along with his brother Aristobulus II, last of the Maccabean dynastic rulers. Under his vacillating leadership, Judaea fell into vassalage to Rome. When his father died in 76, Hyrcanus was appointed High Priest, and on his mother's death in 67 he assumed rulership. After a troubled reign of three months his warlike brother Aristobulus drove him from power.

JOHN OF BEVERLEY, Saint

(656-721) Bishop of York, Yorkshire, one of the most popular medieval English saints. He founded a monastery at Inderawood, later called Beverley, where he retired.

JOHN OF DAMASCUS, Saint

(645-749) Eastern monk and theological doctor of the Greek Orthodox church whose treatises on the veneration of sacred images placed him in the forefront of the 8th century Iconoclast Controversy and whose theological synthesis made him a pre-eminent intermediary between Greek and medieval Latin cultures.

JOHN OF EPHESUS

(507-586) Monophysite bishop of Ephesus and foremost early historian and leader of Syriac Monophysite Christianity, a sect adhering to the heretically defined doctrine that Christ's divine nature operated exclusively in Jesus, reducing his human element to insignificance.

JOHN OF MATHA, Saint

(1160-1213) Co-founder of the Order of the Most Holy Trinity for the Redemption of Captives, a Roman Catholic mendicant order originally dedicated to free Christian slaves from captivity under Muslims, but now devoted to the ministry, principally in parishes.

JOHN OF MERECOURT

(14 century) French Cistercian monk, philosopher and theologian whose skepticism about certitude in human knowledge and whose limitation of the use of human reason in theological statements established him as a leading exponent of medieval Christian nominalism and voluntarism.

JOHN OF NEPOMUK

(1345-1393) Patron saint of the Czechs, murdered during the bitter conflict of church and state that plagued Bohemia in the latter 14th century.

JOHN OF ST. THOMAS

(1589-1644) Philosopher and theologian whose comprehensive commentaries on Roman Catholic doctrine made him a leading spokesman for post-Reformation Thomism, a philosophical theological school of thought named after its foremost theorist, St. Thomas Aquinas (1225-1274).

JOHN OF THE CROSS, Saint

(1542-1591) Great Spanish poet and mystic. A Carmelite, John founded a reformed Carmelite order under the inspiration of his friend St. Teresa of Avila. He is remembered chiefly for his beautiful mystical poetry which includes *The Dark Night of the Soul, The Ascent of Mount Carmel,* and *The Living Flame of Love.* Canonized in 1726, he was made a Doctor of the Church in 1926. His feast is 24 November.

JOHN PAUL I

(1912-1978) Albino Luciani; pope from August 26 - September 28, 1978. A native of Forno di Canale in northern Italy, he was ordained to the priesthood in 1934. For 10 years he taught in the seminary of Belluno, then became vicar general of that see in 1954. Named bishop of Vittoria Veneto in 1958, he was distinguished for his concern for the poor and illiterate. In 1969 he became patriarch of Venice and was elevated to the cardinate in 1973.

Elected the first day of the conclave following the death of Paul VI, he chose the name John Paul I, marking the first time in history a pope had chosen a double name, and the first time since the 10th century that a new name had been elected.

JOHN PAUL II

(1920-) Karol Jozef Wojtyla; Polish-born pope elected in 1958. His election as pope to succeed John Paul I came on the second day of the papal conclave and was greeted by surprise, since he is the first non-Italian pope since Adrian VI (1522-23).

A personable world traveler, he has maintained a theologically conservative position on such controversial issues as birth control and abortion. He survived an assassination attempt in 1981.

He has shown himself to be a strong and magnetic personality, dedicated to the ideas and implementation of Vatican Council II. He has expressed particular interest to further the functioning of episcopal collegiality and to provide human rights, especially religious freedom.

JOIADA

In the Old Testament, son of Paseah who helped repair the Gate of the Old City when Nehemiah had Jerusalem's wall rebuilt (Nehemiah 3:6).

JOIAKIM

In the Old Testament, son and successor of post-exile High Priest Joshua (Nehemiah 12:10, 12, 26). According to Josephus he held office at the time Ezra returned. However, by the time of Nehemiah's arrival later (455 BC), Joaikim's son Eliashib had become High Priest (Nehemiah 3:1).

JOIARIB

In Judaism, a paternal house of priests (1 Chronicles 24:6-7). Representatives of this house (or another priest with the same name) returned with Zerubbabel to Jerusalem, where they remained down through the time of Ezra, Nehemiah and High Priest Joshua's successor Joiakim (Nehemiah 12:1-6; 19, 26).

JOKMEAM

In biblical times, an Ephraimite city given to the Kohathites (1 Chronicles 6:66-68). The name is also applied to a region under the jurisdiction of Ahilud's son Baana, one of Solomon's 12 deputies (1 Kings 4:12).

JOKSHAN

In Judaism, a descendant of Abraham by Keturah and the progenitor of Sheba and Dedan (Genesis 10:30).

JOKTHEEL

In biblical times, the Edomite city of Sela, which was conquered by Judean King Amaziah and renamed Joktheel (2 Kings 14:1, 7). It has been linked with Umm el-Bayyarah, an acropolis located some 50 miles south of the Dead Sea.

JONAH

A prophet from Gath-hepher (2 Kings 14:25), a border city in the territory of Zebulun (Joshua 19:10-13). In fulfillment of God's word spoken through Jonah, Israel's King Jeroboam II succeeded in restoring "the boundary of Israel from the entering in of the Hamath clear to the sea of the Arabah" (2 Kings 14:23-25). So it appears that Jonah served as a prophet to the ten-tribe kingdom during the reign of Jeroboam II. He is evidently the same person God commissioned to proclaim judgment against Nineveh (Jonah 1:1-2) and, therefore, also the writer of the book bearing his name.

JONAH, Book of

Fifth book of the minor prophets, unique in its entirely narrative form. Jonah is portrayed as so intolerant of Gentiles that he disobeys God's command to convert the city of Nineveh. He sails away and in a storm is swallowed by a "great fish", now usually identified as "whale". He prays for deliverance and is vomited out on dry land. He goes to Nineveh and prophesies against the city, causing the king and all the inhabitants to repent.

JONAH, Sign of

When Jesus was asked for a sign (Matthew 12:38-42; Luke 11:29-32), he gave the sign of Jonah. His meaning seems to be that just as Jonah and his preaching were a sign to the Ninevites, so Jesus and his preaching will be sign enough (Matthew 12:41; Luke 11:32).

JONATHAN

In the Old Testament 1 and 2 Samuel, eldest son of King Saul. He is known for his intrepidity and fidelity to his friend, the future king David. Saul, Jonathan, and Jonathan's brothers were killed in a battle against the Philistines at Mount Gilboa.

JORAM

In the Old Testament, son of King Toi of Hamath. Joram was sent with costly gifts made of gold, silver and copper, along with his father's congratulations, to King David when the latter defeated Hadadezer the king of Zobah. David, in turn, accepted and sanctified the gifts to God (2 Samuel 5:5-11).

The name is also applied to a king of Israel for 12 years; son of Ahab. Usually he is identified by the longer form of his name Jehoram (2 Kings 3:1).

JORDAN RIVER

The main river of the Promised Land forming a natural border between most of east and west Palestine (Joshua 22:25). It is the lowest river in the world, flowing southward from Syria across Israel and flows about through the Sea of Galilee and the Ghor valley to the Dead Sea. It is an important source of water in an arid region.

This is the formidable river that the Bible mentions more than 200 times and that divided Palestine into its two parts. Lot chose the Jordan Valley for his territory (Genesis 13:8-13). Under the leadership of Joshua the Israelites

miraculously crossed the river on dry land (Joshua 3:7-17). The Midianites crossed the Jordan as they fled from Gideon (Judges 7:24). It was along the banks of the Jordan that Elijah was taken up to heaven and left his spirit upon his disciple Elisha 2 Kings 2:6-15).

In the New Testament John the Baptist preached in the region of the Jordan (Luke 3:3), and he baptized Christ there (Luke 3:21). Today at a point not far from Jericho is a small Christian shrine commemorating Christ's baptism in these waters.

JORIM

In the Bible, a descendant of David through Natyhan, and an ancestor of Jesus' mother Mary (Luke 3:29-31). Jorim may have lived while Uzziah was king of Judah.

JOSECH

A forefather of Jesus' mother Mary. Josech was a distant descendant of David through Nathan, and the fourth generation after Zerubbabbel, placing him about the end of the Hebrew scripture era (Luke 3:23-31).

JOSEPH, Husband of Mary

He was a carpenter, living in Nazareth, who espoused Mary who proved to be with child. He wanted to quietly separate from her, but was assured from an angel that she was conceived under divine influence (Matthew 1:18). Because he was a descendant of David, he then went with Mary to Bethlehem for a census (Luke 3:23).

Most what we know about Joseph is from the gospel accounts, especially of Matthew and Luke, where he is described as a just and holy man. He has long been held in veneration by the Roman Catholic Church, is honored as her universal patron on the feast of St. Joseph, March 19th, and as a special patron of working people on the feast of St. Joseph the Worker, May 1st.

JOSEPH, Son of Jacob

In the Old Testament, son of the patriarch Jacob and his wife Rachel. As

Jacob's name became synonymous with all Israel, so that of Joseph was eventually equated with all the tribes that made up the northern kingdom.

His jealous brothers sold him into slavery in Egypt. There he won favor with Pharaoh by correctly interpreting his dreams with the help of God, and was eventually made chief minister. He forgave his brothers and Jacob was invited to come to Goshen, where a settlement was provided for the family and their flocks.

JOSEPH-BASSHEBETH

In the Old Testament, the head one of David's three most outstanding mighty men (2 Samuel 23:8). Each of the three mighty men had one of his deeds credited to him, so if the overpowering of the 800 were attributed to someone else, there would be no deed credited here to Josheph-Basshebeth.

JOSEPH OF ARIMATHEA, Saint

(circa 30) According to all four gospels, a secret disciple of Christ, whose body he buried in his own tomb. Designating him as "member of the council," Mark (15:43) and Luke (23:50-53) suggest membership of the town-council in Jerusalem. Virtuous and rich, he held a high office, and he boldly gained Pontius Pilate's permission to obtain Christ's body.

JOSEPHISTS

An obscure sect that appeared in parts of France, Germany, and Italy in the late 12th century. Because it was alleged that adherents spurned marriage but allowed full indulgence of the passions outside that state, the sect is often listed as a branch of the Cathari. The sect was condemned by Gregory IX in 1231.

JOSHAH

In the Old Testament, one of the Simeonite chieftains who, in the days of King Hezekiah, conquered a portion of territory from the Hamites and Meunim in order to have more pasture ground (1 Chronicles 4:24, 38-41).

JOSHUA

In the Old Testament, son of Nun; an Ephraimite who ministered to Moses and was later appointed as his successor (Exodus 33:11; Deuteronomy 24:9; Joshua 1:1-2). He is portrayed as a bold and fearless leader, one who was confident in the certainty of God's promises, obedient to divine direction and determined to serve God in faithfulness. His original name was Hushea, but Moses called him Joshua or Jehoshua (Numbers 13:8, 16). The Bible record, however, does not reveal just when Hoshea came to be known as Joshua.

JOSHUA, Book of

Sixth book of the Old Testament, named after Joshua, personally appointed successor to Moses (Deut. 34:9). He was a charismatic warrior who led Israel in the conquest of Canaan after the exodus from Egypt.

The book can be divided into three sections: the conquest of Canaan (1-12), the distribution of the land among the Israelite tribes (13-22), and Joshua's farewell address and death (23-24).

JOSIAH

In the Old Testament king of Judah (circa 641-609 BC), who set in motion a reformation that bears his name, radically stamping out idolatry (2 Kings 22-23:20). Josiah was the grandson of Manasseh, king of Judah, and ascended the throne at the age of eight after the assassination of his father, Amon, in 641. Circa 621 the pious king launched a program of national renewal, centered on the Temple. His death in the battle at Megiddo was a great loss for Judah (2 Kings 23:29).

JOSIPHIAH

In Judaism, a member of the paternal house of Bani whose son Shelomith, as head of the paternal house, went to Jerusalem with Ezra in 468 BC (Ezra 8:1, 10).

JOTBAH

In Judaism, the home of Haruz, Judean King Amon's maternal grandfather (2

Kings 21:19). Jotbah is often identified with modern Khirbet Jefat, circa nine miles north of Nazareth.

JOTHAM

In the Old Testament, a descendant of Judah designated as a "son" of Jahdai (1 Chronicles 2:47).

JOZABAD

In the Old Testament, a warrior who joined David at Ziklag; a Gederathite (1 Chronicles 12:1-4). The name is also applied to a commissioner appointed by King Hezekiah to assist in the caring of the tithes, contributions and holy things brought in by the people; no doubt a Levite (2 Chronicles 31:12, 13).

JOZACAR

In the Old Testament, a servant of King Jehoash of Judah, who, with his companion Jehozabad, killed their ruler in reprisal for the death of Zechariah and apparently other sons of High Priest Jehoiada. However, Jehoash's son and successor Amiziah, in turn, avenged his father's death by striking down Jozacar and his accomplice. Jozacar was the son of Shimeath, an Ammonitess.

JUBAL

In the Old Testament, son of Lamech and Adah; descendant of Cain. As "founder of all those who handle the harp and the pipe," Jubal may have invented both stringed and wind instruments, or perhaps he "founded" a profession, which gave considerable impetus to the progress of music (Genesis 4:17-21).

JUBILEES, Book of

A pseudepigraphical work (one resembling in style and content authentic biblical literature, but noncanonical) most notable for its chronological schema, by which events described in Genesis on through Exodus 12 are dated by "jubilees" (49 years) which are in turn composed of seven weeks of years, each year consisting of 364 days. The proposal for the adoption of such a calendar, which deviates from the one in use in Palestine, is indicative of the Halakhic (legal) character of the work. The institution of a jubilee calendar supposedly ensured the observance of Jewish religious festivals and holy days on the proper dates and by setting Jews apart from their gentile neighbors emphasized the Old Testament picture of Israel as the covenant community of God.

JUDAH

The southernmost of the three traditional divisions of ancient Palestine; the other two were Galilee in the north and Samaria in the center. No clearly marked boundary divided Judah from Samaria, but the town of Beersheba was on the traditional southernmost limit. The region presents a variety of geographical features, but the real core of Judah was the upper hill country, extending south from the region of Bethel to Beersheba and including the area of Jerusalem, Bethlehem, and Hebron.

JUDAH

One of the 12 tribes of Israel, named after Judah, who was the fourth son born to Jacob and his first wife, Leah.
After the Israelites took possession of the Promised Land, the tribe of Judah settled in the region south of Jerusalem and in time became the most powerful and most important tribe. Not only did it produce the great kings David and Solomon but also, as it was prophesied, the Messiah came from among its members.

JUDAH BEN SAMUEL

(1145-1217) Mystic and semilegendary pietist, a founder of the fervent, ultrapious movement of German Hasidism and author of a number of works on medieval Judaism.

JUDAH HA-LEVI

(1075-1141) Jewish Hebrew poet and religious philosopher. His poetic works were the culmination of the development of Hebrew poetry within the Arabic culture sphere.

JUDAH HA-NASI

(135 - 220) Member of a small group of Palestinian masters of the Jewish Oral Law, parts of which he set down as the Mishna (Teaching). The Mishna became the subject of interpretation in the Talmud, the fundamental rabbinic compendium of law, lore, and commentary.

JUDAISM

The religion of the Jewish people, the oldest of the world's monotheistic faiths. Judaism claims only some 16 million adherents in the world today, but it has been one of the greatest historic influences on the development of Western civilization. It is the parent religion of Western civilization and of Islam; both faiths accept the Jewish belief in one God and the ethical message of the Hebrew Bible, the Old Testament.

The essence in Judaism is the belief in one God. At daily prayers and services Jews repeat the words of Deuteronomy 6:4, "Hear O Israel: the Lord our God, the Lord is one."

Abraham, father of the Jewish people, made a covenant with God that he and his descendants would carry the message of one God to the world. This covenant, the burden of special service to God, is Judaism's reason for being, and the chosen people is the subject of the Hebrew Bible, the foundations of Judaism. The Torah, or the Law, is the first part of the Bible, known as the Five Books of Moses, or the Pentateuch. The Torah includes the history of the Jewish people from the creation through the death of Moses. It contains the Ten Commandments and the ritual laws and ethical precepts which form the structure of the Jewish religion. In the later books of the Old Testament, particularly in the prophets, the bond between God and the Jewish people, is reemphasized and the universalist message of Judaism is developed.

The Torah is not only the first five books of the Bible, it is all Jewish law, tradition, learning and observance. In the centuries after the Bible was completed, its text was explained and adapted by a set of traditions and interpretations known as the oral law. When the Temple and the hereditary priesthood were destroyed in AD 70, there was a danger that the oral law would be lost; therefore it was recorded in a work known as the Mishnah. Later religious teachers discussed and interpreted the Mishnah, forming a commentary called the Gemara. These two works together made up the Talmud, an inexhaustible storehouse of tradition, guidance and instruction, second only to the Bible in its authority.

Although there have been numerous sects and mystical movements in the history of Judaism, and although Jewish philosophers since the Middle Ages have sought to formulate the essentials of the faith, Judaism has little formal dogma or strict doctrine. The very nature of God remains largely undefined, and many thinkers have maintained that even His attributes are beyond human understanding. Although Judaism holds that man will be rewarded for good deeds and punished for evil, there are many interpretations of how this is to be fulfilled. Post-biblical Judaism formulated a belief in eternal life based on the biblical promise of the resurrection of the dead, and some Jewish thinkers even spoke of Heaven and hell; but these beliefs have remained matters of individual conviction, not of doctrine.

According to Judaism, the individual himself has the full ability to choose between good and evil. In contrast to Christianity, Judaism believes that man is not born into sin, but is provided with good and evil inclinations - and is himself the master of both. Judaism also differs from Christianity in maintaining that the coming of the Messiah, or of a Messianic Kingdom of justice, is still in the future and will usher in a period of peace and brotherhood among men.

Judaism is rich in law, custom and ritual which give sacred meaning to every aspect of daily life. Dietary laws, the Kosher preparation of food, is only one of the ways in which holiness is brought into even the simple act of eating. Every meal is surrounded by a framework of prayers. While formal prayers take place three times each day,m observance of the precepts of the Torah outside the synagogue is a matter of even greater obligation.

Because there has been no single ecclestical authority for the past 1900 years, Jews have differed about their religion and still remained Jews. Differences over ritual observance are the chief characteristics of the groups within Judaism today.

Reform or liberal Judaism began in the 19th century in answer to the challenge of rationalism. In the United States today there are circa one million Reform Jews. They believe that each generation has the right to adapt or discard traditions it finds no longer meaningful. Judaism is conceived as an evolutionary faith in which God's will is progressively revealed. Much of Reform synagogue service in America is in English, and the compatibility of Judaism with modern secular values is emphasized. With the spread of Reform Judaism, the leaders of traditional Judaism, who had formerly been considered the religion's sole representatives, were forced to formulate their beliefs and observances. Orthodox Judaism accepts the totality of the Bible and oral law as divine revelation and holds strictly to all dietary laws and codes of conduct. Religious services are conducted solely in Hebrew, and men and women sit in separate parts of the synagogue. Most of the world's Jewry is Orthodox.

JUDAS ISCARIOT
(died circa AD 30) One of the disciples, responsible for the receipt of money and distribution to the poor (John 12:4-6). For 30 pieces of silver (Matthew 26:14-16) he identified Jesus to the soldiers at Gethsemane by a kiss of greeting (Matthew 26:49). He later repented and hanged himself (Matthew 27:3-10).

JUDAS MACCABEUS
(died 160 BC) Jewish leader of the Hasmonean dynasty. He defeated Antiochus IV, a Seleucid king seeking to force paganism on the Jews, and in 165 BC reconsecrated the Temple. This event is commemorated in the festival of Kahakkah.

JUDE, Letter of
Brief New Testament letter written to a general Christian audience by Jude, a servant of Jesus Christ and brother of James. Thus probably a brother of Jesus (Mark 6:3). The letter, dated circa 75, mainly deals with false teachings. He urges the Christians to stay in God's love (Jude 1:17-21).

JUDE, Saint
One of the Apostles, possible author of the New Testament Epistle of Jude, which combats heresy. Jude is an anglicized form of Judas, to distinguish him from Judas Iscariot.

JUDEA
Well-known land in biblical times. The exact boundaries of this region of Palestine are uncertain. Seemingly Judea embraced an area of approximately 50 miles from east to west and more than 30 miles from north to south. Samaria lay to the north and Idumea to the south. The Dead Sea and the Jordan Valley formed the eastern boundary. However, when Idumean territory was included in Judaea, the southern boundary appears to have extended from below Gaza in the west to Massada in the east.

JUDGES
The judges to whom the title of the book refers were charismatic leaders in the time between Joshua and the accession of Saul. A period characterized by people withdrawn from God (17:6). The main body of the book consists of narratives about the judges. Covering

The Judas kiss.
"And he that betrayed him had given them a token, saying, Whomsoever I shall kiss, that same is he" (Mark 14:44).
Lithograph by Gustave Doré (about 1860).

several centuries, it was compiled around 1020 BC.

JUDGES, Book of

Seventh book of the Old Testament. It recounts the exploits of military leaders, known as "judges" between the time of Joshua and the birth of Samuel. Israel's successive apostasies from God are punished by enemy oppression, until God sends a judge to deliver the people. The main judges are Barak, Deborah, Gideon, Abimelech, Jephtha and Samson.

JUDGMENT

According to Catholic teaching, there is a distinction between General Judgment and the particular judgment. The General, or Last of Final Judgment, is the judgment of the human race by Jesus Christ (see Matthew 25:31; Thessalonians 2:3-10) who, "will come in glory to judge the living and the dead" (Nicene Creed). The particular judgment is the judgment that takes place immediately after an individual's death and determines whether the individual is worthy of heaven (after purification in purgatory, if necessary) or hell.

JUDITH

Book of the Old Testament. During an Assyrian invasion a young Jewish widow, Judith, seduces the Assyrian general Holofernes in order to murder him. She shows his head to the Jewish army, which routs its leaderless enemy.

JULIAN OF ECLANUM

(380-455) Bishop of Eclanum who is considered to be the most intellectual leader of the Pelagians, promulgatory of a heretical doctrine minimizing the role of the divine grace in man's salvation. Julian systematized Pelagian theology and wrote several works (several of which are now lost) that gained him prestige above his Pelagian contemporaries. His writings are known primarily through extensive quotations from bishop St. Augustine of Hippo, who refuted him.

JULIAN THE APOSTATE

(331-363) Roman emperor from 361, the last emperor to oppose Christianity. Julian was brought up as a Christian in Asia Minor, but subsequently abandoned Christianity for paganism. His troops proclaimed Julian Emperor in 361. On his accession Julian tried to revive paganism, but he did not persecute the Christians. In 363 he was killed in a battle by the Persians.

JULIUS I, Saint

(Died 352) Pope from 337 to 352. Julius was chiefly known for his stand against Arianism, a movement which denied the divinity of Christ. He convened the Council of Sardica (342 or 343), where the anti-Arian stand of the Council of Nicaea was upheld.

JULIUS II

(1443-1513) Pope from 1503 to 1513. A Franciscan, Julius was primarily interested in restoring the temporal power of the papacy. He recovered control of the Papal States from the French and from his political rival Cesare Borgia. In 1511 he formed the Holy League against France. He convened the Fifth Lateran Council in 1512. A patron of literature and art, Julius commissioned notable works by the architect Bramante and the artists Raphael and Michelangelo.

JULIUS III

(1487-1555) Giovanni Maria Clocchi del Monte; pope from 1550 to 1555. Aware that a reform of the church was urgent, he appointed a commission that recommended resumption of the Council of Trent, which Julius reopened on May 1, 1551. He attempted to stop cardinals from receiving too many benefices and to restore monastic discipline.

JUM'A, al-

The title of the 62nd sura of the Koran; it means "Friday." The sura belongs to the Medinan period and has 11 verses. The title of the sura is drawn from verse 9 which counsels the believers, when they hear the call to prayer on Friday to hurry to "the remembrance of God" and to cease trading.

JUM'AH

Friday of the Muslim week and the special noon service on Friday that all adult, male, free Muslims are obliged to attend. The jum'ah which replaced the usual noon ritual prayer, must take place before a sizable number of Muslims (according to some legal scholars, 40) in one central mosque in each locality.

Mohammed's choice of Friday as the Muslim day of communal worship was probably based on the pre-Islamic function of Friday as market day, a natural occasion for dispersed local tribes to gather in a central location.

The influence of the Jewish and Christian sabbath was also felt in the institutionalization of the Muslim Friday, though in Islam it was not a day of rest but a convenient setting for the special religious service.

JUNO

In Roman religion, chief goddess and female counterpart of Jupiter, closely resembling the Greek Hera with whom she was universally identified. Juno was connected with all aspects of life of women, most particularly married life.

JURISDICTION, Ecclesiastical

The power to rule and govern that is vested in the church in the persons of certain of its officials. Although in its present sense, as distinguished from the power of order and differentiated from purely administrative function, the term is hard to find before the 13th century, the reality that it expresses arises from the nature of the church as established by Christ.

It is clear from the ordinary teaching of the church that it considers itself a society completely master of its own social action and that it consequently possesses jurisdiction, the power for direction of social life in a juridically perfect society.

JUROJIN

In Japanese mythology, one of the Seven Gods of Luck, particularly associated with longevity. He is supposed to have lived on earth as a Chinese Taoist sage. He is often depicted as an old man with a white beard, wearing a scholar's headdress and sometimes accompanied by a stag.

JUSTICE

In Roman Catholicism, one of the principal (cardinal) moral virtues; in the strictest sense, it is the virtue by which one person renders to another that which is his or her due, or the virtue which urges one to give to others what is theirs by right (cumulative justice). Justice is required not only between persons but also between individual persons and the community (legal justice) and likewise between the leaders of the community and the community itself (distributive justice).

JUSTIFICATION OF FAITH

Pauline doctrine that justification is given freely by God on the grounds of Christ's Atonement and by imputation of his righteousness. Justification is God's declaration that a person is righteous. The sinner is justified through believing in Jesus Christ, not by his own works. The reformers, especially Luther, emphasized the doctrine in opposition to the popular medieval Roman Catholic belief in justification by works. It is no longer controversial.

JUSTIN MARTYR, Saint

(circa 100-165) Christian theologian who conducted a school of Christian studies in Rome; he was martyred under Marcus Aurelius. His *Apology* defended Christianity against charges of impiety and sedition.

JUVENAL, Saint

(387-458) Bishop of Jerusalem from 422 to 548 who elevated the see of Jerusalem - before under the metropolitan rule of Caesarea - to a patriarchate.

JUXON, William

(1582-1663) Anglican priest, archbish-op of Canterbury, and minister to the condemned King Charles I on the scaf-fold. As England's lord high treasurer, Juxon was the last English clergyman to hold both secular and clerical offices in the medieval tradition of clerical state service.

KA

Ancient Egyptian conception designating part of a human being or of a god. It seems originally to have designated the protecting divine spirit of a person, and later the personified sum of physical and intellectual qualities constituting an "individuality."

KA'BAH

Small shrine located near the center of the Great Mosque in Mecca, considered by Muslims everywhere to be the most sacred spot on earth. Muslims orient themselves toward the central shrine of the Islamic faith during the five daily prayers, bury their dead facing its meridian, and cherish the ambition of visiting it on pilgrimage, in accord with the command of God in the Koran.

KABBALA

Esoteric Jewish mysticism as it appeared in the 13th and following centuries; the term is also a general designation for various systems of Jewish mysticism. Kabbala has always been essentially an oral tradition in that initiation into its doctrines and practices is conducted by a personal guide to avoid the dangers inherent in mystical experiences.

KABIR

(1440-1518) Indian mystic and poet who attempted to bridge or unite Hindu and Muslim thought and preached the essential unity of all religions and the essential equality of all men. He was a forerunner of Sikhism, established by hid disciple Nanak.

KABIRPANTHIS

Those who follow the path of Kabir, the great 15th century devotional poet of India. Although Kabir worked for a synthesis of Hindu and Muslim teachings and preached the equality of all men before God, after his death his devotees split into several separate branches.

KABZEEL

In biblical times, a city in the southern part of Judah (Joshua 15:21). It is sometimes identified with Khirbet Hora, about ten miles north-east of Beersheba.

KACHINA

Term for Pueblo Indian spirits of nature and of the dead. Dancers dressed as kachinas summon these supernatural beings. Kachina cults among Hopi and Zuni have persisted from prehistoric times, their ceremonies, masks, and accessories preserved in kachina figurines and costumes; highly symbolic in organic and geometric designs in brilliantly colored wood, horsehide, feathers, and cloth.

KADDISH

In Jewish doxology exalting and glorifying the holy name of God, and usually recited in Aramaic at the end of the synagogue services. Its name derives from the Aramaic word "hallowed," as in its opening phrase: "Hallowed be the great Name of the Lord"; and may have originated with the Jewish communities in Babylon, where it served as a closing doxology to end haggadic discourse.

KADESH

In biblical times, an Israelite wilderness encampment situated at the extremity of Edomite territory near the "way to Shur," perhaps the modern

Darb el-Shur extending from Hebron to Egypt (Genesis 16:7, 14).

KADMIEL

In the Old Testament, a Levite returning to Jerusalem (with Zerubbabel), accompanied by members of his family (Ezra 2:1-2; Nehemiah 7:6-7). "Kadmiel and his sons" helped supervise the Temple reconstruction (Ezra 3:9).

KADMONITES

In biblical times, a people listed among other nations whose lands God promised to Abraham's seed (Genesis 15:18-21). They were evidently a pastoral or nomadic tribe, like the Kenites and Kenizzites with whom they are mentioned (Genesis 15:19). The exact location of their territory is uncertain, although it is suggested that they inhabited the Syrian desert between Palestine-Syria and the Euphrates River.

KAFIRUN, al-

The title of the 109th sura of the Koran; it means "The Infidels." The sura belongs to the Meccan period and has 6 verses. Its title derived from the first verse which reads: "Say, oh infidels." The sura encapsulates the belief that religions should be freely chosen and held, and stresses the unswerving allegiance of the Prophet Mohammed to the worship of the One True God.

KAFUR

Arabic word for camphor. A cup of Kafur, sometimes identified by tradition as a river in Paradise, will be drunk by the pious of Surat al-Insan in the Koran. However, the Koran itself, in verse 6 of this sura, describes Kafur as a fountain or spring.

KAHF, al-

The title of the 18th sura of the Koran; it means "The Cave." The sura belongs mainly to the Meccan period but contains some Medinan verses. In all there are 110 verses. The title of the sura is drawn from a major piece of Koranic narrative which occupies verses 9-26 and gives the story of "The Companions of the Cave." According to this, a number of young men seek refuge in a cave, fleeing religious persecution. They fall asleep and awake after a considerable period has elapsed. The story has parallels in the Christian tradition with the Seven Sleepers of Ephesus.

KAHIN

An ancient Semitic tribal priest, custodian of a sanctuary, or seer, probably not set apart by ordination, who in Arabia and Palestine served as a prophet or officiant at religious functions.

K'AI FENG JEWS

Now extinct religious community in Honan Province, China, whose adoption of Judaism and careful observance of its precepts over many centuries has long intrigued scholars.

KAILASA

In Hinduism the paradise of Siva, in Buddhism, Kuvera's abode. Kailasa is a mountain in the Himalayas, north of Manasa Lake. There Siva, the great Yogi, sits deep in meditation in mystical stillness maintaining the world, his long hair in a topknot where the crescent moon is fixed and from which flows the sacred waters of the Ganges.

KAIN

In the Old Testament, a name employed in a proverbial utterance of Balaam to refer to the tribe of the Kenites (Numbers 24:22).

KAIVALYA

In the dualist and evolutionist Samkhya system of Hindu philosophy, a state of liberation achieved by recognizing the separateness of two eternal ontological orders in the nature; that of material nature and of the soul.

KALACAKRA TANTRA

The chief text of a divergent, syncretistic and astrologically oriented school of Tantric Buddhism that arose in north-western India in the 10th century. As such, the work represents the final phase of Buddhist Tantrism in India, just prior to the Muslim invasion, but it has remained prominent in Tibet down to modern times.

KALAKACARYAKATHA

A noncanonical work of the Svetambara sect of Jainism, a religion of India. Four separate episodes of Kalaka's career are generally covered in the many versions. The stories do not relate to a single person but to three separate teachers each known by the name Kalaka.

KALAM

Arabic word for speech. The word also had the more technical sense in medieval Islam of "scholastic theology," Included under the general heading of kalam may be placed many of the great debates of Islamic theology.

KALI

Indian goddess who, from alternate points of view, is both one of Siva's consorts, and one of his principal manifestations as his energy or "other self." She is usually depicted in black, frequently with a sword and bedecked with skulls or several heads, symbolizing the destructive aspects of her activity as personification of death or time. Sometimes, however, emphasis lies on her destruction of the elements of an enslaved human condition; in this sense she is a liberating force, personifying the path to liberation, enlightenment, moksha.

KALLAI

In the Old Testament, a priest in the days of the High Priest Joiakim. He was the head of the paternal house of Sallai and returned to Jerusalem with Zerubbabel in 537 BC after the Babylonian exile (Nehemiah 12:1, 12, 20).

KALPA

In Buddhism, the length of a day and night of Brahma, the "Unrolling and rolling up" of the universe as described in the Pali Canon. It is given in Hindu chronology as 4,320,000,000 years.

KALPA-SUTRAS

Manuals of Hindu religious practice which emerged within the different schools of the Veda (earliest sacred literature of India). Each explains the procedures of its school and as it applied to three different categories:
▲ the sacrificial ritual;
▲ the domestic ritual;
▲ the conduct of life.

They are written in the short aphoristic style of the sutra (literally "thread") so that they could be committed easily to memory.

KAMA

In Buddhism and Hinduism, desire of the senses, especially sexual desire. Kama is one of the four asavas or mental defilements, and is the first of the six factors of existence, the elimination of which is essential for liberation from rebirth.

KAMI

Objects of worship in Shinto, a religion of Japan. The term kami is often understood to mean "gods," or "deities," but includes other forces of nature, both good and evil, which, because of their superiority or divinity become objects of reverence and respect. Creator spirits, great ancestors, and both animate and inanimate things, such as plants, rocks, birds, beasts, and fish, may all be treated as kami.

KAMISON

In the Byzantine churches a vestment similar to an alb, but with wider sleeves, worn by minor clerics or acolytes.

KAMMATTHANA

In Theravada Buddhist tradition, one of the objects of mental concentration or stage of meditation employing it.

Theravada Buddhism classifies men's dispositions into six:
▲ covetousness;

- ▲ anger;
- ▲ stupidity;
- ▲ trustfulness;
- ▲ wisdom;
- ▲ reason.

Each type as its appropriate objects for mental concentration among the kammatthanas.

KAMMAVIPAKA

In Buddhism and Hinduism, a term described as maturing or ripening of past causes under the law of Karma. Hence the results of deeds which have ripened.

KAMON

In biblical times, the burial place of judge Jair (Judges 10:5). Two locations east of the Jordan are commonly presented for ancient Kamon. One is Qamm, about eleven miles south-east of the Sea of Galilee, but its ruins give no evidence of habitation before Roman times. The other suggestion is the site of the less impressive ruins of undetermined antiquity at Qumeim, more than one mile farther south.

KANAH

In the Old Testament, a torrent valley that served as a boundary between Ephraim and Manasseh (Joshua 16:8). Today it is usually linked with the Wadi Qanah. This small stream rises in the hill country a few miles south-west of Nablus (thought to be ancient Shechem) and, as the Wadi Ishkar, flows in a south-westerly direction and then joins the Yarkon River, which empties into the Mediterranean Sea north of Tel Aviv. However, some scholars believe that in Joshua's day the lower course of the Wadi Qanah perhaps flowed directly into the Mediterranean at a point about eight miles farther north.

KANISHKA RELIQUARY

(2nd century AD) Important cylindrical bronze, covered and inscribed, from Shah-ji-ki-Dheri, Ghandara. On the cover in relief is a garland-bearing yakshas, a Buddha and a royal figure around the body. The inscription upon cleaning referred to an unidentified monastery.

KANON

One of the main forms of Byzantine liturgical chant; it consists of nine odes, based on the nine biblical canticles of the Eastern Christian Church. The kanon originated in Jerusalem after the Council in Trullo (691-692) to replace the biblical canticles in the morning office.

KANPHATA YOGIS

An order of religious ascetics in India that venerates the Hindu deity Lord Siva; its members are distinguished by the large earrings they wear in the hollows of their ears. Two characteristics of their monasteries are the continuous fire, called dhuni, and the tombs of dead yogis in their monastery compounds. The dead ascetics are buried seated in postures of meditation, symbolic of their permanent liberation.

KAPLAN, Mordecai Menahem

(1881-1975) Theologian and United States religious leader who founded the influential Reconstructionist movement in Judaism. Reconstructionism was an attempt to adapt Judaism to modern-day realities that Kaplan believed created the necessity for a new conception of God. Thus Kaplan found God revealed in the creative forces within man and the cosmos that are antithetical to evil. He did not believe in the supernatural God that exists outside nature and the relationship of which to evil is beyond man's ken, a mystery that is also self-justifying.

KARAITES

Jewish sect of about 15,000 members centered in Ramla, Ashdod and Beersheba. They reject rabbinical traditions and rulings, and have their own religious courts. After independence, the community has been reduced to only one family. Living in the Jewish Quarter of Jerusalem's Old City, they had to move due to the capturing of the area by the Jordanians. Shortly afterwards, Karaites from Egypt settled in the country and they founded the new colonies.

In principle, the Bible is the Karaites' sole source of creed and law, but apart from its fundamental strand on Oral Law, Karaite creed does not differ in its essentials from that of rabbinical Judaism.

KAREAH

In the Old Testament, a man of Judah whose sons Johanan and Jonathan were chiefs of military forces in Judah. This was at the time Gedaliah was commissioned by the king of Babylon over the Judeans not taken into Babylonian exile following Jerusalem's destruction in 607 BC (2 Kings 25:21-23).

KARKOR

In biblical times, the campsite east of the Jordan from which the remaining forces of Midianite Kings Zebah and Zalmunna were routed by judge Gideon's surprise military maneuver (Judges 8:10-11). Karkor's exact location is today unknown. Some geographers, however, tentatively identify it with Qarqarm located a 100 miles each of the Dead Sea. Whether Gideon's tired foot soldiers traveled that distance in pursuit of the enemy may be subject to doubt (Judges 8:4-5).

KARMA

In Buddhism and Hinduism important term of which the root means "action." Derivatives of the term mean action and the appropriate result of that action. It is also used in the sense of the law of cause and effect. As applied to the moral sphere it is the Law of Ethical Causation, through the operation of which a man builds his character, makes his destiny, and works out his salvation.

Karma is not limited by time or space, and is not strictly individual; there is a group karma, family karma, national karma, etc.

The doctrine of rebirth is an essential corollary to that of Karma, the individual coming into physical life with a character and environment resulting from his actions in the past. His character, family, circumstances and destiny are all, therefore, his Karma, and according to his reaction to his present destiny he modifies and builds his future.

Karma does not, in itself, bind to the wheel of re-birth; the binding element is personal desire for the fruit of action. Liberation is therefore achieved by elimination of desire for self.

Karma has come to be regarded as a kind of potential power gained as a result of each deed done in one's past. That is, each of our acts results in either good or bad, suffering or pleasure, depending upon the act, and it has an influencing power upon our future and this is regarded as one's Karma. It is believed that if a good deed is repeated, good will be accumulated, and its potential power will function upon the future as a beneficial influence. There are three kinds of deeds: physical, oral, and mental, in this concept.

KARMA-PA

A branch of the third-largest Buddhist sect in Tibet. The Karma-pa school was founded by Dus-gsummkhyen-pa, who established its principal monastery in 1185 at Mtshur-phu in central Tibet.

KARMATIANS

A branch of the Ismaili Shiites. The sect is named for one of its earliest leaders, Hamadan Qarmat. Through its egalitarian propaganda, the movement was able to attract wide support against the Abbasid government. The open activity of Hamadan Qarmat was begin in 890, but from the earliest beginning the movement was run as a highly organized secret society, and its true leaders have never been known. Their esoteric doctrine is heavily influenced by Gnosticism and late Neoplatonism and may in part have been influenced by Fatimid theology. The Karmatians are thought to have had considerable influence on later secret societies in Islam and perhaps on the Freemasons in Europe.

KARMA-YOGA

Hindu term meaning doing one's duty without thought of reward or punishment.

KARNAK

Site of a complex of ruins which is the Great Temple of Amon, the largest enclosure in Egypt, growing by accretion (2060 - 7th century BC), the courtyards and pylons added by successive pharaohs. Karnak is known for the magnificent Hypostyle Hall (338 by 170 feet), having two rows of papyrus columns in the nave and 122 smaller bundle-bud columns in the aisles, with a sacred lake south of the earliest structures.

A festival hall with clerestory, set transversely to the axis of the Temple of Amon, built by Thutmose III, later served as a Coptic church. An avenue of sphinxes leads to temples of Amenhotep III and Ramses II. Colossal architecture at Karnak is not marred by deterioration in later styles.

KART

A Cheremis sacrificial priest who was either a lifetime representative of a clan or a temporary official chosen by lot to oversee common sacrificial feasts of an entire village or several villages. The kart was chosen on the basis of respect and for his knowledge of ritual; because his position afforded great honor it was not generally refused. The kart's functions included saying prayers, lighting ceremonial fires for the sacrificial meals and blessing the offerings.

KARTER

(3rd century AD) Influential High Priest of Zoroastrianism (a religion founded by the 6th century BC prophet Zoroaster). The aim was to purge Iran of all other religions, especially the eclectic Manichaeism. On more than 700 cliffs he proclaimed the fundamentals of the religion of Zoroaster, such as "Heaven exists and hell exists; virtue is rewarded in heaven, wickedness is punished in Hell." Heaven and hell are basic to Zoroastrianism. Karter seems to have been extremely ambitious and single-minded in his goal to uphold his concept of Zoroastrianism.

KARTTIKEYA

Hindu god of war, son of Siva and Parvati, also called Skanda or Kumara (youth).

KARUNA

In Buddhism, mercy or compassion; one of the four sublime states, or spiritual moods, that both laymen and monks are exhorted to develop constantly. Karuna and the other states are regarded as states of mind, virtues to be exemplified, and also objects of meditation.

KASB

In Islam, medieval theological doctrine of "acquisition," often associated with, but probably not invented by, al-Ashari. According to this doctrine God creates any action but man "acquires" it. This was a valiant attempt by medieval Islamic theologians to solve an age-old problem: how did one reconcile, on the one hand, God's total omnipotence and omniscience with, on the other hand, man's free will and responsibility for his own actions?

KASHF

In Islamic mystic literature, the knowledge that mystics acquire through personal experience and direct vision of God. The truths revealed through kashf cannot be transmitted to those who have not shared with them the same experience.

KASHRUT

In Judaism, regulations that prohibit the eating of certain foods and require that other foods be prepared in a specific manner. Most prescriptions regarding kashrut are found in the Old Testament books of Leviticus,

Deuteronomy, Genesis, and Exodus. Some efforts have been made to establish a direct relationship between these laws and health, but for the observant Jews no other motive is required than the fact that God has so ordained.

KASYAPA

Most famous disciple of Buddha Sakayamuni. In early sculpture and painting Kasyapa is paired with Amanda in attendance upon the Buddha. Kasyapa, wrinkled for age and status, appears with Amanda in early Chinese Buddhist art.

KATHENOTHEISM

One after the other, classification for a stage between polytheism and monotheism, i.e., a stage in which one of many gods is conceived as supreme.

KAWTHAR, al-

The title of the 108th sura of the Koran; it means literally "The Abundant." The sura belongs to the Meccan period and has three verses. Its title is drawn from the first verse in which God states that he has given man al-Kawthar. The remaining two verses urge man to pray to God and offer sacrifice. The man who hates the Prophet Mohammed will remain without offspring.

KEDAR

In the Old Testament, one of the 12 sons of Ishmael (Genesis 25:13-15). The name is also applied to an Arab tribe descended from Ishmael's son Kedar and classed with "the sons of the East." A nomadic and pastoral people, having herds of sheep, goats and camels (Isaiah 60:6; Jeremiah 49:28-29), the Kedarites evidently inhabited the Syro-Arabian desert east of Palestine in the north-western part of the Arabian Peninsula. The reference to "the settlements that Kedar inhabits" (Isaiah 42:11), while possibly referring to temporary encampments, may instead indicate that a portion of them were somewhat settled. Perhaps because of their importance among the Arab tribes, the name of Kedar in later times came to apply to desert tribes in general.

KEDEMAH

In Judaism, a son of Ishmael, named last in order at Genesis 23:15 and 1 Chronicles 1:31. He was one of the twelve chieftains produced by Ishmael.

KEDEMOTH

In biblical times, the name applied to a city east of the Jordan and apparently also to the wilderness surrounding it. From the wilderness of Kedemoth Moses sent messengers to Amorite King Sihon, requesting permission to pass through his land (Deuteronomy 2:26-27). Originally given to the Reubenites, Kedemoth was latter assigned to the Merarite Levites (Joshua 13:15-18; 1 Chronicles 6:77-79). Geographers generally favor as a possible identification Kasr ez-Za'feran, situated about ten miles north-east of what is thought to be the site of ancient Dibon.

KEGON

A Buddhist philosophical tradition introduced into Japan from China during the Nara period (710-784). Although the Kegon school no longer be considered an active faith teaching a separate doctrine, it continues to administer the famous Todai-ji monastery at Nara.

KEHELATHAH

In the Old Testament, one of the places where the Israelites encamped while wandering in the wilderness (Numbers 33:22-23).

KELITA

In Judaism, one of the Levites of Ezra's day who recognized their guilt in taking foreign wives and therefore sent them away in 468-467 BC. The name is also applied to a Levite whose descendant, if not himself, attested by seal the "trustworthy arrangement" of Nehemiah's time (Nehemiah 9:38; 10:1-10).

KEMUEL

In Judaism, a son of Abraham's brother Nahor and his wife Milcah, and hence Abraham's nephew. He had a son named Aram (Genesis 22:20-21).

KEN, Thomas

(1637-1711) Anglican bishop, hymn writer, one of the seven bishops who in 1688 opposed King James II's Declaration of Indulgence, designed to promote Roman Catholicism.

KENATH

In biblical times, a site east of the Jordan captured by Nobah, probably a Manassite, who thereafter called it by his own name (Numbers 32:42), but the designation "Nobah" perhaps did not stick for later "Kenath" is reported to have been taken by Geshur and Syria (1 Chronicles 2:23).

KENITE

Member of a people residing in Canaan or its vicinity in the days of Abraham. They plied their trade while traveling in the region of the Arabah (desert rift valley extending from the Sea of Galilee to the Gulf of Aqaba) from at least the 13th century to the 9th century BC.

KENIZZITE

In biblical times, member of a non-Israelite people in or near Canaan whose territory was promised by God to Abraham's seed (Genesis 15:18-19). The Kenizzites evidently moved into the Negeb from the south-east, possibly spreading over part of Edom as well as what became southern Judah, doing so prior to the Israelite conquest of the Promised Land.

KENNETH, Saint

(515-599) Monastic founder, and missionary who contributed to the conversion of the Picts; one of the most famous Celtic saints popular in Scotland and Ireland.

KENOSIS

A Greek word meaning "emptying," used to express the abasement of the Son of God in the Incarnation. The origin of the term is an early Christian hymn, probably borrowed by Paul from the Palestinian church. The emptying did not involve a temporary abandonment of his divine nature, but a concealment of the divine attributes under the weakness of his assumed humanity.

KENOTIC THEORIES

Explanation which interpret the Incarnation to mean that in becoming man the Second Person of the Trinity, the Logos, emptied himself of his divine attributes. The general concept of a kenosis connected with the Incarnation occurs in theologians from patristic times, but as a specific theory it derives from G. Thomasius and other German Lutherans of the 19th century.

KEREN-HAPPUCH

In the Old Testament, the third and youngest of the daughters born to Job after his great test and suffering had ended and God had blessed him (Job 42:12-14).

KERIOTH

In the Old Testament, a place mentioned in two prophecies against Moab (Jeremiah 48:24; Amos 2:2). The meaning of its name may indicate that the city was comprised of several small towns. Kerioth's exact location is uncertain. Some scholars tentatively suggest Saliya, a site about 24 miles due east of the central part of the Dead Sea. Others believe that Kerioth is perhaps the same as Ar. This view seems to find some support in the fact that Ar and Kerioth, although figuring as principal cities (compare Amos 2:1-3; Deuteronomy 2:9, 18), do not appear together in lists of Moabite towns.

KEROS

In Judaism, founder of a family of Nethinim, some of whose descendants were among those returning to Jerusalem and Judah with Zerubbabel after the Babylonian exile (Ezra 2:1-2, 43-44; Nehemiah 7:6-7, 46-47).

KERYGMA

From the Greek word for "proclamation;" in the Christian sense, it refers especially to the preaching of the good news of salvation, the proclaiming of the essential elements of God's salvific plan in Christ, the passing on of the "core message."

KERYGMATIC THEOLOGY

A description of theology as receiving its origin, form, and purpose from the preaching of the good news of salvation. In the Greek of the New Testament, kerygma refers to the proclamation of what God has done in Christ for the salvation of men. Dialectic theology, or crisis theology, has been called kerygmatic because of an exclusive concern for the proclamation of God's word and self-revelation in Christ, the only saving knowledge for man.

KETAV ASHUR

The Hebrew script developed during the Second Temple era (6th-2nd centuries BC) and in use up to the present day.

KETURAH

In Judaism, a wife of Abraham and the mother of six of his sons, Zimran, Jokshan, Medan, Midian, Ishbak and Shuah, ancestors of various north Arabian peoples dwelling to the south and east of Palestine.

It was only because their reproductive powers were miraculously revived that Abraham and Sarah were able to have a son, Isaac, in their old age (Hebrews 11:11-12). Evidently, such restored powers enabled Abraham to become father to six more sons by Keturah when he was even more advanced in age.

KEYS

The symbol of spiritual power and authority conferred on Peter and his successors by Jesus Christ: "I will give you the keys of the kingdom of heaven" (Matthew 16:19). The "power of the keys" is an expression used by Roman Ctaholics to describe the authority of the Bishop of Rome, the pope, over all the faithful and all the churches.

KEZIAH

In the Old Testament, the second of the three daughters of Job born after his severe trial and subsequent restoration and blessing by God (Job 42:14).

KHADIJA BINT KHUWAYLID

(554-619) First wife of the Prophet Mohammed and also revered as the first Muslim after him. She was a member of the tribe of Quaraysh. A widow of considerable wealth, for whom Mohammed had originally worked, she married the Prophet when she was aged 40 and he aged 25. While she remained alive, the Prophet did not take any other wives. Khadija bore the Prophet six children, two boys, both of whom died very young, and four girls.

KHALIFA

Caliph, head of the Islamic Community. The Arabic word in early Islamic history meant literally "successor" or "deputy" (i.e., of the Prophet Mohammed). This technically elective office combined in theory a spiritual and secular function, though in practice, under such dynasties as the Umayyads, it was the latter function which was generally prominent at the expense of the former.

KHALSA

The dominant brotherhood of Sikhism, a religion in India. Most Sikh boys and girls undergo initiation into the Khalsa upon reaching puberty. The ceremony is conducted by five members of the Khalsa, who mix sweets in water with a double-edged dagger while reciting hymns. The initiates are all asked to drink the preparation from the same cup and are given new names with the suffix Singh ("lion"). Sikh girls on initiation are given the surname Kaur ("lioness").

KHARIJITES

Members of an early Islamic sect, the origins of which are confused and obscure. Kharijism, whose beliefs were by no means uniform, divided into a number of sub-sects, some increasingly fanatical and exclusivist, teaching, for example, that grave sinners would go to hell and that they thereby placed themselves outside the community; that non-Kharijites were kafirs and could thus be killed.

KHILAFAT MOVEMENT

A force that arose in India in the early 20th century as a result of Muslim fears for the integrity of Islam.

KHITAN

Arabic word for circumcision. It is a widespread custom in Islam but is not mentioned in the Koran. Circumcision was probably practiced in pre-Islamic Arabia and tradition teaches that the great prophet Ibrahim was circumcised when he reached his 80th year. The age today at which boys are circumcised varies from country to country. Female circumcision is also practiced in some areas of the Islamic world, particularly those influenced by African custom. The barbarity of clitoridectomy, more properly called khafd in Arabic, owes nothing to Islam.

KHMER REPUBLIC

Formerly a constitutional monarchy in south-eastern Asia. The Khmers, fore-bears of today's Cambodians, developed a Hindu-Buddhist civilization that flourished from the first to the eighth century AD. Its great temples with their striking wall sculptures were disclosed by discoveries in the mid-18th century. The state religion, as well as that of the vast majority of the people, is Buddhism of the Hynayana type, blended with animistic practices.

KHORRAM-DINAN

Esoteric Islamic religious sect whose leader Babak led a rebellion in Azerbaijan from 816 until 837. The doctrinal beliefs of the Khorram-dinan are not altogether clear. Although the sect accepted the general principles of Islam, its members believed in transmigration of the soul and placed special emphasis on the Zoroastrian dualism of light and dark.

KHUTBA

Arabic word for sermon, address; in particular the sermon delivered during the Friday prayer in the mosque. During the khutba blessings are invoked on the ruler and thus, in medieval times, in the absence of modern methods of communication like radio and TV, the khutba could serve to announce a change of khalifa or even dynasty to the assembled congregation.

KIBZAIM

In the Old Testament, an Ephraimite city given to the Kohathite Levites (Joshua 21:20-22).

KIDDUSH

Jewish prayer and ceremonial ritual. At the meal on the eve of Sabbath or festival the head of the household chants the kiddush (prayer of sanctification of the day), while holding a cup of wine in his right palm; on the table in front of him are two loaves of hallah, bread covered with cloth, symbolizing the two portions of manna gathered on the eve of Sabbath during Israel's wilderness wandering.

KIDRON, Torrent valley of

In biblical times, a deep valley that separates Jerusalem from the Mount of Olives and runs first south-eastward and then southward along the city. Waterless even in the winter, except in cases of especially heavy rain, the Kidron valley starts some distance north of Jerusalem's walls. At first a broad and shallow valley, it continues to narrow and deepen. By the time it is opposite St. Stephen's gate near the former Temple area, it is approximately 100 feet deep and 400 feet wide. To the south of the former temple area the Kidron valley is joined by the Tyropean valley and the valley of

Hinnom respectively. From then on it continues south-eastward across the arid wilderness of Judah to the Dead Sea. The modern name applied to the valley's lower course is Wadi en-Nar ("fire wadi"), indicating that it is hot and dry most of the time.

KINDI, al-

(died circa 866) The "Father of Islamic Philosophy" who paved the way for his successors like al-Farabi. During his lifetime his library was temporarily confiscated and he was beaten. He believed that philosophy and theology were compatible and he remained, at heart, a Koranic Muslim, despite the accusations levelled at him in his own age.

KINGDOM

Basically, a royal government; also the territory and peoples under the rule of a king or, less frequently, a female monarch or queen. Often the kingship was hereditary. The sovereign ruler might bear other titles such as Pharaoh or Caesar.

Kingdoms of ancient times, as today, had various symbols of royalty. There was generally a capital city or place of the king's residence, a royal court, a standing army (though perhaps quite reduced in size at times of peace). The word "kingdom," as used in the Bible, does not of itself reveal anything definite as to the governmental structure, the territorial extent, or the authority of the monarch. Kingdoms ranged in size and influence from the mighty world powers such as Egypt, Assyria, Babylon and Medo-Persia, on down to small city-kingdoms such as those in Canaan at the time of the Israelite conquest (Joshua 12:7-24).

KINGDOM OF GOD

The expression and exercise of God's universal sovereignty toward His creatures, or the means or instrumentality used by Him for this purpose (Psalms 103:19). The phrase is used particularly for the expression of God's sovereignty through a royal administration headed by His Son.

The Kingdom of God is a rich biblical term, often translated as "the reign of God"; the coming of the kingdom of Gad was foretold in the Old Testament and was especially revealed in the very person of Christ, Son of God and Son of Man (see Mark 1:15; Matthew 4:17); in the words, works, and miracles of Christ, the kingdom is described (see, for example, Luke 11:20 and Matthew 12:38).

The mission of the church, in the words of Vatican Council II, is "of proclaiming and establishing among all peoples the kingdom of Christ and of God, and she is, on earth, the seed and the beginning of that kingdom. While she slowly grows to maturity, the church longs for the completed kingdom and, with all her strength, hopes and desires to be united in glory with her king."

KINGS, Books of

Two Old Testament books that recount the fate of the monarchy in Israel after the death of David. The first two chapters of 1 Kings complete the story of David, begun in the preceding books of Samuel, and tell of the accession of his son Solomon. This is followed by the reigns of kings of Judah and Israel from the beginning of the divided monarchy circa 930 BC until the fall of the kingdom of Israel in 721 BC. 2 Kings tells of the reigns of kings of the surviving southern kingdom of Judah until its eventual collapse in 586 BC.

KING'S HIGHWAY

The road by which Moses promised to travel peacefully through the land of Edom and the land of Sihon, king of Heshbon. Both refused his request, and so the Israelites were forced to avoid Edom and to fight and defeat Sihon. The King's Highway was probably the main route north to south along the heights east of the Jordan, between Damascus and the Gulf of Aquaba.

KIR

In ancient times, the place from which the Aramaeans came to Syria, although

not necessarily their original home (Amos 9:7). The prophet Amos indicated that the Aramaeans would return to Kir, but as exiles. This prophecy was fulfilled when Tiglath-pileser III, after having been bribed by Judean King Ahaz to do so, captured Damascus, the Aramaean capital, and led its inhabitants into exile at Kir (2 Kings 16:7-9).

KIRIATH

In ancient times, a city of Benjamin usually thought to be the same as Kiriath-jearim. Some scholars believe that the name "Kiriath-jearim" appeared in the original text at Joshua 18:28, as it does in the Alexandrine manuscript.

KIRIATHAIM

In ancient times, a city east of the Jordan, built or rebuilt by the Reubenites (Numbers 32:37; Joshua 13:15-19). At a later period the city came under Moabite control. It is mentioned in the prophecies of Jeremiah (48:1) and Ezekiel (25:9) as a city of Moab that would experience calamity. Geographers usually identify Kiriathaim with modern el-Qereiyat, circa six miles north-west of the suggested location of biblical Dibon.

KIRIATH-JEARIM

In ancient times, a Hivite city associated with the Gibeonites (Joshua 9:17), also known as Baalah (Joshua 15:9). The city later came to belong to Judah and bordered on Benjaminite territory (Joshua 15:1, 9; 18:11-14).

KIR OF MOAB

In ancient times an important city of Moab, probably a onetime capital. The Aramaic Targum consistently refers to Kir (of Moab), Kir-hareseth and Kir-heres as Kerak, indicating that these are but alternative names for the same place. "Kir of Moab" is therefore usually identified with modern Kerak (Isaiah 15:1). This city is situated on a small plateau over 3,000 feet above sea level and circa eleven miles east of a point just below the Dead Sea peninsu-

la El-Lisan. Steep valleys separate most of Kerak from the loftier neighboring mountains.

Towards the close of the 10th century BC the allied forces of Israel, Judah and Edom attacked Kir-hareseth. Although the latter city evidently was not taken, the battle went hard against the king of Moab. For some unstated reason, he, along with 700 warriors, sought to break through the battle lines in order to reach the king of Edom but was unsuccessful. As a last resort it appears that the king of Moab publicly sacrificed his own firstborn son, probably to appease the god Chemosh (2 Kings 3:5-9).

KISH

In the Old Testament, a Merarite Levite who was the son of Mahli and brother of Eleazar. As Eleazar died without sons, having had only daughters, the sons of Kish took these heiresses as wives. One of the "sons of Kish" was Jerahmeel (1 Chronicles 23:21-22; 24:29).

The name is also applied to a Benjaminite; the son of Jeiel and his wife Maacah (1 Chronicles 8:29, 30). His brother Ner was the grandfather of Saul, Israel's first king (1 Chronicles 9:35-39).

KISHON, Torrent valley of

In ancient times, a stream identified as the Nahr el-Muqatta. The Kishon winds its way in a north-westerly direction through the Plain of Esdraelon and, after flowing through a narrow gorge between Mount Carmel and a spur of the Galilean hills, enters the Plain of Acco before finally emptying into the Mediterranean.

In the time of Barak and Deborah the torrent valley of Kishon figured in the deliverance of the Israelites from Canaanite oppression.

KISMET

Turkish adaptation of an Arabic word, qismah or qismat, meaning portion, lot, or destiny and having to do with the fate that befalls or is allotted each individual in life. It is to be distinguished from the Calvinistic doctrine of predestination and from the more general religious belief that the universe is guided by a divine intelligence or purpose.

KITRON

In ancient times, a city from which the Zebulunites failed to expel the Canaanite inhabitants (Judges 1:30). Kitron is identified by some geographers with Tell el-Far, circa seven miles south-east of Haifa. This ancient city may be the same as Kattah (Joshua 19:15).

KITTIM

In the Old Testament, one of the four "sons" of Javan (Genesis 10:4).

KNESET HA-GEDOLA

An elite group of 120, or perhaps 85, Jewish religious leaders who, after returning (538 BC) to their homeland from the Babylonian exile, initiated a new era in the history of Judaism.

They convened at least once under the leadership of Ezra and Nehemiah to sign a document swearing to observe the law of Moses (Nehemiah 9:38), but it is not certain that a formal organization ever existed. Tradition credits this group - which should perhaps extend to several succeeding generations - with having established norms for Judaism that have persisted to the present day.

KNIGHTHOODS, orders of

Originally, in medieval Europe, religious societies of knights, bound by monastic vows, whose main duty was to fight the Muslims.

KNIGHTS OF COLUMBUS

International fraternal benefit society of Roman Catholic men, founded by Michael J. McGivney and chartered by the state of Connecticut in 1882. Besides supplying a wide range of insurance benefits and the opportunity for social intercourse, the organization has been active in a great number of religious, educational, war relief, and social welfare programs.

KNIGHTS OF SAINT JOHN

Officially, Order of the Hospital of St. John of Jerusalem; also known as Hospitallers, Knights of Rhodes, or of Malta religious order founded by papal charter (1113) to tend sick pilgrims in the Holy Land.

It became a military order as well in 1140, and after the fall of Jerusalem was based successively on Cyprus (1291), Rhodes (1309), and Malta (1530) to provide a defense against Muslim seapower. Expelled from Malta by Napoleon in 1789, the Knights have been established at Rome since 1834.

KNIGHTS TEMPLARS

Military Christian order of knights whose name was taken from the earliest headquarters of the order in the crusader's palace at Jerusalem on the site of the Temple of Solomon. Founded circa 1118, the purpose of the order was the protection of pilgrims on their way to holy shrines. It took a leading part in the Crusades and grew rapidly in numbers and in wealth, founding centers in all Christian countries. Accused of heresy, corruption and immorality by Philip IV of France, the order was suppressed by the pope in 1312.

The modern order reappeared in the 18th century and today survives in the United States as one of the major branches of Freemasonry. It has circa 400,000 members.

KNOWLEDGE OF GOD

Human beings are capable of knowing God through the exercise of reason, but such knowledge is extended through grace and revelation.

KOA

In biblical times, a people or region mentioned with Pekod and Shoa at Ezekiel 23:23 and foretold to supply part of the enemy forces that would assault unfaithful Jerusalem and Judah. Koa was probably located east of Babylonia and has been generally linked with the Kutu, a people who resided east of the Tigris on the steppes between the upper Adhaim and Diyala Rivers. The Kutu are frequently coupled with the Sutu in Assyrian inscriptions, such records showing them as fighting against Assyria.

KOAN

In Zen Buddhism, succinct statements or questions that pose mental dilemmas and are used as meditations discipline for novices. The effort to "solve" a koan is intended to exhaust the analytic intellect and the egoistic will, readying the mind to entertain an appropriate response on the intuitive level. There are said to be 1,700 koan in all.

KOGOSHUI

One of the sacred texts of the Shinto religion of Japan. The work was composed by Imbe Hironari and presented to emperor Heizei in 807. It consists of commentaries on ancient words and practices and contains material emitted from the two earlier written classics.

KOHATH

In the Old Testament, a son of Levi and grandfather of Moses. His descendants were known as the Kohathites and formed one of the three groups of Levites.

KOLAIAH

In the Old Testament, father of the false prophet Ahab who was among the Jews in babylonian exile before Jerusalem;s destruction in 607 BC (Jeremiah 19:21).

KOL NIDRE

Important Jewish holiday; Kol means "all" and Nidre means "vows." The words of the Kol Nidre prayer state that all vows and oaths not carried out are hereby cancelled and made void. To understand the meaning of this prayer, some knowledge of Jewish history is important. In the days of Inquisition in 15th century Spain and Portugal, Jews were often forced to give up their faith. Though they became Christians outwardly, these Jews, who are called Marranos, secretly continued to observe Jewish customs. In the Kol Nidre prayer that begged God to forgive them for their vows which they knew they could not keep because they practiced their religion in secret. Kol Nidre released them from the vows they had been pressed to make. Kol Nidre refers only to vows made by man to God. Other promises made in the course of everyday life cannot be done away with by reciting a prayer.

Actually, the Kol Nidre prayer goes back much further than the Inquisition. In fact it is first mentioned in the ninth century. But it came to have a greater and deeper meaning in the evil days when Jews were forced to give up their faith.

KOLYBA

A word of uncertain origin signifying a cake of boiled wheat with almonds, pistachios, and raisins mixed with sugar and spices. It is blessed and dedicated to the dead and distributed to the faithful on the first Saturday of Lent. At a funeral a similar cake is brought to the church by the family of the deceased during the last office celebrated from his soul.

KONKO-KYO

A religious movement founded in the 19th century, a prototype of the "new religions" that proliferated in the post-World War II period in Japan. The movement was founded by Kawate Bunjiro, a farmer who lived in present-day Okayama Prefecture. He believed that he was appointed by the deity Konko to act as a mediator between God and mankind. The mediator takes on the pain and sufferings of his followers and transmits them to God.

KOPPERS, Wilhelm

(1886-1961) Roman Catholic priest and cultural anthropologist who advocated a comparative, historical approach to the study of religious phenomena.

KORAH

In the Old Testament, one of Esau's three sons by his Hivite wife Oholibamah; born in Canaan prior to Esau's withdrawal to the mountainous region of Seir (Genesis 36:2, 5-8; 1 Chronicles 1:35).

The name is also applied to a Kohathite Levite of the family of Ishar (Exodus 6:16-21). During Israel's wilderness trek he rebelled against the authority of Moses and Aaron, doing so in league with the Reubenites Dathan, Abiram and On and 250 "chieftains of the assembly" or "men of fame" (Numbers 16:1-2). They contented that "the whole assembly are all of them holy and God is in their midst," asking, "Why, then, should you lift yourselves up above the congregation of God?" (Numbers 13:3-11). Korah, his assembly, and High Priest Aaron were told to present themselves before God, all supplied with fire holders and burning incense (Numbers 16:16-17).

KORAHITE

In the Old Testament, a descendant of Korah, who rebelled in Moses' day. The Korahites were a paternal house of the Kohathite Levites and descended from Korah through his three sons Assir, Elkanak and Abiasaph (Exodus 6:18-24; Numbers 16:1-3).

KORAN

Also spelled Qur'an; literally "Recitation". The Koran is Islam's holiest book, being the uncreated word of God revealed through Jibril (Gabriel) to the Prophet Mohammed. The text consists of 114 chapters, each called a sura in Arabic, arranged so that the longest ones come first. Each sura is classified as Meccan or Medinan according to whether the sura was revealed to Mohammed in Mecca or Medina. Each sura is divided into verses, a single one of which is called in Arabic an aya.

Muslims believe that the Koran is inimitable. Stylistically, much of the text resembles a kind of rhymed prose called saj' in Arabic.

The Koran is far more than a religious scripture. Since it was the first major book written in Arabic, and formed a point of unity for all Arabs as well as for the diverse peoples they conquered, it is in a sense the foundation of the great Islamic civilization of the past, as well as the molder and preserver of the Arabic language. Since it was forbidden to recite the Koran in any other language than Arabic, the language was perpetuated in its purest form with no corruption from the languages of the many peoples who were converted to Islam. The Koran today is the inspiration and guide for millions of Muslims. It is the supreme authority of the Islamic tradition.

KORE

In the Old Testament, a Kohathite Levite "of the sons of Asaph" and a descendant of Korah (Exodus 6:16-21).

KOREAN RELIGION

The religious beliefs and practices of the people of the Korean peninsula, including native folk traditions and the sophisticated religions introduced from abroad. Although Buddhism, Taoism, Confucianism, Christianity and Shinto have exerted extensive or, at times, only peripheral influences on Korean culture, the substrata of folk traditions, especially shamanism (a belief system centering on religious personages with healing and psychic transformation powers) and tribal religions, remains a source for the many new religions that have arisen in the 19th and 20th centuries.

The most primitive indigenous religion of Korea was characterized by animism, a belief in spirits, and ancestor worship. The early Koreans worshiped natural phenomena such as the sun, moon, some stars, high mountains, and wide rivers; they venerated good spirits and propitiated evil ones. Equally pervasive was a recourse to magic, especially through the shaman or witchdoctor. Women acted as sorceresses, after resorting to dancing dervishes or trances to communicate with occult powers.

But despite all their beliefs in a multitude of good and evil spirits, the ancient Koreans held the ideas of a Supreme Being. Known as Hananim, a name derived form the words for heaven and master, he was the Supreme Ruler of the universe and of the spirit world. There were no idolatrous rites in his worship, but no personal devotion either, since the worship of this awesome deity was entrusted to the king alone.

KOSHER

In Judaism, the fitness of an object for ritual purposes. Though generally applied to foods that meet the requirements of the dietary laws, kosher is also used to describe, for instance, such things as the Torah scroll, ritual water, and the ritual ram's horn.

KOZ

In the Old Testament, a descendant of Judah. Koz "became father to Anub and Zobelkah and the families of Aharhel the son of Harum (1 Chronicles 4:1, 8).

KRIYATANTRA

In Buddhist mysticism, one of the four traditional kinds of Tantras, basically ritualistic and devotional in character.

KRISHNA

The most widely revered and most popular of all Indian divinities, worshipped as the eighth incarnation of the Hindu god Visnu and also as a supreme god in his own right.

KSHATRIYA

At the time of the Buddha the Aryan clans in India recognized four social grades called varnas, the highest being the Brahmin or priest. Next comes the Kshatriya, the warrior-ruler; then the Vaishya, or merchant; and lastly, the Sudra or people of non-Aryan descent. The lines of demarcation between each varna were variable and undefined; the complexity and rigidity of the modern caste system was unknown.

KUAN TI

Chinese god of war. His immense popularity with the common people rests in the firm belief that Kuan Ti's control over evil spirits is so great that even actors who play his part in dramas share his power over demons.

KUBALA

The goddess of the Syrian city of Carchemish. In religious texts of the Hittite Empire (circa 1400-1190 BC) she played a minor part and appeared mainly in the context of Hurrian deities and rituals.

KUBERA

In Hindu mythology, the king of yaksas (nature spirits) and the god of wealth. He is associated with the earth, mountains, all treasures such as minerals and jewels that lie underground, and riches in general.

KUFR

Arabic word for infidelity, unbelief, atheism.

KUNDALINI

In Buddhism, the fiery serpent-power which lies coiled in its chakra at the root of the spine. At a late stage in spiritual development it moves up through the other six cakras to open the 1,000-petalled Lotus in the brain. It is a doctrine of esoteric Yoga and no part of Buddhist teaching. Attempts to rouse this tremendous power before training in the hands of a master sufficiently advanced leads to complete insanity.

KUFR

Arabic word for infidelity, unbelief, atheism.

KUO TZU-I

In some parts of China, the god of happiness and riches, whose great moment in life has been a favorite subject of Chinese artists.

KUROZUMI-KYO

A religion regarded as one of the prototypes of the contemporary "new religions" of Japan, named after its founder, Kurozumi Munetada (1780-1850). The believers venerate the Shinto sun goddess Amaterasu as the supreme god and creator of the universe and consider the other traditional Shinto gods or sacred powers to be her manifestations.

KUSALA

In Buddhism, term meaning wholesome, in contrast to akusala, unwholesome. The terms are used to describe acts whose karmic effect will be to assist or retard progress in the development of the mind, or to produce pleasant or painful results.

KUSHAIAH

In the Old Testament, a Levite of the family of Merari and the father or ancestor of Ethan, one of the group of Levite singers and musicians of David's day (1 Chronicles 15:16-17).

KUSHAPA

A prayer which the East Syrian celebrant is directed to say in a low voice and kneeling. In practice, the Nestorian celebrant says it rather with his knees bent in such a way that he is almost sitting on his heels.

KUVERA

God of wealth, appearing in later Vedic literature, well-known in Buddhism, lord of precious jewels and metals, guardian of the North, living in the jeweled city of Alaka, near Mount Kailasa, commanding gnomes and fairies. The many-jeweled Kuvera rides a lion or horse, and with fierce expressions exerts power over the nagas who guard the earth's treasures.

L

LABADISTS

Members of the Reformed sect founded in Hereford, Westphalia, circa 1670 by Jean de Labadie. They believed that the Bible could be understood only by the immediate inspiration of the Holy Spirit, denied the real presence, rarely celebrated the Eucharist, and held that marriage with an unregenerate person was not binding. After the death of their last preacher in 1732 the sect dwindled and its remaining members scattered.

LABAN

A Gershonite Levite from whom several paternal houses originated (1 Chronicles 23:7-9).

LABDACIDS

In Greek mythology, the royal house of the Labdacids was named after Labdacus, the grandson of Cadmus (who was the founder of Thebes). Oedipus was descended from Cadmus, the first king of Thebes.

LACTICINIA

Such foods as butter, or cheese, that derive from milk and were at times forbidden according to some ecclesiastical or monastic rules.

LADDER

The only biblical reference to a ladder is in Genesis 28:12, where the Hebrew term sul-lam' applied to a ladder Jacob beheld in a dream. The patriarch saw a ladder (or perhaps what looked like a rising flight of stones) stationed upon the earth, with its top reaching up to the heavens. God's angels were ascending and descending on the ladder and a representation of God was above it (Genesis 28:13). This ladder with the angels upon it indicates the existence of communication between earth and heaven and that angels minister in an important way between God and those having His approval.

When Jesus said to his disciples, "Most truly I say that you men, you will see heaven opened up and the angels of God ascending and descending to the Son of man," he may have had in mind Jacob's vision (John 1:51).

LADY CHAPEL

Chapel attached to a church and dedicated to the Blessed Virgin. As the development of the chevet, or radiating system of apse chapels, progressed during the 12th and 13th centuries, it became customary to give the one dedicated to the Blessed Virgin the most important position, directly behind the high altar.

LAEL

A Levite and the father of Eliasaph, the chieftain of the paternal house of the Gershonites during Israel's trek in the wilderness (Numbers 3:24).

LAETARE SUNDAY

Fourth Sunday in Lent in the Western Christian church, from the first word ("rejoice") of the introduction of the liturgy.

LAG BE-OMER

Jewish festival on the 18th day of the month of Iyar. Like many Jewish holidays, it tells of the Jewish people's fight for freedom against the dark forces of oppression, commemorating the life in Palestine and the battles for independence.

The name of the holiday means the 33rd day of the omer, which was a measure the Palestinian farmers used for measuring their grain. The days between Passover and Shavuot were known to the farmer ancestors of the Jews as omer days, for this was the time when the Jews gathered their harvest. They are also known as sefirah, or counting days. Jews counted the days from Passover to Shavuot to know when to celebrate the end of the harvest season.

The days between Passover and Shavuot are a solemn period on the Jewish calendar. They recall the suffering which the Jews endured under Roman persecution. No joyous celebrations, like weddings and parties, are held during the sefirah days. But Lag Be-Omer comes to break the series of solemn days. Lag Be-Omer is the one joyous day of the sefirah days, for, according to folklore, Bar Kochba won a great victory on the 33rd day of the omer days. Another story tells that a plague which was raging among Akiba's students suddenly stopped on that day. For this reason, Lag Be-Omer is also called Scholar's Holiday.

LAGRANGE, Marie-Joseph

(1855-1938) Theologian and outstanding Roman Catholic biblical scholar. In Jerusalem he founded (1892) a journal, the *Revue Bibliques,* and in 1903 began a series of scholarly commentaries to the Bible, the *Etudes Bibliques,* to which he contributed three volumes on the historical method of Old Testament criticism, on the Book of Judges, and on the Semitic religions.

LAHAD

A descendant of Judah and the second named of Jahath's two sons (1 Chronicles 4:1-2).

LAHMI

The brother of Goliath the Gittite (1 Chronicles 20:5).

LAHMU AND LAHAMU

In Mesopotamian mythology, twin deities, the first gods to be born from the chaos created by the merging of Apsu (the watery deep surrounding the earth) and Tiamat (the personification of the salt waters). Lahmu and Lahamu were rather vague deities who do not seem to have played any significant part in subsequent myths.

LAICISM

An attitude that passes beyond the reaction of anticlericalism to a positive and explicit interference into areas regarded as the monopoly of the clergy's influence and competence.

LAICIZATION

In general a juridic process leading to a rescript that allows one in holy orders to return to the lay status in the church. In current usage the term usually connotes the contemporary phenomenon whereby a priest's resignation from the priesthood is canonically accomplished.

LAIMA

In Baltic religion, the goddess of Fate, generally associated with the linden tree. Together with Dievs, the sky, and Saule, the sun, Laima determines the length and fortune of human life.

LAISH

In the Old Testament, a man from Galli, the father of Palti, to whom Saul gave as a wife his daughter Michal, previously the wife of David (1 Samuel 25:44).

LAITY

Members of a religious faith as distinct from its clergy. All members of the church belong to the people of God, the Christian faithful. According to the Code of Canon Law: "The Christian faithful are those who, inasmuch as they have been incorporated in Christ through baptism, have been constituted as the people of God; for this reason, since they have become shares in Christ's priestly, prophetic and royal office in their own matter, they are called to exercise the mission which God has entrusted to the church to fulfill in the world, in accord with the condition proper to each one" (Canon 204).

Among the Christian faithful the laity are all the faithful except those in holy orders (clergy) and those who belong to a religious state approved by the church (religious). According to Vatican Council II's Decree on the Apostolate of the Laity, the special mission of the laity is to renew the temporal order and to witness to Christ in a special way amid secular affairs.

LAIUS

In Greek mythology, one of the members of the royal house of the Labdacids, kings of Thebes. Laius married Jocasta, daughter of Menoiceus and sister of Creon. Time passed, however, and Laius and Jocasta had no sons. So the king went to the oracle, as was the custom then. The oracle told him that the couple would indeed have a son, but that he would bring great misfortune upon Thebes, killing the king, his father, and marrying his mother.

After this time, Laius kept well away from his wife. But Jocasta wanted a child more than anything else in the world, and so she got Laius drunk at a feast and spent the night with him. As soon as he discovered that the queen was with child, Laius began to think of ways of ridding himself of a baby which was a threat both to him and his country.

As soon as the little boy was born, he pierced the infant's legs at the ankles, passed a chain through the holes and tied his legs together. Then he ordered a faithful shepherd to expose the baby in the forest of Mount Cithairon, where it would die of hunger and cold or might be devoured by some wild beast. But the shepherd took pity on the crying baby and, when some horse traders in the service of King Polybus of Corinth came through the forest, he gave him to them without saying who he belonged to.

The horse traders took the baby to Polybus and his wife, who - childless themselves - were only too glad to look after him. Queen Merope gave the boy the name Oedipus which means "swollen-footed," because his legs had swelled up where Laius had pierced them to put on the chains (see Oedipus).

LAKSANA

In Hindu philosophy, a feature that defines one thing from other things; by extension, the definition itself.

Laksana also refer to the conception common to Hinduism, Buddhism, and Jainism of those characteristics that distinguish the "great man," destined to become either a universal emperor or a great spiritual leader, such as Buddha.

LAKSHMI

Hindu goddess of beauty and fortune. Lakshmi clothed in jewels stands in the trinhanga (three-bending) pose, carrying her symbol - the lotus flower.

LAKSMANA

In Hindu mythology, half-brother of Rama, the incarnation of Visnu. Laksmana followed his brother, Prince Rama, into exile and aided him in his fight against Ravana's demon army.

LAKSMI-NARAYANA

Syncretistic Hindu god, combination of Laksmi (goddess) and Narayana (a form of Visnu).

LALITAVISTARA

A legendary life of the Buddha, apparently a Mahayana tradition recasting of a Sarvastivada work that shows much about the development of the Buddha legend.

LAMA

In Tibetan Buddhism, a spiritual leader. Originally used to translate guru and thus applicable only to heads of monasteries or great teachers, the term is now extended out of courtesy to any respected monk or priest.

LAMAISM

Monastic religion of Tibet, suppressed by the Chinese communists in the 1960s but still found in Bhutan, Sikkim, southern Siberia and

Mongolia. Basically a form of Buddhism, it was influenced by the animist religions of ancient Tibet, where it was first introduced circa 649, and by Tantrism, a mystic Hindu cult. It includes demon worship and is characterized by the chanting of prayers and hymns, the endless recitation of magical formulas, which are often inscribed on walls and prayer wheels, and by the use of drums and long horns. Its name comes from the monks or lamas (superior beings) of Tibet, whose high priest is the Dalai Lama. Second in the hierarchy is the Tashi or Panchen Lama.

Emphasis is placed on an awareness of the essential identity of the human being and the universe, related as microcosm to macrocosm. The scriptural canon of Lamaism assumed its present shape in the 13th and 14th centuries through the work of the scholar Bu-ston (1290-1364.

LAMANITES

According to Mormon belief, a legendary people who were the forefathers of the indigenous Americans. They formed part of an Israelite migration to America led by the prophet Lehi circa 600 BC. A group headed by his son Laman rebelled and became savage wanderers, the ancestors of the Indians.

LAMB

In Israelite religion the lamb appears to have been the dominant sacrificial victim, the sacrifice of which was prescribed for the major feasts (Num. 28:26-27), the daily offerings (Exodus 29:38-42), and other occasions (Leviticus 3:6).

The central symbol and sacrifice in the Passover (Exodus 12:11-12), the lamb also symbolized innocence (2 Sam. 12:3) or evoked sympathy as in the consoling words addressed to exiled Israel (Isaiah 40:11).

LAMB OF GOD

A title given to Jesus in several books of the New Testament (John, Acts, 1 Peter, Revelation) and used in the Christian liturgies. The title evokes the twofold idea of the Servant of Yahweh, who is compared to a lamb (Isaiah 53:7), and the paschal lamb.

LAMBERT, Franz

(1486-1530) Protestant convert from Roman Catholicism and leading reformer in the German province of Hessen. After a meeting with Luther in Wittenburg, he returned to Strasbourg in 1524 to preach Reformation doctrines to the French-speaking population.

LAMBETH QUADRILATERAL

Four points that constitute the basis for union discussions of the Anglican Communion with other Christian groups:
▲ acceptance of Holy scripture as the rule of faith;
▲ the Apostles' and the Nicene creeds;
▲ the sacraments of baptism and the Lord's Supper;
▲ the historic episcopate.

The fourth point, episcopacy (church government based on bishops) has been the principal block to union of Anglican and Protestant churches.

LAMECH

The son of Methushael and a descendant of Cain (Genesis 4:17-18). His lifetime was overlapped by that of Adam. Lamech was the first polygamist of Bible record, having two wives at the same time, Adah and Zillah (Genesis 4:19). By Adah he had sons named Jabal and Jubal (Genesis 4:20-21). By Zillah, Lamech became the father of Tubal-cain.

LAMENNAIS, Robert de

(1782-1854) Priest and philosophical and political writer who attempted to combine political liberalism with Roman Catholicism after the French Revolution.

LAMENTATION

A theme in Christian art showing the Virgin Mary, St. John the Apostle, St. Mary Magdalene, St. Joseph of Arimathea, and other figures mourning over the body of the dead Christ. The subject has no source in the gospels or the Apocrypha; it is an imaginary scene that gained popularity with accounts of the meditations of late medieval mystics of the lives of Christ and the Virgin.

LAMENTATIONS OF JEREMIAH

Old Testament book, consisting of five poems, lamenting the destruction of Jerusalem by the Babylonians (586 BC). The poems, written by Jeremiah, are independent units, but their mood and content provide a unity to the book as a whole. The poet celebrates God's righteousness but bewails the injustice of the nation.

In the first chapter, beginning with verse twelve, Jeremiah personifies Jerusalem, God's covenant "woman" Zin, as speaking. She is now desolate, as though widowed and bereft of her children, a captive woman put into forced labor as a slave.

In chapter two, Jeremiah himself speaks. In chapter three, Jeremiah pours out his feelings, transferring them to the figure of the nation as an "able-bodied man."

In chapter four, Jeremiah continues his lament. In the fifth chapter, the inhabitants of Jerusalem are pictured as speaking. The expressions of acknowledgment of sin, the hope and confidence in God, and the desire to turn to the right way, as portrayed throughout were not the actual feelings of the majority of the people. However, there was a remnant like Jeremiah. So the view expressed in the book of Lamentations is a true evaluation of Jerusalem's situation as God saw it.

LAMPSTAND

In biblical references, the lampstand of the tabernacle and temple (Exodus 25:31-40). A specific Hebrew term, menorah, refers to the lampstand. The menorah became a symbol of Judaism, particularly after the fall of Jerusalem (70); the menorah of Herod's Temple is depicted on the Arch of Titus in Rome. In Revelation 1:12-20 lampstands are symbols of the churches.

LANCE, Liturgical

In the Byzantine rite a small knife which is used to cut the Phosphora (altar bread) into particles for use at the Divine Liturgy. It usually has the shape of a lance in order to recall the instrument used to pierce the side of Jesus on the cross.

LANCE, the Holy

The spear claimed to be that mentioned in John 19:34 which pierced the side of Jesus. According to legend this lance was discovered at the time of the finding of the holy cross. From the sixth century there is ample record of the veneration of such a lance at Jerusalem.

LANDMARKISM

A Baptist movement that stressed the independence of local churches, denied that the New Testament refers to a universal church, and claimed that the Baptist Church is the only true church. The movement originated in the United States in 1850.

LANDO

(837-914) Pope from July/August 913 to early 1914. He reigned during one of the most difficult periods in papal history.

LANG, John Dunmore

(1799-1878) Anti-Catholic Australian ecclesiastic and an anti-convict but eventually radical political leader, founder of the Australian Presbyterian Church, and an influence in shaping early colonial settlement.

LANKAVATARA-SUTRA

A distinctive and influential philosophical discourse in the Mahayana Buddhist tradition that is said to have been preached by the Buddha in Lanka, usually understood as Sri Lanka.

LAN TS'AI-HO

In Chinese mythology, one of the Eight Immortals of Taoism whose true identity is much disputed. He is depicted as a young man invariably carrying a flute, or a pair of clappers and occasionally wearing one shoe. He is one of the several Chinese symbols of immortality.

LAOCOON

In Greek legend, a seer and a priest of the god Apollo.

LAODICEA

A city in the western part of Asia Minor, the ruins of which lie near Denizli, over ninety miles east of Ephesus. Known earlier as Diospolis and Rhoas, Laodicea was probably refounded in the third century BC by the Seleucid. Situated in the fertile valley of the Lycus River, Laodicea lay at the junction of major trade routes and was linked by roads with cities such as Ephesus, Pergamum and Philadelphia.

In the first century AD a Christian congregation existed at Laodicea and apparently met in the home of Nympha, a Christian sister there. The effects of Paul's work at Ephesus likely reached as far as Laodicea (Acts 19:10). Although not ministered there personally, Paul was nevertheless concerned about the Laodicean congregation and even wrote a letter to them.

LAO TSUE

("Old Master") Chinese philosopher, born circa 604 BC, who is generally regarded as the founder of Taoism. His actual existence is uncertain. We know of him through legends and through a history written in the first century BC. According to tradition, he wrote the Tao To Ching, the work on which the Taoist religion is based, and was a librarian at the Chou court.

His teachings (Tao means "The Way") urge man to live in harmony with nature and the universe, without struggle. Good government means letting men live their lives in peace. Everyone should dedicate himself to the service of others.

LAPSED CATHOLICS

Those who, while presumably not rejecting the faith, have fallen away from the practice of their religion, particularly from attendance at Mass and fulfillment of the Easter precept of at least annual reception of the sacraments. The number of non-practicing Catholics, judged on the basis of a drop in Sunday Mass attendance, has increased in the latter part of the 20th century.

LA SALLE, Saint Jean-Baptiste de

(1651-1719) Educator and founder of the Brothers of the Christian Schools, first Roman Catholic congregation of male non-clerics devoted solely to schools, learning, and teaching.

LASHA

A place mentioned in the earliest Canaanite boundary description (Genesis 10:19). Its exact location is uncertain. Many place Lasha near Callirhoe, near the eastern shore of the Dead Sea.

LASSHARON

A royal Canaanite city whose king was defeated by the Israelites under Joshua (Joshua 12:7-18). Lassharon is often linked with the district called Sarona, situated, according to Eusebius, between Mount Tabor and the Sea of Galilee.

LAST DAYS

In Bible prophecy, "last days" or comparable expressions such as "final part of the days" were used to designate a future time (Ezekiel 38:8, 16); Daniel 10:14). The content of the prophecy fixes the starting point of the "final part of the days" when the foretold events begin to occur. Those living at the time of the prophecy's fulfillment could therefore be spoken of as living in the "last days" or the "final part of the days." Depending upon the nature of the prophecy, this may be a period covering just a few years or many centuries and can apply to widely separated time periods.

LAST JUDGMENT

The judgment of all men by God at the end of the world. The dead will be

The Last Supper.
"Therefore, when he was gone out, Jesus said, Now is the Son of man glorified, and God is glorified in him" (John 13:31).
Lithograph by Gustave Doré (about 1860).

raised and, with those then living, assembled before God to be judged by what they have done: the unrighteous thrown into hell with Satan, the righteous admitted to heaven (Matthew 25:31-36).

LAST JUDGMENT

A theme in Christian art illustrating the events surrounding the final judgment of mankind at the end of the world.

LAST SACRAMENTS

The term used to designate those sacraments (penance, anointing of the sick, and the Eucharist as viaticum) which are received by a person near death. The phrase, last rites of the church, is often used equivalently.

Penance and anointing of the sick are administered conditionally if the recipient is unconscious. Included with the administration of the last sacraments is a prayer invoking a plenary indulgence upon the sick person.

The Vatican Council II document *Constitution of the Sacred Liturgy* requires that viaticum be received after penance and the anointing of the sick. Although not generally understood as such, baptism, confirmation, and matrimony can be classified as last sacraments insofar as they may be administered to a person near death, e.g., when a priest witnesses a sacramental marriage to convalidate a civil marriage when one partner is dying.

LAST SUPPER

The final Passover meal held by Jesus and his disciples in Jerusalem before his crucifixion (See also Mark 14:15; Luke 22:12). In it he distributed bread and wine to them, instituting the Christian sacrament of Holy Communion. Leonardo da Vinci's well-known fresco of the Last Supper is in Milan.

According to Catholic teaching, it was this occasion that Jesus instituted the Holy Eucharist and the holy priesthood. The church celebrates the Lord's Supper on Holy Thursday evening.

LAT, al-

Arabian goddess of pre-Islamic times to whom a stone cube at at-Ja'if (near Mecca) was held sacred as part of her cult.

LATERAN

District of south-eastern Rome, name given to the church by Emperor Constantine I in 311. The Lateran Palace - the papal residence until 1309 - was demolished and replaced in the 16th century. The basilica of St. John Lateran is the cathedral church of the pope as bishop of Rome.

The monumental facade (1733-36) by Alessandro Galilei, though related to Maderno's facade at St. Peter's, is more severe, and heavily contrasted between columns, and darkly recessed arcades. San Giovanni in Fonte, the Lateran baptistery, retains its original early Christian character, though restored.

The interior has two concentric naves separated by eight porphyry columns, and supporting an architrave, with an inscription from Sixtus III (fifth century), from which rise smaller columns supporting a cupola.

LATERAN COUNCIL, First (1123)

Ecumenical council of the Roman Catholic Church held in the Lateran Palace in Rome during the reign of Pope Calixtus II. The council promulgated a number of canons (probably 25), many of which merely reiterated decrees of earlier councils.

LATERAN COUNCIL, Second (1139)

Ecumenical council of the Roman Catholic Church held in the Lateran Palace in Rome, convoked by Pope Innocent I to condemn as schismatics the followers of Arnold of Brescia, a vigorous reformer and opponent of the temporal power of the pope, and to end the schism created by the election of Anacletus II, a rival pope.

LATERAN COUNCIL, Third (1179)

Ecumenical council of the Roman Catholic Church held in the Lateran

Palace in Rome convoked by Pope Alexander III, condemning the heretical Cathari (or Albigenses). Christians were authorized to take up arms against vagabond robbers.

LATERAN COUNCIL, Fourth (1215)

Ecumenical council of the Roman Catholic Church held in the Lateran Palace in Rome, convoked by Pope Innocent III, attended by more than 400 bishops, 800 abbots and priors. The primary aims of the council were reform of the church and the recovery of the Holy Land. The council rules on such vexing problems as the use of church property, tithes, judicial procedure, and patriarchal precedence. It ordered Jews and Saracens to wear distinctive dress and obliged Catholics to make a yearly confession and to receive Communion during the Easter season.

LATERAN COUNCIL, Fifth (1512-1517)

Ecumenical council of the Roman Catholic Church held in the Lateran Palace in Rome, convoked by Pope Julius II, restoring peace among warring Christian rulers and sanctioning a new concordat with France. In dogmatic decrees the council affirmed the immortality of the soul end repudiated declarations of the councils of Constance and Basel that made church councils superior to the pope.

LATERAN TREATY

Concordat between the papacy and the government of Italy, signed 1929 in the Lateran palace and confirmed by the 1949 Italian constitution. It established Roman Catholicism as Italy's state religion and Vatican City as an independent sovereign state.

LATIMER, Hugh

(1485-1555) English Protestant who advanced the cause of the Reformation in England through his vigorous preaching and through the inspiration of his martyrdom.

LATIN CHURCH

Part of the Catholic Church that follows the Latin Rite in the liturgy, has its own canon law, and is subject to the bishop of Rome as the patriarch of the West.

LATIN FATHERS

The four great Fathers of the Western church:
▲ Ambrose of Milan;
▲ Augustine of Hippo;
▲ Gregory the Great;
▲ Jerome.
These were the first officially designated Doctors of the church as well by Boniface VIII in 1295. More broadly used to include other premedieval writers, the term would include:
▲ Bede the Venerable;
▲ Cyprian of Carthage;
▲ Hilary of Poitiers,
▲ Isidore of Seville;
▲ Leo I the Great.

LATIN RITE

One of the 18 canonical rites recognized in the Roman Catholic Church - the other 17 are Oriental. Canonical rites means not only the liturgical rite but also the canonical discipline and spiritual heritage of a church. In this canonical sense the Latin Rite coincides with the Latin church.
Liturgically there are other Latin rites besides the Roman; for example, the particular rites of religious orders such as Carthusians, Cistercian, and Dominican.

LATITUDINARIANISM

A word used derisively in the latter part of the 17th century for a school of thought within the Church of England that tended to regard formal expressions of doctrine, worship, or government to be of little importance as compared with man's inner, rational, or mystical experience.

LATREILLE, Pierre-Andre

(1762-1833) Roman Catholic priest, who wrote some important theological treatises, but was also a well-known professor of zoology and a world-renowned entomologist.

LATTER DAY SAINTS, Reorganized Church of Jesus Christ of

Mormon religious group which split from the main body of Mormons after the death of the founder, Joseph Smith, when leadership passed to Brigham Young in 1847. The group chose Joseph Smith III as their leader, a post he held from 1860 to 1914. The group's beliefs are based on the Bible and the Book of Mormon. Community life is an important aspect of the religion. Its headquarters are at Independence, Missouri, and many American members live in the midwest.

LATTER RAIN REVIVAL

Early name for the Pentecostal movement within United States Protestantism. It began in the late 19th and early 20th centuries in Tennessee and North Carolina and took its name from the "latter rain" referred to in Joel 2:23. The Bible passage states that the former (fall) rain and the latter (spring) rain were poured down from God. The latter rain referred to a second period, when people would again receive the Holy Spirit and speak in tongues as a sign that the Second Coming of Christ would soon occur.

LAUDA

Hymn of praise; a type of Italian poetry or nonliturgical devotional song in praise of the Virgin Mary, Christ, or the saints.

LAUDS

In Roman Catholicism, the morning prayer in the office of the Liturgy of the Hours, forming one of the chief or "hinge" hours of each day. Vespers is considered the other hinge hour of prayer.

LAURA

A term that came into use in 4th century Palestinian monasticism to denote a colony of monks who lived in separate huts grouped around a church where they assembled for Divine Liturgy and other services and who were subject to a common spiritual father. This type of monasticism spread into many countries of the East and West.

LAURENTIUS

(445-517) Antipope in 498 and from 501 to 505 whose disputed papal election gave his name to the Laurentian schism, a split in the Roman Catholic Church.

LAURENTIUS OF CANTERBURY, Saint

(547-619) Second archbishop of Canterbury, missionary who pioneered in establishing the Anglo-Saxon church. Like Augustine, Laurentius endured persecution by and hostilities from the Britons while fruitlessly trying to convince the Celtic Christians to obediently follow Roman customs.

LAVABO

Opening word of the psalm that a priest recites when he performs the ritual hand washing in the course of mass.

LAVIGERIE, Charles-Martial-Allemand

(1825-1892) Cardinal and archbishop of Algiers and Carthage whose dream to convert Africa to Christianity prompted him to found the Society of Missionaries of Africa, or White Father. The Society was finally approved by Pope St. Pius in 1908.

LAW

In Christianity, a divine commandment, or a revelation of the will of God; collectively the whole body of God's commandments or revelations; the will of God, whether expressed in scripture, implanted in instinct, or deduced by reason.

As used in Catholic theology, the term "law" is used in several senses, the most important of which are:

▲ eternal law;
▲ natural law;
▲ divine positive law;
▲ ecclesiastical law;
▲ civil law.

LAW, Civil

In Roman Catholicism, usually defined as an ordinance of reason promulgated by authority for the common good; ideally, every civil law should be consistent, just, observable, and useful.

LAW, Divine positive

In Roman Catholicism is the eternal law of God manifested in a fuller and clearer way through divine revelation: through "the law and the prophets" in the Old Testament and "in these final days, he has spoken to us by a Son" (Hebrews 1:2).

LAW, Ecclesiastical

In Roman Catholicism, the norm that governs the church organized as a social and visible structure.

LAW, Eternal

In Roman Catholicism, the plan of divine wisdom as it directs all activity and change toward a final end; the eternal and universal law whereby, in the words of Vatican Council II, "God orders, directs and governs the whole world and the way of the human community according to a plan conceived in his wisdom and love."

LAW, Natural

In Roman Catholicism, that is, the sharing of the rational creature in the eternal law of God, for as Vatican Council II expresses it, "God has enabled man to participate in this law of His so that, under the gentle disposition of divine providence, many may be able to arrive at a deeper and deeper knowledge of unchangeable truth."

LAW, William

(1686-1761) Author of influential works on Christian ethics and mysticism. His chief contribution lies in his delineation of the Christian ethical ideal for human life and its actualization through the disciplined practices of private mysticism. His *Practical Treatise Upon Christian Perfection* (1726) and his *Serious Call to a Devout and Holy Life* (1728), considered his best work, both espouse a mild mysticism within the bounds of the normative Christian tradition.

LAW OF CONSCIENCE

The Bible shows this results from persons having "the law in their hearts." Those not under a direct law of God, such as the Law given through Moses, are shown to be "a law to themselves," for their consciences cause them to be "accused or even excused" in their own thought (Romans 2:14-15). Many just laws in pagan societies reflect this conscience, originally placed in their forefather Adam, and passed down through Noah.

LAW OF FAITH

The "law of faith" is contrasted with "that of works." Man cannot attain the righteousness by his own works or those of the law of Moses, as though earning righteousness as pay for works, but righteousness comes by faith in Jesus Christ (Romans 3:27-28; 9:30-32).

LAW OF GOD

The apostle Paul speaks of the Christian's fight as influenced by two factors, the "law of God," the "law of mind" or the "law of that spirit which gives life" on one side and "sin's law" or the "law of sin and of death" on the other. Paul describes the conflict, saying that fallen flesh infected with sin is enslaved to "sin's law" (Romans 7:21-8:13).

LAW OF MOSES

Although the Bible repeatedly mentions "the law of Moses" (Joshua 8:31-32; Kings 2:3; 2 Chronicles 23:18), it also acknowledges Jehovah as the actual lawgiver, and Moses as only His instrument and representative in giving the Law to Israel (2 Chronicles 34:14).

LAW OF NATURE

In one sense, this is the moral law that is knowable by all humans and that is universally binding. In another sense, this is the law that contains the physical ordering of the universe, such as the law of gravity.

LAW (AL-) AL-MAHFUZ

In Islam, the Preserved Tablet; a tablet in Heaven on which is to be found the original text of the Koran. The Koran itself specifically refers to the Tablet in the 22nd and last verse of the Surat al-Buruj.

LAW TO ADAM

In the garden of Eden, Adam and Eve were commanded by God as to their duties:

1 to fill the earth;
2 to subdue it;
3 to have in subjection all other living creatures of earth, sea and air (Genesis 1:28).

They were given laws as to their diet, granting them the seed-bearing vegetation and fruit as food (Genesis 1:20; 2:16). However, Adam was given a command that prohibited eating from the tree of the knowledge of good and bad (Genesis 2:17); this was transmitted to Eve.

LAWRENCE, Saint

(178-258) One of the most venerated Roman martyrs, celebrated for his Christian valor. He was among the seven deacons serving Pope St. Sixtus II, whose martyrdom preceded Lawrence's by a few days. The Basilica of St. Lorenzo, Rome, was built over his burial place. His feast day is August 10th.

LAWRENCE OF BRINDISI, Saint

(1559-1619) Doctor of the Church and one of the leading polemicists of the Counter-Reformation in Germany. He fought against the rise of German Protestantism and founded Capuchin houses at Madrid and Munich.

LAWS TO NOAH

Noah was given commandments relative to the building of the Ark and the saving of his family (Genesis 6:22).

After the flood he was given laws allowing fish to be added to man's diet; declaring sacredness of life and, therefore, of blood, in which is the life; prohibiting the eating of blood; condemning murder and instituting capital punishment for this crime (Genesis 9:3-6).

LAXISM

A moral system never theoretically proposed as such, but implied in certain solutions of some 17th century moral theologians that went to extremes in favoring the liberty of the individual against any but the most certain demands of law.

LAYING ON OF HANDS

Ritual act first practiced in Judaism and adopted by Christianity. In the Hebrew Bible it is associated with three interrelated ideas:

▲ consecration (i.e., setting apart for the service of God);
▲ transmission of a divine gift;
▲ identification (the means whereby an offerer was linked with the sacrifice.

In the New Testament the same ideas are present.

The early church continued these uses and added two more: the laying on of hands for the blessing of the catechumens (i.e., those preparing for baptism) and for the reconciliation of penitents and heretics. In the New Testament it is a gesture of blessing (Mark 10:16) or of healing (Matthew 9:18); it is also used as a sign of the Holy Spirit's being received (Acts 8:15-17), or of conferring a special mission (Acts 6:1-6).

In the Roman Catholic Church the laying on of hands by the bishop is an essential part of the sacrament of holy orders to symbolize the reception of the Holy Spirit.

The raising of the confessor's hand before the imparting of absolution is also a trace of the laying on of hands as a symbol of reconciliation. Outside of the ritual of the sacrament, it is part of the blessing of monks, and abbots, and of the consecration of virgins.

LAYL, al-

The title of the 92nd sura of the Koran; it means "The Night." The sura belongs to the Meccan period and has 21 verses. Its title is drawn from the reference to the night in the first verse. Its title begins with three distinct formal oaths: By the night, by the day and by God himself, the Creator. It goes on to promise a happy end to the generous and pious man but the opposite to the miser. Riches will not help the latter when he dies. The sura is particularly significant as it stresses the doctrine that it is good deeds and good faith which will bring a person to Paradise.

LAYLAT AL-MI'RAJ

In Islam, the Night of the Ascension (of the Prophet Mohammed). A popular festival celebrates this event on the 27th of the Muslim month of Rajab.

LAYLAT AL-QADR

In Islam, the Night of Power (or Decree) which is believed to be the night between the 26th and 27th of Ramadan, or the 27th night. The Night has a very special significance in the Muslim calendar because it is the anniversary of that night when the Koran was first revealed to the Prophet Mohammed. In Surat al-Qadr, this Night is described as "better than 1000 months." Tradition holds that requests made to God during Laylat al-Qadr will be granted.

LAZA

In Islam, literally "flame," "blazing fire." Laza is one of the seven ranks of hell to which tradition later consigned the Christians. The word only occurs once in the Koran in Surat al-Ma'arij. Here in verse 15, Laza is described as a great furnace which will burn off the sinner's scalp and swallow up the miser and those who turned their backs on the truth.

LAZARUS

The story of Lazarus is known from the gospel according to John (11:44-46). Lazarus was the brother of Martha and Mary and lived at Bethany, near Jerusalem. When Lazarus died, he was raised by Jesus from the dead after he had been entombed for four days. By this, many Jews came to believe in Jesus as the Messiah.

Lazarus is also the name given by Luke (16) to the beggar in the parable of the rich man and Lazarus. It is the only proper name attached to a character in the parables of Jesus.

LAZARUS, Moritz

(1824-1903) Jewish philosopher and psychologist, a leading opponent of anti-Semitism in his time. The fundamental principle of Lazarus' philosophy stated that truth must be sought not in metaphysical or a priori abstraction but in psychological investigation and, further, that his investigation cannot confine itself successfully to the individual consciousness but must be devoted primarily to society as a whole.

LEAH

In the Old Testament, first wife of Jacob (later Israel) and the ancestor of five of the 12 tribes of Israel. Leah was the mother of six of Jacob's sons and one daughter; the sons were: Reuben, Simeon, Levi, Issachar, Zebulun, and Judah; Judah was the ancestor of King David and of Jesus. The daughter was named Dinah (Genesis 29:32-35).

Leah and her children accompanied Jacob when he left Paddan-aran and returned to Canaan, the land of his birth (Genesis 31:11-18). Before Jacob met Esau en route, he protectively divided off the children to Leah and to Rachel and their maidservants, putting the maidservants and their children foremost, followed by Leah and her children, with Rachel and Joseph to their rear (Genesis 33:1-7).

Leah's children accompanied Jacob into Egypt, but the Bible account does not say that she did so (Genesis 46:15). The time, place and circumstances of her death are not furnished, but she may have died in Canaan. Whatever the case, the patriarch had her body taken to the family burial place, the cave in the field of Machpelah. Jacob's instructions respecting his own remains show that it was his desire to be buried where Abraham and Sarah, Isaac and Rebekah, and Leah had been buried (Genesis 49:29-32).

LEAP OF FAITH
Metaphor used by the 19th century Danish philosopher Kierkegaard to describe commitment to an objective uncertainty, specifically to the Christian God.

LEBANAH
In the Old Testament, founder of a family whose sons or descendants were among the Nethinim returning with Zerubbabel from Babylonian exile (Ezra 2:1-2; Nehemiah 7:46-18).

LECTIONARY
In Christianity, a book containing portions of the Bible appointed to be read on particular days in the year. In the Roman Catholic Church, it contains a three-year cycle of scripture readings for Sundays and solemn feasts, a two-year weekday cycle, a one-year cycle for the feasts of saints, and readings for ritual Masses and Masses for particular intentions.

LECTISTERNIUM
Ancient Greek and Roman rite consisting of a meal offered to gods and goddesses whose representations were laid upon a couch or pulvinar in the attitude or reclining.

LEDA
In Greek legend, usually believed to be the daughter of Thestius, king of Aetolia, and wife of Tyndareus, king of Lacedaemon. She was also believed to be the mother of Zeus.

LEGATE, Bartholomew
(1575-1612) English religious fanatic and preacher in a sect called the Seekers. Found guilty of heresy in 1612, he was burned at the stake.

LEGATE, Papal
In the Roman Catholic Church, a cleric sent on a mission, ecclesiastical or diplomatic, by the pope as his personal representative.

LEHABIM
A name appearing in the Bible at Genesis 10:13 and 1 Chronicles 1:11 among the descendants of Ham through Mizraim. Since the Hebrew name is a plural form, many scholars hold that a tribe taking its name from one of Mizraim's sons is generally identified with the Libyans and at least seems to have constituted one of the tribes inhabiting Libya in ancient times.

LEHI
The scene of one or, possibly, two Israelite victories over the Philistines. At Lehi, Samson struck down a 1,000 Philistines with the jawbone of an ass. Subsequently he called the state Ramath-lehi ("the lofty place of the jawbone"), probably to memorize the victory Jehovah had given him there (Judges 15:9-19). Originally, though, Lehi may have gotten its name from the shape of its crags.

LEIB-OLMAI
A Lapp forest deity considered the guardian of wild animals, especially bears.

LEIGHTON, Robert
(1611-1684) Scottish Presbyterian minister and devotional writer who attempted to reconcile proponents of the Presbyterian form of church government with their episcopal opponents.

LELEK
Originally associated with breath or the life principle, which was manifested in the form of vapor. Lelek belongs to a family of nondetachable Finno-Ugaric souls closely associated with the body as a living entity, the loss of which meant death.

LE MAISTRE DE SACY, Isaac-Louis

(1613-1684) French Jansenist theologian, a spiritual director of the celebrated Jansenist abbey of Port-Royal. He was the principal author of the translation of the New Testament.

LEMUEL

In the Old Testament, an unidentified king of ancient times whose words are recorded in Proverbs (Chapter 31). His identity has been the subject of considerable discussion, some commentators suggesting that Lemuel was another name for Solomon. The words of King Lemuel constitute "the weighty message that his mother gave to him in correction" (Proverbs 31:1).

LENITY

A quality of the virtue of clemency; mildness of spirit that inclines to tempering the redress of grievances or the infliction of punishment. This quality may apply either in the case of a judge's passion sentence, or of a private person's redressing a wrong done him or her. In either case, as belongs to virtue, lenient mitigation still observes the requirements of what is right, but in the given circumstances rightly forgoes severity.

LENT

In the Christian church, a period of penitential preparation for Easter. In the Western church it begins on Ash Wednesday, six and a half weeks before Easter, and provided for a 40-day fast, in imitation of Christ's fasting in the wilderness. In the Eastern church it begins eight weeks before Easter.

LEO I, Saint

(400-461) Also called "The Great." Pope from 440 to 461 who suppressed heresy and established his authority in both the West and East. He persuaded the barbarian leaders Atilla (in 452) and Genseric (in 455) not to destroy Rome.

LEO II, Saint

(609-683) Pope from 681 to 683. He ratified the decision of the sixth ecumenical Council of Constantinople (Istanbul, 68) to condemn Monothelitism, a heresy concerning the will of Christ, as well as the conciliatory policies of Pope Honorius I.

LEO III, Saint

(751-816) Pope from 795-816. He crowned Charlemagne "Emperor of the Romans" in Rome on Christmas Day, 800, thus allying church and state. While the relations between Pope and Emperor were relatively amiable, Charlemagne controlled imperial administration and ecclesiastical reform. Upon Charlemagne's death in 814, the hatred of the Roman nobility against Leo reasserted itself. He had some conspirators executed and submitted an account of his action to Louis, who had succeeded his father. Leo died soon afterward.

LEO IV, Saint

(1777-855) Pope from 847 to 855. A Benedictine monk, he took a firm hand against abuses by important ecclesiastics. He censured the powerful archbishop Hincmar for excommunicating an imperial vassal without papal approval.

LEO V

(840-903) Pope from July to September 903. Elected while a priest to succeed Pope Benedict IV, Leo's pontificate occurred in the darkest period of papal history. He was deposed and murdered, presumably strangled, by the antipope Christopher, who was, in turn, executed by Pope Sergius III in 904.

LEO V THE ARMENIAN

(756-820) Byzantine emperor responsible for inaugurating the second iconoclastic period in the Byzantine empire. In 815 Leo deposed the Orthodox patriarch Nicephorus and convoked a synod for the same year that reimposed the decrees of the iconoclast synod of Hieria of 754, which had opposed the religious use of images (icons).

LEO VI

(850-928) Pope from May to December 928. He was elected by the senatrix Marozia, then head of the powerful Roman Crescentii family, who deposed and imprisoned Leo's predecessor, Pope John X. His principal act was the regulation of the jurisdiction of the hierarchy in Dalmatia.

LEO VII

(871-939) Pope from 936 to 939. He encouraged reform of the German clergy and forbade archbishop Frederick of Mains to enforce the conversion of Jews to Christianity.

LEO VIII

(901-965) Pope from 963 to 965. He was a layman and some scholars regard Leo as an antipope until after emperor Otto compelled his acceptance.

LEO IX, Saint

(1002-1054) Bruno of Egisheim; head of the medieval Latin church (1049-1054), during whose reign the papacy became the focal point of western Europe, and the great East-West Schism of 1054 became inevitable.

LEO X, Saint

(1475-1521) Giovanni de Medici; pope from 1513-21, who made Rome a center of the arts and literature and raised money for rebuilding St. Peter's by the sale of indulgences - a practice attacked by Martin Luther at the start of the Reformation.

He was one of the most extravagant of the Renaissance popes, who made Rome a center of European culture but depleted the papal treasury and by his response to the developing Lutheran movement, contributed to the dissolution of the unified Western church.

LEO XI

(1535-1605) Alessandro Ottaviano de Medici; pope in April 1605. Elected to succeed Clement VIII on April 1, 1605, he died within the month.

LEO XII

(1760-1829) Annibale Sermattei della Genga; pope from 1823 to 1829. Although he reduced expenditure, thus reducing taxation, the precarious economic situation remained unchanged. In doctrinal matters, Leo strove to prevent the infiltration of liberal ideas and to strengthen the efficiency of the Inquisition.

LEO XIII

(1810-1903) Gioacchino Pecci; pope from 1878-1903. He worked to reconcile Roman Catholicism with science and liberalism and generally applied Christian principles to the religious and social questions of his time. His *Rerum Novarum* on the condition of the working class, strengthened Roman Catholicism's link with the working-class movement and helped counter anticlericalism at home and abroad.

LEONTIUS OF BYZANTIUM

(485-543) Byzantine monk and theologian who provided a breakthrough of terminology in the 6th century Christological controversy over the mode of union of Christ's human nature with his divinity. He did so through his introduction of Aristotelian logical categories and Neoplatonic psychology into Christian speculative theology. His work initiated the later intellectual development of Christian theology throughout medieval culture.

LEPANTO, Battle of

Naval engagement (October 1571) between the allied Christian forces and the Ottoman Turks during an Ottoman campaign to acquire the Venetian island of Cyprus. The Venetians had formed an alliance with Pope Pius V.

LESHY

In Slavic mythology, the forest spirit; a sportive spirit who enjoys playing tricks on men, though when angered he can be treacherous.

LETHE

In Greek mythology, daughter of Eris. It is also the name of a water or plain in the infernal regions. Orphism, an ancient Greek mystical religious movement, distinguished a spring of memory (Mnemosyne) and one of oblivion (Lethe).

LETTERS

The writing and sending of letters, either of an official, a business or a personal nature, was a widely used means of communication in ancient times (2 Samuel 11:14; 2 Kings 5:5-7; 10:1-2; 2 Chronicles 30:1; Ezra 4:7; Isaiah 37:14; Jeremiah 29:1; Acts 9:1-2). Confidential letters were usually sealed (1 Kings 21:8).

Letter writing was often done by professional scribes. As in the Persian court, such scribes were usually on hand to take down official government correspondence (Esther 8:9; Ezra 30:6). Scribes were also to be found in the marketplaces near city gates, where they could be engaged by the populace to write letters to record business transactions.

In the first century AD, letters from Paul, James, Peter, John, Jude and the governing body in Jerusalem contributed to the growth and preservation of the unity and cleanness of the Christian congregation (Acts 15:22-31; 2 Corinthians 7:8-9; 10:8-11).

LETTERS (NEW TESTAMENT)

The letters or epistles form a large part of the New Testament. These letters are commonly divided into two general categories: the Pauline letters and the Catholic letters.

The Pauline letters were written by St. Paul himself or by his disciples; they were written not long after the death and resurrection of Christ (roughly between 54 and 80), they are rich first-hand sources of the development of Christian theology and practice. Included in the Pauline Letters are:

▲ Romans,
▲ 1 Corinthians,
▲ 2 Corinthians,
▲ Galatians,
▲ Ephesians,
▲ Philippians,
▲ Colossians,
▲ 1 Thessalonians,
▲ 2 Thessalonians,
▲ 1 Timothy,
▲ 2 Timothy,
▲ Titus,
▲ Philemon.

The letter to the Hebrews is by an unknown author.

The Catholic letters (so named because they were thought to be addressed not so much to particular communities but to a more general or universal audience) were written by various authors from approximately 65 to approximately 95.

Included in the Catholic letters are:

▲ James,
▲ 1 Peter,
▲ 2 Peter,
▲ 1 John,
▲ 2 John,
▲ 3 John,
▲ Jude,
▲ Revelation.

LETUSHIM

In the Old Testament, a name appearing among the descendants of Abraham through Dedan, one of his sons by Keturah (Genesis 25:1-3). Many scholars believe that a tribe or people is meant. In view of their relationship to Dedan, this tribe is likely located in the Arabian Peninsula, but precise identification is impossible.

LEUCOTHEA

In Greek mythology, a sea goddess customarily identified with Ino, daughter of the Phoenician Cadmus.

LEUMMIM

In the Old Testament, a name appearing among the descendants of Abraham through Dedan, one of his sons by Keturah (Genesis 25:1-3). Many scholars believe that a tribe or people is meant. In view of their relationship to Dedan, this tribe is likely located in the Arabian Peninsula, but precise identification is impossible.

LEVELERS

A religious, political party of Puritans. The name, applied from 1647, was intended as a term of derision. The Levelers sought to abolish the monarchy, all class privileges, and any established church and to create a democratic republic with complete political and religious equality for all. In 1649 Oliver Cromwell took strong measures against the movement; the Levelers had disappeared by 1660. Their ideas influenced Quaker emphasis on human equality

LEVI

Jacob's third son by his wife Leah, born in Paddan-aram (Genesis 35:23-26). At his birth Leah said: "Now this time my husband will join himself to me, because I have born him three sons." The boy was therefore called Levi, the meaning of this name evidently being linked with Leah's hope for a new bond or affection between her and Jacob (Genesis 29:34). Levi became the father of Gershom, Kohath and Merari, founders of the three principal divisions of the Levites (Genesis 46:11; 1 Chronicles 6:1).

LEVIATHAN

In the Bible, the name of a primordial monster or, as in the book of Job, a sea monster, perhaps a whale.

LEVITA, Elijah

(1469-1549) Grammarian whose writings and teaching furthered the study of Hebrew in European Christendom at a time of widespread hostility toward the Jews.

LEVITATION

Rising of a human body in the air, apparently defying gravity. Levitation of witches and of spiritualist mediums is called transvection. The levitation of saints is usually static whereas that of witches has the dynamic purpose of transportation. Theological debate raged long over whether transvection was illusion or fact, but levitation has been subject to less controversy.

LEVITE

Member of the tribe of Levi. It is also the title of the portion of the tribe which was set apart for religious service. The functions of the tribe of Levi was to preserve the law of God and to transmit it to posterity (Deuteronomy 17:18). They were not given land when Canaan was divided, but were allotted revenues from certain towns.

LEVITICUS

Third book of the Bible, the name of which designates its contents as a book (or manual) primarily concerned with the priests and their duties. Some topics are ceremonial purity, the people's holiness and offerings. The rules should help the people to be holy (11:45). In principle, Leviticus is a collection of religious and moral laws concerning sacrifices, the installation of priests, the ritual of the Day of Atonement, Yom Kippur and the basic moral instructions sometimes called "the Holiness Code."

Not a very long period is covered by the book of Leviticus, most of it being devoted to listing God's ordinances rather than recounting various happenings over an extended period of time. Thus not more than a month can be covered by the events given in the book.

The tabernacle erection on the first day of the first month in the second year of Israel's departure from Egypt is mentioned in the final chapter of Exodus, the book preceding Leviticus (Exodus 40:17). Then, the book of Numbers (immediately following the Leviticus account) in its first verses (1:1-3) begins with God's command to take a census, stated to Moses "on the first of the second month in the second year of their coming out of the land of Egypt."

LIANG SHU-MING

(1893-1980) Neo-Confucian philosopher who attempted to demonstrate the relevance of Confucianism to China's problems in the 20th century. A believer in the unity of thought and action, Liang became a leader in an attempt at peasant organization.

LI AO

(767-844) Scholar and official who helped re-establish Confucianism at a time when it was being severely challenged by Buddhism and Taoism.

LIBATION

A sacrificial offering made to the gods or to the dead by the pouring out wholly or in part of some liquid such as wine, milk, honey, oil, or a mixture of these. A libation could be of a private or of a public character; it could be employed alone or in conjunction with other sacrifices; it could be used to solemnize an oath, to seal a treaty, or simply as an offering at the beginning of a meal.

LIBELLATICI

A term used to describe those Christians who, during the persecution of Decius (249-251), used a questionable strategy to evade the penalties imposed by the imperial government on those who refused to offer sacrifice or to give other indication of their adherence to the pagan gods and their loyalty to the emperor.

They used bribery to obtain from local officials certificates (libelli) falsely testifying that they had offered sacrifice. After the persecution church authorities condemned the subterfuge, but with less severity than the apostasy of those who had offered the required sacrifice.

LIBERAL CATHOLIC CHURCH

A sect that combines theosophy, Roman Catholic sacraments, and freedom of belief and interpretation. churches were established in the beginning of the 20th century in England and the United States. The church headquarters are in London.

LIBERALISM, theological

A form of religious thought that establishes religious inquiry on the basis of a norm other than the authority of tradition. It was an important influence in Protestantism from about the mid-17th century through the 1920s.

LIBER AND LIBERA

In Roman Religion, a pair of deities of uncertain origin. Liber came to be identified with Dionysus. Liber and Libera (his female counterpart) formed a triad with Ceres.

LIBERTAS

In Roman religion, personification of liberty and personal freedom. Libertas was given a temple on the Aventine Hill about 238 BC; later, two other temples were built for her, and a statue of Libertas was set up in the Forum.

LIBNAH

In the Old Testament, a royal Canaanite city taken by Joshua before the conquest of Lachish (Joshua 10:29-32). Libnah was one of cities in the territory of Judah given to the sons of Aaron (Joshua 15:21; 21:13).

LIBNI

A grandson of Levi and the son of Gershom (Exodus 6:17; 1 Chronicles 6:17). He was the founder of a Levitical family (Numbers 3:18-21) and was evidently also called Ladan (1 Chronicles 23:6-7).

LI CHI

One of the Five Classics of Chinese Confucian literature, the original text of which is said to have been compiled by Confucius (551-479 BC). In general, Li Chi, underscores moral principles in its treatment of such subjects as royal regulations, development of rites, ritual objects and sacrifices, education, music, the behavior of scholars, and the doctrine of the mean.

LIEH-TZU

(circa 4th century BC) One of the three primary philosophers who developed the basic suppositions of Taoist thought and the presumed author of the Taoist work Lieh-tzu.

LIFE PHILOSOPHIES

A term sometimes used to designate the thought of several French, German, and English philosophers who emphasized a surging vibrant principle of life that abstract concepts, scientific theories, and metaphysics tend to belie and ignore. Their biological explanation of life tends toward vitalism, an alternative to materialism and organicism that holds for a substantial entity present in living things, fundamentally distinguishing it from inanimate things. Henri Bergson and Hans Driesch are the most explicitly vitalistic of these philosophers.

LIGASARIRA

Hindu philosophical conception of transmigration, part of the body complex that accompanies the body soul from life to life. Ligasarira comprises the higher psychophysical organs of:
▲ buddhi ("consciouness");
▲ ahamkara ("organ of subjectification");
▲ manas ("mental coordinating organ of sense impressions");
▲ prana ("breath, vitality").

LIKHI

In the Old Testament, a man of the tribe of Manasseh who is named third in the list of Shemida's sons (1 Chronicles 7:19).

LINUS

A Christian in Rome named by the apostle Paul as sending greetings to Timothy (2 Timothy 4:21). Irenaeus (born circa 130) and others after him have identified this Linus with an early overseer of Rome who bore the same name, but this identification rests merely on tradition.

LION'S PIT

In the Bible, the place of execution into which the prophet Daniel was thrown but from which he was later removed unharmed, having enjoyed angelic protection (Daniel 6:7-13). This pit had an opening that could be covered with a stone (Daniel 6:17). It was evidently a sunken or underground place, for Daniel was "lifted up and out of the pit" (Daniel 6:23).

LITANY

From the Greek word meaning "supplication," a litany is a form of prayer in which a person makes fixed responses to a series of petitions. Examples of litanies are the Litany of the Saints and the Litany of the Precious Blood.

The term also refers to a procession with accompanying petition, e.g., the Greater Litanies of April 25 and the Lesser Litanies on the 3 days before the Ascension. As a prayer form, the litany is known in most religions. The psalms contain several litanies, e.g., Psalm 135.

The early Christian church seems to have employed a litany with the response Kyrie eleison (Lord have mercy) which was incorporated into the Mass and subsequently shortened to the response alone. In the Eastern liturgies, this response occurs very frequently.

LITERAL INTERPRETATION, Biblical

A hermeneutical (interpretive) principle and method employed to arrive at the simple, primary meaning of a biblical text intended by the original author.

LITERARY CRITICISM, Biblical

The study of the Bible that is concerned with the historical circumstances out of which the biblical books developed (their authorship, the sources used, the date and place of origin, the purpose of their composition) and the literary form, or genres, in which they were written.

LITTLE BROTHERS OF JESUS

Roman Catholic religious congregation inspired by the example of Charles-Eugene de Foucauld, a French military officer and explorer who experienced a religious conversion in 1886, while serving in Morocco, and later lived as a hermit among the Tuareg tribesmen.

The congregation was founded in 1933 in south Oran, Algiers. The congregation lived in small groups in ordinary dwellings among the poor laboring classes. In the early 1990s there were circa 300 Little Brothers.

LITTLE SISTERS OF JESUS

Roman Catholic religious congregation inspired by the example of Charles-Eugene de Foucauld, a French military officer and explorer who experienced a religious conversion in 1886, while serving in Morocco, and later lived as a hermit among the Tuareg tribesmen.

The Congregation was founded in 1939 at Touggourt, Algiers. They earn their living by manual labor in the same type of jobs their neighbors hold. Their hope is that their presence among the people will influence the acceptance of Christianity. In the early 1990s there were circa 900 Little Sisters.

LITURGICAL ART

Images, signs, and symbols created for the purpose of giving glory to God.

LITURGICAL BOOKS, Roman Catholic

The official books used in liturgical services conducted in accordance with the Roman Rite. Such books may be published only by the authority of the Holy see or by competent or local authority with the approval of the Holy see. The general revision of service books was entrusted to the Concilium established by Paul VI in 1964 to implement the liturgical reform pre-scribed by Vatican Council II.

LITURGICAL MOVEMENT, Protestant

Many Protestant Christians are striving to bring about the corporate worship of their respective communities in which a way in which there is active, intelligent, and salutary worship by all present.

The response of the various Protestant churches to the liturgical movement depends upon their historical back-ground and theological emphasis. Although the reformers reacted against the abuses of the Middle Ages, they also accepted some of its presupposi-tions. One of these presuppositions was the dominant and almost exclusive role played by the minister in the worship service.

The liturgical movement therefore has attempted to reinstate the active role of the faithful. The roots of this move-ment are the historicism and romanti-cism that developed in the mid-19th century.

The Anglican Oxford movement with its emphasis on the sacraments, Eucharist, ceremony and chant pro-duced scholars and prayer books. The Lutherans lead by Wilhelm Loehe (1808-72) and Theodor Kliefoth (1810-95) paved the way for the revision of the Common Service.

The Reformed churches' recognition of the values of the liturgical movement came through the formation of the Church Service Society (1865) and produced the Book of Common Order (1928), with its subsequent revisions. These standardized liturgies have influ-enced the prayer forms of the free churches. Slowly but surely those with a less structured liturgy have adopted some of the recent structures.

The principal agent for the promotion of liturgical reform has been the ecu-menical movement, which has had to face the major problems separating Christians. The agreement among bib-lical theologians and exegetes regard-ing the meaning of worship in the New Testament has laid the basis for the introduction of newer communal forms of worship into the Protestant church-es. In many communions the present is a period of liturgical experimentation.

LITURGICAL MOVEMENT, Roman Catholic

A movement in Roman Catholicism from the early 1900s to encourage congregational participation in the mass, after a long period during which passivity or engagement in individual devotions has been customary. Results include; more frequent communion; simplified services; and translation of the mass out of Latin, especially since the Second Vatican Council (1963).

LITURGICAL RENEWAL

This can be defined as the contemporary movement toward a revivifying reform in the Roman Catholic Church's liturgical life. Liturgical renewal in the late 20th century is the heir and successor of periodic reform movements in the history of the church and of many more recent prophetic pioneers.

Because the liturgy is the chief realization and actualization of the church, any effort to return to the sources, to purify the church's life, to achieve a kind of rejuvenation must deal with the liturgy.

This is true of church reform movements since the fourth century, including the extensive reformation, advanced, recognized, and approved by Vatican Council II. The Constitution on the Sacred Liturgy was the first of that Council's teaching documents and was clearly influential in its subsequent work. That document teaches that liturgical renewal must be a permanent and constant part of the church's work, because as man and society change the liturgy must adapt itself to them, must be able to speak to them and for them.

The ideal of a changeless liturgy, which had gained some currency in the churches in communion with Rome during the rigid post Reformation centuries, was exposed in the council's teaching as indefensible both theologically and historically.

But, because of those centuries, the early stages of liturgical renewal are a somewhat complicated and multi-levelled process. Tradition is an important factor in liturgy, so the most authentic tradition must be ascertained. This is a kind of purification, a clearing away of historical accidents, so that the genuine development and structure of each rite can be seen clearly. The beginnings of this century's renewal under Pius X and Pius XII involved this kind of activity, and Vatican Council II mandated the same restoration for all liturgical rites, a work carried in by the postconciliar liturgical commission in Vatican City.

Another part of the process of renewal is the practical pastoral work for adult education and total community involvement in the liturgy. Because of the communal and hierarchic nature of liturgy, everyone present in a liturgical assembly is an actor - each with his own role - and there is no audience.

A liturgical tradition in the West which has ignored the fact adds a special urgency to the educational effort and to the work of solidity for everyone's active engagement and participation in liturgical celebrations.

LITURGICAL RITES

Liturgical rites are those fixed patterns of ceremonial movement, and verbal formulas which have been fixed by law and tradition and are expressive of Christianity as it exists in specific areas of the world.

The two great families of liturgical rites in the church are Eastern and Western rites. For the first four centuries the rituals of these respective liturgies were not as detailed as they are today. In the fourth century, because of Arianism, apocryphal literature, and the ignorance of many clerics, the ritual became more uniform. Liturgical books evolved, along with standardized forms of celebration which centered around the local metropolitan and patriarchal see.

Eastern Liturgical Rites

In the East are the Syrian liturgies of West and East Syria. The East Syrian centers around Edessa. It is Semitic in tone and survives in the liturgies of the Nestorians, Chaldeans, and Malabar Christians of India.

The West Syrian liturgies evolved from the liturgies of Jerusalem and the primitive rite of Antioch. The result was the so-called liturgy of St. James, which survives among the Jacobites, Melchites, and Maronites. In Vigils, singing, and magnificent processions are some of its outstanding characteristics.

The Byzantine rite, whose center is Constantinople, received its primary liturgical impetus from Antioch in the fourth century. By the ninth century, it was the rite used throughout the Eastern Empire. The tradition of Alexandria, the rival of Antioch, is still found in the Coptic and Ethiopian rites.

Western Liturgical Rites

The Western rites are generally divided into two principal families: the Gallican and Roman. The origin of the Gallican rites is disputed; four general types can be enumerated:

▲ Old Spanish (Mozarabic);
▲ Celtic of Ireland and Scotland;
▲ Milanese;
▲ Gallican properly so called, which emerged with the Roman Rite at the time of Charlemagne.

The Roman Rite's origin is also difficult to ascertain. But the essential formularies of the rite were developed by the fifth, or at the latest, the seventh century. The present Roman Rite is an amalgam of Gallican, Eastern, and Roman traditions.

LITURGICAL YEAR

The Western liturgical year begins with four Sundays (Sabbaths) of Advent, which prepare for Jesus Christ's coming at Christmas.

Advent is followed by Epiphany, celebrating his revelation to the gentiles. Several weeks later, Ash Wednesday introduces the 40 days of fasting in Lent. This leads to Good Friday (commemorating Jesus' crucifixion) and Easter Sunday (celebrating his resurrection).

Five Sundays then lead to Ascension Day (commemorating Jesus' reception into heaven). Next comes White Sunday (Pentecost, the day of the reception of the Holy Spirit by the Apostles) and the following Sunday celebrates the Trinity.

The liturgical year of the Orthodox churches has certain differences, i.e., it begins on September 1; Epiphany commemorated the Baptism of Jesus and Pentecost is the feast of the Holy trinity as well as the descent of the Holy Spirit.

LITURGY

Originally liturgy in the Greek-speaking world referred to a voluntary work done for the people such as a play, road building, or the outfitting of warships. In the Greek Septuagint the term generally refers to priestly worship in the temple services.

The New Testament seldom uses the term, and when used it generally refers to Old Testament practice. The usage of the early fathers and that of the New Testament, where the context is properly Christian, would describe the liturgy as a service of worship where each member of the Christian community according to his role offers to God within and on behalf of the community. The word vanished from use in the West. The Renaissance saw the reappearance of the word, which now was used to describe the church's worship. The term usually conveys the meaning of public worship performed in a place that serves as a church according to the circumstances of time and place.

Liturgy has the characteristics of being:

▲ Christian, for the ability to function in the liturgy is founded upon one's baptism;
▲ hierarchical, because according to one's sacramental character he or she performs a work for the community;
▲ communal, because it is a public ecclesial act;
▲ sanctifying, because it is a means of being caught up into Christ's paschal mystery;
▲ didactic, because it is expressive of and speaks to the faith of those celebrating.

In Roman Catholicism, liturgy is the whole of the public worship of the church, including the celebration of the sacrament and sacrifice of the Eucharist, the celebration of the other sacraments, and the Liturgy of the Hours and the Divine office, which is a set form of hymns, psalms, readings, and prayers recited at particular times of the day. Vatican Council II, in its Constitution on the Sacred Liturgy, teaches that: ".... it is through the liturgy, especially the divine Eucharistic sacrifice, that the work of redemption is exercised. The Liturgy is thus the outstanding means by which the faithful can express in their lives, and manifest to others, the mystery of Christ and the real nature of the true church."

LITURGY OF THE EUCHARIST

One of the major parts of the Roman Catholic Mass. This liturgy focuses on the central act of sacrifice in the consecration and on the Eucharistic banquet in Holy Communion. The Liturgy of the Eucharist begins with the presentation of the gifts of bread and wine and prayers of offering by the priest; then follows the Eucharistic Prayer or Canon, the central portion of which is the act of consecration by which the bread and wine are changed into the Body and Blood of Christ.

LITURGY OF THE WORD

One of the major parts of the Roman Catholic Mass. This liturgy features the proclamation of the Word of God; on Sundays and other feasts there are three readings (usually including a first reading from the Old Testament, a second reading from the New Testament, and the third reading from one of the gospels); on other days there are two readings, the final one is always from one of the gospels. Between the readings is a responsorial psalm, and an acclamation is sung before the reading of the gospel.

After the scripture readings there is a homily on the scriptural and liturgical theme of the Mass with an application to one's Christian life; then follows the Creed on Sundays and other feasts, after which come the general intercessions or prayers of the faithful.

LIUDGER, Saint

(744-809) Frisian who preached Christianity among his own people and was afterward active in ecclesiastical organizations in Saxony.

LIVING BUDDHA

A misnomer for a class of Tibetan Lamas known as Tulkus, who are given the high title of Rimpoche ("Precious One"). They are not Buddhas, or necessarily of high spiritual attainment in their own right, but are used, or overshadowed by, and in some cases incarnations of some spiritual entity which in the same way used a previous holder of the office in question, such as the abbot of a monastery. The Dalai Lama and the Panchen Lama are the best known examples of the practice, which is not confined to Tibetan Buddhism.

LLYR, Children of

In Celtic mythology, a family of gods in constant conflict with the Children of Don. In Welsh tradition, Llyr and his son Manawydan, were associated with the sea, though myths about them differed.

LO-AMMI

In the Bible, the name of the second son borne by Hosea's wife Gomer. God commanded that the child be given this meaningful name (meaning "not my people") to show that he had disowned faithless Israel (Hosea 1:8-9). It has been suggested that this boy was not Hosea's offspring but a child of Gomer's adultery (Hosea 1:2).

LOD

In biblical times, a city with dependent towns built either by the Benjaminite Elpaal or his "son" Shemed (1 Chronicles 8:1, 12). After the Israelites returned from Babylonian exile Lod was one of their most westerly settlements (Ezra 2:22; Nehemiah 7:37; 11:35). It is thought to be the same as Lydda, where Peter healed Aeneas (Acts 9:32-38).

Its location anciently placed the city at the intersection of what is considered to have been the principal route between Egypt and Babylon and the main road from Joppa to Jerusalem.

LOIS

In the Bible, Timothy's grandmother and apparently the parent of his mother Eunice. That she was not Timothy's grandmother is indicated by the Syriac rendering "thy mother's mother." Lois is commended by Paul, who indicated that she was a Christian woman having "faith without hypocrisy" (2 Timothy 1:5).

LOISY, Alfred Firmin

(1857-1940) Biblical scholar and philosopher of religion, generally considered the father of Modernism, a movement within the Roman Catholic Church aimed at revising its dogma relative to revolutionary advances in science and philosophy.

LOKA

In Hindu philosophy, the universe or any particular division of it. The most common division of the universe is the tri-loka, or three worlds; heaven, earth, atmosphere.

LOKAKASA

In Jainism (Indian religion), the abode of unliberated beings.

LOKAPALAS

In Hindu and Buddhist mythology, the guardians of the four cardinal directions. The Hindu protectors, who ride on elephants, are Indra, who governs the east, Yama the south, Varupa the west, and Kubera the north.

LOKI

In Norse mythology, a cunning trickster who had the ability to change his shape and sex.

LORD

A customary title of God in the Old Testament, one of the titles given to Jesus in the New Testament, still frequently used in the prayers of the Roman Catholic Church (for example, at the beginning - "Lord, Jesus Christ" - or at the conclusion - "through Christ our Lord").

LORD'S DAY

In biblical usage the word "day" may denote a period of time far longer than twenty-four hours (Genesis 2:4; John 8:56) Contextual evidence indicates that the "Lord's Day" of Revelation 1:10 is not a particular twenty-four-hour day. Since it was "by inspiration" that John came to be "in the Lord's Day," the reference could not be the same particular day of the week. It would not have been necessary for John to have been inspired to come no specific day of the week. Therefore, the "Lords's Day" must be that future time, during which events that John was privileged to see in vision would occur.

LORD'S PRAYER

The chief Christian prayer, taught by Christ to his disciples. Addressed to God the Father, it contains seven petitions, the first three for God's glory, the last four for man's bodily and spiritual needs. It appears in two forms in the New Testament, the shorter version, part of Luke 11:2-4 and the longer version, part of the Sermon on the Mount, in Matthew 6:9-13. In both contexts it is offered as an example of how to pray.

The closing doxology, used by most Protestants ("For thine is the kingdom" etc.), was added to the Roman Catholic version after the Second Vatican Council (1962-65).

LORD'S SUPPER

The final Passover meal held by Jesus and his disciples in Jerusalem before his crucifixion. In it he distributed bread and wine to them, inaugurating the important ordinance (Luke 22:14-23, 1 Corinthians 11:23-25). The Lord's supper is the token of the New Covenant (2 Corinthians 3:6), in which the promised forgiveness is fulfilled (Jeremiah 31:34).

LO-RUHAMAH

In the Bible, name for a girl borne by Gomer, the wife of Hosea. Gold told the prophet to give the child this name

because He would "no more show mercy again to the house of Israel." God thus indicated his rejection of Israel as a whole
(Hosea 1:6-8).

LOT

In the Old Testament, son of Abraham's brother Haran. he lived in the city of Sodom. Warned that both Sodom and Gomorrah were to be destroyed because of their wickedness, he fled with his wife and two daughters. Told not to look back, his wife disobeyed and was turned into a pillar of salt (Genesis 11:14-19).

LOTAN

In the Old Testament, a son of Seir the Horite and one of the sheiks of Edom (Genesis 36:20, 29). His sons were Hori and Hemam and his sister was named Timna (Genesis 36:22; 1 Chronicles 1:38-39).

LOTUS

A favorite Buddhist symbol; rooted in the mud, it rises though the water and opens in the air to receive the sun. Padmasana, the lotus posture in meditation and art, is the Dhyanasana, with both soles upward on the other thigh and the figure seated on an opening lotus.

LOTUS-EATERS

In Greek mythology, people on an island near the coast of Africa, who played an important role in the wanderings of Odysseus. After the destruction of Troy, Odysseus set out for home with Agamemnon's fleet, but the ships were scattered in a storm. Odysseus ran aground on the coast of Thrace, where the Cicones lived. They were allies of Troy, and so Odysseus overcame and looted Ismarus, one of their cities, sparing only Maron, the priest of Apollo, who made him a gift of 12 jars of sweet intoxicating wine.

The landing and the attack on the city of the Cicones cost Odysseus the lives of six men from each of his ships. Now they sailed south again, to the sea of Cythera, near Cape Maleas. Their next stop was an island off the coast of Africa. The people of the country welcomed Odysseus and his companions when they landed to reconnoitre, offering them lotus fruit which they themselves ate. But when the sailors of the ships of Odysseus ate the fruit they forgot their homelands and their wish to return there. In the end, Odysseus had to use force to get them to re-embark.

LOURDES

World-famous center of roman Catholic pilgrimages in south-western France where, on February 11, 1858, the Virgin Mary is said to have appeared to the 14 year old peasant girl Bernadette Soubirous. The Rosary church and a statue of the Virgin mark the site and its holy pilgrims annually. The huge underground Basilica of St. Pius X, opened in 1958, is the world's second-largest Roman Catholic church after St. Peter's, Rome.

LOYOLA, Ignatius de, SAINT

(1491-1556), Spanish founder of the Society of Jesus (the Jesuits), a religious order that was a major force in the Catholic Counter-Reformation and has provided some of the finest Roman catholic theologians.

A Basque nobleman and soldier, he was born at Loyola castle in Guipuzcoa province and christened Inigo Lopex de Recalde. While recovering from a serious wound received at the siege of Pamplona (1521), he read religious books that completely changed his life. At the convent of Manresa (1522-23), aided by self-denial, prayer and meditation, eh was inspired to write his famous *Spiritual Exercises*.

After travel and study at various Spanish universities, he went to Paris for further studies (1528) and there, with six followers, including St. Francis Xavier, formed the Society of Jesus (1534), which was formally approved by Pope Paul III (1540). Loyola was the first general and was the author of its Constitutions (1547-50). He instituted the strict discipline from which Jesuits derived strength and unity. Schools and missionary work abroad were his great interest.

LUCIFER

(1) The devil, (2) the planet Venus as the morning star. In the Bible, the term "day star" is applied to the boastful king of Babylon who was doomed to be cast down: "How art thou fallen from heaven, O day star, son of the morning (Isaiah 14:12). In early translations "Lucifer" was used instead of "day star," and this was misunderstood as a reference to the fallen angel. Lucifer thus came to be another name for Satan.

LUCIUS

In the New Testament, a Christian "relative" of Paul who was with him in Corinth during his third missionary tour when the apostle wrote his letter to the Romans. Lucius is a name of Latin origin. He joined in sending greetings to Christians in Rome (Romans 16:21).

LUCY, Saint

(circa 245-301) A martyr at Syracuse, Sicily, probably during the emperor Diocletian's persecutions. She is mentioned in the canon of the Roman mass. Her feast day is December 13th.

LUCY, Richard de

(1102-1179) Founder of Lesnes Abbey in penance for his part in the events leading to Becket's murder.

LUD

In the Old Testament, a descendant of Ham through Mizraim (Genesis 10:6; 1 Chronicles 1:8-11). The people descended from Lud are evidently the "Litem" noted for their proficiency with the bow who were incorporated in Egyptian military forces (Jeremiah 46:8).

LUDMILLA, Saint

(860-921) Celebrated Slavic martyr and patroness of Bohemia, where she pioneered in establishing Christianity.

LUGUS

One of the most important pagan Celtic gods and one of the deities whom Julius Caesar identified with the Roman god Mercury. His cult was widespread throughout the early Celtic world.

LUKE

The author of the third gospel and the Acts of the Apostles. Luke was a gentile and worked as a physician, probably in Antioch. Being Paul's friend, he accompanied him on his missionary journeys. The gospel, written for gentiles, is based on eyewitness accounts (Luke 1:1-4). Luke is first mentioned in the letters of the apostle Paul as his "coworker" and as the "beloved physician".

LUKE, Gospel of

Third of the four New Testament gospels (dated circa 60 AD). It is composed by Luke, the beloved physician (Colossians 4:14), a close associate of the apostle Paul. Luke's gospel is written for gentile converts: it traces Christ's genealogy for example, back to Adam, the father of the human race, rather than to Abraham, the father of the Jewish people. Containing five great songs, Luke's gospel is clearly good tidings of great joy.

LUMBINI

Birthplace of the Siddhartha Gautama, who became the Buddha. The site is now in Nepal Therai, marked by a pillar erected by the Emperor Asoka, circa 250 BC. It is one of the holy places of Buddhism.

LUMPA CHURCH

A tribal religious movement in Zambia, Central Africa. which, though all-African, has had many conflicts with the government. Magic and witchcraft are confessed and renounced, followed by baptism.

LUQMAN

Wise man known to the Arabs in the Jahilliyya whose wisdom is vaunted in early Arabic poetry. In the Koran an entire sura is named after him. Here he is celebrated as a figure who believes in one God, and the provider of good advice to his son. Luqman is not mentioned in any other part of the Koran.

LUQMAN

The title of the 31st sura of the Koran; a proper name sometimes likened to, or even identified with, the Greek Aesop. The sura belongs to the Meccan period and contains 34 verses. Its title is drawn from verses 12 and following which portray Luqman being granted wisdom by God and then counselling his son to remain a monotheist and giving other good advice. In verse 17, for example, he exhorts his son to observe the prayer ritual and to command the good and forbid evil. The sura begins with three of the mysterious letters of the Koran and goes on to announce that the verses which follow are from the Wise Book. God's power is apparent in the creation of the pillarless Heavens and His provision of life-giving water to the earth. His words are infinite and could not be encompassed or exhausted even if all the trees on earth became pens dipped in seven seas (of ink).

LUSSY, Melchior

(1529-1606) Roman Catholic partisan and champion of the Counter-Reformation in Switzerland who was one of the most important Swiss political leaders in the latter half of the 16th century.

LUSTRATION

Any of various processes in ancient Greece and Rome whereby individuals or communities rid themselves of ceremonial impurity or simply from the profane or ordinary state, which made it dangerous to come into contact with sacred rites or objects.

LUT

Arabic word for Lot; one of the messengers, whose story is recorded in several suras of the Koran. He is sent by God to warn his people; their crimes include sodomy. His people's city is destroyed but Lut and nearly all his family are saved; only Lut's wife, who lingers, is destroyed.

LUTHER, Martin

(1483-1546) German Reformation leader and founder of Lutheranism. Following a religious experience he became an Augustinian friar, was ordained in 1507, and visited Rome (1510), where he was shocked by the worldliness of the papal court.

While professor of scripture at the University of Wittenberg (from 1512), he wrestled with the problem of personal salvation, concluding that it comes from the unmerited grace of God, available through faith alone. When Johann Tetzel toured Saxony (1517) selling indulgences, Luther denounced the practice in his historic 95 theses, for which he was fiercely attacked.

In 1520 he published *To the Christian Nobility of the German Nation*. It denied the pope's final authority to determine the interpretation of scripture, declaring instead the priesthood of all believers, and it rejected papal claims to political authority, arguing for national churches governed by secular rulers. In December 1520 he publicly burned a papal bull of condemnation and a copy of the canon law; he was excommunicated in 1521.

He was outlawed but, protected by Frederich III of Saxony, he retired to the Wartburg Castle. There he translated the New Testament into German in six months and began work on the Old Testament. His hymns have been translated into many languages, and he wrote two catechisms (1529), the basis of Lutheranism.

LUTHERAN

Supporter of the Protestant church founded by Martin Luther (1483-1546), German leader of the Reformation. Luther, a scholar and a priest, believed that faith rather than Catholic ritual would save people from sin and enable them to receive the grace of God. The largest Protestant sect in the world today, Lutheranism is the state church in the Scandinavian countries and is strong in Germany.

In the 18th century German immigrants founded Lutheran churches in the mid-Atlantic American colonies, and the Evangelical Lutheran Church is now the fourth largest Christian sect in the United States.

LUTHERAN CHURCH, Missouri Synod

Branch of Protestantism with headquarters in St. Louis, organized to maintain evangelical Lutheranism. It was founded by German immigrants in 1847 and operates a number of colleges, seminaries and foreign missions.

LUTHERAN CHURCHES

Largest of the three classical Protestant churches of the 16th century Reformation. Historical circumstances led to the formation of the Lutheran churches, founded by Martin Luther in Germany initially as a movement for doctrinal reform within the medieval Latin church. They have preserved the early doctrinal tension and conflict between a conservative element (preservation of the ancient faith) and a revolutionary element (a radical trust in God who justifies man).

LUTHERAN CHURCH IN AMERICA

The largest of the main American Lutheran bodies. There are some 6,500 Lutheran congregations in the United States, Canada and the Caribbean, grouped into 35 synods or regional districts. The church body was organized in 1963 by uniting four existing Lutheran organizations. It operates seminaries, missionary colleges and relief programs.

LUTHERAN COUNCIL IN THE UNITED STATES OF AMERICA

A cooperative agency for four Lutheran churches whose membership includes circa 95 percent of all Lutherans in the United States, established January, 1967, as a successor to the National Lutheran Council.

LUTHERAN FREE CHURCH

Denomination organized in 1897 at Minneapolis, Minnesota, by a group that left the United Norwegian Lutheran Church because of disagreements over church government.

Over the years its own church government became more centralized, but it was cautious in considering actual union with other Lutheran groups. In 1963, however, the Lutheran Free Church became part of the American Lutheran Church, organized in 1960 by the merger of three Lutheran churches.

LUTHERANISM

Branch of Protestantism based on the doctrines and teachings of Martin Luther. The Lutherans form the largest Protestant church in the world; in the 1990s the Lutheran World Federation estimated that there were between 90 and 100 million Lutherans.

Doctrine

Lutherans regard the Bible as "the only source and infallible norm of all church doctrine and practice." They believe than man can be saved only by faith, made available through the redeeming Jesus Christ on the cross. They recognize only two sacraments: baptism, essential for regeneration, and the Eucharist (the Lord's Supper or Sacrament of the Altar). They reject the doctrine of transubstantiation.

The most important statements of their faith are the two catechisms that Luther wrote (1529) and the unaltered Augsburg Confession (1530). These three, with three with the Apology of the Augsburg Confession, Schmalkald Articles and the Formula of Concord, are included in the Book of Concord (1580).

Although Luther retained altars and vestments and provided an order of service, he was more concerned with faith than form, and did not require his followers to accept a rigid organization or to observe set practices. Lutheran organization and church services therefore vary greatly. Some Lutheran groups are headed by bishops; in others, each local congregation may have autonomy. Some have very formal services; in others, the keynote is simplicity. Preaching and congregational singing are important features of most Lutheran services.

The Churches

Lutheranism is still strong in Germany, where it began in the 1500s. The Lutheran churches of Germany are part of the German Evangelical Church. Lutheranism is the established national faith of Denmark, Iceland, Norway, Sweden and Finland.

In America there were Dutch Lutherans among the settlers on Manhattan Island in 1625. But the first Lutheran congregation was formed by the Swedes at Fort Christina (now Wilmington, Delaware) in 1638. Today there are more than 10 million Lutherans in the United States, where they constitute the fourth-largest Christian group. The three major synods are the Lutheran Church in America, the American Lutheran Church, and the Lutheran Church Missouri Synod. Other Lutheran bodies include the Wisconsin Evangelical Synod.

LUTHERAN WORLD FEDERATION

National cooperative agency of Lutheran churches, organized at Lund, Sweden, in 1947. It developed from the Lutheran World Convention, which was held in the 1920s and 1930s. It is a free organization of churches and cannot dictate to or interfere in the autonomy of the member churches. Its various activities include mission, social welfare, and educational programs.

LUTHER'S LARGE CATECHISMUS

Manual of religious instruction published by Martin Luther in 1529. This catechism contains the same subjects as the small catechism, but was intended primarily for use by the clergy in the preparation of their sermons and in religious instruction. It included many of Luther's sermons.

LUTHER'S SMALL CATECHISMUS

Manual of religious instruction published by Martin Luther in 1529. It is a basic textbook of religious instruction for Lutherans since its publication, and it has been considered as possibly the most influential book produced by any of the reformers. To the three principal parts contained in earlier catechisms, the Apostles' Creed, the Lord's Prayer, and the Ten Commandments, Luther added discussions of the sacraments of Baptism and the Lord's Supper.

LUZ

In the Old Testament, the earlier name of the town of Bethel, evidently given it by the Canaanite inhabitants. Jacob applied the name "Bethel" (house of God) to the site where he received a dream containing a divine revelation: a place were Abraham had previously camped (Genesis 28:16-19).

Originally the site of Bethel was distinct from the town of Luz, being situated to the east of Bethel in the direction of Ai (Genesis 12:8). It appears that the name "Bethel" eventually superseded that of Luz, at the latest by the time of the Israelite conquest of Canaan (Judges 1:22).

LYCAON

In Greek mythology, a legendary king. Traditionally, he was an impious and cruel king who tried to trick Zeus, the king of gods, into eating human flesh. The god was not deceived and in wrath caused a deluge to devastate the earth.

LYCAONIA

In biblical times, a region in Asia Minor where the Lycanonian language was spoken (Acts 4:6-11). The exact boundaries of Lycaonian are uncertain and fluctuated considerably throughout its history.

Basically, in the period during which Lycaonia figured in the biblical record, it lay in the southern part of the Roman province of Galatia, and was bounded by Pisidia and Phrygia on the west, Cappadocia in the east and Cilicia on the south.

The apostle Paul visited Derbe and Lystra, two cities of Lycaonia, during the course of his first and second missionary journeys. He may also have stopped there on his third missionary tour as he traveled from "place to place through the country of Galatia" (Acts 14:6, 20, 21).

LYDIA

A woman mentioned in the Bible (Acts 16:14-15) and considered among the first persons in Europe to accept Christianity as a result of the apostle Paul's activity at Philippi in circa 50. Originally she lived at Thyatira, a city in Asia Minor known for its dying industry. Later, at Philippi in Macedonia Lydia sold purple, either the dye or garments and fabrics colored therewith.

LYONS, Cuncils of

The 13th and 14th ecumenical councils of the Roman Catholic Church. The first council of Lyons, convoked by Pope Innocent IV in 1245 renewed the church's excommunication of Holy Roman Eperor Frederick II.

The second council of Lyons, convoked by Pope Gregory X in 1274 acknowledged the supremacy of the pope. A profession of faith, which included sections of purgatory, the sacraments, and the primacy of the pope, was approved by the Orthodox representatives and some 200 Western prelates, and reunion between the Orthodox and Western church was formally accepted.

LYSANIAS

The district ruler or patriarch of Abilene when John the Baptist began his ministry (AD 19), during the 15th year of Tiberius Caesar's rule (Luke 3:1).

LYSTRA

In biblical times, a city of Lycaonia, a region in the south-central part of Asia Minor. It was to Lystra in the Roman province of Galatia that the apostle Paul and Barnabas came after being forced to leave Iconium because of an attempt to have them stoned.

The native inhabitants, however, continued to speak the Lycaonian language. After Paul healed a man lame from birth, the crowds concluded that he and Barnabas were incarnated gods, Hermes and Zeus. Barely were they able to restrain the people from sacrificing to them. Later, however, Israelites from Iconium and Pisidian Antioch so stirred up the inhabitants of Lystra against Paul that they stoned him, leaving him for dead. Afterward, when surrounded by fellow Christians, Paul got up, entered Lystra and then, accompanied by Barnabas, left the next day for Derbe (Acts 14:1; Acts 14:5-20).

M

MAACATHITE
In the Old Testament, inhabitant of the Aramaean kingdom of Maacah (Deuteronomy 3:14; Joshua 12:5), one of these being Eshtemona.

MAADAI
In the Old Testament, an Israelite among the "sons of Bani," who had accepted foreign wives but sent them away in Ezra's days after the Israelites returned from Babylonian exile (Ezra 10:25-34).

MA-AD, al-
In Islam, the Hereafter, a synonym of al-akhira. The term also encompasses all the things which will happen on the Day of Resurrection.

MAADIAH
In the Old Testament, a priest and head of a paternal house accompanying those returning from Babylon with Zerubbabel (Nehemiah 12:1-5).

MAAI
In the Old Testament, a priest and musician who descended from Asaph and played an instrument of song at the inauguration of Jerusalem's wall in Nehemiah's time (Nehemiah 12:36).

MA'AMADOT
24 groups of Jewish laymen that witnessed, by turns of one week, the daily sacrifice in the Second Temple of Jerusalem as representatives of the common people. Thou public sacrifices were terminated when Jerusalem was destroyed in AD 70, daily prayers called ma'amadot are still recited privately by many pious Jews.

MAARATH
In biblical times, a town assigned to the tribe of Judah (Joshua 15:21). A site near the village of Beit Ummar in the hill country of Judah, circa seven miles north of Hebron, is considered to be the probable location.

MA-ARIJ, al-
The title of the 70th sura of the Koran; it means "The Ascents" or "The Stairs." The sura belongs to the Meccan period and has 44 verses. Its title reflects verse 3 where God is described as "The Lord of the Ascents." The majesty of God is vividly and beautifully emphasized at the beginning of the sura with a reference to the angels ascending to God in a day whose measure is deemed to be "fifty thousand years." The terrors of the Day of Judgment are described. The wicked will go to hell while the trustworthy and pious will be honored in paradise.

MA'ARIVE
Jewish evening prayers recited after sunset; the name derives from one of the opening words of the first prayer.

MAASAI
In the Old Testament, a priest and descendant of Immer, who returned from Babylonian exile (1 Chronicles 9:10-12).

MAASEIAH
In Judaism, a Levite musician of the second division who played a stringed instrument when the ark of Jehovah was brought from the house of Obed-edom to Jerusalem in David's day (1 Chronicles 15:17-20).
The name is also applied to one of the "chiefs of hundred" who entered the covenant with High Priest Jehoiada in connection with establishing Jehoash

as Judah's rightful king in place of the usurper Athaliah (2 Chronicles 23:1).

MA'ASE MERKAVA

An idiomatic expression in esoteric Jewish mysticism for mystical speculations centered on the divine chariot (Merkava) seen in vision by Ezekiel (Ezekiel 1).

MAATH

In the Bible, one of Jesus' ancestors listed in his genealogy as given by Luke (Luke 3:23).

MAAZ

In the Old Testament, one of Judah's descendants through Jerahmeel and Ram (1 Chronicles 2:3, 25-27).

MAAZIAH

One of the priests, or a forefather of one, who attested by seal the "trustworthy arrangement" of Nehemiah's time (Nehemiah 9:38; 10:1).

MACAULEY, Catherine Elizabeth

(1787-1841) Founder of the Sisters of Mercy, a congregation of nuns engaged in education and social service. It has become one of the largest English-speaking congregations with circa 25,000 nuns.

MACCABEES, Books of

Books of the Old Testament apocrypha, which tell the story of the Maccabees or Hashmoneans, Jewish rulers oft he 2nd and 1st centuries BC who fought for the independence of Judea from Syria. Maccabees I, a prime historical source, was written circa 100 BC; Maccabees II is a devotional work of low historical value, written before AD 70.

The father of the Maccabaean family, Mattathias, defied the Syrian king, refused to worship Greek gods and fled to the hills with his sons. One of these, Judas Maccabaeus, organized resistance, defeated the Syrian army and captured Jerusalem and the Temple in 164 BC, a victory celebrated by Hanukkah, the Festival of lights. The

kingship passed through several generations but lost power when Pompeiy captured Jerusalem in 53 BC.

MACCABEES, First Book of

An apocryphal work (non-canonical for Jews and Protestants) omitted from the Hebrew Bible but included in the Septuagint (Greek translation of the Old Testament). The book presents an historical account of political, military and diplomatic events from the time of Judea's relationship with Antiochus IV Epiphanes of Syria (ruled 175-164 BC) to the death of Simon Maccabeus, High Priest in Jerusalem (142-13 BC).

MACCABEES, Fourth Book of

A pseudepigraphical work on the supremacy of religious reason that has not been included in either the Hebrew or Christian biblical canons. It is a philosophical treatise with the theme that obedience to religious law gives reason control over the emotions. The book has very scanty historical information and belongs to the Maccabees series only because it deals with the beginning of the persecution of Jews by Antiochus IV Epiphanes of Syria (ruled 175-164 BC). It does not deal with the Maccabean revolt itself.

MACCABEES, Second Book of

The only extant source for the history of Palestinian Jews in the decade prior to the reign of Antiochus IV Epiphanes (ruled 175-164 BC). It focuses on the Jews' revolt against Antiochus and concludes with the defeat of the Syrian general Nicanor in 161 BC by Judas Maccabeus, the hero of the work. In general, the chronology coheres with that of the First Book of Maccabees. Both books are non-canonical for Jews and Protestants.

MACCABEES, Third Book of

An apocryphal work (non-canonical) not included in either the Hebrew of the Christian biblical canons, although it is found in some manuscripts of the Septuagint (Greek translation of the Old Testament). It has no relation to the other three books of Maccabees. The book, of an unknown author, purports to be a historical account of the repressing and miraculous salvation of Egyptian Jewry during the reign of Ptolemy IV Philopator (221-205 BC), who supposedly threatened the Jews with loss of citizenship after Palestinian Jews refused to permit him to enter the sanctuary of the Temple of Jerusalem.

MACCABEUS, Judas

(circa 240-161 BC) Famous Jewish guerilla leader who defended his country from invasion by Seleucid King Antiochus IV Epiphanes, resisted the imposition of Hellenism upon Judea, and preserved the Jewish religion.

MACEDONIA

A country lying north of Greece. The ancient kingdom of Macedonia achieved hegemony over the Greek world in the 4th century BC. The history of Paul's journey through Macedonia is given in Acts 16:10-17:15.

MACEDONIANISM

A 4th century Christian heresy that denied the full personality and divinity of the Holy Spirit. According to this heresy, the Holy Spirit was created by the Son and was thus subordinate to the Father and the Son.

The name of Macedonius, a Semi-Arian, became associated with the heresy some 20 years after his deposition in 360 as bishop of Constantinople.

MACHBANNAI

In the Old Testament, a Gadite mighty man who joined David's band at "the place difficult to approach in the wilderness" and became one of the heads of his army (1 Chronicles 12:8-14).

MACHBENAH

In the Old Testament name appearing in a list of Caleb's descendants through his concubine Maacah, her son Sheva being called the "father of Machbenah

and father of Gibea (1 Chronicles 2:48-49).

MACHEN, John Greshom

(1881-1937) Scholar who joined in forming the doctrinally conservative Presbyterian church in America (1936); later named the Orthodox Presbyterian church.

MACHI

In the Old Testament, a Gadite and the father of Geuel, one of the twelve Israelites sent to spy out Canaan (Numbers 13:1-2, 15-16).

MACHIR

In the Old Testament, the first-named son of Manasseh by his Syrian concubine. Machir founded the family of Machirites and is called "the father of Gilead." His wife was Maacah, and he had sons within Joseph's lifetime (Genesis 50:23); Numbers 26:29).

MACHIRITES

A family of the tribe of Manasseh founded by his son Machir (Numbers 26:29).

MACHNADEBAI

A post-exile Israelite among those who sent away their foreign wives in Ezra's time (Ezra 10:25, 40-44).

MACHPELAH

In the Old Testament, the name used with reference to a field and a cave in the vicinity of Hebron, purchased by Abraham from Ephron the Hittite for 400 silver shekels as a burial place for Abraham's wife Sarah and at least five others: Abraham, Isaac, Rebekah, Jacob and Leah (Genesis 23:14-19; 25:9; 49:30). The designation "Machpelah" evidently also applied to the surrounding area (Genesis 23:17).

MACKENNA, Alexander

(1835-1904) English Congregational churchman and secretary of the Free Church federation, who joined the movement (1892) to merge Britain's independent Protestant churches.

MACKENZIE, Charles Frederick

(1825-1862) Anglican priest and the first bishop in the British colonial territory of Central Africa. He aroused opposition among settlers by his view that native Christians should participate in full equality with white Christians in all church affairs.

MACLEOD, Norman

(1812-1872) Influential liberal Presbyterian minister of the Church of Scotland who took advantage of the controversy over church reform during 1833-1843 to implement policies of the splinter church of 1843, the Free Church of Scotland, while yet remaining within his own denomination.

MADAI

In the Old Testament, the third-listed son of Japheth (Genesis 10:2; 1 Chronicles 1:5). He is believed to be the progenitor of the Medes.

MADDERAKKA

The Lapp goddess of childbirth. She is assisted by three of her daughters: Sarakka, the cleaving woman; Uksakka, the door women; and Juksakka, the bow woman, who watch over the development of the child from conception through early childhood.

MADHHAB

Arabic term with various meanings such as "deology," "doctrine," "creed," and "movement." It indicates one of the major schools of law.

MADHVA

(1199-1278) Hindu philosopher, exponent of Dvaota; dualism, or belief in a basic difference in kind between God and individual souls. His followers are called Madhvas.

MADHYAMIKA

An important school in Mahayana Buddhist tradition. It takes its name "intermediate" from the fact that it sought a middle position between the realism of the Sarvastivada and the idealism of the Yogacara schools.

MADMANNAH

In the Old Testament, one of the descendants of Judah through Caleb. Caleb's concubine Maacah is stated to have borne "Shaaph the father of Madmannah" (1 Chronicles 2:49). However, most scholars consider the term "father" to be used here in the sense of "founder" and consider Madmannah in this text to correspond with a town in the southern part of the territory of Judah (Joshua 15:21).

MADMENAH

In biblical times, a site in the path of the Assyrian advance toward Jerusalem (Isaiah 10:24).

MADON

In biblical times, a royal Canaanite city that leagued itself with Hazor against the Israelites and was subsequently defeated (Joshua 11:1-12). Madon is usually identified with Qarn Hattin, circa 5_ miles north-west of Tiberias.

MADONNA

Name given to the Virgin Mary, especially as depicted in works of art. The Madonna is often shown with the infant Jesus or, in the Pieta, mourning over his body taken down from the cross. Among the many artists who have painted Madonnas are Raphael, Bellini, Botticelli, Correggio, Titian, Rubens and Murillo. Sculptors of Madonnas include Andrea Della Robbia, Leonardo da Vinci and Michelangelo.

MADRASAH

A Muslim institution of higher education. The madrasah functioned until the 20th century as a theological seminary and law school, with a curriculum centered on the Koran.

MAENAD

In Greek religion, one of the female attendants who shared in the nocturnal orgiastic rites of Dionysus, the wine god. The Maenads were women who personified the orgiastic spirits of nature. During the Dionysian orgies they were overcome by a mania for dance, song and frenetic merry-making. This happy company was constantly around Dionysus, creating high spirits wherever they went.

MAFATIH AL-GHAYB

Literally "Book of Great Commentary", a commentary on the Koran by Fakir ad-Din ar-Razi, completed from 1279 to 1289.

MAGADAN

An area near the Sea of Galilee to which Jesus withdrew after his miraculous feeding of 4,000 men (Matthew 15:39; Mark 8:10).

MAGBISH

In the Old Testament, either a name of a person or a place. Among those returning from babylonian exile were 156 "sons of Magbish" (Ezra 2:1, 30).

MAGDIEL

In the Old Testament, a descendant or, perhaps, one of the sheiks of Edom (Genesis 36:40-43). Magdiel may have also been the name of a place and a tribe.

MAGGIDIM

Itinerant Jewish preachers who flourished especially in Poland and Russia during the 17th and 18th centuries. Since rabbis at that time preached only on the sabbaths preceding Passover and Yom Kippur, Maggidim were in great demand throughout the year to instruct, encourage, and sometimes admonish their congregation.

MAGI

The wise men who were led by the stars to pay homage to the infant Jesus in Bethlehem. They brought gifts of gold, frankincense, and myrrh, and by tradition are named Gaspar, Melchior, and Balthasar.

MAGI PLAYS

Liturgical dramas featuring the visit of the Wise Men to the infant Christ. These plays were highly spectacular productions because of the splendid pageantry of the Magi and their retinues, together with the ostentation of Herod's court. The latter figure became the dominant character of these plays in his role of angry and jealous tyrant, a part coveted by a talented actor and applauded by the spectators, who expected him to "out-herod Herod," in Hamlet's phrase.

MAGIC

The practice of manipulating or controlling the course of events by supernatural means. Throughout history, magic has been practiced in an attempt to avoid evil and ensure good fortune. Good health, fertility and success in hunting and warfare were all believed to be achievable through magic. Unseen forces were also believed to be responsible for man's spiritual well-being: in the Middle Ages the Christian concept of the struggle between God and the Devil for man's soul was tied up with the ancient belief in good and evil spirits.This idea persisted into the 17th century, when witchcraft was believed to be the work of the Devil and witches were persecuted as the Devil's instruments.

Magical beliefs are linked with the ancient practice of animism, and even today many people explain the world by ascribing powers of good and evil to various spirits, whom they try not to offend. Magic formed the basis of many folk mythologies and primitive religions. Practices such as fortune telling were a part of Greek and Roman culture, and in the Middle Ages magical beliefs flourished.

In Buddhism, belief in the efficacy of rites and ceremonies (as means of attaining liberation) is one of the ten Fetters to be cast off in following the Path.

MAGISTERIUM

A Latin word meaning "teaching authority"; according to Catholic doctrine, this teaching authority is vested in the pope, the successor of St. Peter and the head of the church, and in the bishops together and in union with the pope.

The teaching authority is at times infallible, and then demands from the Christian faithful the assent of faith. At other times this teaching authority, though not explicitly infallible, does express authentic Christian Catholic teaching and demands from the Christian faithful the loyal submission of the will and the intellect,

Vatican Council II explains this matter in this way: "Bishops who teach in communion with the Roman pontiff are to be revered by all as witnesses of divine and Catholic truth; the faithful, for their part, are obliged to submit to their bishops' decision, made in the name of Christ, in matters of faith and morals. This loyal submission of the will and intellect must be given, in a special way, to the authentic teaching authority of the Roman pontiff, even when he does not speak ex cathedra in such wise, indeed, that his supreme teaching authority be acknowledged with respect, and that one sincerely adheres to decisions made by him, conformably with his manifest mind and intention, which is made known principally either by the character of the documents in question, or by the frequency with which a certain doctrine is proposed, or by the manner in which the doctrine is formulated".

MAGNANIMITY

The virtue, recognized by Aristotle and other philosophers of antiquity, that regulates and controls a man's appetite for honor and glory. The virtuous man will not strive for a greatness that is beyond his powers, but neither will he allow timidity or disinterest to discourage the attempt to make his accomplishment measure up to the greatness of his potential.

MAGPIASH

In the Old Testament, one of the heads of the people whose descendant, if not himself,m attested by seal the "trustworthy arrangement" of nehemiah's day (Nehemiah 9:38, 40:20).

MAGUPAT

Ancient Zoroastrian priestly grade.

MAGUSAIOI

A Greek word coined to designate the Hellenized Magi, to whom a copious literature in Greek dealing with astrology, magic, and Oriental cult lore is attributed. While definite contacts were made between Greek and Iranian thought especially in Asia Minor in the Hellenistic Age, pseudo-scientific works had any real knowledge of Iranian religion or cosmic speculation.

Under the influence of this literature the term magus among the Greeks after Alexander, and among the Romans, came to designate as astrologer, magician, or scorerer.

MAHABALIPURAM

Religious center in India, founded by a 7th century Hindu Pallava King. It contains many surviving 7th and 8th century temples and monuments.

MAHABBHARATA

One of the two major epics in India, valued for both its high literary merit and its religious inspiration. The epic is believed to be based on actual events presumed to have taken place sometime between 1400 and 100 BC. Above all, the Mahabbharata is an exposition of codes of conduct; the proper conduct of a king, of a warrior, of a man living in times of calamity, of a person seeking to attain emancipation from rebirth.

The Mahabbharata has been retold in written and oral vernacular versions throughout South and Southeast Asia, and has always enjoyed immense popularity.

MAHA BODHI SOCIETY

Organization to encourage Buddhist studies in India and abroad. The society was founded in Sri Lanka (1891) by a monk.

MAHAKALA

A form of the Hindu god Siva (Shiva) in his aspect of time, the great destroyer; also widely worshipped in the northern Buddhist pantheon as a fierce protective deity.

MAHALALEL

In the Old Testament, a descendant of Seth through Enosh and Kenan; hence Seth's great-grandson (genesis 5:6-17). In Luke's genealogy of Jesus he is referred to by the name Mahalaleel (Luke 3:37-38).

The name is also applied to a descendant of Judah through Perez and the ancestor of Athaiah, a resident of Jerusalem after the return from Babylonian exile (Nehemiah 11:4).

MAHALATH

In the Old Testament, Ismhael's daughter, the sister of Nebaioth and one of the women Esau took as a wife (genesis 28:9). She is probably the same person as the Basemath of Genesis (36:3). The name is also applied to a granddaughter of David through his son Jerimoth. She became one of the wives of Rehoboam (2 Chronicles 11:18).

MAHA MAYA

The mother of Gautama Buddha, wife of Raja Suddhodana. According to Buddhist legend, she dreamt that a white elephant with six tusks entered her right side, which was interpreted to mean that she had conceived a child who would become either a world leader of a Buddha.

MAHAMUDRA

In Tantric Buddhism, the final goal, that of the union of all apparent dualities. Mudra, in addition to its more usual meaning of "sign" or "symbol," has in Tantric Buddhism the esoteric meaning of female partner, which in turn symbolizes prajina (wisdom).

MAHANAIM

In biblical times, according to tradition, a site east of the Jordan were Jacob, after parting from Laban, encountered a company of angels. Jacob than called the place "Mahanaim" (Genesis 32:1-2). The

meaning of the name ("two camps") may allude to Jacob's company as having become two camps, or to the camp of angels and the camp of Jacob (Genesis 32:7, 10). Apparently sometime later a city was built on the site. In the fifteenth century BC this city was first assigned to the Gadites and then to the Levite Merarites (Joshua 19:24-26; 21:34-38).

MAHANEH-DAN

In biblical times, a place once described as lying "between Zorah and Eshtaol" (Judges 13:25) and another time as being located west of Kiriath-jearim (Judges 18:11-12).

MAHA PARINIBBANA SUTTA

In Buddhism, a long Sutta containing a description of the Buddha's passing and much of his teaching.

MAHAPURUSA

A belief common to Hinduism, Jainism, and Buddhism that from time to time supermen are born into the world who can be distinguished by certain physical marks on their bodies. Such men are destined to become either spiritual leaders (such as Buddhas) or the Jaina spiritual leaders.

MAHARAI

In Judaism, a mighty man of David's military forces and a Netophathite (2 Samuel 23:8; 1 Chronicles 11:26). He was a descendant of Zerah, and was later put in charge of the division of 24,000 ministering to the king during the 10th month (1 Chronicles 27:1, 13).

MAHASANGHIKA

Early Buddhist school of the Hinayana. Some of its Canon and other Scriptures survived the Muslim invasion of India, and famous works such as the Lalitavistara and Mahavastu belong to this school.

MAHASIDDHA

In the Tantric, or esoteric, traditions of India and Tibet, a person who by the practice of meditative disciplines had attained siddha (miraculous power); a great magician.

MAHA-SIVARATRI

The most important sectarian festival of the year for Indian devotees of the Hindu god Siva (Sivha). The 14th day of the dark half of each lunar month is specially sacred to Siva, but, when it occurs in the month of Magha (January-February) it is a day of particular rejoicing.

MAHASUKHAKAYA

In Sanskrit: "existence in absolute bliss," state defined by Tantric or esoteric Buddhist theology.

MAHATH

In the Old Testament, a Kohathite Levite and ancestor of Samuel and Heman the singer at the house of God (1 Chronicles 6:31-35).

The name is also applied to one of the Kohathite Levites who aided in cleansing the temple in King Hezekiah's day (2 Chronicles 29:12-15). Evidently the same person was made a commissioner under Conaiah and Shimei in charge of "the contribution and the 10th and the holy things" at the temple (2 Chronicles 31:12-13).

MAHATMA

A name of honor which should be reserved for those of high spiritual attainment, such as the Rishis of India, or Masters of the Wisdom, but nowadays often used for a national saint like Mahatma Gandhi.

MAHAVAIROCANA-SUTRA

Text of late Tantric or esoteric Buddhism and a principal scripture of the large Japanese sect known as Shingon (True World). The text received a Chinese translation in circa 725 and its esoteric teachings were propagated a century later in Japan. These teachings, also called cosmotheism, center upon the supreme cosmic Buddha, whose body forms the universe.

MAHAVASTU

An important legendary life of the Buddha, produced as a late canonical work by the Mahasanghika school of early Buddhism and presented as a historical introduction to the vinaya, the monastic discipline section of the canon.

MAHAVIHARA

Buddhist monastery founded in the late 3rd century BC in Anuradhapura (Sri Lanka). Until the 10th century it was a great cultural and religious center and the chief stronghold of orthodox (i.e., Theravada) Buddhism. The centralized authority and pre-eminence of the Mahavihara gradually disintegrated until, by the 11th century, it has ceased to be a viable force in religious life.

MAHAVITE

In Judaism, a designation applied to Eliel, one of the mighty men of David's military forces (1 Chronicles 11:26, 46).

MAHAYANA

In Buddhism, School of the Great Vehicle (of salvation). The Mahayana gradually developed from the primitive teaching, and no sharp line of demarcation has ever existed; the doctrines of the Mahasanghika School contain all the basic elements of the developed Mahayana. The teaching of the Mahayana is more distinctly religious, making its appeal to the heart and intuition rather than to the intellect. It seeks the spiritual interpretation of the verbal teaching, and endeavors to expound that teaching in a variety of forms calculated to appeal to every type of mind and every stage of spiritual development.

That this method is but a concession to man's limitations, an accommodation to truth to the intelligence of the hearer, must be borne in mind when considering certain Mahayana teachings.

The Mahayana type of Buddhism spread to Tibet, China, Korea, Japan etc., while the Trevada type spread to Burma, Sri Lanka, Thailand, etc.

MAHAZIOTH

In Judaism, a Kohathite Levite and last mentioned of the fourteen sons of Heman. Mahazioth became head of the 23rd service group of Temple musicians as organized by David (1 Chronicles 25:4-6).

MAHDI

In Islamic eschatology, a messianic deliverer who will fill the earth with justice and equity, restore true religion, and usher in a short golden age lasting seven, eight, or nine years before the end of the world. Because the Mahdi is seen as a restorer of the political power and religious purity of Islam, the title has tended to be claimed by social revolutionaries in Islamic society.

MAHDI, al-

In Islam, term meaning "the One who is Rightly Guided." The Mahdi is a figure of profound eschatological significance in Islam and a title often claimed by diverse leaders throughout Islamic history. His just rule will herald the approach of the end of time. Both Sunnis and Shiites adhere to the belief in the Mahdi, though Shiism has developed the doctrine perhaps rather more deeply.

MAHR

In Islam, term with several meanings such as dowry, bridal gift, bride-price, bride-wealth. Islamic law enjoins that the bridegroom give a bride a gift when the marriage contract is instituted. In the period of Jahiliyya the Mahr was given to the bride's father or male guardian. However, the Koran decreed that it should be the wife who received the Mahr and that it was hers to keep, even in the event of a future divorce. If the marriage is dissolved before it has been consummated, the prospective bride is still entitled to half of the dowry. The amount of Mahr varies considerably; the Shari'ia does not stipulate a maximum amount and so it has happened sometimes that greedy families have felt to ask for a Mahr much larger than the other family can bear. But however high or low the amount, the Mahr is legally an integral and necessary aspect of the marriage contract.

MA'IDA, al-

The title of the 5th sura of the Koran; it means "The Table." The sura belongs to the Medinan period and contains 120 verses; its title is drawn from the Miracle of the Table which is described in verse 112 and following. Here Jesus' disciples challenge Jesus and ask if his Lord can send down the requested table at Jesus' prayer, but warns that those who disbelieve thereafter will be severely punished. This sura is a particularly long and rich one; it contains, inter alia, a number of prohibitions, instructions on how to perform the prayer, the story of the two sons of Adam and reference to the Ka'ba.

MAHLAH

In the Old Testament, one of the daughters of Zelophead of the tribe of Manasseh. Mahlah and her sisters requested their father's inheritance, since he had no sons but only five daughters. Moses ruled that the daughters of Zelophehad should receive it (Numbers 26:28-33). A subsequent order required Mahlah and the other daughters of Zelophead to marry within the tribe of Manasseh, to prevent the inheritance from passing to another tribe. Accordingly, Mahlah and her sisters "became the wives of the sons of their father's brothers" (Numbers 36:1-6, 10-12).

MAHLI

In Judaism, Levi's grandson, a son of Marari and brother of Mushi (Exodus 6:16-19). Mahli was the father of Eleazar and Kish and the family head of the Mahlites (Numbers 3:20-33; 1 Chronicles 23:21-29).

MAHLITES

In Judaism, Levites who were descendants of Marari's son Mehli (Numbers 3:17, 20, 33).

MAHLON

In the Old Testament, son of Elimelech and Naomi. During a famine in the days of the judges, he moved with his parents from Bethlehem in Judah to Moab. There Mahlon married the Moabitess Ruth, but died childless (Ruth 1:1-5; 4:10). Ruth returned to Judah with her mother-in-law, and complying with the law of Levite marriage, married Boaz (Ruth 4:9-10; Deuteronomy 25:5-6). The resulting family line produced David and led to Jesus Christ (Ruth 4:22; Matthew 1:5-16).

MAHSEIAH

In the Old Testament, ancestor of Jeremiah's associate Baruch and of Seraiah the quartermaster (Jeremiah 32:12, 51-19).

MAIA

In Greek mythology, the eldest of the Titan Atlas' seven daughters (the Pleiades) by Pleione, one of the 3,000 daughters of Oceanus (the river that encircles the earth). Maia was the mother of Zeus and Hermes.

MAIMBOURG, Louis

(1610-1686) Jesuit and historian who wrote critical works on Calvinism and Lutheranism and a defense of Gallican liberties - the belief that the Roman Catholic Church should maintain some independence from papal control.

MAIMONIDES

Or Moses Ben Maimon (1135-1204) Jewish rabbi, physician and philosopher, born at Cordoba, Spain. He is known to Jews as Rambam (from the initials of rabbi Moses ben Maimon). Guided by his father and the finest Arabic scholars, he studied medicine, theology and Greek philosophy. Religious persecution forced his family to emigrate to Egypt, where he became physician to the sultan Saladin. His major works include his commentary on the Mishna: *Sefer ha-Mizvoth (Book of Precepts)*, a legal summary anticipating his master-work *Mishneh Torah*

(Second Law), a monumental rationalization of traditional law. His greatest philosophical treatise *Moreh Nevochim (Guide for the Perplexed)* determined the course of Jewish thought and also profoundly influenced Christian thinking. Maimonides is one of the outstanding figures of Judaism, and perhaps the greatest Jewish philosopher.

MAITHIL BRAHMIN

A caste of Brahmins in India, well-known for their orthodoxy and interest in learning. They observe a complicated pattern of marriage among five hierarchically ordered groups, each of which may take a wife from the group below it.

MAITREYA

The future Buddha. According to Buddhist tradition, there have been many Buddhas in the past and will be many more to come. Maitreya resides at present as a bodhisattva ("Buddha-to-be") in the Tusita heaven and when the teaching of Gautama Buddha have completely decayed he will descend to earth and again preach the dharma ("law").

MAKAZ

In the Old Testament, a place under the jurisdiction of one of Solomon's 12 deputies (1 Kings 4:7-9). Makaz is often identified with Khirbet el-Mukheizin, some ten miles west-north-west of the suggested location Beth-shemesh.

MAKKEDAH

In biblical times, a royal Canaanite city in the Shephelah. It was in the cave of Makkedah that the five kings who had allied themselves against the Gibeonites hid and were then temporarily trapped until their execution. Thereafter this cave became their common tomb, and the Israelite army under Joshua captured the city of Makkedah and devoted it to destruction. At the time of the division of the Promised Land Makkedah was granted to the tribe of Judah (Hoshua 10:5-29).

The exact site of Makkedah is unknown. It has been tentatively identified with Khirbet el-Kheishum, circa a mile and a half north-north-east of the suggested location of Azekah. Extensive ruins and nearby caves mark the site.

MAKTAB
Muslim elementary school. Until the 20th century, boys were instructed in Koran recitation, reading, writing, and grammar. During the 20th century government-supported primary schools have tended to supplant the maktab in Muslim countries.

MAKTESH
In biblical times, a section of Jerusalem near the Fish Gate and the second quarter. At the time of Judah's calamity the inhabitants of Maktesh were foretold to howl, since commercial activities would cease there.

MALABAR CHRISTIANS
(St. Thomas Christians) A group mostly found in Kerala State (Southwest India). Considered heretics by the Portuguese, though traditionally aligned with Rome since the 6th century, they broke with Rome in 1653. The majority reverted to Catholicism in 1661, but some joined the Syrian Orthodox Church.

MALABAR LITURGY
Persian or Chaldean missionaries brought the gospel to the Malabar Coast of India and with it their own liturgical traditions. Under the influence of Portuguese missionaries, however, this liturgical tradition underwent much Latinization.

In 1962 a purified Malabar Qurbana (sacrifice or liturgy) restoring fully Eastern traditions of the Malabar Liturgy (including Eastern vestments, fermented bread, communion under both species, etc.) was promulgated.

In the pastoral renewal initiated by Vatican Council II, further adaptation and reforms were considered necessary. This resulted in 1968 in the promulgation of another Malabar Qurbana for experimental use.

After the vesting of the priest (during which one of the canonical Hours may be sung) the Liturgy opens with an invocation of the triune God and the solemn recitation of the Our Father. A few psalms and prayers in dialogue between priest and congregation precede the Liturgy of the Word with the Epistle and Gospel.

The Creed is solemnly recited, the gifts are prepared upon the altar, and the priest invites all the faithful to join him in praising God. Then follows the solemn antiphons - commemorations of the Blessed Virgin, of St. Thomas, and other saints, and of the living and the dead - and the eucharistic prayer (Canon) opens with the Kiss of Peace and the traditional dialogue.

As in all Eastern liturgies, the narration of the institution (Consecration) is followed by the anamnesis and the invocation of the Holy Script (epiclesis). The anaphora (Canon) is concluded with two psalms recited by priest and congregation together.

MALABARESE CATHOLIC CHURCH
A Chaldean-rite church of India that united with Rome after the Portuguese colonization of Goa at the end of the 15th century.

MALACHI, Book of
The 12th of the Old Testament minor prophets. Written by Malachi circa the 5th century BC, it prophesies judgment for insincerity and negligence in worship at the coming of the Messiah. The book consists of six distinct sections, each in the form of a question-and-answer discussion. Malachi calls for fidelity to God's covenant. Faithfulness will be rewarded; unfaithfulness will bring a curse.

MALACHY, Saint
(1094-1148) Celebrated archbishop and papal legate who is considered to be the dominant figure of church reform in 12th century Ireland.

MALAKBEL

West Semitic sun god and messenger god, worshipped primarily in the ancient Syrian city of Palmyra; he was variously identified by the Greeks with Zeus and Hermes.

MALALAS, John

(491-578) Byzantine chronicler of Syrian origin. His *Chronographic* in 18 books begins with the Creation and continues certainly to 565. The greater part of it stresses the importance of Antioch and has a monophysite (a Christian heresy) flavor.

MALAMATIYAH

Muslim mystic group that flourished in Persia during the 8th century. The doctrines were based on the reproach of the carnal self and a careful watch over its inclinations to surrender to the temptations of the earthly world.

MALANKAR RITE

One of the Eastern Catholic rites proper to those Catholics of South India who use the Syro-Antiochene ritual and are distinguished from the Indians of the Malabar rite. Syrian tradition prevailed in Christian India until the 16th century, when the Portuguese arrived and tried to impose the Latin Rite and to establish a Latin hierarchy.

Because of the suppression of their traditions, the majority of Malabar Christians refused further obedience to the Latin hierarchy. They appealed to the Jacobite patriarch of Antioch, and in 1772 they received a valid hierarchy with the consecration of the fifth successor of Thomas Parambil as Dionysius I. They all call themselves Syrian Jacobites. Their submission to the Jacobite patriarch of Antioch was not taken too seriously at times and several attempts at reunion were made. The 20th century brought another discussion between the patriarch of Antioch and metropolitan Dionysius V. At stake was the independence of the Indian Jacobites, under their catholicos. This split the church into two groups, one in obedience with the patriarch, the other in favor of their own catholicos.

In order to overcome their state of isolation after excommunication by the Antiochene patriarch, the catholicos faction opened official discussions with Rome in 1925 which resulted in the reunion of two bishops, Mar Ivanios and Mar Theophilus, a few clergy, and laity. In 1932 Pope Pius XI erected the separate Malankar Rite province of the Trivandrum. In 1995 there were some 250,000 Malankar Catholics in two jurisdictions.

MALANKARESE CATHOLIC CHURCH

An Antiochene-rite member of the Eastern Catholic Church, composed of former members of the Syrian Orthodox Church of Kerala, India, who united with Rome in 1930.

MALCAM

In the Old Testament, a Benjaminite and a son of Shaharaim by his wife Hodesh (1 Chronicles 8:1-9). The name is also applied to the principal idol god of the Ammoinites (2 Samuel 12:30; 1 Chronicles 8:1-9), also called Malcham.

MALCHIEL

In the Old Testament, grandson of Asher and a son of Beriah (Genesis 46:17). He is called "the father of Birzaith" (1 Chronicles 7:31) and was a family head in Israel (Numbers 26:45).

MALCHIELITES

In the Old testament, a family of Asherites that descended from Malchiel (Numbers 26:44-45).

MALCHIJAH

In the Old Testament, a Levite who descended from Gershom and who was an ancestor of the Levitical musician Asaph (1 Chronicles 6:39-43).

The name is also applied to another Israelite "of the sons of Parosh" among those accepting foreign wives but dismissing them in Ezra's days (Ezra 10:25).

A priest of the name Malchijah participated in the inauguration ceremonies
for Jerusalem's wall as rebuilt under
Nehemiah's supervision (Nehemiah
12:40-42). he may have been the same
person as a priest who stood at Ezra's
left hand when the copyist read the law
before the Israelites in reestablishing
Jerusalem (Nehemiah 8:4).

MALCHIRAM

In the Old Testament, one of the sons
of King Jeconiah (Jehoiachin) as a
prisoner in Babylon (1 Chronicles
3:17-18).

MALCHI-SHUA

In the Old Testament, one of King
Saul's sons (1 Samuel 14:40; 1
Chronicles 8:33). He was struck down
in battle by the Philistines at Mount
Gilboa (1 Samuel 31:2; 1 Chronicles
10:2) and his corpse (along with those
of his brothers Jonathan and Abinadab
and that of his father Saul) was fastened by the Philistines on the wall of
Beth-shan. However, valiant men of
Israel retrieved the bodies, burned
them in Jabesh and buried their bones
there (1 Samuel 31:8-13).

MALCHUS

According to biblical tradition, the
High Priest's slave who accompanied
Judas iscariot and the crowd to
Gethsemane, where Jesus Christ was
arrested (John 18:10; Matthew 26:51;
Mark 14:47). Peter struck off Malchus'
right ear with a sword, but Jesus miraculously healed it (Luke 22:50). Another
slave of the High Priest, Caiaphas, a
relative of Malchus, later recognized
Peter, and this led to the Apostle's third
denial of Jesus Christ (John 18:26-17).

MALICE

A cause of sin on the part of the will:
its fixed sinful intent either as present
in a single act or as a habitual disposition towards a sinful way of acting.

MALKA

The Nestorian leaven, traditionally
handed down from the saints Addai
and Mari, added to the dough used in
making eucharistic bread. It is renewed
on Holy Thursday by adding to the
remaining malka of the previous year.
The term is also applied to that part of
the baking actually used for consecration.

MALKUT

In Jewish kabbalistic speculations, one
of the divine potencies emanated from
the hidden God.

MALLOTHI

In the Old Testament, a Kohathite
Levite and one of the 14 sons of the
singer Heman (1 Chronicles 25:4-5).
The family served as musicians under
the direction of their father, Heman.
When David organized the divisions of
the Levites to serve in turn at the house
of God, the 19th lot fell to Mallothi,
who assumed the headship of that division of twelve musicians (1 Chronicles
26:1-10).

MALLUCH

In Judaism, a Merarite Levite and a
forefather of the Levitical singer Ethan
(1 Chronicles 6:44-47). The name is
also applied to an Israelite "of the sons
of Bani" among those who has accepted foreign wives but who dismissed
them in Ezra's time (Ezra 10:31-32).

MALLUCHI

In Judaism, a priestly family whose
representative served in the days of
High Priest Joiakim, and in the days of
Ezra and Governor Nehemiah
(Nehemiah 12:12-14).

MAMERTINE PRISON

The name of Carcer Tullianum, the
oldest prison in Rome, located on the
eastern side of the Capitoline Hill.
Built, according to tradition, by Ancus
Marcius, 4th king of Rome (640-616
BC), the prison, including a small
underground circular section and a spa-
cious rectangular section above
ground, was last renovated during the
reign of Tiberius. Among those who
were imprisoned or died there were

Jugurtha, Lentulus, and Vercingetorix. An early Christian tradition claims that Peter and Paul were also detained here.

MAMLUKS

Major dynasty of late medieval Islam which flourished between 1250 and 1517 in Egypt. The Arabic word mamluk means "one who is owned," "a slave," and reflected the origins of the dynasty in Circassian and Turkish slave soldiers. Their rule in Egypt ushered in a golden age of Egyptian Islamic art and architecture.

MAMRE

In Judaism, an Amorite chieftain who, along with his brother Aner and Eshcol, supported Abraham in defeating King Cherdolaomer and his allies. The basis for their support was evidently the confederacy into which they entered with Abraham (Genesis 14:13, 24).

MAN, Religious Doctrines of

Interpretations of the nature of man that reflect's man's experience of the holy or sacred. It is sometimes claimed that religious experience releases insights into human nature that the secular man cannot achieve. In particular, many Christian theologians have held that the Bible affords a revelation of man as well as of God, and have taught that man, as the crown of God's creation has been endowed with a special mark of God's presence and action, also called "the image of God."

MANAEN

In biblical tradition, a man who was among the prophets and teachers in the congregation at Antioch. He had been educated with the district ruler Herod (Antipas) (Acts 13:1).

MANAF

Pre-Islamic deity in ancient Arabia. The Quraysh and other tribes like Tamim, had a great devotion to this goddess before the rise of Islam.

MANAHATH

In the Old Testament, a descendant of Seir through Shobal (Genesis 36:20-23). The name is also applied to a site to which certain "sons of Ehud" inhabiting Geba were exiled at an unspecified time (1 Chronicles 8:6).

MANAHATHITES

In the Old Testament, certain Judeans descended from Caleb and Salma who apparently constituted part of the population of Manahath (1 Chronicles 2:50-54).

MANAS

In Buddhism, term denoting mind; the rational faculty in man. The term is used for that aspect of consciousness concerned with the relation of subject and object. Manas is essentially a dual phenomenon, its lower aspect being concerned with and directed towards the worlds of sense, constituting the perishable Skandhas; the higher, attracted to and illuminated by Buddhi, the faculty of intuition.

MANASSEH

In the Old Testament, Joseph's first-born son and the grandson of Jacob. After Joseph became Egypt's food administrator, Pharaoh gave him Asenath, the daughter of Potiphera, the priest of On, as a wife and she bore Joseph two sons, Manasseh and Ephraim.
Manasseh had sons by a Syrian concubine (1 Chronicles 7:14), and Joseph lived long enough to see the sons of Manasseh's son Machir (Genesis 50:22-23).

MANASSEH

One of the 12 tribes that in biblical times comprised the people of Israel. The tribe was named after one of the younger sons of Joseph, himself a son of Jacob. Among the most illustrious members of the tribe of Manasseh was Gideon, a God-fearing warrior who served as judge for 40 years.

MANASSEH, Prayer of

An apocryphal work (non-canonical for Jews and Protestants), one of a collection of songs appended to the Old Testament book of Psalms in several manuscripts of the Septuagint (the Greek version of the Hebrew Bible) and, like the Psalms, used during Jewish religious services.

The Prayer of Manasseh, best known of the collection, is a penitential prayer written as an extension of 1 Chronicles 33:11-13, wherein Manasseh, successor to Hezekiah as king of Judah in the 7th century BC, represents his idolatrous worship of gods other than Jehovah.

MANASSEH BEN ISRAEL

(1604-1657) Rabbi and Kabbalist, founder of the Jewish community in England. Manasseh's studies in Kabbala, the influential body of Jewish mystical writings, had convinced him that the Messiah would return to lead the Jews back to the Holy Land only if they were first dispersed elsewhere. He was therefore interested in obtaining their readmission to England, where a ban on Jewish residence had existed since the edict of Edward I in 1290.

MANDAEANISM

An ancient Near Eastern religion still surviving in Iraq and Iran, the central figure of which is fertility worship. The religion's followers call themselves Mandaiia, which means Gnostics. They were heretical Christian dualists who flourished in the 2nd and 3rd centuries AD.

MANDALA

In Tantric Hinduism and Buddhism, a symbolic diagram used in the performance of sacred rites and as an instrument of meditation. It is basically a representation of the universe, a consecrated area that serves as a receptacle for the gods and as a collection point of universal forces.

MANDAPA

The open assembly hall before the shrineroom in the Hindu temple, simplest and most beautiful examples of which were in the 10th and 11th centuries at Khajurabo.

MANDATUM

It was customary in eastern countries in ancient days to wash the road dust from the feet of a guest. In imitation of this gesture of courtesy Jesus washed the feet of the Apostles at the Last Supper. Today, in an optional foot-washing rite during the Holy Thursday Liturgy after the homily, a presider goes to select people, pours water over each one's feet, and dries them with a towel.

Any number of persons who are representative of the assembly are chosen for the rite. This ceremony is called Mandatum because of the scripture "I give you a new commandment ...." (John 13:34). Washing the feet of another is an important gesture of humility and charity that brings about reconciliation and symbolizes Jesus' call to service.

MANDELKERN, Solomon

(1846-1902) Hebrew poet and grammarian whose Hebrew-Latin concordance to the Hebrew Bible appeared in 1896 and excelled all earlier attempts.

MANDYAS

The name of two types of garment in the Byzantine church.

1 A black, hoodless monastic cape, part of the angelic habit of the advanced Byzantine monk and worn on solemn occasions.

2 the choir mantle of bishops in the Byzantine church. It is made of purple or blue silk, open in the front but fastened at the neck and again beneath the knees.

Four richly embroidered squares sometimes depicting pictures or symbols of the Evangelists are found at the fastenings. Horizontal stripes of red and white come forth from these squares to symbolize the life-giving streams of true doctrine.

The mandyas is also worn by prelates such as the archimandrite or hegumenos of a monastery but is black in color. The episcopal mandyas usually has a long train which is carried by a train bearer and may be ornamented at the bottom with tassels or little bells reminiscent of the decorations of the ephod of the Jewish High Priest.

MANES

In Roman theology, collective Latin name for the spirits of the dead. It was probably a euphemistic title, meaning "Good People."

MANGAL-KAVYA

Eulogistic verse in honor of a popular god or goddess in Bengal (India). It tells the story of how a particular god or goddess succeeded in establishing his or her worship on Earth

MANICHAEISM

Religion founded by Mani (circa 216 - circa 276), a Persian sage who preached from circa 240 and claimed to be the Paraclete (intercessor) promised by Christ. Mani borrowed ideas from Buddhism, Christianity, Gnosticism, Mithriaism and Zoroastrianism. Manichaeism contained an elaborate cosmic mythology of salvation. Man was created by Satan, but had particles of divine light in him, which has to be released. St. Augustine was a Manichee in his youth. In the Middle Ages, Manichaeism doctrine surfaced among the Bogomils and Cathari.

The early history of Manichaeism was one of persecution. From its beginnings it was proscribed in the Roman Empire by a succession of emperors. The Fathers of the Church (notably Augustine, once a Manichaean himself) wrote against it for centuries. It was the target of pagan critics.

Nevertheless, Manichaeism continued in many places. In China, for example, it persisted until the time of Ghengis Khan (13th century). Later forms of gnostic religion such as the Cathari and Albigensian heresies carried much of the Manichaean doctrine in the 13th century in the West.

MANIPLE

An oblong strip of cloth which hangs over the wrist or forearm in equal folds. Its use in liturgical services is no longer obligatory. It began as a linen cloth which was much like a handkerchief, became stylized as a formal item of dress, and after Constantine (died 337) was a symbol of rank. It spread throughout Europe between the 7th and 9th centuries. In the 12th century it became a badge of the subdiaconate.

MANJUSRI

In Mahayana Buddhism the Bodhisattva ("Buddha-to-be") personifying supreme wisdom.

MANNA

In the Old Testament, the main food of the Israelites during their forty-year trek in the wilderness (Exodus 16:35). According to biblical tradition, manna appeared on the ground with the evaporation of a layer of dew that developed in the morning, so that "upon the surface of the wilderness there was a fine flaky thing, fine like hoarfrost upon the earth," When the Israelites first saw it, they said, "What is it?" or, literally, "Man hu" (Exodus 16:13-15; Numbers 11:9). This is the probable origin of the name the Israelites themselves beginning to call the food "manna" (Exodus 16:31).

MANNERISM

A debated style in art (circa 1520-1580), originating in Italy as a perversion, some say, of the rational ideals of the High Renaissance, and noted for its pronounced emotional aesthetical feelings accompanied by a disturbing combination of distortions such as the crowding of compositions, attenuation of figures, exaggeration of poses, ambiguity of space, and acidity of color.

MANNING, Henry Edward (1808-1892)

A member of the Oxford Movement, which sought a return of the Church of England to the high-church ideals of the 17th century, who converted to Roman Catholicism and became archbishop of Westminster.

MANNING, James

(1738-1791) Baptist clergyman who founded Brown University, Providence, and served as its first president.

MANNIX, Daniel

(1864-1963) Roman Catholic prelate who became one of Australia's most controversial political figures during the first half of the 20th century. He became archbishop of Melbourne in 1917. His demands for state support of Roman Catholic educational institutions and his opposition to drafting soldiers for World War I made him a subject of controversy.

MANOAH

In Judaism, a Danite man of the Shephelah town of Zorah (Joshua 15:33) and the father of judge Samson.

MAN OF LAWLESSNESS

An expression used by the apostle Paul at 2 Thessalonians 2:3, in warning of the great anti-Christian apostasy that would develop before the "day of Jehovah."

MANSEL, Henry Longueville

(1820-1871) Philosopher and Anglican theologian and priest remembered for his exposition on moral and metaphysical doctrines. His contention that the human mind could not attain to any positive conception of the nature of God or His fondness provoked considerable controversy and he was accused of agnosticism.

MANSFIELD, Ernst, GRAF VON

(1580-1626) Roman Catholic missionary who fought for the Protestant cause during the 30-year War (1618-48).

MANTELLETTA

A sleeveless garment, fastened at the neck but open in front, worn liturgically by cardinals, bishops, abbots, and papal prelates. Round in form, it reaches to just below the knees and is of the same color as the individual's cassock. It seems originally to have been a mantle or cape, covering the rochet.

MANTRA

In Buddhism, a magical formula or invocation used in Tantric Buddhism in Tibet and in the Shingon School of Japan. The practice is based on a scientific knowledge of the occult power of sound.

A mantra is characterized by a series of sounds or words (sometimes a scriptural verse; most often the sounds are meaningless to all but the initiated) imparted by a guru or teacher to his disciple as part of initiation. Its recitation is used psychologically as support for meditation and concentration; it is further believed to possess a metaphysical or cosmic power enabling the devotee to be united with, or at least interiorly "in tune" with, a universal force, a divine being, or ultimate reality.

MANU

In the mythology of India the first man, and the legendary author of an important Sanskrit code of law.

MANUAL OF DISCIPLINE

In Judaism, one of the most important documents produced by the Essene community of Jews, who settled at Qumran in the Judaean desert in the early 2nd century BC to follow their own purist form of Judaism. The document contains an introduction to the sect's religious and moral ideals; a description of its admission ceremony and a long cathechetical discourse on its mystical doctrine of the primordial spirits of truth and perversity.

MANUAL OF THE MOTHER CHURCH

Also called church Manual of the First Church of Christ, Scientist, the fundamental law of the Church of Christ, Scientist, established in minute detail the polity, form of worship, and other particulars of the Christian Science movement.

It is composed of a series of bylaws, which cannot be in any way altered or repealed since the death of Mary Baker Eddy and which are binding and normative for all branch Churches of Christ, Scientist.

The Christian Science Board of Directors, as Mrs. Eddy's representatives and legal successors, are permitted to act only within the scope of the Manual, and its terms are binding on them as on any other member. The Manual was first published in 1895 and was periodically revised until 1906; it has preserved Mrs. Eddy's legislation intact since that time and prevented alteration or dissension within the Christian Science movement.

MANUSCRIPT ILLUMINATION

Term applied to many types of decoration of manuscript pages. Beginning in the 6th century, Byzantine artists, adapting methods used in Hellenistic illumination of ancient Greek classics, provided a rich counterpart to Byzantine church painting and mosaic.

In Europe from the 7th to the 9th centuries, Anglo-Irish art produced masterpieces in the Lindisfarne gospels and the Book of Kells, remarkable for a complex, intricate fantasy of decorated initials. On the continent great Carolingian manuscripts include the Vivian Bible from the school of Tours, and the 9th century Utrecht Psalter whose illustrations consist of extraordinary lively and expressive drawings without color.

German manuscripts of the Ottonian period, chiefly from the island of Reichenau, are characterized by lavish use of color and gold appropriate to their regal style. The flowering of monasticism during the Romanesque period helped to spread the art of illumination.

The work of high medieval artists on the manuscript page, complemented - in inventiveness and subtlety - Gothic stained glass and sculpture.

MAOCH

In the Old Testament, father of Achish, king of the Philistine city of Gath, with whom David and his 600 men found refuge from Saul (1 Samuel 27:1-3). He may be the same person as the Maacah of 1 Kings 2:39, though such identification is not positive. The name Maacah is quite similar to Maoch and it is possible that Achish, who was ruling when David was outlawed, was still the Philistine king of Gath at the commencement of Solomon's rule.

MAON

In the Old Testament, a descendant of Caleb through Shammai. Maon may have been the father of Beth-sur's inhabitants or the principal man or founder of that city (1 Chronicles 2:42-45).

MAPPO

In Japanese Buddhism, the age of the degeneration of the Buddha's law, which some believe to be the current age in human history.

MAQAMAT

Arabic word with a wide variety of meanings such as "sites," "places," "ranks," and "saints' tombs." In tasawwuf the word acquired the specific technical sense of mystical stages in the progress along the sufi road which are achievable by man.

MARA

In the Old Testament, name suggested by Eimelech's widow for herself to express the bitterness she experienced due to being bereaved of her husband and her sons Mahlon and Chilion. Naomi had left Bethlehem with a husband and two sons (Ruth 1:1-2), but returned from Moab as a saddened, childless widow. Mara means bitter.

MARA

In Buddhism, the Buddhist "Lord of the Senses" who was the Buddha's tempter on several occasions.

MARABOUT

A Muslim holy man or saint, a term used particularly in northern Africa. It is derived from the Arabic murabit, one who lives in a ribat or (generally fortified) monastery and dedicates his life to asceticism and the spread of Islam by means of the sword.

Such communities were particularly common in northern Africa where all to often jihad served as little more than a pretext for slaving. Nonetheless, the heads of such communities are especially revered by the people for their sanctity and are commonly believed to have some supernatural gifts. The term marabout is used in French and thence English to designate a solitary Muslim ascetic.

MARAH

One of Israel's early encampments in the Sinai Peninsula. It was named "Marah" (bitterness) because of the unpalatable water found there (Exodus 15:23; Numbers 33:8).

MARBECK, John

(1510-1585) Composer and organist known for his setting of the Anglican liturgy.

MARCAN HYPOTHESIS

In general, the agreement among scholars that Mark is one of the primary sources of Matthew and Luke. All but about 50 verses of Mark turn up in Matthew; more than half of Mark (about 350 verses) was taken over by Luke.

The priority of Mark is, however, variously explained. One of such theories (Vaganay) questions this priority, at least in the absolute sense. The author believes that all three Synoptics were Greek translations of the original Aramaic Matthew. But the more general opinion is that Mark is an original and independent work on which the other two drew, each adapting the Marcan material in accordance with his individual style and purpose.

Another hypothesis similar to the one proposed above, suggests that Mark was preceded by a smaller pro-Mark. This suggestion is made with a view to explaining the omission of at least a part of it by Matthew. Were these omissions purposeful or were the passages in question not included in the version of Mark on which they depended? This hypothesis has not won many adherents.

MARCELLINUS, Saint

(234-304) Pope probably from 294 to 304. His pontificate saw a long tranquil period terminated by a renewal and bloody persecution of Christians, the last of its kind, by the Roman emperor Diocletian.

MARCELLUS I, Saint

(234-309) Pope from 308 to 309. The penances he imposed on apostulates resulting from the persecutions of Christians by the Roman emperor Diocletian led to rioting. In 309 he was banished from Rome.

MARCIONISM

The teaching of Marcion, a Christian from Asia Minor, who settled in Rome circa 144. He maintained that Christianity was a completely new revelation, quite unrelated to the Old Testament (Bible) or to Jewish religion. He published the first known Canon of Christian scripture, edited in conformity with his beliefs.

MARCIONITE PROLOGUES

Introductory paragraphs prefacing the Epistles of Paul in many Vulgate manuscripts. They are called Marcionite because they are generally considered to be the work of Marcion, whose phraseology and ideas they reflect, e.g., the exaltation of Paul at the expense of the other Apostles and the abomination of "Jewish" teachings. They appear to have been written originally in Greek.

The Pastoral Epistles, which Marcion

rejected as non-canonical, also have prologues, but these betray no heretical ideas and are probably the work of another hand.

MARCIONITES

A semi-Gnostic sect that flourished in the 2nd century AD. The aim of this sect derives from Marcion of Asia Minor who, sometime after his arrival in Rome, fell under the influence of Cerdo, a Gnostic Christian.

MARDI GRAS

Festive day celebrated in France on the Tuesday before Ash Wednesday, which marks the close of the pre-Lenten season. In the United States, the festival is celebrated in New Orleans.

MARDUK

In Mesopotamian religion, the chief god of the city of Babylon and the national god of Babylonia. Originally he seems to have been a god of thunderstorms. All nature, including man, owed its existence to him; the destiny of kingdoms and subjects was in his hands.

From Marduk's universal sovereignty, the earthly sovereignty of the kings of Babylon was derived, and it was the king - at least in the later periods of the Babylonian history - who assumed the personality of Marduk in the annual cultic drama of the battle between Marduk and the forces of chaos, intended to assure order in the world for the coming year.

MARESHAH

In Judaism, a descendant of Judah who is called the "father" of Hebron (1 Chronicles 2:3, 42). While it might be concluded that Mareshah was the ancestor of the inhabitants of the city of Hebron, this is unlikely since the Hebron here mentioned has sons and thus was evidently a person (1 Chronicles 2:43).

The name is also applied to one of a group of nine cities in the Shephelah region of Judah (Joshua 15:44). Mareshah occupied a position of strategic importance beside one of the val-

leys forming a natural route from the coastal plain up into the mountains and to Hebron.

In the post exile period, Mareshah became known as Marissa and continued to be a site of considerable importance, though it became a Sidonian colony and later an Idumaean stronghold. It was finally destroyed by the Parthians in 40 BC.

MARGA

In Hinduism, the path, or way, of reaching salvation. Traditionally, three means are enumerated:

▲ jnana-marga, the way of knowledge, involving the study of philosophic texts and contemplation;

▲ karma-marga, the way of action, the proper performance of one's religious and ethical duties;

▲ bhaki-marga, the way of devotion and self-surrender to God.

MARGARET OF ANTIOCH, Saint

(3rd or 4th century) Virgin martyr and one of the 14 Auxiliary Saints, or Holy Helpers (a group of saints jointly commemorated on August 8), who was one of the most venerated saints during the Middle Ages.

During the reign of the Roman emperor Diocletian (284-305), Margaret allegedly refused marriage with the prefect Alybrius at Antioch and was consequently beheaded after undergoing extravagant trials and tortures.

MARGARET OF SCOTLAND, Saint

(1045-1093) Queen consort of Malcolm III and patroness of Scotland. In spite of her leanings toward a religious life, she married Malcolm III, king of Scotland from 1057 or 1058 to 1093. Through her influence over her husband and her court, she promoted, in conformity with the Gregorian reform, the interest of the church and of the English population.

MARGOLIOUTH, David Samuel

(1858-1940) Arabic scholar and minister of the Church of England whose pioneer efforts in Islamic studies won him a near-legendary reputation among Islamic peoples and Oriental scholars of Europe.

MARIA LEGIO

The largest African independent church with a Catholic background, which had a meteoric rise in the 1960s. Maria Legio originated with two Catholics of the Luo tribe, Simeon Ondeto and Gaundencia Aoko, who underwent prophetic experiences that directed them to reject traditional magic and divine healers and to form an African church to be named Maria Legio (after the Catholic Legion of Mary), which offered free healing by prayer and exorcism of evil spirits.

MARIANISTS

Religious congregation of the Roman Catholic Church founded by William Chaminade at Bordeaux (France) in 1817. There is a male and female congregation. To the usual religious vows of poverty, chastity, and obedience, the Marianists add a fourth vow of stability, faithfulness to the congregation, and special consecration to Mary. As an outward sign of this fourth vow, they wear a gold ring on the right hand.

MARIANNE

(about 57-29 BC) Jewish princess, a popular heroine in both Jewish and Christian tradition, whose marriage (37 BC) to the Judean King Herod the Great united his family with the deposed Hashmonean royal family and helped legitimize his position.

MARILLAC, Saint Louise de

(1581-1660) Cofounder with St. Vincent de Paul of the Daughters of Charity of St. Vincent de Paul, a congregation of laywomen dedicated to teaching and hospital work. It is - with some 40,000 followers, the largest congregation of women of the Roman Catholic Church.

MARINUS, Saint

Early 4th century Dalmatian and the traditional founder of San Marino.

MARINUS I

(812-884) Pope from 882 to 884. Pope John VIII appointed him ambassador to Constantinople, to negotiate the schism following Photius' condemnation. As pope, he continued discussing the issue of Photius.

MARINUS II

(877-946) Pope from 942 to 946. He worked for church reform, contributing mainly to discipline and monasticism.

MARIOLATRY

Giving to Mary the worship due to God. It is sometimes used as a term of reproach by Protestants contending that the honor Catholics pay to Mary is improper and should be directed only to God.

Catholic theology, however, distinguished latria, worship paid to God, from dulia, honor given to the saints, and hyperdulia, veneration given to Mary. Controversy has centered around whether common devotional practices directed toward Mary violate the prohibition against honoring her with latria, particularly among uneducated worshipers who may be unaware of the theological distinctions.

MARIOLOGY

In Christian, especially Roman Catholic, theology, the study of doctrines concerning Mary, the mother of Jesus; the term also refers to the content of these doctrines.

MARITAIN, Jacques

(1882-1973) Influential Roman Catholic philosopher, respected both for his interpretation of the thought of the medieval Scholastic St. Thomas Aquinas and for his own Thomist Philosophy.

MARK

Author of the second gospel. According to Acts, his mother's house in Jerusalem was a center of Christian life (12:12). Mark accompanied Barnabas (his cousin) and Paul on their missionary journeys (Acts 12:24).

Mark is the John Mark mentioned in the book of Acts and the John of Acts 13:5, 13.

He was evidently an early believer in Jesus Christ. His mother's home was used as a place of worship by the early Christian congregation, which may mean that both she and Mark became Jesus' followers before Christ's death (Acts 12:12). Since Mark alone mentions the sanctity clad young man who fled on the night of Jesus' betrayal, there is reason to believe that Mark himself was that young man (Mark 14:51-52). So it seems likely that Mark was present when the holy spirit poured out on the some 120 disciples of Christ on Pentecost 33 (Acts 1:13-15; 2:1-4).

John Mark is associated with Peter in Babylon, for he is mentioned as sending greetings in the Apostle's first letter (written about 62-64). Peter calls him "Mark my son," perhaps indicating the strong bond of Christian affection that existed between them (1 Peter 5:13).

MARK, Gospel of

Second of the four gospels, composed by John Mark in Rome. He was an associate of Paul and a disciple of Peter, whose teachings the gospel may reflect. It is the shortest of the four gospels, presumably written during the decade preceding the destruction of Jerusalem in 70. Mark's explanations of Jewish customs and his translations of Aramaic expressions suggest that he was writing for Gentile converts.

MARK, Saint

(263-336) Pope from January 18 to October 336. He is credited with giving the bishops of Ostia the right to consecrate new popes.

MARKS OF THE CHURCH

Four essential characteristics of the church that mark it as a true church of Christ. These are that, according to Roman Catholicism, the church is one, holy, catholic, and apostolic.

MARONITE CHURCH

One of the largest Eastern rite communities of the Roman Catholic Church, and the most numerous religious group in modern Lebanon; it is the only Eastern rite church that has no non-Catholic or Orthodox counterpart. They trace their origin to St. Maron, or Maro, a Syrian hermit of the late 4th and early 5th centuries, and St. John Maron, or Joannes Maro, patriarch of Antioch in 685-707, under whose leadership the invading Byzantine armies of Justinian II were routed in 684 making the Maronites a fully independent people.

MARONITE LITURGY

A form of Eastern Christian worship derived from the Syro-Antiochene rite. The oldest anaphora, called Shara, has some affinities with the East Syrian (Chaldean) anaphora of the apostles Addai and Mari. The anaphora used are those of the Twelve Apostles, of James the Apostle, of John the Evangelist, of Mark the Evangelist, of Pope Sixtus, of John Marun, and that of the Holy Roman Church.

MARONITES

A sect of Eastern Christians who in the 7th century espoused monotheism. In the 12th century they became affiliated with the Roman Catholic Church, Although some Maronites have settled in Cyprus, Syria and Egypt, their largest community is still in Lebanon, where their immediate spiritual head under the pope, the Maronite patriarch, also resides.

MAROTH

In biblical times, a town mentioned by the prophet Micah in his prophecy foretelling Jehovah's punishment of Jerusalem and Judah (Micah 1:12). The location is undetermined, some would identify it with Maarath (Joshua 15:59).

MARPRELATE CONTROVERSY

A brief but famous pamphlet war (1588-89) carried on by English Puritans using secret presses. They attacked the episcopacy as profane, proud, paltry, popish, pestilent, pernicious, presumptuous prelates. The identity of the authors, who signed themselves as Martin Marprelate, gentleman is still a mystery.

MARRANOS

Organized Jews in Spain and Portugal as distinguished from openly practicing Jews. Current use, however, applies the term to anyone connected with Judaism either by blood or practice. Since 1917 Jews have been proselytizing in northern Portugal among a backward group of Christians that, though without known ties with Judaism, may be a relic of the Marranos who from 1600 to 1800 formed a rich merchant league with centers in Constantinople, Salonika, Venice, Ferrara, Livorno, Antwerp, Amsterdam, Hamburg, London and Mexico. By 1800 most European countries permitted the open practice of the Jewish religion; in Spain and Portugal the Inquisition had by then eliminated Marranism.

MARRIAGE, Christian

One of the seven sacraments defined thus by the Roman Catholic Church: "The matrimonial covenant, by which a man and a woman establish between themselves a partnership of the whole of life, is by its nature ordered toward the good of the spouses and the procreation and education of offspring; this covenant between baptized persons has been raised by Christ the Lord to the dignity of a sacrament" (Canon 1055). In light of this teaching, the Christ emphasizes that "a matrimonial contract cannot validly exist between baptized persons unless it is also a sacrament by that fact."

Marriage is marked by two essential properties: "The essential properties of marriage are unity and indissolubility, which in Christian marriage obtain a special firmness in virtue of the sacrament" (Canon 1056).

Marriage is effected by true consent: "Marriage is brought about through the consent of the parties, legitimately manifested between persons who are capable in law of giving consent; no human power can replace this consent" (Canon 1057). This consent "is an act of the will by which a man and a woman, through an irrevocable covenant, mutually give and accept each other in order to establish marriage" (Canon 1057).

Because true consent is so fundamental to the church's understanding of marriage, there is an entire section of canon law dedicated to defining and explaining it (Canons 1095-1107). In brief, this consent must be rational, free, true, and mutual; it can be invalidated by an essential defect, substantial error, the influence of fear or force, or the presence of a condition or intention contrary to the true nature of marriage.

MARRIAGE TRIBUNAL

An ecclesiastical court before which is brought cases concerning the validity of marriage.

MARTHA

According to biblical tradition, the friend of Jesus and the sister of Mary and Lazarus of Bethany (Luke 10:38-42; John 11:1-46; 12:1-9). As the busy housewife she came to symbolize the active life, while Mary sat at Jesus's feet listening to his words, and thus came to represent the contemplative life centered on love of God.

MARTIN, Saint

(255-316) Patron Saint of France, the father of monasticism in Gaul, and the first great leader of Western monasticism. As bishop, Martin made Marmoutier (France) a great monastic complex to which European ascetics were attracted and from which apostles spread Christianity throughout Gaul.

MARTIN I, Saint

(587-655) Pope from 649-655 who summoned a great council of bishops which condemned heresies about the true nature of Christ. For defying the Emperor Constans II, he was imprisoned and eventually sent to the Crimea, where he died.

MARTIN IV

(1212-1285) Simon de Bris; pope from 1281-1285 who supported Charles I of Naples who wanted to restore the Latin Empire of Constantinople. He excommunicated the Byzantine Emperor Michael VIII (1281) and, after the Sicilian Vespers, Peter III of Aragon.

MARTIN OF TOURS, Saint

(323-397) Bishop of Tours. Son of a pagan, he served in the Roman army but after a vision of Christ sought a religious life. Bishop of Tours from circa 372, he encouraged monasticism and opposed execution of heretics.

MARTYR

Person who willingly gives his life or makes great sacrifices rather than give up his beliefs, religious or otherwise. The name comes from a Greek word meaning "witness." Most religious faiths have their martyrs. The first recorded Christian martyr was St. Stephen who, about 36 was accused of blasphemy and stoned to death in Jerusalem (Acts 7:8-60). Many social and political movements have also their martyrs.

MARTYRDOM

In the Old Testament and frequently in the New Testament the Greek martus means witness; but Paul uses the term to designate Stephen at the precise moment of his death (Acts 22:20). The suffering of Jesus in his Passion is the martyr's model; in fact, the early church popularly called Christ himself the first martyr.

In the *Epistle of Clement* the indifference of pain that characterizes many martyrs is ascribed to their confidence in Christ rather than to their belief in the truth of his teaching.

Theology defines martyrdom as the voluntary undergoing of death to bear witness to a cause, most properly speaking, to Christ's truth. How extensive is this truth will vary according to different views on the universitality of grace; some will see instances of it in those who have laid down their lives for any righteousness, thus Socrates and John the Baptist; others will require a more explicitly Christian certificate to be attached to this heroism, and this, quite understandably, will be expected for official commemoration in the ecclesiastical calendar.

The cause for which they died may have been the simple gospel tidings, such as we may have imagine to have been the case with Thomas the Apostle, or for order in the church (thus Thomas More), or the church's freedom (Thomas of Canterbury).

MARTYROLOGY

A chronological list of the feast days of saints with all the names given for each date. A martyrology gives some biographical information for some saints listed. The best-known martyrology is the Roman martyrology, which first appeared at the end of the Middle Ages.

MARY

The mother of Jesus, living in Nazareth. The chief events of her life related in the gospels are her betrothal to Joseph, the birth of Christ (Luke 2:7) and her witnessing his crucifixion (John 19:25-27).

The last mention of her (Acts 1:14) includes her in the company of those who devoted themselves to prayer after the ascension of Jesus into heaven. She was a faithful and humble woman (Luke 1:38).

Virgin Mary is placed above the saints for devotion in Roman Catholicism, the Orthodox Church, and among Anglo-Catholics. Special doctrines about her include the teaching that she is "ever-virgin," God-bearer and that her body was taken into heaven (the Assumption).

The Immaculate Conception (that she was conceived without sin) was defined dogmatically for Roman Catholics in 1854. This is generally rejected by the Orthodox Church. Protestantism has generally rejected this theology and devotion, but some Protestants now express more interest and sympathy.

MARY, Blessed Virgin

Catholic teaching on the Blessed Virgin Mary is very rich. Mary was the daughter of Joachim and Anne, a native of Nazareth who could trace her lineage to the royal house of David.

The Catholic Church teaches that Mary conceived without sin, that she remained sinless throughout her life, that she was truly the Mother of God, that she was always a virgin, and that she is able to make intercession for us before God.

In his encyclical *Munificentissimus Deus* of November 1, 1950, Pius XII aptly summarized Roman Catholic doctrine about Mary: "The revered Mother of God, from all eternity joined in a hidden way with Jesus Christ in one and the same degree of predestination, immaculate in her conception, a most perfect virgin in her divine motherhood, the noble associate of the divine redeemer who has won a complete triumph over sin and its consequences, was finally granted, as the supreme culmination of her privileges, that she should be preserved free from the corruption of the tomb and that, like her Son, having overcome death, she might be taken up body and soul to the glory of heaven where, as queen, she sits in splendor at the right hand of her Son, the immortal King of the ages."

He stressed the four great privileges of Mary that have been formally defined:

▲ her divine maternity - that she is truly the mother of God and true man;

▲ her Immaculate Conception - that from the first moment of her own conception she was preserved free from all stain of original sin;

▲ her perpetual virginity - that she was a virgin before, during, and after the birth of Christ;

▲ her Assumption - that after the completion of earthly life she was assumed body and soul into the glory of heaven. The Roman Catholic Church honors Mary with many liturgical feasts, the most notable being:

▲ the Immaculate Conception, December 8;

▲ the Nativity of Mary, September 8;

▲ the Annunciation, March 25;

▲ the Purification, February 2; and

▲ the Assumption, August 15.

MARY, In the Bible

Although the thrust of Old Testament messianism is Christological, some passages refer also to the mother of the Messiah: the alma-mother of Emmanuel (Isaiah 7:14); the woman whose offspring crushes the serpent's head (Genesis 3:15). Modern scholars do not agree on the precise biblical sense in which such passages refer to Mary.

Facts about Mary in the New Testament are relatively few but usually significant. Most of the material is concentrated in the independent gospel traditions of Matthew 1-2 and Luke 1:26-2:52.

Mary, a virgin at Nazareth, is espoused to Joseph. He certainly, she possibly, is of Davidic descent (Luke 1:26-27). The couple were not yet living together (Matthew 1:28-25) when Mary's consent to become the mother of the Messiah, "Son of the Most High," is solicited by an angelic messenger.

She is puzzled, she had resolved (vowed?) to remain a virgin. When assured that the conception would be effected by God, she humbly agrees (Luke 1:26-28). Joseph's subsequent predicament concerning the pregnancy is also resolved by an angelic messenger (Matthew 1:28-23).

After the Annunciation Mary visits her relative Elizabeth and gives voice to the Magnificat (Luke 1:39-56). In response to the census decree, Joseph takes Mary to Bethlehem, where she brings forth Jesus "her firstborn Son" (Luke 2:1-7). Neighboring shepherds visit the newborn child, and Mary ponders the significance of all that is happening (Luke 2:8-20).

40 days after the birth, Mary and Joseph take the infant to the Temple for her rite of purification and his presentation that the infant would be a sign of contradiction (Luke 2:22-38).

Later, Magi from the East visit the child and Mary, and offer gifts in homage (Matthew 2:11). Then, to protect the boy from harm at King Herod's hands, Joseph takes him and Mary to Egypt until notice of Herod's death (Matthew 2:13-15), after which they return to Nazareth, where they settle down (Matthew 2:19-23; Luke 2:39).

When Jesus is 12 years old he visits Jerusalem at Passover with Mary and Joseph but remains there unknown to them as they begin the return trip. After searching several days they find him with the teachers in the Temple but do not comprehend the reasons he gives for his actions (Luke 2:41-50).

Further references to Mary are infrequent. During the public ministry of her son, she is responsible for his first miracle, the changing of water into wine at a wedding feast in Canaan (John 2:1-11), after which she accompanies him, to Capernaum (John 2:12). People know her as the mother of Jesus (Mark 3:31). In two enigmatic passages she is apparently praised by her son as a model of faith (Luke 11:27-28). She stands beneath the cross on Calvary and is entrusted by her crucified son to the care of the beloved disciple (John 19:25-27).

She is last found in the community at prayer in the upper room after the Ascension (Acts 1:14). Paul's writings contain but one passing reference to her (Galatians). Many scholars find a final significant reference to Mary in the "woman" of Revelation 12.

MARY, Roman Catholic Theology

In his encyclical *Munificentissimus Deus* of November 1, 1950, Pope Pius XII aptly summarized Roman Catholic doctrine about Mary: "The revered Mother of God, from all eternity joined in a hidden way with Jesus Christ in one and the same degree of predestination, immaculate in her conception, a most perfect virgin in her divine motherhood, the noble associate of the divine redeemer who has won a complete triumph over sin and its consequences, was finally granted, as the supreme culmination of her privileges, that she should be preserved free from the corruption of the tomb and that, like her Son, having overcome death, she might be taken up body and soul to the glory of heaven where, as queen, she sits in splendor at the right hand of her Son, the immortal King of the ages."

He stresses the four great privileges of Mary that have been formally defined:

▲ her divine maternity - that she is truly the mother of God, because she is the mother of Jesus Christ, who is true God and true man;

▲ her Immaculate Conception - that from the first moment of her own conception she was preserved free from all stain of original sin;

▲ her perpetual virginity - that she was a virgin before, during, and after the birth of Christ;

▲ her Assumption - that after the completion of her earthly life she was assumed body and soul into the glory of heaven.

The pope also referred to other Marian beliefs not formally defined, e.g., that Mary is queen of heaven and earth, sharing her Son's dominion in a real but analogous, subordinate way; and that she is associated with her Son in the Redemption.

Catholic tradition sees Mary's role in the Redemption as twofold. She is coredemptrix, in that she cooperated indirectly and subordinately with her Son in the objective redemption, willingly devoting her whole life to the service of her Son, and suffering and sacrificing with Him beneath the cross. She is mediatrix of all graces because of her cooperation in subjective Redemption, using her maternal intercesssion in the application of Redemption's grace to mankind.

MARY, GOSPEL OF

Gnostic-influenced apocryphal gospel of the early Christian era not accepted into the New Testament canon.

MARYAM

Arabic word for Mary, the name of the mother of Isa in the Koran. She figures prominently at the beginning of the 19th sura which is named after her Surat Maryam. However, she is also mentioned in many other places, always with great respect. Maryam is the only women who is called by her proper name in the Koran.

MARYAM

The title of the 19th sura of the Koran. The sura belongs to the early Meccan period apart from two verses and has a total of 98 verses. The title of the sura is drawn from verses 16-34 which describe the announcement to Maryam, the mother of Isa, by Jibril of the forthcoming birth of Isa as well as the actual birth of the latter and the speech of Isa while still a baby in the cradle. The sura, which begins with five of the mysterious letters of the Koran, also refers to the Zakariyya, his son Yahya, the story of the prophet Ibrahim and his idol-worshipping father, Musa, Harun, and Idris.

MARY MAGDALENE

In the New Testament, the woman of Magdala from whom Jesus cast out seven demons (Luke 8:2). She became his devoted follower and was present at his death and burial. Mary was the first person to see the risen Jesus (John 20:18).

MARY OF THE INCARNATION

(1566-1618) Mystic whose activity and influence in religious affairs inspired most of the French ecclesiastics of her time.

MASAD, al-

The title of the 111th sura of the Koran; it means "The Palm Fibers." The sura belongs to the Meccan period and has 5 verses. Its title is drawn from the fifth verse which makes reference to the palm fibers around the neck of Abu Lahab's wife. Basically, this entire short sura is a majestic condemnation of an uncle of the Prophet Mohammed called Abd al-Uzza, known as Abu Lahab, who opposed the Prophet. The sura warns that Abu Lahab's riches will not help him and that he and his wife will burn in hell.

MASADA

Ancient mountaintop fortress in southeast Israel, site of the Jews' last stand against the Romans in the revolt of 66-73. It occupies the entire top of a great mesa near the south-east coast of the Dead Sea.

MASH

In the Old Testament, a descendant of Shem through Aram (Genesis 10:22-23).

MASHAL

In Judaism, a city of Asher assigned to the Gershonites; apparently an alternate name for Mishal (Joshua 21:27, 30; 1 Chronicles 6:71-74). The exact location is unknown.

MASHRIQ AL-ADHKAR

Baha'i temple or house of worship. It is a none-sided construction, in keeping with the Baba'i belief in the mystical properties of the number 9. Free of ritual and clergy, the mashriq is open to adherents of all religions and offers a simple service consisting of readings from the sacred baba'r writings and the holy books of other faiths.

MASIH, al-

In Islam, literally "The Messiah." This is a title frequently born by Isa in the Koran. However, the latter does not explain this title. Some commentators identify the word as foreign, and a variety of explanations have been put forward. What is clear is that the Koran does not use the word in the precise sense of Judaic or Christian usage.

MASJID

Arabic word for mosque. The word means literally "a place of bowing down." The word masjid on its own often indicates a fairly simple mosque. A jami or masjid jami, on the other hand, indicates a rather larger mosque in a central location which often has a public function as a focus and place for the Friday Prayer.

MASONRY

Or Freemasonry, one of the oldest and largest fraternal organizations in the world. Members of the fraternity participate in elaborate allegorical and symbolic rituals. Freemasonry exists to promote brotherhood and morality. members may be of any religion, though most are Christians.

MASS

A term mainly in Roman Catholicism for the eucharist. Protestantism rejected it because of the association with the notion of eucharistic sacrifice, although Luther constructed a "German Mass." Anglo-Catholics have revived the term and the associated doctrines in Anglicanism.

The *Canon of the Mass* refers to the prayer consecrating the "elements" (bread and wine). "High Mass" involves elaborate ceremonial, music and several assistants, by contrast with the more common "Low Mass" - a distinction, however, which ended with Vatican Council II. The Catholic Mass consists of two main parts:

▲ the Liturgy of the Word;
▲ the Liturgy of the Eucharist.

In addition, there are introductory rites (greeting, penitential rite, the Glory of God hymn on certain occasions, opening prayer) and concluding rites (final greeting, blessing, dismissal).

MASS FOR THE PEOPLE

The celebration of the Holy Eucharist for the intention of the faithful. Pastors and diocesan bishops are required by canon law to offer Mass for the people on Sundays and other holy days of obligation.

MATER MATUTA

In Roman religion, goddess of the ripening of grain. Her worship in Italy was widespread and of ancient origin. Her temple at Rome, located in the Forum Boarium, was dedicated in 395 BC.

MATRED

In the Old Testament, mother of Mehetabel, the wife of Edomite King Hadar (Genesis 36:31; 1 Chronicles 1:50).

MATRITES

In Judaism, a Benjaminite family of which King Saul of Israel was a member (1 Samuel 10:21).

MATSYA

In Hinduism, first of the ten avataras (incarnations) of the Hindu god Visnu (Vishnu). In this appearance Visnu saved the world from a great flood.

MATSYENDRANATHA

(flourished 10th century) First human guru, or spiritual teacher, of the Natha cult, a popular Indian religious movement combining elements of Hinduism, Buddhism, and Hatha Yoga, a form of yoga that stresses breath control and physical postures.

MATTAN

In Judaism, a priest of Baal who was killed before the altars at the house of that false god. This occurred when the people, led by Johoiada the priest, pulled down the house of Baal, as well as destroying his altars and images. At that time the usurper Athaliah was put to death and Jehoash was installed as Judah's king (2 Kings 11:16-21; 2 Chronicles 23:17).

MATTANAH

One of Israel's encampments between the Arnon torrent valley and the territory of Sihon the Amorite (Numbers 21:12-21).

MATTANIAH

In Judaism, a Levite, a son of Heman of Asaph's family. He was selected by lot to head the ninth service group of Levitical musicians as arranged by David (1 Chronicles 25:1-16).

The name is also applied to a Levite of the sons of Asaph living in the time of King Jehoshaphat (2 Chronicles 9:15). It may be another Mattaniah or the representative of that house that is mentioned in Nehemiah 12:8.

MATTATHA

In the Old Testament, a man of the tribe of Judah who was a son of Nathan and grandson of David. He was an ancestor of Jesus, according to Christ's maternal genealogy reported by Luke (Luke 3:23, 31).

MATTATHIAS

(283-166 BC) Jewish priest and landowner of Modein near Jerusalem, who in 167 BC defied the decree of Antiochus IV Epiphanes of Syria to Hellinize the Jews; he fled to the Judean hills with his five sons and waged a guerilla war against the Syrians, being succeeded by his son Judas Maccabeus.

MATTHAT

According to biblical tradition, a distant ancestor of Jesus Christ through Mary. He is called "the son of Levi" and was one of the persons listed in Jesus' maternal genealogy of the period between Zerubbabel and David (Luke 3:29).

The name is also applied to a closer ancestor of Jesus through Mary. Her father Heli is referred to as the "son" of this Matthat, who was probably Mary's grandfather (Luke 3:23-24).

MATTHEW

According to biblical tradition, one of the 12 apostles, surnamed Levi, the author of the first gospel. He was a tax-collector, working for the Romans, before Jesus called him (Matthew 9:9). Because Matthew's occupation was one that earned distrust and contempt everywhere, the scribes of the Pharisees criticized Jesus on seeing him eat with tax collectors and sinners.

Thereupon Jesus answered: I came not to call the righteous, but sinners (Mark 2:15-17).

After the Passover of 31, Jesus selected the 12 Apostles, and Matthew was one of them (Mark 3:13-19; Luke 6:12-16). Though the Bible makes various references to the Apostles as a group, it does not mention Matthew by name again until after Christ's ascension to heaven. Matthew saw the resurrected Jesus Christ (1 Corinthians 15:3-6), received parting instruction from him and saw him ascend to heaven. After this he and the other Apostles returned to Jerusalem. The Apostles were staying in an upper chamber there, and Matthew is specifically named as being among them. Some 120 disciples received the holy spirit on the day of Pentecost, 33 (Acts 1:14-15; 2:1-4).

MATTHEW, Gospel of

First of the four New Testament gospels, written by Matthew, one of the 12 disciples. He is described in the text as a tax collector (10:3). The gospel, the fullest of the four, was written probably circa 50 for Jewish Christians. Being written especially for Jews, it explains that the gospel was not a rejection of the Old Testament. It is rather an outworking of the great promises of the old covenant. By many Old Testament quotes Jesus is proved to be the predicted Messiah (5:17).

MATTHIAS

According to biblical tradition, the disciple who was chosen to replace Judas Iscariot after Judas betrayed Jesus (Acts 1:21-26). It is generally believed that Matthias ministered in Judaea and then carried out missions to foreign places.

MATURIDIYAH, al

A Muslim orthodox school of theology named after its founder Abu Mansur Muhammad al-Maturidi (867-935). The school is characterized by its reliance on the Koran without reasoning or free interpretation.

MATZA

Unleavened bread eaten by the Jews at the time of their exodus from Egypt. Because matzas could be quickly baked, they were also served to unexpected guests.

MATZEVA

A stone pillar erected on elevated ground beside a sacrificial altar. It was considered sacred to the god it symbolized and had a wooden pole to signify a goddess. After conquering the Canaanites, early Israelites used these symbols as their own until their use was outlawed as idolatrous (Deuteronomy 16:21).

MA'UN, al-

The title of the 107th sura of the Koran; the Arabic word here has been variously translated as "Charity," "Benevolence," and "Alms." Some of the sura's 7 verses were revealed in Mecca and others in Medina. The title of the sura is drawn from the seventh verse which refers to the prevention of al-ama'un. The sura begins with the question; have you seen the man who denies the Judgment to come?

MAUNDY THURSDAY

The Thursday before Easter, commemorating Christ's washing of the disciples' feet and institution of Holy Communion at the Last Supper.

MAURICE, Saint

(222-286) Early Christian soldier and his comrades whose alleged martyrdom inspired a cult still practiced today in Switzerland and northern Italy. The unbroken chant is still a tradition at the Abbey of St. Maurice.

MAURISTS

A congregation of French Benedictine monks founded in 1618 and devoted to strict observance of the Benedictine rule and especially to historical and ecclesiastical scholarship.

MAWLA

Arabic word for client. In early islamic history this word indicated a non-Arab convert to Islam who became the "client" of an Arab. Although, in theory, all Muslims in the early Islamic state were supposed to be treated as equals, in practice the mawali or clients were often treated as second-class citizens by comparison with those of Arab stock.

MAWLAWIYYA

Arabic word for whirling dervishes. This is an important sufi order, originating in Turkey, whose name derives from the title borne by their inspirer, the Persian mystical poet Rumi or Mawlana. The whirling dance of the Mawlawiyya which is performed with music during their dhikr, and for which the order has become famous, attempted to emulate or symbolize the motion of the spheres, according to one interpretation.

MAWLID

Arabic word for birthday, anniversary. The feast of the Prophet Mohammed's birthday is an occasion of happy celebrations in the Muslim world.

MAWLID AL-NABI

The birthday of the Prophet Mohammed. It is celebrated with much festivity in the Islamic world on the 12th day of the Islamic lunar month of Rabi al-Awwal.

MAYA

In Buddhism, term used in the sense of illusion. Philosophically, whereas that alone which is changeless and eternal is real, the phenomenal universe, subject to differentiation and impermanence, is maya.

MAYMUNA

A widow married by the Prophet Mohammed on his return from pilgrimage in 629.

MAZDAK

Religious leader who developed Mazdakism, a dualistic sectarian religion in Persia during the Sassanid dynasty from the late 5th century AD.

MAZDAKISM

A dualistic religion that developed in Persia (Iran) as an offshoot of Manichaeism, a Gnostic religion. Mazdakism was a reform movement seeking an optimistic interpretation of the Manichaean dualism (Light and Darkness, Good and Evil, etc). According to this belief, there exist two original principles, Good (or Light) and Evil (or Darkness). Light acts by free will and design; Darkness, blindly and by chance. By accident the two became mixed, producing the world. The god of Light, who is to be worshipped, is enthroned in paradise, having before him four powers: perception, intelligence, memory, and joy.

MEAL, Sacred

A sacred meal is regarded as the sharing of food and drink as (sign of) communion with the Holy, generally regarded as their source, based on the fact that food in human society is a symbolic reality as well as an object of consumption.

Anthropologically, there are two major types:

▲ theophagy (god-eating), related to cannibalism (e.g., Aztecs's) and

▲ theoxenia, community meals with the gods, perhaps derived from meals shared with ancestors.

Sacred and ordinary meals are difficult to distinguish in the Old Testament because of the interrelation of the "sacred" and "secular," except that the former have a more elaborate ritual. The sacred meal, a dinner in God's presence to acknowledge him as source of blessings, takes various forms.

Theophagy is unknown; only in some offerings and sacrifices is there an indication of a divine meal, food offered to God. Communion meals (God as participant) are common (e.g., Passover); part of the sacrifice is offered to God and the rest is shared by the participants.

Covenant meals, signifying fellowship and solemnizing an agreement, celebrate god as the source of the bond of sharing and union. In the New Testament, a banquet often symbolizes the messianic age and Jesus' meals with sinners anticipate the kingdom-meals.

In Christian theology the meal provides a paradigm of sacramental as an effective symbol of the invisible transcendent, and thus a ritual impetus to communal living and social action. The Eucharist centers on bread and wine, already signs, but moves beyond the gifts of creation to celebrate salvation in an eschatological perspective, with the Eucharistic Prayer or Canon articulating the meaning of the community's experience. Thus a meal as sign of fellowship and participation in the mystery of life, acknowledged as God's gift is context for Christian Eucharist.

MEARAH

In biblical times, a Sidonian city or district that remained to be conquered after Israel's campaign under Joshua's leadership ended (Joshua 13:2-4). Two locations have been suggested as possible identifications. One is the village of Mogheiriyeh, circa 6 miles north-east of Sidon. The other is Mughar Jezzin, a district of caves atop the Lebanon range and east of Sidon.

MEBUNNAI

In Judaism, a Hushathite mighty man in David's army (2 Samuel 23:27). Apparently he is the same person as the Sibbecai mentioned in 2 Samuel 21:18 and 1 Chronicles 11:29.

MECCA

Called in Arabic Makka; the holiest city in Islam whose history is inextricably bound up with that of the Prophet Mohammed himself. He lived there for much of his life. Muslims turn towards Mecca in prayer and undertake the pilgrimage (Hajj) to that city, not only because of its prophetic and historical associations, but because it contains the Ka'ba. The Koran was first revealed to Mohammed near this city and it was from Mecca that he made his famous migration (Hijra) to Medina in 622.

Mecca probably originated and developed as a major city in pre-Islamic times because of its strategic position on the great trade routes running from the Yemen empire to the Byzantine and Persian empires. The city today is within the modern Kingdom of Saudi Arabia and the Saudi king likes to refer himself as "The Servitor of the Two Sanctuaries."

MECHERATHITE

A biblical term pertaining to a person or place named Mecherah, to which Hepher, one of David's mighty men, was linker either by descent or former residence (1 Chronicles 11:26, 36).

MECHITARISTS

A congregation of Roman Catholic Armenian monks, widely recognized for their contribution to the renaissance of Armenian philology, literature, and culture early in the 19th century and particularly for the publication of old Armenian-Christian manuscripts. The Armenian Academy at San Lazzaro, set up in Rome by the Venetian Mechitarists in the early 19th century, quickly became a center of Armenian learning.

MECONAH

In biblical times, a town in southern Judah apparently near Ziklag and large enough to have dependent or "daughter" towns (Nehemiah 11:25-28).

MEDAD

In Judaism, one of the 70 older men of Israel selected to assist Moses during the wilderness trek. While Nedad and Eldad had not gone to the tent of meeting with the others, "they were among those written down." Hence, when God took away some of the spirit that was upon Moses, putting it upon each of the 70 older men, these too received it

and began acting as prophets in the camp (Numbers 11:16-17; 24-26). Though Joshua suggested restraining Medad and Eldad, Moses said: "Are you feeling jealous for me? No, I wish that all of God's people were prophets, because God would put his spirit upon them! (Numbers 11:27-29).

MEDAN

In the Old Testament, one of Abraham's six sons by his concubine Keturah (Genesis 25:1-2). The Arabian tribe that descended from Medan has not been identified, and where it settled is unknown. However, "Medan" may be represented in "Badan," a place south of Tema taken by Assyrian King Tiglath-pileser II in the eight century BC, and the Arabic "m" and "b" are frequently interchanged.

MEDEA

In Greek mythology, an enchantress who helped Jason, leader of the Argonauts, to obtain the Golden Fleece from her father, King Aeetes of Colchis. She was perhaps a goddess and had the gift of prophecy. She married Jason and used her magic powers and advice to help him.

MEDEBA

Biblical place represented by modern Madeba, a town located on a low, gently sloping hill circa 12 miles east of the northern end of the Dead Sea. The ancient "King's Road" linked it with other cities east of the Jordan. Situated on a treeless but fertile plain or plateau averaging 2,300 feet in elevation, Medeba itself lies at an altitude of 2,540 feet above sea level. In the plain, the "tableland of Medeba," flocks of sheep and goats find pasturage (Joshua 13:9, 16).

After the Israelites defeated Amorite King Sihon, Medeba came to be in the territory given to the tribe of Reuben (Joshua 13:8-16).

MEDES

According to biblical tradition, an Aryan race, hence of Japhetic stock and evidently descended from Japheth's son Madai (Genesis 10:2). They were closely related to the Persians in race, language and religion. As a people, the Medes do not begin to appear in biblical history until the eight century BC, while the first mention of them in available secular records dated from the time of the Assyrian King Shalamaneser III, a contemporary of King Jehu (905-876 BC). Sometime between the dispersion of peoples resulting from the confusion of languages at Babel (Genesis 11:8-9) and the reign of Shalamaneser III, the Medes had entered into the Iranian plateau region. Archaeological and other evidence is viewed as indicating their presence there from about the middle of the second millennium BC onward.

Although it was dominated variously by the Parthians and by the Seleucid Empire, Greek geographer Strabo indicated that a Median dynasty continued in the first century BC. At Jerusalem, Medes along with Parthians, Elamites and persons of other nationalities were present at Pentecost in AD 33. Since they are spoken of as "Jews, reverent men, from every nation," they may have been descendants of those Jews exiled to cities of the Medes following the Assyrian conquest of Israel, or perhaps were proselytes of the Jewish faith (Acts 2:1-5).

MEDIATION

In general the interposition between persons at variance to pacify them; in Catholic theology: the process of reconciling God and man. The role applied primarily to Christ, secondarily and by analogy to his mother and the church. Christ's mediatorship has three phases:

▲ Being God and man, he is in a middle position between the parties to be reconciled.

▲ By his atoning and meritorious sacrifice on the cross, he brought about man's redemption, i.e., restored man to God's friendship lost through his sin (Hebrews 7:27).

▲ By interceding for man in heaven, he now makes available the fruits (graces) in his redemption (Hebrews 7:25).

Christ's mediation is primary, self-sufficient, independent, of infinite value. In this sense he is the only mediator (1 Timothy 2:5). The mediator role of all others is secondary, insufficient by itself, of finite value, drawing all its efficacy from Christ's redemption.

Mary has been hailed as mediatrix since at least the 8th century. The term first referred either to her exalted rank in the hierarchy of creation, owing to her divine motherhood, or to the influential prayer in man's behalf. In the 14th century she began to be styled Coredemptrix, a word widely used since, and found in papal documents.

According to most Catholic theologians, Mary is Coredemptrix, not merely because she gave man the Redeemer, but also because, in the restricted sense, her lifelong cooperation with Christ, mainly through her sufferings, was accepted by God as having atoning and meritorious value for man's Redemption.

MEDINA

Anglicized form of the Arabic al-Madina meaning "The City." It is the second holiest city in Islam after Mecca. Its early name was Yathrib. Medina is frequently characterized by the epithet "The Radiant." Like the city of Mecca the early history of Medina is closely bound up with that of the Prophet Mohammed. It was to this city that he made his famous Hijra in 622. It was there that, very early on, the "Constitution of Medina" was formulated.

A walled city, its chief building is the mosque containing the tombs of Mohammed, his daughter Fatima and the caliph Omar. The mosque also has a famous library. Founded by Jewish settlers circa 2,000 years ago, and long known as Yathrib, Medina stands in a fertile oasis noted for its dates, gains and vegetables.

MEDITATION

Profound and generally peaceful consideration of truths that are thought to have great importance in ordering and living one's life. Meditation is especially esteemed and practiced regularly by persons who have dedicated themselves to religious pursuits.

Meditation is a central theme in Buddhism, being the surest way to purification. Right Mindfulness, the seventh step on the Eightfold Path, implies constant control of thoughts; the consequent right concentration, complete control of all the mental processes, results in Samadhi, the attainment of spiritual insight and tranquility.

MEDIUM

One whose organism is sensitive to the vibrations from the spirit world, and through whose instrumentality intelligences in that world are able to convey messages and produce the phenomena of spiritualism.

Spiritualists do not maintain that the medium must be the recipient of extraordinary supernatural gifts; their view is rather that the medium acts in accordance with given laws of nature. They also feel that only certain individuals are naturally endowed with the necessary psychic powers and even they must carefully cultivate their sensitivity in spiritual impulses.

MEDIUMSHIP

In Buddhism, a phenomenon that may be positive or negative. The former is rare, for it involves an advanced pupil, highly trained for the purpose, who allows his Master to take possession of the lower vehicles or personality while the pupil retains full consciousness.

Negative mediumship causes permanent damage to the medium, for as control of the lower principles is loosened by the invasion of some discarnate entity or elemental it becomes much easier for evil entities of any kind to take possession, and increasingly hard for the medium to resume responsibility.

MEGALOSCHEMI

In the Orthodox curch monks who have normally passed through the grades of rasophore and microschemos and have accepted the highest state of monasticism which involves stricter fasting and prayer as well as a greater commitment to silence than is required of the other monks.

In Russian practice the habit is given to the second grade of monks but in Greek practice it is reserved for the megaloschemi together with a special monastic headdress, signifying the mystic cross that the monk takes upon himself when he vows poverty, chastity, obedience, and a life of asceticism.

MEGIDDO

In biblical times, one of the royal cities of the Canaanites, later in the possession of the tribe of Manasseh (Judg. 1:27). It lies circa 18 miles south-east of Haifa in northern Israel. Megiddo's strategic location at the crossing of two military and trade routes made the city very important. It controlled a commonly used pass on the trading route between Egypt and Mesopotamia, and it also stood along the north-west-south-east route that connected the Phoenician cities with Jerusalem and the Jordan River valley.

MEHETABEL

In the Old Testament, daughter of the woman Matred and wife of Edomite King Hadar (Genesis 36:31-39). The name is also applied to an ancestor (probably the grandfather) of the Shemaiah hired by Tobiah and Sanballat to try to induce Nehemiah to sin out of fear (Nehemiah 6:10-14).

NEHIDA

In the Old Testament, ancestor of a family of Nethinim whose "sons" or descendants returned to Judah from Babylonian exile with Zerubbabel in 537 BC (Ezra 2:1-2, 43, 52; Nehemiah 7:54).

MEHIR

In Judaism, a man of the tribe of Judah who was the son of Chelub (Caleb) and "father of Eshton" (1 Chronicles 4:1-11).

MEHOLATHITE

In the Old Testament, the designation for Adriel (a son-in-law of Saul) and his father Barzillai (1 Samuel 18:19; 2 Samuel 21:8). It probably denotes that they were from the town of Abel-meholah.

MEHUJAEL

In the Old Testament, great-grandson of Cain. Mehujael was the father of Methushael and the grandfather of Lamech (Genesis 4:17-18).

MEHUMAN

In biblical times, one of the court officials of Persian King Ahasuerus (Xerxes I), who ruled in the days of Mordecai and Esther. Nehuman was named first among the seven court officials ordered by Ahasuerus to bring Queen Vashti into his presence (Esther 1:10-11).

MELATIAH

In the Old Testament, a Gibeonite who assisted in repairing part of Jerusalem's wall under Nehemiah's supervision in 455 BC (Nehemiah 3:7).

MELCHIZEDEK

In the Old Testament, a figure of importance because he was both king and priest. He was connected with Jerusalem, and was revered by Abraham, who paid a tithe to him. He appears as a person only in the story of Abraham rescuing his kidnapped nephew, Lot, by defeating a coalition of Mesopotamian kings under Cherdorlaomer. Psalm 110, in referring to a future Messiah of the Davidic line, shows the priest-king Melchizedek as a prototype of the Messiah. In the letter to the Hebrews Melchizedek is also seen as the foreshadow Christ (Hebrews 7:1-5). Just as the Old Testament assigns no birth or death to Melchizedek, so is the priesthood of Christ eternal.

MELCHIZEDEK PRIESTHOOD

In the Church of Jesus Christ of Latter-day Saints, the higher of two priesthoods. It is concerned with spiritual rather than secular matters. According to Mormon belief it was originally conferred in 1829 on the prophet Joseph Smith and on Oliver Cowdery directly by the Apostles Peter, James, and John.

MELEA

According to biblical tradition, a maternal ancestor of Jesus Christ who lived long after King David (Luke 3:31).

MELEAGER

In Greek mythology, the leader of the Calydonian boar hunt, a famous joint undertaking of the heroic age.

MELETIOS PEGAS

(1549-1601) Greek Orthodox patriarch of Alexandria who strove by theological arguments and ecclesiastical diplomacy to maintain the exclusive leadership of Greek Orthodoxy throughout Eastern Christendom during the 16th century.

MELETIUS OF ANTIOCH

(310-381) Theologian and bishop of Antioch, leader of the Meletian Schism, an orthodox, anti-Arian movement that was the focus of the 4th century Arian controversy concerning the theological terminology designating God as one nature in three Persons.

MELETIUS OF LYCOPOLIS

(285-357) Bishop of Lycopolis, near Thebes, Egypt, who formed an ascetical, schismatic church holding a rigorous attitude in readmitting apostates who had compromised their faith in pagan persecutions, particularly the violent repression decreed by the Eastern Roman Emperor Diocletian (284-305).

MELKITE CHURCH

One of the most ancient Catholic churches of the Byzantine Rite in the Near East. The name is derived from the Aramaic title melek, king and was coined during the 5th century theological and political dispute and applied to those Christians of Syria and Egypt who refusing Monophysitism and accepting the definition of faith of the Council of Chalcedon (451), remained in communion with Rome, and in that specific historical incident, with the imperial see of Constantinople as "king's men."

In 1724, thanks to the initiative of archbishop Eftimios Saifi, the legitimate native Melkite patriarch Cyril VI Tanas publicly reasserted the abiding communion of the Roman and Antiochene (Melkite) churches. However the Greek Orthodox Church immediately installed a Greek bishop in the patriarchal see of Antioch, creating an Eastern Orthodox hierarchy for the so-called Syrian Antiochene Church.

Melkites follow the Byzantine Rite, which is proper to the Church of Constantinople. Liturgical languages are basically Greek and Arabic but also any language of the local Melkite community.

MELVILLE, James

(1556-1614) Scottish Presbyterian reformer and educator whose *Diary* (1556-1601) became a popular chronicle of the religious events of his day.

MEMNON

In Greek mythology, son of Tithonus and Eos and king of the Ethiopians. He was a post-Homeric hero, who, after the death of Trojan warrior Hector, went to assist his uncle Priam, the last king of Troy, against the Greeks.

MEMPHIS

In antiquity the premier city of Egypt. Standing at the junction of Upper and Lower Egypt, circa 15 miles south of Cairo, it was the royal residence during most of the 3rd and 4th dynasties and occasionally up to the 6th. It was rebuilt by the pharaohs of the 18th and 19th dynasties.

MEMUCAN

In biblical times, the chief spokesman for the seven Medo-Persian princes on the occasion that Vashti refused to obey King Ahasuerus (Esther 1:13-15). Memucan's opinion was that Vashti had wronged not only the king but also the princes and the people of the empire, and, therefore, she should be removed as queen, so that all wives of the empire might learn to be obedient to their husbands. The king and the other princes agreed with Memucan, and a royal decree to this effect was written among the unchangeable laws of the Medes and Persians (Esther 1:16-22).

MENAHEM

In Judaism, son of Ghadi and king of Israel for ten years (circa 791-780 BC). Upon learning that Shallum had assassinated King Zechariah, Menahem went from Tirzah to Samaria and killed the assassin there. He then assumed rulership. Evidently during the early part of his reign Menahem struck down Tiphsah and all that was in it and its territory out from Tirzah, because it did not open up. The town was apparently reluctant to open its gate to him (2 Kings 15:10-17).

MENAT

In Egyptian religion, protective amulet, usually hung at the back of the neck as a counterpoise to the necklace worn in the front.

MENDELSSOHN, Moses

(1729-1786) Jewish philosopher, critic, Bible translator and commentator whose prestige contributed to the efforts of Jewish communities to assimilate to the German bourgeoisie.

MENDICANT ORDERS

Religious orders of men committed to an evangelical poverty that originally prohibited individual and in some cases even communal ownership of property. These orders emerged, mainly in the 13th century, when clerical affluence was common enough to give scandal and various doctrinally suspect sects were intensely concerned with the practice of poverty.

The absolute prohibition of communal ownership proved so impractical, however, that most of the mendicant orders have abandoned it or sought certain concessions in favor of individual poverty but community control of the order's resources.

Under the impetus of Vatican Council II, the mendicant orders are seeking through new experimental constituents to express the ideals of their founders.

MENESS
In Baltic religion, the moon, the god whose monthly renewal of strength is imparted to all growing things.

MENNA
According to biblical tradition, a distant maternal ancestor of Jesus Christ, not far removed from David (Luke 3:31).

MENNONITE BRETHREN CHURCH IN NORTH AMERICA
Denomination established by Mennonite Brethren immigrants from Russia who began arriving in the western United States in the 1870s.

MENNONITE CHURCH
Largest and oldest of the Mennonite churches located in North America. It developed from groups of Mennonites and Amish who left Germany and Switzerland and settled in eastern Pennsylvania in the late 17th and 18th centuries.

MENNONITES
Protestant sect originating among the Anabaptists of Switzerland. They became influential, particularly in the Netherlands, and are named for the Dutch reformer Menno Simons. They base their faith solely on the Bible, believe in separation of church and state, pacifism, and baptism only for adults renouncing sin. Despite persecution, the sect spread and now totals circa 655,000. They are known for their strict simplicity in their life and worship.

MENNONITE WORLD CONFERENCE
An international organization of Mennonites that meets every five years for fellowship and discussion of items of mutual concern.

MENNO SIMONS
(1496-1561) Priest whose leadership of the Dutch Anabaptists during its formative first years-has been of significant influence in the Mennonite church and in pacifism to the present time.

MENOLOGY
A term applied to a number of types of liturgical books used in the Eastern church. It is at times used as the equivalent of menaion, one of the 12 volumes (for each month of the year) that taken together correspond to the Proper of the Saints in the Roman Breviary, but with the addition of hymns and references to the saints honored each day.

Most frequently the term is simply applied to a collection of the historical notices read in the daily liturgy. It may also be applied to the lists for scriptural readings arranged according to the days of the months found at the beginning of manuscripts of the gospels or other lectionaries.

Most properly it is used for long lives of the saints of the Greek church arranged according to the month of the ecclesiastical year, which begins with September and ends with August. The most famous monologion of this type is that of Simeon Metaphrastes, compiled towards the end of the 10th century.

MENORA
Multibranched ritual candelabrum used by Jews during the eight-day festival of Hanukkah. The menora is an imitation of the seven-branched candelabrum of the tabernacle that signified, among

other things, the seven days of creation. The cup atop the central shaft, somewhat elevated to signify the sabbath, was flanked by three lights on each side.

MEN SHEN

In Chinese mythology, the two door gods whose separate martial images are posted on the two halves of the front doors of private homes to guarantee protection from evil spirits.

MEONOTHAI

In Judaism, a descendant of Judah who "became father to Ophrah," being either the paternal ancestor of a person named Ophrah or the founder of a place bearing that name (1 Chronicles 4:1, 14).

MEPHAATH

According to biblical tradition, a city originally assigned to the Reubenites but subsequently granted to the Merarite Levites (Joshua 13:15-18; 1 Chronicles 6:77-79). In Jeremiah's days, circa eight centuries later, Mephaath was under Moabite control (Jeremiah 48:21-24). The city is usually identified with modern Jawah, circa seven miles south of Amman.

MEPHIBOSHETH

According to biblical tradition, one of King Saul's two sons by Rizpah the daughter of Aiah (2 Samuel 21:8). He was among the seven descendants of Saul that David gave to the Gibeonites to atone for Saul's attempt to annihilate them. The Gibeonites exposed Mephibosheth and the six other members of Saul's household "on the mountain before god," after putting them to death "in the first days of the harvest, at the start of the barley harvest" (Numbers 25:4). However, Rizpah acted to keep the fowls and wild beasts away from them, and David later had their bones gathered and buried them with those of Saul and Jonathan in the burial place of Kish (2 Samuel 21:1-14).

MERAB

According to biblical tradition, the older of King Saul's two daughters (1 Samuel 14:49). Saul had evidently promised to give one of them in marriage to the man who would defeat Goliath (1 Samuel 17:25) and it may have been for that reason that he offered Merab to David. After his encounter with Goliath, David proved to be a prudent and successful fighter against the Philistines, so much so that Saul "was scared of him," while the people of Israel and Judah loved him (1 Samuel 18:15-16). In offering Merab to David as a wife, Saul urged him on to continued valor, while thinking to himself, "Do not let my hand come to be upon him, but let the hand of the Philistines come to be upon him," hoping for David's death in battle. David, in humility, hesitated to accept the offer to become the son-in-law of the king. As matters turned out, Saul did not keep his promise, Merab never becoming David's wife. The account states that the younger daughter, Michal "was in love with David," which may imply that Merab was not. At any rate, it came about that at the time for giving Merab, Saul's daughter, to David, she herself had already been given to Adriel the Meholathite as a wife (1 Samuel 18:17-20).

Merab bore five sons to Adriel. However, David later gave these sons and two other members of Saul's household to the Gibeonites, who put all seven to death. This was done to atone for Saul's having tried to annihilate the Gibeonites (2 Samuel 21:1-10).

MERAIOTH

According to biblical tradition, a priest identified as "the son of Ahitub, a leader of the house of the true God" and who appears to be the father of Zadok (1 Chronicles 9:10-11).

The name is also applied to the founder of a priestly paternal house, the head of which was Helkai in the days of Joiakim (Nehemiah 12:12-15). Meraioth, the name of this house of a generation following the Jews' return from Babylonian exile, may be a variation of "Meremoth," the name of one of the priests accompanying Zerubbabel to Jerusalem in 57 BC (Nehemiah 12:3).

MERARI

In Judaism, son of Levi and brother of Gershon (Gershom) and Kohath (Genesis 46:11; 1 Chronicles 6:1, 16). Since Merari is mentioned in third place among Levi's sons, he may have been the youngest. He was one of the 70 members of Jacob's household "who came into Egypt" (Genesis 46:8-26). Merari had two sons, Mahli and Mushi (Exodus 6:19; 1 Chronicles 6:19), and was the founder of the Merarites, one of the three main Levite families (Numbers 26:57).

MERARITES

One of the three major families of Levites, descending from Levi's son Merari through Mahli and Mushi (Exodus 6:16-19; Numbers 3:20). The first census of the Israelites in the wilderness listed 6,200 Merarite males from a month old upward, 3,200 of these being from 30 to 50 years of age and entering the service group "for the service in the tent of meeting" (Numbers 3:33-34; 4:42-45). Their chieftain then was Zuriel and their encampment was on the north side of the tabernacle (Numbers 3:35). During the wilderness trek the three-tribe division of Judah was first to pull away from an encampment. Then the Gershonitea and Merarites "as carriers of the tabernacle pulled away," followed by the three-tribe division of Reuben and then the Kohathite Levites (Numbers 10:14-21).

In the division of the Promised Land under Joshua, 12 cities were assigned to the Merarites, four each from the tribal territories of Reuben, Gad and Zebulun (Joshua 21:7, 34-40; 1 Chronicles 6:63).

MERCURY

In Roman religion, god of merchandise and merchants, commonly identified with the Greek Hermes. His worship was introduced early, and his temple at the Aventine Hill in Rome was dedicated in 495 BC.

MERCY

The virtue that inclines one to compassion for those who suffer and inspires one to do what is possible to alleviate their misery. Already in the Old Testament Yahweh is described as the God of mercy. Out of pity He frees the Israelites from the Egyptians (Exodus 3:7). On Mount Sinai He reveals Himself as the Merciful One (Exodus 34:6). The prophets continuously remind the people of this characteristic of their God (e.g., Hosea 11:8) who wills the conservation of sinners. The mercifulness of Yahweh reaches out to all human beings (Isaiah 58:6-11).

The New Testament reveals the astounding dimensions of that mercy - the Son of God becomes man in order to share the misery of human lot and to rescue men from it.

MERED

According to biblical tradition, a son of Ezra, mentioned in the genealogy of the tribe of Judah. Mered had an Egyptian wife, Bithiah the daughter of Pharaoh, by whom Mered had sons (1 Chronicles 4:1, 17-18). The "Jewish" wife mentioned in verse 18 may have been another wife of Mered.

MEREMOTH

According to biblical tradition, one of the head priests accompanying Zerubbabel from Babylon to Jerusalem in 537 BC (Nehemiah 12:1-7). A priestly paternal house of the next generation is named "Meraioth" and it is possible that Meremoth was its founder (Nehemiah 12:15). The names are rather similar as written in Hebrew characters.

The name is also applied to the son of Urijah and a prominent priest in the days of Ezra and Nehemiah. When Ezra and a Jewish remnant came to Jerusalem from Babylon in 468 BC, Meremoth was among the priests into whose hands they proceeded to weigh out the silver and the gold and the utensils in the house of God (Ezra 8:31-34). Meremoth was a descendant of Hakkoz, some of whose descendants could not establish their genealogy (Ezra 2:61-61). But that the division of the family to which he belonged could verify its lineage is evident, since Meremoth shared in priestly functions. He also took part in doing repair work on Jerusalem's wall under Nehemiah's supervision (Nehemiah 3:3-4, 21).

MERES

In biblical times, one of the seven princes whom Ahasuerus consulted when Vashti disobeyed him (Esther 1:14).

MERIBAH

In the Old Testament, a place in the vicinity of the Israelite wilderness encampment at Rephidim. It was there that Jehovah provided a miraculous supply of water when Moses struck the rock in Horeb with his rod. Moses then called the site "Massah" (testing, trial) and "Meribah" (quarrelling, strife, contention). These names were commemorative of Israel's quarreling with Moses and its testing of God on account of the lack of water (Exodus 17:1-7).

MERIBATH-KADESH

In biblical times, a southern limit of Israel's territory as seen by Ezekiel in a vision (Ezekiel 47:13, 19; 48:28). The name alludes to Israel's quarreling with God at the "waters of Meribah" while dwelling at Kadesh (Numbers 20:1-13).

MERIB-BAAL

In the Old Testament, grandson of King Saul, son of Jonathan and the father of Micah (1 Chronicles 8:33-34). This is apparently another name for Mephibosheth. Others had two names such as Eshbaal, also called Ish-bosheth (Compare: 2 Samuel 2:8 with 1 Chronicles 8:33).

MERIT

In Catholic theology, broadly speaking, a good work worthy of reward; strictly speaking, that aspect of a good work by which it is deserving of reward. The Catholic doctrine on merit, formulated at the Council of Trent (1545-1549, 1582) against the Protestant rejection of good works as cause of men's justice, only means to express what the gospel (e.g., Matthew 5:1-12;) and Paul (e.g., 2 Timothy 4:7-8) taught about the reward awaiting the followers of Christ.

MERKAVA

In Judaism, the object of contemplation for early Jewish mystics whose esoteric approach to God was based on Ezekiel's vision of the divine throne (Ezekiel 1). Merkava mysticism began to flourish in Palestine the 1st century AD, but from the 7th to 11th century its center was in Babylon.

MERODACH

The Hebrew form for Marduk, the most important Babylonian god. The Babylonian Kings Merodach-baladan (Isaiah 39:1) and Evil-merodach (2 Kings 25:27) were undoubtedly named after this god. With the rise of Babylon to prominence, because of King Hammurabi's making it the capital of Babylonia, Merodach likewise increased in importance.

The attributes of earlier gods came to be assigned to him, and it is thought that the babylonian priests altered the mythological accounts to make Merodach the slayer of Tiamat and the creator of the world and man.

Babylonian texts identify Marduk (Merodach) as the son of Ea (the god presiding over the watery element), the consort of Sarpanitu and the father of Nebo.

Jeremiah the prophet, with respect to Babylon's fall, foretold that Merodach would "become terrified," This came true in the sense that Merodach proved to be unable to preserve the dignity of the Babylonian World Power and, since the conquerors of Babylon were worshipers of other deities, his future became very uncertain, filled with foreboding (Jeremiah 50:2).

MERODACH-BALADAN
In biblical times, the "son of Baladan" and King of Babylon who sent letters and a gift to King Hezekiah of Judah following that king's recovery from illness (Isaiah 39:1). He is called "Berodach-baladan" at 2 Kings 20:12, but this difference is generally considered to be the result of a scribal error, or else to represent an attempt at transliterating an Akkadian consonant with a sound somewhere between that of "m" and "b."
Toward the close of his rule of approximately 12 years over Babylon, Merodach-baladan saw his main support from Elam cut off by an Assyrian victory over that kingdom, and thereafter he was attacked and forced to flee from Babylon.

MERON
In biblical times, name for a village and nearby mountain, in upper Galilee, northern Israel. Nearby is a perennial spring, the likeliest location of the "waters of Meron," site of Joshua's victory over the pagan kings of Palestine under Jabin, king of Hazor (Joshua 11).

MERU, Mount
In Hindu mythology, a golden mountain that stands in the center of the universe; the axis of the world. It is the abode of gods, and its foothills are the Himalaya, to the south of which extends Bharatavarsa, the ancient name for India. The roof tower crowning the shrine in a Hindu temple represents Meru.

MESHA
In the Old Testament, firstborn son of "Caleb the son of Herzon" of the tribe of Judah. Mesha was the father (or founder) of Ziph (1 Chronicles 2:18, 42).

The name is also applied to the king of Moab in the time of Kings Jehoshaphat of Judah and Ahab, Ahaziah and Jehoram of Israel.

MESHACH
In biblical times, the Babylonian name given by Nebuchadnezzar's chief court official to Daniel's companion Mischael. The meaning of this new name is uncertain, but is sometimes equated with "Who is what Aku is?" similar to Mischael ("Who is what God is"). The new names given to Mischael and three other prominent captives apparently incorporated the names of Babylonian deities in place of God's name or title (Daniel 1:7).

MESHECH
In the Old Testament, one of the sons born after the Flood to Japheth, the son of Noah (Genesis 10:2; 1 Chronicles 1:5). The name evidently extended to his descendants and the land of their settlement. The prophet Ezekiel regularly mentions Meshech along with Tubal, indicating that they were located to the north of Palestine. They are described as exporting slaves and copper to Tyre and as being warlike and as either allies or subjects of "Gog of Magog" in his prophesied vicious campaign against "the mountains of Israel" (Ezekiel 27:13; 32:26). Meshech is mentioned independently of Tubal at Psalm 120:5, evidently as representing an aggressive, barbarous people.

MESHELEMIAH
In Judaism, a Kohathite Levite and ancestral head of a division of Kohathites. he "had sons and brothers, capable men, eighteen," who were assigned with him as gatekeepers of the sanctuary during King David's reorganization of the priestly and Levitical services (1 Chronicles 26:1-3).

MESHEZABEL
In Judaism, a man of Judah of the family of Zerah and whose "son" Pethahiah "was at the side of the king

for every matter of the people" (Nehemiah 11:24).

MESHILLEMOTH

In the Old Testament, an Ephraimite whose "son" Berechiah was one of the headmen of Ephraim who persuaded the Israelites of King Pekah's day to release the captives they had taken in a successful military campaign against Judah (2 Chronicles 28:6-8, 12-15).

MESHOBAB

In the Old Testament, a chieftain of the tribe of Simeon who had a large household and who participated in the seizure of pasturelands from the Hamites and the Meunim near Gedor in the days of King Hezekiah of Judah (1 Chronicles 4:34-42).

MESHULLAM

In the Old Testament, a family head in the tribe of Benjamin who lived in Jerusalem; son of Elpaal (1 Chronicles 8:1, 17-18). The name is also applied to the father or ancestor of High Priest Hilkiah of King Joshua's reign (1 Chronicles 9:11; Nehemiah 11:11). Meshullam himself had perhaps acted as High Priest.

MESHULLEMETH

In Judaism, daughter of "Haruz from Jotbah" who became the wife of Judean King Manasseh and the mother of King Amon (2 Kings 21:19-20).

MESLAMTAEA

In Mesopotamian religion, city god of Cuthah in Akkad. His temple in Cuthah was called Emeslam or Meslam.

MESONYTIKON

Greek term meaning literally the midnight service, nocturnes, or vigils. It is only celebrated in monasteries, since neither in structure nor in content is it a parochial service. The service begins with the blessing of the one presiding and the usual Trisagion prayers. Psalm 50 is then read, followed by Psalm 118 on weekdays, and Kathisma of Psalms 64-69 on Saturdays, and the Canon and Troparia of the Holy Trinity on Sundays. The Nicene Creed is then repeated, followed by the Lord's Prayer.

MESOPOTAMIA

(Greek: Land between the Rivers) Region between the Tigris and Euphrates in western Asia, now known as Iraq. Marked by a network of irrigation canals it had a very high degree of civilization.

MESOPOTAMIAN RELIGION

The religion of the inhabitants of Mesopotamian in historical times, from the early third millennium BC down into the Persian and Hellenistic periods, shows a fundamental unity in continuity, despite modifications and differences of emphasis depending on differences of race, on the shifting influences of local traditions, and an evolution in time.

The matrix was Sumerian, and the waves of new Semitic inhabitants succeeding one another seem to have accepted the religious system already existing upon their arrival, modifying it slightly according to their own religious temperaments.

While much of the practice and symbolism of the third millennium is known, it is only with the early second millennium that the religious thought clearly emerges. Gods and goddesses in the developed pantheon were of various types. Some were high gods, omnipotent but distant, like An (Anum), Enhil, and Enki (Ea).

Others were numinous powers in natural phenomena; some of these, like the astral gods Sin and Shamash (Moon and Sun) or Naru (River), were confused with the phenomena themselves, while others, like Dumuzi or Tammuz, the power behind the fertile and infertile periods of the natural cycles, were personified without possibility of such material confusion.

In the south the important gods were for the most part originally gods of particular cities; in the north they were rather nature-gods with cosmic functions.

As Mesopotamian theology evolves, the attributes of various gods were often blended and transferred. West Semitic and other foreign gods tended to be absorbed into one or another of the local gods.

The number of divinities, already high, was augmented by the throngs of anonymous gods called igigi and anunnaki, by various types of evil and good demons belonging to the divine world as ministering spirits, and by the personal gods.

These latter groups of inferior divine beings are antecedents of the angels serving as heavenly courtiers and of the guardian angels, found in later Judaism and thence in Christianity. The high gods were responsible for the origins of the cosmic universe and for the continuing existence of that universe and its structure.

The Babylonians regarded their divinities as somewhat quiet, orderly beings dwelling peacefully in their temples among the people. The more turbulent Assyrians regarded them as far more capricious and violent beings inspiring awe and dread, and performed cultic acts not only in temples but also on mountain tops, in sacred groves, and near the sources of streams, for the aspect of nature religion remained stronger in the Assyrian north.

The personalities and actions of the gods, portrayed in narratives accounting for the reasons things are as they are - creation, cycles of fertility and infertility in nature, cultic practices - are the substance of Mesopotamian myth.

The tension between transcendence and immanence was not keenly felt in Mesopotamia. Just as a high god was lord and king in his heavenly palace, surrounded by ministering inferior divinities, so on earth he was lord and king in his temple, surrounded by the ministering temple personnel, receiving homage from the people, receiving their petitions, appearing periodically in splendid processions, daily clothed, given food, and otherwise treated like an earthly king.

His immanence in the temple was thus handled as a reflection of his transcendence in a higher world, where he was also a mighty lord in the palace of heaven.

MESOPOTAMIAN RELIGION, Bible sources

The notion of the earthly temple in Mesopotamian religion as an imitation of the heavenly one can be found in the Bible (Exodus 25:9; Exodus 26:30; Hebrews 8:5), and the idea of the Temple in Jerusalem as a place where Yahweh holds court, listening to and acting upon the petitions of the people can be found in 1 Kings 8:10-51, with a corrective note in favor of transcendence in 1 Kings 8:27).

It is in this contact of the temple as the god's palace, where he is treated like an earthly king, that the Mesopotamian liturgical system must be understood. Hymns of praise differed from the laudatory songs sung by court musicians only in the matter of divine epithets and attributes; prayers of petition were analogous to the petitions of clients asking favors in the royal court.

Incense perfumed the god's quarters, libations and sacrifices provided his daily food. There was no equivalent of the west Semitic holocaust, for part of the sacrificial food was always received by certain elements of the temple personnel; yet, there was no real equivalent of the Hebrew sacrifice of communion either, for participation in the god's meal was limited to the temple personnel and, upon occasion, the king - the ordinary people who offered sacrificial food having no share therein.

There was no sacrifice of expiation for sin, although the ritual for the Jewish Day of Atonement in Leviticus 16 has certain material parallels in Mesopotamian non-sacrificial, magic practice.

MESOPOTAMIAN RELIGION, Practices

Mesopotamian religious practice was not limited to the strictly liturgical. It contained much apotropaic magical practice which, far from being condemned, entered the official cult itself and gave it much of its meaning. Sickness and misfortune were felt to depend upon the displeasure of their high gods, or, far more often, to be the result of the influence of evil demons.

While prayer and sacrificial offerings often sought to assure divine good will, the ritual cleansings, exorcisms, and incantations that played so important a role in Mesopotamian life sought to turn away the harmful influences of demons in everything from toothache to marital problems.

The Ancient Near Eastern mind's ability to envisage personal identity as a fluid thing explains such practices as transferring a sick man's personality (by ritual formula) to an animal, who was then killed, so that the besetting demon, transferring the animosity in all its fury from the sick man to the animal substitute, might leave the sick man in peace and the malady might depart; the killing of the animal was magical, not sacrificial. These magical practices, and divinitory practices too, formed part of the regular round of services available at a temple.

As in monarchical Israel, the temple, palace of the god, was associated with the palace of the earthly king, and the connection between temple and dynasty was close. The king, representative of god before the people and of the people before god, was ultimately responsible for the state cult, and in Assyria he was himself reckoned as the supreme member of the complex temple personnel.

In ritual drama the king himself enacted the role of the god. The same notion of personal identity as a fluid thing was extended to the numinous, so that in ritual drama the king took on numinous power, activated it externally, and, since he also enjoyed fluid identification with the entire kingdom, made the numinous power effectively present throughout the land.

Thus, in the rite of sacred marriage the king, representing Dumuzi, assured the powers of fertility throughout the land; representing Marduk in the battle drama of the Babylonian New Year festival, he vanquished chaos and assured cosmic order for the coming year; the people's lament for Damuzi (see Ezekiel 8:13-14) associated the people themselves in the cycle of vanishing and reappearing fertility.

MESSIAH

(Hebrew: anointed one, Greek: christos) Foretold by Israelite prophets, especially Isaiah, the ruler whom God would send to restore Israel and begin a glorious age of peace and righteousness (Isaiah 7-11). He would be a descendant of king David. Christians recognize Jesus of Nazareth as the Messiah (Mark 14:61-62), but his role as suffering for mankind was alien to Jewish hopes of a political deliverer.

Today many Orthodox Jews still believe in the eventual coming of a Messiah, while others prefer the concept of a Messianic Age. In Christian belief, Jesus Christ is recognized as the Messiah, and the period of his earthly life is sometimes called the Messianic Age.

MESSIANIC JEWS

Small group of Jews that differ from the majority in that they accept Jesus christ as the Son of God and all that he has said as written in the New Testament. They have formed their own denomination within the Christian church as they still have major differences with some interpretations of the teachings of Jesus Christ in relation to their understanding of the Old Testament and the status of the Jewish people.

MESSIANIC MOVEMENTS

Variety of movements with a markedly eschatological or utopian-revolutionary character or message. Though messianic movements occur throughout the world, they apparently are especially characteristic of the Jewish and Christian traditions.

METHODISM

A section of the Evangelical Revival (Revivalism) led by John Wesley (1703-91) and George Whitefield (1714-70). Wesley taught justification of faith and Christian perfection (Salvation), using lay preachers to develop a chain of fellowship associates. After separating from Anglicanism, English Methodism suffered many divisions, but it was largely reunited in 1932.

The name Methodist was first used in 1729 for members of the Holy Club, a small group at Oxford University founded by Charles Wesley and led by his brother John, which conducted its meetings "by rule and method." But Methodism as an evangelical movement dates from 1738 when John Wesley, influenced by a deep religious experience and by his contact with the Moravian Brethren in Georgia, began his preaching.

Doctrine

Methodism is evangelical; it seeks to convert non-methodists to the Methodist beliefs. John Wesley described Methodism as "the religion of the Bible," and the Bible remains the fundamental authority of belief and practice. Methodists believe in salvation through faith and work, and in God's forgiveness of personal sin. Public affirmation of belief in Jesus Christ the Savior and faithful membership of the church are especially important.

METHODIST CHURCH, The

In Britain, Protestant church that developed from the Methodist revival movement that began within the Church of England. It broke with the Church of England in 1795.

METHODIST REVIVAL

The 18th century religious movement begun and sustained by John Wesley.

METHUSELAH

Old Testament patriarch whose life span (recorded in Genesis 5:27) was 969 years. In the New Testament he is mentioned in the gospel of Luke. There (3:23-28) the lineage of Joseph is traced back 75 generations, through David and Saul, and Abraham, Isaac, and Jacob, to Methuselah and thence to Seth and Adam.

METHUSHAEL

In the Old Testament, a descendant of Cain through Enoch. Methushael was the son of Mehujael and the father of Lamech (Genesis 4:17-18).

METROPHANES KRITOPOULOS

(1589-1639) Greek Orthodox patriarch of Alexandria, Egypt and Byzantine theological scholar whose discussions with European Protestants concluded with his writing an exposition of Eastern Orthodox doctrine in an attempt at Christian unity.

METROPOLITAN

In the Roman Catholic, Eastern Orthodox, and Anglican churches, the head of an ecclesiastical province.

METROPOLITAN CHURCH ASSOCIATION, The

Wesleyan group organized in Chicago in 1894 as the Metropolitan Holiness Church and chartered under the present title in 1899.

METTA

In Buddhism, love, active good will. Metta is the first of the four Brahma-Viharas in which the force of love is radiated to all beings.

MEUNIM

On the basis of the name, the Meunim are considered to have been an Arabian people residing in and around Ma'an, a city circa twenty miles south-east of Petra.

During Hezekiah's reign (745-716 BC) a band of Simeonites struck down the tent-dwelling Meunim in the vicinity of Gebor (1 Chronicles 4:24, 39-41).

MEZAHAB

In the Old Testament, parent of Matred and ancestor (or, perhaps, ancestress) of Mehetabel, the wife of Hadar (Hadad), the last named of the kings of Edom (Genesis 36:31, 39; 1 Chronicles 1:50).

MEZUZAH

Hebrew for doorpost; consisting of a small case of metal or wood containing a roll of parchment. Upon the tiny scroll two passages are found from Deuteronomy 6:5-9 and 11:13-21. They are in Hebrew, written in the manner of Torah script. The first is a famous passage which begins: Hear, O Israel, the Lord our God, the Lord is one.

When Jews move into a new home, the first thing done is to fasten a mezuzah to the upper part of the right doorpost of each room. By doing this an announcement is made that they are proud members of the Jewish people and aware of the long and honorable heritage.

MIBHAR

In the Old Testament, son of Hagri and one of the mighty men of David's military forces (1 Chronicles 11:26, 38).

MIBSAM

In Judaism, one of the sons of Ishmael and founder of a family (Genesis 25:13; 1 Chronicles 1:29).

MICAH

Judean prophet of the late 700s BC during the reign of Kings Jotham, Ahaz and Hezekiah of Judah; a contemporary of Isaiah. The exact duration of his prophetic activity is uncertain. His prophesying apparently closed by the end of Hezekiah's reign, when the composition of the prophet's book was completed (Micah 1:1; Isaiah 1:1).

Micah was a native of the village of Meresheth, south-west of Jerusalem (Jeremiah 26:18). As a resident of the fertile Shepelah, the prophet was well acquainted with rural living, from which he was inspired to draw meaningful illustrations (Micah 2:12; 4:12; 7:1-14). Micah prophesied during very turbulent times when false worship and

moral corruption flourished in Israel and Judah. While the devastation of Judah and Jerusalem in 607 BC occurred many years after Micah's day, he probably lived to see the foretold destruction of Samaria (2 Kings 25:1-21).

MICAH, Book of

The sixth of the 12 Old Testament books that bear the names of the minor prophets. The Judaean prophet Micah was active during the first half of the 8th century BC. His main theme is justice. His warnings are directed against idolaters, priests and prophets who use their profession for financial gain, and leaders who abhor justice. At the time of Jeremiah he was known for being the prophet who foresaid Jerusalem's destruction and could not be killed (Jeremiah 26:18-19).

The book of Micah candidly portrays the wrongs of Israel and Judah. While foretelling desolation for Samaria and Jerusalem on account of their transgressions (Micah 1:5-9; 3:9-12), it also contains promises of the restoration and divine blessings to follow (Micah 4:1-8; 5:7-9; 7:15-17).

MICAIAH

In Judaism, son of Imlah and a prophet of the northern kingdom of Israel during King Ahab's reign (1 Kings 22:8). While King Jehoshaphat of Judah was visiting Ahab, the Israelite king invited him to join in a military campaign against the Syrians to regain possession of Ramoth-gilead. Before accepting, Jehoshaphat asked that the word of God be sought. So Ahab summoned 400 prophets and asked them: "Shall I go against Ramoth-gilead in war, or shall I refrain?" They answered in the affirmative. However, Jehoshaphat wanted more assurance, whereupon Ahab reluctantly sent for Micaiah, the prophet who had always prophesied bad for him. The dispatched messenger urged Micaiah to speak words like those of one of the other prophets. At first Micaiah did so, but Ahab placed him under oath to speak "truth in the name of God," At that, Micaiah said: "I certainly see all the Israelites scattered on the mountains like sheep that have no shepherd" (1 Kings 29:1-17). At the end of the prophesy Micaiah was placed in the house of detention, and Ahab went to war. Ahab never returned, because during the battle at Ramoth-gilead, "there was a man that bent the bow in innocence," the arrow struck the Israelite king, and he gradually died (1 Kings 22:18-37; 2 Chronicles 18:17-34).

MICHAEL

One of the seven archangels. He is repeatedly mentioned as the leader of the heavenly hosts and the warrior helping the children of Israel. In Acts 12:7-12 he fights the dragon (Satan). His feast day is September 29th.

Michael is, with Gabriel (Daniel 8:16) and Raphael, one of the three angels whose name is given in the Bible. Michael is identified in Daniel (10:13) as an archangel, i.e., a chief prince, because he is deputed to be guardian over Israel.

In the New Testament Jude 9, in a passage derived from a now-lost part of the Assumption of Moses, alludes to a struggle between Michael and Satan over Moses' body. In Revelation 12:7-12 he is the leader of the angels in victory over the dragon and the dragon's angels. Michael is the first of the archangels to have an individual liturgical cult in the church before the 9th century.

MICHAELMAS

Feast day of Michael the archangel, which in the Middle Ages was a holiday of obligation. In the present liturgical calendar the feast of Michael, together with the Archangels Gabriel and Raphael, is celebrated on September 29th.

MICHAL

In Judaism, King Saul's younger daughter who became the wife of David. Saul had offered his older daughter Merab to David as a wife, but gave her to another man. Michal, however, "was in love with David," and Saul offered her to David if he could produce the foreskins of a hundred Philistines, thinking that David would meet death in attempting to kill that many enemy warriors. David accepted that challenge, presented Saul with 200 Philistine foreskins, and was given Michal as a wife. But, thereafter, "Saul felt still more fear because of David" and became his lasting foe (1 Samuel 14:19; 18:17-29). Later, when Saul's hatred for David reached a peak, Michal helped David escape the king's wrath. During David's long absence, Saul gave her in marriage to Palti the son of Laish from Gallim (1 Samuel 19:11-17).

When Abner later sought to conclude a covenant with David, David refused to see him unless he brought Michal with him. David, by messenger, presented his demand to Saul's son Ish-bosheth, and Michal was taken from her husband Palti and returned to David (1 Samuel 3:12-16).

MICHELANGELO

(1475-1564) One of the world's most famous artists. Sculptor, painter, architect and poet, he was an outstanding genius of the Italian Renaissance. His most famous work is the ceiling of the Sistine Chapel in the Vatican.

In 1489 Lorenzo de Medici, virtual ruler of Florence, became Michelangelo's patron. There the boy studied sculpture under Bertoldo, a pupil of Donatello, and came into contact with the poets and philosophers of Lorenzo's court. His earliest surviving sculptures (Madonna of the Steps, Battle of the Centaurs) data from this time.

When Lorenzo died (1492) and the Medici fell from power, Michelangelo went to Bologna. In Rome (1496-1501), he established his reputation as a leading sculptor with the statue of Bacchus and his poignant Pieta, a large marble statue of the Virgin Mary with the dead Christ.

Back in Florence (1501-1505) he produced the first of his mature sculptures, the huge David, and worked with Leonardo da Vinci designing frescoes for the city hall.

He was called to Rome by Pope Julius II to design the latter's tomb, a project never completed as he intended due to endless changes and interruptions. But he later produced his famous Moses and two other statues for the much-altered tomb.

The Sistine Chapel ceiling, his master-piece, was completed in 4_ years (1508-1512). Never before had an artist painted such an area (1,000 square feet) with so unified and spiritu-ally majestic a theme, or so brilliantly portrayed the human figure. These frescos of Old Testament scenes, prophets, sibyls and ancestors of Christ, inspired and influenced genera-tions of painters.

MICHMASH

In biblical times, a site identified with modern Mukmas on a hill circa 2,000 feet above sea level and some seven miles north-east of Jerusalem. It lies north of the Wadi Suweinit, considered to be the "ravine pass of Michmash" (1 Samuel 13:23). Joined by other wadis from the south-west and north-west Suweinit extends from the mountain-ous region of Ephraim to the Jordan valley.

The prophecy of Isaiah mentions Michmash as the place where the con-quering Assyrian would "deposit their articles" (Isaiah 10:24-28). After the Israelite return from Babylonian exile in 537 BC Michmash was apparently reoccupied by Benjaminites (Ezra 2:1-2, 27; Nehemiah 7:31; 11:31).

MICHMETHATH

In biblical times, a site on the boundary between Ephraim and Mannasseh. It is often identified with Khirbet Juleijil, less than two miles south-east of the suggested site of ancient Shechem. This agrees with the biblical statement that Michmathath was "in front of Shechem" (Joshua 16:5-6; 17:7).

MICHRI

In the Old Testament, a Benjaminite and ancestor of Elah who resided in Jerusalem after the Babylonian exile (1 Chronicles 9:1-3, 7-8).

MIDDIN

In Judaism, a place in the Judean wilderness (Joshua 15:20). Middin is perhaps identified with Khirbet Abu Tabaq situated in the low-lying plain called el-Buqe'ah (the valley of Achor) near the north-western end of the Dead Sea.

MIDDLE AGES

The period in Western European histo-ry between the 5th and 15th centuries, or from the fall of the Roman Empire to the dawn of the Renaissance. The centuries preceding the 11th century are often referred to as the Dark Ages; in general the Middle Ages fall into two roughly equal halves - a period of decline in the earlier centuries and a period of resurgence in the later years.

Role of the Church

The distinctive feature which united the earlier and the later centuries, and which above all characterizes the Middle Ages as "medieval," is the dominant role of the Catholic church. The church survived the decay of the Roman imperial system to act as the great unifying institution of what became known as "Christendom." As the Rome of the Caesars had once been acknowledged as the capital of the empire, so now the Rome of the popes was acknowledged as the spiritual cen-ter of Christian civilization.

Modern Western civilization is secular. Religion is regarded as a primitive matter for the individual conscience and we tend to look to the law and the governments we elect for guidance in our lives. Medieval Europe was very different. The church was the only organization to exert authority over more than a single country. From end to end of Europe the pope's agents, the bishops, and beneath them the parish priests, collected taxes to support the work of the church, preached sermons that told people what to believe and how to behave, and provided secular rulers with literate scribes to keep records and advice them on the conduct of affairs. The monasteries, independent communities of monks who had dedicated their lives to the service of God, performed many functions which are nowadays regarded as the role of government, including care of the poor and sick, the upkeep of bridges and the maintenance of schools.

In the dark days of the 5th to 10th centuries it was the church and the monasteries which had preserved the writings of the Greeks and Romans and kept alive Latin as the international language of scholarship and government. No aspect of man's lifer was considered to be outside the sphere of the church's jurisdiction - merchants were to charge a "just price," warriors were to observe the "truce of God;" everyone was to be baptized, married and buried by the church. Art and culture, in particular, were patronized almost solely by the church and were devoted to religious purposes.

Indeed, the supreme artistic achievement of the Middle Ages, the Gothic cathedral, was a symbol of the control exerted by the church over men's minds, efforts and purses. Soaring heavenward, the delicately carved stonework, vigorous sculpture and brilliantly-colored stained glass represented the will of medieval man to assert the reality of salvation and heaven in a world too obviously bound in violence, poverty and disease.

By the 16th century an obscure German priest named martin luther had set Europe aflame with his criticisms of the Catholic church, Gutenberg's printing press was enabling people to read the Bible and the writing of the ancients for themselves, gunpowder had made the knight in armor obsolete, and beyond the Atlantic Columbus had discovered a New World. These developments marked the close of the Middle Ages and the dawning of the modern world.

MIDIAN

In the Old testament, one of Abraham's sons by his concubine Keturah; the father of Ephah, Epher, Hanoch, Abida and Eldaah (Genesis 25:1-1; 1 Chronicles 1:32-33). Before his death, Abraham gave presents to Midian and the other sons of his concubines and then sent them to the land of the East (Genesis 25:5-6).

MIDIANITES

According to biblical tradition, the descendants of Abraham's son Midian, being collectively designated as "Midianites" (Numbers 31:2-3). Being descendants of Abraham, The Midianites likely spoke a language that closely resembled Hebrew. Gideon, for instance, apparently had no difficulty in understanding the Midianites (Judges 7:13-15). There is also a possibility, however, that Gideon learned the tongue of the Midianites, Israel having been under their domination for seven years (Judges 6:1). Primarily the Midianites were nomadic tent dwellers (Judges 6:5-6). But in Moses' day they are also reported as residing in cities (Numbers 31:9-10). At that time they were quite prosperous, having asses and animals of the flock and herd numbering into the tend of thousands (Numbers 31:32-34). Their riches included gold ornaments having a total weight of more than 312 pounds troy (191 kilograms) (Numbers 31:50-52).

MIGDAL-EL

A fortified city in the territory of Naphtali (Joshua 19:35-38). One possible identification that has been suggested for Migdal-el is Mujedil. This site is on a hill circa 10_ miles east-south-east of Tyre.

MIGDOL

In biblical times, an Egyptian site used as a reference point in describing the location of Israel's last encampment at Pihahiroth before crossing the Red Sea. They were to encamp "before Pihahiroth between Migdol and the sea in view of Baal-zephon" (Exodus 14:2;

Numbers 33:5-8). Scholars generally hold that Migdol is likely to be an Egyptian pronunciation for the Hebrew migh-dal' meaning "tower" and that it doubtless refers to a military post or watchtower on the Egyptian border. However, there is evidence that there were several such Migdols along the Egyptian border; even today there are three different villages bearing the name Mishtul, the present form of Migdol in Egyptian (of Coptic derivation).

MIGRON

A location "at the outskirts of Gibeah" were King Saul was encamped when Jonathan and his armor-bearer killed circa 20 men from the Philistine outpost near Miriam situated over half a mile south-south-west of Mukmas (Mickmash), is often presented as a possible identification, but the identification is not at all conclusive.

At Isaiah 10:28 Migron is foretold to be one of the cities through which the Assyrians would pass on their way toward Jerusalem.

MIHNAH

Islamic courts of inquisition established in 833 by the Abbasid caliph al-Ma'mun to impose the Mu'ttazili doctrine of a created Koran on his subjects.

MIHRAB

Indented niche within a mosque indicating the direction of the prayer towards Mecca. Mihrabs are frequently decorated with beautiful calligraphy, tiles and mosaics and constitute an area of the mosque where the artist feels free to give full expression to his combined religious fervor and artistic zeal.

MIJAMIN

In Judaism, descendant of Aaron selected by lot to head the sixth division of priestly services in King David's day (1 Chronicles 24:1-9). The name is also applied to one of the heads of the priests who returned from Babylon with Zerubbabel (Nehemiah 12:1-7). He may have founded the paternal house of Miniamin mentioned at Nehemiah 12:17 (where the name of the head of that house appears to have been an inadvertent scribal omission in the Hebrew text).

MIKA-IL

Arabic word for Michael, one of the great Islamic angels. He is mentioned once in the Koran in company of Jibril. Tradition shows him and Jibril instructing Mohammed and both were characterized as wazir (literally "minister") by the Prophet. Mika-il watches over places of worship.

MIKLOTH

In Judaism, father of Shimeah and descendant of the Benjaminite Jeiel of Gibeon (1 Chronicles 8:29-32). The name is also applied to the leader appointed for the king's service during the second month in the division commanded by Dodai the Ahohite (1 Chronicles 27:1-4).

MI-KOSHI

In the Shinto religion of Japan, a palanquin used to carry the shrine kami (god or sacred power) in possession during a festival.

MIKTAM

A Hebrew word of obscure meaning and uncertain etymology contained in the superscriptions of six psalms ascribed to David (Psalms 16, 56-60). Miktam may designate a song or psalm intended to cover or atone for sin, guilt or uncleanness, Atonement seems to be implied because David's miktam psalms contain lamentations to an extent, though they also reflect gratitude for God's aid and confidence in him. The "writing" King Hezekiah composed "when he got sick and revived from his sickness" was possibly also a miktam (Isaiah 38:9-20).

MILALAI

In the Old Testament, a Levite musician who marched in one of the inaugural processions on Jerusalem's rebuilt wall in Nehemiah's day (Nehemiah 12:31-36).

MILAN, Edict of

A proclamation that permanently established religious toleration for Christianity within the Roman Empire. It was the outcome of a political agreement concluded in Milan between the Roman emperor Constantine I and Licinius in 313.

MILAN CATHEDRAL

Late Gothic structure in Italy begun 1386. Though nearest to a true Gothic cathedral in Italy it is actually through a succession of French and German architects a compromise between the ad quadratum of Master Jean Vignot of Paris and ad triangulatum of the German school, witnessing also, to the Italian rejection of dominant vertically, in a lack of height and absence of towers, yet in abundance of delicate pinnacles, evidencing an Italian delight in the elaborate ornament of Late Gothic style. Milan's is the largest cathedral after St. Peter's, with five aisles and an aisled transept; the Baroque facade by Tiobaldi (1607), is truly Italian in its alternating Greek pedimental and Roman arched window frames. The stained glass in the choir dates from the 19th century.

MILCAH

In the Old Testament, daughter of Abraham's brother Haran, wife of his brother Nahor (her uncle) and the sister of Lot (Genesis 11:27-29). Bethuel, one of Milcah's eight children became father to Rebekah (Genesis 22:20-23).

MILETUS

A city on the west coast of Asia Minor that is now in ruins. It lies near the mouth of the Maeander (Menderes) River and anciently had four harbors. By the seventh century BC the Ionians seem to have made Miletus a prosperous commercial center having numerous colonies on the Black Sea and in Egypt. The woolen goods of Miletus

came be widely known.

As time passed, the city declined in importance. This is attributed to the silting of its harbor facilities by the Maeander River. Ancient Miletus seems to have been situated on a promontory extending from the south side of the Lamnian Gulf. But today the ruins of the city lie circa five miles inland, and what was once the Lamnian Gulf is a lake.

It was to Miletus that apostle Paul came, probably in 56. Because of wanting to get to Jerusalem by Pentecost if at all possible and not wishing to spend time unnecessarily in Asis Minor, Paul, apparently at Assos, decided to take a vessel that bypassed Ephesus. But he did not neglect the needs of the congregation there. From Miletus, doubtless by means of a messenger, Paul sent for the older men of the Ephesus congregation. The additional time it took for word to reach them and for them to come to Miletus (perhaps a minimum of three days) apparently was less than might have been involved had Paul gone to Ephesus (Acts 20:14-17).

At an unspecified time after his first imprisonment in Rome, Paul seems to have returned to Miletus. Trophimus, who had earlier accompanied him from Miletus to Jerusalem, became ill, necessitating Paul's leaving him behind (Acts 20:4; 21:29; 2 Timothy 4:20).

MILLENNIARISM

A belief that Christ will establish a kingdom on earth for a 1,000 year period. Based upon a single passage, Revelation 20:1-10, this concept has given rise to varied speculation and hope since the 1st century.

According to the passage, Satan was to be bound for 1,000 years, and those who had not worshiped the beast or his image, "came to life again, and reigned with Christ a thousand years."

Since this is an apocalyptic book filled with imagery, there is need for caution about accepting literally the idea of a 1,000 year reign. Taken in context, the passage probably refers to the time

between Christ's Resurrection and the
end of the world, when Christ raises
the dead, judges the world, and creates
a new heaven and a new earth.

Post-millenniarism is the view that
Christ's return, after the gospel has
gradually permeated the world and
after a Christian society has been
established, will last 1,000 years, during which the Jews will be converted.
Finally, there will be an apostasy, a terrible conflict, and Christ will intervene
to destroy the world after having raised
and judged the dead. There are also a-
millenniasists who do not take the idea
of a millennium literally.

MILTIADES, Saint

(256-314) Pope probably from 311 to
314. He became the first pope after the
edicts of toleration by the Emperor
Galerius (ending the persecution of
Christians), Maxentius (restoring
church property to Miltiades), and
Constantine I the Great (favoring
Christianity). He is considered a martyr
because of earlier sufferings under the
Roman Emperor Maximian.

MIMOUNA

Jewish festival celebrated on the day
after the last day of Pesah. It has been
celebrated by the North African Jewish
communities for generations.
Mimouna's exact origins are unknown.
One theory is that it is an Arabization
of the Hebrew word emunah, meaning
faith, or belief, in the coming of the
Messiah and the redemption of the
Jews. Certainly the theme of Mimouna
is confidence in God and patience in
awaiting the Messiah.

MINARET

Tower of a mosque, one of the distinctive features of Islamic architecture,
from the gallery of which Muslims are
called to prayer by a muezzin (official
caller). A mosque usually has one or
more of these towers. The earliest
minarets, built during the 7th century,
were low and square. Later forms were
slender and tall, and either octagonal or
cylindrical.

MINBAR

Pulpit; key piece of furniture in the
mosque, from which the Friday khutba
or sermon is preached by the mosque
Imam. The minbar in a large mosque is
often a very high and ornate structure,
intricately carved from beautiful
woods.

MINDFUL AND SELF-POSSESSED

A key term in all schools of Buddhism.
It is defined as a state of mind which in
the monk or self-dedicated layman
should be permanent, in which the
Goal and the Way to it are constantly in
view. This unremitting inward pressure
of mind alone leads to enlightenment.

MIND OF THE CHURCH

1 In regard to matters of divine faith the
phrase, further illumined by Vatican
Council II, refers to the living understanding in the church of the deposit of
faith, the content of divine revelation.
The mind of the church is the mind of
the believers in the ecclesial community. For the very faith that makes them
believers rests immediately on God's
own infallible word; faith can never be
anything but a principle of right understanding; there exists as well as
enlightening the mind of the church the
Holy Spirit and his charismatic gifts,
including infallibility.

2 In regard to matters pertaining to the
implications of the truths of faith, or to
actual circumstances of the life of the
faithful, the "mind of the church" connotes a guiding indicator, a point of
reference for Christian prudence. The
directives of official teaching are worthy of religious assent and obedience
of the faithful.

MINIAMIN

In Judaism, one of the Levites serving
under Kore in office of trust for the distribution of the holy contribution
among their brothers at priests' cities in
King Hezekiah's day (2 Chronicles
31:14-15). The name is also applied to
one of the priestly paternal houses
existing in the time of High Priest
Joiakim (Nehemiah 12:12-17).

MINISCULE

A type of biblical Codex distinguished from the earlier unical type by being written in a cursive hand. The earliest minuscule goes back to AD 835 and the latest to the 17th or 18th century. Over 2,500 such manuscripts of the New Testament have been catalogued, and in the modern system of reference to the New Testament are designated by the word Codex plus an Arabic numeral.

MINISTRY

The work and service performed by a minister, servant or attendant responsible to a superior authority. In ancient Israel, the Levites served as God's ministers. Prophets were also used to minister in a special way (Deuteronomy 10:8; 21:5).

MINISTRY, Christian

The office held by those Christians who are set apart by ecclesiastical authority to be ministers in the church. The type of ministry varies in the different churches. That which developed in the early churches and is retained by the Roman Catholic, Eastern Orthodox, Old Catholic, Anglican, and some other churches is episcopal and is based on three orders, or offices, of bishop, priest, and deacon.

MINISTRY, Roman Catholic

From the word minister which means "to render service", in the viewpoint of Catholic theology, there is one essential ministry - the ministry of Jesus Christ; his ministry is extended, however, through the members of his Body, the church. In the church, the term is used in a variety of ways, among which are the following:

▲ The ordained ministry: the service of the people of God by those who have received the sacrament of holy orders (that is, bishops, priests, deacons) and who have specific functions determined by the teaching of the church itself.

▲ Non-ordained ministry: the service of the people of God undertaken by baptized Catholics either with a formal commission from the church (for example, lector, catechist, acolyte, Eucharistic minister) or without a formal commission from the church (for example, performing the corporeal and spiritual works of mercy).

Vatican Council II calls attention to both the variety and the unity of ministries in the church: "In the church not everyone marches along the same path, yet all are called to sanctify and have obtained an equal privilege of faith through the justice of God (see also 2 Peter 1:1).

"Although by Christ's will some are established teachers, dispensers of the mysteries and pastors for the others, there remains, nevertheless, a true equality between all with regard to the dignity and to the activity which is common to all the faithful in the building up of the Body of Christ."

MINNI

According to biblical tradition, an ancient kingdom that was divinely summoned to fight against Babylon. At that time Minni was allied with the kingdoms of Ararat and Ashkenaz, all under control of Cyrus (Jeremiah 51:27-29).

The exact location of this ancient kingdom and its people is uncertain. Some map makers have placed it in the region between Lake Van and the Araxes River, to the north-east in eastern Armenia. But most commentators are of the opinion that it lay in the general area south-east of Lake Van, either in the region of the upper Great Zab, a tributary of the Tigris River, between Lake Van and Lake Urmina, or more to the south of Lake Urmina.

MINNITH

In the Old Testament, one of the 20 Ammonite cities Hephthah subdues after making his vow to God (Judges 11:30-33). Centuries later "wheat of Minnish" is mentioned as an item of Tyre's trade (Ezekiel 27:2, 17). The exact location of Minnith is not known. One of a number of possible identifications is Khirbet Hanizeh, circa four miles north-east of Heshbon.

MINOS

In Greek mythology, legendary king of Crete. Androgenos, son of Minos, was a charismatic young man and outstanding athlete who came to Athens in order to compete in games organized by Aegeas. The young prince from Crete succeeded in beating all the other competitors. Envious of his success, Aegeas sent him against the bull of Marathon, which slew Androgenos.

The news of the death of his son reached Minos as he was sacrificing on Paros. As soon as the feast was over, he summoned his fleet and sailed to attack Athens. The war lasted some time and ended with the defeat of Athens, which Minos compelled to pay him a tribute of blood: each year, seven youths and seven maidens were sent to Crete and fed to the monstrous Minotaur.

Minotaur was a monster with a human body and the head of a bull. He was the son of Pasiphae, the wife of Minos and a bull that Poseidon has sent to Minos. Minos, shamed by the birth of this monster, called on the architect Daedalus to built the labyrinth as a palace in which the terrible Minotaur was incarcerated and fed on human bodies.

MIQAT

In Islam, literally, "time of appointment," or "meeting point." The term has the special sense of the place where, or the time at which, pilgrims to Mecca gather.

MIRACLE

The English word "miracle" is defined as "something that exercises wonder or astonishment, a wonderful thing, a marvel; an effect in the physical world which surpasses all known human or natural powers and is therefore attributed to supernatural agency." In the Hebrew scriptures the word moh-pheth' sometimes translated "miracle," means "a great and splendid deed" or "splendid and conspicuous deed." In the Greek scriptures the word dynamis, "power" is rendered "powerful work," "ability," "miracle" (Matthew 22:15; Luke 6:19).

In Christianity, miracle is regarded as a wonderful event, exceeding the known laws of nature, due to divine intervention. Only God has power to work miracles (though he may delegate it). Miracles are immediate acts of God: normal events are ordered by God mediately through natural law. In the Bible, miracles that occur are associated with redemption, culminating in those wrought by Jesus Christ, and, above all, in his resurrection. Often miracles are called "signs" or "powers", bringing out the deeper meaning.

In Buddhism, happenings resulting from the violation of natural law by an extra-cosmic being or beings are unknown. Control of the physical world by physical methods is possible to a limited extent. Control of nature by super-physical methods through the development of the individual is possible to much greater extent, but these methods are not supernatural and therefore not miraculous.

MIRACLE PLAYS

Religious dramas having the lives of the saints as subject, and concentrated upon the marvelous works or the great sufferings, credited to these heroic persons. The earliest surviving miracle plays are in Latin, and date from the 12th century renaissance in France and Germany.

Although the precise development of this genre is still uncertain, whether from tropes or directly from existing vitae, the materials are very similar to those in the lessons read on saints' days in the Office of Matins.

MIRACLES OF CHRIST

The gospels recount a large number of miracles performed by Jesus Christ: for example, miracles of healing, miracles of raising the dead, and miracles exhibiting control of natural forces.

In the New Testament sense, they are signs and wonders - events that are naturally unexplainable - which serve as a motive of credibility by manifesting the power of christ and inviting those who witness them to faith in Christ himself (see John 2:11).

MARRIAGE
In Islam, term indicating ascension, specifically of the Prophet Mohammed from Jerusalem through the Seven Heavens, after the Night Journey from Mecca to Jerusalem. In Paradise Mohammed entered God's presence. The Night Journey and Ascension into Paradise are covered in some detail in the Koran.

MIRIAM
In the Old Testament, daughter of Amram and his wife Jochebel, both of the tribe of Levi; sister of Moses and Aaron (Numbers 26:59; 1 Chronicles 6:1-3). Though not specifically named in the account, she was undoubtedly the one termed "his sister" who watched to see what would become of the infant Moses as he lay in the ark placed among the reeds of the river Nile (Exodus 2:3-4). After Pharaoh's daughter discovered the baby, "felt compassion" for it and recognized that it was "one of the children of the Hebrews," Miriam asked if she should summon a Hebrew woman to nurse the child. Being told to do so by Pharaoh's daughter, the maiden went and called the child's mother (Jochebed), who was thereafter employed to care for Moses until he grew up (Exodus 2:5-10).

MIRMAH
In Judaism, a paternal head of the tribe of Benjamin and son of Shaharaim by his wife Hodesh (1 Chronicles 8:1, 8-10).

MIRROR
In Chinese thought the mirror does not receive or absorb the image as in Western culture, but rather intercepts, arrests, and throws back the thing reflected. Therefore mirrors are protective. They are hung before houses at dead-end lanes or streets, turning away objects that might collide with them. Mirrors are placed in tombs to turn away evil or harm for the dead. Taoists placed mirrors to collect dew which they considered the Elixir of Life.

MISHAEL
In the Old Testament, a Kohathite Levite and son of Uzziel (Exodus 6:18-22). After Aaron's sons Nadab and Abihu, according to biblical tradition, were executed by God for offering illegitimate fire, Mishael and his brother Elzaphan carried their bodies outside the camp (Leviticus 190:1-5).

MISHAL
In biblical times, a border city of Asher given to the Gershonite Levites, apparently also called Mashal. Probably Mishal was situated not far from Mount Carmel (Joshua 19:24-26; 1 Chronicles 6:74). However, the exact location is unknown.

MISHAM
In the Old Testament, son of the Benjaminite Elpaal. Misham and his brothers built Ono and Lod and its independent towns (1 Chronicles 8:1-12).

MISHMA
In the Old Testament, a son of Ishmael and chieftain of an Arabian clan (Genesis 25:14-16; 1 Chronicles 1:30-31).

MISHMANNAH
In the Old Testament, one of the valiant Gadite army men who joined David's forces at Ziklag. He is listed fourth among the heads of David's army (1 Chronicles 12:1, 10, 14).

MISHNA(H)
One of the two sections of the Talmud, is the collection of Jewish law, compiled by the scholar Judah ha-Nasi and completed in the 4th century AD. It is divided into six "orders" dealing, among others, with laws relating to the Sabbath and festivals, marriage and

divorce, civil and criminal proceedings, ritual sacrifices and ceremonial.
The mishnah is a milestone in Jewish history. It explained many passages in the Torah in the light of daily problems of living. But the compact style of the mishnah needed interpretation and expansion. That task was undertaken by the gemara.

MISPERETH
One of the prominent leaders among the Jews returning with Zerubbabel from Babylonian exile in 537 BC (Nehemiah 7:6-7).

MISREPHOTH-MAIM
In biblical times, a point to which the Israelites pursued the armies of northern Canaanite kings allied with Jabin after having defeated them to the water of Merom (Joshua 11:1-8). When the Promised Land was divided into inheritance portions, the area extending from Lebanon to Misrephoth-maim remained to be conquered (Joshua 13:2-6).

MISSAL
Book containing all necessary prayers and ritual directions for the cerebration of Mass in the Roman Catholic Church throughout the year. Since Vatican Council II the missal consists of two books:
▲ the Roman Missal, which contains the texts for the celebration of the Mass;nd
▲ the Lectionary for Mass, containing a three year cycle of Scripture readings and chants for sundays and a two-year cycle of first readings and Gospels for the weekday liturgy. Readings for other feasts and for votive Masses are also included.

MISSIONS, Christian
Organized efforts for the propagation of the Christian faith. Ultimately, the origin of mission is found in the idea of God acting in history for the salvation of mankind. This universalism was found in prophetic Judaism and culminated in the conviction of the early church that God was in Christ reconciling the world to Himself. The gospel, being both the message of Jesus and the message of the early Christians about Jesus, was directed to all men. Jesus himself had commissioned his Apostles to make disciples of all nations.

MISSIONS, Religious
Organized attempts to spread religious faith and convert others to belief. Those who carry out the propagation of faith from their own convictions are called missionaries. Although missionary persuasion has been a provision of many religions throughout the ages, the preponderance of religious missions have been undertaken by Buddhists, Muslims and Christians.
The spread of religions
In the 3rd century BC, monks spread Buddhism to the peoples of India, China, Japan, Korea and other countries of Asia. Muslim missions and military conquests have widely disseminated Islam from the time of Mohammed to the present throughout the Middle East, Africa, south-east Asia and India. But the most familiar concept of missions in the past few centuries is largely associated with the efforts of Christianity.
Early Christianity was spread by Paul, Peter, Thomas, Barnabas and other earlier followers of Christ until the conversion of the barbarians who later dominated Europe. From their midst came the brave missionaries who penetrated to northern Europe, supplanting the worship of pagan gods with the ritual and ethical teaching of Christianity. From Constantinople, the eastern Christian church established missions in the Balkans and Russia, and eventually some missions reached Central Asia and China.
The proselytizing zeal of the Islamic conquerors, as they poured out of Arabia and built a vast empire, challenged the Christian hold on some parts of the world during the Middle Ages. But as Europe revived and the age of exploration and colonization began, the missionary efforts of the Roman Catholic Church followed

closely in the path of explorers, soldiers and traders, particularly in the New World, but also in Asia, where the Jesuits were active. By the 18th century Protestants also became active in missionary work.

MISSIONS IN AMERICA

America has always been the scene of wide missionary activity - from early Spanish, Portuguese and later French attempts to convert Indians in both North and South America to the wandering Mormons preaching to both natives and immigrants in the 19th century. One of the most massive missionary efforts in the United states were undertaken by Protestant evangelists, particularly the Methodists and Baptists, to convert and educate the freed slaves. Many American Protestant churches sent missionaries further afield to Australia, Asia, Africa and the Pacific islands in the 19th and 20th centuries. These missions, concentrated not only on conversion but also on providing education and health care. The best known permanent "home missions" in the United States, Great Britain and Commonwealth countries are those of the Salvation Army, who have come to rely greatly on Christian charity and example as on preaching, to reach the homeless and forgotten in their own lands.

Today the established churches are once again initiating evangelism in their own countries and the term "foreign missions" has been replaced by that of "world missions." Although traditional Christian missionary efforts seem to have passed their greatest peak, the Christian faith now exists in nearly every nation of the world primarily due to the groundwork of the pioneer missions.

MITHKAH

In the Old Testament, one of Israel's wilderness encampments (Numbers 33:28-29). Its location is not known to day. If Mithkah is correctly defined as "sweetness," the name may allude to the good water of the region.

MITHNITE

In Judaism, a term applied to Joshaphat, one of the mighty men in David's military forces. It is not known whether "Mithnite" refers to his place of origin or is his family designation (1 Chronicles 11:26, 43).

MITHRA

God of ancient Persia and India, the "Heavenly Light" of Zoroastrianism. He became the chief Persian deity, and his worship spread rapidly throughout the Middle East. His cult became one of the great religions of the Roman Empire, where he was called Mithras, and was especially popular in the Roman Army.

MITHRAEUM

Temple of Mithras, an Indo-Iranian god whose cult was widespread throughout the Roman Empire. The temple was an artificial cave, with naves and aisles. Mitraea have been found in Syria, Asia Minor, and Spain.

MITHRAINISM

The worship of Mithra, the Iranian god of the sun, justice, contract, and war in pre-Zoroastrian Iran. Mithraism, until its rapid decline in the 200s AD, was the chief rival of Christianity, which it resembled in some way. It was a personal faith, based on the struggle between good and evil. Its faithful were promised a lifer after death, and its secret rites (restricted to men) included baptism and a sacred feast. The seventh day was kept holy, and December 25 was celebrated as Mithras' birthday.

MITHREDATH

In biblical times, the treasurer of Cyrus who, under royal command, turned over some 5,400 temple utensils of gold and silver to the Israelites for return to Jerusalem (Ezra 1:7-11).

The name is also applied to an opposer of the post-exilic Temple reconstruction who shared with others in writing a letter to the Persian King Artaxerxes falsely accusing the Jews (Ezra 4:7).

MITRE

A liturgical headdress worn by Roman Catholic bishops and abbots and some Anglican and Lutheran bishops.

MITYLENE

In biblical times, the principal city of Lesbos, an island in the Aegean Sea off the west coast of Asia Minor. While on route to Jerusalem in the spring of 56, the apostle Paul sailed to Mitylene from Assos, a seaport on the mainland of Asia Minor circa 28 miles to the north-north-west (Acts 20:14). The fact that no mention is made of Paul's going ashore may imply that the ship merely anchored at Mitylene, perhaps because the needed northern winds had abated. On the following day the ship continued south-south-west toward Chios (Acts 20:15).

MITZWA

In Judaism, any commandment, ordinance, law, or statute contained in the Torah and , for that reason, to be observed by all practicing Jews.

MITZWOT MA'ASIYOT

In Judaism, the totality of external religious practices whose observance is regarded by Orthodox Jews especially as a hallmark of genuine piety.

MIXED MARRIAGE

In Roman Catholicism a mixed marriage is called a marriage between a Catholic party and a party who is not catholic. The basic discipline of the Catholic Church in regard to mixed marriage is explained in the Code of Canon Law: "Without the express permission of the competent authority, marriage is forbidden between two baptized persons, one of whom was baptized in the Catholic Church or received into it after baptism and has not left it by formal act, and the other of whom is a member of a church or ecclesial community, which is not in full communion with the Catholic Church" (Canon 1124).

The express permission called for in this Canon may be granted by the local ordinary (bishop) for a just and reasonable cause; according to Canon 1125, he is not to grant this permission, however, unless the following conditions have been fulfilled:

1 The Catholic party declares that he or she is prepared to remove dangers of falling away from the faith and makes a sincere promise to do all in his or her power to have all the children baptized and brought up in the Catholic church;

2 The other party is to be informed at an appropriate time of these promises which the Catholic party has to make, so that it is clear that the other party is truly aware of the promise and obligation of the catholic party.

3 Both parties are to be instructed on the essential ends and properties of marriage, which are not to be excluded by either party.

The Catholic party is bound to the form of marriage (that is, marriage in the presence of the local ordinary (bishop) or the pastor or a priest or deacon delegated by either of them, who assists, and in the presence of two witnesses); but for serious reasons the local ordinary has the right to dispense from the form in individual cases. It is the responsibility of the Catholic party to request this dispensation in due time before the marriage.

MIZPAH

In biblical times, a region inhabited by Hivites and situated at the base of Mount Hermon (Joshua 11:3). At least part, if not all of this area, may also have been called the "valley plain of Mizpah" (Joshua 11:8). The "land of Mizpah" possibly was the region around Banyas to the south of Mount Hermon or the plain east of Mount Hermon along the Wadi et-Tem.

MIZRAH

Plaque in a wall facing east in a Jewish home decorated with beautiful flowers and the word mizrah. The members of a Jewish household turn toward it when they pray, so that they face the Land of Israel, the ancient home of the Jewish people, and its capital Jerusalem, where the Temple stood.

MIZRAHI

A religious movement within the World Zionist Organization, with emphasis on religious education within the framework of nationalism; its traditional slogan was "the Land of Israel, for the people of Israel, according to the Torah of Israel."

MIZRAIM

In the Bible, person listed second among the sons of Ham (Genesis 10:6). Mizraim was the progenitor of the Egyptian tribes (as well as some non-Egyptian tribes) and the name came to be synonymous with Egypt (Genesis 10:13-14; 50:11).

Many scholars hold that Mizraim is a dual form representing the duality of Egypt (that is, Upper and Lower Egypt), but this is conjectural. The names of Mizraim's descendants are apparently plural forms: Ludim, Anamim, Lehabim, Nephtuhim, Pethrusim, Casluhim and Caphtorim (Genesis 10:13-14; 1 Chronicles 1:11-12). For this reason it is usually suggested that they represent the names of tribes rather than individual sons.

MIZZA

In Judaism, a descendant of Esau through Reuel and a sheik of Edom (Genesis 36:17; 1 Chronicles 1:34-37). Izzah was Esau's grandson, as he is included among "the sons of Basemath, Esau's wife," who was Ishmael's daughter and the mother of Reuel (Genesis 36:2-13).

MNASON

In biblical times, a native of Cyprus and "an early disciple." Paul and those with him were to be entertained in Mnason's home as the apostle returned from his missionary journey in circa 56. Some disciples from Caesarea accompanied Paul's group on the way from Caesarea to Jerusalem, to bring them to Mnason (Acts 21:15-17).

MNEMOSYNE

In Greek mythology, one of the Titans and daughter of Uranus (Heaven) and Ge (Earth); and, according to Hesiod, the mother (by Zeus) of the nine Muses,

MOAB

In the Old Testament, the son of Lot by his older daughter. Like his half-brother Ammon, Moab was conceived after Lot and his daughters left Zoar and began dwelling in a cave of the nearby mountainous region. Moab became the forefather of the Moabites (Genesis 19:30-38).

MOABITE

Member of a West-Semitic people who lived in the Transjordan plateau of Palestine and flourished in the 9th century BC. Their ancestral founder was Moab, a son of Lot, who was the Israelite patriarch Abraham's nephew. Their idol was called Chemosh.

MOADIAH

During biblical times, a priestly paternal house of which Piltai was the head in the days of Joaiakim (Nehemiah 12:12, 17). It has been suggested that "Moadiah" is a variation of the name "Maadiah" and that Moadiah is the same person as the priest Maadiah who accompanied Zerubbabel to Jerusalem after the Babylonian exile (Nehemiah 12:1-5).

MOGEN DAVID

A Jewish symbol composed of two overlaid equilateral triangles that form a six-pointed star, also called the star of David.

MOGGALLANA

One of the Buddha's chief disciples, being renowned for his supernormal powers; also the name of a famous Buddhist philosopher.

MOHA

In Hinduism, term meaning release; release from the round of birth and death. The term is used in Buddhism as synonymous with Nirvana.

MOHAMMED

(570-632) Also spelled Mohammed; Muhammad b. Abd Allah, the Prophet and founder of Islam and that faith's most important and significant messenger. He received his first revelation of the Holy Koran via the angel Jibril (Gabriel) when he was circa forty years old. He began to preach the messages he received - messages of the Oneness of God, the need of repentance, the certainty of a Day of Judgment - and encountered much opposition in his native city of Mecca, especially from the merchant classes who perceived a triple threat to their selfish mores, trade and polytheistic religion. Mohammed was eventually forced to make his famous Hijra to the city of Medina in 622 where he was welcomed. He set about establishing himself there, achieved a position of power, fought three major battles with the Meccans and finally returned in triumph to Mecca in 630. He died two years later in 632.

Mohammed, a human being who never claimed divinity, was both a prophet and a statesman and these two epithets neatly sum up the two principal features of his life. Through his prophethood he founded a great religion, that of Islam; through his statesmanship he laid the foundations for what would be later become a great Islamic empire under such dynasties as those of the Umayyads and the Abbasids.

Mohammed is buried in Medina and his tomb is frequently visited by Muslim pilgrim,s after the Hajj.

MOKSHA

Hindu term for liberation. Originally conceived as liberation from the oppressive weight of karma (one's deeds and their consequences) and from the endless round of samsara (rebirth), it later became synonymous with realization: liberation form a limited and conditions human existence.

It is conceived as the fourth and final goal (varga) of human existence, transcending pleasure (kama), wealth (artha), and even, at least for some, duty (dharma).

The positive content of moksha varies with diverse Hindu philosophies. The traditions generally agree, however, that some form of moksha may be achieved through any of the four paths (usually margas):

▲ knowledge or realization (jnana marga);

▲ love or devotion (bhakti marga);

▲ action (originally ritual actions but later through any deed, especially one's duty, done with the whole of one's being: marka marga);

▲ and finally through yoga, although here the goal is usually termed samadhi, a consummate inwardness.

MOLADA

In biblical times, one of the cities in southern Judah allotted to Simeon. Moladah remained in the hands of this tribe at least down till David's reign (Joshua 15:21, 26; 19:1; 2 Chronicles 4:24-31). After the exile Judeans resettled the site (Nehemiah 11:25-26).

MOLID

In Judaism, a man of Judah and descendant of Hezron through Jerahmeel. Molid was the son of Abishur by his wife Abihail (1 Chronicles 2:4-9; 25-29).

MOLINOS, Miguel de

(1628-1696) Priest condemned for advocating an extreme form of Quietism, a doctrine that came to be considered heretical by the Roman Catholic Church. It asserts, in general, that Christian perfection is achieved when the soul is in a passive state, at which time it is capable of being entered by the divine spirit.

MOLOCH

A deity to whom child sacrifices were made throughout the ancient Middle

East. The name derives from combining the consonants of the Hebrew "melech" (king) with the vowels of boshet (shame). Boshet was often used in the Old Testament as a variant name for the popular god Baal (Lord). The laws given to Moses by God expressly forbade the Jews to do what was done in Egypt or Canaan (Lev. 18:21).

MOLTEN SEA

Copper Sea; when in biblical times, the temple was constructed during Solomon's reign, a "molten sea" replaced the portable basin of copper sued with the earlier tabernacle (Exodus 30:17-21; 1 Kings 7:23-44). Built by Hiram, a Hebrew-Phoenician, it was evidently called a "sea" because of the large quantity of water it could contain. This vessel, also of copper, was "ten cubits (circa 15 feet) from its one brim to its other brim, circular all around; and its height was five cubits (circa 7.3 feet), and it took a line of thirty cubits (44 feet) to circle all around it" (1 Kings 7:23).

MONARCHIANISM

A Christian heresy that developed during the 2nd and 3rd centuries. It opposed the doctrines of an independent, personal subsistence of the Logos, affirmed the sole deity of God the Father, and thus represented the extreme monotheistic view.

MONASTERY

A place of residence where a community of men or women reside under a common rule. In general, a monastery is made up of a church, a chapter house, a cloister, refectory, work area, and individuals cells or a dormitory.

MONASTICISM

Way of life, usually communal and celibate, always ascetic, conducted according to a religious rule. It is found in all major religions. Christian monasticism originated in loosely organized communities of hermits in the 4th century who retreated to the Egyptian desert in search of perfection. The monk's original aim was personal salvation, although later his sanctity was also thought to benefit those in ordinary life. His central activities are the daily "hours" of prayer and work. He is supported by a life under special rules, including the vows of poverty, chastity, and obedience. The rule of St. Benedict (450-543) has been of primary influence in Western monasticism.

In Orthodox Christian monasticism all monks and nuns belong to one spiritual family. There are no separate "orders" as in the Western church. Orthodox monastic life is centered on prayer (contemplation) and self-discipline, and takes several forms.

MONASTICISM, Buddhist

A movement of Buddhist groups pledged to poverty and chastity and historically forming the organizational center of Buddhism, though lay Buddhist associations have emerged in recent years.

Buddha is said to have outlined monastic rules for the man who followed him as disciples, and at the request of his foster mother to have founded an order for nuns.

The community of Buddhist monks is known as the Sangha, with the Buddha and the Dharma (Buddha's teaching) one of the three valued components of Buddhism.

For those who joined Buddha's monastic order the traditional caste distinctions were eliminated. Any male might join, provided he was not sick, disabled, a criminal, a soldier, a debtor, or a minor lacking parental consent.

Monks were required to wear the yellow robe, shave their heads, carry the begging bowl, meditate daily, make an initiate's confession, and obey certain precepts. Monasteries have been the intellectual centers of Buddhism, and taking a strong role in society they have sometimes been important political centers. Prior to the 1950 takeover by China the monks of Tibet held total political power.

Generally Buddhist laymen support the monks in return for religious instruction, with laymen commonly spending some months at a monastery.

MONASTICISM, Early Western

Organized ascetism began in the West somewhat later than in the East. Individuals who had gone on pilgrimages to the Desert Fathers in Egypt and to monasteries in other parts of the East brought back to the West ideals of abnegation which they followed at home single or in small groups.

An impetus was given to the movement by Athanasius, bishop of Alexandria, during his numerous exiles at the hands of the Arians. When he came to Rome in 339 to plead his case before a Roman synod, a young Roman of high station, was so impressed by his reports of Egyptian monasticism that she and her companions made her house on he Aventine into a kind of convent.

About 356 Athanasius wrote a life of Anthony of Egypt, which he intended as an ideal pattern of the ascetical life. The biography was soon translated into several languages. Augustine testifies to the influence exerted by the Latin version of Evagrius of Antioch.

Martin of Tours founded the first monastery in Gaul in 361. When he had to leave his retreat upon his election of bishop, he chose a cell near Tours in which to dwell. The influx of numerous disciples gave rise there in 372 to the famous monastery at Tagaste. Later at Hippo he lived in common with his clergy under rule, a practice that had already been followed by Ambrose (died 397) and Eusebius (died 371), whose community may be regarded as the prototype of the secular canons of the Carolingian reform.

This penetration of monastic life into the ranks of the clergy who served the local churches was a characteristic of Western monasticism in contradiction to the forms it took in the East.

Eastern ideas were freshly introduced into monasticism with the return of John Cassian from years spent studying Eastern institutions. His express purpose was the reform of Gallic monastic life. To this end he founded a double monastery at Marseilles in 415 and composed for his followers a number of books.

The greatest of the Western founders was Benedict of Norse, who drew upon Cassian and other sources to write. Circa 530-540 he published the first detailed piece of monastic legislation specifically for the West. The copying of manuscripts he fostered was imitated in other monasteries and helped in preserving the classical culture of Europe.

MONASTICISM, Later Western

The Anglo-Saxon missionaries who carried Christianity back to the Continent in the late 7th and the 8th centuries were Benedictines. It was only natural that the new centers they founded should be Benedictine also.

In time the Benedictine rule became normative, sometimes with borrowing from older, more austere rules; and the legislation of Charlemagne (817) made it obligatory for all monks and nuns in the Carolingian domain.

In Spain and the Celtic lands, however, other rules continued to be used for several centuries. The rise of feudalism made abbeys into fiefs and abbots into feudal lords with accompanying obligations and privileges. Schools and scriptoria claimed much of the monks' time.

The first attempt to reduce extramonastic interests was made by Benedict of Aniane. He presided over the monastic Synod of Aachen (817), which decreed the elimination of external work, the lengthening of the Divine Office, and many other changes; but only when Cluny adopted the Synod's legislation (910) did the reform came alive.

Up to that time each monastery had been wholly autonomous, the rule being the only link among them. Now all Clunian houses were made dependent upon a central policy administered by the abbot of Cluny. Reforms occurred also in other places in Europe. Some reforms among the Benedictines emphasized eremitic and contemplative ideals.

The ills attendant on commendation, the Great Western Schism, wars, and the Black Death so weakened monasticism that Reformation attacks upon it were almost mortal. Yet renewal and reform, continued. Two of the most notable reforms were those of the Maurists in 1621 and of the Cistercians at La Trapped in 1664, the origin of the Trappists.

A characteristic of the reform movements of more recent centuries is a tendency to group monasteries into congregations with uniform observance and central government. In 1893 a loose federation of all Benedictine congregations was formed with headquarters at St. Anselmo in Rome.

MONASTIC THEOLOGY

A formula that designates the monastic approach to theology and not the study of monastic life. It has been in current use since 1953, the 8th centenary of the death of St. Bernard of Clairvaux, but the type of theology it indicates existed long before. During the Middle Ages it was the business of contemplatives within the cloister, generally monks.

Though distinct from scholastic theology as studied in the town schools, it was not opposed, but complementary, to it. In the 12th century, it was exemplified by the writings of Benedictines, Cistercians, and Canons Regular.

Because it was in fact the prolongation of the patristic thought of the ancient church into the mid-13th century, it may be called medieval patristics. Its value is not to be overestimated, yet it has been acknowledged by historians.

The stress it lays on the unity among Bible, patristic thought, and liturgy makes it akin to the theology of the Orthodox church. Its emphasis on the union that should exist between reflection and spiritual experience gives it some relationship with certain trends of Protestant theology. It thus has ecumenical value.

MONERGISM

The teaching that God is the sole cause of man's salvation; the opposite of synergism. The term has been applied especially to the Gnesiolutherianism of those who invoked Luther's teaching on justification and the abiding sinfulness of man against the synergistic controversy of Melanchton. Calvinism, particularly as articulated in the Synod of Dort (1618), may also be classified as monergistic in opposition to Arminianism.

MONISM

A generic philosophical term used to designate any position in metaphysics that reduces all objective reality to a single principle which alone exists, or any position in epistemology that reduced all knowledge to one fundamental kind.

MONK

A man who separates himself from society and lives either alone (a hermit or anchorite) or in an organized community t devote himself full time to religious life.

MONOPHYSITE CHURCHES

Branches of the Eastern church, formed in the 6th century by schismatic adherents of monophytism: the Armenians, Coptic and Jacobite Churches. Their doctrine is now essentially orthodox.

MONOPHYSITISM

(from Greek monos, *one,* and physis, *nature*)

Heretical doctrine that in the Person of Christ there is but one (divine) nature. It arose in opposition to the orthodox council of Chalcedon (451). A confused controversy resulted, and despite reconciliation attempts the schism hardened.

MONOTHEISM

Belief in one God, contrasted with polytheism, pantheism or atheism. Monotheism recognizes a single, supreme and personal deity, the creator and ruler of the universe. Classical monotheism is held by Judaism, Christianity and Islam; some other religions, such as early Zoroastrianism and later Greek religion, are monotheistic to a lesser degree.

MONOTHELITES

7th century Christians, who, while otherwise orthodox, maintained that Christ has only one will. They were attempting to solve the problem of the vital unity of Christ's Person on the basis of the firmly established doctrine of the two natures, divine and human, in the Person of Christ.

MONSTRANS

The sacred vessel which holds the consecrated host when it is exposed for adoration or carried in procession; it is constructed of precious metal and in such a way that the consecrated host is clearly visible.

MOODY BIBLE INSTITUTE

Originally called the Chicago Bible Institute, a Fundamentalist Protestant institution founded by Dwight L. Moody in 1889.

MOON WORSHIP

Adoration or veneration of the moon, a good in the moon, or a personification or symbol of the moon. The sacredness of the moon has been connected with the basic rhythms of life and the universe.

MOORE, Clement Clarke

(1779-1863) Scholar of Hebrew and teacher. He was instrumental in the establishment of the General Theological Seminar in New York.

MORALITY

Standard of human behavior determined either subjectively or objectively and based on what is considered ethically right or wrong.

In Catholic moral theology, morality is usually defined as the relationship between the human act and the norm of morality; the goodness or badness of a human act deriving from its conformity to or lack of conformity to the norm established by God. The objective norm of morality is especially the eternal law of God, embracing both the natural law and the divine positive law. The subjective norm of morality is the conscience of the individual person formed in harmony with the divine norm.

MORAL RE-ARMANENT

Movement founded by the American Lutheran Frank N.D. Buchman (1878-1961) in the 1920s which from 1929 called itself the "Oxford group." Concentrating on the affluent and influential, it operates through small groups cultivating the "Four Absolutes" (honesty, purity, unselfishness, love).

MORAL THEOLOGY

Love for God and man may be said to be the root principle of Christian morality. It came to be regarded as the chief 'theological virtue; (with faith and hope) as contrasted with the "cardinal" (i.e., fundamental) virtues (prudence, temperance, fortitude, and justice) derived from classical ethics.

Modern Christians have been influenced by the complexities of contemporary societies; by concern for social morality; and by non-Christian moral reflection.

MORAVIAN BRETHREN

The Bohemian Brethren were "renewed" by the Lutheran court Zinzendorf in Germany (1722) under pietist influence and later became an independent church.

MORAVIAN CHURCH

A Protestant communion founded in the 18th century but tracing its origin to the 15th century Hussite Unitas Fratrum (Unity if Brethren) in Bohemia and Moravia. It is principally a product of German pietism.

MORDECAI

In Judaism, important person who returned to Jerusalem and Judah in 539 BC after the seventy years of exile in Babylon (Ezra 2:1-2). Mordecai was a prominent Israelite and leader who assisted Zerubbabel and was distinguished in the initial genealogical enrolment of the reestablished community in Judah (Nehemiah 7:5-7).

The name is also applied to the son of Jair the son of Shimei the son of Kish, a Benjamite (Esther 2:5), an older cousin and guardian of Esther (Esther 2:7). Mordecai is portrayed solely in the Bible book of Esther. The book recounts his prominent part in the affairs of the Persian Empire during the years of approximately 484 to 474 BC. Evidence points to him als the writer of the book of Esther.

MORE, Henry

(1614-1687) Poet and philosopher of religion whose affinity for the metaphysics of Plate places him among a group of thinkers known as the Cambridge Platonists.

MOREH

In biblical times, a well-known landmark in Abraham's time near Shechem and seemingly continued to such for centuries afterward (Genesis 12:6; Deuteronomy 11:30).

The name also applied to a hill, in the vicinity of which the Midianites were defeated by Gideon (Judges 7:1). This hill is generally thought to be the bare gray ridge of Jebel Dahi circa five miles north of the suggested site for the well of Harod.

MORESHED

In the Old Testament, the home of the prophet Micah (Jeremiah 26:18; Micah 1:1). Tell el-Judeideh, circa twenty-two miles southwest of Jerusalem and about the same distance northeast of Gath, has been suggested as possible identification. The composite name Moresheth-gath (Micah 1:14) implies that the city was at times dominated by that Philistine city, since the philistines controlled places other than their five major cities (Gath being one of the five) (1 Samuel 6:18; 27:5).

MORGAN, William

(1545-1604) Anglican bishop of the Reformation whose translation of the Bible into Welsh helped standardize the literary language of his country.

MORIAH

In biblical times, the name of the rocky eminence on which Solomon built a magnificent temple. Earlier his father David had purchased the site from the Jebusite Araunah (Ornan) in order to erect an altar there, as this was the divinely indicated means for ending a scourge resulting from David's sin in connection with the taking of a census (2 Samuel 24:16-25; 1 Chronicles 21:15-28).

Ancient Jewish tradition links the temple site with the mountain in the "land of Moriah" where Abraham, at God's command, attempted to offer u[p Isaac (Genesis 22:2). This would make the "land of Moriah" that Abraham traveled from the vicinity of Beer-sheba, and, on the third day, he saw from a distance the divinely designated place for the sacrifice (Genesis 21:33-34). This could be said regarding Mount Moriah. Mount Moriah evidently was a sufficient distance from the Salem of Abraham"s time so that the attempted sacrifice of Isaac did not take place in full view of the city"s inhabitants. There is no record that these witnessed the incident or tried to interfere. That the site was somewhat isolated centuries later may be inferred from the fact that in David"s day there was a threshing floor on Mount Moriah. However, no mention is made of any buildings on the site (2 Chronicles 3:1). Today the Islamic mosque known as the Dome of the Rock is situated atop Mount Moriah.

MORISCOS

Name given to those Spanish Muslims and their descendants who became baptized Christians, from the pejorative form of Spanish moros, 'Moors' or 'Muslims.'

MORISON, James

(1816-1893) Theologian and founder of the Evangelical Union, whose followers were also called Morrisonians. He won many converts to his view that Christ's atonement saved not only believers but all men as well.

MORMON, Book of

Work (first published in 1830) accepted as holy scripture, in addition to the Bible, in the Church of Jesus Christ of Latter-day Saints. It relates the history of a group of Hebrews who migrated from Jerusalem to America circa 600 BC, led by the prophet Lehi. According the Book of Mormon, one group, the Lamanites, forgot their beliefs, became savages, and were the ancestors of the American indians. The other group, the Nephites, developed culturally and built great cities but were eventually destroyed by the Lamanites circa 400. Before this occurred, however, jesus had appeared and taught the Nephrites. The history and teachings were abridged and written on gold plates by the prophet Mormon.

MORMONISM

The Church of Jesus Christ of Latter-Day Saints. The Mormons' visionary founder Joseph Smith (1805-44) in the United States claimed to have translated the revealed Book of Mormon, which supplements the Bible. Brigham Young (1805-77) led the sect to Salt Lake City (1847). The church is ruled by an elaborate hierarchy. Baptism and marriage can be contracted vicariously for the dead to "seal" them in the faith. Mormons avoid stimulants and give two years' free service to the church.
There are no professional priests. The priesthood consists of Aaronic (lesser) and Melchizedek (higher) grades. Heading the church is the First Presidency (a President and two counselors) - part of the body called the "General Authorities." which also includes the Council of Twelve Apostles and their assistants, the patriarch to the church, and the seven-member First Council of the Seventy.

MORMON TABERNACLE

(1867) Latter-Day Saints tabernacle in Salt Lake City, Utah.

MORMON WAR

(1857) A conflict between the government of the United States and the Mormon government of Utah.

MORONI

According to the teaching of the Church of Jesus Christ of Latter-Day Saints, an angel or resurrected being who appeared to Joseph Smith on September 21, 1823, to inform the Mormon founder that he had been chosen to restore God's church on earth.

MORPHEUS

In Greek mythology, one of the sons of Somnus, the god of sleep.

MORRISON, Robert

(1782-1834) Presbyterian minister, translator, and the London Missionary Society's first missionary to China; he is considered the father of Protestant mission work there.

MORTAL SIN

From the Latin word meaning "deadly," the term mortal is synonymous in Catholic teaching with "grave" and "serious." A moral sin is a personal sin involving a fundamental choice against God in a serious way, a free and willing turning away from his love in a grave matter; or, in the words of Thomas Aquinas, "when our acts are so deranged that we turn away from our last end, namely God, to whom we should be united by charity, then the sin is mortal."
Traditional Catholic theology has emphasized three conditions for mortal sin:
▲ that the matter be grave or serious;
▲ that there be sufficient reflection or advertence or awareness of the seriousness of the choice one is making;
▲ that there be full consent of the will, that is, that one freely chooses to do what one knows is seriously wrong even though one could stop from doing it.

According to Catholic theology, mortal sin brings about the loss of sanctifying grace or friendship with God; grace and friendship are regained especially through the sacrament of penance, for individual and integrated confession and absolution constitute the only ordinary way by which the faithful person who is aware of serious sin is reconciled with God and with the church.

MORTIFICATION

From the Latin word which means "death"; the Christian ideal (see Luke 9:23-24; Galatians 5:24) of "dying to self" through the deliberate restraint of unruly passions and appetites; the struggle against one's evil inclinations so as to bring them in conformity with the will of God. Spiritual writers often distinguish between external mortification (that is, the discipline of the senses by way of fasting, abstinence, control of the tongue, modesty of the eyes) and internal mortification (that is, control over errant passions, emotions, and feelings).

MORTUARY TEMPLE

In ancient Egypt, places of worship of deceased kings as well as places where services were held to deliver food and objects to the dead monarch.

MOSERAH

In Judaism, the place where Israelites were encamped when Aaron died (Deuteronomy 10:6). It is evidently near Mount Hor (whereon Aaron died), but its exact location is unknown (Numbers 33:38). Some scholars tentatively locate Moserah seventeen miles west-southwest of Jebel Madurah.

MOSES

Hebrew lawgiver, leader and prophet who led the Israelites out of Egypt. The infant Moses, hidden to save him from being killed, was found and raised in Egypt by the pharaoh's daughter.

After killing a tyrannical Egyptian, he fled to the desert. From a burning bush, God ordered him to return and demand the Israelites' freedom under threat of the plagues.

After 40 years in the wilderness, he brought the Jews to the Jordan River, the eastern border of canaan, the promised land. He is believed to have lived some time during the period 1500-1200 BC. The only source of his story is the bible. Tradition names him as the author of the Pentateuch (the first five books of the Old Testament), but this is discounted by scholars.

His life

The Book of Exodus tells of the birth of Moses in Egypt, of Levite parents, at a time when the Pharaoh (Egyptian king) had ordered the killing of all male Israelite babies; and how he was discovered by Pharaoh's daughter in an ark (open chest) in rushes by the Nile and reared to manhood in the Egyptian court. It tells also of his flight to the Medianite Jethro after killing an Egyptian overseer for maltreating a slave; and how God spoke to him through the burning bush, commanding him to return to Egypt and liberate the Israelites.

This he did, but the Pharaoh did not free the Israelites until Egypt had suffered through ten terrible plagues. Moses then led the Israelites across the Red sea, which engulfed the pursuing troops of the reneging Pharaoh, and at Mount Sinai received the Ten Commandments from God for whose worship he built the Tabernacle.

The story is continued in the Book of Numbers, Leviticus and Deuteronomy, which record the years in the wilderness (a punishment fort the Israelite rebellion against God and Moses, during which Moses, inspired by God, formulated the Law; the arrival at the banks of the Jordan; and the death of Moses in Moab, after God had allowed him to see the summit of Mount Nebo.

Moses' importance is not confined to his achievements as lawgiver, prophet and leader of the Exodus. He is also an outstanding figure in history as the creator of a united Israelite people, bound together by a common religion based on the covenant that God made with him.

MOSES, Assumption of

A pseudepigraphical work (a non-canonical writing that in style and content resembles authentic biblical literature), originally written in Hebrew or Aramaic.

The book does not mention the actual ascension of Moses, but the Letter of Jude, when discussing the battle between Satan and the archangel Michael for possession of Moses' body, refers to the *Assumption of Moses*. It is thus clear that this work must have described the actual assumption in chapters that have been lost. Several passages, moreover, are incomplete.

MOSES (BEN SHEM TOV) DE LEON

(1250-1305) Jewish Kabbalist and probably the author of *Sefer ha-zoar* ("The Book of Splendor"), the most important work of Jewish mysticism; for a number of centuries its influence rivalled that of the Old Testament and the Talmud.

MOSES DE KHOREN

Traditionally held to be a 5th century author, he had been dated as late as the 9th century. He is the only Armenian historian to treat of events in this century long before its conversion to Christianity.

MOSQUE

A Muslim place of worship corresponding to a Christian church or Jewish synagogue. The name is derived from the Arabic masjid, meaning "a place for prostration" (in prayer). Devout Muslims attend their mosques on Friday (the Muslim Sabbath) and on other occasions, but can say their prayers wherever they happen to be.

The features of a mosque include one or more minarets; a courtyard with fountains or wells for ceremonial washing; an area where the faithful assemble for prayers led by the imam; a mihrab (niche) indicating the direction of Mecca; a nimbar (pulpit) and sometimes, facing it, a maqsurah (an enclosed area for important persons).

MOSQUE OF ISLAM

The primal community institution of the Nation of Islam, or Black Muslims. The Mosque forms a vital part of Muslim life as every member must attend two meetings each week without fail and at risk of suspension. Meetings, without rites or ceremonies, consist of a lengthy sermon or discourse delivered by the minister. The Mosque is administered by a minister, who heads a body of officers consisting of captains, secretary, treasurer, and investigator.

MOST HOLY

In biblical times, the innermost room of the tabernacle and, later of the temple. This compartment in the tabernacle was apparently cubical, each of its three dimensions being ten cubits (circ 14.6 feet); the dimensions of the Most Holy in the temple by Solomon were twice those of the tabernacle, so that it was eight times as large in volume (Exodus 25:15-23; 1 Kings 6:16-20; 2 Chronicles 3:8).

MOTHER GODDESS

A widely used term to designate a variety of feminine deities and maternal symbols of creativity, birth, fertility, sexual union, nurturing, and the cycle of growth.

MO TZU

(circa 470-390 BC) Chinese philosopher who preached universal love as the means of regenerating the war-torn world in which he lived. This is ion contrast with Confucianism, which starts from particular affections, especially within the family. Mo Tzu lived simply, conducting a school in which he inculcated his teachings. He was the founder of a religious cult that did not, however, outlive him long. His thought is guided by a general method that examines statements both as to their validity and their practical effects.

MOUNTAIN OF MEETING

According to biblical tradition, an expression appearing at Isaiah 14:13, where the king of Babylon is depicted as saying in his heart: "Above the starts of God I shall lift up my throne, and I shall sit down upon the mountain of meeting, in the remotest parts of the north."

Some scholars hold that this "mountain of meeting" was some distant northerly eminence that Babylonians regarded as the dwelling place of gods.

In Isaiah's time there was only one mountain, Mount Zion (which name evidently came to include the temple site at Mount Moriah), where god representatively met with his people (Isaiah 8:18; 24:23). It could appropriately be termed the "mountain of meeting" because at the sanctuary there all mature Israelite were to appear before the face of God three times each year (Exodus 23:17). Psalm 248:1,2 further confirms this identification byu giving Mount Zion a northerly location, harmonizing with the "mountain of meeting" being in "the remotest parts of the north."

MOUNT OF OLIVES

Multi-summited limestone ridge just east of the Old City of Jerusalem, and separated from it by the Kidron Valley.Frequently mentioned in the Bible and later religious literature, it is holy both to Judaism and Christianity.

First mentioned in the Bible as the "ascent of the Mount of Olives (2 Samuel 15); itis referred to in the Book of Zechariah in the prophecy of the end of days (Zechariah 14).

The Mount of Olives is often mentioned in the New Testament; from it, Jesus entered Jerusalem at the beginning of the last week of his life (Matthew 21:1; Mark 11:1).

According to ancient Jewish tradition, the messianic era will commence on the Mount of Olives; for this reason, its sloped have been the most sacred burial ground in Judaism for centuries.

MOUSEION

Originally a Greek temple dedicated to the Muses or a place where the arts were studied or practiced.`Specifically it refers to the Mouseion of Alexandria, Egypt.

MOZA

In Judaism, a descendant of Judah and son of Caleb by his concubine Ephah (1 Chronicles 2:46). The name is also applied to a Benjamite and descendant of King Saul. He was the son of Zimri and father of Binea (1 Chronicles 8:33-37).

MOZAH

In biblical timers, a Benjamite city (Joshua 18:21, 26). The ancient site is considered to be at or near Qaluniya, a village circa three miles west-north-west of Jerusalem. Jar handles stamped with the name "Mozah" have been found at Jericho and Tell en-Nasheh.

MOZARAB

Word deriving from the Arabic musta'rib which means literally "one who has become Arabized." The Norarabs were Christians living under Musoim rule in medieval Islamic Spain who adopted the mores of their masters but maintained, nonetheless, their Christian faith.

MOZARABIC ART

Artistic tradition of the Mozarabs, Christians who lived in the Iberian Peninsula after the Arab invasion of 711.

MPADI, Simon-Pierre

(1900-1973) Messianic Zairese religious leader and the organizer of a militant, separist African church. Mpadi exploited African bitterness over the racism of the white Christian missions to create a movement but, though short-lived, had significant effects on the growth of nationalist political and cultural feelings in Zaire.

MUADHDHIN

In Islam, the person who gives the call to prayer from the minaret of a mosque. In the Islamic world, particularly in large cities like Cairo, it is becoming more infrequent for this to be done in person, loudspeakers having replaced in many mosques the need for a muadhdhin's physical presence.

MUDANG

A Korean priestess who employs magic to effect cures, to tell fortunes, to soothe spirits of the dead, and to repulse evil. Her counterpart, the male shaman, is called a paksu; both, however, are also known by numerous other names in various parts of Korea.

MUDDADTHIR, al-

The title of the 74th sura of the Koran; it means "The Shrouded One." The sura belongs to the Meccan period and has 56 verses. Its title is taken from the first verse in which the Prophet mohammed is addressed formally as "Oh Shrouded One." This is one of the most important suras of the Koran for it constitutes the initial command to Mohammed to begin preaching the revelation. It warns too, of the torments of hell, guarded by nineteen keepers, whose inhabitants will include those who did not pray nor feed the poor.

MUDEJARS

Name for those Muslims who remained in Spain after the Christian reconquest (11th-15th centuries AD) of the Iberian Peninsula. In return for the payment of a poll tax, the Mudejars were a protected minority, allowed to retain their own religion, language, and customs.

MUDRA

Ritual gestures of the hands used in symbolic mahic, especially in the Buddhist tantric schools of Tibet. They are used in conjunction with Mantras and Yantras as aids to meditation. Buddha images are found in a variety of Mudra positions.

MUFASSIR

Exegete, interpreter, especially of the Koran.

MUFTI

In Islam, one who delivers, or is qualified to deliver, a fatwa. He may or may not hold the rank of qadi. The mufti constitutes a living bridge from pure Islamic jurisprudence to everyday Islamic life. In some cities and countries there exists (or has existed) the office of Grand Mufti.

MUGGLETON, Lodowick

(1609-1698) Puritan religious leader and anti-Trinitarian heretic whose followers, known as Muggletonians, that he was a prophet. After claiming to have had spiritual revelations, beginning in 1651, he and his cousin John Reeve announced the,selves as the two prophetic witnesses referred to in revelation 11:3.

MUHAMMAD, Prophet

See: Mohammed.

MUHAMMAD

The title of the 47th sura of the Koran. The sura belongs to the Medinan period and has 389 verses. Its title is drawn from the second verse which talks about belief in what has been revealed to the Prophet mohammed. The sura begins by warning that the deeds of the unbelievers will be in vain. However, the reverse is true of the deeds of those killed in the path of God; they will enter Paradise. God will protect the believer but the unbeliever will have no protector. Paradise contains rivers of milk, wine and honey by contrast with the boiling water which will be fed to the wicked in hell.

MUHAMMAD AL-BAQIR

(676-743) Fifth Shiite Imam. He was the grandson of the second Shiite Imam, al-Hasan. He was not political active but his imamate saw the development of certain Shiite rituals and legal attitudes.

MUHAMMAD AL-MAHDI AL-HUJJAH

(812-887) 12th and last imam (supreme Muslim leader), venerated by the Twelves, the main body of Shi 'ah Muslims, who believe he is still aline and will reappear to save the world.

MUHARRAM, al-

First month of the Islamic lunar calendar; often called the Muslim "Month of Mourning" because of the commemoration of the martyrdom of al-Husayn at the battle of Karbala, on the tenth day of the month.

MUHASIBI, al

(789-857) Eminent Muslim mystic and theologian renowned for his psychological refinement of pietistic devotion and his role as a precursor of the doctrine of later Muslim orthodoxy,

MUHKAMAT

In Islam, literally meaning "strengthened," "precise." In the exegesis of the Koran it is applied to those words or passages in the Koran which are "clear" and "intelligible."

MU'IZZ-UD-DIN MOAHAMMAD OF GHUR

(1123-1206) The Ghurid conqueror of the north Indian plain, and one of the founders of Muslim rule in India.

MUJADDID

In Islamic tradition, one of the succession of historical figures who, though less important that prophets, bring about an uprising of faith and keep religious values alive in the interim between prophetic advents.

MUJADILA, al-

The title of the 58th sura of the Koran; it means "The Woman who Disputes." The sura belongs to the Medinan period and contains 22 verses. Its title is drawn from the first verse which states that God has heard the speech of the woman who disputes with you in the matter of her husband. The reference here, and in the following verses, is to a pre-Islamic prelude to divorce, and concerns an actual case brought to the attention of Prophet mohammed. The remainder of the sura threatens dire punishments to those who are unbelievers and hypocrites.

MUJAHADAH

A Sufi (Muslim mystic) term meaning self-mortification. It is one of the major duties that a Sufi must perform throughout his mystical journey toward union with God. The Sufis maintain that God can be satisfied only through the believer's disregard and his carnal self. Thus, all acts of penance and austerity, such as prolonged fasts and abstinence from the comforts of life, have become part of the mujahadadh doctrine.

MUJTHID

In Islam, one entitled to give an independent judgment on a point of theology or law.

MUKAMMAS, David al-

(913-976) Philosopher and polemist, regarded as the father of Jewish medieval philosophy. While considered a Jewish scholar by both Jews and Muslim, it is not entirely clear whether al-Mukammas returned fully to Judaism. Faulting Christianity for the impurity of the monotheism, he also attacked Islam; he maintained that the style of the Koran did not prove its divine origin.

MULK, al-

The title of the 67th sura of the Koran; it means "The Sovereignty". The sura belongs to the Meccan period and has 30 verses. Its title is drawn from the first verse in which blessing is called down upon God in whose hand is "the sovereignty." He is the Creator of the Seven Heavens. Unbelievers will be tormented in Jahannam but those who fear God will be well rewarded. Those who are cast into hell will beasked whether or not a warner came to them. They will respond in the affirmative but admit they rejected such warners.

MULLAH

Title given in Muslim countries to religious leaders, teachers in religious schools, those versed in the canon law, leaders of prayer in the mosques, or reciters of the Koran. The word is often used to designate the entire class that upholds the traditional interpretation of Islam.

MULTIPLE SOULS

A widely distributed notion, especially in central and northern Asia and Indonesia, that an individual's life and personality are made up of a complex set of psychic interrelations.

MU'MINUN, al-

The title of the 23rd sura of the Koran; it means "The Believers." The sura belongs to the Meccan period and has 118 verses. Its title is taken from the first verse which proclaims the triumph of the believers. God has created man from clay and ultimately fashioned him into a human being. The early verses recall God's blessings which he has showered on his creation before proceeding to outline in some detail the histories of Nuh, Musa and Harun. Maryan and her son Isa, we are told, have been made a sign by God, who has led them to a safe place.

MUMTAHANA, al-

The title of the 60th sura of the Koran; it means "The Woman who is Tested." The sura is Medinan and contains 13 verses. Its title comes from, the tenth verse which advises that believing females among new muhajirum should be tested as to their true beliefs.

MUNAFIQUIN, al-

The title of the 63rd sura of the Koran; it means "The Hypocrites." The sura belongs to the Medinan period and contains 11 verses. Its title is drawn from the first verse which tells the Prophet Mohammed that God is well aware that the hypocrites do not mean what they say when they acknowledge Mohammed as the prophet of God. The hypocrites do not understand that God is the real owner of all wealth and treasure in Heaven and on earth.

MUNI

In ancient India, a religious ascetic who observed silence. A muni was both respected and feared for his supernatural powers, attained after the most severe disciplines, such as mediating between fires of fasting.

MUNKAR AND NAKIR

In Islam, the angels of the grave. These two angels, who play a significant role in the afterlife of man, are described principally in the tradition literature and do not appear in the Koran by name, although it impossible that the Koran does refer to the Punishment of the Grave.

MUPPIM

In Judaism, one of the "sons" of Benjamin (Genesis 46:21). he is evidently identical with Shephupham (Numbers 26:39), Shephuphan (1 Chronicles 8:5) and Shuppim (1 Chronicles 7:12).

MURATORIAN CANON

A late 2nd-century AD Latin list of New Testament writings regarded as canonical (scripturally authoritative), named for its discoverer Lodovica Antonio Muratori, an Italian scholar who published the manuscript in 1740.

MURJA'A AL-

In Islam, those who adhered to a belief in "postponement." These were people in early Islam who, while differing on other points, agreed that the Muslim who committed grave sin did not cease to be a Muslim (contrary to the view of the Kjarijites). For the murji'a any decision about the grave sinner was postponed and left to God. It must be noted here that the concept of postponement had profoundly political origins and connotations as well.

MURJI'AH

One of the earliest Islamic sects to believe in the postponement of judgment on committers of serious sins, recognizing God alone as being able to decide whether or not a Muslim had lost his faith.

MURRAY, John Courtney

(1904-67) Roman Catholic priest and theologian who was a principal author of the Declaration on Religious Liberty at the Second Vatican Council.

MURSALAT, al-

The title of the 77th sura of the Koran; it means "Those who have been Sent." The sura belongs to the Meccan period and has 50 verses. Its title is drawn from the first verse which commences by swearing by "Those who have been sent." These have been interpreted as angels but also as winds or rain clouds.The sura begins with a description of the Last Day and goes on to issue dire warnings to those who have made accusations by lying. The good, however, will be well awarded in Paradise.

MURUGAN

Chief deity of the ancient Tamils of South India, later identified in part with the Hindu god Skanda. He probably originated as a fertility god, and his worship is said to have included orgiastic dancing.

MUSA

Arabic word for Moses. he is a major prophet and messenger in the Koran. He is portrayed in several places proclaiming his mission in front of Pharaoh. Of particular interest is the meeting of Mnusa and the sage identified as al-Khadir. The Koran records Musa as performing nine signs or miracles, including the division of the sea. The text also presents Musa's religion as that of the Prophet mohammed; the former is thus a precursor of the latter.

MUSAR MOVEMENT

A religious development among Orthodox Jews of Lithuania during the 19th century that emphasized personal piety as a necessary complement to intellectual studies of the Torah and Talmud.

MUSHAHADAH

In Sufi (Muslim mysticism) terminology, the vision of God obtained by the illuminated heart of the seeker of truth. Through mushahadah, the Sufi acquires real certainty (yaqin), which cannot be achieved by the intellect or transmitted to those who do not travel the Sufi path.

MUSHI

In Judaism, grandson of Levi and son of Merari (Exodus 6:16-19). Mushi became father of three sons and founded a family called the "Mushites" (1 Chronicles 23:33).

MUSHITES

In Judaism, a Levite family that descended from Mushi the son of Merari (Numbers 3:17, 20-23).

MUSLIM

In Islam, literally, "submitter," "one who submits (i.e. to the will of God)." A Muslim is one who professes and practices the faith of Islam, worshipper of the one God (Allah) whose laws and dogmas are explained in the Koran, a holy book set down according to their prophet Mohammed. Islam, the Muslim religion, embraces more than 70 millions, mainly in the Middle East, North Africa and central southeast Asia. Muslims form a majority in the populous nations of Pakistan, Malaysia and Indonesia and they constitute a large minority in India.
Beginnings
The first Muslims are members of two pagan tribes who inhabited the northern and southern regions of the Arabian peninsula. Circa 100 BC the most powerful, the Quraysh, conquered the strategic city of Mecca, located on an important trade route between Yemen, Syria and Egypt. Mohammed, a member of the Quraysh tribe, was borne in Mecca, and spent nearly 40 years of his life there, until he experienced the vision that called him to be the prophet of the one God. The Meccans were idol-worshippers and rejected Mohammed's preaching, but by the

time of his death in 632, the converts he made had established the islamic religion forcefully in the Arab world. It a remarkably short time the Muslims began to create what was to become one of the world's great empires.

MUSLIM BROTHERHOOD

Religiopolitical organization founded in 1928 in Egypt. Emphasis was on the return to the Koran (Islamic sacred scriptures) and the Hadith (traditions relating to life and sayings of the prophet Muhammad) as quidelines for a healthy, modern Islamic society.

MUSLIM CIVIL WARS

Major struggles for power that disrupted the Orthodox, Umayyad, Abbasid, and Spanish Umayyad caliphates. The various Muslim civil wars occurred in the period of 683-1031.

MUSLIM IBN AL-HAJJAJ

(817-875) Scholar who was one of the chief authorities on the Hadith, accounts of the sayings and deeds of the Prophet Muhammad.

MUSNAD

In Islam, literally, "based," "founded." The word is used in hadith criticism to characterize a tradition whose complete isnad links it directly, usually to the prophet Mohammed.

MUSTA-LIANS

Adherents to the branch of Islam of the Isma'ilis.

MUSUBI

The power of becoming or creation, a central concept in the Shinto religion of Japan. A number of deities are associated with Musubi.

MUT

In Egyptian religion, a sky goddess and great divine mother. Originally she was a vulgar goddess of Thebes; but during the 18th dynasty she was married to the god Amon and as such became, with their adopted son Khons, a member of the Theban Triad. During the New Kingdom the marriage of Amon and Mut became one of the great celebrations held annually at Thebes.

MUT'AH

In Islam, temporary marriage. This is permitted by the law of the Ithna Asharis, but not sanctioned elsewhere in Islam. The temporary marriage is contracted for a fee, rather than a dowry, which a woman receives.

MUTAFFIFIN, al-

The title of the 83rd sura of the koran; it means "Those who give Short Measure." The sura belongs to the Meccan period and has 36 verses. It is considered that this was the last sura to have been revealed in Mecca before the Hjjra took place. The title of the sura is taken from the first verse. The sura condemns unfair business and trading practices and promises the joys of Paradise to the pious.

MUTASHABIHAT

Arabic term, literally "ambiguous," "unclear." The word is used in the exegesis of the Koran, as an epithet applied to those words and passages in the Koran which are not clear or which are obscure, as opposed to those which are characterized as muhkamat.

MUTAWWIF

Pilgrim guide in Mecca whose function is to guide the visiting pilgrim through the complex rituals of the Hajj.

MU'TAZILAH, al-

General Arabic term for political and religious neutralists; by the 10th century, used specifically of an Islamic school of speculative theology that flourished in Basra and Baghdad (8th-10th centuries).

MUTH-LABBEN

An expression included in the superscription of one of David's psalms (Psalm 9). Some commentators suggest that it indicated to the musical director the name or perhaps the opening words of a familiar song that furnished the melody to be used in singing this psalm.

MUZAMMIL, al-

The title of the 73rd sura of the Koran; it means "The Mantled One." The sura belongs mainly to the Meccan period and has 20 verses. Its title is taken from the first verse which translates as "Oh Mantled One" (i.e. Mohammed). The reference is made to Mohammed's request to his wife Khadija to wrap him up in a mantle after his receiving the vision of Jibril. The sura praises god as Lord of the East and the West and stresses that Mohammed has been sent to his people in the same was as Musa was sent to Pharaoh.

MYO-O

In Buddhist mythology of Japan, fierce protective deities, corresponding to the Sanskrit Vidyaraja ("king of knowledge"), worshipped mainly by the Shingon sect.

MYRA

In biblical times, a major city in the province of Lycia. Situated near the coast of southwest Asia Minor, Myra occupied a hill over two miles inland on the river Andracus. The site is now known as Dembre. Ruins include rock-hewn tombs and a large theater with well-preserved decorations.

MYRON

The Greek name for the chrism consecrated by the bishop at the Mass of Chrism on Holy Thursday, and used throughout the diocese for the administration of confirmation and to consecrate churches and altars.

MYSIA

In biblical times, a region in the northwestern part of Asia Minor. Its boundaries appear to have fluctuated, but basically Mysia was bounded from west to north by the Aegean Sea, the Hellespont and Propontis (Sea of Marmara).

While on his second missionary journey, Paul, accompanied by Silas and Timothy, endeavored to go to Bithynia but "the spirit of Jesus did not permit them. So they passed Mysia by and came down to Troas (Acts 15:40; 16:1-3).

MYSTAGOGY

Initiation into the mystery of Christ through special instruction in the sacramental life which takes place immediately after initiation into the Christian community.

MYSTERIES OF FAITH

Doctrines of faith, such as they Blessed Trinity and the Incarnation, that are products of divine revelation but cannot be totally understood by reason alone.

MYSTERIOUS LETTERS OF THE KORAN

Twenty-nine suras of the Koran begin with single letters, or groups of letters, from the Arabic alphabet. They occur after the Basmala (invocation) but before any other words. A large number of theories, over the centuries, have been put forward to explain these letters. Such theories include the idea that each letter is the first of an epithet characterizing God, and the idea that each letter has a numerical (mystical) value, among others. Others explain the letters by reading them as mnemonics or as abbreviated tables of content. Others simply state that "God knows best what is meant by this.

MYSTERY

As used in Roman Catholic theology, a mystery is a divinely revealed truth whose existence cannot be known without revelation by God and whose inner essence cannot be wholly understood by the human mind even after revelation; for example, the mystery of the Trinity, the mystery of the Eucharist.

A mystery, in this sense, is said to be above reason but not contrary to reason; even though it cannot be fully understood, it can be understood to some degree, and for that reason the church encourages all to reflect upon and study the mysteries God has revealed.

MYSTERY RELIGIONS

Secret cults of the Greco-=Roman world that offered to individual initiates a way to have religious experiences not provided by the official public religions.

MYSTICAL BODY OF CHRIST

A designation for the Christian church made popular by Pope Pius XII in his encyclical *Mystici Corporis* (1943). It signifies a supernatural reality that unites all Christians with Christ, who is their head.

MYSTICISM

Belief than man can experience a transcendental union with the divine in this life through meditation and other disciplines. It is at the core of most eastern religions, though it may be only loosely linked with them. The path of this union is usually seen as three stages: cleansing away of physical desires; purification of will; enlightenment in metaphors, especially of love and marriage.

Mysticism is important in most forms of christianity. The goal is union and communion with God in love and by intuitive knowledge in prayer; mystical experience may be expressed only in metaphors, especially of love and marriage.

In Buddhism, an awareness of the essential Oneness of the universe and all in it, achieved by a faculty beyond the intellect. There is a mysticism in the Theravadan but in the Mahayana it appears in many forms, and great mystical works are freely used in the monasteries. In a sense Zen Buddhism is itself a school of mysticism, for its first and final precept is: "Look within, thou art Buddha."

MYTHOLOGY

Study and interpretation of myths, or the collected myths of a particular people or area. Many people, including the ancient Egyptians, the Indians and the Aztecs, have elaborate mythologies. Western civilization has been especially influenced by the Greek and scandinavian mythologies, particularly in its literature.

Myths are stories of gods, semi-divine heroes and supernatural events. They can thus be distinguished from fables, which are intended to teach moral precepts and sagas, which are concerned with human beings and not deities. But some mythologies are a mixture of proper myths, often with religious significance, and traditional stories with some basis of fact

Myths probably began in the awe felt by primitive peoples, in the absence of scientific knowledge, for such natural phenomena as the rising and setting of the sun, and in their attempts to explain everything around them. The sun was the powerful giver of light and warmth; it must surely be a god. The winds must surely also be the work of gods or goddesses.

In this way every natural thing - sun, moon, stars, seas, rivers and so on - and emotions such as love and hate were ascribed to gods and goddesses. The belief that a god has human form and personality is called anthropomorphism. Its roots lie in animism, and man's need for some visual concept of his deities.

Since there were many gods and goddesses, it was natural to regard one as supreme over all the others. In Greek mythology, the king of the gods was Zeus (the Roman Jupiter); god of the sky whose weapon was the thunderbolt, he was widely worshiped in connection with most human activities.

Some theological scholars have drawn attention to the similarity between certain myths and stories in the Bible. For example, in Greek mythology Deucalion survives the great flood sent by Zeus and is therefore identified by some with Noah. Babylonian myths also repeat the story of the flood. Such instances, they say, show that certain biblical stories reflect related myths, or share a common source with them. The title of the 107th sura of the Koran; the Arabic word here has been variously translated as "Charity," "Benevolence," and "Alms." Some of the sura's 7 verses were revealed in Mecca and others in Medina. The title of the sura is drawn from the seventh verse which refers to the prevention of al-ama'un. The sura begins with the question; have you seen the man who denies the Judgment to come?

N

NAAMATHITE

In the Old Testament, a designation applied to Job's companion Zophar (Job 2:11; 20:1) and identifying his family or the place of his residence. Djebel-el-Nah-ameth in north-west Arabia has been presented as a possible location for Zophar's home.

NAAMITES

In the Old Testament, a family of Israelites descended from Benjamin's grandson Naaman (Numbers 26:38-40).

NAARAH

In biblical times, a city on the boundary of Ephraim (Joshua 16-18) thought to be the same as Naaran (1 Chronicles 7:28).

NAARAI

In Judaism, son of Ezbai and a mighty man in David's military forces (1 Chronicles 11:26-27). He may be identical with "Paarai the Arbite" mentioned at 2 Samuel 23:35, in what seems to be a parallel list.

NAARAN

In biblical times, an Ephraimite border city (1 Chronicles 7:20, 28).

NABA, al-

The title of the 78th sura of the Koran; it means "The News." The sura belongs to the Meccan period and has 70 verses. The title comes from the second verse which refers to "the great news." The sura begins with physical references to the earth and the Heavens created by God and this is followed by a description of the Day of Judgment. The wicked will drink foul things in hell while the good will enjoy the physical delights of Paradise.

NABAL

According to biblical tradition, a wealthy Maonite sheep owner who pastured and sheared his flocks in Carmel of Judah. He was also known as a Calebite, that is, a descendant of Caleb (1 Samuel 25:2-3). Few Bible characters are so contemptuously described as is Nabal. Nabal's flocks of 3,000 sheep and 1,000 goats had been protected from marauding bands by David's men. After showing this kindness and not being guilty of any misappropriations, David requested Nabal to prove some material assistance for him and his men at shearing time, a traditional time of feasting and hospitality. Nabal refused and "his heart came to be dead inside him, and he himself became as a stone," perhaps indicating some type of paralysis (Deuteronomy 28:28). Circa ten days later Nabal was struck dead by God (1 Samuel 25:2-38).

NABATEANS

Arab people whose kingdom in what is now Jordan flourished from the 3rd century BC until its conquest by the Romans (AD 106). Originally nomadic, the Nabateans were influenced by Aramaic civilization to adopt a settled life. Although they spoke Arabic, they used Aramaic on their coins and inscriptions.

NABI

Arabic word for prophet. Islam teaches that Mohammed was the Last or Seal of the Prophets. A total of 28 prophets are named in the Koran. Several are mentioned in Surat Maryam where each is characterized as a nabi or rasul or both. Every rasul is necessarily a nabi; however, the reverse is not true.

NABONIDUS

In biblical times, last supreme monarch of the Babylonian Empire and father of Belshazzar. On the basis of cuneiform texts he ius believed to have ruled some 17 years (556-539 BC).

NABOTH

In biblical times, a Jezreelite vineyard owner and victim of a wicked plot by Queen Jezebel. Naboth's vineyard in Jezreel was within sight of King Ahab's palace. Naboth declined Ahab's offer to buy the vineyard or to exchange it for a better vineyard somewhere else, because God had prohibited sale in perpetuity of a family inheritance (1 Kings 21:1-4). Ahab's wife Queen Jezebel, however, schemed to have two witnesses falsely accuse Naboth of blaspheming God and the king. Thereby Naboth and his sons were put to death (2 Kings 9:26), enabling Ahab to take possession of the vineyard. Because of these murders, Elijah foretold that the dogs not only would eat up Jezebel but would also lick up Ahab's blood. Their offspring would similarly be cut off (1 Kings 21:5-23). This divine pronouncement was carried out (1 Kings 23:34-38).

NABU

A major god in the Assyro-Babylonian pantheon. He was patron of the art of writing and a god of vegetation.

NABULUS

In biblical times, city of central Palestine. As a Canaanite city it was important in ancient Palestine. Its ruins are under the stratified mound of Tell al-Balajah, just east of the present city, named Shechem. After king Solomon's death, the ten northern tribes of Israel revolted in Shechem against his son, Rehoboam, and installed Jeroboam as king in his place (1 Kings 12:1-10). After the Assyrian conquest of the northern Kingdom of Israel (722 BC) the city declined; it was resettled by the Samaritans, who established their sanctuary on adjacent Mount Gerizim, and was important in the Hellenistic period,

but was destroyed by the Maccabean ruler Hyrcanus (ruled 135-104 BC).

NACON

According to biblical tradition (2 Samuel 6:6), the name of the threshing floor where Uzzah died for grabbing hold of the ark of the covenant. The parallel account at 1 Chronicles 13:9 says "Chidon," probably indicating that one writer mentioned the name of the place, the other that of its owner, or that one name is an altered form of the other.

NADAB

In Judaism, the first-born son of Aaron and Elisheba (Exodus 6:23; 1 Chronicles 6:3). Nadab was born in Egypt and made the great exodus with Israel. He with his next young brother Abihu and 70 other Israelites were called with Aaron and Moses up into Sinai, where they saw a vision of God (Exodus 24:1, 9-11). Nadab and his three brothers were all installed into the priesthood with their father (Exodus 28:1; 40:12-16). Within a month, however, Nadab and Abihu abused their office by offering illegitimate fire. Just what made the fire illegitimate is not stated, but it was probably more than just getting intoxicated (suggested by the immediate prohibition to priests not to drink wine or intoxicating liquor when on duty). However, intoxication may have contributed to their wrongdoing. For their transgression they were killed by fire from God and their bodies were disposed outside the camp (Leviticus 10:1-11; Numbers 26:60-61). Nadab and Abihu died before they had fathered any sons, leaving their brothers Eleazar and Ithamar to found the two priestly houses (Numbers 3:2-4; 1 Chronicles 24:1-2).

According to biblical tradition, the name is also applied to the son of Jeroboam and second king of the northern ten-tribe kingdom of Israel. Nadab rules parts of two years (circa 976-975 BC) during which he continued the calf worship instituted by his father. While besieging Gibbethon, a former Levite city (Joshua: 21-20-23) taken over by the Philistines, Nadab was assassinated by Baasha, who then killed off all remaining members of Jeroboam's house in order to secure the throne for himself (1 Kings 14:20; 15:25-31).

NAFS

In Islam, term with various meanings such as soul, spirit, human being, person, self, mind.

NAGA

In Hindu and Buddhist mythology a class of semidivine beings, half-human and half-serpentine. They are considered to be a strong, handsome race who can assume either human or wholly serpentine form, potentially dangerous, but in some ways superior to men.

NAGARJUNA

(AD 150-231) Buddhist monk-philosopher and founder of the Madhyamika (Middle Path) school whose clarification of the concept of "emptiness" is regarded as an intellectual and spiritual achievement of the highest order. He is recognized as a patriarch by several later Buddhist schools.

NAGGAI

According to biblical tradition, ancestor of Jesus Christ listed in his genealogy as given by Luke (Luke 3:23-25).

NAGUAL

Personal guardian spirit believed by some Meso-American Indians to reside in an animal or bird. The nagual is similar to the West African bush soul and to the ancient Roman individual genius.

NAGUALISM

A widespread belief among North, Central, and South American Indians that certain individuals have the power to transform themselves into animals in order to perform evil activities.

NAHALAL

In biblical times, a city in Zebulun assigned to the Merarite Levites (Joshua 19:10-15). Rather than driving out the Canaanites inhabiting this city as divinely instructed, the Zebulunites subjected them to forced labor (Judges 1:30; 2:2).

NAHALIEL

In the Old Testament, a place where the Israelites encamped not long before their flight with Amorite King Sihon (Numbers 21:19-24).

NAHAMANI

In Judaism, one who returned with Zerubbabel from Babylonian exile (Nehemiah 7:6-7).

NAHARAI

In Judaism, a Beerothite and one of Joab's armor-bearers. Naharai was among the mighty men of David's military forces (2 Samuel 23:24, 37; 1 Chronicles 11:26).

NAHASH

In biblical times, king of the Amminites at the same time Saul began his reign. Nahash brought his army against Jabesh in Gilead. Israel rallied around Saul, went to Jabesh and defeated Nahash (1 Samuel 11:1-11).

The name is also applied to the father of David's half-sister Abigail and possibly the father of Zeruiah. He was the grandfather of Abishai, Joab, Asahen and Amasa (2 Samuel 17:25; 1 Chronicles 2:16). Abigail is called "the daughter of Nahash," but she and her sister are nowhere called daughters of Jesse, David's father.

NAHATH

According to biblical tradition, Sheik of Edom, son of Reuel and grandson of Esau and his wife Basemath, Ishmael's daughter (Genesis 36:2-4).

The name is also applied to a Levite, descendant of Kohath, and ancestor of Samuel (1 Chronicles 6:16, 22-28).

NAHBI

In Judaism, son of Vophsi of the tribe of Naphtali. He was one of the 12 men Moses sent for spying out the land of Canaan and was among those returning with a bad report (Numbers 13:1-3; 31-33).

NAHL, al-

The title of the 16th sura of the Koran; it means "The Bees." The vast majority of the sura belongs to the late Meccan period; it contains 128 verses. The title of the sura is drawn from verse 68 which refers to God's advice to the bees that they should find dwellings in the mountains and trees and building materials. The sura lauds God's blessings on His creation, proclaims His Oneness, and described Paradise awaiting the pious. Much pain awaits those who do not believe in the signs, or verses of God. The sura also forbids the consumption of pork, dead meat, blood, and what has been killed in a name other than God's name.

NAHMANIDES

(1195-1270) Spanish Talmudist, commentator on the Bible, and Jewish religious leader, whose writings reflect Kabbalistic beliefs.

NAHOR

In Judaism, father of Terah and grandfather of Abraham. Nahor was a son of Serug and descendant of Shem (1 Chronicles 1:24-27).

The Genesis account of Terah and Abraham leaving Ur of the Chaldeans does not include Nahor's name in the list of travelers (Genesis 11:31). It does seem, however, that he may have come later, for Abraham's servant, seeking a wife for Isaac, traveled to Haran, where Terah took up dwelling and where he died, and where Nahor's grandson Laban lived when Jacob went to him (Genesis 11:31-32; 12:4; 27:43). Abraham's servant came "to the city of Nahor," either to Haran itself or to a place close by, perhaps the Nahur frequently mentioned in various Mari tablets of the second millennium BC (Genesis 24:10). And when Jacob parted company from Laban, Laban called on "the god of Abraham and the god of Nahor" to judge between them (Genesis 31:53).

NAHSHON

In Judaism, wilderness chieftain of the tribe of Judah. Nahshon was the son of Amminadab and among other lister fifth generation after Judah (1 Chronicles 2:3-10). His sister was Aaron's wife (Exodus 6:23). Nahshon formed a link in the line of descent that led to David and Jesus, becoming father to Salmon, who married Rabah, and grandfather of Boaz, who, in turn, married Ruth (1 Chronicles 2:11-15; Ruth 4:20; Matthew 1:4-6).

As chieftain of Judah, the leading tribe of Israel, Nahshon assisted Moses with the first wilderness registration of fighting men. He presented Judah's contributions to the tabernacle service when the altar was inaugurated, and headed Judah's army of 74,600 that led Israel's line of march (Numbers 1:2-7; 2:3-4; 6:2-17).

NAHUM

According to biblical tradition, an Israelite prophet of the seventh century BC and the writer of the book bearing his name. Nahum may have been in Judah at the time he recorded his prophecy (Nahum 1:15). His being an Elkoshite evidently means that he was a resident of Elkosh, possibly a city or village of Judah (Nahum 1:1).

The name is also applied to a post-exilic ancestor of Jesus Christ in the line of his earthly mother Mary (Luke 3:25).

NAHUM, Book of

The seventh of the Old Testament minor prophets, the oracles of the prophet Nahum. It graphically describes the fall of Nineveh, the capital of the Assyrian Empire (612 BC). Nahum sees this as God's punishment, caused by the cruelty of the Assyrians. The book contains many types of material, among which are a hymn, oracles of judgment, satire, a curse, and funeral laments.

Nahum portrays the panic-stricken palace, the fainting hearts, the preparation for the siege of Nineveh (capital of Assyria). Nahum's book is so sharp in its details that it must have been written during or shortly after this historic event.

NAIADS

In Greek mythology, the nymphs of flowing water - springs, rivers, fountains, lakes. Like the other classes of nymphs, they were extremely long-lived, although not immortal.

NAIN

According to biblical tradition, a Galilean city where Jesus Christ resurrected the only son of a widow (Luke 7:11-17). Nain appears to be represented by the village of Nein on the northwestern side of Jebel Dahi. It is situated in the general area indicated by Jerome and Eusebius for the ancient site. Overlooking the Plain of Esdraelon, Nain lies in an attractive natural setting.

In AD 31, during his first preaching tour of Galilee, Jesus Christ came to Nain from the vicinity of Capernaum (Luke 7:1-11). A distance of 23 miles separated the two locations. The "gate" may simply have been an opening between the houses by which a road entered Nain, there being no evidence that a wall ever surrounded the city. It was probably at the eastern entrance of Nain that Jesus and his disciples met the funeral procession, which was perhaps headed for the hill-side tombs lying to the south-east of modern Nain. Moved with pity for the now childless widow, Jesus approached the bier and resurrected the widow's son. News of the miracle spread throughout the region and even reached Judea. The event may also be alluded by the words "the dead are being raised up," forming part of Jesus's reply to the messengers later sent by the imprisoned John the Baptist (Luke 7:11-22).

NAJM, al-

The title of the 53rd sura of the Koran; it means "The Star." The sura is Meccan and has 62 verses. The title comes from an oath in the first verse. The early verses of the sura are a major source of detail about the famous Mi'raj of Mohammed. A number of major prophets like Musa, Ibrahim and Nuh are also mentioned.

NAME OF GOD

From a biblical viewpoint, the name signifies more than the external person; it describes also his or her basic personality; thus the name of God was held in such high reverence that they did not even say "Yahweh" but used "Adonai" (the Lord) instead. Likewise, the first Christians held the name Jesus in great reverence (see Philippians 2:9-10).

The second commandment inculcates this spirit of reverence: "You shall not make wrongful use of the name of the Lord your God, for the Lord will not acquit anyone who misuses his name" (Exodus 20:7).

NAML, al-

The title of the 27th sura of the Koran; it means "The Ants." The sura is Meccan and has 93 verses. Its title is drawn from the 18th verse which portrays an ant advising his brethren to seek refuge in their homes lest they be inadvertently crushed by Sulayman and his armies. The sura begins with two of the mysterious letters of the Koran, makes reference to the staff of Musa being turned into a snake, and then goes on to relate the story of Sulayman who can speak the language of the birds. The hoopoe bird brings him news of the ruler of Sheba and Sulayman has a notable encounter with her. The sura is full of prophetic history and it goes on to give details of the stories of Salih and Lut.

NANSHE

In Mesopotamian religion, Sumerian city goddess of Nina (modern Surghul).

NANTES, Edict of

Law promulgated at Nantes in Brittany on April 13, 1598 by Henry IV of France, which granted a large measure of religious liberty to his Protestant subjects, the Huguenots. The edict upheld Protestants in freedom of conscience and permitted them to hold public worship in many parts of the kingdom, though not in Paris.

NANTOSUELTA

A pagan Celtic goddess worshipped primarily in Gaul; she was sometimes portrayed together with the god Sucellus. One of her attributes was the raven, which thus linked her with the Irish goddess Morrigan and her two companions.

NAOMI

According to biblical tradition, mother-in-law of Ruth, who was an ancestress of David and of Jesus Christ (Matthew 1:5). Naomi was the wife of Elimelech, an Ephrathite of Bethlehem in Judah, in the days of the judges. During a severe famine she and her husband and their two sons, Mahlon and Chilion, moved to Moab. There Elimelech died. The sons then married Moabite women, Orpah and Ruth, but circa ten years later these sons died childless (Ruth 1:1-5).

NAPHISH

In Judaism, the 11th listed of Ishmael's twelve sons (Genesis 25:13-16); 1 Chronicles 1:29-31). As chieftain he also headed an Ishmaelite tribe that took his name and presumably resided in territory bordering on the eastern and north-eastern frontier of the Promised Land. In the days of Saul The Israelite tribes of Reuben, Gad and the half tribe of Manasseh living east of the Jordan successfully made war on the Hagrites and their confederates, including the tribe of Naphish, and captured a great quantity of livestock and people (1 Chronicles 5:10, 18-22). It is possible, as some scholars suggest, that these Naphish captives were put to work as Nethenim slaves of the sanctuary, and that after the return from Babylonian exile their descendants were called the sons of Nephushesim or Nephusim (Nehemiah 7:46; Ezra 2:43-50).

NAPHTALI

In Judaism, the second son born to Jacob by Rachel's maidservant Bilhah in Paddan-aram (Genesis 35:25-25); 1 Chronicles 2:1-2). Since Bilhah had substituted for her mistress Rachel, Nephtali like his other full brother Dan, was considered by the barren Rachel as her own son. Although her sister Leah by then already had four sons (Genesis 29:32-35), Rachel was elated over her success in getting a second son through her maidservant (Genesis 30:2-8).

Later, Naphtali himself became the father of four sons, Jahzeel (Jahziel), Guni, Jezer and Shillem (Shallum) (Genesis 46:24; 1 Chronicles 7:13). When the dying patriarch Jacob related to his sons what would happen to them in the "final part of the days," his statement about Naphtali. though one of the briefest, was favorable (Genesis 49:1-2; 21).

NAPHTALI, Tribe of

One of the 12 tribes that in biblical times constituted the people of Israel who later became the Jewish people. The tribe was named after the younger of two sons born to Jacob and Bilhah, a maidservant of Jacob's wife Rachel.

About a year after the Israelites left Egypt, the fighting men of this tribe from twenty years old upward numbered 53,400 (Numbers 1:42-43). While in the wilderness, the tribe of Naphtali, under the leadership of its chieftain Ahira, encamped north of the tabernacle alongside the tribes of Asher and Dan.

As part of the three-tribe division of the camp of Dan, the tribe of Naphtali, along with Dan and Asher, was last in the order of march and occupied the important position of rear guard (Numbers 1:15-16; 2:25-31).

By the time a second census was taken circa four decades after the exodus from Egypt, the number of able-bodied men in the tribe had dropped to 45,400 (Numbers 26:50). Along the men lost to the tribe was Nahbi, one of the ten spies who brought back a bad report and discouraged Israelites from entering the Promised Land (Numbers 13:14, 31-33; 14:35-37).

After finally crossing the Jordan and sharing in the conquest of Jericho and Ai under Joshua's leadership, Naphtali was one of the tribes "standing for the malediction" in front of Mount Ebal (Joshua 6:24-25; 8:30-35; Deuteronomy 27:13). When the time came for apportioning the land into tribal inheritances, Pedahel, as divinely appointed representative of the tribe of Naphtali, assisted Joshua and Eleazar the priest in this (Numbers 34:16-17; Joshua 19:51).

NAPHTUHIM

According to biblical tradition, name of a man listed among the descendants of Mizraim, the son of Ham (Genesis 10:6-14; 1 Chronicles 1:11-12). As with the other names in this list, scholars usually take the apparent plural form to indicate a tribe or people. Assuming the name to derive from some geographical relationship, scholars often associate Naphtuhim with an Egyptian phrase meaning "those of the Delta," and on this basis the Naphtuhim are included among the inhabitants of Lower (northern) Egypt.

NAQSHBANDIYAH

Orthodox fraternity of orthodox Islamics (Sufis) found in India, China, and Malaysia. The order has no mass support, for its litanies are subdued and emphasize repetition of the ritual prayer to oneself.

NAR, al-

Arabic name for hell. The commonest of all names for hell appears many times in the Koran where hell is always described in very physical terms.

NARASIMHA

Fourth of the ten incarnations (avataras) of the Hindu god Visnu (Vishnu).

NARCISSUS

In biblical times, head of a household ion Rome. When Paul wrote his letter to the Romans, he requested that his greetings be given to "those from the household of Narcissus who are in the Lord" (Romans 16:11).

NAS, al-

The title of the 114th and last sura of the Koran; it means "The People" or "Mankind." The sura belongs to the Meccan period and has 6 verses. Its title comes from the first verse which counsels that one should say "I seek refuge with the Lord of mankind." The remaining five verses are a completion of the invocation. They describe God as the King and God of mankind and then specify that the evil from which refuge is sought is that of the Devil, called "The Tempter" and "The one who leaves when God"s name is mentioned," who whispers in men"s hearts, as well as the evil of the Jinn and men.

NASHIM

In Judaism, the third of the six major divisions of orders of the Mishna (codification of Jewish oral laws), which was given in its final form early in the 3rd century AD by Judah ha-Nasi. Nashim covers principally aspects of married life.

NASI

In the Talmud, the president of the Great Sanhydrin, who shared jurisdiction with the presiding judge; together they were known as the "pairs" (zugot).

MASIKH AND MANSUKH

Doctrine of abrogation in the Koran according to which a verse revealed later may abrogate one revealed earlier;

this resolves the problem of any apparent conflict. The Arabic word masikh designates the "abrogating" verse while mansukh indicates that the verse has been "abrogated."

NASR, al-

The title of the 110th sura of the Koran; it means "The Help." The sura belongs to the Medinan period and has 3 verses. It was the last Koranic sura to be revealed to the Prophet Mohammed and is characterized as Medinan. The title is taken from the first verse which speaks of when God's help and victory arrives. At that time God is to be praised and His forgiveness sought.

NATARAJA

The Hindu god Siva (Shiva) in his form as the cosmic dancer, represented in metal or stone in most Siva temples in South India.

NATHA CULT

A popular all-India religious movement that strives for immortality by transforming the human body into an imperishable divine body. It combines esoteric traditions from Buddhism, Sivism (worship of the Hindu deity Siva), and Hatha Yoga (stresses physical discipline), with a liking for the occult.

The Natha cult is essentially made up of yogis whose aim is to achieve sahaja, defined as a state of neutrality transcending the duality of human existence.

NATHAN

According to biblical tradition, prophet who rebuked King David, in his famous parable on the ewe lamb, for abducting Bath-sheba (2 Samuel 12:1-14). He secured Solomon's succession as King of Israel (1 Kings 1). The Book of Samuel may have been partly based on his lost history of David and Solomon (1 Chronicles 29:29; 2 Chronicles 9:29).

The name Nathan is also applied to a son of David by his wife Bath-sheba, born to him in Jerusalem (2 Samuel 5:13-14; 1 Chronicles 3:5). Through Nathan and his descendants the natural lineage of Messiah is traced, from David down to Jesus, evidently through his mother Mary (Luke 3:32-31).

NATHANAEL

According to biblical tradition, one of the earliest disciples of Jesus (John 1:45-51), generally identified with St. Bartholomew. Cana of Galilee was his home. Jesus appeared to him and others at the Sea of Galilee after rising from the tomb (John 21:2).

As one of the Twelve, Nathanael was in constant attendance throughout Jesus' ministry, being trained for future service (Matthew 11:1; 19:25-28; Mark 4:10; 11:11; John 6:48-67). After Jesus' death and resurrection, Nathanael and others of the Apostles went back to their fishing, and it was while they were approaching shore in their boat one morning that Jesus called to them. Nathanael, unlike Peter, stayed in his boat until it got to shore, and then, joining the rest for breakfast he took in the meaningful conversation between Jesus and Peter (John 21:1-23). He was also present with the other Apostles when they met together for prayer and on the day of Pentecost (Acts 1:13-14; 2:42).

NATHAN-MELECH

In Judaism, a court official of Judah whose dining room was situated in the porticoes of the Temple. While taking steps against false worship, King Josiah made the horses that Judean kings had given to the sun "cease from entering the house of God by the dining room of Nathan-melech" (2 Kings 23:11).

NATIONAL ASSOCIATION FOR PASTORAL RENEWAL

A contemporary American Roman Catholic reform group.

NATIONAL ASSOCIATION OF EVANGELICALS

A fellowship of various evangelical Protestant groups in the United States founded in 1942 and signed by 147 evangelical leaders. It comprises more than 40 denominations, many independent religious organizations, local churches, and individual Christians. All members must subscribe to a Statement of Faith that requires belief in the Bible "as the inspired, the only infallible, authoritative word of God" and commitment to a well-defined category of fundamental Christian doctrines.

NATIONAL ASSOCIATION OF FREE WILL BAPTISTS

An association of Baptist churches organized in Nashville, Tennessee, in 1935. The group continues to emphasize Arminian rather than Calvinist doctrine, and they believe that salvation is available to all who accept Christ.

NATIONAL BAPTIST CONVENTION, U.S.A.

An association of African-American Baptist churches that until 1917 had the same history as the National Baptist Convention of America. It has a mission program and carries on home-mission and other programs.

NATIONAL BAPTIST CONVENTION OF AMERICA

One of two large African-American Baptist churches that trace their origin to 1880. The Convention carries on mission, benevolence, youth, and other work.

NATIONAL CONFERENCE OF CHRISTIANS AND JEWS

United States organization founded in 1928 to fight prejudice, intolerance and bigotry and to promote interface harmony. The conference sponsors brotherhood/Sisterhood Week.

NATIONAL COUNCIL OF THE CHURCHES OF CHRIST IN THE USA

Organization of 32 Protestant and Eastern Orthodox churches (with combined membership of 40 million), founded in 1950 to promote interdenominational cooperation and understanding. It has educational, ecumenical, political and relief programs, and has allied itself with many other church bodies and missionary societies.

NATIONAL COVENANT

A solemn agreement inaugurated by Scottish Presbyterians on February 28, 1638, in the Greyfriars' churchyard, Edinburgh.

NATIONAL THEOLOGY

Knowledge of God acquired by natural reason aided by divine revelation. Natural theology seeks to establish, for example, the fact that God exists and to derive analogous knowledge of His nature from the study of the visible world that He created.

NATURAL LAW

In Roman Catholicism, the law inherent in the very nature of rational creatures whereby they rightly order their basic conduct with respect to God, others, and themselves. Paul speaks of "the law .... written on their hearts" (Romans 2:15). Thomas Aquinas defines the natural law as "the participation of the rational creature in the eternal law of God" and argues that all men and women, through the light of reason, are able to arrive at a basic moral code, embracing at least the principle that good must be done and evil avoided.

NATURAL WORSHIP

A working concept limited primarily to those involved in or influenced by the modern, especially Western, study of religion and concerned with the veneration of individual natural phenomena.

NATURE MYSTICISM

Form of mysticism in which the divine or sacred is perceived in natural forms and phenomena. The visible and sensible world, experienced in this special way, is central in this kind of mysticism.

NAVAJO RELIGION

Basic religious concepts of the Navajo Indians, the most populous of all Indian groups in the United States.

Some of the many myths related the emergence of the first people from various worlds beneath the surface of the Earth; other stories justified the numerous rites that were performed. Most rites were primarily for curing bodily and psychiatric illness. In other ceremonies there were simply prayers or songs.

NAVE

Central and principal part of a church, extending from the entrance to the transepts (transverse aisle crossing the nave in front of the sanctuary in a cruciform church) or, in the absence of transepts, to the chancel (area around the altar).

NAZARENE

In the New Testament, a title applied to Jesus and, later, to those who followed his teachings (Acts 24:5). Originally the term designated any native of Nazareth, a town in Galilee.

It was natural and not particularly unusual to speak of Jesus as the Nazarene, since from infancy (less than three years of age) he was raised as the local carpenter's son in the city of Nazareth, a place circa 62 miles north of Jerusalem. The practice of associating persons with the places from which they came was common in those days (2 Samuel 3:2-3; 17:27; 23:25-37; Acts 13:1; 21:29).

NAZARENE, Church of the

A large United States Holiness denomination.

NAZARENES, The

The members of the "Lucas Brotherhood," or Brotherhood of St. Luke (the patron saint of painting), an association formed by a number of young German painters in 1809 in a return to the medieval spirit in art.

NAZARETH

Historic city of Lower Galilee, northern Israel, where Jesus Christ lived as a youth. The first reference is in the New Testament. Nazareth is a place of Christian pilgrimage; the town has many shrines and churches.

It is difficult to say with certainty how prominent Nazareth was in the first century. The most common view of commentators is that Nazareth was then a rather secluded, insignificant village. The principal biblical statement used to support this view is what Nathanael said when he heard that Jesus was from there: "Can anything good come out of Nazareth?" (John 1:46). This has been taken by many to mean that Nazareth was looked down upon, even by the people of Galilee (John 21:2). In addition, it is claimed by some that Nazareth was not directly on the main trade routes of the area. It was not mentioned by Josephus, though he referred to nearby Japhia as the largest fortified village of all Galilee, leading to the idea that Nazareth was eclipsed by its neighbor.

NAZI'AT, al-

The title of the 79th sura of the Koran; it means "The Removers." The sura belongs to the Meccan period and has 465 verses. The title comes from an oath in the first verse; the "removers" are the angels who remove evil men's souls. The sura begins with a series of five formal oaths and goes on to stress the doctrine of the resurrection of the body in the Last Day. The sura concludes by underlining that only God knows when the Last Day will be.

NAZIRITE

Among the ancient Israelites, a person who made a special vow either for life or a period. His separation was most commonly marked by his uncut hair and his abstinence from wine during the time of his consecration. Making a vow this way also existed in New Testament times (Acts 21:23).

NEAH

In biblical times, a city mentioned in a description of Zebulun's territorial boundaries (Joshua 19:10-16). Neah's location is uncertain.

NEAPOLIS

In biblical times, a city of Greece at the northern end of the Aegean Sea that served as a seaport for Philippi. It is generally linked with modern Kavalla. This city occupies a rocky promontory at the head of the Gulf of Kavalla. Its harbor is situated on the western side, and Kavalla itself lies circa ten miles south-east of the ruins of Philippi. Latin inscriptions indicate the city's dependence on Philippi in Roman times, and portions of an aqueduct there appear to be of Roman construction.

It was at Neapolis that the apostle Paul first entered Europe in response to a call to "step over into Macedonia." From there her went to Philippi, this possibly taking him three or four hours as he crossed the mountain range between the two cities (Acts 16:9-11). Circa six years later Paul doubtless passed through Neapolis again (Acts 20:6).

NEBAI

In the Old Testament, one of the "heads of the people" whose descendant, if not himself, attested by seal the "truthworthy arrangement" of Nehemiah's day (Nehemiah 9:38; 10:14-19).

NEBAIOTH

In Judaism, the firstborn of Ishmael's 12 sons and founder of one of the prominent Arabian tribes (Genesis 25:13-16; 1 Chronicles 1:29-31). Nebaioth's sister Nahalath married their cousin Esau (Genesis 28:9; 36:2). The descendants of Nebaioth are not identified as living in any definite locality; they were probably nomads, moving about as bedouins with their flocks. In the time of Isaiah the "flocks of Kedar (Kedar was Nebaioth's brother) and the "rams of Nebaioth" were associated together in a prophecy fore-

telling how such animals would serve as approved sacrifices on God's altar (Isaiah 60:7).

NEBALLAT

In biblical times, a place settled by Benjaminites after the Babylonian exile (Nehemiah 11:31-34). Neballat is generally identified with Beit Nebala. Situated on a low hill circa four miles northeast of modern Lydda, Beith Nebala overlooks the south-eastern end of the Plain of Sharon.

NEBAT

In biblical times, an Ephraimite and father of King Jeroboam I, the first ruler of the ten-tribe kingdom of Israel (1 Kings 11:26; 2 Kings 14:23-24).

NEBO

Major god in the Assyro-Babylonian religion. He was patron of the art of writing and a god of vegetation. In the Old Testament, the worship of Nebo is denounced by Isaiah (46:1).

NEBO

In biblical times, a Moabite city that came under the control of Amorite King Sihon sometime before the Israelites entered the Promised Land (Isaiah 15:2). Subsequent to Israel's defeating Sihon, the Reubenites rebuilt Nebo (Numbers 32:37-38).

NEBUCHADNEZZAR I

The most important king of the second Isin dynasty which rose to power after the Kassites (circa 1150 BC). His reign (circa 1125 BC to circa 1104 BC) was marked by the conquest of Elam, a country north-east of the Persian Gulf, and by successful resistance to the Assyrians.

NEBUCHADNEZZAR II

King of the Chaldean Empire (reigned 604-562 BC). He was known for his military might, the splendor of his capital, Babylon, and his important part in Jewish history. He was the oldest son and successor of Nabopalassar, founder of the Chaldean Empire. On expeditions in Syria and Palestine he received the submission of local states, including Judah, and captured the city of Ashkelon. In 597 he also captured Jerusalem, deporting King Jehoiachin to Babylon. Further deportation of prominent citizens took place in 582. Nebuchadnezzar rebuilt Babylon, making it the finest city of the times. Its hanging gardens were one of the seven wonders of the world. The Book of Daniel records his bouts of madness.

NEBUSHAZBAN

In biblical times, the Rabsaris, chief court official, in the forces of Nebuchadnezzar that destroyed Jerusalem in 607 BC. Nebushazban was one of the several princes that directed the release of Jeremiah (Jeremiah 39:13-14).

NEBUZARADAN

In biblical times, chief of the bodyguard and principal figure in Nebuchadnezzar's forces at the actual destruction of Jerusalem in 607 BC. It does not appear that Nebuzaradan was present during the initial siege and breakthrough of Jerusalem, for it was about a month later that "he came to Jerusalem," after King Zedekiah had been brought to Nebuchadnezzar and blinded (2 Kings 25:2-8; Jeremiah 39:2-3; 52:6-11).

NECHO II

(flourished 7th century BC) King of Egypt and a member of the 26th dynasty, who unsuccessfully attempted to aid Assyria against the Neo-Babylonians. When Josiah, king of Judah, and an ally of the Neo-Babylonians, was slain in battle at Megiddo, Necho replaced Joshiah's chosen successor with his own nominee and imposed tribute on Judah. In 606 the Egyptians routed the Neo-Babylonians, but at the great Battle of Carchemish the Neo-Babylonian crown prince, Nebuchadnezzar, defeated Necho's troops and forced their withdrawal from Syria and Palestine.

NECHUNG ORACLE

The state oracle-priest of Tibet who, until the conquest of Tibet in 1959 by the People's Republic of China, was consulted on all important occasions.

NEDABIAH

In Judaism, last-named son of King Jeconiah (Jehoiachin), born during Jeconiah's exile in Babylon (1 Chronicles 3:17-18; 2 Kings 24:15). Nedabiah was a descendant of David of the tribe of Judah and an uncle of Zerubbabel, the post-exile governor (1 Chronicles 3:1, 17-19).

NEGEB

Arid region, southern part of Israel, occupying almost half of Palestine west of the Jordan. Biblical references such as Psalms 126 point to the semi-arid character of the region from early recorded times (Psalms 126:3-5).

NEHELAM

In biblical times, perhaps the home of the false prophet Shemaiah (Jeremiah 29:24-31). But a location by this name is unknown. Therefore some have suggested that "of Nehelam" may be a family designation. Others believe that Jeremiah's family Nehelam was perhaps a play on the Hebrew word ha-lam meaning "to dream" (Compare Jeremiah 23:25).

NEHEMIAH

(6th century BC) Jewish leader of the return from the Babylonian captivity. As described in the Old Testament Book of Nehemiah (written with the Book of Ezra by the author of the Chronicles), he rebuilt Jerusalem;s walls and enforced moral and religious reforms.

NEHEMIAH, Book of

One of the historical Old Testament books, written by Nehemia (5th century BC). Nehemiah was the cupbearer of the Persian king Artaxerxes I at a time when Judah in Palestine had been partly repopulated by Jews released from their Babylonian captivity.

Distressed at news of the desolate condition of Jerusalem, Nehemiah obtained permission from Artaxerxes to journey to Palestine. There he became the leader of the returned Jews. He rebuilt Jerusalem's walls and reformed abuses and revived the worship of God.

Nehemiah stands out as a sterling example of faithfulness and devotion. He was unselfish, leaving behind a prominent position as cupbearer in the courtyard of Artaxerxes to undertake the rebuilding of Jerusalem's walls. As there were many enemies, Nehemiah willingly exposed himself to danger in behalf of his people and true worship. Not only did he direct the work of repairing the wall of Jerusalem, but he also had an active personal share in the task. He wasted no time, was courageous and fearless, relied fully on God and was discreet in what he did. Zealous for true worship, Nehemiah knew God's law and applied it. He was concerned about building up the faith of his fellow Israelites.

Though enforcing God's law zealously, he did not domineer over others for selfish benefit, but showed concern for the oppressed. Never did he demand the bread due the governor. Instead, he provided food for a considerable number of persons at his own expense (Nehemiah 5:14-19).

NEHUSHTA

In biblical times, daughter of Einathan of Jerusalem and wife of King Jehoiakim. When the first captives were taken to Babylon, Nehushta was taken along and likely remained there the rest of her life (2 Kings 24:6-12).

NEIEL

In biblical times, a city of Asher (Joshua 19:24-27), perhaps to be identified with Khirbet Ya'nin. This site lies circa ten miles east-south-east of Acre (Acco).

NE'ILA

In Judaism, the last of the five Yom Kippur services, the most sacred of the yearly liturgy, expressed in melodies of great solemnity. When the shifar (ritual ram's horn) sounds, the synagogue service ends and the day-long fast is over.

NEKHABED

In Egyptian religion, vulture- or serpent-goddess, the protectress of Upper Egypt and especially its rulers, often portrayed as spreading her wings over the pharaoh, while grasping in her claw the royal ring or other emblems.

NEKODA

In Judaism, the forefather of a group of Nethinim who returned from Babylonian exile in 537 BC (Ezra 2:1, 43, 48).

NEMBUTSUHER

In Buddhism, the invocation Namu Amida Butsu and the act of repeating it, by which rebirth into Amida's Paradise at death may be, according to the tenets of the Pure Land School, assured.

NEMESIS

In Greek religion, the name of two divine conceptions. The first was a goddess (perhaps of fertility), worshipped at Rhamnus in Attica, who was very similar to Artemis.

The second divine entity of this name was an abstraction - i.e., indignant disapproval of wrongdoing, particularly the disapproval of the gods at human presumptions, and, also, the eventual personification of that disapproval.

NEMESIUS OF EMESA

(flourished late 4th century) Christian philosopher, apologist, and bishop of Emesa. A man of extensive culture, Nemesius integrated elements from various sources of Hellenistic philosophical and medical literature.

NEMUEL

In Judaism, first listed of Simeon's five sons and family head of the Nemuelites (Numbers 26:12-14; 1 Chronicles 4:24). In the list of those who came into Egypt with Jacob he is called Jemuel (Genesis 46:8-10; Exodus 6:15).

NEMUELITES

In Judaism, a family of Simeon descended from Nemuel (Numbers 26:12).

NEO-LUTHERANS

Mid-19th century German Pietist group.

NEOPHYTE

Term used by early Christians in the figurative sense of "one recently baptized." The term occurs in the New Testament (1 Timothy 3:6) and is translated in various English Bibles as "neophyte," "novice," "convert," "newly baptized," or "recent convert."

NEOPLATONISM

A school of philosophy that developed the work of Plato and dominated philosophy from the third until the sixth century. Plotinus (3rd century) and Proclus were the founders of Neoplatonism. They extended Plato's theory of forms, according to which everything has an unchanging form at its root, into a theory that forms are the only ultimate reality. These forms exist in a Divine Mind beyond heavens.

Plotinus rejected the dualism of two separate realms of being (good and evil, material and transcendent, universal and particular) in favor of the all-embracing concept of One. The One is incomprehensible but overflows to create the Divine Mind or Logos (word). The Divine Mind contains all the forms that lie behind reality. Below is the World Soul, which mediates between mind and matter. The longing of man is to rise upward toward union with the One. Neoplatonic philosophy greatly influenced Christian theology during the first three centuries of the Christian era through St. Augustine and others. It revived at the time of the Renaissance and has influenced many later mystical movements.

NEOPTOLEMUS

In Greek mythology, the son of Achilles and killer of Priam, King of Troy. In the legend of the Trojan War his presence was required to capture the city after Achilles' death. Neoptolemus entered Troy in the wooden horse and killed King Priam at Zeus' altar as Troy fell.

NEPHEG

According to biblical tradition, son of Izhar and brother of Korah and Zichri. Of the tribe of Levi, he was a cousin of Moses and Aaron (Exodus 6:16-21).

NEPHTOAH

In biblical times, name associated with a spring on the boundary between Judah and Benjamin (Joshua 15:1, 9; 18:11, 15). This spring is usually identified with the one at Lifta, to the east of Kiriath-jearim and circa two miles northwest of Jerusalem.

NEPHUSHESIM

In Judaism, a family head of Nethinim, some of whose descendants returned from Babylonian exile with Zerubbabel, 537 BC (Nehemiah 7:6-8; 46; Ezra 2:43). Possibly he was of Ishmaelite ancestry through the Naphish tribe (Genesis 25:13-15; 1 Chronicles 1:29-31).

NEREUS

In the New Testament, a brother who, with his sister, was included in Paul's greetings to the Roman congregation (Romans 16:15). The name is also found on Roman inscriptions listing some of the emperor's household, as well as in legend.

NEREUS

In Greek religion, sea god called by Homer "Old Man of the Sea"; noted for his wisdom, gift of prophecy, and ability to change his shape.

NERGAL

A Babylonian deity especially worshipped at Cuthah, a city repeatedly referred to in ancient inscriptions as the "city of Nergal." The people of Cuth (Cuthah), whom the king of Assyria settled in the territory of Samaria, continued worshipping this deity (2 Kings 17:24-33).

NERI

In the Old Testament, a descendant of King David through Nathan in the royal lineage of Jesus. According to Luke, Sheatiel was "the son of Neri," yet Matthew says Jeconiah was the father of Shealtiel (Matthew 1:12; Luke 3:27). Apparently Shealtiel married Neri's daughter, thus becoming his son-in-law. It was not uncommon in Hebrew genealogical listings to speak of a son-in-law as a son. Hence, both accounts are correct.

NERI, Saint Philip

(1515-1595) One of the outstanding mystics during the Counter-Reformation and founder of the Congregation of the Oratory (Oratorians), a congregation of secular priests and clerics.

NERIAH

According to biblical tradition, son of Mahseiah, and father of both Baruch, Jeremiah's secretary, and Seraiah, the one who read the denunciation of Babylon to that city (Jeremiah 32:12; 36:4-14).

NERO

(AD 37-68) Roman Emperor, notorious for his crimes and cruelty. He had many Christians tortured and burned to death; he had his mother Agrippina murdered (AD 59) and his wife Octavia executed (62) so that he could marry Poppaea Sabina. Historians doubt his responsibility for the fire than destroyed half of Rome (64).

NESTORIANS

Members of an ancient Christian sect named after Nestorius, patriarch of Constantinople (AD 428-431), whose teachings they followed. Nestorius was condemned as a heretic and deposed because he believed that Jesus Christ was born as a man, not divine, and therefore that the Virgin Mary was not the mother of God.

Nestorianism flourished in the Middle East for the next 800 years, and its missionaries even penetrated India and China. It was largely destroyed by the Tartar hordes of Tamerlane during the late 1300s, and by Turkish and Kurdish persecution in the 1800s and 1900s. The modern Nestorian church (the East Syrian and Assyrian Church) has few followers, mainly in Iraq and Syria, and bears only traces of the ancient Nestorianism. Its beliefs and rites are very close to those of the Eastern Orthodox Church. Its leader bears the title "Catholicos of the East."

NETHANEL

According to biblical tradition, chieftain of the tribe of Issachar; son of Zuar (Numbers 1:8, 16). In this office, he supervised the wilderness census for Issachar, presented their gift when the tabernacle altar was inaugurated, and led their army of 54,400 (Numbers 2:5-7; 7:11-23).

The name is also applied to a priest who played a trumpet before the ark of the covenant in the procession that accompanied it to Jerusalem (1 Chronicles 15:24).

NETHANIAH

In Judaism, third named of Asaph's four sons chosen for musical service at the sanctuary. Of the 24 divisions, Nethaniah headed the fifth (1 Chronicles 25:1-12).

The name is also applied to a Levite of the corps composed of priests. Levites and princes who were sent out by King Jehoshaphat in the third year of the reign to teach God's law in the cities of Judah (2 Chronicles 17:7-9).

NETHINIM

In Judaism, non-Israelite temple slaves or ministers (1 Chronicles 9:2; Ezra 8:17). Representatives of 35 Nethinim families were among those returning from Babylonian exile with Zerubbabel in 537 BC (Ezra 2:1-2; 43-54; Nehemiah 7:46-56; the sons of Akkub, Hagab and Asnah, however, are not mentioned by Nehemiah, perhaps because their names did not appear on the official list used by him in compiling his account. They may have been combined under other family names.) Also, in 468 BC, some of the Nethinim accompanied Ezra from Babylon to Jerusalem (Ezra 7:1-7). Thereafter certain Nethinim shared in repairing Jerusalem's wall (Nehemiah 3:26). They also joined with the Israelites in a covenant to keep themselves free from marriage alliances with foreigners (Nehemiah 10:28-30).

NETI, Neti

In Buddhism, literally "Not this, not this" being all that can be said of the Absolute. The ultimate negation of all philosophy of those matters which transcend the intellect. It is a phrase denoting the only possible description of the point where thought ends and no-thought, no-mind, takes over.

NEUMANN, John Nepomucene

(1811-1860) Bishop of Pennsylvania, a leader in the Roman Catholic parochial school system in the United States, and the first US Catholic bishop proposed for canonization.

NEUMANN, Therese

(1898-1962) German stigmatic. At the age of 20 she underwent a severe nervous shock after the outbreak of a fire and later suffered from hysterical paralysis, blindness, and gastric troubles for several years. In 1926 a blood-colored serum began to ooze from her eyes, and during Lent of the same year the stigmata (wounds resembling these of Christ in hands, feet, and side) appeared. Throughout the next 30 years these continued to bleed on many Fridays, especially during the last two weeks of Lent, and were accompanied by trances and other striking phenomena that attracted many visitors. The controversy about the supernatural or purely neurotic origin of the phenomena continues.

NEW APOSTOLIC CHURCH

Organized in Germany in 1863 as the Universal Catholic Church, by members of the Catholic Apostolic Church who believed that new apostles must be appointed to replace deceased apostles and rule the church until Christ returns. The present name was adopted in 1906.

NEW COVENANT

A sacred agreement between God and his people established by Jesus Christ and completing the Old Covenant established between God and Moses.

NEW JERUSALEM

Expression occurring two times and in the highly symbolic book of Revelation (Revelation 3:12; 21:2). Near the end of that series of visions, and after seeing "Babylon the Great" destroyed, the apostle John says: "I saw also the holy city, New Jerusalem, coming down out of heaven from God and prepared as a bride adorned for her husband (Revelation 21:2). Obviously this city is not one erected by men and consisting of literal streets and buildings constructed in the Near East on the site of the ancient city of Jerusalem, which was destroyed in AD 70.

NEWMAN, John Jenry

(1801-1890) English churchman who was one of the great religious forces of his day. He was a teacher and Church of England clergyman at Oxford University when he was converted to Catholicism in 1845. He became a cardinal in 1879.

Newman helped found the Oxford movement (1833), which worked to restore traditional beliefs and practices in the Church of England. After becoming a Roman Catholic Priest (1846), he founded an oratory, a male religious community

NEW TESTAMENT

Being the second part of the Bible, it is the fulfillment of the promise of the Old Testament. Its books are arranged in logical narrative order, the gospels telling the life of Jesus and his teachings; the Acts detailing the work of Christ's followers in proclaiming the Christian faith; the Epistles teaching the meaning and implications of the faith, and Revelation prophesying future events. The New Testament is written in everyday 1st-century Greek. The earliest copy fragments date from the early 2nd century.

The Gospels (lives of Christ) are named for their traditional authors: Matthew, Mark, Luke and John. The Epistles are evangelical letters, written to local churches of individuals. Thirteen are ascribed to Paul; the others (except the anonymous Hebrews), are named for their traditional authors.

NEWTON, John

(1725-1807) A leader of the Evangelical revival, to which his main contribution came through his devotional letter writings.

NEZIAH

In Judaism, forefather of a group of Nethenim who returned with Zerubbabel after the Babylonian exile (Ezra 2:1-2; Nehemiah 7:46, 56).

NEZIB

In biblical times, a Judean site in the Shephelah (Joshua 15:20-23). It is usually identified with Khirbet Beit Nesiz, some seven miles north-west of Hebron.

NEZIQIN

In Judaism, the fourth of the six major divisions, or orders, of the Mishna (codification of Jewish oral laws), which was given its final form early in the 3rd century AD. Neziqin deals principally with legally adjudicated damages and financial questions.

NGO VAN CHIEU

(1878-1926) Founder of the Vietnamese religion Cao Dai, the doctrine of the Third Revelation. The religion contains elements of Confucianism, Taoism, Buddhism, and Roman Catholicism.

NIBHAZ

A deity of the Avites, whom the king of Assyria settled in the territory of Samaria following the deportation of the Israelites after the fall of the ten-tribe kingdom (2 Kings 17:24-31). Aside from a brief Scriptural reference to Nibhaz, nothing can be said with certainty about the nature or form of this god.

NIBSHAN

In biblical times, a city in the Judean wilderness (Joshua 15:20, 60-61). The exact location of Nibshan is unknown. But it is tentatively identified with Khirbet el-Marqari, located on a level ridge some seven miles south-east of Jerusalem.

NICAEA, Councils of

The first and second Ecumenical Councils. The first Nicaean Council, called in 325 by the Emperor Constantine, condemned Arianism and drew up the Nicene creed. The denunciation of the Arian doctrine that Christ was not the equal of God, was an important event in the church's development. The second Nicaean Council in 787 ruled in favor of the restoration of images in churches. The council declared that icons deserved reverence and veneration, but not adoration.

NICENE CREED

Either of the two early creeds. The first was issued by the first Council if Nicaea (325) to state orthodoxy against Arianism. The second was perhaps issued by the Council of Constantinople (381); much longer, it is used at Holy Communion in both

Eastern and Western churches.

Additional discoveries of documents in the 20th century, indicated that the situation was more complex, and the actual development of Niceno-Constantinopolitan Creed has been the subject of scholarly dispute. Most likely it was issued by the Council of Constantinople even though this fact was first explicitly stated at the Council of Chalcedon in 451. It was probably based on a baptismal creed already in existence, but it was an independent document and not an enlargement of the Creed of Nicaea.

NICEPHORUS I, Saint

(758-829) Greek Orthodox theologian and patriarch of Constantinople (806-815) whose chronicles of Byzantine history and writings in defense of Byzantine veneration of icons provide data otherwise unavailable on early Christian thought and practice.

NICETAS STETHATOS

(1001-1080) Byzantine mystic, and theologian who played the principal theorist role in the 11th century Greek Orthodox-Latin church controversy concluding in the definitive schism of 1054.

NICHIREN

(1222-1282) Militant Japanese Buddhist prophet who contributed significantly to the adaptation of Buddhism to the Japanese mentality and who remains one of the most controversial and influential figures in Japanese Buddhist history.

NICHIREN BUDDHISM

A school of Japanese Buddhism named after its founder, the 13th century militant prophet, Nichiren. It is one of the largest schools of Japanese Buddhism; numbering more than 35 million subjects.

NICHIREN-SHO-SHU

A sect of the Nichiren school of Japanese Buddhism that has had phenomenal growth since 1950, mainly because of intensive conversion efforts of its associated lay religious group, the Soka-gakkai.

NICHOLAS, Saint

(4th century) One of the most popular saints commemorated in the Eastern and Western churches, multifariously honored as a patron; now traditionally associated with the festival of Christmas. Nothing certain is known about his life except that he was probably bishop of Myra in the 4th century.

NICHOLAS I THE GREAT, Saint

(819-867) Pope from 858 to 867. He supported the patriarch St. Ignatius of Constantinople, who was uncanonically replaced by the scholar Photius. Consistently urging the supremacy of Rome, he fully endorsed the papal inheritance of sacerdotal and royal functions as conferred by Christ on St. Peter and the delegation of temporal power to the emperor for the protection of the church. He reacted against Carolingian domination in ecclesiastical matters and claimed the right to legislate for the whole of Christendom.

NICHOLAS I THE MYSTIC

(852-925) Byzantine patriarch of Constantinople (901-907; 912-925), who contributed measurably to the attempted reunion of the Greek and Roman churches and who fomented the tetragamy controversy, or the question of a fourth marriage for the Eastern Orthodox.

NICHOLAS II

(989-1061) Pope from 1058 to 1061; a major figure in the Gregorian reform. At the Lateran Council of April 1059, a milestone in papal history, Nicholas promulgated his famous bull on papal elections; he did so in reaction to the disorders that interrupted his own election.

NICHOLAS III

(1225-1280) Giovanni Gaetano Orsini; pope from 1277 to 1280. He issued the important bull of 1279, temporarily settling the Franciscan struggle over the interpretation of perfect poverty, The Conventuals and the Spirituals.

NICHOLAS IV

(1277-1292) Girolamo Masci; pope from 1288 to 1292. He issued a bull against the Apostolici, various Christian sects that sought to re-establish the life and discipline of the primitive church by a literal observance of continence and poverty.

NICHOLAS V

(1254-1333) Pietro Rainalducci; last imperial antipope, whose reign in Rome rivalled the pontificate of Pope John XXII at Avignon. Having little support, Nicholas' cause proved fruitless.

NICHOLAS OF AUTRECOURT

(1300-1350) Philosopher and theologian known principally for developing the medieval school of Skepticism to its extreme logical conclusions, which were condemned as heretical. Philosophically, Nicholas' extreme Nominalism precluded the possibility of knowing anything as a permanent concept, allowing only the conscious experience of an object's sensible qualities.

NICHOLAS OF CUSA

(1401-1464) Influential philosopher who stressed the incomplete nature of man's knowledge of God and of the universe.

NICHOLAS OF HEREFORD

(1345-1417) Theological scholar and advocate of the English reform movement within the Roman Catholic Church who later recanted his unorthodox doctrine and aided in repressing innovators.

NICHOLAS OF LYRA

(1270-1349) Nicolaus Lyranus; author of the first printed commentary on the Bible and one of the most influential exegetes (biblical interpreters)

NICODEMUS

In Judaism, a Pharisee and a teacher of Israel, a ruler of the Jews (that is, a member of the Sanhedrin), who is mentioned only in John's Gospel. Nicodemus was impressed with the signs that Jesus performed in Jerusalem at Passover time in AD 30. Consequently, he visited Jesus one night, and confessed that Jesus must have come from God. Probably out of fear of the Jews he chose the cover of darkness for his first visit.

About 2_ years later, following the Festival of Booths, the Pharisees sent officers to lay hold of Jesus. On the officers' return empty-handed, the Pharisees belittled them for making a report favorable to Jesus, whereupon Nicodemus spoke up, saying: "Our law does not judge a man unless first it is heard from him and come to know what he is doing, does it?" For this the others ridiculed him (John 7:45-52). After Jesus' death, Nicodemus came along with Joseph of Arimathea, that fearful disciple, bringing a 100-pound roll of myrrh and aloes, an expensive offering, with which to prepare Jesus' body for burial (John 19:38-40). There is no Scriptural evidence for or against the traditions that say Nicodemus later became a disciple.

NICODEMUS THE HAGIORITE

(1748-1809) Greek Orthodox monk and author of ascetical prayer literature influential in reviving the practice of Hesychasm, a Byzantine method of contemplative prayer and mysticism.

NICOLAS, Saint

4th century patron saint of children, scholars, merchants, and sailors and probably bishop of Myra in Lycia, Asia Minor. In many European countries he traditionally visits children and gives them presents on his feast day (December 6th). The custom as brought to America by the Dutch, whose Sinter Klaas (Sinterklaas) became the Santa Claus of Christmas.

NICOLAUS

In the New Testament, one of the seven qualified men whom the congregation recommended to the Apostles for appointment as food distributors to ensure just and fair treatment among the early Jerusalem congregation following Pentecost AD 33. Nicolaus is the only one of the seven called " a proselyte of Antioch," which suggests that he may have been the only non-Jew of the group, the Greek names of others being common even among natural Jews (Acts 6:1-6).

NICOLE, Pierre

(1625-1695) Theologian and author, whose writings supported Jansenism, a movement within Roman Catholicism emphasizing original sin and God's sovereignty.

NICOPOLIS

In biblical times, a city where the apostle Paul decided to spend the winter during one of his trips and to which he urged Titus to come (Titus 3:12).

Of the various ancient cities named Nicopolis, the Nicopolis of Epicurus located in a peninsula in north-western Greece seems to fit the biblical reference best. Being a prominent city, it would have been a good place for Paul to declare the good news, and it was conveniently situated for both Paul (apparently then in Macedonia), and Titus (in Crete). It may be that Paul was arrested in Nicopolis and then taken to Rome for his final imprisonment and execution.

NIDANA

In Buddhism, links; term used to describe the processes by which a being comes into existence, and which bind him to the Wheel of Life. The links are:

1 On Avijja: ignorance.
2 On the Sankharas: the karmic results of such illusion.
3 On Vinnana: individual consciousness.
4 On Nama-Rupa: mind, and its expression in form.
5 On Salayatana: the six organs and their appropriate functions.
6 On Phassa: touch, the sense, the object, and the sense impression.
7 On Vedana: feeling, sensation.
8 On Tanha: thirsty, craving for personal experience.
9 Upadana: grasping, clinging to existence.
10 Bhjava: becoming and re-becoming.
11 Jati: birth, the final outcome of karma.

There is little authority for regarding the links as fixed in number or connected by any rule of logical sequence. The relation between them is of mutual dependence rather than causal sequence.

"That this becomes; this ceasing to be, that ceases to be" - this is the Buddhist teaching, and the Nidanas are but some grouping of the factors involved in this tremendous process.

NIEBUHR

Family name of two eminent American Protestant theologians, Reinhold and Helmut Richard Niebuhr.

Reinhold Niebuhr, after serving as pastor of the Bethel Evangelical Church in Detroit, Michigan, became professor of Applied Christianity at Union Theological Seminary (1930-1960). He was an active socialist in the early 1930s and preached what became known as the "social gospel," but after World War II turned back to traditional Protestant values, relating them to modern society. His *Nature and Destiny of Man* (1941-43) greatly influenced American theology.

Helmut Richard Niebuhr (1894-1962) was professor of theology at Yale Divinity School from 1954. His works include *The Kingdom of God in America* (1937) and *Radical Monotheism and Western Culture* (1960).

NIEMOELLER, Friedrich Gustav Emil Martin

(1892-1981) Prominent anti-Nazi theologian and pastor, founder of the Bekennende Kirche ("Confessing church") and a president of the World Council of Churches. Increasingly disillusioned with the prospects for demilitarization, both in his own country and in the world, Niemoeller became a controversial pacifist. Lecturing widely, he spoke freely in favor of international reconciliation and against armaments. In 1961 he was elected one of the six presidents of the World Council of Churches.

NIFO, Agostino

(1473-1538) Renaissance philosopher noted for his development from an anti-Christian interpreter of Aristotelian philosophy into an influential Christian apologist for the immortality of the individual soul.

NIGHT OF THE SENSES

The spiritual purification of sense faculties so that the person may be more completely directed toward God. This may be accomplished actively when an individual strives with grace and through various privations to use his senses in total conformity to God's will. On the other hand, the passive night of the senses is a product of purgative, contemplative prayer in which a man perceives his own unworthiness and God's infinite holiness, thereby accommodating his senses to the soul's spiritual élan.

NIGHT OF THE SOUL

The spiritual purification of the soul by which it is perfectly united with God through love. It is a phenomenon experienced only by those who are advanced in the spiritual life.

NIGUN

Wordless song sung by Hasidic Jews (members of a pietistic movement that began in the 18th century) as a means of elevating the soul to God. Because they lacked words, the nigunim were felt to move the singer beyond the sensual and rational toward the mystic.

NIHILISM

In Buddhism, the philosophic doctrine than denies a substantial reality to the phenomenal doctrine. Buddhism takes the middle path between the realists, who maintain the universe to be real, and the non-realists, who deny all reality.

NIKAH

In Islam, marriage, marriage contract. The Koran permits a Muslim male to marry up to four wives, provided that he feels able to treat them all equitably. However, as a result of the interpretation of certain verses of the Koran, polygamy is now banned in many Islamic countries. The Koran also specifies certain forbidden degrees of kindred within which a Muslim may not marry. The marriage need not be contracted in a mosque nor does it have to be in the presence of a religious official. It is thus more a civil than a religious affair. The dowry is an important part of the marriage contract.

NIKE

In Greek religion, the goddess of victory, daughter of the giant Pallas and of the internal river Styx.

NILE

The longest river of Africa and second of the world, rising in highlands south of the equator. It flows northward through north-eastern Africa to drain into the Mediterranean Sea.

The Egyptians worshiped the Nile as a God of fertility under the name of Hapi. This god was depicted as basically male but with large feminine breasts, the head crowned with aquatic plants and a fisherman's girdle being around the plump waist. Festivals, with accompanying sacrifices, were held annually in his honor at the beginning of each inundation period.

Some scholars suggest that Pharaoh's going out to the Nile, mentioned at Exodus 7:15, related to some morning devotional act, but it may have been merely for a morning walk or to examine the height of the river.

NILUS OF ANCYRA, Saint

(365-430) Greek Byzantine abbot and author of extensive ascetical literature that influenced both Eastern and Western monasticism. He also participated in the prevalent theological controversies concerning the Trinity and the person and work of Christ.

NI'MATULLAHIYYA

Major Sufi Shiite order named after Shah Ni'matullah (1130-1431). It gained particular popularity in Iran and also in India.

NIMRAH

In biblical times, a town east of the Jordan built or rebuilt by the Gadites; a shortened form of Beth-nimrah (Numbers 32:3-5).

NIMRAH

In Judaism, an important waterway, also called Wadi Nimrim. In prophesies directed against Moab, Isaiah and Jeremiah refer to the "waters of Nimrim (Isaiah 15:5-9; Jeremiah 48:34-35). On the basis of the fertility of the surrounding region, some identify the waters of Nimrim with the Wadi Nimrim, whose waters flow into the Jordan north of the Dead Sea.

NIMROD

According to biblical tradition, son of Cush, who was the principal progenitor of the dark-complexioned branch of the human family (1 Chronicles 1:10; Jeremiah 13:23). Nimrod was the founder and king of the first empire to come into existence after the Flood.

The beginning of Nimrod's kingdom included the cities of Babel, Erech, Accad and Calneh, all in the land of Shinar (Genesis 10:10). Therefore it was likely under his direction that the building of Babel and its tower began.

In appears that after the building of the Tower of Babel Nimrod extended his domain to the territory of Assyria and there built, among other cities, Nineveh (Genesis 10:11-12).

NIMSHI

In Judaism, father of Jehoshaphat and grandfather of Jehu (1 Kings 19:16; 2 Kings 9:2). The name had been found inscribed on a fragment of ancient pottery excavated in Samaria.

NINETY-FIVE THESES

Propositions for debate concerned with the question of indulgences, written in Latin and posted by Martin Luther on the door of the Schlosskirch, Wittenberg on October 31, 1517. The event was eventually considered the beginning of the 16th century Protestant Reformation.

NINEVEH

One of the oldest and most populous city of the ancient Assyrian Empire, situated on the east bank of the Tigris opposite modern Mosul (in Iraq).

Excavations of its ruins, dating from the 19th century uncovered precious treasures of Assyrian art and a great hoard of cuneiform writings that have opened up the languages and history of ancient Akkadia, Sumeria, Babylon, and the whole Mesopotamian region.

In biblical lore Nineveh was the symbol of oppressive arrogance that was bound to be punished by God (Nahum) and, in the parable of Jonah (John 1-2), it became the vast, pagan city that did penance and worshiped God in response to Jonah's preaching, in contrast to the unrepentant in Israel.

NINGIZHZIDA

In Mesopotamian religion, Sumerian deity, city god of Gishbanda. He was originally a tree god, for his name apparently means reproductive.

NINIAN, Saint

(282-360) Bishop and church founder, first Christian missionary to what is now Scotland, where he began the conversion of the southern Picts.

NINIGI

Grandson of the Japanese sun goddess Amaterasu, whose descent to earth established the divine origin of the Yamato clan, the Imperial House of Japan. He is said to have been the great-grandfather of the first emperor, Jimmu Tenno.

NINLIL

In Mesopotamian religion, member of the Sumero-Akkadian pantheon, city goddess of Tummal.

NINMAR

In Mesopotamian religion, Sumerian deity, city goddess of Guabba. She was apparently a bird goddess, and her emblem, a bird, probably represents her original nonhuman form.

NINSUN

In Mesopotamian religion, Sumerian deity, city goddess of Kullab. She was mostly represented in cow form and was considered the divine power behind, and the embodiment of, all the qualities the herdsman wished for his own cows.

NINURTA

In Mesopotamian religion, city god of Girsu; the farmer's version of the god of the thunder and rainstorms of the spring.

NINUS

In Greek mythology, king of Assyria and the founder of Nineveh.

NI-O

In Japanese Buddhist mythology, protector of the Buddhist faith, who makes a dual appearance as the guardian on either side of temple gateways.

NIOBE

In Greek mythology, the daughter of Tantalus and wife of King Amphion of Thebes; she was the typical sorrowful woman, weeping for the loss of all her children.

NIRANKARIS

A reform movement within Sikhism, a religion of India. It was founded by Dayal Das (1778-1855), who belonged to a half-Sikh, half-Hindu community in Peshawar. He believed that God is formless, or nirankar.

NIRGRANTHAS

The name by which the early jaina religious community of India were referred to by their Buddhist and Hindu contemporaries.

NIRGUNA

A concept of primary importance in the orthodox Hindi philosophy of Vedanta, raising the question of whether the supreme being, Brahman, is to be characterized as without qualities or as possessing qualities.

NIRJARA

In Jaina religious belief of India, the destruction of karman (merit and demerit). Nirjara is accomplished by physical and spiritual austerities as fasting, mortification of the body, confession and penance, meditation and study, and indifference to the body and its needs.

NIRMALAS

An ascetic order of the Sikhs, a religious group of India. Nirmalas ("those without blemish") at first wore only white garments but later adopted the ocher robes worn by Hindu ascetics and shared some other practices such as birth and death rites with Hindus.

NIRMANAKAYA

In Buddhism, the body of transformation, by which the Buddha remains in contact with phenomenal existence for the helping of humanity on its pilgrimage.

NIRODHA

In Buddhism, extinction, also cessation. The term is used in the sense of stopping of undesirable conditions. As the cessation or annihilation of all the attributes of finite existence, it equates with Nirvana.

NIRVANA

The supreme goal of Buddhist endeavor; release from the limitations of existence. The word is derived from a root meaning extinguished through lack of fuel, and since rebirth is the result of desire, freedom from rebirth is attained by the extinguishing of all such desire. Nirvana is, therefore, a state attainable in this life by the right aspiration, purity of life, and the elimination of egoism. This is cessation of existence, as we know existence; the attainment of being (as distinct from becoming). The Buddha speaks of it as "unborn, unoriginated, uncreated, unformed," contrasting it with the born, originated, created and formed phenomenal world. Those who have attained the state of Nirvana are called buddhas. Gautama Siddhartha had attained this state and became a Buddha at 35. However, it is now believed that it was only after he had passed away that he reached such a state of perfect tranquility, because some residue of human defilement would continue to exist as long as his physical body existed.

NISA, al-
The title of the 4th sura of the Koran; it means "The Women." The sura belongs to the Medinan period and has 176 verses. Its title reflects much of the subject matter of the sura which was revealed around the time of the Battle of Uhud and its aftermath. Orphans are to be treated fairly, women may receive the dowry and rules for inheritance are prescribed. Punishment is also prescribed for sexual sin and a list of forbidden degrees of kindred is given. Wilful murder will be punished forever in hell. Much of this sura may fairly be described as a "woman's right document" in view of its concern for females. Towards the end of the sura a firm statement denies that Isa was killed or crucified; this is one of the key texts in any understanding of the Islamic view of the crucifixion.

NISIBIS, School of
The intellectual center of East Syrian Christianity (the church of the East, or Nestorian Church) from the 5th to the 7th century. The School stresses the independence of the divine and human natures of Christ so that it appeared as though the natures were in effect two persons loosely joined in a moral union.

MISPRAPANCA
In a number of schools of Buddhist philosophy, ultimate reality, which is not possible to express verbally. The term is usually used to describe the manifoldness of worldly phenomena.

NISROCH
A deity worshipped by Sennacherib the king of Assyria. It was in the temple of Nisroch that Adrammelech and Sharezer murdered their father Sennacherib (2 Kings 19:36-37; Isaiah 37:38). Certain identification of Nisroch with a known Assyrian deity is not possible. A number of authorities suggest identifying Nisroch with the fire-god Nusku, who, it was thought, assisted in bringing defeat to the enemy in warfare and served as messenger of the gods as well as a dispenser of justice.

NISSABA
In Mesopotamian religion, Sumerian deity, city goddess of Eresh on the ancient Euphrates river. She was goddess of the grasses in general, including the reeds and cereals.

NIVRITTI
In Buddhism, completion. The term is used in the sense of involution as opposite to evolution.

NIVARANA
In Buddhism, hindrances; the five factors which blind our vision from the truth. They are: lust, ill-will, torpor, worry and skeptical doubt.

NIYYA
In Islam, intention. Islamic moral theology, and, indeed, Islamic ritual, places considerable emphasis on a man's intention. A well-known hadith states that actions are judged by the intentions associated with them and

that every man will receive what he intended.

NO

In ancient times, a prominent city and onetime capital of Egypt, located on both banks of the upper Nile circa 330 miles south of Cairo. The Greeks knew it as Thebes, the name commonly used today.

Even though administrative control shifted to other sites, No-amon (Thebes) continued to be a wealthy and prominent city, the center of the powerful priesthood of Amon, whose chief priest ranked next to the Pharaoh himself. But in the seventh century BC Assyrian aggression spread into Egypt during the rule of Assyrian King Esarhaddon. His son and successor Assuroanipal renewed the conquest, reaching Thebes and thoroughly sacking the city. It is evidently to this devastation that the prophet Nahum referred when warning Nineveh, Assyria's capital, about a destruction of similar magnitude (Nahum 3:7-10).

NOADIAH

In Judaism, son of Binnui and one of the three Levites who, on the fourth day following arrival in Jerusalem, 468 BC, helped inventory the silver, gold and utensils for the Temple (Ezra 8:32-33).

NOAH

The son of Lamech and ninth in descent from Adam. He was the patriarch who, because of his blameless piety, was chosen by God to perpetuate the human race after his wicked contemporaries had perished in the Flood (Genesis 6:10-15). Consequently the entire surviving human race descended from Noah's three sons Shem, Ham and Japheth.

Jesus also uses the story of the Flood that came on a worldly generation of men "in the days of Noah" as an example of baptism, and Noah is depicted as a preacher of repentance to the men of his time.

NOAHIDE LAWS

A Jewish Talmudic designation for seven biblical laws given to Adam and to Noah before the revelation on Mount Sinai and consequently binding on all mankind.

Using Genesis 2:16 as a starting point of exegesis, the Babylonian Talmud listed the first six commandments as prohibitions against idol worship, blasphemy, murder, adultery, and robbery and the positive command to establish courts of justice. After the Flood a seventh commandment, given to Noah, forbade the eating of flesh cut from a living animal (Genesis 9:4).

NOB

In biblical times, a city evidently in the territory of Benjamin and close to Jerusalem. While there is some question as to the precise location of Nob, Nehemiah 11:31-32 and Isaiah 10:28-32 indicate that it was near Anathoth and possibly close to a hill from which one could see Jerusalem.

When David fled from Saul, he went to High Priest Ahimelech, who was at Nob, "the city of priests," and received from Ahimelech some shewbread as food for his men, and Goliath's sword, which was being kept there.

NOBAH

According to biblical tradition, an Israelite, probably of the tribe of Manasseh, who captured Kenath and its dependent towns. Thereafter he named the city after himself (Numbers 32:42).

NOBREGA, Manuel da

(1517-1570) Founder of the Jesuit mission of Brazil and leader of the order's activities there from 1549 to 1570.

NODAB

In Judaism, one of the confederated groups overwhelmingly defeated with God's help by the tribes of Reuben, Gad and the half tribe of Manasseh (1 Chronicles 5:18-22).

NOGAH

In Judaism, son of King David, born to him in Jerusalem (1 Chronicles 3:5-7; 14:3-6).

NOHAH

In Judaism, the fourth-listed son of Benjamin (1 Chronicles 8:1-2). Since he is not named among those listed in Genesis chapter 46, he was probably born in Egypt.

NOMINALISM

A term with two meanings, one ontological and the other historical.

1 From an ontological point of view, nominalism is a philosophical doctrine concerning the problem of universals. It holds that only individual things exist. In opposition to Platonism, which explains the similarity of two individuals by saying that they share a common property or nature, i.e., by assuming the existence of a universal, nominalism holds that if individuals similar to one another may be said to share anything at all, this can only be a spoken or written name or a mental image, i.e., another individual.

2 Historically, nominalism is a term applied to certain movements in early and late scholasticism, whose representatives were called nominales. Their doctrines included, among others, ontological nominalism in the broad sense, i.e., not excluding conceptualism.

NO-MIND

Phrase used to translate various terms in Zen Buddhism. It describes a state of consciousness before the division into duality created by thought takes place. Yet this unconscious is at the same time conscious, a mind unconscious of itself. This is a paradox without meaning save as achieved in direct spiritual experiences. It is the purpose of Zen training to achieve and maintain this state of mind.

NONAE CAPROTINAE

In Roman religion, festival honoring the goddess Juno, celebrated principally by female slaves on July 7th.

ON-CHRISTIAN RELIGIONS

From a Roman Catholic point of view, Vatican Council II issued a Declaration on the Relation of the Church to Non-Christian Religions; in that Declaration, the Council Fathers referred specifically to the religion of Hindus, Buddhists, Muslims, and especially Jews.

According to that Declaration: "The Catholic Church rejects nothing of what is true and holy in these religions. She has a high regards for the manner of life and conduct, the precepts and doctrines which, although differing in many ways from her own teaching, nevertheless often reflect a ray of that truth which enlightens spiritual heritage," the Council encouraged "mutual understanding and appreciation" between them.

In a summary statement Vatican Council II eloquently insisted that "the church reproves, as foreign to the mind of Christ, any discrimination against people or any harassment of them on the basis of their race, color, condition in life and religion."

NONCONFORMISTS

(Dissenters) Those who will not conform to the doctrine or practice of an established church; especially the Protestant dissenters from the Church of England (mainly Puritans) expelled by the Act of Uniformity (1622). They now include Baptists, Brethren, Congregationalists, Methodists, Presbyterians and Quakers.

NONRESISTANCE

A doctrine developed by the 16th century Swiss Anabaptists and particularly associated with the Mennonites. Nonresistance is the renunciation of any coercive means, whether employed by individuals or society, to redress wrongs or to achieve objectives; pacifism and conscientious objection are allied but not synonymous terms.

Historically, the practice of nonresistance has varied among the Mennonites with regard to military service. Because of persecution in their early history, those who were not martyred fled to isolated settlements in the Swiss Alps, the steppes of Russia, and later to the frontiers of North America. Nonresistance, nonparticipation, and nonconformity developed as characteristics that to this day continue among such conservative Mennonites as the Amish.

NOSTRADAMUS

(1503-1566) French astrologer, famous for his prophesies. His real name was Michel de Notredame, and he was court physician to King Charles IX. In 1555 Nostradamus published a book or prophesies in verse entitled *Centuries*. Although the prophesies are vague enough to allow many interpretations, he is considered to have predicted the manner in which the French King Henry II would die four years later (1559), and this made his reputation.

NORUZ

In Zoroastrianism, the New Year. Throughout the day, persons greet one another with the rite of hamazor, in which the right hand of one person is passed between the palms of the one greeting him. Words of greeting and good wishes are then exchanged.

NORWAY, Church of

The established (state-supported) Lutheran church in Norway, which changed from the Roman Catholic faith during the 16th century Protestant Reformation.

NOTES, Theological

Technical formulas that express the binding character and certitude of doctrinal teachings of the Catholic church. They are called notes because they distinguish one doctrine (or its aspect) from another in terms of human knowledge; and they are theological because they belong to the science of theology as a systematic analysis of divine revelation.

NOTIONAL ACTS

Also called origins, are acts related to the Trinitarian notions; they are the acts implied in the two immanent Trinitarian processions as revelatory of the Trinity and the Persons and are four in number:
▲ active generation;
▲ passive generation;
▲ active spiration;
▲ passive spiration.
Between active and passive generation, on the one hand, and active spiration on the other, there is no relation of opposition, and so no real distinction between them. The existence of notional acts in God, of course, is not to be understood to imply any imperfection in him.

NOTRE-DAME DE PARIS

(1163-1320) Cathedral built on the site of two 9th century Carolingian churches, St. Étienne and Notre-Dame, begun (1163) by Bishop Maurice de Sully, the choir and transepts erected 1163-1182, bays of the nave and finally the facade and towers added 1190-1245.
It is a five-aisled basilica with deep choir and double ambulatory; the elevation was effected in four stages: open arcades (ground story), tribune galleries, windows, and clerestory.
Impressive sculpture of the western facade in portals of the Virgin, Last Judgment, and St. Anne, moves from early Gothic, through monumental 13th century style, to the more naturalistic mode insinuating the "precious" style of Reims (circa 1250).
On the interior the fine 14th century Virgin at the transept comes from a chapel in the cloister. Tombs, choir stalls, and lecterns date from the 17th and 18th centuries.

NOVENA

A word signifying "nine" and referring to a public or private devotion that extends for nine consecutive days or, in less common usage, for nine consecutive weeks, with the devotion being held on a particular day for those nine weeks. The church approves of such devotional practices, provided that there is no superstition connected with the number nine and that such externals are used as a help to prayer.

NOVICE

In Roman Catholicism, according to the Code of Canon Law, novices are those who begin a period of trial and formation in the novitiate of a religious institute in order to "better recognize their divine vocation" and to "experience the institute's manner of living" (Canon 646). The novice helped to discern his or her vocation, and is formed both in the essentials of the Christian life and in the charisma and spirit of the particular institute (Canon 652). This period must last for 12 months and may be extended to 24 months; at the end of it the novice either leaves or is admitted to temporary vows of poverty, chastity, and obedience.

NOVITIATE

The period of at least 1 full year of religious formation required before admission of a candidate to religious profession. The religious house or part of it, where the probationary period is passed is also called the novitiate.

NUH

(*Noah*) Arabic name for Noah; Koranic messenger (rasul) sent to warn his people who reject him. They are drowned in a great Flood while Nuh is saved in the Ark. The story of Nuh is related at some length in the Koran in Surat Hud.

NUH

The title of the 71st sura of the Koran. The sura belongs to the Meccan period and has 28 verses. The title is drawn from the first verse in which God states that He has sent Nuh to his people. The sura is devoted almost entirely to the story of Nuh; he comes to warn his people and tells them to seek forgiveness from God. Nuh is refused and the wicked are drowned in the Flood. The sura concludes with Nu praying to God that the latter should not leave one unbeliever on the Earth.

NUMBERS

The fourth book of the Old Testament. Its title refers to the counting of Israel's people, mentioned twice. Numbers is basically the history of the Israelites as they wandered in the wilderness. The book contains Israel's history between the departure from Sinai and before their occupation of Canaan, the Promised Land. It describes their sufferings and their numerous complaints against God. The Israelites are described as being faithless and rebellious, but God provided for and sustained his people.

NUMBERS AND NUMBER SYMBOLISM

A usage of varying importance in all cultures. In some it is distinctly magical, philosophical and religious. In others, it is hard to determine the predominate emphasis. Mystic and/or symbolic meaning has enhanced the significant of certain numbers such as 1, 2, 3, 4, 7, 10, 12, 40, 70, 100.

The number 1 is the Monad of Pythagoras, the One of Plato and in the Bible God as the "Wholly Other" (Deuteronomy 6:4; John 17:11). The number 2 brings together pairs or opposites in terms of their relationship to one another e.g., sun-moon, day-night, yang-yin.

The number 3 is associated with perfection in God and the most common of all symbolic numbers e.g., the Divine Triads:

▲ Zeus, Athena, Apollo (Greece);
▲ Jupiter, Juno, Minerva (Rome);
▲ Osiris, Isis, Horus (Egypt);
▲ in the Bible, God's perfection in act (Genesis 18:2).

The number 4 is the symbol of completeness e.g.:

▲ the 4 cardinal virtues of Plato;
▲ the seasons of the year;
▲ the four beatitudes (Luke 6:20-22).

In the Bible 7 is associated with a full series; it has special reference to cult and sacred objects (feasts, sacrifices, the Sabbath). The number 10 meant completeness to the Pythagoreans whereas in the Bible as a symbol of totality there is an uneven usage (10 Plagues of Egypt, 10 Commandments). The number of 12 reflected cosmic order and government for instance, the 12 tribes of Israel and the Twelve

Apostles, 12 as the symbol of the people of God passim in the Bible.

The number 40 is significant in the Bible and Islamic Literature. In the former it frequently is associated with periods of man's struggle with all manner of evil and ultimate victory through God, e.g., the Flood (Genesis 7:17), Israelites 40 years in the desert (Numbers 14:33), Christ in the desert (Matthew 4:2).

NUMINOUS

The special, nonrational aspect of sacred or holy reality in religious experience.

NUN

A term commonly used to designate a woman who is a member of a religious order or group. Within Roman Catholicism, vows of poverty, chastity, and obedience are taken by women entering the religious life. According to Roman Catholic canon law, only women living under solemn vows are nuns; those living under simple vows are more properly called sisters.

In Eastern Orthodoxy, nuns are almost entirely of the contemplative type and do not participate actively in the life of the secular world.

In Buddhism the number of nuns has never been large. It is said that the Buddha was very reluctant to allow women to form communities, though he finally gave his consent. The women lived apart from the monks and were always considered inferior to them.

NUNCIO

A Vatican representative accredited as an ambassador to a civil government that maintains official diplomatic relations with the Holy see.

NUPTIAL MASS

The Mass at which a Catholic is married; it includes a choice of readings, prayers, and blessings that have special relevance to Christian marriage. The nuptial blessing is a formal blessing of the newlywed couple and is given after the Our Father at the nuptial Mass.

NUR, al

The title of the 24th sura of the Koran; it means "The Light." The sura is Medinan and has 64 verses. Its title is taken from verse 35 which described God as the Light of the Heavens and the earth in one of the most famous and mystically beautiful of all Koran verses, called "The Light Verse." The sura lays down a number of legal and other injunctions; for example, 100 lashes are prescribed for adultery, women are to dress modestly; prayer is to be performed; zakat is to be paid to the Messenger of God. These are just a few of the regulations which are laid down in what is a very wide-ranging sura from the point of view of its legal content.

NUSAYRIS

Members of a syncretic group also called Alawis, those who followed Ali b. Abi Talib. Their name derived from one of their important early leaders Mohammed ben Nusayr (9th century). Their beliefs have much in common with those of the Isma'ilis. There are Nusayris in Syria, Turkey and Lebanon.

NYAYARUSARINO VIJNANAVADINAH

One of the principal divisions of the Yogacara school of Mahayana Buddhism. The school is characterized by its exclusive concentration on the theory of knowledge; it does not deal with the question of how to transcend beyond empirical reality.

NYMPHIA

According to biblical tradition, a Christian woman living in or near Laodicea or Colossae in whose house a congregation held meetings, and to whom Paul sent greetings (Colossians 4:15).

NYX

In Greek mythology, female personification of night but also a great cosmogonical figure, feared even by Zeus, the king of gods.

OANNES

In Mesopotamian mythology, an amphibious being who taught mankind wisdom. He had the form of a fish with the head of a man under his fish's head and under his fish's tail the feet of a man.

OATES, Titus

(1649-1705) Renegade Anglican priest who fabricated the "Popish Plot" of 1678. Oates's allegations that Roman Catholics were plotting to seize power caused a reign of terror in London and strengthened the anti-Catholic Whig Party.

OBADIAH

In biblical times, a prophet and writer of the fourth of the so-called "minor" prophetical books. Nothing personal is known of this prophet of the seventh century BC.

The name is also applied to the household steward of King Ahab. Even though King Ahab and Jezebel practiced wickedness, Obadiah greatly feared God, hiding one 100 prophets "by 50 in a cave" when Jezebel had ordered them all slaughtered. During the divinely imposed drought foretold by Elijah, Obadiah's master Ahab divided certain territory with him and each was searching for grass to feed the livestock, when Elijah met up with Obadiah, who out of great fear, hesitated to go until given assurance that the prophet would not leave, for Ahab would surely kill his servant if this report proved false (1 Kings 18:1-16).

OBADIAH, Book of

The fourth of 12 Old Testament books that bear the names of the minor prophets. With only one chapter consisting of 21 verses, it is the shortest of all biblical books and is the record of "the vision of Obadiah". Probably written in the 6th century BC it foretells the triumph of Israel over its rival Edom. The book also announces that the Day of Judgment is near for all nations, when all evil will be punished and the righteous renewed. The final verses prophesy the restoration of the Jews to their native land.

OBAKU

One of the three Zen sects in Japan (founded in 1644 by the Chinese priest Yin-yuan); it continues to preserve elements of the Chinese tradition in its architecture, religious ceremonies, and teachings.

OBAL

In the Old Testament, the eighth listed of Joktan's thirteen sons, each of whom founded one of the 70 post-flood families; descendant of Shem. Exactly where the tribe of Obal settled is uncertain, but similar names occur in Yemenite south-west Arabia (Genesis 10:21, 25-30; 1 Chronicles 1:20-22).

OBED

In Judaism, a descendant of Judah; the father of Jehu and the son of Ephlal of the family of Jerahmeel (1 Chronicles 2:3, 25, 37-38). .

The name is also applied to a Levite of the family of Korah; the grandson of Obed-edom and the son of Shemaiah. He served as a gatekeeper at the house of God (1 Chronicles 26:1-7).

OBED-EDOM

According to biblical tradition, a Gittite at whose home the ark of the covenant was kept for three months after its near upset and the accompanying death of Uzzah. For the duration of its stay there, Obed-edom and his household were blessed by Jehovah, and when David learned of this he took it as an indication that Jehovah favored bringing the sacred chest on to Jerusalem (2 Samuel 6:109-12; 1 Chronicles 13:13-14).

OBEDIENCE

The moral virtue which inclines one to submit to the law of God in all of its manifestations, including (in Roman Catholicism) the eternal law, the natural law, the divine positive law, ecclesiastical law, and civil law. Obedience is also one of the evangelical counsels or vows which religious publicly profess in the church.

OBEDIENCE, Religious

Voluntary submission to the authority of another for religious motives. In monastic orders it is a requirement for admission and a test of one's qualifications. In a broader sense, religious obedience is adherence to God's precepts.

OBERAMMERGAU PASSION PLAY

Play given once every ten years in the Upper Bavarian village of Oberammergau. Begun in 1634, the tradition is said to have been maintained in fulfillment of a vow made by villagers during an outbreak of plague.

OBOTH

In biblical times, an Israelite encampment between Punon and Iye-abarim. Its location is today unknown (Numbers 21:10-11; 33:43-44).

O'BRYAN, William

(1778-1868) Methodist churchman who founded the Bible Christian Church (1815) as a dissident group of Wesleyan Methodists desiring effective biblical education, a Presbyterian form of church government, and the participation of women in the ministry.

OBSERVANCE, Religious

Ibada; term denoting devotional action, or observance required by the Islamic faith. The ibada contrasts with the mu'amalat, the former being basically the rituals enjoined by Islamic law, and the latter the social obligations enjoined by the same law, embracing such aspects of it as inheritance and contracts.

OCCASIONS OF SIN

In Roman Catholicism, extrinsic circumstances (persons, places, or things) which tend to lead one to sin. Theologians make a number of distinctions about occasions of sin, the most important of which are occasions that are voluntary (that is, of one's own choosing and therefore easily avoidable) and occasions that are necessary (that is, those that frequently lead one to sin) and occasions that are remote (that is, those that seldom lead one to sin.

There is a definite moral obligation to avoid voluntary proximate occasions of sin; and to take precautions against those which are remote. Most moral theologians hold that to place oneself in a voluntary proximate occasion of sin is itself a sin.

OCCULTATION

Islamic term (Ghayba), also meaning absence, concealment, invisibility.

OCCULTISM

A general designation for various theories, practices, and rituals based on esoteric knowledge, especially alleged knowledge about the world of spirits and unknown forces of the universe.

OCHRAN

In Judaism, an Asherite, whose son Pagiel was appointed chieftain of the tribe of Asher after the exodus from Egypt (Numbers 1:13-16; 7:72; 10:26).

ODANTAPURI

A celebrated Buddhist center of learning, north-east of Nalanda, identified with modern Bihar (India). It was founded in the 7th century AD by Gopala, the first ruler of the Pala dynasty. It also served as a model and inspiration for Tibetan Buddhists.

ODED

In the Bible, father of the prophet Azariah (2 Chronicles 15:1). The name is also applied to a prophet of Samaria during the overlapping reigns of Pekah of Israel and Ahaz of Judah (761-758 BC). After Israel and Syria delivered a smashing defeat to Judah, 200,000 captives from the southern kingdom were brought toward Samaria. Oded, however, intercepted the victorious army and warned them of God's wrath if they enslaved their brothers. Four Ephraimite leaders supported Oded, and the captives were cared for and repatriated (2 Chronicles 28:5-15).

ODIN

In Scandinavian mythology, king of the gods. He was god of wisdom, learning and magic, but above all, god of war. He made the world of the body of the giant Ymir, man from the ash tree and woman from the elm.

He lived with other gods in Asgard, holding court in the hall of Valhalla with the dead heroes brought by the Valkyries. His wife was Frigg; his children included Thor and Balder.

In Germany he was known as Wotan or Woden, and identified with the Roman god Mercury, whose day became Wotan's day (Wednesday).

ODO OF CLUNY, Saint

(879-942) Second abbot of Cluny, who gained for Cluniac monasteries exemption from all but papal authority.

ODYSSEUS

Ulysses; one of the most famous Greek heroes. His wanderings after the Trojan War, in which he took a prominent part, are the subject of Homer's epic, the Odyssey.

OEDIPUS

In Greek mythology, King of Thebes, whose doom-laden life inspired dramatic masterpieces by Sophocles (Oedipus Rex, Oedipus in Colonus) and a new term in psychology (Oedipus Complex).

Oedipus was fated to kill his father and marry his mother without knowing that they were his parents. His father Laius, King of Thebes, had been warned that he would be killed by his own son; and when his wife Jocasta gave birth to Oedipus, Laius exposed him on a mountain to die. But the infant was found and taken by Polybus, King of Corinth, and his wife Merope, who raised him as their son. They called him Oedipus ("Swellfeet") because his feet had been pierced when he was abandoned on the mountain.

Later, Oedipus was warned by the Delphic oracle that he would kill his father and marry his mother. Thinking this referred to Polybus and Merope, he fled to Thebes. On the way, he quarrelled with, and killed, a stranger, who was Laius.

He saved Thebes from the Sphinx by answering her riddle, was made king, and married the widowed Jocasta. When plague came, he was told that it would not abate until Laius' murderer had been driven from the city. Oedipus then discovered that he was the murderer. In a frenzy, he blinded himself. Jocasta hanged herself, and Oedipus, driven from Thebes, died at Colonus.

OFFICE, Divine

The liturgy of the Hours; according to Vatican Council II, this is the public prayer of the church for praising God and sanctifying the day. "The Divine office, in keeping with ancient Christian tradition, is so devised that the whole course of the day and night is made holy by the praise of God. Therefore, when this wonderful song of praise is correctly celebrated by priests and others deputed to it by the church, or by the faithful prayer together with a priest in a approved form, then it is truly the voice of the Bride herself addressed to her Bridegroom. It is the very prayer which Christ himself together with his Body addresses to the Father" (Constitution on the Sacred Liturgy).

OG

In biblical times, the powerful Amorite king of Bashan (1 Kings 4:19) whom the Israelites defeated before crossing into the Promised Land. Og was one of the giant Raphaim. In fact, his immense iron bier (perhaps a sarcophagus or possibly a bed frame) measured some 13 feet by 6 feet. He and Sihon ruled the Amorites east of the Jordan (Deuteronomy 3:11-13). The domain of Og extended from Mount Hermon to the Jabbok River, territory east of the Jordan that included 60 fortified cities and numerous rural towns (Deuteronomy 3:3-5, 8-10; Joshua 12:4-5). His two principal cities were Edrei and Ashtaroth (Deuteronomy 1:4; Joshua 13:12).

The defeat of Og at the hands of Israel came toward the end of Israel's 40 year wandering, just before they encamped on the plains of Moab. After defeating Sihon, Israel clashed with Og's forces at Edrei and, in an overwhelming God-given victory, killed off Og and all his army and took possession of his cities and towns (Numbers 21:33-22:1).

The victory brought fright to the inhabitants of Canaan and was a contributing factor prompting Rahab and the Gibeonites to seek peace with Israel and was remembered even many centuries later (Deuteronomy 31:4; Nehemiah 9:22; Psalms 135:10-12; 136:17-22).

OGMIOS

One of the Celtic gods of Gaul identified with the Roman Hercules. He was portrayed as an old man with swarthy skin and armed with a bow and club. He was also a god of eloquence and in that respect he was represented as drawing along a company of men whose ears were chained to his tongue.

OHAD

In Judaism, the third-listed son of Simeon (Genesis 46:10; Exodus 6:15). His name does not appear as founder of a family in the later registration list (Numbers 26:12-14).

OHEL

In Judaism, a son of Governor Zerubbabel and descendant of David (1 Chronicles 3:19-20).

OHOLIAB

In Judaism, chief assistant of Benzalel in constructing the tabernacle; of the tribe of Dan, son of Ahisamach. Oholiab was "a craftsman and embroiderer and weaver in the blue thread and the wool dyed reddish purple and coccus scarlet material and fine linen" (Exodus 31:6; 35:34; 38:23).

OHOLIBAMAH

According to biblical tradition, a Canaanite wife of Esau. She bore him three sons, Jeush, Jalam and Korah, all of whom became sheiks of Edom. Oholibamah was a daughter of Anah and grand-daughter of Hivite Zibeon (Genesis 36:5-8; 14-18).

OILS, Holy

In Roman Catholicism, a general term for the various kinds of oils for religious purposes, especially:

1 the oil of catechumens used at baptism;
2 the oil of chrism used at baptism, at confirmation, at the ordination of a priest or bishop, on the dedication of churches and altars; and
3 oil of the sick used in the anointing of the sick.

The oils are usually blessed by the bishop at the Mass of Chrism on Holy Thursday (though in case of necessity they may be blessed at another time or by a priest if the bishop is not available).

Traditionally, olive oil has been the oil of preference, but for a good reason the church allows other oils (from plants, seeds, or coconuts).

OLD BELIEVERS

Russian religious dissenters who refused to accept the liturgical reforms imposed upon the Russian Orthodox Church by the patriarch of Moscow Nikon (1652-1658). Numbering millions of faithful in the 17th century, the Old Believers split into a number of different sects, of which several survived into modern times.

OLD CATHOLIC CHURCHES

A term used to describe well-organized local churches that claim to have maintained the essentials of Christian doctrine and the historic succession of the episcopate, but not in communion with the bishop (pope) of Rome. They refuse to accept the infallibility of the pope and also reject fast days, indulgences, the veneration of saints, and a celibate clergy.

OLD CATHOLICS

Members of a splinter church of the Roman Catholic Church that began in Germany (1847) under the leadership of the theologian Johann Joseph von Doellinger (1799-1890). Its members do not accept the doctrine of papal infallibility proclaimed at Vatican Council I (1870). Old Catholics follow Roman Catholic ritual, but their priests are allowed to marry and confession is optional.

OLDER MAN

Term not only used for persons of advanced age (Genesis 18:11; Deuteronomy 28:50; 1 Samuel 2:22; 1 Timothy 5:1-2), or the older of two persons (Luke 15:25), but also applied in a special way to those holding a position of authority and responsibility in a community or nation. The use of this term in this latter sense by far predominates in both the Hebrew and the Greek scriptures.

OLD MAN OF THE MOUNTAIN

Hassan i Sabbah (died 1124), leader of the Assassins of Alamut, scholar, administrator and ascetic. He lived an ascetical life, executing both his less rigorous sons.

OLD TESTAMENT

A collection of 39 books of writings sacred to both Judaism and Christianity. With the 27 books of the New Testament it makes up the Bible. The Old Testament is the first part of the Bible, describing God's Covenant with Israel. It is traditionally divided into three parts: the Law (first 5 books), the Prophets and the Writings. The Former Prophets are the earlier historical books, the Latter are the three major prophets and the minor prophets. The Writings include the later historical books, Daniel and the poetic and "wisdom" books. The Old Testament is an inspired record of God's dealings with his people in preparation for the coming of Christ.

The Jewish Canon was fixed by the 1st century AD and is followed by the Protestant churches; the Greek Septuagint version, containing also the Apocrypha, was followed by the Vulgate and hence the Roman Catholic Church.

The standard masoretic text of the Hebrew Old Testament is now largely confirmed for most books by the Dead Sea scrolls (almost 1000 years earlier).

The Old Testament is traditionally divided into three parts:

▲ the Law;

▲ the Prophets (the Former Prophets being the earlier historical books, the Latter being the three major prophets and the minor prophets);

▲ the Writings, including the later historical books, Daniel and the poetic and "wisdom" books.

Christianity regards the Old Testament as an inspired record of God's dealings with His people in preparation for the coming of Christ, containing in embryo much New Testament teaching.

OLD TESTAMENT, Former Prophets

Underlying traditions date from the 12th century BC; these books of the Old Testament were probably completed between 600 and 500 BC. The high points of this section are unquestionably the choosing of David and of Zion, the inauguration of Solomon, and the building of the Temple.

The rest of the tradition material incorporated - the stories of heroes, judges, and prophets, the accounts of wars, and the annals of the kings, etc. - all tend to be secondary.

But a further level of interpretation has been superimposed upon the whole complex by Deuteronomist editors in such a way that it now displays a recurrent pattern of sin, chastisement, repentance, and deliverance until the increase in sin, for which the later kings are chiefly blamed, finally leads to the ruin and exile of 587 BC.

OLD TESTAMENT, Latter Prophets

Composition of this part of the Bible was from 750 BC (Amos) to the third century BC (the minor prophets). The message here is primarily and basically concerned with the judgment of Yahweh. This is to fall either on the people or on specific classes for their sins (chiefly pre-exilic Prophets) or else upon those who ill-treat the Israelites or triumph over their misfortunes (chiefly post-exilic prophets).

But the prophets also predict the survival and restoration of an Israel purged and renewed. This is to be achieved through a "righteous remnant" led by a divinely inspired Messiah (First Isaiah) through a new covenant greater and more glorious than the old one, which the people have so radically betrayed (Jeremiah), in a new and more glorious land reorganized and repeopled after the exile with a new Zion and a new temple at its center to supply it with miraculous fruitfulness and healing (Ezekiel).

All this is to take place when the people return from Babylon in a new and glorious exodus (Deutero-Isaiah). Salvation and restoration are to come through a supreme charismatic figure, a "prototype" Israelite who is to proclaim Yahweh's Law to all the Gentiles, to suffer vicariously for his people's sins, and at last to receive glory and honor from all. The basic themes of judgment and restoration are continued with variations in the minor prophets.

OLD TESTAMENT, The Law

The Evolution of the Law or Pentateuch shows remarkable characteristics. Its heart and center is constituted by two broad complexes of tradition. The first of these commemorates the events of the exodus and the entry into the promised land, and is epitomized in the ancient cultic "credo" as preserved, for instance in Deuteronomy 26:5-10.

The second tradition complex is centered upon the covenant. It displays the basic structure of the Hittite vassal treaty: a solemn proclamation of Yahweh's name is followed by a reminder of his past favors as a motive for the people's gratitude and future faithfulness. This leads on to the solemn proclamation of Yahweh's will in law and the sealing of the covenant, in which the people commit themselves to obey this law. A list of blessings for obedience and cursings for disobedience is then appended. Into this structure various further law codes associated with the covenant are later inserted.

These two basic complexes are then united and further expanded by the inclusion of a number of previously independent units and complexes of tradition - some very ancient - relating to the patriarchs and centered primarily upon the promise of land and seed.

This patriarchal history too is seen as oriented toward the covenant promises as the goal of Yahweh's plan and purpose, in which his own glory and his people's happiness are to be achieved.

A further stage in the process of development is the prefixing of one version of the primordial history (Genesis 1-11), which makes the implementation of the divine plan begin not merely with the promise of Abraham but with the Creation of the world.

Finally, the whole body of tradition acquires a fresh level of interpretation when the 10thcentury Yahwist writer, who was probably attached to Solomon's court, aligns the whole with the accession of Solomon himself and the glories of his kingdom. These are now seen as implementing and fulfilling Yahweh's plan and purpose right from the Creation onwards.

OLD TESTAMENT, the Writings

Sources date from the tenth century; composition extended to the second century. These are obviously more heterogenous in character, and their function in the Old Testament as a whole is correspondingly more difficult to define. Broadly speaking, however, they do not express God's dynamic will and plan for his people in the same direct sense as do the Law and the Prophets, but rather the people's own reaction to that will and their inspired reflections upon the significance of its workings.

The Psalms, most of which were composed in the context of the Temple and its cult, express, in a manner recognized as sacred in the ancient Near East, the basic attitudes of the prayer with which Israel responds to, appeals to, or praises her covenant God.

Proverbs, Sirach, and Wisdom teach that the wisdom that enables man to live harmoniously and happily in all departments of human life comes from God and is a charisma bestowed upon his people by him. Job and Ecclesiastes, without solving it, reflect on the problem of evil as it bears upon the individual Israelite's relationship with his covenant God.

The deuterocanonical books were all composed in the last two pre-Christian centuries.

OLGA, Saint

(890-969) Princess who was canonized as the first Russian Saint of the Orthodox church. She was the widow of Prince Igor I. Her efforts to bring Christianity to Russia were carried out by her grandson, the grand prince St. Vladimir; together they mark the transition between pagan and Christian Russia.

OLIPHANT, Laurence

(1829-1888) Author and mystic, whose quest to establish a Jewish state in Palestine -"fulfilling prophecy and bringing on the end of the world" - won him support of both Jewish and Christian officials but was thought by some to be motivated either by commercial interests or by a desire to strengthen Britain's position in the Near East.

OLIVES, Mount of

A ridge of hills each of Jerusalem which overlooks the city. On the western slope is the Garden of Gethsemane where Jesus went with his disciples after the Last Supper. The Mount includes the traditional site of Christ's Ascension.

Notable events of Bible history are associated with the Mount of Olives. King David, barefoot and weeping, ascended the Mount of Olives as he fled from his rebellious son Absalom (2 Samuel 15:14, 30-32). King Solomon built high places for idolatrous worship there (1 Kings 11:7), King Josiah later made these unfit for worship (2 Kings: 23-13). In the first century AD Jesus Christ often met with his disciples in the Garden of Gethsemane, located on or in the vicinity of the Mount of Olives (Matthew 26:30; John 18:1-2). When at Jerusalem, Jesus and his disciples customarily spent the night at Bethany on the eastern slope of the Mount of Olives, undoubtedly in the home of Martha, Mary and Lazarus (Matthew 21:17; Mark 11:11; Luke 21:37). Apparently from Bethphage, near Bethany, Jesus seated on the colt of an ass, commenced his triumphal ride over the Mount of Olives to Jerusalem (Matthew 21:1; Mark 11:1; Luke 19:29). And it was at the Mount of Olives that he explained to his disciples what the "sign of his presence" would be (Matthew 24:3; Mark 13:3). Finally, after his resurrection, Jesus ascended from there into the heavens (Acts 1:9-12).

OLYMPUS, Mount

Highest mountain in Greece, rises 9,571 feet at the eastern end of the 25 miles range along the Thessaly-Macedonia border. The summit is snowcapped for most of the year. The ancient Greeks long believed that

Olympus was the home of Zeus and other major gods (the Olympians), who lived on nectar and ambrosia in their splendid, mountaintop palaces. But later the Olympus of the gods was placed somewhere in the heavens, the earthly Mount Olympus having become too well known to the Greeks.

OM

Term used in Tibetan Buddhism meaning mantra. The invocation "Om Mani Padme Hum" is found throughout Tibet and is usually translated as "Hail to the Jewel in the Lotus."

OMAR

In the Old Testament, second-listed son of Esau's firstborn Eliphaz; a sheik of Edom (Genesis 36:10-15).

OMAYYADS

A dynasty of caliphs who ruled the early Muslim empire from Damascus from 661 to 751. The Omayyad caliphate was essentially Arabic in character. Thus the caliph relied heavily on the Syrian army (comprised substantially of Arab tribesmen from the desert) to maintain himself in power and extend his empire. For this reason the Omayyad caliphate is sometimes described as the Arab Kingdom. Replaced by the Abbasids of Baghdad, the last Omayyad fled to Spain and in 756 set up the Caliphate of Cordoba, which lasted until 1031.

OMEN

Anything viewed as giving some indication about the future; a situation or occurrence thought of as portending good or evil (Gnesis 30:27; Numbers 24:1). Looking for omens, as a form of divination, was specifically prohibited by God's law to Israel (Leviticus 19:26; Deuteronomy 18:10). But apostates like Judan King Manasseh did look for omens (2 Kings 17:17). Since this practice is condemned in the sriptures, evidently faithful Joseph's comment about use of his silver cup to read omens was merely part of a ruse (Genesis 44:5, 15).

OMOTO

A religious movement of Japan that had a large following in the period between World War I and World War II. The teaching of Omoto is based on divine oracles transmitted through a peasant woman, Deguchi Nao, whose healing powers attracted an early following. Her first revelation in 1892 foretold the destruction of the world and the appearance of a messiah who would usher in the new heaven on earth.

OMRI

In biblical times, sixth king of the northern ten-tribe kingdom of Israel. Nothing of Omri's ancestry is recorded, not even the name of his father or tribe. Omri founded the third dynasty of Israel (those of Jeroboam and Baasha preceded), his son Ahab and grandsons Ahaziah and Jehoram succeeding him, all four totalling some 46 years 951-905 BC on the throne).

Omri came to the throne, not by inheritance, but by the sword. he had been chief of Israel's army under King Elah (and perhaps under his predecessor Baasha) when Zimri, chief of half the chariots, overthrew Elah, took the kingship for himself and wiped out the house and friends of Baasha. As soon as this was reported to the Israelite army, at the time camped against the Philistines at Gibbethon, "all Israel," doubtless the tribal heads "in the camp," made Omri their king. At once they withdrew from Gibbethon and stormed Zimri's capital Tirzah. Zimri, seeing the hopelessness of his cause, burned down the king's house over himself, tragically ending his even-day rule (1 Kings 16:8-20).

Religiously Omri continued the downward trend of the northern kingdom; he continued Jeroboam's idolatry; in fact, he "kept doing what was bad in the eyes of God and came to do worse than all who were prior to him" (1 Kings 16:25). Some 200 years later, through Micah God condemned Israel for following "the statutes of Omri" (Micah 6:16).

ON

According to biblical tradition, the name of a person and a place. On was a son of Peleth and a principal man of the tribe of Reuben (Numbers 16:1). He was among those raising a protest against Moses and Aaron, but his name does not appear among the rebels in their later speeches to Moses nor when they were punished by God with destruction (Numbers 16:2-3); This may be due to his playing a very subordinate part in the rebellion or it may even indicate that he withdrew from it following Moses' initial rebuking of the conspirators.

The name On is also applied to an ancient and renowned city in Egypt, located circa ten miles north-east of Cairo, on the east bank of the Nile and near the point where the river's waters divide to begin the formation of the Delta region.

On first appears in the Bible records as the city of Potiphera, priest of On, whose daughter Asenath was given to Joseph as his wife (Genesis 41:45-50). In the course of time the priesthood of On became very wealthy, rivaling the priesthood of Memphis in this respect and being surpassed only by the priesthood of Thebes (biblical No-amon). Connected with its temple to the sun, a school was operated for training priests and for the teaching of medicine. Greek philosophers and scholars were drawn there to learn the priestly theology and On became celebrated as a center of Egyptian wisdom. The city was destroyed by King Nebuchadnezzar when he overran Egypt (Jeremiah 43:10-13).

ONAM

In Judaism, last of the five listed sons of Horite sheik Shobal, and grandson of the Horites' forefather Seir (Genesis 36:20-23; 1 Chronicles 1:40).

The name is also applied to a son of Jerahmeel and a link in the Jerahmeelite genealogy in the tribe of Judah; his mother's name was Atarah (1 Chronicles 2:26-28).

ONAN

According to biblical tradition, a son of Judah, his second by his Canaanite daughter of Shua (Genesis 38:2-4; 1 Chronicles 2:3). After Onan's childless older brother Er was put to death by God for wrongdoing, Onan was told by Judah to perform brother-in-law marriage with Er's wife Tamar. If a son was produced, he would not be the founder of Onan's family, and have the firstborn's inheritance for himself. When Onan had relations with Tamar, he "wasted his semen on the ground" rather than giving it to her. This was not an act of masturbation on the part of Onan, for the accounts says "when he did have relations with his brother's wife" he spilled his semen. Apparently it was a case of "coitus interruptus," in which Onan purposely prevented ejaculation of his semen into Tamar's genital tract. For his obedience to his father, his covetousness and his sin against the divine arrangement of marriage, not for self-abuse, Onan, himself also childless, was put to death byu God (Genesis 38:6-10; Numbers 26:19).

ONE AND MANY

Phrase used in Buddhism to denote that there is no final distinction between the One and the Many, both being relative aspects of the Absolute behind all duality. One in All and All in One is a statement of spiritual experience, not to be intellectually analyzed.

ONEG SHABBAT

Jewish phrase for Sabbath Joy. On Saturday afternoon is has become a custom in Israel to gather for Sabbath discussion, song, and refreshment. This tradition is only a generation old. It was originated by the outstanding Hebrew poet of modern times, Hayyim Nahham Bialik. The custom has since taken root in America and in many synagogues the Oneg Shabatt is a regular Sabbath feature, ending in the Se'udag Shelishes (the third meal of Sabbath), evening prayer, and Havdalah.

ONEIDA COMMUNITY

A utopian religious community that developed out of a Society of Inquiry established by John Humphrey Noyes and some of his disciples in Putney, Vermont, in 1841. At the height of its development the community was organized into 48 departments that carried out the various activities of the settlement. Those who were to produce children were carefully chosen and paired. Hostility mounted in the surrounding communities to the Perfectionists' marriage arrangements, and in 1879 Noyes advised the group to abandon the system. Noyes and a few adherents went to Canada where he died in 1886.

ONENESS OF GOD

Term used in Islam, belief in Oneness or Unity, monotheism. It is one of the most fundamental Islamic doctrines.

ONESIMUS

According to biblical tradition, a runaway slave whom Paul helped to become a Christian. Onesimus has been a servant to Phelemon, a Colossian Christian, but had run away from Colossae to Rome. He may even have first robbed his master in order to make the journey (Colossians 4:9). In is quite possible that he had met or at least heard of Paul through Phelemon; for, though no visit of Paul to Colossae on the missionary tour is specifically mentioned, Paul did travel through the general area and was acquainted with Phelemon (Acts 18:22-23). At any rate, in some unstated way, Onesimus became associated with Paul in Rome and soon became a Christian.

ONESIPHORUS

In the New Testament, a Christian referred to in Paul's second letter to Timothy (2 Timothy 4:19). In contrast with others in the district of Asia who turned away from Paul, Onesiphorus remained a loyal supporter and, when in Rome, diligently hunted to find Paul in spite of the risk to himself. He was not ashamed of Paul's prison bonds, but rendered the apostle good service, as he had done in Ephesus. Paul greatly appreciated this loyalty and prayed that Onesiphorus and his household would receive of God's mercy (2 Timothy 1:15-18).

The fact that Paul sent greetings to the household of Onesiphorus rather than to Onesiphorus himself (2 Timothy 4:19) does not necessarily indicate that he was no longer alive, though such might be true. He may simply have been away from his family at the time, or may even be included in the general greeting sent to his households of believers.

ONO

In biblical times, a city built either by Benjaminite Elpaal or by his "sons" (1 Chronicles 8:1, 12). After the Babylonian exile Ono was reoccupied by Benjamites (Ezra 2:1, 33). Kefr 'Ana, circa seven miles east-south-east of Joppa, is thought to preserve the city's ancient name. This location would place Ono just a few miles from the suggested sites of ancient Lod and Hadid. The "valley plain of Ono" (Nehemiah 6:2) possibly denotes the wide valley in which modern Kefr 'Ana lies.

OPHIR

According to biblical tradition, the name of a person and a place. Ophir is the name of a descendant of Shem through Arpachshad, Shelah, Eber and Joktan; the 11th of Joktan's 13 sons (Genesis 10:22-29). Ophir was probably born circa 200 years before Abraham, who was a descendant of his paternal uncle Peleg (Genesis 10:25; 11:18-26). As in the case of his brothers, it appears that Ophir also headed one of the Shemite tribes that were numbered among the descendants of Noah (Genesis 10:31-32).

The name Ophir is also applied to a place renowned as a source of much gold of the finest quality. Thus already in Job's time "precious ore in the dust" and "pure gold" were spoken of in parallel with the "gold of Ophir" (Job

22:24; 28:15). The precise location of Ophir cannot be determined today with certainty. Most likely Ophir was located in a region of south-western Arabia in the vicinity of modern Yemen.

OPHITES

A Gnostic sect - i.e., a group of religious dualists who believed that matter was evil and the spirit good and that salvation was attained through esoteric knowledge, or gnosis.

OPHNI

In biblical times, a city of Benjamin (Joshua 18:21-24), commonly linked with the Gophna mentioned by Josephus.

OPHRAH

A city of Benjamin (Joshua 18:21-23). Its relative location may be inferred from the narrative about Israel's encounters with the Philistines during Saul's reign. The most probable location of to the north of Michmash (1 Samuel 13:16-18).

The name is also applied to the home of Gideon and the place where God's angel commissioned him to save Israel out of Midian's palm (Judges 6:11-32). After his victory over the enemy forces, Gideon made an ephod from the contributed spoils and exhibited it to Phrah. Subsequently this ephod became an object of idolatrous veneration (Judges 8:24-27). Later, after Gideon's death and burial at Ophrah, his ambitious son Abimelech "killed his brothers ... 70 men , upon one stone, but Jonathan the youngest ... was left over" (Judges 8:32; 9:5).

OPPERMAN, Daniel C.

(1890-1959) United States Pentecostal leader and one of the organizers of the Pentecostal conference in Hot Springs, Arkansas, in 1941.

OPUS DEI

A Roman Catholic organization of laymen and priests whose members seek personal Christian perfection and strive to implement Christian ideals in their chosen professions. There are separate organizations for men and women under a president general, who resides in Rome. Priests comprise only a small percentage of the 70.000 members living in some 90 countries.

ORACLE

In ancient times, the reply given by a god to someone seeking his advice. His response was usually given through a priest or priestess (also called oracles). But sometimes the god spoke through the rustling of a sacred laurel or the movement of a sacred bird or animal. In ancient Egypt. the oracle of Amon in the Siwa oasis was very highly regarded. There, the response came in the shaking appearance of the god's statue. Oracles were always associated with particular places. The two most famous oracles of ancient Greece were those of Apollo at Delphi and of Zeus at Dodona. Zeus also had an oracle at Olympia. Inquirers seeking the aid of the Delphi oracle first made sacrifices and then, crowned with laurel leaves, submitted their questions on tablets made of lead. The responses, sometimes obscure, were considered infallible, and were delivered by a priestess called Pythia, who writhed wildly as she spoke. At Dodona, the responses often came through sacred oaks and doves.

ORATORIANS

Roman Catholic congregation formed circa 1575 in Rome by St. Philip Neri. Members, organized in autonomous congregations, are secular priests who take no vows. John Newman founded oratories in Birmingham (1848) and London (1849). A separate society was founded in 1611 in Paris by Pierre de Berulle.

ORATORY

A place of worship divided into public, semipublic, and private classifications. Oratories are not meant for public use, but for religious communities, schools, families, or individuals.

ORCHARD, William Edwin

(1877-1955) Ecumenical priest who strove for a closer understanding between Protestants and Roman Catholics. He worked in England and the United States.

ORCUS

In Roman religion, the kingdom of the dead or its ruler. He was too menacing and insubstantial to have a cult or to be represented in the visual arts.

ORDERIC VITALIS

(1075-1142) Monk of St. Evroul in Normandy. He wrote important works on the history of Roman Catholic religion.

ORDERS, Religious

A general term commonly used to describe what in the laws of the Roman Catholic Church are called "institutes of consecrated life"; this consecrated life is thus described in the Code of Canon Law: "Life consecrated by the profession of evangelical counsels is a stable form of living by which the faithful, following Christ more closely under the action of the Holy Spirit, are totally dedicated to God who is loved most of all, so that, having dedicated themselves to His honor, the upbuilding of the church and the salvation of the world by a new and special title, they strive for the perfection of charity in service of the Kingdom of God and, having become an outstanding sign of the church, they may foretell the heavenly glory" (Canon 573).

There are in the Roman Catholic Church a large number of institutes of consecrated life; they have different purposes and charisms, stemming from the intention of the founders and the different gifts of grace that have been given to them. All of these institutes of consecrated life have goals and norms expressed in their constitutions and all are in some way under the competent authority of the church.

ORDINARIATE

An ecclesiastical unit similar to a diocese but which is not based on geographic boundaries. Most often used to refer to military dioceses.

ORDINARY

A title for a certain class of officeholders, among them bishops, major religious superiors, vicars general, and so on.

ORDINATION

In the Christian church, the ceremonial appointment to one of the orders of the ministry. The ordination of bishops is usually called consecration. Regarded by the Roman Catholic Church as a sacrament, ordination is performed in Episcopal Churches by a bishop, and in Presbyterian churches by the presbytery. The rite includes prayer and the laying on of hands, traditionally in a eucharistic context.

OREB

According to biblical tradition, a prince of Midian. Oreb and Zeeb were in the Midianite Army of Kings Zebah and Zalmunna that Gideon and his 300 put to flight. The two princes were captured and put to death by men of Ephraim and their heads were brought to Gideon (Judges 7:24, 25).

ORESTES

In Greek mythology, son of Agamemnon and Clytemnestra of Argos. After Clytemnestra had killed Agamemnon, he was sent away from Argos. Ordered by Apollo to avenge the crime, he killed his mother and her lover, Aegisthus. Pursued by the Furies, he was told to steal the image of Artemis from Tauris to atone for the murders. He did this with the help of Iphigenia.

ORIENTAL JEWS

A popular designation for approximately 1.5 million Diaspora Jews who have lived for the most part in North Africa and the Middle East and whose ancestors did not reside in either Germany or Spain. They are thus distinguished from who other major groups of Diaspora Jews - the Ashkenazim ("German") and the Sefardim ("Spanish"). Each of the groups has a distinctive liturgy.

ORIGINAL JUSTICE

A term used to describe the pre-sinful state of Adam and Eve before the Fall.

ORIGINAL SIN

In Christian doctrine, the state of sinfulness in which all mankind is born, and which is the root cause of all actual sins. When Adam disobeyed God, the whole human race fell in solidarity with him and inherited his sin and guilt, losing supernatural grace and communion with God, and our free will was made spiritually inoperative (Romans 5:14-15).

In Catholic theology, original sin is washed away in baptism. Original sin is not a personal sin actually committed by each individual but, rather, in the words of Pope Paul VI, "it is human nature so fallen, stripped of the grace that clothed it, injured in its natural powers and subjected to the dominion of death, that is transmitted to all men, and it is in this sense that every man is born in sin" (Credo of the People of God).

Original sin means, therefore, that each descendant from Adam is created without sanctifying grace and is subject to concupiscence (that is, the tendency of fallen human nature to act contrary to reason and grace) as well as the punishment of death.

Yet human nature is not completely corrupt or incapable of good choices; fallen human nature is capable of receiving sanctifying grace through the death and resurrection of Jesus Christ.

ORIGINAL SIN, Contemporary thought

In contemporary theology, the classical theories are widely repudiated. The presupposition of monogenism and of a pristine state of human perfection are regarded as unwarranted by biblical exegesis as original or hereditary not because of origin from Adam, but as inherited from mankind; it is a sin of the race, "the sin of the world" (John 1:29).

This sin is not simply an imitation of the Genesis episode through personal sins; it is a sin by propagation in the sense that by birth every man comes under the power of iniquity pervading human history and environment. There is in humanity a unity of sinfulness, which every man and the community of man have ratified by personal sins.

The sin of the race is upon every man not through a biological lineage, but through the toll of his human heritage, an environment of accumulating guilt. Being born into a community of sin, each man is heir to sin and needs salvation.

ORIGINAL SIN, Nature

The decrees of Trent did not resolve continuing differences among Roman Catholic theologians as to whether original sin consists essentially simply in the absence of an original righteousness or in concupiscence. Canon 5 states that all that is of sin, not just its imputation, is taken away by baptism; concupiscence is not sin in a proper sense.

Canon 2 refers to a loss of sanctity and righteousness, as well as death and other penalties, derived to all men from Adam's sin. The moral plight of man, however, does not mean loss of free will; nor does it mean complete incapacity for moral good.

For Luther original sin is the "capital sin," looming larger than actual sins; it is an abiding condition of blindness, rebellion, and concupiscence besetting human nature; its dominance makes critical the need of grace saving through faith.

The Calvinistic tradition speaks of human total depravity; Arminianism rejected this idea and extolled man's power to consent to grace. Holiness teaching on sanctification also extols the moral capacities of man; concupiscence is not an insuperable sinfulness. Rationalist and liberalist tendencies in theology, of course, did not recognize any basic deterioration in human nature.

ORIGINAL SIN, Scripture

As a history of salvation the whole Bible and especially the New Testament proclaims the universal need of saving grace (see Titus 2:11), and this the universality and community of human sinfulness.

The account of the Fall in Genesis (Genesis 2-3) points out in particular that God created man good; it was man who by sin introduced moral evil. The idea of racial community, as well as of hereditary guilt and punishment enter the biblical range of vision, namely that the present human plight is connected with man's introduction of sin into God's work; the account does not say more.

The central New Testament text Romans chapter 5, is similar. It contrasts the universal, baneful presence of sin and death in the world, introduced by Adam's sin, with the universal saving grace of Christ.

The text points to the appearance and universality of sin in man's world; the Vulgate reading of verse 12, "in which (Adam) all have sinned," is not faithful to Paul's own words ("because all men have sinned").

ORIGINAL SIN, Source

The articulation of the universal sinfulness of mankind as a sin through origin from Adam came with Augustine. His teaching was reflected in the second canon of the Council held at Carthage in 418 against Pelagianism and in canons 1 and 2 of the Second Council of Orange, held in 529. These canons were revised and incorporated at the Council of Trent in the decree on original sin, which stands as the normative statement of Roman Catholic teaching. The decree speaks of a particular person, Adam, sinning and losing grace and other gifts not only for himself but for all mankind, and of his passing on not only punishment but also sin to his descendants. The sin is described as one in kind because of its one source and as present in each person because of descent from Adam, not because of a personal act imitating his sin.

The classical Protestant confessions of faith for the most part simply assumed the explanation of man's sinful condition as a "birth sin." The Lutheran Augsburg Confession states that all men begotten after the common source of nature are born with sin.

The Reformed confessions repeat that original sin is "an hereditary evil" but also introduce the idea of a covenant by which Adam acted for all, and his sin was this imputed to all.

For Anglicanism the Thirty-nine Articles speak of "the fault and corruption of the nature of every man that naturally is engendered of the offspring of Adam."

Pelagianism was a denial of the hereditary sin of mankind. Unitarian rationalism rejected the concept of the Fall and of hereditary guilt. The Anabaptists and Menonnite traditions with their stress on salvation as a personal experience paid little heed to original sin.

Mormons, or Latter-day Saints, simply reject original sin. Even where the churches officially maintained the traditional acceptance of original sin, actual adherence to the doctrine diminished. Under the influence of enlightenment, rationalism, and higher biblical criticism, Protestants, except for fundamentalists, largely dismissed the doctrine.

ORISHA OKO

A god of the Yoruba people of southwestern Nigeria and eastern Dahomey.

ORNAN

In Judaism, a Jebusite from whom David bought the threshing floor that later became the site for a temple (1 Chronicles 21:18-28).

ORPAH

According to biblical tradition, the Moabite wife of Chilion, and, like Ruth, a daughter-in-law of Naomi.

ORPHEUS

In Greek mythology, Orpheus of Thrace was one of the protagonists in the Argonaut adventure. He is also the central figure in a highly symbolic myth with more religious features about it than any other of its time.

The son of Oeagrus and (probably) the muse Calliope, Orpheus was a charismatic musician, poet and singer. Apart from being a superb performer on the lyre, he was credited with inventing the cithara, the ancient guitar.

The most familiar myth about Orpheus is that which tells of his descent into Hades in search of his beloved wife Euridice. Euridice was a beautiful nymph of the woods. One day, she was running away from the attentions of Aristaeus, along the bank of the river, when she trod on a poisonous snake. It bit her, and she died. Orpheus, inconsolable, descended into Hades to find her and bring her back to life.

His music charmed the entire underworld, and all the souls in torment there forgot their punishments for a little while. Sisyphus, Tantalus, the Danaids and all the others rested from their eternal tortures to listen with delight to the music.

Hades and Persephone agreed to let Euridice go, but on one condition: that as Orpheus was ascending to the upper world once more, with Euridice behind him, he must not turn around to look at her until they were safely out of the underworld.

But just before they emerged in the sunlight, Orpheus' anxiety to make sure that the shade of Euridice really was behind him overcame him, and he turned around to make absolutely sure the gods of the underworld had not tricked him. Then everything was lost for ever; Euridice joined the dead with no hope of return, and Hades turned a deaf ear to the pleas of the tragic figure of Orpheus.

After that time, there are many tales of Orpheus the inconsolable widower. he is said to have turned his back on worldly things, refusing to re-marry, avoiding women and their love for three years. According to tradition, his only companions were Thracian boys, to whom he taught the "Orphic life": abstinence from the consumption of meat, and initiation into music and the experiences which Orpheus himself had had in the underworld.

ORTHODOX

True Christian doctrine and its adherents as opposed to heterodox or heretical doctrines and their adherents. The word was first used in the early 4th century by the Greek Fathers. Because almost every Christian group believes that it holds the true faith, the meaning of ;orthodox" in a particular instance can be correctly determined only after examination of the context in which in appears.

ORTHODOX CHURCHES

The family of Christian churches that developed out of the Eastern church, remaining orthodox when the Nestorians and Monophysite churches separated. They finally broke with Rome in the Great Schism of 1054.

Each church is independent, but all are in full communion and acknowledge the honorary primacy of the ecumenical patriarch of Constantinople; some are patriarchates, others are governed by synods.

The ancient patriarchates of Constantinople, Alexandria, Antioch and Jerusalem are dwarfed by the more recent churches of Russia, Serbia, Romania, Bulgaria, Georgia, Cyprus and others. There are now approximately 105 million Orthodox worldwide, including circa 6 million in the United States.

Since the large-scale Slavic immigration to the eastern United States in the 1880s, there has been a substantial Orthodox community in America. With the stimulus of the Russian revolution in 1917, the expulsion of Greeks from Asia Minor in 1921, and the many refugees who fled to the United States to escape World War II, the Orthodox church in America grew to the abovementioned number of 6 million. This now comprises eight main churches (Greek, Russian, Syrian, Serbian, Bulgarian, Rumanian, Albanian and the Russian synod in exile.

Orthodoxy accepts the first seven ecumenical councils, but often prefers not to define dogma very closely; it is characterized by monasticism, veneration of icons and the importance of the laity. It rejects papal claims, the immaculate conception and purgatory and does not require clerical celibacy. The leading figure in the Orthodox church is the Ecumenical Patriarch of Constantinople.

ORTHODOX JEWISH CONGREGATIONS OF AMERICA, Union of

Official federation of Jewish Orthodox synagogues in the United States and Canada; its counterpart organization for rabbis is the Rabbinical Council of America.

ORTHODOX JUDAISM

The religious tenets of those Jews who adhere most strictly to traditional beliefs and practices. Jewish Orthodoxy resolutely refuses to accept the position of Reform Judaism that the Bible and other sacred Jewish writings contain not only eternally valid moral principles but also historically and culturally conditioned adaptations and interpretations of the Law that may be legitimately discarded in modern times.

In Orthodox Judaism, therefore, both the Written Law (Torah, first five books of the Old Testament) and the Oral Law (codified in the Mishna and interpreted in the Talmud) are immutably fixed for all times and remain the sole norm of religious observance.

ORTHODOX RABBIS OF THE U.S AND CANADA, Union of

An organization founded in New York City in 1902 to foster traditional Orthodox practices such as strict observance of the sabbath and the dietary laws.

ORTHODOXY

Correct religious belief, according to an authoritative norm; i.e. tradition, doctrine, dogma, or creed.

ORTHODOXY, Feast of

Feast celebrated on the first Sunday of Lent by the Eastern Orthodox Church and Eastern Catholics of the Byzantine Rite to commemorate the return of icons (sacred images) to the churches (843) and the end of the long iconoclastic controversy.

OSIRIS

God of the underworld in ancient Egypt, brother and husband of Isis, through whom every Egyptian hoped to gain immortality. His cult spread widely through the Mediterranean and was popular in imperial Rome. Legendary King of Egypt before 3200 BC, he is said to have introduced agriculture and other benefits. He was slain by his evil brother Set, who cut his body into 14 pieces and reunited them. Later Horus, son of Isis and Osiris, killed Set and ruled in Egypt, while Osiris ruled over the souls of the dead.

OSMUND, Saint

(1021-1099) Norman priest and bishop of Salisbury, who organized a cathedral chapter of secular canons similar to Norman chapters, which was copied by other English cathedrals. His liturgical reforms became the basis for the later "Old Sarum" liturgy used throughout the British Isles.

OSWALD, Saint

(605-641) Anglo-Saxon king of Northumbria from 633 to 641, who restored Christianity to his kingdom and gained ascendancy over most of England.

OSWALD OF YORK, Saint

(925-992) Anglo-Saxon archbishop who was a leading figure in the 10thcentury movement of monastic and feudalistic reforms. As an ecclesiastical landlord, he practiced the leasing of land to certain men and to their heirs on condition that they perform various services for him.

OTHNI

In Judaism, son of Shemaiah and grandson of Korahite Obed-edom, appointed as a Levitical gatekeeper before the sanctuary. Othni and his brothers were "rulers of the house of their father ... capable, mighty men" (1 Chronicles 26:1-4; 6-8).

OTTOMANS

Major dynasty which occupied a prominent position in the Near and Middle East from 1281 until 1924 and founded a great empire. They took their name from an early leader in the 134th century called "Uthman."

OXFORD MOVEMENT

19thcentury religious movement aiming to revitalize the Church of England by reintroducing traditional Catholic practices and doctrines. It started in 1833 in Oxford; its leaders, John Keble, J.H. Newman and, later, Edward Pusey, wrote a series of *Tracts of the Times* to publish their opinions. They became known as the "Tractarians." Despite violent controversy over the Romeward tendency of some culminating in Newman's con-

version to Roman Catholicism (1845) - and over ritualism (from 1850), the movement has had great influence in the Anglican Church.

Newman was responsible for the movement's *Tracts of the Times,* writing many of them himself. Working for a revival of traditional doctrine and custom, the movement suffered a severe blow when Newman became a Roman Catholic (1845).

OZEM

According to biblical tradition, the fourth-listed son of Jerahmeel in the tribe of Judah (1 Chronicles 2:250.

The name is also applied to the sixth-name son of Jesse and older brother of David; tribe of Judah (1 Chronicles 2:13-15).

OZNI

In Judaism, a son of Gad of the tribal family of Oznites numbered in the second wilderness registration of Israel (Numbers 26:15-16). Ozni is called Ezbon in the first list of Gad's sons, some of whose names are written somewhat differently in Numbers (Genesis 46:16).

OZNITES

A family of the tribe of Gad founded by Ozni (Numbers 26:15-16).

P

PAARAI

In Judaism, an Arbite and one of the mighty men of David's military forces (2 Samuel 23:8) He may be identical with the Naara mentioned at 1 Chronicles 11:37, in what appears to be a parallel list.

PACHOMIUS, Saint

(290-346) Founder of Christian cenobitic(communal) monasticism, whose Rule (book of observances) for monks established the definitive character for the major monastic institutions of Eastern and Western Christian civilization. His name is from Coptic Egyptian and means Eagle or Falcon.

PACIFISM

The moral conviction that all war is intrinsically evil and that it is forbidden by the gospel; historically, this position (sometimes called "absolute pacifism") has been a minority position among Christians, the more common position being that of the "just-war theory;" in recent times, the moral position that opposes not all war but the use of nuclear weapons is sometimes called "relative pacifism."

PADDAN

According to biblical tradition a region around the city of Haran in northern Mesopotamia (Genesis 28:6-7). Though some consider Paddan and Aram-naharaim to be identical, it seems more likely that Paddan was a part of Aram-naharaim (Genesis 24:10;

25:20). This may be inferred from the fact that Aram-naharaim (meaning 'Aram of the two rivers") included mountainous territory, something that could not be true of Paddan, if its name is correctly understood to mean "plain" (Numbers 23:7; Deuteronomy 23:4). The patriarch Abraham resided temporarily at Haran in Paddan (Genesis 12:4; 28:7). Later from among the offspring of his relatives there, his son Isaac and then his grandson Jacob got their wives (Genesis 22:20-23; 25:20). Jacob personally spent 20 years at Paddan in the service of his father-in-law (Genesis 31:17-18). While there, he became father of Dinah and eleven sons. His 12th son Benjamin, was born in Canaan (Genesis 35:16-18).

PADILLA

(1498-1567) First Christian missionary martyred within the territory of the present United States. In 1540-41 he accompanied the Spanish explorer Francisco Vazquez de Coronado in his fruitless quest for a legendary kingdom of riches called Quivira, probably in modern Kansas. He was killed by Wichita Indians.

PADMASAMBHAVA

(706-765) Indian Buddhist mystic who introduced Tantric Buddhism to Tibet and who is credited for establishing the first Buddhist monastery there.

PADON

In Judaism, paternal head of a family of Nethinum. "The sons of Padon" returned with Zerubbabel from Babylonian exile (Ezra 2:1-2; Nehemiah 7:46-47).

PAEAN

In Greek religion, the physician of the gods. It is not known whether he was originally a separate deity or merely an aspect of Apollo.

PAGIEL

According to biblical tradition, wilderness chieftain of the tribe of Asher; son of Ochran (Numbers 1:13-16). He assisted Moses in taking the first census of Israel, presented Asher's offering at the inauguration of the tabernacle altar, and took the military command of the tribe (Numbers 1:4-19; 2:27-28; 7:72-77).

PAGODA

Towerlike, storied structure of stone, brick, or wood built by Buddhists, that is usually associated with a temple complex. The pagoda derives from the stupa of ancient India, which was a dome-shaped funeral mound erected over the remains, or relics, of a holy man or king.

The pagoda, like the stupa, was at first thought of as an architectural diagram of the cosmos. The great pillar that runs up the core of the structure is symbolic of that invisible world axis joining the centers of earth and heaven. The cosmic diagram, thus fixed in architectural forms, was thought to be animated by the precious relics enshrined within.

PAHATH-MOAB

According to biblical tradition, founder of a family in Israel. If he was an official of Moab, as his name may imply, it was probably during the time when Moab was under Judah's domination. His holding such a position remains uncertain, however, as nothing is said of him personally in the Scripture record.

Pahath-moab's descendants noted in Ezra and Nehemiah are all post-exilic. Some of them comprised the second most numerous family to return with Zerubbabel in 537 BC (Ezra 2:1-6; Nehemiah 7:11). By the time of Ezra's return in 468 with more descendants of Pahath-moab accompanying him, some of the first group had taken foreign wives, but responded to Ezra's admonition to dismiss them (Ezra 8:1-4; 10:30).

PA-HSIEN

A heterogenous group of holy Taoists, each of whom earned the right to immortality and had free access to the Peach Festival of Hsi Wang Mu, Queen Mother of the West. Though unacquainted in real life, the eight are frequently depicted as a group - bearing gifts for instance, to Shou Hsing, god of longevity, to safeguard their position as immortals.

PALAMAS, Saint Gregory

(1296-1359) Orthodox monk, theologian, and intellectual leader of Hesychism, a monastic mystical method of prayer. After a civil war in the Byzantine Empire, Palamas was appointed bishop of Thessalonica (1347). In 1368, nine years after his death, he was acclaimed a saint and named "Father and Doctor of the Orthodox Church."

PALESTINE

Name of a territory on the eastern Mediterranean coast, occupied in biblical times by the kingdoms of Israel and Judah. Often called the biblical Holy Land, its name is derived from the Philistines who once lived on its lowland coast. This famous cradle of Judaism and Christianity comprises an area little bigger than the American State of Vermont, located at the eastern end of the Mediterranean Sea, between Egypt and Syria. It is only about 150 miles long from Mount Hermon in the north to the Dead Sea in the south, and 80 miles across at its widest, between the Mediterranean Sea and the Arabian Desert. From west to east it features a coastal plain, a western plateau, the Jordan Valley and the Jordanian plateau. The river-fed lowlands are largely fertile, but much of the uplands are hot rocky desert. Most of Palestine now belongs to Israel, the rest to Jordan, Lebanon and Syria. The Palestinian Authority under chairmanship of Yasser Arafat governs in a semi-independent way the Gaza Strip and the area of Jericho as of 1994.

PALESTINE, Early Church

Despite the fact that Jerusalem was the cradle of Christianity, the site of the first church (49 or 50 AD), and an object of solicitude to the other churches of the Roman world, as is indicated by the collections taken up for its poor (Acts 24:17; Romans 15:26; 1 Corinthians 16:1-2), the church in Palestine never attained the prominence that might have been expected.

This was due to the continued hostility of the Jews, to the twofold destruction of Jerusalem by the Romans (in 70 and 135 AD), and especially to the Gnostic and Judaizing tendencies within the Christian communities themselves that eventually led many of them into heresy.

The daily increase of converts (Acts 2:47) after the descent of the Holy Spirit upon the Apostles soon brought their number to 5,000 men (Acts 4:4) Though these primitive Christians followed most of the customs of the Mosaic Law, their preaching and meeting together for their own services aroused the anger of the Jews and led to the eventual stoning of Stephen (circa 34).

Many of the Christians then fled to the country districts of Judea and Samaria, thus introducing the new faith into those areas. Some 10 years later James the Younger, the first bishop of Jerusalem, suffered a similar fate by order of the Sanhedrin (circa 63).

His successor, Simeon, saved his flock by taking them across the Jordan to Pella before the investing of Jerusalem by the Roman army under Vespasian and Titus. Some of these must have returned to the Holy City after the reestablishment of peace, and some of their descendants may have been able to remain there after the expulsion of the Jews (135) though many migrated to Kokhaba in Transjordania, to Nazareth, and to Beroea (modern Aleppo) in northern Syria.

The Judaeo-Christians of Palestine retained a strong attachment to the relatives of Christ. Their stubborn retention of Jewish customs and attempts to impose these upon converts from paganism, however, and the development of their own literature (notably the Gospel according to the Hebrews, which resembles that of Matthew) separated them from the general run of Christians.

By the mid-2nd century many converts from paganism would not associate with them; and by the end of the century there were some who were obviously heretical in their beliefs and came to be known as Ebionites or Nazarenes. Their rigorisms possibly be traced to the conversion of the Essenes to Christianity after the destruction of Qumran.

Both Eastern and Western monasteries were erected in Palestine in the early fourth century, the latter largely under the initiative of St. Jerome. In the same century the Holy Land became an extremely popular place of pilgrimage; and its liturgy, a description of which has been preserved in the *Peregrinatio ad loca sancta* of Etheria from the end of the fourth century, has a wide influence throughout the church because of the pilgrims who took part of it.

PALESTINE, History

Paleolithic men occupied Palestine 200,000 years ago. Later came Mesolithic cultures, and by 7000 BC waves of Semites began entering Palestine, where the so-called Canaanites built a Bronze Age civilization (300-1500 BC). Soon after 2000 BC Hebrew tribesmen led by Abraham reached Canaan from Mesopotamia. Then came invasion by the Hyksos (around 1900 BC) and counter-invasion by Egypt's Thutmose III (1479 BC).

The Egyptians enslaved many Hebrews (or Israelites) in Egypt, but under Moses' leadership they returned by about 1200 BC to join other Hebrews still in Palestine, and waged successful wars against the Canaanites, as well as the Philistines who had recently settled south-western Palestine from the Aegean area. The need to fight against common enemies caused what was originally a loose confederation of Israelite tribes to form a powerful kingdom in about 1020 BC. The first king, Saul, was succeeded by David, who strengthened Israelite unity, expanded the kingdom and made Jerusalem the national capital. However, heavy taxes and labor conscription imposed by David's son Solomon caused unrest, particularly among the northern tribes. As a result, the monarchy split into two separate kingdoms: Israel in the north, and Judah in the south. (The name Judah - later Judea - gave rise to the term "Jew.")

Both kingdoms began compiling the histories of their ancestors, centering the narrative upon the One God, Yahweh (Jehovah). Early Judaism was further developed and refined by the religious leaders called prophets. But while Judaism was thus taking shape among the Jews, Israel was overrun by Assyrians (721 BC), and Judah by Babylonians (597 BC). Many Jews were deported to Babylonia, to be returned only after Persia's Cyrus the Great had conquered Babylonia in 539 BC. More conquests placed Palestine successively under Alexander the Great (332-323 BC), the Ptolemaeoi of Egypt (323-198 BC), and the Seleucids of Syria (198-168 BC). Then Judas Maccabeus began a national revolt which established the Jewish Hashmonean dynasty (143-37 BC) in Palestine.

Palestine than came under Roman rule (63 BC - AD 395). The period saw the birth of Christianity in Palestine through Jesus' teachings, but also political repression, climaxed by the Roman's destruction of Jerusalem in AD 70 followed by massive Jewish emigration. Control than passed to the Byzantines (395-611, 628-633), Persians (611-628) and Arabs, whose conquest in the 630s began 1,300 years of Muslim rule, first by the Arab Empire, then by the Seljuk Turks, and finally by the Ottoman Empire (1517-1918). The Crusades of the Middle Ages built shaky Christian states in Palestine which soon collapsed.

Jewish immigration to Palestine, mainly from Russia and Rumania, began as early as 1855. Zionism was greatly advanced by the British government's Balfour Declaration, promising the Jews a national home in Palestine. But the British has previously promised the Arabs their own independent state in south-west Asia (1915-1916). The British claim that Palestine was one of the areas excluded from this promise has never been accepted by the Arabs.

After World War I, Palestine was administered by the British under mandate of the League of Nations (1923-1948). The steadily increasing flow of Jewish immigrants, especially after the rise of Nazism in Germany, led to growing Arab discontent. After World War II, with both Arab and Jewish terrorists active, Britain asked the United Nations to find a solution. A special UN commission recommended partition into Jewish and Arab states, with Jerusalem as an international zone. This was accepted by the Jews, but rejected by the Arabs, On May 14, 1948, the day before British mandate was due to end, the Jews proclaimed the state of Israel.

PALI

One of the basic languages in which the Buddhist tradition is preserved. It is the language used in Trevada Buddhism. The oldest type of Buddhist canons are believed to have been written in this language. As this is a kind of Prakrit, a dialect of Sanskrit, there is not a big difference between Pali and Sanskrit.

PALLADIUM

In Greek religion, an image of the goddess Pallas (Athena), especially the archaic wooden image of the goddess that was preserved in the citadel of Troy as a pledge of the safety of the city.

PALLADIUS

(363-431) Monk who took up ascetical life, first at the Mount of Olives, outside Jerusalem, the scene of Christ's passion, then in Egypt in the Nitriaj desert, to avail himself of the advice of the 4th century pioneer monks Macarius and Evagrius Ponticus. Returning to Palestine in 399 because of poor health, he was named bishop of Heleopolis in Bithynia, near modern Istanbul.

PALLU

In the Old Testament, second-named son of Jacob's firstborn Reuben (Genesis 46:9; 1 Chronicles 5:3). Pally founded the family of Pallutes in the tribe of Reuben (Exodus 6:14; Numbers 26:5). His is possibly the same son of Reuben called Peleth at Numbers 16:1.

PALLUITES

In the Old Testament, a Reubenite family descended from Pallu (Numbers 26:5).

PALMS, Blessed

Palm or other branches blessed and distributed to the faithful on Passion (Palm) Sunday, the sixth Sunday of Lent; the blessed palms are carried in procession to commemorate the triumphant entrance of Jesus into Jerusalem (Matthew 21:1-9) shortly before he died.

PALM SUNDAY

The Sunday before Easter and the first day of the Holy Week, commemorating Christ's triumphal entry into Jerusalem riding on an ass, when palm leaves were spread in his path. Palm leaves are blessed and carried in procession.

PALTI

In Judaism, a Benjaminite chieftain selected as one of the twelve spies to preview the land of Canaan in 1512 BC. He was a son of Raphu (Numbers 13:2-9; 29-33).

PALTIEL

In Judaism, representative of Issachar at the time the tribes divided the Promised Land into inheritance portions; son of Azzan (Numbers 34:17-18).

The name is also applied to the son of Galim, who after the outlawing of David, took his daughter Michal, David's wife and gave her in marriage to Palti (Paltiel) (1 Samuel 25:44). After becoming king, David demanded of Abner and Ish-bosheth that Michal be returned to him. This greatly grieved Paltiel, who followed her, weeping until Abner ordered him to go home (2 Samuel 3:13-16).

PALTITE

In biblical times, term used with reference to Helez, one of David's mighty men and generally believed to refer to a native of Beth-pelet (2 Samuel 23:8, 26).

PAMADA

In Buddhism, heedlessness, mental sloth as the opposite of right mindfulness.

PAMPHYLIA

In biblical times, a small Roman province on the southern coast of Asia Minor visited by Paul on his first missionary journey. Though the size of the province may have varied over the years, Pamphylia is commonly viewed as having been a strip along the coastline some 75 miles long and up to 30 miles wide. It was bounded by the provinces of Lycia on the west, Galatia on the north and the Kingdom of Antiochus on the east.

The inhabitants are thought to have been a mixture of a native tribe with Greeks, some even suggesting Pamphylia to mean "of every race." Evidently Jews or proselytes were in the area, for on Pentecost AD 33 persons from Pamphylia were in Jerusalem and were amazed to hear the disciples speaking in their "own language" (Acts 2:6-10).

PAN

A Greek deity who was the son of Cronus or Hermes and the god of pastoral fertility. He is usually represented with the horns, ears and lower quarters of a goat and the head and torso of a man. Pan lived in Arcadia, where he was the god of wood and pastures, the protector of shepherds who could control the fecundity of the flocks. He liked to sport with nymphs and sometimes frightened them with his appearance.

Pan's background is far from clear. He was born in Arcadia, and may have been the son of Cronus (with Rhea) or Hermes. According to one myth, when the Nymph who was his mother gave birth to him and saw what a monster she had brought into the world, she abandoned him. But Hermes found him, wrapped him in the skin of a hare and took him to Olympus. The gods found him appealing, and allowed him to stay with them. He was a particular favorite of Dionysus, who took him travelling.

Pan fell in love with many of the Nymphs but was often rejected - as was the case with Peuce, who turned herself into a pine-tree to elude him. He loved the beautiful Echo, the Nymph of springs and forests, but when she did not return his love he dismembered her. It is said Echo loves Narcissus hopelessly and died of grief leaving only her voice behind. Pan's greatest success in these escapades was with Selene whom he deceived by turning himself into a sheep.

PANATHENAEA

In Greek religion, an annual Athenian festival of great antiquity and importance. The festival consisted solely of the sacrifices and rites proper to the season in the cult of Athena, the city protectress.

PANCARATA CULT

An early Hindu group that worshipped the deified sage Narayana (who came to be identified with Lord Visnu) and that, in merger with the Bhagavatas, formed the earliest sectarian movement within Hinduism. The group was a forerunner of modern Vaisnavism, or the worship of Visnu.

PANCHEN LAMA

Second to the Dalai Lama among the Great Lamas of the Gelupga School of Tibetan Buddhism. His seat is in the Tashilhumpo monastery at Shigatse; hence the common but inaccurate description of him as the Tashi Lama.

On the death of the title holder a new Lama is found in the body of a small child, as in the case of the Dalai Lama, and no lama is recognized as such by the people until examined and approved by a Tibetan commission appointed for this purpose. As the present user of the title has not been so examined he is not yet accepted by the people as the 9th Panchen Lama.

PANDARUS

In Greek legend, son of Lycaon, a Lycian. In the Iliad he broke the truce between the Trojans and the Greeks by treacherously wounding Menelaus, the king of Sparta.

PANDHARPUR

Religious and administrative town (Sholapur district, India), visited throughout the year by thousands of Hindu pilgrims.

PANDORA

In ancient Greek mythology, the first woman on earth. She was made from earth and water by Hephaestus on the orders of Zeus and given a box which the gods told her never to open. Unable to contain her curiosity she opened it and released all the evils that plague mankind. When she closed the lid the only thing that had not escaped was Hope.

PANEGYRIS

In Greek religion, an ancient assembly that met on certain fixed dates for the purpose of honoring a specific god. The meetings included prayers, feasts, and processions.

PAN-ISLAMISM

The ideal of an Islam united under a caliph who could oppose the advance of Christian powers in Muslim lands, propagated by Muslim leaders in the 19th century. It originated mainly as a result of European encroachments on Muslim lands in the 19th century and partly in Islam's realization of its own stagnation.

P'AN KU

Central mythological figure in Chinese Taoist legend of creation. P'an Ku, the first man, is said to have come forth from chaos (an egg) with two horns, two tusks, and a hairy body.

PANTHEISM

Religious or philosophical viewpoint in which God and the universe are identified, stressing God's immanence and denying his transcendence. Religious pantheists see finite beings as part of God; others deify the universe, nature being the supreme principle. Pantheism is found in Hinduism, Stoicism, Idealism and notably in Spinoza's thought; Christian mysticism may tend to it.

In Buddhism, no form of pantheism exists, for it lacks the duality of thought implied in the God-concept and that which the God creates. In Buddhism, the One and All are not different but exist in absolute self-identity.

The American transcendentalists, such as Ralph Waldo Emerson, were pantheistic in outlook, as are many members of the present-day religious revival.

PANTHEON

A temple dedicated to the worship of all the gods. In its modern sense the term has come to mean a building where a nation's heroes are buried or honored.

The most famous pantheon is a remarkably well-preserved ancient temple still standing in Rome. It is a cylindrical building with a perfect hemisphere dome, 142 feet in diameter, that represented a considerable engineering feat in its day and shows the Roman mastery of interior volume and space at its most dramatic. Completed in its present form by the Emperor Hadrian in about 120 AD, the Pantheon was later dedicated as a church and has thus served continuously as a place of worship for nearly 2000 years.

PANTOCREATOR

In Christian art, a representation of Christ as the almighty, combining in one person the Creator and the Savior. The type of Pantocreator is derived from early Christian (about 2nd century - 6th century) representations of Christ as judge, which, in contrast to the youthful early Christian image of Christ, depict him as an older bearded figure.

PAPACY

The papal system; the pope's office or tenure. "Pope" (father) is now normally used of the bishop of Rome as head of Roman Catholicism and "vicar of Christ" on earth. His authority is held to descend from Jesus Christ through the Apostle Peter as first bishop of Rome. The Vatican City still gives the pope status as an independent ruler.

The Pope claims to be the shepherd of all Christians. This claim is not accepted outside the Roman Catholic Church. The entire tradition of papal supremacy seems to rest on a single biblical source, that of Christ's words to St. Peter, "Thou art Peter and upon this rock I will build my Church" (Matthew 16:18-19).

PAPAL BULL

Papal letter containing a weighty pronouncement and bearing a leaden seal (bulla). It may grant a favor, issue a reprimand, or proclaim the canonization of a saint. It is considered more important than an encyclical.

PAPAL STATES

States of the church lands in central Italy held by the popes as temporal rulers (756-1870). Their legendary origin was the grant of Rome "and all the provinces and cities of Italy" to Pope Sylvester I (314-335) by Constantine I, the first Christian emperor.

But the real founder of the Papal States

was the Frankish King Pepin the Short, who defeated the Lombards and gave Pope Stephen II the city of Ravenna and other places (756). Charlemagne and later emperors made gifts. By the early 1200s the Papal States covered some 16,000 square miles and stretched across central Italy from coast to coast.

During the Resorgimento, the papal states were popularly annexed by king Victor Emmanuel II of Sardinia (1860), who became king of a united Italy in 1861. But Rome itself, protected by the French, remained under papal rule until the fall of the French Emperor Napoleon III in 1870.

Refusing to accept the situation, Pope Pius IX and his successors lived as voluntary "prisoners" in the Vatican until 1929, when relations with Italy were restored by the Lateran Treaty, which created the independent Vatican City state.

PAPHOS

In biblical times, a city on the west coast of the island of Cyprus. Here Paul, after working his way across the island with Barnabas and John Mark, encountered the sorcerer Bar-Jesus (Elymas), who opposed their preaching to Sergius Paulus the proconsul. For this he was made temporarily blind by Paul, miraculously. Witnessing this act, Sergius Paulus was converted to Christianity (Acts 13:6-13).

PARABLE

Short narrative by which moral or spiritual relations are set forth. The most famous parables are in the New Testament. In them, Jesus uses the form to illustrate his message to his followers by telling a fictitious story that is nevertheless true-to-life. There are also parables in the Old Testament (2 Samuel 12:1-9, 2 Samuel 14:1-13).

Jesus Christ's parables (such as the sower and the seed, the good Samaritan, the prodigal son) are particularly well known; each illustrates one aspect of his message about God's dealings with human beings.

PARACLETE

A word meaning "Consoler," "Defender," or "Advocate," it is used in the gospel of John to refer either to Christ himself, who fulfilled this role for the disciples, or to the Holy Spirit who continues to fulfill this role in the community of the church (See John 14:16).

PARADISE

Originally the Garden of Eden. Later it became an appellation for a place of rest and refreshment in which the righteous dead enjoy the glorious presence of God.

Throughout many of the prophetic books of the Bible divine promises are found regarding the restoration of Israel from the lands of its exile to its desolated homeland. God would cause that abandoned land to be tilled and sown, to produce richly and to abound with humankind and animalkind; the cities would be rebuilt and inhabited and people would say: "That land yonder which was laid desolate has become like the Garden of Eden" (Ezekiel 36:6-11; Isaiah 51:3; Jeremiah 31:10-12). However, these prophesies also show that paradise conditions related to the people themselves, who, by faithfulness to God, could now "sprout" and flourish as "trees of righteousness," enjoying beautiful spiritual prosperity like a "well-watered garden," showered by bounteous blessing from God due to having this favor (Isaiah 51:11; Jeremiah 31:12;).

These and other parts of the scriptures undoubtedly provide the key for understanding Paul's description of the vision (evidently had by him, since it forms part of his defense of his own apostleship) referred to at 2 Corinthians 12:1-7. Taken away to the "third heaven", the vision viewer entered "paradise" and heard unutterable words. That this paradise visioned could refer to a spiritual state among God's people, as in the case of fleshy Israel, can be seen from the act that the Christian congregation was also God"s "field under cultivation," his spiritual vineyard, rooted in Jesus Christ and bearing fruit to God's praise (1 Corinthians 3:9; John 15:1-8). Paul's vision must logically have applied to some future time, so as to constitute a "revelation" (2 Corinthians 12:1).

PARADOX

Term with specific meaning in Buddhism because truth is regarded as in non-duality, and thus beyond the condition of the opposites. Any statement, therefore, is only partially true, its opposite being also partially true. In Zen teaching it is taught that A is A because A is not-A.

PARAH

In biblical times, a city of Benjamin (Joshua 18:21-23). Parah is usually identified with Khirbet el-Farah, about 5.5 miles north-east of Jerusalem. A nearby spring furnishes water for the Old City of Jerusalem.

PARAMANU

In Buddhism, the smallest conceivable thing.

PARAMARTHA SATYA

In Buddhism, term denoting the absolute as distinct from the relative truth. Several Buddhist schools admit this distinction.

PARAMESVARA

(1347-1424) Founder of Malacca (now Malaysia), which after conversion to Islam became the most powerful and wealthy maritime trade center in 15th century South-east Asia.

PARAMITAS

In Buddhism, term denoting perfection; the six (or ten stages of spiritual perfection followed by the Bodhisattva in his progress to Buddhahood. They consist of the practice and highest possible development of:
1 Dana, charity.
2 Sila, morality.
3 Kshanti, patience.
4 Virya, vigor.
5 Dhyana, meditation.

6 Prajna, wisdom.
The following four are sometimes added:
7 Skilful means of teaching.
8 Power of obstacles.
9 Spiritual aspiration.
10 Knowledge.
These last four, are mostly regarded as amplifications of Prajna, wisdom.
The term is also used in the sense of "to cross over to the other shore" meaning to reach the Buddha Land by means of practicing various Buddhist disciplines. The traditional Japanese Higan weeks in spring and autumn are derived from this Buddhist concept.

PARAVRITTI

In Buddhism, the turning about or sudden revulsion at the deepest seat of consciousness. This is the Buddhist moment of conversion.

PARIKALPITA

In Buddhism, term denoting falsely imagined, referring in particular to the Yogacara teaching to the effect that all phenomena have no reality.

PARILIA

Ancient Roman festival celebrated annually in honor of the god and goddess Pales, the protectors of herds and flocks. The festival, basically a purification rite for herdsmen, beasts, and stalls, was to first celebrated by the early kings of Rome, later by the chief priests.

PARINAMA

In Hindu philosophy, an organic change of a particular object into something else that has the same degree as reality. The stock example is milk turned into curds.

PARINAMANA

In some forms of Buddhism, the transfer of merits from a buddha, or Bodhisattva, to an ancient being.

PARINIRVANA

In Buddhism, the state of Nirvana achieved by one who has completed the incarnation in which he achieved Nirvana and will not be reborn on earth.

PARISH

In Roman Catholicism, according to the Code of Canon Law, "A parish is a definite community of the Christian faithful established on a stable basis within a particular church; the pastoral care of the parish is entrusted to a pastor as its own shepherd under the authority of the diocesan bishop" (Canon 515).

Though a parish is generally territorial, embracing all the faithful within a certain territory, it is also possible that other types of parishes be established "based upon time, language, the nationality of the Christian faithful within some territory or even upon some other determining factor" (Canon 518).

PARIS PSALTER

10th century illuminated manuscript from Constantinople that is one of the finest examples of miniature painting produced during the second Golden Age of Byzantine art.

PARIVARTA

In Buddhism, the "turning over" of merit acquired by good deeds of an individual to the benefit of another being, or of all beings.

PARMENAS

According to biblical tradition, one of the seven recommended to the Apostles and appointed by them to ensure a just daily distribution of food supplies in the Jerusalem congregation after Pentecost of 33 (Acts 6:1-6).

PARNACH

In Judaism, a Zebulunite whose son Elizaphan was the tribal representative in dividing the Promised Land (Numbers 34:17-25).

PARNASSUS, Mount

Mountain in Greece, in ancient times a sacred mountain. Situated in Phocis, north of Delphi, Mount Parnassus rises 8,061 feet. It was sacred to Dionysus and Apollo, and was the dwelling place of the Muses.

PAROCHIAL EDUCATION

Education offered institutionally, by a religious group; especially, in the United States, education in elementary and secondary schools that are maintained by Roman Catholic parishes.

PAROCHIAL SCHOOLS

In the United States, refers to elementary and secondary educational institutions operated by a religious body. The Roman Catholic Church operates the great majority of such institutions, followed by the Lutheran system, the Jewish day schools and a small number of small systems operated by various Protestant groups. Most of these parochial systems were established in the 19th century and continued to grow and provide facilities for increasing numbers of students.

PAROSH

In Judaism, founder of a family in Israel. There were 2,172 of his descendants who returned to Jerusalem with Zerubbabel in 537 BC (Ezra 2:1-3; Nehemiah 7:8). By the time that Ezra arrived in 468 BC with 150 "sons of Parosh" led by Zechariah, some of their family already in Jerusalem had taken foreign wives, whom they later sent away (Ezra 8:1-1;). Pedaiah, one of the family, repaired a section of Jerusalem's wall (Nehemiah 3:25). The head of the Parosh family attested to the later covenant agreeing to keep the law of God (Nehemiah 9:38; 10:1).

PAROUSIA

The Second Coming of Christ to earth (See 1 Corinthians 15:23), when his triumph over evil will be complete and his kingdom definitively established.

PARSEES

Religious group centered in Bombay and the north-western part of India, who practice Zoroastrianism. Their ancestors came from Persia in the 8th century to escape Muslim persecution. They now number about 125,000. The parsees, many of whom are traders, are among the wealthiest and best educated groups in india. They worship at fire temples.

PARTHENON

The best known of all Greek temples, dominating the Acropolis at Athens and dedicated to the city's patron goddess, Athena Parthenos (Athena the Maiden). The Parthenon was built between 447 and 438 BC and its decoration and sculptures, supervised by Pheidias, took several more years to complete. This Doric temple is generally considered the greatest achievement of classical architecture, not only for its carefully calculated proportions and sense of repose, but also for the sculptures and friezes that once decorated the building. The best preserved of these are the "Elgin Marbles," now in the British Museum.

The Parthenon was converted into a Christian church and later into a Turkish mosque, but it remained in a remarkable state of preservation until 1687, when a Venetian general attacking Athens bombarded the Acropolis and set off a powder magazine in the Parthenon, completely wrecking the roof and interior.

PARTHIANS

In biblical times, inhabitants of Parthia. Jews and proselytes from Parthia are listed first among those visitors attending the festival of Pentecost in AD 33. God's holy spirit poured out on the group of about 120 Christian disciples enabled them to proclaim the good news in the language or dialect of those Parthians, some of whom doubtless responded favorably, became Christians, and likely spread the message among their own people upon returning to Parthia (Acts 1:15; 2:1-14). The natural Jews from Parthia were part of the dispersion; the "proselytes" (Acts 2:10) were non-Jews who had become converts to Judaism.

ARTICULAR CHURCH

A term used to describe the local church, which is the diocese or a community of Christian faithful under the guidance of their bishop ordained in apostolic succession.

PARUAH

In Judaism, father of the Jehoshaphat who served as Solomon's food deputy in the territory of Issachar (1 Kings 4:7).

PARYUSANA

A popular eight-day festival in Jainism, a religion in India. Paryusana closes the Jaina year. Jainas make confessions to the meetinghouse so that no quarrel is carried over into the new year, and many lay members temporarily live the lives of monks, an observance called posadha.

PASACH

In Judaism, family head in the tribe of Asher; son of Paphlet (1 Chronicles 7:30-40).

PASCHAL

A phrase referring to the passion, death, and resurrection of Jesus Christ, the Lamb of God, by which he brought about salvation for all humankind; also, our way of participating in the dying and rising up of Jesus (See 2 Corinthians 4:10-12).

PASCHAL I, Saint

(756-824) Pope from 817 to 824, whose pontificate was continually embroiled in the problem of relating the papacy to the recently founded Frankish Empire under Charlemagne's son and successor, Louis I the Pious, who forcibly imposed on the church an unprecedented reform and reorganization of monasteries and dioceses while concurrently arranging the empire and trying to reconcile the safeguarding of Christian order and unity.

PASCHAL II

(1039-1118) Pope from 1099 to 1118. Although he fostered the crusade cause and followed his predecessor's great policies of church reform, his pontificate was dominated by the Investiture Controversy - the long conflict between popes and secular rulers over whose authority was supreme in the church regarding the right of investiture for major church offices.

PASCHAL III

(1101-1168) Guido of Crema; Antipope from 1164 to 1168, one of the original supporters of Antipope Victor IV, whom he succeeded in 1164, becoming the second antipope set up by the Holy Roman emperor Frederick I Barbarossa.

PASCHAL CANDLE

Easter candle, marked with a cross, Alpha and Omega, and the numerals of the current year, which stands as a symbol of Christ rising from the dead. The paschal candle is lit at the opening of the Easter Vigil.

PASCHAL CONTROVERSIES

In the Christian church, disputes concerning the correct date for observing Easter (Greek: pascha). The earliest controversy was over the question of whether Easter should always be celebrated on a Sunday or on the actual day of the Jewish lunar month (14th of Nisan), when the Resurrection took place.
Later controversies concerned the different methods of calculating the paschal moon, until in the 6th century the computations of Dionysius Exiguus were generally accepted in the West.

PASCHAL LAMB

In Judaism, the lamb sacrificed at the first Passover on the eve of the exodus out of Egypt, the most momentous event in Jewish history.

PASCHAL PRECEPT

Church law which requires the reception of the Eucharist during the Easter season, also called the Easter duty.

PASCHASIUS RADBERTUS, Saint

(785-860) Theologian, and major author of important works on the Eucharist. For Paschasius, the bread and wine on the altar become, after consecration, Christ's true flesh and blood. Others regarded these phenomena are symbolical of Christ's blood and body.

PASEAH

According to biblical tradition, a descendant of Judah in the line of "Chelub the brother of Shulah" (1 Chronicles 4:1-12). The name is also applied to a forefather of a family of Nethinim, some of whom returned from the Babylonian exile with Zerubbabel in 539 BC (Ezra 2:1-2, 43).

PASHHUR

In biblical times, a prince in the delegation of Zedekiah sent to inquire of Jeremiah concerning the future of Jerusalem (Jeremiah 21:1-2). Pashhur also petitioned the king for permission to put Jeremiah in the cistern (Jeremiah 38:1-6).
The "sons of Pashhur" were a paternal house of priests, 1,247 of whom returned from exile with priest Jeshua in 537 BC (Ezra 2:1-2; 36-38); Nehemiah 7:41). Six of these married foreign wives but sent them away after Ezra arrived in 468 BC (Ezra 10:22-24).

PASSION

Musical setting of the gospel texts describing the crucifixion. From early plain songs developed medieval music-drama and Renaissance music forms. Among the first works were those of Scheutz, who influenced J.S. Bach, composer of the famous St. John and St. Matthew passions for soloists, choirs and orchestra.

PASSION

The sufferings which Jesus Christ underwent in order to redeem mankind.

The Passion applied especially to his last days on earth, the agony in the garden of Gethsemane, the betrayal, arrest and trial, the crucifixion and death. Christ's Passion is commemorated by the Christian church every year in great solemnity. Passiontide, the last two weeks of Lent, begins on the fifth Sunday in Lent, Passion Sunday, and extends to the day before Easter, Holy Saturday.

Actually, the term passion has several religious and philosophical meanings.

1 In material logic it is one of Aristotle's ten categories of real being; it is the condition of being acted upon or of being affected by an external agent; hence the correlatives action-passion.

2 In psychological philosophy it means the feeling induced by being acted upon.

3 It is sometimes used in a broad sense to include spiritual and intentional reception of activity; thus the mind is affected by what it knows, the will by what it desires.

4 It its most proper sense it is synonymous with emotion and implies the causal production of an effect in the sensitive appetite of an animal, human or otherwise. By common usage, passion in this sense refers especially to strong emotions of desire or anger.

5 The psychosomatic alteration implied in the preceding sense may spell either gain or loss: gain, as in pleasure after hope deferred; loss, when it means suffering or undergoing an evil. This is passion in its most pointed sense; it is used of the endurance of martyrdom, and above all of martyrdom's chief exemplar, the Passion of Christ.

PASSION, Bible

A cursory glance at the general outline of the four gospels discloses that the Passion narrative unquestionably constitutes their most important part. In Mark the Passion accounts for almost a third of the text. It is, moreover, noteworthy that the four Gospels agree more closely in the sequence of events of the Passion story than they do in any other portion of their contents.

This indicates that the Evangelists are depending on a fixed form of telling the story of the last days that was already a tradition in the preaching of the primitive church.

The fact of Christ's Passion is of such fundamental significance for the church's faith and preaching that the whole story of how the event of the Crucifixion took place was recounted - it was not enough to proclaim it as the object of that faith and confession.

The reason for this attention to the Passion is, first of all, because together with the Resurrection the Passion is the central theme of the apostolic kerygma. The Gospel narratives are theologically structured to show that, contrary to contemporary Jewish expectations, Christ's death for man's sins is "in accordance with the Scriptures" (1 Corinthians 15:3-5).

Second, the Passion narrative holds a privileged place in Christian worship. Traces of it are found in the hymns of Philippians (Philippians 2:6-11); 1 Timothy 3:16; 1 Peter 1:18-21, and in the heavenly liturgy of Revelation 5:6-14, while explicit references to the Passion are made in the rites of eucharist and baptism.

Thus, the Passion narrative presents Jesus' self-sacrifice in the apostolic writings (e.g., Romans 8:17; 2 Corinthians 1:5, Philippians 3:10; 1 Peter 4:13).

PASSION IN DEVOTION

While always a part of the Christian experience, the remembrance of the Passion has been marked by different emphases throughout history. Some emphases have been legitimate developments, while others have shown signs of distorting the paschal mystery. Already in Scriptures, the characteristics of a Passion devotion are present, even if not dominant. The amplitude of the Passion narratives is witness to the reverent reflection of the first Christians on this mystery. Giving a glimpse into his own heart, Paul marvels at him "who loved me and who sacrificed himself for my sake"

(Galatians 5:24), carrying his cross (Luke 9:23), suffering with him (Romans 8:17).

The reality of this discipleship unto blood finds poignant expression in the plea of Ignatius of Antioch to the Romans while looking forward to his martyrdom: "Permit me to follow the example of the Passion of my God" (Romans 6:3).

The great Fathers of the Church exhibit a genuine personal devotion to Christ in the mystery of his sufferings in their sometimes surprisingly render sermons on the Passion. But it is in the 12th century that the writings of St. Bernard turned hearts toward the mysteries of the earthly life of Jesus, especially those of his birth and Passion.

The popular preachers of the mendicant orders expanded the trend. The reticence of the Gospels was supplemented with imaginative and dramatic embellishments culled from, apocryphal gospels and personal fancy.

Emotional elements were very prominent but at their best were so channeled that a genuine experience of faith was nurtured by the experience of felt compassion. This pre-reformation era gave rise to the cult of the wounds of the Savior, the pierced heart, and the precious blood of Jesus. The devotion of the Way of the Cross became popular.

There were also aberrations. Liturgical life was at a low ebb, and devotional experience tended to become divorced from sound theology, especially Christology. He who made himself loving sacrifice for out sin would become in popular thought, preaching, and ultimately in a new theology their scapegoat, the object of God's wrath accepting alienation from God in the place of sinners.

A compassion for the sufferings of the Savior risked blocking out his glorious victory, abetting a pessimistic view, and even opening the way to enthusiastic excesses like those of the Flagellants.

A devout awareness of the Passion of Christ is essential if the integral paschal mystery is to be lived in a renewed church pledged to walk the road Christ walked: "a road of poverty and obedience, of service and self-sacrifice to the death, from which death He came forth a victor in his Resurrection" (Vatican Council II statement).

PASSION IN THEOLOGY

The fact of the Passion confronts the believer with the full mystery of the Incarnation. This man, who is in his person the consubstantial Son of the Father, is fully a man like other men. The Passion narrative catalogs the reality of his bodily suffering: he sweated blood, was scourged, crowned with thorns, and crucified; he experienced torturing thirst, and gasped a last breath in death.

Even more significantly, he experienced the psychological tortures of anguish, revulsion, and dread in anticipation of his death, sorrow over the disloyalty of his friends, sadness at the rejection of his people, and instinctive conflict with the severe demands of his Father's will.

Theology has wrestled with the mystery of the psychology of the suffering God-man from the beginning. An earlier theology attributed a perfection of human knowledge to Christ that made the full reality of this suffering struggle hard to account.

Contemporary theology tends rather to limit the impact of Christ's divine being on his human mode of knowing and acting in a way that accounts better for his being "tempted in every way that we are, though he is without sin (Hebrews 4:15).

PASSION PLAY

Usually a dramatic presentation of the Crucifixion of Christ and the events leading up to it. The Passion Play of the death of the god Osiris was also an important ritual in ancient Egyptian religion. Passion plays often formed part of the Mystery Play cycles of the Middle Ages. The most famous extant passion play is that presented every 10 years at Oberhammergau, southern

Germany, in thanksgiving for the deliverance of the town from plague in 1633.

PASSIONS

Feelings, emotions, or movements of the sensitive appetite that dispose a person to act or not to act in regard to something believed to be good or evil. According to this definition, there are eleven passions:

- ▲ love,
- ▲ hate,
- ▲ desire,
- ▲ aversion,
- ▲ joy,
- ▲ sadness,
- ▲ hope,
- ▲ despair,
- ▲ courage,
- ▲ fear,
- ▲ anger.

PASSOVER

Ancient major Jewish festival celebrating the Israelites' escape from Egyptian slavery. At that time each family slew a paschal lamb and sprinkled its blood on the doorposts, and the destroying angel passed over (Exodus 12). During Passover unleavened bread (matzah) is eaten; no leaven at all may be used, a reminder of the hasty departure. Jesus gave a new meaning to the Passover, known as the Lord's Supper.

Preparing for the holiday begins in every home many days before Passover. Everything in the house is scrubbed and polished. Carpets are cleaned, floors are scrubbed, fresh curtains are hung. Just before Passover, all-year-round kitchen utensils are put away, to be replaced by those specially reserved for Passover.

Then comes the matzah - enough to last through Passover. Matzah are the only kind of bread permitted in a Jewish home on Passover. The Bible does not tell exactly how matzah are prepared, but the Talmud gives details as to the ingredients used (wheat flour and water), the proper thickness of the cakes, and other information.

PASTOR

A title, from the Latin word meaning "shepherd," applied in general to Christian clergymen serving a local church or parish.

PASTOR AETERNUS

A papal decree issued July 1870, that outlines the conditions for a formal statement on faith or morals to qualify as an infallible pronouncement.

PASTORAL COUNSELING

Personalized advice given to individuals for their general spiritual development or to solve spiritual problems.

PASTORAL LETTERS

Those writings of the New Testament that are principally concerned with the responsibilities of church leaders and church discipline, namely:

- ▲ the First Letter of Paul to Timothy;
- ▲ the Second Letter of Paul to Timothy;
- ▲ the Letter of Paul to Titus.

PASTORAL LITERATURE

That which presents the society of shepherds as one freed from the complexity and corruption of city live.

PATARA

In biblical times, the Lycian seaport where the apostle Paul and his associates, likely in 56 transferred to a boat sailing for Phoenicia (Acts 21:1-2). Patara is today represented by ancient ruins at the village of Gelemish on the mountainous south-western coast of Asia Minor and lies several miles east of the mouth of the Xanthos River.

At Acts 21:1 certain ancient manuscripts add "and Myra" after Patara. If this addition is correct, then the ship on which Paul sailed from Miletus either passed Patara or put into port there, with the actual transfer to another boat taking place at Myra, not Patara.

PATHRUSIM

In the Old Testament, person listed fifth among the offspring of Mizraim, the son of Ham (Genesis 10:6, 13; 1 Chronicles 1:11-12). The name is apparently the plural form of Pathros (Ezekiel 29:14). This would indicate that the tribe of Pathrusim settled or became dominant in Upper Egypt.

PATIMOKKHA

The 227 disciplinary rules binding on the Bhikkhu and recited on Upsatha days for purposes of confession.

PATMOS

In biblical times, an island where the Apostle John was exiled "for speaking about God and bearing witness to Jesus" (Revelation 1:9). While there, he received the Revelation. According to ancient tradition, John, having been condemned to dwell on the island of Patmos in the 15th year of Domitian's reign (circa 95), was released after the death of the ruler.

PATRIARCH

The title used chiefly in the Old Testament to describe the father, husband or most venerable male of a family or tribe - in particular the founders of the Hebrew nation, Abraham, Isaac and Jacob. Early Christians used the title for major church leaders, and it was later given to the bishops of eminent sees, especially in the Eastern Orthodox Church. From about the 6th century, the bishops of Rome, Antioch, Jerusalem and Alexandria became known as patriarchs. The Roman pontiff was understood to be the first patriarch, but this title was absorbed in his higher rank as head of the entire church.

The patriarch is the father and head of his church or rite, with ordinary powers over metropolitans, bishops, clergy, religious, and faithful. However, he is only the first among otherwise equal bishops.

The authority of a Catholic is greater than that of an Orthodox patriarch, despite the fact that the Orthodox patriarch as such is independent of any higher ecclesiastical authority. The law covering the Catholic Eastern patriarchies is laid down in writings of the Vatican Council II.

Although he is head of his church, the patriarch can exercise his authority only together with his hierarchy. Affairs of lesser importance he resolves alone - e.g., dispensations and encyclical letters. For more important matters the advice and consent of the permanent synod is needed - e.g., they dispense the entire patriarchate, establish exarchies, etc. The election of bishops, the establishment of dioceses and the transfer of bishops, etc. are reserved to the patriarchal synod under the presidency of the patriarch, although in all these matters the initiative is in his hands.

The patriarch is elected by a synod composed of all the bishops of the patriarchate. Confirmation of a secular ruler may be needed in Orthodox churches, Catholic patriarchs can be enthroned at once and then only request ecclesiastical communion with the pope.

Catholic Patriarchal Titles

The pope, as bishop of Rome is patriarch of the West. The patriarch of Alexandria is known as the patriarch of the Copts. Antioch has Byzantine (Melchite), Maronite, and Syrian patriarchs; the Melchite patriarch of Antioch has also the personal title of patriarch of Alexandria and Jerusalem. At Baghdad there is the Chaldean patriarch of Babylon; in Lebanon there is the Armenian patriarch of Cilicia.

Orthodox Patriarchal Titles

The archbishop of Constantinople is the Byzantine and ecumenical patriarch (i.e., of the entire Byzantine empire) and the first prelate of the Eastern Orthodox Churches. There is also an Armenian patriarchate of Constantinople. At Alexandria there is a Byzantine pope and patriarch, and a Coptic patriarch. Antioch has Byzantine and Syrian patriarchs; Jerusalem, Byzantine and Armenian.

The patriarchal title is also accorded to the heads of the following churches:
▲ Bulgarian (1245, reestablished 1953);
▲ Serbian (1346, reestablished 1920);
▲ Russian (patriarch of Moscow and all Russia, 1589);
▲ Rumanian (1925).

PATRIARCHS, Biblical

The title is applied to the great figures of Israel's history, but is more generally restricted to the three, Abraham, Isaac, and Jacob whose stories are related in Genesis 12-50. The substance of these accounts is the migration of Abraham from Mesopotamia to Canaan, his wandering in the hill country, the birth and marriage of Isaac, the birth and marriages of Jacob, his 12 sons, the taking of Joseph to Egypt and the later descent of the whole family to that land.

As they now stand, the stories of the patriarchs serve as an introduction to the story of Israel. They have undergone some theological transformation to that end. The covenantal observations and particularly the promises of a great prosperity and of future possession of the land are the principal areas of this transformation by the three traditions (Yahwist, Elohist, and Priestly) responsible for the material.

Varying cultic and moral emphases can also be attributed to these traditions. For the most part, however, the authors respected their sources and presented them as they found them. But before they adopted them, the stories had already experienced a long period (some 800 years or more) of oral transmission, during which elaboration took place. This is not history in the modern sense of the word.

Nevertheless, archeology and other sciences have shown that the patriarchal narratives are an authentic reflection of the period attributed to them, the first half of the second millennium, BC.

Originally independent stories about individuals, peoples, and holy places, they were gradually developed as cycles of stories centering on an individual patriarch and preserved at various sanctuaries. These were then taken over by the later Israelites when they conquered the land and were affixed to their history of salvation.

Because of the elaboration and adaptation, it is impossible to answer specific questions about the historical character of particular events and persons. But the evidence would justify the theological use made of the stories of Israel.

The exodus from Egypt has definite historical antecedents in the movements of the patriarchs in Canaan some 400 years earlier. Israel's faith saw these as under the direction of the same God that brought it out of the land of Egypt.

PATRIARCHY

A hypothetical social system based on the absolute authority of the father or an elderly male over the family group.

PATRICK, Saint

(Circa 385-461) Missionary bishop who evangelized Ireland and later became its patron saint. It is difficult to separate the facts from the legend concerning St. Patrick. Born a Roman citizen and member of a Christian family, he was carried off by pagan Irish raiders from his home on Britain's west coast. After six years of slavery he escaped, but was later called in a dream, to evangelize Ireland. He trained for the priesthood in France and returned to Ireland, tradition says, in 432. He was by no means the first Irish Christian missionary, but he was the first to make any impact, especially in the north, center and west. He made his first major group of converts at Tara, the seat of the high kings, after he defied the pagan priests by kindling the easter fire on a hilltop. His *Confession* tells of the struggles with colleagues and his preaching successes. By 444 he had not only built up a large organization with an archiepiscopal seat at Armagh, but he had also Christianized most Ireland. He was among the most successful Christian missionaries in all church history. His feast day, celebrated by Irishman everywhere, is March 17.

PATRISTIC LITERATURE

The writings of the Fathers (bishops and teachers) of the early Christian church from the late 1st to the early 8th century. Both orthodox and heretical writings are included because some

Christian writers were of questionable orthodoxy, others deliberately left the church, and the orthodox Fathers cannot be properly understood in isolation from their heterodox contemporaries.

PATROBAS

In the New Testament, a Christian of the congregation in Rome whom Paul greets in his letter (Romans 16:14).

PATROLOGY

The scientific study of the writings of the Fathers of the church; also called patristics.

PATRON SAINT

A saint whose projection and intercession for a person, a society, a church, or a place is dedicated. The choice is often based on the basis of some real or presumed relationship with the persons of places involved,

PAUL

Original name Saul of Tarsus born in Cilicia (now in Turkey). Being a 1st century Jew, he had been a bitter enemy of the Christian church, but later he became its leading missionary. Paul paid his last visit to Corinth and then went to Jerusalem, where he was arrested. After being imprisoned at Caesarea for two years, he appealed to the emperor. He arrived in Rome and was kept in custody awaiting trial, during which time he wrote several letters. He probably died by decapitation in 68.

Missionary journeys

After the Apostles has been persuaded by Barnabas of the authenticity of his conversion he began to preach and was generally accepted by the early Christians. He then went into seclusion for circa 13 years to deepen his faith before embarking on his remarkable missionary career. His first missionary tour was to Cyprus and Asia Minor. On his return, he joined in the debate over the condition on which Gentiles and Jews respectively were admitted to the church and resolved to direct his efforts to the gentiles. His secondary missionary expedition took him again to Asia

Minor and on to Greece, where he was especially successful. His third, equally far-ranging journey brought him full circle to Jerusalem where he clashed with the fanatical Jewish religious hierarchy and was subsequently imprisoned for two years as a troublemaker. Having invoked his right as a Roman citizen to appeal to the emperor, he was sent to Rome, probably 62. After two years' house-arrest he was executed.

Writings

The ancient church recognized 13 of the New Testament epistles (letters) as having been written by Paul. Galatians, Romans and Corinthians (1 and 2) certainly were; the rest are the subject today of dispute among scholars. During his lifetime Paul became the dominating figure of the apostolic age of the Christian church. Since his death his writings have had an incalculable influence on Christian belief and practice, and he remains a major fountainhead of Christian doctrine, particularly since the Reformation.

PAUL I, Saint

(698-767) Pope from 757 to 767. He vigorously protested Constantine's revival of iconoclastic (destruction of images) persecution. The ensuing iconoclastic persecution caused an expulsion of many Greek monks, for whom Paul provided refuge in Rome. His feast day is June 28th.

PAUL II

(1417-1471) Pope from 1464 to 1471. Seeing the advancing Turks as a major threat to Christendom, Paul in 1468 began fruitless negotiations with the Holy Roman Emperor Frederick III to mount a crusade against them. He is responsible for founding the first printing presses at Rome, where he had built the celebrated Palace of St. Mark, his principal residence from 1466.

PAUL III

(1468-1549) Pope from 1534 to 1549. His personal laxity prior to his ordination caused great criticism and he was accused of using his position to advance his family, the Farnese. However, he became a major reformer who established the order of Jesuits, revived the Inquisition in 1542 and convoked the Council of Trent in 1545. He also excommunicated Henry VIII, following the split that resulted in the formation of the Church of England. Yet he was also a humanist scholar and patron of Michelangelo.

PAUL IV

(1476-1559) Pope from 1555. he increased the powers of the Roman inquisition, enforced segregation of the Jews in Rome and introduced strict censorship. His fanatical reformism proved self-defeating by creating widespread hostility.

PAUL V

(1552-1621) Pope from 1605, he was one of the Borghese family. He was uncompromising in dogma and doctrine, but progressive in encouraging missions and public works.

PAUL VI

(1897-1978) Pope elected in 1963, he continued the modernizing reforms of his predecessor. John XXIII, confirmed the Roman Catholic Church's ban on contraception and became the first pope to travel widely.

PAUL, Acts of

An apocryphal (noncanonical and unauthentic) Christian writing of the late 2nd century that purported to be an account of the apostle Paul's travels and teachings. It was composed of a presbyter of a church in Asia Minor who, though claiming to have written "out of love for Paul," was deposed from his church for sanctioning the right of women to teach and baptize.

PAUL AND THECLA, Acts of

An apocryphal (noncanonical) writing that was popular in the early Christian church; it described Paul the apostle's activities in Asia Minor and his alleged encounter with a lion he had previously baptized.

PAULICIANS

A dualist Christian sect that originated in Armenia in the mid-7th century. It combined the dualism of Marcionism, a heretical movement in early Christianity, and of Manichaeism, a Gnostic religion founded in the 3rd century by the Persian prophet Mani. The identity of Paul, after whom the Paulicians are called, is disputed.

PAULINE LETTERS

New Testament writings traditionally attributed to the apostle Paul. Some are now known to have been written by someone else.

PAULINUS, Saint

(584-644) Missionary who converted Northumbria to Christianity; he became the first bishop of York and was later made archbishop of Rochester.

PAULINUS OF NOLA, Saint

(353-431) Bishop of Nola and one of the most important Christian Latin poets of his time. Some 50 of his extant letters correspond with famous contemporaries, including Augustine and Jerome.

PAULIST FATHERS

Officially the Society of Missionary Priests of St. Paul the apostle, an evangelical order of Roman Catholic priests in the United States, founded by Isaac Hecker (1858).

PAUL OF SAMOSATA

(212-298) Christian philosopher-theologian and bishop of Antioch, whose condemnation of a heretic for rejecting Christ's absolute divinity became a prototype of doctrinal controversies in the church for three centuries.

PAUL OF THEBES, Saint

(230-341) Traditionally regarded as the first Christian hermit. He lived a life of prayer and penitence in a cave, dying at the reputed age of 111. Jerome considered Paul to be the first Christian hermit, an honor in modern times generally accorded to St. Anthony of Egypt.

PAUL OF THE CROSS, Saint

(1694-1775) Italian mystic who founded the Passionist order of monks in 1720, and an order of the same name for nuns in 1770.

PEACE

A term among Catholic Christians in several senses, among them:

▲ right relationship between God and human beings, a fruit of fidelity to the covenant, a result of reconciliation;

▲ right relationship between and among individuals and communities. Christ is the Prince of Peace (See Isaiah 9:5) and came to bring peace (Luke 2:14) and reconciliation (see Ephesians 2:14-17).

True peace can be achieved only by extending the reign of Christ to all human relationships.

PEACE, Sign of

The sign of peace used at Mass today to symbolize renewal in Christ was originally a kiss. The form of this gesture in the Mass is left to the local episcopal conferences.

PEACE OF GOD AND TRUCE OF GOD

Agreements as the basis for the Christian peace movement that arose in the late 10th century in medieval Europe, designed to abolish violence and private warfare and to guarantee protection to pilgrims and travelers.

PECTORAL CROSS

A cross, sometimes made of precious metal and adorned with jewels, that is worn on a chain or silken cord by abbots, bishops, cardinals, and the pope.

PEDAHEL

In Judaism, a chieftain of Naphthali and, according to biblical tradition, appointed by God to help divide the Promised Land among the tribes; son of Ammihud (Numbers 34:16-17).

PEDAHZUR

In Judaism, a man in the tribe of Manasseh whose son Gamaliel was appointed chieftain of their tribe after the Exodus (Numbers 1:10-16; 10:23).

PEDAIAH

Name applied to several persons in biblical times. Pedaiah was the father of Joel; during David's reign he was prince of the half of the tribe of Manasseh, dwelling west of the Jordan (1 Chronicles 27:20-22).

Pedaiah was also the name of the third-named son of King Jekoiachin (Jeconiah) born during the Babylonian exile. Pedaiah became father to post-exilic Governor Zerubbabel and was therefore a vital link in the line leading to Jesus (1 Chronicles 3:17-19). Because of some unrecorded circumstances, Zerubbabel is also called the "son" of Pedaiah's brother Shealtiel. Shealtiel may have adopted Zerubbabel if Pedaiah died when the boy was young; or, if Shealtiel died before fathering a son. Pedaiah may have performed brother-in-law marriage, fathering Zerubbabel in the name of his brother Shealtiel (Ezra 5:2; Matthew 1:12).

PEKAH

In biblical times, king of Israel for a 20-year period (778-758 BC), contemporaneous with Judean kings Azariah (Uzziah), Jotham and Ahaz. Earlier Pekah had served as adjutant to Israelite King Pekehiah. But in the 52nd year of Uzziah's reign, Pekah the son of Remaliah, with the cooperation of 50 men of Gilead, assassinated Pekahiah and seized the kingship over Israel in Samaria (2 Kings 15:25-27). During Pekah's reign idolatrous calf worship continued (2 Kings 15:28). This ruler also formed an alliance with Rezin the king of Syria. Toward the close of Judean King Jotham's reign (which began in the second year of Pekah) both Pekah and Rezin caused trouble for Judah (1 Kings 15:32-38).

PEKAHIAH

In biblical times, king of Israel in Samaria, son and successor of Menahem. His brief reign of two years (circa 780-778 BC) was marked by the same idolatrous calf worship introduced by Jeroboam and permitted to Menachem. Pekahiah's adjutant, Pekah, conspired against him, killed him and began to reign in his place (2 Kings 15:22-26).

PEKOD

In biblical times, apparently the name of an area in the vicinity of Babylon. According to biblical tradition, men of Pekod were to be included in the military forces to execute God's judgment on unfaithful Jerusalem (Ezekiel 23:4, 22-26). Later, Pekod itself was to be devoted to destruction (Jeremiah 50:21).

PELAGIA OF ANTIOCH, Saint

(296-311) 15-year old Christian virgin who, probably during the persecution of Christians by the Roman Emperor Diocletian, threw herself from a housetop to save her chastity and died instantly. Her feast day is June 9.

PELAGIANISM

Christian heresy based on the teachings of the British theologian Pelagius (circa 353 - circa 425); an ascetic movement chiefly of aristocratic laity. Pelagius held that men are not naturally sinful and have free will to take the first steps to salvation of their own efforts. This challenged the basic Christian doctrines relating to grace, original sin and Christ's atonement. Pelagianism was opposed by St. Augustine and condemned by the Council of Ephesus in 441. A middle position, semi-pelagianism, was dominant in Gaul until condemned by the Council of Orange (529).

PELAGIUS I

(496-561) Pope from 556 to 561. During his pontificate, his major aim was church unification, and his power was set by the imperial government. In addition to his ecclesiastical labors, he was faced with the problem of alleviating the drastic aftermath of the Gothic invasions and wars.

PELAGIUS II

(529-590) Pope from 579 to 590. His pontificate was continuously troubled by the Lombards, a Germanic people living in northern Italy, who were besieging Rome. The Lombard problem was crucial because it threatened not only Rome but also the Italian peoples, for whom the papacy was responsible as a result of temporal power granted the papacy in 554 by the Byzantine Emperor Justinian I.

PELAIAH

In Judaism, a Levite who assisted Ezra in reading and explaining the law to the Israelites assembled in Jerusalem's public square. He is probably the same Levite
(unless a representative of the family that is meant) who attested to the covenant of faithfulness put forward shortly thereafter (Nehemiah 8:1-8; 10:1-10).

PELATIAH

In biblical times name for several persons. Pelatiah is one of four Simeonite chieftains who led 500 men against Mount Seit and struck down the remnant of the Emalekites, likely under Hezekiah's reign (1 Chronicles 4:41-43).

The name is also applied to the son of Benaiah; a prince of Israel whom Ezekiel saw in vision. Pelaiah, along with Jaazaniah, was "scheming hurtfulness and advising bad counsel" against Jerusalem. Ezekiel was inspired to utter a prophecy against the people of Israel, after which Pelatiah died (Ezekiel 11:1-13).

The name of Pelatiah is also applied to a family head represented in the signatures to the covenant promising not to take foreign wives (Nehemiah 9:38).

PELEG

In Judaism, a son of Eber and father of Reu in the line from Shem to Abraham, and therefore an early ancestor of Jesus. Peleg founded one of the post-Flood families (Genesis 11:16-19).

PELET

According to biblical tradition, a son of Jahdai listed in the Calebite division of Judah's genealogy (1 Chronicles 2:47). The name is also applied to one of the ambidextrous Benjaminite mighty men who joined David at Ziklag; son of Azmaveth (1 Chronicles 12:1-3).

PELETH

According to biblical tradition, a Reubenite whose son On joined Dathan, Abiram and Korah in their rebellion (Numbers 16:1).

The name is also applied to a descendant of Judah through Jerahmeel (1 Chronicles 2:33).

PELETHITES

In biblical times, loyal fighters for King David, always mentioned with the Cherethites. When David fled from Jerusalem because of Absalom's rebellion (which a major portion of the army supported), the Pelethites went along with David across the Kidron (2 Samuel 15:18-23). They also helped put down the rebellion of Sheba (2 Samuel 20:7), and later supported David's choice of Solomon as his successor, rather than siding with Adonijah as Joab did (1 Kings 1:38, 44).

The Cherethites and Pelethites were not part of the regular army. but were a separate division in the service of King David, for Joab is called the head of the army, but, separately, Benaiah was over the Cherethites and Pelethites (2 Samuel 8:18; 1 Chronicles 18:17).

PELEUS

In Greek mythology, king of the Myrmidons of Thessaly; he was most famous as the husband of Thetis (a sea nymph) and the father of the hero Achilles, whom he survived.

PELIAS

In Greek mythology, son of the god Poseidon by Tyro. As King of Thessaly he sent Jason in search of the Golden Fleece while he killed Jason's father, mother and brother. Jason, helped by Medea, persuaded Pelias' children to dismember and stew their father, saying that it would restore his lost youth.

PELOPIDS

In Greek mythology, a royal house which took its name from Pelops, the son of Tantalus. It was the leading force in the towns of the Peloponnese, which were then at their peak.

PENANCE

Penance may be defined as a series of external actions that accompany conversion and are indicative of internal repentance. Penance is associated with, but should not be identified with, the central biblical and prophetic concepts of conversion and repentance.

Each of these latter concepts is meant to include the whole movement that the two of them together clearly denote. One comes from Hebrew language and culture, the other from Greek, and each has a different emphasis.

Conversion, to turn back, involves action: a concrete change to a new way of life; a turning in one's track and going in a new direction. Repentance, change of mind, involves a feeling of regret or remorse which leads to a trusting obedience to God.

Unfortunately, it was once considered acceptable to translate one or the other of these concepts by the phrase "do penance," which is hopelessly inadequate. There is in fact no biblical word for penance which comes from the Latin poena, which means pain or punishment.

The reality of this Latin concept can be found in scripture, however. In the confession of sin and the penitential prayer that accompanied conversion or repentance, it was normal to fast, to keep a long vigil or prayer, to wear sackcloth and ashes, to weep and rend one's garments, to sleep on the ground, to pluck hairs from the head and beard, to offer sacrifice for sin, and give alms. This was a normal concomitant of the remorse that accompanies and leads to conversion.

Penance is also described as the sacrament for the forgiveness of sins. In early centuries it was elaborate, severe, public; and allowed only once in a lifetime. The medieval system involved private confession to a priest. This system continues today.

PENANCE, New Rite of

For the new Roman Ritual three forms for celebrating the sacrament of penance, approved by Paul VI and promulgated in its Latin version by the Sacred Congregation for Divine Worship (1973).

Use in the various regions of the church begins when an appropriate vernacular version has been readied by the episcopal conferences and approved by the Holy See. The new rite was developed in response to the directive of Vatican Council II.

The general inspiration of the new rite is an intent that it should express the pastoral (rather than the juridic) and reconciliatory meaning of the sacrament of penance. The particular new emphasis it gives is on the ecclesial aspects of sin and repentance: separation from God by sin is also a diminution of the inner unity of the church community, since this rests on the union in charity of each member with Christ and thereby with one another.

The rite of reconciliation with God should also express reconciliation and healing with the body of Christ. The three forms of the rite approved consist in:
▲ Form I: the reconciliation of the individual penitent by the priest-confessor, and the comminatory Forms II, III.
▲ Form II culminates in individual confession and absolution.
▲ Form III is a generalized confession and general absolution.

The rite of the individual reconciliation should include the greeting of the penitent by the confessor, appropriate readings and prayers, before confession and absolution; and the whole rite should make clear the ecclesial aspect by underlying that it is the ministry of the ecclesial community that is being exercised.

PENANCE, Practices of

Penance, as understood in Judaic and Christian religions, consists most essentially in an interior consciousness of sin and a change of heart in which the sinner regrets and turns from his sinful deeds and is converted to God.

There is frequently, but less essentially, some external manifestation of the inner change of heart. This commonly takes the form of a confession of guilt and the performance of certain difficult or humiliating works which
1 testify to the depth and sincerity of the interior conversion of the heart and
2 are a voluntary assumption, at least in symbolic form, of the punishment the sinner acknowledges himself to have merited by the violations of God's law.

Practices of penance are works undertaken in this spirit. In popular usage the term also embraces works of the same kind performed less by way of penalty than for ascetical purposes (i.e., to establish mastery over the disorderly inclinations of sinful nature) or out of a motive of love that wishes to share in the sufferings of Jesus.

Among the commoner forms the practice of penance has taken are:
▲ fasting;
▲ abstinence;
▲ abstemiousness;
▲ continence;
▲ poverty;
▲ isolation;
▲ privation of sleep;
▲ manual labor;
▲ the infliction upon self of discomfort and pain.

The penitential spirit has existed in the church from the earliest times, but at some periods it has been more strongly emphasized than at others, and cultural or other historical circumstances account for considerable differences in the forms in which it has expressed itself. In the contemporary church there has been a great reduction in the number of obligatory penances.

PENANCE, Recent Development

Penance is regarded as a sacrament of the new law by the Greek and Russian

Orthodox Churches and since the time of the Oxford Movement by the Anglo-Catholics and some Episcopalians. A growing number of Lutherans, particularly in Germany, are reviving the early Lutheran practice of private confession to the minister, or pastor, followed by absolution.

In Southern France the community of Taizé (a Calvinist Foundation) has not only introduced the practice of private confession and absolution, but many of the members regard penance as a sacrament.

Among Catholics there is a growing awareness that sin is not only an offense against God but ordinarily presupposes reconciliation with the church. Liturgical expression of this awareness is to be found in the growing practice of introducing some of the more communal and public features of the ancient liturgy of penance.

PENANCE, Sacrament of

In Roman Catholicism, one of the seven sacraments of the church described thus in the Code of Canon Law: "In the sacrament of penance the faithful, confessing their sins to a legitimate minister, being sorry for them, and at the same time proposing to reform, obtain from God forgiveness of sins committed after baptism through the absolution imparted by the same minister; and they likewise are reconciled with the church which they have wounded by sinning" (Canon 959).

It is the teaching of the church that "individual and integral confession and absolution constitute the only ordinary way by which the faithful person who is aware of serious sin is reconciled with God and with the church; only physical or moral impossibility excuses the person from confession of this type, in which case the reconciliation can take place in other ways" (Canon 960). Only a priest is the minister of the sacrament of penance; the priest cannot validly absolve, however, unless he possesses the faculty to do so either from the law of the church or from competent authority. The confessor

acts as both judge and healer in the sacrament of penance; he is to act with prudence and in fidelity to the magisterium of the church. The Confessor's obligations under the sacramental seal are stated thus: ".... it is a crime for a confessor in any way to betray a penitent by word or in any manner or for any reason" (Canon 983).

PENANCE, Theological reflections

The Montanist and Novatianist schisms of the third century offer indirect proof that Catholics at the time believed that the church had the power on earth of ministering divine pardon. The sacramental aspect of penance is evidenced by the parallel repeatedly drawn between baptism and penance.

The sacramental nature of the priest's reconciliation as well as its necessity is given eloquent expression by Augustine in an exhortation to his clergy to remain at their posts during the Vandal invasion: "How great a crowd of both sexes and all ages is accustomed to gather in the church, some demanding baptism, others reconciliation, others the discipline of penance itself, all seeking consolation and the administration of the sacraments. But if ministers are lacking, how great will be the destruction that follows those who leave this life either unregenerate or bound?" (Augustine Sermons 329.3).

This early emphasis on the importance of the priest's reconciliation was obscured by early scholastic teaching on the necessity of sorrow motivated by love as the operative element in the sacrament of penance.

The absolution of the priest came to be regarded as a simple declaration that the sinner was already reconciled by God through perfect contrition, or as the remission of the temporal punishment due to sin.

PENANCE, Works of

Acts performed in satisfaction for personal sins or the sins of others. They can include prayers, alms, good works, acts of denial, service to one's neighbor, and so forth.

PENINNAH

According to biblical tradition, a wife of Elkanah, who produced many children, in contrast with Elkanah's other wife, Hannah. Nonetheless, Peninnah was loved less than Hannah, and so she ridiculed Hannah's barenness, especially at the time of the family's annual visits to the tabernacle (1 Samuel 1:1-8).

PENITENTIAL BOOKS

Manuals used by priests of the Western church, especially during the early Middle Ages, in administering ecclesiastical penance.

PENNSYLVANIA DUTCH

Refers principally to descendants of German-speaking immigrants from the Rhineland and Switzerland who came to Pennsylvania during the late 17th and 18th centuries. The word Dutch is a corruption of Deutsch, meaning German, and does not imply derivation from the Netherlands. Primarily emigrating in search of religious freedom, the original settlers were mainly Lutheran and reformed Protestants, but included such Pietist sects as Amish, Mennonites and Moravians, who still retain their original culture.

PENRY, John

(1559-1593) Welsh Puritan, author of some of the most famous early Puritan treatises, most of which are violent and anti-episcopal in tone.

PENTATEUCH

(meaning "five books") First five books of the Old Testament, called the Torah or the Law by Jews. The books are Genesis, Exodus, Leviticus, Numbers and Deuteronomy. They contain the story of the creation, the forming of the Hebrew nation and the exodus from Egypt, and provide the earliest compilation of Hebrew laws. Traditionally ascribed to Moses, the Pentateuch is actually a compilation of historical and religious materials dating from the earliest Hebrew times to the 6th century BC.

PENTECOST

The 50th day inclusively after Easter, commemorates the descent of the Holy Spirit upon the Apostles, marking the birth of the Christian church (Acts 2:1-4).

Pentecost is a liturgical solemnity celebrated 50 days after Easter to commemorate the descent of the Holy Spirit upon the Apostles and the baptism of some 3,000 new Christians (See Acts 2:14); it is considered "the birthday of the church," the day of its empowerment to bring the Good News of Jesus Christ to all nations.

PENTECOSTAL ASSEMBLIES OF JESUS CHRIST

Unitarian "Jesus only" Pentecostal group that arose out of controversies over baptismal ritual with the Pentecostal movement beginning circa 1915. The Assemblies merged to form the United Pentecostal Church in 1945.

PENTECOSTAL CHURCHES

Protestant religious bodies of the fundamentalist and revivalist tradition that emphasize holiness, baptism in the Holy Spirit and miraculous occurrence. Although Pentecostal churches vary widely in theology and practice, all derive their inspiration from the story of the descent of the Holy Ghost upon the Apostles at Pentecost (Acts 2:1-4). These passages refer to "speaking in tongues" (speaking in a language one has never heard and cannot know), which is taken to be proof of the entrance of the Holy Spirit into the speaker's body. The largest churches in the group are the Assemblies of God, the United Pentecostal Church, and the Pentecostal Church of God in America.

PENTECOSTAL CHURCH OF GOD OF AMERICA

Church organized in Chicago in 1919, accepting Pentecostal beliefs including divine healing and the Baptism of the Holy Spirit accompanied by the sign of speaking in tongues.

PENTECOSTAL FELLOWSHIP OF NORTH AMERICA

Cooperative organization established in Chicago in 1948 by eight Pentecostal denominations for the purpose of interdenominational Pentecostal cooperation and fellowship.

PENTECOSTALISM

Pentecostalism is that form of Christianity teaching the "Pentecostal experience," namely, that baptism with the Holy Spirit is accompanied and manifested by glossolalia (tongues speaking) and divine healing and that the charismatic gifts of the early church, a continuing Pentecost, should be ordinary occurrences in Christian Life.

Many of the typical elements in Pentecostalism were taught by the 19th century Catholic Apostolic Church. The actual Pentecostal movement, however, began in the United States in the early 1900s, as an outgrowth of the Holiness movement.

Prominent at the origins of 20th century Pentecostalism were the Apostolic Faith Movement (1901) of C. P. Parham and the Azusa Street Revival (1906). Some groups in the East originated as break-offs, over tongues speaking, from the Christian and Missionary Alliance.

The intense spirit of evangelism, in the form, of faith mission, spread the movement. There has been traditionally little formal organization in the Pentecostal bodies, and this has often led to internal disputes and divisions.

In recent years, however, large Pentecostal bodies have developed some set form of church government. The early deliberate downgrading of education has also changed among the larger Pentecostal groups. There are Pentecostal churches, or, as they are often called, Assemblies, in all of the states of the U.S..

Many smaller units of less than a few hundred members exist throughout the country. Certain more extravagant cults in the South, e.g., snake-handlers, use the Pentecostal name but are disowned by official Pentecostal bodies. The Neo-Pentecostalism of recent years refers to the search for the Pentecostal experience by small groups within other Christian churches; it has no formal connection with Pentecostalism.

PENTECOSTALISM, Doctrine

Pentecostals agree in their distinctive doctrines, the Pentecostal experience and divine healing and in their fundamentalism; in other matters there is wide diversity. At times some Pentecostals are accused of diminishing belief in the Trinity, and of misunderstanding the doctrine of justification by faith.

In keeping with their Holiness origin they are Arminian. Pentecostal dispensationalism means that these last days are a period for the preaching of charismatic gifts to a morally depraved generation.

Baptism and the Lord's Supper are recognized as ordinances; but the first (water baptism) is seen only as a pledge of regeneration already obtained, and the second, as a purely symbolic rite.

Many Pentecostal groups reject infant baptism (while practicing at times the dedication of children to the Lord); some observe footwashing. Pentecostals forbid smoking, drinking, dancing, gambling, and frivolous entertainment. This type or Puritanism has been effectively applied against abuse of alcohol - a widespread vice in more than one nominally Catholic nation - and to cure addicts, and has become one of the secrets of their missionary penetration.

Ecclesiologically Pentecostals are heirs to the concept of Pietism; the church is not an instrument of sanctification but rather a holy club in which the members help one another and thereby sanctify the community itself.

They have admirably developed the sense of koinonia, mutual brotherhood and friendship. Congregationalism, emphasis on the autonomy of the local church, has been a traditional ideal for church polity.

In practice, with the increase of organization, the governing of many denominations has become more centralized through the adoption of elements from Presbyterian or Methodist polity. Pentecostal authorities often have the power to act in a stern way to enforce church discipline.

PENTECOST CYCLE

A festival period of the ecclesiastical year which is allotted to the celebration of Pentecost with its vigil and its octave. It was not liturgically distinct, but was rather the conclusion of the Easter cycle.

The Sundays after Pentecost, numbered according to their succession from that feast, did not pertain in any proper sense to the Pentecost cycle, for they had no intrinsic relationship to Pentecost or to one another.

Presently the weeks and Sundays after Pentecost (or Whitsunday) is the celebration of the Holy Spirit's gift of the new law and of his formation of the new people. It is celebrated 50 days after Easter.

The Jewish Pentecost, also celebrated 50 days after the Passover, marked the completion of the wheat harvest and commemorated the reception of the law by Moses.

First evidence of the Christian feast comes from the mid-second century and from the fourth century there are indications of the beginnings of the Pentecost cycle. The Ascension broke from its original unity with Pentecost and became the feast of the 40th day after Easter. At the same time Pentecost became, in the West, a feast of the Holy Spirit.

Its vigil has been celebrated from the fourth century, and on that occasion baptism was administered to those prepared for it who had not been baptized at the Easter vigil. Although there is some indication of an octave of Pentecost in the fourth century, it was only in the seventh that the octave was unified under one theme, i.e., that of recalling the first Pentecost and celebrating the Spirit's continuing work among Christians.

PENTEKOSTARION

An Eastern Orthodox worship book, used from Easter to the Sunday of the Holy Fathers, that connotes a feeling of joy, over against the penitential mood of the odes of the Triodion, the service book of worship used during Lent.

PENUEL

Name used for a person and a site or place. Penuel is a family head in the tribe of Benjamin who lived in Jerusalem; son of Shashak (1 Chronicles 8:1; 25:28).

Penuel is the name of a place near the ford of the Jabbok River where, according to biblical tradition, Jacob wrestled with the angel; hence he called the place Peniel (Penuel) because there he "had seen God face to face" (Genesis 32:22-31).

In the time of the Judges, Gideon asked the men of Penuel for food in order that his forces might continue after the kings of Midian, but the Penuelites refused, for which reason Gideon later destroyed their tower and killed all their men (Judges 8:4-17).

PEOPLE OF THE BOOK

Islamic concept (Ahl al-Kitab). The name initially referred to the Jews and the Christians whose scriptures like the Torah and the Gospel were completed in Muslim belief by the Islamic revelation of the Koran. The term was later broadened to cover adherents of other religions like Zoroastrianism. Differences on the same subject between the Koran and, for example, the gospels are accounted for by the doctrine of corruption according to which Christians are believed to have corrupted or distorted the original Gospel; text. Koranic references to the People of the Book are a mixture of the friendly and the hostile. In early Islamic history the People of the Book had a protected status provided that they paid the poll tax.

PEOPLE OF THE CAVE

Islamic concept (Ashab al-Kahf); also called the Companions of the Cave. This title is frequently given to a gang of youths who fell asleep in a cave, and awoke many years later, described in the sura of the Koran banned after the episode, Surat al-Kahf. The story is paralleled in the Christian tradition by that of the Seven Sleepers of Ephesus.

PEOR

In biblical times, in the account of King Balak's efforts to get the prophet Balaam to curse Israel, the third vantage point to which Balaam was conducted is said to be the "top of Peor, which looks toward Jeshimon" (Numbers 23:28). From here Balaam could see the tents of Israel spread about on the Plains of Moab below (Numbers 22:1; 24:2).

PEREGRINUS LAZIOSI, Saint

(1260-1345) Patron saint of cancer victims, who was himself miraculously cured of cancer. His feast day is May 1st.

PEREZ

In the Old Testament, one of the twin sons of Judah by his daughter-in-law Tamar. At birth, Perez' brother Zerah started to emerge first, but withdrew and Perez came out first, producing a perineal rupture of Tamar (Genesis 38:24-30). Perez retained priority over his brother and is always listed ahead of him, and his house became the more famous of the two (Ruth 4:12). Perez and his own two sons, Hezron and Hamul, are listed among those of Jacob's lineage coming into Egypt, where all three became heads of individual families in Judah (Genesis 46:8, 12). Aside from this no personal information about him is recorded.

PERGA

In biblical times, a prominent city of the Roman province of Pamphylia. The ruins of ancient Perga are believed to be near the modern village of Murtana,
circa eight miles inland from the southern coast of Asia Minor and some five miles west of the Cestrus River. It appears that anciently, according to the Greek geographer Strabo, this river was navigable as far north as Perga. However, nearby Attalia on the coast of Pamphylia seems to have served as Perga's harbor and, in time, even displaced Perga in importance (Acts 14:24-26).

PERGAMUM

In biblical times, a Mysian city in the northwestern part of Asiatic Turkey (Asia Minor) and the location of one of the seven congregations to which the apostle John addressed letters as recorded in the Revelation (Revelation 1:11; 2:12-17). The city was circa 50 miles north of Smyrna and fifteen miles from the coast of the Aegean Sea. Close to the site of ancient Pergamum (or Pergamos) lies modern Bergama. Pergamum was originally a fortress on a steep, isolated hill between two rivers. In time the city spread into the valley below, and the hill became the acropolis.

PERGAMUM ALTAR

Hellenistic altar to Zeus erected between 180 and 160 BC on the acropolis at Pergamum in commemoration of the victory of Attalus I over the Gauls.

PERIDA

In Judaism, forefather of a family of Solomon's servants, some of whom returned to Jerusalem with Zerubbabel (Nehemiah 7:6-7). The name is spelled Peruda at Ezra 2:55.

PERIZZITES

In the Old Testament, one of the tribes that inhabited the land of Canaan before Israelites occupied it (Genesis 13:3-7; Exodus 3:8, 17). They are not mentioned in the list of 70 families after the Flood, which names "the families of the Canaanite" (Genesis 10:15-18). Their ancestry is unknown.

PERJURY

Calling on God to witness to what one knows to be a lie; a public bearing of false witness when one is under oath. It dishonors God, is a violation of truth, and brings about many compromises in the application of justice.

PERMISSIVENESS

An attitude that allows for great personal latitude in moral decision making. In its excess this belief rests on an erroneous conception of human freedom.

PERPETUAL HELP

An ancient and well-loved picture of the Madonna and Child; it is a Byzantine picture and belongs to the "sorrowing" style meant to highlight the meaning of Christ's Passion and death; in the picture, on a background of gold, Mary's head is titled toward Jesus, her hand loosely clasping his hand; Jesus seems frightened as he gazes into the future; his sandals seems to be falling from his foot; two angels in the upper corners of the picture carry the instruments of Christ's Passion; the original picture was entrusted to the Redemptorists by Pope Pius IX in 1866 and is now enshrined in the Redemptorist Church of San Alfonso in Rome; to honor Mary, the Redemptorists have established the worldwide Archconfraternity of Our Mother of Perpetual Help.

PERSECUTION, Religious

Extreme harassment of individuals or groups because of their religious beliefs. Religious persecutions have affected members of all the major religions and range from restrictions on employment and living quarters to exile and even death by torture.

PERSEUS

In Greek mythology, son of Zeus and Danae, hero of Argos. His grandfather, Acrisius, once asked an oracle if he would ever have sons. The oracle replied that it would be the destiny of his daughter Danae to have a son who would kill him. In order to prevent this prophecy from coming true, Acrisus had Danae shut up in an underground cave with brass walls.

But Zeus managed to squeeze through a crack in the cave - after transforming himself into a shower of golden rain - and formed a union with the lovely Danae. She gave birth to a son, whom she managed to bring up in secret for some months. When Acrisus found out about the baby, he refused to believe that Zeus had had anything to do with it; he killed Danae's wet-nurse, whom he suspected of complicity in the affair, and put his daughter and grandson in a wooden ark and set them adrift on the sea.

The waves washed them up on Seriphos, where the fisherman Dictes, brother of Polydectes, tyrant of the island, found it. Dictes took Perseus and his mother, and it was in his house that the boy grew into a brave young man blessed with talents and gifts of all kinds. At one point King Polydectes fell in love with Danae, but he was never able to meet her because Perseus kept his mother well-guarded and the king felt unable to bring pressure to bear.

Many years later, Perseus put his adoptive father Dictes on the throne and set out for Argos, his home, to meet his father. But as soon as Acristus heard of the approach of his grandson, he fled - yet he did not escape his fate. Later, he was present as spectator at games in Larisa arranged by King Tentamides, at which Perseus was a competitor in the discus. When Perseus' turn came to throw, the discus slipped from his hand and hit Adrisus on the head, killing him. Perseus was grieved to learn who the dead man had been, and buried him with every honor.

PERSIS

In the New Testament, a beloved Christian in Rome whom Paul greets and commends for her many Christian works (Romans 16:12).

PERSONALITY

In Buddhism, term with a very special meaning, the false belief in the permanence of any aspect of the total self as different from the rest. This is one of the fundamental Buddhism doctrines on which all Schools are agreed.

PESA

Jewish feast of Passover (Exodus 12:17-18, 12:24-27; 34:18), celebrated throughout the Jewish world during the month of Nisan. It recalls and relives the events in the history of the Jews in Egypt and their exodus, led by Moses. Lasting a full week, Pesah results in most of the Jewish stores (including the foodstores and markets) being closed or opened for limited hours.

The holiday commences with the Seder meal on the eve of the festival. During this first meal, the story of the Passover is read. Special foods are served. For example, Ashkenazim exclude rice, while Sephradim make a point of including it. Matzah (unleavened bread) is the principal ingredient for all Pesah dishes, as it is forbidden to eat, and even to keep, leavened products in Jewish households at this time.

The Samaritans celebrate their version of Pesah on Mount Gerizim near Nablus. To them this is the authentic Mount Sinai as well as the site of Abraham's sacrifice of his son, Isaac. Here they sacrifice a lamb, watched by a crowd of onlookers, as they have done for over 2,500 years.

PESHAT

The designation for the simple, obvious, literal meaning of a biblical text in the hermeneutical (interpretive) principles and methods used by Jewish rabbis.

PESHITTA

The version of the Bible used in the Syrian Christian Churches. Written without elaborate critical apparatus (which is the reason for this version being named the Peshitta), this translation is a revision of the Old Syriac version in accordance with Greek textual principles.

PESSIMISM

The philosophical doctrine that the Universe is fundamentally evil. Buddhism is not pessimistic but asserts that sorrow or evil is due to ignorance of the true nature of reality and false conceptions of self. The Noble Eightfold Path teaches the way out of sorrow into the enlightenment and peace of Nirvana.

PETER

In Christianity, one of the most important Apostles. His original name being Simon, he received from Jesus the name Peter (Rock). He was a Galilean fisherman when Jesus called him to be a disciple (Matthew 4:18). Peter was a dominating but impulsive figure, and denied Jesus after his arrest (Luke 22:56-58). Later he played a leading role in the early church, especially in Jerusalem. He presided over the appointment of Matthias as an apostle to take the place of Judas, who had betrayed Christ and later died. It was Peter who first "raised his voice" and preached at Pentecost, the day when the disciples were filled with the Holy Spirit. By tradition, he died a martyr at Rome and is said to have been crucified upside down at his own request, because he felt himself unworthy to die in the same manner as Christ. Where he died is not known for certain, and has aroused some controversy between Protestants and Roman Catholics. The latter believe Peter to have been the first head of the church in Rome, where he died. In 1950 Pope Pius XII announced that a tomb found under the church of St. Peter in Rome had definitely been identified as that of the saint.

PETER, Apocalypse of

An apocryphal (noncanonical and unauthentic) Christian writing dating from the first half of the 2nd century. The unknown author, who claimed to be Peter the Apostle, relied on the canonical Gospels and on Revelation

St. Peter denying Christ.
"And Simon Peter stood and warmed himself. They said therefore unto him, Art not thou also one of his disciples? He denied it, and said,. I am not" (John 18:25).
Lithograph by Gustave Doré (about 1860).

to John to construct a conversation between himself and Jesus regarding events at the end of the world.

PETER, Gospel of

An apocryphal (noncanonical and unauthentic) Christian writing of the mid-2nd century, the extant portion of which covers the condemnation, crucifixion, and Resurrection of Jesus. Because the work reflects the view that Christ's body had only the appearance of reality, Serapion, bishop of Antioch (circa 190), believed it was written by a member of the heretical Docetist sect. Modern scholars are more inclined to attribute it to a Syrian Christian Gnostic because the gospel does not view the crucifixion as an act of atonement.

PETER, Letters of

Two New Testament letters written by the Apostle Peter. The first is written to encourage persecuted Christians in Asia Minor. The Christians are urged to repay evil with goodness and to love one another.

The second letter refers to the Second Coming of Christ and the evils preceding this great event. The writer warns against false teachers, whose conduct is as immoral as their words are deceptive.

PETER CHRYSOLOGUS, Saint

(406-450) Archbishop of Ravenna (Italy), whose orthodox discourses earned him the title of doctor of the church. His short sermons stress the fundamental Christian doctrines and the duties of Christian life in keeping with the needs and ideals of the times.

PETER CLAVER, Saint

(1581-1654) Jesuit missionary to South America who, in dedicating his life to the aid of Negro slaves, and earned the title of apostle of the Negroes.

PETER MARTYR, Saint

(1205-1252) Vigorous preacher, and religious founder who, for his militant reformation, was assassinated by the Cathari, heretical Christians proclaiming that good and evil have two separate creators.

PETER NOLASCO, Saint

(1189-1256) Founder of the order of Our Lady of Ransom (Mercedarians, or Nolascans), a religious institute originally designed to ransom Christian captives from the Moors; today, the Mercedarians, whose numbers have declined, are engaged mostly in hospital work.

PETER OF ALCANTARA, Saint

(1499-1562) Franciscan mystic who founded an austere form of Franciscan life known as the Alcantarines or Discalced (i.e., barefooted) Friars Minor. He founded convents that were unique for their isolation and discomfort.

PETER OF CASTELNAU

(1145-1208) Cistercian martyr, apostolic legate, and inquisitor against the Albigenses (heretical Christian sect in southern France during the 12th and 13th centuries) whose assassination led to the violent Albigensian Crusade.

PETER THE HERMIT

(circa 1050-1115) French monk and preacher, one of the instigators of the First Crusade to wrest the Holy Land from the Muslims. There are many legends about this colorful ex-soldier and pilgrim, but his historical importance has been much exaggerated. After an evangelical journey through france on mule-back, he did lead a large rabble army as far as Asia Minor, where it was cut to pieces by the Turks and deserted by Peter, who had meanwhile joined a knightly army which was besieging Antioch. Later he founded a monastery in the Low Countries.

PETER THE VENERABLE

(1092-1156) Outstanding French abbot of Cluny whose spiritual, intellectual, and financial reforms restored Cluny to its high place among the religious establishments of Europe. He wrote hymns and poems and left circa 200 letters of considerable historiographical interest.

PETHAHIAH

In biblical times, the paternal house selected for the 19th of the 24 rotating priestly divisions that David organized (1 Chronicles 24:5-7, 44).

The name is also applied to one of the Levites who joined in proposing the "trustworthy arrangement" to the returned exiles in which they reviewed the history of God's dealings with their nation, confessed their sin and agreed to renew true worship (Nehemiah 9:5-8).

PETHOR

In biblical times, the home of Balaam, the prophet who attempted to curse Israel. Pethor was situated "by the River," apparently the Euphrates (Numbers 22:5; Deuteronomy 23:4). It is generally identified with the "Pitru" of Assyrian inscriptions. Pitru lay on the Sajur River, a western tributary of the Euphrates to the south of Carchemish.

PETHUEL

In Judaism, father of the prophet Joel (Joel 1:1).

PETRI, Laurentius

(1499-1573) Swedish churchman, who was appointed the first Protestant bishop of Uppsala in 1531. His church order of 1571 defined the practice of the church, particularly its relation to government.

PETRI, Olaus

(1493-1552) Churchman who, with his brother Laurentius, played a decisive role in the reformation of the Swedish church. He provided most of the literature for the Swedish Reformation movement, including a Swedish New Testament, hymnbook, church manual, the Swedish liturgy, and many homiletical and polemical writings.

PETRINE THEORY

The basis of Roman Catholic doctrine on papal primacy, resting partly on Christ's bestowing the "keys of the Kingdom" on Peter (the first pope, according to Catholic tradition), and partly on Christ's words: "Thou art Peter, and upon this Rock I will build my church."

PETRUS AUREOLI

(1280-1322) Theologian and archbishop, who promoted an individualistic empiricism (i.e., the attitude of the mind that emphasizes the part played by experience in knowledge against that played by reasoning), supported by a doctrine of universals, or general words that can be applied to more than one particular thing.

PETURSSON, Hallgrimur

(1614-1674) Lutheran pastor and greatest religious poet of Iceland.

PEULETHAI

In biblical times, the eighth of Obededom's sons, listed as a gatekeeper (1 Chronicles 26:1-5).

PHAETHON

In Greek mythology, son of Helios the sun-god. Many versions have him as the son of Auge and Cephalus, but in the most common myth he is the offspring of Helios and the Oceanid Clymene, who brought him up without his father knowing of his very existence. When Phaethon reached adolescence, his mother revealed the truth about father and son. Young Phaethon wanted proof of his paternity, however, and asked his father to let him drive the chariot of the sun. Helios refused, at first, but eventually gave in, bombarding the young man with instructions and advice.

To begin with, Phaethon took the route Helios used every day, but when he had gained height he took fright at the drop beneath him. The proximity of the signs of the Zodiac scared him, too, and he changed course. The chariot began to veer wildly about the sky, sometimes coming so low it was in danger of setting fire to the earth, and sometimes soaring so high it nearly scorched the stars. To put an end to this menace, Zeus set loose a thunderbolt and shot Phaethon down into the river Eridanus, where his sisters, the Heliads, buried him with all the honors due to the dead.

PHAG-MO-GRU

Tibetan monastic order that in the 14th century liberated Tibet from Mongol control and re-established centralized native rule in the country for the first time in 500 years.

PHAGS-PA

(1235-1280) Tibetan scholar and religious figure who established Tibetan Buddhism as a theocracy.

PHALA

In Buddhism, term denoting fruits or fruition. It is a technical term for the state of consciousness following attainment of Vipassana, insight.

PHANUEL

In Judaism, a descendant of Asher, whose daughter Anna was a prophetess at the Temple in Jerusalem when Joseph and Mary brought Jesus there (Luke 2:36).

PHARAOH

Originally, the royal palace in ancient Egypt, the word came to be used as a synonym for the Egyptian king. The word meant, literally, "great house" - the palace, which became associated with the king in much the same was as "Holy See" came to be used as synonym for the Pope. The early Egyptians believed Pharaoh to be a god, specifically the personification of the god Horus and later of the god Amos. He was an absolute ruler responsible alike for the temporal and spiritual needs of his people. Thus he owned all the land, and headed the government, the clergy and the army.

He lived a life quite apart from his subjects.

In Islam, it is a translation of Fir-awn; a figure frequently encountered in the Koran, especially in his dealing with Musa (Moses) and Harun. Notable encounters include that in which Musa performs various miracles before Pharaoh, and the conversion to Musa's God, and subsequent crucifixion of Pharaoh's magicians.

PHARISEES

An ancient Jewish group devoted to strict observance of the holy law and strongly opposed to pagan practices and to the Sadducees (Acts 23:8). Their piety consisted mainly in forms and outward observances.

The Pharisees flourished before the Christian era in Palestine, whose spiritual descendants fashioned rabbinical Judaism.

They formed brotherhoods whose members encouraged one another in devotion to the law. Their interpretation of the law adapted it to changing conditions; they were the only religious party in Israel capable of surviving the catastrophe of AD 70. Jesus Christ agreed with them on resurrection, angels and demons, but his association with "sinners" and his free attitude towards the law incurred their disapproval. Several Pharisees joined the primitive Jerusalem church.

Popular tradition has made "Pharisee" a synonym for hypocrisy and self-righteousness but this view, which is largely derived from the New Testament, does not take account of the fact that Jesus did not attack the Pharisees as a group, but only the hypocrites among them.

PHARMAKOS

In Greek religion, a human scapegoat used in certain state rituals. In Athens, for example, a man and a women were selected as scapegoats each year.

PHARPAR

In biblical times, name for one of the two "rivers of Damascus" that Naaman

The Pharisee and the Publican.
"The Pharisee stood and prayed thus ... God, I thank thee, that I am, not as other men are ... And the publican smote upon his breast, saying, God be merciful to me a sinner" (Luke 18:11, 13).
Lithograph by Gustave Doré (about 1860).

considered superior to "all waters of Israel" (2 Kings 5:12). The fact that Naaman mentioned the Pharpar second may indicated that it was the smaller stream. This river is usually linked with the Nahr el-'A'waj. Besides the Nahr Barada (identified with the Abanah), it is the only other independent stream in the Damascus area. But the volume of the 'A'waj is about one-quarter that of the barada, The smaller streams that unite to form the 'A'waj take their rise on the eastern slopes of Mount Hermon and merge circa 19 miles southwest of Damascus. From this point the river winds its way through a deep rocky channel until finally losing itself in a swamp to the south-east of Damascus.

PHASA

In Buddhism, contact. The term is used in the sense of the mental impression from contact with sense-objects.

PHICOL

In biblical times, army chief of Philistine King Abimelech. Phicol accompanied Abimelech when covenants were concluded with both Abraham and Isaac (Genesis 21:22; 26:26-31). As these two meetings were more than 75 years apart, however, "Phicol" might well be a title or name used for whoever held this office rather than their being one man in the position for so long.

PHILADELPHIA

In ancient times, a city in western Asia Minor having a Christian congregation to which one of the seven letters contained in Revelation was written (Revelation 1:11; 3:7-13). The Lydian city of Philadelphia was situated on a hilly plateau south of the Cogamis River, circa 30 miles southeast of Sardis and 50 miles north-west of Laodicea. It was built in the second century BC by Eumenes II, king of Pergamum, or his brother Attalus II (Philadelphos), after whom the city was named.

The city lay at the head of a broad sea-coast. Roads connected it with the coast, Pergamum to the north and Laodicea to the south-east. The city served as a doorway to the heart of Phrygia.

Evidently there were Israelites living in Philadelphia, Revelation 3:9 mentioning "those from the synagogue of Satan who say they are Jews." Perhaps these worked against the faithful Christians in the city by trying to win back Christians who were Jews by birth or to persuade them to retain or take up again certain practices of the Mosaic law. The attempt was unsuccessful, Jesus commending the Christians for their endurance. He encouraged them to "keep on holding fast" (Revelation 3:9-11).

PHILEMON

In the New Testament, a Christian slave owner associated with the congregation at Colossae. His house in this city of south-western Asia Minor served as a meeting place for the congregation there. Philemon proved himself to be a source of refreshment to fellow Christians and an example in faith and love. The apostle Paul regarded him as a beloved fellow worker (Philemon 1, 2, 5-7).

PHILEMON, Letter to

Brief New Testament letter written by Paul the apostle. The letter is written to a wealthy Christian of Colossae, Asia Minor, whose slave Onesimus had run away. At Rome Onesimus was converted and he was induced by Paul to return to his master. Paul, writing from prison, expresses affection for the newly converted slave and asks that he be received in the same spirit that would mark Paul's own arrival. The letter was probably composed in Rome circa 61.

PHILEMON AND BAUCIS

In Greek mythology, a pious Phrygian couple whose hospitality received Zeus and Hermes when their richer neighbors turned away the two gods, who were disguised as wayfarers. As a reward they were saved from a flood that drowned the rest of the country.

PHILETUS

A first-century apostate from Christianity whom Paul implicates with Hymenaeus as false teachers concerning the resurrection, and subverters of the faith (2 Timothy 2:17,18).

PHILIP, Acts of

Apocryphal (noncanonical) book of the New Testament.

PHILIP, Gospel of

An early Christian writing composed about the end of the 2nd century and generally considered to be apocryphal (unauthentic). It is but one of many such writings that circulated in the early church and were rediscovered in modern times. A 5th century Coptic version is extant, but the original Greek is lost.

PHILIP, John

(1775-1851) Controversial missionary in South Africa who championed the rights of the Africans against the European settlers.

PHILIP, the Apostle

One of the earliest disciples; one of the 12 apostles. Mentioned only by name in the apostolical list of the gospels, he is a frequent character in the Gospel according to John. He came from Bethesda, answered Jesus' call and was instrumental in the call of Nathanael whom he brought to Jesus (John 1:45).

PHILIP, the Evangelist

In the early Christian church, one of the seven deacons appointed to tend the Christians of Jerusalem, thereby enabling the apostles to freely conduct their missions. His energetic preaching, however, earned him the title of Philip the Evangelist and led him to minister successfully in Samaria, in Palestine. where he converted, among others, the famous magician Simon Magus (Acts 8:11-13). Later, on the road from Jerusalem to Gaza, he instructed and baptized a court official from Ethiopia. His missionary journey ended at Caesarea (Acts 8), where he raised his four daughters, reputed to be prophets, and where, circa 58, he entertained the apostle Paul and his companions on their last journey to Jerusalem.

PHILIPPI

In biblical times, principal city of the district of Macedonia, at the time of the apostle Paul's second missionary tour. It was located in the eastern part of the district, at the northern end of the Aegean Sea, not far from the district of Thracia. Paul, coming by boat from Troas, landed at Philippi's seaport town, Neapolis, and traveled circa ten miles north-west along the Via Egnatia or Egnatian Way, the great commercial and military road from Asia to Rome, which ran through a mountainous pass some 1,600 feet above sea level and down into the Philippian plain (Acts 16:11-12).

PHILIPPIANS, Letter to the

New Testament letters written by Paul from prison in Rome (circa 62) to the Christians at Philippi, whom he himself had converted. Apprehensive that his execution was close at hand, Paul explains that he was imprisoned for preaching the gospel of Christ. Paul exhorts his readers to remain steadfast in their faith and to imitate the humility of Christ. He also quotes an early hymn on Christ's humility.

PHILIPPICUS BARDANES

(654-713) Byzantine emperor whose brief reign (711-713) was marked by his quarrels with the papacy and his ineffectiveness in defending the empire from Bulgar and Arab invaders.

He was an advocate of the Monothelite heresy, the belief in a single will of Christ. Even before entering Constantinople, he had ordered the picture of the Third Council of Constantinople (which had condemned Monothelitism in 680) to be removed from the palace and the names of those the council had condemned restored.

PHILISTINES

One of the sea peoples who settled on the southern coast of Palestine in the

12th century BC, about the time of the arrival of the Israelites. The Philistines came from Caphtor (Jeremiah 47:4), now probably Crete. Expanding into neighboring areas they soon came into conflict with the Israelites. With their superior arms and military organization the Philistines were able to occupy part of the Judaean hill country. They were finally defeated by the Israelite King David (10th century) and thereafter their history was that of individual cities rather than of a people.

PHILO JUDEAS

(circa 20 BC - AD 50) Alexandrine Jewish philosopher whose attempt to fuse Greek philosophical thought with Jewish biblical religion had a profound influence on Christian and Jewish theology.

PHILOKLIA

A prose anthology of Greek monastic texts that was part of a movement for spiritual renewal in Eastern monasticism and Orthodox devotional life in general.

PHILOLOGUS

In biblical times, a Christian whom Paul greets in his letter to the Romans (Romans 16:15). The same name is found on inscriptions associated with the household of Caesar.

PHILOPONUS, John

(534-587) Greek Christian philosopher, theologian and scholar whose writings expressed an independent Christian synthesis of classical Hellenistic thought, which in translation contributed to Syriac and Arabic cultures and to medieval Western thought. In order to defend the Christian dogma of personal immortality, Philoponus broke with the common Aristotelian and Stoic interpretation of a single universal mind operative in all men and taught that each person possesses an individual intellect.

PHILOTHEUS COCCINUS

(1302-1379) Theologian, monk, and patriarch of Constantinople. He was a leading protagonist of Byzantine quietist mysticism and principal opponent of the Greek Orthodox movement for union with the Roman church.

PHILOXENUS OF MABBUG

(440-523) Syrian bishop, and theologian, who was the leader of the Jacobite Monophysite church, a heterodox group teaching a single, divine nature in Christ, subsuming his humanity

PHINEHAS

In Judaism, son of Eleazar and grandson of Aaron. His mother was a daughter of Putiel and his son's name was Abishua (Exodus 6:25; 1 Chronicles 6:4).

During his lifetime Phinehas served in various capacities. He was the priestly representative in the army that executed, according to biblical tradition, God's vengeance upon Midian (Numbers 31:3-6). When it was thought that three tribes were forsaking God's worship, he headed a group of investigators (Joshua 22:9-33). He was chief of the tabernacle gatekeepers (1 Chronicles 9:20). After the burial of his father in the Hill of Phinehas, he served in the office of the High Priest (Joshua 24:33; Judges 20:27-28). His name is prominent in several post-exilic genealogies (1 Chronicles 6:4, 50; Ezra 7:5; 8:2).

PHLEGYAS

In Greek mythology, son of the war god, Ares, and who, as their king, gave his name to the savage Phlegyas in Thessaly.

PHOEBE

In the New Testament, one of the Roman Christians whom Paul greets in his letter (Romans 16:14).

PHOEBE

A Christian sister of the first-century Cenchreae congregation. Paul, in his letter to the Christians at Rome, "recommends" this sister to them, and calls on them to render her any needed assistance as one who "proved to be a defender of many, yet of me myself" (Romans 16:1-2). It may be that Phoebe delivered Paul's letter in Rome or else accompanied the one who did.

PHOENICIA

In ancient times, name for a strip of coastland along the eastern shore of the Mediterranean between Syria and Palestine that was bounded on the east by the Lebanon mountains. The plains were well watered by a number of streams originating in the mountain range that formed the natural boundary along the eastern frontier.

The Phoenicians were among the great seafaring peoples of the ancient world. Their ships were very seaworthy for their size. They were high at the stern, of wide beam, and could be powered by both sails and oars (Ezekiel 27:3-7). In the time of David and Solomon the Phoenicians were famous as cutters of building stones and as woodsmen skilled in bringing down the stately trees of their forests (2 Samuel 5:11; 1 Kings 5:6-10; 1 Chronicles 14:1).

As Canaanites, the Phoenicians practiced a very base religion centered around the fertility god Baal, and involving sodomy, bestiality and ceremonial prostitution, as well as abhorrent rites of child sacrifice.

The Phoenician city of Baalbek (some 40 miles north-east of Beirut) became one of the great centers of polytheistic worship in the ancient world, in Roman times great temples to various gods and goddesses being erected there, the ruins of which can be seen today.

In the spring of 31, certain residents of Phoenicia demonstrated faith by traveling inland to Galilee to listen to Jesus and to be cured of their ailments (Mark 3:7-10; Luke 6:17). A year or so later Jesus visited the coastal plains of Phoencia and was so impressed by the faith of a Syro-Phoenician woman living there that he miraculously cured her demon-possessed daughter (Matthew 15:21-28; Mark 7:24-31).

When persecution broke out in Judea following the martyrdom of Stephen, some Christians fled to Phoenicia. There, for some time, they proclaimed the good news to Jews. But following the conversion of Cornelius congregations began to spring up along the Phoenician coast, as in the other parts of the Roman Empire.

The apostle Paul visited some of these congregations in Phoenicia during the course of his travels, the last recorded visit with believers there being at Sidon on his way to Rome as a prisoner in 58 (Acts 11:19; 21:1-7).

PHOENIX

In biblical times, name for a harbor in Crete (Acts 27:12). The grain boat on which Paul was traveling as a prisoner to Rome attempted to sail from Fair Havens to Phoenix for winter anchorage. Seized by a storm, it was subsequently wrecked on the island of Malta (Acts 27:13-28:1). As to the location of Phoenix, the Acts narrative indicates only that it was west of Fair Havens on the southern side of Crete, and that it provided safe winter anchorage.

PHOENIX

In Greek mythology, son of Amyntor, king of Thessalia, Hellas. After a violent quarrel Amyntor cursed him with childlessness, and Phoenix escaped to Peleus (king of Myrmidons in Thessaly), who made him responsible for the upbringing of his son Achilles.

PHORONEUS

In Greek legend, an early king of Argos and the son of Inachus. Phoroneus was considered the first mortal king. Traditionally Phoroneus and two river gods had to decide between the sea god, Poseidon and Hera, the goddess of marriage and the wife of Zeus, as the deity of the land. They chose Hera, and Poseidon took his vengeance by depriving the Argos region of water.

PHOTIAN SCHISM

A 9th century controversy between Eastern and Western Christianity that was precipitated by the opposition of the Roman pope to the appointment by the Byzantine Emperor Michael II of the lay scholar Photius to the patriarchate of Constantinople, and also involved Eastern and Western ecclesiastical jurisdictional rights in the Bulgarian church.

PHRYGIA

In biblical times, name for a country or region in central Asia Minor. The geographical boundaries of Phrygia fluctuated greatly over the years, so it is difficult to define the area encompassed unless one refers to a specific period.

It is commonly believed that the Phrygians spread south from Greece toward the close of the second millennium BC and gained control of much of central and western Asia Minor north of the Taurus Mountains, from the Halys River to the Aegean Sea.

Archeological evidence points to Gordion as their capital and King Midas as one of their prominent rulers. A noteworthy aspect of the religion of the people of early Phrygia is the worship of a mother-goddess (Rhea Cybele).

On his second missionary tour Paul and his companions, coming northwest through Cilicia and Lycaonia, "went through Phrygia and the country of Galatia, because they were forbidden by the holy spirit to speak the word in the district of Asia" (Acts 12:41; 16:1-6). So they entered the eastern part of old Phrygia (this by Paul's time being Galatian Phrygia), but instead of continuing west through the province of Asia (containing Asian Phrygia) they went north toward the province of Bithynia and then west to Troas.

Paul's third tour took him through Galatian Phrygia and Asian Phrygia. He left Antioch in Pisidia and "went from place to place through the country of Galatia and Phrygia" (Acts 18:23).

PHYGELUS

In the New testament, one from the district of Asia who "turned away from" Paul (2 Timothy 1:15).

PHYI-MCHOD

In Tibetan Buddhist ceremonies, the seven offerings of external worship, presented before the tranquil deities. They are basically the seven ways of honoring a distinguished guest - by offering water for drinking, water for washing, flowers, incense, lamps, perfume, and food.

In the regular, daily attendance on the deities, the seven offerings are often represented by seven small bowls filled with water, though special ceremonies and festivals require the full offerings.

PHYLACTERY

In Jewish religious practice, a small black-leather, cube-shaped case containing four Torah texts written on parchment, which, in accordance with Deuteronomy 6:8, are to be worn by male Jews of 13 years and older as constant reminders of God and the obligation to keep the Law during daily life.

PIBESETH

In biblical times, a city mentioned along with On (Heliopolis) at Ezekiel 30:17 in a prophecy directed against Egypt.

Pibeseth or Bubastis was the seat of the worship of the goddess Bastet or Bast, a feline goddess often represented with the head of a cat. The presence of a large burial ground for cats near the city testifies to the prominence of her worship there. An annual festival was held in honor of Bastet, drawing thousands of adherents from all parts of the land.

While Pibeseth was the capital of the eighteenth district of Lower Egypt, it reached its greatest political prominence with the line of Libyan rulers over Egypt begun by Pharaoh Shishak, a contemporary of Solomon and

Rehoboam (1 Kings 11:40; 14:25-26). Pibeseth was a royal city of Shishak. Ezekiel's prophecy relates to the Babylonian conquest of Egypt when Pibeseth would be overrun. The Persians later destroyed the city, and today only ruins remain of the ancient site.

PICUS

In Roman mythology, ancient Roman woodpecker, sacred to the god Mars. It was widely reverenced in ancient Italy and developed into a minor god. Picus was an agricultural deity associated particularly with the fertilization of soil with manure.

PIETA

Subject in art representing the Virgin Mary supporting the body of the dead Christ after the deposition. It originated in northern Europe in the 14th century and was popular in the Italian Renaissance and carved three times by Michelangelo.

PIETISM

A movement in Lutheranism (17th century) stressing practical and inward religion rather than dogmatic theology. Most pietists remained within the church, using primate meetings and education; others founded sects. Pietism influenced Moravian Brethren and the Evangelical Revival.

Pietism was responsible for the development of a number of separate denominations, notably the Herrnhuters, or Moravians. Through the Moravians Pietism affected John Wesley and Methodism, but the primary importance for church history of the Pietist movement lay in its impact upon the older Protestant communions, the Lutheran and Reformed.

After the conflicts between Pietism and orthodoxy had subsided, many elements of both combined forces in opposition to rationalism and the Enlightenment. Accepting the validity of the Pietist critique but lamenting the emotionalism into which Pietistic religion had often fallen, the defenders of Lutheran confessional orthodoxy during the 19th century all showed the effects of the reformation it had wrought.

Perhaps the most visible effect of Pietism within the churches was the revival of a zeal for the missions. Neither Luther nor the high Lutheran orthodoxy of the 17th century had succeeded in organizing a missionary movement - partly because of the paralysis caused by the abolition of the religious orders, partly because of political reasons, but also partly because of failure to accept the demands of the missionary imperative. Pietism corrected this lack in Lutheranism, fostering the formation of missionary societies in the various Lutheran lands and territories. It also took up the task of eliciting vocations to the missions among theological students and clergy.

As a result, the evangelical Christianity exported by these missionaries and planted in pagan cultures bore (and often still bears) marks of its Pietist origins: a moral seriousness, a concern for individual conversion, and a stress upon the use of the Bible, especially upon its private study; but also a tendency to underemphasize the presence and power of God within the structures of nature and of human culture.

PIETY

In Roman Catholicism regarded as a gift of the Holy Spirit which fosters in us duty, respect, and loyalty toward our parents, family, and country.

PIETY, Forms of

Expressions of fervor in the practice of religion. The forms of piety may include participation at the Holy Mass and other liturgical services, as well as acts of veneration of the saints.

PIHAHIROTH

In biblical times, the last camping site of the Israelites before crossing the Red Sea (Numbers 33:7-8). After having encamped at "Etham at the edge of the wilderness" (Exodus 13:20) Moses, according to biblical tradition, received instructions from God to "turn back and encamp before Pihahiroth between Migdol and the sea in view of Baal-zephon (Exodus 14:1-2).

Pihahiroth was near the Red Sea and at some point where the only route of escape from the advancing Egyptian forces would be through the sea itself. The sea at that point would also have to be of sufficient depth to allow for the waters to be "split apart" to form the passage through "the midst of the sea." with the waters forming a "wall" on both sides (Exodus 14:16-21). Many modern scholars favor the theory of a crossing in the shallow Bitter Lakes region, which begins circa 15 miles north of present-day Suez. Older scholars either associate Pihahiroth with the plain lying between Jebel Atakah and Jebel el Galala or with the narrow strip of that plain running along the south-eastern foot of Jebel Atakah, circa 12 miles south-east of Suez.

PILATE, Pontius

Roman procurator of Judea (AD 26-36) who ordered the crucifixion of Christ, afterwards washing his hands to disclaim responsibility (Matthew 27:24). Hated by the Jews, he was recalled to Rome after his behavior had provoked a riot which had to be put down by troops.

PILDASH

In Judaism, sixth named of the eight sons of Abraham's brother Nahor by his wife Milcah (Genesis 22:21-23).

PILGRIMAGE

Journeys of devotion, penance, thanksgiving, or the fulfillment of a vow. Divine grace is felt to be especially potent in places visited by Jesus Christ or saints or by Mary; where they have appeared in visions; or where their relics are kept.

Abuses of pilgrimage were criticized by reformers, and pilgrimages were abolished in Protestantism. They remain popular in Roman Catholicism and the Orthodox church, especially to holy icons and monasteries.

Pilgrimage is an important concept in Islam. Hajj is one of the five arkan (pillars of Islam). All Muslims, provided a number of conditions including good health and financial ability are present, have a duty to make a pilgrimage to Mecca at least once in their lifetimes. This major pilgrimage must be made in the month of Pilgrimage, the last month of the Muslim lunar calendar, between the 8th day of the month and the 12th or 13th. A minor pilgrimage to Mecca, which does not count towards fulfillment of the religious duty and is called in Arabic an umra, may be made at any time and requires less ceremonial.

PILGRIMAGE, Buddhist

Though not required for followers of the religion, pilgrimage attracts Buddhists in large numbers to centers and shrines associated with the Buddha or his disciples.

Paramount among these are the four sites associated with the four great events of the Buddha's life:

1 Lumbini (Nepal); an Asokan pillar and a small temple mark the site of the Buddha's birthplace;

2 Bodh Gaya (India); prominent railings dating from the 1st century BC and the Mahabodhi temple, a restoration of earlier restorations of a structure probably erected in the 2nd century AD;

3 The Deer Park (Isipatana) at Sarnath (India); an Asokan pillar and a stupa denote the place where Buddha preached his first sermon;

4 Kusinagara (India); a stupa and a shrine commemorate the site of the Buddha's parinircana, or death.

PILGRIMAGE, Christian

Journey to a saint's shrine or other sacred place, undertaken for a variety of motives: to gain supernatural help; as an act of thanksgiving or penance; for the sake of devotion.

PILGRIMAGE OF GRACE

A rising in the northern counties of England, the only overt immediate discontent shown against the Reformation legislation of King Henry VIII. The pilgrimage achieved nothing and received no support from other parts of the country.

PILGRIM FESTIVALS

In Judaism, the three occasions on which male Israelites were required to go to Jerusalem to offer sacrifice at the Temple and bring offerings of their produce from the fields.

PILGRIMS

Those who journey to a holy place either for penance or to seek divine help. Since antiquity pilgrimages have been a part of all major religions. The ancient Greeks visited Delphi and Eleusis, and Christians have made their way to shrines in the Holy land since the 3rd century. Muslims go to Mecca for the Hajj as they have for 13 centuries, Hindus flock to Benares to bathe in the holy Ganges, and Buddhists visit the Temple of the Tooth at Kandy in Sri Lanka. In modern times many members of the Roman Catholic Church make holy pilgrimages, especially to Rome and to Lourdes.

PILGRIMS'S PROGRESS

Religious allegory by the English writer John Bunyan (published between 1678 to 1684), a symbolic vision of the good man's pilgrimage through life, at one time second only to the Bible in popularity.

PILHA

In Judaism, a family head of Israel or a representative of a family of that name attesting the post-exilic "trustworthy" arrangement (Nehemiah 9:38; 10:1, 14, 24).

PILLARS OF ISLAM

Arkan, literally meaning supports, basic elements. The pillars are in alphabetical order:
1 Hajj (Pilgrimage to Mecca);
2 Salat (The Prayer Ritual);
3 Sawm (Fasting during Ramadan);
4 Shahada (The Profession of Faith);
5 Zakat (Almsgiving).

PILTAI

In Judaism, post-exilic head of the priestly paternal house of Moadiah in the days of Joshua's successor Joiakim (Nehemiah 12:12-17).

PINON

In biblical times, one of the sheiks of Esau (Edom) (Genesis 36:40-43; 1 Chronicles 1:51-52). Some think that these names are a listing of places or settlements rather than individuals or that the names came to apply to a particular region or city ruled by the sheiks.

PIR

In Islam, term denoting a wise guide, spiritual master, saint, or old man.

PIRAM

In biblical times, the Amorite king of Jarmuth at the time Israel entered the Promised Land. Piram joined with four other Amorite kings in a conspiracy against the Gibeonites, who had made peace with Joshua. In the battle that followed, Piram and the other kings took refuge in a cave at Makkedah, which the Israelites sealed up until the fighting was over. Piram and the others were then slain, hung on stakes until evening and entombed in the same cave (Joshua 10:1-27).

PIRATHON

In biblical times, a town of Ephraim in the mountain of the Amalekite. Evidently an inhabitant of Pirathon was known as a "Pirathonite," as were Hillel and, later, Benaiah, one of David's mighty men. Hillel's son Judge Abdon was buried there (Judges 12:13-15; 1 Chronicles 11:31). Far'ata, circa six miles west-southwest of the suggested location for Shechem, has been suggested as a possible identification.

PIRE, Dominique Georges

(1910-1969) Dominican who won the Nobel Peace Prize in 1958 for his aid to European displaced persons from World War II.

PIRITHOUS

In Greek mythology, the companion and helper of the hero Theseus in his adventures, including the descent into Hades to carry off Persephone, the daughter of the goddess Demeter. They were detained in Hades until the Greek hero Heracles rescued Theseus but not Pirithous.

PISA, Council of

In Roman Catholic Church history, a council convened in 1409 with the intention of ending the Great Schism, when rival popes, each with his own Curia, were set up in Rome and Avignon. The council deposed the two existing popes, and elected a third, Alexander V.

PISACA

In the mythology of India a fiend or evil spirit, either male or female. It is regarded as the ghost of a liar, adulterer, madman, or animal and is said to drink blood and to rend human flesh.

PISIDIA

In biblical times, name for an interior region of southern Asia Minor. It was a mountainous section, taking in the western portion of the Taurus range, lying north of Pamphylia and south of Galatian Phrygia. The region is believed to have been about 120 miles from east to west and circa 50 miles in breadth.

The people of Pisidia were wild and warlike, forming tribal bands of robbers. These mountaineers were difficult to control and slow to be affected by Hellenic or Roman culture. The Romans assigned Galatian King Amyntas the task of subjugating them, but he died before accomplishing it. Pisidia became part of the Roman province of Galatia in 25 BC.

The apostle Paul passed through Pisidia on his first missionary tour, traveling from coastal Pamphylia over the mountains to Pisidian Antioch (Acts 12:13-14). He also passed through Pisidia on the return trip (Acts 14:21-24). The bandits and the rushing mountain rivers of the area might well have been a basis for Paul's statement that he had been in "dangers from rivers, in dangers from highwaymen" (2 Corinthians 11:26).

PISTOIA, Synod of

A diocesan meeting held in 1786 that was important to the history of Jansenism, a nonorthodox, pessimistic, and rigoristic movement in the Roman Catholic Church. The Synod was aimed at a reform of the Tuscan church along the lines advocated by the Jansenists and the Gallicans, who sought to restrict the authority of the pope.

In 1794 Pope Pius VI condemned 85 propositions of Pistoia.

PITHOM

In the Old Testament, name of two storage cities built by the enslaved Israelites in Egypt, the other being Ramses (Exodus 1:11). The name Pithom is generally thought to have some relation to the Egyptian name Pr-Tem, meaning "house of (the god) Tem."

PITHON

In Judaism, name for a descendant of Saul through Jonathan and Merib-baal (1 Chronicles 8:33-35).

PITI

In Buddhism, rapture; as a high degree of enthusiasm. The term is used in the sense of a joyful state of consciousness; a mental factor in the Abhidhamma analysis of mind.

PITTSBURGH PLATFORM

Jewish manifesto of religious principles enunciated by Reform rabbis at the Pittsburgh Conference in 1885.

PIUS I

(81-155) Bishop of Rome from circa 140 to 155. He combatted Gnosticism - a religious movement teaching that matter is evil and that emancipation comes through spiritual truth attained only by revelatory esoteric knowledge.

The claim that Pius is martyred is unsubstantiated. His feast day is July 11.

PIUS II

(1405-1464) Aeneas Silvius Piccolomini; pope from 1458-1464; outstanding humanist and astute politician who tried to unite Europe in a crusade against the Turks at a time when they threatened to overrun all of Europe. He died disappointed after valiant but futile efforts to unite rival factions in Europe.

PIUS III

(1440-1503) Francesco Todeschini Piccolomini; pope during 1503, who was consecrated on October 1, 1503, but died soon after. In honor of Pius II he founded the Piccolomini Library adjoining the Siena Cathedral. He was a virtuous man who might have accomplished much as pope had he lived.

PIUS IV

(1499-1565) Giovanni Angelo de Medici; pope from 1559 to 1565, who concluded the Council of Trent. Several important works that the Council recommended or initiated but could not effectually carry out were given to Pius for completion; among these were drafting the Index of Forbidden Books and reforming the catechism, missal, and breviary.

PIUS V

(1504-1572) Antonio Ghislieri; pope from 1566 to 1572. With some severity he restored a degree of discipline and morality to the papacy in the face of a Protestant challenge, and organized the Spanish-Venetian expedition which defeated the Turks at Lepanto in 1775.

PIUS VI

(1717-1799) Giannangelo Braschi; pope from 1775 to 1799, drained the Pontine Marshes and completed st. peter's. The French Revolution led to the occupation of the papal territories and Pius' death in captivity.

Under Pius, the papacy, crushed by the Revolution, had reached perhaps its nadir since the Middle Ages, partly because of his inability to adopt a suitable policy. The revolutionary leaders in France and the preceding reformative monarchs were not primarily anti-clerical; Pius failed to realize that the church could not remain untouched by the enormous changes happening in Europe. He was unable to handle Joseph's Febronianism as well as the cataclysm that ensured from the French Revolution, which destroyed his temporal authority and presaged a new epoch for the papacy.

PIUS VII

(1741-1823) Pope from 1800 to 1823. He restored order in the papal states when the French troops were withdrawn and in 1801 concluded a Concordat with Napoleon, whom he consecrated as Emperor in 1804. He was later forced to sanction Napoleon's annexation of the papal states. Upon his restoration (1815) he suppressed brigandage and secret societies and restored the Jesuits.

PIUS VIII

(1761-1830) Francesco Saverio Castiglioni; pope from 1829 to 1830. He was generally broad-minded and conciliatory. He accepted the July revolution (1830) in France that deposed Charles X in favor of Louis-Philippe. Pius encouraged French ecclesiastics to endorse the new regime, hoping it would secure amiable ties with the papacy.

PIUS IX

(1792-1878) Giovanni Maria Mastai-Ferretti; pope from 1846 to 1878. He began the longest papal reign in 1848 with liberal reforms, but became an extreme reactionary in both politics and dogma (1854), and papal infallibility was proclaimed in 1870 by the First Vatican Council. In 1871 the new kingdom of Italy passed the *Law of Guaranties* defining relations between the state and the papacy, but Pius refused to accept the position.

PIUS X

(1835-1914) Guiseppe Melchiorre Sarto; Pope from 1903 to 1914, whose staunch political and religious conservatism dominated the early 20th-century church. He led the reaction against Christian democracy because he could not tolerate the idea of some Catholics making their social work a matter independent of the hierarchy and conducting it in an increasingly political direction. He opposed the contemporary trend in European countries where Christians reacted against doctrines of materialism by forming their own social movements or popular action groups. Accordingly, he formally condemned the Italian priest Romulo Murri's popular action movement in 1903 and the pioneering Christian Democrat Marc Sagnier's Sillon movement in France.

His revival of the Gregorian plainsong and his recasting of the breviary and of the missal were important liturgical reforms. His decision to adapt and systematize canon law led to the publication of a new code in 1917.

PIUS XI

(1857-1939) Ambrogio Damiano Achille Ratti; pope from 1922 to 1939, one of the most important modern pontiffs whose motto "the peace of Christ in the Kingdom of Christ" illustrated his unremitting work to construct a new Christendom based on world peace. He made great efforts to organize the laity, first in Italy and then throughout the whole church, calling for "specialized movements" and particularly encouraging Catholic Action, a Christian youth organization for the working classes.

PIUS XII

(1792-1958) Eugenio Pacelli; pope who reigned from 1939 to 1958, was an active diplomat in a difficult period and undertook a considerable amount of humanitarian work during World War II although he was criticized for refusing to condemn Nazi policy towards the Jews. His encyclical *Mediator Dei* led to changes in the mass.

Pius dealt with contemporary moral and theological issues in innumerable addresses and in several encyclicals. In his final years of ill health, the power of his conservative curia increased.

PIYYUT

In Judaism, one of several types of liturgical compositions or religious poems, some of which have been incorporated into Jewish liturgy and have become virtually indistinguishable from the mandatory services, especially on sabbaths and on Jewish religious festivals.

PLAGUE

In biblical times, the original-language words rendered "plague" or "scourge" often designate blows dealt by God as a punishment for rebellious murmuring (Numbers 16:41-50), refusal to comply with His will (Zechariah 14:12-18), the profane use of something sacred (1 Samuel 6:1-6), touching his anointed ones (Genesis 12:17) and unfaithfulness or violations of his law (Leviticus 26:21; Numbers 14:36).

A plague could also result from the natural outworking of a person's sin (Proverbs 6:32-33). It could be an affliction, such as the "plague of leprosy" (Leviticus 13:2), or an adversity resulting from time and circumstance (Psalms 38:11).

The plagues visited upon Egypt in the time of Moses were, according to biblical tradition, manifestations of His great power and caused His name to be declared among the nations (Exodus 9:14-16).

PLAGUES OF EGYPT

in the book of Exodus, the 10 disasters inflicted on Egypt by God when the pharaoh refused Moses' demand that the Israelites be freed. They were: the rivers turned to blood, frogs, lice, flies, murrain, boils, hail, locusts, darkness, and finally the death of all firstborn. After the last plague, from which the Israelites were protected by the Passover, they were allowed to leave.

PLAINCHANT

Term referring to Gregorian chant and, by extension, to other similar religious chants. Its principle is defined as unmeasured rhythms and monophony (single line of melody) of Gregorian chant.

PLANUDES MAXIMUS

(1260-1310) Greek Orthodox scholar, who established a monastery for laymen. He wrote on the traditional Byzantine dogma that the Spirit relates exclusively to the Father, and thus refusing to accept the Trinitarian dogma (one God in three persons).

PLATO

(circa 427-347 BC) Athenian philosopher, perhaps the greatest thinker of all time. In 385 he founded his philosophy school in the grove of the hero Academus. It was therefore called the Academy. The most famous of his students was Aristotle who later set up a school of his own.

Plato stands at the center of Greek philosophy. In him the various strands of pre-Socratic philosophy came together. Heraclitus had held that everything is in constant motion while Parmenides had taught that reality was frozen into permanent rest. Plato combined these two notions showing what was valuable in both of them. Reality, according to Plato, is a process. To say, for example, that grass is green does not imply that grass is an unchanging thing, but that which we attribute to it, the property of being green, is stable and unchanging. This idea that different things, such as dry grass or green grass, can be called by the same name, grass, because they have features in common, is an important element in the theory of ideas or forms.

The theory of forms or ideas, however, presents one insurmountable difficulty: how are the qualities to be linked with the individual objects that they qualify? Because of this problem, Plato later abandoned the theory and concentrated on examining the way in which certain very general features (such as identity and difference, what came later to be called categories) functioned in reasoned argument. It was from such beginnings that Aristotle later developed his logical theories. Plato also laid down the principles of the method of hypothesis and deduction.

He had a major impact on certain religious philosophies. During the early Middle Ages much of Plato, as seen through Neoplatonic and Aristotelian eyes, dominated Christian philosophy through the writings of Boethius and Augustine. In the 17th century a group of English philosophers at Cambridge University, known as the Cambridge Platonists, revived Platonic studies in England in an attempt to harmonize reason and religion.

PLATONISM

A family of philosophic movements that derive their ultimate inspiration from the Dialogues of Plato and embrace his belief in absolute values rooted in a realm of unchanging and eternal realities independent of the world perceived by the senses.

PLATONISM, Islamic

The influence of the ideas of Plato on Islam. Generally speaking, the thought of Plato had less impact on the development of Islamic philosophy than that of Aristotle or Plotinus. Plato's greatest areas of influence were perhaps those of ethics and morals, and in such classifications as the tripartite division of the soul. Plato's *Republic* was translated into Arabic in the 9th century. The Platonic themes of the body prison for the soul and Socrates as a hero who knows how to die bravely, appear in such Arabic works as the Epistles of the Ikhwan al-Safa.

PL KYODAN

A religious movement of Japan founded in 1946 by Miki Pokuchika, who based it on the pre-World War II sect Hito-no-michi. PL Kyodan teaches that "life is art," including within the scope of art all human activity. The goal of man is joyful self-expression, but when man forgets God because of his own egocentricity, his manifestations of selfishness bring misfortune and suffering down upon himself.

PLOTINUS
(circa 205-270) Greco-Roman philosopher, probably from upper Egypt, the founder and chief representative of Neoplatonism. The period of his greatest influence began circa 244 when he settled in Rome where his school attracted wide following. His philosophy, based on Plato, subsequently exercised a considerable influence on Christian theology, particularly on St. Augustine even though Plotinus himself opposed Christianity.

PLUNKET, Oliver
(1629-1681) Roman Catholic primate of all Ireland and the last man to suffer martyrdom for the Catholic faith in the United Kingdom.

PLUTO
In classical mythology, the god of the underworld, brother of Zeus and Poseidon. He was often called Hades by the Greeks, who depicted him as a shadowy figure ruling over the infernal regions and the dead with his wife Persephone. As Pluto, however, he was seen as a benevolent deity linked with agriculture and the riches of the earth, including gold and silver.

PLUTUS
In Greek religion, god of abundance or wealth, a personification of Ploutos (Greek, "riches").

PLYMOUTH BRETHREN
Christian (Protestant) body that originated in England through the work in particular of J.N. Darby (1800-82), a former priest in Anglicanism. The original teaching of the Brethren was strongly biblical, and influenced by Calvinism.
The chief types of Brethren are the "Open" and "Exclusive". The Exclusive's severe standards lead them to reject many aspects of modern life and to restrict social contacts with non-Brethren, even members of their own family.

POCHERETH-HAZZEBAIM
In Judaism, head of a family whose descendants were among "the sons of the servants of Solomon" returning from the Babylonian exile under the leadership of Zerubbabel (Ezra 2:1-2; 55-57; Nehemiah 7:59).

POCH'ONGYO
An indigenous Korean religion, founded by Kang Il-sun (1871-1909). Incantations are said to induce trembling and to produce a trancelike sense of selflessness, which is a sign of the ascent of God; diseases are cured, and the future is revealed. More recently, meditation on the Tao, has been emphasized as the path to self-enlightenment and as an effective means of inducing a state of selfless trance, the highest of all goals.

POGROM
A mob attack, either approved or condoned by authorities, against the persons and properties of a religious, racial, or national minority. The term is usually applied to attacks on Jews.

POLAND, Orthodox Church of
An autocephalous (ecclesiastically independent) member of the Eastern Orthodox communion, established in 1924.

POLDING, John Bede
(1794-1877) First Raman Catholic bishop in Australia, where he became the first archbishop of Sydney. In 1844 and 1859 he convoked synods in Melbourne and in Sydney, where he founded St. John's College.

POLISH NATIONAL CATHOLIC CHURCH OF AMERICA
An Old Catholic Church that arose in the late 19th and early 20th centuries among Polish immigrants in the United States, who left the Roman Catholic Church.

POLITICS

Activities revolving around public affairs that concern all members of a community. The role of the church in the political orders is to defend the dignity of the human person. The church may also comment on those political issues that have moral implications.

POLUDNITSA

In Slavic mythology, the female field spirit, generally seen either as a tall woman or a girl dressed in white. The poludnitsa customarily appears in the field at noon, when the workers are resting from their labors. Any human who dares upset her traditional visit risks his health and his life.

POLYCARP, Saint

(124-178) Greek bishop of Smyrna, the leading 2nd-century figure in Roman Asia by virtue of his intermediary position between the apostolic and patristic ages and his work during the initial appearance of Christianity's fundamental theological literature.

POLYCARP, Martyrdom of

A letter that described the death by burning of Polycarp, bishop of Smyrna in Asia Minor, sent to the Christian church in Philomelium, Asia Minor, from the church in Smyrna. It is the oldest authentic account of an early Christian martyr's death.

POLYGAMY

Concept that plays a major role only in Islam. The Koran permits a Muslim male to marry up to four wives, provided that he feels able to treat them all equitably. However, as a result of the interpretation of certain verses of the Koran, polygamy is now banned in countries like Tunisia and Algeria.

POLYTHEISM

The belief in or worship of more than one god. Most polytheistic religions are quite old and most still exist in regions longest isolated from the rest of society, such as in Africa and parts of Polynesia. The worship of one god, in fact, seems to be a more recent development historically, since most cultures contain traces of a polytheistic past. Commonly, polytheism deifies the major forces of nature and life - such as rain and thunder, love and death, the moon and the harvest. Modeled after man, these gods are rarely meant to exemplify perfection, as in monotheism, and although generally immortal and possessed of supernatural power are usually possessed of human weakness as well. Polytheistic systems generally envisage a community of gods ruled by one chief god.

It is a heinous sin forbidden in the Koran. The Arabic word means literally "sharing": man is forbidden to share his worship of God with that of any other creatures, and to ascribe partners to God as sharers of His Divinity. Polytheism is the one since which the Koran mentions that cannot and will not be forgiven. This is because it denies God's very existence.

PONTIANUS, Saint

(167-236) Pope from 230 to 235, known only for the summoning of a Roman synod that conformed the condemnation of Origen, one of the chief theologians of the early Greek church, whose influence continued despite Pontianus' condemnation.

PONTUS

In biblical times, name for a district of northern Asia Minor along the Euxine (Black Sea). After being under Persian influence for a time, the separate kingdom of Pontus was set up in the fourth century BC. There was a succession of kings called Mithradates, and close ties with Rome developed.

The first-century Jewish writer Philo said that Jews had spread to every part of Pontus. Jews from Pontus were present on Pentecost AD 33 (Acts 2:9). Possibly some of these Jews from Pontus who heard Peter's speech became Christians and returned to their home territory. Some 30 years later, Peter addressed his first canonical letter to "temporary residents scattered about in Pontus" and other parts of Asia Minor (1 Peter 1:1). Since he mentioned "older men" who were to shepherd the flock, Christian congregations likely existed in Pontus (1 Peter 5:1-2). The Jew named Aquila who was a native of Pontus traveled to Rome and then to Corinth, where he met the apostle Paul (Acts 18:1-2).

POPE

An ecclesiastical title expressing affectionate respect (from the Latin: pappa), formerly given, especially from the 3rd to the 5th century, to any bishop and sometimes to simple priests; the title is still used in the East for the Orthodox priests, but, since about the 9th century, reserved in the West exclusively for the bishop of Rome (see table page 832-833),

POPLARS, Torrent Valley of

At Isaiah 15:7 the prophet described the escaping Moabites as fleeing with their goods across the "torrent valley of the poplars." If their flight was to the south, as it seems likely to have been this torrent valley would appear to refer to the "torrent valley of Zered" (Numbers 21:12; Deuteronomy 2:13), which acted as the frontier boundary between Moab and Edom to the south. The torrent valley of Zered is generally identified with the Wadi el-Hesa, which flows into the southern end of the Dead Sea. In its lower course it is called the Seil el-Qurahi and as such passes through a small plain that is somewhat swampy in places and could thus be a suitable place for polars to have grown.

PORATHA

In the Old Testament, one of Harman's ten sons (Esther 9:9-10).

POSEIDON

The Greek god of the sea and water, the brother of Zeus, later identified by the Romans with their god Neptune. Poseidon was often portrayed carrying a trident which he used to raise storms and cause earthquakes. Bulls were sacrificed to him to appease his vengeful spirit. His mythical offspring were numerous, and they included such strange creatures as Pegasus, the winged horse, and the one-eyed giant Polyphemus.

Poseidon's amatory exploits involved many of the goddesses and a respectable number of mortal females, on whom he bestowed numerous children. Among them (with the mothers in brackets) were: Triton (Amphitrite); Polyphemus (Thoosa), Antaeus (Mother Earth), Orion (Euryale), Pelias and Neleus (Tero), Pegasus and Chrysaor (Medusa), and Atlas (Cleito).

POSSESSION, Diabolical

The state of a person whose body, mind, or organs are controlled by a demon or demons. The New Testament records several instances of diabolical possession.

POTHIER, Dom Joseph

(1923-1991) French monk and scholar who, together with his contemporaries, reconstituted the Gregorian chant.

POTIPHAR

In biblical times, an Egyptian court official and chief of Pharaoh's bodyguard. He was Joseph's master for a time and, it appears was a man of wealth (Genesis 37:36; 39:4). Potiphar purchased Joseph from the traveling Midianite merchants, and, observing what a good servant Joseph was, eventually put him in charge of his whole house and field (Genesis 39:1-6).

POTIPHERA

In biblical times, Joseph's father-in-law, whose daughter Asenath bore Manasseh and Ephraim (Genesis 41:45; 46:20). Potiphera was the priest, likely of the sun-god Ra, officiating at On, a center of Egyptian sun worship.

POVERTY

A term used by Christians in several senses, among them:

▲ The state of being destitute or in need of the basic necessities of life; this state is opposed to human dignity and is the result of an unjust distribution of the goods of the world, and is seen as a moral and social evil.

▲ The state of being "poor in spirit," having the attitude of Christ toward material possessions, that is, seeing them as gifts of God for one"s support, the support of one's family, and the support of those in need.

▲ One of the evangelical counsels or vows professed by religious men and women in the church.
It involves the voluntary renunciation of the right to own property or, at least, the renunciation of the independent use and disposal of what one owns, the living of the common life, whereby one gives to the community what one earns and receives from the community what one needs.
In the Roman Catholic Church the details of the vow of poverty are regulated by the Code of Canon Law and by the constitutions of each religious institute.

PRACTITIONER

In Christian Science, one who is certified in the public ministry of healing by spiritual means.

PRADAKSINA

In Buddhism, keeping to the right; ritual circumambulation of a Stupa or holy object, keeping the object or person to the right. The same was observed in European pilgrimage at a shrine. In the same way visitors to the Buddha kept to the right as they approached and sat down on his left.

PRAJNA

In Buddhism term meaning wisdom; one of the six Paramitas. Prajna is the mental function which enables one to perceive life without error and to distinguish between what is true and what is false. One who has acquired this perfectly is called a Buddha. Therefore, this is the most refined and enlightenment wisdom, distinct from ordinary human intelligence.

PRAJNA-PARAMITA

Buddhist literature (literally meaning "Wisdom which has gone beyond"), compiled in India over many centuries, beginning in the first century BC.

PRAJNA-PARAMITAHRDAYA-SUTRA

Brief distillation of the essence of Prajna-paramita writings, much produced throughout Asia and frequently recited in Zen Buddhist monasteries. True to its title, it summarized, in contrast to other brief wisdom sutras that tend to water it down for easier consumption.

PRAJNAPTI

In Buddhist philosophy, a concept important especially in the Madhyamika and Viijnanavada. It described by a word the denotation of a thing. According to Buddhist philosophers of these schools, the names generally admitted conceptions used in our everyday language do not correspond to any substantial existence, as is supposed by realists.

PRAKRITI

In Buddhism, primordial matter, as one of the pairs of opposites into which the Oneness of the universe divides on manifestation, the other being Purusha Spirit. According to Buddhist philosophy even this duality is "falsely imagined," for this Matter is the crystallization of Spirit, and Spirit is the ultimate sublimation of Matter.

PRAMANA

A fundamental concept of Indian philosophy, describing the means of obtaining accurate and valid knowledge about an object. The principal three means of knowledge are:

▲ perception;
▲ inference;
▲ word.

POPES

CHRONOLOGICAL LIST IF POPES.
The names of antipopes are in italics.

POPE	YEAR	POPE	YEAR	POPE	YEAR
St. Peter	42	St. Leo	440	St. Gregory III	731
St. Linus	67	St. Hilary	461	St. Zachary	741
St. Anacletus	76	St. Simplicius	468	Stephen II	752
St. Clement I	88	St. Felix III	483	St. Paul	757
St. Evaristus	97	St. Gelasius I	492	*Constantine*	*767*
St. Alexander I	105	Anastasius II	496	Philip	768
St. Sixtus I	115	St. Symmachus	498	Stephen III	768
St. Telesphorus	125	St. Hormisdas	514	Adrian I	772
St. Hyginus	138	St. John I	523	St. Leo III	795
St. Pius I	140	St. Felix IV	526	Stephen IV	816
St. Anicetus	155	Boniface II	530	St. Paschal	817
St. Soter	166	*Dioscorus*	*530*	Eugene II	824
St. Eleutherius	175	John II	533	Valentine	827
St. Victor I	189	St. Agapitus I	535	Gregory IV	827
St. Zephyrinus	199	St. Silverius	536	*John*	*844*
St. Callistus I	217	Vigilius	537	Sergius II	844
St. Hippolytus	*217*	Pelagius I	556	St. Leo IV	847
St. Urban I	222	John III	561	Benedict III	855
St. Pontian	230	Benedict I	575	Anastasius	855
St. Anterus	235	Pelagus II	579	St. Nicholas I	858
St. Fabian	236	St. Gregory I	590	Adrian II	867
Novatian	*251*	Sabinian	604	John VIII	872
St. Lucius I	253	Boniface III	607	Marinus I	882
St. Stephen I	254	St. Boniface IV	608	St. Adriane III	884
St. Sixtus II	257	St. Adeodatus	615	Stephen V	885
St. Felix I	269	Boniface V	619	Formosus	891
St. Eutychian	275	Honorius I	625	Boniface VI	896
St. Caius	283	Severinus	640	Stephen VI	896
St. Marcellinus	296	John IV	640	Romanus	897
St. Marcellus I	308	Theodore I	642	Theodore II	897
St. Eusebius	309	St. Martin I	649	John IX	898
St. Melchiades	311	St. Eugene I	654	Benedict IV	900
St. Sylvester I	314	Adeodatus II	672	Leo V	903
St. Marcus	336	Donus	676	*Christoph*	*903*
St. Julius I	337	St. Agatho	678	Sergius III	904
Liberius	352	St. Leo II	682	Anastasius III	911
Felix II	*355*	St. Benedict II	684	Landus	913
St. Damasus I	366	John V	685	John X	914
Ursinus	*366*	Conon	686	Leo VI	928
St. Siricius	384	*Theodore*	*687*	Stephen VII	928
St. Anastasius I	399	Paschal	687	John XI	931
St. Innocent I	401	St. Sergius I	687	Leo VII	936
St. Zosimus	417	John VI	701	Stephen VII	939
St. Boniface I	418	John VII	705	Marinus II	942
Eutalius	418	Sisinnius	708	Agapitus II	946
St. Celestine I	422	Constantine	708	John XII	955
St. Sixtus III	432	St. Gregory II	715	Leo VIII	963

POPE	YEAR	POPE	YEAR	POPE	YEAR
Benedict V	964	*Paschal III*	*1164*	Alexander VI	1492
John XIII	965	*Callistus III*	*1168*	Pius III	1503
Benedict VI	973	*Innocent III*	*1179*	Julius II	1503
Boniface VII	*974*	Lucius III	1181	Leo X	1513
Benedict VIII	974	Urban III	1185	Adrian VI	1522
John XIV	983	Clement III	1187	Chement VII	1523
John XV	985	Gregory VIII	1187	Paul III	1534
Gregory V	996	Celestine III	1191	Julius III	1550
John XVI	*997*	Innocent III	1179	Marcellus II	1555
Sylvester II	999	Honorius III	1216	Paul IV	1555
John XVII	1003	Gregory IX	1227	Pius IV	1559
John XVIII	1004	Celestine IV	1241	St. Pius V	1566
Sergius IV	1009	Innocent IV	1243	Gregory XIII	1572
Benedict VIII	1012	Alexander IV	1254	Sixtus V	1585
Gregory	*1012*	Urban IV	1261	Urban VII	1590
John XIX	1024	Clement IV	1265	Gregory XIV	1590
Benedict IX	1032	Gregory X	1271	Innocent IX	1591
Sylvester III	1045	Innocent V	1276	Clement VIII	1592
Benedict IX	1045	Adrian V	1276	Leo IX	1605
Gregory VI	1045	John XXI	1276	Paul V	1605
Clemens II	1046	Nicholas III	1277	Gregory XV	1621
Benedict IX	1047	Martin IV	1281	Urban VIII	1623
Damasus II	1048	Honorius IV	1285	Innocent X	1644
St. Leo IX	1049	Nicholas	1288	Alexander VII	1655
Victor II	1055	St. Celestine V	1295	Clement IX	1667
Stephen IX	1057	Boniface VIII	1294	Clement X	1670
Benedict X	*1058*	Benedict XI	1303	Innocent XI	1676
Nicholas II	1059	Clement V	1305	Alexander VIII	1689
Alexander II	1061	John XXII	1316	Innocent XII	1691
Honorius II	1061	*Nicholas V*	*1328*	Clement XI	1700
Clemens III	1080	Benedict XII	1334	Innocent XII	1721
Victor III	1086	Clement VI	1342	Benedict XIII	1724
Urban II	1088	Innocent VI	1352	Clement XII	1730
Paschal II	1099	Urban V	1362	Benedict XIV	1740
Theodoric	*1100*	Gregory XI	1370	Clement XIII	1758
Albert	*1102*	Urban VI	1378	Clement XIV	1769
Sylvester IV	1105	*Clement VII*	*1378*	Pius VI	1775
Gelasius II	1118	Boniface IX	1389	Pius VII	1800
Gregory VIII	*1118*	*Benedict XIII*	*1394*	Leo XII	1823
Callistus II	1119	Innocent VII	1404	Pius VIII	1829
Honorius II	1124	Gregory XII	1406	Gregory XVI	1831
Celestine II	*1124*	*Alexander V*	*1409*	Pius IX	1846
Innocent II	1130	*John XXI*	*1410*	Leo XIII	1878
Anacletus II	*1130*	Martin V	1417	St. Pius X	1903
Victor IV	*1138*	Eugene IV	1431	Benedict XV	1914
Celestine II	1143	*Felix V*	*1439*	Pius XI	1922
Lucius II	1144	Nicholas V	1447	Pius XII	1939
Eugene III	1145	Callistus III	1455	John XXIII	1958
Anastasius IV	1153	Pius II	1458	Paul VI	1963
Adrian IV	1154	Paul II	1464	John Paul I	1978
Alexander III	1159	Sixtus IV	1471	John Paul II	1978
Victor IV	*1159*	Innocent VIII	1484		

PRAMANA-VARTTIKA

(literally: Explanation of Evidence) Perhaps the foremost work on Buddhist logic and epistemology, written in the 7th century, when logic had become a dominant concern in Buddhist thought and Buddhism itself was losing ground in India.

PRANA

A central conception in early Hindu philosophy, particularly as expressed in the Upanishads, in which a person's breath was held to be the principle of vitality and was thought to survive as his "last breath" for eternity or till a future life.

PRANAYAMA

In the Yoga-system of Indian philosophy, fourth of the eight stages intended to lead the aspirant to samadhi, a state of perfect concentration. The immediate goal of pranayama is to reduce breathing to an effortless, even rhythm, thus helping to free the individual's mind from attention to bodily functions.

PRANIDHANA

In Buddhism, a vow, an earnest wish; a vow to oneself, as self-dedication. The term is used in the sense of the Bodhisattva's vow to same mankind before benefiting from his own enlightenment.

PRAPATTI

In Hinduism, the devotee's passive surrender to the grace of God. It is an outgrowth of the path of bhakti, which required that the devotee actively seek the grace of God by love and devotion.

PRATISANDHI

In Buddhism, term literally meaning "Combination on return." The phrase denotes birth and rebirth as a reunion of parts; the first moment of consciousness on rebirth.

PRATYAHARA

In the Yoga-system of Indian philosophy, fifth of the eight stages intended to lead the aspirant to samadhi, the state of perfect concentration. The goal of pratyahara is to arrest the reaction of the senses to external objects, thus helping to isolate and free the mind from the involuntary intrusions caused by sensory activity.

PRATYAYA

In Buddhist philosophy, an auxiliary indirect cause, as distinguished from a direct cause. A seed, for example, is a direct cause of a plant, while sunshine, water, and earth are auxiliary causes of a plant.

PRATYEKA BUDDHA

The solitary sage of Indian life whose ideal was incompatible with that of the Bodhisattva, in that he "walked alone," and having attained his enlightenment, passed into Nirvana, indifferent to the woes of men.

PRAVRITTI

In Buddhism, literally flowing forth, infolding; hence evolution as the opposite of Nirvritti, involution. The term is also used in the sense of the rising up or appearance of consciousness as reaction to sense stimuli.

PRAYER

The way in which adherents to a religion personally address their god. Prayer may be in the form of praise, supplication or thanksgiving, and people of deep faith place great trust in its power to achieve good. In many Christian denominations it is custom to kneel to pray, whether in public or in private. Roman Catholics often pray to the Virgin Mary or the saints, asking their intercession before God. Christ told his followers that it was better to pray in private than to make a public display of prayer and warned against the repetition of meaningless formulae (Matthew 6). He gave Christians their most important prayer, the Paternoster or Lord's Prayer.

In Islam, the word for prayer is salat, performed by the practicing Muslim five times a day. This should not take place at the time of the actual rising or setting of the sun. Although the Koran mentions prayer many times, the obligation to pray five times per day derives from hadith rather than the Koran. The Prayer Ritual is one of the five arkan or Pillars of Islam.

PRAYER, Discursive

Often referred to as meditation, a reasoned kind of prayer in which one applies the mind to some truth or faith and, through that application, comes to embrace the truth more firmly and relate it to daily life.

The purpose of discursive prayer is twofold, to develop in oneself clearer and firmer convictions about some truth and, as a result, to turn to God and the things of God with an ever stronger love and devotion.

In the concrete, the combination of reasoned and affective action influences the one praying to make his or her prayer practical by resolving on some course of action which is seen to be needed.

The subject, the matter mediated on, may be anything which has an appeal to the reason, e.g., the fatherliness of God, an event from the life of Jesus, such as his acceptance of the cross, his compassion for sinners, etc. The choice of the subject matter is to be indicated by one's needs and one's capacities; hence, beginners are advised to accentuate what will have an imaginative appeal, as scenes from the life of the savior, especially those susceptible of a moral application to self, e.g., a virtue to practice or a vice to avoid.

All agree that the heart of discursive prayer, which is the usual type of prayer for those who are in the earlier stages of spiritual life, is the so-called "affective acts," i.e., acts having a volitional content, such as sorrow for sin, or gratitude to God.

PRAYER, Islamic

Salah or prayer constitutes one pillar of Islam and is considered the foundation of religion. Any Muslim who fails to observe his prayers and has no reasonable excuse is committing a grave offense and a heinous sin. This offense is so grave because it is not only against God, which is bad enough, but it is also against the very nature of man.

It is, according to Islam, an instinct of man to be inclined to adore the great beings, and to aspire to lofty goals. The greatest being and the loftiest goal of all is God. The best way to cultivate in man a sound personality and actualize his aspiration in a mature course of development is the Islamic prayer.

It is difficult for anyone to impart in words the full meaning of prayer in Islam, but the following points are regarded as being essential characteristics of prayer:

▲ a lesson in discipline and willpower;
▲ a practice in devotion to God and all worthy objectives;
▲ a vigilant reminder of God and constant revelation of His goodness;
▲ a seed of spiritual cultivation and moral soundness;
▲ a guide to the most upright way of life;
▲ a safeguard against indecency and evil, against wrong deviation and stray;
▲ a demonstration of true equality, solid unity, and brotherhood;
▲ a course of inner peace and stability;
▲ an abundant source of patience and courage, of hope and confidence.

Kinds of prayer

The following are the various kinds of prayer:

1 *Obligatory prayer* (Fard), which includes the five daily prayers, the Friday's noon congregation and the funeral prayer. Failure to observe these prayers is a serious and punishable sin, if there is no reasonable excuse.

2 *Supererogatory prayer* (Wajib and Sunnah), which includes the prayers accompanying the obligatory services, and the congregations of the two great festivals (Eeds). Failure to observe these is a harmful negligence and a reproachable conduct.

3 *Optional prayer* which includes all voluntary prayers at any time of the day or the night. Two periods have a special preference: the later part of the

night until just before the breaking of the dawn and the mid-morning period.

Times of prayer

Every Muslim, male or female, must offer at least five daily prayers in time, if there is no lawful reason for exemption, combination, or temporary delay. They are:

1 The *early morning prayer (Salatu-l-Fajr),* which may be offered any time after the dawn and before sunrise, a total period of about 2 hours.

2 The *noon prayer (Salatu-z-Zuhr).* This prayer may be offered any time after the sun begins to decline from its zenith until it is about midway on its course to setting.

3 The mid-afternoon prayer *(Salatu-l-'Asr),* which begins right after the expiration of the noon prayer time and extends to sunset.

4 The *sunset prayer (Salatu-l-Maghrib).* The time of this prayer begins immediately after sunset and extends until the red glow in the western horizon disappears. Normally it extends over a period of one hour and 20 to 30 minutes.

5 The *evening prayer (Salatu-l-'Isha'),* which begins after the red glow in the western horizon disappears (nearly one hour and 30 minutes after sunset) and continues till a little before the dawn.

PRAYER, Theology of

Theologically, in Roman Catholicism, prayer is a personal communion with the Father in the Son (Incarnate) through the Holy Spirit, a functioning in man of his participation in divine life. And while it is, psychologically, essentially of the mind (the practical intellect), in the full context of faith it is moved by love (the desires of charity) and is a direct and explicit expression of hope.

It has been treated by theologians chiefly (with sacrifice, adoration, devotion) as an act of the virtue of religion, yet it is realized in some way in all exercise of the theological virtues.

As a distinct "exercise" in religious life, prayer is a simple and unique activity; yet it is intimately involved in the totality of spiritual life. It has been called the "central phenomenon of religion."

While all prayer belongs to the domain of the vocative and all prayer, as such, is (in the literal sense) mental, commonly prayer is termed vocal where there is a fixed formula of approach to God; it is termed mental where the approach is a free, spontaneous (yet properly discerning) expression of the desires.

The types of prayer commonly distinguished (discursive, affective, contemplative) represent the forms that prayer takes according to the growth or stages of the spiritual life. Thus, discursive prayer (meditation) is usually that of one entering seriously upon a life of prayer; affective prayer develops with the loving understanding gained through familiarity with divine realities in meditation; contemplative (a simple, loving intuition or attention) characterizes the prayer of one who has deepened in union with God in love.

The life of prayer develops not in isolation, but as an integral element of the spiritual life and involves the necessary renouncement of self interest and sincere commitment to the divine will. Prayer thus tends to pervade all activities and circumstances of life.

PRAYER CARPET

In Islam, sajjada, carpet or rug for the practicing Muslim. The word acquired an extra dimension in tasawwuf where the head of a tariqa might bear a title like "Master of the Prayer Carpet."

PRAYER GROUPS

An assembly of people whose purpose is both to pray together and to grow in the practice of prayer.

PRAYER WHEEL

Revolving metal cylinder containing a mantra or passages from the scriptures, used in Tibet and in other places where Tibetan Buddhism is found. The prayer wheel is mounted on a short handle. Materials vary from wood and copper to beautifully wrought ivory and silver. The purpose is not for prayer, but to hold the attention of the senses while the mind, in uninterrupted "mindfulness," concentrates on the subject of meditation in hand.

PREACHING

In its primary Christian meaning, preaching is the act of proclaiming God's saving word. The term also denotes the art of pulpit oratory, which has its own history.

In the first sense, the English term preaching stands for several New Testament terms:

▲ kerussein, to herald, proclaim;
▲ euangelizesthai, to announce the good news;
▲ marturein, to witness, as used in the Johannine writings.

These are central in the dynamics of Christianity: by preaching Christianity had its beginnings, its growth, and its continuation, whatever the forms it has taken.

The fact should not be obscured by exaggerating a contrast between preaching in the Roman Catholic Church and in the churches of the Reformation.

PREACHING, First Millennium

New Testament literature indicates that the one who preaches announces his message with authority; he is commissioned; John the Baptist, for instance, was herald for Jesus, proclaiming the good tidings of the redemption (Mark 1:38; Luke 4:18). Preaching describes the whole ministry of Jesus and the Apostles (Mark 1:2; John 1:23; Acts 6:2-4; 1 Corinthians 1:17). When Jesus preached in towns and villages "to the whole world" as he had told them (Matthew 24:14; Luke 24:46).

No complete record of apostolic sermons remains, but Acts gives many reports of preaching in which the Apostles' proclamation of the kingdom is revealed (Acts 2:14-40; Acts 3:12-26; Acts 10:28-43). Paul preached in connection with the celebration of the Eucharist (Acts 12:7). Preaching is presented as the saving act of God (Mark 1:15; Luke 4:16-21), and its subject matter is the whole work of salvation through Christ.

In post-apostolic times Justin Martyr mentioned (circa 150) preaching as part of the regular liturgical service. The discourses of Polycarp (died circa 116) to his people of Smyrna are referred to by Tertullian (died circa 220) and also by Irenaeus (died circa 202), whose own sermons, collected in the 4th century by Eusebius, are no longer extant.

Among the earliest surviving preached sermons is a prolix homily on wealth by Clement of Alexandria (died circa 210), based on Mark 10:17-31. By the 4th century preaching had become an integral part of Christian worship, as the collected sermons of the great preachers attest.

Preachers of East and West were trained rhetoricians, particularly proficient at the exegetical sermon, a running commentary on the sacred scripture used in the day's liturgy.

Famed in the East were the Cappadocians, Gregory of Nazianzus (died circa 390) and Basil the Great (died 379), together with John Chrysostom (died 407) and in the West Ambrose (died 397) and Augustine (died 430). The latter often preached several times a day and composed a work on preaching.

Gregory the Great (Pope Gregory I, died 604) wrote a series of homilies that were widely read in the following centuries and gave directions for preaching in one of his books. In the Dark Ages after the barbarian invasions preaching fell into disuse, and the sermon was almost restricted to monastery churches, where homiliaries, collections of patristic sermons, like that of Paul the Deacon (720-800), were employed.

The Carolingian reforms of the 9th century improved both clerical education and preaching, notably by collections of sermons made by Alcuin and Rabanus Maurus.

PREACHING, Reformation Churches

Protesting against a special sacrificing priesthood, sacramentalism, and papal teaching authority, the Reformers asserted the primacy of the word of God as present in scripture, sermon, and sacraments.

Early reformers designated themselves simply "the preachers." Both the Augsburg Confession and the Thirty-nine Articles defined the church as existing where the gospel is rightly preached and the sacraments rightly administered.

The preaching of the word was proposed as the instrument through which justification comes about and the Holy Spirit is given. The Reformed tradition especially extolled preaching as the primary function of the ministry. While Anabaptists - the radicals of the Reformation - and later the Quakers rejected any special ministry, the influence of preaching nevertheless had a paramount influence on their history.

The high value set on preaching as characteristic of the Reformation was exemplified by Luther, Zwingli, and Calvin. A close alliance between the biblical and the preached word was observed through the expository sermon, closely following the scriptural text. The original esteem for preaching the word has never been lost in Protestantism.

Conviction that the living word of God is present in the act of preaching inspired the Puritans of England and New England, the evangelists John Wesley and George Whitfield, and preachers on revivalism. Almost every Protestant church has had its beginning with a great preacher; throughout Protestant history the major figures and the most significant movements are closely connected with preaching.

The content and quality of preaching has naturally reflected theological trends. The original Reformation zeal for the living word of God has sometimes stiffened into letter-bound biblicism. Within the century after the Reformation, both Lutheran and Reformed pulpits became platforms for a scholastic orthodoxy, in which emphasis was placed upon correct formulation of doctrine.

In reaction, Pietism developed themes and style inculcating an individualistic experience of salvation, an emphasis carried on in Wesleyan and revivalistic preaching. The impact of the Enlightenment and of rationalism turned sermon emphasis away from distinctive Christian dogma in favor of ethical and naturalistic explanations of the gospel.

This trend was continued and compounded in the 19th and 20th centuries by liberal theology; preachers sought to present an enlightened view of biblical themes accommodated to evolutionary theory, and stressed the subjective appeal of religious truths.

PREACHING, Roman Catholic

One Roman Catholic reaction to the Reformation was a strong reaffirmation of church doctrine on the sacraments and the Mass. The Catechism of the Council of Trent was designed as a doctrinal guide, especially for preaching. Since Trent there has been a conscientious fulfillment of the preaching ministry, at the parish Sunday Masses, in special sermons, particularly during Lent, and in the development of the parish mission, novenas, and retreats. In these centuries there also have been throughout the church powerful preachers, sometimes brilliant pulpit orators.

The most significant factor in Roman Catholic preaching since the reforms of Trent, however, has been a new, or newly stated, evaluation of preaching. The formulation of a Roman Catholic theology of the word was slow to come. There has been a sense of the obligation to preach; the sermon has been used for doctrinal instruction, moral exhortation, and for polemical or apologetic purposes.

Vatican Council II in the *Decree on the Liturgy* recognized the evangelizing, instructional, and exhortatory functions of preaching. But the Council described preaching in its fullest significance as "a proclamation of God's wonderful works in the history of salvation, that is, the mystery of Christ, which is ever made present and active within us, especially in the celebration of the liturgy."

These and other teachings have led to a richer theology of preaching, to an appreciation of the union between word and sacrament and of preaching as essentially the present celebration of the mystery of salvation.

PRECEPT

In Buddhism, a concept used in the sense of moral precepts, which pledge those who take them not to:

1 take life,
2 steal,
3 indulge in sensuality,
4 lie,
5 become intoxicated by drink or drugs,
6 eat at unseasonable times,
7 attend worldly amusements,
8 use perfumes or wear ornaments,
9 sleep on a luxurious bed,
10 possess gold or silver.

The first five precepts were originally binding on all who entered the Sangha; later, another group of five precepts were added. It became the custom of the pious laymen to take the first five, and these are now considered as the minimum moral code to be followed by all who call themselves Buddhists. Precepts are not commandments, they are aspirations or vows.

PRECEPT

In Christianity, an order given to an individual by an ecclesiastical superior. A precept usually enjoins a person to do or refrain from doing something.

PRECEPTS OF THE CHURCH

Obligations imposed on Catholics by the law of the church, traditionally six are listed:

1 to participate in Mass on all Sundays and holy days of obligation;
2 to fast and abstain on days designated by the church;
3 to confess one's sins once a year;
4 to receive Holy Communion during Eastertime;
5 to contribute to the support of the church;
6 to observe the laws of the church governing marriage.

PRECOGNITION

Supernormal knowledge of future events, with emphasis not upon mentally causing events to occur but upon predicting those the occurrence of which the subject claims has already been determined.

PRECONSECRATED OFFERINGS, Liturgy of the

A communion service used during Lent in Eastern Orthodox and Eastern rite Catholic churches; the consecration is omitted, and bread and wine reserved from the previous Sunday's liturgy is distributed to the faithful.

PREDESTINATION

The theological doctrine that salvation is individually conferred upon some at birth; in other words, that some human beings are predestined from birth to be saved and reach a state of grace, and - in most interpretations - the others are therefore predestined to damnation. A number of Christian theologians, including St. Augustine, St. Thomas Aquinas and Martin Luther, have dealt with some form of predestination in their writings, but the doctrine is most commonly associated with the teachings of John Calvin.

The Koran contains verses which may be interpreted in favor of both free will and predestination. An example of the latter is verse 27 of Surat al-Ra'd: "God leads astray whomsoever He wishes, and guides to Him whoever repents."

PREFECT

In biblical times; an official lower than a satrap in the Babylonian government. The title is used at Daniel 2:48 in conjunction with the "wise men." It seems that these "wise men" were classed as to their official functions. Daniel, besides being one of the three high officials of Nebuchadnezzar, was appointed chief prefect over all the "wise men" (Daniel 2:48; 3:2-3).

PREHISTORIC RELIGION

The religious beliefs and practices of early man, Since this is a phenomenon of preliterate times, there are no written records of it, and all statements about it depend on a complex body of theory, concepts, and data and on inferences and reconstructions from archaeological remains.

PRELATE

An ecclesiastical dignitary of high rank. In the modern Roman Catholic Church, prelates are those who exercise the public power of the church. In the Church of England it is restricted to bishops.

PRE-LENT

Season in the Christian church Year lasting for three and a half weeks before Ash Wednesday (the beginning of Lent). The three Sundays of the season, called Septuagesima, Sexagesima, and Quinquagesima, fall roughly 70, 60 and 50 days before Easter.

PREMONSTRATENSIANS

A Roman Catholic religious order founded in 1120 by St. Norbert of Xanten. The order combined the contemplative with the active religious life and in the 12th century provided a link between the strictly contemplative life of the monks of the preceding ages and the more active life of the friars of the 13th century.

PRESANCTIFIED, Liturgy of the

A service of worship in Eastern Orthodox and Eastern rite churches in communion with Rome that is celebrated on Wednesdays and Fridays of Lent and the first three days of Holy Week.

PRESBYTERIAN

A form of church government developed by John Calvin and other Reformers during the 16th century Protestant Reformation and used with variations by Reformed and Presbyterian churches throughout the world. According to this government system the church is a community or body in which Christ is head and all members are equal under him. The ministry is given to the entire church and is distributed among many officers. All who hold office do so by election of the people whose representatives they are. The church is to be governed and directed by assemblies of officeholders, pastors, and elders chosen to provide just representation of the church as a whole.

PRESBYTERIANISM

The English-speaking version of Reformed churches, deriving from the doctrine and church organization of Calvinism. The Presbyterian hierarchy of church courts is staffed with ministers and "elders."

The Westminster Confession is the classic standard of faith. The eucharist has traditionally been celebrated rather infrequently, but with searching preparatory services. Presbyterianism is the established church in Scotland and is strong in Northern Ireland. Migrants from these two countries carried it to the United States, where it is now a major group of churches.

Presbyterian churches believe in the principle of reform, simplicity of ceremony and liturgy, the importance of baptism and communion, and the Bible as an authority (rather than revelation or proclamation). Presbyterian doctrine and practice varies among its sects, but they have in common a specific system of church government. This is representative government by presbyters or elders. The lay elders (elected by church members) and the minister of a Presbyterian church sit on its board (in sessions, or consistories). Sessions in turn send members to distinct presbyteries, or classes, which in turn send representatives to regional synods, or assemblies. A General Assembly meets once a year (elected by the presbyteries). Each church is also served by deacons and trustees, who share in its local responsibilities.

PRESBYTERY

In Western architecture, that part of a cathedral or other large cruciform Christian church that lies between the chancel, or choir, and the high altar, or sanctuary.

PRESENTATION OF THE VIRGIN MARY

Feast celebrated in the Roman Catholic and Eastern churches on November 21. The feast commemorates a visit by the three-year old Mary to the Temple in Jerusalem, where she was consecrated to the service of God.

PRESERVED TABLET

In Islam, a tablet in Heaven on which is to be found the original text of the Koran. The Koran itself specifically refers to the tablet in the 22nd verse of Surat al-Buruy.

PRESUMPTION

A condition seen as the opposite of hope whereby a person expects to gain eternal life either totally without help from God or solely on God's power without personal effort.

PRETA

The "hungry ghosts," shown in the lower segments of the Tibetan wheel of life. This is the purgatory where men in between lives are for a while tortured by their own unsatisfied desires. But no Buddhist hell lasts longer than the causes which created it.

PRETERNATURAL GIFTS

Exceptional gifts enjoyed by Adam and Eve before original sin. Among these gifts were immunity from suffering and death, integrity, control of the passions, and superior knowledge.

PRIAM

In Greek mythology, the last King of Troy who reigned during the period of its destruction by the Greeks at the climax of the Trojan War. After the sack of Troy, Priam took refuge on an altar of Zeus, but was slain by Pyrrhus, son of Achilles.

PRIAPUS

In Greek religion, a god of animal and vegetable fertility whose cult was originally located in the Hellespontine regions. He was represented in caricature of the human form, grotesquely misshapen, with an enormous phallus. Priapus looked rather like Pan. The sources call him a son of Dionysus by the Nymph Chione or of Dionysus and Aphrodite, or Hermes, or even of Zeus. He grew up in Lampsacus, which he was reputed to have founded.

The excessively large penis of Priapus, ever at the ready for reproduction (and for punishment), was intended to impose his will on those whom he protected and controlled. According to another view, this feature was a projection and representation of the male organ as the bringer of life and creation.

PRIEST

Title sometimes given to that member of a religion who leads his people in worship or who is empowered to perform its sacred rites.

The original meaning of the word kohen' is not known, but its significance as used in the Bible can be clearly understood from an examination of the many texts in which the word appears, together with their context. A fine definition is given at Hebrew 5:1 "Every High Priest taken from among men is appointed in behalf of men over the things pertaining to God, that he may offer gifts and sacrifices for sins." The priest "comes near to Jehovah" (Exodus 19:22), representing God to the people he serves, instructing them about God and His laws and, in turn, representing the people before god, approaching God in their behalf, offering sacrifices and interceding and pleading for them (Numbers 16:43-50; Hebrew 6:20; 7:25).

In English usage, the word priest is commonly employed to describe high functionaries of ancient faith (such as the High Priests of the Incas, or of the ancient Greeks or even of early

Judaism) and Buddhism, which maintain a priestly class. The title is, however, most commonly associated with the Roman Catholic and Eastern Orthodox Churches, whose priests are formally trained members of a complex hierarchy who may minister to a community of souls or enter orders devoted to study, spiritual advancement and service.

PRIESTHOOD

An official religious institution that mediates and maintains a state of equilibrium between the sacred and profane aspects of human society. The priesthood is composed of ritual experts learned in a special and sometimes secret knowledge of the techniques of worship and accepted as religious and spiritual leaders of their societies.

PRIESTS' CITIES

In biblical times, cities in the Promised Land that were set aside as places of residence for the Aaronic priests and their families. Of the 48 cities given to the tribe of Levi by Israel's other tribes, thirteen particularly belonged to the Kohathite priests of Aaron's family (Joshua 21:1-42). The tribes of Judah and Simeon gave them nine cities and four were given by the tribe of Benjamin. Thus, "all the cities of the sons of Aaron, the priests, were 13 cities and their pasture grounds" (Joshua 21;4; 9-19). These cities were Hebron, Libnah, Jattir, Esthtemoa, Holon, Debir, Ain, Juttah, Bethshemesh, Gibean, Geba, Anathoth and Almon, all except Juttah and Gibean again being named at 1 Chronicles 6:54-60.

David sent word to priests in their various cities to gather together when he was about to bring the ark to Jerusalem (1 Chronicles 13:1-5). And specific reference is made to the appointment of men to distribute contributed portions to their priestly brothers in priests' cities during King Hezekiah's reign (2 Chronicles 31:11-19).

PRIMACY, Papal

In the Roman Catholic Church, the doctrine that, as the successor of St. Peter, who was head of the Apostles, the pope, as bishop of rome, has full and supreme power of jurisdiction over the universal church in matters of faith and morals, as well as in church discipline and government.

The charisma of the pope as head of the church is described on the Code of Canon Law in this way: "The Roman Pontiff by virtue of his office, not only has power in the universal church but also possesses a primacy of ordinary power over all particular churches by which the proper, ordinary and immediate power which bishops possess in the particular churches entrusted to their care is both strengthened and safeguarded" (Canon 333).

PRISCA, Priscilla

In the Old Testament, name for a woman, the shorter form of the name is found in Paul's writings, the longer form in Luke's. Such a variation was common in Roman names.

Priscilla was the wife of Aquila, with whom she is always mentioned. The two showed fine Christian works and hospitality, not only to individuals, but also by having congregation meetings in their home in both Rome and Ephesus.

Because of Emperor Claudius' decree, Aquila and his wife left Rome and went to Corinth in 50. Not long after their arrival Paul joined them in tent-making (Acts 18:2-3). They traveled on with Paul to Ephesus, remained there for a time, and were instrumental in "expounding the way of God more correctly" to the eloquent Apollos (Acts 18:18-19). Returning to Rome for a time (Romans 16:3-5), they later traveled back to Ephesus (2 Timothy 4:19). There personal contact with Paul extended from about AD 50 to Paul's death, some 15 years or so later, during which association they "risked their own necks" for the apostle's soul (Romans 16:3-4).

PROCESSION, Christian

Organized body of people advancing in formal or ceremonial manner as an element of Christian ritual or as a less official expression of popular piety. Public processions seem to have come into vogue soon after the recognition of Christianity as the religion of the empire of Constantine in the 4th century.

PROCHORUS

In biblical times, one of the seven certified men full of spirit and wisdom appointed to assure equal treatment in the daily distribution of food in the first-century Christian congregation at Jerusalem (Acts 6:1-6).

PROFESSION, Religious

The public act by which one embraces the religious state by pronouncing the vows of poverty, chastity, and obedience and promising to live according to the rules and constitutions of a particular religious community.

PROFESSION OF FAITH

In Islam, shahada, one of the five arkan (Pillars of the Islam). The Profession runs as follows: "There is no God but God and Mohammed is the Messenger of God."
In Christianity, a public recitation of the central doctrines of the faith, usually during the liturgy. Also, an obligation of those who hold high church office to make a solemn declaration of faith before taking office.

PROGRESSIVE NATIONAL BAPTIST CONVENTION

Association of African-American Baptist churches, organized in 1961 at Cincinnati, Ohio.

PROKOP HOLY

(1380-1434) Bohemian warrior-priest, foremost leader of the Hussite Reformation forces in the later period of the Hussite wars.

PROKOPOVICH, Feofan

(1681-1736) Orthodox theologian and archbishop of Novgorod, who reformed the Russian Orthodox Church by a Lutheran theological orientation and a political integration with the state that was to last two centuries.

PROMETHEUS

In Greek mythology, a semi-god. One of the Titans and a brother of Atlas, Prometheus was surely a great benefactor of mankind. According to one account he created man out of clay and water. After Zeus mistreated man, Prometheus stole fire from the gods and gave it to man. In another account, Prometheus warned man of a universal flood which threatened his extinction. In retaliation for his displaying too much sympathy with man, Prometheus was condemned by Zeus to perpetual torment by being tied to Mound Caucasus with an eagle devouring his liver, which grew again as fast as it was eaten. He was eventually rescued by Hercules.

PROMISES

A voluntary and spontaneous action by which a person contracts to do or not to do something for another's benefit. Promises are binding on the basis of truth because truth requires actions to mirror words.

PROMOTOR OF THE FAITH

In the Roman Catholic Church, an office within the sacred Congregation for the Causes of Saints whose job it is to investigate any objections raised against a cause of beatification and to make sure that the procedures are followed.

PROPAGATION OF THE FAITH, Society for the

Organ of the papacy for the collection and distribution of money to support Roman Catholic missions throughout the world. The society was organized in 1822.

PROPHECY

Biblical revelation based on the idea of God communicating to certain chosen individuals through prophetic inspiration. The contents of the prophet's message and style in which it is couched differ from prophet to prophet.

Though the biblical tradition traces the origins of Israelite prophecy to Moses (Numbers 11:24-30; 12:2-8), not much is heard of prophets until the late period of the judges and the early monarchy, when they are mentioned in connection with the Philistine wars as stimulating religious and patriotic fervor.

The prophets of this period were ecstatic prophets living and traveling in groups (see 1 Samuel 10:6-13). Such prophets are given the name "sons of the prophets" (see 1 Kings 20:35; 2 Kings 2:3-20). The ecstatic experience during which they prophesied was often induced by mutual excitation through dance and music.

These prophets often served as disciples or apprentices under some noted prophet, but could also live apart as private individuals (2 Kings 4:1-4). In either capacity, they can often be found attached to sanctuaries as "cult prophets" (2 Kings 22:14-17; Amos 7:10-17) or serving the king as "court prophets" (2 Samuel 7:1-3).

Apparently they wore a distinctive garb of haircloth (2 Kings 1:8; Zechariah 13:4) and often bore other distinguishing marks. Ecstaticism continued to some degree throughout the entire history of Israelite prophecy, for Samuel is represented on one occasion as leading a band of ecstatic prophets (1 Samuel 19:20-24) and both Elijah and Elisha are habitually associated with the "sons of the prophets". Jeremiah 29:26 shows that ecstatic prophecy was common in Jeremiah's time and Ezekiel certainly received many of his prophecies in ecstatic trance.

In the early Christian church prophets played a prominent part. They were recognized as mouthpieces of the Holy Spirit. Some travelled from place to place. Responsible teachers insisted that the validity of the prophets' claim should be tested by the content of their utterances. The chief literary product of New Testament prophecy is the Revelation of John.

PROPHECY, Classical

By classical prophecy is meant the prophecy of those whom the Old Testament regards as exemplifying what is distinctive about the Israelite prophets, that is, the prophecies of Amos, Hosea, Micah, Isaiah, Nahum, Zephaniah, Habakkuk, Jeremiah and Ezekiel.

The basic source of what constitutes a prophet are found in the accounts of the call of the major prophets (Isaiah 6:1-13; Jeremiah 1:4-19; Ezekiel 1:1-3, 21; Amos 3:7-8). These accounts with other passages reveal:

▲ that the prophet is delegated to speak on behalf of Yahweh (Isaiah 6:8-9; Jeremiah 1:9);

▲ that the prophetic vocation is compelling even though the prophet is reluctant or untalented (Amos 3:7-8; Jeremiah 1:7-8);

▲ that God communicates His word to the prophet (Isaiah 6:9; Jeremiah 1:7-9; Ezekiel 2:8);

▲ that this communication involves visual and auditory experiences.

PROPHECY, Post-exilic

While Jeremiah and Ezekiel at the beginning of the exile and Second Isaiah at the end of the exile provide a new vision of divine plan to inspire the people, the post-exilic prophets lack much of the vigor and spontaneity of the pre-exilic prophets.

The diversity of Third Isaiah, Haggai, Zechariah, Malachi, Obadiah, Joel, the prophet of Zechariah (Zechariah 9-11) is mainly one of styles which are often frankly derivative and lacking the freshness of the earlier prophetic oracles.

The themes are very common, typical of a people living in a Judaism where Temple and Torah had become the enduring realities that would ensure unity. Prophecy itself helped to ensure the conditions under which the people of God could survive for many generations.

It did so by responding to the needs that Jeremiah and Ezekiel had already foreseen before the exile, by insisting on individual responsibility and fidelity to the Law. The prophets often opposed the priesthood for its neglect of the precepts of the moral law, but opposition was not a matter of jealous rivalry, for at its best the priesthood did the same work or part of the same work as the prophets, namely, transmitting the moral will of the God of Israel.

Priesthood did so by the traditions of the religious law preserved in the sanctuaries; prophecy accomplished the task by the communication of the living word, which was always consistent with the law even if expressed in its own way.

Similarly, despite some strong statements against abuses in the Israelite sacrificial system (Amos 5:21-27; Hosea 6:6; Isaiah 1:2-17), it cannot be maintained that the prophets were against either religious ritual or sacrifice in principle.

In terms of span, Israelite prophecy and the monarchy coincided almost exactly. Paradoxically, prophecy was instrumental in establishing this institution for which prophetic enthusiasm was at best lukewarm. Nonetheless, the prophets never initiated any countermovement to replace the monarchy with another form of government.

While the monarchy existed, the prophets insisted upon a return of the old covenant precepts which had been relegated to the realm of private morality by regal legislation and the changes in the structure of the society that accompanied the monarchy.

PROPHECY, Theology

The prophetic theology centered itself in the one God who had chosen the people of Israel and had communicated His will to this people in the Law. It was in the light of this election that the prophets foretold judgment and salvation for the people, criticized empty forms of worship, and called the people to their social responsibilities.

While it is difficult to confine Jesus to the category of prophets, the New Testament bears witness to the fact that there were prophets in the early Christian communities (Acts 11:27; 1 Corinthians 13:2; Ephesians 3:5; 1 Timothy 1:18; Revelation 22:6-8).

The Christians were particularly conscious that the spirit of prophecy had returned to them as a community, which they claimed as evidence that they were indeed God's elect and chosen community.

While prophets were among the charismatic leaders of early Christianity (Romans 12:6; 1 Corinthians 12:10; Ephesians 2:20), prophecy itself was submerged in the development of the hierarchical offices at the close of the first century.

PROPHECIES OF SAINT MALACHY

Supposed prophecies that list characteristics attributed to 102 popes and 10 antipopes, erroneously ascribed to St. Malachy, Bishop of Armagh. Actually this list was a forgery by an unknown writer in the 16th century and while some characteristics are fitting, others are widely distorted.

PROPHET

One who is divinely inspired to communicate God's will to his people, and to disclose the future to them. In the church prophecy is recognized as a gift of the Holy Spirit (1 Corinthians 12:8-10).

Islam teaches that Mohammed was the Last or Seal of the prophets. A total of 28 prophets are named in the Koran. Several are mentioned in Surat Maryam where each is characterized as a nabi or rasul or both. Every rasul is necessarily a nabi; however the reverse is not true.

PROPHET, The

(1768-1834) North American Shawnee Indian religious revivalist, who worked with his brother Tecumseh for an

Indian confederacy to resist US encroachment in the North-west.

PROPHET DANCE

North American Plateau Indian ritual of the early 19th century during which the participants danced in order to hasten the return of the dead and the renewal of the world, particularly the world as it was before European contact.

PROPHETS, The Lives of the

A pseudepigraphicl work (a noncanonical writing that in style and content resembles authentic biblical literature) consisting of folk stories and legends about the lives of the major and minor biblical prophets and a number of other prophetic figures from the Old Testament books of 1 Kings, 2 Chronicles, and Nehemiah.

The book was written in the first century AD by a Jew, but the versions that have been preserved all show signs of Christian editing, especially of the messianic material and icons.

PROSELYTE

In biblical terminology, term meaning "stranger," or "one who has come over to Judaism, convert." Throughout Israelite history non-Jews became proselytes, in effect saying about the Jews what Moabitess Ruth said to Naomi: "Your people will be my people, and your God my God" (Ruth 1:16; Joshua 6:25; Matthew 1:5). Solomon's prayer at the inauguration of the Temple reflected God's open and generous spirit toward those of many nations who might want to serve Him as proselytes (1 Kings 8:41-43).

Non-Jews mentioned by name who evidently became proselytes included Doeg the Edomite (1 Samuel 21:7), Uriah the Hittite (2 Samuel 11:3, 11) and Ebed-melech the Ethiopian (Jeremiah 38:7-13). When the Jews in Mordecai's time received permission to stand and defend themselves, "many of the peoples of the land were declaring themselves Jews" (Esther 8:17).

PROSPER OF AQUITAINE, Saint

(390-463) Polemicist famous for his defense of Augustine of Hippo and his doctrine on grace, predestination, and free will that became a norm for the teachings of the Roman Catholic Church.

PROTESTANT ASSOCIATION

Term used to describe the political and economical domination of Ireland in the 18th and 19th centuries by a Protestant Anglo-Irish minority.

PROTESTANT EPISCOPAL CHURCH

See: Episcopal Church, Protestant.

PROTESTANTISM

Forms of Christianity originating in the Reformation. The term derives from the "protestation" of the German princes (1529) against Roman Catholicism. Protestants stressed the authority of the Bible and justification of faith against what they felt to be the errors of Rome. Numerous different types developed such as Lutheranism, Calvinism, and many later forms. Anglicanism may be regarded as containing Protestant and "reformed Catholic" elements which are not "Roman."

The Protestant Reformation, which under the leadership of Martin Luther, John Calvin, Huldreich Zwingli and John Knox spread throughout Northern and Central Europe, enshrined certain common principles which still characterize Protestantism today. They include the acceptance of the Bible as the supreme authority in matters of doctrine, the priesthood of all believers, and the doctrine of justification by faith alone (that is not by good works or any dispensation by the church).

Once it had severed its links with the Roman Catholic Church, Protestantism developed varying forms of church government and doctrinal emphases ranging from Lutheranism to Presbyterianism to Anglicanism, each of which regarded itself as returning to the beliefs and practices of the New

Testament Church. After Protestantism had been embraced by the majority of people in north-west Europe, the Protestant missionary movement of the 19th century spread its doctrines to many parts of the world, especially to Africa, China and India.

Protestantism in America

Prior to the arrival of the Central European and the Irish and Italian Catholics, Protestantism was the pre-eminent religion of early America. From the New England Congregationalists to the Dutch Reformed Church of New Amsterdam; from the Southern Episcopalians to the French Reformed Church of South Carolina; and from the Quakers of Pennsylvania to the Swedish Lutherans of Delaware, Protestantism helped to shape early America. By 1990 there were about 260 separate forms of Protestantism in America.

At least three major doctrinal movements have developed in American Protestantism during the 19th and 20th centuries. They are *fundamentalism,* which is a very literal belief in the Bible; *liberalism,* a concentration on the social implications of the Bible and a minimizing of its supernatural elements; and *neo-orthodoxy,* which is a return to a belief in the Bible as a reliable rather than literal document.

PROTESTANT ORTHODOXY

Specific phase in the Lutheran and Reformed theology after the 16th century Reformation. The two movements shared many features as a result of the largely common political, cultural, social, and intellectual matrix that included not only the Lutheran and Reformed communities but also the bulk of European Catholicism at the time.

The central aspects of Protestant Orthodoxy included:

▲ the primacy of God's Word;

▲ the forgiveness of sins exclusively by divine grace for Christ's sake through faith as the core of the biblical message;

▲ the vital roles of baptism, absolution, the eucharist, and the sacred ministry.

PROTEUS

In Greek mythology, the patron of sea creatures who is mentioned in many myths. In the Odyssey he is encountered as the god of the sea who nurtured the marine animals of his liquid kingdom while Herodotus refers to him as the king of Egypt.

PROVERB

A succinct and pithy saying in general use, expressing commonly held ideas and beliefs. Proverbs are part of every spoken language, related to such other forms of folk literature as riddles and fables and originating in oral tradition.

PROVERBS, Book of

Book of the Old Testament, an example of the "wisdom literature", mainly written by Solomon. Its eight sections consist of numerous pithy proverbs, and mostly unconnected moral maxims. The different sections belong to different periods ranging from the 9th to the 2nd century BC. The book is among the earliest examples of Jewish wisdom writings, a literary form which also flourished in other parts of the Ancient World such as Egypt, Syria and Mesopotamia. Other examples of Jewish wisdom literature are Job and Ecclesiastes.

PROVIDENCE, religious doctrines and myths

Those conceptions and accounts of the divine reality on which man bases his belief in a benevolent divine intervention in human affairs and the affairs of the world he inhabits.

PROVINCE

In biblical times, term originally indicating the sphere of authority of a Roman administrator. When Rome expanded its conquests beyond the Italian peninsula, the territory or geographical limits of the rule of a governor came to be called a province.

When Paul was delivered to Felix at Caesarea, the governor "inquired from what province he [Paul] was, and ascertained that he was from Cilicia" (Acts 23:34). Tarsus, Paul's birthplace was in the Roman province of Cilicia (Acts 22:3).

PRUDENCE

A moral virtue which inclines a person to choose the most suitable means for attaining one's good purposes or for avoiding evil; it demands mature deliberation, taking advice if necessary, a wise judgment, and right execution of what one has decided.

PSALMODY

Singing of psalms in worship. In biblical times professional singers chanted psalms during Jewish religious services. Occasionally, the congregation interpolated a short refrain between the chanted verses.

PSALMS, Book of

Collection of 150 songs in the Old Testament, used as the hymn book of the Jews. Many psalms are composed by David. The songs contain praise, personal testimonies and thanksgiving to the Lord, as well as far-reaching predictions.

The poetry of the book of Psalms consists of parallel thoughts or expressions. Distinctive are the acrostic or alphabetic psalms (Psalms 9, 10, 25, 34, 37, 111, 112, 119 and 145). In these psalms the initial verse or verses of the first stanza begins with the Hebrew letter aleph, the next verse(s) with behth, and so on through all or nearly all of the letters of the Hebrew alphabet. This arrangement may have served as a memory aid.

Of the 150 psalms, 73 are attributed to David, 11 to the sons of Korah (one of these [Psalm 88] also mentioning Heman), 12 to Asaph (evidently denoting the house of Asaph), one to Moses, one to Solomon, and one to Ethan the Ezrahite. Additionally, Psalm 72 is "regarding Solomon." From Acts 4:25 and Hebrews 4:7 it is evident that Psalms 2 and 95 were written by David. Psalms 10, 43, 71 and 91 appear to be continuations of Psalms 9, 42, 70 and 90 respectively. Therefore, Psalms 10 and 71 may be attributed to David, Psalm 43 to the sons of Korah, and Psalm 91 to Moses. This leaves over 40 psalms without a specific composer named or indicated.

The individual psalms were written over a period of about 1,000 years, from the time of Moses until, after the return from Babylonian exile.

The Dead Sea psalms scroll provides evidence of the accurate preservation of the Hebrew text. Although about 900 years older than the generally accepted Masoretic text, the contents of this scroll (41 canonical psalms in whole or in part) basically correspond to the text on which most translations are based.

PSALM TONE

Melodic recitation formula used in the singing of the psalms and canticles of the Bible, followed by the Gloria Pater (Glory Be to the Father) during the chanting of hours, or divine office.

PSALTERY

Musical instrument related to the dulcimer and consisting of strings stretched over a flat soundbox, and plucked. Of Near Eastern origin, it enjoyed great popularity in the West in the 13th-15th centuries.

PSELLUS, Michael Constantine

(1018-1078) Theologian and Byzantine statesman whose advocacy of Platonic philosophy as ideally integrable with Christian doctrine initiated a renewal of Byzantine classical learning that later influenced the Italian Renaissance.

PSEUDIGRAPHA

(Greek; writings falsely ascribed) Uncanonical books excluded from the Apocrypha and generally pseudonymous. Such Jewish works, written largely from circa 150 BC to circa AD 100, include the Book of Enoch, Assumption of Moses and Apocalypse of Baruch. Christian pseudepigrapha, also called New Testament Apocrypha, include numerous gospels, Acts of most of the apostles, and numerous epistles; they are mostly fanciful and heretical.

PSEUDO-DIONYSIUS THE AREOPAGITE

(circa 506-567) Probably a Syrian monk who, known only by his pseudonym, wrote a series of Greek treatises and letters for the purpose of uniting Neoplatonic philosophy with Christian theology and mystical experience.

PSYCHIANA

A religious movement that emphasized spiritual healing, prosperity, and physical and material happiness, founded in 1929 by Frank R. Robinson (1886-1948). The emphasis of the movement was the availability of the power of God to all. The power could be used by individuals to meet all their physical and material needs.

PSYCHICAL RESEARCH

The scientific study of such alleged occurrences as thought transfer, foretelling the future, hauntings involving appearances of ghosts and movements of objects, and messages received through mediums from the spirits of those who have died.

PTOLEMAIS

In biblical times, later name of Acco. The apostle Paul stopped at this seaport city near Mount Carmel on his way to Jerusalem circa 56.

PUAH

In Judaism, name for an Israelite midwife who, together with midwife Shiphrah was commanded by Pharaoh to kill all the male babies born to the Israelites. However, because she feared God she preserved the baby boys alive and was blessed with a family of her own.

PUBLIUS

In biblical times, a wealthy land-owning resident of Malta who kindly entertained Paul and those with him for three days after their shipwreck on the island. Paul, in turn, healed Publius' father of fever and dysentery (Acts 28:7-8).

PUDGALA

Nearest approach in Buddhism to Western theory of soul.

PUJA

In Buddhism, a gesture of worship or respect, usually that of raising the hands, palms together, the height of the hands indicating the degree of reverence.

In Hinduism, ceremonial worship, ranging from brief daily rites in the home to elaborate temple ritual. The components of a puja vary greatly according to the sect, community, part of the country, time of day, needs of the worshipper, and religious text followed.

PUL

In biblical times, the name given a king of Assyria at 2 Kings 15:19 and 1 Chronicles 5:26. During the reign of Menehem, king of Israel, Pul entered Palestine and received tribute from Menahem. The identity of Pul was long an open question. However, most authorities now conclude that Pul and Tiglath-pileser III of Assyria were the same, since the name of Pul (Pulu) is found in the dynastic tablet known as the "Babylonian King List A."

PULPIT

In Western architecture, elevated and enclosed platform of a Christian church, from which the sermon is delivered during a service.

PUNNA

In Buddhism, a primary obligation of both monks and laymen, acquired in order to build up a better karman (the effects of good and bad deeds) and thus to achieve a more favorable future rebirth.

PURGATORY

In Roman Catholic theology, a state through which the souls of the dead ("friends of God" who have nevertheless failed to merit Heaven's absolute grace in life) pass in order to endure a process of purification. This consists of suffering to such a degree as completely to purge the soul of mortal sin and guilt. The soul may then pass on to heaven. The punishment (generally characterized by fire) may be shortened by the sacrifice of the Mass.

The purification in purgatory is altogether different from the punishment of the damned. The faithful are encouraged to pray for the souls in purgatory, especially on the feast of All Souls, November 2.

PURIFICATION RITES

Religious or sociocultural practices of a wide variety of types and forms found in all known cultures and religions, based on concepts of purity and pollution, that attempt to reestablish lost purity or to create a higher degree of purity in relation to the sacred or holy.

PURIFICATION RITES, Caste

Sanctions applied by a Hindu caste group to its offending members, which upon completion allow the group to resume normal social and ritual intercourse.

PURIM

Jewish feast of Lot, celebrated on the 14th day of Adar, recalling the story about hunger for power, and the hatred born of the Jews' refusal to assimilate and their unwillingness to compromise religious principle by bowing before secular authority. Despite such a serious, if highly relevant, theme, the holiday has a carnival atmosphere. Jews are required to get so drunk that they cannot distinguish between the words "bless Mordechai" and "curse Haman." The most popular of the Purim foods are Haman's Ears, or Oznei Haman. A fried, three-cornered pastry filled with apricots or other fruits and covered in poppy seeds, it is supposed to look like Haman's ears

PURITANISM

Originally an English 16th century movement to "purify" the Church of England. At first Puritans attacked vestments (ceremonial garments especially used for the eucharist) and ceremonies. Some, however, adopted Presbyterianism and others accepted the Book of Common Prayer (Anglicanism), with modifications.

The English Puritans

During the reign of Elizabeth I the Puritans, though strongly represented in both the Church of England and in Parliament, were restrained from introducing many of their ideas by the Queen. Under James I many more Anglican Puritans were driven into Separatism and exile, and with the accession of Charles I in 1625, Puritanism was systematically repressed under the direction of Archbishop William Laud. During the Protectorate of Oliver Cromwell, a staunch Puritan, they enjoyed considerable influence over the republican government. But with the restoration in 1660, the English Puritans (for the most part) left the Church of England and joined the Separatists or nonconformists.

The American Puritans

Puritans were among the pioneers of the North American colonies and have had lasting effects on religion and society in the United States. During the reign of James I some of the Puritan Separatists were among the Pilgrims who settled Plymouth Colony in New England in 1620. But the major body of Puritans, a group of congregationalists, founded the strongest New England colony of all at Massachusetts Bay ten years later. Puritans also founded other New England colonies and in varying degrees influenced all the English colonies in North America.

PURITY OF HEART

A term that refers to those who have attuned their minds and wills to the demands of God's holiness in the areas of charity, chastity, and love of truth.

PURPOSELESSNESS

In Buddhism motive must be steadily purified and purged of self-interest. Finally, as taught in the Zen school, the goal is seen as purposelessness. The spiritual as distinct from the social-moral life is sufficient unto itself and needs no goal or purpose by which to shape the means of the present moment.

PURUSA

In the Samkhya and Yoga schools of Hindu philosophy, the soul, or self. Purusa is made up of an indefinite number of soul nomads, which in their essence are pure consciousness.

Purusa is also, in one of the early creation myths related in the Vedas, the primal man from whose body the universe was created.

PURUSHA

In Buddhism, spirit, as one of the basic pairs of opposites into which the Oneness of the universe divides on manifestation, the other being Prakriti.

PUT

In biblical times, name for a "son" of Ham (Genesis 10:6; 1 Chronicles 1:8). Although Put is mentioned elsewhere in the Bible, none of his individual offspring are named. Often his descendants lent military support to Egypt (Jeremiah 46:9; Ezekiel 30:4-6).

PUTEOLI

In the first century AD, a chief port south-east of Rome. Paul arrived at Puteoli on his way to stand before Caesar in Rome circa 59 (Acts 28:13). With the help of a southern wind his ship arrived "on the second day" at Puteoli from Rhegium, a place some 100 statute miles to the south-south-east.

PYANOPSIA

In Greek religion, the festival in honor of Apollo, held at Athens on the 7th of the month Pyanopsion (October). Two offerings, a hodgepodge of pulse (edible seeds) and a branch of olive or laurel bound with wool and some other items were old pieces of rustic magic.

PYRRHUS

According to biblical tradition, a Beroean whose son Sopater accompanied Paul through Macedonia on part of his third missionary journey (Acts 20:3-4).

PYTHAGOREAN BROTHERHOOD

An association or cult founded in the 6th century BC and dedicated to the Muses and to the god Apollo. The exact purposes of the cult are unknown.

QABIL AND HABIL

Arabic names for Cain and Abel. The two sons of Adam are mentioned, though not by these names, in the Koran which tells the well-known story of the first murder.

QADA

In Islam, term denoting divine decree, divine judgment, divine will, the function of God as judge.

QADAR

Arabic word often translated as destiny, fate, divine predestination of divine determination. Quadar is specifically used in the sense of divine application of qada in time, according to the most widespread interpretations.

QADAR, al-

The title of the 97th sura of the Koran; it means "The Power" or "The Decree." The sura belongs to the Meccan period and has 5 verses. Its title is drawn from the reference to Laylat al-Qadr in the first verse.

QADARIYYA

School of theology in early Islam which championed the idea of man's free will. The Koran contains verses which both back the idea of predestination and that of man's free will. The Qadariyya arose in early Islam as a result of the debates about man's exact freedom to act. The partisans of a free will doctrine received what was, in effect a nickname, Qadaris, because they talked about qadar, its opposite. The whole question of free will became one of the key issues in medieval Islamic theology.

QADDI

A Jewish expression of praises to God usually recited in Aramaic at the end of principal sections of all synagogue services.

QADI

Arabic term for judge. Some people refused to become judges in early and medieval Islam lest their judgment lead them to condemnation in hell fire. The institution dates from the time of the Umayyads.

QADIRIYA

Major Sufi order named after Abd al-Qadir who, when more than 50 years old, established a reputation by his preaching in Baghdad. The order has been described as the first major one in the history of tasawwuf. Although never the most popular of the orders, the Qadiriyya none the less spread widely all over the Near and Middle East and also established itself in parts of India.

QAF

The title of the 50th sura of the Koran; Qaf is one of the letters of the Arabic alphabet. The sura belongs to the Meccan period and contains 45 verses. The title is drawn from the first letter of verse 1, who whole of which reads: "Qaf, by the Glorious Koran." The sura retails some of God's blessing and mentions various peoples to whom God has sent His messengers. Hell awaits the sinners and Paradise the pious. In a famous statement in verse 16, which underlines His immanence, God declares that He is nearer to man than the latter's jugular vein.

QALAM, al-

The title of the 68th sura of the Koran; it means "The Pen." The sura belongs to the Meccan period and has 52 verses. Its title is drawn from an oath in the first verse "By the Pen." The sura begins by reassuring Mohammed that he is not mad and, after telling the story of the selfish owners of the garden, whose desire to gather its fruit is frustrated, the sura concludes with a reference to the story of Yunus.

QAMAR, al-

The title of the 54th sura of the Koran; it means "The Moon." The sura belongs mainly to the Meccan period and contains 55 verses. Its title is drawn from the first verse which refers to the Hour approaching and the moon splitting. This is interpreted either as a reference to the end of the world, or to an eclipse. A number of disbelieving peoples, like those of Nuh, Ad and Thamuc, who ignored the warnings of God's messengers and in consequence are punished by God, are mentioned.

QARI'A, al-

The title of the 101st sura of the Koran; it means "The Sudden Misfortune" and the reference here us to the time of the Last Judgment. The sura belongs to the Meccan period and has 11 verses. Its title is drawn from the first 2 verses which may be translated as "The Misfortune! What is the Misfortune?" The sura goes on to provide a brief description of the end of the world and the Judgment with scales.

QASAS, al-

The title of the 28th sura of the Koran; it means "The Story." The sura belongs to the Meccan period and has 88 verses. The title of the sura is drawn from the reference to a story in verse 25. The sura begins with three of the Mysterious Letters of the Koran and tells the story of Musa in considerable detail, referring to Pharaoh several times. At the end of the sura which also covers a variety of other matters, man is warned not to be an idolater, and told that all things will perish except the face of God who will judge all men.

QASIM, al-

Son of Prophet Mohammed and Khadija, who died in infancy aged two.

It was because of him that Mohammed was sometimes called Abu 'l-Qasim.

QEDESHA

In ancient times, one of a class of sacred prostitutes found throughout the ancient Near East, especially in the worship of the fertility goddess Astarte. Prostitutes, who often played an important part in official temple worship, could be either male or female.

QIBLA

In Islam, direction of prayer towards the Ka'ba in Mecca. This is indicated in a mosque by the mihrab. Originally, the direction of prayer was towards Jerusalem but it was changed towards Mecca after the Hijra. This change is recorded in the Koran in surat al-Baqara which notes that the original qibla towards Jerusalem was designed as a test for the faithful, and specifically urges them to turn towards "The Sacred Mosque" in Mecca.

QISAS

In Islam, term denoting retaliation. Pre-Islamic blood revenge was replaced by the concept of just retaliation in Islam.

QIYAMA, al-

The title of the 75th sura of the Koran; it means "The Resurrection." The sura belongs to the Meccan period and has 40 verses. Its title is drawn from the first verse which contains an oath "by the Day of Resurrection." Some of the signs of this day are itemized. At the end man is reminded of God's power to raise the dead.

QIYAS

In Islam, term denoting analogy, analogical reasoning. This was one of the four main sources of law for al-Shaffi'i. It implies an extension or elaboration of the basic guidelines and principles which may be derived from the three other major sources of law enunciated by al-Shafi'i.

QODASHIM

In Judaism, the fifth of the six major divisions, or orders of the Mishna (codification of Jewish oral laws), which was given its final form early in the 3rd century by Judah ha-Nasi. Qodashim deals primarily with rites and sacrifices that took place in the Temple of Jerusalem, destroyed in 70 and never rebuilt.

QUADRATUS, Saint

(107-165) Earliest known apologist for Christianity. He wrote a number of treatises in response to sharp attacks on the Christian religion.

QUAKERS

An early nickname for members of the Society of Friends, founded by George Fox (1624-91) and others. Quakers reject such externals as sacraments, in favor of the "inner light" of Jesus Christ in the soul. Worship is largely silent. Social concern has always been strong. In recent times Quakers have been noted for their tolerance of different religious views, Christian and non-Christian.

Origin

The group was founded in 17th-century England by George Fox. Having experienced what he called the "Inner Light," Fox set out on an evangelistic crusade in the period of religious fervor following the English Civil War, and by 1660 had about 40,000 followers. However, the "Quakers," so named by a scornful judge who said they "quaked in fear," met with continual persecution for their rejection of the trappings of all organized churches. They started emigrating to the New World in about 1655 but met with no better fate in Puritan New England. Three were hanged on Boston Common between 1659 and 1661 and others driven out. Finally William Penn, under fox's direction, led the "Holy Experiment" to Pennsylvania, where he established a Friends' haven in 1681. From that point on the church's main growth took place in America.

American Quakers

The Friends had a tremendous impact on American history, through their pacifism, charity, local programs of prison reform, humane treatment of the mentally ill, relief projects and stern antislavery stand. Throughout this history two divergent attitudes have caused periodic crises among their informally organized membership. Fox, in promulgating the "Inner Light," had stressed three factors;

▲ Christ's immediacy to and within man, and therefore the irrelevance of church, temple and clergy;

▲ the absolute relevance of Christ to everyday life;

▲ the need for simplicity, sincerity and meditation.

The more mystical Quakers therefore tended toward Quietism and meditation. Others felt that following the dictates of their conscience inevitably led them into the world and tended to social activism and/or evangelism. Dress and manner also caused some divisions, as some clung to the simple attitude and garb of earlier days, while others believed that simplicity could be as well expressed in modern dress and speech.

As the early Friends rejected the organized church and its trappings - including liturgy and clergy - they decided to come together at "meetings." Meetings for worship, held in "Meeting Houses," characteristically began in silence. Any member who then felt spiritually moved to speak would stand and offer his message to the meeting as a whole. There was no set service and no single speaker. Some alterations in the traditional meeting have occurred, particularly in the United States, to admit such additions as hymns and sermons; but Friends today still follow this meeting form to a greater or lesser extent.

Several Quaker meetings in an area may combine to form a Quaker Meeting, which meets four times a year, and a large number of meetings may form a Yearly Meeting. There are seven Yearly Meetings in the United States for about 15,000 Friends.

QUARREL

In biblical terminology, word with several meanings: a dispute (Deuteronomy 17:8); controversy (Jeremiah 25:31); ore case of law (Jeremiah 11:20). The Scriptures counsel against becoming involved in quarrels or disputes without cause, labeling this as an act engaged in by someone stupid (Proverbs 3:30; 18:6).

QUARTERMASTER

In biblical times, possibly the officer in charge of rations and supplies for the troops. A literal translation is "prince of the resting place," and may mean the one in charge of the king's caravan when on a campaign or journey. Seraiah as quartermaster for King Zedekiah of Judah accompanied him on the trip to Babylon in the fourth year of Zedekiah's reign, carrying with him Jeremiah's written prophecy against Babylon. After reading it aloud in that city, Seraiah pitched it, tied it to a stone, into the Euphrates, as a symbol of Babylon's future fall, never to rise again (Jeremiah 51:59-64).

QUBBAT AL-SAKHRA

The Dome of the Rock; the principal Islamic shrine in Jerusalem, built over the area of the rock on the Temple Mount from which the Prophet Mohammed made his Mi'raj.

QUEEN

In the modern sense, a title given either to a wife of a king or a female monarch. In the Bible the title has a usage to women outside the kingdoms of israel and Judah. The Hebrew word most nearly expressing the idea of "queen" as it is understood today is malkah'. But it was rare in the Orient for a woman to possess ruling authority.

The queen of Sheba may have been one with such power (1 Kings 10:1; Matthew 12:42).

QUEEN OF HEAVEN

The title of a goddess worshipped by apostate Israelites in the days of Jeremiah. Although the women were primarily involved, apparently the entire family participated in some way in worshipping the "queen of the heavens." The women baked sacrificial cakes, the sons collected the firewood and the fathers lit the fires (Jeremiah 7:18; 44:15). That the worship of this goddess had a strong hold on the Israelites is reflected by the fact that those who had fled down to Egypt after the murder of Governor Gedaliah attributed their calamity to their neglecting to make sacrificial smoke and drink offerings to the "queen of heavens." The prophet Jeremiah, though, forcefully pointed out the wrongness of their view (Jeremiah 44:15-30).

QUESNEL, Pasquier

(1634-1719) Controversial theologian who led the Jansenists through the persecution by King Louis XIV of France until they were papally condemned.

QUETZALCOAT

("The Feathered Serpent") One of the major deities of the ancient Mexican pantheon. Representations of a feathered snake occur as early as the Teothihuacan (3rd to 8th centuries AD) on the central plateau of Mexico.

QUIET, Prayer of

A form of interior prayer described by St. Teresa as a spiritual delight in the presence of God, the first step in mystical union with God.

QUIETISM

A mystical religious movement within the Roman Catholic church which began in Spain, then spread to Italy and France in the late 17th century. Reacting against what they saw as bureaucratic, militant aspects in 17th century Catholicism, Quietists like Archbishop Francois de Salignac de la Mothe Fénelon (1651-1715) argued in favor of a passive life of prayer and contemplation guided by God's direct communication with the individual conscience. By denying the necessity of an organized church they provoked papal condemnation in 1699, and the movement collapsed. The Society of Friends, or Quakers, separately developed a quietistic philosophy during this period.

QUINISEXT COUNCIL

Council convened in 692 by the Byzantine Emperor Justinian II to issue disciplinary decrees related to the second and third councils of Constantinople (553 and 680-681 respectively). The Council prepared over 100 canons which were directed against Western church customs and legislation. The Western church and the pope were not represented at the Council.

QUIRINIUS

Roman governor of Syria at the time of the "registration" ordered by Caesar Augustus that resulted in Jesus' birth taking place in Bethlehem (Luke 21:1-2). His full name was Publius Sulpicius Quirinius.

QUIRINUS

In Roman religion, a major deity ranking close to Jupiter and Mars. Their families constituted the three major priests at Rome. He bore a similarity to Mars, the god of war, and some believe that he was only another form of that deity.

QUMRAN

A locality, north-west of the Dead Sea, which provided a home for an ascetic Jewish community between 130 BC and 70. The place became world famous for the discovery of its library, stored in 11 caves overlooking Wadi Qumran. Portions of about 500 books survive. About 100 are copies of Hebrew Scripture; others include commentaries, rule-books, hymnals, and apocalyptic studies. The so-called Dead Sea scrolls were made public in 1991 by the Biblical Archaeological Society.

QU'RAN

See: Koran.

QURAYSH

The Arab tribe of the prophet Mohammed, from which the early caliphs came and in whose dialect the Koran is written.

QURAYSH

The title of the 106th sura of the Koran. The sura belongs to the Meccan period and has 4 verses. It takes its title from the reference to the tribe of Quraysh in the first verse. The sura orders Quraysh to serve God who has fed them and protected them.

QURBAN

In Islam, term denoting the specialist ritual sense of sacrifice.

QURRA

In Islam, a professional class of reciters of the text of Muslim sacred scripture, the Koran. In the early Islamic community, Mohammed's divine revelations had often been memorized by his Companions (disciples), a practice derived from the pre-Islamic tradition of preserving poetry orally.

QUTB

In Islam, the Head of the saints, although other saints have been honored by the title as well. Popular belief holds that the idea of a qutb originated with the famous Egyptian Sufi

RAAMAH

In Judaism, a son of Ham's firstborn, Cush, and brother of Nimrod. Raamah and his two sons Sheba and Dedan founded three of the 70 post-Flood families (Genesis 10:6-8; 1 Chronicles 1:9). Many centuries later the tribal descendants of Raamah, Dedan and Sheba all carried on trade with Ryre (Ezekiel 27:20-22). Just where the tribe springing from Raamah resides is uncertain, but the city of Raamah near Ma'in in south-west Arabia mentioned in a Minaean inscription is likely.

RAAMIAH

In biblical times, name of a person who returned to Jerusalem with Zerubbabel. The name is an alternate form of Reelaiah (Nehemiah 7:7; Ezra 2:2).

RAAMSES

Alternate spelling for Ramses.

RABANUS MAURUS

(780-856) Archbishop, Benedictine monk and theologian whose work so contributed to the development of German language and literature that he received the title Praeceptor Germanniae ("Teacher of Germany"). Rabanus wrote a wealth of treatises and compendiums for the clergy and laity. He also wrote commentaries on almost all the books of the Bible. Of special note are his annotations on the Old Testament Pentateuch.

RABAT

Town, west central Malta, adjoining Medina, west of Valletta. There are many Roman ruins, including a partially restored villa housing a museum. Extensive early Christian catacombs are beneath the town; and there are several cave churches and medieval churches and monasteries.

RABAUT, Paul

(1718-1794) Protestant minister and reformer, one of the leaders of the Huguenots (French Protestants).

RABB, al-

In Islam, the Lord. Strictly speaking, this title should only be applied to God who is called "The Lord of the Worlds in the Fatiha. The hadith literature forbids a slave calling his master "My Lord."

RABBAH

In biblical times, name for a city in the southwestern extremity of the ancient kingdom of Ammon after its loss of territory to the Amorites. Rabbah is the only city of the Ammonite kingdom that is named in the biblical record, so it is assumed to have been the capital. It lay circa 23 miles east of the Jordan. The city was on the northern bank of a tributary of the upper Jabbok, and was thus in position to benefit from the rich fertility of that region. Also, it was an important link in the trader route between Damascus and Arabia.

"Rabbah of the sons of Ammon" is first mentioned in the Bible as being the location of the iron bier of Og, king of Bashan (Deuteronomy 3:11). When the Israelites came to the Promised Land, the tribe of Gad received Amorite land "as far as Aroer, which is in front of - or perhaps to the north-east of - Rabbah" (Joshua 13:25).

RABBI

Derivative of the Hebrew word rav, meaning "great, master, chief." "Rab" is used in the composition of several names, such as Rabsaris (chief attendant), Rabshakeh (chief cupbearer), and Rabmag (chief prince or magician)

(2 Kings 18:17; Jeremiah 39:3, 13).
The designation "rabbi" can be used in a de facto sense as "teacher." But among the Jews, shortly before the birth of Jesus, it came to be used also as a form of address and as a title of respect and honor, the title being demanded by some of the learned men, scribes, teachers of the Law. They delighted to be called "rabbi" as an honorary title. Jesus Christ condemned such title seeking and forbade his followers to be called "rabbi,"as he was their teacher (Matthew 23:6-8).

RABBINICAL ASSEMBLY OF AMERICA
An organization of United States and Canadian rabbis (founded in 1900), most of whom are graduates of the Jewish Theological Seminary of America, in New York City. The Assembly promotes the goals of Conservative Judaism, though various standing committees, such as those for prayer and worship, education, and social action.

RABBINICAL COUNCIL OF AMERICA
Organization of Orthodox Jewish rabbis, almost all of whom have received their rabbinical training in the United States and, consequently, do not speak Yiddish. The council's chief aims have been to promote the study and practice of Orthodox Judaism, to defend the basic rights of Jews in all parts of the world, and to support the State of Israel.

RABBINICAL JUDAISM
The normative form of Judaism that developed after the fall of the Temple of Jerusalem (AD 70). Originating in the work of Pharisaic rabbis, it was based on the legal and commentative literature in the Talmud, and set up a` mode of worship and a life discipline that were to be practiced by Jews all over the world down to modern times.

RABBULA
(350-435) Reforming bishop of Edessa (Turkey), advocating the orthodox Alexandrian position in the 5th century Christological controversy with the Antiochian school of Nestorianism, a heretical teaching that denied in Christ the union of the divine with the human nature.

RABI'A AL-ADAWIYYA
(713-801) Perhaps the most famous of all female Sufis. She spent her entire life in Basra. Enslaved as a child, she began an ascetical life on regaining her freedom. She attracted many disciples and became famous for her mystical teachings and emphasis on love of God. She refused marriage preferring instead to be the beloved of God. Perhaps her most famous saying was that in which she prayed to God that, if she worshipped Him our of fear of hell, then He should consign her there; and if she worshipped Him hoping for Paradise, then He should exclude her from there; but if she worshipped Him for His own sake alone, then He should not keep His eternal beauty from her.

RABMAG
In biblical times, the title of a major official of the Babylonian Empire at the time that Jerusalem was destroyed in 607 BC. The title has been identified on monuments recently excavated. Nergal-sharezer the Rabmag was one of the men in the special tribunal of high Babylonian princes who sat in judgment in Jerusalem's Middle Gate after the city fell to Nebuchadnezzar and who arranged for Jeremiah's release from prison (Jeremiah 39:3-14).

RABSARIS
In biblical times, the title of a chief court official in the Assyrian and Babylonian Empires. The Rabsaris was one of the committee of three high Assyrian dignitaries that was sent by the king of Assyria to demand the surrender of Jerusalem in King Hezekiah's time (2 Kings 18:17).

RABSHAKEH
In biblical times, the title of a major Assyrian official (2 Kings 18:17). Like

the titles "Rabmag" and "Rabsaris," Rabshakeh as a title comes from two Assyrian words rab and saqu, which, when combined, mean "chief cupbearer," "chief of the officers" or a general, a high officer of state.

While Sennacherib the King of Assyria was laying siege to the Judean fortress of Lachish he sent a heavy military force to Jerusalem under the Tartan, the commander-in-chief along with two other high officials, the Rabsaris and the Rabsakeh (2 Kings 18:17); the entire account appears also at Isaiah chapters 36 and 37.

RACAL

In biblical times, one of the places to which David sent spoils from his war with the Amalekites (1 Samuel 30:18, 26, 29).

RACHEL

In the Old Testament, daughter of Laban, younger sister of Leah, and Jacob's first cousin and preferred wife (Genesis 29:10, 16, 30). Jacob fled from his murderous brother Esau, traveling to Haran in Paddan-aram, in the "land of Orientals" (Genesis 28:5; 29:1). Rachel, a girl "beautiful in form and beautiful in countenance," served as a shepherdess for her father and she met Jacob at a well near Haran. Jacob was received into his uncle's household and one month later agreed to serve Laban seven years in order to marry Rachel, with whom he was now in love. His love did not weaken during the seven years and so these "proved to be like some few days" to him.

On the wedding night, however, his uncle substituted the older daughter Leah, who evidently cooperated in carrying out the deceit. Accused of trickery by Jacob on the following morning, Laban appealed to local custom as an excuse for his conduct. Jacob agreed to work another seven years for Laban (Genesis 29:4-28).

RACISM

A theory that holds that some human beings are inherently superior and others essentially inferior because of race. From the viewpoint of Catholic moral teaching: "Racism is a sin; a sin that divides the human family, and violates the fundamental human dignity of those called to be children of the same father .... It is the sin that makes racial characteristics the determining factor for the exercise of human rights."

RAD, al-

The title of the 13th sura of the Koran; it means "The Thunder." The sura belongs to the Medinan period and has 43 verses. Its title is drawn from verse 13 where the thunder is described as praising God. The sura begins with four of the mysterious letters of the Koran and has much to say about the wonders of God's creation. There is a stress on the unity of God and Paradise is promised for the virtuous with hell as the abode of the wicked and the infidels.

RADEGUNDA, Saint

(521-587) Queen of Merovingian king Chlotar I, who left her husband to become a nun and later founded a monastery near Poitiers (France). She was one of the first of the Merovingian saints.

RADHA SOAMI SATSANG

An esoteric religious sect of India that has followers among both Hindus and Sikhs. The sect was founded in 1861. Adherents believe that human beings could only perfect their highest capabilities through repetition of the sabd ("sound"), or nam ("name"), of the Lord. This practice is known as surat sabd yoga (the union of the soul with the current of sound that comes from God).

RAFIDI

In Islam, term in the sense of rejector. It is a general term of abuse used by Sunnis and Shiites, especially in medieval times.

RAGA

In Buddhism, greed, passion. The term is used in the sense of uncontrolled lust

of every kind. Raga forms with Dosa and Moha the three cardinal blemishes of character.

RAGNAROK

In Scandinavian mythology, the name for the end of the world of gods and men.

RAHAB

According to biblical tradition, a prostitute of Jericho who became a worshipper of God. Two Israelite spies came to Jericho and took up lodging at Rahab's home (Joshua 2:1). The duration of their stay there is not stated, but Jericho was not so big as to take a long time to spy it out.

Rahab's two guests were recognized as Israelites by others, who reported the matter to the king. However, Rahab quickly hid the men among the flax stalks drying on the roof so that when the authorities got there to pick the men up she was able to direct them elsewhere without arousing their suspicions. In all of this Rahab demonstrated greater devotion to the God of Israel than to her own condemned community (Joshua 2:2-7).

RAHBANIYAH

In Islam, the monastic state whose admissibility in Islam is much disputed by Muslim theologians. Many believe that Islam does not prohibit monasticism as a form of asceticism but condemns it only when it imitates Christian monasticism's traditional removal from the secular world.

RAHIM, al-

Arabic word for the compassionate. It is one of the 99 beautiful names of God.

RAHMAN, al-

Arabic word for the merciful. It is one of the 99 beautiful names of God.

RAHMAN, al-

The title of the 55th sura of the Koran; it means "The Merciful" and the reference, of course, is to God. The sura belongs to the Medinan period and has 78 verses. Its title is drawn from the first verse which reads "The Merciful." The sura goes on to say that God has taught the Koran and created man. It describes God's blessings to man and also the jinn, provides a vivid description of Paradise and its delights, and threatens Jahannam (Hell) for the wicked.

RAHNER, Karl

(1904-1987) German Roman Catholic theologian, distinguished for his attempt to integrate an existential philosophy of personalism with Aristotelian-Thomastic realism.

RAHULA

In Buddhism, a fetter; the name of the Buddha's son, born shortly before he left his home on his quest for enlightenment. Rahula entered the Sangha at about the age of 15 and became one of the 12 "Elders."

RAIMUNDO, Don

(1086-1152) Archbishop and leading prelate of the 12th century Spanish church. He stimulated the teaching of Spanish Arab literature and made it available to Christians.

RAKKATH

In biblical times, a fortified city of Naphtali (Joshua 19:32-35). It is today often identified with Tell Eqlatiyeh, located on the Sea of Galilee a short distance north of Tiberias.

RAM

According to biblical tradition, a descendant of Judah through Perez and Hezron who lived while Israel was in Egypt. Though Ram was apparently not the first son of Hezron, Ram's genealogy, leading to the Davidic line, is listed first among the three sons of Hezron (1 Chronicles 2:4-17). Having Nahshon, Boaz and David among his descendants, Ram was an ancestor of Jesus (Numbers 1:7; Ruth 4:18-22; Matthew 1:2-4).

RAMA

A traditional hero of Hinduism who has also been worshiped as a deity since medieval times. According to the Ramayana Epic, Rama was prince and later king of the old northern kingdom of Kosala. Rama experienced adventures in which he revealed qualities of justice and grace that have long endeared his image to Hindus. Particularly in northern india, many people eventually developed a religious cult in which Rama figured as an incarnation of the god Vishnu.

RAMADAN

The ninth month of the Muslim lunar calendar and also the Muslim month of fasting. Because the Islamic calendar is lunar rather than solar, Ramadan falls at different times every year. By fasting in Ramadan - and fasting at this time is one of the five arkan (Pillars of the Islam) - Muslims mark the revelation of the Koran in this month. The fast lasts every day, according to the koran, from the time when a believer can distinguish between a white and a black thread (or, according to another interpretation, when he can perceive the first white streak of dawn on a black sky). During the fast the believer must abstain from food, drink and sexual intercourse. Those who are sick, women who are pregnant and those making long journeys are exempted from fasting. The mosques in Ramadan are full of worshippers performing extra prayers. The month concludes with one of the great feast days of the Muslim calendar, Id al-Fitr.

RAMAH

In biblical times, name for a number of cities or high places in Israel.
1 A city in the territory of Benjamin (Joshua 18:25).
2 An enclave city of the tribe of Simeon in the Negeb (Joshua 18:1, 8).
3 A fortified city in Naphtali's territory (Joshua 19:32-36).
4 A city in the territory of Asher listed only in Joshua 19:24, 29.
5 The hometown of the prophet Samuel and his parents (1 Samuel 1:1).

RAMAKRISHNA

(1836-86) Hindu mystic and teacher. Raised as a high-caste Brahman, he served in a Hindu temple founded by a low-caste Sudra, thus emphatically rejecting caste discrimination. After studying both Islam and Christianity, he became convinced that all religions seek one ultimate reality, and that Rama, Allah and Jesus are one deity with different names. By his saintly example of active benevolence he inspired many followers from different faiths. His influence was considerably extended by his disciple, Swami Vivekananda, who founded the Ramakrishna mission.

RAMANA MAHARISHI

(1879-1950) Hindu philosopher and yogi, whose position on monism (the identity of the individual soul and the creator of souls) and maya (illusion) parallels that of Sankara (700-750). He believed that death and evil were maya, or illusion, which could be dissipated by the practice of vicara, by which the true self and unity of all things would be discovered.

RAMANANDA

(1309-1400) North Indian Brahman, fifth in succession of the famous philosopher-mystic Ramanuja and founder of the bhakti (devotional) cult of the god Rama, which flourished in the 14th century and is still popular in parts of northern India.

RAMANANDIS

In Hinduism, followers of Ramananda, a Hindu religious and social reformer of the 15th century, who worship the Rama incarnation of Lord Vishnu (Vishnu) as the one true God. The ascetics among the Ramanandis, have numerous monasteries in North India.

RAMATHAIM-ZOPHIM

In biblical times, the home of Eikanah, father of Samuel, in the mountainous region of Ephraim (1 Samuel 1:1).

RAMATHITE

In Judaism, a designation for Shimel, the vineyard keeper of King David (1 Chronicles 27:27). It indicates that he was from one of the several towns named Ramah, but there is no way of determining which one).

RAMATH-LEHI

In the Old Testament, the name Samson gave the site in Judah where he struck down a 1,000 Philistines with the moist jawbone of an ass (Judges 15:16-18).

RAMATH-MIZPEH

In biblical times, one of the cities east of the Jordan given to the tribe of Gad (Joshua 13:24-26). Evidently, Ramath-mizpeh was near Betonim. One location that has been suggested for Ramath-mizpeh is Khirbet Sar, some nine miles north of Heshbon.

RAMATIRTHA

(1873-1906) Hindu religious leader known for the highly personal and poetic manner in which he taught what he styled "Practical Vedanta," using common experiences to illustrate the divine nature of man.

RAMESES

In biblical times, Ra was the name for sun-god. When Jacob's family moved into Egypt they were assigned to live in "the land of Rameses" (Genesis 47:11). Since elsewhere they are spoken of as residing in the land of Goshen (Genesis 47:6), it appears that Rameses was either a district within Goshen or was another name for Goshen (Genesis 47:6).

Later, the Israelites were enslaved and put to building cities "as storage places for Pharaoh, namely Pithom and Rameses (Raamses)" (Exodus 1:11). Many scholars suggest that Rameses (Raamses) was so named for the district of Rameses in which they assume it was located.

When the exodus from Egypt began, Rameses is given as the starting point. Most scholars assume that the city is here meant, perhaps being the rendezvous site where the Israelites gathered from various parts of Goshen. But Rameses may here refer to a district, and it may be that the Israelites pulled away from all parts of the district, converging on Succoth as the place of rendezvous (Numbers 33:3-5).

RAMESSEUM

Funeral temple of Ramses II (1304-1237), erected on the west bank of the Nile at Thebes in Upper Egypt. The temple was dedicated to the god Amon

RAMIAH

In the Old Testament, name of an Israelite, one of the "sons of Parosh" who sent away their foreign wives and sons at the encouragement of Ezra (Ezra 10:10-11, 25).

RAMIRO II THE MONK

(1087-1154)King of Aragon from 1134 to 1137. He was a bishop-elect of Barbastro and a monk.

RAMOTH

In biblical times, a Levitical city in the territory of Issachar (1 Chronicles 6:71-73)

RAMOTH-GILEAD

In biblical times, a strategic city in the territory of Gad east of the Jordan. The city was also called by its shortened name Ramah (2 Kings 8:28-29); 2 Chronicles 22:5-6). It was one of the Levite cities on that side of the river (1 Chronicles 6:80), and it was selected as one of the cities of refuge (Deuteronomy 4:43; Joshua 20:8). Solomon appointed a deputy in Ramoth-gilead to care for providing food for the king from cities in Gilead and Bashan (1 Kings 4:7, 13).

RAMPOLLA MARIANO

(1843-1913) Italian prelate who played a notable role in the liberalization of the Vatican under Leo XIII. Cardinal Rampolla assembled the ideas for the encyclical Rerum Novarum ("New Things"), issued by Pope Leo in 1892, emphasizing the obligations of governments and employers to the working class.

RAM RAIYAS

A group of dissenters within Sikhism, a religion of India. They are descendants of Ram Rai, the eldest son of Guru Har Rai (1630-31). Their only significant dispute with other Sikh groups is on the question of the succession of leadership since the time of their founder.

RAMSAY, Arthur Michael

(1904-1992) Anglican archbishop of Canterbury, theologian, and advocate of Christian unity. His meeting with Pope Paul VI (March 1966) marked the first encounter between the leaders of the Roman Catholic and Anglican churches since their separation in 1534.

RAPHA

In Judaism, a son of Benjamin, called his fifth at 1 Chronicles 8:1-2. His name is absent from the list of those who went into Egypt (Genesis 46:21), and from the listing of the Benjamin's tribal families (Numbers 26:38-40). This may indicate that, regardless of where Rapha was born, he died son with no descendants, or else they were absorbed into a different family.

RAPHAEL

An archangel. In Jewish tradition he is the third of the archangels, after Michael and Gabriel. He is believed to have special powers of healing, and deliverance from danger. He is mentioned in the Book of Tobit, in the Old testament Apocrypha as saying, "I am Raphael, one of the seven holy angels." Raphael is set among the Roman Catholic and Eastern Orthodox saints, and his feast day traditionally falls on October 24th.

RAPHAH

In Judaism, a descendant of benjamin through Saul; also called Rephaiah (1 Chronicles 8:33-37).

RAPHU

In Judaism, a Benjaminite whose son Palti was one of the twelve to spy out the land of Canaan (Numbers 13:9, 16).

RAPPITES

A religious communal group founded in the early 19th century by circa 600 German Pietists under the leadership of George Rapp. Protesting the growing rationalism of the Lutheran church, the group decided to leave Germany for America, where they settled in western Pennsylvania. Shortly after coming to the United States, the Rappites renounced marriage, and eventually all persons lived in celibacy. Rapp died in 1847, and thereafter the colony membership dwindled.

RASH JUDGMENT

Attributing sins or faults to a person without sufficient reason; unfounded suspicion of another's conduct. It is a violation of justice and charity.

RASHNU

In Zoroastrianism, the deity of justice, who together with Mithra, the god of truth, and Sraosha, the god of religious obedience, determines the fates of the souls of the dead.

RASUL

Arabic word for messenger, envoy, apostle. Mohammed is called in the Shahada, the Koran and elsewhere, "The Messenger of God," Rasul Allah. His absolute humanity is stressed in the Koran in terms of his being a Rasul and it is stressed in the same verse that there were other messengers before him.

RATANA, Tahupotiki Wiremu

(1870-1939) Maori political and religious leader who founded the Ratana religious movement that dominated

Maori politics after it gained its first parliamentary seat in 1931. He founded the Ratana Church, which developed a ritual and doctrine that required a belief in God and rejected tohugas (Maori priest-healers) and modern medicine.

RATANA CHURCH

The greatest religious awakening among the New Zealand Maoris for over a century, and a national political influence through its support of the Labour Party, especially during the period 1943-63.

RATIONALISM

A view requiring that all claims to truth be proven on a scientific basis. Rationalism stands in opposition to any religious tradition based on divine revelation and was condemned by Vatican Council I.

RATNA

In Buddhism, jewel. The three Jewels of Buddha are Dhamma, Sangha and Ratna.

RATRAMUS

(802-868) Theologian, priest, and monk at the Benedictine abbey in the 9th century eucharistic controversy who was posthumously condemned.

RAVANA

In Hindu mythology, a ten-headed demon king. He is described as having 10 heads and 20 arms and is vividly portrayed in Rajasthani painting of incidents of the Ramayana.

RA'Y

Arabic word for opinion, idea. In Islamic law ra'y has the sense of personal opinion, individual judgment, or speculation not based on a recognized source of law.

RE

God of the sun and of creation, one of the most important in the Egyptian pantheon. He was thought to travel across the sky in his solar boat each day, and during the night to make his passage in another boat through the underworld, where, in order to be born again for the new day, he had to vanquish the evil deity Apepi.

REAIAH

In the Old Testament, a son of Shibal and descendant of Judah (1 Chronicles 4:1-2). It may be that Haroeh at 1 Chronicles 2:52 is the same person.

The name Reaiah is also applied to a Reubenite, presumably an ancestor of persons taken into exile by Tiglath-pileser (1 Chronicles 5:5-6).

REAL PRESENCE

The teaching of the Roman Catholic Church, as defined by the Council of Trent, that "in the sacrament of the most Holy Eucharist is contained truly, really, and substantially the body and blood, together with the soul and divinity, or our Lord Jesus Christ, and consequently the whole Christ."

REBECCA

In the Old Testament, the wife of Isaac and mother of Esau and Jacob. Rebecca was selected by a servant of Abraham, Isaac's father, to be his son's wife. Later, she devised the plot by which Jacob, her favorite son, deprived Esau of his father's blessing.

REBIRTH

An Indian doctrine with the Buddha embodied in his own teaching in a modified form. To be distinguished from transmigration, for the latter implies the return to earth in a new body of a distinct entity which may be called a soul. In Buddhism rebirth is the corollary of Karma; i.e., no immortal entity passes from life to life, but each life must be considered the karmic effect of the previous life and the cause of the following life. The karma which causes man to return to this world in a cycle of rebirths is the result of desire.

RECHABITES

In biblical times, descendants of Rechab the Kenite through Jehonadab.

(Jeremiah 35:6; 1 Chronicles 2:55). During Jehonadab's time it seems that at least some of the Rechabites lived in the northern kingdom, for it was there that Jehonadab joined Jeru (king 905-876 BC) in opposing Baal worship and "all who were left over of Ahab's in Samaria" (2 Kings 10:15-17). Jehonadan laid a command on his family (whether before or after the experience with Jehu is not stated) to live in tents, not sowing seed or planting vineyards and not drinking wine, because they were alien residents in the land (Jeremiah 35:6-10).

In the final part of Jehoiakim's reign (628-618 BC) a number of Rechabites dwelt in Judah. When Nebuchadnezzar came against the land, the Rechabites entered Jerusalem for protection from the Chaldeans and Syrians.

RECOLLECTION

The practice of being aware of the presence of God or of "walking in the presence of God" so that one may grow in love and fidelity to Him.

RECONCILIATION

The act of reestablishing a damaged or destroyed relationship between two parties. Reconciling humankind to God was, according to Roman Catholic theology, the primary work of Jesus Christ and is an essential part of the good news (*See* 2 Corinthians 4:17-19). According to Catholic teaching, reconciliation with God after one has gravely sinned against Him and reconciliation with the church wounded by sin are basic results of the sacrament of penance.

RECONCILIATION ROOM

A place in most Catholic churches set aside for celebrating the sacrament of penance; the penitent is given the option of confessing anonymously behind a screen or conversing with the priest face to face.

RECONSTRUCTIONISM, Jewish

The view that Judaism is in essence a religious civilization, the religious ele-ments of which are purely human, naturalistic expressions of specific culture. Because Reconstructionism rejects the notion of a transcendent God, who made a covenant with the chosen people, it does not accept the Bible as the inspired word of God.

RECORDER

In biblical times, a highly responsible officer in the royal court of Israel. His duties are not described in the Bible, but it appears that he was the official chronicler of the kingdom, furnishing the king with information on developments in the realm and also reminding him of important matters for his attention, supplying advice thereon.

REDEMPTORISTS

A community of Roman Catholic priests and lay brothers founded by St. Alfonso Maria de Liguori at Scale, Italy, in 1732. Its special concern is the preaching of the word of God, especially to the poor, through various means, but particularly parish missions and retreats.

RED SEA

As a modern geographical designated "Red Sea" refers to the body of water separating north-eastern Africa from the Arabian Peninsula and including the two arms known as the Gulf of Suez and the Gulf of Aqabah, the Red Sea measures some 1,400 miles in length, has a maximum width of circa 220 miles and an average depth of approximately 2,000 feet.

It is part of the great geological fault known as the Rift Valley. Due to a fast rate of evaporation the waters of this sea are quite salty. Along the eastern coast are high mountain ranges, whereas rocky tablelands and low hills occupy the western coast.

According to biblical tradition, it was the waters of the Red Sea that God miraculously divided to let the Israelites pass through on dry land, but drowned Pharaoh and his military forces who came in pursuit (Exodus 14:21-15:22; Deuteronomy 11:4;

Joshua 2:10; Nehemiah 9:9). The biblical passages relating this incident use the Hebrew expression yam ("sea") and yam suph ("sea of rushes or reeds, bulrushes). On the basis of the literal meaning of yam suph, certain scholars have argued that the Israelites crossed a more swampy place, such as the Bitter Lake region, and not the Red Sea (principally the western arm, the Gulf of Suez, where others believe the crossing likely occurred).

It is not known why the Red Sea was designated yam suph by the Israelites. Since the Hebrew term suph can also designate seaweeds (Jonah 2:5), there is a possibility that the Red Sea got its name from such plants.

REELAIAH

In Judaism, one whose name occurs with those of such prominent men as Zerubbabel and Joshua at the beginning of the list of those returning from Babylon to Jerusalem in 537 (Ezra 2:1-2).

REFORMATION

A movement for theological and moral reform in the Western Christian church primarily during the 16th century. Theologically, it was an attempt to recover what was considered to be the teaching of the Bible and early Christianity. Martin Luther's "theses" triggered the German Reformation in 1517. The more radical Huldreich Zwingli (1484-1531) reformed the church in Zurich at about the same time. In the next generation John Calvin in Geneva initiated another major Reformation tradition.

REFORMATION, Beginnings

Criticism of the Roman Catholic Church by its own members began in the late 14th century in England, where the Lollards, led by John Wycliffe, attacked the powers and privileges of the priesthood, demanded a Bible in English and questioned the supreme authority of the pope. Similar criticisms were made in Bohemia in the early 15th century by Jan Hus and his

followers. Both the Lollards and the Hussites were crushed, but during the 14th and 15th centuries anticlericalism, often allied to nationalism, grew steadily. The kings of France and England, for instance, passed a series of laws to limit papal control over church land in their respective countries. The Papacy itself lost considerable prestige, first from being forced to spend 70 years at Avignon under the patronage of the French king, and later from the 50 year long Great Schism when there were sometimes up to three claimants to the papal office. By the early 15th century the Conciliar Movement arose, aiming to replace the pope's authority over the church with that of a General Council of Bishops and senior churchmen. The attempt failed, but not for any want of unpopularity on the part of the papacy.

Meanwhile, alongside the general decline in power and standards within the medieval church there grew up the positive forces of humanism and the spirit of the Renaissance, both of which stimulated the reform movement. Humanism encouraged a study of Greek and Hebrew texts and a new critical spirit, while the Renaissance stressed the importance of the individual and questioned the concept of automatic obedience to the church. The introduction of printing into Western Europe not only spread criticism but also enabled the new theology to circulate widely. For in the end, whatever the social, economic and political forces at work, the Reformation was a preeminently religious revival in the late 15th century.

REFORMATION, Calvin

In Geneva, John Calvin, a French theologian, struggled for several years to gain authority over the religious and political life of the city. When he and his followers finally triumphed, in 1541, he began to establish an entirely new form of priestly government which controlled not only public affairs but even the most everyday details of people's lives, enforcing the strictest morality by severe punishments. From that time until his death, Calvin was virtual dictator of Geneva. His influence was felt not only in the city but throughout Europe, for he was not simply an able ruler but also a great preacher, teacher and a distinguished scholar. His greatest work of scholarship, which was to become one of the most influential documents in European history, was the famous *Institutio Christianae Religionis,* first published in 1536 usually known as the *Institutes.*

By providing a summary of biblical theology which could be understood by laymen as well as clergy, Calvin inspired Protestants as far away as the Netherlands and Scotland. The Protestants there often found their followers (as they did in France and Germany) among the prosperous merchants and craftsmen of the towns. This expanding new urban group, whose material prosperity was accompanied by a growth in political and social influence, soon began to challenge the landowners and the Catholic church which had for so long sustained the feudal system. At the core of Calvin's teachings was the doctrine of predestination, the belief that God had ordained, from the beginning of time, which souls were to be saved and which damned. Each man was therefore unable to affect his prospects of salvation by "good works" and had to place his hopes upon the grace of an omnipotent God.

It is difficult to trace the progress of the Calvinist Reformation in detail because the religious movements which drew their inspiration from Calvin became almost inseparable from a complex series of political struggles. France, for instance, was ravaged by nearly half a century of "Wars of religion," which ultimately led to toleration for the Huguenots, the French Protestants.

In the Low Countries the Protestant movement became linked with the national revolt which freed the Dutch from their subordination to Catholic Spain. In Germany, the Thirty Years' War of 1618-1648 brought terrible hardships to the common people, but confirmed the survival of Lutheranism in northern Germany under Swedish patronage, despite Catholic efforts to dislodge it. In Scotland the Calvinists, led by John Knox, managed to engineer a reform movement which abolished the authority of the pope in Scotland. They also produced a confession of faith (the Scottish Confession of 1560) which helped to galvanize most of Scotland behind the reformers (also ending an alliance between Catholic France and Scotland which had lasted for nearly 300 years.)

REFORMATION, England

Events in England, by contrast, were determined largely by internal political and cultural forces, rather than by external rivalries and influences. In England it was the king himself, Henry VIII, and not an obscure reformer, who took the initiative, denying the authority of the Pope and dissolving the monasteries. But Henry's motives were almost purely political. He denied the pope's authority and made himself head of the church in England because he wished to divorce his wife in order to be able to remarry and beget a legitimate male heir to the throne. He dissolved the monasteries (whose corruption provided him with a respectable pretext) largely because he wanted to seize the wealth to bolster his sagging financial resources. Both actions were part of his general policy of extending the authority of the royal government into every sphere of national life.

In matters of doctrine, however, Henry remained a traditional Catholic, having been awarded the title "Defender of the Faith" by the pope for his book *The Assertion of the Seven Sacraments,* in which he defended the doctrines of the church against Luther. But there was a powerful and growing faction within the English church which favored the new continental doctrines. Even the loyal Catholic, Sir Thomas More, had criticized the general state of the Roman Catholic Church and had, together with other distinguished English scholars, welcomed to England the great Dutch humanist scholar Erasmus, who gave a significant impetus to the New Learning.

Under Henry VIII's pious son, Edward VI, the Protestant faction gained supreme power through the person of Lord Protector, Edward Seymour, Duke of Somerset. Thanks to him, Thomas Cranmer, the archbishop of Canterbury, was able to introduce a new (Protestant) Prayer Book in 1549. Somerset's successor, John Dudley, Duke of Northumberland, tried to bring in a more extreme form of Protestantism.

Under Edward VI's successor, his sister Mary, an attempt was made to reverse the whole current of religious life and bring England back to the Catholic religion and under the authority of the pope. The association of Catholicism with Spain, England's arch-enemy, was enough to defeat this policy, despite a campaign of persecution which resulted in the burning of 300 Protestants who refused to renounce their beliefs. Upon her accession in 1558, Queen Elizabeth I finally established a moderate form of Protestantism as the doctrinal basis of the English church. Not for another century, however, would the religious settlement of Europe as a whole be stabilized.

REFORMATION, Luther

When Martin Luther, a German monk, protested against the low moral standards of Rome and such abuses as the sale of indulgences (pardons for sins) to pay for the building of St. Peter's cathedral in Rome, he was scarcely doing anything new. Like many critics in the previous century and a half, he called for a return to the purity and simplicity of the primitive church. Luther went further than that. His study of the writings of Augustine, and of Paul's Epistle to the Romans, led him to challenge the accepted Catholic doctrine which emphasized salvation through the sacraments and the media-

tion of the priest. In Luther's view, salvation was "by grace through faith" from which good works derived as a natural expression. Luther also strongly challenged the doctrine of papal supremacy on biblical and historical grounds.

Later he attacked the doctrine of transubstantiation, which claimed that during the Mass the water and wine, which represented the body and blood of Christ, were actually transformed by the sacrament into the body and blood of Christ, who was therefore present at every Mass. Luther argued, on the contrary, that the wafer and wine were merely outward signs or symbols. He also rejected the rule that priests should not marry. As well as making these attacks on fundamental aspects of basic Catholic doctrine, he went on to demand the abolition of papal power in Germany and a radical reform of monastic orders.

Luther's action in nailing 95 of his "theses" (or arguments) on the door of the church at Wittenberg in 1517, marked a turning point in the history of Christianity. Within a fortnight he was known throughout Germany. In 1520, at the Diet of Worms, Luther was declared an outlaw. A gifted preacher as well as an outstanding scholar, Luther's ideas spread rapidly, aided by the introduction of printing. Meanwhile the economy of Europe was expanding, and the growth of new cities and of an urban middle class was undermining the old order by its adoption of capitalist principles, notably of usury.

Besides Luther's ideas on freedom, the harsh economic conditions of the early 1520s led to a great peasant rising in many parts of Germany. The people demanded an end to serfdom as well as many religious reforms, including the freedom to elect their own priests. In their fury against the existing order they attacked and burned castles and monasteries alike. Far from encouraging this movement, however, Luther condemned it and supported the princes in the suppression of the rebels. Luther's attitude in this crisis won him princely support for his reform movement, even if it did cost him much of his personal popularity. As a result, the rulers of Saxony, Hessen, Brandenbrug and Brunswick and the kings of Denmark and Sweden (already opposed to both the major supranational institutions of their day, the Catholic church and the Holy Roman Empire) ordered the churches in their lands to follow "Lutheran" doctrines and practices.

REFORMATION, Zwingli

Meanwhile in Switzerland a similar "Protestant" or protest movement had been gathering pace under the leadership of the Swiss divine, Huldreich Zwingli. Like Luther, Zwingli came through study and experience to believe that the Catholic church was a corrupt institution and that many of its beliefs were mistaken. Zwingli upheld his views in a public debate with a special representative sent by the pope to refute his criticisms, and thereafter (with the support of the civic authorities of Zürich) he carried out a series of religious reforms in that city. Under his influence images and pictures were removed from churches, the Mass itself was abolished, and the authority of the pope and his bishops rejected. Unlike Luther, Zwingli held radical views on social matters, and he soon won a large following in many Swiss cantons. But Zwingli's death in battle against the Catholic cantons in 1531 made certain that the leadership of the reformist movement would pass from Zürich to Geneva.

REFORMATION DAY

Anniversary of the day Martin Luther posted his "95 theses" on the door of the church in Wittenberg, Germany (October 31, 1517), considered the beginning of the Reformation.

REFORMED CHURCHES

A group of Protestant religious bodies originating in Europe after the Reformation. These churches are generally Calvinist in theology and Presbyterian in organization. Unlike the Presbyterians, however, they tend to maintain a set liturgy. Most of these churches are in Switzerland, Germany, the Netherlands, France, Hungary and the Czech Republic.

A branch of the Dutch Reformed Church was established in New Amsterdam (New York) in 1628. The church grew with immigration and became the Reformed Church in America in 1867. Today the synod includes more than 1,000 churches and over 350,000 members. A schism of the original Dutch Reformed Church created the Christian Reformed Church in 1822. The Hungarian Reformed Church in America represents some 30 churches; the Reformed Church in the United States about 15 churches and the Protestant Reformed churches of America about 20 churches.

REFORMED EPISCOPAL CHURCH

A Protestant church in the United States, formed in 1873 as a result of a division in the Protestant Episcopal Church. Tensions has developed within the American church as it responded to the influence of the Oxford Movement within the Church of England, which emphasized the church's Catholic heritage. The struggle between those influenced by the Oxford Movement (high churchmen) and the Evangelicals (low churchmen), who emphasized the Protestant heritage of the church, went on in the Protestant Episcopal Church for a generation.

REFORMED LEAGUE

A voluntary association of German Reformed churches founded at Marburg in 1884 to aid Reformed churches and to conserve the Reformed heritage in Germany. It was organized by Reformed pastors and elders who met to commemorate the 400th anniversary of the birth of the Reformer Huldriech Zwingli.

REFORM JUDAISM

A religious movement that has abandoned many traditional Jewish beliefs, laws, and practices on the grounds that they were not directly revealed by God and may, therefore, be disregarded if observance is incompatible with modern times. Reform Judaism thus sets itself in opposition to Orthodox belief by challenging the binding force of ritual laws and customs set down in the Bible and in certain books of rabbinic origin (e.g., the Talmud) long considered authoritative.

REGEM

In the Old Testament, first-named son of Jahdai in the Calebite branch of Judah's genealogy (1 Chronicles 2:3).

REGEM-MELECH

In the Old Testament, one of two leading men sent by the people of postexilic Bethel to "soften the face of Jehovah" and to inquire about continuing the customary fasting. This was more than two years before the rebuilt Temple was completed (Ezra 6:15).

REGENSBURG BOOK

Religious doctrinal compromises discussed during the colloquy of Regensburg (1546) as the basis of solution to Protestant-Catholic separatism. The compromises, involving secret negotiations between liberal Catholics and the Protestant reformer Martin Buber, were rejected by both sides.

REHABIAH

In Judaism, grandson of Moses, only son of Eliezer and founder of a family of Levites that still existed when David was king (1 Chronicles 23:15-17; 24:21).

REHOB

In the Old Testament, father of Hadadezer the king of Zobah against whom David warred victoriously (2 Samuel 8:3-12).

The name is also applied to one of the Levites or the forefather of one attesting by seal a covenant in the time of Nehemiah and Ezra (Nehemiah 10:1-11).

REHOBOAM

In biblical times, son of Solomon by his Ammonite wife Naamah. He succeeded his father to the throne in 997 BC at the age of forty-one and reigned for 17 years (1 Kings 14:21; 1 Chronicles 3:10). Rehoboam had the distinction of being the last king of the united monarchy and the first ruler of the southern two-tribe kingdom of Judah and Benjamin, for shortly after he was crowned king at Shechem by all Israel, the united kingdom of David and Solomon was divided. Ten tribes withdrew their support of Rehoboam and made Jeroboam their king, as has been foretold by the prophet Ahijjah (1 Kings 11:29-31; 2 Chronicles 10:1).

REHOBOTH

In the Old Testament, the name that Isaac gave to a well (Genesis 26:22). Though its exact location is unknown, many geographers have identified Rehoboth with Ruheibeh, some 19 miles south-west of Beer-sheba. In naming the well Isaac said that now God had given ample room, he and his shepherds could be fruitful without interfering with, or getting interference from, others.

The name is also applied to a city of unknown location from which came Saul, an early Edomite king (Genesis 36:31, 37; 1 Chronicles 1:43-48). In both references to it, the place is called "Rehoboth by the River." Generally in the Bible the designation "the river" means the Euphrates.

REHOBOTH-IR

In biblical times, a suburb of ancient Nineveh. The exact location is not now known. It was built by Nimrod (Genesis 10:10-11).

REHUM

In Judaism, one of those listed at the head of the register of exiles who returned from Babylon to Jerusalem with Zerubbabel and Joshua (Ezra 2:1-2). The name is also applied to a priest listed among those who returned with

Zerubbabel (Nehemiah 12:1-3).
Rehun is also called the "chief government official" of the Persian Empire residing presumably in Samaria who took the lead in writing a letter to King Artaxerxes falsely accusing the Israelites concerning their intentions for rebuilding Jerusalem. The imperial reply ordered Rehum and his compatriots to go to Jerusalem and forcibly put a stop to the Israelites' rebuilding work on the Temple (Ezra 4:8-24).

REIMARUS, Hermann Samuel

(1694-1768) Philosopher and man of letters of the Enlightenment who is remembered for his Deism, the doctrine that human reason can arrive at a religion more certain that religions based on revelation.

REINCARNATE LAMAS

In Tibetan Buddhism, the belief that a great spiritual teacher is successfully reborn after his death in order to continue his teachings and may be so identified; the major system of succession for heads of religious orders and monasteries.

REINCARNATION

A belief in the rebirth of the soul in one or more successive existence, which may be human, animal, or, in some instancess, vegetable. Usually found in the Asian religions and philosophies, the belief in reincarnation, sometimes referred to as the transmigration of souls, metempsychosis, or palingenesis, also has been found in the religions and philosophical thought of primitive religions, in some Near Eastern religions, and Gnosticism.

REINKENS, Josef Hubert

(1821-1896) German bishop, and leader of the Old Catholic Church, a dissident group separating from the Roman Catholic Church because of opposition to the doctrine of papal infallibility pronounced by the First Vatican Council (1869-70).

REIYU-KAI

A Japanese lay religion (founded in 1925 by Kubo Kakuttaro) based on the teachings of Nichiren school of Buddhism. The Reiyu-Kai stresses devotion to the ancestors and the efficacy of the horizon (the central scripture of the Nichiren school of Buddhism). The Reiyu-kai has no clergy but relies on volunteer lay teachers.

REKEM

In the Old Testament, a king of Median, one of five such who were slain for having seduced Israel with immorality. The five, presumably vassals of the Amorites, were also called "dukes of Sihon" (Numbers 31:8; Joshua 13:21).

RELATIVISM

A view that holds that moral norms differ from culture to culture or that the rightness or wrongness of an action varies depending on the situation and one's motives. The Catholic view is that certain actions are always wrong despite cultural, psychological, or social conditions.

RELIC

In the strict sense, the mortal remains of a saint; in the broad sense, the term also includes objects that have been in contact with the saint.
A relic is part of the physical remains of a saint or an object closely associated with a saint; according to Catholic teaching, authentic relics are worthy of veneration by the faithful; the relics of martyrs and other saints are placed in the altar stone of a fixed altar; according to the church law: "It is absolutely forbidden to sell sacred relics" (Canon 1190).

RELICS

In Buddhism, veneration of relics began immediately after the Parinibbana of the Buddha, religious pilgrimages being made to the ten Stupas erected over his ashes, and to the four Holy Places. Stupas were also erected over the ashes of Arhats, and these became objects of veneration.

The famous "tooth relic" is preserved at the Dalada Maligawa Temple, near Kandy, where its vicissitudes have been bound up with Sinhalese history for over 2,000 years.

RELIGION

Since his beginning, man has explained the mysteries of birth and death, the cycles of nature and the phenomena around him by the power of some supernatural being or beings. Around this fundamental belief in the existence of supernatural forces, man has elaborated thousands of rituals, myths, tales and parables, dogmas, creeds, ethical systems and organizations ranging from simplistic to highly complex.

Man's religious beliefs have so profoundly permeated his relationship to life, that he has fought more wars for beliefs than for territory, defense or gain. Despite the vast differences between peoples and cultures the world over, the impulse to religion, in one form or another, has characterized them all. Most religions have been expressed with sacred symbols, idols, objects, writings and incantations, have invested certain men with power of mediation, and have attempted to reconcile human experience with the invisible power or powers by setting out and following certain codes of conduct. Many, but not all, religions that have lasted into modern times conceive of the supernatural as one supreme power or powers by setting out and following certain codes of conduct. Many, but not all, of the ancient religions of mankind have imagined a great variety of gods abiding in both animate and inanimate nature.

No human activity might seem so blameless as practicing one's particular religious beliefs. Yet some of the world's bloodiest wars have been fought in the names of the two great world faiths, Christianity and Islam. In and after the 7th century AD, both faiths came into conflict as militant Muslim Arabs proclaiming a holy war overran much of the Byzantine Empire and crushed the Visigoths in Spain. Later the Christians countered with the medieval Crusades. But some of the worst fighting has been between different factions of the same religion, for instance between Sunnite and Shiite Muslims and among Christians (the continuing fighting between Protestants and Roman Catholics in Northern Ireland is a tragic example). Thus ideological disputes between the Orthodox church and the Roman Catholic Church helped provoke the notorious Fourth Crusade; while enmity between Roman Catholicism and Protestantism spawned such horrors as the Thirty Years' War and the Massacre of St. Bartholomew's Day.

RELIGION, Animism

Animism is the belief that inanimate objects and animals have souls. It is the general belief in spirits which, in primitive peoples, was extended to included spirits other than those of human beings. This belief was based on such human experiences as trances or dreams. Researchers have found contemporary primitive peoples to be similar to early man in their acceptance of the belief that inanimate objects are potentially animate, and that objects as well as animals possess personal traits. Animists often believe, too, that spirits are capable of good or evil: for example, that persons suffering from physical or mental disease are possessed of evil spirits.

Anthropologists have interpreted the term animism more generally to describe the belief that natural phenomena are endowed with personalities as well. The term animalism has sometimes used by anthropologists to describe an earlier, more primitive state of animism which ascribes individual souls or spiritual qualities to all things. Common to almost all primitive cultures, animism remains important also in certain advanced religions such as Shintoism. Modern psychologists have noted the existence of an animistic state during early childhood.

RELIGION, Earliest Forms of Belief

Since no real written records exist prior to the third millennium BC, man's earliest beliefs can only be deduced from anthropology and the inferential knowledge of scholars. From these sources we learn that the Old Stone Age people buried their dead in a ritualistic way with food and utensils beside them, demonstrating a belief that man would live again after death. Paleolithic man carved small figures of women with featureless faces but exaggerated maternal attributes, implying belief that Woman was the source of life (a belief amplified in later ancient religion as the Great Mother Goddess). Animals, too, were depicted in countless cave drawings of reindeer, horses and cattle, many of them shown as speared or trapped, apparently in order to gain power over them as a magical means for success in hunting.

Sky gods were a prevalent form of early belief. The powers of the sun, moon, stars, rain, thunder and lightning were often given human appearance and qualities, making them familiar as well as remote and superhuman. People also venerated fire. Much supernatural power was ascribed to it, and fire gods took many forms. The development of agriculture brought belief in various fertility and water gods and the need to make sacrifices to win their cooperation. Domestication of animals produced veneration of fecundity, and in many countries the bull was made its sacred symbol or god.

No strict division exists between early and later forms of belief. Millions of people in Africa, South America, Australia, the Pacific Islands and other places not influenced by the missionaries of scriptural religions, still believe in earth, sky and animal gods. Without written histories we cannot be certain to what extent these rites of magic, ceremonies or sacrifice and intricacies of belief have changed or developed. But we do know that the worship of ancestors, whose souls may be contained in an animal, the use of magic to command spirits of both evil and good, and the existence of various taboos (prohibited acts) all appear to be timeless manifestations of human imagination applied to belief in the supernatural.

RELIGIONS, Major

Today, there are eight main bodies of religious belief distributed throughout the world. Today animism and tribal religions are confined to the more remote or peripheral areas of the world in Asia, tropical Africa and the more inaccessible parts of South and Central America.

Hinduism is confined to India. Buddhism spread greatly north and east of its origins and now prevails in Tibet and Mongolia, parts of China and the South-east Asian countries, Sri Lanka is also largely Buddhist. Confucianism and Taoism are confined to China, Shinto to Japan. Islam holds the hot dry lands of the Old World, North Africa, the Sahara and southward into the grasslands, Arabia and the Middle East, south-central Asia and Afghanistan and Pakistan. But it also spread to very different environments, to East Bengal and many of the islands and peninsulas of South-east Asia. An enclave in Albania reminds us of Muslim inroads into Europe. All these lands are Sunni, except Iran, which is Shiite.

Eastern Orthodox Christianity dominates Eastern Europe and Russia. In the remainder of Europe the north is predominantly Protestant, the south mainly Roman Catholic. Central and South America, early conquered by Spanish and Portuguese, are Roman Catholic. North America, originally colonized mainly from northern Europe, remains predominantly Protestant, although Roman catholics form the largest single Christian group by far.

Christianity

Christianity has three major divisions: The Roman Catholic Church, with approximately 600 million members; the Protestant church with approximately 400 million members; and the Eastern Orthodox Church with some 150 million members. This total of over a billion is spread over almost the entire world and divided into about 350 denominations.

It was founded in the first century AD on the teachings of Jesus of Nazareth, as recorded in the New Testament. Jesus had been hailed by Jews in Palestine as their Messiah, the Christ. The name Jesus and Christ became linked and his followers became known as Christians. His message was of the brotherhood of man and of a compassionate God, whose kingdom would come, offering the chance of salvation and eternal life to those who had faith in him and followed his teachings. Despite many conflicting interpretations and disputes concerning such questions as the nature of Christ's being as both man and God, the possibilities of redemption and the authority of the church, these beliefs remain the binding foundation of all Christianity.

Judaism

The religious beliefs and practices of the Jews, who were the first people to worship one God, became the fount of all monotheism. Their teachings were founded in the Torah (the Five Books of Moses), contained in the Hebrew Bible. Like its offshoot, Christianity, Judaism is ethical and spiritual. Moses was its precursor, who revealed God's will to his "chosen people," and its creeds centers upon this special revelation and relationship to God.

After Jerusalem was destroyed by the Romans in AD 70, the dispersion, or "Diaspora," of the Jews began. Centuries of persecution failed to shake their faith, though the lack of a geographic base and a Temple eliminated the priests and established the authority of rabbis (teachers). The emphasis for the individual Jew lay on the duty to observe the laws and rituals and adhere closely to the ethical principles. There are about 16 million Jews in various parts of the world today, more than a third of whom live in the United States, where there are three divisions: Orthodox, Conservative and Reformed.

Hinduism

Hinduism is the traditional religion of India, going back to 2500 BC and including a complex caste system and social customs gathered through the ages. It has over 500 million followers and believes in a supreme and eternal spirit, Brahman, who is both cause and effect of all that is. It works through the Trimurti, a triad of principal gods: Brahma (the creator), Vishnu (the preserver) and Shiva (the destroyer). Hindus believe in the transmigration of souls and Karma. When the soul is at last pure, it achieves oneness with Brahman. There are many rites and ceremonies and a great profusion of temples of worship.

Islam

The second-largest monotheistic religion (next to Christianity), has over 500 million members and was founded by the prophet Mohammed in Arabia in the 7th century. Mohammed was considered the only spokesman of the one, beneficent but inscrutable God, Allah. Islam means submission to the will of God. Its followers are called Muslims. Islam shares many Christian tenets, but has no organized church. Muslims are individually responsible for their religious life, which is based on "The Pillars of Faith" (five daily prayer obligations) and one pilgrimage a lifetime to the Holy City of Mecca. Their sacred book is the Koran (or Qu'ran), written in Arabic and containing Allah's revelations to Mohammed. Islam is divided between Sunni and Shiite, the latter tracing their spiritual authority from the son-in-law of Mohammed.

Buddhism

Originally an outgrowth of Hinduism, Buddhism was founded on the teachings of Gautama Buddha (about 563-483 BC), the "Enlightened One." It has about 200 million followers in Asia, the majority today in China. Buddha taught the Noble Eightfold Path (right views, right intention, right speech, right action, right livelihood, right effort, right mindfulness and right concentration) as the means to nirvana, or the extinction of desire which finally breaks the chain of karma and ends the wheel of rebirth. While symbolized in many idols and divided by superstition and conflicting interpretations, Buddhism's lofty ethical teaching explains its growing strength. It is monastic, but has no church. Buddhism has two main divisions, Hinayana and Mahayana. The first is predominant in Vietnam, Thailand, Laos, Cambodia, Burma and Sri lanka; the second is the religion of China, Korea, Japan and Mongolia. Tibetan Buddhism and Zen Buddhism are offshoots of Mahayana.

Confucianism

Until 1912 the most popular religion of China, this body of beliefs and practices grew from an elaboration and imaginative implementation of the basic moral teachings of Confucius (circa 550-478 BC), called the "Primal Sage." Confucianism, has an estimated following of 400 million. Bared of its connection with ancestor worship, nature gods and sacrificial rites, it is a lofty system of human ethics incorporating the Golden Rule, and gives answers to many important moral questions. These are contained in a body of Chinese classics collected by Confucius and including the *Annals of Lu,* which may contain his own writings, and *The Analects,* his discussions and sayings as compiled by his disciples.

Taoism

Taoism is a religion of many sects supposedly founded by Lao Tse (the "Old Master"), said to have been born in 640 BC. Taoism has about 60 million followers in China. It is based on a mixture or myth and a harmonious theory of man's place in the world, contained in a great work called the *Tao Te Ching* or "The Way and its Power." Today that is considered more likely the work of a number of unknown authors of the 4th century BC rather than that of Lao Tse (or Tsu), whose existence is in doubt. Taoist doctrine has been obscured by the addition of superstition and alchemy, but in its essence it stresses humility, kindness and living in harmony with nature. The word Tao means a road, a path, a way, that followed, leads to God; though God is ultimately indefinable.

Shinto

Essentially a worship of nature, Shinto has always been indigenous to Japan (although now existing in compromise with Buddhism) and has some 80 million followers. It endows countless aspects of nature with "spirit" power, including the sun, earth, sea and river, wind, animals, trees, large rocks and mountains. "Superior and extraordinary beings" include heroic ancestors and emperors, who as traditional descendants of the most powerful sun goddess, Amaterasu-Omikami, are worshiped as gods. Emperor worship was disestablished in 1947, but state Shinto has over 100,000 temples and shrines in beautiful settings for the worship of other spirits. Sect Shinto consists of 150 sects and has both church and educational organizations.

All those, and many other less widespread religions today have lasted many centuries despite the pace of political and scientific change. True, some have shown signs of being "creeds outworn," but others, and monotheism in particular, have continued to be vital forces that can accommodate themselves to fit modern concepts of God and man without losing their essential message. Perhaps this is because man's need to know the answer to the question "why" can never be satisfied by science, while his need to accept his own destiny as an individual implies the necessity to accept a higher power.

RELIGIONS, Phenomenology of

The descriptive analysis of religious phenomena. The leading phenomenologists of religion analyze the various manifestations (phenomena) of religion in an attempt to discover similarities and differences in the forms of religious expression. When similar forms are analyzed, such scholars seek to discover common needs or experiences that give rise to these forms.

RELIGIOUS EDUCATION

This term generally refers to instruction in the history and creed of a particular church and faith. American law and tradition provide for separation of church and state, and religious training is no longer given in US public schools.

Most early American schools, however, were built and run by various churches for the traditional purpose of educating the young in Christian life and preparing older students for the ministry and other high office. Some of the oldest, however, were actually "town schools," operated by the Congregational Church but controlled by the local colonial government. The concept of free public education maintained by the government grew up gradually in various states. Only slowly did the schools' primary purpose come to be educating "good citizens" rather than "good Christians."

Beginning with the Supreme Court's McCollum case decision in 1948, religious training was formally removed from American primary and secondary schools. Since that time religious education below the university level has been confined to parochial schools, sunday schools, vacation Bible schools, and Hebrew schools. Special catechism or confirmation classes leading to the formal adoption of church membership are also conducted separately by Protestant and Roman Catholic churches.

In other countries, where the vast majority of the population adheres to one official religion, religious instruction may be assumed by the state schools.

RELIGIOUS EXPERIENCE

Either certain special experiences involved in what is believed to be an encounter with the holy or divine, or the apprehension of a holy or divine dimension in any or all experience.

RELIGIOUS LIFE

In Roman Catholicism, according to the Code of Canon Law, a person who belongs to a religious institute, that is, "a society in which members, according to proper law, pronounce public vows either perpetual or temporary, which are to be renewed when they have lapsed, and live a life in common as brothers or sisters" (Canon 607).

RELIGIOUS SOCIETY OF FRIENDS

Fellowship of three yearly meetings of Friends: Iowa, Ohio, and North Carolina. Beginning in 1845, several yearly meetings of Friends separated because of differences brought about by the preaching of the English Friends minister Joseph John Gurney, who stressed the authority of the Bible. The conservative yearly meetings continue to follow traditional Friends customs and worship patterns.

RELIGIOUS YEAR

A liturgical or ritual calendar based on the lunar or solar systems that, in all the religions of the world, both ancient and modern, sophisticated and preliterate, recalls through ritual reenactments the activities of God, the gods, or mythical ancestors or other mythical beings, and also historical or legendary events, that give meaning and coherency to the beliefs and practices of the adherents of a religion.

RELIQUARY

A container used to display one or more relics.

REMALIAH

In Judaism, father of Israelite King Pekah (2 Kings 15:25).

REMETH

In biblical times, name of a boundary city of Issachar (Joshua 19:17-18). It appears to be the same as Jarmuth and Ramoth.

RENNYO

(1415-1499) Japanese Buddhist leader and eighth monastic patriarch of the Shinran temple at Kyoto (Japan), the center of Reformed Japanese Buddhism.

RENUNCIATION

In Buddhism, sacrifice of self-interest; the only kind of sacrifice recognized as of any value in treading the Path. The two great renunciations in the life of Buddha were:
1 the renunciation of home, family and kingdom, and
2 the renunciation of Nirvana at the enlightenment in favor of teaching the good law.

REPENTANCE

From the English word "repent" meaning "to change one's mind with regard to past (or intended) action, conduct, etc., on account of regret, or dissatisfaction.

In many biblical texts this is the meaning of the Hebrew na-hham'. Nahham' can mean "to regret, to mourn, to repent" (Ezekiel 13:17; Genesis 38:12; Job 42:6).

According to biblical tradition, the cause making repentance necessary is sin, failure to meet God's righteous requirements (1 John 5:17). Since all mankind was sold up into sin by Adam, all his descendants have had need of repentance (Psalms 51:5; Romans 3:23).

In Islam, repentance is the translation of tawba. The Arabic verb taba, said of a man, indicates "to repent;" when it is said of God it means "to forgive." Polytheism is the only sin which will not be forgiven. Otherwise those who turn to God in repentance will be forgiven.

REPHAEL

In the Old Testament, a son of Obed-edom's firstborn Shemaiah. He was assigned with his brothers as a gate-keeper caring for the storehouses on the southern part of the sanctuary (1 Chronicles 26:4-8).

REPHAIAH

In Judaism, second-named son of Tola and head of a paternal house in the tribe of Issachar (1 Chronicles 7:1-2). The name is also applied to at least two other persons in the Bible.

Rephaiah is one of the four sons of Ishi who, likely during Hezekiah's reign, led 500 Simeonites against the Amalekites who had escaped into Mount Seit. The Simeonites than took over this territory (1 Chronicles 4:41-43). Rephaiah is also the name of a descendant of David and Zerubbabel (1 Chronicles 3:5-9).

REPHAIM

In biblical times, name for a people living east of the Dead Sea. The Moabites who dispossessed them, referred to the Rephaim as Emim ("frightful creatures"). The Amminites called them Zamzummim (perhaps meaning "gibberish") (Deuteronomy 2:10-19). When King Cherdolaomer of Elam came west to fight five rebellious kings near the Dead Sea (taking Lot captive), he defeated the Rephaim in Ashteroth-karnaim (Genesis 14:1-5). This located the Rephaim at that time in Bashan east of the Jordan.

Shortly thereafter, according to biblical tradition, God said that he would give Abraham's descendants the Promised Land, which included territory where the Rephaim lived (Genesis 15:18-20).

REPHAIM, Low plain of

In biblical times, name for a broad plain or valley near Jerusalem. Presumably it got its name from the tall people named the Rephaim who must have lived there at one time. It is listed as a boundary between the territories of Judah and Benjamin (Joshua 15:1, 8: 18:11). At its northern end was a mountain that faced the Valley of Hinnom. The traditional identification of the low plain of Rephaim is the plain of the Baqa'. It descends for about three miles from Jerusalem south-west toward Bethlehem. Near its south-western end it narrows into the Wadi el Werd.

The plain's fertility (Isaiah 17:5) and its proximity to Jerusalem and Bethlehem would have made it desirable to the Philistines (2 Samuel 23:13-14). After David had been anointed as king over Israel the Philistines made raids in the low plain of Rephaim. David followed God's directions, however, and was victorious over them (2 Samuel 5:17-25; 1 Chronicles 14:8-17).

REPHAN
In biblical times, an astral deity mentioned by Stephen in his defense before the Sanhedrin (Acts 7:43).

REPHIDIM
In biblical times, one of the places where the Israelites encamped on their journey from the Red Sea to Mount Sinai. Upon leaving the wilderness of Sin, they encamped at Dophkah, then Alush and finally Rephidim (Exodus 17:1; Numbers 33:12-14). Lacking water at Rephidim, the people complained and quarreled with Moses. According to biblical tradition, Moses took some of the older men to "the rock of Horeb" (evidently the mountainous region of Horeb, not Mount Horeb) and struck a rock with his rod. Water flowed, apparently reaching to the people encamped at Rephidim (Exodus 17:2-7).

The exact location of Rephidim is uncertain. The various locations offered by geographers have been determined in accord with their understanding as to the route the Israelites traveled from the wilderness of Sin to Mount Sinai. Many modern geographers identify Rephidim with a site in Wadi Refayied, not far to the northwest of the traditional location of Mount Sinai. Adjacent to the Wadi is a hill of the same name, on which Moses might have stood with arms elevated during the battle wi the Amalekites.

RESCUE MISSION
A religious organization established to provide spiritual, physical, and social assistance for those in need. It originated in Great Britain in the city mission movement among evangelical laymen and minsters in the 19th century. The work of rescue missions resembles that of settlement houses, institutional churches, and charitable societies, but rescue missions usually also emphasize religious conversion through evangelistic preaching services.

RESEN
In biblical times, name for a city in Assyria built by Nimrod between Nineveh and Calah. Its location is otherwise unknown (Genesis 10:10-12).

RESHEPH
In Judaism, an Ephraimite; one of Joshua's ancestors (1 Chronicles 7:22-27).

RESHEPH
Ancient West Semitic god of the plague and of the underworld, the companion of Anath, and the equivalent of the Babylonian god Negral.

RESISTANCE
In moral theology, the right of the citizen in conscience not to follow the directives of civil authorities when they are contrary to the demands of the moral order or the fundamental rights of other persons. In New Testament teaching, there is a sharp distinction between serving God and serving "Caesar" or the political community when it opposes the law of God (See Matthew 22:21, Acts 5:29).

RESURRECTION
The raising of a dead person to life. The resurrection of Jesus Christ on the third day after his death and burial lies at the basis of Christian faith. In recognizable but glorified bodily form Jesus appeared to several groups of disciples; though skeptical, they became convinced that he had overcome death (1 Corinthians 15:3-8). Believers will participate in Christ's resurrection, culminating in the general bodily resurrection of the dead at the Second Coming of Christ (Romans 8:11).

Resurrection also plays a role in Islam. Pre-Islamic Arabia believed that the souls of the dead lived on in some kind of shadowy existence beyond the grave. However, there was no concept of any resurrection of the body. The

The Ressurrection.
"And the angel answered and said unto the woman, Fear not ye: for I know that ye seek Jesus, which was crucified. He is not here: for he is risen, as he said. Come, see the place where the Lord lay" (Matthew 28:5,6).
Lithograph by Gustave Doré (about 1860).

Koran later taught that there would be a resurrection of both bodies and souls, something at which many of the pagan Arabs scoffed. Many Islamic philosophers held, contrary to the teaching of the Koran, that only souls would be resurrected. The Koran contains much information about the Day of Resurrection as well as its terrors and judgments

RESURRECTION, Greco-Oriental

Prominent motif in Iranian texts. Both a personal judgment after death and an eschatological judgment are mentioned. The soul is thought to hover near the dead body for 3 days before it is judged on the 4th day on the "Bridge of the Requiter." Good souls gain heaven, evil ones hell.

Some texts mention a "place of the mixed," which receives those whose good deeds equal their evil ones. Ohrmazd, the power of light and good, rules hell. Since history is conceived as a continual struggle between Ohrmazd and Ahriman, the final resurrection coincides with Ohrmazd's definitive triumph. which is more a rehabilitation of the cosmos than a final judgment.

The savior Saoshyans raises bodies from the elements and reunites them with their souls. After enduring a 3-day ordeal in molten metal, all drink the elixir of immortal life (Haoma), which Saoshyans prepares from the fat of a sacrificed bull.

Despite many parallels, direct Iranian influence on Christian thought is generally doubted. Less convincing are purported parallels with Ancient Near East "dying-and-rising gods." Antecedents of Christian beliefs are best sought in the Jewish tradition, which evinces by the second century BC belief in resurrection.

RESURRECTION OF CHRIST

Central doctrine of the Christian church based on the belief that Jesus Christ was raised from the dead on the third day after his crucifixion and that through his conquering of death all believers will subsequently share in his victory over "sin, death, and the devil." The celebration of this event, called Easter, or the festival of the Resurrection, is the major feast day of the church. The accounts of the Resurrection of Jesus are found in the four gospels - Matthew, Mark, Luke, and John - and various theological expressions of the early church's universal conviction and consensus that Christ rose from the dead are found throughout the rest of the New Testament, especially in the letters of the apostle Paul.

In situating the resurrection of Jesus in the singularly exclusive experience of divinely chosen witnesses, the New Testament does not deny historical and theological dimensions of the prophetic witnesses to "God raising Jesus" (Acts 2:32; Acts 3:15; Acts 5:30; Acts 13:30) had such dimensions.

The material in the kerygmatic speeches of Peter and Paul in Acts (see above) and of the resurrection narratives at the conclusion of each gospel reflects the preoccupation of early Christianity with the theological and historical questions that naturally arise from the proclamation of the resurrection.

The kerygmatic speeches in Acts are mainly preoccupied with the theological implications of the resurrection. Outside of the sheer appeal to the Twelve as witnesses, the speeches are not concerned with the historical aspects of the resurrection event.

They include no data on the empty tomb or on the disciples' experience of the risen Jesus. Their theological concern is to validate the crucifixion and death of Jesus as well as his resurrection by appeal to the prophetic quality in the literature of the Old Testament.

RESURRECTION OF THE DEAD

The resurrection of the dead is described in the Bible as the restoration to personal existence, of deceased human beings. In the history of Old Testament thought, belief in the resurrection of the individual was a slow development.

Throughout the prophetic period from

the 8th to the 6th centuries the concept of human immortality was entertained, but not the concept of individual resurrection. At death the life principle, or spirit, of man was thought to be consigned to a nether lower world, variously termed the Pit, the nether world, or Sheol.

This state was not truly human existence, since in the Hebrew concept of man the separation of the life principle from the body destroyed the unity of the person (Isaiah 38:17; Ezekiel 26:20).

The Old Testament texts that speak of resurrection (Hosea 6:1-2; Isaiah 26:19; Ezekiel 37:1-14) are, in the opinion of the majority of Old Testament scholars, a reflection on the future national restoration of Israel as a people that would be faithful to Yahweh.

The book of Job, composed after the completion of Israel's main prophetic tradition (sometime after 600 BC, perhaps as late as 300 BC), does not envision individual resurrection as a solution to the inequities of reward and punishment its author observes as an anomaly of human life (see Job 3:16; Job 7:9; Job 14:7-22); hence the author of Job is not aware of an Israelite tradition of individual resurrection.

In the first book of Daniel, written circa 164 BC, there appears in the Old Testament a categorical declaration of individual resurrection (Daniel 12:1-3). The author's horizon, however, is not one of universal resurrection, but only of a limited number of just and unjust, who will rise to everlasting life or punishment. This conviction seems to have arisen in the context of the Seleucid persecution of Judaism under Antiochus IV Epiphanes, when many Jews suffered martyrdom rather than repudiate their religious laws.

By the first century BC belief in individual resurrection was generally current in Judaism, although it is not clear that all Jewish sects accepted it. The attitude of the Dead Sea Scrolls leaves the attitude of the Qumran sectaries uncertain.

If they followed Essene doctrine as described by Josephus, they believed in the immortality of the human spirit, but not in individual resurrection. The Sadducees are known to have been strong opponents of resurrection (Acts 23:8; Acts 26:8), while the Pharisees, whose teaching dominated popular belief, were equally strong adherents of the doctrine.

The gospels reveal that Jesus not only accepted the current belief in individual resurrection, but declared it to be a doctrine necessitated by the promises of God to the patriarchs, which could be fulfilled for them and their descendants only by resurrection (Mark 12:18-27).

The New Testament doctrine of individual resurrection was the result of the belief of Judaism, the teaching of Jesus, and the event of his own resurrection as an act of God brought about for man's salvation (Acts 4:12).

Baptism incorporates the believer into the existence of Jesus and sets in motion first a moral resurrection (Romans 6:1-4; Ephesians 5:14) that is to culminate in the glorious resurrection of the just.

The objection that the disintegration of the human body makes individual resurrection impossible is answered by Paul in terms of God's creative power, which produces a "spiritual body" for a new kind of existence in a resurrected life (1 Corinthians 15:35-44; Mark 12:24-25).

RETALIATION
Pre-Islamic blood revenge was replaced by the concept of just retaliation in Islam.

RETREAT
A special period of prayer, reflection, and solitude for deepening one's relationship with God and renewing one's living of Christian life; priests and religious are required by church law to spend some days in retreat each year, and laypeople are strongly encouraged to do so.

REU

In Judaism, son of Peleg and father of Abraham (1 Chronicles 1:24-27). He was, according to biblical tradition, an ancestor of Jesus Christ (Genesis 11:18-21; Luke 3:35).

REUBEN

In Judaism, the firstborn of Jacob's twelve sons. His mother was Jacob's less favored wife, Leah, who named her boy Reuben because, to quote her, "God has looked upon my wretchedness, in that now my husband will begin to love me" (Genesis 29:30-32; Exodus 1:1-2; 1 Chronicles 2:1). Reuben and his five full brothers (Simeon, Levi. Judah, Issachar, Zebulun) constituted half of the original tribal heads of Israel; the other six (Joseph, Benjamin, Dan, Naphtali, Gad, Asher) were Reuben's half brothers (Genesis 35:23-26).

Some of Reuben's good qualities displayed themselves when he persuaded his nine brothers to throw Joseph into a dry well instead of killing him. Reuben's purpose being to return secretly and deliver Joseph out of the well (Genesis 37:18-30). More than 20 years later when these same brothers reasoned that the spy charges against them down in Egypt were due to their mistreatment of Joseph, Reuben reminded the others that he had not shared in their plot on Joseph's life (Genesis 42:9-22). Again, when Jacob refused to let Benjamin accompany his brothers on their second trip to Egypt, it was Reuben who offered his own two sons as surety, saying: "You may put [them] to death if I do not bring [Benjamin] back to you" (Genesis 42:37).

In the symbolic books of Ezekiel and revelation, Reuben is mentioned in significant order along with the other tribes. Immediately adjacent to the holy strip on the north was Judah, with Reuben bordering next to Judah on the north (Ezekiel 48:6-22). In John's vision of the sealing of the twelve tribes of spiritual Israel, Reuben is not given the leading place, but is named second, after the tribe of Judah (Revelation 7:4-5).

REUBEN, Tribe of

In Judaism, name for one of the 12 tribes of Israel that in biblical times comprised the people of Israel who later became the Jewish people. The tribe was named after the oldest of Jacob's sons born of Leah, his first wife.

REUBENI, David

(1455-1532) Jewish adventurer whose grandiose plans inspired the messianic visions of the martyr Solomon Molcho (died 1532), with whom he took part in one of the strangest episodes of Jewish history. Reubeni claimed to be a prince descended from the tribe of Reuben (hence his name) of a Jewish state in Arabia.

REUEL

In Judaism, second-named son of Esau, by Ishmael's daughter Basemath. Reuel's own four sons became Edomite sheiks (Genesis 36:2-27; 1 Chronicles 1:35-37).

The name is also applied to Moses' father-in-law, a priest in Midian (Exodus 2:16-21).

REUMAH

In Judaism, concubine of Abraham's brother Nahor. She gave birth to four sons (Genesis 22:20-24).

REVELATION

The Greek word (apokalypsis) thus translated denotes "an uncovering" or "an unveiling" and is often used regarding revelations of spiritual matter or of God's will and purposes (Luke 2:32; 1 Corinthians 14:6; Revelation 1:1). The Bible also speaks of the "revealing of God's righteous judgment" (Romans 2:5), the "revealing of the sons of God" (Romans 8:19) and the "revelation of Jesus Christ" and "of his glory" (1 Peter 1:13; 4:13).

REVELATION (TO JOHN)

Last book of the New Testament. It is the only book of the New Testament classified as prophetic literature rather than didactic or historical. Disclosing the future of the world, it makes use of visions, symbols, and allegory. The book was written by John, at Patmos in the Aegan Sea (about 95). The described victory of God over Satan typifies similar victories over evil in ages still to come and God's final victory at the end of time.

REVELATION, Primitive

1 Primitive being taken to mean "original" in a historical sense, the expression means the knowledge of supernatural truths given to the first man at his creation; or the knowledge of all necessary truths given by God's revelation, then passed down to all as the object of the "common sense," i.e., consensus of all mankind.

The first meaning was included in the common theological understanding of the endowments of the first man; the second meaning is associated with Traditionalism. In this usage there is also the connotation of a progressive loss of originally possessed knowledge.

2 Primitive being taken to mean "rudimentary" by comparison to the explicit revelation that is the object of Christian belief, the expression means God's self-manifestation implicit in the right moral and religious conceptions of those lacking knowledge of Christian revelation.

Such a primitive revelation is a necessary postulate, on the grounds of the biblical account of God's dealings with men before the call to Israel; and of the truth that God makes possible to every human being a grace-relationship with himself. Whatever the explicit, conscious terms in which one not a believer in the Christian sense, relates to or turns away from God, those terms are the manner in which God presents himself as the object of a salvific choice.

REVELATION, Sources of

In Roman Catholic teaching the sources of revelation are scripture and apostolic tradition. Prior to the era of Vatican Council II this teaching was designated the "two-source" understanding of the way divine revelation is communicated.

Against the reformers' teaching, sola scriptura, the Council of Trent declared that the revealed truth and manner of life contained "in written books and in the unwritten traditions" handed down, as it were, from the Apostles and preserved in the church.

Vatican Council I in its dogmatic constitution on faith quoted the Tridentine teaching. Vatican Council II in its dogmatic constitution Dei Verbum on revelation expressed a more unified understanding of how revelation is communicated. The document continues to speak of both sacred Scripture and sacred tradition.

Theological reflection on the theme of scripture and tradition is especially guided by the Council's more dynamic understanding of tradition; that understanding is reflected in this statement: "The church in her teaching, life, and worship perpetuates and hands down to all generations all that she is, all that she herself believes. This tradition which comes from the Apostles develops in the church with the help of the Holy Spirit. For there is a growth in the understanding of the realities and the words which have been handed down" (Writings Vatican Council II).

REVELATION, Theological Implication of

Revelation, in general, is the act or an instance of revealing, especially the supposed disclosure of knowledge to humankind by a divine or supernatural agency. The term is used in the sense of truths by God, either directly to prophets or by inspiring scripture. Whether propositional or embodied in God's "mighty acts," it is the basis of revealed theology as opposed to natural theology. Protestants hold that revelation is sufficiently contained in the Bible; Roman Catholics and Orthodox regard tradition as revelatory.

Buddhism recognizes no revelation in the sense of a disclosure of truth to mankind by favor of a deity. Revelation of truth is attained by each individual for and by himself by the removal of error from the mind and its consequent illumination or enlightenment.

REVELATION AND EVENT

At the center of the biblical view of revelation, both in the Old Testament and in the New Testament, is the conviction that God makes himself known through happenings. Above all, it was in the exodus from Egypt that the Old Testament believer saw a special manifestation of God's relation to the people of Israel.

Here it was that the covenant between the Lord and Israel has been established; the Law has been given to Moses; and the promises sworn to Abraham about the land had been fulfilled.

In the New Testament the revelation of God reached its consummation and climax when "the Word became flesh and dwelt among us, full of grace and truth; we have beheld his glory, glory as of the only Son from the Father" (John 1:14).

The biblical theology of the 19th and 20th centuries, both Protestant and Roman Catholic, has rediscovered this emphasis upon the deeds of God in human history as the bearers of his communication by his mighty acts.

REVELATION AND RELIGION

From the earliest days of the church, the Christian claim to be in possession of divine revelation has had to take into account of the rival claims of other faiths. Although some theologians have found it possible to dismiss the problem by denying to other religions any true knowledge of God, most interpreters of the question have distinguished between those truths that have been known outside the historical revelation of God - be it through remnants of primitive revelation or through reason or through other means - and those that can be known only through the supernatural act of God's self-disclosure.

It is missionary work, too, the church has proceeded on the assumption that the grasp of the divine already present among non-Christians did not need to be unlearned, but needed to be corrected and completed by the Christian message.

REVELATION AND SCRIPTURE

Whether as event or as truth, the revelation of God is recorded in the Bible; on this all Christians agree. Where they disagree is on the question whether all revelation is contained in scripture.

Protestants have generally maintained that scripture, and scripture alone, records the word and will of God for men. Roman Catholics have assigned to the tradition of the church a role in the proper interpretation of divine revelation; some have asserted that all revelation is contained in scripture, at least implicitly, and needs tradition to give it authoritative expression; others have treated tradition as in fact a "second source" of revelation.

In practice, these differences have often been less sharp than they are in theory; for Protestant theology has continued to confess such dogmas as the Trinity, which are not stated in so many words in the Bible; and Roman Catholics have striven to find biblical warrant even for such dogmas as the Immaculate Conception and the Assumption, despite the acknowledgment that scripture does not teach them in so many words.

REVELATION AND TRUTH

Earlier generations of theologians often tended to define revelation in the category of truth rather than in the category of event. Revelation is the disclosure of that is supernaturally true about God. For the very events that serve as bearers of revelation become this by virtue of the word of God that is spoken in them and to them.

Other nations have emigrated from the captivity of their oppressors, what made the exodus of Israel from Egypt a revelation was the truth about God that was spoken by him through his servant

Moses in the Torah.

The revelation of Christ was not simply an event, but "grace and truth came from Jesus Christ" (John 1:17). Because this truth has taken the form of doctrines, revelation has often been interpreted as the delivery of accurate and reliable information, stated in the proposition and dogmas of faith.

REVIUS, Jacobus

(1586-1658) Dutch Calvinist poet long esteemed only as a theologian but later acknowledged as the greatest Christian lyricist of his period.

REVIVALISM

In the broadest sense, any instance of renewed religious fervor within a Christian group, church, or community. In common usage, it refers primarily to concerted efforts in some Protestant churches to revitalize the spiritual ardor of their members and win new adherents.

The best historical explanation for the recurrent nature of revivalism is based upon the inevitable need for theological and ecclesiastical reorientation from generation to generation.

REZIN

In biblical times, king of Syria who reigned in Damascus during parts of the reigns of King Jotham (777-762 BC) of Judah and his son King Ahaz (whose reign ended about 746 BC).

Evidently near the end of Jotham's reign Rezin joined with Pekah the king of Israel in warring against Judah (2 Kings 15:36-38). During the warfare, which continued into the reign of Ahaz, the Syrians, evidently under Rezin, captured many Judeans and took them to Damascus (2 Chronicles 28:5). Also, Rezin wrested from Judah Elath, a city on the Gulf of Aqabah, clearing out the Israelites and restoring the city to the Edomites (2 Kings 16:6). The combined Syro-Israelite forces laid siege to Jerusalem, intending to make "the son of Tebeel" its king, but they were unable to capture the city (2 Kings 16:5).

Tiglath-pileser warred against Damascus, capturing it and putting Rezin to death. Syria thus came under Assyrian domination (2 Kings 16:9).

REZON

In biblical times, a resister of King Solomon. This son of Eliada had been in the service of Hadadezer the king of Zobah, from which David took over Damascus. Rezon abandoned Hadadezer, however, and organized a marauder band. At some undisclosed time, Rezon himself took up reigning over Syria from Damascus, and especially from the time of Solomon's apostasy to the end of his reign Rezon gave vent to his abhorrence of Israel (1 Kings 11:23-25; 1 Chronicles 18:3-6). If, as some suggest, he was the person called Hezion at 1 Kings 15:18), this would make him founder of the Syrian dynasty that had extensive dealings with Israel.

RHADAMANTHUS

In Greek mythology, the son of Europa and Zeus, and brother of Minos and Sarpedon. When Minos ruled Crete he and Rhadamanthus gained such a reputation for the fair administration of justice that they were both made judges of the dead in Hades.

RHEA

In Greek religion, ancient goddess, probably pre-Hellenic in origin. A daughter of Uranus and Gaea (Heaven and Earth), she married her brother Cronus, who, warned that one of his children would be fated to overthrow him, swallowed his children Hestia, Demeter, Hera, Hades, and Poseidon soon after they were born. Rhea concealed the birth of Zeus in a cave on Mount Dicte in Crete.

RHEGIUM

A city in southern Italy today called Reggio or Reggio Calabria. The ship on which the apostle Paul was traveling as a prisoner made a stop at Rhegium when he was on his way to appear before Caesar in Rome, about 59.

Rhegium is situated on the Strait of Messina, which separated the mainland of Italy and Sicily. Just north of Rhegium the ship on which Paul was traveling would have had to navigate past the promontory Scylla on the Italian side of the strait and the whirlpool Charybdis on the Sicilian side, both considered hazardous by ancient mariners. A day after their arrival ar Rhegium a southern wind sprang up and this moved them safely through the strait and north-north-west Puteoli (Acts 28:13).

RHESA

In the Old Testament, son, that is descendant of Zerubbabel and ancestor of Jesus Christ (Luke 3:23-27).

RHODA

In biblical times, a member of the Christian congregation in Jerusalem at the time of the Apostle Peter's miraculous release from prison in AD 44. Rhoda was a servant girl, presumably in the household of Mark's mother Mary. At least she was pone of those who spent the night there praying for Peter. Answering a knock at the door of the gateway, and recognizing Peter's voice, Rhoda was so overcome with joy that, instead of letting him in, she ran back inside to tell the others. All the while Peter kept knocking until they finally let him in (Acts 12:3-5; 12-16).

RHODES

An island off the south-western corner of Turkey and one of the largest in the Aegean Sea, measuring some 45 miles long by 20 miles wide. Its capital city is also called Rhodes. A ship on which the apostle Paul was traveling came from Cos to Rhodes near the close of the apostle's third missionary journey in the spring of 56 (Acts 21:1).

RIBA

Arabic word for usury, the charging of interest on a loan. This is forbidden by Islam and condemned in the Koran. Despite this the course of history shows that the observance of this pro-

hibition has often fallen short of the ideal.

RIBAI

In Judaism, a Benjaminite of Gibeah whose son Ittai was one of David's "thirty" famous warriors (2 Samuel 23:24; 1 Chronicles 11:31).

RIBLAH

In biblical times, name for a town north of Israel "in the land of Hamath" (Jeremiah 52:9). The site generally accepted for Riblah is on the east bank of the Orontes River, circa 36 miles north-east of Baalbek, in the valley between the Lebanon and Anti-Lebanon mountains. Evidently Pharaoh Nechok encamped at Riblah after defeating King Josiah, circa 629 BC. He was at that time marching north to fight against the Babylonians, who by then dominated Assyria. Jehoahaz succeeded Josiah, but after three months Nechoh had Jehoahaz brought to him at Riblah before taking this king captive to Egypt (2 Kings 23:29-34).

Riblah was a strategic location for a military camp. It dominated a north-south trade and military route between Egypt and the Euphrates. Water was readily available, and food and fuel could be obtained from the surrounding valley and forests.

RICHARD OF CHICHESTER, Saint

(1198-1253) Bishop of Chichester, who was an expert on canon law. He later became archbishop of Canterbury.

RIDDA

Apostasy from the Islamic faith. After the death of the Prophet Mohammed a War of the Ridda or Apostasy War broke out in Arabia, many tribes believing that their contract and contact with Islam has ended with the death of the Prophet. The majority of these tribes were defeated during the rule of Mohammed's successor, Abu Bakr.

RIDWAN

In Islam, angel in charge of al-Janna. At the Last Judgment it will be his task to adorn Paradise and set out robes of honor for the Prophet Mohammed. On the same occasion Ridwan will also feed the blessed faster as they are resurrected from their graves.

RIFA'IYAH

Fraternity of Muslim mystics, known in the West as howling dervishes, found primarily in Egypt and Syria. The order preserved its stress on poverty, abstinence and self-mortification. It also performs the ritual prayer essential to all Sufi orders in a distinct manner: members link arms to form a circle and throw the upper parts of their bodies back and forth until ecstasy is achieved.

RIGHTS, Human

According to Catholic social teaching, each human person is endowed by God with certain fundamental and inalienable rights; perhaps the most complete enumeration and explanation of these rights is contained in Pope John XXIII's Peace on Earth (Pacem in Terris, 1963); among the more important listed are :
▲ the right to life;
▲ the right to bodily integrity;
▲ the right to the means necessary for the development of life;
▲ the right to security in sickness or old age;
▲ the right to respect for one's person and good reputation;
▲ the right to a share in the benefits of one's culture;
▲ the right to the free exercise of religion;
▲ the right to freedom of choice to one's state in life;
▲ the right to the ownership of private property;
▲ the right to freedom of movement (emigration and immigration);
▲ the right to an active part in public affairs;
▲ the right to just juridical protection.

RIHLA

In Islam, term used in the sense of travel, journey, travelogue; a well-known hadith attributed to the Prophet Mohammed urges the believer to seek knowledge even as far as China. This provided the religious impetus in medieval Islam for the tradition, undertaken by many of the great hadith collectors and scholars, of travel in search of knowledge. A primary impulse also in undertaking a rihla was the performance of the Hajj and this gave rise to a whole genre of travel or rihla literature.

RIMMON

In biblical times, name of several persons and cities.

Rimmon is the name of the Benjaminite father of Baanah and Rechab, the murderers of Saul's son Ish-bosheth; from Beeroth north of Gibeah (2 Samuel 4:2-9).

Rimmon is also the name of a city of the tribe of Simeon in the area surrounded by the tribe of Judah (Joshua 19:1-7).It is mentioned as a southern point in Zechariah 14:10. The name Rimmon is also applied to a Levite enclave city of the Merari family on the eastern border of the land of Zebulun (Joshua 19:10-13). Location is believed to be the present-day Rummaneh, about six miles north of Nazareth.

The name Rimmon is another context applied to an eminence to which 600 men of the tribe of Benjamin retreated as survivors of the battle near Gibeah, in which all Israel rose up against the Benjaminites to revenge the rape and murder of the concubine of a Levite (Judges 20:45-47). They remained there until approached by peace envoys (Judges 21:13).

Rimmon is also the name of a Syrian god. The Syrian army chief Naaman, after being cured of his leprosy, acknowledged Jehovah as the true God but expressed concern over his having to accompany the king of Syria into the temple of Rimmon and there bow down with the king before the idol of Rimmon, as the king would be leaning upon Naaman's army (2 Kings 5:15-18). Rimmon is generally identified with Ramman, a god known to have been venerated in Assyria and Babylonia.

RIMMON-PEREZ

In Judaism, one of Israel's wilderness camping sites, mentioned between Rithmah and Libnah (Numbers 33:19-20). The location has not been definitely determined, though certain geographers suggest Neqb el-Biyar, some 12 miles west of the northern end of the Gulf of Aqabah.

RINNAH

In Judaism, one of the "sons" of Shimon listed among the descendants of Judah (1 Chronicles 4:1, 20).

RINZAI

One of two major Zen Buddhist sects in Japan; it stresses sudden, abrupt means of obtaining transcendental wisdom, or Enlightenment. Among the practices are shouts or blows delivered by the master on the disciple, question-and-answer sessions, and meditation on paradoxical statements, all intended to accelerate a breakthrough of the normal boundaries of consciousness and to awaken insight that transcends logical distinctions.

RIPHATH

In biblical times, the name of the son of Gomer and grandson of Japheth (Genesis 10:2-3; 1 Chronicles 1:6). Riphath is listed among those from whom the various nations and peoples were spread about in the earth following the flow (Genesis 10:32). The only historical reference regarding his descendants is that of Josephus, of the first century BC, who claims that the early inhabitants of Paphlagonia (along the south side of the Black Sea in northwestern Asia Minor) were anciently called "Ripheans."

RISSAH

In biblical times, an Israelite campsite mentioned between Libnah and Kehelathah (Numbers 33:21-22). Rissah's location is not certain, though some have connected it with Kuntilet el-Jerafi, some fifteen miles north-northwest of the northern end of the Gulf of Aqabah.

RITES

A term used to describe the forms and ceremonies in liturgical worship; the words and actions that belong to a religious ceremony, for example, the rite of baptism. The term is used also to group various communities within the Catholic Church in accordance with their official ritual usages, for example, Roman rite Catholics and Byzantine rite Catholics.

RITES CONTROVERSY

A 17th-18th century argument originating in China among Roman Catholic missionaries about whether the ceremonies honoring Confucius and family ancestors were too tainted with superstition as to be incompatible with Christian belief.

RITHMAH

In biblical times, one of Israel's encampments in the wilderness (Numbers 33:18-19). Its site is now unknown.

RITUAL

Early buddhists deprecated ritual, and the Southern School still makes little use of ceremony. The Tantric Schools of Tibet and the Shingon of Japan use elaborate rituals.

RITUAL, The

A book, previously called Roman Ritual and now called the Book of Blessings, that contains the prayers and ceremonies, other than the Mass, that are used in the administration of the sacraments and other functions.

RIZIA

In the Old Testament, a warrior and family head in the tribe of Asher (1 Chronicles 7:39-40).

RIZPAH

In the Old Testament, a concubine of King Saul; daughter of Aiah (2 Samuel

3:7). After Saul's death, his son Ish-bosheth alienated General Abner by calling him to account form having relations with Rizpah, an act he construed as intimating seizure of the throne. As a consequence, Abner defected to David (2 Samuel 3:7-21).

ROBERTSON, Frederick William

(1816-53) Church of England clergyman who became widely popular among the working class because of the oratory and psychological insight in his ethico-political sermons preached in the 1840s.

ROBIGALIA

In Roman religion, festival in which the god of mildew or wheat rust, Robigus, was asked not to hinder the crops.

ROGATION DAYS

In the Roman Catholic Church, festivals devoted to special prayers for the crops, comprised of the Major Rogation on April 25th and of Minor Rogations on the three days before Ascension Day (40th day after Easter). The time and manner of the celebration of rogation days is left up to the conference of bishops.

ROGELIM

In biblical times, name of a town in Gilead and home of David's friend Barzillai (2 Samuel 17:25-29) Some geographers tentatively place Rogelim at Tell Barsina, less then sixteen miles southeast of the Sea of Galilee.

ROGERS, William

(1819-1896) Educational reformer, known as "Hang-Theology Rogers" because of his proposals that doctrinal training be left to parents and the clergy.

ROHGAH

In biblical times, name for the second-listed son of Shemer in the genealogy of Asher (1 Chronicles 7:30-34).

ROKYCANA, Jan

(1390-1471) Bohemian priest, archbishop, and follower of Jan Hus. He was a chief organizer of the papally denounced Hussite church. The Hussites differed from Roman Catholics in particular by asserting that the Eucharist should be given to the laity in both elements and bread, rather than in bread only.

ROLLE, Richard

(1300-1349) Early English mystic and author of mystical and ascetic tracts. Throughout his writings the life of contemplation and solitude is exalted. Strict physical self-control is urged, but spiritual progress consists in the development of love of God.

ROMAMTI-EZER

In Judaism, a son of Heman selected by lot during David's reign to head the last of the 24 Levitical groups of musicians at the sanctuary (1 Chronicles 25:1-9).

ROMAN CATHOLIC CHURCH

A worldwide body of Christians led by the Pope at Rome and a hierarchy of priests who administer Church rites. The Church embodies and proclaims a set of religious doctrines and beliefs which Roman Catholics accept as divinely ordained. With nearly 650 million members, the Roman Catholic Church is by far the largest Christian community. It also has more members than Islam, the world's largest non-Christian religion. Roman Catholicism has played a major part in the religious, political, economic, military and cultural history of Europe and the Americas, and Roman Catholic missionaries have done much to spread Christian ideals and civilization to the rest of the world.

For most of its history, the Roman Catholic Church has been not just the major form of Christian faith but the chief patron of Western culture. Early Christian art and architecture has left impressive remains in Italy. Later, architects building Roman Catholic churches were inspired to create the styles we know as Romanesque, Renaissance, and Baroque. Inside monasteries, medieval monks produced beautiful manuscript illumination. Artists from Giotto to Michelangelo decorated church walls and ceilings with brilliant frescoes depicting biblical themes. Michelangelo, Bernini and others also produced outstanding chapel sculptures.

In music, Roman Catholicism gave rise to plainsong and to brilliant settings of the Mass, from the vocal polyphony of Palestrina to the rich complexity of Johann Sebastian Bach. Above all, perhaps, the Roman Catholic Church preserved literacy at a time when Western Europe was culturally at its lowest ebb.

ROMAN CATHOLIC CHURCH, History

The rise of the Roman Catholic Church can be traced through popes Clement I (90-99), Leo I (440-461) and Gregory the Great (590-604). Their efforts strengthened the pope's claim to be head of all Christian churches, created a strong church administration, led to the setting up of bishoprics answerable to Rome and the evangelization of much of Western Europe on Roman lines. The church was reinforced by the growth of international monastic orders, starting in Italy with the Benedictine Order, founded circa 529 by St. Benedict.

During these early centuries Roman orthodoxy was hammered out with the help of councils, attended by church leaders throughout Christendom, and through the writings of influential theologians known as Church Fathers, including Saint Augustine.

The expanding Roman church became a temporal power under Pope Stephen II (752-757), whose receipt of northern Italian lands from their Frankish conquerors marked the birth of the papal states. By the early Middle Ages, Roman Catholic prelates controlled huge estates throughout Western Europe in the name of the church.

During the Middle Ages, the church was powerful enough to influence all aspects of life in Western Europe - including the arts (by inspiring great medieval cathedrals, paintings and music), education (clerics were often the only literate members of society), agriculture (through land clearance by diligent monks), and warfare (by promoting the Crusades).

But meanwhile the Roman Catholic church had begun facing major crises. A schism beginning in the 9th century led to a permanent rift with the Eastern Orthodox Church. During the 16th century, Protestantism was adopted by much of northern Europe and this led to a devastating series of religious wars in France and Germany. Later, anticlericalism based largely on nationalism, atheism and agnosticism weakened the Roman church's influence in many countries.

There was also long-standing opposition to its influence in secular affairs, beginning early in the Middle Ages with a long struggle between popes and Holy Roman emperors. This was ended by the Concordat of Worms in 1122 which defined the spiritual and temporal roles of pope and emperor. Gradually, too, powerful nations began absorbing church lands, culminating in 1860 in the loss of the papal States to emergent Italy, followed in 1870 by the loss of Rome. It was halted only in 1929 with the Italian recognition of the vatican as the Papal State.

While many of these events severely weakened the Roman Catholic church, some also helped to rejuvenate it. For instance, Protestant accusations of ecclesiastical corruption helped to inspire the Counter-Reformation and, in the present century, the growing threat of scientific skepticism towards religion in general has helped bring the Roman Catholic Church and its Christian rivals closer together resulting in a strong ecumenical movement.

ROMAN CATHOLIC CHURCH, Organization

The pope is at the apex of a great pyramid of churchmen. To help him govern the Roman Catholic Church he appoint a body of cardinals who make up the sacred college, and who are called cardinal bishops, cardinal priests and cardinal deacons. Their tasks are to administer church affairs under the pope's guidance, and to elect a successor when he dies, usually from among themselves.

Detailed church administration is divided among a number of so-called congregations, headed by cardinals, and comprising ecclesiastical committees specializing in different aspects of the church's work. For instance, the Congregation of the Consistory deals with the formation of new dioceses, and the Congregation of Rrites investigates evidence for the canonizing of new saints.

Other church officials include those responsible for church affairs in particular areas. Archbishops supervise archdioceses, while bishops supervise dioceses, and their parish priests form the immediate link between the ecclesiastics and the laymen, the mass of those who make up the church. Because the Roman Catholic Church has long believed that priests can best serve God if they remain unmarried, almost all clergy are celibate, except those of certain Eastern rites.

ROMAN CATHOLIC CHURCH, Papacy

Roman Catholicism depends upon the place of the popes as Christ's earthly representatives, forming an unbroken line of successors to the Apostle St. Peter. By virtue of holding office as bishop of Rome, the pope has the same special powers which Christ granted to Peter. Because Catholics consider that the pope speaks with this special authority, they believe that his official pronouncements on faith and morals represent God's intentions and cannot be theologically wrong. The foundations of Catholic belief are the Apostles' Creed, Nicene Creed, Athanasian Creed and the Creed of Constantinople.

ROMAN CATHOLIC CHURCH, Sacraments

Priests are set apart from laymen by receiving the sacrament of Holy Orders, which is held to place them in Christ's service, and to give them the spiritual authority which they need for their appointed tasks. These include administering six other sacraments:

▲ baptism,
▲ confirmation,
▲ the Holy Eucharist,
▲ penance,
▲ marriage,
▲ anointing the sick.

Roman Catholics consider all sacraments to be vital for their spiritual welfare. *Baptism,* usually of infants, is given to wash away original sin, and formally marks a person's entry into the Christian faith. *Confirmation* reinforces baptism at a later age by conferring the Holy Ghost. Taking the *Holy Eucharist* or Communion involves periodically eating and drinking consecrated wine and bread, believed to have been transubstantiated (changed) into the body and blood of Christ and forming a kind of spiritual nourishment. *Penance* involves inward regret for committed sins, confessing these sins to a priest, who is sworn not to divulge them, and receiving God's forgiveness from the priest on accepting penitential acts which the priest prescribed. *Marriage* sanctifies the union between a man and women and is considered indissoluble. *Anointing the sick* removes sin from the repentant soul in face of death.

Penance and anointing the sick are sacraments not normally recognized in Protestant churches. Apart from the concept of transubstantiation and papal infallibility, other aspects of Roman Catholicism which set it apart from most Protestant churches include its stress on regularly hearing the service of the mass, the Roman Catholic church's most sacred ceremony; belief in the role of saints, especially the

Virgin Mary, as intercessors between man and Christ; and belief in purgatory as a place where the souls of the dead are purified before passing to heaven.

ROMAN CATHOLICISM

A Christian church characterized by its uniform, highly developed doctrinal and organizational structure that traces its history to the Apostles of Jesus Christ in the first century AD.

Roman Catholicism may also be described as Christians in communion with the papacy. It is the largest church of Western Christianity, spread elsewhere by European colonization and missions. Church organization is by an authoritative hierarchy under the papacy. Worship is markedly sacramental, centered on the mass. Doctrine is drawn from scripture and tradition, and defined infallibly as "dogma" through Councils and the papacy.

ROMAN EMPIRE

The ancient state, centered on the city of Rome, covered the whole area around the Mediterranean Sea. At the time of its first emperor, Augustus (reigned 31 BC-AD 14), Jesus was born. Under Tiberius (14-37 AD) occurred the ministry of Jesus and John the Baptist. Caligula (37-41) was succeeded by Claudius (41-54). During Claudius' reign Paul travelled spreading the gospel. Under Nero (54-68) Rome was burned and Christians were persecuted. After Nero's death Vespasian became emperor (69-79) during whose reign Jerusalem was destroyed. After him TItus (79-81) and Domitian (81-96) reigned, attended with persecutions of Christians.

ROMANIA, Orthodox Church of

The largest of the Orthodox churches in the Balkans. The present Orthodox church of Romania was founded in 1925 as a patriarchate uniting the Romanian Orthodox population of the former Austro-Hungarian Empire with the autocephalous (ecclesiastically independent) Romanian church, created in Moldavia and Walachia in 1865

and recognized by Constantinople in 1885.

ROMANIAN CATHOLIC CHURCH

An Eastern Catholic church with the Byzantine rite, in communion with Rome. In 1698 the bishop of Alba Iulia and the majority of the clergy negotiated a union between the Orthodox of Transylvania and Rome, on condition that their traditional rites be preserved intact.

ROMAN RELIGION

The religious beliefs, practices, and institutions of the Romans from the 7th century BC to the early 4th century AD, when Christianity became the official religion of the Roman Empire. Based on a mutual trust between god and man, the object of Roman religion was to secure the cooperation, benevolence and "peace" of the gods, which was obtained by the meticulous attention to ceremonial and cultic acts.

ROMAN RELIGION, Characteristics

In comparison with the polytheistic anthropomorphism of the early Greeks, the religion of the early Romans was of a "primitive" character. The gods they worshiped had definite functions to perform but were themselves poorly defined and practically devoid of any legends.

They were little more than the unseen forces behind the varied phenomena of nature, which had to be honored or placated with suitable prayers, offerings, and sacrifices to secure the well-being of individuals, families, and the state itself.

This is evident from the frequent use of the word numen in connection with the gods. The word may be variously translated as "life," "spirit," "will," or "power" and may be compared with the Melanesian "mana," which has similar animistic connotations.

Only in later centuries, after the Romans had come into contact with the Greeks of southern Italy, did their gods acquire a definite personality and mythology. Through a process known as the interpretatio Romano, they came to identify their own gods with those of Greece and to assimilate the myths of the Greeks.

ROMAN RELIGION, Pantheon

At the head of the early Roman pantheon was a triad of three gods, who has even in historical times their own priests. The first of these was Jupiter. The second was Mars, originally a god of agriculture but later of war. The third, of Sabine origin, was probably at first the god of the popular assembly, but he later became identified with Romulus, the founder of Rome.

Allied with these major powers were others such as Vulcan (god of fire), Neptune (god of water), and Janus (god of the outer door and of beginnings), and a host of lesser deities or spirits whose names were largely derived from the objects or activities with which they were connected.

▲ Faunus and Silvanus were guardians of the woods;
▲ Terminus of the boundary stones;
▲ the Lares were deities of the farm who were later introduced into the house;
▲ the Penates were the gods of the storeroom;
▲ Vesta was the goddess of the hearth;
▲ Robigus was responsible for the rust on wheat and could be placated with the sacrifice of a red-haired dog;
▲ Pomona watched over the ripening fruit;
▲ Messor watched over the harvest;
▲ Cunina tended a child in its cradle;
▲ Statulinus helped the child to stand.

In addition to a countless number of spirits of this sort, it was quite commonly believed that every man has his guiding Genius and every woman a corresponding Juno.

During the Etruscan domination of Rome, the original triad of Jupiter, Mars, and Quirinus was replaced by that of Jupiter, Juno, and Minerva; and a great temple was erected to them upon the Capitoline hill.

Juno was an old Italian goddess of women and Minerva another Italian goddess of arts and crafts whom the Etruscans had adopted for themselves. From the Greeks the Romans received Castor, Pollux, and Apollo, and an identification of Venus with Aphrodite, Neptune with Poseidon and Ceres with Demeter.

Imitating Greek customs, they deified Romulus, the founder of their city in the fourth century BC and later their living rulers, the emperors.

In an attempt to secure the assistance of more potent deities, the Romans also turned to the East. The first official import of this kind was occasioned by the disasters of the Second Punic War.

In order to rid Italy of Hannibal, upon the advice of a Sibylline oracle, they brought the black stone of the goddess Cybele from Pessinus to Rome in 204 BC. Later they added to their religious observances the worship of the Egyptian Isis and Osiris, the Syrian Astarte and Adonis, and the Iranian Mithras, who became extremely popular with the soldiers throughout the empire.

ROMAN RELIGION, Sources

Because of the nature of the sources - ancient calendars, data furnished by poets, historians, and encyclopedists of the late republic and early empire - knowledge of the beliefs of the early Romans is limited and ambiguous.

From the Indo-Europeans the Romans obtained their knowledge of a great sky- and weather-god Jupiter, etymologically connected with the Greek "Zeus" and the Sanskrit "Dyaus," and their practice of offering bloody sacrifices and of celebrating special rites for the dead. From the earlier inhabitants of Italy, the Romans came to know the gods of the Lower World and how to propitiate them with offerings of flowers and milk and of the first fruits of the land.

ROMAN RELIGION, Worship and Honors

Just as the worship of the Roman family was primarily the concern of the head of the household, the pater familias, so the worship of the state was primarily the duty of the rulers, whether these were kings, as in the first centuries, or consuls during the republic, or emperors during the principate.

But they were assisted in this by a large number and variety of priests. In the first century BC there were, e.g., four priestly colleges and a number of sodalities, most of which went back to early times.

The college of pontiffs consisted of a rex sacrorum, 12 flamines, 6 Vestal virgins who tended the fire at the state hearth, and 15 pontiffs proper so called, who were the experts in sacral law.

The other three colleges consisted of the augurs, 15 experts in reading the auspices; others who were consulted on the introduction of foreign cults; and people who supervised a feast of Jupiter celebrated on the Capitoline.

The gods were honored in various ways, with prayers, vows, dances, races, games, and above all, with sacrifices, which could be simple or very elaborate. Male animals were offered to the gods and female to the goddesses. Light-colored animals were sacrificed to the celestial deities, and black to the infernal. The sacrifices were regularly offered by the magistrates but with the assistance of priests who recited the proper verbal formula for them to follow.

Despite the fact that the Romans in their official dealings with their gods adopted a legalistic attitude and expected a quid pro quo, they were on the whole deeply convinced of the need of keeping the pax deorum through the exact performance of their official cult acts.

In the second century BC, the Greek historian Polybius praised the Romans for their religious convictions and declared that it was their fear of the gods which maintained the unity of the Roman state. Fear of offending foreign gods was a partial cause of their general toleration of the beliefs of conquered nations, but they were at the same time convinced that those who do not worship the religion of Rome should recognize the ceremonies of Rome.

Failure on the part of the early Christians to do so led to frequent persecutions and eventually to the collapse of Roman religion itself.

ROMANS, Letter to

The longest of Paul the apostle's New Testament writings, composed at Corinth in circa 57. It was addressed to the Christian church at Rome, whose congregation Paul hoped to visit for the first time on his way to Spain.

In the letter Paul demonstrates the universal sinfulness of the human race and the need for divine righteousness. He declares that righteousness no longer comes through observance of the Mosaic Law, not even for Jews, because God now manifests His righteousness through Christ. His righteousness is the source of righteousness for all mankind. Paul, however, cautions his readers that righteousness is not a license to sin.

ROME

Located on the Tiber River in central Italy, Rome was one of the great cultural centers in antiquity. It was not only the first city of the Roman Empire, but the largest and most impressive city of the day. In Paul's time its Cchristian church consisted mainly of converted Gentiles, since Claudius banished the Roman Jews.

ROMUALD, Saint

(950-1027) Ascetic who founded the Camaldolese Benedictines (Hermits). The most significant monastery founded by Romuald was Camaldoli (circa 1012), near Arezzo (Italy). It became the mother house of the new order, which combined cenobitic and eremitical elements with strict silence.

ROSARY

Bead-string used in some religions. Buddhists were using the rosary long before it can be suggested the cult came from Christianity. The Tibetan and Chinese form is of 108 beads; the Japanese use a smaller type, held over the hand. The purpose is the same, to help concentration on the subject for meditation, and to help "mindfulness."

ROSARY, Catholic

The rosary is a popular devotion among Catholics, including meditation on the main mysteries of salvation as well as the recitation of certain vocal prayers. The mysteries are divided into five as follows:

▲ the Joyful Mysteries:
  ▲ the Annunciation,
  ▲ the Visitation,
  ▲ the Nativity,
  ▲ the Presentation in the Temple,
  ▲ the Finding in the Temple;
▲ the Sorrowful Mysteries:
  ▲ the Agony in the Garden;
  ▲ the Scourging;
  ▲ the Crowning with Thorns;
  ▲ the Carrying of the Cross;
  ▲ the Crucifixion;
▲ the Glorious Mysteries:
  ▲ the Resurrection;
  ▲ the Ascension;
  ▲ the Descent of the Holy Spirit;
  ▲ the Assumption of Mary into Heaven;
  ▲ the Coronation of Mary.

Meditation on each mystery is accompanied by the vocal praying of one Our Father, ten Hail Mary's, and one Glory to the father. To help in praying the rosary, a string of beads is usually used. The church strongly recommends the praying of the rosary, especially the family rosary.

ROSCELIN

(1050-1125) Philosopher and theologian known as the originator of nominalism, a doctrine that holds that all universals are nothing more than a verbal expression.

ROSE OF LIMA, Saint

(1586-1617) Patron saint of South America and the first person born in the Western Hemisphere to be canonized by the Roman Catholic Church. She became a dominican of the Third Order. She chose strict enclosure and contemplation and withdrew to the seclusion of a hut in the family garden, where she endured a life of severe austerity; she wore a crown of thorns, practiced fasting, slept on a bed of broken glass and potsherds, and experienced numerous visions, particularly of the devil.

ROSH

In the Old Testament, a son of Benjamin listed among those who went into Egypt with Jacob's household, or who were borne shortly thereafter (Genesis 46:21-26). The omission of his name from later lists of Benjaminite families may indicate that he died childless, or that his sons merged with a different tribal family.

ROSH HASHANAH

One of the two days of the Jewish calendar known as Days of Judgment or Days of Awe (Leviticus 23:24, Numbers 29:1; Nehemiah 8:2-3). The other day is Yom Kippur. On these days, Jews are called upon to account to God. Purely religious in character, they are mainly celebrated in the synagogue. As for all Jewish holidays, prayer services begin the eve of the holiday and in the case of Rosh Hashanah continue for two days. A special feature during the prayers is the blowing of a shofar, to remind Jews to obey God's command.

Characteristic foods eaten on Rosh Ha-Shanah include pomegranates, over which the blessing of the first fruits of the New Year is recited; apples dipped in honey or other honeyed foods to augur a sweet year; and tongue or fish heads to mark the "head of the year," a direct translation of Rosh Ha-Shanah.

ROSH HODESH

In Judaism, the start of the Hebrew month, a minor festival on which fasting and mourning are not allowed. The modern observance consists principally in preserving the ancient custom of reciting a blessing on the sabbath preceding Rosh Hodesh and in singing or reciting an abbreviated form of the Hallel psalms on Rosh Hodesh itself.

ROSHI

In Buddhism, term meaning the old teacher. Roshi is the name given to the Zen Master of a monastery who takes the pupil-monks and laymen in San-Zen and gives them Zen instruction. He may be at the same time the abbot. but in large monasteries the two offices are frequently distinct, the abbot concentrating on administration while the roshi confines himself to practical instruction in Zen.

ROSICRUCIANS

Members of an international secret fraternity. They trace their origin to ancient Egypt, circa 1500 BC, but the order itself was probably founded in medieval Europe. The society is highly secret in all respects and little is known about it. It appears to be generally religious in nature and concentrates on study through a mixture of ancient and modern methods.

ROSS, William David

(1877-1971) Scottish rationalistic moral philosopher and critic of Utilitarianism, who proposed a form of "situation ethics" or "institutionism" based on intuitional knowledge rather than on metaphysical concepts of what is good.

RSABHANATHA

First of the 24 Tirtthankaras, or saviors, of Jainism, a religion of India. His name is attributed to the series of 14 auspicious dreams seen by his mother before his birth in which the bull (rsabha) appeared first. He is one of the most honored of the Jaina saints, having been the first to preach the Jaina faith.

RTA

(literally meaning in Sanskrit: truth) In the earliest sacred scriptures of India (Vedas), the concept of cosmic order, which led in later Hinduism to the development of the doctrines of sharma (duty) and karman (causal laws governing rebirth). Rta is the physical order of the universe, the order of the sacrifice, and the moral law of the world.

RUBRICS

From the Latin term meaning "red text," rubrics are directions for liturgical actions or gestures that are printed in red in order to distinguish them from the spoken texts which are printed in black.

RUDRA

In Hinduism, a relatively minor Vedic god and one of the names of Shiva, a major god of later Hinduism.

RUFINUS, Tyrannius

(345-411) Theologian and translator of Greek theological works into Latin at a time when knowledge of Greek was declining in the West. His own writings include a commentary on the Apostles' Creed that exemplified contemporary catechetical instruction and provided the earliest continuous Latin text of the creed.

RUFUS

In the New Testament, son of the Simon who was compelled to help carry Jesus' torture stake, and brother of a certain Alexander (Mark 15:21; Luke 23:26).

RUH

In Islam, term denoting spirit, soul, life breath. Jibril in Surat Maryam is described as "Our (i.e. God"s) Spirit".

RUM, al-

The title of the 30th sura of the Koran; it means "The Byzantine Greeks." The sura belongs to the Meccan period and has 60 verses. Its title is taken from the second verse which reads: "The Byzantine Greeks have been defeated." This is probably a reference to the Persian capture of Jerusalem from the Byzantines in 614. This is one of the very few references in the Koran to contemporary history. The sura begins with three of the Mysterious Letters of the Koran and goes on to talk of the Hour and God's sign.

RUMAH

In the Old Testament, home of Zebidah (and her father Pedaiah), a wife of King Josiah of Judah and the mother of Jehoiakim (2 Kings 33:34-36). Its location is uncertain. The best possibility seems to be Khirbet Rumeh, which bears a similar name.

RUPA

In Buddhism, term for form. Form implies limitation, and form as recognized by the lower mind persists into the lower heaven worlds. The higher heaven worlds are called formless (arupa) because the mind is free from the limitations of particular forms. Desire for life in the worlds of form is the sixth fetter to be cast off, and aruparaga the seventh.

RUPA-SKANDHA

In Buddhism, the first of five skandhas, or aggregates, that comprise all things. The rupa-skandha is the aggregate of all the forms - i.e.,
▲ perceptible things, comprising the four elements: earth, water, fire, and wind;
▲ the organs or faculties of the senses and their domains;
▲ the sexes;
▲ vitality;
▲ volitions of body and speech;
▲ the element of space;
▲ the properties of material objects, such as softness, flexibility, lightness, mass, continuity, aging, and transitoriness;
▲ all that can be regarded as nourishment.

RUSALKA

In Slavic mythology, lake-dwelling soul of a child who died unbaptized or of a virgin who was drowned.

RUSSELL, Charles Taze

(1852-1916) Founder of the International Bible Students Association, forerunner of Jehovah's Witnesses. Of Presbyterian and Congregationalist background, Russell renounced the creeds of orthodox Christian denominations and in 1872 organized an independent Bible study class in Pittsburgh. In 1879 he started a Bible journal later called Watchtower, and in 1884 founded the Watchtower Bible and Tract Society.

RUSSIA, Orthodox Church of

The largest autocephalous (ecclesiastically independent) Eastern Orthodox church in the world; its membership is circa 40 million. The church showed a considerable revival in the 1990s.

RUSSIAN CATHOLIC CHURCH

An Eastern Catholic church of the Byzantine Rite, in communion with Rome since the early 20th century.

RUSSIAN CHANT

The monophonic (i.e., only one melody in unison) chant of the liturgy of the Russian Orthodox Church. The Russians accepted Christianity from the Greeks (officially in 988), and thus nearly all forms of medieval Russian chant are of Byzantine origin.

RUTH

In biblical times, Moabite heroine of the Old Testament book of the same name. She married Mahlon after the death of his father Elimelech and while Mahlon, his mother Naomi and his brother Chilion were living in Moab, a famine having provided the occasion for the family to leave their native Bethlehem in Judah. Ruth's brother-in-law Chilion was married to the Moabitess Orpah. Eventually the two brothers died, leaving behind childless widows. Later Naomi, accompanied by her two daughters-in-law, proceeded to return to Judah (Ruth 1:1-7; 4:9-10).

RUTH, Book of

Old Testament book, named for its central character, the Moabite woman Ruth. Widowed during a famine in the time of the Judges (circa 1000 BC), Ruth followed her Judahite mother-in-law, Naomi, to Bethlehem. She survived by gleaning barley from the fields of her husband's next-of-kin, Boaz, who eventually married her. Their great-grandson was David.

RU'YAT ALLAH

In Islam, vision of God, sight of God, in Paradise. The possibility and modality of the beatific Vision gave rise to considerable controversy in medieval Islam. Al-Ash'ari for example, taught that the vision of God in Paradise was a reality, though its modality was beyond man's comprehension, thereby vehemently opposing the idea of the Mu'tazila that God would not be visible in a literal sense to men.

RYOBU SHINTO

A general term used to refer to the pattern of coexistence that developed in Japan between Buddhism and the indigenous religion, Shinto; more specifically, the syncretic school that combines Shinto with the teachings of the Shingon sect.

RYONIN

(1072-1132) Japanese Buddhist leader, who founded the Yuzu Nembitsu sect of the Pure Land school of Amida Buddhism as a branch of the older Tendai sect.He initiated the renewal of Buddhist thought in the Kamakura era of government (1192-1333), when other new schools such as Zen and Nichiren Buddhism also arose.

S

SA'A, al-

In Islam, term to designate the Last Day, the Hour or Resurrection. In the Koran, verse 107 of Surat Yusuf talks of "The Hour" taking the unwary unbeliever by surprise. Islamic eschatology has elaborated a profusion of detail about "The Hour" and the "Signs of the Hour," which signal its imminent coming.

SA'ADIA BEN JOSEPH

(882-942) Jewish exegete, and polemicist whose influence on Jewish literary and communal activities made him one of the most influential scholars of his time.

SABA

The title of the 34th sura of the Koran (Arabic name for Sheba). Sheba was a major seat of South Arabian civilization in ancient times. The sura belongs to the Meccan period and has 54 verses. Its title is drawn from verse 15 which relates the story of the destruction of the great Ma'rib Dam. The sura goes on to stress that Mohammed has been sent as a herald and a warner.

SABA, Saint

(439-532) Christian Palestinian monk, champion of orthodoxy in the 5th century Christological (nature of Christ) controversies and founder of the Great Laura monastery of Mar (Saint) Saba. The renowned community of contemplative monks in the Judean desert near Jerusalem became a prototype for the subsequent development of Eastern Orthodox monasticism.

SABATIER, Auguste

(1839-1901) Protestant theologian, who helped revolutionize biblical interpretation by applying method of historical criticism and who also promoted the development of liberal theology and the Roman Catholic Modernist movement.

SABAZIUS

In Greek religion, a Phrygian or Thracian deity frequently identified with Dionysus, the wine god, and sometimes with Zeus, the chief god.

SABBATARIANISM

Doctrine of those Christians who believe that Sunday (the Christian sabbath) should be observed in accordance with the Fourth Commandment, which forbids work on the sabbath because it is a holy day.

SABBATH

A day of holiness and rest observed by Jews from sunset on Friday to nightfall of the following day; seventh day of the Hebrew week. The Jews observe it as the day of rest laid down in the fourth commandment to commemorate the Creation (Exodus 20:8-11). It starts at sunset on Friday and ends at sunset on Saturday. Christians adopted Sunday as the Sabbath (Hebrew: rest) to commemorate the Resurrection (Acts 20:7).

An sabbaths, a Sidra, or Torah portion is read. Torah readings are also held at new moon, holiday, and fast-day afternoon services. Congregants are honored by being called up to the reading. This act of going up is called an Aliyah.

The section from the Prophets recited at the conclusion of the reading from the Torah is called Haftarah. Each portion of the Torah has a specific Haftarah of its own; there is some connection between the Torah reading and the Haftarah.

SABBATH, Manichaean

Manichaean ritual observance of Sunday, involving abstinence from sex and food.

SABBATH, Special

A number of sabbaths during the Jewish religious year that have distinctive designations. Four occur between the end of the Shevat (fifth month of the Jewish civil year) and the first day of Nisan (seventh month of the Jewish civil year).

SABBATH YEAR

Counting from 1473 BC, the year that Israel, according to biblical tradition, entered the Promised Land, a sabbath year was to be celebrated "at the end of every seven years," actually on every seventh year (Deuteronomy 15:1-2) The sabbath year evidently began with the trumpet blast on Ethanim (Tishri), the Day of Atonement. However, some hold that, while the Jubilee year started with the Day of Atonement, the sabbath year started with Tishri 1st.

There was no cultivaiton of land, sowing or pruning, nor any gathering in of the crops grown, but what grew of itself was left in the field, open to the owner of the field as well as to his slaves, the hired laborers and the alien residents to eat. This was a merciful provision for the poor and, additionally, for the domestic animals and wild beasts, as these would also have access to the produce of the land during the sabbath year (Leviticus 25:1-7).

The sabbath year was called "the year of release" (Deuteronomy 15:9; 31:10). During that year the land enjoyed a complete rest or release lying uncultivated (Exodus 23:11).

Every year of release, during the Festival of Booths, all the people were to assemble, men and women, little ones and the alien residents, to hear the law read (Deuteronomy 31:10-13).

The land would have enjoyed 121 sabbath years besides 17 Jubilee years prior to the captivity if Israel had kept the Law properly. But the sabbath years were only partially kept. When the people went into exile in Babylon, the land remained desolate for 70 years "until the land had paid off its sabbaths" (2 Chronicles 36:20-21; Leviticus 26:34-43).

SABDA

In Hindu philosophy, term referring to the authority of the Veda (most ancient sacred scriptures) as a means of obtaining correct knowledge of things supersensual.

SABEANS

In biblical times, the designation of a band of raiders who attacked the property of Job of the land of Uz. These Sabeans took Job's cattle and she-asses and slaughtered his attendants (Job 1:14-15). Job also mentions "the traveling company of Sabeans" at Job 6:19. The name of the Sabeans are also applied to tall people linked in Isaiah 45:14 with laborers of Egypt and merchants in Ethiopia as ones who would recognize Jehovah and His people.

SABELLIANISM

A Christian heresy that was a more developed and less naive form of Modalistic Monarchianism. It was propounded by Sabellius (187-249) who was possibly a presbyter in Rome.

SABINIAN

(540-606) Pope from 604 to 606. His cautious administration of the papal granaries during a winter famine probably explains the later untrustworthy legend of his parsimony.

SABTAH

In the Old Testament, a son of Gush and brother of Nimrod; progenitor of one of the 70 post-Flood families (Genesis 10:7-8; 1 Chronicles 1:9-10). Sabtah's descendants apparently settled in southern Arabia, perhaps in one of the places later bearing a name similar to his.

SABTECA

In the Old Testament, fifth-named son of Cush and father of one of the 70 post-Flood families (Genesis 10:7, 32). His descendants likely settles in southern Arabia or perhaps Ethiopia, the exact location being unknown.

SACAR

In Judaism, Hararite father of David's warrior Ahiam (1 Chronicles 11:26). The name is also applied to the fourth son of Obed-edom and one of the gatekeepers during David's reign (1 Chronicles 26:1-4).

SACCIDANANDA

In Hinduism, a customary formula used to express the all-encompassing nature of Brahman (ultimate reality).

SACHEVERELL, Henry

(1674-1724) English preacher and a fanatical High church Anglican. He played a significant role in politics because his impeachment by the Whigs enabled the Tories to win control of the government.

SACHIA

In Judaism, the head of a paternal house in the tribe of Benjamin; son of Shaharaim by his wife Hodesh (1 Chronicles 8:1-10).

SACRA CONVERSAZIONE

A theme in Italian Renaissance art showing the Madonna and Child surrounded by a group of saints who are unrelated historically and who seem by their attitudes to be conversing with one another.

SACRAMENT

A religious rite, especially associated with the Christian church, in which a sacred or spiritual power is believed to be transmitted through material elements that are viewed as channels of divine grace.

The Latin word sacrament means "something holy." In Christian theology it is "the invisible form of an invisible grace" (St. Augustine) or a holy ordinance instituted by Christ, symbolizing and transmitting sanctification of the spirit. Sacraments are material signs believed by Christians to have been ordained by Jesus Christ to symbolize and convey spiritual gifts (e.g., bread and wine in the eucharist convey the presence and power of Christ). To be valid, a sacrament should have the correct "matter" (material sign), "form" (formula of administration), and "intention" (to do what the church intends). This guarantees that grace (salvation) is conveyed, whatever the personal character of the priest.

The sacraments are means and channels of the grace of God. In this understanding of their function and nature, two historic misunderstandings must be avoided. The communication of divine grace through the sacraments is not to be thought of in a mechanical or an automatic sense, as though grace were a measure of sacred stuff distributed in so many doses through sacraments.

As the gift and favor of a personal God, grace cannot be reduced to magic or to material; nor can the connection between sacrament and grace be made arbitrary or accidental, as though the recipient of the sacrament could not depend upon the presence of grace in it, but had to wonder each time whether it was in fact being proffered there.

The scholastic formula "God is bound by the sacraments but not to the sacraments" seeks to ensure both that the personal relationship to God is not degraded into magic and that the objective availability of divine grace in the sacrament is not jeopardized.

As means and channels of grace, the sacraments convey to those who rightly receive them the benefits of the death and resurrection of Christ, uniting them to this work. Although it is more explicit in the case of baptism than in that of other sacraments, this union with the saving work of Christ in his death and resurrection characterizes the sacraments: "We were buried therefore with him by baptism into death, so that as Christ was raised from the dead by the glory of the father, we too might walk in newness of life" (Romans 6:4).

As means of grace, the sacraments are more than symbols or signs, but they are never less. Their very nature as actions that point beyond their intrinsic meaning to an ultimate significance is bound up with their being "signs".

The laying on of hands that takes place in confirmation or in holy orders in an ancient rite is by no means confined to Christianity; in Genesis 48:14 it was part of the patriarchal blessing. But within the context of Christian sacraments this ceremony becomes a sign of the grace being conferred in and through the sacramental transaction.

Similarly, there have been ceremonial washings and sacred meals in many religions, so that Christian baptism and the Christian Eucharist may attach themselves to a widespread, if not indeed universal, phenomenon of religious experience.

Yet they are special "signs" because they point not only to some timeless truth about the cosmos but to the events in the life of Jesus by which the salvation of the human race was achieved. Locked as he is into a world of self-experience, man cannot look beyond this world without signposts that, appearing within the empirical realm, nevertheless show the way to another realm. The sacraments have a special role among such signposts, and the rituals surrounding their celebration have sought to enhance their importance as signs, their significance.

It belongs to the nature of sacraments that they are properly carried on within the church. As the body of Christ, who is himself the fundamental mystery (or sacrament) of salvation, the church participates in his sacramental character and dispenses his sacramental gifts.

Thus there have been many writers, both in the scholastic period and again in the modern, who have not hesitated to designate both Christ and the church as "sacraments." Without becoming involved in dogmatic nomenclature, one may nevertheless see in this recognition that the sacraments, to be effective, are simultaneously grounded in the person and work of Christ and set into the context of the church.

This emphasis protects them from an individualistic (and often magical) distortion. Infant baptism, for example, is not a magical incantation over an individual child but the responsible action of the Christian community and of the parents of the child, assuming the responsibilities of Christian nurture of which baptism is the first and most important step.

As the dispenser of the sacraments, the church through them invites and welcomes men to participation in the life of God Himself; as the "sign" of the Incarnation and of the Redemption, the church employs the other "sign" instituted by its Lord.

The specific number of the sacraments, about which so much of the polemic between Protestant and Roman Catholic theology has argued, is not the central issue it has sometimes appeared to be. Theologians of impeccable orthodoxy have maintained, on the basis of a particular definition, that there are more than seven (for instance, 14) or fewer than seven (for instance, two or three).

The seven traditionally identified as sacraments are:

▲ baptism;
▲ confirmation;
▲ Eucharist;
▲ penance;
▲ sacrament of the sick (formerly called extreme unction);
▲ holy orders, and
▲ matrimony.

Protestants have usually restricted the number to baptism and the Eucharist. Luther was willing to call absolution a sacrament as well. Both the problem of a proper definition and the question of a biblically validated institution by Christ have played a part in the debate about the number of the sacraments.

SACRAMENT, Most Blessed

A term for the Holy Eucharist that expresses the fact that this is the sacrament of sacraments.

SACRAMENTAL CONFESSOR

The priest who has received from a bishop the jurisdiction permitting him validly to absolve sins in the sacrament of penance. The role of the priest as sacramental confessor derives from the role in Christian antiquity of the bishop who directed the liturgical rite of reconciliation of sinners.

The bishop was informed of serious sins of Christians. When such Christians presented themselves for public penance, the bishop would assign the satisfactory works whose nature and duration were determined by the seriousness of the sin. Reconciliation by the bishop followed completion of the satisfactory works.

SACRAMENTALISM

Emphasis on the sacraments as central to the Christian life; often a pejorative term applied to the value allegedly set on sacraments as external acts apart from faith and inward appreciation of their meaning.

The term is particularly used to discredit the theory that sacraments confer grace ex opere operatio, and suggests that this implies a devotion to sacraments that neglects God, Who acts through them, and turns from faith in Christ himself to dependence on the performance of the signs of his action.

Those who affirm the objective effectiveness of sacraments, however, mean that it is God's action that causes this effectiveness, and that the sacraments being Christ's presence; they agree that actual reception of this effectiveness and presence is in proportion to the faith of the recipient.

SACRAMENTALS

In the Roman Catholic Church, sacred signs instituted by the church to dispose the faithful to receive the chief sanctifying effects of the sacraments and to render various occasions in life holy.

SACRED

In Buddhism, there is no division of life into the dualism of sacred and pro-fane, or good and evil. Veneration is shown for holiness, especially for the basic virtue of altruism.

SACRED HEART, Promises of the

In Roman Catholicism 12 promises communicated by Christ to St. Margaret Alacoque:

1 all graces necessary to their state in life;
2 peace in their homes;
3 comfort in all afflictions;
4 secure refuge in life and death;
5 abundant blessings on all their undertakings;
6 infinite mercy for sins;
7 tepid souls turning fervent;
8 fervent souls mounting in perfection;
9 blessings everywhere a picture or image of the Sacred Heart is mounted;
10 gift to priests of touching the most hardened hearts;
11 promoters' names written in the Sacred Heart of Jesus;
12 grace of final penitence to those who receive Holy Communion on nine consecutive First Fridays.

SACRED HEART OF JESUS

The physical heart of Jesus as a sign and symbol of his immense love for human beings for whom he accomplished the work of redemption; the Roman Catholic Church celebrates the solemnity of the Sacred Heart on the Friday after the second Sunday after Pentecost; the church encourages the faithful to practice approved devotion in honor of the Sacred Heart.

SACRED KINGSHIP

A religio-political concept that views the ruler as an incarnation, manifestation, mediator, or agent of the sacred or holy (the transcendent or supernatural realm).

SACRED PLACE

Site where the divine or sacred is especially present, a point of juncture between the transcendent and earthly spheres.

SACRED SCRIPTURES

The revered texts, or holy writ, of the religions of the world.

SACRED TIME

Mythical or religious time, as distinguished from profane time, the ordinary time and secular calendars.

SACRED OR HOLY

The power, being, or realm understood by religious persons to be at the core of existence and of transformative effect on their lives and destinies.

SACRIFICE

A religious rite in which an object is offered to a divinity in order to establish, maintain, or restore a right relationship of man to the sacred order.

From a religious viewpoint, the form of worship by which a duly authorized minister offers a victim in recognition of God's supreme dominion; in the Old Testament true and authentic sacrifices were offered, but they were imperfect "for it is impossible for the blood of bulls and goats to take away sins" (Hebrews 10:4); in the New Testament Christ himself is the perfect sacrifice, with his own blood "obtaining eternal redemption" (Hebrews 9:12).

SACRILEGE

A violation or contemptuous treatment of a person, place, or thing that is publicly dedicated to the worship of God; in essence it amounts to a personal affront against God.

SACRISTY

A room annexed to a church used to store sacred vessels and other materials used in the liturgy, and to provide a place for priests and other ministers to vest and prepare for liturgical celebrations.

SACROSANCTA

Decree by the Council of Basel in the 15th century, asserting the supremacy of conciliar power over that of the pope.

SAD

The title of the 38th sura of the Koran; it is the name of one of the letters of the Arabic alphabet. The sura belongs to the Meccan period and has 88 verses. It takes its title from the letter Sad which appears in the first verse and which, in this context, is one of the Mysterious Letters of the Koran. The sura surveys some of those people who disbelieved the messengers sent to them. It tells at some length the story of Dawud who is asked to give judgment between two disputants, provides information from the life of Sulayman and refers to some of the trials of Ayyub. Several other prophets are mentioned as well. Towards the end of the sura the story of Iblis is told with his refusal to bow down to God's new creation Adam.

SADDHA

In Buddhism, the initial acceptance of the Buddha's teachings, prior to the acquisition of right understanding and right thought.

SADDHARMAPUNDARIKA-SUTRA

In Buddhism, one of the earlier Mahayana texts venerated as the quintessence of truth by the Japanese Tendai and Nichiren sects, regarded by many others as a religious classic of great beauty and power and one of the most important works in the Mahayana tradition, the form of Buddhism predominant in East Asia.

SADDUCEES

Aristocratic ultraconservative Jewish religious group in Roman Judea, opposed to the pharisees. They rejected the Pharisaic Oral Law and based their faith on the written Mosaic Law (Acts 23:8). They were in constant conflict with the Pharisees on the content and extent of God's revelation to the Jewish people. Their great influence ended with the destruction of the Temple at Jerusalem (70). The Sadducees stressed the notion of freewill and the individual's responsibility to be held accountable for his actions.

SADHANA

In Hindu and Buddhist Tantrism, a spiritual exercise by which the practitioner evokes a divinity, identifies with it, and reabsorbs it into himself - a primary form of meditation in the Tantric Buddhism of Tibet.

SADHU

In India, any religious ascetic or holy man. The class of sadhus includes not only genuine saints of many faiths but also men (and occasionally women) who have left their homes in order to concentrate on physical and spiritual disciplines.

SAFF, al-

The title of the 61st sura of the Koran; it means literally "The Row" or "The Rank." The sura belongs to the Medinan period and has 14 verses. Its title is drawn from the fourth verse which notes that God must love those who fight in His way "in ranks." The sura condemns hypocrisy among the believers, goes on to quote Ida prophesying the coming of Mohammed, and urges men to strive or fight for God.

SAFFAT, al-

The title of the 37th sura of the Koran; it means "The Rangers," i.e. the angels ranged in front of God. The sura belongs to the Meccan period and contains 182 verses. Its title is drawn from the first verse which takes the form of an oath: "By the rangers in line." The sura goes on to stress the Oneness of God and His ability to raise bodies from the dead at the end of time. The torments of hell await the wicked while the blessed will enjoy the delights of Paradise. Nuh called on God and was saved by Him while others drowned. Ibrahim is flung into the flames and also asked to sacrifice his son Isma'il. In both cases he is rescued or reprieved by God. The whole sura, as can be seen, is full of prophetic history.

SAFI OD-DIN

(1253-1334) Mystic and founder of the Safavid order of mystics in Iran. He was a Sunni of the Shafi'i school, one of the four schools of Sunni law.

SAFIYYA BINT HUYAY

One of the wives of the Prophet Mohammed. She was a Jewess, captured at Khaybar, but was freed on conversion to Islam.

SAHABA

Companions, i.e. of the Prophet Mohammed. The word is used variously to denote both the Prophet's close friends and associates, and, more loosely, anyone who saw the Prophet while the latter was alive.

SAHAJIYA

Sakta cult of the Hindu Vaisana movement, arising in the Bengal in the 16th century and stressing the natural nondualistic qualities of the senses.

SAHIFA

Arabic word designating any revealed writings to the prophetic predecessors of Mohammed.

SAHIH

In Islam, term denoting the highest level of trustworthiness in a tradition.

SAINT

Term that has become to signify a holy person who personifies the best qualities of the particular religion to which he subscribes. In the Roman Catholic Church a saint is a believer possessed of extraordinary piety and virtue whose dedication to God sometimes reaches the point of martyrdom for the faith. When the Roman Catholic Church officially recognizes a person as a saint, and thus worthy of veneration, he is said to be canonized. before the 6th century the term saint meant any member of the Christian church, and many Protestants still employ the term saint in a New Testament sense of any believer who has been sanctified by the grace of God.

SAINT BARTHOLOMEW'S DAY, Massacre of

The destruction of several thousand French Huguenots (Protestants) which began on August 24, 1572. The growing influence of the Huguenots in France prompted Catherine de Médicis, mother of King Charles IX, to plot the assassination of the Huguenot leaders, notably Gaspard de Coligny. When an attempt on Coligny's life misfired, Charles, fearful of Huguenot power, ordered the death of all the leading Huguenots. Thus, on St. Bartholomew's Day, tens of thousands of Huguenots were dragged from their beds and brutally murdered. Although by August 25 the government ordered the killing to cease, the carnage continued in the French provinces right into October. The massacre touched off two more decades of religious warfare, which was only ended by the Edict of Nantes.

SAINT CATHERINE'S

Greek Orthodox monastery situated on Mount Sinai more than 5,000 feet above sea level in a narrow valley north of Jabal in the Sinai peninsula. The monastic foundation is the smallest of the autonomous churches that together compose the Eastern Orthodox Church.

SAINT PATRICK'S DAY

March 17, celebrated as the anniversary of the death (circa 461) of St. Patrick, Ireland's patron saint. Irishmen celebrate St. Patrick's Dayu by wearing leaves of chamrock (Ireland's national plant) and by staging colorful parades.

SAINT PETER'S, New

Present basilica of St. Peter's in Rome, that was begun by Julius II in 1506 and was finally completed in 1615 under Paul V as a three-aisled Latin-cross plan church with a dome at the crossing directly above the high altar, which covers the shrine of St. Peter the Apostle. The church has functioned as a chief pilgrimage center in Europe and also was the scene of papal ceremonies and of the Vatican ecumenical councils.

SAINT PETER'S, Old

First basilica of St. Peter's in Rome, a five-aisled basilican plan church with apsed transept at the west end that was begun between 326 and 333 at the order of the emperor Constantine and finished circa 30 years later. The shrine of St. Peter in the apse of the transept was encased by Constantine in blue-veined marble. Old St. Peter's was torn down in the early 16th century and replaced by New St. Peter's.

SAINT'S PLAY

A term often used by modern scholars to describe those vernacular plays of the Middle Ages which presented the lives and martyrdom of the saints. The saint's plays are also often known as miracle plays, as distinct from mystery plays, the latter taking as their subject episodes from the Old and New Testament.

SAINTS, Devotion to

The ancient Christian practice of offering honor to those who are recognized as especially close to God. Both the Council of Trent and Vatican Council II stated the antiquity and rightness of this practice.

Its dogmatic basis is the article of the Creed confessing belief in the Holy Spirit as sanctifier, through whose action the holiness effected in some members serves the building up of others in the body of Christ.

Theologically, devotion is the concern of the virtues of both religion and charity. As it means a joyful readiness to honor and serve God, devotion includes honoring Him in the reflection of His goodness through the saints.

That prompts a pietas towards them as they are sources of spiritual good in the family of the Father. Devotion also engages charity in that this means a union in love with God that loves as he loves; because their sanctity is a sign of a special divine love toward him, the saints are a particular object of charity as love of neighbor.

The manifestation of piety and charity toward the saints includes reliance on their intercession; but devotion toward them takes on also a particular meaning: a looking toward them as examples in the hope of imitating their reflection of the grace of Christ. This is particularly true of veneration for their founder by religious; and of devotion to patron saints for their particular way of reflecting Christ's holiness.

SAINTS, Legends of the

Accounts of the saints' lives of martyrdom, written for inspirational reading. The Latin legenda means simply writings that "should be read," and does not in itself denote fanciful tales. In fact, however, the legend writer's concern was not history; and the legends contain many nonfactual elements and evince an easy transference to their subject of feats or data from other legends, since certain accomplishments were taken as ideals of saintliness. The works of the historian Eusebius of Caesarea incorporated many pre-existent Acts of the martyrs.

SAINTS, Veneration of

The ancient tradition of honoring and invoking the saints, explained by Vatican Council II: "The church has always believed that the apostles and Christ's martyrs, who had given the supreme witness of faith and charity by the shedding of their blood, are closely united with us in Christ; she has always venerated them, together with the Blessed Virgin Mary and the holy angels, with a special love, and has asked for the help of their intercession."

SA'IR

In Islam, one of the seven ranks of hell. According to tradition Sa'ir is the blazing inferno in which Sabaeans will burn.

SAIVA-SIDDHANTA

An important medieval school of Hinduism. The name is used for the South Indian religious system of Saivism (worship of the god Siva).

SAIVISM

Cult of the Indian god Siva, with Vainavism and Saktism, one of the three principal forms of modern Hinduism. Saivism includes such diverse movements as the highly philosophical Saiva-siddhanta, the socially distinctive Lingayats, ascetic orders such as the dasnami sannyasins, and innumerable folk variants.

SAIVO

The Lap underworld. The deceased lead happy lives with their families and ancestors; they build tents, hunt, fish, and in every way act as they did on earth.

SAJDA, al-

The title of the 32nd sura of the Koran; it means "The Prostration." The sura belongs to the Meccan period and has 30 verses. Its title is drawn from verse 15 where reference is made to those believers in God's signs who prostrate themselves in prayer before God when reminded of them. The sura begins three of the Mysterious Letters of the Koran and goes on to refer to God's creative power and might. Those who believe and do good works will abide in Paradise while the wicked will burn in hell.

SAJJADA

Arab word for carpet, prayer rug, prayer carpet. The word acquired an extra dimension in tasawwuf where the head of a tariqa might bear the title like "Master of the Prayer Rug".

SAKER, Alfred

(1814-1880) English missionary who established the first British missionary in the Cameroons. He founded the city of Victoria, Cameroon, and translated the Bible into Douala, the local language.

SAKKOS

An outer liturgical vestment worn by bishops of the Eastern Orthodox Church. It is a short, close-fitting tunic with half sleeves, buttoned or tied with ribbons on the sides, and usually heavily embroidered.

SAKRA

In Buddhist mythology, the chief of the devas (gods), who presides over the Tavatimsa heaven, or the Heaven of the 33 gods. He is identified as the Hindu god Indra, who is said to have become a convert to the teachings of the Buddha.

SAKTISM

Worship of the Hindu supreme goddess, Sakti. Saktism is, together with Vaisnavism and Saivism, one of the major forms of modern Hinduism, especially popular in Bengal and Assam. Sakti is conceived of either as the paramount deity, or as the consort of a male diety, generally Siva.

SAKYA

The name of the tribe or clan to which Gautama the Buddha belonged. The tribe was at the time subject to the Kosalas, whose capital was Sravasti.

SALADIN

(1138-1193) Muslim leader who crushed the Christian crusaders in Palestine. Born in Mesopotamia of Kurdish origin, he began an army career, and became Vizier (circa 1169), then Sultan of Egypt (1174), where he restored orthodox Sunnite Islam and established his own hereditary Ayyubid Dynasty. Directing his army northward from Egypt, he reclaimed Syria and most of Palestine (including Jerusalem) from the Christian crusaders, and ultimately forced a stalemate on England's King Richard I (1192) during the Third Crusade, which was provoked by his success. This left the Muslims masters of all of Palestine, including Jerusalem. Saladin's magnanimity to prisoners, tolerance of Christian pilgrims, and encouragement of Christian-Muslim trade earned him a favorable reputation among both peoples.

SALAFIYYA

In Islam, term to designate the early generation after Mohammed, i.e., groups as the sahaba and the tabi'un, whose example constituted a religious paradigm for later generations. The Salafiyya tried, among other things, to identify a via media between the strict tenets of Islam and the ideas of secular society and modern science.

SALAMIS

In biblical times, name for an important city of Cyprus. Paul, Barnabas and John Mark "published the word of God" there near the start of Paul's first missionary tour in 47. How long they stayed in the city is not stated. Apparently there was a large Jewish population in Salamis as it had more than one synagogue (Acts 13:2-5).

SALAT

The prayer and its accompanying ritual, performed by the practicing Muslim five times a day. This should not take place at the time of the actual rising or setting of the sun. Although the Koran mentions prayer many times, the obligation to pray five times per day derives from hadith rather than the Koran. The prayer ritual is one of the five arkan or Pillars of Islam.

The five prayers are named as follows:
1 The morning prayer (Salat al-Subh)
2 The midday prayer (Salat al-Zuhr)
3 The afternoon prayer (Salat al-Asr)
4 The evening prayer (Salat al-Maghrib)
5 The night prayer (Salat al-Isha).

SALECAH

In biblical times, name for a city at the eastern limit of Bashan, and part of the domain of Og. Taken by Israel under Moses, Salecah came to be inhabited by Gadites (Deuteronomy 3:8-10; Joshua 12:4-5). It is usually identified with Salkhadm situated in a southern extension of Jebel el-Druze, some 70 miles east-south-east of the southern end of the Sea of Galilee.

SALESIAN SISTERS

One of the largest Roman Catholic religious congregations of women, founded in 1872 at Mornese (Italy) by St. John Bosco and St. Mary Mazzarello. The Sisters followed St. John Don Bosco's norms for education, reason, religion, and amiability and the employment of all that is humanly useful in character formation. The Sisters number circa 20,000 in 55 countries.

SALESIANS OF DON BOSCO

A Roman Catholic religious congregation of men devoted to the Christian education of youth. Their founder, St. John Bosco formulated the principles of education, reason, religion, and amiability and the employment of all that is humanly useful in character formation - academic studies, manual skills, work, clubs, and athletic games.

SALIH

Arabian prophet sent to warn the tribe of Thamud. The latter not only rejected Salih's message but they hamstringed the she-camel which had been sent as a "proof" and a "sign" from God, i.e,, of friendship and covenant.

SALII

In ancient Italy, a priesthood usually associated with the worship of Mars, the god of war. The priests, probably representing a section of the early Roman army, wore the archaic Roman war dress. Characteristic was the primitive chant as a community prayer on behalf of the Roman state.

SALIM

In biblical times, a place mentioned at John 3:23 to help locate Aenon, where John the Baptist baptized persons, Hence, Salim must have been well known at the time. Today its situation and that of Aenon are both uncertain.

SALIM, Hadji Agus

(1884-1954) Indonesian nationalist and religious leader who played a key role during the 1920s in moderating the messianic and communist element in the Muslim nationalist movement.

SALJUQS

Also spelled Seljuks, major dynasty in medieval Islamic history. They originally came from the steppe country to the north of the Caspian Sea. They established themselves in Persia in 1038 and gradually extended their rule over Persia and Iraq, gaining control of Baghdad in 1055.

SALLAI

In Judaism, a name for four different persons.

1. In the list of Benjaminites who lived in Jerusalem following the Babylonian exile (Nehemiah 11:4-8).
2. A priestly paternal house in the days of High Priest Jeshua's successor Joiakim (Nehemiah 12:12, 20).
3. A post-exilic Benjaminite resident of Jerusalem; son of Meshullam (1 Chronicles 9:3-7; Nehemiah 11:7).
4. A priestly family head who returned to Jerusalem with Zerubbabel (Nehemiah 12:1-7). In the list at verse 20 of later paternal houses, the name Sallai appears at the corresponding place.

SALMA

In the Old Testament, forefather of those who settled in places such as Bethlehem, Netophah and Atroth-beth-joab (1 Chronicles 2:51-54). Salma was a son of Hur in the Calebite branch of Judah's geneaology (1 Chronicles 2:4-9).

SALMON

In Judaism, son of Judah's chieftain Nahshon, likely born during the 40-year wilderness trek. Salmon married Rahjab of Jericho, by whom he fathered Boaz. He was, therefore, a link in the genealogical line leading to David and Jesus (Numbers 2:3; Matthew 1:4-5; Luke 3:32).

SALMONE

In biblical times, name for a promontory of Crete, generally identified with

Cape Sidero at the eastern extremity of the island. Apostle Paul sailed past Salmone in 58 on his way to Rome for trial. However, strong winds apparently did not permit the vessel, en route from Cnidus, to sail north of Crete past the southern tip of Greece and on to Rome southward the craft past Salmone and thereafter had some protection from the wind while sailing along Crete's southern shores (Acts 27:7).

SALOME

(1st century AD) Grand-daughter of Herod the Great. Her dancing so pleased her stepfather Herod Antipas that he promised her anything she wanted. Prompted by her mother Herodias, she asked for John the Baptist's head, which was presented to her on a platter (Mark 6:21-29).

SALT, City of

In biblical times, a Judean city in the wilderness (Joshua 15:61-62). It is sometimes tentatively connected with Khirbet Qumran, by the north-western shore of the Dead Sea.

SALT, Valley of

In biblical times, a valley where, on two occasions, the Israelites defeated the Edomites (2 Samuel 8:13; 2 Kings 14:7). Its precise location is uncertain, but scholars have generally recommended either of two locations, one near Beer-sheba and the other to the south of the Salt Sea.

SALT SEA

One of the biblical designations for the large lake or sea now generally known as the Dead Sea. The Salt Sea forms the southern termination of the Jordan River.

SALU

In Judaism, a Simeonite whose son Zimri was executed for immorality on the plains of Moab (Numbers 25:14).

SALVATION

Man's deliverance from the power of sin. It is freely offered to all men, but is conditional upon repentance and faith in Jesus Christ (John 3:16). All history is a divine plan of salvation, consequent on Adam's fall, achieved in the incarnation, death and resurrection of Jesus Christ, and consummated at the Last Judgment.

Salvation means atonement. Jesus Christ is called Savior in Christian language because he achieved salvation by his life, death, and resurrection. Western Christian theology has frequently defined this salvation in the language of vicarious satisfaction.

By his death on the cross Christ satisfied the injured justice of God and thus made atonement for human sin. In Greek theology the emphasis has been on the resurrection of Christ as not only the declaration of salvation but its means as well.

Christ triumphed over the spiritual enemies of man - sin, death, and the devil - and grants salvation as Christus Victor. These emphases are by no means mutually exclusive, but they do stress different aspects of the saving work of Christ.

This definition of salvation underlies such biblical statements as Titus 2:11-14: "The grace of God has appeared for the salvation of all men .... our blessed hope, the appearing of the glory of our great God and Savior Jesus Christ, who gave himself for us to redeem us from all iniquity."

Salvation means conversion. Thus Christians of the evangelical tradition speak of "the day I was saved" as the day when, through an experience of repentance and conversion, they became Christian believers. The etymological meaning of salvation is "health" and in the New Testament, being saved means being restored to spiritual health and living a healthy life.

In this sense, salvation is a state of

being, brought about by the saving work of Christ and conferred upon the individual through the gifts of the Holy Spirit. As a new life in Christ, it is also a following in his steps.

The joy and courage that are components of salvation in this sense of the word are described not only in the New Testament but also and especially in the Old Testament, as in Psalm 27:1-4: "The Lord is my light and my salvation; whom shall I fear? One thing have I asked of the Lord, that will I seek after; that I may dwell in the house of the Lord all the days of my life, to behold the beauty of the Lord. and to inquire to his temple."

Salvation means immortality. In some Christian traditions, this understanding of salvation as the life that will commence only after death has largely overshadowed the other meanings of the word, especially the second. There is good New Testament warrant for interpreting salvation as immortality - though not for restricting it to this meaning.

When Paul says that "salvation is nearer to us now than when we first believed" (Romans 13:11), salvation is being used for the eschatological hope of the return of Christ at the Second Coming and the beginning of life in heaven. But the same apostle, quoting the Book of Isaiah, "Behold, now is the acceptable time; behold, now is the day of salvation" (2 Corinthians 6:2).

The solution to this apparent contradiction is to be found in the biblical use of such terms as "eternal life," which refers to an existence that begins here and now within human history but reaches its consummation and perfection only at the end of history. For it is only there that the enemies of salvation are completely abolished and their power taken away.

SALVATION, Theology of

Salvation is a basic human hope expressed in many different religions. It is deliverance through religion from the perils of human existence. For primitive man these perils were encountered in his contest with nature, which threatened human survival in many ways, and only the appeasement of nature spirits or of various other divinities keep a man from coming to harm.

Salvation constitutes the major theme of the Hebrew Old Testament. The God of the Hebrews was a saving God, and the history of Israel a salvation history. Its great focal point was the exodus, the deliverance of the Hebrew people from the slavery of Egypt.

The historical experience was above all else the foundation of the Israelites' conviction that Yahweh-Elohim was a saving God. Projected backward in time, it was the same God who delivered the patriarchs from earlier perils; projected forward into the future, the exodus event as a guarantee that Yahweh-Elohim would continue to save Israel from all the perils of social and political upheavals.

Gradually the conviction of God's salvific intervention in the history of Israel evolved into the themes of the Messianic end-time. This would be the final time of God's kingdom on earth established by the Messiah. It would be a time of peace and justice, not only for the people of Israel, but for all nations through Israel.

The idea of salvation in the earlier stage of the Old Testament was concerned with deliverance from immediate perils such as battles, famines, migrations, invasions, and captivity. Only gradually was the hope projected to a future and final salfivic establishment of God's kingdom. The salvation hope of the Israelite centered in the main about the strength of this nation, his own happiness, and a long life. Salvation as a projection into the afterlife was not a part of Old Testament theology.

The New Testament theology focused on Jesus as the Messiah. Jesus proclaimed the immediacy of the kingdom of God. The end-time was begun through the prophetic agency of Jesus. Although New Testament salvation thought retains shades of national liberation from the Romans, a major shift had taken place.

Jesus was preached, not as a national liberator, but as a deliverer from sin and death; and salvation was something to be finally and perfectly realized in the after-life. Jesus through his death-to-sin had established for all men the possibility of eternal life. The perils of human existence in this life were seen as the necessary consequence of human sinfulness. However, through faith in Jesus, human sinfulness could be overcome and death would resolve itself into a glorious after-life.

Later Christian theologies confirmed the association between salvation and resurrection. The Resurrection of Jesus was the sign that death and sin had been overcome, the forces of evil had been defeated. Sin and death would continue as part of human existence, but complete deliverance would finally come to those who believed in the redemptive power of Jesus.

SAMA'

In Islam, a mystical or spiritual concert; the Sufi practice of listening to music and chanting to reinforce ecstasy and induce mystical trance. Sufis maintain that melodies and rhythms prepare the soul for a deeper comprehension of the divine realities and better appreciation of divine music.

SAMADHI

In Buddhism, contemplation on reality; the state of even-mindedness when the dualism caused by thought has ceased to ruffle the surface of the ocean of truth. The term is used in the sense of the distinction between the mind, the object and their relationship is transcended. Samma Samadhi is the last step on the Noble Eightfold Path and a prelude to Nirvana. But the final step is a large one, from duality to non-duality.

SAMANTABHADRA

In Mahayana Buddhism, the bodhisattva, representing kindness or happiness. He is represented seated on an elephant with three heads and six tusks. In Tantric Buddhism he is regarded as the manifestation of Vairocana Buddha.

SAMAPATTI

In Buddhism, term denoting spiritual exercises used in meditation.

SAMARIA

In biblical times name for a city in the central region of ancient Palestine. It is bounded by Galilee on the north and by Judaea on the south; on the west is the Mediterranean Sea and on the east the Jordan River. The city was built circa 800 BC by King Omri as the capital of the northern kingdom (Israel) and named for Shemer, owner of its hilltop site. Conquered by the Assyrians (772 BC), the city was completely destroyed by the Hasmonean ruler Hyrcanus I (108 BC). It was rebuilt by Herod the Great (30 BC) and named Sebaste (Augusta) in honor of Octavian. Tradition makes it the burial place of John the Baptist.

SAMARITAN CANON

The version of the Pentateuch (Genesis, Leviticus, Numbers and Deuteronomy considered as a unit) that the Samaritans, an almost extinct sect of Judaism, consider to be the only canonical scriptures of Judaism.

SAMARITANS

In biblical times, inhabitants of the ancient district of Samaria. Originally non-Jewish colonists from Assyria, they intermarried with the Israelites and accepted the Jewish Torah. Jews who returned to their homeland after the Babylonian captivity would not accept the help of the Samaritans in the building of the second Temple of Jerusalem. Consequently, in the 4th century BC, the Samaritans built their own temple in Shechem. They were not socially accepted - hence the significance of the good Samaritan in Luke's gospel (10:25-37).

The Samaritan priesthood dominates life in the community. These men are the sole interpreters of the law and the

The good Samaritan.
"But a certain Samaritan ... had compassion on him, and went to him, and bound up his wounds, pouring in oil and wine, and set him on his own beast" (Luke 10:33,34).
Lithograph by Gustave Doré (about 1860).

SAMARITANS

calendar, which is a vital part of their faith as it governs the observation of their festivals. Unlike the Jews who have the Bible and the Talmud, the Samaritans have a faith whose beliefs are relatively simple to outline. After Moses, Joshua is the only prophet to be held in high esteem. It could be said that the Samaritan doctrine is that anything not covered in the Five Books of Moses cannot be regarded as valid. They regard the Ten Commandments as nine, adding a tenth of their own stipulating the sanctity of Mount Gerizim.

The Samaritan way of life results from an interpretation of biblical laws which is usually stricter than that of the most ultra-orthodox Jews. They observe Sabbath in similar style to the Jews, and also have the same circumcision rules. During their menstrual period, women are obliged to remain separated from their families for seven days, and the men must look after them.

SAMATA

In Buddhism, expression meaning sameness, as in sameness of mind.

SAMATHA

In Buddhism, tranquility of mind; rather in the negative sense of withdrawal.

SAMBHOGAKAYA

The "Bliss Body" of the triune Buddha. In this phrase the Buddha is considered as communicating the Dharma to the Bodhisattva, as distinct from Nirmanakaya, his manifestation in the ordinary world of samsara.

SAMBODHI

In Buddhism, the insight, wisdom, and assimilation of truth essential to the attainment of the three higher stages of Arhatship. The seven successive factors which lead to Sambodhi are:
▲ mindfulness,
▲ investigation of the Dhamma,
▲ zeal,
▲ joy,
▲ tranquility of mind,
▲ concentration,
▲ equanimity.

Samma sambodhi is the supreme spiritual insight of a Buddha.

SAMGAR-NEBO

In biblical times, the name or title of one of the Babylonian princes who entered Jerusalem right after a breach was made in the walls in the summer of 607 BC (Jeremiah 39:3).

SAMGHA

Buddhist brotherhood, consisting of monks, nuns, laymen, and laywomen. In early times, it consisted of homeless monks and nuns. Later, when the Mahayana movement arose, those who aimed at the state of Bodhisattva, regardless of being layman or monk, joined together in the brotherhood. It is regarded as one of the three treasures of Buddhism.

SAMJNA-SKANDHA

In Buddhist philosophy, one of five skandhas, or aggregates that comprise all empirical phenomena. Samjna-skandha refers to mental activity that conceptualizes the image of the object caught by internal organs.

SAMKARSANA

In Hindu theology, form of the god Vishnu, applied to Balarama, the elder brother or Krsna, who was conceived in the body of Devalu and transferred to the womb of Rohini.

SAMKYA

One of the philosophical schools of India said to have influenced the development of Buddhism. Its doctrines include the three Gunas, the evolution of this threefold:
▲ Nature from Prakriti;
▲ The Atman or Purusha;
▲ The Life of Nature's Form.

SAMLA

In the Old Testament, the fifth-named king of Edom who reigned before a king ruled Israel. Samla was from Masrekah (Genesis 36:31-37; 1 Chronicles 1:47-48).

SAMMA

In Buddhism, term meaning supreme; the highest point or summit. It its relative meaning it is used to describe each step of the Noble Eightfold Path, being usually translated as "Right." Here is means the highest state possible for any given individual to attain, according to his mental and moral development and his environment. In its absolute sense it means "supreme."

SAMMATIYA

An ancient Buddhist school or group of schools that held a distinctive theory concerning the pudgala or person. They believed that though an individual does not exist independent from the five skandhas, or components that make up his personality, he is at the same time something greater than the mere sum of his parts.

SAMOS

In biblical times, name for an island in the Aegean Sea near the west coast of Asia Minor. Apostle Paul apparently stopped briefly at Samos on the return from his third missionary tour (Acts 20:15).

According to the biblical record, the ship Paul was on when returning to Jerusalem stopped at Chios, sailed some 65 miles down the coast of Asia Minor and "touched at Samos, and on the following day arrived at Miletus" (Acts 20:15). The ship Paul was on evidently docked briefly at Samos and then traveled on to Miletus.

SAMOTHRACE

In biblical times name for a mountainous island located in the northeastern Aegean Sea, having a city of the same name on its northern side. Paul's ship came "with a straight run" to the island of Samothrace from Troas in northwest Asia Minor in the spring of 50 during his second missionary journey. There is, however, no indication that he went ashore (Acts 16:11). The modern-day island lacks a good harbor, though it offers a number of places for safe anchorage.

SAMPADA

In Buddhism, attainment as desirable attainment. The five significant attainments are:
▲ faith;
▲ morality;
▲ learning;
▲ liberality;
▲ wisdom.

SAMPRADAYAS

In Hinduism, traditional schools of religious teaching, transmitted from one teacher to another. From about the 11th century onward, several sects emerged out of the Vaisnavism (worship of the god Visnu), which continue to the present day.

SAMSARA

In Buddhism, Hinduism, and Jainism the most commonly used term for the central Indian conception of metempsychosis. It is a term with the basic meaning of reincarnation; the perpetual repetition of birth and death from the past through these six illusory reals: hell, hungry spirits, animals, asura or fighting spirits, men, and heaven. Unless enlightened, one cannot be freed from this wheel of transmigration. Those who are free from this can be called Buddhas.

SAMSKARA

In Buddhism, the second link in the chain of Nidanas and one of the five Skandhas. In the Nidanas this arises because of Avidya, ignorance, and in turn gives rise to consciousness.

In the five Skandhas, or analysis of the personality, the Samskaras are placed below consciousness. In either case the collection of mental contents contains complexes, conditioned reflexes and mental habits of all kinds, including subconscious habits and memories. Indeed, the term seems to include all contents of the mind at any one moment which will condition the functioning of consciousness and be influenced in turn by that functioning.

SAMSKARAS

In Hinduism, term denoting personal sacraments traditionally observed at every stage of a Hindu's life, from the moment of conception to the final scattering of his or her funeral ashes.

SAMSKARA-SKANDHA

In Buddhist philosophy, one of the five skandhas or aggregates that comprise all that exists. The samskaras consists in "fabricated" - i.e., configured - composites of any kind that make up the elements of the psyche, conscious or unconscious.

SAMSON

(circa 1070-1010 BC) Israelite hero portrayed in the Old Testament book of Judges (13-16). He was a Nazirite and a legendary warrior whose exploits show the weight of Philistine pressure on Israel during much of the early, tribal period of Israel in Canaan. The book of Judges ranks him with other divinely inspired warriors who delivered the community to establish themselves as its judges.

SAMUDAYA

In Buddhism, term meaning origin; the second Noble Truth, that the origin of suffering is Tanha, craving, selfish desire.

SAMUEL

(flourished 11th century BC). Religious hero in the history of Israel, being priest, judge, prophet and military leader. His greatest distinction was his role in the establishment of the monarchy of Israel. By the revelation of God, he anointed Saul king and installed him before all Israel. Because of Saul's disobedience to God, Samuel later anointed David as king.

SAMUEL, Books of

Two Old Testament books that are principally concerned with the origin and early history of the monarchy of ancient Israel. The books are written anonymously in the 10th century BC. The work bears the name of Samuel because he is the first of its principal figures and was instrumental in the selection of the first two kings. 1 Samuel treats Samuel as prophet and judge and Saul as king. 2 Samuel presents David as king.

SAMUEL OF NEHARDEA

(177-257) Babylonian rabbi and scholar, disciple of Judah ha-Nasi, who became head of the religious academy of Nehardea on the Euphrates.

SAMVARA

In mystical Buddhism, a fierce protective deity. He is an emanation of the Buddha Aksobhya, and wears a figure of that god in his headdress. Two of his 12 arms are crossed on his breast, one holds the four-faced head of Brahma.

SAMVRTI-SATYA

In Buddhist thought, the truth based on the common understanding of ordinary people. It refers to the empirical reality usually accepted in everyday life and can be admitted for practical purposes of communication.

SAMYE DEBATE

Held at the first Tibetan Buddhist monastery near Ilasa during a two year period (792-794), between Indian and Chinese teachers of the doctrine. The debate centered on the question of whether enlightenment was attained gradually, through activity, or suddenly, without activity.

SAMYOJANA

In Buddhism, term meaning Fetters. There are ten so-called fetters binding things to the Wheel of Becoming.
1 Belief in a permanent self.
2 Skeptical doubt.
3 Clinging to rules and rituals, a special form of Upadana.
4 Sensuous craving.
5 Ill-will.
6 Craving for the world of form.
7 Formless world.
8 Conceit.
9 Restlessness.
10 Ignorance.

SANBALLAT

In the Old Testament, a Horonite who opposed Nehemiah's efforts to repair the wall of Jerusalem (Nehemiah 2:10). He is thought to be the Samballat mentioned in a papyrus found at Elephantine (Egypt), which identifies him as the governor of Samaria and the father of Delaiah and Shelemiah.

SANCTIFYING GRACE

According to Catholic teaching, a created participation or sharing in the life of God himself; friendship with God.

SANCTUARY

In religion, a sacred place, set apart from the profane, ordinary world. In Christianity and Judaism, a sanctuary is defined as a place set apart for the worship of God or of gods, a holy place (1 Chronicles 22:19; Isaiah 16:12; Ezekiel 28:18). The Hebrew noun rendered "sanctuary" is drawn from a verb meaning in a physical sense "to be bright, to be new or fresh, untarnished or clean." The Bible often uses the term in a moral sense to designate that which is holy or sacred.

A "sanctuary" need not necessarily be a special building, for the one at Shechem referred to at Joshua 24:25-26 may simply have been the site where Abraham had centuries earlier erected an altar (Genesis 12:6-7). However, frequently the expression "sanctuary" designates either the tabernacle (Exodus 28:10; 2 Chronicles 36:17) or the Temple at Jerusalem (1 Chronicles 28:10; Ezekiel 24:21). As applied to the tabernacle, "sanctuary" could mean the entire tent and its courtyard, or the furniture and utensils of the sanctuary (Numbers 10:21).

SAN FRANCISCO

Franciscan monastery and church in Assisi (Italy), begun after the canonization in 1228 of St. Francis of Assisi and completed in 1253. The lower church is where the saint is buried.

SANGHA

An assembly, the monastic order founded by the Buddha, the members of which are called Bhikkhus or Bhikkhunis. It is the oldest monastic order in the world. The act of admission to the order is called pabbajja (renouncing the world). The hair of the head and beard is shaved, the yellow robe (consisting of three garments) is donned, and the Tisarana is recited. The candidate is then a novice. The ordination ceremony takes place before a chapter of senior Bhikkhus and Theras. No oaths are taken, and the Bhikkhu is free to leave the order at any time if he desires to do so. The Bhikkhu possesses only his robes, alms-bowl, razor, needle and water-strainer. He eats only one meal a day, no food being taken after mid-day.

In the Mahayana, monasteries are training colleges rather than retreats. The monks keep a strict discipline. Ordained temple priests may now marry.

SANGHAMITTHA

(3rd century BC) Sister of Mahinda who by tradition was responsible for converting Sri Lanka (then named Ceylon) to Buddhism; she founded an order of nuns.

SAN GIOVANNI IN LATERANO

Basilican church built by the emperor Constantine I (circa 313); the first major Christian church constructed in Rome. In the 17th century the church was renovated.

SANGITIPARYANA

One of the several Sanskrit sections - called padas - of the Buddhist sacred scripture Abhidharma Pitaka.

SANHEDRIN

Ruling councils of the Jews in Roman-occupied Palestine. The Great Sanhedrin was made up of 71 Sadducees and Pharisees, presided over by the High Priest. It served as a civil and religious court and was thus responsible for the trials of Christ and several of the Apostles. There were also local or provincial sanhedrins of lesser jurisdiction and authority.

SANKAPPA

In Buddhism, mindedness free from sensuous desire, ill-will and other such taints; the second step on the Noble Eightfold Path. Sankappa may be extended to right intent or motive; not only the state of mind but the purpose for which the Path is trodden.

SANKARA

(701-750) Philosopher and theologian, most famous exponent of the Advaita Vedanta school of philosophy, and the source of the main currents of modern Indian thought. He wrote commentaries on the Brahma-sutra and on the principal Upanisads, affirming his belief in one eternal, unchanging reality (Brahman) and the illusion of plurality and differentiation.

SAN KUAN

In Chinese mythology, the Three Officials:
- ▲ Tien Kuan, official of Heaven who bestows happiness;
- ▲ Ti Kuan, official of earth who grants remission of sins;
- ▲ Shui Kuan, official of water who averts misfortune.

SANNO ICHI-JITSU SHINTO

A school of Japanese religion, a synthesis of the indigenous Shinto and the Tendai school of Buddhism, dating from the late Heian (794-1185) to the early Kamakura (1192-1333) period. Sanno is the name of the Shinto mountain god who resides on Mount Hiei (headquarters of the Tendai Buddhist school) and who is considered by members of the religion to be a manifestation of the Buddha Sakyamuni and also identical with the chief Shinto divinity, the sun goddess Amaterasu.

SANNYASIN

In Hinduism, one who has renounced the world, a religious ascetic. In the tradition concept of asrama, which divides a man's life into four stages, the renunciation of all material possessions to wander homeless without family ties was assumed only by those individuals who had fulfilled all prior obligations and had reached the fourth and final stage.

SANRON

A school of Buddhist philosophy introduced into Japan from China in the Nara period (710-784). The Sanron teaching is derived from the Indian Madhyamika school of philosophy and because of its denial of the reality of both the subjective and objective world sometimes was characterized as nihilistic. Although Sanron has ceased to exist as a religious sect, its beliefs continue to be studied in Japan and China.

SANSANNAH

In biblical times, name for a town in the southern portion of the territory of the tribe of Judah (Joshua 15:21). A comparison of Joshua 15:31 with parallel lists of cities of Joshua at 19:5 and 1 Chronicles 4:31 indicates that it may be the same as Hazar-susah.

SANSIN

A Korean guardian spirit residing in mountains, whose cult has been closely associated with mountain tigers and is still fostered in Korean Buddhist temples.

SANSKRIT

The classical literary language of ancient India; one of the Indo-European family of languages. It is divided into Vedic and Classical Sanskrit. The scriptures of the mahayana tradition have been written in this language which style is called Buddhist Hybrid Sanskrit.

Its earliest (Vedic) texts go back to circa 1,500 BC and include the sacred texts of the Hindu religion, known as the Rigveda (or simply Veda). The Sanskrit language was developed by the Aryan invaders of India in prehistoric times. As the language of the conquerors, and the literary vehicle of the dominant Hindu culture, it spread throughout the Indian subcontinent. At a later stage, when it became the language in which the Buddhist religion first spread, it became common in South-east Asia. Eventually, Sanskrit gave rise to the various Indo-Aryan languages of modern India (Hindi or Urdu amongst them) and is clearly an ancestral relative of most of the languages of Europe (Romance, Germanic, Slavonic, Celtic, Greek).

SANTA CLAUS

Christmastide gift-bringer, said to maintain residence at the North Pole with a company of elves. He appears yearly with gifts for good children and coal or switches for bad ones, which he carries on a flying sleigh pulled by eight reindeer and delivers via the chimney. The tradition derives from the feast in honor of St. Nicholas, and was brought to the New World by Dutch settlers as the legend of Sinter Klaas. The celebrations were gradually moved from his feast day (December 6) to Christmas, and the familiar white-haired, jolly figure was described by the American Clement Moore, in "A Visit from St. Nicholas" in 1822.

SANTA MARIA MAGGIORE

Early Christian church in Rome built (begun 432) by Pope Sixtus II on the site of an ancient Roman basilica. It was enlarged in the 5th century and remodelled in part during the Renaissance. The mosaics are outstanding examples of early Christian art and are the earliest surviving example of the use of an Old Testament cycle for architectural decoration.

SANTANA

In Buddhism, term in the sense of continuity; the individual stream of consciousness.

SAOSHYANS

In Zoroastrianism, final savior of the world and quencher of its evil; last and most important of three saviors, all posthumous sons of Zoroaster.

SAPH

In Judaism, one of four giantlike Rephaim who fought with the Philistines against Israel, only to be put to death by David's mighty men. Saph, or Sippai, was slain by Sibbecai (2 Samuel 21:18; 1 Chronicles 20:4).

SAPPHIRA

In biblical times, the wife of Ananias who entered a conspiracy with her husband that resulted in their death. They sold a field of their possession and hypocritically pretended to bring the full value to the Apostles, as other Christians in Jerusalem were doing to meet the emergency that developed after Pentecost of 33.

The sin of Ananias and Sapphira was, not that they did not give the entire amount of the price of the possession sold, but that they lyingly claimed to do so, evidently to receive plaudits of men rather than to honor God and to do good toward his congregation (Acts 4:34-35).

SAPTAMATRKAS

In Hinduism, a group of seven mother-goddesses, each of whom is the sakti, or female counterpart of a god.

SAQAR

In Islam, one of the seven ranks of hell; the scorching fire to which tradition assigns the Zoroastrians. The word is used to indicate hell four times in the Koran.

SARACENS

Name given by medieval Christians to the Arab, Berber and Turkish Muslims who overran what had once been Christian territory in South-west Asia, North Africa, Spain and Sicily. They also raided European coasts and harassed Christian shipping in the Mediterranean. The term came from the Greco-Roman Saraceni, describing hostile nomadic Arab tribes of the Syrian Desert.

SARAH

In the Old Testament, the wife of the Hebrew patriarch Abraham, and the mother of Isaac. Although Abraham had also fathered Ishmael by the Egyptian woman, Hagar, God acknowledged Sarah's son as Abraham's only true heir.

Her original name was Sarai (Genesis 11:29; Isaiah 51:2). She was ten years younger than Abraham (Genesis 17:17) and married him while they were living in he Chaldean city of Ur (Genesis 11:28-29). She continued barren until her reproductive powers were miraculously revived after she had already stopped menstruating (Genesis 18:11; Romans 1:19).

Sarah may have been in her 60s when she left Ur with Abraham and took up residence in Haran. At the age of 65 she accompanied her husband from Haran to the land of Canaan (Genesis 12:4-5). There they spent time at Shechem, in the mountainous region east of Bethel and various other places before famine forced them to go to Egypt (Genesis 12:6-10).

Though advanced in years, Sarah was very beautiful in appearance. Therefore, Abraham had earlier requested that, whenever necessary in the course of their travels, Sarah identified him as her brother, lest others kill him and then take her (Genesis 20-13). In Egypt this resulted in Sarah's being taken into the household of Pharaoh on the recommendation of his princes. But divine intervention prevented Pharaoh from violating her. Thereafter he returned Sarah to Abraham, requesting that they leave the land. He also provided safe conduct for Abraham and his possessions (Genesis 12:11-20).

Possibly she was pregnant when she and her husband began residing at Gerar. According to biblical tradition, Sarah had the joy of giving birth to Isaac. Some 32 years later Sarah died, and Abraham buried her "in the cave of the field of Machpelah" (Genesis 23:1, 19-20).

SARAPH

In the Old Testament, a descendant of Shelah of the tribe of Judah, one who took a Moabite wife for himself. Perhaps, according to alternate readings, Saraph ruled in (or for) Moab (1 Chronicles 4:21-22).

SARCOPHAGUS

Stone coffin of the ancient Greeks, made of a particular limestone believed to consume the flesh of the corpse (The Greek words sacra means flesh, and phagein: to eat). Materials other than limestone were used, and the term "sarcophagus" applied generally to any coffin made of stone, granite, porphyry or terra-cotta. They were sometimes the size of a casket and at other times in the form of a tomb. Usually highly decorated, they were at one and the same time a coffin and a monument. Sarcophagi are to be found among the ancient Greeks, Romans, Etruscans, Phoenicians and Egyptians.

SARDICA, Council of

An ecclesiastical council of the Christian church held at Sardica (modern Sofia) in 342. It was convened by the joint emperors Constantius II and Constans I to attempt a settlement of the Arian controversies. In fact, the council merely embittered still further the relations between the two parties and those between the Western and Eastern halves of the Roman Empire.

SARDIS

In biblical times, name for the ancient capital of Lydia (in western Asia Minor) and a center of the worship of an Asiatic goddess, linked either with Artemis or with Cybele. Situated on the east bank of the Pactolus River (a tributary of the Hermus), Sardis lay circa 30 miles south of Thyatira and circa 48 miles east of Smyrna.

The Jewish historian Josephus indicates that in the first century BC there was a large Jewish community in Sardis. By the latter part of the first century AD the Christian congregation that had been established at Sardis needed to "wake up" spiritually. However, there were also persons associated with this congregation who had not "defiled their outer garments" (Revelation 31:1-6).

Prominent ruins at the ancient site of Sardis include those of the temple of Artemis and a Roman theater and stadium.

SARGON II

One of Assyria's kings (ruled 721-705 BC). He extended and consolidated the conquests of his presumed father, Tiglath-pileser III. Sargon is the Hebrew rendering of Assyrian Sharrukin, a throne name meaning "the king is legitimate". Historians refer to him as Sargon II, an earlier king, not of Assyria, but of Babylon, being designated as Sargon I.

Sargon is mentioned by name but once in the Bible (Isaiah 20:1). In the early part of the past century the biblical reference to him was often discounted by critics as of no value. From 1843 onward, however, archaeological excavations produced the ruins of his palace at Khorsabad and the inscribed records of his royal annals. Though Sargon II is now one of the best known of the Assyrian kings, the picture presented by the ancient records is by no means complete. The beginning of Sargon's reign is generally considered to coincide with the fall of Samaria in the sixth year of Judean King Hezekiah's rule (740 BC) and Sargon is often credited with having completed the conquest of that city begun by Shalmaneser V (2 Kings 18:10). During his reign Sargon erected a new capital circa 15 miles northeast of Nineveh, near the present-day village of Khorsabad.

SARID

In biblical times, name for a city on the border of Zebulun (Joshua 19:10-12).

It appears to be represented by Tell Shadud, some six miles north-north-east of Megiddo.

SARIPUTTA

One of the two chief disciples of the Buddha, also called Upatissa. He is regarded as second only to Buddha in "turning the Wheel of the Law." His ashes were found with those of Moggallana in one of the Stupas at Sanchi.

SARIQA

Arabic word for theft. The prescribed punishment in the Koran is the amputation of a hand. Shari'a law prescribed the corroborating testimony of witnesses or the thief's own confession, and insists that they have some value.

SARSECHIM

In biblical times, a Babylonian prince who was among the first to enter Jerusalem after the army broke through the walls in the summer of 607 BC (Jeremiah 39:2-3). His position and duties are not disclosed though "Sarsechim" may have been a title, possibly meaning "chief of the slaves."

SARVASTIVADA

An important early Buddhist school of philosophy. A fundamental concept in Buddhist metaphysics is the assumption of the existence of dharmas, cosmic factors and events that combine momentarily under the influence of a person's past deeds to form a person's life flux, which is considered his personality and career. While like all Buddhists, the Sarvastivadins are idealists and consider everything empirical an illusion, they maintain that the dharma factors are eternally existing realities.

SASANA

In Buddhism, doctrine; the Dhamma as taught by Buddha.

SA-SKYA-PA

Tibetan Buddhist sect that takes its name from the great Sa-skya monastery founded in 1073, 50 miles north of Mount Everest. The sect follows the teachings of the noted traveller and scholar Brog-mi (992-1072).

SASTHI

A folk deity of Hinduism who is goddess of vegetation, reproduction, and infant welfare. The name is derived from the sixth day after the birth of a child. Worship is ordinarily offered to Sasthi in her role as a custodian of infant welfare.

SAT

In Buddhism, being, or more correctly Be-ness, for, although in one sense its opposite is Asat, no-being, it is also a term for that which lies beyond all duality.

SATAN

The prince of evil spirits and adversary of God, known as the devil.

SATI

In Buddhism, term denoting attentiveness; the seventh step on the Noble Eightfold Path. The system of mindfulness built about the concept is mainly analytical, in contemplating the divers factors in the body, the sensations, the thought-processes and phenomena, but goes further in a higher synthesis of consciousness in Samadhi.

SATI-PATTHANA

In Buddhism, term in the sense of awareness of attentiveness. It is a system of mind development by the analysis of consciousness based on the Sati-Patthana Sutta of the Pali Canon. Contemplation on body, feelings, mind, and mind-objects is taken to the minutest detail, with the interrelation of states of consciousness arising from such contemplation. Thereafter the mind is reintegrated towards the experience of Samadhi.

SATRAP

A viceroy or governor of a province in the Babylonian and Persian Empires appointed by the king as a chief ruler of a jurisdictional district. The title means: "protector of the realm." Daniel mentioned satraps as serving under Nebuchadnezzar in the Babylonian Empire (Daniel 3:1-3). After the Medes and Persians conquered Babylon, Darius set up 120 satraps over his entire kingdom (Daniel 6:1). Ezra had dealings with satraps in the time of King Artaxerxes of Persia (Ezra 8:36). In the days of Esther and Mordecai the satraps supervised 127 jurisdictional districts under the Persian king Ahasuerus (Esther 1:1).

Being the king's official representatives, they were responsible to him and had quite free access to his presence. Consequently, they wielded considerable influence and power as civil and political chiefs. They collected taxes and remitted to the royal court the stipulated tribute.

SATUM

In Zoroastrianism, a ceremony in praise of the dead.

SATYA

In Buddhism, term meaning truth, which may be absolute (Paramartha), or relative (Samvitri).

SATYAGRAHA

In Hinduism, term denoting a cheerful, nonviolent resistance to some specific evil.

SATYRS AND SILENI

In Greek mythology, creatures of the wild, part man and part beast, who in classical times were closely associated with the god Dionysus. The occurrence of two different names for the creatures has been explained by two rival theories: that Silenus was the Asian Greek and Satyr the mainland name for the same mythical being or that the Sileni were part horse and the Satyrs part goat.

SAUL

First king of Israel, circa 1025 BC. The son of Kish of the tribe of Benjamin, he was anointed by Samuel, after the

Conversion of Saul.
"And he fell to the earth, and heard a voice saying unto him, Saul, Saul, why persecutest thou me? (Acts 9:4).
Lithograph by Gustave Doré (about 1860).

SAUL

tribes decided to unite under a king. His reign was generally successful, but he killed himself after a defeat by the Philistines. His rival David succeeded him.

The young man Saul lived during a turbulent time of Israel's history. Philistine oppression had reduced the nation to a helpless state militarily (1 Samuel 9:16; 13:19-20), and the Ammonites under King Nahash threatened aggression (1 Samuel 12:12). Whereas Samuel had faithfully judged Israel, his sons were perverters of justice (1 Samuel 8:1-3). Viewing the situation from a human standpoint and, therefore, losing sight of God's ability to protect his people, the older men of Israel approached Samuel with the request that he appoint a king over them (1 Samuel 8:4-5).

A special occasion occurred for anointing Saul as king. With his attendant, Saul looked for the lost she-asses of his father. Since the search proved to be fruitless, he decided to return home. But his attendant suggested that they seek the assistance of the "man of God" known to be in the nearby city. This led to Saul's meeting Samuel (1 Samuel 9:3-19). In his first conservation with Samuel, Saul showed himself to be a modest man (1 Samuel 9:20-21). After eating a sacrificial meal with Saul. Samuel continued speaking with him. The next morning Samuel anointed Saul as king. Samuel gave him three prophetic signs, all of which were fulfilled that day (1 Samuel 9:22-10:16).

Later, at Mizpah, when chosen as king by lot (1 Samuel 10:20-21), Saul bashfully hid among the luggage. Found, he was presented as king, and the people approvingly shouted: "Let the king live!" Escorted by valiant men, Saul returned to Gibeah.

SAURAS

A Hindu sect widely dispersed throughout India in the Gupta and medieval periods; its members worshiped Suruya, the sun, as the supreme deity. Suruya as the son was worshipped by Indians from the Vedic period onward for his help in destroying sins and bestowing blessings.

SAUTRANTIKA

One of the ancient schools of Buddhism that emerged in India (circa 2nd century BC), so called because of its reliance on the sutras, or words of the Buddha, and its rejection of the authority of the Abhidharma, a part of the canon.

SAVA, Saint

(1176-1236) Monk and patronal founder of the Serbian church, whose ecclesiastical policy in recognizing the jurisdiction of the patriarch of Constantinople ensured the adherence of Serbian Christianity to Eastern Orthodoxy.

SAVELLI, Luca

(1201-1266) Roman scholar who in 1234 led a revolution against Pope Gregory IX to further the commercial interests of the Roman middle class.

SAVIOR

An important figure in the various religions of the world who brings salvation, healing, integration of the personal self with the divine self, or redemption. Among the many savior figures have been the Buddha in Buddhism, the Christ in Christianity, the Saoshyans in Zoroastrianism, and many other salvatory personages.

SAWM

In Islam, the fast of the month of Ramadan, one of the five obligatory "pillars" of Islam. The sawn is observed during the entire month, because it is traditionally the period during which the Koran, Islamic sacred scripture, was sent down to earth.

SAYADAW

Teacher, Burmese Buddhist title of rank and respect. The term is in theory reserved for heads of monasteries but sometimes used as an honorary title for a very distinguished Thera.

SCAPULAR

An outer garment worn by members of some religious orders, consisting of a shoulder-wide strip of cloth reaching almost to the floor front and back and symbolizing the yoke of Christ; also an adaptation of this (two small pieces of cloth connected by strings) worn around the neck by persons who do not belong to the religious order.

SCAPULAR MEDAL

A medal with an image of the Sacred Heart on one side and the Blessed Virgin on the other. It may be worn on a chain or carried in place of the scapular in which the wearer is invested.

SCEVA

In Judaism, a Jewish "High Priest." His seven sons were among "certain ones of the roving Jews who practiced the casting out of demons." In one instance, in the city of Ephesus, they tried to exorcise a demon by saying: "I solemnly charge you by Jesus whom Paul teaches." The wicked spirit responded by saying: "I know Jesus and I am acquainted with Paul; but who are you?" The man obsessed by the spirit then leaped upon Sceva's seven sons and drove them out of the house naked and wounded. This resulted in magnifying the name of the Lord and caused many to give heed to the good news that Paul was preaching (Acts 19:13-20).

SCHECHTER, Solomon

(1847-1915) Outstanding authority on the Talmud, researcher who discovered important ancient documents, and leader of the United States Conservative Judaism.

SCHEFFLER, Johannes

Polish mystic, Roman Catholic polemicist, and poet whose religious songs celebrating the soul's union with God are found in Roman Catholic and Protestant hymnals.

SCHISM

In Christianity, a break in the unity of the church. In the early church, schism was used to describe those groups that broke with the church and established rival churches. Until the 16th century Protestant Reformation, the most significant schism was the East-West schism that divided Christendom into Western (Roman Catholic) and Eastern (Orthodox) branches. It began in 1054 because of various disputes and actions, and it has never been healed.

In early Christianity the term was used by Paul to designate the factions in the church at Corinth that threatened its unity (1 Corinthians 1:10; 1 Corinthians 11:18). The Fathers speak of schism as any sinful splitting off of a group from the Catholic church without the added element of heterodoxy. Yet most of them felt that error was somehow connected with schism, so they do not always clearly distinguish between schism and heresy. In arguing against Donatius, Augustine held that some sort of error is at the root of schism. In the East St. Basil distinguished between:

▲ heretics, who have left the faith itself and are completely lost to the church;

▲ schismatics, who because of ecclesiastical causes or problems separate from one another in a way that does not preclude reunion;

▲ dissident groups, such as disgruntled clergy who refuse to obey the bishop without necessarily forming a rival church.

The malice of schism, according to the Fathers, consists in defying the one Spirit by leaving the one Body of Christ and setting up a rival altar and a rival Eucharist. Thomas Aquinas stressed schism as a violation of a counter church challenging the unique role of the Roman Catholic Church.

Schism was originally discussed in the context of a local church and was described as the separation from the bishop, the center of unity. In the medieval West, schism was seen more in the framework of the universal church, with particular reference to the pope, and gradually became to be defined as disobedience to the Holy see.

The Orthodox churches, however, still generally look upon schism as internal, to the local or national church and tend to speak of Roman catholics as heretics rather than as schismatics.

SCHISM, East-West

East-West schism may be defined as the breaking off of communion between the Eastern and the Western churches, represented chiefly by the sees of Constantinople and of Rome, and the resultant state of separation, or schism, which still exists between the Orthodox and the Roman Catholic Churches.

Its extremely complex origin involve so many factors that one cannot assign a precise date to its beginning or fix upon any one cause, much less try to determine the blame for it. Perhaps more than any other event, this schism has caused the most serious harm to the Christian church in both East and West. In theory the disruption of ecclesiastical communion was signified by removing a prelate's name from the diptychs, but because of poor communications and other factors, several popes were not commemorated in Constantinople. By itself then, removing the name did not constitute schism. A more accurate criterion is the existence of rival patriarchs, Greek and Latin, although this occurred at different times and under different circumstances in the various patriarchates. The schism really began when the heads and members of both churches believed that they were no longer in communion with one another.

Religious and political conflicts had occasioned several schisms between Rome and Constantinople, but each time unity had been restored. In the 11th century political problems in southern Italy apparently caused the removal of the pope's name from the diptychs of Constantinople. About the middle of that century the Byzantine patriarch Michael Cerularius tried to undermine a papal-imperial entente by launching an attack on Roman usages.

This provoked the reform-minded cardinal Humbert to retaliate with an equally absurd list of trivial accusations against the Greeks. The farce ended with Humbert dramatically excommunicated by a Byzantine synod shortly thereafter.

Scarcely noticed by contemporaries, this unworthy episode was not the beginning of the schism as has usually been claimed. In 1089 Emperor Alexius I Comnenus insisted on the pope's name being replaced in the diptychs, since the Byzantine clergy did not know why it had been erased.

Certainly at the time of the First Crusade schism did not exist. Early in the 12th century, though, both Latin and Greek patriarchs laid claim to the sees of Jerusalem and Antioch. Relations between the Latins in the East and the Greeks gradually deteriorated so that by the end of the century the Byzantine canon lawyer, Theodore Balsamon, asserted that the Western church was clearly in schism.

But it was popular animosity erupting in violence and culminating in the Latin capture of Constantinople in 1204 that made the rupture irreparable. Probably the establishment and papal recognition of a Latin patriarch in Constantinople marks the final step in the schism.

The Greco-Latin council of Nymphaeum in 1234 was clearly a meeting between representatives of two separated churches. In 1245 Pope Innocent IV spoke of the schism having occurred "in our own time, only a few years ago." About the same time the other Eastern churches seem to have aligned themselves with the Byzantine churches. Subsequent attempts at reunion have been unsuccessful or have been concerned only with small groups.

SCHISM, Maintenance of

Differences in language, culture, liturgy, political circumstances, tradition, and customs facilitated the schism and have helped to maintain it; but they were not its causes.

Divergence on such dogmas as the procession of the Holy Spirit and purgatory was not, as has sometimes been stated, the principal cause of the schism. Although filling volumes of controversy and polemics, the Eastern and Western viewpoints on these matters are certainly reconcilable.

Studies on the schism have often hopelessly jumbled theological and nontheological factors, yet a basic theological issue underlies the whole situation. Unfortunately this difference was never seriously discussed; in both East and West the study of ecclesiology is a comparatively recent development.

The Byzantine theology of the church was merged in that of its union with the empire, and such matters as relations between bishops came to be regarded as mere administrative problems. As a result bishops seemed unaware of the dogmatic implications of the Roman primatial claims or else replied with ambiguous rhetoric.

Eventually the Western concept of the primacy became more definite, universal and absolute, while the Byzantine church thought only of its autonomy within the imperial framework. There developed, then, two decidedly different views of the structure of the church. After the fall of Byzantium, these attitudes remained fixed both in the West and in the several autocephalous Orthodox churches in the East.

That these two attitudes are not irreconcilable is evidenced by current endeavors to reexamine the notions of primacy and collegiality. Participation of many of the Eastern churches in the World Council of Churches, dialogue with Rome and with the Anglican Communion have marked the path of progress toward unity between East and West.

SCHISM OF 1054

The date of an event arbitrarily set by church historians for the separation between the Eastern Christian churches, led by the Byzantine patriarch Michael Cerularius of Constantinople, and the Western churches, led by Pope Leo IX of Rome.

SCHISMATIC CHURCH

A body of Christians formally and wilfully separated from the universal church, e.g., the Novationists and Donatists in early Christianity.

Roman Catholic Theology regards those churches that do not profess communion with the pope as schismatic or, if the cause of separation is doctrinal, heretical. Traditionally, the designation was applied by Roman Catholics to the Orthodox churches, although the fact that Vatican Council II did not use the notion of schism in its documents suggests that it does not apply to any of the larger contemporary churches, since the characteristic note of culpability is lost.

Anglican and Protestant theologians use the term to refer to the various divisions within the church, i.e., the Protestant, Catholic, Anglican, and Orthodox Communions.

SCHMUCKER, Samuel Simon

(1799-1873) Controversial Lutheran theologian and educator, principal exponent of a reformed American Lutheran Church, joined in establishing the General Synod (1820) that coordinated the various Lutheran Churches in the United States.

SCHOLASTICISM

Originally a philosophy and theology developed in medieval Europe which was based on reason and Christian revelation. Roughly speaking, it lasted from the 12th century to the time of the great Franciscan scholars in the late 14th and 15th centuries. Scholastic philosophers drew on the works of non-Christians such as Aristotle and Plato as well as on Christian theology, and attempted to reconcile the two. Perhaps the most famous of the scholastic philosophers is St. Thomas Aquinas, whose great system, set out in Summa Theologica, combines Aristotelian metaphysics with Catholic theology. However, scholasticism was by no means a unified movement, and the scholastics often took sharply conflicting positions in their philosophical battles. The principal medieval scholastic philosophers included John Duns Scotus, Peter Abelard, St. Bonaventura, Albertus Magnus and William of Ockham.

SCHWABACH, Articles of
Early Lutheran confession of faith, written in 1529 by Martin Luther and other Wittenberg theologians and incorporated into the Augsburg Confession by Philipp Melanchton in 1530.

SCHWENCKFELD, Kaspar
(1489-1561) Theologian, and preacher who led the Protestant Reformation in Silesia, founded the movement called Reformation by the Middle Way, and established societies that in the United States survive as the Schwenckfelder church.

SCIENTOLOGY
Religio-scientific movement originated in the early 1950s by L. Ron Hubbard in the United States. Scientology introduced the role of the soul and life energy in the physical universe, which is conceived as MEST (matter, energy, space, time). The subject is heavily structured with axioms and a language of its own.

SCILLITAN MARTYRS
12 African Christians from Scilla in Numidia who were tried in Carthage under Emperor Marcus Aurelius. The Acts of their martyrdom is the earliest authentic document on Christianity in North Africa and represents the earliest specimen of Christian Latin. The African Christians were executed on July 13, 180, by order of the proconsul Saturinus.

SCOTLAND, Church of
The national church in Scotland, which accepted the Presbyterian faith during the 16th century Reformation.

SCOTLAND, Episcopal Church in
An independent church within the Anglican Communion. It developed out of the 16th century Protestant Reformation. The development of Protestantism in Scotland went through confusing periods, with the Presbyterian Party sometimes in control and the Episcopal Party sometimes in control. The Episcopal Church is the direct descendant of the Episcopal churches of the 17th century that remained loyal to the episcopal tradition, and its bishops are the direct successors of those consecrated to Scottish sees after the Restoration.

SCOTLAND, Free Church of
Denomination organized in 1843 by dissenting members of the Church of Scotland.

SCOTS CONFESSION
The first confession of faith of the Scottish reformed Church, written primarily by John Knox (1514-1472), the Scottish Reformer, and adopted by the Scottish Parliament in 1560.

SCRIBE
In biblical times, a professional copier of books by hand, before the development of printing. The work of scribes was of particular importance at royal or imperial courts. The name was also given to the Hebrew teachers of the Law (Torah) in ancient times, who were called sopherim. The first of these interpreters of scripture was Ezra (circa 400 BC), who led the Jews after their Babylonian exile. For some 200 years thereafter the scribes revised and transmitted the text of the Old Testament, and developed and extended the basis of oral law. The scribes referred to in the New Testament were a later group of teachers and jurists called Hakhamim ("sages").

SCRIPTURAL DRAMA

Term often used by modern scholars to describe that drama in the vernacular (dating from the Middle Ages) that took as its subject episodes from the Old and New Testament and from the apocryphal books of both.

SCROLL

The form of an ancient book, often made of papyrus, vellum or leather. See Dead Sea crolls.

SCRUPLE

A fear arising in the mind by which a person sees a sin when there is none.

SCRUPULOSITY

A religious-moral-psychological state of more or less severe anxiety, fear, and indecision; an unreasonable and morbid fear of sin, error, and guilt.

SCYLLA

In Greek mythology, a sea monster which resembled a woman from the waist up, the remainder being composed of six fierce and monstrous dogs. She lived in a cave on the Italian side of the Strait of Messina, and she devoured passing sailors.

Scylla and Charybdis were two immortal and irresistible monsters who beset the narrow waters traversed by the hero Odysseus in his wanderings; later localized as the Strait of Messina.

SEAL OF CONFESSION

The secrecy demanded of the confessor in the sacrament of penance; no reason whatever justifies the breaking of this seal, and the church reserves grave penalties for any confessor who would dare to do so.

SEBA

In biblical times, name for a people of East Africa. At Isaiah 43:3 Seba is linked with Egypt and more particularly with Ethiopia (Cush), as being given as a ransom in place of Jacob. In a similar listing Isaiah 45:14 has "Sabeans" in place of "Seba," indicating that the people of Seba were called Sabeans. These verses suggest that Seba bordered on or was included in Ethiopia. This is supported by Josephus, who says that the name applied to the city of Meroe on the Nile and to the large section (Isle of Meroe) between the Nile, Blue Nile and Atabara Rivers. The reference of these Sabeans as "tall men" (Isaiah 45:14) is borne out of Herodotus, who speaks of the Ethiopians as "the tallest and handsomest men in the whole world."

SEBASTIAN

(1554-1578) King of Portugal from 1557, a fanatically religious ruler who lost his life in a crusade against the Muslims in Morocco. After his death, which many of his people disbelieved, he came to symbolize freedom from Spanish oppression.

SEBASTIAN, Saint

(Died circa 228) Early Christian martyr. He was a Roman captain in the praetorian guard of Emperor Diocletian. When he proclaimed himself a Christian, Diocletian has him tied to a tree and used by his archers as a target and then, when Sebastian miraculously escaped death, had him beaten to death in the amphitheater. Sebastian's martyrdom was a favorite subject for Renaissance religious paintings and his intervention was invoked against the plague. His feast day is observed on January 20th.

SEAL

In Buddhism, the seal of transmission, the Heart-Seal of the Buddha. The term is used the describe what each of the Patriarchs of Chinese Zen handed to his successor. Seal is the wordless transmission from Guru to Chela, from Master to pupil, of that which nevertheless cannot be transmitted, for it is the Bodhi-dharma, the wisdom that has gone beyond, that dwells for ever, waiting to be revealed, in each aspect of all-mind.

SEBEK

In Egyptian religion, crocodile god whose chief sanctuary in Fayyum province included a live sacred crocodile, Petsuchos, in whom the god was believed to be incarnate.

SECOND COMING OF CHRIST

The future return of Christ in glory, when it is understood that he will set up his kingdom, judge his enemies, and reward the faithful, living and dead (1 Thessalonians 4:13-18).

SECOND EVE

In Christianity, a title given to Mary that parallels the title Second Adam given to Christ. Christ and Mary are thus viewed as representatives of the human race who make amends for the sins of Adam and Eve, depicted in Genesis as the parents of the human race.

SECRECY

A secret is something known only to a certain person or persons (either because of their profession or because they have promised to keep a secret) and purposely kept from the knowledge of others; something that for one reason or another should not be made known to other people. The possessor of a secret has a moral responsibility to conceal his or her knowledge of the secret unless grave harm would come to the holder of the secret, to the community, or to an innocent third party. There is no exception to the confessional secret.

SECT

Term used to denote bodies regarded as heretical. As a neutral technical term in sociological analysis of Christianity, however, a "sect" denotes a body with certain doctrines of Christian tradition at the expense of others; personal conversion as a condition of membership; and condemnation of the values and institutions of ordinary society.

This is contrasted with the "church" type of Christianity, which is characterized by: a comprehensive or balanced range of teaching; membership including whole nations or requiring only minimal qualifications; and a high degree of accommodation to the values and institutions of society at large.

SECUNDUS

In biblical times, a Thessalonian Christian who accompanied Paul through Macedonia into Asia Minor on the return leg of the apostle's third missionary journey, in the spring of 56. How far Secundus went with Paul is not stated (Acts 20:3-5).

SECULAR INSTITUTES

In Roman Catholicism, according to the Code of Canon Law, "A secular institute is an institute of consecrated life in which the Christian faithful living in the world strive for the perfection of charity and work for the sanctification of the world especially from within" (Canon 710). Persons who belong to an institute of consecrated life profess the evangelical counsels of chastity, poverty, and obedience according to the constitutions of their particular institute.

SECULARISM

A philosophy of life that in theory or in practice rejects the value of the supernatural in human life; it professes that human existence and destiny belong to this world only, with no reference to eternal realities.

SEDER

In Judaism, term meaning order or arrangement. The arrangement of foods at the Seder reminds the Jews of the many-sided meaning of Passover, the great festival that marks the birth of a free people thousands of years ago.

SEEING

Technical term in Zen Buddhism; to see is to see all things in their state of Tathata. This is not a matter of physiology or psychology but of personal spiritual experience. To see that all is well as it is, in its "isness," is liberation from the bonds of self and separateness and illusion.

SEEKERS

A radical sect that arose during Puritan attempts to reform the Church of England in the 17th century. Several Seekers became Friends (Quakers) or Baptists.

SEFARDIM

Originally, Jews who lived in Spain from the Middle Ages until their mass expulsion in 1492. Thereafter, they settled in many other European countries, Turkey, Palestine, and North Africa. Of the estimated 600,000 Sefardic Jews in the world today, many now reside in the State of Israel.

SEFER HA-BAHIR

In Judaism, a largely symbolic commentary on the Old Testament. The basic motif is the mystical significance of the shapes and sounds of the Hebrew alphabet. The influence of the Bahir on the development of nascent Kabbala (esoteric Jewish mysticism) was profound and lasting.

SEFER HASIDIM

In Judaism, a highly valuable account of the day-to-day religious life of medieval German Jews known as Hasidim. The original Hasid is described in terms of asceticism, humility, serenity, altruism, and strict ethical behavior.

SEFER HA-TEMUNA

In Judaism, an anonymous work in Hebrew that imbues the letters of the Hebrew alphabet with a mystical significance and claims that there are invisible parts of the Torah (first five books of the Bible). The book first appeared in Spain in the 13th century.

SEFER HA-ZOHAR

In Judaism, a 13th century book, mostly in Aramaic, whose influence on esoteric Jewish mysticism makes it a classic text of Kabbala. Because the mystery of creation is a recurrent theme in the Zohar, there are extensive discussions of the ten divine emana-

tions, which reputedly explain the creation and continued existence in the universe.

SEFER TORAH

In Judaism, the first five books of the Old Testament written in Hebrew by a qualified calligraphist on vellum or parchment and enshrined in the ark of the law in synagogues.

SEFER YETZIRA

In Judaism, the oldest known Hebrew text on white magic and cosmology; it contends that the cosmos derived from the 22 letters of the Hebrew alphabet and from the ten divine emanations. Taken together, they were said to comprise the "32 paths of secret wisdom" by which God created the universe.

SEFIROT

In Judaism, the speculations of esoteric Jewish mysticism (Kaballa), the ten emanations, or powers, by which the Godhead was said to become manifest.

SEGUB

In the Old Testament, the youngest son of Hiel the Bethelite. In fulfillment of Joshua's curse, Segub lost his life when his father rebuilt Jericho during the reign of King Ahab (Joshua 6:26; 1 Kings 16:34).

SEIR

In biblical times, name for the mountainous region between the Dead Sea and the Gulf of Aqabah (Genesis 36:8, 30; Deuteronomy 2:1, 8). In Abraham's time Horites inhabited Seit (Genesis 14:6). Later, Abraham's grandson Esau established interest in Seit, while his twin brother Jacob resided at Paddan-Aram (Genesis 32:3). But it seems that Esau did not complete the move to Seit until sometime after Jacob returned to Canaan (Genesis 36:6-9). Finally, Esau's descendants, the Edomites, dispossessed the Horiotes (Deuteronomy 2:4-5; Joshua 24:4) and the land came to be called Edom. However, the older name "Seir" was also applied to the descendants of Esau and to the area where they lived (Numbers 24:18; 2 Chronicles 25:11).

SEIRAH
In biblical times, the place to which Ehud escaped after assassinating Moabite King Eglon. Its exact location, some place in the mountainous region of Ephraim, is not known today (Judges 3:26-27).

SEKHMET
In Egyptian religion, a fierce goddess of war and the destroyer of the enemies of the sun god Re. Sekhmet was considered the Eye of Re and was placed as the serpent on Re's head.

SELA
In biblical times, name for a location on the boundary of Amorite territory after the Israelites took possession of the Promised Land (Judges 1:36). The site is unknown today. Some would identify this Sela with the one in Edom (2 Kings 14:7), but there is no evidence that Amorite territory ever extended so far south into the region controlled by the Edomites. The name is also applied to a major fortified Edomite city that was captured by Judean King Amaziah and renamed Joktheel (2 Kings 14:7). Sela may be the unnamed "fortified city" referred to at Psalm 108:10.

SELAH
A transliterated Hebrew expression found frequently in the Psalms and also appearing in Habakkuk, chapter 3. Although it is generally agreed to be a technical term for music or recitation, its exact significance is unknown. It is held to mean a "pause, suspension, or holding back," either of the singing of the psalm for a musical interlude or of both singing and instrumental music or silent meditation.

SELED
In Judaism, a son of Nadab in the Jerahmeelite division of Judah's genealogy. Seled died without sons (1 Chronicles 2:25, 30).

SELEUCIA
In biblical times, name for a fortified Mediterranean port town serving Syrian Antioch and located circa 16 miles south-west of that city. The two sites were connected by road; and the navigable Orontes River, which flowed past Antioch, emptied into the Mediterranean Sea a few miles south of Seleucia.

Accompanied by Barnabas, Paul sailed from Seleucia at the start of his first missionary journey, in 47 (Acts 13:4). Though thereafter unnamed in the Acts account, Seleucia likely figured in events narrated therein (Acts 14:26; 15:30-41).

SELF
The doctrine of "no-soul" (anatta) is basic to all schools of Buddhism. The illusion that the separated "self" is permanent and has interests of its own is the cause of suffering and the barrier to enlightenment.

SELF-CONTROL
A fruit of the Holy Spirit marked by the quality of having one's desires under the control of the will and enlightened by right reason and faith.

SELF-DEFENSE
The moral right to use force against an unjust aggressor.

SELF-IDENTITY
In Buddhism, the ultimate foundation of the Mahayana. To be distinguished from mere identity, in which there are still two objects. In self-identity there is just one object or subject, one only, and this identifies itself in order to see itself reflected in itself. Self-identity is the logic of pure experience. In self-identity there are no contradictions whatever.

SELF-KNOWLEDGE
The act of understanding one's self, useful as a means of resisting temptation and in a full examination of conscience.

SELIHOT

Special Jewish prayer on the Saturday before Rosh Hashanah. After the clock has struck 12, Jews go over to the synagogue to say Selihot. Services begin after midnight, and this is a time to recite special prayers of repentance and asking forgiveness. Selihot are also said during the rest of the Ten Days of Repentance.

SELJUKS

The Turkish dynasties originating in Central Asia that swept into the Near East in the 11th century and created an empire that stretched from the borders of India to the Mediterranean Sea. The Seljuks were descended from Turkmen tribesmen who had been converted to Islam. They gained control of the caliphate of Baghdad and advanced far into Asia Minor, threatening the Byzantine Empire. This was one of the major factors bringing about the Crusades.

SEMACHIAH

In Judaism, a Levite grandson of Ebed-edom assigned as a gatekeeper to the south of the sanctuary during David's reign. Semachiah and his fleshly brothers are commended for their capabilities (1 Chronicles 26:1-8).

SEMEIN

In Judaism, a descendant of David and ancestor of Jesus' mother Mary (Luke 3:26).

SEMELE

In Greek mythology, the daughter of King Cadmus of Thebes. Hera, the jealous wife of Zeus, tricked her into persuading the god to appear in all his glory. Semele was burnt to death by the sight, but Zeus rescued their unborn son, Dionysus (Bacchus).

SEMINARY

A place where candidates for the priesthood (called seminarians) pursue their academic, apostolic, and spiritual formation.

SEMI-PELAGIANISM

A term introduced into the theological discussions of the 17th century that designated the doctrine of an anti-Augustine movement that flourished from circa 430 to circa 530. Unlike the Pelagians, who denied original sin and believed in perfect human free will, the Semi-Pelagians believed in the universality of original sin as a corruptive force in man.

SEMITES

In biblical times, a people once believed to have descended from Shem, the son of Noah, Today the term is used in a linguistic rather than a racial sense and refers to all those people who speak Semitic languages. This group includes such ancient peoples as the Babylonians, Assyrians and Phoenicians. Today the Arabs and most Ethiopians speak Semitic languages. Since Hebrew is also a member of this language group, the Jews were sometimes classed as Semites, and hostility towards Jews is thus known as anti-Semitism.

SENAAH

In the Old Testament, over 3,000 "sons of Senaah" returned from exile in Babylon with Zerubbabel in 537 BC (Ezra 2:1-2). Senaah may be the same as Hassenaah (Nehemiah 3:3).

Many of the names in the lists of Ezra 2 and Nehemiah 7 are apparently places rather than people, and Senaah is accordingly thought by some to be a place a few miles north of Jericho, where Eusebius and Jerome mention a tower "Magdalenna."

SENEH

In biblical times, name for a "toothlike crag" facing Geba and lying to the south of another crag called by the name Bozez; both crags being situated between the towns of Michmash and Geba and figuring in the accounts of Jonathan's attack on the Philistines (1 Samuel 14:4-5).

SENIR

In biblical times, the Amorite name for Mount Hermon (Deuteronomy 3:9). Since 1 Chronicles 5:23 mentions "Senir and Mount Hermon," the name "Senir" may also have been used to denote a part of the Hermon or Anti-Lebanon range. Senir was a source of juniper timbers (Ezekiel 27:5).

SENNACHERIB

In ancient biblical times, King of Assyria (705-681 BC), Sennacherib was the son and successor of Sargon II, from whom he inherited an empire that extended from Babylonia to southern Palestine and into Asia Minor. Because of his attack on Jerusalem, Sennacherib receives prominence in the Bible. Isaiah regarded Sennacherib as Gods's instrument; the prophet did not condemn the King's military activities as such, though punishment was decreed for his arrogance in not acknowledging the divine source of his power.

SENTENCES

A 12th century compendium of contemporary theological and philosophical thought, by Peter Lombard.

SEORIM

In Judaism, head of the fourth of the 24 priestly service divisions selected by lot during David's reign (1 Chronicles 24:5-8).

SEPHAR

In biblical times, name for one limit of the territory in which descendants of Joktan resided. The Bible says, "And their place of dwelling came to extend from Mesha as far as Sephar, the mountainous region of the East" (Genesis 10:29-30). One extremity was Mesha, apparently in north Arabia, making it probable that Sephar was in the south. One suggested location is the Yemenite city of Zafar (once the capital of the Himyarite kings), about a 100 miles north-east of the southern end of the Red Sea. Another location is a coastal city in Mahra, on the Arabian Sea. But the exact location of ancient Sephar remains uncertain.

SEPHARAD

In biblical times, name for a site from which Jerusalem's exiles were due to return. Its exact location is unknown, but of several suggestions a likely possibility is Saparda, mentioned in certain Assyrian annals as a district of Media. The Assyrians once exiled people of Israel's northern kingdom to "cities of the Medes" (2 Kings 17:5-6).

SEPHARVAIM

In biblical times, name for a city from which the king of Assyria brought people to dwell in Samaria after the Israelites had been taken into exile (2 Kings 17:24). Earlier, Sepharvaim and its king appear to have experienced defeat at the hands of the Assyrians (2 Kings 19:13; Isaiah 37:13). Being mentioned along with places in Syria and Babylonia, Sepharvaim was perhaps in one of these areas.

SEPHARVITES

People of the city of Sepharvaim. After 740 BC at least some of the inhabitants of Sepharvaim were taken by the Assyrians as colonists to Samaria. The Sepharvaim brought with them a peculiar religion, which included the sacrificing of their sons to the gods Adrammelech and Anammelech (2 Kings 17:24-33; Isaiah 36:19).

SEPTUAGINT

The Greek translation of the Hebrew Bible, begun at Alexandria in the 5th century BC for the benefit of the Greek-speaking Jewish community in that city. Since the first century AD Septuagint has been the standard version of the Hebrew Bible for Greek-speaking Christians.

In addition to all the books of the Hebrew canon, the Septuagint contains the extra books known to Protestants and jews as the Apocrypha and to Roman Catholics as deuterocanonical books. The Hebrew canon has three divisions: law, prophets, and writings. The Septuagint has four divisions: law, history, poetry, and prophets, with the books of the Apocrypha inserted where appropriate. This division has continued in the Western church in the old Latin version, the Vulgate, and in most modern Bible translations, except that in Protestant versions the Apocrypha are either omitted or grouped separately.

SERAH

In Judaism, name for a daughter of Asher among "the souls of the house of Jacob who came into Egypt" (Genesis 46:7; Numbers 26:46).

SERAIAH

Name for several persons mentioned in the Old Testament.

Seraiah is the name for the secretary in King David's administration (2 Samuel 8:15-17). Unless there were several changes in the personnel of this office he is elsewhere called Sheva of Shavsha.

The name is also applied to the quartermaster of King Zedekiah; son of Neriah and brother of Baruch (Jeremiah 33:121). In the fourth year of Zedekiah, 614 BC, Seraiah accompanied Zedekiah to Babylon. Jeremiah had given him a scroll containing prophetic denunciations of Babylon, instructing him to read it alongside the Euphrates River, then tie a stone to the scroll and pitch it into the river, thus illustrating the performance of Babylon's fall (Jeremiah 51:59-64). Seraiah likely passed on to the Israelites already captive there some of the thoughts from the prophecy.

The name is also mentioned for the chief priest when Babylon destroyed Jerusalem in 607 BC. Though Seraiah was slain at Nebuchadnezzar's order, his son Jehozadak was spared and taken captive to Babylon (2 Kings 25:18-21). Through Seraiah's son Jehozadak, the High-Priestly line from Aaron continued, Jehozadak's son Jeshua holding this office on the Jews' release and return (1 Chronicles 6:14-15; Ezra 3:2).

Seraiah is also called the "father" of Ezra, but in view of the 139 years between Seraiah's death and Ezra's return, there were probably at least two unnamed generations in between them, a type of omission common in biblical genealogies (Ezra 7:1).

Seraiah is also the name given to a priest who returned from exile with Zerubbabel. In the following generation, Meraiah represented his paternal house (Nehemiah 12:1, 12). The Seraiah included among the signers of the covenant in the days of Ezra and Nehemiah may also have been a representative of the same family, or another priest of this name (Nehemiah 10:1-8). Seraiah, again possibly one of this paternal house of a priest of the same name, lived in Jerusalem after the walls were rebuilt (Nehemiah 11:1-11).

SERAPH

Celestial being variously described as having two or three pairs of wings and serving as a throne guardian of God. Often called the burning ones, seraphim in the Old Testament appear in the Temple vision of the prophet Isaiah as six-winged creatures praising God (Isaiah 6:2).

SERED

In the Old Testament, name for the first-named son of Zebulun and founder of the Seredites, a Zebulunite tribal family (Genesis 46:14).

SEREDITES

In the Old Testament, name for a Zebulunite family founded by Sered (Numbers 26:26).

SERGIUS

(1867-1944) Theologian and patriarch of Moscow and the Russian Orthodox Church who, by his leadership in rallying the church membership in a united effort with the Soviets to repel the German invasion of 1941, obtained government recognition of the Orthodox Church as a religious bureau within the then prevalent Socialist system.

SERGIUS I, Saint

(639-701) Pope from 687 to 701, one of the most important 7th century pontiffs. He rejected several canons of the Council in Trullo (692), for which Justinian commanded his arrest and transportation to Constantinople, but the Romans and the militia of Ravenna forced Justinian to abandon his attempt against the Pope.

SERGIUS I

(556-638) Greek Orthodox theologian and patriarch of Constantinople (610-638). He strove in the Christological controversy to achieve doctrinal unity throughout Eastern Christendom by submitting a compromise formula, later condemned as unorthodox, emphasizing Christ's unique divine source of vital operation and single faculty of will.

SERGIUS II

(776-847) Pope from 844 to 847. His pontificate was marked by the brutal raid on the Roman walls by the Saracens, who pillaged the basilicas of St. Peter and St. Paul. Sergius was accused of failing to provide protection.

SERGIUS III

(844-911) Pope from 904 to 911, considered one of the worst pontiffs in history. He restored the Lateran basilica, which had collapsed from an earthquake during the time of the Cadaver Synod.

SERGIUS IV

(955-1012) Pope from 1009 to 1012. While temporally weak, Sergius was particularly noted for his aid to the poor and for granting privileges to several monasteries.

SERGIUS AND BACCHUS, Saints

(died circa 303) Among the oldest authenticated and most celebrated Christian martyrs commemorated in the Eastern and Western churches. They were supposedly favorites of the Roman emperor Maximian, whose wrath they incurred by refusing to sacrifice to the pagan god Jupiter because they were Christians.

SERGIUS OF RADONEZH, Saint

(1314-1392) Monk whose spiritual doctrine and social programs made him one of Russia's most respected spiritual leaders and whose monastery of the Trinity became the Russian center and symbol of religious renewal and national identity.

SERGIUS PAULUS

In biblical times, name of the proconsul of Cyprus when Paul visited there on his first missionary journey, circa 47. Luke is correct in calling him "proconsul," since the administration of Cyprus was at that time under the Roman Senate rather than the emperor. Sergius Paulus resided in Paphos, on the western coast of the island. He was "an intelligent man," and earnestly seeking to hear the word of God, he summoned Barnabas and Paul. As they spoke to the man, Elymas (Bar-Jesus), a Jewish sorcerer, "began opposing them, seeking to turn the proconsul away from the faith." But Paul, filled with holy spirit, told this opposer of the good news that he would be struck with temporary blindness. He was. On observing this powerful work of God's spirit, the proconsul became a believer, "as he was astounded at the teaching of God" (Acts 13:6-12).

SERMON ON THE MOUNT

A discourse delivered by Jesus as found in Matthew chapters 5-7. The sermon was addressed to disciples and a large crowd of listeners to guide them in life. It treats a new discipline based on a law of love, even to enemies, as opposed to the old law of retribution. In the Sermon on the Mount are found many of the most valuable homilies and sayings, including the Beatitudes and the Lord's Prayer. It has been called the "Magna Carta of Christianity" and contains the teaching of Jesus on true discipleship.

SERUG

In Judaism, a descendant of Shem, son of Reu and great-grandfather of Abraham, therefore an ancestor of Jesus. Serug became the father of Nahor at the age of thirty (Genesis 11:10, 20-23; 1 Chronicles 1:24-27).

SERVANT OF GOD

Jesus Christ as Servant of the Lord who came in fulfillment of the servant poems in the Book of Isaiah.

SESSHIN

Period of intensive meditation in a Rinzai Zen monastery, sometimes lasting a week, during which the monks sit in meditation for a large proportion of the day and night with frequent visits to the Roshi.

SET

(or Seth) Ancient Egyptian god, often depicted as a creature with an ass's head and the snout of a pig. At one time regarded as an important royal deity, Set later became the personification of evil as the murderer of the fertility god Osiris. Horus, the son of Osiris, fought and defeated Set.

SETH

According to biblical tradition, the son of Adam and Eve born when Adam was 130 years old. Eve named him Seth because, as she said, "God has appointed another seed in place of Abel, because Cain killed him." Seth may not have been the third child of Adam and Eve. According top Genesis 5:4, Adam had "sons and daughters," some of whom may have been born before Seth.

SETHUR

In Judaism, name of the Asherite chieftain appointed with representatives of the other tribes to spy out Canaan; son of Michael (Numbers 13:2-13).

SETON, Elizabeth Ann Bayley

(1774-1821) Roman Catholic founder of the American Sisters of Charity (1812) and the first American-born canonized by the Roman Catholic Church. A widow with five children, she became a convert to Roman Catholicism in 1805. Declared blessed in 1963, she was canonized in 1975.

SEVEN GODS OF LUCK

Group of seven popular Japanese deities, all of whom are associated with good fortune and happiness. The seven are drawn from various sources but have been grouped together from at least the 16th century.

SEVENTH-DAY ADVENTISTS

The largest group within the religious body of Adventists, which in 1844 adopted the observance of Saturday, the seventh day, as the Sabbath. Today the Seventh-Day Adventists support about 450 colleges and secondary schools, and over 280 medical units, in all parts of the world. Over 40 publishing houses produce literature in many different languages and braille, for worldwide dissemination. In 1990 there were more than 4,000 churches in the United States with a total membership of circa 500,000.

SEVERUS OF ANTIOCH

(465-538) Greek monk-theologian and patriarch of Antioch who, as the erudite founder of a heretically leaning (in matters of Christology) Byzantine sect, inspired its ascendancy. His writings testify of the high culture underlying his theological perspective and independent religious tradition.

SHAALBIM

In biblical times, name for a city whose Amorite inhabitants were subjected to forced labor by the house of Joseph (Judges 1:35). Later, Shaalbim was included in one of the districts annually providing Solomon's household with food (1 Kings 4:7-9). It is generally understood to be the same as Shaalabbin, a border city of Dan (Joshua 19:40-42).
Ancient Shaalbim is usually identified with modern Selbit, which appears to preserve the biblical name. It is situat-

ed about 16 miles west-northwest of Jerusalem and relatively near the suggested site of other places mentioned with Shaalbim in the Scriptures.

SHAALBONITE

In Judaism, the designation of Eliahba, one of David's warriors, presumably indicating one from the city of Shaalbim (2 Samuel 32:8, 32).

SHAALIM

In biblical times, name for a "land" Saul passed through when searching for the lost she-asses belonging to his father Kish (1 Samuel 9:3-4). Due to the difficulty in determining Saul's exact route, the situation of Shaalim is not definitely known. Some scholars have equated the "land of Shaalim" with the "land of Shual" in 1 Samuel 13:17. At any rate, a location in Ephraim seems best suited to the context.

SHAAPH

In Judaism, name for a son of Caleb (the son of Hezron) by his concubine Maacah. Shaaph was the founder or "father" of those who settled Madmannah (1 Chronicles 2:9, 42-49). The name is also applied to the last-named of Jahdai's six sons listed among the descendants of Caleb the son of Hezron in the tribe of Judah (1 Chronicles 2:9, 42).

SHAARAIM

In biblical times, name for a city of Judah in the Shephelah (Joshua 15:20). After David's killing of Goliath and due to the Israelite pursuit, the Philistine dead were scattered from "Shaaraim as far as Gath and Ekron" (1 Samuel 17:52). Shaaraim was in the vicinity of the "low plain of Elah" (where Goliath died) and Azekah (Joshua 15:35; 1 Samuel 17:1-2).

SHAASHGAZ

In the Old Testament, the guardian of King Ahasuerus' concubine; his Eunuch in charge of the second house of women (Esther 2:14).

SHABBAT HA-GADOL

Special sabbath on the Saturday before Passover. Just before the afternoon services, the rabbi gives his holiday sermon, in which he usually explains the complicated laws of hametz. He may also present rabbinical interpretations of the exodus from Egypt, the Song of Songs, or of anything else associated with Passover.

SHABBAT HAZON/NAHAMU

Special sabbaths before and after Tisha Be-Av; the Saturday before Tisha Be-Av is called Shabbat Hazon and the following Saturday is called Shabbat Nahamu. These names refer to the portion of the Prophets read in the synagogue on each of these sabbaths. On the first sabbath, the reader chants from the first chapter of Isaiah, which begins with the Hebrew word Hazon (vision, or prophecy). The chapter foretells the gloomy events which were to face Israel after the destruction of the Temple.
Tied up with the feeling of mourning was the hope for happier days to come. Therefore, the sabbath after Tisha Be-Av is called Shabbat Nahamu (comfort). On that day, the 40th chapter of Isaiah is chanted in the synagogue, the chapter beginning with Nahamu (comfort).

SHABBAT SHUVAH

Sabbath between Rosh Hashanah and Yom Kippur. It received its name from the first word of the prophets which is read on that day.

SHABBAT ZAKHOR

Sabbath before Purim (Zakhar means remember). An extra passage of the Bible is read, which says, "Remember what Amalek did to you when you came from Egypt." The Haftarah, the portion of the Prophets that is recited, is from the book of Samuel and tells of Saul's war against Agag, king of the Amalekites.

SHABBETAINISM

A 17th century messianic movement within Judaism that, in its extreme form, espoused the sacredness of sin.

SHABBETAI TZEVI

(1626-1676) The most important of the false messiahs that have appeared from time to time within Judaism. A mass movement grew up around him that threatened rabbinical authority in Europe and the Near East and gave rise to the rumor that Shabbetai would seize the Turkish throne.

A sect of Muslim Sabbatians survived him, and, within Judaism, his influence periodically erupted as in the 18th century messianic movement of Jacob Frank.

SHADKHAN

In Judaism, term denoting one who undertakes to arrange a Jewish marriage. Such service was virtually indispensable during the Middle Ages when custom frowned on courtships and numerous Jewish families lived in semi-isolation in small communities.

SHADRACH

In biblical times, the Babylonian name of a Jewish exile elevated to a high position in the government of Babylon. Shadrach, Meshach, and Abednego, the three companions of Daniel, are always mentioned together, and Shadrach is always listed first, perhaps, because their corresponding Hebrew names, Hananiah, Mishael and Azariah, always appear in alphabetical order according to the Hebrew characters.

SHADRAFA

Ancient West Semitic benevolent deity. He was often represented as a youthful, beardless male, standing on a lion above mountains, wearing a long, trailing garment and a pointed hierdress.

SHAFA'A

In Islam, term denoting intercession, mediation. While many Muslim theologians, particularly under the influence of Wahhabi teaching, have disapproved of the idea of the invocation of, or intercession with or via, the saints popular Islam, with its cult of the saints and veneration of their tombs, has never lost the idea. Mohammed will intercede with God for sinners on the Day of Judgment.

SHAHADA

In Islam, profession of faith. This is one of the five arkan (Pillars of Islam). The profession runs as follows: "There is no God but God and Mohammed is the Messenger of God."

SHAGEE

In biblical times, a Hararite whose son Jonathan was one of David's mighty men (1 Chronicles 11:26, 34).

SHAHARAIM

In Judaism, a Benjaminite who lived in Moab for a time and whose three named wives bore him many sons, some of whom became family heads (1 Chronicles 8:8-11).

SHAHARIT

In Judaism, the first of three periods of daily prayer observed mostly by Orthodox Jews; the other daily services are minha and ma'ariv. They are all ideally recited in the synagogue so that a quorum can be formed to pray as a corporate body representing "Israel."

SHAHAZUMAH

In biblical times, name for a boundary site of Issachar (Joshua 19:17-22). Some modern geographers would place it at Tell el-Muqarqush, about five miles east-south-east of Mount Tabor.

SHAKERS

Religious body more properly known as "The United Society of Believers in Christ's Second Appearing." The name "Shakers" was once a term of opprobrium, referring to the ecstatic quavering which possessed them in spiritual exaltation. The sect originated in early 18th century England, and was brought to America in 1774 by "Mother" Ann Lee, who represented herself as the female manifestation of the Second Coming. A number of Shaker communes were established in the late 18th and early 19th centuries. Their members wore uniforms, abstained from drinking alcohol and eating meat and maintained absolute celibacy. They were also fine craftsmen whose industrial and furniture designs were widely adopted. Isolation and celibacy have since reduced their membership to a few hundred.

SHAKTI

In Hinduism, term in the sense of power or energy; a practice of Hindu Tantra. The power of the Hindu deities as shown in art as a female companion of "power" in sexual union.

SHALISHA

In biblical times, name for a "land" or district Saul journeyed through while searching for his father's she-asses (1 Samuel 9:3-4), likely the area in which Baal-shalishah was located (2 Kings 4:42). The latter site is identified with Kefr Thilth, about 13_ miles northwest of Gilgal.

SHALLUM

Name for several people in biblical times.

1 Shallum was the son of Shaul, grandson of Simeon and father of Mibsam (1 Chronicles 4:24-25).

2 Shallum is also the name of a head gatekeeper of the sanctuary who at one time was stationed at the king's gate to the east; a descendant of Korah. Though the name appears mainly in lists of those returning from Babylon and living in Jerusalem (1 Chronicles 9:2-3; 17-19; Ezra 2:1; Nehemiah 7:45), references such as to "the dining room of Maaseiah the son of Shallum the doorkeeper" in Jeremiah's time (Jeremiah 35:4) might indicate that the name appearing in the post-exilic lists refers to a paternal house or family of doorkeepers descended from an earlier Shallum.

The name is also applied to the 16th king of the ten-tribe kingdom; son of Jabesh. In a conspiracy Shallum killed Zechariah, the last of Jehu's ruling descendants, and became king in Samaria for one lunar month (circa 791 BC), only to be murdered by Menahem (1 Kings 15:8-13).

SHALMAN

In biblical times, the name of the despoiler of the house of Arbel whom Hosea mentions when prophesying against the faithless northern kingdom of Israel. Though neither Shalman nor Arbel are otherwise mentioned in the Bible, Hosea's incidental but emphatic reference to them suggests that the incident was apparently fresh in the mind of his audience (Hosea 10:14).

SHALMANESER

In ancient times, name of five different Assyrian monarchs; only two of them appear to have had direct contact with Israel: Shalmaneser III and V.

SHALMANESER III

Assyrian king who succeeded his father Ashurnasirpal. He is considered to have ruled for about 35 years; 31 of those years appeared to have been employed in warring campaigns to maintain and extend Assyrian dominion. Shalmaneser III made repeated thrusts to the west against the Aramaean kingdoms in Syria.

The name of King Jehu of Israel (about 904-876 BC) appears on the "Black Obelisk" of Shalamaneser III accompanying a relief depicting what appears to be an ambassador of Jehu kneeling before the Assyrian king and bringing him presents.

This tribute is not mentioned in the Bible account concerning Jehu, and, while such action may quite possibly have been taken by the Israelite king in view of the conditions described at 2 Kings 10:31-33, it should not be assumed that the egotistical Assyrian monarchs were beyond the expressing of gross misrepresentations, both in their inscriptions and in their engraved reliefs.

SHALMANESER V

King of Assyria (reigned 727-722 BC) who subjugated ancient Israel and undertook a punitive campaign to quell the rebellion of Israel's King Hoshea (2 Kings 17:3).

SHAMANISM

The cult, found in many parts of Buddhist Asia and elsewhere, which centers around an intermediary whose psychic powers are so developed that he can link the ordinary daily world with the world of spirits.

In principle, Shamanism refers to religious practices and beliefs directed by an equivalent of the Siberian shaman. This figure is a kind of priest-magician, witch doctor or medicine man, who presides over the tribe's rituals and manipulates good and evil spirits to influence the course of events.

SHAMASH

In Mesopotamian religion, the sun god of the Semitic pantheon. He was identified with the Sumerian sun god Utu, whose temple was called Ebabbar and whose picture sign was a disc rising from two mountains in the east to indicate the rising sun.

SHAMGAR

In Judaism, a deliverer of Israel between the judgeships of Ehud and Barak. Only one heroic deed of Shamgar is recorded, the slaying of 600 Philistines with a cattle goad, but he is accredited thereby with "saving Israel" (Judges 3:31).

SHAMIR

In biblical times, name for a city in the mountainous region of Judah (Joshua 15:20). The ancient name appears to be preserved at Khirbet Somerah, though the actual site is thought to have been at nearby el-Bireh, some 12_ miles south-west of Hebron. The name is also applied to a residence and burial site of Judge Tola in the mountainous region of Ephraim (Judges 10:1-2). Shamir may have been situated at or near the later location of Samaria.

SHAMMA

In Judaism, a leading member of the tribe of Asher; son or descendant of Zophah (1 Chronicles 7:36-40).

SHAMMAH

Name of several persons during the time of King David.

1 The name of an older brother of King David, also called Shimea(h) and Shimei (1 Chronicles 2:13; 2 Samuel 13:3). As the third son of Jesse, Shammah was the third possible choice rejected from being anointed as king by Samuel (1 Samuel 16:6-9).

2 The name for one of David's top three warriors; son of Agee the Hararite. On one occasion, Shammah defended a whole field against the Philistines, striking down many of them (2 Samuel 23:13-17).

3 A name applied to one of David's 30 mighty men; a Harodite (2 Samuel 23:8, 25).

SHAMMUA

In biblical times, name of the chieftain representing the tribe of Reuben whom Moses sent into the Promised Land as a spy; son of Zaccur. He joined nine other spies in discouraging the Israelites from having faith that God would clear Canaan of their enemies (Numbers 13:2-4).

The name is also applied to a son of David among those borne by Bath-sheba, therefore a full brother of King Solomon (2 Samuel 5:13-14; 1 Chronicles 14:3-4).

SHAMS, al-

The title of the 91st sura of the Koran; it means "The Sun." The sura belongs to the Meccan period and has 15 verses. Its title comes from the first verse which begins with the oath "By the sun ...." The sura continues with a series of oaths and briefly tells the story of the people of Thamud who hamstringed the she-camel sent to them by God as a sign.

SHAMSHERAI

In biblical times, name for the head of a forefather's house that lived in Jerusalem; son of Jeroham in the tribe of Benjamin (1 Chronicles 8:1; 26-28).

SHAPHAM

In Judaism, the second in charge of the tribe of Gad in Bashan sometime prior to the reign of Jeroboam II in the ninth century BC (1 Chronicles 5:11-17).

SHAPHAN

In the Old Testament, name for the son of Azaliah and a royal secretary. King Josiah, in 642 BC, sent Shaphan and two other officials to High Priest Hilkiah with instructions for Temple repairs. On this occasion Hilkiah turned over to Shaphan "the very book of the law," possibly even the original, recently found in the Temple.

SHAPHAT

In biblical times, a chieftain representing the tribe of Simeon as one of the spies who spent 40 days in the Promised Land; son of Hori (Numbers 13:2-5).

SAPHIR

In the Old Testament, name for a place, evidently in Judah, the inhabitants of which were included in Micah's prophecy of judgment due to come upon Judah and Jerusalem (Micah 1:11). In this section of the prophecy, Micah makes a frequent play on words in his usage of the place-names. The present tentative is with Saphir is with Kirhbet el-Kom, a site on a hill dominating the Wadi es-Saggar, about ten miles west of Hebron.

SHAREZER

In biblical times, name of the son of Assyria King Sennacherib. Sharazer and his brother Adrammalech killed their father with the sword while he was bowing down to his idol god, after which they fled to the land of Ararat (2 Kings 19:7; 35-37; Isaiah 37:38).

The name Sharazer is also applied to the first named of two representatives of post-exilic Bethel sent, about two years before the Temple rebuilding was completed, to inquire about the propriety of fasting (Ezra 6:15).

SHARH, al-

The title of the 94th sura of the Koran; it means "The Laying Open" or "The Expanding." The sura belongs to the Meccan period and has 8 verses. Its title is taken from the first verse which asks: "Did we not lay open your heart for you?" Some commentators suggest that this refers to the incident in the childhood of the Prophet Mohammed during which the Prophet's heart was laid open by angels and a clot of sin was removed. The sura seeks to console the Prophet by reminding him that he has a high reputation and that the difficulty he has suffered will bring its rewards.

SHARI'A

The Holy Law of Islam.

SHARIRA

An indestructible substance in pellet form said to be found in ashes of great saints on cremation.

SHARON

In biblical times, the maritime plain between the plain of Dor (south of Carmel) and the plain of Philistia. From its northern border by the Crocodile River, Sharon extends southward for about 40 miles to the area of Joppa and varied in width from about 10 to 12 miles.

According to 1 Chronicles 5:16, the tribe of Gad dwelt in "Gilead, in Bashan and in its dependent towns and in all the pasture lands of Sharon."

SHARONITE

In biblical times, a person from the plain of Sharon. Shitrai, the man in charge of David's herds in Sharon, was called a Sharonite (1 Chronicles 27:29-31).

SHASHAI

In Judaism, one of the post-exilic sons of Binnui who took foreign wives for themselves, but, in response to Ezra's urging, sent them away (Ezra 10:10-11).

SHASTRA
In Islam, a discourse or philosophical analysis of the contents of a Sutra, which thus becomes a commentary.

SHATH
A Sufi (Muslin mystic) term for the divinely inspired statements that Sufis utter in their mystical state of fana (annihilation of the self).

SHATTARIYAH
A Sufi (Muslim mystic) order named after the Indian Sufi Master 'Abd Allah Shattari (1378-1428). He stressed the "self," personal deeds, personal attributes that made one godlike, and union with God himself.

SHAUL
In biblical times, sixth-named king of ancient Edom; successor of Samlah and predecessor of Baal-hanan (Genesis 36:31-38). The name Shaul is also applied to the last-named son of Simeon, born of a Canaanite woman (Genesis 46:10).

SHAVEH, Low plain of
In biblical times, name of "The King's Low Plain," where Abraham, victorious over Chedorlaomer and his allies, was met by the king of Sodom and received a blessing from Melchizedek, king of Salem (Genesis 14:17-24). Centuries later, Absalom erected his monument in the "Low Plain of the King," apparently the same place and likely near Jerusalem (2 Samuel 18:18).

SHAVUOT
One of the oldest of all Jewish festivals. Shavuot means "weeks" and it falls exactly seven weeks after the second day of Passover, on the sixth and seventh days of the month of Sivan. Another, non-Jewish, name for Shavuot is Pentecost, which in Greek means "50th," because it takes place on the 50th day after the beginning of Shavuot.

Shavuot is a triple holiday, a three-fold celebration which commemorates:
▲ the giving of the Torah on Mount Sinai;
▲ the harvesting of wheat in Israel and;
▲ the ripening of the first fruit in the Holy Land.

The rabbis declared the Shavuot to be the most pleasant of all Jewish holidays. In a way, it fits in very well with Passover and brings that great festival to a glorious conclusion. For on Passover the Jews were freed from slavery and on Shavuot the freed slaves were made into free men by the Ten Commandments. It was on Shavuot that God spoke to Moses atop Mount Sinai and gave the Israelites the Ten Commandments.

SHAYKH
In Islam, old man, chief, title of resp[ect for Islamic religious leader; master of a suffi order.

SHAYTAN
In Islamic myth, an unbelieving class of jinn (spirits created of smoke). It is also the name of Iblis, the devil, when he is performing demonic acts.

SHEALTIEL
In Judaism, a descendant of King David and ancestor of Jesus in the tribe of Judah. Shealtiel is called the son both of Jehoiachin (Jeconiah) and of Neri. Both Shealtiel and his brother Pedaiah are called the father of post-exilic Governor Zerubbabel.

SHEARIAH
In Judaism, name of a descendant of Saul and Jonathan; one of Azel's six sons (1 Chronicles 8:33-38).

SHEAR-JASHUB
In the Old testament, name of the first son of Isaiah. Shear-jashub went along when Isaiah delivered a prophetic message to King Ahaz at the time of Israelite King Pekah's invasion of Judah between 761 and 759 BC (Isaiah 7:1-3). Isaiah and his sons were to

serve as signs and miracles from Jehovah in Israel; hence Shear-jashub's name foretold that "a mere remnant would return" from Babylonian exile (Isaiah 8:18).

SHEBA

Kingdom of the Sabeans in pre-Islamic south-western Arabia, frequently mentioned in the Bible. The Sabeans were a Semitic people who, at an unknown date, entered southern Arabia from the north, imposing their Semitic culture on an aboriginal population. Sheba was rich in spices and agricultural products and carried on a wealth of trade by overland caravan and by sea.

SHEBANIAH

In the Old Testament, name of a priestly paternal house that Joseph represented in the day of High Priest Jeshua's successor Joiakim (Nehemiah 12:12-14).

The name is also applied to one of the Levites, or a representative of a Levitical family, contemporaneous with Ezra and Nehemiah, who led the Israelites in a prayer of confession, after which they proposed and sealed a covenant of faithfulness (Nehemiah 9:4-5; 10:1-10).

SHEBARIM

In biblical times, name of the place to which men of Ai chased the Israelites, when they were unable to stand before the enemy after Achan's sin (Joshua 7:5). The site is unknown, except that it was near Ai.

SHEBUEL

In Judaism, name of a Levitical son or descendant of Moses' son Gershom (1 Chronicles 23:15-16). Shebuel's paternal house was enrolled when David reorganized the Levitical services (1 Chronicles 24:20), being given duties that included caring for the stores (1 Chronicles 26:24).

The name is also applied to one of the sons of Heman and an expert musician selected by lot to head the 13th division of sanctuary musicians (1 Chronicles 25:4-9).

SHECANIAH

Name of several important persons in Judaism and early biblical times.

1 Shecaniah is a descendant of Aaron whose paternal house was selected by lot as 10th of the 24 priestly divisions that David organized (1 Chronicles 24:1-11).

2 Shecaniah is also the name of one of those entrusted with equal distribution of the tithes and other contributions in the priests' cities during Hezekiah's reign (2 Chronicles 24:1-3).

3 The name is also mentioned of a descendant of David through Zerubbabel who lived several generations after the Babylonian exile. He was a son of Obadiah and father of Shemaiah (1 Chronicles 3:5-10).

SHECHEM

An ancient and important city of Palestine, located between the mountains Ebal and Gerizim. After the Babylonian captivity Shechem became Samaria's capital.

The name Shechem is also mentioned for the son of Hivite chieftain Hamor (Genesis 33:19; Joshua 24:32). After Jacob settled near the city of Shechem, his daughter Dinah began associating with females of that city. The man Shechem, described as being the "most honorable of the whole house of his father," saw Dinah and "lay down with her and violated her." Then he fell in love with Dinah and wanted to marry her. But Jacob's sons were enraged about the affair and, "with deceit," said that they could make marriage arrangements only with circumcised men. This was agreeable to Shechem and his father Hamor and they convinced the Shechemites to get circumcised. However, before the males of Shechem could recover from being circumcised, Jacob's sons, Simeon and Levi, attacked the city, killing Hamor, Shechem and all the other men (Genesis 34:1-31).

SHECHEMITES

In biblical times, the descendants of Manasseh through Shechem (Numbers 26:29-31).

SHEERAH

In the Old Testament, a daughter of Ephraim, or of his son Beriah. She is mentioned as building or founding lower and upper Beth-horon and Uzzen-sheerah, though this may have been done by some of her descendants (1 Chronicles 7:22-24).

SHEHARIAH

In Judaism, head of a Benjaminite family living in Jerusalem; son or descendant of Jeroham (1 Chronicles 8:1, 26-28).

SHEIK

In biblical times, a title usually given to the Edomite and Horite tribal chiefs, the sons of Esau and the sons of Seit the Horite (Exodus 15:15).

Seven sheiks of the Horites are listed, all "sons of Seit" (Genesis 36:20-30). The sheiks of Edom were 14 in number: seven grandsons from Esau's first-born Eliphaz the son of his wife Adah, four grandsons from his son Reuel the son of his wife Basemath, and three of his sons by his wife Oholibamah (Genesis 36:15-19). The clans that developed from the sheiks came to bear their names as clan names.

SHEKHINA

A Jewish theological designation for the presence of God. It was first used in the Aramaic form, shekinta, in the interpretive Aramaic translations of the Old Testament known as Targums, and it was frequently used in the Talmud, Midrash, and other post-biblical Jewish writings.

SHELAH

In the Old Testament, name of a son of Arpachshad and grandson of Shem. Shelah and one of his sons, Eber, founded one of the 70 post-Flood families; through Eber ran the genealogical line that led from Shem to Abraham and finally to Jesus (Genesis 10:22-24; 11:12-15).

The biblical record also mentions the name of Shelah for the third son of Judah by his Canaanite wife (1 Chronicles 2:3). Tamar should have been given in Levirate marriage to Shelah, but was not (Genesis 38:1-5). Shelah's descendants, some of whom, with their places of settlement, are listed by name, formed the tribal family of Shelanites. Some of these returned from Babylonian exile (Numbers 26:20; 1 Chronicles 4:21-23).

SHELANITES

In biblical times, a family of Judah founded by Shelah (Numbers 26:20).

SHELEMIAH

Name of various important persons during biblical times. Shelemiah is the name of a Levitical gatekeeper assigned by lot to the east of the sanctuary during David's reign (1 Chronicles 26:14). The name is also mentioned as the father of Irijah, the officer in charge of Jerusalem's gate of Benjamin; son of Hananiah (Jeremiah 37:13).

The name Shelemiah is also found as belonging to a priest, and one of those whom Nehemiah, on his second visit to Jerusalem, entrusted with the stores and distribution of the tithes to their proper recipients (Nehemiah 13:6-13).

SHELEPH

In biblical times, the second-named son of Joktan and founder of one of the early post-Flood families (Genesis 10:26; 1 Chronicles 1:20).

SHELOMI

In the Old Testament, an Asherite whose chieftain son was appointed to help divide the Promised Land among Israel's tribes (Numbers 34:17-18).

SHELOMITH

In biblical times, name for several persons mentioned in the Old Testament. Shelomith is the name of a Danite daughter of Dibri whose son by an

Egyptian was put to death in the wilderness (Leviticus 24:10-14).

Shelomith is also the name of a Kohathite Levite of the family of Izhar (1 Chronicles 23:12). Shelomith is also found as the name of a son of Josiphiah and head of the paternal house of Bani. He came, accompanied by 160 males, to Jerusalem with Ezra (Ezra 8:1, 10).

SHELOMOTH

In Judaism, name of the head of a paternal house among the descendants of Levi's son Gershon (1 Chronicles 23:6-9). The name is also connected to a Kohathite Levite of the family of Izhar (1 Chronicles 23:12).

SHEM

In the Bible, name of one of Noah's three sons (Genesis 6:10). Although the three sons are consistently listed as "Shem, Ham and Japheth," there is some uncertainty as to their relative positions according to age. The fact that Shem is mentioned first is of itself no definite indication that Shem was Noah's first-born, since Shem's own firstborn son (Arpachshad) is listed third in the genealogical record (Genesis 10:22; 1 Chronicles 1:17).

According to biblical tradition, when Shem and his brother Japheth covered over their father's nakedness at the time of Noah's being overcome by wine, they showed not only filial respect but also respect for the one who God has used to effect their preservation during the Flood (Genesis 9:20-23). Thereafter, in the blessing Noah pronounced, indication was given that the line of Shem would be particularly favored by God and would contribute to the sanctification of God's name (Genesis 9:26). It was from Shem, through his son Arpachshad, that Abraham descended, and to him was given the promise concerning the deed in whom all the families of the earth would receive a blessing (1 Chronicles 1:24-27; Genesis 12:1-3). Noah's prediction concerning Canaan's becoming " a slave" to Shem was fulfilled by the Semitic subjugation of the Canaanites as a result of the Israelite conquest of the land of Canaan (Genesis 9:26).

SHEMA

In Judaism, name of a head of a Benjaminite household that settled in Aijalon and one of those who chased away the inhabitants of Gath (1 Chronicles 8:12-13).

SHEMAIAH

In the Old Testament, name mentioned for a number of important persons.

Shemaiah is the name of a Simeonite whose distant descendant joined the expedition that seized grazing territory from Canaanites in the days of Hezekiah (1 Chronicles 4:24, 37-41).

The name of Shemaiah is also mentioned as the secretary of the Levitical house of Elizapham. He and 200 of his brothers, having sanctified themselves, were in the procession that brought the ark of the covenant to Jerusalem (1 Chronicles 15:4, 11-16).

Shemaiah is also the name of a prophet during the reign of Solomon's son Rehoboam. Following the revolt of the ten northern tribes in 997 BC, Shemaiah pronounced God's words forbidding an attempt by Rehoboam to reconquer them (1 Kings 12:21-24; 2 Chronicles 11:1-4). Shemaiah also penned one of the written records of Rehoboam's reign (2 Chronicles 12:15).

SHEMARIAH

In the Old Testament, one of the ambidextrous Benjaminite warriors who joined David while a fugitive at Ziklag (1 Chronicles 12:1-5).

The name Shemariah is also applied to one of the sons of Binnui who had taken foreign wives but sent them away (Ezra 10:38-44).

SHEMBE'S NAZARITE CHURCH

South African independent church, founded by Isaiah Shembe, a Zulu prophet-healer who founded the church in 1911. The church is Zionist in nature and stresses divine healing.

SHEMER

In biblical times, a descendant of Asher, perhaps his great-grandson. Four sons of Shemer are named (1 Chronicles 7:30-34).

The name is also mentioned as the owner of the hill of Samaria, possibly a tribe rather than an individual, for "Samaria" means "belonging to the clan Shjemer." Israelite King Omri bought the mountain for two talents of silver and began ruling from there in 945 BC.

SHEMINI ATZERET

A Jewish religious festival on the eighth day of Sukkot, considered by some an independent celebration immediately following Sukkot.

SHEMIRAMOTH

In Judaism, a Levite musician who accompanied the ark of the covenant from Obed-edom's house to Jerusalem and was afterward stationed to play before its tent (1 Chronicles 15:17-25).

SHENAZZAR

In Judaism, fourth-named son of Jehoichin (Jeconiah), born during his exile in Babylon (1 Chronicles 3:17-18).

SHEOL

In biblical times, the common grace of all mankind. While the Greek teaching of the immortality of the human soul infiltrated Jewish religious thinking in later centuries, the Bible record shows that Sheol refers to a place of unconsciousness in mankind's common grave (Ecclesiastics 9:4-10). Those in Sheol neither praise nor mention God (Psalms 6:4-5; Isaiah 38:17-19). Yet it cannot be said that it simply represents "a condition of being separated from God," since the scriptures render such a teaching untenable by showing that Sheol is "in front of" him, and that God is in effect "there" (Proverbs 15:11; Amos 9:1-2). Throughout the entire scriptures Sheol is continually associated with death and not life (1 Samuel 2:6; Isaiah 28:15-18).

SHEPHAM

In biblical times, a site on the eastern border of the Promised Land, apparently no great distance from Riblah (Numbers 34:10-11). Its location is now unknown.

SHEPHATIAH

In biblical times, name applied to a number of important persons. Shephatiah is one of the Benjaminite warriors who defected from Saul to David at Siklag (1 Chronicles 12:1-5).

Shephatiah is also the fifth son born to David while he was ruling in Hebron. Sephatiah's mother was Abital (2 Samuel 3:2).

Shephatiah is also the name of one of the princes of Judah who, on securing King Zedekiah's permission to kill Jeremiah, had him thrown into a cistern; son of Mattan (Jeremiah 38:1-6).

The name Shephatiah is also the name of a family of the "sons of the servants of Solomon; who also returned from Babylon with Zerubbabel. Biblical records show the name Shephatiah as being the founder of a family in Israel of which 372 males returned to Jerusalem with Zerubbabel in 537 BC, and 80 more, headed by Zebadiah, with Ezra in 468 (Ezra 2:1-4; Nehemiah 7:9).

SHEPHELAH

In biblical times, a designation that is usually applied to the region of low hills between Palestine's central mountain range and the coastal plains of Philistia (Deuteronomy 1:7; Joshua 9:1; Judges 1:9). The Shephelah was one of the regions of the territory assigned to Judah (Joshua 15:33-44).

The valleys that divide the rolling foothills of this region served as natural routes for east-west travel. The Shephelah is fertile, and a temperate climate prevails there. Anciently this region was noted for its many sycamore trees and olive groves (1 Kings 10:27; 2 Chronicles 1:15).

SHEPHUPHAM

In Judaism, a Benjaminite who founded the tribal family of Shephamites (Numbers 26:38-39).

SHEREBIAH

In biblical times, name of a Levite descended from, Mehali; "a man of discretion" who summoned to join Ezra on his journey to Jerusalem in 468 BC (Ezra 8:17-18). He is probably the same person as the "chief of the priests" mentioned in Ezra 9:24, one of those entrusted with transporting to Jerusalem the valuable things contributed for temple use (Ezra 8:25-30).

SHESHACH

In biblical times, probably a symbolic name for Babylon (Jeremiah 25:26; 51:41). The name Sheshach may also imply humiliation, for which Babylon was due.

SHESHAI

In Judaism, name for the son of Anak and brother of Ahiman and Talmai. They inhabited Hebron at the time the 12 Israelite spies visited the Promised Land (Numbers 13:22-28). When Joshua's forces were exterminating the Anakim from the land many years later, it was Caleb's special privilege to drive Sheshai and his brothers out of Hebron (Joshua 11:21; 14:10-15).

SHESHAN

In Judaism, name for a descendant of Judah through Jerahmeel. Sheshan had no sons, so gave his daughter (probably Ahlai) in marriage to his slave Jarha in order to continue his line of descent (1 Chronicles 2:31-35).

SHESHBAZZAR

In biblical times, an appointee of King Cyrus over the first exiles returning from Babylon. As he led the Jews back, Sheshbazzar brought with him the gold and silver utensils that Nebuchadnezzar had looted from the Temple. On arrival in Jerusalem, he laid the foundations of the second Temple (Ezra 1:7-11; 5:14-16).

SHETHAR

Name of one of the seven princes of Persia and Media consulted by King Ahasuerus when Queen Vashti refused to obey him (Esther 1:13-15).

SHEVA

In biblical times, father of Machbenah and Gibea. As these are names of towns, however, Sheva was perhaps the father of those who settled there or was himself the founder of these towns. Sheva's father Caleb, headed one of the three major divisions of Judah's descendants through Hezron (1 Chronicles 2:9, 48-50).

SHIBAH

In biblical times, name of a well that Isaac's servants dug, or redug, at Beersheba (Genesis 26:32-33). They reported finding there after concluding a covenant of peace with Abimelech the king of Gerar; hence, Isaac named the well "Shibah" (meaning "seven" and referring to an oath or statement sworn to by seven things) (Genesis 26:26-33).

SHIKKERON

In biblical times, name of a site on the boundary of Judah (Joshua 15:1, 11). The modern location is uncertain, but some tentatively identify it with Tell el-Ful, some three miles north-west of the suggested site of Ekron, with which it is mentioned in the Joshua account.

SHILHIM

In biblical times, name for a city in the southern part of Judah (Joshua 15:21, 32). It seems to be the same as Sharuhen, listed among the cities in Judah's territory belonging to Simeon (Joshua 19:1-6).

SHILLEM

In Judaism, last named of Naphthali's four sons listed among "the names of Israel"s sons who came into Egypt' (Genesis 46:8, 24). He founded the tribal family of Shillemites (Numbers 26:49-50).

SHILOH

Canaanite town east of the main road from Jerusalem to Bethel. It became the central sanctuary site of the Israelite confederacy during the period of the judges (12th-11th century BC). After the Israelite conquest of Canaan, the tabernacle and the ark of the covenant were captured by the Philistines (c. 1050 BC) in a battle with the Israelites at Ebenezer and Shiloh was soon thereafter destroyed.

According to biblical tradition, the name Shiloh has also a different meaning. In pronouncing a blessing upon Judah, the dying patriarch Jacob said: "The scepter will not turn aside from Judah, neither the commander's staff from between his feet, until Shiloh comes; and to him the obedience of the people will belong" (Genesis 49:10). Beginning with the rule of the Judean David, power to command (the commander's staff) and regal sovereignty (the scepter) were the possessions of the tribe of Judah. This was to continue until the coming of Shiloh as the permanent heir. Similarly, before the overthrow of the kingdom of Judah, God indicated to the last Judean king, Zedekiah, that rulership would be given to one having the legal right (Ezekiel 21:26-27).

SHIMABARA REBELLION

(1637-1638) Uprising of Japanese Roman Catholics, the failure of which virtually ended the Christian movement in 17th century Japan and furthered government determination to isolate Japan from foreign influences. The revolt began as a result of dissatisfaction with the heavy taxation and abuses of local officials on the Shimabara-hanto (peninsula).

SHIMEA

In biblical times, name of an ancestor of temple musician Asaph in the Levitical family of Gershon (Gershom) (1 Chronicles 6:39-43).

SHIMEAM

In biblical times, name for the son of Mikloth, who, it appears, lived in Jerusalem. This Benjaminite was related to King Saul's ancestors (1 Chronicles 9:35-39).

SHIMEI

Name of several important persons during biblical times. The name Shimei is applied to the second-named son of Gershon (Gershom), grandson of Levi (Exodus 6:16-17; Numbers 3:17-18). Several Shimeite families of Levites descended from him (Numbers 3:21-26). The name Shimei is also found to belong to a Benjaminite whose nine sons (or descendants) were heads of forefathers' houses living in Jerusalem (1 Chronicles 8:1, 19-21).

Elsewhere the name Shimei is used for a loyal supporter of King David who refused to join Adonijah's consipracy (1 Kings 1:8). He is presumably the same Shimei appointed as King Solomon's food deputy in Benjamin's territory (1 Kings 4:7, 18).

The name Shimei is also applied to a Benjaminite from the village of Bahurim. Shimei, the son of Gera, of a family in King Saul's house, harbored a grudging spirit toward David for years after Saul's death and the removal of the kingship from his house. Shimei found an occasion to vent his long-contained wrath when David and his party fled from Jerusalem on account of Absalom's rebellion. Just a little east of the Mount of Olives, Shimei walked along throwing stones and dust down at them and cursing David. Abishai asked David's permission to kill Shimei, but David refused, hoping that perhaps God would turn Shimei's curse into a blessing (1 Kings 2:8-9).

SHIMEITES

In biblical times, descendants of Shimei, the son of Gershon and the grandson of Levi (Exodus 6:16-17).

When the first census in the wilderness was taken, the Shimeites and Libnites ("the families of the Gershonites") had registered ones totaling 7,500 (Numbers 3:20-22). The Shimeites were encamped with the Libnites behind the tabernacle, that is, to the west. As Gershonites, their Levitical duties included transporting, erecting and maintaining the tabernacle tent and its coverings, as well as the hangings of the courtyard, the screens (both to the entrance of the courtyard and to the tent) and the tent cords (Numbers 3:23-26).

SHIMENAWA

In the Shinto religion of Japan, a sacred rope made of twisted rice straw hung with paper of cloth strips, which is strung together before the presence of a god or is otherwise used to demarcate a sacred area.

SHIMEON

In Judaism, one of the eight sons of Harim whom Ezra encouraged to dismiss their pagan wives and sons (Ezra 10:10-11, 31-34).

SHIMRATH

In Judaism, name for a Benjaminite family head in Jerusalem; one of the nine sons of Shimei (1 Chronicles 11:26, 46).

SHIMRI

In biblical times, Simeonite ancestor of one of the chieftains who expanded the tribe's territory in the days of Hezekiah (1 Chronicles 4:24, 37-41).

The name is also found to belong to a Merarite son of Hosah included among the Levitical gatekeepers selected by lot to the assignment west of the sanctuary. Though Shimri was not Hopsah's firstborn, his father appointed him head of the paternal house (1 Chronicles 26:10-16).

SHIMRON

In biblical times, name for a son of Issachar (Genesis 46:13; 1 Chronicles 7:1). He was among "Israel's sons who came into Egypt." His descendants, the Shimonites, formed one of the families of Issachar (Genesis 46:8).

The name is also applied to a town whose king joined the confederation of northern Canaanites that Joshua defeated at the waters of Merom (Joshua 11:1-8). Shimron was included in the tribal allotment of Zebulun (Joshua 19:10, 15). The most commonly suggested location of ancient Shimron is Tell Semuniya, a short distance west of Nazareth, a site, however, rejected by a few scholars.

SHIMSHAI

In biblical times, name for a scribe in the administration of Rehum, the chief government official of the Persian province "beyond the river," which included Jerusalem. Shimshai joined in writing a letter to the Persian ruler Artaxerxes in an effort to stop the Israelites from their rebuilding work in Jerusalem, which was resumed during the reign of his successor King Darius Hystaspes (Darius I of Persia (Ezra 4:8-24).

SHIN

The largest of the popular Japanese Pure Land sects that hold that salvation is obtainable through faith in the Buddha Amida.

SHINAB

In biblical times, name of the king of Admah, one of the five monarchs in the southern Red Sea area who rebelled in his 13th year of vassalship to Chedorlaomer. The rebellion, however, was unsuccessful (Genesis 14:1-10).

SHINAR

In biblical times, the original name of the area between the Tigris and Euphrates Rivers later called Babylonia. It was there that Nimrod assumed kingship of Babel, Erech, Accad and Calneh, and where construction of the temple-tower of Babel was aborted (Genesis 10:9-10; 11:2-8). Later, the king of Shinar, Amraphel, was one of the confederates that took

Abraham's nephew Lot captive (Genesis 14:1-12). This territory was still called by its original name in the days of Joshua (Joshua 7:21). It is referred to by the prophets Isaiah, Daniel and Zechariah.

SHINBUTSO SHUGO

In Japan the amalgamation of Buddhism with the ancient religion Shinto.

SHINGAKU

A religious and ethical movement in Japan founded by Ischida Baigan (1685-1744). It pays particular devotion to the Shinto sun goddess Amaterasu and to Shinto tutelaru deities, but also uses in its popular ethics the teachings of Zen Buddhism and Neo-Confucianism.

SHINGON

An esoteric Buddhist sect that has had a considerable following in Japan since its introduction from China in the 9th century. Its emphasis is in attempting to reach the eternal wisdom of the Buddha that was not expressed in words, thus, not in his public teaching. The sect believes that this wisdom may be developed and realized through special ritual means employing body, speech, and mind, such as the use of symbolical gestures, mystical syllables, and mental concentration.

SHINRAN

(1173-1262) Buddhist philosopher and religious reformer who established the Jodo Shinshu (True Pure Land sect), the largest school of Buddhism in Japan today.

SHINSEN

In the Shinto religion of Japan, food offerings presented to the kami (god, or sacred power). The dishes may vary according to the shrine, the deity honored, and the occasion of worship.

SHINSHOKU

In Japanese Shintoism, the priest, whose main function is to officiate at all shrine ceremonies on behalf of and at the request of worshippers. He is not expected to lecture, preach, or to act as spiritual leader to his parishioners; rather his main role is to ensure the continuance of a satisfactory relationship between the kami (god, or sacred power) and man.

SHINTO

The ancient indigenous religion of Japan which has been severely modified by both Confucianism and Buddhism. Shinto differs from most of the major world religions in having no founder, no official scriptures and thus no dogma to speak of. Yet it has transmitted down the centuries a definite ethos, which in the 20th century was harnessed to reinforce Japanese nationalism on a militaristic course. Shinto is derived mainly from the Chinese Shen-Tao and the Japanese Kamino-Michi, both meaning "way of the gods." After the 6th century, Shinto developed quite distinct from both Buddhism and worship of the native gods, kami.

Doctrine

Essentially the worship of nature. Shinto venerates countless diverse spirits, among them the sky, the earth, the sea, crops, rocks, and mountains, animals and in particular "superior and extraordinary beings," such as emperors and national heroes of the past - the greatest of them being the Sun-goddess Amaterasu Omikami (the "Heaven-Shining August Goddess"), from whom the Imperial Family is considered to descend. In 1946, however, Emperor Hirohito disavowed his divinity and General Douglas MacArthur

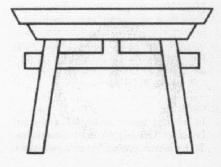

ended the use of state funds to support Shinto.

Contemporary Shinto

Shinto has many thousands of shrines, from great temples to myriads of small ones, sometimes just huts at the roadside where deities of all kinds are worshiped. They are characteristically set in peaceful surroundings, emphasizing the beauties of nature, and are never of stone but are made of simple unpainted wood. They contain symbols, perhaps a mirror and jewels, but seldom an image. Priests perform rituals to light handclasps and followers ring a bell, call, bow and repeat Shinto prayers.

Twofold Shinto)a compromise between Buddhism and Shinto, and Sect Shinto, which comprises 130 sects, each founded on a historical character) is today the most active and organized Shinto movement, with churches and schools, official recognition, and about 25 million followers. The newer sects of Shinto are strong advocates of world brotherhood.

SHION

In biblical times, name of a city of Issachar (Joshua 19:17-19). 'Ayun esh-Sha'in, a few miles east of Nazareth, may preserve the name Shion and suggest its ancient situation.

SHIPHI

In biblical times, name for a Simeonite whose son was one of the tribal chieftains that extended their pasture grounds during Hezekiah's reign (1 Chronicles 4:24, 37-41).

SHIPHTAN

In biblical times, father of Kemuel, the chieftain representing Ephraim when the Promised Land was divided among the tribes of Israel (Numbers 34:17-24).

SHIRK

In Islam, term to designate idolatry, polytheism. This is a heinous sin condemned in the Koran. The Arabic word means literally "sharing." Man is forbidden to share his worship with God with that of any other creatures, and to ascribe partners to God as sharers of His Divinity. Polytheism is the one sin which the Koran tells us cannot and will not be forgiven. This is because it denies God's very existence.

SHISHAK

An Egyptian king, known as Sheshonk (I) from Egyptian records. Shishak, regarded as the founder of the "Libyan dynasty," is generally credited with a rule of about 21 years. His son Osorkon succeeded him to the throne. When Jeroboam fled to Egypt to escape the wrath of King Solomon, Shishak ruled there (1 Kings 11:40). Some years later, in the fifth year of Solomon's successor Rehoboam (993/992 BC), Shishak invaded Judah with an mighty force of chariots and horsemen. He captured fortified cities in Judah and then came to Jerusalem. According to biblical tradition, God did not allow him to bring Jerusalem to ruin, for Rehoboam and the princes of Judah humbled themselves upon receiving a message from the prophet Shemaiah. Shishak, however, did strip the city of its treasures (2 Chronicles 12:1-12).

SHITTIM

In biblical times, name of a location on the desert plain of Moab to which the encampment of the Israelites extended from Beth-jeshimoth (Numbers 25:1; 33:49; Joshua 2:1). Evidently "Shittim" is a shortened form of the name Abel-shittim. It is commonly identified with Tell el-Kefrein, a low hill about five miles north-east of Beth-jeshimoth, near the north-eastern corner of the Dead Sea.

SHIV'A

In Judaism, a period of seven days of prescribed mourning that commences with the burial of a parent, a spouse, a child, or brother or sister and concludes early on the seventh day. Shiv'a is not observed on the intervening sabbath and automatically terminates if a major religious festival occurs.

SHOBACH

In biblical times, army chief of Syrian King Hadadezer. In directing an army of Syrians hired by the Ammonites to fight against David, Shobach lost the battle and his life along with 40,700 of his men (2 Samuel 10:15-19).

SHOBAI

In Judaism, a Levite founder of a family of temple gatekeepers. Some of his descendants returned from, Babylonian exile with Zerubbabel (Ezra 2:1-2; 40-42; Nehemiah 7:45).

SHOBAL

In biblical times, a Horite sheik, son of Seit, and himself father of five sons (Genesis 36:20-29). The name is also found to apply to a son of Hur descended from Caleb of the tribe of Judah. A number of descendants are credited to Shobal, including the inhabitants of Kiriath-jearim and other towns (1 Chronicles 2:50-53).

SHOBEK

In Judaism, an Israelite or the head of a family represented in the attestations of the "trustworthy arrangement" put forward during Nehemiah's governorship (Nehemiah 9:38; 10:1, 14, 24).

SHOBI

In Judaism, name for a loyal subject of King David. Shobi and two others brought much-needed supplies to David, when Absalom's rebellion caused the king and his party to flee Jerusalem (2 Samuel 17:17-29).

SHOFAR

In Judaism, special ram's horn. The shofar is blown every day in the month of Elul, except on the sabbath. It provides the most impressive moment of the morning service of Rosh Hashanah. Not a whisper is heard as the shofar is raised for the hallowed sounds.

The shofar is made of a ram's horn. The horn is boiled in water until it gets soft. The inside is than hollowed out and the horn flattened somewhat. But it is not flattened too much for then air could not be blown through it. The mouthpiece is then carefully shaped and the horn is put aside to harden.

In biblical times, the shofar was used to herald great moments. It proclaimed the ascent of a king upon the throne, it announced the jubilee every 50th year, the sabbath and festivals. In wartime, it signalled the army.

SHOHAM

In Judaism, a Merarite Levite involved in David's reorganization of the Levitical services; son of Jaaziah (1 Chronicles 24:27-31).

SHOMER

In biblical times, name for a descendant of Asher whose four sons were chieftains and family heads (1 Chronicles 7:30-40).

SHOMYO

Classical chant of Buddhism in Japan. Both the Tendai and Shingon sects maintain the tradition and use its theoretical books and notation systems as the basis for other forms of Buddhist singing.

SHONIN

In Buddhism, a superior man; title to honor used from early times for a Buddhist monk or superior attainment.

SHOU HSING

In Chinese mythology, the second of three stellar gods known collectively as Fu-Shou-Lu. Though greatly revered as the god of longevity, Shou Hsing has no temples.

SHOZOKU

Vestments worn by the Shinto priests of Japan during the performance of religious ceremonies. Most of the costumes appear to date from the Heian period (795-1185) and originated as dress of the noblemen, the colors and cut often determined by court rank.

SHRINE SHINTO

A form of Shinto religion of Japan that focusses on worship in public shrines, in contrast to folk and sectarian practices. More than 80,000 shrines, about 98 percent of those formerly administered by the government, have formed themselves into an Association of Shinto Shrines.

SHRINE OF OUR LADY

Holy places where apparitions of the Blessed Virgin Mary are believed to have taken place; because of their reputation as places where moral and physical miracles have been granted, they are centers of Roman Catholic pilgrimages. Among the outstanding shrines of the Blessed Virgin Mary, the following four (in alphabetical order) are especially noteworthy:

Fatima, Portugal

Between May 13 and October 13, 1917, Mary appeared six times to three children near Fatima, north of Lisbon. After intense study, church authorities pronounced these apparitions worthy of belief in 1930. The message of Mary at Fatima included an exhortation of frequent recitation of the rosary, works of mortification on behalf of sinners, the consecration of the people of Russia to her under the title of the Immaculate Heart, and the observance of the first Saturday of each month by receiving Holy Communion in reparation of sin.

Guadalupe, Mexico

In 1531, Mary appeared four times to Juan Diego on Tepeyac Hill near Mexico City; a life-size figure of Mary was miraculously painted on Juan Diego's mantle; this painting is now enshrined in the basilica of the shrine; the church has accepted the apparition as authentic and celebrates the feast of Our Lady of Guadalupe (The "Mother of the Americas") on December 12.

La Salette, France

In September 1846, Mary appeared to two peasant children; in 1851 church authorities declared the apparition worthy of belief, and devotion to Our Lady of La Sallette was approved. The chief message of Our Lady was the necessity of penance on the part of the faithful.

Lourdes, France

Between February and July, 1858, Mary (identifying herself by saying, "I am the Immaculate Conception") appeared 18 times to a young woman, Bernadette Soubirous. After four years of intense study, church authorities approved the apparitions as authentic in 1862. Mary's message was a solemn exhortation to prayer and penance for the conversion of the peoples. The feast of Our Lady of Lourdes is celebrated on February 11.

SHROUD OF TURIN

The cloth or winding sheet housed in the cathedral of Turin, Italy, is thought by many to have covered the body of Jesus in the tomb. This shroud bears an imprint of a crucified man and has been subject of many investigations. The Catholic Church, however, has made no ruling on the authenticity of the relic.

SHROVE TUESDAY

The day before Ash Wednesday. It is traditionally a day id feasting, marked by such carnivals as the Mardi Gras of New Orleans. The faithful confess (or are "shriven") on this last day before Lent.

SHUA

In Judaism, Canaanite father of Judah's wife, and grandfather of Er, Onan and Shelah (Genesis 38:2-5).

SHUAH

In Judaism, the sixth and last-named son of Abraham by his second wife Keturah (1 Chronicles 1:32). Shuah and his five brothers received gifts from Abraham and were sent out of his household toward the East (Genesis 25:1-6). Shuah's descendants, the Shuhites, are thought by some to have lived along the Euphrates between two of its tributaries, the Balikh and Khabur. The only Shuhite named in the Bible is Job's companion Bildad (Job 2:11).

SHUAL

In biblical times, name for a region associated with Ophrah, presumably to the north of Michmash. The Philistines encamped at Michmash made raids in the direction of Shual (1 Samuel 13:16-17).

SHU'AYB

Arabian prophet sent to warn the people of Madyan to worship the one true God and against sharp business practices; they rejected his message and were punished accordingly by earthquake.

SHUHAM

The only son of Dan mentioned in the Bible. He was forefather of the Shuhamites, the only tribal family enrolled for Dan, and which numbered 64,400 at the end of the 40-year wilderness wandering (Numbers 26:42-43).

SHUHITE

Evidently a descendant of Shuah, a son of Abraham by his wife Kenturah (Genesis 25:2; 1 Chronicles 1:32). Job's companion Bildad is the only Shuhite mentioned in the Bible (Job 2:11; 25:1).

SHULAMMITE

In biblical times, the designation for the beautiful country girl who is the principal character of The Song of Solomon (6:13). Likely this title portrays her as from the city of Shuen (modern Solem).

SHULHAN 'ARUKH

A 16th century codification of Jewish religious law and practice that is still the standard reference work for Orthodox observance.

SHUMATHITES

In Judaism, name for one of the families of Kiriath-jearim, likely descendants of Judah through Caleb and Shobal (1 Chronicles 2:19, 50-53).

SHUNAMMITE

In biblical times, an inhabitant of Shunem. Abishag, the nurse of David in his old age, is called a "Shunammite" (1 Kings 1:3-15).

SHUNEM

In biblical times, name of a city in the territory of Issachar (Joshua 19:17-18) and not far from Jezreel and Mount Gilboa (1 Samuel 28:4). Shunem is linked with modern Solem on the south-western slope of Nebi Dahi and overlooking the low plain of Jezreel. The place lies about three miles north of Zer'in (Jezreel) and some five miles north of the western end of the traditional site of Mount Gilboa.

SHUNI

In Judaism, third-named of Gad's seven sons. Shuni accompanied Jacob into Egypt, and, as his own offspring expanded in numbers, they formed the tribal family of the Shunites (Genesis 46:8; Numbers 26:15).

SHUPPIM

In the Old Testament, a descendant of Benjamin, perhaps through Bela and Iri (1 Chronicles 7:6-12). The name is also found to apply to a gatekeeper appointed to the west of the sanctuary (1 Chronicles 26:16).

SHUR

In biblical times, name for a place or region described as "in front of Egypt," that is, on or to the east of Egypt. The context located Shurt in the north-western portion of the Sinai Peninsula (Genesis 25:18). After Israel crossed the Red Sea, Moses led them from the shores of the sea into the "wilderness of Shur" (Exodus 15:22).

SHURAH, al-

The title of the 42nd sura of the Koran; it may be translated as "The Counsel." The sura mainly belongs to the Meccan period and contains 53 verses. Its title comes from verse 38 which refers to those who organize themselves by shura. The sura begins with five of the mysterious Letters of the Koran, goes on to emphasize God's power and omniscience, and makes reference to such great figures as Nuh, Ibrahim, Musa and Isa. The mercy of His creation and His signs are mentioned and the sura concludes by noting that all things return to God.

SHUSHAN

In biblical times, name for an ancient city, the ruins of which lie on the Karkheh River, about 225 miles east of Babylon. Shushan or a fortified part of the city, "Shushan the castle," was the setting for one of the visions of the prophet Daniel (8:2), the scene for the events narrated in the book of Esther (1:2-6; 2:3-8) and the place where Nehemiah served as cupbearer during the reign of Artaxerxes (Nehemiah 1:1).

There is evidence that Shushan was the capital of ancient Elam. In the seventh century BC, King Asenappar of Assyria conquered Shushan and transported inhabitants of the city to Samaria (Ezra 4:9-10). Under Persian domination, Shushan was a royal city. In the fourth century BC, Shushan fell to Alexander the Great and eventually witnessed decline. Today only a mound of ruins occupies the site.

SHUSHAN PURIM

In Judaism, the day after Purim. According to the Book of Esther, the Jews of Shushan celebrated the victory over Haman a day later than did the other Jews because they were engaged in battle an additional day.

SHUSHIGAKU

Most influential of Neo-Confucian schools in Japan that developed during the Tokugawa period (1603-1867). The school followed the tradition of the Chinese philosopher Chu Hsi.

SHUTHELAH

In biblical times, a son of Ephraim and forefather of the tribal family of Shuthelahites (1 Chronicles 7:20; Numbers 26:35-37).

SHUTHELAHITES

In biblical times, the family descendants of Shuthelah; included among the registered ones in the tribe of Ephraim at the time of the second census in the wilderness (Numbers 26:35-37).

SIBBECAI

In Judaism, one of David's mighty men, a Hushahite (1 Chronicles 11:26-29). Sibbecai, in a war with the Philistines at Gob, slew Saph, one of the giantlike Rephaim, thereby subduing the enemy (2 Samuel 21:18). When David organized the monthly rotational service of the nation's forces, Sibbecai was placed in charge of the eighth division (1 Chronicles 27:1, 11).

SIBMAH

In biblical times, name of a town east of the Jordan, taken by Israel from Amorite King Sihon and assigned to the Reubenites, who desired it because of surrounding pastureland. Apparently it was also called Sebam (Numbers 32:2-5; Joshua 13:15-21). Originally a city of the Moabites, it reverted to them in an undisclosed time, and was noted for its vineyards and summer fruitage (Isaiah 16:8-14; Jeremiah 48:32). The exact location is now unknown though it is mentioned with Heshbon and Nebo (Numbers 32:3), and Jerome said that it was only about 500 paces from Heshbon.

SICKLE

One of the most ancient of harvesting tools, consisting of a metal blade, usually curved, attached to a short wooden handle.

SIDDHA

According to Jainism (a religion of India), a perfect being. By right faith, right knowledge, and right conduct, a siddha has freed himself from the cycle of rebirths. Since he is bodyless, he resides in a state of perpetual bliss in the siddha-sila, which is located at the top of the universe.

SIDDHARTHA

The personal name of Gautama, who became the Buddha. It means "he whose aim is accomplished."

SIDDHAS

A list of eighty-four Perfected Ones (siddha) common to the Buddhist and Shaivite tradition found in Buddhism of Tibet. Their biographies are told in the Tibetan Canon, covering the seventh to the eleventh century. They have in common a dedication to the life of helping others, as taught by their various masters.

SIDDHI

In Buddhism, spiritual powers, of two kinds, the lower and merely psychic, and the higher, the fruits of long periods of spiritual training. The former are involved in self; the latter are only available to those in whom self is dead.

SIDDIM, Low Valley of

In biblical times, name for a valley linked in the Bible with the Salt (Dead) Sea (Genesis 14:3). There, in Abraham's day, the rebellious kings of Sosom, Gomorrah, Admah, Zeboiim and Zoar battled with Elamite King Chedorlaomer and his three Mesopotamian allies. Defeated, the kings of Sodom and Gomorah fled, only to have some of their troops fall into the "pits upon pits of bitumen" that filled the area (Genesis 14:4, 8-10).

SIDDUR

The Jewish prayer book, which contains the entire Jewish liturgy, for homes as well as synagogues. Its prayers and benedictions breathe Old Testament sentiments of praise, thanksgiving, petition, intercession, acknowledgement of sin, and prayers for forgiveness; numerous versicles from the Psalms express these religious feelings.

SIDON

In biblical times, Sidon was the progenitor of the Sidonians. The seaport town of Sidon was named after their forefather, and for many years it was the principal city of the Phoenicians, as the Greeks called the Sidoneans. Today the city is known as Saida.

A port city favored with two of the few harbors on the Phoenician coast, Sidon became a great trading center where overland caravans met and exchanged their wares for goods brought in vessels plying the shipping lanes of the Mediterranean. Among the Sidoneans were wealthy merchants, skilled sailors and hardy rowers (Isaiah 23:2; Ezekiel 27:8-9).

SIDONEANS

In biblical times, descendants of Sidon. Religiously, the Sidoneans were depraved, lewd sex orgies in connection with the goddess Ashtoreth being a prominent part of their worship. The Israelites, allowing the Sidoneans to remain among them, were eventually ensnared into worshipping their false gods (Judges 10:6-13). Some of the foreign wives that Solomon married were Sidoneans, and these caused the king to go after the disgusting fertility goddess Ashtoreth (1 Kings 11:1-6).

SIFAT ALLAH

In Islam, the attributes of God. Muslim theology classically distinguished between the basic attributes of the Essence (like God's eternity, self-subsistence and permanence), and others. Much medieval theological debate concerned itself with the exact relationship between all the attributes and God's Essence; were they identical with the Essence or separate? If the latter was the case, what were the implications for the doctrine of God's unity. One conclusion to the debate was that

God's attributes were eternal and subsisted in His Essence, but they were not God nor other than God.

SIGN OF THE CROSS

A gesture in the form of a cross by which one professes his or her faith in the Holy Trinity; it is made in several ways:

▲ one "blesses oneself," for example at the beginning and end of one's prayers, by touching the fingers of one's right hand to one's forehead, breast, left shoulder, and right shoulder while saying, "In the name of the father, and of the Son, and of the Holy Spirit";

▲ one forms a small cross on one's forehead, lips, and breast before the proclamation of the Gospel;

▲ one authorized to give blessings in the church makes a large cross with the right hand over the person or object to be blessed.

SIGNS OF THE TIMES

A phrase used in Vatican Council II's Pastoral Constitution on the church in the Modern World which declares that "the church has always had the duty of scrutinizing the signs of the times and of interpreting them in the light of the gospel."

SIKHARA

In Indian temple architecture, the superstructure of spire above the sanctuary and also above the mandapas (halls); the most dominant and characteristic feature of the Hindu temple in North India.

SIKHS

A religious community of nine million who are chiefly concentrated in East Punjab, north India. The religion of the Sikhs, which combines elements both from Hinduism and Islam, was founded by guru Nanak in the 15th century. The word "sikh" derives from the Sanskrit shishya, disciple. In the 19th century, under the leadership of Ranjit Singh, the Sikhd developed a powerful state before the British government assumed direct control throughout India.

SIKHISM

The Sikh religion is recorded in their sacred book, Adi Granth, in the Punjab language. There is no professional priesthood, and officially no recognition of the caste system. However, the Sikhs have been much persecuted and have in consequence developed militant characteristics. Each "initiated" male Sikh adopts a pattern of wearing uncut hair and beard, shorts, a steel comb, a steel bangle on the right wrist and a steel dagger.

The authority of Adi Granth replaced the Vedas; Gurakhi replaced Sanskrit as the sacred language. While idolatry was forbidden, veneration of the Granth, the Holy Book, was often idolatrous. Although maintaining great reverence for the true name of God, the Sikhs rejected the ceremonial repetition of names. By abolishing sacrifice, they eliminated the class of priests. By rejecting nonviolence, they lost scruples against killing and eating animals. The history of the patriarchal period of Sikhism reflects a gradual shift, under the increasing hostility of the Muslims, from the pacifism of Nanak toward the political and militaristic character the movement acquired under Gobind Singh. Nanak, considered an incarnation of God with the 16 avatara signs of Rama and Krishna, is believed to be incarnated in the other gurus.

By instituting the Khalsa or Sikh Council of those who were pure of faith, and establishing the Granth as the lasting sacred book of the Sikhs, he eliminated the need for future gurus. He began worship of the terrible goddess, Durga, and imparted some of his violent and martial personality to the movement.

Sikh nationalism continues today in the Punjab, finding expression in the deathless movement. Akali, Yet, other strains of Sikhism which retain the influence, character, and teaching of Nanak have survived, as have sects which are dedicated to the continued study and theology of Adi Granth.

SIKKHA

In Buddhism, term used in the sense of training; the training of the would-be Buddhist in the higher realms of Sila (morality), Samadhi and Panna, a threefold division of the Noble Eightfold Path.

SILAS

Early Christian prophet and missionary, companion of the apostle Paul. Acts 15:22 first mentions him as one of the leading men among the brethren. The Christian community at Jerusalem sent him to Antioch where he is identified as a prophet (Acts 15:32) preaching to the Antiochene Christians. On many journeys Silas accompanied Paul, spreading the gospel.

SILHAK

School of thought that emerged amid the chaotic conditions of 18th century Korea and was dedicated to a practical approach to statecraft, instead of the blind and uncritical following of Confucian teachings that had been the practice of the day.

SILOAM

In biblical times, name of a pool in Jerusalem where Jesus Christ had a blind man wash in order to receive sight (John 9:6-11). Little is known about this pool as it then existed, though its general location apparently is marked by the present Birket Silwan, just south-west of the city of David. Likely this is also the approximate site of King Hezekiah's "pool" or reservoir adjoining the conduit he constructed to carry the waters of Gihon (2 Kings 20:20; 2 Chronicles 32:30).

SILSILA

In Islam, chain of spiritual authorities or leaders.

SILVANUS

In Roman religion, the god of the countryside, similar in character to Faunus, the god of animals, and normally depicted in the guise of a countryman.

SILVERIUS, Saint

(465-537) Pope from 536 to 537, a victim of intrigues of the Byzantine empress Theodora. He was deposed by a Byzantine general and sent to Palmyra where he died of murder or starvation.

SIMEON

The second son of Jacob's twelve sons; so named because, as his mother Leah said, "Jehovah has listened, in that I was hated and so he gave me also this one" (Genesis 29:32-35; Exodus 1:1-4).

When his father Jacob was encamped near Shechem, Simeon, together with his next younger brother Levi, displaced a vengeful anger that was unreasonably harsh and cruel. Arbitrarily, without their father's knowledge and consent, they set about to avenge the honor of the younger sister Dinah by slaughtering the Shechemites, bringing ostracism upon the whole family (Genesis 34:1-31).

Simeon was later involved in wrongdoing when he and his brothers planned to kill Joseph (Genesis 37:12-28). Whether Simeon as second oldest, was or was not the ringleader in this plot on Joseph's life is not stated. Years later, when Joseph as a good administrator of Egypt was testing out his brothers, Simeon was selected by Joseph to be bound and imprisoned until the other brothers brought Benjamin down to Egypt (Genesis 42:14-24).

SIMEON, Charles

(1759-1836) Church of England clergyman and biblical commentator who from Cambridge led the Evangelical movement in reaction to the liturgically and episcopally oriented High church party.

SIMEON, Tribe of

One of the 12 tribes of Israel that in biblical times comprised the people of Israel who later became the Jewish people. The tribe was named after the second son born to Jacob and his first wife, Leah. During Israel's wilderness journey Simeon encamped with Reuben and Gad on the south of the tabernacle, the three-tribe division being headed by Reuben. On the march this same tribal arrangement was maintained, with Shelumiel serving as Simeon's chieftain, both of the camp and of the army (Numbers 1:4-6; 2:10-15).

SIMEON BEN YOHAI

(2nd century AD) Member of a select group of Palestinian rabbinic teachers, one of the most eminent disciples of the martyred rabbi Akiba ben Joseph, and, according to many Orthodox scholars, aurhot of Zokar, the most important work of Jewish mysticism.

SIMEONITES

In biblical times, the descendants of Jacob's second son Simeon. After about 40 years of wandering in the wilderness the male population among the Simeonites who were 20 years old and upward and who were qualified for military service numbered only 22,200, constituting the smallest of the 12 tribes. They were divided into five principal families; the Nemuelites, Janimites, Jachinites, Zerahites and Shaulites (Numbers 25:14; 26:1-12; Joshua 21:4).

SIMEON METAPHRASTES

(898-950) Byzantine hagiographer whose Menologion, a ten-volume collection of the lives and martyrdom of early Eastern saints, achieved wide popularity because of Simeon's Byzantine rhetorical style.

SIMON

Name of a number of important [persons in biblical times. Simon was an apostle of Jesus Christ, distinguished from Simon Peter by the term "Canaanaean" (Matthew 10:4; Mark 3:18). While it is possible that Simon once belonged to the Zealots, a Jewish party opposed to the Romans, it may instead have been due to his religious zeal that he was called "the zealous one" or "the zealot" (Luke 6:15; Acts 1:13).

Simon is also the name for the half brother of Jesus (Matthew 13:55; Mark 6:3). Though he was still an unbeliever prior to the festival of tabernacles in AD 32 (John 7:2-8), he may have become a disciple later, Jesus' fleshy brothers were among the crowd of about 120 disciples in Jerusalem during the season of Pentecost, AD 33, although Simon is not specifically named as being present (Acts 1:14-15). The name Simon is also supplied to a Pharisee at whose house Jesus dined and where a sinful woman showed him great kindness and resp[ect, greasing his feet with perfumed oil (Luke 7:36-50).

According to biblical tradition, Simon was a resident of Bethany, spoken of as a "leper" (perhaps one cured by Jesus), in whose house Jesus and his disciples, as well as the resurrected Lazarus and his sisters Mary and Martha, has a meal. There Mary anointed Jesus with costly perfumed oil (Matthew 26:6-13; Mark 14:3-9; John 12:2-8).

SIMON

Name of a number of important persons in biblical times. Simon was an Apostle of Jesus Christ, distinguished from Simon Peter by the term "Canaanaean" (Matthew 10:4; Mark 3:18). While it is possible that Simon once belonged to the Zealots, a Jewish party opposed to the Romans, it may instead have been due to his religious zeal that he was called "the zealous one" or "the zealot" (Luke 6:15; Acts 1:13).

Simon is also the name for the half brother of Jesus (Matthew 13:55; Mark 6:3). Though he was still an unbeliever prior to the festival of tabernacles in 32 (John 7:2-8), he may have become a disciple later, Jesus' fleshly brothers were among the crowd of about 120 disciples in Jerusalem during the season of Pentecost, 33, although Simon is not specifically named as being present (Acts 1:14-15).

The name Simon is also applied to a Pharisee at whose house Jesus dined and where a sinful woman showed him great kindness and resp[ect, greasing his feet with perfumed oil (Luke 7:36-50).

According to biblical tradition, Simon was a resident of Bethany, spoken of as a "leper" (perhaps one cured by Jesus), in whose house Jesus and his disciples, as well as the resurrected Lazarus and his sisters Mary and Martha, had a meal. There Mary anointed Jesus with costly perfumed oil (Matthew 26:6-13; Mark 14:3-9; John 12:2-8).

SIMONIANISM

A doctrine expressed by followers of Simon Magnus (1st century AD), who was called the first Gnostic teacher. The Gnostics were religious dualists who generally taught that matter was evil and the spirit good and that salvation was attained through esoteric knowledge, or gnosis.

SIMON MAGNUS

(1st century AD) a practitioner of magical arts in biblical Samaria, who, according to the New Testament (Acts 8:9-24) after becoming a Christian, offered to purchase from the apostles Paul and John the supernatural power of transmitting the Holy Spirit, thus giving rise to the term simony as the buying or selling of sacred things or ecclesiastical office. He was identified in early Christian literature as the founder of post-Christian Gnosticism.

SIMON STYLITES, Saint

(390-459) The first known Christian monk to practice the austere asceticism of dwelling atop a column to pursue meditation interrupted only by charitable social concerns.

SIMONY

Intentional buying or selling of something spiritual (for example, grace, a sacrament) or something closely connected with the spiritual (for example, a relic); both the law of God and the law of the church forbid such buying and selling because it is a violation of the honor due to God and the things of God.

SIN

In Christianity, violation of the will of God being attributable to human pride, self-centeredness, and disobedience. Every man is a sinner (Psalms 51:5-10), not capable to live like God wants him to. Bearing his punishment for that is impossible to do. That's why Jesus died for mankind, bearing man's sins and punishment on the cross (Romans 5:8-11).

In Christian mythology Adam was the first man, who lost his superior nature by disobedience to God and so "fell" from grace. This fall story has been challenged in the light of science and history, but the basic belief has been maintained in man's bias to sin as a falling short of God's purpose for him.

Other concepts of sin include serving what is seen as the will of the devil; practicing the Seven Deadly Sins (pride, covetousness, lust, envy, gluttony, anger and sloth); the breaking of the Ten Commandments given to Moses, or of the further injunctions of Christ.

The deepest insight of Christian faith into the nature of sin has been the recognition that sin is an act of severing, or at least of jeopardizing, the intimate relation between creator and creature. As the positive form of that relation is never simply one of conformity to the prescriptions of a book of rules but is always one of fellowship with God Himself, so the negation of that relation is inevitably defined in personal terms.

A vivid metaphor for the violation, especially prominent in the prophecy of Hosea but audible in large parts of the Old Testament, is that of the unfaithful wife who was, by a deliberate and wanton act, cut herself off from her loving husband. This personal dimension of sin attends even the expressions of guilt brought on by the remembrance of a moral wrong.

Thus Psalm 51:4, attributed to David after his adultery with Bath-sheba, makes clear that the sin has violated a relation with God: "Against thee, thee only have I sinned." Conversely, the forgiveness of sins is not merely the removal of moral guilt, but the restoration, by God himself as the injured party, of this personal relationship.

In Buddhism, no original sin in man is being recognized, save those results of his own past causes which have not yet "ripened." The effects of any new act which is Akusala, unwholesome, will be borne by the causer under the law of Karma.

Thus sin may be seen as a complex philosophical and theological concept bound up in the nature of man, existence and evil, or as the violation of certain laws derived from custom, biblical interpretation, revelation and current modes of thought.

SIN, Personal

The scholastic psycho-theological analysis of personal or actual sin is picked up from the old Greek controversy as to whether moral failure could be resolved into an unfortunate mistake due to ignorance, as Socrates thought, or whether it also introduced a culpable defect of affectivity, as Aristotle thought.

It worked with a delicate psychology of human activity, and was constantly alert to the setting of biblical revelation and to Augustine's teaching on transgression of divine and indeed eternal law.

Nature

A sin is an evil in acting, not in being. It is a failure of an activity to reach its purpose, an action that miscarries or goes amiss. The notion by extension may be applied also to non-intelligent beings, which do not always succeed in their natural activities.

However, sin takes on a special sense when applied to human acts, namely of doing wrong, not right, and through our own fault. It should be conceived in terms less of substantives and adjectives than of verbs and adverbs; less of a right or a wrong in juridical sense, than of acting well-directly or ill-directly toward God who is the ultimate aim of human life. This theological reference is essential for a moral meaning, and in particular for that of sin.

Basic source

How does it come about that a man fails? It does not spring from the nature of things, not even from the nature of freedom, which lies in the ability, not to be uncompelled by any particular good.

It is a consequence of the present human predicament. In his environment, the only object which a man's will can love, without any hesitation, is goodness, subsistent and complete. However, this is not immediately presented to him as a thing, namely God clearly seen; it exercises its appeal in the pervasive abstraction called happiness, the concrete exemplification of which is broken up into bits and pieces. Were the objects that take man to God the only attractions, were those which lead him away simply distasteful, there would be no problem. As it is, since God Himself is an imperative held only as a principle in the darkness of faith or as an influence in the light of reason, and since the objects that take man to Him on occasion prove very tedious than those which take him away, he is very open to deflection from his course. Along these lines the problem of moral evil can be represented as the problem of too many and conflicting goods.

Causes

Sin rises from a creature who is radically reversible, liable to topple or overturn. That he does so is because of some factor either energetic enough to upset the balance of the whole or inhibiting the action of forces that would maintain it. These causes are both inside and outside man.

The sinner of whom we speak is man, not a hypothetical state of pure nature, which has never been historical, but in a state of fallen nature; even when he is forgiven through Christ and lives in God's friendship, he still bears the wounds of original sin, is not yet restored to the integrity of original justice.

The mainspring of sin is the human will, yet the trouble is not exclusively there, but may lie in the mind or sensorium: indeed the true interior cause is the whole personality as the source of voluntary activity.

God is in no sense the cause of sin, either directly or indirectly, though from him comes all that is positively real in the act. We should not be in a hurry to blame the parents of the human race, for original sin, which is racial nor personal, is our sin as well as theirs, and is to be distinguished from the first actual sin they committed.

Though some sins bring a brood of other sins, and are called capital sins by Gregory the Great, there is no intrinsic connection between the vices as there is between the virtues; there effect is anarchic, and it is reassuring to be taught that we can refer to the kingdom of evil only in metaphorical sense.

SIN IN THE BIBLE

The complexity of the Old Testament conception of sin is reflected in the number of words for sin in Hebrew, each of which expresses a slightly different aspect of it.

Old Testament

▲ Hattat indicates a failure to attain what is due, a missing of the mark;

▲ Awon connotes distortion or "twisting out of the true," and conveys the idea of crookedness or deformity, a turning aside from, the true way laid down for man by God which alone can bring him to the happiness he needs and longs for;

▲ Pesah signifies rebellion;

▲ Ma'al means infidelity, a failure to fulfill one's personal obligations to another, especially those incurred by the covenant with Yahweh freely entered into by the people;

▲ Seker, a lie, conveys that element of falsity which is present in all sin, for all sin implies being false to one's true nature or one's position in relation to God. Sin is also called folly in the sense of being the outcome of a culpably stupid decision that can only lead to disaster.

Sin can only bring trouble, and that not upon the perpetrator alone but on his or her descendants and family and all those connected with him or her. Thus, for instance, the sin of one individual, Achan, brings disaster and defeat upon the Israelite army (Joshua 7). This aspect of sin is expressed by the word awen, which includes in its meaning not only the sin itself but its evil effects. Hebrew writers, especially Jeremiah, are acutely aware of how deeply rooted sin is in the heart of man, which is prone to evil from the very first. "Behold I was brought forth in iniquity and in sin did my mother conceive me" (Psalms 51:5).

The writings of Qumran and the traditions of the rabbinical schools, too, reflect this preoccupation with the yeser hara, the evil inclination which is innate in man. But at least according to the Jewish tradition of the Pentateuch, this disposition to sin was no part of man's original rebellion of the first parents and intensified by the proliferation of sin in the primordial history of the world so that the inclination to sin became universal and endemic (Genesis 3-11).

New Testament

In the synoptic gospels, little is said about the nature of sin as such, though here, too Jesus insists that it has its origin in the heart (Matthew 15:18-19), Mark 7:20-22), and that it consists in going astray and voluntarily separating oneself from God.

This is the plain meaning of the relevant part of the parable of the Prodigal Son (Luke 15:18-21). Sin is disobedience and rebellion (Matthew (7:23), and the effect of obstinate and unrepented sin will be final exclusion from the kingdom of God.

In the Johannine writings it is, perhaps, significant that sin is spoken of in the singular rather than the plural. Christ has come to take away the sin of the world (John 1:29-33). Jesus takes the collective burden of guilt upon himself in order to reconcile the world of God and to bring it back from its state of Godlessness (1 John 3:4) and subjugation to the prince of this world.

For there is a radical opposition between the works of Satan and the world of God, the children of Satan and the children of God; and it is this that chiefly characterizes the Johannine theology of sin.

All sin is regarded as a lie and proceeds from the father of lies (John 8:44). As such it is radically opposed to the truth which Jesus himself represents and embodies; and it seeks to murder this truth (John 8:44). This murderous intention is characteristic of sin as such. It manifests itself in hatred of one's brother just as love of one's brother is a sign that one is engrafted into the truth and endowed with eternal life (1 John 3:10; John 13:35).

SIN, Mesopotamian

In Mesopotamian religion, the moon god. Son of Enlil, he was head of the secondary cosmic triad of the Akkadian pantheon, its two lesser members being his son and daughter, Shamash and Ishtar.

SINAI, Mount

Mount Sinai is renowned as the principal site of divine revelation in Jewish history, where God appeared to Moses and gave him the Ten Commandments (Exodus 20). Sometimes called mount Horeb, it is probably located in the south-central Sinai Peninsula, Egypt.

SINAI PENINSULA

Wedge-shaped, mountainous peninsula between the Gulf of Suez and the Gulf of Aqaba, the northern arms of the Red Sea. Its southern peaks, over 8,000 feet high, are traditionally regarded as the place where Moses received the Ten Commandments. But scholars have not agreed on the location of the biblical Mount Sinai.

SINAN, Rashid ad-Din as-

(1112-1192) Leader of the Syrian branch of the Assassins (a Sufi sect) at the time of the Third Crusade. He was known as the Old Man of the Mountain.

SINIM, Land of

According to biblical tradition, a country from which, it was foretold, scattered Israelites would come, to dwell in and rehabitate their homeland (Isaiah 49:12). References to the north and west in the same verse suggest that Sinim was south or east of Palestine.

SINITE

In biblical times, name of a branch of Canaan's descendants and one of the 70 post-flood families (Genesis 10:15-17; 1 Chronicles 1:15). Several Lebanese locations of similar name are noted in various ancient writings, but the exact place where the Sinites settled remains uncertain.

SINS AGAINST THE HOLY SPIRIT

Sins considered especially repugnant to the third Person of the Trinity. These six sins are:

▲ despair;

▲ presumption;
▲ envy;
▲ obstinacy in sin;
▲ final impenitence;
▲ deliberate resistance to the known truth.

SIPHMOTH

In biblical times, name of a Judean city to which David sent a "gift blessing" of the spoils of his victory over the Amalekites. While a fugitive, he and his men had free access to the city (1 Samuel 30:26:31).

SIRAH, Cistern of

In biblical times, place where Abner was when Jacob's messengers had him return to Hebron, where he was subsequently murdered (2 Samuel 3:26-27). Siorah may correspond to 'Ain Sarah, a spring or well about 1_ miles northwest of Hebron.

SIRAT (AL-) AL-MUSTAQIM

In Islam, The Straight Path, the Right Path. The phrase has been interpreted as indicating the Islamic Faith or that which pleases God.

SIRENS

In Greek mythology, beings represented as birds with the heads of women, who lured voyagers to their death by their sweet songs. In order to hear their singing and survive, Odysseus had himself lashed to the mast while his sailor's ears were stopped with wax. The Sirens were said to be two, later three, in number, and some legends placed them on the west coast of Italy near Naples.

SIRHINDI, Shaykh Ahmad

(1564-1624) Mystic and theologian largely responsible for the reintroduction of orthodox Islam into India and leader of a movement against syncretistic beliefs that prevailed in the Mughal Empire.

SIRICIUS, Saint

(334-399) Pope from 384 to 399. His famous letters - the earliest surviving texts of papal decretals - focus particularly on religious discipline and include baptism, consecration, ordination, penance, and continence. He designated Easter and Pentecost as days of baptism and established that consecrations must be conducted by several bishops rather than by one.

SIRION

In biblical times, the old Sidonian name for Mount Hermon, called Senir by the Amorites. The names "Sirion" and "Senir" appear in the Ugaritic texts found at Ras Shamra in northern Syria, and in the documents from the Turkish village Boghazkevi, thus corroborating the Bible's exactness.

SISERA

In the Old Testament, army chief under Canaanite King Jabin. Sisera, who lived at Harosheth rather than at Jabin's city Hazor, is more prominent in the account than King Jabin. Sometime after Judge Ehud had overthrown Moabite domination, Sisera and Jabin came to oppress Israel for 20 years (Judges 4:1-3; 1 Samuel 12:9).

SISMAI

In Judaism, a descendant of Judah through Jerahmeel and Sheshan; son of Eleasah and father of Shullam (1 Chronicles 2:3-5. Sismai possibly lived during the period of the Judges.

SISTERS OF CHARITY

The title of numerous Roman Catholic congregations of noncloistered women who are engaged in a wide variety of active works, especially teaching and nursing. Many of these congregations follow ma life based upon that of St. Vincent de Paul, but modified for the Daughters of Charity, according to the specific constitutions of the institute.

SISTERS OF MERCY

A Roman Catholic religious congregation founded in Dublin in 1831 by Catherine Elizabeth McAuley. By 1822 she had developed a program for instructing and training poor girls, distributing food and clothing to the needy, and performing other works of mercy.

SISTINE CHAPEL

The most famous of the many chapels of the Vatican Palace in Rome, renowned for its magnificent frescoes by Michelangelo and other artists. The chapel was named after Pope Sixtus VI, who began its construction in 1473. It is used by the Sacred College of Cardinals when it meets to elect a new pope. Michelangelo's paintings of the Creation and other Old Testament scenes crowd the chapel's ceiling, and a vast fresco depicting the Last Judgment adorns the wall behind the altar.

SISYPHUS

In Greek mythology, the cunning king of Corinth who was punished in Hades by repeatedly having to roll a huge stone up a hill only to have it always roll down again as soon as he had brought it to the summit.

Once when Zeus sent Thanatos ("Death") to take Sisyphus, the latter reacted by fettering him in chains so that for a period no one died. When Zeus freed Thanatos, Sisyphus again behaved slyly. He persuaded his wife not to inter him in the traditional way. When he reached Hades, the Lord of the Dead asked him why he was there without a proper funeral. Sisyphus then denounced his wife for disrespect and asked for permission to return to life to bring her to her senses. Thus he lived on to a great old age. But when he at last was truly dead, Hades severely punished him.

SITA

In Hindu mythology, the consort of Rama, and the embodiment of wifely devotion and self-surrender. Her abduction by the demon king Ravana and subsequent rescue are the central incidents in the great Hindu epic the Ramayana.

SITHRI

In Judaism, a Levite living during the Israelite slavery in Egypt; son of Uzziel and cousin of Moses (Exodus 6:18-22).

SITNAH

In biblical times, a well that Isaac's servants dug in the vicinity of Gerar and Rehoboth. It was named Sitnah because of their dispute over it with the shepherds of Gerar. Sitnah's exact location is not known (Genesis 26:19-22).

SIVA DAYAL SAHEB

(1818-1878) Founder of the esoteric Hindu sect Radha Soami Satsang. The sect believes that human capabilities are most fully developed by secret disciplines aimed at uniting the individual soul, the sound made by the worshipper in repeating the name of the lord, and the sound heard internally, which emanates from God. The usual Hindu divinities are not worshipped, but great veneration is accorded a guru, or spiritual leader.

SIXTUS I, Saint

(62-125) Pope from 115 to 125. He ruled the church under the Roman Emperor Hadrian. His martyrdom is unproved.

SIXTUS II, Saint

(178-258) Pope from 257 to 258, who was martyred by the Emperor Valerian. He restored relations with those churches that had been severed by Stephen because of the conflict on rebaptism.

SIXTUS III, Saint

(367-440) Pope from 432 to 440. In 433 he witnessed the restoration of church peace after he helped settle a Christological dispute following the Council of Ephesus (431) between patriarchs St. Cyril of Alexandria and John of Antioch. He sponsored important building projects in Rome, including a reconstruction of the Liberian Basilica.

SIXTUS IV

(1414-1484) Francesco della Rovere; pope from 1471-1484. He built the Sistine Chapel and was the second founder of the Vatican Library. But his nepotism and the heavy taxation caused by his munificence made him highly unpopular.

Neither a crusader nor curial politician, Sixtus aimed at the aggrandizement of his family and of the papal states, subordinating his duties as the church's head in a manner characteristic of his era. His beneficiaries were members of his own family, whom he greatly enriched and who involved him in messy disputes, perhaps the worst of which was a conspiracy against Lorenzo de Medici.

SIXTUS V

(1521-1590) Pope from 1585 to 1590. Enterprising and autocratic, he restored order to the anarchic papal states and made the pope one of the richest princes in Europe. He also reformed the College of Cardinals and the entire administrative system of the papacy, helping to implement the goals of the Counter-Reformation.

SKANDHA

In Buddhism, the five causally conditioned elements of existence forming a being or entity. In the personal sense, the Skandhas are the elements which make up the personality in the sphere of Samsara. The five Skandhas are inherent in every form of life, either in an active or a potential state. In man, all five elements are active:

1 Rupa;
2 Vedana;
3 Sanna;
4 Sankhara;
5 Vinnana.

All are subject to the characteristics of existence, Anicca, Dukkha, Anatta. They form the temporal or phenomenal nature of man, and the belief that this collection constitutes a separate self or ego is the heresy of sakkayaditthi.

SKULL CULT

Veneration of human skulls, usually those of ancestors, by various prehistoric and some modern primitive people. The skulls are cleaned and set up for worship long after death. Prehistoric man also paid special attention to animal skulls, such as that of the cave bear, often placing him under a platform of rocks. This is believed to have served as a type of hunting magic, whereas the human skulls were honored with the reverence accorded to heroic ancestors.

SLAVIC RELIGION

The religious beliefs and practices of the ancient Slavic peoples of eastern Europe. Although the sources of information about the pre-Christian beliefs of the Slavs are all late and by Christian hands, it is known that their pantheon of deities had neither a center nor a hierarchy; each supernatural being was active in its own particular sphere without contact with other deities.

SLOTH

In Roman Catholicism, one of the capital or deadly sins; it is a kind of spiritual laziness or boredom in regard to the things of God, frequently leading to a neglect of one's spiritual duties.

SMET, Pierre-Jean de

(1801-1873) Jesuit missionary whose pioneering efforts to Christianize and pacify Indian tribes west of the Mississippi River made him their beloved "Black robe" and cast him in the role of mediator in the United States' government's attempt to secure their lands for settlement by whites.

SMON-LAM

Most important Tibetan Buddhist celebration of the year, held annually as part of the New Year festivals in Llasa.

SMRTI

That class of Hindu sacred literature based on human memory, as distinct from Vedic literature, which is considered to be revealed.

SMRTYUPASTHANA

In Buddhist philosophy, one of the preparatory stages of meditation practiced by Buddhist monks aiming for enlightenment. It consist of keeping something in mind constantly.

SMYRNA

An ancient city on the west coast of Asia Minor; now called Izmir. Early settled by the Greeks, it was destroyed about 580 BC by Lydian king Alyattes. More than two centuries later. Alexander the Great planned to rebuild it as a Greek city, this being done by his successors on another site. Smyrna thereafter became an important commercial city. Later becoming part of the Roman province of Asia, Smyrna, with its fine public buildings, was noted for its beauty. It has a temple of Tiberus Cesar and therefore promoted emperor worship.

Smyrna was the second of the seven Christian congregations in Asia Minor to which Jesus Christ directed the Apostle John to write a message (Revelation 1:11). Despite their poverty and tribulation, Christians of the congregation in Smyrna are encouraged not to fear the things they will yet suffer, but to be "faithful even to death" in order to receive "the crown of life" (Revelation 2:8-11).

SMITH, Joseph

(1805-1844) Founder of the Mormon Church. Smith was born in Vermont, but when he was 11 moved to Palmyra, NY, where he began to experience visions. The result was the Book of Mormon, published in 1829 and transcribed, he said, from golden plates which came to him through the angel Moroni. The next year he founded the Church of Jesus Christ of Latter-Day Saints at Fayette, New York. Moving west to Kirtland, Ohio, and by 1838 to Missouri, Smith organized his church and attracted many followers. But internal dissensions, disastrous

Mormon business ventures and friction with non-mormons finally prompted Smith to found his own Mormon city of Nauvoo in Illinois. The church flourished and so did Nauvoo, but Smith caused further dissension by promulgating the doctrine of polygamy and announcing his candidacy for the presidency in 1844. That year his enemies had him jailed for conspiracy in Carthage, Ill, where he and his brother were murdered by a mob. Nevertheless Smith's church, led by Brigham Young, became one of the great religions of America.

SOCIAL DOCTRINE OF THE CHURCH

The Roman Catholic Church's teaching is a body of doctrine, on economic and social matters, articulated by the church as it encounters events in the course of history. The church makes moral judgment about these matters when the salvation and rights of the person demand it.

SOCIAL JUSTICE

A part of the cardinal virtue of justice; according to Catholic social teaching, it is that aspect of justice which urges the individual member of a social group to seek the common good of the whole group rather than just his or her own individual good; it presumes, in the explanation of Pope Pius XII, "a social conscience that calls individuals to their social duties, urges them to take into account in all their activities their membership in a community, to be preoccupied with the welfare of their neighbors and with the common good of society." Social justice strives to bring authentic moral values to the organization of society and to the social institutions (educational, economic, political) by which society functions.

SOCINIANS

A religious group that arose in the 16th century and accepted Jesus as God's revelation but considered him merely a man, divine by office rather than by nature and rejected the doctrine of the

Trinity. The movement originated in Italy with the work of Laelius Socinus and his nephew, Faustus Socinus. The church flourished in Poland and Socinian groups survived in Europe until the 19th century.

SOCINUS, Faustus

(1539-1604) Theologian whose anti-Trinitarian teachings, attacked by the Inquisition, led to the founding of the Socinian sect and were influential in the development of Unitarianism. He attained a predominant influence in the Minor (or anti-Trinitarian) church, centered at the colony of Rakow in Poland.

SOCINUS, Laelius

(1525-1562) Theologian whose anti-Trinitarian doctrine was developed into Socinianism by his nephew Faustus Socinus. Central to his teaching was the attainment of eternal life through study of divinely revealed scripture. He saw Christ as a real man, though without sin, who by his sufferings taught men how to bear their own sufferings.

SOCO(H)

In biblical times, name for a Judean city in the Shephelah, seemingly referred to as both Soco and Socoh (Joshua 15:20-35). The Philistines collected their army together at Socoh and then camped at nearby Ephesdammim before Goliath's encounter with David (1 Samuel 17:1). Years later this Soco was apparently among the cities that Rehoboam strengthened (2 Chronicles 11:5-7). Nevertheless, Soco, along with its dependent towns, was captured by the Philistines more than 200 years later, during King Ahaz's rule (2 Chronicles 28:16-18). It seems to be represented by the ruins at Khirbet 'Abbnad, some 16.5 miles south-west of Jerusalem.

The name Socoh is also applied to a place under the administration of one of Solomon's deputies (1 Kings 4:7-10). The suggested identification of it with Tell er-Ras, circa 10.5 miles north-west of Samaria, seems to fit the account, as the proposed sites of both Arubboth and Hepher are nearby.

In the genealogy of Judah, Heber is called "the father of Soco" (1 Chronicles 4:18). Soco could be a personal name of Heber's descendant; or, the text could indicate that Heber was the founder of the city of Soco or its population.

SODEN, Hermann, FREIHERR VON

(1852-1914) Biblical scholar, who established a new theory of textual history of the New Testament. He argued that all extant New Testament texts derived from an original 2nd-century document (which he reconstructed), but were altered by the intrusion of the Diatessaron version by the late-2nd-century Gnostic Christian Taitan.

SODOM AND GOMORRAH

Notoriously sinful cities in the Old Testament book of Genesis. They are now possibly covered by the shallow waters south of Al-Lisan, a peninsula near the southern end of the Dead Sea in Israel. Sodom and Gomorrah constituted, along with the cities of Admah, Zeboiim, and Zoar, the five "cities of the plain" (Genesis 13:12). Both cities were destroyed by brimstone and fire because of their wickedness (Genesis 19:24).

SOFER, Moses

(1762-1839) Famous Halakist (interpreter of Jewish religious law) and a leading Orthodox rabbi who founded a prestigious yeshiva that became a center of vigorous opposition to the newly established movement of Reform Judaism.

SOFERIM

In Judaism, scholars who interpreted and taught biblical law and ethics from circa the 5th century BC to circa 200 BC. Understood in this sense, the first of the soferim was Ezra, even though the word previously designated an important administrator connected with the Temple but without religious status.

SOL

In Roman religion, name of two distinct sun gods at Rome. The original Sol, or Sol Indiges, had a shrine on the Quirinal and an annual sacrifice on August 9. Although the cult appears to be native, the Roman poets equated him with the Greek sun god Helios.

SOLAR DEITIES

Gods that are sovereign, steady, and all-seeing. Inextricably connected with sovereign activities, the sun often is a prime attribute of or identified with the Supreme Deity or the king.

SOLIDARITY

The term refers to the principle of social charity as a direct result of the unity of humankind before God. Solidarity implies that special attention be given to those who are powerless, excluded from a fair share of distributed goods, and who are facing unjust conditions.

SOLOMON

(Ruled circa 965-925 BC) Son and successor of David and traditionally regarded as the greatest king of Israel. He maintained his dominions with military strength and established Israelite colonies to handle military, administrative, and commercial matters. The crowning achievement of his vast building program was the famous Temple at his capital, Jerusalem. Marrying many foreign women, his empire became under influence of other religions, thus preparing the break-up of the monarchy under his son Rehoboam.

At home he introduced taxation and forced labor, which enabled him to finance a massive building program. The magnificence of his court and his foreign alliances, each cemented by marriage, brought many heathen and idolatrous worshipers to the court, creating an atmosphere of toleration which was thought to conflict with ancient Hebrew religious law.

SOLOMON, Psalms of

A pseudepigraphical work resembling in style and content authentic biblical literature, but noncanonically comprising 18 psalms that were originally written in Hebrew, although only Greek and Syriac translations survive. Like its canonical counterpart, the Psalms of Solomon contains hymns, poems of admonition and instruction, and signs of thanksgiving and lamentation. Many of the psalms were probably written between 63-30 BC. The compositions reflect the anguish felt by Jews on the fall of Jerusalem and satisfaction at the ousting of the Hasmonean rulers.

SOLOMON, Wisdom of

An outstanding example of the "wisdom" genre of religious literature, which commends a life of introspection and reflection on human existence, especially from an ethical perspective. It is an apocryphal work (noncanonical for Jews and Protestants) but is included in the Septuagint (Greek translation of the Old Testament). The original text was most probably written in Greek, fragments of which were discovered in the Essence library, at Qumran.

SONG OF SOLOMON

A book of the Old Testament, sometimes known as the Song of Songs. At one time thought to be the work of Solomon, it is now considered to have been written at a later date.

SONG OF SONGS

This Old Testament book is a collection of love poems. The book is commonly interpreted as describing the love of God for His people. The poetic drama, involving three characters - a girl, a shepherd lover and King Solomon - has been interpreted by some Christians as an allegory of Christ's love for the church. Written in a gracefully repetitive style, it contains elaborate and erotic imagery.

SON OF MAN

A term variously used in the Old and New Testaments and in intertestamental literature to designate:

1 a human being, such as in the Old Testament Book of Ezekiel;
2 an apocalyptic-eschatological figure, such as in the First Book of Enoch;
3 a title conferred on and used by Jesus of Nazareth as the messianic (salvatory) initiator of the eschatological Kingdom of God, such as in the gospels of Matthew, Mark, Luke, and John.

SONO MAMA

In Buddhism, colloquial meaning "just as it is." As a Zen term it is used in the sense of the suchness or isness of all things which ever is before "things" are born.

SOPATER

In biblical times, a Beroean Christian associated with Paul in Greece at the time of Paul's third missionary journey. Sopater was a son of Pyrrhus and may be the same person as Sosipater in Rome to whom Paul sent greetings (Acts 20:2-6; Romans 16:21).

SOPHERETH

In the Old Testament, apparently name for an ancestor of a family ("the sons of Sophereth") among the "sons of the servants of Solomon" who returned from the Babylonian exile (Ezra 2:55; Nehemiah 7:57). Some scholars suggest that the sons of Sophereth were a staff of scribes or copyists, as is suggested by the meaning of the name. The meanings of some of the other names in the list might allow for reference to an occupation, while others do not.

SOPHIA

In Gnosticism, the female emanation of the pleroma, the fullness of the godhead, responsible for the coming into being of the Demiurge, the creator of the material world.

SOPHRINIUS

(560-638) Patriarch of Jerusalem, monk, and theologian who was the chief protagonist for Orthodox teaching in the doctrinal controversy on the essential nature of Christ and his volitional acts

SORCERY

A kind of magic that invokes evil spirits in order to attain some end. Such occult intervention is against the first Commandment.

SOREK, Torrent valley of

In biblical times, name for a location of the home of Deliah, where Samson was seduced to reveal the secret of his strength, leading to his capture, blinding and imprisonment by the Philistines (Judges 16:4-21). The name Sorek seems to be preserved in that of Khirbet Suriq, about 16 miles west of Jerusalem, situated on the northern side of the Wadi es-Sarar and opposite the proposed location of Beth-shemesh.

SOSIPATER

In biblical times, name for a companion of Paul when in Corinth, whom the apostle described as "my relative," and whose greetings are sent from Corinth in Paul's letter to the Romans (Romans 16:21). He is possibly the same person as Sopater, mentioned at Acts 20:4 as associated with Paul in Greece.

SOSTHENES

In biblical times, the presiding officer of the Corinthian synagogue during Paul's visit to Corinth; possibly the successor of Crispus, who became a Christian. When Proconsul Gallio declined to hear the Jews' charges against Paul's religious teaching, the crowd took Sosthenes and beat him. (Acts 18:8, 12-17).

SOTAPANNA

In Buddhism, phrase meaning "He who entered the stream." It is the first of the Four Paths to liberation.

SOTER, Saint

(82-175) Pope from 166 to 175. He continued Pope Anicetus' attack against Montanism, a heresy overemphasizing prophecy and rigid moral norms.

SOTERIA

In Hellenistic religions, any sacrifice or series of sacrifices performed either in commemoration or in expectation of deliverance from a crisis. Sixteen Soteria festivals are known; the most famous was that at Delphi, which celebrated the defeat of the Celts in 279-278 BC.

SOTERIOLOGY

That aspect of religion which is concerned with salvation. It is especially important in Buddhism and Christianity.

SOTO

Largest of Zen Buddhist sects in Japan. It follows the method of quiet sitting and meditation, as a means of obtaining enlightenment. It was founded in China in the 9th century and transmitted to Japan by Dogen, in 1244.

SOUL

In common usage, an immaterial principle or aspect that, with the body, constitutes the human person.

In Christianity, the soul is regarded as the spiritual or immaterial part of a human being, often regarded as immortal. It is a term usually avoided by e.g. Buddhists. Buddhism does not admit an immortal, unchanging entity created by a Deity, the destiny of which may be eternal happiness or eternal misery according to the deeds of the personality it ensouls. The soul is then in this respect, the character created by experience in the phenomenal worlds, becoming more and more enlightened by following the Path, or more degraded by departing from it.

In Roman Catholicism, the soul is being defined as that part of the human person that animates the body; the principal of spiritual activities such as thinking and willing; according to Catholic teaching, the human soul is individually created for each person by God and infused at the time of conception and is immortal.

SOUL, Biblical

Soul in the Bible should be regarded as the principle of life. Thus, in traditional Catholic philosophy, the human soul is the principle of human life. In Hebrew the word nephesh is often translated "soul."

But such phrases as "Save my soul, O Lord" could as easily be translated: "Save my life ... ", or possibly, "Save my neck" or even "Save me." The Hebrew intuition of man was that of a unity, an indivisible being, not as having a body, but as being a living body; not as having a soul, but as being a living soul.

In the classic text in Genesis 2:7, God breathed on the clay he had fashioned, and man became "a living soul" (nephesh), meaning "a living being." To speak of the body means itself as bodily and physically present to others; to speak of the soul means self as the subject of appetite or emotion.

To speak of the heart, means this same self as the subject of thought, decision, and volition. To speak of the spirit, means the same self again as graced with life, vitality, and energy.

There is a dichotomy that can emerge between spirit and flesh. The first refers to man when God turns to him, smiles on him, and imparts life to him; the second means man in his fragility and confusion, left to die when God turns his face away and withdraws the gift of life.

The Greek versions continue this dichotomy of soul (psyche) and body (soma), in which the former is by nature immortal. This is a departure from the Greek New Testament, which is faithful to Jewish apocalyptic tradition: that if man overcomes death, it is because God wills it, not because of an immortal soul that of its nature necessarily survives death. In the New Testament as in Jewish apocalyptic, one hopes for the resurrection of the just as the gracious act of God.

SOUL, Human

An important anthropological term referring to the inner, vital, or spiritual principle in man. This term has a complex history and a great variety of meanings.

Nonphilosophical thought and intuition in all cultures and civilizations point to some mysterious reality in man that is relatively independent of his body or that is an intrinsic force or principle of movement and life, including perception, volition, and intellection.

In philosophy and religion the views on human soul have a wide range.

1 Materialism reduces it to the manifestations or epiphenomena of living matter and denies any possibility of an immaterial, spiritual, or immortal principle or substance in man.

2 An extreme dichotomy in different views holds a spiritual and immaterial principle or soul (spirit) in man that is imprisoned in the human body (matter) for its sins and that can be redeemed from it either by some purification or expiration (Orphism, Neoplatonism, Manichaeism) or by loss of its individuality (usually after many transmigrations or metempsychoses) and merger with an Absolute (Brahmanism, primitive Buddhism).

3 The Thomistic view mediates between the two extremes and is most commonly accepted. According to this hylomorphic presentation man is one being substantially composed of two metaphysical parts: body and rational soul (matter and form), which is man's one substantial form and which performs all vegetative, sensitive, and intellective functions.

It as a whole informs the whole body and each part of it. It is essentially and quantitatively simple and completely immaterial, i.e., a subsistent and spiritual form that is naturally incorporeal, incorruptible, indivisible, and immortal. It does not have existence before the body, but is created with it and for it by God.

In theology, there is no unanimous Christian teaching on the human soul. The solemn magisterium teaches that the Trinitarian God created man "constituted, as it were, alike of the spirit and then body"; "that man has one rational and intellectual soul".

Recent development of biblical anthropology initiated a return from an excessive Hellenic dichotomy to the primitive Christian view concerning the unity of man (which has priority before his parts and dimensions) in his origin (creationism), life, and final destiny (resurrection).

SOUL-BODY RELATIONSHIP

The Old Testament ascribes equal importance to "flesh" (Hebrew basar) and "spirit" or "breath" (Hebrew: nefes, ruah). God did not create body and spirit but a human (Genesis 2:7; Psalms 63:1). Such a view supported the concept of bodily resurrection that later emerged (Daniel 12; 2 Maccabees 7).

Only when Platonic thought influenced later Judaism was the body seen as a limiting vehicle from which the soul yearned to be freed through contemplation (Wisdom 9:15; Ecclesiastes 12:7).

The New Testament books teach that to be human is to be embodied by their emphasis upon the incarnation and bodily resurrection of Christ, in which believers share as members of Christ's body (John 1:14; 1 Corinthians 6:14-15). At the same time the body is contrasted with the soul as the mortal with the immortal (Matthew 10:28).

Paul (1 Thessalonians 5:25), and such apostolic fathers as Justin Martyr, distinguished spirit (pneuma), soul (psyche), and body (soma). The body is not evil in itself; it can be the medium of the sin of an individual. Only when the psychic flesh (sarx) becomes spiritual does the body become incorruptible (Romans 6-8; Galatians 5).

During the medieval period the Aristotelian doctrine of holymorphism prevailed; every physical being is constituted of matter and form; the soul is the substantial form of the human body. Adapting such philosophical insights Thomas Aquinas reiterated the substantial unity of the human being.

The union is such that it is contrary to the nature of the soul to be without the body.

Matter is a condition of possibility for the human spirit, which cannot know and love without the body. Whatever is in the intellect was in the senses. Love or fellowship cannot be actualized without the mediation of language, signs, and gestures.

A certain tension between the bodily and spiritual dimensions must be respected. One achieves personhood not by appetitive spontaneity but by an active self-transcendence interior to finite beings. One becomes a person by rising above natural necessities and inertia, by consciously opting for the openness that leads beyond the finite self. Although the body can be identified with concupiscence, understood either as a natural drive to possess or as an inertia preventing the achieving of spiritual self-transcendence, it is also the only means by which the soul or spiritual dimension can fulfil or concretely realize the human potential.

SOUL LOSS

The departure of the soul from the body and its failure to return, which in many preliterate cultures, is believed to be the cause of illness. Though the soul may wander inadvertently when its owner's guard is relaxed - e.g., in sleep or when sneezing or yawning - the most common cause of soul loss is its enticement and capture by an enemy through witchcraft.

SOUL OF THE CHURCH

A phrase used in several senses.

1 Primarily it refers to the Holy Spirit. In keeping with the theme that the church is the mystical body of Christ, the Holy Spirit, who is the Spirit of Christ, is described in this image as vivifying and sanctifying the members of Christ's body. The expression in modern times was taken up by Leo XIII in Divinum illud munus (1897), developed at length by Pius XIII in Mystici corporis (1943), and incorporated into the ecclesiology of Vatican Council II.

2 Some theologians have distinguished the uncreated soul, the Holy Spirit, from the created soul of the church, charity. Charity is received from Christ and is the source of conformity with Christ, i.e., it is derived from the sacraments of Christ and is directed toward the fullness of ecclesial unity.

3 After Vatican Council II some theologians spoke of those who lived in grace and charity but outside visible membership in the church as belonging to the soul of the church.

SOUTHCOTT, Joanna

(1750-1814) Religious enthusiast reared in the Anglican and Methodist biblical tradition of the of the east Devonshire village of Gittisham. She attracted a following because of allegedly transcribing divinely inspired messages relating to the imminent Second Coming of Christ as given in the New Testament book of Revelation.

SOUTHERN BAPTIST CONVENTION

The largest Baptist group in the United States organized at Augusta (Georgia), in 1845 by Southern Baptists who disagreed with the antislavery attitudes and activities of Northern Baptists.

SOUTHERN CHRISTIAN LEADERSHIP CONFERENCE

Civil rights organization founded by Martin Luther King Jr. and others in 1957. King led the conference until he was assassinated in 1968, when its presidency was taken by the Rev. Ralph D. Abernathy. Originally meant to coordinate Southern civil rights crusades, the organization broadened its base in the 1960s to include such projects as the Memphis sanitary workers' strike, the Poor Peoples's March on Washington and Operation Breadbasket in Chicago.

SPENCER, Philipp Jakob

(1635-1705) Theologian, and a leading figure in German Pietism, a movement among 17th and 18th century

Lutherans that stressed personal improvement and upright conduct as the most important manifestations of Christian faith.

SPINOZA, Benedict de
(1632-1677) Independent Rationalist philosopher and religious thinker, who formulated one of the most consummate metaphysical systems in Western philosophy. He was accused of atheism throughout the 18th century, despite the deep religious feeling in his writings.

SPIRIT
In various religions, a supernatural power or unseen deity thought to have control over the destinies of man and generally believed to be susceptible to the influences of shamans or priests.

SPIRITISM
Also called spiritualism, it is the belief that the living can communicate with spirits and with the deceased by way of a human medium or inanimate objects, such as a Ouija board. In Roman Catholicism, practices derived therefrom are a violation of the first Commandment of the Decalogue and opposed to the virtue of religion.

SPIRITS, discernment of
In Christianity, the process of determining whether a person is truly acting under the influence of divine grace (the good spirit) or, on the contrary, has knowingly or unknowingly been led astray by the devil (the bad spirit).

SPIRITUAL ASSEMBLIES
In the Baha'i faith, administrative units on the local, national, and world levels that conduct an extensive work of missions, publications, education, and general philanthropy.

SPIRITUALIST GROUPS
Religious organizations, generally small and of short duration, that make communication with those who have died, or "passed into the higher life," the center of their beliefs.

SPIRITUAL LIFE
A term used by Christians to refer to the interior life of sanctifying grace, by which one shares in the life of the triune God (see John 14:23) and becomes a temple of the Holy Spirit, and to describe the efforts of the individual Christians to cultivate that life by participating in the sacraments, prayer, works of penance, and charity.

SPIRITUALS
An extreme group within the Franciscans, a mendicant religious order founded by St. Francis of Assisi in 1209, that espoused the austerity and poverty prescribed in the original rule of St. Francis.

SPIRITUAL WORKS OF MERCY
They are to counsel the doubtful, instruct the ignorant, admonish sinners, comfort the afflicted, forgive offenses, bear wrongs patiently, and pray for the living and the dead.

SPURGEON, Charles Haddon
(1834-1892) Fundamentalist Baptist minister and celebrated preacher, whose sermons were widely translated. He founded a ministerial college and an orphanage. An ardent Fundamentalist, he distrusted the scientific approach of modern biblical criticism.

SRAOSHA
In Zoroastrianism, divine being, messenger of Ahura Mazda; embodiment of the divine word. Depicted as a strong and holy youth whose heavenly abode is a thousand-pillared house, he has, in addition, a protective role.

SRAUTA-SUTRAS
Hindu ritual manuals for the use of the priests engaged in the performance of the grander Vedic sacrifices, those requiring three fires and the services of a number of specialized priests.

SRAVAKA
In Buddhist, literally a hearer, hence a pupil or beginner. When he undertakes

the practice he becomes a Sramanera, or Samanera.

SRI-NATHAJI

A unique representation of the Hindu god Krishna, the main cult image of the Vallabhacaryas, an important devotional sect of India. The image is enshrined in the main temple of the cult at Nathdwara, where it is accorded an elaborate service of worship daily.

SRIVAISNAVAS

A prominent sect of Hindus most numerous in South India who pay allegiance to Lord Vishnu and follow the teachings of Ramanuja. Ramanuja is a qualified monism that maintains that the ultimate reality is a personal god whom the individual soul can unite in loving devotion.

SRUTI

The most reverend body of sacred literature in Hinduism. Sruti works are considered divine revelation, heard and transmitted by earthly sages, as contrasted to Smrti, or that which is remembered.

STACHYS

In biblical times, one in the Christian congregation at Rome in circa 56 whom Paul speaks of as "my beloved," and to whom he sends his greetings (Romans 16:9).

STANISLAW, Saint

(1030-1079) The patron saint of Poland, who became bishop of Cracow in 1072. He denounced and finally excommunicated King Boleslaw II and was slain by the revengeful monarch. St. Stanislaw was canonized in 1253 and his feast day is May 7th.

STARETS

In Eastern Orthodoxy, a monastic spiritual leader. In Eastern Christian monasticism, which understood itself as a way of life that aimed at a real experience of the future kingdom of God, the starets was one who had already achieved this experience. Thus he

became the charismatic spiritual guide who could aid others in attaining spiritual progress and success.

STAR OF BETHLEHEM

Celestial phenomenon mentioned in Matthew as leading "wise men from the East" to the birthplace of Jesus Christ. Whether the reference is legendary is not known. Some Christians have held the star to be miraculous.

STATE SHINTO

The prewar suprareligious nationalist cult of Japan, which focussed on ceremonies of the Imperial household and public Shinto shrines. State Shinto was abolished in 1945.

STATIONAL CHURCHES

Churches in the city of Rome where the early popes would celebrate the liturgy on at least one special day. Examples of stational churches include St. Mary Major at Midnight Mass on Christmas and St. John Lateran for Easter.

STATIONS OF THE CROSS

A series of 14 crosses, usually accompanied by pictures or images portraying final events in the Passion of Christ. The stations are usually ranged around the inside walls of a church or chapel. The devotion stems from the early Jerusalem Christian practice of visiting the scenes of Christ's Passion. The origin of the devotion in its present form, however, is not clear.

The stations are wooden crosses, often inserted in paintings or sculptures, and may be attached to the walls of a church or oratory or erected outdoors. The stations must be lawfully erected and blessed by one who has the authority to do so.

STEPHANAS

In biblical times, name of one of the mature members of the congregation at Corinth, the capital of the Roman province of Achaeia in southern Greece. Paul personally baptized Stephanas' household as the "first fruits" of his ministry in that province (1 Corinthians 1:16; 16:15). Some five years later, circa 55, Stephanas, together with two other brothers from Corinth, visited Paul in Ephesus, and it may have been through them that Paul learned of the distressing conditions about which he wrote in his first canonical letter to the Corinthians (1 Corinthians 1:11; 5:1; 11:18). Also, it may have been by their hands that this letter was delivered to Corinth (1 Corinthians 16:17).

STEPHEN

In biblical times, the first Christian martyr. Though his name is Greek, he was one of the faithful Jewish remnant that accepted and followed the Messiah (Acts 7:2).

Stephen's name first appears in the biblical record in connection with the appointment of men to special service responsibilities in the Christian congregation at Jerusalem (Acts 6:1-4). Stephen received an appointment to a ministry in a special way. He may have already been an "older man" or "overseer," along with the six others appointed over "this necessary business," the distribution of food supplies. These men were "full of spirit and wisdom," which this particular emergency required, for it was, not only the mechanical distribution of food supplies, but also a matter of administration.

While taking care of these appointed ministerial duties, Stephen vigorously continued his Christian preaching. Stephen boldly recounted God's dealings with the Jews from the time of their forefather Abraham, and concluded with powerful accusations against his own audience of religious leaders. As they were cut to the heart by the accusations and began to gnash their teeth at him, Stephen was favored by God with a vision of God's glory and of Jesus standing at God's right hand. At this description of the vision, the assembly shouted and rushed upon him with one accord and threw him outside the city. Then, laying their garments at the feet of Saul, they stoned Stephen to death. Certain reverent men came and gave him a burial and lamented his death. Great persecution broke out then against the Christians, scattering them, though the Apostles remained in Jerusalem (Acts 6:8-8:2).

STEPHEN I

(192-257) Pope from 254 to 257. He threatened to excommunicate bishops in Africa (including Cyprian) and in Asia Minor unless they discontinued the practice of rebaptizing heretics. During that time, the Roman Emperor Valerian began his persecution of the Christians, during which Stephen died.

STEPHEN II

(689-752) Pope during 752. He was elected on March 23, 752, to succeed Pope St. Zachary but died of apoplexy a few days later. Because he had not been consecrated he is not listed in the catalog of the popes.

STEPHEN III

(690-757) Pope from 752 to 757, first sovereign of the newly founded papal states. The central act of his pontificate was to free the papacy from Byzantium and to ally it with the Franks against the Lombards.

STEPHEN IV

(720-772) Pope from 768 to 772. He approbated the worship of icons for the Western church and extended the rights of cardinal bishops for the Western church.

STEPHEN V

(741-817) Pope from 816 to 817. Immediately after his consecration he ordered the Romans to swear fidelity to the Carolingian Emperor Louis I the Pious, whom he informed about his election.

STEPHEN VI

(816-891) Pope from 885 to 891, whose pontificate witnessed the disintegration of the Carolingian Empire and intermittent struggles for the

Italian crown. To alleviate a famine, he used his father's wealth, for the papal treasury was depleted.

STEPHEN VII

(815-897) Pope from 896 to 897, whose reign plunged the papacy to the nadir of its existence in the Middle Ages and possibly throughout its entire history.

STEPHEN VIII

(857-931) Pope from 929 to 931. Except for some grants he made to Italian and French monasteries, the history of his pontificate is practically unknown.

STEPHEN IX

(867-942) Pope from 939 to 942. His political efforts were directed toward supporting the last Carolingian, King Louis IV. He formally recognized Louis, threatening to excommunicate those who rebelled against him. He also supported the important Cluniac reform of monasticism in Europe.

STEPHEN X

(999-1058) Frederick of Lorraine; pope from 1057 to 1058. During his brief pontificate the general church reform begun by Leo gained impetus. He convoked a Roman synod to denounce simony, zealously enforced clerical celibacy, and centralized the reform.

STERILITY

The inability to generate children because of some physical defect. In Roman Catholicism, according to the Code of Canon Law, "Sterility neither prohibits nor invalidates marriage."

STEWARDSHIP

The religious conviction that every gift of nature and grace comes from God and that the human person is not absolute master of his or her gifts and possessions but, the trustee (steward) of them (see 1 Peter 4:10); they are given "in trust" for the building of the kingdom.

STIGMATA

In the religious sense, the reproduction on a living person's body of wounds or scars corresponding to those of the crucified Christ - i.e., on the hands and feet, near the heart, and sometimes on the head or shoulders and back. Although cases of Protestants and non-Christians are known, most stigmatics are Roman Catholic mystics, and of these the majority are women. Stigmata have been explained as psychophysical repercussions of ecstatic trance.

STIPEND, Mass

An offering made to a priest on the occasion of requesting a Mass to be offered for one's personal intentions; according to the Code of Canon Law: "In accord with the approved usage of the church, it is lawful for any priest who celebrates or consecrates Mass to receive an offering to apply the Mass according to a definite intention" (Canon 945), but at the same time priests are urged to "celebrate Mass for the intention of the Christian faithful, especially of the needy, even if no offering has been received" (Canon 945).

The faithful who make such an offering "contribute to the good of the church and by their offering take part in the concern of the church for the support of its ministers and works" (Canon 946). The Code of Canon Law also insists that "any appearance of trafficking or commerce is to be entirely excluded from Mass offerings" (Canon 947) and has strict regulations governing this entire matter.

STOICISM

The school of philosophy, so-called because its founder, Zeno of Citium, taught in a painted stoa, or covered colonnade, in the central square in Athens circa 300 BC. The stoics maintained that logos, the essence of all matter, animate or inanimate, is found in its purest form in rational intelligence. All events in nature are accessible to reason, and all men are bound together by their possession of reason.

Martyrdom of St. Stephen.
"And he kneeled down, and cried with a loud voice, Lord, lay not this sin to their charge.
And when he had said this, he fell asleep" (Acts 7:60).
Lithograph by Gustave Doré (about 1860).

STEPHEN

The wise man lives rationally and virtuously, submitting to the dictates of fortune with patient endurance. In this way he rises above the effects of misfortune and chance, ultimately achieving spiritual freedom.

The modern Puritanical tradition, and preoccupation with the problems of fate and free will, are in part derived from Stoicism.

STOLE

An ecclesiastical vestment worn by Roman Catholic deacons, priests, and bishops and by some Anglican, Lutheran, and other Protestant clergy. It is a band of silk 2 to 4 inches wide and circa 8 feet long. In the Roman Catholic Church it is a symbol of immortality. It is generally considered the unique badge of the ordained ministry and is conferred at ordination.

STORAGE CITIES

In biblical times, cities especially designed as government storage centers. Reserves of provisions such as grain, as well as other things, were preserved in warehouses and granaries built at these locations.

Under Egyptian oppression, the Israelites were compelled to build "cities as storage places for Pharaoh, namely, Pithom and Raamses" (Exodus 1:11). Storage cities were also built by Solomon (1 Kings 9:17-19; 2 Chronicles 8:4-6). Later, as King Jehoshaphat prospered, "he went on building fortified places and storage cities in Judah" (2 Chronicles 17:11; 1 Chronicles 27:25).

STRACHAN, John

(1778-1867) Educator and clergyman who, as the first Anglican bishop of Toronto, was responsible for organizing the church in Canada as a self-governing denomination within the Anglican community.

STRAIGHT

In biblical times, a street in Damascus, Syria (Acts 9:10-11). During the Roman period, it was a major thoroughfare approximately one mile long and circa 100 feet wide. Then divided by colonnades into three sections, its center lane was used by pedestrians and the two outside lanes were for mounted and vehicular traffic moving in opposite directions.

In a vision, Jesus directed the disciple Ananias to the home of Saul on "the street called straight" to restore Saul's sight (Acts 9:3-12, 17-19).

STREETER, Burnett Hillman

(1874-1937) English theologian and biblical scholar, best remembered for his original contributions to knowledge of biblical origins.

STUPA

A Buddhist commemorative monument usually housing sacred relics associated with the Buddha or other saintly persons; an architectural symbol of the Buddha's parinirvana, or death.

STYX

In Greek mythology, a river which the souls of the dead had to cross to reach Hades. The Styx was sacred even to the gods, and oaths sworn on its waters were inviolable. It was often personified as a nymph, a daughter or Oceanus and Tethys.

SUA

In biblical times, the first-named son of Zophah, of the tribe of Asher. He was one of the paternal heads among some 26,000 select, valiant and mighty men of Israel's army (1 Chronicles 7:30-40).

SUBHADDA

Disciple of Gautama Buddha, the 6th-5th century BC founder of Buddhism.

SUBHAH

A string of Muslim prayer beads whose 100 units represent the names of God.

SUBSIDIARITY

An article of Catholic social teaching first proclaimed by Pope Pius IX in 1931. This principle cuts two ways.

First, that a larger institution should not interfere with a smaller institution. Second, larger institutions have an obligation to support smaller institutions in positive ways.

SUBSTANCE

A philosophical term that designates the pure existence of a thing considered separately from the accidents, or outward appearances. The Roman Catholic Church uses the term substance to designate the divine Being in its unity and to describe the transubstantiation of the bread and wine into the body and blood of Christ.

SUCATHITES

In the Old Testament, name for a Kenite family of scribes who lived at Jabez (1 Chronicles 2:55).

SUCELLUS

A powerful and widely worshipped pagan Celtic god; his iconographic symbols were usually his mallet and libation saucer, indicative of the powers of protection and provision.

SUCCOTH

In biblical times, name of a place where, after his meeting with Esau, Jacob built himself a house and made covered stalls for his herd; hence the name Succoth (meaning covered stalls) (Genesis 33:16-17). The statement that his next stopping place, Shechem, was "in the land of Canaan" implies that Succoth was not in Canaan proper.

Other references also indicate a location east of the Jordan River, since they likely refer to the same place. Thus, Succoth is named as one of the cities in the inheritance of the tribe of Gad east of the Jordan (Joshua 13:24-27). Gideon, pursuing remnants of Midianite forces, crossed the Jordan and came to Succoth, where the city princes refused his request for food for his troops, as did the men at nearby Penual. On his return trip, Gideon obtained the names of 77 princes and elders of Succoth and punished them for their failure to support his God-directed military action (Judges 8:4-16). When the Temple was built by Solomon, the copper items were cast in the District of the Jordan, between Succoth and Zarethan (1 Kings 7:46).

SUCCOTH-BENOTH

A deity worshipped by the Babylonians whom the king of Assyria brought into the cities of Samaria after his taking the Israelites of the ten-tribe kingdom into exile (2 Kings 17:30).

SUDRA

Sacred shirt used in Zoroastrianism and Parsi initiation rite.

SUDRA

The fourth and lowest of the traditional varnas, or social classes, of Hindu India, traditionally artisans and laborers.

SUFFERING

Emotional, physical, spiritual, or mental pain. Seen by the Roman Catholic Church as a consequence of original sin.

SUFI

Islamic mystic. The term should not be used, or appropriated, by those mystics who are not Muslims or who do not root their mysticism in the Koran.

SUFISM

Muslim mystic movement which began in the late 10th and early 11th centuries, in Syria, Mesopotamia and Persia. Sufism stresses personal communication with God. Its greatest exponent was the philosopher Al-Gazel.

SUICIDE

According to Buddhist doctrine a man cannot avoid suffering by taking his life, nor does he escape from the "Wheel of Life" by so doing. The destruction of the physical body merely transfers the entity to other spheres of existence, and rebirth into the physical follows. Physical life is considered of great importance, as it is only here that the Way of Liberation can be followed, and enlightenment attained. Taking one's life is, therefore, waste of opportunity. Voluntary sacrifice of one's life for the welfare of others is considered meritorious, the motive being altruistic.

SUIKA SHINTO

An academic school of the Shinto religion of Japan, founded by Yamazaki Ansai (1618-1682), who was a scholar of the Chu Hsi school of Neo-Confucianism. Suika Shinto teaches the unity of man and God, an attitude of careful observance of rules and precepts, as the highest of the scriptures.

SUKKIM

In ancient times, a component force of the army of Egyptian King Shishak, who invaded Judah during Rehoboam's reign (2 Chronicles 12:2-3). Some scholars believe the Sukkim are referred to on certain ancient Egyptian texts and that they were of Libyan origin.

SUKKOT & SIMHAT TORAH

Jewish Feast of Tabernacles and Rejoicing in the Law (Exodus 34:22; Numbers 28:26; Leviticus 23:34; Deuteronomy 16:9-10 and 13), celebrated in the month of Tishri. The Festival of Sukkot has both religious and cultural significance. Most Jews, religious or not, live for seven days in home-made sukkot (shelters), to remind them of the Israelites living in the wilderness after the exodus. The sukkot can be erected on the balconies of apartments and houses, in gardens and even in hotels and restaurants. The major requirement is that the roof is made only of leafy branches to enable the sky to be seen. The agricultural significance is symbolized by the "four-species" used - the palm branch, the myrtle, the wilklor and the citron. Special blessings are recited during the holiday.

The eighth day of the Feast of Tabernacles is Simhat Torah, Rejoicing in the Law. The cycle of reading the Torah in the synagogues has just been completed and another is immediately begun, after the scrolls have been carried around the congregation in seven encirclements accompanied by singing and dancing.

SULAYMAN

Arabic word for Solomon. he is a prophet and king, epitome of wisdom and arcane knowledge, frequently mentioned in the Koran. Here is he portrayed as knowing the language of the birds and insects, and dealing with the Queen Bilqis. Reference is also made to his death in Surat Saba and this is elaborated in tradition; the jinn continue to build the Temple after he dies, and only realize he is dead when the staff on which his dead body leans is eaten through by a worm, and King Solomon's body falls over.

SUMMANUS

In Roman religion, an obscure god whose name ("Highest") suggests that he began as an epithet of Jupiter. Later he developed into a Jupiter of the night, having jurisdiction over the nocturnal sky and thunderbolt.

SUN DANCE

The most spectacular and important religious ceremony of the Plains Indians of 19th century North America. Ordinarily held by each tribe once a year in early summer, it was an occasion when all could gather with guests from other tribes and reaffirm their basic beliefs about the universe and the supernatural through words, ceremonies, and symbolic objects.

SUNDAY SCHOOL

A school for religious education, usually for children and young people and usually a part of a church or parish. The movement has been important primarily in Protestantism.

SUNNA

In Islam, term to designate trodden path. It developed from meaning "customary practice" to indicating the specific actions and sayings of the Prophet Mohammed himself.

SUNYATA

In Buddhism, important term in the sense of non-substantiality. This is the concept that everything has neither substance nor permanence and is one of the fundamental points in Buddhism. Since everything is dependent upon causation, there can be no permanent ego as a substance. But, one should neither adhere to the concept that everything has substance, not that it does not. Every being, human or non-human, is in relativity. Therefore, it is foolish to hold to a certain idea or concept or ideology as the only absolute. This is the fundamental undercurrent in the Prajna scriptures of Mahayana Buddhism.

SUPEREROGATION

Actions which develop one's spiritual life but which exceed the demands of morality.

SUPERSTITION

Either the worship of God in an unworthy manner (for example, by bizarre cultic practices) or attributing to persons or objects a power which belongs to God alone (for example, astrology, spiritism). Superstition is regarded by many religious authorities as a violation of true religion.

SUPH

In biblical times, name for one of the locations mentioned to indicate where Moses spoke to the Israelites in the 40th year of their wilderness wandering (Deuteronomy 1:1). Though its exact site is unknown, Suph apparently was a place east of the Jordan. It is sometimes identified with Khirbet Sufa, circa four miles south-south-east of Madaba.

SUPHAH

In biblical times, name for a region of valley, probably in the vicinity of the Arnon River (Numbers 21:14).

SURA(H)

Chapter of the Koran. Each chapter is divided into a number of verses and the chapters are characterized as either Meccan or Medinan according to their place of revelation. The Koran is arranged so that, after the Fatiha, the longest chapters appear first.

SUSANNA

In biblical times, name for one of the many faithful women, who, out of their own belongings, cared for the needs of Jesus and his 12e apostles during Jesus, Galilean ministry of 31 (Luke 8:1-3).

SUSI

In Judaism, father of Gaddi, who represented the tribe of Manasseh in spying out the Promised Land (Numbers 13:2, 11).

SUTRA

See: Sutta

SUTTA (SUTRA)

In Buddhism, literally a thread on which jewels are strung. It is a term applied to that part of the canon containing the dialogues or discourses of the Buddha. In the Mahayana School no serious claim is made that its Sutras are the words of the Buddha, and the authors are unknown. All save one, however, are put into the mouth of the Buddha, the exception being the Platform Sutra of Hui-neng.
With the addition of explanatory texts, Sutras play an important role in the Hindu, Buddhist and Jain religions.

SVABHAVA

In Buddhism term applied cosmically in the sense of "own-nature", basic substance of the universal Mulaprakriti or root essence, thus equating with Tathata.

SYCHAR

In biblical times, name for a city in Samaria and the site of Jacob's fountain. It was "near the field that Jacob gave to Joseph his son" in the vicinity of Shechem (John 4:5-6).

SYENE

In the Old Testament, name for a city apparently situated at the southern extremity of ancient Egypt (Ezekiel 29:10). As may be inferred from the possible meaning of Syene, the city may have served as a "market" or "trading post." It is identified with Aswan, situated on the east bank of the Nile opposite Elephantine and some 430 miles south of Cairo.

SYLVESTER I, Saint

(260-335) Pope from 314 to 335. Under him the Council of Nicaea (325) defined the articles of the Christian faith. He is said to have cured Constantine the Great of leprosy and baptized him.

SYLVESTER II

(940-1003) Pope from 999 to 1003. He was the first Frenchman to be elected Pope and was scientifically inclined, credited with the introduction of clocks and Arabic numerals.

SYLVESTER III

(978-1046) Pope during 1045. He was elected pope in January 1045 by a Roman faction that had driven Pope Benedict IX out of Rome. When Benedict returned the following April, he expelled Sylvester and his supporters.

SYLVESTER IV

(1046-1111) Antipope from 1105 to 1111. He was elected as successor to the antipope Albert. He was never widely supported.

SYMBOLON

A Greek word designating half of a broken object. When the broken parts were placed together, they verified the bearer's identity. Thus a symbol of faith as a sign of recognition and communion. This same Greek word means a "collection" or "Summary". Thus a gathering of the principal truth of the faith, as in a creed, is a symbol of faith.

SYMEON

In biblical times, name for an ancestor of Jesus' mother Mary (Luke 3:30). The name is also found to belong to one of the prophets and teachers of the Antioch, Syria, congregation who laid their hands on Barnabas and Paul after the holy spirit had designated these two for missionary work (Acts 13:1-3).

SYNAGOGUE

(Greek: house of assembly), Jewish place of worship. The synagogue became the center of communal and religious life after destruction of the Temple in Jerusalem (AD 70) and dispersal of the Jews. It serves as a place not only for liturgical services but also for assembly and study.

The synagogue was known under three names:

▲ Bet Ha-T'filah or House of Worship;
▲ Bet Ha-Midrash or House of Study;
▲ Bet Ka-Knesset or House of Assembly.

On sabbath and holiday afternoons, the rabbi of the community would speak. Teachers and preachers from foreign countries brought news from abroad. A meshulah or messenger from Palestine would sometimes bring news of the Holy Land to the community. The weary traveler came there to find lodging, and the Jewish custom of reciting the Kiddush on Friday night in the synagogue is a result of that age-old practice of hospitality.

A child was given its name in the synagogue and a bridegroom came there to offer prayers on the sabbath before his wedding. The custom still exists that sympathy is to be given to mourners by turning toward them with words of comfort as they enter the synagogue on Friday night.

The synagogue also housed the heder, or school for children, and the higher school of learning or yeshiva. The synagogue was a real community house, where town meetings were held, and charity was collected and distributed. When disputes arose, they were settled at trials in the synagogue. Friends met in the synagogue and used its library for reading and study. The officers of the synagogue were also the leaders in the community.

As the Jewish people settled in various countries, officials often sought to curb Jewish life by issuing decrees against building new synagogues or making them higher than mosques or churches. The Emperor Justinian even tried to interfere in the worship by directing which Greek translation of the Bible was to be used. Sometimes it even served as a fortress, as in France and Germany during the Crusades. During the period of the Inquisition in Spain, the Marranos, who were forced to pretend that they were Christians, made their synagogues in cellars or caves, so that prayers should not be heard by spies.

With the dawn of modern times, the ghettos vanished and many Jewish communities built synagogues of beauty and grandeur. But the chief purpose of every synagogue, whether it was majestic or humble, was the same: to provide a place where men might worship God in democratic fashion.

SYNOD

A representative ecclesiastical assembly, often including both clergy and laymen, and usually constituting a governing body for an association of churches. The synod is particularly important to the organization of the Lutheran and Presbyterian churches.

SYNOD OF BISHOPS

In Roman Catholicism, according to the Code of Canon Law, "The Synod of bishops is that group of bishops who have been chosen from different regions of the world and who meet at stated times to foster a closer unity between the Roman pontiff and the bishops, to assist the Roman pontiff with their counsel in safeguarding and increasing faith and morals and in preserving and strengthening ecclesiastical discipline, and to consider questions concerning the church's activity in the world" (Canon 342).

SYNOPTIC GOSPELS

Synoptic is from a Greek word meaning "seeing the whole together" and is applied to the gospel of Matthew, Mark, and Luke because they present a similar view of the life and teaching of Jesus.

SYNTYCHE

In the New Testament, a Christian woman at Philippi whom Paul commended for her integrity and whom he exhorted to "be of the same mind in the Lord" with a Christian sister named Euodia.

SYRACUSE

In biblical times, name for a city with a fine harbor, on the south-east coast of the island of Sicily. The apostle Paul stayed at Syracuse for three days toward the close of his trip to Rome in 59. The layover there may have been necessary because of having to wait for suitable sailing wind (Acts 28:12).

SYRIA

Country, in biblical times commencing on the northern frontier of Palestine, extending northward to the skirts of Taurus. Its capital is Damascus.

SYRIAN CATHOLIC CHURCH

An Eastern Catholic Church of the Antiochene rite, in communion with Rome since the 17th century. The Christians of Syria have been Monophysites since the 5th century; that is, they rejected the rulings of the Council of Chalcedon (451) and insisted on the existence of only one nature in Christ.

SYRIAN CHANT

Generic term of the vocal music of the various Syrian Christian churches. Although the responsorial chanting (alternating between a soloist and a choir) found in Eastern and Western liturgies may have originated in Hebrew Temple ritual, it is considered probable that antiphonal singing (alternation between two choirs) is of Syrian origin.

SYRIAN ORTHODOX CHURCH

A body of Syrian Christians who acknowledge only one nature of Christ; it is administered by the Syrian Orthodox patriarch of Antioch.

SYRTIS

The Greek name of two gulfs located within the large indentation on the coast of northern Africa. The western gulf (between Tunis and Tripoli) was called Syrtis Minor (now the Gulf of Gabes). Just to the east was Syrtis Major, the modern Gulf of Sidra.

When the apostle Paul was being taken to Rome as a prisoner, the ship in which he traveled was seized south of Crete by a north-easterly gale. The crew, therefore, feared that the ship would be run aground on the "Syrtis," evidently the quicksands or sandbanks of the Gulf of Sidra (Acts 27:14-17).

TAANACH

In biblical times, an enclave city of Manasseh in the territory of Issachar (Joshua 17:11; 1 Chronicles 7:29) that was assigned to the Kohathite Levites (Joshua 21:20, 25). Under the command of Joshua, the Israelites defeated the king of Taanach (Joshua 12:7, 21). But the Manassites failed to drive out the Canaanites from this and other cities. Eventually, however, these Canaanites were put to forced labor (Judges 1:27-28). In the time of Judge Barak the forces of Jabin the king of Hazor, led by his army chief Sisera, were defeated at Taanach (Judges 5:19).

TAANATH-SHILOH

In biblical times, name for a site on Ephraim's border (Joshua 16:5-6). It is often identified with modern Khirbet Ta'nan el-Foqa, circa six miles southeast of the suggested location of ancient Shechem.

TABBATOH

In Judaism, forefather of a family of Nethinim; some of whose descendants returned to Jerusalem with Zerubbabel (Ezra 2:1-2; Nehemiah 7:46).

TABEEL

In Judaism, father of a man whom the kings of Israel and Syria intended to place on the throne in Jerusalem if they captured Judah's capital. The name of the son is not given. The incident occurred during the period when the reigns of Ahaz and Pekah overlapped (between circa 762 and 758 BC) (Isaiah 7:5-6).

The name is also found to be of a joint author of an Aramaic letter sent to Persian king Artaxerxes opposing the Israelites' reconstruction work in Jerusalem and resulting in a halt of Temple rebuilding (Ezra 4:7, 24).

TABERAH

In biblical times, name of an Israelite encampment in the wilderness of Sinai, the precise location of which is uncertain. On account of Israel's complaining there, God sent a fire that consumed some of the people at the extremity of the camp. But, when Moses supplicated God, the blaze sank down, or was extinguished. This incident gave rise to the name "Taberah," meaning "burning, conflagration, blaze" (Numbers 11:1-3; Deuteronomy 9:22).

TABERNACLE

A portable temple carried by the Israelites during their nomadic period. Its design, by direction of God, is described in Genesis 25-28. The inner chamber contained the ark of the covenant, which held the Ten Commandments. The Tabernacle no longer served a purpose after the erection of Solomon's Temple in Jerusalem in 950 BC.

TABERNACLE, Catholic

A receptacle for the exclusive reservation of the Most Holy Eucharist. According to the Code of Canon Law, it "should be placed in a part of the church that is prominent, conspicuous, beautifully decorated, and suitable for prayer" (Canon 938). Moreover, it should be "immovable, made of solid and opaque material, and locked so that the danger of profanation may be entirely avoided" (Canon 938).

A special lamp (often called the sanctuary lamp) "to indicate and honor the presence of Christ is to burn at all times before the tabernacle in which the Most Holy Eucharist is reserved" (Canon 940).

TABOR, Mount

Historic elevation of northern Israel, in Lower Galilee near the edge of the Plain of Esdraelon. Though comparatively low it dominates the level landscape around it, hence the expression "like Tabor among the mountains" (Jeremiah 46:18).

Its chief Old Testament association is as the site of the triumph of the Israelite General Barak over the Canaanite leader Sisera, under the inspiration of the judge and prophetess Deborah (Judges 4).

TABRIMMON

In biblical times, name for the father of Syrian King Ben-hadad I; son of Hezion (1 Kings 15:18).

TADMOR

In The Old Testament, a wilderness location where Solomon did building work (2 Chronicles 8:1-4). Tadmor is commonly identified with the city known to the Greeks and Romans as Palmyra. Its ruins lie in an oasis on the northern edge of the Syrian desert circa 130 miles north-east of Damascus. A nearby city is still called Tudmur by the Arabs. If correctly identified with Palmyra, Tadmor may have served as a garrison city for defending the distant northern border of Solomon's kingdom and also as an important caravan stop.

TAFSIR

In Islam, term denoting exegesis, interpretation, commentary, especially relating to the Koran. Classical Koranic tafsir concentrated on such matters as grammar, identification or provision of proper names, textual ambiguities, provision of more information on central characters, lexicography, philology etc., all with the intention of clarifying the Koranic words themselves. Ima'ili exegesis differed somewhat in its desire to seek a hidden sense beneath the apparent sense.

TAGHABUN, al-

The title of the 64th sura of the Koran; it means "The Mutual Disillusion" or "The Mutual Cheating." The sura belongs to the Medinan period and has 18 verses. Its title comes from verse 9 which refers to the day of resurrection as "The Day of Mutual Disillusion." On this day men's expectations will be turned upside down. The believers will enter Paradise while the disbelievers who denied God's signs will enter hell. The believers are warned to beware of enemies even among their wives and children.

TAGORE, Denbendranath

(1817-1905) Hindu philosopher and religious reformer, active in the Brahmo Samaj (Society of Brahma) that purged the Hindu religion and way of life of many abuses. Tagore, in his zeal to erase idolatry as well as divisive and undemocratic practices, finally rejected the whole of the Vedas, ancient Hindu scripture, claiming that no set of writing, however, venerable, can furnish complete and satisfying guidelines to human activity. Man's brain and heart alone must rule.

TAHA

The title of the 20th sura of the Koran; it consists of two letters of the Arabic alphabet T and H. The sura belongs to the Meccan period and contains 135 verses. The title is drawn from the first verse which comprises simply the above-mentioned letters. The early part of the sura has much to say about Musa, Pharah, the Children of Israel and Harun. Later, reference is made to the terror of the Day of Judgment, the rebellion of Iblis and the temptation of Adam and Eve.

TAHAJJUD

In Islam, the recitation of the Koran and prayers during the night. Tahajjud is generally regarded as tradition and not obligation. In some Muslim countries an official nighttime call for prayer has been instituted.

TAHANNUTH

In Islam, devotional or pious practice of some kind. The Prophet mohammed

used to occupy himself with tahannuth in a cave on Mount Hira around the time of the revelation of the Koran.

TAHARA

In Islam, ritual purification, ritual purity, ritual cleanliness. Islam places much stress on the concepts of inner and outer purity.

TAHATH

In Judaism, name for a descendant of Ephraim through Shuthelah (1 Chronicles 7:20). The name is also applied to a Kohathite Levite, forefather of Samuel and Heman (1 Chronicles 6:22-38).

TAHCHEMONITE

In the Old Testament, a designation for one of David's mighty men (2 Samuel 23:8).

TAHPANES

In biblical times, name for a city in Egypt regularly mentioned with other cities of northern Egypt, such as Noph, On, and Pibeseth.

During the last years of the Judean kingdom, the prophet Jeremiah consistently warned against political alliances with Egypt or reliance on Egypt for help against the rising power of Babylon. Noph and Tahpanes are spoken of as "feeding on [Judah and Jerusalem] at the crown of the head" due to the apostasy of the Israelites. Any support from Egypt was doubtless obtained at a high cost to the royal leaders of Judah; but they would become ashamed of Egypt, even as they had become ashamed of Assyria (Jeremiah 2:1-2, 14-19).

TAHPENES

In the Old Testament, name of the wife of the Egyptian pharaoh, contemporary with David and Solomon. Tahpenes' sister was given in marriage to Hadad, a resister of Solomon. Tahpenes raised Genubath, the child of his marriage, with her own children in the house of Pharaoh (1 Kings 11:19-20).

TAHRIF

In Islam, word to designate corruption, distortion, alteration, especially as applied to sacred texts. Muslims invoke the concept of tahrif to account, for example, for the disparity between the data about Jesus in the New Testament and that in the Koran; Islam believes that Christians have altered the original text of a proto-gospel now lost.

TAHRIM, al-

The title of the 66th sura of the Koran; it means "The Prohibition." The sura belongs to the Medinan period and has 12 verses. It draws its title from the first verse which asks the Prophet Mohammed why he has forbidden to himself something lawful in the eyes of God, i.e., honey. The sura goes on to warn both believers and disbelievers of the pains of hell and concludes by surveying a number of disbelieving and believing women. Maryam is among the latter.

TAHTIM-HODSHI

In the Old Testament, name for a site on the route of the census takers sent out by David (2 Samuel 24:4-6). The exact location of Tahtim-hodshi is not known. However, it is mentioned between Gilead and Dan-jaan, placing it in the northern part of the Promised Land.

T'AIGO WANGSA

(1301-1382) Buddhist monk, founder of the T'aigo sect of Korean Buddhism. He established a new Buddhist administration office. Though he became head of the office, his reform attempt did not bear tangible fruit, and the T'aigo sect has remained relatively small.

TAJ MAHAL

A tomb at Agra, northern India, the world's supreme example of Mogul architecture. It was built, from 1632 to 1654, by the Mogul emperor Shah Johan as a tribute to his favorite wife,

Mumtaz-i-Maha; (Taj Mahal is a corruption of her name). The Taj Mahal complex is contained within a 634-yard by 334-yard rectangle by the River Jumna. The white marble tomb itself stands on a 312-feet square marble plinth, 23 feet high, and is decorated with religious texts and inlaid with semiprecious stones. The dome and pinnacle rise to a height of 243 feet. The whole complex took more than 20,000 workmen 22 years to complete.

TAIMITSU

A Japanese Buddhist Tendai sect, based on the esoteric teachings of the 9th century master Jikaku Daishi.

TAIT, Archibald Campbell

(1811-1882) Anglican priest, bishop of London, and archbishop of Canterbury. He is remembered primarily for his efforts to develop the see of London and to moderate tension in the Church of England at the height of the Oxford Movement, which sought to revive pre-Reformation forms of piety in the interest of Anglo-Catholicism.

TAKATHUR, al-

The title of the 102nd sura of the Koran; it means literally "The Growth" or "The Multiplication" but the title has also been rendered as "The Rivalry" or "The Worldly Gain." The sura belongs to the Meccan period and has 8 verses. Its title is drawn from verse 1 where it is stated that "Multiplication preoccupies you." According to one interpretation this is directed at clans which have boasted about their numbers, one even enumerating the dead in its calculations.

TAKBIR

In Islam, praise, glorification, the declaration or expression "God is Most Great." The latter is a much used part of the salat.

TAKKANA

In Judaism, a regulation promulgated by rabbinic authority to promote the common good or to foster the spiritual development of those under its jurisdiction. Among the most far-reaching ordinances of the Middle Ages was a takkana against polygamy issued in the 11th century by rabbi Gershom ben Judah.

TAKUAN

(1573-1645) Japanese Zen Buddhist priest responsible for the construction of the famous Todai-ji temple.

TAKWIR, al

The title of the 81st sura of the Koran; it means "The Winding Up" or "The Darkening." The sura belongs to the Meccan period and has 29 verses. Its title is drawn from the first verse which begins with a description of the Day of Resurrection with the words "When the sun is wound up/darkened." The sura refers to the occasion when Mohammed saw the angle Jibril in his glory, standing on the horizon, for the first time. There is also an interesting reference in verses eight and nine to the pre-Islamic custom of burying female children alive.

TALAQ, al-

The title of the 65th sura of the Koran; it means "The Divorce." The sura belongs to the Medinan period and contains 12 verses. Its title is drawn from the first verses which deal with the subject of divorce and supplement the data in Surat al-Baqara. The sura concludes by linking good deeds with entry to Paradise and wicked deeds to a parallel end in hell.

TALHA

(died 656) A very early convert to Islam and companion of the Prophet Mohammed. Talha belonged to the Taym clan of the tribe Quraysh.

TALITHA CUMI

According to biblical tradition, the Semitic expression used by Jesus Christ at the time he resurrected Jairus' daughter (Mark 5:41).

TALLIT

In Judaism, prayer shawl in the style of the upper garment worn in ancient Palestine. In those days the rabbis wore special robes as a sign of distinction. When Jews spread to other lands, the Tallit came to be used for religious services.

TALMAI

In the Old Testament, name of the son of Anak, and brother to Ahiman and Sheshai, who dwelt in Hebron when the land was spied out by the Israelites (Numbers 13:22-33). The name is also found to apply to a son of Ammihud, king of Geshur (2 Samuel 13:37). Palmai's daughter bore Absalom to David (2 Samuel 3:3; 1 Chronicles 3:2). After having Amnon killed for violating his sister Tamar, Absalom fled to his grandfather Talmai (2 Samuel 13:28-38).

TALMON

In Judaism, head of a post-exilic Levitical family of gatekeepers. After having returned from Babylon with Zerubbabel, he "and his brothers" were chosen to live in Jerusalem (1 Chronicles 9:13, 17).

TALMUD

From the Hebrew talmed, or study, series of religious Jewish books, consisting of two separate parts. One part is the Mishnah, which comes from shanah, to repeat, or study. The Mishnah contains all the Jewish laws that have been handed down since the time of the Bible. The other part is the Gemara (from the Aramaic gemar, meaning study or teaching) which is an explanation of the Mishnah. The Talmud contains all Jewish religious laws, but it is more than a law book. It is also a history book and a story book about the development of the Jewish people.

TAMAGUSHI

In Shinto religion of Japan, a type of offering presented in formal worship of the maki (god, or sacred power). It consists of a branch of the sacred tree to which are attached strips of paper or cloth.

TAMAR

In the Old Testament, name of the daughter-in-law of Jacob's son Judah. Tamar married Judah's first son Er, but he was put to death for his wickedness, leaving Tamar a widow. She was then given Onan, but, according to biblical tradition, God put him to death for failure to perform brother-in-law marriage, and Tamar still remained a childless widow. Judah procrastinated in giving her his third son; so as to conceal her identity she disguised herself as a prostitute in order to get Judah himself to have relations with her, cleverly taking his seal ring, cord and rod as security. When Judah learned that Tamar was pregnant, he at first wanted her stoned and then burned. But on learning that through her maneuvering to get an heir he had become the father, Judah exclaimed "She is more righteous that I am." In the difficult birth that followed Tamar produced twins, Perez and Zerah (Genesis 38:6-30). The Messianic lineage is traced through her son Perez (Ruth 4:12, 18-22; 1 Chronicles 2:4; Matthew 1:3).

The name is also found to apply to the beautiful daughter of Absalom likely named after her aunt (2 Samuel 14:27). Like her father, she was very attractive in appearance. She may have married Uriel, which would have made her the mother of Rehoboam's favored wife Maacah (2 Chronicles 11:20-21).

TAMBOURINE

A percussion instrument comprising a skin stretched across a hoop fitted with bells or "jingles" which rattle as it is tapped or shaken. Originating in the Middle East, it is used in folk music and in some orchestral scores.

TAMMUZ

In ancient Mesopotamia god of fertility embodying the powers for a new life in nature in the spring.

TAMMUZ, fast of

In Judaism, a minor Jewish observance that inaugurates three weeks of mourning that culminate in the 24-hour fast of Tisha be-Av.

TANABE HAJIME

(1885-1962) Philosopher of science who attempted to synthesize Buddhism, Christianity, Marxism, and scientific thought.

TANCRED

(1045-1112) One of the leaders of the First Crusade. He played a prominent part in most of the major battles of the Crusade, and after the capture of Jerusalem (1099) he received the title of prince of Galilee.

TANHUMA

A commentary on the Pentateuch (the first five books of the Old Testament), named after the late-4th century-Palestine religious scholar Tanhuma bar Abba.

TANHUM BEN JOSEPH OF JERUSALEM

(1398-1471) Rabbinic scholar noted for his biblical commentaries in Arabic for a lexicon to Maimonides' code of Jewish law, the Mishne Torah.

TANHUMETH

In Judaism, the Netophathite father of Seraiah, a military leader of the Jews left in Jerusalem after the deportation to Babylon (2 Kings 25:23; Jeremiah 40:8).

TANTALUS

A king and son of Zeus in Greek mythology. Tantalus stole nectar and ambrosia from heaven and was sentenced to stand in a pool whose water he could not drink when he was thirsty, while branches of fruit hung just out of reach. Hence, the word "tantalize."

TANTRAS

A name commonly given to the texts dealing with the esoteric practices of some Hindu, Buddhist, and Jaina sects. Tantras refer to a class of post-Vedic Sanskrit treatises similar to the Paranas (medieval encyclopedic collections of myths, legends, and other topics). Tantras are, theoretically, considered to treat of theology, yoga, construction of temples and images, and religious practices but in reality tend to deal with the more practical side of popular Hinduism.

TANZIH

In Islam, considering or declaring God to be above and beyond anthropomorphic elements or description. Tanzih stresses the remote and transcendent aspect of God, while its opposite, tashbih, emphasizes, sometimes too much in the view of some Islamic theologians, the immanent aspect of God. These two Koranic concepts are neatly summarized in the Koranic assertion, on the one hand, that God has no like and, on the other, the statement that God is nearer to man than his own jugular vein.

TAO

Chinese term having three separate meanings. In the sense of a Way, it implies Way of Heaven; in the sense of leader-follower or one who follows a leader, it implies a pilgrim of the Way, and in its third sense, that of to tell or proclaim, it echoes the Buddha's injunction to his Bhikkhus to "proclaim the Doctrine glorious ...."

Tao is the central concept of the Tao Te Ching, the classic of Taoism, the teaching of Lao-tzu in the sixth century BC. With its gentle mysticism it has been called the mother of Zen Buddhism, the fierce and masculine father being Bodhidharma.

TAOISM

One of the tripod or three religions of China, founded by Lao Tzu circa 600 BC. Its principles are derived mainly from the Tao Te Ching and from the writings of Chuang Tzu who lived some 200 years later.

Taoism is action through inaction, opposition to violence through quietism; it is total inward harmony with nature, and union with Tao makes the spirit immortal.

TAPAS

Austerities, renounced by the Buddha in the course of his search for enlightenment as being useless.

TAPHAT

In Judaism, name of a daughter of King Solomon and wife of one of his 12 deputies (1 Kings 4:7-11).

TAPPUAH

In the Old testament, name of one of Hebron's sons and a descendant of Caleb (1 Chronicles 2:42-43). The name is also found to apply to a town in the Shephelah region assigned to the tribe of Judah (Joshua 15:20-34). It is thus distinct from Beth-tappuah in the Hebron area.

TAQDIR

In Islam, term denoting predestination. The Koran contains verses which may be interpreted in favor of both free will and predestination.

TAQIYAH

In Islam, the practice of concealing one's belief and foregoing ordinary religious duties when under threat of death or injury to oneself or one's fellow Muslims.

TAQIYYA

Dissimulation of one's religion, especially in time of persecution or danger. The practice was permitted by Shiism and also by the Druze religion.

TAQLID

In Islam, the unquestioning acceptance of the legal decisions of ancient scholars as authoritative.

TARA

The Tibetan Goddess of Mercy; the wisdom of Avalokiteshvara who manifests in the Dalai Lama. When King Sron-tsan-Gampo arrived with two Buddhist wives from China and Nepal in the seventh century they converted him to Buddhism and Tibet became a Buddhist country. The two queens were thenceforth regarded as the White Tara and the Green Tara respectively. The White Tara is depicted in art as having eyes in her forehead, hands and feet in order to see and thus help all suffering; the Green Tara is seated with one foot down. Other Taras were added to the pantheon later.

TARALLAH

In biblical times, name for a Benjaminite city, the location of which is today unknown. It is listed, however, with other cities situated in the mountainous region north of Jerusalem (Joshua 18:25-28).

TARAWIH

In Islam, extra prayers undertaken on a voluntary basis during the nights of the month of fasting, Ramadan.

TARGUM

An Aramaic translation of the Bible, or some part of the Bible, usually supplemented by a commentary. Such works were well known and used by Jews several centuries before the Christian era; those that were regarded as especially authoritative were accorded nearly equal status with the Hebrew version.

TARIKI

In Buddhism, term used in the sense of salvation by "other power," usually the personification of the absolute in Amida. The term should be distinguished from Jiriki, meaning salvation by one's own efforts as advocated in the Theravada.

TARIQ, al-

The title of the 86th sura of the Koran; it means "The Night Star." The sura belongs to the Meccan period and contains 17 verses. Its title is drawn from the oath in verse 1: "By the heaven and night star." The sura refers to God's power to raise man from the dead on Judgment Day, and counsels patience with the unbelievers.

TARSHISH

According to biblical tradition, one of Javan's four sons born after the Flood (Genesis 10:4; 1 Chronicles 1:7). He is included among the 70 family heads from whom the nations were "spread about in the earth" (Genesis 10:32). As in the case of Javan's other sons, the name Tarshish came to apply to a people and region. There are some indications of the direction in which the descendants migrated during the centuries following the Flood.

The prophet Jonah, commissioned by God to go to Nineveh in Assyria, tried to escape his assignment by going to the Mediterranean seaport of Joppa and buying passage on "a ship going to Tarshish" (Jonah 1:1-3). Thus Tarshish must obviously have been in or on the Mediterranean in the opposite direction from Nineveh and evidently was better reached by sea than by land.

TARTAK

In ancient times, a deity worshiped by the Avvites, whom the king of Assyria settled in the territory of Samaria after his taking the Israelites of the ten-tribe kingdom into exile (2 Kings 17:31). Aside from the brief reference to Tartak in the Bible, nothing can be stated with any certainty concerning the nature of this deity. According to the Talmud,

Tartak had the form of an ass. Based on the conclusion that the name "Tartak" may be comparable to the Pahlavi (Persian) word Tar-thakh (intense darkness, hero of darkness), it has been suggested that Tartak may have been a demon of the lower regions.

TARTARUS

In Greek mythology, a region of hell where man was punished for his worst crimes. It was said to be as far below Hades as earth was below Heaven, and that a falling stone would take nine days to reach it. Zeus put the rebellious Titans in Tartarus.

TASAWWUF

Sufism, the mysticism of Islam. This is the inner dimension of Islam and has been neatly described as "the Science of the Heart." There is no such thing as a Sufism apart from Islam though there are, of course, many religions with their own mystical dimension. The word "Sufism" is, however, exclusively Islamic since the Sufis sought - and seek - to found their spirituality in and upon the Koran. The Sufis often tried to be above sect. accepting the one which ruled in the country where they lived.

TASBIH

In Islam, glorification, praising of God i.e., by saying the Arabic phrase Subhana Allah which means "Praise be to God."

TASHBIH

Arabic word for anthropomorphism, describing God in human terms. The whole problem of how God should be described and the nature of His attributes precipitated much debate in medieval Islam.

TASHLICH

Hebrew word for "you will cast." On the afternoon of the first day of the New Year (or on the second day if the first is a sabbath) many Jews gather near a flowing body of water to "cast all sins into the depths of the sea."

Often crumbs of bread, symbol of sins and of broken promises, are thrown into the moving water.

TASNIM

Arabic word for nectar; a spring in Paradise. Its waters will be drunk by those "brought near" (i.e., to God).

TATHAGATA

A title of the Buddha, used by his followers, and also by himself when speaking of himself. The correct interpretation of the word is uncertain; Buddhist commentaries present as many as eight explanations. The most generally adopted interpretation is "one who has thus gone" or "one who has thus arrived," applying that the historical Buddha was only one of many who have in the past and will in the future experience enlightenment and teach others how to achieve it.

TATHAGATA-GARBHA

A Buddhist concept of an inherent Buddha-nature within all living things.

TATHATA

In Buddhism, term used in the sense of "thusness" or "suchness." The term is employed in Mahayana for the ultimate and unconditioned nature of all things.

TATTENAI

Name of the governor of the Persian province "beyond the River" during the reign of Darius I. The Israelites again started to rebuild the Temple in Darius' second year (520- BC), Tattenai and his colleagues came to Jerusalem to conduct an inquiry. The Israelites appealed to Cyrus' original decree; so Tattenai wrote to Darius asking if such a decree had been issued, as the Israelites contended. The answer received confirmed Cyrus' decree and their validity of the Temple work, and warned Tattenai not to interfere, but to render material assistance to the Israelites. This Tattenai proceeded to do (Ezra 4:24; 6:13).

TAUROBOLIUM

A bull sacrifice from about 160 onward in the cult of the Great Mother of the gods. Celebrated primarily among the Romans, the ceremony enjoyed much popularity and may have been introduced by the Roman emperor.

TAURT, Beautiful Feast of

Ancient Egyptian festival named after Taurt, the hippopotamus goddess, whose temple was near the great temple of Amon-Re at Karnak. The festival and processions lasted nearly a month, during which the population of Thebes went on holiday and merrymakers thronged the Nile banks.

TAWBA

In Islam, word designating repentance. The Arabic verb taba, said of a man, indicates "to repent"; when it is said of God it means "to forgive." Thus tawwab means both "repentant" (a man) and "forgiving" (God).

TAWBA, al-

The title of the 9th sura of the Koran; it means "The repentance." The sura belongs to the Medinan period and has 129 verses. Uniquely in the Koran it lacks the Basmala at the beginning. The sura draws its name from verse 104 which refers to God accepting repentance from His servants. The sura distances the Muslims from the polytheists, refers to various peoples to whom God has sent messengers, counsels the Prophet Mohammed to fight unbelievers and hypocrites (who are both destined for hell) and contains a number of references to war and fighting. Towards the end of the sura, the asking for forgiveness for this idolatrous father of Ibrahim is noted.

TA'ZIYAH

A commemoration - among the Shi'ah, a branch of Islam acknowledging 'Ali, the fourth caliph, and his descendants as the only legitimate successors of Mohammed - of the murder of Husayn, son of Ali' in 680.

TEBAH

In Judaism, name of the first-named son of Abraham's brother Nahor by his concubine Reumah (Genesis 22:23-24). His descendants may be connected with the town of Betah (2 Samuel 8:8; 1 Chronicles 18:8).

TEBALIAH

In Judaism, name of a Merarite Levite, the third-listed son of Hosah and a gatekeeper in the time of David (1 Chronicles 26:1-16).

TE DEUM LAUDAMUS

("Thee, God, We Praise"), perhaps the most famous of all hymns of the Gregorian chant repertoire, traditionally sung in Roman Catholic Churches on occasions of public rejoicing. According to legend, it was improvised antiphonally (by alternating voices) by St. Ambrose and St. Augustine at the latter's baptism.

TEFILLIN

In Judaism, small square box with special meaning. When a Jewish boy reaches the age of 13, he is expected to put on Tefillin, or phylacteries, during morning weekday prayers. The custom arises from the biblical commandment: "And thou shalt bind them for a sign upon the arm, for frontlets (or head-garments) between thine eyes."
Each of the two teffilin is a little square box made of parchment with a strong strap, or Retzuah, attached. One box, called the "Shel Rosh," is worn above the forehead, and the other, the "Shell Yad," is worn on the left arm. Both contain strips of parchment on which are inscribed passages from the Bible. The headpiece has the letter Shin stamped on it; the knot of the armpiece forms the letter Yud. The strap of the head phylactery is tied in the back into a knot shaped like a Daled.

TEHINNAH

In Judaism, name of a descendant of Chelub in the genealogies of Judah. He is also identified as the father of Ir-nahash, probably meaning that he was the founder of such a community (1 Chronicles 4:11-12).

TEILHARD DE CHARDIN, Pierre

(1881-1955) French Jesuit theologian, philosopher and noted paleontologist who studied Peking Man. He is best known through his writings, especially *The Phenomena of Man* and *The Divine Milieu,* which ingeniously attempt to reconcile Christianity and science (in particular evolution). Because his views were considered unorthodox his ecclesiastical superiors banned him from teaching or publishing them. He spent the years 1923-1946 in China as an explorer and paleontologist. From 1951 he lived in the United States.

TEKLA-HAYMANOT

(1245-1312) Ethiopian saint who was the most famous religious figure in Ethiopia. Distinguished by both his piety and his political acumen, Tekla-Haymanot was the founder of one of the two great monastic communities of Ethiopia and the restorer of the ancient Solomonic dynasty of kings.

TEKOA

In biblical times, name for a town in the territory of Judah that is commonly identified with Khirbet Taqu'a, lying at the elevation of circa 2,700 feet. To the east stretches the wilderness of Judah, of which the "wilderness of Tekoa" (where the Amonites. Moabites and the forces from Mount Seir suffered a crushing defeat during Jehoshaphat's reign) was apparently a part (2 Chronicles 20:20-24). King Rehoboam, David's grandson, rebuilt and fortified Tekoa, and for centuries thereafter the city evidently served as an outpost in the Judean defense system (2 Chronicles 11:5,6).

TEKOITE

An inhabitant of Tekoa (2 Chronicles 11:6; Jeremiah 6:1). The term is applied to Ikkesh, the father of David's warrior Ira (2 Samuel 23:26; 1 Chronicles 11:28); likewise to a wise woman who, at the behest of Joab, feigned widowhood before David in a scheme to accomplish Absalom's return from bBanishment (2 Samuel 14:2-9). After the return from Babylonian exile, Tekoites were among those who shared in repairing Jerusalem's walls, though their "majestic ones" took no part in the work (Nehemiah 3:7, 27).

TEL-ABIB

In biblical times, name for a place by the river Chebar in the land of the Chaldeans where Ezekiel and other Israelites were exiled. Its exact location is unknown (Ezekiel 1:1-3; 3:15).

TELAIM

In biblical times, name for a site, apparently in Judah, where Saul numbered his forces before striking the Amalekites (1 Samuel 15:1-4). Telaim appears to be the same as telem, listed in the southern Judean cities, and is usually believed to have been located circa 26 miles west-southwest of the southern end of the Dead Sea (Joshua 15:21-24).

TELAKHON

One of the oldest Buddhist-influenced prophet cults among the Karen hill people of Burma. In their mythology, the restoration of their lost Golden Book of their white younger brothers heralds the millennium. It banned traditional animal sacrifice, practiced a strict ethic, and maintained Karen culture.

TEL-ASSAR

In biblical times, name of a place inhabited by "the sons of Eden" mentioned along with Gozan, Haran and Rezeph, sites in northern Mesopotamia (2 Kings 19:12). Sennacherib boasted, through his messengers, that the gods worshiped by the people of these places had been unable to deliver them from the power of his forefathers. Due to the reference to "the sons of Eden," Tel-assar is generally associated with the small kingdom of Bit-adini along the Upper Euphrates.

TELEM

In biblical times, name of a gatekeeper among those dismissing their foreign wives in the days of Ezra (Ezra 10:17-24). The name is also found to apply to a city in other southern part of Judah (Joshua 15:21-24). It may be represented by Tell Umm es-Salafeh, some 26 miles west-south-west of the southern end of the Dead Sea. It is possibly the same as Telaim, though the two names could have different meanings.

TEL-HARSHA

In Judaism, name of a Babylonian site from which certain persons unable to establish their genealogy as Israelites came to Judah with the exiles in 537 BC (Ezra 2:1; Nehemiah 7:6).

TEL-MELAH

In Judaism, name of a Babylonian site from which certain persons unable to establish their genealogy as Israelites came to Judah with the exiles in 537 BC (Ezra 2:1; Nehemiah 7:6).

TEMA

In biblical times, name for both an important person and place. The name Tema is applied to the son of Ishmael, and the place where Tema's descendants settled (Genesis 25:13-15; 1 Chronicles 1:29-30).

The name Tema is probably also the same as modern Taima, an oasis located circa 250 miles south-east of Ezion-geber, where two major caravan routes crossed (Job 6:19). Tema, along with nearby Dedan is mentioned in the prophecies of Isaiah (21:13-14) and Jeremiah (25:15-23). In this latter prophecy Tema was specifically named as among the places whose inhabitants would be compelled to drink of God's "cup of the wine of rage." Babylonian King Nabonidus apparently established a second capital in Tema, leaving Belshazzar at Babylon in charge during his absence.

TEMAH

In Judaism, name of the forefather of a family of Nethinim who returned from Babylon to Jerusalem with Zerubbabel (Ezra 2:1-2; 43, 53; Nehemiah 7:55).

TEMAN

According to biblical tradition, name of a descendant of Esau through his first-born Eliphaz (Genesis 36:10; 1 Chronicles 1:35-36); an Edomite sheik (Genesis 36:15-16).

The name is also linked by some scholars with Tawilan, a few miles east of Petra. It was evidently an Edomite city or district ("the land of the Temanites"), where the descendants of Teman resided (Genesis 36:34; Jeremiah 49:7; Amos 1:11-12). The place became noted as a center of wisdom (Jeremiah 49:7).

TEMANITE

In biblical times, a term generally understood to refer to a native of Teman in Edom. An early Edomite king, Husham, came from the "land of the Temanites," and Eliphaz, one of Job's three companions, as a Temanite (Genesis 36:31-34; Job 2:11). That Eliphaz came from Teman in Edom is suggested by the understanding that the land of Uz, where Job lived, was near Edom. Some scholars, however, believe that the Eliphaz mentioned in the book of Job, was not from Teman, but from Tema, a place identified with an oasis on the Arabian peninsula circa 250 miles south-east of Ezion-geber (Jon 6:19)

TEMPERANCE

One of the cardinal virtues; it moderates and regulates the desire for pleasure, especially but not exclusively in regard to the pleasures of eating, drinking, and sex.

TEMPLE

A building set apart for the worship of God or an idol.

TEMPLE, Jerusalem

The first Israelite temple was built by Solomon (950 BC). Phoenician architects constructed it on a common Near Eastern plan: from east to west one proceeded through the courtyard, vestibule, nave ("holy place") to the inner sanctuary ("holy of holies") where stood the ark, the symbol of Yahweh's presence (God).

In 587 BC it was destroyed by the Babylonians. The site lay derelict for 70 years, until a new Temple of modest proportions was built by permission of the Persian king. Under Herod (19 BC) it was greatly enlarged and beautified. In its outer court Jesus Christ taught when he visited Jerusalem. It was destroyed by the Romans in 70.

TEMPLE SCROLL

One of the Dead Sea scrolls, discovered in 1947, containing a minute description of the Second Temple.

TEMPORAL PUNISHMENT

In Roman Catholicism, the punishment still due to venial or mortal sins already forgiven; it is "temporal" as opposed to "eternal," that is, the punishment of hell. Temporal punishment may be remitted in this life by the practice of penance and other virtues, in the next life in purgatory.

TEMPTATION

In Roman Catholic theology, an attraction or enticement to sin, arising from within a person or from without (that is, from the world, the flesh, or the devil). It is not of itself a sin but an opportunity or occasion of proving one's fidelity to God. Catholic moral teaching encourages the Christian to deal with temptation by prayer for grace and prudent action.

TEN COMMANDMENTS

The moral laws, engraved on two tablets of stone. It was delivered by God to Moses on Mount Sinai (Exodus 20:2-17). Jesus summarized the Ten Commandments in two great laws (Mark 12:30-31). They are recognized

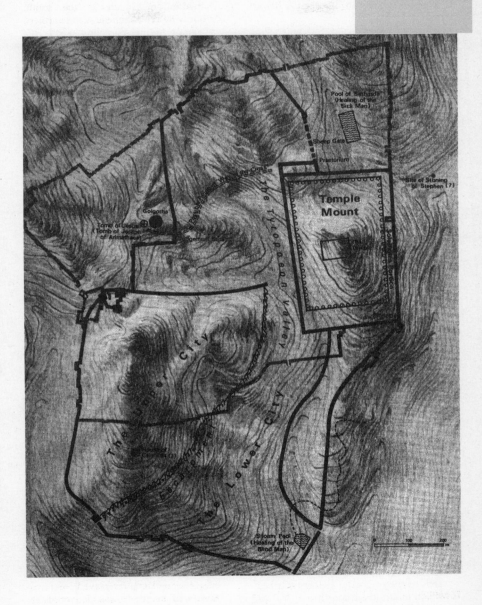

The Temple Mount in Jerusalem at the time of Jesus.

by both Jews and Christians. Simplified, the Ten Commandments are:

1 You shall have no other gods before me;
2 You shall not make for yourselves graven images;
3 You shall not take the name of the Lord your God in vain;
4 Remember the sabbath day, to keep it holy;
5 Honor your father and your mother;
6 You shall not kill;
7 You shall not commit adultery;
8 You shall not steal;
9 You shall not bear false witness against your neighbor;
10 You shall not covet that which belongs to your neighbor.

TENDAI

An important Buddhist sect introduced into Japan from China that flourished during the Heian period. It takes its name from a mountain in south-east China, T'ien t'ai, which was a center of its teachings. Attempts were made to incorporate within the framework of the Lotus Sutra, T'ien t'ai doctrine, Zen meditation, vinaya discipline, and esoteric cults. The Tendai School also encouraged an amalgamation of Shinto and Buddhism in the Ichi-jitsu (One Truth).

TENKALAI

One of the two Hindu subsects of the Sirvaisnavas, an important religious movement in South India. The Tenkalai believe that the process of final deliverance begins with God and that the devotee need not make any effort beyond surrendering himself to God's will. It uses as an illustration the helplessness and complete dependence of a kitten being carried by its mother.

TEN LOST TRIBES OF ISRAEL

Tem of the original 12 Hebrew tribes, which, under the leadership of Joshua, took possession of Canaan, the Promised Land, after the death of Moses. In 930 BC the ten tribes formed the independent Kingdom of Israel in the north and the two other tribes, Judah and Benjamin, set up the Kingdom of Judah in the south. Following the conquest of the northern kingdom by the Assyrians in 721 BC, the ten tribes were gradually assimilated by other people and thus disappeared from history.

TENRI-KYO

A Japanese messianic healing cult, the largest and most successful of the modern Shinto sects in Japan. The goal of Tenri-kyo is a happy life free from disease and suffering. The center of religious activity is the jiba, a sacred recess in the sanctuary of the main temple in Tenri city. The world is said to have been created here, and from the jiba salvation will finally be extended to the entire world.

TENSHO-KOTAI-JINGU-KYO

One of the "new religions" of Japan that have emerged in the post-World War II period, commonly known as the Dancing Religion. It was founded by Kitamura Sayo (1900-1967), a peasant woman of Yamaguchi Prefecture, whose charismatic preaching took the form of rhythmic singing and dancing. She had a revelation in 1945 that she was possessed by a Shinto deity.

TENT

A collapsible shelter made of cloth or skin and supported by poles. Tents were one of the earliest types of man-made dwellings (Genesis 4:29; 9:21) and were commonly used by nomadic peoples in the Middle East (Genesis 9:27). In biblical times, larger tents were usually divided into at least two compartments by means of hanging tent cloths. The "tent of Sarah" mentioned at Genesis 24:67 may refer to her compartment or to a tent that she alone occupied, and women sometimes were assigned their own tents (Genesis 13:5; 31:33). Probably mats were used on the ground inside the tent.

TENT OF MEETING

According to biblical tradition, an expression applied both to the tent of Moses (Exodus 33:7) and to the sacred tabernacle erected in the wilderness (Exodus 39:32; 40:2-7, 26-35). For a time, until the erection of the tabernacle, the tent of Moses served as a temporary sanctuary. It was called the "tent of meeting," evidently because the people had to go there to inquire about God (Jehovah) and thus, in effect, they met God (Jehovah) there (Exodus 33:7-11).

TERAH

According to biblical tradition, Abraham's father, the eighth generation from Shem (Luke 3:34; Genesis 11:10-24; 1 Chronicles 1:24-26). Terah, through his sons Abraham, Nahor and Haran, became a forefather of numerous tribes (Genesis 11:27; 22:20-24; 1 Chronicles 1:28-42). Terah began having children at 70. While Abraham is listed first, this appears because he is the most famous of Terah's sons rather than the first-born. Sarah was Abraham's half-sister, likely a daughter of Terah by a different wife (Genesis 20:12). Terah's first-born was most likely Haran, whose daughter was old enough to marry Terah's other son Nahor (Genesis 11:29).

TERAPHIM

In biblical times, family god or idols (Genesis 31:30-34). Although in the plural, the designation "teraphim" can also apply to a single idol. At least some of these idols may have been the size and shape of a man (1 Samuel 19:13-16). Others must have been much smaller, able to fit inside a woman's saddle basket (Genesis 31:34). The teraphim were, on occasion, consulted for omens (Ezekiel 21:21).

In Israel the idolatrous use of teraphim existed in the day of the judges as well as the kings (Judges 17:5; 18:14). It is not likely, though, that the teraphim served for purposes of inheritance in Israel, in view of God's express command against the making of images (Exodus 20:4). Also, the prophet Samuel spoke of teraphim in parallel with uncanny power, comparing the use of both to pushing ahead presumptuously (1 Samuel 15:33) and the teraphim were among the appendages of idolatry cleared out of Judah and Jerusalem by faithful King Josiah (2 Kings 23:24).

TERESA OF AVILA, Saint

(1515-1582) One of the patron saints of Spain. She was a Spanish nun and mystic who reformed the Carmelite Order to restore its original severity and asceticism. Her autobiography and other writings are considered classics of spiritual literature. She was canonized in 1622, and in 1970 Pope Paul issued a proclamation at St. Peter's cathedral in Rome, according her the title "Doctor of the Roman Catholic Church."

TERESH

In biblical times, one of two doorkeepers in the Persian palace who conspired against King Ahasuerus. Upon learning of the plot, Mordecai informed Queen Esther who, in turn, revealed it to the king. Teresh and his accomplice were hanged on a stake, and the incident was entered in the royal records (Esther 2:21-23; 6:1-2).

TERPSICHORE

In Greek religion, one of the nine Muses, patron of lyric poetry and dancing.

TERTULLUS

In the New Testament, a public speaker who presented the Jews' case against Paul before Governor Felix in Caesarea. Of what Luke recorded, much of Tertullus' statement personally praises Felix, with only a very brief accusation against Paul, attempting to implicate him with the frequent seditions against Rome (Acts 24:1-8).

TESTAMENTUM DOMINI

One of a series of writings that claim to set forth the fundamental rules of the early Christian church. Originally written in Greek, probably in the 4th-5th century, it survives in a 7th century Syriac translation.

TEUTATES

One of the three important Celtic gods referred to by the Roman poet Lucan in the 1st century AD. According to later commentators, victims sacrificed to Teutates were killed by being plunged headfirst into a vat filled with an unspecified liquid, which may have been ale, a favorite drink of the Celts.

TEXTUAL CRITICISM, biblical

The study of existing biblical manuscripts and textual traditions in order to reconstruct as closely as possible the original biblical text.

TEZCALIPOCA

A god of the Great Bear constellation and of the night sky, one of the major deities of the Aztec pantheon.

THADDEUS

According to biblical tradition, an apostle of Jesus Christ (Matthew 10:2-3; Mark 3:18). He appears to be called elsewhere "Judas the son of James" (Luke 6:16; John 14:22; Acts 1:13).

THALIA

In Greek religion, one of the nine Muses, patron of comedy. In her hands she carried the comic mask and the shepherd's staff.

THANATOS

In ancient Greek religion, the death principle, sometimes deified; in modern psychoanalytic theory, the death instinct.

THARGELIA

In Greek religion, one of the chief festivals of Apollo at Athens, celebrated on the 6th and 7th of Thargelion (May-June). Basically a vegetation ritual upon which an expiatory rite was grafted, the festival was named after the first fruits or the first bread from the new wheat.

THEBEZ

In biblical times, name of a city having a strong tower. When Abimelech had taken Thebez and was attempting to assault the tower where the populace had sought refuge, a woman pitched an upper millstone upon him from atop the wall. His skull shattered by the blow, Abimelech had his attendant put him to death so that no one could say: "It was a woman that killed him" (Judges 9:50-54; 2 Samuel 11:21).

THEISM

The view that all limited or finite things, though fully real in their own right, are dependent in some way upon, whole yet distinct from, one supreme or ultimate being, of which one may also speak in personal terms. In religion, one speaks of this being as God.

THEISM, Finitistic

The doctrine that God, at least in some respects, is limited, usually in his power and knowledge.

THEISM, Neoclassical

The belief that God includes the changing world as a part of himself and is, consequently, in part temporal, and that His perfection thus includes the surpassing of Himself. The basic uniqueness of the neoclassical view lies in its concept of divine perfection.

THEISM, Temporalistic

The doctrine that God is temporal; it constitutes a radical departure from the classical idea of God.

THEMIS

In Greek religion, personification of justice, goddess of wisdom and good counsel, and the interpreter of the gods' will. Themis is actually the goddess of justice. She looked after moral order among gods and men. She protected the weak and ill-treated. Themis possessed the gift of divination, and had her own oracle at Delphi before it was taken over by Apollo, to whom she passed on her oracular skills.

Themis was the daughter of Uranus

and Mother Earth, and the sister of Cronus, Rhea, Mnemosyne, Oceanus and the other Titans. Her union with Zeus produced the Horae ("hours"), Einomia ("order of law"), Dice ("justice") and Eirene ("peace"), who looked after the works of men, along with the three Fates. The first of the three Fates, Clotho, spun the thread of human life; the second, Lachese, shared out joy and sorrow, and the third, Atropos, cut the thread to bring life to an end.

THEOCRACY
Political rule by clergy, priests, or other religious officials deemed representatives of God.

THEODICY
The justification of God, which is concerned with reconciling the goodness and justice of God with the observable facts of evil and suffering in the world.

THEODORE, Saint
(602-690) Seventh archbishop of Canterbury and the first archbishop of the whole English church. His administrative importance especially rests on his improvement of the English church's permanent organization, including division of dioceses that had represented ancient kingdoms.

THEODORE I
(583-649) Pope from 642 to 649. He devoted most of his pontificate in combatting Monothelitism, a heresy maintaining that Christ had only one will. He refused to recognize the uncanonically installed patriarch Paul of Constantinople.

THEODORE II
((823-897) Pope for 20 days in the year of his death.Because of the intrigue in Rome of the Cadaver Synod, it is possible that Theodore was murdered for his acts.

THEODORE OF MOPSUESTIA
(350-428) Controversial theologian, considered the greatest exegete - or biblical interpreter - of his time and the spiritual head of the exegetical School of Antioch. He wrote commentaries on the Lord's Prayer, the Nicene Creed, the sacraments, and most of the biblical books. Theologically, Theodore insisted that Christ's person had two natures: divine and human. Basing his Christological issue on a psychological analysis of personality, he believed that the human and divine nature were some kind of union, as between body and soul.

THEODORE OF RHAITHU
(507-567) Theologian-monk of a monastery at Rhaithu (Sinai Peninsula), considered the last of the Neo-Chalcedonian authors. His writings sought an orthodox formulation of Christological doctrines (on the nature of Christ). He thereby proposed to integrate the authoritative expression of Christ's coexisting human and divine essences as decreed by the Council of Chalcedon (451).

THEODORE STUDITES, Saint
(759-826) Abbot and leading opponent of Iconoclasm, the doctrine opposing the veneration of religious images, which severely disturbed relations between the Byzantine and Roman churches.

THEODOSIUS OF ALEXANDRIA
(478-566) Theologian, and leader of a heterodox independent Christian church in Egypt and Syria, reputed for its asceticism and mystical prayer. His extant works include Coptic sermons and expositions of moderate Monophysite doctrine addressed to leading Byzantine figures.

THEODOSIUS OF PALESTINE, Saint
(423-529) A principal proponent of orthodoxy in the Christological (nature of Christ) controversy and one of the fathers of Palestinian monasticism. With his patriarchal colleague, St. Saba, Theodosius induced the monastic and lay population of Palestine to resist the attempts of influential Eastern

churchmen and Byzantine princes to impose the heresy of Monophysitism, the doctrine that Christ comprised only a divine nature that subsumed his humanity.

THEODOTION

(2nd century AD) Hellenistic Jewish scholar and linguist who compiled a Greek version of the Old Testament that provided a more accurate reading that the ancient Semitic or Hebrew text and served as a response to Christian biblical interpretation.

THEODOTUS

(2nd century AD) Principal exponent at Rome of the heresy of Adoptionism, the teaching that Christ was essentially a man favored ("adopted") by God and not intrinsically divine.

THEODOTUS OF ANCYRA

(376-446) Byzantine theological, bishop of Ancyra, and a leading advocate in the Christological question (on the nature of God) at the Council of Ephesus (431).

THEODOTUS THE GNOSTIC

(flourished 2nd century AD) A principal formulator of Eastern Gnosticism, a system of religious dualism (belief in rival deities of good and evil) with a doctrine of salvation by gnosis (Greek: esoteric knowledge).

THEOGNOSTOS OF ALEXANDRIA

(245-299) Greek theologian, prominent head of Alexandria's Catechetical school. at that time the intellectual center for Hellenistic Christianity.

THEOLEPTUS OF PHILADELPHIA

(1250-1326)Greek Orthodox metropolitan of Philadelphia (now Alasehir, Turkey) and writer on Christian asceticism. His opposition to the union of Eastern and Western churches and his advocacy of a controversial school of Eastern monastic mysticism involved him in the political and theological turmoil of his age.

THEOLOGICAL VIRTUES

The three virtues of faith, hope, and charity that are God-given (infused with the gift of sanctifying grace) and God-directed (that is, God Himself is their direct object). These virtues enable us to know and love God in Himself and lead to union with Him, in mind and heart.

THEOLOGY

The study of God or gods, either by reasoned deduction from the natural world, or through revelation, as in the scriptures of Christianity, Islam, or other religions. The themes of theology are God, man, the world, salvation, and eschatology.

One should distinguish the original definition from certain related notions. Revelation, the source of theology, is God's act of disclosing Himself by His "word" and mighty deeds in history, with respect both to His mysteries, which are quite beyond our own powers to attain, and to the "natural truths of religion," which we might come to ourselves but for our congenital muzziness of mind and heart, the legacy of original sin.

Faith is our reception of this revelation, our utter cleaving to God's truth, which even when considered as an act of the mind according to the analysis of the schoolmen, still more of course, when taken in its full Pauline and in its Lutheran sense, is an assent breaking free from all bounds of thought.

Holy scripture is the record of revelation. Articles of faith are the dogmas or creedal declarations made by the Christian church to safeguard our authentic witness to God; they are not what we believe "in," but rather what we believe "through"; nevertheless they are permanent, not interim, structures for the corporate faith of the church.

So theology is to be defined essentially, if rather generically, as the overspill of divine faith into all the levels of human reasonableness; its wit, humor, poetic imagery, sense of analogy, power of coordination, openness to be taught, and search for reasons why, whence, how, and what it is all about.

It engages all that makes the theologian other than God and other than the angels and the beasts. We are not to suppose that God is a theologian Himself, or that angels are - except, according to Augustine, as a minor and evening avocation.

The term theology does not occur in the scriptures. The earthly Christians jabbed at it because of its pagan associations, preferring gnosis until that was spoilt for them. It was generally adopted by the Greek Fathers from the time of Origen, though it referred to the study of divinity, whereas the term economy (oikonomia) denoted that of the humanity of Christ, and the restoration of friendship between God and man in the Word made flesh.

It is not prominent in Augustine, and though it appeared in Erigena's influential translation of the Dionysian *De mystica theologia,* it was not until Abelard that it was popularized in Latin; even with him it stood for a dialectical discipline. The term adopted by Thomas Aquinas was *sacra doctrina,* holy teaching, and despite the title of his Summa, the word theology appears only fugitively in that work, and then in its Aristotelian sense.

THEOLOGY, Christian

The first question, which defines the scope of Christian theology, remains a locus classicus. Important is its inclusion of symbol, myth, metaphor, indeed of all the genialities of human communion with God's world. Nevertheless, Thomas Aquinas was of too Aristotelian temper to leave matters at that; accordingly, he sought how theological investigation could adopt intellectual processes, not merely dialectical but also scientific, and form a body of knowledge, an episteme which worked with its own proper severity of discourse and could conduct an argument or dialogue in which human reasons communicated in a civilis conservatio.

From this sprang the divisions of theological disciplines. Henceforth theology was to be regarded - disapprovingly by those acquainted only with physico-mathematical models - as truly a science. The effort of scholasticism to this effect can be caricatured, and not altogether unfairly, for a naked deductivism, but in Thomas Aquinas at least it sprang from his view that revelation was published to the people of God, that a people, not just a race-group or caste-group and so forth, really communicate when there is an agreed currency of thought and values, and that only on this agreement can there be a progressive development.

This is not an argument for any one school of theology, but for a thinking theology, and one prepared to elaborate and explain. Such a science is no more to be ripped from its living roots than are the political and legal institutions of a state from the deeper and more indeliberate factors of a country's social unanimity.

Indeed, theology is the church thinking aloud, and here, it may be remarked, the people, not the professionals, have sometimes led the way - the distinction is not that between laity and clergy.

Accordingly, Christian theology takes place within the household of the faith. To look at divine revelation from outside, in so far as that be possible, would not be theology, but a detached and critical philosophy of religion, and the same may be said about "natural theology," when treated merely as a part of natural, moral, and metaphysical philosophy out of its context in salvation history.

For this reason theology is single in its root, whatever its ramifications. The growth may seem luxuriant and wild, for like scripture it takes in the jungle as well as the cultivated patches of human experience, yet all is from and for the revelation of God.

It is on God Himself that Thomas Aquinas centers his theological science, and though not unsympathetic to earlier views fixing on the sacraments, the works of salvation, of the mystical body, it is not preoccupationally kerygmatic or eschatological. It springs from faith, and faith is a prelude to the beatific vision, and of both God Himself is the object.

THEOLOGY, Practical

This may be comprehensively called, quite simply, moral theology, and shades back according to the old tradition, now being recovered, into contemplative theology, for as anyone who has fallen in love knows, and that without being bemused, it is difficult to draw the line between a state of being and a condition of being.

A manualist tradition tended to cut it off from its sources, and even to commit to canon law, too closely for the health of either. Then also a past vogue made three disciplines:

▲ moral theology, how to avoid sin;
▲ ascetical theology, how to advance in virtue;
▲ mystical theology, how to respond to the rarer and miraculous manifestations of grace.

It is the compartmentation, not the nomenclature that is criticized. But an emphasis on diverse functions can, of course, break a single science into appropriate sections, and so can diverse applications; thus we have

▲ pastoral theology;
▲ educational theology;
▲ inner-city theology.

Affective theology as a rhetoric belongs here, but as engaged really with the heart of the matter it is part of contemplative theology, and, not least, of systemic theology, which might be expected on a superficial view.

All the above rough headings should mark no exclusion: a biblical and historical theologian will need to be dogmatic theologian and work back to origins from meanings as they are present in the mind of the church, and a scholastic theologian will be all the better for a well-informed sense of history.

THEOLOGY, Systematic

The discipline concerned with a reasoned reflection on and interpretation of the main tenets of Christian faith; the equivalent of what in Catholic curricula is called dogmatic as distinct from moral theology.

The designation systematic usually distinguishes this branch of theology from biblical theology, from positive theology, which includes patristics and symbolic theology (study of the confessions of faith), or from historical theology.

In its strongest meaning systematic theology implies both a faith or confessional commitment and the choice of an intellectual or philosophical system, i.e., the acceptance and discursive application of an epistomological and ontological viewpoint as best suited to defend, articulate, and elaborate upon the articles of belief.

The term philosophical theology has a narrower usage, signifying at times natural theology or at times a theology developed exclusively through philosophical categories. Systematic theology incorporates elements from scripture, the Fathers, symbols of faith, and historical theology.

THEOPASCHITISM

The view that it was Christ's divine nature that suffered on the cross; part of the theology of some Monophysites who hold that Christ had only one nature.

THEOPHANES THE CONFESSOR

(752-818) Byzantine monk, theologian, and chronicler, a principal adversary of the heterodox Iconoclasts (destroyers of religious images). The annals he wrote constitute the leading source for 7th and 8th century Byzantine history.

THEOPHANY

A manifestation of deity in sensible form. The term has been applied generally to the appearance of the gods in the ancient Greek and Near Eastern religions but has in addition acquired a special technical usage in regard to biblical materials.

THEOPHILUS

In the New Testament, name of a person to whom Luke addressed both his gospel and the Acts of Apostles (Luke 1:3-4; Acts 1:1). His being called "most excellent" may indicate a high position of some kind, or may simply be an expression of high esteem. Theophilus apparently was a Christian, having been orally taught about Jesus Christ and his ministry. Luke's written statement served to assure him of the certainty of what he had learned previously by word of mouth.

THEOPHILUS OF ANTIOCH

(109-180) Syrian saint, sixth bishop of Antioch, and Christian apologist. He probably was the first to express a trinity, or triad, in the divine existence: God, his Word (Logos), and his Wisdom. He upheld the divine mystery of the Trinity by an original use of the Stoic distinction between the intrinsic and extrinsic (revealed) Word in the divine mind.

THEOSOPHY

A religious movement founded in 1875 in New York by Madame Elena Blavatsky, a Russian, and others. Based on the closely guarded secret teachings of great Hindu "Masters" in the Vedas and Vedanta, it shares many Hindu beliefs, particularly the concept of reincarnation or transmigration of souls. It holds that there are seven planes of existence: physical, astral, mental, spiritual, ethereal and two divine. Theosophy also claims to represent "a body of truths" underlying all religion.

In Buddhism, the term theosophy stands for wisdom religion, or wisdom of the Gods. Sometimes is the term incorrectly rendered as the "Wisdom of God." It is used in the sense of the substratum of truth on which all religions are based; the source from which they derive whatever truth they contain. The term is also used in the sense of the esoteric interpretation of all religious doctrines and dogmas.

THERA

In Buddhism, an "elder" in the Sangha; a senior member of the Order who, by length of years as a respected Bhikkhua or by exceptional qualities of character, is generally accorded this honorary title.

THERAPEUTAE

Severe ascetics who, probably in the 1st century AD, settled on the shores of Lake Mareotis near Alexandria (Egypt). Individual members lived in relative seclusion, seeking wisdom through allegorical interpretations of the scriptures. They spent the day in spiritual exercises, with prayer at dawn and in the evening. Some ate every second day, others only once a week; all abstained from wine and meat.

THERAVADA

Southern tradition of Buddhism. Thera means elder or older. Theravada is the school of elders which was historically a group of conservative senior monks who advocated a strict adherence to the precepts as opposed to another group of rather freer progressive monks (whose beliefs were to develop later in Mahayana, that is the modern tradition). This kind of opposing trends in Buddhist Orders is said to have started in an early period, a few centuries after the dease of the Buddha, when Mahadeva, a progressive monk, insisted upon the freer interpretation under the five categories of the Buddhist precepts. This provoked the split into Therevada and Mahasamghika which was the fountainhead of later Mahayana.

THESEUS

In Greek mythology, the hero of Athens, who occupied a position equivalent to that of Heracles for the Dorians. His father was Aegeas, king of Athens, and his mother was Aethra, daughter of king Pittheus of Troezem. However, in many versions, his true father is Poseidon, and there are numerous myths surrounding his birth. The best-known relates how after two barren marriages Aegeas sent to the Delphic Oracle for advice. The oracle told him not to untie the mouth of his wineskin before he returned to Athens lest one day he should die of grief. Unable to understand the words of the oracle, Aegeas decided to travel home via Troezen, to consult King Pittheus, who was known for his wisdom. Whether Pittheus understood the oracle or not, he wanted his daughter to be the mother of the son whom the king of Athens wished for so dearly.

After becoming an adult, Theseus went to Athens. At this time, Aegeas had just married the sorceress Medea. She knew in advance who Theseus was as he progressed towards Athens. Without giving a way any details to the king, she managed to inspire in him a fear of the young hero, whose beauty had already become legendary. She managed to convince Aegeas to offer Theseus a poisoned drink. But as the youth went to cut a piece off sacrificial animal with his sword - perhaps intentionally - Aegeas recognized the weapon he left with king Pittheus. He stepped forward and stopped him from raising the poisoned cup, recognizing as he did so his son. Aegeas poured out the contents of the cup and exiled Medea from his country.

Among the feats of Theseus in Attica was to catch the fearful bull which Heracles had brought from Crete. Some sources place this incident before Theseus' recognition by his father and some after, but however that may be the beast had been roaming the plain of Marathon destroying crops and human lives. Theseus managed to catch it, bind it with chains and sacrifice it to Apollo.

THESSALONIANS, Letters to

Two New Testament letters written by Paul from Corinth circa 52 and addressed to the Christian community he had founded in Macedonia.

The first letter was written after Timothy, his co-worker, returned from Thessalonia to report that the new converts had stood fast in the Lord despite persecution. In answer to a question that disturbed the community, Paul explained that everyone, both the living and the dead, will share Christ's Resurrection at the time of his Second Coming. The second letter was written shortly after the first. The letter explains that the final day will not arrive until after the Antichrist appears.

THESSALONICA

Important port and commercial center in Macedonia, situated at the Termean Gulf. It was founded in 316 BC and named for a sister of Alexander the Great.

Paul established a Christian congregation in Thessalonica about the year 50. For three sabbaths Paul preached in Thessalonica's synagogue, and as a result some Jews and a great multitude of Greek proselytes became believers and associated themselves with Paul and Silas and among them were "not a few of the principal women" (Acts 17:1-4). How long Paul remained there is not disclosed; although he had the authority, as an apostle, to receive material help from those to whom he ministered spiritual things, he set the example that "one should eat food he himself earns" (1 Corinthians 9:4-18; 2 Thessalonians 3:7-12). This was probably partly because of the tendency toward idleness that some there had.

In less than a year after leaving Thessalonica, Paul, by now down in Corinth, wrote his first letter to the Thessalonians. He had sent Timothy to comfort and encourage them and had received Timothy's good report.

Over the years Paul no doubt revisited Thessalonica, on occasions when passing through Macedonia in the course of his travels (Acts 20:1-3). And certain Thessalonians who are mentioned by name, Aristarchus and Secundus, were traveling companions of Paul (Acts 20:4; 27:2).

THESSALONIANS

THEUDAS

In the New Testament, name of a rebel who started an insurrection with a following of about 400 men sometime before 6. By using this Theudas as his first example of a movement that caused no more trouble after its leader was put the death, the Pharisee Gamaliel persuaded the Sanhedrin not to bother the youthful Christian congregation so soon after Jesus' death (Acts 5:34-40).

THIRTY-NINE ARTICLES

Together with the Book of Common Prayer, these are the theological formulas that make up the doctrine of the Church of England. They were derived from the 42 Articles drawn up by Archbishop Cranmer in 1553 and were approved by Queen Elizabeth I in 1571. In the United States, the 39 Articles form part of the Protestant Episcopal prayer book.

THOMAS

One of the 12 apostles, known as "Doubting Thomas" because he would not believe Christ's resurrection until he put his fingers in Christ's wounds (John 20:24-29).

Thomas appears to have been somewhat impetuous in expressing his feelings or in voicing his doubts. However, upon having his doubts removed, Thomas did not hesitate to make acknowledgment of his belief.

When Jesus proposed returning to Judea that he might awaken Lazarus from death, Thomas declared: "Let us also go, that we may die with him" (John 11:16). Since the Judeans had shortly before this time sought to stone Jesus (John 11:7-8), Thomas perhaps had in mind encouraging the other disciples to accompany Jesus even though this might result in their joining Lazarus and/or Jesus in death.

Thomas showed a dubious attitude in response to Jesus' comment about going away to prepare a place for the Apostles, saying" "Lord, we do not know where you are going. How do we know the way?" (John 14:2-6).

Similarly, after hearing about Jesus' resurrection, Thomas stated: "Unless I see in his hands the print of the nails and stick my finger into his side, I will certainly not believe." Eight days after Thomas had the opportunity to do this when Jesus again appeared to the disciples. But whether Thomas actually did feel the wounds on this occasion is not stated. He was nevertheless convinced and exclaimed: "My Lord and my God!" Jesus than mildly reproved him, saying: "Happy are those who do not see and yet believe" (John 20:24-29).

There are several ancient Indian churches called the "Christians of St. Thomas." Thomas' feast day is celebrated on December 21st in the Roman church and July 3 in the Eastern Orthodox calendar.

THOMAS À BECKET, Saint

See: Becket, Thomas à

THOMAS À KEMPIS

(1380-1471) German religious writer (his real name was Thomas Hamerken van Kempen). An Augustinian friar at Zwolle in the Netherlands, he is famous above all for his book, *The Imitation of Christ,* perhaps one of the most widely known pieces of devotional literature. It is divided into four books, dealing respectively with general admonitions useful for a spiritual life, admonitions pertaining to inward things, internal consolation, and Holy Communion. Because of its gentle and humane approach, it has remained immensely popular.

THOMAS AQUINAS, Saint

(1224-1274) Christian philosopher who developed his own conclusions from Aristotle, theologian whose major works form the classical systematization of Latin theology (Thomism), and poet whose eucharistic hymns are used in the church's liturgy. He is recognized by the Roman Catholic Church as its foremost philosopher and theologian.

His genius was to relate faith and reason, theology and philosophy. he wrote many books, the chief one was his *Summa Theologica,* a broad exposition of theology as related to philosophical principles.

THOMISM

The philosophical system of St. Thomas Aquinas and his followers. It has had a contemporary revival, usually called Neo-Thomism. A central theme of Thomism is the study of different areas in which faith and reason operate. For example, the Thomist view as regards the existence of God is that this can be established by reason alone. On the other hand a specifically orthodox Christian tenet, such as the three-fold nature of God, must be grasped by faith and remains inaccessible to reason by itself. Thomism has long been the official philosophical doctrine of the Roman Catholic Church.

THOR

Deity common to all the early Germanic people, a great warrior represented as a red-bearded, middle-aged man of enormous strength, an implacable foe to the harmful race of giants but benevolent toward mankind. His figure was generally secondary to that of the god Odin, who in some traditions was his father.

THOTH

Greek form of the name of the Egyptian god Djhowtey, whose cult was centered in the town of Khumunu (Upper Egypt). Through his early representation as the moon god he became the god of reckoning and of learning in general. Thoth's sacred animals were the ibis and the baboon; numerous mummified bodies of these animals were found in cemeteries near Hermopolis and Thebes.

THREE SIGNS OF BEING

Famous Buddhist Trilogy, a fundamental doctrine in the Theravada, pointing out that all manifested things without exception are inseparable from Anicca (change), Dukkha (suffering or imper-

fection), and Anatta, which negatively means possessing no separate and immortal soul or spiritual entity, and positively implies the oneness and in severability of life, the live-force of the universe, however different and fleeting its forms.

THREE WEEKS

A period of Jewish mourning running from the 17th day of Tammuz, the fourth month of the Jewish religious year, to the 9th month of Av, the fifth month. The observance commemorates the days between the first breaching of the walls of Jerusalem in 586 BC by Babylonian troops under Nebuchadnezzar to the subsequent destruction of the First Temple of Jerusalem.

THREE WISE MEN

In the Gospel of Matthew, noble [pilgrims "from the East" who followed the star of Bethlehem, where they paid homage to the Christ child. Eastern tradition sets their number at 12, but Western tradition sets their number at 3, probably based on the three gifts of "gold and frankincense and myrrh" (Matthew 2:11) that they brought the child.

THUNDER CULT

Prehistoric beliefs and practices that at times seem directed toward one aspect of the supreme sky god and at other times appear to be concerned with a separate thunder deity. The thunder cult became prominent in western Europe during the Neolithic Period.

THURIBLE

Vessel used in the Christian liturgy for the burning of aromatic incense strewn on lighted goals. Censers of terra-cotta or metal were widely used in Egypt, in the ancient Near East civilizations, including the Jewish, and in the classical world. They were destined chiefly for religious worship, originally above all in funeral rites.

THURSTAN

(1078-1140) Archbishop of York whose tenure was marked by disputes over precedence with the see of Canterbury and with the Scottish bishops. He developed the parochial system and extended generous patronage toward the religious orders.

THYARIA

In biblical times, name of a city rebuilt early in the third century BC by the former general of Alexander the Great, Seleucus Nicator. It was situated some 40 miles inland from the Aegean Sea along a tributary of the Hermus River in western Asia Minor. Thyaria's Christian congregation received a message written by the hand of the Apostle John (Revelation 1:11).

Thyaria today is called Akhisar and is located circa 157 miles south-southwest of Constantinople and some 230 miles east of Athens. In the days of the Roman Empire it was an important city halfway along the road between Pergamum and Sardis in the region of Lydia, within the Roman province of Asia.

The city was never a great metropolis or a center of special political significance or importance; but it was a wealthy industrial center, noted for its numerous crafts, including weaving, dyeing, brass-working, tanning and pottery making.

The polytheistic religion of the Thyarians was just another variety of the more ancient Babylonian cult. Pergamum was very near, and to this city Chaldean priests had emigrated, where they had established a religious center. The local chief deity was Tyrinbos, who in time became identified with the sun-god Apollo, the brother of the goddess Diana or Artemis.

When and by whom Christianity was first introduced to the Thyarians is not known. There is no record of Paul or other evangelists ever visiting the city. Possibly the message reached there during the two years (circa 53-55) that Paul was active in Ephesus some 70 miles south-west of Thyaria, for during that time "all those inhabiting the district of Asia heard the word of the Lord, both Jews and Greeks" (Acts 19:10). What is known is that some 40 years later there was a rather vigorous congregation of Christians in Thyaria (Revelation 1:10-11).

TIARIA

A triple crown worn by the pope, the symbol of his sovereign power. It is worn by (or carried in front of) the pope at some non-liturgical functions such as processions. Beehive-shaped, it is circa 15 inches high, made of silver cloth, and ornamented with three diadems, with two streamers, known as lappets, hanging from the back.

TIBERIAS

City in north-eastern Israel, on the western shore of the Sea of Galilee. It was founded by Herod Antipas tetrarch of Galilee under the Romans, in AD 18, and named for the reigning emperor Tiberius.

It was some 11 miles around the sea from Capernaum and six miles above where the Jordan leaves that body of water. Here Herod the tetrarch made his residence. Nearby, to the south of the city, were famous warm springs. The city is mentioned only once in the Bible (John 6:23).

TIBERIUS

Second Roman emperor who reigned AD 14-37, being an adopted son of Augustus. In his last years he became a tyrannical recluse, inflicting a reign of terror against the major personages of Rome.

Tiberius lived until March 37, and hence was emperor foe the entire period of Jesus' ministry. It was therefore Tiberius' image that was on the tax coin that was brought to Jesus, "Pay back Caesar's things to Caesar" (Mark 12:14-17; Matthew 22:17-21). Tiberius extended the law of laesa majestas (injured majesty) to include, in addition to seditious acts, merely libelous words against the emperor, and presumably on the strength of this law the Jews pressured Pontius Pilate to have Jesus killed (John 19:12-16). Tiberius later called Pilate to Rome because of Jewish complaints against his administration, but Tiberius died and Caligula succeeded him before Pilate arrived.

TIBETAN BUDDHISM

A distinctive form of Buddhism that evolved from the 7th century AD in Tibet. Based mainly on the rigorous intellectual disciplines of Madhyamika (Middle Way) and Yogacara (Practice of Union) philosophy, and utilizing the symbolic ritual practices of Vajrayana (Tantric Buddhism), Tibetan Buddhism also incorporated the vinayam or monastic disciplines, of early Theravada Buddhism and shamanistic features of the indigenous Tibetan religion, Bon.

TIBHATH

In biblical times, name of a city north of Palestine from which David took a great quantity of copper after striking down Hadadezer, king of Zobah, at Hamath, some 140 miles north of Dan (1 Chronicles 18:3, 8).

TIBNI

In Judaism, a contender for the kingships of the ten-tribe kingdom of Israel following the seven-day rule of Israel's fifth king Zimri in 951 BC. The populace was divided over whether Tibni or Omri should now be king. Four years later, during which time civil war presumably raged, the issue was finally settled; Tibni lost to Omri's supporters and met death. He was a son of Ginath (1 Kings 16:15, 21-23).

TIDAL

In biblical times, name of the king of Goiim and an ally or vassal of Elamite King Chedorlaomer when they and two other monarchs subjugated five kings near the Dead Sea. Following 12 years of domination, the five defeated kings staged a rebellion. Tidal, Chedorlaomer, and the others came west to put it down, and in doing so took spoil and captives, including Abraham's nephew Lot. Abraham pursued the oppressors and recovered the prisoners and pillaged goods, but there is no indication that Tidal or those kings with him were captured or slain (Genesis 14:1-17).

T'IEN MING

In Chinese Confucian thought, the notion that the right of emperors to rule was conferred directly by heaven. The continuation of the mandate was believed to be conditioned by the personal behavior of the ruler, who was expected to posses i ("righteousness") and jen ("benevolence").

T'IEN-T'AI

A rationalist school of Buddhist thought that takes its name from the mountain in south-east China where its founder and greatest exponent, Chih-i, lived and taught in the 6th century. The school also travelled to Japan where it was known as Tendai. The basic philosophical doctrine is summarized as the triple truth:

1 all things lack ontological reality;
2 they nevertheless have a temporary existence;
3 they are simultaneously unreal and temporarily existing - the middle, or absolute truth, which includes and yet surpasses the others.

The three truths are considered to be mutually inclusive and each contained within the others.

TIGLATH-PILESER III

One of the greatest conquerors and rulers of Assyria, reigning 745-727 BC. He first conquered a people and then deported them to another part of his empire. In this way he made rebellion almost impossible. By his many conquests and cruelties Assyria became a dreaded world power.

TIGRIS RIVER

It rises in the mountains of Armenia, and pursues a meandering course, uniting and flowing as one into the Persian Gulf.

TIKVAH

In Judaism, name of the father-in-law of Huldah the prophetess; son of Harhas (2 Kings 22:14). The name is also found to apply to the father of a certain Jahzeiah who lived in the time of Ezra (Ezra 10:10-15).

TILAKA

In Hinduism, a mark generally made on the forehead, indicating a man's sectarian affiliation. The marks are made by hand or a meta, with ash from a sacrificial fire, sandalwood paste, turmeric, cow dung, clay, charcoal or red lead, and among some cults are made on 2, 5, 12 or 32 parts of the body also.

TILLEMONT, L.S. Le Nain de

(1637-1698) Ecclesiastical historian who was one of the earliest scholars to provide a rigorous appraisal of preceding historical writings.

TILLICH, Paul Johannes

(1886-1965) German-American theologian and philosopher who attempted to relate traditional Christian beliefs to the problems faced by modern man and to the concerns of classical and modern philosophers. Born in Prussia, he taught at various German universities until 1933, when his opposition to the Nazi regime drove him to emigrate to the United States. Tillich held that man's questions about the meaning of existence can be "correlated" with traditional Christian doctrine and that the resulting synthesis can be expressed in the terms of modern existentialist philosophy and depth psychology.

TILLOTSON, John

(1630-1694) English prelate and preacher, who reluctantly accepted the archbishopric of Canterbury (1691) after the deposition of Archbishop Bancroft, who refused to swear allegiance to William and Mary while James II still lived.

TILOKA

In Buddhism, the three worlds, a phrase meant to embrace all manifestations. The worlds are:

1 Kamaloka, the field of the five senses.
2 Rupa-loka, the plane of invisible yet existing form corresponding to certain of the Jhanas or planes of meditation.
3 Arupa-loka, the formless world corresponding to the higher levels of the Jhanas.

TIMAEUS

In the New Testament, name of the father of Bartimaeus the blind beggar healed by Jesus (Mark 10:46).

TIMNA

In biblical times, name of a concubine of Esau's son Eliphaz and mother of Amalek (Genesis 36:10-12). In the genealogy at 1 Chronicles 1:36, there are first enumerated five sons of Esau's son Eliphaz; next are added, "Timna and Amalek."
The name is also found to be the first name found in the list of 11 "sheiks of Esau" or Edom (Genesis 36:40-43; 1 Chronicles 1:51-56).

TIMNAH

In biblical times, name of a location at the boundary of Judah and Dan (Joshua 15:1, 10; 19:40-43). Today it is often identified with a place preserving some similarity to the ancient name, Khirbet Tibnah, circa two miles west of the suggested site of Beth-shemesh.
Samson selected a Philistine woman of Timnah for marriage "when looking for an opportunity against the Philistines," who then ruled over Israel. En route to the city, he killed a lion bare-handed at the vineyards of Timnah (Judges 14:1-6). In the time of King Ahaz, the Philistines captured Timnah and its dependent towns (2 Chronicles 28:16-19).
The name is also found to apply to a city in the mountainous region of Judah. Scholars identify this Timnah

with modern Tibnah, circa two miles north-north-west of the possible site of Gibeoan. Apparently, near this Timnah Judah planned to shear his sheep, and at Enaim (which was on the road to Timnah) he had relations with Tamar, mistaking her for a harlot (Genesis 38:12-18).

TIMNAH-HERES

In biblical times, location of Joshua's inheritance and later burial in the mountainous region of Ephraim, north of Mount Gaash (Judges 2:8-9).

TIMNITE

A person of Timnah; in its only occurrence the term is applied to Samson's father-in-law (Judges 15:6).

TIMON

In the New Testament, one of the seven men "full of spirit and wisdom" appointed by the Apostles to care for the "daily distribution" in the infant Christian congregation. In spite of his Greek name, he was likely a Jew by birth (Acts 6:1-6).

TIMOTHY

(died circa 97) Disciple of Paul the apostle, whom he accompanied on his missions. On his second visit to Lystra, Paul discovered Timothy, taking him as a colleague but first circumcising him (Acts 16:1-3). Timothy worked with Paul and Silas and helped found churches, notably in Corinth, Thessalonica, and Philippi. He was solely in charge of the Christians at Ephesus, possibly the site of his release (Hebrews 13:23).

Timothy's name is included in the salutation of letters written by Paul to the Philippians (1:1), Colossians (1:1) and Philemon (1:1) during the apostle's first imprisonment at Rome. It appears that Timothy personally endured imprisonment at Rome sometime within the period bwteen the writing of the letter to the Philippians and the one to the Hebrews (Philippians 2:19; Hebrews 13:23).

Although having to contend with frequent illness because of stomach trouble (1 Timothy 5:23), Timothy willingly expended himself on behalf of others. His fine qualities endeared him to the apostle Paul, who very much desired Timothy's association when facing imminent death (2 Timothy 4:6-9). Being relatively young, Timothy may have been diffident and hesitant about asserting his authority (1 Timothy 4:11-14).

TIMOTHY, Letters to

Two New Testament writings addressed to Timothy between 63 and 67. They (and the letter of Paul to Titus) have been called pastoral epistles, because all three deal principally with church administration and the growth of heresies.

The first letter to Timothy insists on the need to shun unorthodox teachings and dangerous speculations and stress the qualities expected of deacons. It exhorts Timothy to fulfill his duties faithfully and to instill in his congregation traditional beliefs, notions of proper conduct, and respect for one another. The second letter is Paul's final message (4:6-8), written in circa 68. Paul urges Timothy to guard the truth and to share his suffering as a soldier of Christ. Timothy is asked to visit soon, even though Paul believes he is on the point of being sacrificed.

TIN, al-

The title of the 95th sura of the Koran; it means "The Fig." The sura belongs to the Meccan period and contains 8 verses. Its title is drawn from the first verse which has the oath "By the fig and the olive." The sura goes on to warn of what awaits the unbeliever and concludes by stressing the greatness of God's justice.

TINTERN ABBEY

Famous ecclesiastical ruin, in the Welsh border county of Gwent, on the west bank of the River Wye, founded by Cistercian monks in 1131. Although

the cruciform church is without a roof and the nave is damaged, many details of a style transitional from Early English to Decorated Gothic are preserved.

TIPHSAH

In biblical times, name of a place at the extreme north of Solomon's kingdom (1 Kings 4:24). Scholars generally identify it with Dibseh on the Euphrates River, some 60 miles east-south-east of Aleppo and almost that same distance from the confluence of the Euphrates and Balikh Rivers.

The name is also found to apply to a place, apparently in the vicinity of Tirzah, that was struck down by Israel's King Menahem (circa 791-780 BC) (2 Kings 15:16). Its exact situation is not known. Khirbet Tafsah, circa seven miles south-west of ancient Shechem, bears a similar name, but appears to be too far from the assumed site of Tirzah to be the location of this Tiphsah.

TIRATANA

The Three Jewels or Gems of Buddhism: the Buddha, the Dhamma, and the Sangha.

TIRAS

In Judaism, name of one of the seven sons of Japheth (Genesis 10:2; 1 Chronicles 1:5). The people descended from Japheth's sons were later "spread about in their lands, each according to its tongue" (Genesis 10:5).

TIRATHITES

In biblical times, name of a Kenite family of scribes living at Jabez (1 Chronicles 2:55).

TIRESIAS

In Greek mythology, a blind Theban seer, who played an active part in the tragic events concerning Laius, the king of Thebes, and his son Oedipus.

TIRSHATHA

The Persian title for the governor of a jurisdictional district. The officials mentioned in the Bible by the title Tirshatha ruled over Judah, one of the Persian provinces. Zerubbabel was evidently the Tirshatha mentioned in Ezra 2:63 and Nehemiah 7:65. Later when Nehemiah became governor he was the Tirshatha and is referred to as such at Nehemiah 8:9.

TIRTHANKARA

In Jainism (religion of India), a savior who has succeeded in crossing over life's stream of rebirths and has made a path for others to follow.

TIRTHAYATRA

A Hindu pilgrimage undertaken to a holy river, mountain, or place made sacred through association with a deity or saint. The Hindu pilgrim undertakes his journey to a sacred spot as an act of devotion, to carry out a vow, to appease a deity in the face of misfortune, or to seek prosperity. Upon reaching the tirtha he will usually bathe, circumambulate the temple or holy place, make an offering, carry out a rite such as the sraddha ceremony performed in honor of dead ancestors, have his name recorded by the priests who specially cater to the needs of pilgrims, and listen to the evening expositions of music and religious discourses.

TIRTHIKA

In Buddhism, literally a lord-user. A term used in Buddhism to apply to members of the other schools, with the implication of unbelievers.

TIRZAH

In biblical times, name for a person and a city. Tirzah is the name of one of the five daughters of the Manassite Zelophehad; a contemporary of Moses and Joshua (Numbers 26:29; 27:1-7).

The name Tirzah is also found to apply to a city in Samaria, the exact location of which is uncertain. Under the command of Joshua, the Israelites defeated the king of Tirzah (Joshua 12:7, 24). Centuries later, Jeroboam, the first king of the northern kingdom, transferred his residence to Tirzah (1 Kings 12:25).

Tirzah evidently continued to be the capital of the northern kingdom during the reigns of Jeroboam's son Nadab (1 Kings 15:25-28).

TISARANA

The threefold refuge in Buddha, Dhamma and Sangha, which follows the invocation to the Buddha in Pansil and precedes the five-fold vow of Pansil or Pancha-Sila.

TISCHENDORF, Konstantin von

(1815-1874) German biblical critic who made extensive and invaluable contributions to biblical textual criticism, and is especially famous for his discovery of the important *Codex Sinaiticus* of the Bible.

TISHAH BE-AV

Jewish fast day with a complex history, falling on the ninth day of the summer month of Av.

According to the Talmud, many sad happenings took place on Tishah Be-Av. On that day it was decreed that the Israelites should wander through the wilderness for 40 years. On that day the First Temple was destroyed in 586 BC by Nebuchadnezzar and the Second Temple in 70 by Titus. On that day the fortress city of Betar fell to the Romans in 135. And on that day, shortly afterwards, Bar Kochba and his men were massacred.

In the Middle Ages, on Tishah Be-Av, King Edward I of England signed the decree expelling Jews from England in 1290; they were not re-admitted until the 17th century. And on Tishah Be-Av in 1492, over 150,000 Jews were hounded from Spain, where they had lived peacefully for centuries, by the cruel command of King Ferdinand and Queen Isabella.

To commemorate the destruction of the two Temples, the rabbis ordered a day of mourning and of fasting on Tishah Be-Av. On Tishah Be-Av evening and on the following morning, passages of lamentations are read from the Book of Jeremiah, and mourning candles are lit. In the synagogue, shoes are taken off and the congregants seat themselves on the floor or on overturned chairs and benches. Ekhah is the first word of lamentations, and they are said to be the saddest chant in all of Jewish religious music. Towards the end of the services, poems by Yehudah Halevi, "sweet singer of Zion," are recited. These verses sing of the restoration of Zion, a hope that has been cherished by every generation of Jews.

TITANS

In Greek mythology, the name given to the children of Uranus (Heaven) and Gaea (Earth). It is not certain how many there were, but they included Cronus, Hyperion, Oceanus, Iapetus and Coeus. They were all of gigantic height and possessed great strength. Cronus eventually overthrew Uranus, and the Titans controlled the world until the Olympians, under Cronus' son Zeus, rebelled and defeated them.

TITHE

A custom dating back to Old Testament times and adopted by the Christian church whereby lay people contributed a 10th of their income for religious purposes, often under ecclesiastical or legal obligation. The money (or its equivalent in crops, farm stock, etc.) was used to support the clergy, maintain churches, and assist the poor. Tithing was also a prime source of subsidy for the construction of many magnificent cathedrals in Europe.

TITUS

According to biblical tradition, a fellow-laborer of Paul the apostle, for whom he was secretary. Titus was specially entrusted with organizing the alms collection for poor Christians of Judea and acted as a commissioner for Paul at Corinth. He also organized the churches in Crete.

TITUS, Letter of Paul to

A New Testament writing addressed to one of Paul's close companions, organizer of the churches in Crete. It, and the two letters of Paul to Timothy, have been called pastoral letters because they deal principally with heresies and church discipline. The letter urges Titus to appoint worthy elders to positions of responsibility, to preach sound doctrine, and to exemplify in his own life the virtues that are expected of all Christians.

TLALOC

The Aztec rain god; his name means He Who Makes Things Sprout. Representations of the rain god wearing a particular mask, with large round eyes and long fangs, date at least to the Teotihuacan culture of the highlands (3rd to 8th centuries AD). His characteristic features were strikingly similar to those of the Maya rain god Chac of the same period.

TOB-ADONIJAH

In biblical times, one of the Levites whom Jehoshaphat, in the third year of his reign, sent out to teach God's law in the cities of Judah (2 Chronicles 17:7-9).

TOBIAH

In biblical times, name of the forefather of some returned exiles who were unable to establish their Israelite genealogy (Ezra 2:1; Nehemiah 7:61-62).

The name is also applied to an opponent of Nehemiah. Tobiah was "the servant," likely some official under the Persian king (Nehemiah 2:19). Both he and his son Jehohanan married Jewish women, and Tobiah also related to High Priest Eliashib. This put Tobiah in a position of advantage for undermining Nehemiah's authority, in that many Jews looked up to and spoke highly of Tobiah (Nehemiah 6:17-19).

When Nehemiah arrived in Jerusalem, Tobiah and his associates were displeased with Israel's brightened prospect (Nehemiah 2:9, 10). At first they merely derided and mocked the Jews (Nehemiah 2:9-10), but when the wall rebuilding made progress, they became angrier. However, various conspiracies - to kill off the Jews, and an attempt to get Nehemiah to violate the sanctity of the Temple (Nehemiah 6:1, 10-13) - all failed. Even after the walls were completed, Tobiah through correspondence with his sympathizers in Jerusalem, attempted to intimidate Nehemiah (6:16-19).

On his second arrival from Babylon, when Nehemiah found a dining room in the Temple court reserved for Tobiah, he promptly threw Tobiah's things out (Nehemiah 13:4-9).

TOBIJAH

In Judaism, name of one of the Levites whom Jehoshaphat dispatched to teach God's law in the cities of Judah in 934 BC (2 Chronicles 17:7-9).

The name is found also to apply to one of the returned Jewish exiles from whom gold and silver were taken to make a crown for High Priest Jeshua (Zechariah 6:10-14).

TOBIT

An apocryphal work (noncanonical for Jews and Protestants) not included in the Hebrew Bible but fully accepted in the Greek translation (Septuagint); it is a religious folktale that takes as its historical setting the account in 2 Kings of Israel's defeat and exile to Assyria.

The book is primarily concerned with the problem of reconciling evil in the world with divine justice. Like Job, Tobit and Sarah are pious Jews unaccountably afflicted by malevolent forces, but their faith is finally rewarded, and God is vindicated as both just and omnipotent. Other major themes are the need for Jews living outside Palestine to observe religious law strictly and the promise of the restoration of Israel as a nation.

TOGARMAH

According to biblical tradition, a son of Gomer the son of Japheth, hence a great-grandson of Noah (Genesis 10:1-3; 1 Chronicles 1:4-6). The name apparently came to apply as well to the region occupied by his descendants. In Ezekiel's dirge concerning Tyre, Togarmah is mentioned as the source of "horses and steeds and mules," for which Tyre traded certain goods (Ezekiel 27:2, 14). The same prophet lists Togarmah among Gog or Magog's allies and gives its situation as among the people's of "the remotest parts of the north" (Ezekiel 38:6).

TOHU
In Judaism, name of an ancestor of Samuel (1 Samuel 1:1).

TOI
In biblical times, name of the king of Hamath. On learning that David had defeated their mutual enemy Hadadezer the king of Zobah, Toi immediately sent his son with congratulations and gifts. These David sanctified along with his battle spoil (2 Samuel 8:9-12; 1 Chronicles 18:9-11).

TOLA
In Judaism, name of the first-named son of Issachar, who accompanied Jacob's household into Egypt (Genesis 46:8, 13). Tola's sons and some of his grandsons founded populous tribal families in Issachar, collectively known as Tolaites (Numbers 26:23).
The name is also found to apply to a judge of Israel; the son of Puah. Tola was a descendant of Issachar, but he lived, and was later buried, in the mountainous region of Ephraim. No experiences of his 23 year judgeship are recorded (Judges 10:1-2).

TOLAITES
In biblical times, a family of the tribe of Issachar founded by Tola (Numbers 26:23).

TOLEDO, Councils of
10 councils of the Catholic church in Spain, held in Toledo from 400 to 702. Though ecclesiastical in nature, the councils were often important in Spanish civil and political affairs. Nearly all were convoked by kings, sometimes with the primary purpose of gaining political support from the Spanish church.

TOLERATION, Edict of
Law (issued October 1781) promulgated by the Holy Roman Emperor Joseph II granting limited freedom of worship to non-Roman Catholic Christians and removing civil disabilities to which they had previously been subject in the Austrian domains, while maintaining a privileged position for the Catholic church.

TOLERATION, Religious
The intellectual and practical acknowledgment of the right of others to live in accordance with religious beliefs that are not accepted as one's own.

TOLERATION ACT OF 1689
Law granting freedom of worship to Nonconformists (dissenting Protestants); one of a series of measures that firmly established the Glorious Revolution in England. It allowed Nonconformists their own places of worship and their own teachers and preachers, subject to acceptance of certain oaths of allegiance.

TONGUES, gift of
Speech in an unknown or fabricated language uttered by individuals as a spiritual gift. It first appeared at Pentecost and was common in the early church, its use regulated by Paul (1 Corinthians 14:18-19).

TOPHEL
In biblical times, name of a site mentioned with others as an aid in locating the place where Moses addressed the Israelites (Deuteronomy).

TOPHET
In biblical times, name of a place outside Jerusalem. There, for a considerable period, unfaithful Israelites, including Ahaz and Manasseh, engaged in child sacrifice. Finally, King Josiah made it unfit for worship (1 Kings 23:16; 2 Chronicles 28:3; Jeremiah 7:31-33). Tophet probably occupied a section of the eastern part of the Valley of Hinnom near the gate of the Potsherds (Jeremiah 19:2, 6).

TORAH

(Hebrew: law, teaching), the Pentateuch (first five books of the Bible) kept in the ark of every synagogue. In a wider sense it is the whole body of oral and written Jewish teaching, similar to the Old Testament.

The scrolls of the Torah, fundamental to Jewish faith and practice, are kept in the ark of the covenant chest in the synagogue. They are carried in procession and are read or chanted at services. Moses was believed to have received the law from God on tablets of stone.

TORRENT VALLEY

Description of the Promised Land, which reads in Deuteronomy 8:7: "a land of torrent valleys of water, springs and watery deeps issuing forth in the valley plain and in the mountainous region." Some of the streams are fed by springs and are therefore perennial, whereas others are torrents during the rainy season but dry up completely during the rainless season (1 Kings 17:7; 18:5). Faithful Job compared the treacherous dealings of his brothers toward him to a winter torrent that dries up in the summer (Job 6:15).

TOSEFTA

A collection of oral traditions related to Jewish Oral Law. In form and content the Tosefta is quite similar to the Mishna, the first authoritative codification of such laws, which was given its final form early in the 3rd century AD by Judah ha-Nasi. Both the Tosefta and the Mishna represent the work of Jewish scholars who, for the most part, lived in Palestine and spent some 200 years gathering, evaluating, correlating, and selecting the most important traditions of material that developed from the time of Ezra (circa 450 BC).

TOWER OF DAVID

Monument in Jerusalem, created over the ruins of the Hasmonean and Herodian periods.

TRACHONITIS

In biblical times, name for that region which, together with Ituraea, was under the administration of Philip, the Roman district ruler during the ministries of John the Baptist and Jesus (Luke 3:1). The northern limits of Trachonitis were some 25 miles south-east of Damascus in the north-eastern part of Bashan.

Trachonitis is mentioned only once in the Bible, though Strabo and Josephus make several references to this region. From such secular sources it is learned that Roman Emperor Augustus included Trachonitis in the kingdom territory given to Herod the Great. Upon Herod's death his son Philip received Trachonitis as part of his tetrarchy over which he ruled down to his death.

TRADITION

The aggregate of customs, beliefs, and practices that give continuity to a culture, civilization, or social group and thus shape its views; taken in this sense, laws and institutions are also part of tradition. In certain religions, tradition signifies essential doctrines or tenets that are not explicitly set down in sacred scriptures but are accepted as so orthodox and authoritative that they have equal authority with sacred writings and are sometimes used to interpret them.

TRADITION, Roman Catholic

According to Catholic teaching, one of the sources (together with sacred scriptures) of divine revelation. It is, as Vatican Council II points out, the Word of God which has been entrusted to the apostles of Christ the Lord and the Holy Spirit. Unlike many Christian communities that teach scripture alone is the source of divine revelation, the Catholic Church professes that "sacred tradition and sacred scripture form one sacred deposit of the Word of God, which is committed to the church" (Dogmatic Constitution on Divine Revelation).

TRANSCENDENCE

In religious philosophy, the notion of God as a being beyond and independent of the universe and to whom the concepts of human discourse are not applicable. In Oriental religions the notion has the special meaning of transcending consciousness and allows of a limited human communication with the divine.

TRANSCENDENTALISM

19th century American philosophical and literary movement that centered upon the theories of Waldo Emerson and included such prominent New England writers and reformers as David Henry Thoreau, Margaret Fuller, Amos Bronson Alcott and William Channing. These people felt that the utilitarian and materialist philosophy of the 18th and early 19th century was backward looking and morally bankrupt. Their own outlook, by contrast, was inspired by the German idealist school as expressed in the transcendental theories of Immanuel Kant, but more particularly as interpreted by the English-speaking poet and critic Samuel Coleridge.

This philosophy, based on the primacy of consciousness, emphasized the will and the power of inspiration. Thus the transcendentalists sought to strengthen the cultural development of the individual and to promote social change in the direction of greater freedom. In particular, they felt that the traditional and established forms of Christian religion (Emerson had first been a Unitarian minister) were stale and outworn. Instead they put forward an idealist outlook that taught men to see God directly in nature. They also sponsored or inspired as number of social and literary experiments in line with their impetus for reform.

TRANSFIGURATION

A Christian term referring to the occasion upon which Jesus Christ took three of his disciples, Peter, James, and John, up on a mountain, where Moses and Elijah appeared and Jesus was transfigured, his face and clothes becoming white and shining a light (Luke 9:29).

TRANSFIGURATION, Feast of

Festival of the Transfiguration (August 6) is one of the major feast days of the Orthodox church. It is not known when the festival was first celebrated, but it was kept in Jerusalem by the 7th century and in most parts of the Byzantine Empire by the 9th century. It was gradually introduced into the Western church and was placed on the liturgical calendar by Pope Callistus III in 1457.

TRANSMIGRATION OF SOULS

Belief that the soul travels to a new body after death. As the belief is usually expressed, the journey of the soul from body to body is seen as a progression toward or away from an ultimate heaven goal. Thus the soul may move into a person of higher or lower caste or even downward into the body of an animal or insect, according to the worth it has gained in its past life. Transmigration of the soul is a belief of Brahmanism, Buddhism and a number of ancient religions.

TRANSUBSTANTIATION

The Roman Catholic doctrine that in the Eucharist bread and wine are transformed into the body and blood of Christ. The belief that the transformation takes place, not in appearance, but in essence, is an essential feature of the communion sacraments.

TRAPPISTS

Popular name for the members of the Order of Cistercians of the Strict Observance, a Roman Catholic monastic order. It originated in 1664 at the abbey of La Trappe, Normandy, as a reform movement within the original Cistercian Order. Well known for its strict disciplines, the order values the contemplative life and rigid observance of monastic offices.

TREATISE ON THE POWER AND PRIMACY OF THE POPE

One of the confessional writings of Lutheranism, prepared in 1537 by Philipp Melanchthon, the German reformer. The first section of the treatise considers the papal claim of supremacy within the church and over secular kingdoms and the necessity for Christians to believe this claim in order to be saved. Melanchthon declared the papal claim to be false and without basis in scripture or history. In the second section, the proper role and power of bishops were considered. Melanchthon discussed what he considered abuses of the papal office and recommended that the office be eliminated.

TRENT, Council of

19th ecumenical Council of the Roman Catholic Church (1545-1563), highly important for its sweeping decrees on self-reform and for its dogmatic definitions that clarified virtually every doctrine contested by Protestantism. Pope Pius IV confirmed the council's decrees in 1564 and published a summary of its doctrinal statements; observance of disciplinary decrees was imposed under sanctions. In short order the catechism of Trent appeared, the missal and breviary were revised, and eventually a revised edition of the Bible was published.

Trent set in motion a number of Catholic reforms in regard to the liturgy. The religious education of the faithful, the training of candidates for the priesthood, and the devotional life of the church. Its influence was, for the most part, widespread and positive, and it is considered one of the most important of the church's ecumenical councils.

TRIDUUM

A three-day series of public devotions, similar to a novena except for the shorter time period.

TRIKAYA

The Mahayana (Buddhist) doctrine of the three bodies. Originally the doctrine of the basic unity of the reality underlying manifestation, the phenomenal or Nirmanakaya and the nominal or Sambhogakaya, being aspects of the one ultimate reality, one in essence with Tathata.

As applied to the development of Buddhahood and Bodhisattvahood, the doctrine teaches that each aspirant for Buddhahood may, oan attaining the goal, renounce final Nirvana and keep in touch with humanity by dwelling in the Mirmanakaya, through which he may function at will on any of the phenomenal planes of existence.

TRIMURTU

In Hinduism, a triad made up of the three great gods, Brahma, Vishnu, and Shiva. In a division of the cosmic functions, Brahma is regarded as the creator, Vishnu the preserver, and Shiva the destroyer. Yet the apparent polytheism of India has been qualified by the believer's search for a single deity to whom he could pay personal devotion. Thus, scholars consider the trimurtu as an attempt to reconcile different monotheistic approaches with one another.

TRINITY

In Christian theology term denoting the unity of Father, Son, and Holy Spirit as three persons in one Godhead. The three Persons are each fully God: coequal, eternal and consubstantial, yet are distinct (Matthew 28:19). It is a mystery, being known by revelation and being above reason though not unreasonable.

The doctrine of the Trinity was first proclaimed by the council of Nicaea in 325. Almost all Christian churches express belief in the Trinity in some form, although some theological disagreement exists about the nature of this unity.

Although rooted in Jewish monotheism, Christian belief in the divinity led to the development of the doctrine of the Trinity. This states that the one God reveals Himself in the three "persons" of Father, Son (Jesus Christ), and Holy Spirit. These three persons are nevertheless regarded as one "substance." The doctrine was eventually defined by early councils and theologians as "three persons in one substance."

TRIPITAKA

The three branches of the Buddhist scriptures, Dharma, are meant by this term. They are Sutras which contain the Buddha's teachings; Vinayas, which contain his disciples; and Abhidharmas, which contain various commentaries and essays on Buddhist doctrines and precepts. Later, Buddhist writings by Chinese and Japanese High-Priests were also included in the Buddhist canons.

TRI-RATNA

The three components of the Buddhist and Jaina creed. In Buddhism, the tri-ratna signifies the Buddha, the dharma (doctrine, law) and the sangha (the monastic order, or community of believers). In Jainism the three jewels are understood as samyag-darsana ("right faith"), samyag-jnana ("right knowledge"), and samyak-caritra ("right conduct").

TRISALA

Mother of Mahavira, the most recent of the Jaina saints of India. Trisala was, like the mother of the Buddha, a member of the Ksatriya, or warrior caste.

TRI-SIKSA

In Buddhism, the three types of learning required of those who seek to attain enlightenment. The threefold training comprises all aspects of Buddhist practices: moral conduct (sila), meditation (samadhi) and wisdom (prajna).

TRI-SVABHAVA

In Buddhism, the states of the real existence that appear to a person according to his stage of understand-

ing. Together with the doctrine of store-consciousness, it constitutes the basic theory of the Vijnanavada school of Buddhist philosophy.

TRITON

In Greek mythology, a merman, demigod of the sea, who was the son of the seagod Poseidon, and his wife, Amphitrite.

TROPHIMUS

In the New Testament, a coworker of the apostle Paul; an Ephesian gentile Christian (Acts 21:29). Trophimus became a Christian perhaps during Paul's extended Ephesian ministry on his third missionary journey. Afterward Trophimus was one of Paul's traveling companions on the return leg of the trip through Macedonia into Asia Minor and on to Jerusalem (Acts 20:3-5, 17, 22). There Trophiomus was seen with Paul, and when Paul took several others along with him into the temple grounds the Jews thought that Trophimus, a gentile, went beyond the Court of the Gentiles, thereby defiling the temple. On this false assumption they mobbed Paul (Acts 21:26-30). Some years later, after Paul's first imprisonment, Trophimus traveled with him again. But when they got to Miletus, not far from Trophimus's hometown, Trophimus became sick and was unable to continue (2 Timothy 4:20).

TRUE CROSS

A Christian relic, reputedly the wood of the actual cross on which Jesus Christ was crucified. Legend relates the True Cross was found by St. Helena, mother of Constantine the Great, during her pilgrimage to the Holy Land circa 326.

TRUSTEEISM

In the history of the Roman Catholic Church in the United States, a controversy during the late 18th and early 19th centuries regarding lay control of parish administration. Legislation in various states had recognized elected representatives of the laity (trustees) as the legal administrators of parishes. The assertion by the bishops of their prerogative in this respect tended to confirm for Protestants the authoritarian character of Catholicism.

TRYPHAENA

In the New Testament, name of a Christian woman in Rome whom Paul greets in his letter and commends for her hard labor (Romans 16:12). Tryphaena and Tryphosa, with whom she is listed, may have been fleshly sisters, for it was not unusual for family members to have names derived from the same root word, as in this case. Both names were common among women of Caesar's household; but the record is silent as to whether these two women belonged to that household.

TRYPOSA

In the New Testament, name of a Christian woman of Rome greeted and commended by Paul (Romans 16:12).

TSAO CHUN

In Chinese mythology, the Furnace Prince whose magical powers of alchemy produced gold dinnerware that conferred immortality on the diner.

TSAO SHEN

China's widely worshipped god of the Kitchen (God of the Hearth) who reports to Heaven on family conduct and has it within his power to bestow poverty or riches on individual families.

TUATHA DE DANANN

In Celtic mythology, a race inhabiting Ireland before the arrival of the Milesians (the ancestors of the modern Irish). They were believed to have been skilled in magic.

TUBAL

In the Old testament, name of one of the seven sons of Japheth (Genesis 10:2; 1 Chronicles 1:5). The name is thereafter used as referring to a people or land and usually is associated with Meshech, the name of another of Japheths's sons. Tubal, along with Javal and Meshech, engaged in trading with Tyre, dealing in slaves and copper articles (Ezekiel 27:13). Tubal was included in Ezekiel's dirge over Egypt as being among the "uncircumcised" ones with whom the Egyptians would lie in Sheol, because of the terror they had wrought (Ezekiel 32:26-27). They are also included among those uniting with "Gog and the land of Magog" who is called the "head chieftain of Meshech and Tubal" and who comes storming out of "the remotest parts of the north" in a fierce attack against God's people (Ezekiel 38:2-3; 39:1-2). Tubal thus lay to the north of Israel but not is distant as to be out of commercial contact with Tyre in Phoenicia.

TUBAL-CAIN

In the Old Testament, name of a son of Lamech by his second wife Zillah; therefore, a descendant of Cain and half brother of Jabal and Jubal. He had a sister named Naamah (Genesis 4:17-22). Tubal-cain was "the forger of every sort of tool or copper and iron," which can be taken to mean that he either invented, founded or was prominent in the occupation.

TUESDAY

The third day of the week, named for the Anglo-Saxon god of war. The French call Tuesday Mardi, after the Roman god of war, Mars. Mardi gras or shrove Tuesday, marks the beginning of Lent.

TULKU

In Buddhism, a term meaning emanation, a form created and thus a phantom. A difficult subject as many doctrines blend in it; hence divergent descriptions that are all partially true.

1 The Nirmanakaya, itself a doctrine of great complexity. The appearance-on-earth body of Buddha, who has to some extent refused Nirvana to be available to help mankind.

2 The Bodhisattva's power to produce emanations at will as "skilful means," to help humanity towards enlighten-

ment.

3 The overshadowing and partial using by a spiritual power of a human body chosen for the purpose. In this sense Jesus was a Tulku of the Christ-principle.

4 The actual reincarnation of a holy man, whether a great teacher or merely a previous abbot of the monastery.

TUM-MO

In Buddhism, term meaning vital heat, the driving force of the inner self-training. In its highest manifestation the term is cognate with Kundalini and at its lowest a method of inducing physical warmth which enables the trance to mediate naked in the snow at 10,000-15,000 feet.

TUNSTALL, Cuthbert

(1474-1559) Prelate, bishop of Durham, who was a leading conservative in the age of the English Reformation. Learned in humanistic disciplines, he was essentially an official and was friendly with Sir Thomas More.

TUR, al-

The title of the 52nd sura of the Koran; it means "The Mountain." but has also been considered as a proper name indicating the mountain in the Sinai were Musa conversed with God. The sura belongs to the Meccan period and has 49 verses. Its title is drawn from the first verse which reads "By the Mountain." The sura refers to the fires of hell and the joys of Paradise and challenges disbelievers to produce the like of the Koran. The Prophet Mohammed is reassured that he is neither a soothsayer nor mad.

TURBAN

Item of headgear worn by Muslims and others in the Middle East. The Turks became famous for the massive turbans worn by some of their dignitaries in the days of the Ottoman empire.

T'U-TI

A bewildering variety of Chinese gods whose deification and functions are determined by local residents. Their chief characteristic is the limitation of their jurisdiction to a single place - e.g., a bridge, a street, a temple, a public building, a private home, or a field.

TWELVE PATRIARCHS, Testaments of the

A pseudepicraphical work (a non-canonical writing that in style and content resembles authentic biblical literature) composed of 12 separate sections, each of which purports to be the last words of a son of Jacob to his children. The book is an imitation of the "blessing of Jacob" described in chapter 49 of Genesis, but, unlike its model, this work contains lengthy moral exhortations based on the supposed sin or virtue of each patriarch.

Scholars believe that the book was written in the late 2nd or early 3rd century AD by a Christian who used Haggadic works and the Jewish Testaments of Levi and Naphtali as models to embellish the biblical stories.

TWELVE TABLES, Laws of the

First written Roman Law. Inscribed on 12 tables (tablets) circa 450 BC, the laws were set out in the forum and were memorized by every Roman schoolboy. They included both criminal and civil codes, and applied to all citizens. They are of great historical importance both to the development of Roman law and the tradition of written law.

TWELVE TRIBES OF ISRAEL

The 12 family groups into which the ancient Hebrews were divided. They were descended from and named for ten sons of Jacob and two sons of Joseph. Those descended from Jacob's sons were Asher, Benjamin, Dan, Gad, Issachar, Judah, Naphtali, Reuben,

Simeon, Zebulun; the two from Joseph's sons were Ephraim and Manasseh. When the Hebrews finally reached the Promised Land they divided the country among these 12 family groups. A 13th tribe, Levi, had no portion of land set aside for it, dwelling in towns scattered through all the other tribes.

TWENTY-FIVE ARTICLES OF RELIGION

Creed prepared by John Wesley (1703-1791), founder of Methodism, for the Methodist church in America. The creed was accepted at the conference in Baltimore in 1784, when the Methodist Episcopal Church was formally organized.

TYCHE

In Greek religion, the goddess of chance, with whom the Roman Fortuna was later identified; a capricious dispenser of good and ill fortune.

TYCHICUS

In the New Testament, name of one of Paul's aides, a beloved brother and faithful minister and fellow slave in the Lord; from the District of Asia. Tychicus was a m,ember of Paul's party returning from Greece through Macedonia into Asia Minor; but whether or not Tychicus went all the way to Jerusalem is not stated (Acts 20:2-4).

TYNDALE, William

(1494-1536) English biblical translator, and Protestant martyr. His translation later became the basis of the King James Version of the Bible. Seized by the authorities at Antwerp, he was condemned for heresy and burned at the stake.

TYPOLOGICAL INTERPRETATION, Biblical

A hermeneutical (interpretive) method or principle used to establish the relevance of an earlier biblical text for a later period by emphasizing points both of basic similarity and of essential dissimilarity centered on so-called types or antitypes.

TYRANNUS

In the New Testament, a name connected with the Ephesian school auditorium in which Paul preached for two years after having encountered resistance in the Jewish synagogue (Acts 19:9-10).

TYRE

Ancient city of Phoenicia which grew rich by trade. Tyre was famous for its purple dye, cloth, fine glass and cedarwood. It achieved maritime supremacy by circa 1400 BC and later established colonies as far afield as Spain and North Africa.

Probably founded before 1750 BC, Tyre was conquered by Egypt's Thutmose III, but later broke free. Its island site was joined to the mainland by its most powerful king, Hiram (circa 979-945 BC). It rebelled many times, but fell to Nebuchadnezzar II of Babylon (573 BC) after a 13-year siege. Destroyed by Alexander the Great (333 BC), Tyre recovered under the Seleucids and Romans. After a period of Crusader rule (1124-1291), it was destroyed by the Mamelukes.

TZEDAKAH

In Judaism, term meaning righteousness, an integral part of collective and personal existence. Tzedakah is not an event or occasion in the life of a Jew. Yet it is so much a part of the collective and personal existence and has permeated the consciousness of the Jewish people to such an extent, that it is like a golden thread in the rich heritage of the Jewish heritage.

From earliest times, Tsedakah has meant the act of sharing, being kind to the poor, and doing good deeds. The best one-word translation ofs Tzedakah is "righteousness," and that is what it has signified during the ages.

The golden thread of Tzedekah can be traced through Jewish pathways for thousands of years. It makes its appearance in the Bible. Afterwards, the strand of Tzedakah is taken up by the rabbis of the Talmud and those who followed. Still later it played a vital part in the life of the Jewish community in Europe.

TZU-JAN

In Chinese taoism, an ideal state of human existence that results from living in complete harmony with the forces of nature.

U

UDGITA

In Buddhism, the invocation OM, the highest and most concentrated mantric expression into which the essence of the universe, as realized with the human consciousness, is compressed.

UEL

In the Old Testament, name of one of the sons of Bani whom Ezra induced to send away their foreign wives and sons (Ezra 10:10-11, 34, 44).

UGANDA, Martyrs of

A group of 22 brave and remarkable Roman Catholic Africans who were executed during the persecution of Christians under Mwanga, ruler of Buganda (now Uganda) from 1885 to 1887.

UISANG DAISA

(625-702) Buddhist who devoted himself to the propagation of the teaching of the Garland Sutra, which provided ideological support for the political system of the state of Sila (661-935), one of the three kingdoms into which ancient Korea was divided.

UKE-MOCHI-NO-KAMI

In Shinto mythology the goddess of food. She is also variously identified as Waka-uka-no-me.

UKKO

In Finnish folk religion, the god of thunder. He was depicted as having his abode at the center of the heavenly vault, the navel of the sky. Ukko was believed to possess great power, which the religious specialists (shamans) tried to acquire and use for their own purposes.

ULAI

In biblical times, name of a "water-course" flowing through or near Shushan (Susa). In Elam, along the Ulai, Daniel received the vision of the ram and the she-goat. It cannot be determined whether the prophet actually went there from Babylon or was transported to that location in a visionary way (Daniel 8:1-16). Conjectures about the ulai vary considerably, and identification is difficult because rivers in the vicinity seem to have changed course somewhat through the centuries. One view is that the Ulai is the Kerkha River. According to another, it was an artificial canal to the north or north-east of Shushan connecting the Kerkha and Abdizful Rivers.

ULAM

According to biblical tradition, father of Bedan; of the tribe of Manasseh (1 Chronicles 7:14-17). The name is also found to apply to a distant descendant of Saul, of the tribe of Benjamin, whose sons were outstanding archers. Ulam's descendants, "sons and grandsons," numbered some 150 in the time of the chronicler (1 Chronicles 8:33-40).

ULAMA

In Islam, religious scholars, jurists, learned men, imams, judges, ayatollahs and similar people. The ulama were, and are, often referred to as if they formed a coherent professional monolithic group of intellectuals and academics. Though they were, and are, such groups, the "group ethic" should not be overstressed. The ulama were often regarded as custodians of "orthodoxy."

ULLA

In the Old Testament, name for an Asherite whose three sons were tribal family heads and valiant warriors (1 Chronicles 7:39-40).

ULLAMBANA
Buddhist festival based on Chinese and Japanese reverence of ancestors.

ULRICH, Saint
(890-973) Bishop and patron saint of Augsburg, the first person known to have been canonized by a pope.

ULTRAMOUNTANISM
In Roman Catholic Church history, a strong emphasis on papal authority and on centralization of the church. The word, meaning "beyond the mountains," identified those members of the church who regularly looked beyond the Alps (that is, to the popes) for guidance.

UMMA
In Islam, word designating community, people, nation. It was a highly emotive word in early Islamic history in the time of the Prophet Mohammed, and remains so among the Arabs today, many of who dream of, or regard themselves as, a single Arab umma.

UMMAH
In biblical times, name of a city of undetermined location on the boundary of Asher's territory (Joshua 19:29-31).

UMMAH
In the Koran, a community of freemen under God who have the same ethnic, linguistic, or religious affiliation. The distinctively Muslim ummah, comprising the adherents of Islam, came into being with the migration of the Prophet Mohammed to Medina (622) when the Islamic community was formed.

UMRAH
In Islam, a minor pilgrimage to Mecca, which does not count towards fulfillment of the religious duty. An umrah may be made at any time and requires less ceremonial. Before arrival in Mecca, the pilgrim dons white garments and is then in a state of ihram or ritual consecration during which he or she will abstain from sexual intercourse, perfume, the wearing of sewn garments and the cutting of hair and nails.

UNBAPTIZED, Faith of
If, as the Roman Catholic Church professes, baptism is necessary for salvation (see John 3:5), what can be said of the salvation of those who die without baptism?

Briefly, Catholic teaching holds that, in the case of adults, there are two possibilities:

▲ baptism of blood or martyrdom;
▲ baptism of desire.

In the case of infants a rather common theological opinion has been that infants who die without baptism are excluded from heaven but spend eternity in a state of natural happiness called limbo. This theological explanation has never been explicitly taught by the Roman Catholic Church.

Another fairly common theological explanation has been that God in his mercy can supply for the lack of baptism in a way that has not been revealed to us. In a document from the Vatican's Congregation for the Doctrine of the Faith (1980) it is said that the church "knows no other way apart from Baptism for ensuring children's entry into eternal happiness"; but in regard to children who die without baptism , the church "can only entrust them to the mercy of God, as she does in the funeral rite provided for them."

UNCONSCIOUS
In Buddhism, a term used to translate the Chinese wu-hsin, literally "no mind" or "no thought." This does not mean mere vacuity, but rather freedom from attachment to thoughts. This term should be distinguished from the word unconscious of modern psychology.

UNETANEH TOKEF
In Judaism, one of the most important of the hymns and prayers read on Rosh Hashanah and also recited on Yom

Kippur. According to the story that was handed down from one generation to another, rabbi Amnon was pressed time and again by the local bishop to leave his faith and be converted to Christianity. He always refused. Once, instead of refusing he asked for three days in which to consider the decision. When he was left alone, he felt so guilty for having delayed his reply that, when he was called to the bishop, he asked that his tongue be cut out. Instead, the bishop had the rabbi's hands and feet amputated. In this condition, the rabbi was carried to the synagogue for the High Holy Day services. As the kedushah, or sanctification service, was about to begin by cantor and congregation, rabbi Amnon asked permission to offer a prayer he had composed. As soon as the last word had left his lips, the rabbi's life was mercifully ended.

Unetaneh Tokef expresses the idea of holiness and awe which fills the Rosh Hashanah service.

UNIGENITUS
A bull (solemn document) issued by Pope Clement IX in 1713, condemning the doctrines of Jansenism - a dissident movement within French Roman Catholicism.

UNITARIANISM
A liberal Christian faith which rejects the concept of a Trinity and asserts the unity of God the Father. Unitarians emphasize reason, liberty and the humanist element in the worship of God. They have traditionally exercised tolerance towards all other forms of religious worship, and indeed have welcomed religious ideas from non-Christian sources.

Unitarianism first emerged in Hungary and poland in the 16th century and eventually spread to England. In the United States, the faith developed in New England during the 18th century in opposition to doctrinaire Calvinism. In 1961 the American Unitarian Association and the Universalist Church of America merged to form the Unitarian Universalist Association, which today has a membership of circa 250,000.

UNITAS FRATRUM
A religious group inspired by Hussite spiritual ideals that took shape in Bohemia in the mid-15th century that broke away from the Utraquists in 1467. They followed a simple, humble life of nonviolence, using the Bible as their sole rule of faith.

UNITED CHURCH OF CANADA
A union of the Methodist and most Presbyterian and Congregational churches in Canada, formed in 1925. The Union created the largest Protestant body in Canada, with an approximated present congregation of circa 4 million. It attempts to incorporate the best aspects of each denomination it has embraced, and to welcome others to its union. Its tenets are stated in "Doctrine of the Basis of the Union," incorporating the Protestant articles of faith and a Presbyterian form of organization. The United church runs four universities and eight theological colleges of its own, plus several on the campuses of other universities. In addition to a vast network of home services, the church has an active overseas missionary service.

UNITED CHURCH OF CHRIST
A Protestant body formed by the union of the Congregational Church and the Evangelical and Reformed Church in 1961. The union, a major one for which negotiations began in 1942, gives each church strong local autonomy while combining their services, organization and missionary efforts on a national level. The combined church has over two million members in the United States.

UNITED EVANGELICAL LUTHERAN CHURCH
Organized in 1896 in Minneapolis, Minnesota, as the United Danish Evangelical Lutheran Church in North America and the Danish Evangelical

Lutheran Church Association in America. "Danish" was dropped from the church's name in 1946.

UNITED EVANGELICAL LUTHERAN CHURCH OF GERMANY

A union of ten Lutheran territorial churches in Germany, organized in 1948 at Eisenach.

UNITED FREE CHURCH OF SCOTLAND

A Presbyterian church formed in 1900 as the result of the union between the Free Church of Scotland and the United Presbyterian Church.

UNITED METHODIST CHURCH

In the United States, a major Protestant church formed in 1968 in Dallas (Texas) by the union of the Methodist Church and the Evangelical United Brethren Church.

UNITED PENTECOSTAL CHURCH

Organized in St. Louis, Missouri, in 1945 by merger of the Pentecostal Assemblies of Jesus Christ and the Pentecostal Church. It is the largest of the "Jesus Only" groups; it otherwise accepts typical Pentecostal beliefs.

UNITED PRESBYTERIAN CHURCH IN THE UNITED STATES

Church organization created in 1958, when the Presbyterian church in the United States and the United Presbyterian Church of North America merged to become the largest Presbyterian body in the United States. The United Church represents over 9,000 churches, with over 3 million members and maintains one of the world's largest foreign missionary services and sponsors a number of colleges and seminaries.

UNITY SCHOOL OF CHRISTIANITY

A religious movement founded in Kansas City (Missouri), in the late 1880s by Charles Fillmore (1845-1948) and his wife Myrtle (1845-1931). Although Unity prefers to consider itself a nonsectarian educational institution that attempts to teach reli-gious truth, it has essentially become a denomination. Unity ministers must complete a prescribed course of study and be approved by the Unity School of Christianity.

UNIVERSALISM

Theological doctrine according to which, under the hand of a universally loving and merciful God, sinner and saint alike will ultimately be saved. The Universalist Church was formed in the United States by Hosea Ballou and other New England nonconformist churchmen. It is based on the related view that the love of God is all-power-ful and will ultimately redeem all evil whether at the personal level or in soci-ety as a whole. It has an essentially broad and nonsectarian outlook, based on a belief in the universality of true religion, and recognizes the ultimate possible validity of non-Christian as well as Christian belief. In 1961, the church united with the Unitarians in the Unitarian-Universalist Association.

UNKNOWN GOD

Part of an inscription of an altar seen by the apostle Paul while at Athens. The Athenians expressed their fear of deities by building many temples and altars. They even went so far as to deify the abstract, erecting altars to Fame, Modesty, Energy, Persuasion, and Pity. Perhaps fearing that they might possibly omit a god and thereby incur that one's disfavor, the men of Athens had erected an altar inscribed with the words: "To an Unknown God." At the outset of this discourse to the Stoics, Epicureans and others assembled at the Areopagus, Paul tact-fully drew their attention to this altar, telling them it was this God, heretofore unknown to them, about whom he was preaching (Acts 17:18-34).

UNNI

In Judaism, name of a Levite musician who played a stringed instrument in the procession that brought the ark of the covenant to Jerusalem (1 Chronicles 15:3-20). The name is also found to apply to a post-exilic Levite assigned to guard duty under High Priest Jeshua (Nehemiah 12: 1,9).

UPADANA

In Buddhism, clinging to existence; the will to live, that which supports existence. It is the ninth link in the Chain of Causation.

UPADHI

In Hinduism, term in the sense of substratum of existence. The term refers to adventitious limiting conditions, particularly in the schools of logic and Bhedabheda, a school of the orthodox philosophy of Vedanta.

UPAMANA

In Hinduism, the fourth of the means of knowledge, by which man can have valid cognitions. Upamana describes an argument by analogy.

UPALLAYANA

Hindu ritual of initiation, restricted to the three upper varnas, or social classes. It marks the child's entrance upon the life of a student and his acceptance. The ceremony is performed between the ages of about 5 and 24.

UPANISHADS

Speculative elaborations in prose and verse of the Vedas, the most ancient Hindu sacred scriptures. The Upanisads date from as early as 400 BC and form the basis of much of the later Hindu philosophy. The special concern of the Upanishads is with the nature of reality. There is a development of the concept of a single, supreme being, and knowledge is directed towards reunion with it.

UPASAMPADA

Buddhist rite of higher ordination, by which a novice becomes a monk. The ceremony as observed in the Theravada (Way of the Elders) tradition is basically the same as in ancient Buddhism. Ordination is not necessarily permanent, and, in some countries, may be repeated in a man's lifetime.

UPAVITA

A Sanskrit term for the Hindu ritual of investing a young man with the sacred thread; in later usage, the sacred thread itself.

UPAYA

In Buddhism, a term meaning means, device or method. It is a Mahayana term for a practical means to a spiritual end which, like a raft when the river is crossed, should be in due course laid aside.

UPEKKHA

In Buddhism, term meaning equanimity, serenity; the fourth of the Brahama Viharas and their synthesis, the state of mind in which the other three can be practiced without attachment.

UPHAZ

A presently unidentified place where gold was found in ancient times (Jeremiah 10:9; Daniel 10:5).

UQQAL

In the Druze religion, an elite of initiates who alone know Druze doctrine, participate fully in the Druze religious service, and have access to Druze scripture. The religious system of Druzes is kept secret from the rest of their own numbers, who are known as juhhal ("the ignorant"), as well as from the outside world. Admission to uqqal is possible for any Druze man or woman deemed worthy after serious scrutiny.

UR

Important city of ancient southern Mesopotamia (Sumer), situated circa 140 miles south-east of the site of Babylon and circa 10 miles west of the present bed of the Euphrates River.
Ruins of what appear to be private houses excavated at Ur (suggested by scholars as belonging to the period between the 20th and 16th centuries BC) were constructed of brick, were plastered and whitewashed, and had 13 or 14 rooms surrounding a paved courtyard. Among clay tablets found at

the site were some used top teach cuneiform writing. Other tablets indicate that students there had multiplication and division tables and worked at square and cube roots. Many of the tablets are business documents.

From excavations at Ur it thus appears that Abraham made notable material sacrifices when leaving that city. But, in faith, the patriarch was "awaiting the city having real foundations, the builder and creator of which city if God" (Hebrews 11:8-10).

The name Ur is also found to apply to a "father" of Eliphal, one of the mighty men of David's military forces (1 Chronicles 11:26, 35).

URANIA

In Greek religion, one of the nine Muses, patron of astronomy. In some accounts she was the mother of Linus the musician.

URBAN I, Saint

(154-230) Pope from 222 to 230. His pontificate occurred within the reign of the Roman Emperor Alexander Severus, a time of peace for the church.

URBAN II

(1035-1099) Odo of Lagery; pope from 1088 to 1099. He initiated the crusades with the first Council of Clermont in 1095. He also greatly strengthened papal power within the Holy Roman Empire, triumphing over the antipope put forward by Emperor Henry IV.

URBAN III

(1109-1187) Uberto Crivelli; pope from 1185 to 1187. He inherited a diplomatic crisis that harassed his entire pontificate.

URBAN IV

(1200-1264) Jacques Pantaleon; pope from 1261 to 1264. His bull of 1264 ordered the whole church to observe the Feast of Corpus Christi, a festival in honor of the Real Presence of Christ in the Eucharist.

URBAN V

(1310-1370) Guillaume de Grimoard; pope from 1362 to 1370. He helped restore peace in Italy and began to reform the Avignonese Curia, which in 1365 he planned to re-establish at Rome, despite French opposition. He was a man of austere life and great piety. As a patron of learning, he founded new universities at Orange, Cracow, and Vienna.

URBAN VI

(1318-1389) Bartolomeo Prignano; pope from 1378 to 1389). His disputes with his cardinals resulted in their election of an antipope and created a schism within the church which lasted for 40 years.

URBAN VII

(1521-1590) Giambattista Castagna; pope from 1623 to 1644. He enjoyed the longest reign of any of the Urbans. He played a major role in the disastrous Thirty Years' War and attempted to consolidate his power in Italy. he also initiated many foreign missions.

URBAN VIII

(1568-1644) Maffeo Barberini; pope from 1623 to 1644. His involvements in church affairs were multifarious. For the training of missionaries he founded (1627) the Collegium Urbanum, and in 1633 declared China and Japan open again for missionaries. He condemned the doctrines of Jansenism, a French movement that emphasized God's sovereignty and de-emphasized man's free will.

URBANUS

In biblical times, a Roman Christian greeted in Paul's letter (Romans 16:9). The name is frequently found in inscriptions of Caesar's household, but the record is silent as to whether this Urbanus was an imperial servant.

URBI ET ORBI

Literally, this Latin phrase means "to the city and the world," specifically, it refers to the solemn blessing of the pope given to his visible audience in the city of Rome and also to the entire invisible audience of the faithful throughout the world.

URI

In biblical times, name of a descendant of Judah through Perez, Hezron, Caleb and Hur. Uri's son Bezalel was a noted tabernacle craftsman (Exodus 31:2; 35:30; 1 Chronicles 2:4-9).

The name is also found to apply to one of the three Levitical gatekeepers whom Ezra induced to send away their foreign wives and sons (Ezra 10:10-11; 24, 44).

URIAH

In Judaism, name of the Hittite husband of Bath-sheba. He was one of David's foreign warriors (2 Samuel 23:39; 1 Chronicles 11:41). His words, conduct, marriage to a Jewess and residence in Jerusalem, all suggest that he adopted the worship of God as a circumcised proselyte (2 Samuel 11:3-11).

While Uriah was engaged in the battle against Amon at Rabbah, David committed adultery with his wife Bath-she-ba, about which Uriah never learned. David then sent for and had Uriah come to Jerusalem, whereupon the king asked him about the progress of the war and sent him out to go to his home so that his wife's child might appear to be Uriah's. However, Uriah refused to go there because the army was out in the field (Deuteronomy 23:9-11). Even when David made him drunk he still refused to sleep at home (2 Samuel 11:1-13). David's crime against Uriah then doubled, for he returned to the war carrying David's own instructions to Joab to maneuver Uriah's death in battle (2 Samuel 11:14-26).

URIEL

Name of various important men named in the Scriptures. Urial was a Levite descendant of Kohath; son of Tahath (1 Chronicles 6:22-24). Uriel was also the name of a chief of the Kohathites at the time David had the ark of the covenant brought to Jerusalem (1 Chronicles 15:5-15).

The name Uriel is also found to belong to the father of Micaiah (Maacah), who was the wife of King Rehoboam and mother of Abijah (2 Chronicles 13:1-2; 11:21). Maacah was Absalom's grand-daughter. Since Absalom's three sons apparently died young and childless (2 Samuel 14:27), Micaiah must have been the child of Absalom's daughter Tamar, and Uriel not the son but the son-in-law of Absalom.

URIJAH

In the Old Testament, name of a priest during the reign of King Ahaz of Judah. When Ahaz went to Damascus to offer tribute to Tiglath-pileser III, he sent Urijah the design and pattern of the great altar he saw there, telling him to build one like it and later instructing him to use it instead of God's altar; Urijah complied (2 Kings 16:8-16). Though not so identified, he was presumably High Priest, in view of his importance and the absence of any other person so titled at this time.

The name is also found to apply to a priest whose son Meremoth was one of the priests in whose care Ezra entrusted the gold and silver and Temple vessels brought to Jerusalem. Urijah later helped to repair Jerusalem's wall (Ezra 8:33; Nehemiah 3:4, 21).

URIM AND THUMMIM

Two significant biblical terms, literally meaning lights and perfections. The first mention of these terms is found at Exodus 28:30.

As recorded at Leviticus 8:8, Moses, after placing the breastpiece upon Aaron, put the Urim and Thummim in the breastpiece. While the Hebrew preposition here translated "in" can be rendered "upon," the same word is used at Exodus 25:16 in speaking of placing the two stone tablets in the ark of the covenant (Exodus 31:18). Some scholars have proposed the suggestion that the Urim and Thummim were the 12 stones affixed to the breastpiece. That it is not the case is shown by the fact that, in the priestly inauguration ceremony, the completed breastpiece with the 12 stones sewed on it, was put upon Aaron, and then the Urim and Thummim were put in it.

The Aaronic priesthood is referred to at Deuteronomy 33:8-10, which says: "Your Thummim and your Urim belong to the man loyal to you." The reference to those as belonging "to the man loyal to you [Jehovah]" perhaps alludes to the loyalty of the tribe of Levi, from which the Aaronic priesthood came, as demonstrated in connection with the incidence of the golden calf (Exodus 32:25-29).

According to Jewish tradition, the Urim and the Thummim disappeared, together with the ark of the covenant, when Jerusalem was desolated and her Temple destroyed in 607 BC by the Babylonian armies under King Nebuchadnezzar. This view is supported about what is written regarding these objects in the books of Ezra and Nehemiah. There certain men, claimants to priestly descent, but who could not find their names in the public register, were told that they could not eat from the most holy things provided for the priesthood until a priest stood up with Urim and Thummim, and thereafter the Bible makes no further reference to these sacred objects (Ezra 2:61-63; Nehemiah 7:63-65).

URNA

The jewel or small protuberance between the eyes of a Buddha image representing the "third eye" of spiritual vision.

URSULA, Saint

(321-397) Legendary leader of 11 or 11,000 virgins reputedly martyred at Cologne, by the Huns, 4th century nomadic invaders of south-eastern Europe.

URSULINES

A Roman Catholic religious order of women founded at Brescia (Italy) in 1535 by Angela Merici, as the first institute for women dedicated exclusively to the education of girls.

USHPIZIN

In Judaism, according to the Jewish Kabbalistic book the Sefer ha-zohar, seven guests who take turns visiting the homes of all pious Jews to share their dinner at the festival of Sukkot.

USSHER, James

(1581-1656) Scholar and archbishop of Armagh who first distinguished correctly between the genuine and spurious parts of the epistles of St. Ignatius of Antioch, a 2nd-century church father. He wrote widely on Christianity in Asia Minor, on episcopacy, and in doctrinal controversies against Roman Catholicism.

USUAL LIFE

In Buddhism, phrase meaning that we shall not find enlightenment by a study of scriptures and meditation alone, but by a suddenly-acquired awareness that this daily life is the Absolute in action and is Nirvana itself. To achieve this new vision is the purpose of Zen training, and the training is long and arduous.

USURY

In moral theology, the taking of excessive or exorbitant interest on the loan of money. It is a violation of the virtue of justice.

UTHAI

In Judaism, name of a post-exilic resident of Jerusalem; descendant of Judah through Perez (1 Chronicles 9:3-4).

The name is also found to apply to the head of a paternal house among the sons of Bigvai who came with Ezra to Jerusalem in 468 BC (Ezra 8:1, 14).

UTILITARIANISM

A theory of human conduct and ethics that judges actions in terms of the good to which they give rise: an action is right if it produces the greatest happiness for the greatest number. The formula has antecedents going back to Greek philosophy, but in its modern guise utilitarianism first became important with Jeremy Bentham (1748-1832), who actually coined the term. Bentham's general theory of human behavior argued that men always pursue their own greatest pleasure while shunning pain as much as possible.

UZ

Term of several important persons and a place in biblical times. Uz was a son of Aram and great-grandson of Noah through Shem (Genesis 10:22-23; 1 Chronicles 1:17). The name is also found to apply to the first-born son of Nahjor and Milcah; nephew of Abraham (Genesis 22:20-21). Uz is also the name of a son of Dishan, and descendant of Seir the Horite (Genesis 36:21-28).

Uz was the homeland of Job (Job 1:1), likely settled by the Shemite Aram's son Uz and his descendants (Genesis 10:22-23). Its exact location is unknown. Some geographers would locate Uz in the Hauran, but most now favor a location more to the south. Uz seemingly was near Edom, allowing for a later extension of Edomite domain into Uz, or for some later Edomites to be dwelling in the "land of Uz," as indicated at Lamentations 4:21.

UZAI

In Judaism, name of a man whose son Palal helped Nehemiah rebuild Jerusalem's wall (Nehemiah 3:25).

UZAL

In biblical times, name for a person and a place. Uzal is the sixth named of Joktan's 13 sons, and also the tribe descended from Ehoim (Genesis 10:26-29; 1 Chronicles 1:21).

Uzal is also the name of a place referred to in connection with Tyre's traders, at Ezekiel 27:19. According to an Arabic tradition, Uzal, or Azual, was a former name for the centrally located Yemenite capital San'a. An alternate suggestion is Azalla, a town near Medina, about halfway between San'a and the Gulf of Aqabah.

UZZA

In biblical times, a name connected with a garden. King Manasseh and Amon of Judah were buried in the garden of Uzza instead of the usual royal burial places (2 Kings 21:18-26). Neither Uzza nor the garden are otherwise known. Since persons were buried there, the place could not have been in the temple ground and, since the royal palace adjoined the temple, the "house" of Manasseh in the garden of Uzza may have been a summer residence.

UZZA, al-

Pre-Islamic Goddess of Arabia, who has been identified with the Venus star, with a main shrine between al-Ta'if and Mecca. Her name meant "the Mighty." She was worshipped in pre-Islamic times not only by such Arabian tribes as Thaqif and Quraysh but also by the Lakhmids of Hira.

UZZAH

In biblical times, name of a son of Abinadah, undoubtedly a Levite. Uzzah and his brother Ahio led the wagon carrying the ark of the covenant from their house when David wanted it brought to Jerusalem. When the bulls pulling the wagon nearly caused an upset, Uzzah reached out and grabbed hold to steady the ark, for which God struck him dead on the spot. David named the place Perez-uzzah because there God had broken through in a "rupture against Uzzah" (2 Samuel 6:3-8; 1 Chronicles 13:7-11).

UZZEN-SHEERAH

In biblical times, name of a city that Sheerah, an Ephraimite women, built. In what sense she "built" it is not stated; perhaps this was in the sense of her contributing in some major way to the progress and development of this and other places listed (1 Chronicles 7:22-24).Uzzen-sheerah's location is not definitely known. However, some geographers identify it with Beit Sira, less than three miles west-south-west of the suggested site of Lower Beth-horon and circa 13 miles northwest of Jerusalem.

UZZI

Name of several persons in biblical times. Uzzi is a son or descendant of Tola in the tribe of Issachar. Uzzi and several of his descendants became heads of ancestral houses (1 Chronicles 7:1-3). Uzzi, a tribal family head, is also a descendant of Benjamin through Belah.

The name Uzzi is also fund to apply to a descendant of Aaron through Eleazar in the High-Priestly line; possibly great-grandson of Phineas; forefather of the Bible writer Ezra (1 Chronicles 6:3-6; Ezra 7:1-5).

Uzzi is also found to apply to the head of a priestly paternal house of Jedaiah during the time of the High Priest Jeshua's successor Joiakim (Nehemiah 12:2, 12, 19).

UZZIA

In Judaism, name of a mighty man in David's forces. Uzzia was an Ashtarothite, that is, probably from the town of Ashtaroth east of the Jordan (1 Chronicles 11:26; Joshua 9:10).

UZZIAH

In the Old Testament king of Judah (circa 783-742 BC) and son and successor of Amaziah. His reign marked the height of Judah's power. He fought successfully against other nations and exacted tribute from the Ammonites.

Uzziah's strength caused him to become proud, which led to his destruction. He attempted to burn incense in the Temple, an act restricted to priests. When the priests attempted to send him from the Temple, the king became angry and was immediately stricken with leprosy. His son Jothanam ruled for his father until Uzziah died.

UZZIEL

In the Old Testament, last named of Kohath's four sons; grandson of Levi; uncle of Moses and Aaron. Uzziel's three sons became tribal heads in Levi (Exodus 6:16-22; Leviticus 10:4).

The name is also applied to a Levitical musician of the family of Heman, appointed to head David's eleventh musical service division (1 Chronicles 25:4, 18).

Uzziel is also found to be one of four Simeonite sons of Ishi who led 500 men into Mount Seir to wipe out the remnant of Amalekites and take up living there; contemporaries of Hezekiah (1 Chronicles 4:41-43).

UZZIELITES

In biblical times, Levitical descendants of Kohath's fourth son Uzziel (Numbers 3:19). They camped to the south of the tabernacle, and one of the Uzzielites Elizaphan was chieftain of all the Kohathites (Numbers 3:29-30). 112 Uzzielites under Amminadab accompanied the ark of the covenant when David had it brought to Jerusalem (1 Chronicles 15:3-10). Uzzielites were further involved in David's organization of temple service (1 Chronicles 23:6, 20; 24:24; 26:23-24).

V

VADA

In Buddhism, term meaning expression, speech, showing forth.

VADIANUS, Joachim

Swiss religious reformer and one of the most important native Swiss humanists. He used both his political influence and his power as a popular preacher to establish the Reformation in the city of St. Gallen and was primarily responsible for organizing its Reformed church.

VAHANA

In Hindu mythology the animal of man that serves as the vehicle and as the sign of a particular deity. The vahana accompanies, pulls the chariot of, serves as the seat or mount of, his god. The vahana is also used on banners and emblems to identify the god or the cult affiliation of the devotee.

VAIKHANASA VAISNAVAS

A small but important minority of Hindu Vaisnavas (devotees of the Lord Vishnu) in South India who worship according to the ritual prescribed in the Vaikhanasa Samhitas texts.

VAIRAGIN

In India, a religious ascetic who principally worships one or another form of the Hindu god Vishnu. Most vairagins, when not wandering or on pilgrimage reside in monastic communities.

VAIROCANA

In Buddhism, title of a person regarded by Buddhists of the Far East and of Tibet and Java as the supreme Buddha.

VAISANA-SAHAJIYA

An esoteric Hindu cult centered in Bengal that sought religious experience through the world of the senses, specifically human, sexual love.

VAISESIKA

In Hinduism, one of the six orthodox systems, traditionally distinguished in Hindu philosophy, significant for its naturalism, which is not characteristic of most Indian thought. The Vaisesika school attempts to identify, inventory, and classify entities and their relations that present themselves to human perceptions. Typical of the Vaisesika school is the atomist view of the world. Air, fire, water, and earth are each an "atom", without spatial mass, transcendentally independent elemental presences.

VAISNAVISM

In Hinduism, worship of the god Vishnu and of his incarnations, principally as Rama and as Krisna; one of the major forms of modern Hinduism. A major characteristic of Vaisnavism is the strong part played by religious devotion. The ultimate goal of the devotee is to escape from the cycle of birth and death so as to enjoy the presence of Vishnu.

VAISYA

In Hinduism, third highest in ritual status of the four varnas, or social classes, traditionally commoners. The Vaisya share with the priestly Brahmana and the authoritative Ksatriya the distinction of "twice-born," achieving their spiritual rebirth when they assume the sacred thread at the upanayana ceremony.

VAJRAPANI

In Mahayana Buddhism, one of the celestial bodhisattvas ("Buddhas-to-be"), the manifestation of the self-born Buddha Aksobhya. He is believed to be the protector of the nagas (half-man, half-serpent deities) and sometimes assumes the shape of a bird in order to deceive their traditional enemy, the hawk-like Garuda.

VAJRAYANA

In the history of Buddhism, marks the transition from Mahayana speculative thought to the enactment of Buddhist ideas in individual life. The term vajra is used to signify the absolutely real and indestructible in man as opposed to the fictions an individual entertains about himself and his nature; yana is the spiritual pursuit of the ultimately valuable and indestructible.

VAJRAYOGINI

In Buddhism, an important embodiment of intrapsychic phenomena. Vajrayogini emphasizes experience over speculation but uses the terms of speculative philosophical Buddhism in an imaginative way. This practice means that images taken from the ordinary life world of the individual become the means to further a deeper understanding of man's being, which is both action (upaya) and knowledge (prajna), each reinforcing the other.

VAIZATHA

In the Old Testament, name of one of Haman's ten sons (Esther 9:9-10).

VALENTINE, Saint

Early Christian martyr who perished in Rome circa 270. According to various legends he was a Roman priest or bishop. Lovers' greetings cards are called valentines and are sent on the Feast of St. Valentine (February 14th). The date and the customs which are connected with it are believed to have derived from a Roman pagan festival, Lupercalia, which is also associated with love, and with the exchange of gifts, and was held in med-February.

VALENTINIAN II

(371-392) Associated emperor of the West with his half-brother Gratian from 375 to 383. An emperor with very little power, he was under the influence of his mother, Justina. His reign was marked by civil and religious strife, and he was finally murdered, probably by his Frankish general Arbogast.

VALENTINUS

(746-827) Pope for circa 40 days in 827. He was elected pope in August but died a month later. Nothing is known about his pontificate.

VALENTINUS

(123-189) Religious philosopher, founder of Roman and Alexandrian schools of Gnosticism, an eclectic, dualistic system of religious doctrines postulating the evil origin of matter and the revelatory enlightenment, or gnosis (Greek: "knowledge"), of an elite. Valentinian communities, by their expansion and long standing, provided the major challenge to 2nd and 3rd century Christian theology.

VALHALLA

In Norse mythology, the vast and splendid "Hall of the Slain" in Asgard where the souls of heroes fallen in battle were lavishly entertained by the god Odin. On Doomsday (Ragnarok), they were to march out through the 540 doors to fight with Odin against the giants.

VALLABHA

(1479-1531) Hindu philosopher and founder of the important devotional sect the Vallabnacaryas. He advocated that God is worshipped not by fasting and physical austerities but by love of him and of the universe, salvation rises only by virtue of the grace of God. In order to receive divine love, the devotee must surrender himself wholly to God's gift of love.

VALIDATION OF MARRIAGE

In Roman Catholicism, the making valid of a marriage contract that was originally invalid for one of three reasons:

▲ because of the presence of a diriment (invalidating) impediment;
▲ because of a defect of consent;
▲ because of a defect of form.

The procedures for validation in these cases are given in the Code of Canon Law (Canon 1156 through Canon 1160).

VALIDITY

This term entered the vocabulary of the Roman Catholic Church with the Council of Trent. Validity concerns the conditions that have to be followed for some act to be effectual or legal. For example, reception of baptism is a prior condition for validity receiving any of the other sacraments.

VALIDITY OF SACRAMENTS

When applied to sacraments, validity refers to the minimal requirements of matter, form, and circumstances needed for valid administration and to recognize that an action or celebration has resulted in a true sacrament.

For example, the minister must resolve to do what the church intends in celebrating a sacrament. Since the spouses minister the sacrament to each other in marriage, their intention to celebrate the sacrament is an absolutely necessary condition for validity.

VALUES, Moral

The things that are essential to appropriate human living include, for example, the capacity for love. Other moral values consist of such virtues as chastity, fortitude, justice, and temperance.

VAMANA

In Hinduism, fifth of the ten avataras (incarnations) of the god Vishnu (Vishnu). He made his appearance when the demon king Bali ruled the entire universe and the gods had lost their power. The images of Vamana usually show him already grown to giant size, one foot firmly planted on earth and the other lifted as if to take a stride.

VANIR

In Norse mythology, a race of gods responsible for wealth, fertility and commerce and subordinate to the warlike Aesir.

VARAHA

In Hinduism, third of the ten incarnations (avataras) of the Hindu god Vishnu (Nishnu). When a demon Hiranyaksa dragged the earth to the bottom of the sea, Vishnu took the form of a boar in order to rescue it. They fought for 1,000 years. Then Varaha slew the demon and raised the earth out of the water with his tusks.

VARANASI

Formerly Benares or Banaras, an ancient holy Hindu city in India, on the Ganges River in Uttar Pradesh state. Visited annually by some one million pilgrims, it has many temples. Ghats (steps) leading to the river enable the pilgrims to bathe in its waters. It is the seat of Banaras Hindu University.

VARUNA

In the Vedic phase of Hindu mythology the god-sovereign, the personification of divine authority. He is the rule of the sky realm and the upholder of cosmic and moral law, a duty shared with the gods known as the Adityas, of whom he was the chief.

VASHTI

In biblical times, the queen of Ahasuerus (Xerxes I) king of Persia. In the third year of his reign, Ahasuerus called in all the nobles, princes and servants from the jurisdictional districts. At the end of the conference he held a seven-day banquet. On the seventh day Ahasuerus ordered Vashti brought in, but she refused to come to the banquet. Vashti was deposed and, about four years later, Esther the Jewess was selected to become the wife of Ahasuerus and to take the royal office of Vashti (Esther 2:1-17). The explanation for the long lapse of time between Vashti's dismissal and Esther's replacement of her is thought to have been that

Ahasuerus was occupied in preparation for and execution of his unsuccessful invasion of Greece, which took place in the spring of 480 BC.

VATICAN

A name used to describe a number of different realities; for example, the residence of the pope built upon the Vatican Hill in the city of Rome; the various congregations or tribunals through which the pope governs the Roman Catholic Church; the basilica of St. Peter; the sovereign state of 109 acres, established in 1929 by an agreement between the pope and the Italian government, ruled as an independent territory by the pope.

VATICAN CITY

Smallest independent state in the world, covering 108.7 acres near the west bank of the Tiber River within Rome, the capital of Italy. Its ruler is the pope, and it is the spiritual and administrative hub of the Roman Catholic Church throughout the world. It has a population of circa 1,000.

The dominant feature is St. Peter's, the largest Christian church in the world. The Vatican Palace, dating from the 1400s, has 1,400 rooms and covers 13.5 acres; it is the world's largest residential palace, and has many art treasures, including Michelangelo's famous paintings in the Sistine Chapel. Other treasures are housed in the Vatican Museum, whose collection was begun by Pope Julius II (1503). The Vatican Archive and Library contain many rare historical and religious manuscripts and documents as well as some 900,000 volumes. The Library was begun by Nicholas V.

The Vatican also controls important buildings beyond its boundaries. These include St. John Lateran, the cathedral church of the pope as bishop of Rome, and the papal summer palace Castel Gandolfo.

The Vatican has its own coins, postage stamps and broadcasting station, bank, etc. It maintains diplomatic relations with other countries through ambassadorial legates.

For many centuries the popes ruled over large territories in Italy. When those were absorbed into the Kingdom of Italy (1859-1860, 1870), Pope Pius IX and his successors refused to recognize the situation and remained in isolation within the Vatican until 1929. In that year the Lateran Treaty between the vatican and the Italian government resolved "the Roman question." The Pope formally abandoned all claims to the former papal states, and the Italian government recognized the full independence of the Vatican City State.

VATICAN COUNCIL

Name given to the 20th and 21st ecumenical council of the Roman Catholic Church.

VATICAN COUNCIL, First

This council was convoked by Pope Pius IX and began its deliberations on December 8, 1869, attended by 749 cardinals, bishops and heads of religious orders. Its aim was to consider the problems of faith raised by the advances of natural science and technology. An answer to such problems was given in the Constitution of the Faith (Dei Filius), which declared the pope's infallibility in matters of faith and morals when speaking ex cathedra. The outbreak of the Franco-Russian War and the resultant annexation of Rome by the Italians caused the suspension of the Council on October 20, 1870. Though never dissolved, it did not reconvene.

VATICAN COUNCIL, Second

Council called by Pope John XXIII to find means of spiritual renewal for the church in modern times and to commence the movement towards reunification of the Western and Eastern churches. In June, 1960, the Pope established 11 preparatory commissions and two secretariats for the Council. The opening session on October 11, 1962, was attended by 2,540 prelates and by many observers from other denominations. Pope John died on June 3, 1963, shortly after the end of the first session. His successor, Paul VI, presided over another three sessions, the last of which closed on December 8, 1965. The teaching of Vatican II has an enormous impact on the church in all parts of the world.

The Council issued four Constitutions, nine Decrees and three Declarations on various subjects. Among its more important resolutions were the Declarations on Religious Liberty and Non-Christian Religions (which condemned anti-Semitism), and the decision to celebrate the Mass in each congregation's vernacular language. A brief description of the major documents is given below.

Dogmatic Constitution on the Church
The Dogmatic Constitution on the Church sets forth the church's understanding of her own nature. Its first chapter, "The Mystery of the Church," presents the vision of the church at once divine and human, embracing all people of good will, namely, "the People of God" (second chapter). The third chapter describes the bishops of the world as a "college" collectively responsible, under the leadership of the pope, for the work of the church.

The fourth chapter deals in a very positive way with the role of the laity in the church; the fifth with the universal call to holiness; the sixth with religious communities; the seventh with the relationship between the pilgrim church on earth and the "Heavenly Church." Chapter eight, the final chapter, described the role of the Blessed Virgin Mary.

Dogmatic Constitution on Divine Revelation
The Dogmatic Constitution on Divine Revelation sets forth the church's teaching on how God reveals Himself to humankind. The transmission of this revelation is recorded in written form in the scriptures; its transmission by word of mouth is part of the tradition of the church. Both scripture and tradition spring from one and the same source.

Constitution on the Sacred Liturgy
The Constitution on the Sacred Liturgy sets forth the church's teaching on worship as the heart of her life. It instructs that the sacred texts and rites should be drawn up so that they express more clearly the holy things which they signify and that the Christian people, as far a possible, should be able to understand them with ease and take part in them fully, actively, and as befits a community.

Pastoral Constitution on the Church
The Pastoral Constitution on the church in the modern world sets forth the church's sincere effort to speak to all men and women, to shed light on the dignity of the human person and to cooperate in finding solutions to the outstanding problems of our time.

Decrees
The nine decrees addressed the following subjects:
▲ the pastoral office of the bishops;
▲ ecumenism;
▲ the Oriental Catholic Churches;
▲ the ministry and life of priests;
▲ education for the priesthood;
▲ the renewal of religious life;
▲ the missionary activity of the church;
▲ the apostolate of the laity;
▲ the instruments of social communication.

VATICAN COUNCIL II
Vatican Council II statements with their official Latin titles and the dates of promulgation

▲ Constitution of the Sacred Liturgy (Sacrosanctum concilium) December 4, 1963
▲ Dogmatic Constitution on the Church (Lumen gentium) November 21, 1964
▲ Dogmatic Constitution on Divine Revelation (Dei Verbum) November 18, 1965
▲ Pastoral Constitution on the Church in the Modern World (Gaudium et spes) December 7, 1965
▲ Decree on the Instruments of Social Communication (Inter mirifica) December 4, 1963

▲ Decree on Ecumenism (Unitatis redintegratio) November 21, 1964

▲ Decree on Eastern Catholic Churches (Orientalium ecclesiarum) November 21, 1964

▲ Decree on the Bishops' Pastoral Office in the Church (Christus Dominus) October 28, 1965

▲ Decree on the Appropriate Renewal of the Religious Life (Perfectae caritatis) October 28, 1965

▲ Decree on the Apostolate of the Laity (Apostolicam actuositatem) October 28, 1965

▲ Decree on the Ministry and Life of Priests (Presbuterorum ordinis) December 7, 1965

▲ Decree on the Church's Missionary Activity (Ad gentes) December 7, 1965

▲ Declaration on Christian Education (Gravissimum educationis) October 28, 1965

▲ Declaration on the Relationship of the Church to Non-Christian Religions (Nostrae aetate) October 28, 1965.

▲ Declaration on Religious Freedom (Dignitatis humanae) December 7, 1965.

VATICAN PALACE

Papal residence in the Vatican that lies to the north of St. Peter's Basilica. From the 4th century until the Avignonese period (1309-1377) the customary residence of the popes was at the Lateran.

VAYAMA

In Buddhism, term meaning effort. Samma Vayama is the sixth step on the Noble Eightfold Path. The efforts are described as that to destroy such evil as has arisen in the mind, to prevent any more arising; to produce such good as has not yet arisen in the mind, and to increase the good which has arisen. Together these may be described as developing a right motive for all action.

VEDA

The most ancient and sacred of Hindu scriptures, written in early Sanskrit. The word veda signifies "divine knowledge" or "the science," and Hindus believe the Vedas to be eternal truths formulated by inspired teachers. The principal writings - the oldest of which may date from 1500 BC - are the four collections:

▲ Rgveda (praises and hymns);

▲ Samaveda (chants and tunes);

▲ Yajurveda (sacrificial formulas);

▲ Atharvaveda (incantations and formulas to avert evil and sickness).

VEDAN

In biblical times, one of the places with which Tyre had commercial intercourse (Ezekiel 27:19). Its exact location is uncertain. However, two places in the Arabian Peninsula have been presented as possible identifications, Aden and Wadden near Medina, a city near the middle of the western side of the peninsula.

VEDANTA

In Hinduism, the end or consummation of the doctrine of the Vedas. It is one of the six orthodox systems of Hindu philosophy. It teaches the pantheistic doctrine of the Brahman as the reality unifying all phenomena, and the identity of man's real self with that ultimate reality.

VEDAS

Sacred hymns and oblational verses composed in archaic Sanskrit and current among the Indo-European speaking peoples who entered India from the Iranian regions. The hymns (composed from 1500-1200 BC) formed a liturgical corpus that in part grew up around the cult of the soma and the sacrifice and extolled the hereditary deities, who for the most part personified various natural and cosmic phenomena, such as fire, sun, the dawn, the storms, war and rain, honor, divine authority, and creation.

VED-AVA

Among the Mordvins, the water mother, a spirit believed to rule the waters and their bounty. The water spirits belong to a class of nature spirits common to the Finno-Ugaric peoples dependent on fishing for much of their livelihood.

VEDIC CHANT

Religious chant of India, the expression of hymns from the Vedas, the ancient scriptures of Hinduism. The practice dates back at least 3,000 years and is probably the world's oldest continuous vocal tradition.

VEDIC SACRIFICE

The central religious rite of the Vedeic period of ancient India, a form of worship introduced by the invaders who entered India from the Iranian region. The rite was performed by offering edibles (meat, butter, milk, barley cake, animals, juice of the soma plant) to a sacred fire. The fire, deified as Agni, carried the oblations to the gods.

VEDISM

The religion of the ancient Indo-European-speaking peoples who entered India circa 1500 BC from the Iranian region; it takes its name from the collection of sacred texts known as the Vedas.

Characteristic of Vedism was a belief in the efficacy of ritual and in the correspondences between macrocosm and microcosm. The universe was thought to be in continual danger of being destroyed by chaos. Man contributed to the maintenance of the world by performing sacrifice and by offering the gods the invigorating soma drink.

VENERATION OF THE CROSS

In this devotional, a deep reverence and respect is directed toward the cross. In the Good Friday service, the veneration of the cross involves the procession with the cross through the congregation with the invitation to come forward to show some sign of respect for it. The faithful often bow and/or kiss the cross as a sign of reverence.

VENERATION OF IMAGES

Devotion to icons or images is not against the first Commandment which forbids idols. Rather honoring the images and symbols of God and the saints venerates the person portrayed rather than the image itself.

VENIAL SIN

In contrast to mortal (grave, serious) sin, a venial sin may be described, according to Catholic theology, as a less serious rejection of God's live, not a fundamental choice against God, not a complete turning away from him.

It is a failure to love God and others as much as we should, a transient neglect of God and his law. St. Thomas describes it this way: "Although a person who commits a venial sin does not actually refer his or her act to God, nevertheless he or she still keeps God as his or her habitual end. The person does not decisively set himself or herself on turning away from God, but from overfondness for a created good falls short of God. He or she is like a person who loiters, but without leaving the way.

VERMIGLI, Pietro Martire

(1500-1562) Leading Italian reformer whose chief concern was eucharistic doctrine. His eucharistic was close to that of John Calvin, Buber, and Philipp Melanchthon. Vermigli taught the real presence of Christ in a sacrament mode appropriate to the nature of his glorified humanity.

VERNACULAR

The mother tongue or common spoken language of the people is used in liturgical worship. Ordinarily liturgies are in the local languages, except when another language was originated from missionaries or dictated by a conquering nation. Vatican Council II officially approved the vernacular for Catholic liturgy in the Roman Rite.

VERONICA, Saint

According to legend, a woman of Jerusalem who offered her veil to Jesus to wipe the sweat from his face on his way to Calvary. When he returned the veil, it bore a miraculous imprint of his face.

VERONICA'S VEIL

Tradition has it that a woman who has compassion on Jesus on his way to Calvary gave him her veil that he might wipe the perspiration from his face. The imprint of Jesus's face was miraculously made on this veil.

VERTUMNUS

In Roman religion, a god of uncertain origin who later became associated with the changing year and its seasons, its flowers, and its fruits. In the last connection he is found associated with Pomona, the goddess of fruit trees.

Vespers

Early evening prayer or evensong, part of the Divine Office of the Roman Catholic Church. Once included in the regular parish church services, today vespers are more often recited in monasteries and the largest churches.
The evening service of the Divine Office is also known as Evening Prayer or Evensong. It is one of the two principal hours of prayer. In structure it has an introductory verse; a hymn appropriate for the day, feast or liturgical season; two psalms and a New Testament canticle; a reading from Scripture followed by a responsorial hymn; the Magnificat; intercessions, followed by Our Father, the prayer of the day, and a final blessing.

VESTA

In Roman religion, the goddess of the hearth, identified with the Greek Hestia. Her worship was observed in every household along with that of the Penates and the Lares, and her image was sometimes encountered in the household shrine.

VESTAL VIRGINS

The Roman priestesses of the shrine of Vesta, goddess of the hearth fire. The six Vestal Virgins were chosen when very young and served for 30 years. Punishment for breaking their vow of chastity was burial alive. Their chief responsibility was tending the sacred flame of Vesta, the fire that burned perpetually in her temple in the Roman Forum.

VESTIBULE

The part of a Catholic church between the outer church door and the inside through which people pass in order to reach the interior worship space is known as an entrance hall or antechamber. Today the vestibule is often an area which displays books and pamphlets, church bulletins, and parish announcement boards. It is also the place where the procession to begin the celebration of the Eucharist originates and where it returns after it is ended to greet the faithful.

VESTMENTS

Garments used in the celebration of the Eucharist Liturgy and other sacraments. The vestments have their origin in the ordinary dress of the Roman Empire in the first centuries of Christianity, but they have taken on a symbolic meaning also. The principal vestments now in use are:

▲ Amice: a square or oblong piece of linen (or similar material) to which two long tapes are attached at the upper corners. It is worn over the shoulders and is symbolic of "the helmet of salvation."

▲ Alb: a long, white (albus is Latin for white) garment, symbolic of the total purity that should cover one's approach to God.

▲ Chasuble: a long, sleeveless outer garment worn over the alb by a priest or bishop. Traditionally, the chasuble is a symbol of charity.

▲ Cincture: a cord worn around the waist to keep the alb neatly in place.

▲ Humeral veil: a rectangular shawl worn around the shoulders and used to cover the hands. It is used in Eucharistic processions and devotions for holding the ciborium or the monstrance.

▲ Stole: a long, thin band of appropriate material worn around the neck and shoulders, symbolic of "the yoke of the cord"; it is worn by the priest in solemn celebration of all the sacraments (the deacon wearing it over the shoulder only).

▲ Surplice: a waist-length, lace-decorated, wide-sleeved, white, alblike vestment worn over the cassock outside of Mass.

VETALA

In the mythology of India, a vampire-like fiend that enters corpses. Similar in appearance and behavior to the pisaca, another fiend, the vetala is said to be taller, with parched-up belly and projecting cheek bones.

VICAR

A title for an official acting in some special way for a superior, primarily used as an ecclesiastical title in the Christian church. A vicar general is appointed by the bishop as the highest administrative officer of the diocese, with most of the powers of the bishop.

VICARA

In Buddhism, term meaning investigation; sustained mental application, deeper than Vitakka.

VICAR GENERAL

The priest or bishop appointed by the bishop to assist him in the government of his diocese. The duties of the vicar general are specified in canon law. His office ends with that of the bishop.

VICAR OF CHRIST

The pope is the representative of Christ on earth and the visible spiritual head of the church. The title is used exclusively for the bishop of Rome as the successor of Peter.

VICIKICCHA

In Buddhism, term meaning doubt, as wavering uncertainty. It is a hindrance and a fetter to be removed.

VICTOR I, Saint

(123-199) Pope from 189 to 199. He is hailed for asserting Roman authority in the church. Most notably, he imposed the Roman date for Easter over that celebrated by the Quartodecimans, or Asiatic Christians, whom he threatened to excommunicate if they did not follow suit.

VICTOR II

(1018-1057) Gebhard of Dollnstein-Hirschberg; pope from 1055 to 1057. He held a council that condemned clerical marriages and simony (i.e., the buying or selling of church offices).

VICTOR III

(1027-1087) Dauferi; pope from 1086 to 1087. He sent an army to Tunis, where it defeated the Saracens (Arab and Turkish Muslims) and compelled them to pay tribute to Rome.

VICTOR IV

(1089-1164) Octaviano Monticelli; reigning from 1159 to 1164, the first of four antipopes established against Pope Alexander III by the Holy Roman Emperor Frederick I Barbarossa.

VIDYARAMBHA

Sanskrit term for the religious rites marking the commencement of education.

VIGIL

The word vigil comes from the Latin vigilia which means "a watching." A vigil is a prayer watch kept the night before the feast. In the Roman Catholic Church the mother of all vigils is the Easter Vigil which begins after nightfall on Holy Saturday and ends before dawn on Easter Sunday.

Other important vigils during which Mass is celebrated preceding the feast are Christmas, Pentecost, birth of John the Baptist, Sts. Peter and Paul, and the Assumption. The day and evening before certain feasts have a special office in preparation for the feast day.

VIGIL LIGHTS

Small candles placed in glass cups burn before a shrine or replica of a saint as an act of devotion or for a particular intention. Vigil lights are Catholic sacramentals and are symbols of the deep hope of the faithful that their prayers will be answered and that their special needs will be met. These vigil lights symbolize the light of prayer and may burn for only a few hours or as long as a week. It is believed that the flame "keeps vigil" when the person cannot be present.

VIHARA

An early Buddhist monastery consisting of an open court surrounded by open cells, to which access is provided through an entrance porch.

VIJNAPTI-KARMAN

In Buddhist philosophy, a kind of action that manifests itself outside of the actor and is capable of being recognized by others. Among three kinds of action (i.e., those produced by the body, mouth, and mind) usually admitted in Buddhism, bodily ones and verbal ones are classified as vijnapti-karman.

VIKALPA

In Buddhism, term meaning discrimination, as opposed to the intuitive vision which passes beyond it; the false imagination of foolish thinking which imposes a necessary habit of daily life onto the realities of the spirit. Finally, the term is also used in the sense of the products of such foolish thinking, subjective forms which the mind believes to be real.

VINAYA PITAKA

The oldest and smallest of the three sections of the Buddhist canonical Tripitaka and the one that regulates monastic life and the daily affairs of monks and nuns according to rules attributed to the Buddha.

VINCENT DE PAUL, Saint

(Circa 1581-1660) French Roman Catholic priest, founder of the Congregation of the Mission (Lazarists) and cofounder of the Daughters of Charity. Captured by pirates in 1605, he spent two years as a slave in Tunis. He became chaplain general to the galley slaves in France in 1617 and was canonized in 1737.

VINCENTIANS

A Roman Catholic Society of priests and brothers founded at Paris in 1625 by St. Vincent de Paul for the purpose of preaching missions to the poor country people and training young men in seminaries for the priesthood.

VINNANA

In Buddhism, one of the five Skandhas. Vinnana is the normal consciousness, the relation between subject and object. It is the empirical mind, the vehicle by which one recognizes the phenomenal worlds and gains the experience of life. Vinnana is also the consciousness which lies below the threshold of normal experience (the subliminal consciousness), in which the experiences of the past are registered and retained, the results of such experience becoming faculties in the next physical birth.

VIRGIN BIRTH

The birth of Jesus Christ who was conceived by the virgin Mary through the Holy Spirit's power, without a human father (Matthew 1:20-25). It is a fundamental doctrine of orthodox Christianity. The doctrine that Mary was the sole natural parent of Jesus is based on the infancy narratives contained in the gospel accounts of Matthew and Luke, and it was universally accepted in the Christian church by the 2nd century. Except for several minor heretical sects, it was not seriously challenged until the rise of Protestant theological' liberalism in the 19th century. It remains a basic article of belief in the Roman Catholic, Orthodox, and most Protestant churches. Muslims also accept the virgin birth of Jesus.

VIRGINITY

The observance of perpetual sexual abstinence. In the Christian context its motive is "for the sake of the kingdom of heaven" (Matthew 19:12). In speaking of the evangelical counsels, Vatican Council II teaches that "towering among these counsels is that precious gift of divine grace given to some by the father to devote themselves to God alone more easily with an undivided heart in virginity or celibacy (See Matthew 19:11; 1 Corinthians 7:32-34). This perfect continence for love of the kingdom of heaven has always been held in high esteem by the church as a sign and stimulus of love, or as a singular source of spiritual fertility in the world" (Dogmatic Constitution on the church).

VIRTUE

A good habit that enables a person to act according to right reason enlightened by faith and to do so with relative ease and with perseverance despite obstacles. The Christian tradition distinguishes especially between theological virtues and moral virtues. Theological virtues are powers infused by God with sanctifying grace, enabling the person to act on a supernatural level; they are faith, hope, and charity.

The moral virtues are powers which are acquired by repeated human acts aided by the grace of God; there are many moral virtues, but the chief ones are prudence, justice, fortitude and temperance.

The Old Testament progressively discloses the notion of virtue as inner responsiveness rather than external legalistic conformity; this thought also runs strongly in Greek philosophy.

By Aristotle a distinction is drawn between the intellectual and moral virtues. Of the former the fivefold enumeration has become traditional: for matters of theory, insight, scientific knowledge, and wisdom; for matters of practice, prudence, and art.

They suffice to adapt a man to a certain phase in his experience, but not to put him in harmony with the whole business of living, as, e.g., in the case of one who by insight knows what should be done and yet does nothing about it. Consequently moral virtues, dispositions implying a right appetitional attitude or goodwill and qualities of character, are also required before one can speak of a downright good man.

In this Aristotle is criticizing the Socratic reduction of virtue to knowledge and vice to ignorance. Their four main types, prudence, justice, courage, and temperance, have been called cardinal virtues since the days of Saint Ambrose.

It will be noted that prudence holds a place under both headings. This is because it not only is the practical wisdom of knowing what should be done, but also fills the imperative role of carrying it into execution. It differs from art because it is concerned with human doing, not human making, and a moral reference is implied in a human act well done, but not, directly, in a work well made.

VIRTUE, Infused

Some virtues are called infused because they are not acquired as the result of continual practice but are given directly by God. Infused virtues may be either theological or moral.

The theological virtues of hope, faith, and charity and the moral, or cardinal virtues, of prudence, justice, fortitude, and temperance are infused virtues given to a newly baptized person. These virtues bring to fulfillment the gifts the person has, help the individual act in a supernatural way, and incline the person toward good.

VIRTUES, Index of

The index of the virtues according to the Latin Stoics and the patristic moralists who followed them was more detailed and descriptive if less analytical, and the tendency was to treat the life of virtue as a single Gestalt while tracing its various general conditions; thus all courage was temperate and all justice prudent.

It was not until the thought of Aristotle was recovered in the 13th century that the whole field was systematically mapped by Thomas Aquinas, and his work, which coherently relates together without suppressing the mixed teachings tradition, remains the classical typology of the virtues.

Their parts fall into three classes.

▲ First, the components, or the elements that go to make up the virtue; thus memory and circumspection enter into prudence.

▲ Second, the sub-species of a generic type of virtue; thus sobriety and chastity are distinct kinds of temperance.

▲ Third, allied virtues, which are half like and half unlike the main virtues with which they are ranged; thus religion goes with justice in rendering what is strictly due, and yet differs in that it sets up a relationship not between equals.

Of these associated virtues, 22 come up for separate discussion in St. Thomas' *Summa theologiae*. The principle of differentiation is this: where a distinct specific interest is engaged, there a distinct specific virtue may be isolated. For instance, the challenge to the good life from our emotional fears and our desires for pleasure are not the same, hence the distinction between courage and temperance, and within the scope of temperance the distinction scales down to the pleasures of food, drink, and sex and thus provides basis for the difference between abstemiousness, sobriety, and chastity.

Here it should be noticed that the vices, differentiated along the same lines, are more numerous than the virtues, since they may be in conflict with them either by excess or defect; thus rashness and cowardice are against courage and are diametrically opposed to each other.

The moral virtues follow a measured course for right living in this world. Taken as the City of Reason, they are the natural virtues, better called the acquired virtues, since they are not innate but are learned by repeated acts; taken as the City of God already present, then they are the supernatural or "infused" virtues which are among the endowments of sanctifying grace.

Within their respective dimensions these two sets offer counterparts to one another at every point. How far the natural virtues can flourish by themselves or whether the activity of these supernatural virtues is merely that of the natural virtues though oriented towards a higher end are matters of controversy.

Note, however, the norm for a Christian theologian is man as open to grace; pure nature is not a historical condition, but an abstraction serving methodic consideration of the working of natural virtue as the material substructure to the workings of Christian virtues, of the decencies that remain after grace has been lost, and of the dynamism in the growth of virtue.

The enumeration of the virtues in systematic theology may convey the impression, not allayed by the knack in scholastic Latin of deification, that they represent so many different compartments, but in fact they are like shorthand headings to show the versatility of the good life.

Its singleness is well recognized, alike in the patristic teaching on the interpenetration of the virtues, in Aristotle's that the moral virtues are knit together by prudence, and in the general consensus that, unlike the vices which can be quite disjoined, all the virtues are quickened and reach their goal through charity.

VIRTUES, Theological
Those supernatural gifts which, as habitual dispositions of the intellect and will, have God as their immediate object. They are faith, hope, and charity.

Theological virtues are supernatural rather than natural, i.e., they transcend all human virtue and belong to man only insofar as God has called him to divine life. They are distinguished from the intellectual and moral virtues insofar as they relate directly to God; it is He in whom, man must believe and hope, and whom he must love.

VIRYA
In Buddhism, vigor and energy; the fourth of the six Paramitas.

VISITATION
Mary paid a visit to her cousin Elizabeth at Ain Karim after the angel announced to her that she was to become the

Mother of God. When Elizabeth saw Mary she was filled with the Spirit and proclaimed: "Blessed are you among women, and blessed is the fruit of your womb." Mary responded with the Magnificat (See Luke 1:39-56).

VISITATION, Canonical

The official inspection of a religious house made by a bishop, the superior of a religious community or order, or someone delegated by either, to ensure the observance of canon law or for some other purpose is visitation. The bishop in a diocese makes an official visit to all diocesan institutions under his jurisdiction every five years.

VISHNU (VISJNU)

One of the principal Hindu deities, worshipped as the protector and pre-server of the world and restorer of dharma (moral order). He is a syncretic personality who combines many lesser cult figures and folk heroes.

VIVARTA

In the Advaita, or Monist, school of the Hindu philosophic system of Vedanta, a causal change the product of which is of a lower degree of reality than its cause.

VIVEKA

In Buddhism, detachment, either physi-cal, as living in solitude, or mental, mentally detached from being affected by objects of sense.

VLADIMIR, Saint

(circa 956-1015) Russian prince who began the mass conversion of the Russians to the Eastern Orthodox reli-gion. A pagan of Viking origin, he became Grand Duke of Kiev after killing his brother, the former ruler. He became a Christian in 989 and married Anna, sister of Byzantine Emperor Basil II, initiating a period of close cul-tural relations with Constantinople.

VOCATION

In general sense, a call from God to salvation and holiness. Thus Vatican Council II speaks of the universal call (vocation) to holiness for all members of the church. In a specific sense, a call to a particular way of life in the church: to priesthood, religious life (as a priest, nun, or other religious), Christian mar-riage, or a single life in the world.

VOODOO

A folk religion chiefly of Haiti, with West African, Roman Catholic and native West Indian elements. It involves the worship of spirits or saints (loa), and of the dead. Cult groups are headed by a priest or priestess, but there is no dogma or priestly hierarchy. At a voodoo ritual, persons supposedly possessed by spirits carry out various rites, give council or perform cures. Priests may be "divinely" selected mediums and it is believed that they can work charms, lay curses and create zombies or "living dead." Since it is believed that some use their skills for harmful magic, priests also practice protective magic for those who wish it.

VOW

Sacred voluntary promise to dedicate oneself or members of one's family or community to a special obligation that goes beyond usual requirements.
In the ancient Middle East, individuals often made vows to God to perform certain acts in return for a divine favor. Hannah, the mother of the Old Testament judge Samuel, for example, vowed that if God would grant her a son she would devote him to the serv-ice of the Lord.
A Buddhist takes vows when he takes Pansil, but he takes them to himself. Even the more stringent vows taken by a Bikkhu may be given up on leaving the Sangha. The Bodhisattva vow, tak-en by many of the Mahayana School, is to work for humanity and to sacrifice all gain for self until that idea is achieved.

VULGATE

The standard version of the Latin Bible used by the Roman Catholic Church, primarily translated by St. Jerome. In

382 Pope Damasus commissioned Jerome, the leading biblical scholar of his day, to produce a Bible from the various translations then being used. His revised Latin translation of the gospels appeared circa 383. Using the Septuagint version of the Old Testament, he produced new Latin translations of the Psalter, the Book of Job, and some other Old Testament books. Later, he decided that the Septuagint was unsatisfactory and began translating the entire Old Testament from the original Hebrew versions, completing his work circa 405.

W

WAHHAB, Muhammad ibn 'Abd

(1703-1792) Theologian and founder of the Wahhabi movement, which attempted a return to the "true" principles of Islam. His teachings have been characterized as puritanical because they represent the simple Islamic religion of the Arabian Desert and as such constitute a hindrance to the development of Islam away from this origin. He made a clear stand against all innovations in Islamic faith because he believed them to be reprehensible, insisting that the original grandeur of Islam could be regained if the Islamic community would return to the principles enunciated by the Prophet Mohammed.

WAHHABIS

Followers of the strict puritanical teachings of Ibn Abd al-Wahhab. They are sometimes called "Unitarians" and so should not be confused with the Almohads. The Wahhabis embraced a strict fundamentalism in the spirit of Ahmad and some of their ethos still pervades Saudi Arabia today. Among the various things forbidden by the Wahhabis were intercession of the saints, use of the rosary, use of jima in law, visiting the tombs of saints, and tobacco.

WAILING WALL

A section of what is believed to be part of the western wall of the Temple in Jerusalem, rebuilt by Herod the Great (King of Judea, 37-4 BC) and destroyed by the Romans in 70. Since medieval times, Jewish pilgrims have gathered at the wall to pray and bewail their sufferings. The site, close to the Mosque of Omar, was Jordanian territory and barred to Jews from 1948 until 1967, when it was captured by Israel in the Six-Day War.

WAKE

This term describes the custom of remaining awake and on watch with a deceased person. It is usually a period of one or two days before the funeral when mourners may pay their respects to the deceased and offer their condolences to the bereaved.

According to Catholic custom, the wake should also be a time of prayer for the repose of the soul of the deceased and for strength and courage on the part of the bereaved. It is customary in some countries to have a liturgical wake service (a "vigil for the deceased") and/or the praying of the rosary.

WALDENSES

A reforming Christian sect, founded by Peter Waldo of Lyon, France, in the 12th century. Rejecting the wealth and worldliness of the Roman Catholic clergy, the Waldenses took vows of poverty and encouraged celibacy, fasting and a life of prayer and meditation. Excommunicated by Pope Lucius III in 1184 for their heretical beliefs, they further rejected Catholicism, refusing to accept the concept of purgatory, adoration of the crucifix and the sanctity of churches. Their faith was largely based on the literal interpretation of biblical texts.

The Waldenses were severely persecuted during the 12th and 13th centuries, but were saved from gradual extinction by joining forces with Swiss Protestant reformers in the 16th century. Waldensian immigrants from France, Switzerland and Italy settled in the United States in the 1870s. Today there are communities in Missouri, Texas, Utah and North Carolina.

WALI

Is Islam, saint, holy man. While tasawwuf acknowledges a whole hierarchy of saints and ordinary Muslims the world over pay popular devotion to, and intercede at, saints' tombs and shrines, many Muslim theologians have regarded such practices and intercession with suspicion and disquiet. This is particularly the case with those influenced by the Wahhabis.

WALI ALLAH, Shah

(1702-1762) Theologian and founder of modern Islamic thought who first attempted an integrative reinterpretation of Islam. He believed that Muslim polity could be restored to its former splendor by a policy of religious reform that would harmonize the religious ideals of Islam with the changing social and economic conditions of India.

WALTER OF COVENTRY

(1265-1341) English monk or friar, compiler of historical materials. He described the struggle of King John with the church and the English barons.

WAQF

In Islamic law, the legal creation of a pious foundation or endowment whereby the owner relinquishes his right of disposal provided that the usufruct is for charitable purposes. Popularly the word waqf has been applied to the endowment itself. This endowment once made is perpetual and irretrievable.

WAQI'A, al-

The title of the 56th sura of the Koran; it means "The Happening." The sura belongs to the Meccan period and has 96 verses. It draws its title from the first verse. The sura contains descriptions of the delights of Paradise which await the just, and pains of hell for the wicked. God's creative powers are stressed as a signal that man should believe, thank God and glorify Him.

WAR, Morality of

In view of the fact that war involves many evils, including the maiming and killing of other human beings, the question about its morality arose early in the Christian community: Is it possible to justify war from a Christian viewpoint? The answer to this question gradually developed into what is commonly called "the just war theory." Briefly, this theory held that four conditions were necessary for a war to be just:

1 a war must be declared by the lawful authority;
2 there must be a just cause, a serious grievance, for going to war;
3 there must be a right intention, such as true self-defense, not mere vengeance;
4 there must be a right use of means, that is, the war must be carried out in a moral manner.

WARBURTON, William

(1689-1779) Anglican bishop of Gloucester. He advocated tolerance by the state church (Anglicanism) for those whose beliefs and worship were at variance.

WAR OF THE SONS OF LIGHT AGAINST THE SONS OF DARKNESS

One of the most important documents of the Essene sect of Jews that established a community at Qumran in the Judean dessert during the first half of the 2nd century BC. Organized as a theocratic society, the Essenes thought themselves to be the holy elect of Israel, the Sons of Light, who would, at the end of time, engage in a catastrophic war with the Sons of Darkness, the enemies of Israel.

WARS OF RELIGION

In France, a series of conflicts between Catholics and Huguenots (Protestants) in the period 1562-1598.

WARS OF YAHWEH, Book of the

A lost document referred to and quoted in the Old Testament (Numbers 21:14-16). Probably a collection of early Israelite war songs including hymns of victory, curses, mocking songs, and other literary genres recounting the victories of Yahweh, the God of Israel, over His enemies. The book indicates that biblical books rely on both written and oral tradition.

WASHING OF FEET

In the generally warm climate of the ancient Middle East where persons customarily wore open sandals, walked on dry soil and traveled on feet on dusty roads, the Oriental gesture of washing the feet was a welcome and hospitable act that often preceded the eating of a meal.

In the average home of the common people, the host provided needed vessels and water and visitors washed their own feet (Judges 19:21). A wealthier host usually had his slave do the foot washing, and this was considered a menial task.

According to biblical tradition, Abigail indicated her willingness to comply with David's wish that she become his wife by saying: "Here is your slave girl as a maid-servant to wash the feet of the servants of my Lord" (1 Samuel 25:40-42). Especially was it a display of humility and affectionate regard for guests if the host or hostess personally washed the visitor's feet.

Foot washing was not only a host's gesture of hospitality toward his guest (2 Samuel 11:8), but the feet were also customarily washed before retiring to bed. Especially noteworthy was the requirement that Levite priests wash their feet and hands before going into the tabernacle or before officiating at the altar (Exodus 30:17-21).

WASHING OF HANDS

Rather than being plunged into a container filled with water, in ancient times the hands were washed with water poured upon them. The dirty water then ran into a container or basin over which the hands were held (2 Kings 3:11).

According to biblical tradition, the law prescribed that the priests wash their hands and their feet at the copper basis located between the sanctuary and the altar before ministering at the altar or entering the tent of meeting (Exodus 30:18-21). The law also stated that, in case someone slain was found and it was impossible to ascertain who the murderer was, the older men of the city nearest the slain person were to take a young cow, one that had never been worked with or pulled a yoke, to a torrent valley of running water and there break its neck. After this the older men were to wash their hands over the young cow, denoting their innocence in regard to the murder (Deuteronomy 21:1-8). Also, according to the Law, a person was rendered unclean if touched by someone with a running discharge who had not rinsed his hands (Leviticus 15:11).

The scribes and Pharisees in the first century AD attached great importance to hand washing and took issue with Jesus Christ concerning his disciples' overstepping the traditions of men of former times by not washing their hands when about to eat a meal. This involved no ordinary hand washing for hygienic purposes, but a ceremonial ritual. "The Pharisees and all the Jews do not eat unless they wash their hands up to the elbow" (Mark 7:2-5; Matthew 15:2).

The Talmud puts the one eating with unwashed hands on the same plane as one committing fornication, and states that the one lightly esteeming hand washing will perish from the earth.

WASIL IBN 'ATA

(701-748) Muslim theologian considered the founder of the Mu'tazilah sect. He gathered around him many devoted believers and ascetics, whom he often set out as emissaries to spread his doctrines of speculative theology in more distant provinces.

WATER, Liturgical use of

A few drops of water are mingled with the wine to be consecrated at the Roman Catholic Mass. This action symbolized the union of the two natures in Jesus, the unity of Jesus with the people of God, the pain and toil of our lives which become one with the blood of Jesus, or the commingled water and blood that came from Jesus' side at the crucifixion.

Other liturgical uses of water occur at baptism, blessing of bells, consecration of a church, washing of hands after the Offertory, and Mandatum. Holy water is used in fonts at the entrances of the church, for blessings, and in homes.

WENCESLAS, Saint

(circa 907-929) Duke of Bohemia whose efforts to Christianize his people became legendary. Murdered by his brother Boleslav I, he was later canonized. The Christmas Carol Good King Wenceslas, written by J.M. Neale in the 19th century, is based on one of the many legends about him.

WEIZMANN, Chaim Azriel

(1874-1952) First president of the new nation of Israel (1949-1952), who was for decades the guiding spirit behind the World Zionist Organization. His measures were in large measure responsible for bringing Israel into being.

WELL OF MOSES

Late Gothic six-sided well surrounded by six life-size statues of Old Testament prophets by Claus Sluten (constructed 1395-1404). It stands in the cloister of the Chartreuse de Champmol in Dijon (France).

WESLEY, Charles

(1707-1788) English minister, a great hymn writer, author of over 6,000 Methodist hymns. It was he who founded the "Methodists" at Oxford. Ordained in 1735, he worked with his brother John both in Georgia and as a Methodist preacher after 1738.

WESLEY, John

(1703-1791) Founder of the Methodist Church. He was ordained in 1728, and in 1729 assumed leadership of a religious study group at Oxford, nicknamed "Methodists" because of their interest in monastic methods (or discipline). In 1734 he went to Georgia as a missionary. Following his return in 1738, he experienced a conversion to evangelism at a religious meeting in London. For the next 50 years he traveled far and wide, preaching his message of salvation by faith in chapels and at open-air meetings. He organized the local societies and class-meetings which became the basis of the Methodist movement, and trained traveling lay preachers.

WESLEY, Samuel

(1662-1735) English clergyman, who was brought up a dissenter, but joined the Church of England. Rector of Epworth, near Lincoln, from 1695, he was a prolific writer of religious works.

WESLEYAN CHURCH

Conservative US Protestant church, organized in 1968 by the merger of the Wesleyan Methodist Church of America and the Pilgrim Holiness Church. The Wesleyan Church is considered one of the Holiness churches. It stresses entire sanctification, a post-conversion experience that allows the person to live a sinless life. Members of the church promise not to use, produce, or sell tobacco or alcoholic beverages, and membership in secret societies is forbidden.

WESTERN SCHISM

In the history of the Roman Catholic Church, the period from 1378 to 1417, when there were two, later three, rival popes, each with his own following, his own Sacred College of Cardinals, and his own administrative offices.

WESTERN WALL

See Wailing Wall.

WESTMINSTER ABBEY

Great English church at Westminster, London. Officially called the Collegiate Church of St. Peter, it has been the scene of almost every British coronation since William the Conqueror. Edward the Confessor built a church on the site and consecrated it in 1065. In 1245, Henry III began enlarging it in fine Gothic style. Later additions include the fan-caulked chapel of Henry VII, built at the beginning of the 16th century, and the twin western towers of the mid-18th century. It is the traditional burial place of English monarchs and famous men.

WESTMINSTER CONFESSION

A confession of faith of English-speaking Presbyterians. It was produced, along with two catechisms and other directories, by the Westminster Assembly of Puritan clergymen, which was called together by the Long Parliament in 1643, during the English Civil War, and met regularly in Westminster Abbey until 1649.

In effect a theological consensus of international Calvinism, it consisted of 33 chapters, closely reasoned and grave in style, and it provided some latitude among points of view recognized within the orthodoxy of the time. It stated that the sole doctrinal authority is scripture, and it agreed and restated the doctrines of the Trinity and of Christ from the creeds of the early church. Reformed views of the sacraments, the ministry, and the two covenants of works and grace were given.

WHEEL OF LIFE

Important Buddhist symbol. The Tibetans make great use of pictures of the Wheel to bring before mind the nature of existence. The rim shows 12 Nidanas, its six sections portraying the different spheres of existence in which the concatenation of Cause and Effect operates. The six spheres are:

1   The Heaven worlds;
2   The Asura Worlds;
3   The Human worlds;
4   The Animal worlds;
5   The Purgatorial worlds;
6   The Hells.

It is noteworthy that in the lowest hell there is an exit, and that a Buddha is depicted in each of the six worlds, thus indicating that he is ever ready to aid in whatsoever state one may be.

The wheel is depicted as being whirled around by a demon, symbolizing the miseries and limitations of existence. In the center of the wheel are shown the three cardinal sins or unwholesome roots: lust, malevolence, and stupidity-

greed, symbolized by the red cock, the green snake, and the black pig. Outside the wheel the Buddha is depicted to symbolize release from the wheel as summum bonum, and his attainment thereof.

WHEEL OF THE LAW

The Buddha set the Wheel of the Law in motion with his first sermon in the Deer Park near Benares.

WHITBY, Synod of

A meeting held by the Christian church of the Anglo-Saxon kingdom of Northumbria in 663/664 to decide whether to follow Celtic or Roman usages. It marked a vital turning point in the development of the church in England.

WHITE, William

(1748-1836) First bishop of the Protestant Episcopal Church in the United States. He was highly influential in the development of the new church. He wrote on doctrinal matters and assisted in the revision of The Book of Common Prayer for use in the United States.

WILDERNESS

Regions or lands that form the background for many of the biblical accounts and are frequently used in figurative or metaphorical statements.

The nation of Israel making its exodus from Egypt, was guided by God into the wilderness along the Red Sea, causing Pharaoh to assume that they had lost their bearings in that region (Exodus 12:18-20; 14:1-3).

On the other side of the Red Sea, and for the remainder of 40 years, Israel passed from one wilderness section to another, including the wilderness regions of Shur, Sinai, Paran and Zin (Exodus 15:22; 16:1; 19:1; Numbers 10:12; 20:1), at times encamping at oases, such as at Elim, with its 12 springs and 70 palm trees (Exodus 15:27), and at Kadesh-barnea (Numbers 13:26; Deuteronomy 2:14). As has been shown, the conditions in some of the wilderness regions were quite possibly more favorable in the ancient past than at the present time. Still, Moses could speak of Israel's trek through Sinai as "through the great and great-inspiring wilderness, with poisonous serpents and scorpions and with thirsty ground that has no water" (Deuteronomy 1:19; 8:15).

The more barren wilderness regions were either uninhabited (Job 38:26) or places were tent dwellers resided and nomads roamed (1 Chronicles 5:9-10; Jeremiah 3:2). Here were brambles and thornbushes (Genesis 21:14-15), thorny lotus trees and thickets of prickly acacia trees (Exodus 25:10).

WILL

A person seeks that which is or seems to be good through this spiritual power of the human soul. The will tends toward good or away from evil when recognized by the intellect. This faculty or power which enables a person to make a free choice has the capability to intend, choose, consent, desire, hope, hate, love, and enjoy.

WILL OF GOD

God has an infinite capacity to desire the good and hence all human beings should let their lives be guided by this sovereign principle. Because God's will is a mystery, persons who want to conform their lives to it have to search for ways to discover what it is for them.

The will of God is ordinarily understood as the apparent designs of God for a person's entire life or for any segment of that life. The will of God can be known to some degree through natural reason, revelation and the teachings of the church.

Regular prayer, daily reflection, and the help of a spiritual companion are all part of God's ordinary way in showing His will to those who are serious about their spiritual journey. The will of God is not always easy to discern in practice and, at times, it can call for painful sacrifice.

There are varied proven approaches to this process of discovery. Christians have prayed daily since the time of Jesus that the will of God be realized "Your will be done, on earth as it is in heaven" (Matthew 6:10).

WILLIAM OF OCKHAM

(circa 1280-1349) English philosopher and theologian best remembered for the saying that entities ought not to be needlessly multiplied, known as "Ockham's razor." This constituted an attack upon the abstract metaphysics of medieval scholasticism and led to skepticism. He was a Franciscan monk and scholar who held that faith and reason are completely unconnected. He also denied that the pope was entitled to wield temporal power, and held that the king should be independent of the church, a view which foreshadowed the separation of church and state in later centuries.

WILLIBRORD, Saint

(658-739) Anglo-Saxon bishop and missionary apostle of Friesland, and patron saint of Holland. In 690 he and 11 companions were sent to the Low Countries to undertake the Christianization of the Frisians, whose districts had recently been conquered (689) by Pepin II the Young. He went to Rome in 690 for a commission from Pope St. Sergius I and was later sent again by Pepin for the consecration as archbishop of the Frisians, with a see to be established at Utrecht (Netherlands).

In 698 Willibrord established his second missionary base, the important monastery of Echternach. Having extended his apostolate into Friesland, he attempted to evangelize Denmark. He was buried in the abbey church of Echternach, and his feast day is November 7th.

WIMPINA, Konrad

(1460-1531) German theologian at the University of Frankfurt who opposed Martin Luther in the indulgence controversy.

WINE

Alcoholic beverage made from the fermented juice of grapes. The drinking of too much wine is intoxicating (1 Sam. 25:36-37). But a little wine can be good for the health (Tim. 5:23).

WINE, Eucharistic

The wine consecrated during the Eucharist Prayer must be pure grape juice which has been naturally fermented. The wine may be white or red. A few drops of water are added to the wine at the Offertory. The consecrated wine is distributed to the faithful during the Communion rite.

WIRD

In Islam, time used for extra worship; or part of the Koran cited at such a time.

WISCONSIN EVANGELICAL LUTHERAN SYNOD

A conservative Lutheran church in the United States, formed in 1892 as a federation of three conservative synods of German background. The Wisconsin Synod has maintained a strict conservative interpretation of Christian doctrines and the Lutheran confessions and insists on absolute agreement in all matters of doctrine and practice.

WISDOM

One of the gifts of the Holy Spirit that enables a person to have a right appreciation or "taste" for the things of God and to have right judgment in discerning what is true and good.

WITS

In Islam, term designating uneven, odd; voluntary prayer comprising an odd number of raka'at between tare isha and subh prayers.

WITCH OF ENDOR

In the Bible (1 Samuel 28), a woman consulted by King Saul before his defeat and death at Mount Gilboa. At his urging, she raised the spirit of the prophet Samuel from the dead.

WITCHCRAFT

The exercise of supernatural power with the assistance of evil spirits often includes the casting of spells, sorcery, and so on. According to Roman Catholic theology, witchcraft is gravely sinful for those who engage in it because of cooperation with evil spirits and because it is often employed with the intention of causing harm to others.

WITNESS, Christian

As a Christian idea, this word means that the believer gives testimony to his or her faith in Jesus Christ and his gospel in all of his or her thoughts, words, and deeds, even at the cost of personal sacrifice or hostility on the part of others.

WITTENBERG

German city on the Elbe River, southwest of Berlin; first mentioned in 1180 and chartered in 1293; the residence of the Ascanian dukes.

The Reformation started in Wittenberg on October 31, 1517, when Luther nailed his famous 95 theses to the wooden doors of the castle church of All Saints. The doors were destroyed in a fire in 1760, and the church, containing the graves of Luther and the reformers, was seriously damaged then and in 1813-14. It has been restored, and the bronze doors of 1858 bear the Latin text of Luther's Theses.

WOLSEY, Thomas Cardinal

(circa 1475-1530) English prelate and statesman. Born the son of an Ipswich butcher, he rose to prominence as chaplain, first to the archbishop of Canterbury and then to the governor of Calais, at that time an English stronghold. Appointed chaplain to Henry VII in 1507, he skillfully cultivated allies at court and won favor by his diplomatic talent. Under Henry VIII he rose even higher. In quick succession, he became bishop of Lincoln, then archbishop of York and finally cardinal and papal legate. In 1515, Henry appointed him Lord Chancellor of England, and in that position he enjoyed unchallenged authority and lived in magnificent style. As controller of the country's foreign policy, he sought to raise England's influence in Europe and to further his own ambition to become pope. However, when he failed to obtain the pope's sanction for Henry's divorce from Catherine of Aragon, he lost the king's confidence and was dismissed from office in 1529. Though he remained archbishop of York, he lost his estates and was left powerless before the many enemies he had made during his career. Accused of high treason, he set out for London but died on the way at Leicester Abbey, a broken and humbled man.

WONHYO, Daisa

(617-686) Buddhist priest considered the greatest of the ancient religious teachers and one of the Ten Sages of the Ancient Korean kingdom. He was the first to systematize Korean Buddhism, bringing the various Buddhist doctrines into a unity that was sensible to both the philosophers and the common people.

WORD, The

Frequently used term in the scriptures. Translated from the Hebrew (da.var') or the Greek (lo'gos) it usually refers to an entire thought, saying or statement rather than simply to an individual turn of speech. Any message from the creator, such as sounds uttered through a prophet, is "the word of God." In a few places logos ("word") is a title given to Jesus Christ.

WORD OF GOD

An expression used to describe several different realities: notably, Jesus Christ as the Word of God (See John 1:1; John 1:14); and the Bible as containing "the Word of God in the words of men."

WORKER PRIESTS

The idea of worker priests seems to have started with priests who had performed forced labor in Germany during World War II. These priests joined the workforce to evangelize alienated workers. The secular employment of priests is left to the discretion of the local ordinary.

WORLD ALLIANCE OF REFORMED CHURCHES

A cooperative organization, formed in Nairobi, Kenya, in 1970, by merging the International Congregational Council and the Alliance of the Reformed Churches. It encourages fellowship and cooperation among its member churches and promotes their common interests.

WORLD CONVENTION OF CHURCHES OF CHRIST

International agency of the Disciples of Christ. It exercises no authority over its member churches but provides a means for fellowship and mutual activities for the various national churches.

WORLD COUNCIL OF CHURCHES

An international fellowship composed of over 200 Protestant, Anglican, Eastern Orthodox and Old Catholic Churches of circa 100 countries. Founded in Amsterdam in 1948, the Council promotes Christian unity, religious liberty, missionary cooperation and interfaith doctrinal study. It also conducts service projects such as relief for refugees. World headquarters of the Council are in Geneva, Switzerland. The day-to-day affairs of the Council are directed by a Central Committee of 100 members.

WORLD METHODIST COUNCIL

Cooperative organization of Methodist Churches that provides a means for consultation and cooperation on an international level.

WORLD'S CHRISTIAN FUNDAMENTALS ASSOCIATION

Interdenominational Protestant organization founded in 1919, militantly against modernistic theology.

WORLD UNION FOR PROGRESSIVE JUDAISM

An international federation of Reform congregations that seeks to coordinate old and newly established Reform groups in various parts of the world.

WORSHIP

The rendering of reverent honor or homage. According to biblical tradition, true worship of the Creator embraces every phase of an individual's life. The apostle Paul wrote to the Corinthians: "Whether you are eating or drinking or doing anything else, all things for God's glory" (1 Corinthians 10:31).

To a Samaritan woman Jesus Christ said: "The hour is coming when neither in this mountain "Gerizim" nor in Jerusalem will you worship the Father. You worship what you do not know; we worship what we know ... Nevertheless, the hour is coming, and it is now, when the true worshipers will worship the Father with spirit and truth, for, indeed the Father is looking for suchlike ones to worship Him. God is a Spirit, and those worshiping Him must worship with spirit and truth" (John 4:21-24).

WRATH OF GOD

The ancient Israelites used this metaphor of anger to describe God's attitude toward sin. This is an anthropomorphism which occurs in the Old Testament to describe God as punishing sinners (Psalms 2:11). Jesus employs this anthropomorphism when he says: "You brood of vipers! Who warned you to flee from the wrath to come?" (Matthew 3:7). Paul described the Day of Judgment as the "Day of wrath" (Romans 2:5).

WREATH

The Advent wreath is a symbol of preparation for Christmas.

WREN, Sir Christopher

(1632-1723) One of the greatest of all English architects, famous as the designer of St. Paul's Cathedral, London.

Wren's opportunity came after the Great Fire decimated London in 1666. Old St. Paul's was destroyed along with most of the city's parish churches. Wren rebuilt over 50 churches, no two exactly alike. Most of these still stand as monuments to his art. St. Paul's, with its great dome composed of three separate shells, was finally completed in 1710.

Wren's architecture is classical, combining elements from the work of his English predecessor Inigo Jones with what he knew of ancient Roman and of Baroque architecture. His buildings are always clear and rational in plan and in spatial organization, sometimes incorporating ingenious structural innovations. Wren's architecture had a great influence on later English architecture.

WUDU

In Islam, minor ritual washing of parts of the body before prayer. It assumes that ghusl has already taken place. Sand may be used if water is scarce or unavailable.

WULFSTAN, Saint

(1008-1095) Bishop of Worcester from 1062. He ended the capture and sale of slaves at Bristol, rebuilt the cathedral at Worcester and was noted for his preaching and personal ascetism.

WU-WEI

In Chinese Taoism, the principle of yielding to others the most effective response to the problems of human existence. It is characterized by a natural, nonaggressive behavior that compels others (through shame, if for no other reason) to desist voluntarily from violence or overly aggressive conduct.

WYCLIFFE, John

(circa 1320-1384) English religious reformer, a precursor of the reformation, whose ideas has a great influence on subsequent religious thought. He distinguished himself as a scholar and teacher at Oxford University, attacking the church and the authority of its pope and bishops. He stressed the importance of inner, personal religion, denouncing the whole system of confession and penance. In the 1370s he served the court as a pamphleteer and ambassador. Wycliffe's followers were called Lollards, and were led by a body of poor preachers. Following his denial of the doctrine of transubstantiation, he was forced to retire to Lutterworth in 1382. There, he and his followers completed the first translation of the Bible into English.

Y

perfect concentration. An ethical preparation, meant to purify the individual, yama involves the abstinence from injury to others and from lying, stealing, sex, and avarice.

YAD

A Jewish ritualistic object, usually made of silver but sometimes of wood or other materials, that consists of a shaft affixed to a miniature hand with its index finger pointing. It is used to indicate the place that is being tread on a Torah scroll.

YAHWEH

The God of the Israelites, His name being revealed to Moses as four Hebrew consonants YHWH called the tetragrammaton. It especially designates God as a creator of the universe and the source of all life.

YAHYA

Arabic word for John. He is the Koranic counterpart of the New Testament Baptist, and appears in the Koran with prophetic status as the longed-for child of Zakariyya.

YAJNA

In Hinduism, worship based on rites prescribed in the earliest scriptures of ancient India, the Vedas, in contrast to puja, which may include image worship and devotional practices non-Vedic in origin.

YAJUJ AND MAJUJ

In Islamic eschatology, two hostile peoples who will ravage the earth before the end of the world. They are regarded as the Muslim counterparts of the biblical Gog and Magog.

YAMA

In the Yoga system of Indian philosophy, first of the eight stages intended to lead the aspirant to samadhi, or state of

YAMA

In Indian mythology, the lord of death. The Vedas describe him as the first man who died, blazing the path of mortality down which all men have since followed. He is the guardian of the south (the region of death) and presides over the resting place of the dead, which is located in the south under the earth.

YAMANA MOCHITOYO

(1404-1473) Buddhist monk, head of a very powerful warrior clan in western Japan; who fought for central control over the outlying religions of Japan.

YAMIM NORAIM

In Judaism, the High Holy Days of Rosh Hashana (on Tishri 1 and 2) and Yom Kippur (on Tishri 10). Though the Bible does not link these two major festivals, the Talmud does.

YANA

In Buddhism, literally career, vehicle or means of progress; a vehicle of salvation from the wheel of Samsara.

YANTRA

Symbolic diagram conceived in meditation and used for spiritual development in Tibetan Buddhism. In art they are depicted as Mandalas and the like.

YAPANIYA SAMGHA

A minor sect of Jainism, a religion of India. It incorporates features from both the principal sects, the Svetambaras and the Digambaras. Yapaniya ascetics remained naked, kept a broom of peacock feathers, and used the palms of their hands as alms bowls.

YA'QUB

In Islam, Jacob, the father of Yusuf. He appears (for the most part unnamed) in

Surat Yusuf as part of the famous Joseph story. In Surat Maryam Ya'qub is named as one whom God has made a prophet.

YASIN

The title of the 36th sura of the Koran; it consists of two letters of the Arabic alphabet Y and S. The sura belongs to the Meccan period and contains 83 verses. Its title is drawn from the first verse which comprises just these two letters. The sura is often recited at times of distress and approaching death. It contains a parable of a village to which delegates are sent, describes some of the signs of God's power, and refers to the Last Day with the joys of Paradise which the righteous will enjoy and the fires of hell prepared for the unbelievers. It is stressed in verse 79 that the body will be raised from the dead.

YAWN AL-DIN

Arabic phrase meaning "The Day of Faith." It is one of the names in Arabic given to the Day of Resurrection.

YAWM AL-JUM'A

Arabic word for Friday. This is the day of the week when Muslims gather, if at all possible, to perform congregationally the Midday Prayer in the mosque, and listen to a sermon there from an Imam or a prayer leader. Business transactions are suspended during this prayer time.

YAWM AL-QIYAMA

In Islam, the Day of Resurrection, the Day of Judgment, the Last Day. The cataclysmic events and upheavals of this Day are frequently and graphically described in the Koran. This day has many other names in Arabic.

YAZATAS

In Zoroastrianism, angels created by Ahura Mazda to help him maintain the flow of the world order and quell the forces of Ahriman and his demons. They gather the light of the Sun and pour it on the Earth.

YAZIDIS

A religious sect, found in Syria, Armenia and the Caucasus. They believe that they were created quite separately from the rest of mankind, not even being descended from Adam, and they have kept themselves strictly separated from the people among whom they live. They are anti-dualists; they deny the existence of evil (which is merely a word) and therefore also reject sin, the devil, and hell. The breaking of divine laws is expiated by way of metempsychosis (transmigration of souls), which allows for a progressive purification of the spirit.

YEAR, Liturgical

The liturgical year, in the words of Vatican Council II, "unfolds the whole mystery of Christ." The liturgical year begins with the First Sunday of Advent, a season of approximately four weeks, with emphasis on the coming of Christ both at the end of time and into human history. The Christmas season, celebrating the Incarnation of Jesus Christ, begins with the Vigil of Christmas and lasts until the Sunday after January 6.

The period between the end of the Christmas season and the beginning of Lent belongs to ordinary time of the year. The season of Lent, with special emphasis on confession and penance, begins on Ash Wednesday and lasts until the Mass of the Lord's Supper on Holy Thursday. The Easter Triduum begins with evening Mass of the Lord's Supper on Holy Thursday and ends with evening payer on Easter Sunday.

The Easter season lasts from Easter until Pentecost and continues until the beginning of Advent, comprising 33 or 34 weeks. Throughout the liturgical year, the holy church honors with special love the Blessed Mary, Mother of God (for example, on December 8, feast of the Immaculate Conception), and includes days devoted to the memory of martyrs and other saints.

YESHIVA

One of the countless Jewish schools of advanced learning that for centuries have forested religious scholarship to preserve, transmit, and interpret God's revelation to Moses on Mount Sinai. Their history goes back to the First Jewish Commonwealth (circa 1200-586 BC), when ancient sacred writings and traditions were studied and taught in religious academies.

YIDAM

In Buddhism, the deity, or aspect of the absolute, chosen as the protective power for meditation and devotion by Tibetan Buddhists of the Vajrayana School.

YIDDISH LANGUAGE

Language spoken and written by Jews in many parts of the world. In has a long history. From the time of Charlemagne onwards many Jews from France and Lombardy settled in German lands where they developed a form of speech which consisted principally of the Middle High German of the period. This was superimposed on older Latin elements and the original Hebrew and Aramaic of their ancestors. The word "Yiddish" itself is simply an old form of the ordinary modern German word for Jewish.

When the Jews were expelled from Western Europe after 1100, they went east, so that the Yiddish language henceforth existed in a Slavonic setting in Poland and Russia. Although it preserved its Middle High German structure, it absorbed various Slavonic words from the host countries. In the 19th century mass emigration from Eastern Europe began, and Yiddish was spread all over the world by the emigrants.

YIRON

In biblical times, one of the fortified cities in the territory of Naphtali (Joshua 19:32-38). Its location is uncertain, but possibly it was situated at present-day Yarun, ten miles west of the Huleh basin, in Galilee.

YOGA

Word meaning "yoke," in the sense of "that which unites," therefore "union." The Hindu system of discipline the term means the mechanism which brings a man to union. There are two great systems: Hatha Yoga, psycho-physical training along ascetic lines, and Raja Yoga, the development of inner powers by meditation.

YOGACARA

An important idealistic school of Mahayana Buddhism. It attacked both the complete realism of Theravada Buddhism and the provisional practical realism of the Madhyamika school of Mahayana Buddhism.

YOM HA-SHOAH

The Day of Remembrance of the six million Jews killed in World War II. The day is commemorated each year on the 27th day of the Hebrew month of Nisan.

On Yom Ha-Shoah the Jews think of the bravery of men, women, and children whose lives were viciously snuffed out the cruelty of the Nazis while an unfeeling world looked on in silence.

YOM KIPPUR

Jewish holiday known as the Day of Atonement (Leviticus 16:30-31; 23:27-28; Numbers 29-7). It occurs on the 10th of Tishri and ends the 10 days of penitence which begins on New Year's Day. Yom Kippur means 25 hours of complete abstinence from food, drink, sex, cosmetics (including soap and toothpaste), and animal products. The time is spent in prayer and contemplation and sins are confessed. It is the only Jewish holiday that is equivalent to Sabbath in sanctity.

YOSHIDA SHINTO

A religious school of Japan that, while upholding Shinto as the basic faith, teaches the unity of Shinto, Buddhist, and Confucian beliefs. The school emphasizes the virtues of purity and cleanliness.

YOUNG, Brigham

(1801-1877) American Mormon leader who established the Mormon community in Utah. Born in Whitingham, Vermont, he joined Joseph Smith's Church of Jesus Christ of Latter-Day Saints (The Mormons) in 1832 and quickly rose to prominence. After Smith was killed in 1844, Young became leader of the Mormons. When they were driven out of Illinois in 1846, he led the Mormons across the Mississippi to Nebraska and then to the Great Salt Lake valley (Utah) where, as president of the church, he established a thriving colony. He directed irrigation schemes and developed home industries, soon putting his community on a sound commercial footing. In 1850 he became Governor of the newly organized Utah territory and, though replaced in 1857 after repeated clashes with the government, he saw his system survive for many years. In keeping with Mormon polygamy (later forbidden), Young had as many as 27 wives.

YOUNG MEN'S CHRISTIAN ASSOCIATION (YMCA)

Worldwide organization, made up largely of boys and young men, which seeks to promote a healthy way of life based on Christian ideas through learning, physical fitness, social service, religious study and good citizenship. The first American branch of the YMCA opened in Boston, Mass., in 1851.

YOUNG WOMEN'S CHRISTIAN ASSOCIATION (YWCA)

International organization of girls and young women which promotes a Christian way of life through educational and recreational activities. The movement began in England in the early 1850s and by 1858 a YWCA had been established in New York.

YOUTH MINISTRY

A pastoral ministry in the Christian community that tries to discern, address, and respond to the particular needs and challenges encountered by young people and their families in contemporary society. The goal is to help those persons become mature followers of Jesus to live out their baptismal commitments to witness to a Christian way of life.

The team entrusted with youth ministry tries to build relationships with the young people, supports their personal and spiritual growth, seeks to address their real-life needs and questions, and invites the youth and their families into the ministry of the people of God.

YUDHISTHIRA

In Hindu mythology, one of the Pandava brothers, the five sons of King Pandu, who built the city of Indraprastha (on the site of modern Dehli).

YUNUS

Arabic name for Jonah. He was a messenger (rasul) sent to warn a people (the inhabitants of the city of Nineveh). Exceptionally, they listen to his warning. The Koran also portrays Yunus as swallowed by a great fish.

YUNUS

The title of the 10th sura of the Koran. The sura belongs to the late Meccan period and has 109 verses. It takes its title from the reference to Yunus in verse 98. The sura begins with three of the mysterious letters of the Koran and stresses God's creative power. The righteous will be rewarded in Paradise while the wicked will suffer in hell. Later, man is challenged to produce a sura like one of those in the Koran. Towards the end reference is made to Musa and Harun before Fir'awn and the ultimate drowning of the latter.

YUSUF

Arabic word for Joseph.

YUSUF

The title of the 12th sura of the Koran. The sura belongs mainly to the late Meccan period and contains 111 verses. It takes its title from the entire sura which, as the longest piece of extended narrative in the whole Koran, gives the story of Jusuf. The latter, who bears the title of al-Siddiq, ranks as one of the prophets of the Koran. The sura named after him tells how Yusuf relates his dream of 11 stars, the sun and the moon to his father, incurs the jealousy and wrath of his brothers and is eventually sold into Egypt. Here the wife of Qitfir attempts to seduce him. Having been cast into prison, Yusuf interprets the dreams of his fellow prisoners, and is eventually summoned by Pharaoh to interpret the latter's dreams. Pharaoh appoints Yusuf to a position of power in Egypt and he deals with his brothers who visit Egypt for food, eventually revealing himself to them. The sura moves towards its conclusion with Yusuf taking his father and mother in his arms, and placing them on the throne, and finally ends with a panegyric on God, thus tying up the didactic threads of the whole story.

ZAANAN

In biblical times, name of a town mentioned by the prophet Micah as among places due to experience the foretold invasion of Judah (Micah 1:11). Many scholars consider it to be the same as Zenan at Joshua 15:37. The suggested identification is with 'Araq el-Kharba, in the Shephelah region of Judah, circa four miles north-west of Lachish.

ZAANANNIM

In biblical times, name mentioned in connection with a "big tree", a point apparently at the southern boundary of Naphthali's tribal territory (Joshua 19:32-33). Sisera met death in the tent of Heber the Kenite, "near the big tree in Zaanannim, which is at Kedesh" (Judges 4:11-21).

ZAAVAN

In the Old Testament, second-named son of Horite Sheik Ezer and grandson or descendant of Seir the Horite (Genesis 36:20-27).

ZABAD

In Judaism, name of an Ephraimite in the family of Shuthelah (1 Chronicles 7:20-21). The name is also found to apply to a descendant of Judah through Jerahmeel; his great-grandfather was an Egyptian; son of Nathan (1 Chronicles 2:5, 25).

ZABANIYYA, al-

In Islam, principal angelic guardians of hell who appear in the Koran in verse 18 of Surat al-'Alaq; their number is given as 19.

ZABBAI

In the Old Testament, a post-exilic son of Bebai, among those who terminated their foreign marriage alliances, on Ezra's counsel (Ezra 10:28, 44). He was probably the father of the Baruch who did work on Jerusalem's walls (Nehemiah 3:20).

ZABBUD

In the Old Testament, one of the two leaders of the sons of Bigvai, a paternal house members of which went to Jerusalem with Ezra in 468 BC (Ezra 8:1, 14).

ZABDI

In Judaism, name of a descendant of Judah in the family of Zerahites; grandfather of Achan (Joshua 7:17-18). The name is also found to apply to the head of a Benjaminite family dwelling in Jerusalem; son or descendant of Shimei (1 Chronicles 8:19-21).
Zabdi is also known to be the name of an officer of King David's wine supplies in the vineyards; a Shiphmite.

ZABUD

According to biblical tradition, name of a priestly adviser of King Solomon; son of Nathan (1 Kings 4:5). It is not certain but Zabud's father may have been the prophet who was a close adviser of King David (2 Samuel 7:3; 12:1).

ZACCAI

In biblical times, founder of a family in Israel. 760 of his male descendants returned from the Babylonian exile in 537 BC (Ezra 2:1-9).

ZACCARIA, Saint Antonio Maria

(1502-1539) Founder of the Congregation of Clerks Regular of St. Paul, or Barnabites, a religious order devoted to monasticism and to the study of the Pauline letters.

ZACCHAEUS

In biblical times, name of a chief tax collector at Jericho who became one of

Christ's disciples. As such an official, Zacchaeus was likely over the other tax collectors in and around Jericho. The district around Jericho was fertile and productive, yielding considerable tax returns, and Zacchaeus, in the manner of most tax collectors, had probably employed questionable practices in connection with his position to procure part of his notable wealth (Luke 19:1-8).

When Jesus came to Jericho in the spring of 33, just before going to Jerusalem and to his death, Zacchaeus wanted to get a glimpse of him, but being small in stature, he could not see over the crowd. So, running ahead to an advanced position, he resourcefully gained a vantage point by climbing a tree. This interest, of course, impressed Jesus, who told Zacchaeus that he would stay with him while in Jericho. The people objected, however, saying that Jesus was making himself a friend of sinners. Showing a different attitude, Zacchaeus volunteered to restore fourfold whatever he had gotten unjustly, and to give half of his belongings to the poor. Jesus then acknowledged that his household was now in line for salvation (Luke 19:3-10). Also, while visiting Zacchaeus, Jesus spoke the illustration of the minas (Luke 19:11-28).

ZACCUR

In Judaism, name for several important persons. Zaccur was a Reubinite whose son Shammua was one of the 12 spies that Moses sent into the Promised Land (Numbers 13:3-4). Zaccur was also the name of the head of the third group of Levitical musicians; a son of Asaph, a Gershonite (1 Chronicles 25:2, 10). The name Zaccur is also mentioned as belonging to a Levite represented in the signatures to the covenant of faithfulness proposed ruling Nehemiah's governorship. Zaccur may have been there himself, or perhaps one of his descendants signed, in his name (Nehemiah 9:38).

ZACHARIAS, Saint

(687-752) Pope from 741 to 752. He is known in the East for his Greek trans-

lation of the Dialogues of Pope St. Gregory I the Great and for his Catholic attitude toward the Iconoclastic Controversy - i.e., the use of religious images - that culminated in the Byzantine Empire during the 8th and 9th centuries.

ZADOK

In biblical times, name of a priest prominently associated with King David. Zadok was a descendant of Aaron through the High-Priestly line of Eleazar (1 Chronicles 6:3-8, 50-53). He is also called a seer (2 Samuel 15:27). Zadok, as a young man mighty in valor, was one of the tribal chiefs who threw in his support for David's kingship (1 Chronicles 12:27). From that time on he was loyal to David (2 Samuel 8:15-17).

Zadok and Abiathar (whenever the two are mentioned, Zadok is named first) accompanied the ark of the covenant when David had it brought up to Jerusalem, after which Zadok continued to officiate for a time at Gibeon, where the tabernacle was located (1 Chronicles 15:11-14). When Absalom rebelled, Zadok and the Levites started to bring the ark along as they accompanied David in his flight from Jerusalem, but David sent them back to the city, designating Zadok and others to act as intelligence intermediaries (2 Samuel 15:23-29).

After the rebellion was over Zadok and Abiathar were instrumental in securing David's favorable reception in Jerusalem (2 Samuel 19:11-14). When, late in his reign, David organized the Levitical services for the Temple, Zadok and Ahimelech the son of Abiathar both assisted him. Zadok also had the post of leader over the house of Aaron (1 Chronicles 24:3-6; 27:16-17).

ZAHIT

Arabic word for exoteric, outer. That which is zahir in Islam is that which is external, on the surface or obvious.

ZAHIRIS

Adherents of a School of Islamic Law, now long defunct, which stressed an entirely literal and explicit interpretation of both the Koran and the Sunna.

ZAIR

In biblical times, name of a site near or in Edom. In the vicinity of Zair, Judah's King Jehoram, by night, struck down a surrounding military force of Edomites (2 Kings 8:20-22).

ZAKHOR

Hebrew term meaning "remember." Sabbath Zakhor is the sabbath before Purim. An extra portion of the Torah is read. The Haftarah, or portion of the prophets, read on Sabbath Zakhor, describes King Saul's meeting with Agag, ruler of the Amalekites.

ZALAPH

In Judaism, father of at least six sons, one of whom helped Nehemiah to repair Jerusalem's wall (Nehemiah 3:30).

ZALMON

In biblical times, name of a place and a person. Zalmon was the name of an Amorite warrior of David (2 Samuel 23:8, 28).
Zalmon is also mentioned as the name of a mountain near Shechem. From Mount Zalmon, Abimelech and his forces cut wood with which to burn down the vault belonging to the city of Shechem (Judges 9:48-49). As the only mountains near Shechem are Ebal and Gerisim, Zalmon was either a peak or slope of one of these, or else some other less important hill nearby.

ZALMONAH

In biblical times, name of a wilderness site where the Israelites encamped after leaving Mount Hor and before moving on to Punon (Numbers 33:41, 42).

ZALMUNNA

In biblical times, one of the kings of Midian whose forces and allies oppressed Israel for seven years prior to Gideon's judgeship (Judges 6:1). Gideon's small band routed the invaders, and in pursuit of the fleeing forces, captured and put to death both Kings Zebah and Zalmunna (Judges 6:33; 8:4-21).

ZALZALA, al-

The title of the 99th sura of the Koran; it means "The Earthquake." The sura belongs to the Medinan period and has 8 verses. Its title comes from the reference to earthquake (on the Last Day) in the first verse. The second verse makes indirect reference to the doctrine of the resurrection of the body from the dead and concludes that on the Day of Judgment man will see (the record of) his good and bad deeds.

ZALZUMMIM

In biblical times, the Ammonite name for the Rephaim; a people dispossessed by the Ammonites (Deuteronomy 2:19-20).

ZANOAH

In biblical times, name of a Judean city in the Shephelah (Joshua 15:20-36). It was among the cities reinhabited after the Babylonian exile (Nehemiah 11:25, 30). The residents of this Zanoah may have been the ones that did repair work on Jerusalem's southern wall and its Valley Gate (Nehemiah 3:13). This Zanoah is usually identified with Khirbet Zanu', circa three miles south-south-east of Beth-shemesh.

ZAPHENATH-PANEAH

In the Old Testament, name that Pharaoh of Egypt gave to Joseph when elevating him in authority to a position next to himself (Genesis 41:45).

ZAPHON

In Judaism, name of a city assigned to God (Joshua 13:24-27). It is usually identified with Tell el-Qos, circa four miles north of the suggested site of Succoth.

ZAQQUM, Tree of al-

In Islam, bitter smelling and fearsome tree in the pit of hell with flowers which resemble demonic heads. The stomachs of sinners obliged to eat from this tree in hell will be badly burned. The tree is mentioned in the koran. The Zaqqum tree with its bitter fruit and foul smell was not only associated with the infernal regions of hell but also with Arabia.

ZAREPHATH

In ancient times, name of a Phoenician town "belonging to" or apparently dependent upon Sidon in Elijah's day. At Zarephath the prophet was shown hospitality by a poor widow, whose flour and oil were miraculously sustained during a great famine and whose son he, in God's power, subsequently raised from death (1 Kings 17:8-24; Luke 4:25-26).

ZATTU

In Judaism, forefather of a large family that returned to Jerusalem with Zerubbabel in 537 BC (Ezra 2:1-8; Nehemiah 7:13). When Ezra came to Jerusalem, some of their descendants dismissed the foreign wives they had taken (Ezra 10:10-17). Shortly thereafter, a representative of this family or someone else named Zattu, sealed the "trustworthy arrangement" (Nehemiah 9:38; 10:1).

ZAZA

In the Old Testament, name of a son of Jonathan among the descendants of Jerahmeel in the tribe of Judah (1 Chronicles 2:3-5).

ZA-ZEN

Term used in the sense of Zen-sitting; Zen meditation, usually in the Zon-do (the hall, usually a separate building, used in a Zen monastery for Za-Zen meditation). The correct posture is the Dhayanasana, loosely known as the Lotus posture, in which the sole of each foot is upturned on the opposite thigh.

ZEAL

The love of God in action. Zeal is characterized by intense passion and eagerness. Zeal in God's service comes from a realization of the great blessings received through faith and it communicates itself in a desire to proclaim and live the Catholic faith in its fullness.

Zeal is the charity and resulting attempts that enable one to serve God and others in the furthering of the kingdom of Christ, the sanctification of souls, and the furthering of the glory of God by making God better known and loved and thus more faithfully served.

ZEALOT

Member of a Jewish religious and political group in Palestine about the time of Christ. Led by Judas of Galilee and Zadok the priest, they resisted Rome and its collaborator Herod the Great, but later perished in 70 with the destruction of Jerusalem. Simon the Apostle may have been a Zealot (Luke 6:15).

ZEBADIAH

In biblical times name of several important persons mentioned in biblical records. Zebadiah is the name of a Benjaminite, son or descendant of Beriah (1 Chronicles 8:1-16). It is also mentioned as the name of a Benjaminite warrior who joined David's forces at Ziklag; son of Jeroham from Gedor (1 Chronicles 12:1-7).

The name is also found to belong to Joab's nephew and chief of the fourth monthly rotational army division. His being mentioned after his father Asahel, may indicate that he succeeded to the post after Asahel was put to death (2 Samuel 2:23). Or if these monthly courses were organized after Asahel's death, then it could mean that Zebadiah was put over a division named after Asahel (1 Chronicles 21:1-7).

The name is also found for a gatekeeper involved in David's organization of the Levitical services; son of

Mechelemiah, a Kohahite (1 Chronicles 26:1-2).

Zebadiah is also the name of the head of the paternal house of Shephatiah. Zebadiah, son of Michael, led 80 males of his paternal house back to Jerusalem with Ezra in 468 BC (Ezra 8:1-8).

ZEBAH

In biblical times, name of a king of Midian who was a party to oppressing Israel. Zebah and Zalmunna were rulers presumably for the seven years that Midian made raids against Israel, ruining fields and bringing about poverty (Judges 6:1-6). At some unspecified time they also killed members of Gideon's household (Judges 8:18-19).

ZEBEDEE

In the New Testament, name of the father of the Apostles James and John (Matthew 4:21-22; Mark 3:17; Luke 5:10; John 21:2). Zebedee's wife Salome is generally believed to have been the sister of Jesus' mother Mary. This would make Zebedee Jesus' uncle by marriage, and James and John, Jesus' cousins (Matthew 27:56; Mark 15:40; John 19:25).

Zebedee was in the fishing business on the Sea of Galilee and apparently did quite well with it, for there were hired men working with him (Mark 1:16-20). His wife Salome was able to render material services to Jesus (Mark 15:40-41). So while there is no indication that Zebedee himself followed Christ, his family freely did (Matthew 20:20).

ZEBIDAH

In Judaism, name of a wife or concubine of King Josiah and mother of King Jehoiakim. Zebidah was the daughter of Pedaiah from Rumah (2 Kings 23:34-36).

ZEBINA

In Judaism, name of a post-exilic son of Nebo. Zebina and six of his brothers married foreign wives but sent them away, as counseled by Ezra (Ezra 10:43-44).

ZEBOIIM

In biblical times, a site named in connection with the boundary of Canaanite territory (Genesis 10:19). Zeboiim was one of the five city-states of the District that rebelled after 12 years of domination by Chedorlaomer.

ZEBOIM

In biblical times, name of a valley in the territory of Benjamin, near Michmash. In King Saul's day, a band of Philistine pillagers would sally forth from Michmash and "turn to the road to the boundary that looks toward the valley of Zeboim, toward the wilderness" (1 Samuel 13:16-18). Though there is uncertainty about its location, the valley of Zeboim may be the Wadi Abu Daba' south-east of Michmash and some eight miles north-east of Jerusalem.

ZEBUL

In biblical times, name of a commissioner of the city of Shechem, subservient to Gideon's son Abimelech. When a certain Gaal and his brothers came to Shechem and attempted to arouse the city against Abimelech, Zebul informed Abimelech and later challenged the rebel leader Gaal to prove his boasts by fighting. The Shechemite rebels were defeated and Zebul drove Gaal and his brothers from the city (Judges 9:26-41).

ZEBULUN

In Judaism, the sixth son of Jacob's wife Leah. Being the less-loved wife, Leah was especially pleased about the birth of the boy. The name she gave him reflected the hope that her standing with Jacob would be enhanced. Leah exclaimed: "At least my husband will tolerate me, because I have borne him six sons" (Genesis 30:20; Exodus 1:1-3; 1 Chronicles 2:1).

ZEBULUN, Tribe of

One of the 12 tribes of Israel that in biblical times comprised the people of Israel who later became the Jewish people. The tribe was named for the sixth son born of Jacob and his first wife, Leah.

About a year after the Israelites were liberated from enslavement in Egypt, this tribe's able-bodied men from 20 years old upward numbered 57,400 (Numbers 1:1-3; 30-31). A second census taken at the close of Israel's 40 years' wandering in the wilderness revealed an increase of 3,100 registered males (Numbers 26:26-27).

In the wilderness, the tribe of Zebulun, alongside the tribes of Judah and Issachar, camped on the east side of the tabernacle. This three-tribe division was first in the order of march. Eliab the son of Helon served as the chieftain of the Zebulunite army (Numbers 1:9; 2:3-7).

ZEBULUNITE

A member of the tribe of Zebulune (Numbers 26:26-27). Judge Elon was a Zebulunite (Judges 12:11-12).

ZECHARIAH

(circa 500-400 BC) Son of Iddo, who wrote a collection of prophecies. Like his contemporary, Haggai, the prophet urges the reconstruction of Jerusalem and its Temple after Babylonian exile.

The name Zechariah is also found to apply to a Levite whose son assured Jehoshaphat and the people of Judah that God would fight their war for them (2 Chronicles 20:13-17).

The name is also found for the son of King Jehoshaphat. Zechariah and his brothers had all received generous gifts from Jehoshaphat, but the kingship passed to the first-born Jehoram; in order to make his position strong, Jehoram, after his enthronement, killed Zechariah and his brothers and other princes (2 Chronicles 21:1-4).

ZECHARIAH, Book of

The 11th of 12 Old Testament books that bear the names of the minor prophets. The prophet Zechariah was active from 520 to 518 BC. Zechariah's book, and in particular his eight night visions (1:7-6:8), depict the arrival of the Messiah both in his first and second advents and future millennial glory. Other visions announced the rebuilding of the Temple and the world's recognition of Yahweh, Israel's God.

ZEDAD

In biblical times, name of a point at Israel's northern boundary (Numbers 34:8). It tentatively has been identified with Sadad, some 65 miles north-east of Damascus.

ZEDEKIAH

The last king of Judah (ruled 597-587 BC), whose reign ended in the deportation of most of the Jews to Babylon. Originally named Mattaniah, he was the son of Josiah and the uncle of Jehoiachin, the reigning king of Judah. In 597 BC the Babylonians under King Nebuchadnezzar besieged and captured Jerusalem. They deported Jehoiachin to Babylon and set Mattaniah up in his place as regent of the Kingdom of Judah under the name Zedekiah. In the ninth year of Zedekiah's rule a Babylonian army lay siege to Jerusalem after he had conspired to revolt against the Babylonians with Egypt's help. The walls and houses of Jerusalem were destroyed, its Temple was sacked and burned, and the people of Judah, except for the poorest of the land, were deported to Babylon.

ZEEB

In biblical times, a prince of Midian in the forces that Gideon and the Israelites defeated. After their initial loss, Zeeb and his fellow prince Oreb fled, only to be captured and slain by the Ephraimites (Judges 6:33; 7:23-25).

ZEFAT

In biblical times, one of the four holy cities of Judaism (Jerusalem, Hebron, Tiberias, Zefat). First mentioned at the time of the Jewish revolt against Rome (2nd century BC), it is thereafter frequently referred to in rabbinic literature, Strategically situated in scenic hill country, Zefat passed from hand to hand during the Crusades. It achieved renown in the late Middle Ages as the principal center of the Kabbala, the occult theosophy and interpretation of the Scriptures forming the principal mystical system of Judaism.

ZELACH

In biblical times, a city in Benjamin (Joshua 18:21) The bones of Saul and Jonathan were buried at Zela. Earlier. Saul's father Kish had been interred there (2 Samuel 21:14).

ZELOPHEHAD

In Judaism, a descendant of Manasseh through Machit, Gilead and Hepher (Numbers 26:29-33). Zelophehad died during the 40-year wilderness wandering, not with "those who ranged themselves against God in the assembly of Korah, but for his own sin (Numbers 27:3). He had no sons, but was survived by five daughters.

ZELZAH

In biblical times, name of a location in Benjamin. As one of the signs confirming Saul's leadership over Israel, he was to meet and receive a message about his father's lost she-asses from two men "close by the tomb of Rachel in the territory of Benjamin at Zelzah (1 Samuel 10:1-7).

ZEMARAIM

In biblical times, a Benjamite city mentioned with Bethel (Joshua 18:21-22). Its is often suggested that it was near or at Ras ez-Zeimara over three miles north-east of Bethel. Nevertheless the exact location of Zemaraim is unknown.

ZEMARITE

In the Old Testament, a family or tribe that descended from Ham's son Canaan (Genesis 10:15-18).

ZEMIRAH

In the Old Testament, name of a family head in the tribe of Benjamin; son or descendant of Becher (1 Chronicles 7:6-9).

ZEN

Chinese and Japanese school of Buddhism which has been described as the revolt of the Chinese mind against the intellectual Buddhism of India. It evolved from the teaching of Bodhidharma, the 28th Patriarch of Buddhism, who came to China in 520. The word Zen is the Japanese equivalent of the Chinese Ch'an or Ch'an-na, derived from the Sanskrit Dhyana, usually translated as meditation. This, however, gives en erroneous conception of Zen, which cannot be confined to any particular practice. Although meditation is part of Zen training, Zen itself includes every possible form of activity. The Chinese mind wished to apply Buddhism to everyday life, asserting that enlightenment could be found just as much by working in the world as in withdrawing from it.

ZENAN

In biblical times, a town in the Shephelah region of Judah (Joshua 15:33, 37).

ZENAS

In the New Testament, name of an acquaintance of Paul, concerning whom Titus was told 'Carefully supply Zenas .... and Apollos for their trip (Titus 8:13). At the time Zenas was evidently on the island of Crete, but where he and Apollos were going, whether to Nicopolis, where Paul hoped to meet Titus, or to some other place, is not stated (Acts 1:23-29).

ZEN LOGIC

Specific characteristic of logic from, a Buddhist point of view. Zen training is a process of transcending thought, for the intellect functions in duality, and the moment of Zen experience is in non-duality. Normal logic is therefore worse than useless to achieve this experience; it binds the mind in the coils of concept. Only when it is seen that A is A because A is not-A is the mind set free. This logic is the fruit of Zen experience and not a means to it. It can be stated, therefore, but not to be the subject of intellectual argument.

ZEPHANIAH

Name of various important persons in the Bible. Zephaniah was a Levite in the genealogical line from Kohath to Samuel and Heman (1 Chronicles 6:33-38).

Zephaniah was also a prophet during the early part of Josiah's reign, and writer of the book bearing his name. Zephaniah was apparently a great-great-grandson of King Hezekiah (Zephaniah 1:1).

The name Zephaniah is also mentioned for a leading priest during the last decade of the kingdom of Judah; son of Maaseiah. He was twice sent by Zedekiah to Jeremiah, first to inquire about Judah's future and later to request him to pray on their behalf (Jeremiah 21:1-3; 37:3).

ZEPHANIAH, Book of

The ninth of 12 Old Testament books that bear the names of the Minor prophets. The book consists of a series of independent sayings, composed by Zephaniah, probably around 640-608 BC. The dominant theme of the book is the "day of the Lord" which the prophet sees approaching as a consequence of the sins of Judah. A remnant will be saved through purification by judgment.

ZEPHATH

In biblical times, a royal Canaanite city in the southern part of Judah's territory, apparently south of Arad, captured by the combined forces of Judah and Simeon (Judges 1:16-17).

ZEPHATIAH

In biblical times, name of a valley near Mareshah where, according to biblical tradition, God enabled the forces of Judah's King Asa to defeat those of Zerah the Ethiopian (2 Chronicles 14:9-12).

ZEPHYRINUS, Saint

(145-217) Pope from 199-217. He failed to condemn Monarchianism or favor the Logos doctrine (emphasizing the distinction of the Persons of the Trinity) and was regarded as being unskilled in the church's rule.

ZERAH

In biblical times, name of several important persons mentioned in various contexts. Zerah was an Edomite Sheik, son of Reuel, and grandson of Esau and Basemath, Ishmael's daughter (Genesis 36:3-17).

The name is also mentioned as belonging to a son of Judah and Tamar; twin brother of Perez (Genesis 38:27-30). Zerah was one of those "who came to Jacob in Egypt" (Genesis 46:12). His five sons grew into a Judean tribal family (Numbers 26:20).

The name is also mentioned in the Old Testament for an Ethiopian, or Cushite, who led a huge army of a million men and 300 chariots into Judah during Asa's reign, sometime after 967-966 BC. Zerah met defeat and his fleeing forces were pursued and slaughtered "as far as Gerar" (2 Chronicles 14:1, 9-15). Identification of Zerah with any secularly known Egyptian or Ethiopian ruler remains uncertain.

ZERAHIAH

In biblical times, a descendant of Aaron through Eleazar and Phinehad in the High-Priestly line (1 Chronicles 6:3-4).

The name is also mentioned as belonging to the father of Elieho-enai who headed the paternal house of Pahath-moab, 200 males of whom returned to Jerusalem with Ezra in 468 BC (Ezra 8:1, 4).

ZERED, Torrent valley of

In biblical times, a torrent valley at which the Israelites camped on their way around the frontier of Moab, at the end of the 38 additional years of wandering from the time of the rebellion at

Kadesh-barnea (Numbers 21:12; Deuteronomy 2:13-14). While some would place this valley at the Wadi es-Sultani in the desert east of Moab, it is generally identified with the Wadi el-Hesa, the southernmost tributary of the Dead Sea. This valley formed the boundary between Moab and Edom, and, over a 35-mile stretch, it descends some 3,900 feet, entering the Dead Sea at the south-eastern end. The valley is some three and a quarter to four miles across at the top. There is evidence there of a series of Edomite fortresses that served to guard the natural approaches to the south of the Wadi el-Hesa.

ZEREDAH

In biblical times, name of the home-town of Jeroboam, first king of the northern kingdom of Israel (1 Kings 11:26).

ZERESH

In the Old Testament, name of the wife of Haman. Zeresh and Haman's friends proposed that he erect a stake to a height of fifty cubits (circa 73 feet), on which to hang Mordecai (Esther 5:10, 14). But when reversals set in, Zeresh, along with Haman's wise men, said: "If it is from the seed of the Jews that Mordecai is before whom you have started to fall, you will not prevail against him, but you will without fail fall before him" (Esther 6:13).

ZERETH

In the Old Testament, name of the first-named son that Helah bore to Asshur; of the tribe of Judah (1 Chronicles 4:1-7).

ZERI

In Judaism, one of Jeduthun's six sons, all of whom were Temple musicians (1 Chronicles 25:1-3).

ZEDOR

In Judaism, name for an ancestor of King Saul; listed as son of Becorath and father of Ariel; of the tribe of Benjamin (1 Kings 11:26).

ZERUBBABEL

(6th century BC) Governor of Judea under whom the rebuilding of the Jewish Temple at Jerusalem took place. Of Davidic origin, Zerubbabel returned to Jerusalem at the head of a band of Jewish exiles and became governor of Judea under the Persians. Influenced by the prophets Haggai and Zechariah, he rebuilt the Temple.

At Jerusalem, under the direction of Zerubbabel and High Priest Jeshua, the temple altar was erected in the seventh month (Ezra 3:1-2).

ZERUIAH

In biblical times, name for King David's sister and mother of Joab, Abishai and Asahel (1 Chronicles 2:16). Since Zeruiah and her sister Abigail are both called "daughters of Nahash," never daughters of Jesse, it is likely that they were daughters of Jesse's wife by a previous marriage to Nahash, therefore only half sisters of David (2 Samuel 17:25).

ZETHAM

In Judaism, name of a Gershonite Levite descended from Ladan. He headed a paternal house and was assigned to care for the Temple treasures (1 Chronicles 23:7-9).

ZETHAN

In Judaism, name of a descendant of Benjamin through Jediael and Bilhan (1 Chronicles 7:6-10).

ZETHAR

In biblical times, name of one of the seven court officials who Ahasuerus sent to bring Vashti before him (Esther 1:10-11).

ZEUS

The supreme god of Greek mythology (counterpart of the Roman god, Jupiter). Originally god of the sky and weather, he later came to be considered all-powerful, all-knowing and all-seeing. He dispensed justice and mercy, and was the source of oracles. He had several wives; Metis (Widsom),

Themis (on whom he fathered the Seasons and the Fates), Eurynome (mother of the Graces), Mnemosyne (mother of the Muses) and finally Hera. He also had numerous mistresses - both immortal and mortal. He fathered the gods Hermes, Apollo and Dionysus, and the goddess Artemis. His most famous and ancient sanctuary was a sacred oak at Dodona in Epirus, north-western Greece.

Zeus had countless love affairs with other goddesses and mortal women, often arousing the jealousy of Hera. In those relationships Zeus sired many other children, some of whom were gods, and others demi-gods and heroes. Zeus loved and protected all his children, who often attracted the rage of Hera. Apart from the hundreds of women with whom the father of gods and men enjoyed covert love relationships, he was also moved by the beauty of the young Ganymede, a member of the royal family of Troy. The boy was so handsome that he awoke the erotic interest of Zeus, who abducted him to Olympus to serve as his cup-bearer - that is, Ganymede's task was to make sure that Zeus' cup was always full of nectar.

Apart from his passions, Zeus was the god who maintained the balance of justice. His role was not only to punish and avenge, but also to share in the pain of the unfortunate and help to relieve their sufferings by dispensing justice.

ZIBA

In the Old Testament, the servant of Saul's household from, whom David, on inquiry, leaned of Jonathan's lame son Mephibosheth. David brought Mephibosheth to Jerusalem and made Ziba, his 15 sons and 20 servants, all care of Mephibopsheth's inheritance (2 Samuel 9:2-12).

ZIBEON

In Judaism, a sheik in the land of Seir (Genesis 36:20-30). His granddaughter Oholibamah married Esau (Genesis 36:2, 14, 24-25).

ZIBIAH

In Judaism, name of the mother of King Jehoash of Judah, presumably the wife of King Ahasiah, and therefore daughter-in-law of Athaliah (2 Kings 11:1-2).

ZICHRI

In Judaism, name of family heads in the tribe of Benjamin, residents of Jerusalem. They were sons or descendants of Shimei, Shashak and Jeroham respectively (1 Chronicles 8:19-28).

The name is also found to apply to a mighty warrior in the army of the northern kingdom which invaded Judah around 760 BC. Zichi killed three prominent members of King Ahaz's household, including a royal prince (2 Chronicles 28:6-7).

ZIGGURAT

A pyramidal, steeped temple tower, characteristic architectural and religious structure of the major cities of ancient Mesopotamia (modern Iraq) from circa 2200 until 500 BC.

ZIKLAG

In biblical times, name of a Simeonite enclave city in south Judah (Joshua 15:21, 31). Later Ziklag was under Philistine control. Achish, king of Gath, gave it to the fugitive David as a place of residence (and thereafter it became the possession of Judah's kings) (1 Samuel 27:6). The Amalekites raided and burned the city, taking captives, including David's wives Ahinoam and Abigail. After defeating the marauders and recovering the captives and things taken, David, from Ziklag, sent some of the spoil of battle to his friends, older men of Judah in various cities (1 Samuel 30:1-10).

After the Babylonian exile, some of the sons of Judah settled in this city (Nehemiah 11:25-28).

ZILLAH

According to biblical tradition, one of the two wives of Lamech, the first polygamist of Bible record. She was the mother of Tubal-cain and of his sister Naamah (Genesis 4:19-24).

ZILPAH

In the Old Testament, Leah's maidservant and Jacob's secondary wife. Zilpah had been a servant of Leah's father Laban until Leah and Jacob were married and she was given to Leah (Genesis 29:24). After Leah had four sons, and she thought she was through childbearing, she gave Zilpah to Jacob as a secondary wife. Zilpah than bore Gad and Asher, who, in turn, had many sons (Genesis 30:9-13; 35:26).

ZIMMAH

In Judaism, name of a Gershonite Levite (1 Chronicles 6:20). His descendant Joah helped to cleanse the temple in Hezekiah's days.

ZIMRAN

In the Old Testament, first-named of the six sons Keturah bore Abraham. Zimran and his five full brothers were given gifts and sent into "the land of the East" (Genesis 25:1-6; 1 Chronicles 1:32).

ZIMRI

Name of several important persons in biblical times. Zimri is the name of the Simeonite chieftain, son of Salu, who brought Cozbi the Midianitess into the camp of Israel, committing fornication with her in his own tent.

Zimri is also the name of the fifth king of the ten-tribe kingdom of Israel. Zimri ruled in Tirzah for seven days in circa 951 BC. He had previously been chief of half the chariots under King Elah, but when the army was away at Gibbethon, and King Elah had remained behind, Zimri killed him and all the rest of Baasha's house, and made himself king.

Zimri is also the name of a descendant of Saul and Jonathan (1 Chronicles 8:33-36).

ZIN

In biblical times, name for a wilderness through which the Israelites traveled en route to Canaan, but not synonymous with the wilderness of Sin (Numbers 33:11). In the second year after Israel's leaving Egypt, 12 spies reconnoitered the Promised Land, starting out from the wilderness of Zin. At that time the Israelites were encamped at Kadesh (Numbers 13:21-26). Later, after having wandered in the wilderness for years, the Israelites arrived at Kadesh in the wilderness of Zin the second time. This area of the wilderness of Zin was desolate, unsewn, lacking figs, vines, pomegranates and water (Numbers 20:1-5).

The wilderness of Zin was "alongside Edom" (being immediately west of Edom) and at the south-eastern extremity of Judah's assigned territory (Numbers 34:3). Since Kadesh was located in both the wilderness of Zin and Paran (Numbers 13:26), Zin may have been part of the more extensive wilderness of Paran.

ZION

In the Old Testament, the easternmost of the two hills of ancient Jerusalem, the site of the Jebusite city captured by David, king of Israel and Judah. In the Bible Zion is also referred to as the future capital of Israel. The New Testament also refers Zion to the New Jerusalem, the eternal city where believers will be received.

ZIONISM

A Jewish nationalist movement that has had as its goal the creation and support of a Jewish national state in Palestine, the ancient homeland of the Jews. Though Zionism originated in Eastern and Central Europe in the latter part of the 19th century, it is in many ways a continuation of the ancient and deep-felt nationalist attachment of the Jews and of the Jewish religion to Palestine, the Promised Land where one of the hills of ancient Jerusalem was called Zion.

The goals of modern Zionism include the intensifying of Jewish national unity, reinforcing the Israeli identity and welcoming Jews from the diaspora around the world who wish to have a national home.

ZIONIST CHURCHES

Prophet-healing groups in southern Africa; they correspond to the independent churches known as Aladura in Nigeria, "spiritual" in Ghana, and "prophet-healing" in most parts of black Africa.

ZIOR

In biblical times, name of a city in the mountainous region of Judah (Joshua 15:20). It is often identified with Si'ir, some five miles north-north-east of Hebron. Ruins there, however, are believed to date only from the Byzantine period.

ZIPH

In biblical times, name of a city in the southern part of Judah (Joshua 15:21-24). It is usually identified with Khirbet ez-Zeifeh, circa 20 miles south-east of Beer-sheba.
The name is also found to apply to a descendant of Judah through Jehallelel (1 Chronicles 4:15-16).

ZIPHITES

The inhabitants of Ziph in the mountainous region of Judah (Psalm 54).

ZIPHORN

In biblical times, name of a site at the northern border of the Promised Land (Numbers 34:9). Its exact location is not definitively known.

ZIPPORAH

According to biblical tradition, the wife of Moses. Zipporah met Moses at a well, when she and her six sisters were watering their father's flocks. When certain shepherds came on the scene and, as was their custom, attempted to drive the girls away, Moses helped the girls pour, even watering the flocks himself. For this kindness he was invited to the home of Zipporah, and eventually her priestly father Jethro gave her in marriage to Moses (Exodus 2:16-21). Zipporah bore two sons to Moses, Gershom and Eliezir (Exodus 2:22; 18:3-4).

ZIYARAH

In Islam, a visit to the Prophet Mohammed's tomb in the mosque of Medina, Saudi Arabia; also a visit to the tomb of some saint or holy man. Muslims make such visits in the hope of obtaining cures or witnessing a miracle or of obtaining the blessings of the saint.

ZIZ

In biblical times, a pass by which the armies of Moab, Ammon and the Ammonim came against Judah during the reign of Jehoshaphat. It is usually identified with Wadi Hasasa, circa ten miles south-east of the suggested site of Tekoa and some seven miles north-west of En-gedi (2 Chronicles 20:1-2).

ZIZA

In the Old Testament, name of a son of King Rehoboam by Absalom's granddaughter Maacah. When the royal succession was directed to Ziza's brother Abijah, Ziza received gifts of cities, food and wives from Rehoboam (2 Chronicles 11:20-23).
The name is also applied to one of the Simeonite chieftains who expanded their grazing land by annexing Hamite territory and destroying its inhabitants during the reign of Hezekiah; son of Shiphi (1 Chronicles 4:24, 37-41).

ZIZAH

In the Old Testament, name of the second-listed son of Shimei, head of a paternal house of Gershonite Levites assigned to certain duties during David's reign (1 Chronicles 23:6-11).

ZOAN

In biblical times, name of an ancient Egyptian city, built seven years after Hebron, hence already in existence around the time of Abraham's entry into Canaan (Numbers 13:22; Genesis 12:5). The town was probably located in the north-eastern part of the Delta region, circa 35 miles south-west of

Port Said. Better known by its Greek name, Tanis, it was situated on the branch of the Nile called the Tanitic branch, since then filled with silt and reduced to a canal.

ZOAR

In biblical times, name of a city of the "District," evidently once at the edge of a fertile plain (Genesis 13:10-12).

ZOBAH

In ancient times, a Syrian kingdom otherwise known as Aram-Zorah. One of the kings was Hadadezer (1 Kings 11:23). King Saul warred against the kings of Zodah (1 Samuel 14:47). The Ammonites later hired Syrians of Zodah and other troops to fight against David, but all were defeated by his army (2 Samuel 10:6-19); 1 Chronicles 19:6-19).

ZOHAR

In the Old Testament, name of a Hittite whose son Ephraon sold the care of Machpelah to Abraham (Genesis 23:7-9).

The name is also found to apply to the fifth-named son of Simeon and father of a tribal family; one of those numbered among the 70 of Jacob's household who "came into Egypt" (Genesis 46:8; Exodus 6:15).

ZOPHAH

In Judaism, a leading member of the tribe of Asher. E;even "sons" of his are listed (1 Chronicles 7:35-40).

ZOPHAI

In Judaism, name of a son of a certain Elkanah and ancestor of Samuel (1 Chronicles 6:33-35).

ZOPHAR

According to biblical tradition, one of the Job's three "companions"; the Naamathite (Job 2:11).

ZOPHIM

In biblical times, name of a field on the top of Pisgah where Balaam built seven altars, where sacrifices were offered and where the prophet took up one of his proverbial utterances regarding Israel (Numbers 23:14-24).

Zorah
In biblical times, a city in the Shephelah allotted to the tribe of Judah (Joshua 15:20). Situated on the boundary between Dan and Judah, it was inhabited by peoples of Dan (Joshua 19:41).

ZOROASTER

(628-551 BC) Great Iranian religious reformer and founder of Zoroastrianism, or Parseeism. He is said to have received a vision from Ahura Mazda, the Wise Lord, who appointed him to preach the truth. Rather than overthrow the polytheism of Iranian religion, he placed Ahura Mazda at the center of a kingdom of justice that promised immortality and bliss. Ahura Mazda was the highest of the gods and alone worthy of worship.

ZOROASTRIANISM

Ancient pre-Islamic religion of Iran that survives there in isolated areas and more prosperously in India, where the descendants of Zoroastrian Iranian (Persian) immigrants are known as Parsees. The religion contains both monotheistic and dualistic features.

Though Zoroastrianism was never, even in the thinking of its founder, as aggressively monotheistic as, for instance, Judaism, or Islam, it does represent an original attempt at unifying under the worship of one supreme god a polytheistic religion comparable to those of the ancient Greeks, Latins, Indians, and other early people. Its other salient feature, namely dualism, was never understood in an absolute, rigorous fashion. Good and Evil fight an unequal battle, in which the former is assured of triumph. God's omnipotence is thus only temporarily limited. In this struggle man must enlist because of his capacity of free choice. He does so with his body and soul, not against his body, for the opposition between good and evil is not the same as the one between spirit and matter. On the whole, Zoroastrianism is optimistic and has remained so even through the hardship and oppression of its believers.

ZOSIMUS, Saint

(345-418) Pope from 417 to 418. His brief but turbulent [pontificate was embroiled in conflicts involving Gaul, Africa, and Pelagianism, a heretical doctrine that minimized the role of divine grace in man's salvation.

ZUCCHETTO

The small skullcap worn since the 13th century by bishops or other prelates. The color varies according to the rank of the wearer. The pope wears a white zucchetto made of watered silk. The cardinals wear scarlet and bishops wear purple. Priests of nonsignorial rank may wear black wit purple piping. A small brown skullcap is worn by Capuchins. All others may wear simple black, including abbots who do not have episcopal dignity.

ZUAD

Arabic word for asceticism, renunciation of worldly and material things. This is often associated with tasawwuf though it was by no means characteristic of every tariqa or sufi individual.

ZUKHRUF, al-

The title of the 43rd sura of the Koran; it means "The Ornament" or "The Gold." The sura belongs to the Meccan period and contains 89 verses. It takes its title from the reference to gold or ornament in verse 35. The sura begins with two of the mysterious letters of the Koran and goes on to survey details of God's creation. Aspects of the missions of Ibrahim, Musa and Isa follow, and the sura concludes with references to God's power and omniscience.

ZUMAR, al-

The title of the 39th sura of the Koran; it means "The Crowds." The sura belongs to the Meccan period and has 75 verses. Its title is drawn from verse 71 in which the unbelievers will be driven into hell in crowds or droves, and, similarly, the pious will be driven towards Paradise in crowds. The sura begins with reference to the revelation of the Koran and goes on to survey God's benefits to man, as well as His divine power. Reference is later made to the Last Day and the Judgment. Those who enter Paradise will see angels circling the throne of God whom they praise.

ZUPH

In biblical times, name of a "land" outside the territory of Benjamin through which Saul went searching for his father's she-asses. In a city within the land of Zuph, Saul had his first meeting with Samuel (1 Samuel 9:3-6). The exact location of Zuph is not known.

ZUR

In ancient times, one of the fine kings of Midian at the time Israel approached the Promised Land. Zur is also called a "chieftain" and a "head of one of the clans of a paternal house," as well as a "duke of Sihon."

His daughter Cozbi was the Midianitess whom Zimri took for immoral relations and whom Phinehas slew. Zur himself was killed when the Israelites punished Midian for luring some men of Israel into immoral intercourse and false worship (Numbers 25:14-18